AN INTERPRETATION OF THE

QUR'AN

ENGLISH TRANSLATION OF THE MEANINGS
A BILINGUAL EDITION

Translated by
Majid Fakhry

AN INTERPRETATION OF THE

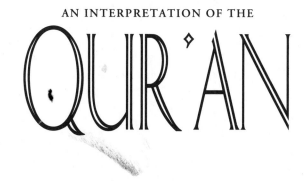

QUR'AN

AN INTERPRETATION OF THE

QUR'AN

ENGLISH TRANSLATION OF THE MEANINGS
A BILINGUAL EDITION

Translated by
Majid Fakhry

NEW YORK UNIVERSITY PRESS
Washington Square, New York

The late Dr Mahmud Zayid
offered valuable assistance with the revision and
annotation of this translation of the work,
prior to his untimely death in 1994.

———

An Interpretation of the Qur'an
English Translation of the Meanings
A Bilingual Edition

Published in the U.S.A. in 2002 by
NEW YORK UNIVERSITY PRESS
Washington Square
New York, NY 10003

Library of Congress Cataloging-in-Publication Data
Koran. English & Arabic.
An interpretation of the Qur'an : English translation of the
meanings : a bilingual edition / translated by Majid Fakhry.
p. cm.
Includes index.
ISBN 0-8147-2723-9 (cloth : alk. paper)
I. Fakhry, Majid II. Title.

BP109 2002
297.1'22521--dc21   4   2002021926

Jacket design by David Rose

Printed in Lebanon

﴿فهرس بأسماء السور وبيان المكّي والمَدَنيّ منها﴾

APPENDIX-I
INDEX OF SÛRAHS — CHAPTERS

Sûrah	No.	Page			الصَّفحَة	رَقمهَا	السُّورَة
Al-Fâtihah	1	5	Makki	مكّية	٥	١	الفَاتِحَة
Al-Baqarah	2	6	Madani	مَدَنيّة	٦	٢	البَقَرَة
Âl-'Imrân	3	54	Madani	مَدَنيّة	٥٤	٣	آل عِمرَان
An-Nisa'	4	80	Madani	مَدَنيّة	٨٠	٤	النِّسَاء
Al-Mâ'idah	5	107	Madani	مَدَنيّة	١٠٧	٥	المَائدة
Al-An'âm	6	127	Makki	مكّية	١٢٧	٦	الأنعَام
Al-A'râf	7	149	Makki	مكّية	١٤٩	٧	الأعرَاف
Al-Anfâl	8	175	Madani	مَدَنيّة	١٧٥	٨	الأنفَال
At-Tawbah	9	185	Madani	مَدَنيّة	١٨٥	٩	التوبَة
Yûnus	10	203	Makki	مكّية	٢٠٣	١٠	يُونس
Hud	11	216	Makki	مكّية	٢١٦	١١	هُود
Yûsuf	12	231	Makki	مكّية	٢٣١	١٢	يُوسُف
Ar-Ra'd	13	244	Madani	مَدَنيّة	٢٤٤	١٣	الرَّعد
Ibrâhim	14	251	Makki	مكّية	٢٥١	١٤	إبرَاهيم
Al-Hijr	15	257	Makki	مكّية	٢٥٧	١٥	الحِجر
An-Nahl	16	263	Makki	مكّية	٢٦٣	١٦	النَّحل
Al-Isrâ'	17	277	Makki	مكّية	٢٧٧	١٧	الإسرَاء
Al-Kahf	18	289	Makki	مكّية	٢٨٩	١٨	الكهف
Maryam	19	301	Makki	مكّية	٣٠١	١٩	مَريَم
Tâ Hâ	20	309	Makki	مكّية	٣٠٩	٢٠	طه
Al-Anbiyâ'	21	321	Makki	مكّية	٣٢١	٢١	الأنبيَاء
Al-Hajj	22	331	Madani	مَدَنيّة	٣٣١	٢٢	الحَجّ
Al-Mu'minûn	23	340	Makki	مكّية	٣٤٠	٢٣	المؤمنون

APPENDIX-I
INDEX OF SÛRAHS — CHAPTERS

Sûrah	No.	Page			الصّفحة	رقمها	السُّورَة
Al-Hujurât	49	522	Madani	مَدَنيّة	٥٢٢	٤٩	الحُجرَات
Qâf	50	525	Makki	مكّية	٥٢٥	٥٠	قى
Adh-Dhâriyât	51	528	Makki	مكّية	٥٢٨	٥١	الذّاريَات
At-Tur	52	532	Makki	مكّية	٥٣٢	٥٢	الطُّور
An-Najm	53	535	Makki	مكّية	٥٣٥	٥٣	النّجْم
Al-Qamar	54	539	Makki	مكّية	٥٣٩	٥٤	القَمَر
Ar-Rahmân	55	542	Madani	مَدَنيّة	٥٤٢	٥٥	الرَّحْمن
Al-Waqi'ah	56	547	Makki	مكّية	٥٤٧	٥٦	الواقِعَة
Al-Hadîd	57	551	Madani	مَدَنيّة	٥٥١	٥٧	الحَديد
Al-Mujadilah	58	556	Madani	مَدَنيّة	٥٥٦	٥٨	المُجَادلة
Al-Hashr	59	559	Madani	مَدَنيّة	٥٥٩	٥٩	الحَشر
Al-Mumtahanah	60	563	Madani	مَدَنيّة	٥٦٣	٦٠	المُمتَحَنة
As-Saff	61	565	Madani	مَدَنيّة	٥٦٥	٦١	الصّف
Al-Jum'ah	62	567	Madani	مَدَنيّة	٥٦٧	٦٢	الجُمُعة
Al-Munâfiqûn	63	569	Madani	مَدَنيّة	٥٦٩	٦٣	المنَافِقون
At-Taghâbun	64	570	Madani	مَدَنيّة	٥٧٠	٦٤	التّغَابُن
At-Talâq	65	572	Madani	مَدَنيّة	٥٧٢	٦٥	الطّلَاق
At-Tahrim	66	574	Madani	مَدَنيّة	٥٧٤	٦٦	التّحْريم
Al-Mulk	67	576	Makki	مكّية	٥٧٦	٦٧	المُلك
Al-Qalam	68	579	Makki	مكّية	٥٧٩	٦٨	القَلَم
Al-Hâqqah	69	582	Makki	مكّية	٥٨٢	٦٩	الحَاقّة
Al-Ma'ârij	70	586	Makki	مكّية	٥٨٦	٧٠	المعَارج
Nûh	71	588	Makki	مكّية	٥٨٨	٧١	نُوح
Al-Jinn	72	590	Makki	مكّية	٥٩٠	٧٢	الجنّ
Al-Muzzammil	73	593	Makki	مكّية	٥٩٣	٧٣	المُزَّمل

APPENDIX-I
INDEX OF SÛRAHS — CHAPTERS

Sûrah	No.	Page			الصّفحة	رقمها	السّورة
Az-Zalzalah	99	630	Madani	مَدَنيّة	٦٣٠	٩٩	الزّلزَلة
Al-'Adiyât	100	630	Makki	مكّية	٦٣٠	١٠٠	العَادِيَات
Al-Qari'ah	101	631	Makki	مكّية	٦٣١	١٠١	القَارِعَة
At-Takâthur	102	632	Makki	مكّية	٦٣٢	١٠٢	التكَاثُر
Al-'Asr	103	632	Makki	مكّية	٦٣٢	١٠٣	العَصر
Al-Humazah	104	633	Makki	مكّية	٦٣٣	١٠٤	الهُمَزة
Al-Fîl	105	633	Makki	مكّية	٦٣٣	١٠٥	الفِيل
Quraysh	106	634	Makki	مكّية	٦٣٤	١٠٦	قُرَيش
Al-Mâ'ûn	107	634	Makki	مكّية	٦٣٤	١٠٧	المَاعون
Al-Kawthar	108	634	Makki	مكّية	٦٣٤	١٠٨	الكَوثَر
Al-Kâfirûn	109	635	Makki	مكّية	٦٣٥	١٠٩	الكافِرون
An-Nasr	110	635	Madani	مَدَنيّة	٦٣٥	١١٠	النّصر
Al-Masad	111	635	Makki	مكّية	٦٣٥	١١١	المَسَد
Al-Ikhlâs	112	636	Makki	مكّية	٦٣٦	١١٢	الإخلاص
Al-Falaq	113	636	Makki	مكّية	٦٣٦	١١٣	الفَلَق
An-Nâs	114	637	Makki	مكّية	٦٣٧	١١٤	النّاس

Introduction

The Qur'an is the sacred scripture of Islam. It consists of 114 Surahs or chapters which are divided into ayat or verses. Most of the Surahs were revealed piecemeal to Muhammad (ﷺ) during the two periods of his Call: the Meccan period (610-622A.D.) and the Medinan period (622-632A.D.).

The Meccan Surahs, which belong to the period of struggle against the Prophet's own tribe of Quraysh in Mecca, are written in an incisive and impassioned style and proclaim in a fiery tone the imminence of the Hour and the horrors of Hell-fire. They summon mankind to heed the divine call with which Muhammad (ﷺ), the Messenger of God, is charged and which centres on the profession of the unqualified oneness and sovereignty of God and the urgency of returning to the true *(hanif)* religion of Abraham, founder of the Sacred Shrine of the Ka'ba in Mecca. This *hanif* religion, having been corrupted over the years by idolatry and other pagan practices, was now being revived and cleansed by Muhammad (ﷺ), whose spiritual call in the Qur'an is described for that reason as reviving or "confirming" the original or pure monotheism of Abraham. Even Jews and Christians, referred to as the People of the Book since they were recipients of a true revelation they are said to have corrupted, are summoned in the Qur'an to adhere to the only true revelation "sent down" to Muhammad (ﷺ).

This revelation, according to the Qur'an, has existed since all time in the Preserve Tablet (Surah 85/22) or the Mother of the Book (Surah 13/39) and was communicated to Muhammad (ﷺ) through the Angel Gabriel (Jibril) in pure Arabic, so as to instruct his own people and through them the rest of mankind. It is believed by Muslims to be the infallible Word of God *(Kalam Allah)*.

The earliest revelation came to Muhammad (ﷺ) at the age of forty, as he was absorbed in meditation in Cave Hira', just outside Mecca. Here, according to Muslim tradition, the angel Jibril spoke to him thus: "Read *(iqra')* in the name of your Lord Who created ..."; hence the name of the Qur'an, reading or recitation. Thereafter the revelations came to the Prophet at different intervals and were written down on palm-leaves, tablets of stone or simply committed to memory by the scribes or "secretaries of revelation", the most famous of whom was Zayd Ibn Thabit.

Following the death of the Prophet in 632 A.D., a copy of the Qur'an based on this written or oral material was compiled by Zayd and entrusted to the care of Hafsah, daughter of the Caliph 'Umar and widow of the Prophet. However, due to the divergent readings of the sacred text and the danger of faulty oral transmission, a definitive edition was compiled in 651 A.D. by order of Uthman, the Third Caliph, and this edition, known as Mushaf Uthman (or Uthman's Codex), has remained ever since the authorized version of the Qur'an, read, chanted and meditated upon by millions of Muslims throughout the world.

The Medinan Surahs, on the other hand, belong to the period of Hijrah (or emigration to Medina), which began in 622 A.D., marking the start of the Muslim calender. For the most part they are written in a prosaic and discursive style, and embody the fundamental principles of Islamic legislation, known as the *shari'ah* or holy law. This legislation covers social, economic and political matters, such as marriage and divorce, inheritance and alms-giving, the relation of Muslim subjects to their rulers and so on. Those subjects are specifically commanded to obey "God, the Messenger and those who wield authority among you" (Surah 4/62) and to submit their differences to God and the Messenger, who was succeeded as head of the Muslim community by the so-called Caliphs, or "successors of the Messenger".

In Medina, originally called Yathrib, Islam became for the first time both a religious and political movement, so that one could speak thereafter of the rise and consolidation of the Muslim community *(Ummah)*, with the Prophet at its head. In that respect, the Prophet now wielded a political authority in addition to his spiritual authority as the Messenger of God, and in this double capacity he was able to confront his erstwhile enemies at Mecca, his native town. After repeated skirmishes outside Medina and a variety of "expeditions" further afield, the Muslims, led by the Prophet, were able to capture Mecca in the eighth year of the Hijrah, or 630 A.D. Thereupon, the Prophet's first move was to enter the Ka'ba, or Sacred Shrine, and destroy the pagan idols - said to number 350 - housed in it, and to institute the rite of pilgrimage to this Sacred Shrine, which Abraham was said to have founded centuries earlier.

The Qur'an has defined clearly the relation of Muslims to other religious communities of the Near East, notably the Sabians, Christians and Jews. The Sabians (Sabi'ah) were recognized as monotheists and, like Christians and Jews, were tolerated (Surah 5/73). However, infidels *(kafirun)* were not, and the Qur'an calls upon Muslims to fight them to the death, unless they embrace Islam. However, it does qualify this stipulation in a variety of ways, one of which is not to initiate aggression against them, "since God does not like the aggressors" (Surah 2/190); the other is toleration, since "there is no compulsion in religion" (Surah 2/257), and the third is "gracious pardon or ransom", once they have been subdued (Surah 47/4).

As People of the Book, Jews and Christians are accorded a special and privileged status in the Qur'an, because "they believe in God and the Last Day" (Surah 2/62), and although accused of having corrupted their scriptures, the Qur'an abounds in references to the Old Testament figures, including Abraham, Isaac, Moses, Jacob, Job and Lot, as well as New Testament figures, including Mary, John (the Baptist), Jesus, son of Mary, and many others. The miracles of Christ are given in full, and, in fact, the Qur'an attributes to Christ a number of other miracles which are not mentioned in the canonical Gospels, but are referred to in the Apocrypha. In addition, a large number of biblical narratives are given in the Qur'an, not for their historical interest but rather for their spiritual or moral interest; they are often intended to illustrate the justice of God's ways and His sovereignty in the world, and to underscore the trials and tribulations to which His prophets or messengers have been subjected throughout history. Those prophets or messengers are said to have been continually shunned or rebuffed, but were never abandoned by God, the Merciful and Compassionate. Muhammad (ﷺ), the last or "seal" of the prophets, was not spared his own share of tribulation, and he is proclaimed as the carrier of the same message of warning or good tidings *(nadhir or bashir)*, which all his predecessors have carried to their own peoples, and which Muhammad (ﷺ) was now summoned by God to revive or confirm.

In addition to the text of the Qur'an itself, a vast exegetical literature grew around it over the years and formed part of an independent science, that of *tafsir*, which together with the science of *hadith*, or Prophetic Traditions, is regarded as the cornerstone of what are known as religious sciences in Islam. The greatest classical commentaries of the Qur'an are those of al-Tabari (d. 923), al-Zamakhshari (d. 1143) and al-Baydawi (d. 1286), to which countless commentaries by modern or contemporary scholars, such as Muhammad 'Abduh (d. 1905) and Sayyid Qutb (d. 1966), may be added.

One of the most widely read books in the world, the Qur'an has been translated into almost all the languages of mankind. A large number of English translations have appeared in modern times, the best known of which are those of J. M. Rodwell, Marmeduke Pickthall, N. J. Dawood, Richard Bell and A. J. Arberry. These translations vary in point of conformity to the Arabic text and are not entirely free from error or deliberate departure from the original, for purposes of literary fluency or elegance. In the present translation in this bilingual edition, we have attempted to give as faithful an English rendering of the Arabic text as possible and to correct the errors or lapses of the above-mentioned translations, while acknowledging that we have profited from some. We have also tried to express ourselves in a simple, readable English idiom. For purposes of accuracy, we have often had to rely on the most authoritative commentaries, especially where the meaning of the text was either obscure or controversial, as the notes will show. These notes are intended to be purely explanatory and have for that reason been kept to a minimum.

In closing, I wish to acknowledge the contribution of my friend and colleague, the late Dr Mahmud Zayid, with whom I worked very closely up to his untimely death. Throughout the early part of the work we constantly exchanged notes, and many of his suggestions or corrections were actually embodied in the final version of the translation. Regrettably, however, Providence decreed that our co-operation be cut short; but I would like this translation to be regarded, none the less, as a joint endeavour, because of the way in which the original project was launched and the mutual understanding we reached in the early stages of the work on questions of procedure, style and classical sources or commentaries to be consulted.

MAJID FAKHRY
June 2000
Washington, DC

Sûrat Al-Fâtihah[1],
(The Opening) 1

1. In the Name of Allah, the Compassionate, the Merciful[2]

2. Praise be to Allah, the Lord of the Worlds,[3]

3. The Compassionate, the Merciful,

4. Master of the Day of Judgement,

5. Only You do we worship, and only You do we implore for help.

6. Lead us to the right path,

7. The path of those You have favoured Not those who have incurred Your wrath or have gone astray.

---

1.   That is, the opening section or chapter of the Qur'an. It has various other names including Umm al-Kitab or the Quintessence of the Book and the Chapter of Prayer, because it is repeated in every one of the five daily prayers. It is also recited on many important occasions.

2.   This verse is one of the most recurrent verses in the Qur'an. Muslims recite it at the commencement of their daily activities.

3.   That is, the whole of creation.

Sûrat Al-Baqarah, (The Cow) 2

In the Name of Allah, the Compassionate, the Merciful

1. Alif, Lam, Mim.[4]

2. This is the Book which cannot be doubted and is a guidance to the God-fearing,

3. Those who believe in the Unseen, perform the prayer and give freely from what We provided for them,

4. And who believe in what was revealed to you and was revealed before you and firmly believe in the life to come.

5. Those are guided by their Lord, and those are the prosperous.

6. Those who have disbelieved, whether you warn them or not, they will not believe.

7. Allah has sealed their hearts and their hearing; their sight is dimmed and a terrible punishment awaits them.

8. There are some who say: "We believe in Allah and the Last Day;" but they are not real believers.

9. They seek to deceive Allah and the believers, but they deceive none other than themselves, though they are not aware of that.

10. In their hearts is a sickness; so Allah has increased their sickness. A painful punishment awaits them because of their lying.

11. And when they are told: "Do not sow mischief in the land", they say: "We are only doing good."

---

4. Those 'abbreviated letters' which preface some, but not all the surahs of the Qur'an are believed by some scholars to be the secret symbols or indices with which the Angel Gabriel (Jibril) opened the revelation of the surahs in question. They often mark the beginning of one surah and the end of another.

12. It is they who make mischief, but they are unaware of that.

13. And when they are told: "Believe as the others have believed", they say: "Shall we believe as the fools[5] have believed?" It is they who are the fools, though they do not know it.

14. And when they meet the believers, they say: "We believe", but when they are alone with their devils[6] they say: "We are with you;[7] we were only mocking."

15. Allah mocks them and gives them the latitude to wander aimlessly in their intransigence.[8]

16. Those are the people who traded away guidance for error; but their trade made no gains and they have not found the right way.

17. They are like one who kindled a fire, but when it lit all around him, Allah took away their light and left them in total darkness unable to see;

18. Deaf, dumb, blind; they shall never return.[9]

19. Or like those who in the midst of a cloudburst from the sky accompanied by darkness, thunder and lightning put their fingers in their ears to guard against thunderbolts for fear of death. And Allah encompasses[10] the disbelievers.

20. The lightning almost takes away their sight; when it flashes they walk on, but when it darkens they stand still. If Allah had willed, He would have taken away their hearing and sight. Surely Allah has power over all things.

أَلَا إِنَّهُمْ هُمُ ٱلْمُفْسِدُونَ وَلَٰكِن لَّا يَشْعُرُونَ ﴿١٢﴾

وَإِذَا قِيلَ لَهُمْ ءَامِنُوا كَمَا ءَامَنَ ٱلنَّاسُ قَالُوٓا أَنُؤْمِنُ كَمَآ ءَامَنَ ٱلسُّفَهَآءُ أَلَآ إِنَّهُمْ هُمُ ٱلسُّفَهَآءُ وَلَٰكِن لَّا يَعْلَمُونَ ﴿١٣﴾

وَإِذَا لَقُوا ٱلَّذِينَ ءَامَنُوا قَالُوٓا ءَامَنَّا وَإِذَا خَلَوْا إِلَىٰ شَيَٰطِينِهِمْ قَالُوٓا إِنَّا مَعَكُمْ إِنَّمَا نَحْنُ مُسْتَهْزِءُونَ ﴿١٤﴾

ٱللَّهُ يَسْتَهْزِئُ بِهِمْ وَيَمُدُّهُمْ فِي طُغْيَٰنِهِمْ يَعْمَهُونَ ﴿١٥﴾

أُوْلَٰٓئِكَ ٱلَّذِينَ ٱشْتَرَوُا ٱلضَّلَٰلَةَ بِٱلْهُدَىٰ فَمَا رَبِحَت تِّجَٰرَتُهُمْ وَمَا كَانُوا مُهْتَدِينَ ﴿١٦﴾

مَثَلُهُمْ كَمَثَلِ ٱلَّذِي ٱسْتَوْقَدَ نَارًا فَلَمَّآ أَضَآءَتْ مَا حَوْلَهُ ذَهَبَ ٱللَّهُ بِنُورِهِمْ وَتَرَكَهُمْ فِي ظُلُمَٰتٍ لَّا يُبْصِرُونَ ﴿١٧﴾

صُمٌّ بُكْمٌ عُمْيٌ فَهُمْ لَا يَرْجِعُونَ ﴿١٨﴾

أَوْ كَصَيِّبٍ مِّنَ ٱلسَّمَآءِ فِيهِ ظُلُمَٰتٌ وَرَعْدٌ وَبَرْقٌ يَجْعَلُونَ أَصَٰبِعَهُمْ فِيٓ ءَاذَانِهِم مِّنَ ٱلصَّوَٰعِقِ حَذَرَ ٱلْمَوْتِ وَٱللَّهُ مُحِيطٌ بِٱلْكَٰفِرِينَ ﴿١٩﴾

يَكَادُ ٱلْبَرْقُ يَخْطَفُ أَبْصَٰرَهُمْ كُلَّمَآ أَضَآءَ لَهُم مَّشَوْا فِيهِ وَإِذَآ أَظْلَمَ عَلَيْهِمْ قَامُوا وَلَوْ شَآءَ ٱللَّهُ لَذَهَبَ بِسَمْعِهِمْ وَأَبْصَٰرِهِمْ إِنَّ ٱللَّهَ عَلَىٰ كُلِّ شَيْءٍ قَدِيرٌ ﴿٢٠﴾

---

5. The ignorant.
6. Their chiefs.
7. We are your co-religionists.
8. Disbelief.
9. Return to the right path.
10. Surpasses them in knowledge and power.

21. O people,[11] worship your Lord who has created you as well as those who came before you so that you may guard against evil;

يَٰٓأَيُّهَا ٱلنَّاسُ ٱعْبُدُوا۟ رَبَّكُمُ ٱلَّذِى خَلَقَكُمْ وَٱلَّذِينَ مِن قَبْلِكُمْ لَعَلَّكُمْ تَتَّقُونَ ﴿٢١﴾

22. Who[12] has made the earth a couch for you, and the heavens a canopy, and Who sent down water from the sky, bringing forth by it a variety of fruits as a provision for you. Therefore do not knowingly set up equals to Allah.[13]

ٱلَّذِى جَعَلَ لَكُمُ ٱلْأَرْضَ فِرَٰشًا وَٱلسَّمَآءَ بِنَآءً وَأَنزَلَ مِنَ ٱلسَّمَآءِ مَآءً فَأَخْرَجَ بِهِۦ مِنَ ٱلثَّمَرَٰتِ رِزْقًا لَّكُمْ فَلَا تَجْعَلُوا۟ لِلَّهِ أَندَادًا وَأَنتُمْ تَعْلَمُونَ ﴿٢٢﴾

23. If you are in doubt as to what We have revealed to Our Servant,[14] then produce a surah similar to it and call upon your witnesses other than Allah,[15] if you are truthful.

وَإِن كُنتُمْ فِى رَيْبٍ مِّمَّا نَزَّلْنَا عَلَىٰ عَبْدِنَا فَأْتُوا۟ بِسُورَةٍ مِّن مِّثْلِهِۦ وَٱدْعُوا۟ شُهَدَآءَكُم مِّن دُونِ ٱللَّهِ إِن كُنتُمْ صَٰدِقِينَ ﴿٢٣﴾

24. If you do not do that, and surely you will not, then guard yourselves against the Fire whose fuel is men and stones, prepared for the unbelievers.

فَإِن لَّمْ تَفْعَلُوا۟ وَلَن تَفْعَلُوا۟ فَٱتَّقُوا۟ ٱلنَّارَ ٱلَّتِى وَقُودُهَا ٱلنَّاسُ وَٱلْحِجَارَةُ أُعِدَّتْ لِلْكَٰفِرِينَ ﴿٢٤﴾

25. Proclaim the good news to those who have believed and have done the good works; they will have gardens under which rivers flow.[16] Every time they get some of the fruits with which they are provided, they will say: "This is what we were provided with before", because they are given each time something that looks like it. They will also have their pure spouses[17] there, and they shall live there forever.

وَبَشِّرِ ٱلَّذِينَ ءَامَنُوا۟ وَعَمِلُوا۟ ٱلصَّٰلِحَٰتِ أَنَّ لَهُمْ جَنَّٰتٍ تَجْرِى مِن تَحْتِهَا ٱلْأَنْهَٰرُ كُلَّمَا رُزِقُوا۟ مِنْهَا مِن ثَمَرَةٍ رِزْقًا قَالُوا۟ هَٰذَا ٱلَّذِى رُزِقْنَا مِن قَبْلُ وَأُتُوا۟ بِهِۦ مُتَشَٰبِهًا وَلَهُمْ فِيهَآ أَزْوَٰجٌ مُّطَهَّرَةٌ وَهُمْ فِيهَا خَٰلِدُونَ ﴿٢٥﴾

26. Surely Allah does not disdain to give as a parable an insect or something bigger. Those

إِنَّ ٱللَّهَ لَا يَسْتَحْىِۦٓ أَن يَضْرِبَ مَثَلًا مَّا بَعُوضَةً فَمَا

---

11.   People of Mecca.
12.   Your Lord.
13.   That is, worship none besides Allah.
14.   The Prophet Muhammad.
15.   That is, the gods you associate with Allah.
16.   That is, rivers flow under its trees and structures.
17.   Spouses who are subject to no impurity.

who have believed know that it is the Truth from their Lord; but those who have disbelieved say: "What does Allah mean by this parable?" By it, He leaves many in error, and guides well many others. And by it, he leaves in error only the sinners.[18]

27. Those who break Allah's Covenant after its confirmation and sever what Allah ordered to be joined, and make mischief[19] in the land - those are the losers.

28. How can you[20] disbelieve in Allah? You were dead[21] and He brought you back to life;[22] then He will cause you to die and then bring you back to life again; then unto Him you will return.

29. It is He Who created for you everything on earth, then ascended to the heavens fashioning them into seven, and He has knowledge of all things.

30. When your Lord said to the angels: "I am placing a deputy on earth", they said: "Will you place one who will make mischief in it and shed blood, while we sing Your praise and glorify Your sanctity?" He said: "I know what you do not know."

31. And He taught Adam all the names. Then He laid them before the angels. He said: "Tell me the names of these if you are truthful."

32. They said: "Glory be to You; we have no knowledge other than what You taught us. You are the All-Knowing, the Wise."

33. He said: "O Adam, tell them their names." When Adam told them their names

---

18. Those who disobey Allah.
19. By committing sins and obstructing faith.
20. The Meccans.
21. Being a life-germ i.e. not living yet.
22. As a child.

9

He[23] said: "Did I not tell you that I know the unseen in the heavens and the earth, and that I know what you reveal and what you conceal?"

34. And when We said to the angels: "Prostrate yourselves before Adam", they all prostrated themselves except Iblis,[24] who refused, out of pride and was one of the disbelievers.

35. Then We said: "O Adam, dwell in Paradise, you and your wife, and eat from it as much as you wish and wherever you wish, but do not approach this tree[25] or you will both be unjust."[26]

36. But Satan caused them to fall down from it and be turned out of the bliss they had been in. And We said: "Go down,[27] being enemies one to the other. And you will have in the earth an abode and sustenance for a while."

37. Then Adam received words from his Lord, Who forgave him. He is indeed the All-Forgiving, the Merciful.

38. We said: "Go down from here[28] all of you. And when in time My Guidance is vouchsafed to you, those who follow My Guidance will have nothing to fear nor will they grieve."[29]

39. And [as to] those who have disbelieved and denied Our Revelations, they are the people of Hell, wherein they will dwell forever.

أَقُل لَّكُمْ إِنِّى أَعْلَمُ غَيْبَ ٱلسَّمَـٰوَٰتِ وَٱلْأَرْضِ وَأَعْلَمُ مَا تُبْدُونَ وَمَا كُنتُمْ تَكْتُمُونَ ۝

وَإِذْ قُلْنَا لِلْمَلَـٰٓئِكَةِ ٱسْجُدُوا۟ لِـَٔادَمَ فَسَجَدُوٓا۟ إِلَّآ إِبْلِيسَ أَبَىٰ وَٱسْتَكْبَرَ وَكَانَ مِنَ ٱلْكَـٰفِرِينَ ۝

وَقُلْنَا يَـٰٓـَٔادَمُ ٱسْكُنْ أَنتَ وَزَوْجُكَ ٱلْجَنَّةَ وَكُلَا مِنْهَا رَغَدًا حَيْثُ شِئْتُمَا وَلَا تَقْرَبَا هَـٰذِهِ ٱلشَّجَرَةَ فَتَكُونَا مِنَ ٱلظَّـٰلِمِينَ ۝

فَأَزَلَّهُمَا ٱلشَّيْطَـٰنُ عَنْهَا فَأَخْرَجَهُمَا مِمَّا كَانَا فِيهِ وَقُلْنَا ٱهْبِطُوا۟ بَعْضُكُمْ لِبَعْضٍ عَدُوٌّ وَلَكُمْ فِى ٱلْأَرْضِ مُسْتَقَرٌّ وَمَتَـٰعٌ إِلَىٰ حِينٍ ۝

فَتَلَقَّىٰ ءَادَمُ مِن رَّبِّهِۦ كَلِمَـٰتٍ فَتَابَ عَلَيْهِ إِنَّهُۥ هُوَ ٱلتَّوَّابُ ٱلرَّحِيمُ ۝

قُلْنَا ٱهْبِطُوا۟ مِنْهَا جَمِيعًا فَإِمَّا يَأْتِيَنَّكُم مِّنِّى هُدًى فَمَن تَبِعَ هُدَاىَ فَلَا خَوْفٌ عَلَيْهِمْ وَلَا هُمْ يَحْزَنُونَ ۝

وَٱلَّذِينَ كَفَرُوا۟ وَكَذَّبُوا۟ بِـَٔايَـٰتِنَا أُو۟لَـٰٓئِكَ أَصْحَـٰبُ ٱلنَّارِ هُمْ فِيهَا خَـٰلِدُونَ ۝

---

23. Allah.
24. Satan.
25. Meaning do not eat from it.
26. By being disobedient.
27. From Paradise to earth.
28. Paradise.
29. Because they will be admitted into Paradise.

40. O Children of Israel, remember the grace which I bestowed on you. Fulfil your covenant[30] and I shall fulfil My Covenant.[31] And Me alone you should fear.

41. Believe in what I have revealed confirming that which is with you[32] and do not be the first to deny it. Do not trade My Revelations for a small price; and Me Alone you should fear.

42. And do not confuse truth with falsehood and do not conceal the truth while you know it.

43. Perform the prayer; give the alms-tax and bow down with those who bow down.

44. Do you command others to be righteous and forget yourselves while you recite the Book? Do you not understand?

45. Seek assistance through patience and prayer. It is hard, except for the truly devout;

46. Who believe that they shall meet their Lord, and unto Him they shall return.

47. O Children of Israel, remember the grace which I bestowed on you, and that I preferred you to all the nations.[33]

48. And guard yourselves against the Day when no soul shall avail any other soul and no intercession will be accepted from it, nor will a ransom be taken from it; and they will not be supported.

49. And [remember] how We saved you from Pharaoh's people who tormented you cruelly, slaying your children but sparing your women. Therein was a great trial from your Lord.

يَٰبَنِىٓ إِسۡرَٰٓءِيلَ ٱذۡكُرُواْ نِعۡمَتِىَ ٱلَّتِىٓ أَنۡعَمۡتُ عَلَيۡكُمۡ وَأَوۡفُواْ بِعَهۡدِىٓ أُوفِ بِعَهۡدِكُمۡ وَإِيَّٰىَ فَٱرۡهَبُونِ ۝

وَءَامِنُواْ بِمَآ أَنزَلۡتُ مُصَدِّقًا لِّمَا مَعَكُمۡ وَلَا تَكُونُوٓاْ أَوَّلَ كَافِرِۭ بِهِۦ وَلَا تَشۡتَرُواْ بِـَٔايَٰتِى ثَمَنًا قَلِيلًا وَإِيَّٰىَ فَٱتَّقُونِ ۝

وَلَا تَلۡبِسُواْ ٱلۡحَقَّ بِٱلۡبَٰطِلِ وَتَكۡتُمُواْ ٱلۡحَقَّ وَأَنتُمۡ تَعۡلَمُونَ ۝

وَأَقِيمُواْ ٱلصَّلَوٰةَ وَءَاتُواْ ٱلزَّكَوٰةَ وَٱرۡكَعُواْ مَعَ ٱلرَّٰكِعِينَ ۝

أَتَأۡمُرُونَ ٱلنَّاسَ بِٱلۡبِرِّ وَتَنسَوۡنَ أَنفُسَكُمۡ وَأَنتُمۡ تَتۡلُونَ ٱلۡكِتَٰبَ أَفَلَا تَعۡقِلُونَ ۝

وَٱسۡتَعِينُواْ بِٱلصَّبۡرِ وَٱلصَّلَوٰةِ وَإِنَّهَا لَكَبِيرَةٌ إِلَّا عَلَى ٱلۡخَٰشِعِينَ ۝

ٱلَّذِينَ يَظُنُّونَ أَنَّهُم مُّلَٰقُواْ رَبِّهِمۡ وَأَنَّهُمۡ إِلَيۡهِ رَٰجِعُونَ ۝

يَٰبَنِىٓ إِسۡرَٰٓءِيلَ ٱذۡكُرُواْ نِعۡمَتِىَ ٱلَّتِىٓ أَنۡعَمۡتُ عَلَيۡكُمۡ وَأَنِّى فَضَّلۡتُكُمۡ عَلَى ٱلۡعَٰلَمِينَ ۝

وَٱتَّقُواْ يَوۡمًا لَّا تَجۡزِى نَفۡسٌ عَن نَّفۡسٍ شَيۡـًٔا وَلَا يُقۡبَلُ مِنۡهَا شَفَٰعَةٌ وَلَا يُؤۡخَذُ مِنۡهَا عَدۡلٌ وَلَا هُمۡ يُنصَرُونَ ۝

وَإِذۡ نَجَّيۡنَٰكُم مِّنۡ ءَالِ فِرۡعَوۡنَ يَسُومُونَكُمۡ سُوٓءَ ٱلۡعَذَابِ يُذَبِّحُونَ أَبۡنَآءَكُمۡ وَيَسۡتَحۡيُونَ نِسَآءَكُمۡ وَفِى ذَٰلِكُم بَلَآءٌ مِّن رَّبِّكُمۡ عَظِيمٌ ۝

---

30. By believing that Muhammad is the Messenger of Allah.
31. By rewarding them.
32. Confirming your Scriptures.
33. The nations which were contemporaneous with the Israelites in their days of triumph.

50. And [remember] how for your sake, We split the sea, rescued you and drowned the people of Pharaoh while you were watching.

وَإِذْ فَرَقْنَا بِكُمُ ٱلْبَحْرَ فَأَنجَيْنَكُمْ وَأَغْرَقْنَا ءَالَ فِرْعَوْنَ وَأَنتُمْ تَنظُرُونَ ۝

51. And [remember] how We promised Moses forty nights;[34] and you took the calf[35] after him, thus becoming evil-doers.

وَإِذْ وَٰعَدْنَا مُوسَىٰٓ أَرْبَعِينَ لَيْلَةً ثُمَّ ٱتَّخَذْتُمُ ٱلْعِجْلَ مِنۢ بَعْدِهِۦ وَأَنتُمْ ظَٰلِمُونَ ۝

52. But We pardoned you after that, so that you might give thanks.

ثُمَّ عَفَوْنَا عَنكُم مِّنۢ بَعْدِ ذَٰلِكَ لَعَلَّكُمْ تَشْكُرُونَ ۝

53. And when We gave Moses the Book and the Criterion[36] so that you might be well-guided.

وَإِذْ ءَاتَيْنَا مُوسَى ٱلْكِتَٰبَ وَٱلْفُرْقَانَ لَعَلَّكُمْ تَهْتَدُونَ ۝

54. When Moses said to his people: "My people, you have wronged yourselves by taking the calf [as god]. Repent to your Creator. Kill yourselves;[37] that would be better for you in the sight of your Creator." Then He forgave you. He is the All-Forgiving, the Merciful.

وَإِذْ قَالَ مُوسَىٰ لِقَوْمِهِۦ يَٰقَوْمِ إِنَّكُمْ ظَلَمْتُمْ أَنفُسَكُم بِٱتِّخَاذِكُمُ ٱلْعِجْلَ فَتُوبُوٓا۟ إِلَىٰ بَارِئِكُمْ فَٱقْتُلُوٓا۟ أَنفُسَكُمْ ذَٰلِكُمْ خَيْرٌ لَّكُمْ عِندَ بَارِئِكُمْ فَتَابَ عَلَيْكُمْ إِنَّهُۥ هُوَ ٱلتَّوَّابُ ٱلرَّحِيمُ ۝

55. And when you said: "O Moses, we will not believe in you until we see Allah with our own eyes", whereupon you were struck by a thunderbolt while you looked on.

وَإِذْ قُلْتُمْ يَٰمُوسَىٰ لَن نُّؤْمِنَ لَكَ حَتَّىٰ نَرَى ٱللَّهَ جَهْرَةً فَأَخَذَتْكُمُ ٱلصَّٰعِقَةُ وَأَنتُمْ تَنظُرُونَ ۝

56. Then We raised you up after you had died, so that you might give thanks.

ثُمَّ بَعَثْنَٰكُم مِّنۢ بَعْدِ مَوْتِكُمْ لَعَلَّكُمْ تَشْكُرُونَ ۝

57. And We caused the clouds to over-shadow you and sent to you manna and quails [saying]: "Eat from the good things We have provided for you." They did not wrong Us; they only wronged themselves.

وَظَلَّلْنَا عَلَيْكُمُ ٱلْغَمَامَ وَأَنزَلْنَا عَلَيْكُمُ ٱلْمَنَّ وَٱلسَّلْوَىٰ كُلُوا۟ مِن طَيِّبَٰتِ مَا رَزَقْنَٰكُمْ وَمَا ظَلَمُونَا وَلَٰكِن كَانُوٓا۟ أَنفُسَهُمْ يَظْلِمُونَ ۝

58. And when We said: "Enter this city[38] and eat wherever you wish from its abundant

وَإِذْ قُلْنَا ٱدْخُلُوا۟ هَٰذِهِ ٱلْقَرْيَةَ فَكُلُوا۟ مِنْهَا حَيْثُ شِئْتُمْ

---

34. At the end of which Moses was to receive the Scriptures.
35. As god and worshipped it.
36. *"Al-Furqan"* which distinguishes right from wrong.
37. Let the innocent kill the evil-doer.
38. Jerusalem or Jericho.

provision", and enter the gate while bowing and say: "Forgiveness." We will [then] forgive you your sins and increase the reward of the righteous.

59. The evil-doers changed what was said to them into something else; and We sent down upon the evil-doers a plague from heaven as a punishment for their transgression.

60. And when Moses prayed for water for his people, We said: "Strike the rock with your staff." Thereupon twelve springs gushed out from it, and each tribe recognized its water trough. [We said:] "Eat and drink from Allah's provision and do not make mischief in the land."

61. And when you said: "O Moses, we will not put up with one kind of food; so pray to your Lord to bring forth for us some of what the earth produces: green herbs, cucumbers, corn, lentils and onions." He said: "Would you exchange that which is better for that which is worse? Come down to Egypt where you will get what you asked for." Humiliation and abasement were inflicted on them and they incurred Allah's wrath. That was because they disbelieved in Allah's Revelations and unjustly killed the Prophets, thus committing disobedience and aggression.

62. The believers,[39] the Jews, the Christians and the Sabians - whoever believes in Allah and the Last Day and does what is good, shall receive their reward from their Lord. They shall have nothing to fear and they shall not grieve.

---

39. The Muslims.

63. And when We made a covenant with you and raised the mountain above you [saying]: "Take what We have given you earnestly and keep in mind what is in it so that you might guard yourselves against evil."

وَإِذْ أَخَذْنَا مِيثَـٰقَكُمْ وَرَفَعْنَا فَوْقَكُمُ ٱلطُّورَ خُذُوا مَا ءَاتَيْنَـٰكُم بِقُوَّةٍ وَٱذْكُرُوا مَا فِيهِ لَعَلَّكُمْ تَتَّقُونَ ٦٣

64. But after that you turned away; and had it not been for Allah's Grace and His Mercy on you, you would surely have been among the losers.

ثُمَّ تَوَلَّيْتُم مِّنْ بَعْدِ ذَٰلِكَ فَلَوْلَا فَضْلُ ٱللَّهِ عَلَيْكُمْ وَرَحْمَتُهُ لَكُنتُم مِّنَ ٱلْخَـٰسِرِينَ ٦٤

65. And you surely know those of you who violated the Sabbath; We said to them:""Be [like] dejected apes."

وَلَقَدْ عَلِمْتُمُ ٱلَّذِينَ ٱعْتَدَوْا۟ مِنكُمْ فِى ٱلسَّبْتِ فَقُلْنَا لَهُمْ كُونُوا۟ قِرَدَةً خَـٰسِئِينَ ٦٥

66. Thus We made that an example to their contemporaries and to those after them, and an admonition to the righteous.

فَجَعَلْنَـٰهَا نَكَـٰلًا لِّمَا بَيْنَ يَدَيْهَا وَمَا خَلْفَهَا وَمَوْعِظَةً لِّلْمُتَّقِينَ ٦٦

67. And when Moses said to his people: "Allah commands you to sacrifice a cow", they replied: "Do you make a mockery of us?" He said: "God forbid that I be one of the ignorant."[40]

وَإِذْ قَالَ مُوسَىٰ لِقَوْمِهِ إِنَّ ٱللَّهَ يَأْمُرُكُمْ أَن تَذْبَحُوا۟ بَقَرَةً قَالُوٓا۟ أَتَتَّخِذُنَا هُزُوًا قَالَ أَعُوذُ بِٱللَّهِ أَنْ أَكُونَ مِنَ ٱلْجَـٰهِلِينَ ٦٧

68. They said: "Call on your Lord to explain to us what [cow] it is." He replied: "He[41] says: 'Let it be neither too old nor too young, but in between.' Therefore, do what you are commanded to do."

قَالُوا۟ ٱدْعُ لَنَا رَبَّكَ يُبَيِّن لَّنَا مَا هِىَ قَالَ إِنَّهُ يَقُولُ إِنَّهَا بَقَرَةٌ لَّا فَارِضٌ وَلَا بِكْرٌ عَوَانٌ بَيْنَ ذَٰلِكَ فَٱفْعَلُوا۟ مَا تُؤْمَرُونَ ٦٨

69. They said: "Call on your Lord to tell us what its colour should be." He replied: "He says: 'Let it be a yellow cow which has a striking colour and which pleases the beholders.' "

قَالُوا۟ ٱدْعُ لَنَا رَبَّكَ يُبَيِّن لَّنَا مَا لَوْنُهَا قَالَ إِنَّهُ يَقُولُ إِنَّهَا بَقَرَةٌ صَفْرَآءُ فَاقِعٌ لَّوْنُهَا تَسُرُّ ٱلنَّـٰظِرِينَ ٦٩

70. They said: "Call on your Lord to tell us what it[42] is; for to us all cows seem to be alike. Thus if Allah wills, we will be rightly guided."

قَالُوا۟ ٱدْعُ لَنَا رَبَّكَ يُبَيِّن لَّنَا مَا هِىَ إِنَّ ٱلْبَقَرَ تَشَـٰبَهَ عَلَيْنَا وَإِنَّآ إِن شَآءَ ٱللَّهُ لَمُهْتَدُونَ ٧٠

---

40. That is, one of the mocking people.
41. Allah.
42. The cow.

71. He said: "He says:[43] 'It is a cow which is neither harnessed to plough the land nor to water the field, but rather sound with no blemish.' " Then they said: "Now you speak the truth." Thereupon they slaughtered it after they had been reluctant to do so.

قَالَ إِنَّهُ يَقُولُ إِنَّهَا بَقَرَةٌ لَّا ذَلُولٌ تُثِيرُ ٱلْأَرْضَ وَلَا تَسْقِى ٱلْحَرْثَ مُسَلَّمَةٌ لَّا شِيَةَ فِيهَا قَالُوا۟ ٱلْـَٔنَ جِئْتَ بِٱلْحَقِّ فَذَبَحُوهَا وَمَا كَادُوا۟ يَفْعَلُونَ ۝

72. And when you slew a man and fell out among yourselves regarding him, Allah brought forth to light what you had concealed.

وَإِذْ قَتَلْتُمْ نَفْسًا فَٱدَّٰرَٰءْتُمْ فِيهَا وَٱللَّهُ مُخْرِجٌ مَّا كُنتُمْ تَكْتُمُونَ ۝

73. We said: "Strike him with a part of it."[44] Thus Allah brings the dead to life, and shows you His Signs so that you may understand.

فَقُلْنَا ٱضْرِبُوهُ بِبَعْضِهَا كَذَٰلِكَ يُحْىِ ٱللَّهُ ٱلْمَوْتَىٰ وَيُرِيكُمْ ءَايَٰتِهِ لَعَلَّكُمْ تَعْقِلُونَ ۝

74. Then your hearts became as hard as stone or harder; for there are stones from which rivers flow, and others which splinter and water comes out from them, and others which tumble down for fear of Allah. Allah is surely not unaware of what you do.

ثُمَّ قَسَتْ قُلُوبُكُم مِّنۢ بَعْدِ ذَٰلِكَ فَهِىَ كَٱلْحِجَارَةِ أَوْ أَشَدُّ قَسْوَةً وَإِنَّ مِنَ ٱلْحِجَارَةِ لَمَا يَتَفَجَّرُ مِنْهُ ٱلْأَنْهَٰرُ وَإِنَّ مِنْهَا لَمَا يَشَّقَّقُ فَيَخْرُجُ مِنْهُ ٱلْمَآءُ وَإِنَّ مِنْهَا لَمَا يَهْبِطُ مِنْ خَشْيَةِ ٱللَّهِ وَمَا ٱللَّهُ بِغَٰفِلٍ عَمَّا تَعْمَلُونَ ۝

75. Do you then hope that they will believe in you when a group of them[45] did hear the Word of Allah, then after they understood it, they knowingly perverted it?

أَفَتَطْمَعُونَ أَن يُؤْمِنُوا۟ لَكُمْ وَقَدْ كَانَ فَرِيقٌ مِّنْهُمْ يَسْمَعُونَ كَلَٰمَ ٱللَّهِ ثُمَّ يُحَرِّفُونَهُۥ مِنۢ بَعْدِ مَا عَقَلُوهُ وَهُمْ يَعْلَمُونَ ۝

76. And when they meet those who have believed they say: "We believe," but when they come together privately, they say: "Will you tell them what Allah has revealed to you[46] so that they might dispute with you concerning it before your Lord? Have you no sense?"

وَإِذَا لَقُوا۟ ٱلَّذِينَ ءَامَنُوا۟ قَالُوٓا۟ ءَامَنَّا وَإِذَا خَلَا بَعْضُهُمْ إِلَىٰ بَعْضٍ قَالُوٓا۟ أَتُحَدِّثُونَهُم بِمَا فَتَحَ ٱللَّهُ عَلَيْكُمْ لِيُحَآجُّوكُم بِهِۦ عِندَ رَبِّكُمْ أَفَلَا تَعْقِلُونَ ۝

77. Do they not know that Allah knows what they conceal and what they reveal?

أَوَلَا يَعْلَمُونَ أَنَّ ٱللَّهَ يَعْلَمُ مَا يُسِرُّونَ وَمَا يُعْلِنُونَ ۝

---

43. Allah.
44. The cow. This could be its tongue or the end of its tail.
45. The Jews.
46. Revealed to you about Muhammad.

78. Among them are illiterate people who know nothing of the Book[47] except illusory desires. Indeed, they are only conjecturing.

وَمِنْهُمْ أُمِّيُّونَ لَا يَعْلَمُونَ ٱلْكِتَٰبَ إِلَّآ أَمَانِيَّ وَإِنْ هُمْ إِلَّا يَظُنُّونَ ۝

79. Woe unto those who write the Book with their hands, then say that it is from Allah in order to sell it for a small price. Woe unto them for what their hands have written, and woe unto them for what they have earned.

فَوَيْلٌ لِّلَّذِينَ يَكْتُبُونَ ٱلْكِتَٰبَ بِأَيْدِيهِمْ ثُمَّ يَقُولُونَ هَٰذَا مِنْ عِندِ ٱللَّهِ لِيَشْتَرُوا۟ بِهِۦ ثَمَنًا قَلِيلًا فَوَيْلٌ لَّهُم مِّمَّا كَتَبَتْ أَيْدِيهِمْ وَوَيْلٌ لَّهُم مِّمَّا يَكْسِبُونَ ۝

80. And they say: "The Fire will only touch us for a few days." Say: "Have you received a pledge from Allah, and Allah does not revoke His Pledge, or are you imputing to Allah what you do not know?"

وَقَالُوا۟ لَن تَمَسَّنَا ٱلنَّارُ إِلَّآ أَيَّامًا مَّعْدُودَةً قُلْ أَتَّخَذْتُمْ عِندَ ٱللَّهِ عَهْدًا فَلَن يُخْلِفَ ٱللَّهُ عَهْدَهُۥٓ أَمْ تَقُولُونَ عَلَى ٱللَّهِ مَا لَا تَعْلَمُونَ ۝

81. Indeed, whoever commits a sin and his sin takes complete hold of him is one of the people of Hell, wherein they will dwell forever.

بَلَىٰ مَن كَسَبَ سَيِّئَةً وَأَحَٰطَتْ بِهِۦ خَطِيٓـَٔتُهُۥ فَأُو۟لَٰٓئِكَ أَصْحَٰبُ ٱلنَّارِ هُمْ فِيهَا خَٰلِدُونَ ۝

82. Those who believe and do good works are the people of Paradise, where they will dwell forever.

وَٱلَّذِينَ ءَامَنُوا۟ وَعَمِلُوا۟ ٱلصَّٰلِحَٰتِ أُو۟لَٰٓئِكَ أَصْحَٰبُ ٱلْجَنَّةِ هُمْ فِيهَا خَٰلِدُونَ ۝

83. When We made a covenant with the Children of Israel (saying): "You shall worship none other than Allah; show kindness to your parents, to the near of kin, to the orphans and to the poor; speak to people; perform the prayers, give the alms-tax." But, with the exception of a few, you did not abide by the covenant and you turned away.

وَإِذْ أَخَذْنَا مِيثَٰقَ بَنِىٓ إِسْرَٰٓءِيلَ لَا تَعْبُدُونَ إِلَّا ٱللَّهَ وَبِٱلْوَٰلِدَيْنِ إِحْسَانًا وَذِى ٱلْقُرْبَىٰ وَٱلْيَتَٰمَىٰ وَٱلْمَسَٰكِينِ وَقُولُوا۟ لِلنَّاسِ حُسْنًا وَأَقِيمُوا۟ ٱلصَّلَوٰةَ وَءَاتُوا۟ ٱلزَّكَوٰةَ ثُمَّ تَوَلَّيْتُمْ إِلَّا قَلِيلًا مِّنكُمْ وَأَنتُم مُّعْرِضُونَ ۝

84. And when We made a covenant with you (saying): "You shall not shed your own blood, nor drive your people away from their homes", you accepted and you bore witness [thereto].

وَإِذْ أَخَذْنَا مِيثَٰقَكُمْ لَا تَسْفِكُونَ دِمَآءَكُمْ وَلَا تُخْرِجُونَ أَنفُسَكُم مِّن دِيَٰرِكُمْ ثُمَّ أَقْرَرْتُمْ وَأَنتُمْ تَشْهَدُونَ ۝

85. Yet there you are killing each other and turning some of your folk from their homes, making common cause against them with sin

ثُمَّ أَنتُمْ هَٰٓؤُلَآءِ تَقْتُلُونَ أَنفُسَكُمْ وَتُخْرِجُونَ فَرِيقًا مِّنكُم مِّن دِيَٰرِهِمْ تَظَٰهَرُونَ عَلَيْهِم بِٱلْإِثْمِ وَٱلْعُدْوَٰنِ

---

47. The Scriptures.

and aggression. But should they come to you as captives you would ransom them. Surely it was unlawful for you to drive them away. Do you, then, believe in one part[48] of the Book and disbelieve in another?[49] The reward of those among you who do that is nothing but disgrace in this world, and on the Day of Resurrection they shall be turned over to the most severe punishment. Allah is not unaware of what you do.

86. Those are the people who have traded the life of this world for the Hereafter. Their punishment shall not be lightened, nor shall they be helped.

87. We have indeed given Moses the Book, and after him We sent one Messenger after another. We also gave Jesus, son of Mary, clear signs[50] and strengthened him with the Holy Spirit. Do you, then, whenever a Messenger brings you what you do not desire, become puffed up with pride accusing some [of them] of lying and killing others?

88. They said: "Our hearts are sealed." Nay, Allah has cursed them on account of their unbelief; for they have very little faith.

89. And when a Book[51] came to them from Allah confirming that which they had,[52] and though they used hitherto to pray for assistance against those who disbelieved; yet when there came to them what they already knew,[53] they disbelieved in it. So may Allah's curse be on the unbelievers.

---

48. Paying the ransom.
49. Killing and driving away their people from their homes.
50. Miracles.
51. The Qur'an.
52. The Torah.
53. That Muhammad would be sent as the Messenger of Allah.

17

90. Evil is that for which they sold their souls when they disbelieved in what Allah sent down, out of envy that He should send down from His Bounty[54] on whomsoever of His servants He pleases. Thus they incurred wrath upon wrath. And there is a demeaning punishment for the unbelievers.

بِئْسَمَا ٱشْتَرَوْاْ بِهِۦٓ أَنفُسَهُمْ أَن يَكْفُرُواْ بِمَآ أَنزَلَ ٱللَّهُ بَغْيًا أَن يُنَزِّلَ ٱللَّهُ مِن فَضْلِهِۦ عَلَىٰ مَن يَشَآءُ مِنْ عِبَادِهِۦ فَبَآءُو بِغَضَبٍ عَلَىٰ غَضَبٍ وَلِلْكَٰفِرِينَ عَذَابٌ مُّهِينٌ ﴿٩٠﴾

91. And when it is said to them: "Believe in what Allah has revealed", they say: "We believe in what was revealed to us", denying thereby what has been revealed thereafter,[55] although it is the Truth which confirms what they have.[56] Say: "Why, then, did you kill Allah's Prophets in the past if you are true believers?"

وَإِذَا قِيلَ لَهُمْ ءَامِنُواْ بِمَآ أَنزَلَ ٱللَّهُ قَالُواْ نُؤْمِنُ بِمَآ أُنزِلَ عَلَيْنَا وَيَكْفُرُونَ بِمَا وَرَآءَهُۥ وَهُوَ ٱلْحَقُّ مُصَدِّقًا لِّمَا مَعَهُمْ قُلْ فَلِمَ تَقْتُلُونَ أَنۢبِيَآءَ ٱللَّهِ مِن قَبْلُ إِن كُنتُم مُّؤْمِنِينَ ﴿٩١﴾

92. Surely Moses came to you with clear signs;[57] then, in his absence you made of the calf a god, and thus you became evil-doers.

وَلَقَدْ جَآءَكُم مُّوسَىٰ بِٱلْبَيِّنَٰتِ ثُمَّ ٱتَّخَذْتُمُ ٱلْعِجْلَ مِنۢ بَعْدِهِۦ وَأَنتُمْ ظَٰلِمُونَ ﴿٩٢﴾

93. And [remember] when We made a covenant with you and raised the mountain over you saying: "Take what We have given you with earnestness and obey." They said: "We have heard. We disobeyed." They were made to imbibe the love of the calf into their hearts because of their unbelief. Say: "Evil is what your faith bid you, if you are true believers."[58]

وَإِذْ أَخَذْنَا مِيثَٰقَكُمْ وَرَفَعْنَا فَوْقَكُمُ ٱلطُّورَ خُذُواْ مَآ ءَاتَيْنَٰكُم بِقُوَّةٍ وَٱسْمَعُواْ قَالُواْ سَمِعْنَا وَعَصَيْنَا وَأُشْرِبُواْ فِى قُلُوبِهِمُ ٱلْعِجْلَ بِكُفْرِهِمْ قُلْ بِئْسَمَا يَأْمُرُكُم بِهِۦٓ إِيمَٰنُكُمْ إِن كُنتُم مُّؤْمِنِينَ ﴿٩٣﴾

94. Say: "If the abode of the Hereafter with Allah is for you alone to the exclusion of all other people, then wish for death if you are truthful."

قُلْ إِن كَانَتْ لَكُمُ ٱلدَّارُ ٱلْءَاخِرَةُ عِندَ ٱللَّهِ خَالِصَةً مِّن دُونِ ٱلنَّاسِ فَتَمَنَّوُاْ ٱلْمَوْتَ إِن كُنتُمْ صَٰدِقِينَ ﴿٩٤﴾

95. But they will never wish for it, because of what they did earlier. Allah knows well the evil-doers.[59]

وَلَن يَتَمَنَّوْهُ أَبَدًۢا بِمَا قَدَّمَتْ أَيْدِيهِمْ وَٱللَّهُ عَلِيمٌۢ بِٱلظَّٰلِمِينَ ﴿٩٥﴾

---

54. Reveal to them.
55. The Qur'an.
56. Their Scriptures.
57. Miracles.
58. The implication here is that they are not believers.
59. Hence the unbelievers.

96. Indeed you will find them of all people the most attached to life, even more attached than those who associated other gods with Allah. Every one of them wishes to live for one thousand years. This long life, however, will not spare them the punishment. And Allah sees what they do.

وَلَتَجِدَنَّهُمْ أَحْرَصَ النَّاسِ عَلَىٰ حَيَوٰةٍ وَمِنَ الَّذِينَ أَشْرَكُوا يَوَدُّ أَحَدُهُمْ لَوْ يُعَمَّرُ أَلْفَ سَنَةٍ وَمَا هُوَ بِمُزَحْزِحِهِ مِنَ الْعَذَابِ أَن يُعَمَّرَ وَاللَّهُ بَصِيرٌ بِمَا يَعْمَلُونَ ۝

97. Say: "Whoever is an enemy of Gabriel - it is he[60] who has instilled it[61] in your heart by Allah's Permission confirming what preceded it,[62] and as a guidance and good tidings to the believers.

قُلْ مَن كَانَ عَدُوًّا لِّجِبْرِيلَ فَإِنَّهُ نَزَّلَهُ عَلَىٰ قَلْبِكَ بِإِذْنِ اللَّهِ مُصَدِّقًا لِّمَا بَيْنَ يَدَيْهِ وَهُدًى وَبُشْرَىٰ لِلْمُؤْمِنِينَ ۝

98. Whoever is an enemy of Allah, His angels, His Messengers, Gabriel and Michael, surely Allah is the enemy of the unbelievers.

مَن كَانَ عَدُوًّا لِّلَّهِ وَمَلَائِكَتِهِ وَرُسُلِهِ وَجِبْرِيلَ وَمِيكَالَ فَإِنَّ اللَّهَ عَدُوٌّ لِّلْكَافِرِينَ ۝

99. Indeed, We have revealed to you clear Signs[63] in which only the wicked will disbelieve.

وَلَقَدْ أَنزَلْنَا إِلَيْكَ آيَاتٍ بَيِّنَاتٍ وَمَا يَكْفُرُ بِهَا إِلَّا الْفَاسِقُونَ ۝

100. Will it be that every time they make a covenant, a group of them will cast it aside? Indeed, most of them do not believe.

أَوَكُلَّمَا عَاهَدُوا عَهْدًا نَّبَذَهُ فَرِيقٌ مِّنْهُم بَلْ أَكْثَرُهُمْ لَا يُؤْمِنُونَ ۝

101. And when a Messenger came to them from Allah confirming what they had, a group of those who were given the Book[64] cast the Book[65] of Allah behind their backs, as if they knew nothing;

وَلَمَّا جَاءَهُمْ رَسُولٌ مِّنْ عِندِ اللَّهِ مُصَدِّقٌ لِّمَا مَعَهُمْ نَبَذَ فَرِيقٌ مِّنَ الَّذِينَ أُوتُوا الْكِتَابَ كِتَابَ اللَّهِ وَرَاءَ ظُهُورِهِمْ كَأَنَّهُمْ لَا يَعْلَمُونَ ۝

102. And they believed what the devils said about Solomon's kingdom. Not that Solomon disbelieved; but the devils did, teaching the people witchcraft and that which was revealed in Babylon to the two angels, Harut and Marut. Yet those two angels did not teach anybody without saying [to him]:

وَاتَّبَعُوا مَا تَتْلُو الشَّيَاطِينُ عَلَىٰ مُلْكِ سُلَيْمَانَ وَمَا كَفَرَ سُلَيْمَانُ وَلَٰكِنَّ الشَّيَاطِينَ كَفَرُوا يُعَلِّمُونَ النَّاسَ السِّحْرَ وَمَا أُنزِلَ عَلَى الْمَلَكَيْنِ بِبَابِلَ هَارُوتَ وَمَارُوتَ وَمَا يُعَلِّمَانِ مِنْ أَحَدٍ حَتَّىٰ يَقُولَا إِنَّمَا نَحْنُ فِتْنَةٌ فَلَا تَكْفُرْ فَيَتَعَلَّمُونَ مِنْهُمَا مَا يُفَرِّقُونَ بِهِ

---

60. Gabriel.
61. The revelation.
62. What had been revealed.
63. Revelations.
64. The Torah.
65. The Qur'an.

"We are a temptation. So do not disbelieve."
Those [who wished] learned from them what
would sow discord between man and wife,
but could not harm anybody with it,[66] except
with Allah's Permission. They learn what
harms them and does not profit them. They
knew that he who bought it will have no
share in the Hereafter. Evil is the price for
which they sold themselves, if only they
knew.

103. And had they[67] believed and feared
[Allah], a reward from Allah would have been
better for them, if only they knew.

104. O believers, do not say:[68] "Ra'ina [listen
to us] but Unzurna [look at us] and listen."[69]
And for the unbelievers a painful punishment
is destined.

105. Neither the unbelievers among the
People of the Book nor the polytheists wish
to see any good[70] sent down to you from
your Lord. Allah favours with His Mercy
whomever He wishes, and Allah's Bounty is
great.

106. Whichever verse We abrogate or cause
to be forgotten, We bring instead a better or
similar one. Do you not know that Allah has
the power over all things?

107. Do you not know that to Allah belongs
the dominion of the heavens and the earth,
and that apart from Allah you have no
guardian or helper?

---

66. With what they learned.
67. The Jews.
68. To Our Messenger.
69. Muhammad, the Messenger of Allah, had an aversion to the Arabic word /ra'ina/, because the Jews frequently used it as
     a term of reproach.
70. Revelation.

108. Or would you rather question your Messenger as Moses was questioned before? He who veers from belief to unbelief has strayed from the Right Path.

109. Many of the People of the Book[71] wish, out of envy, to turn you back into unbelievers after the Truth had become manifest to them. But pardon and overlook, until Allah makes known His Will. Surely Allah has the power over all things.

110. Perform the prayers and give the alms-tax. Whatever good you do for your own sake, you will find it with Allah,[72] surely Allah is cognizant of what you do.

111. They say: "None will enter Paradise except those who are Jews and Christians." Such are their vain wishes. Say: "Bring forth your proof if you are truthful."

112. Indeed, those who submit themselves to Allah, while doing good,[73] will have their reward with Allah.[74] They will have nothing to fear and will not grieve.

113. The Jews say: "The Christians follow nothing [substantial]" and the Christians say: "The Jews follow nothing [substantial]," while both recite the Book. Thus say too, those who know not. Allah will judge between them on the Day of Resurrection regarding what they differ on.

114. And who is more unjust than those who prohibit mentioning the name of Allah in His mosques, and who even seek to destroy

---

71. Jews and Christians.
72. You will be rewarded for it.
73. Believing in the unity of Allah.
74. Their reward will be Paradise.

them. Those people should not have been allowed to enter them except in fear. For them there is disgrace in this world, and terrible punishment in the Hereafter.

115. To Allah belong the East and the West. So whichever way you turn,[75] there is Allah's Face. Indeed, Allah is Omnipresent and Omniscient.

116. And they say: "Allah has begotten a son." Glory be to Him. His is everything in the heavens and the earth; all are obedient to Him.

117. Creator of the heavens and the earth. When He decrees a thing, He only says to it: "Be," and there it is.

118. Those who do not know[76] say: "If only Allah would speak to us,[77] or a sign come to us." Thus said those who came before them.[78] Their hearts are all alike. Indeed, We have made clear the signs for people who firmly believe.

119. We have sent you with the Truth[79] as a bearer of good tidings and as a warner. You are not to be questioned about the people of Hell.

120. Neither the Jews nor the Christians will be pleased with you until you follow their religion. Say: "Allah's Guidance is the [only] Guidance." And were you to follow their desires after the Knowledge that came down to you, you will have no guardian or helper [to save you] from Allah.

إِلَّا خَآئِفِينَ لَهُمْ فِى ٱلدُّنْيَا خِزْىٌ وَلَهُمْ فِى ٱلْأَخِرَةِ عَذَابٌ عَظِيمٌ ۝

وَلِلَّهِ ٱلْمَشْرِقُ وَٱلْمَغْرِبُ فَأَيْنَمَا تُوَلُّوا فَثَمَّ وَجْهُ ٱللَّهِ إِنَّ ٱللَّهَ وَٰسِعٌ عَلِيمٌ ۝

وَقَالُوا ٱتَّخَذَ ٱللَّهُ وَلَدًا سُبْحَٰنَهُ بَل لَّهُ مَا فِى ٱلسَّمَٰوَٰتِ وَٱلْأَرْضِ كُلٌّ لَّهُ قَٰنِتُونَ ۝

بَدِيعُ ٱلسَّمَٰوَٰتِ وَٱلْأَرْضِ وَإِذَا قَضَىٰ أَمْرًا فَإِنَّمَا يَقُولُ لَهُ كُن فَيَكُونُ ۝

وَقَالَ ٱلَّذِينَ لَا يَعْلَمُونَ لَوْلَا يُكَلِّمُنَا ٱللَّهُ أَوْ تَأْتِينَآ ءَايَةٌ كَذَٰلِكَ قَالَ ٱلَّذِينَ مِن قَبْلِهِم مِّثْلَ قَوْلِهِمْ تَشَٰبَهَتْ قُلُوبُهُمْ قَدْ بَيَّنَّا ٱلْءَايَٰتِ لِقَوْمٍ يُوقِنُونَ ۝

إِنَّآ أَرْسَلْنَٰكَ بِٱلْحَقِّ بَشِيرًا وَنَذِيرًا وَلَا تُسْـَٔلُ عَنْ أَصْحَٰبِ ٱلْجَحِيمِ ۝

وَلَن تَرْضَىٰ عَنكَ ٱلْيَهُودُ وَلَا ٱلنَّصَٰرَىٰ حَتَّىٰ تَتَّبِعَ مِلَّتَهُمْ قُلْ إِنَّ هُدَى ٱللَّهِ هُوَ ٱلْهُدَىٰ وَلَئِنِ ٱتَّبَعْتَ أَهْوَآءَهُم بَعْدَ ٱلَّذِى جَآءَكَ مِنَ ٱلْعِلْمِ مَا لَكَ مِنَ ٱللَّهِ مِن وَلِىٍّ وَلَا نَصِيرٍ ۝

_____

75. While praying.
76. Mecca's unbelievers.
77. Tells us that you are His Messenger.
78. To their Prophets.
79. The guidance.

121. Those to whom We have given the Book recite it as it ought to be recited. Those [people] believe in it; but those who disbelieve are the losers.

122. O Children of Israel, remember the grace I bestowed on you, and

remember that I preferred you to all other nations.[80]

123. And guard against a Day when no soul shall avail any other soul, and no ransom will be accepted from it, nor any intercession will benefit it, and they will not have any support.

124. And when Abraham was tried by his Lord with certain commandments which he fulfilled, He said: "I am making you a spiritual exemplar to mankind." Abraham said: "And what about my posterity?" He replied: "My Covenant does not apply to the evil-doers."

125. And [remember] when We made the House[81] a place of residence for mankind and a haven [saying]: "Make of Abraham's maqam [stand] a place for prayer." We enjoined Abraham and Isma'il [saying]: "Purify My House for those who circle it, for those who retreat there for meditation, and for those who kneel and prostrate themselves."[82]

126. And when Abraham said: "My Lord, make this a secure city and feed with fruits those of its inhabitants who believe in Allah and the Last Day." Allah[83] said: "As for those who disbelieve, I shall provide for them for a

الَّذِينَ ءَاتَيْنَٰهُمُ الْكِتَٰبَ يَتْلُونَهُۥ حَقَّ تِلَاوَتِهِۦٓ أُوْلَٰٓئِكَ يُؤْمِنُونَ بِهِۦ وَمَن يَكْفُرْ بِهِۦ فَأُوْلَٰٓئِكَ هُمُ الْخَٰسِرُونَ ﴿١٢١﴾

يَٰبَنِىٓ إِسْرَٰٓءِيلَ اذْكُرُواْ نِعْمَتِىَ الَّتِىٓ أَنْعَمْتُ عَلَيْكُمْ وَأَنِّى فَضَّلْتُكُمْ عَلَى الْعَٰلَمِينَ ﴿١٢٢﴾ وَاتَّقُواْ يَوْمًا لَّا تَجْزِى نَفْسٌ عَن نَّفْسٍ شَيْئًا وَلَا يُقْبَلُ مِنْهَا عَدْلٌ وَلَا تَنفَعُهَا شَفَٰعَةٌ وَلَا هُمْ يُنصَرُونَ ﴿١٢٣﴾

وَإِذِ ابْتَلَىٰٓ إِبْرَٰهِۦمَ رَبُّهُۥ بِكَلِمَٰتٍ فَأَتَمَّهُنَّ قَالَ إِنِّى جَاعِلُكَ لِلنَّاسِ إِمَامًا قَالَ وَمِن ذُرِّيَّتِى قَالَ لَا يَنَالُ عَهْدِى الظَّٰلِمِينَ ﴿١٢٤﴾

وَإِذْ جَعَلْنَا الْبَيْتَ مَثَابَةً لِّلنَّاسِ وَأَمْنًا وَاتَّخِذُواْ مِن مَّقَامِ إِبْرَٰهِۦمَ مُصَلًّى وَعَهِدْنَآ إِلَىٰٓ إِبْرَٰهِۦمَ وَإِسْمَٰعِيلَ أَن طَهِّرَا بَيْتِىَ لِلطَّآئِفِينَ وَالْعَٰكِفِينَ وَالرُّكَّعِ السُّجُودِ ﴿١٢٥﴾

وَإِذْ قَالَ إِبْرَٰهِۦمُ رَبِّ اجْعَلْ هَٰذَا بَلَدًا ءَامِنًا وَارْزُقْ أَهْلَهُۥ مِنَ الثَّمَرَٰتِ مَنْ ءَامَنَ مِنْهُم بِاللَّهِ وَالْيَوْمِ الْٰٔاخِرِ قَالَ وَمَن كَفَرَ

---

80. See comment on verse 47.
81. The Ka'ba.
82. Those who perform the prayers.
83. Having accepted Abraham's prayer.

while,[84] and then subject them to the scourge of the Fire, and what an abominable fate!"

127. And while Abraham and Isma'il raised the foundations of the House, [they prayed]: "Our Lord, accept [this] from us. Surely You are the All-Hearing, the Omniscient."

128. "Our Lord, cause us to submit to You, and make of our posterity a nation that submits to You. Show us our sacred rites, and pardon us. You are, indeed, the Pardoner, the Merciful."

129. "Our Lord, send them a Messenger from among themselves who will recite to them Your Revelations, to teach them the Book[85] and the wisdom, and to purify them. You are truly the Mighty, the Wise."

130. And who would forsake the religion of Abraham except one who makes a fool of himself? We have chosen him in this world and in the Hereafter; he shall be one of the righteous.

131. When his Lord told him: "Submit", he said: "I have submitted to the Lord of the Worlds."

132. And Abraham bequeathed that to his sons, and so did Jacob saying: "O my sons, Allah has chosen the religion for you; so do not die except as submitting people."

133. Or were you present when Jacob was in the throes of death and said to his sons: "What will you worship when I am gone?" They replied: "We will worship your God and the God of your forefathers, Abraham, Isma'il and Isaac - the One God; and to Him we submit."

فَأُمَتِّعُهُ قَلِيلًا ثُمَّ أَضْطَرُّهُ إِلَىٰ عَذَابِ ٱلنَّارِ وَبِئْسَ ٱلْمَصِيرُ ﴿١٢٦﴾

وَإِذْ يَرْفَعُ إِبْرَٰهِـۧمُ ٱلْقَوَاعِدَ مِنَ ٱلْبَيْتِ وَإِسْمَٰعِيلُ رَبَّنَا تَقَبَّلْ مِنَّآ إِنَّكَ أَنتَ ٱلسَّمِيعُ ٱلْعَلِيمُ ﴿١٢٧﴾

رَبَّنَا وَٱجْعَلْنَا مُسْلِمَيْنِ لَكَ وَمِن ذُرِّيَّتِنَآ أُمَّةً مُّسْلِمَةً لَّكَ وَأَرِنَا مَنَاسِكَنَا وَتُبْ عَلَيْنَآ إِنَّكَ أَنتَ ٱلتَّوَّابُ ٱلرَّحِيمُ ﴿١٢٨﴾

رَبَّنَا وَٱبْعَثْ فِيهِمْ رَسُولًا مِّنْهُمْ يَتْلُوا۟ عَلَيْهِمْ ءَايَٰتِكَ وَيُعَلِّمُهُمُ ٱلْكِتَٰبَ وَٱلْحِكْمَةَ وَيُزَكِّيهِمْ إِنَّكَ أَنتَ ٱلْعَزِيزُ ٱلْحَكِيمُ ﴿١٢٩﴾

وَمَن يَرْغَبُ عَن مِّلَّةِ إِبْرَٰهِـۧمَ إِلَّا مَن سَفِهَ نَفْسَهُ وَلَقَدِ ٱصْطَفَيْنَٰهُ فِي ٱلدُّنْيَا وَإِنَّهُ فِي ٱلْءَاخِرَةِ لَمِنَ ٱلصَّٰلِحِينَ ﴿١٣٠﴾

إِذْ قَالَ لَهُۥ رَبُّهُۥ أَسْلِمْ قَالَ أَسْلَمْتُ لِرَبِّ ٱلْعَٰلَمِينَ ﴿١٣١﴾

وَوَصَّىٰ بِهَآ إِبْرَٰهِـۧمُ بَنِيهِ وَيَعْقُوبُ يَٰبَنِىَّ إِنَّ ٱللَّهَ ٱصْطَفَىٰ لَكُمُ ٱلدِّينَ فَلَا تَمُوتُنَّ إِلَّا وَأَنتُم مُّسْلِمُونَ ﴿١٣٢﴾

أَمْ كُنتُمْ شُهَدَآءَ إِذْ حَضَرَ يَعْقُوبَ ٱلْمَوْتُ إِذْ قَالَ لِبَنِيهِ مَا تَعْبُدُونَ مِنۢ بَعْدِى قَالُوا۟ نَعْبُدُ إِلَٰهَكَ وَإِلَٰهَ ءَابَآئِكَ إِبْرَٰهِـۧمَ وَإِسْمَٰعِيلَ وَإِسْحَٰقَ إِلَٰهًا وَٰحِدًا وَنَحْنُ لَهُۥ مُسْلِمُونَ ﴿١٣٣﴾

84.　In this life.
85.　The Qur'an.

134. That was a nation which passed away. Hers is what she has earned and yours is what you have earned. And you shall not be questioned about what they did.

تِلْكَ أُمَّةٌ قَدْ خَلَتْ لَهَا مَا كَسَبَتْ وَلَكُم مَّا كَسَبْتُمْ وَلَا تُسْئَلُونَ عَمَّا كَانُوا يَعْمَلُونَ ﴿١٣٤﴾

135. They say: "If you become Jews or Christians, you shall be well-guided." Say: "Rather, we follow the religion of Abraham, who was upright and no polytheist."

وَقَالُوا كُونُوا هُودًا أَوْ نَصَارَى تَهْتَدُوا قُلْ بَلْ مِلَّةَ إِبْرَٰهِمَ حَنِيفًا وَمَا كَانَ مِنَ ٱلْمُشْرِكِينَ ﴿١٣٥﴾

136. Say: "We believe in Allah, in what has been revealed to us, what was revealed to Abraham, Isma'il, Isaac, Jacob and the Tribes, and in what was imparted to Moses, Jesus and the other Prophets from their Lord, making no distinction between any of them, and to Him we submit."

قُولُوا ءَامَنَّا بِٱللَّهِ وَمَا أُنزِلَ إِلَيْنَا وَمَا أُنزِلَ إِلَىٰ إِبْرَٰهِمَ وَإِسْمَٰعِيلَ وَإِسْحَٰقَ وَيَعْقُوبَ وَٱلْأَسْبَاطِ وَمَا أُوتِيَ مُوسَىٰ وَعِيسَىٰ وَمَا أُوتِيَ ٱلنَّبِيُّونَ مِن رَّبِّهِمْ لَا نُفَرِّقُ بَيْنَ أَحَدٍ مِّنْهُمْ وَنَحْنُ لَهُ مُسْلِمُونَ ﴿١٣٦﴾

137. If they believe in what you have believed, they will be well-guided: but if they turn away, they are indeed dissenting: and Allah will protect you against them; for He is All-Hearing, Omniscient.

فَإِنْ ءَامَنُوا بِمِثْلِ مَا ءَامَنتُم بِهِ فَقَدِ ٱهْتَدَوا وَّإِن تَوَلَّوْا فَإِنَّمَا هُمْ فِي شِقَاقٍ فَسَيَكْفِيكَهُمُ ٱللَّهُ وَهُوَ ٱلسَّمِيعُ ٱلْعَلِيمُ ﴿١٣٧﴾

138. [We take on] Allah's Own Colour;[86] and what colour is better than Allah's? And we do worship Him.

صِبْغَةَ ٱللَّهِ وَمَنْ أَحْسَنُ مِنَ ٱللَّهِ صِبْغَةً وَنَحْنُ لَهُ عَٰبِدُونَ ﴿١٣٨﴾

139. Say: "Do you dispute with us concerning Allah when He is our Lord and your Lord? We have our works[87] and you have your works.[88] To Him Alone we are devoted.

قُلْ أَتُحَاجُّونَنَا فِي ٱللَّهِ وَهُوَ رَبُّنَا وَرَبُّكُمْ وَلَنَا أَعْمَٰلُنَا وَلَكُمْ أَعْمَٰلُكُمْ وَنَحْنُ لَهُ مُخْلِصُونَ ﴿١٣٩﴾

140. Or do you say: 'Abraham, Isma'il, Isaac, Jacob and the Tribes were Jews and Christians?" Say: "Who knows better, you or Allah?" And who is more unjust than he who conceals a testimony which he has received from Allah? Allah is not unaware of what you do."

أَمْ تَقُولُونَ إِنَّ إِبْرَٰهِمَ وَإِسْمَٰعِيلَ وَإِسْحَٰقَ وَيَعْقُوبَ وَٱلْأَسْبَاطَ كَانُوا هُودًا أَوْ نَصَارَى قُلْ ءَأَنتُمْ أَعْلَمُ أَمِ ٱللَّهُ وَمَنْ أَظْلَمُ مِمَّن كَتَمَ شَهَٰدَةً عِندَهُ مِنَ ٱللَّهِ وَمَا ٱللَّهُ بِغَٰفِلٍ عَمَّا تَعْمَلُونَ ﴿١٤٠﴾

---

86. Religion.
87. By which we shall be judged.
88. By which you shall be judged.

141. That is a nation which passed away. It shall reap what it has earned, and you shall reap what you have earned. You shall not be questioned about what they were doing.

تِلْكَ أُمَّةٌ قَدْ خَلَتْ لَهَا مَا كَسَبَتْ وَلَكُم مَّا كَسَبْتُمْ وَلَا تُسْـَٔلُونَ عَمَّا كَانُوا يَعْمَلُونَ ﴿١٤١﴾

142. The ignorant among the people[89] will say: "What caused them[90] to turn away from their former Qibla towards which they used to turn?"[91] Say: "To Allah belongs the East and the West. He guides whom He wills towards the Right Path."

سَيَقُولُ السُّفَهَآءُ مِنَ النَّاسِ مَا وَلَّىٰهُمْ عَن قِبْلَتِهِمُ الَّتِي كَانُوا عَلَيْهَا قُل لِّلَّهِ الْمَشْرِقُ وَالْمَغْرِبُ يَهْدِي مَن يَشَآءُ إِلَىٰ صِرَٰطٍ مُّسْتَقِيمٍ ﴿١٤٢﴾

143. And thus We have made you[92] a just nation, so that you may bear witness unto the rest of mankind, and that the Messenger may bear witness unto you. We did not ordain your former Qibla except that We may distinguish those who follow the Messenger from those who turn on their heels.[93] It was indeed a hard test except for those whom Allah guided. Allah would not allow your faith to be in vain. He is Clement and Merciful to mankind.

وَكَذَٰلِكَ جَعَلْنَٰكُمْ أُمَّةً وَسَطًا لِّتَكُونُوا شُهَدَآءَ عَلَى النَّاسِ وَيَكُونَ الرَّسُولُ عَلَيْكُمْ شَهِيدًا وَمَا جَعَلْنَا الْقِبْلَةَ الَّتِي كُنتَ عَلَيْهَآ إِلَّا لِنَعْلَمَ مَن يَتَّبِعُ الرَّسُولَ مِمَّن يَنقَلِبُ عَلَىٰ عَقِبَيْهِ وَإِن كَانَتْ لَكَبِيرَةً إِلَّا عَلَى الَّذِينَ هَدَى اللَّهُ وَمَا كَانَ اللَّهُ لِيُضِيعَ إِيمَٰنَكُمْ إِنَّ اللَّهَ بِالنَّاسِ لَرَءُوفٌ رَّحِيمٌ ﴿١٤٣﴾

144. Surely, We see your face turned towards heaven.[94] We shall turn you towards a Qibla that will please you. Turn your face then towards the Sacred Mosque;[95] and wherever you are turn your faces towards it. Those who were given the Book[96] certainly know this to be the Truth from their Lord. Allah is not unaware of what they do.

قَدْ نَرَىٰ تَقَلُّبَ وَجْهِكَ فِي السَّمَآءِ فَلَنُوَلِّيَنَّكَ قِبْلَةً تَرْضَىٰهَا فَوَلِّ وَجْهَكَ شَطْرَ الْمَسْجِدِ الْحَرَامِ وَحَيْثُ مَا كُنتُمْ فَوَلُّوا وُجُوهَكُمْ شَطْرَهُ وَإِنَّ الَّذِينَ أُوتُوا الْكِتَٰبَ لَيَعْلَمُونَ أَنَّهُ الْحَقُّ مِن رَّبِّهِمْ وَمَا اللَّهُ بِغَٰفِلٍ عَمَّا يَعْمَلُونَ ﴿١٤٤﴾

145. Were you even to come to the People of the Book with every proof, they will not follow your Qibla, nor will you follow their

وَلَئِنْ أَتَيْتَ الَّذِينَ أُوتُوا الْكِتَٰبَ بِكُلِّ ءَايَةٍ مَّا تَبِعُوا قِبْلَتَكَ وَمَا أَنتَ بِتَابِعٍ قِبْلَتَهُمْ وَمَا بَعْضُهُم بِتَابِعٍ قِبْلَةَ

---

89. Among the Jews and polytheist Arabs.
90. The Prophet Muhammad and the believers.
91. *Qibla* is the direction to which Muslims turn performing the prayers. The first *qibla* was the Aqsa mosque in Jerusalem. In 2 AH/624 AD it was replaced by the Ka'ba in Mecca.
92. The Muslim nation.
93. Return to disbelief.
94. Yearning for guidance through revelation.
95. The Sacred Mosque of Mecca.
96. The Jews and Christians.

بِعَيِّنٍ وَلَئِنِ ٱتَّبَعْتَ أَهْوَآءَهُم مِّنۢ بَعْدِ مَا جَآءَكَ مِنَ ٱلْعِلْمِ إِنَّكَ إِذًا لَّمِنَ ٱلظَّٰلِمِينَ ﴿٧٥﴾

Qibla. Nor will some of them follow the qibla of the others. And were you to follow their desires after all the knowledge that came to you, surely you would be one of the evil-doers.

ٱلَّذِينَ ءَاتَيْنَٰهُمُ ٱلْكِتَٰبَ يَعْرِفُونَهُۥ كَمَا يَعْرِفُونَ أَبْنَآءَهُمْ وَإِنَّ فَرِيقًا مِّنْهُمْ لَيَكْتُمُونَ ٱلْحَقَّ وَهُمْ يَعْلَمُونَ ﴿١٤٦﴾

146. Those to whom We gave the Book know him[97] as they know their own sons; but a group of them will knowingly conceal the truth.

ٱلْحَقُّ مِن رَّبِّكَ فَلَا تَكُونَنَّ مِنَ ٱلْمُمْتَرِينَ ﴿١٤٧﴾

147. The truth is from your Lord. So do not be one of the doubters.

وَلِكُلٍّ وِجْهَةٌ هُوَ مُوَلِّيهَا فَٱسْتَبِقُوا۟ ٱلْخَيْرَٰتِ أَيْنَ مَا تَكُونُوا۟ يَأْتِ بِكُمُ ٱللَّهُ جَمِيعًا إِنَّ ٱللَّهَ عَلَىٰ كُلِّ شَىْءٍ قَدِيرٌ ﴿١٤٨﴾

148. To everyone there is a direction towards which he turns. So hasten to do the good works. Wherever you are, Allah will bring you all together.[98] Surely Allah has power over all things.

وَمِنْ حَيْثُ خَرَجْتَ فَوَلِّ وَجْهَكَ شَطْرَ ٱلْمَسْجِدِ ٱلْحَرَامِ وَإِنَّهُۥ لَلْحَقُّ مِن رَّبِّكَ وَمَا ٱللَّهُ بِغَٰفِلٍ عَمَّا تَعْمَلُونَ ﴿١٤٩﴾

149. From whatever place you come out, turn towards the Sacred Mosque. This is indeed the truth from your Lord. Allah is not unaware of what you do.

وَمِنْ حَيْثُ خَرَجْتَ فَوَلِّ وَجْهَكَ شَطْرَ ٱلْمَسْجِدِ ٱلْحَرَامِ وَحَيْثُ مَا كُنتُمْ فَوَلُّوا۟ وُجُوهَكُمْ شَطْرَهُۥ لِئَلَّا يَكُونَ لِلنَّاسِ عَلَيْكُمْ حُجَّةٌ إِلَّا ٱلَّذِينَ ظَلَمُوا۟ مِنْهُمْ فَلَا تَخْشَوْهُمْ وَٱخْشَوْنِى وَلِأُتِمَّ نِعْمَتِى عَلَيْكُمْ وَلَعَلَّكُمْ تَهْتَدُونَ ﴿١٥٠﴾

150. From whatever place you come out, turn your faces towards the Sacred Mosque. And wherever you all are, turn your faces towards it, lest people should have cause to argue with you, except for the evil-doers among them. Do not fear them, but fear Me so that I may complete My Grace upon you, and that you may be rightly guided.

كَمَآ أَرْسَلْنَا فِيكُمْ رَسُولًا مِّنكُمْ يَتْلُوا۟ عَلَيْكُمْ ءَايَٰتِنَا وَيُزَكِّيكُمْ وَيُعَلِّمُكُمُ ٱلْكِتَٰبَ وَٱلْحِكْمَةَ وَيُعَلِّمُكُم مَّا لَمْ تَكُونُوا۟ تَعْلَمُونَ ﴿١٥١﴾

151. Just as We sent forth to you a Messenger[99] from among you reciting Our Revelations[100] to you, purifying you,[101] instructing you in the Book[102] and the wisdom, and teaching you what you did not know.

---

97. Muhammad, the Messenger of Allah.
98. In the Hereafter.
99. Muhammad, the Messenger of Allah.
100. The Qur'an.
101. From polytheism.
102. The Qur'an.

152. Remember Me[103] then and I will remember[104] you. Give thanks to Me[105] and do not be ungrateful.[106]

153. O you who believe, seek assistance through forbearance and prayer. Allah is with the steadfast.

154. And do not say of those who are killed for the Cause of Allah that they are dead. They are alive, but you are unaware [of them].

155. We will certainly test you with some fear and hunger and with some loss of property, lives and crops. Announce the good news to those who endure patiently.

156. Those who upon being visited by adversity say: "We are Allah's[107] and to Him we shall return."

157. Upon such people are blessings and mercy from their Lord; and those are the well-guided.

158. Surely Safa and Marwa[108] are beacons of Allah.[109] He who performs the proper or the lesser pilgrimage commits no sin if he goes around them.[110] And those who volunteer to do a good deed[111] will find Allah Rewarding, All-Knowing.

159. Those[112] who conceal the clear proofs and guidance We sent down, after making

---

103. By glorifying Me.
104. By rewarding you.
105. By obeying Me.
106. By disobeying Me.
107. Allah's servants.
108. Safa and Marwa are the names of two mountains near Mecca. They were the scene of Hagar's running to and fro in quest of water when she was left alone with Isma'il in the wilderness.
109. They are beacons of Allah's religion.
110. The early Muslims felt at first averse to do that because the pre-Islamic Arabs visited them and touched the two idols which stood there.
111. Without being enjoined to do that.
112. The Jews.

them clear to mankind in the Book,[113] shall be cursed by Allah and the cursers.

160. Except those who repent, mend their ways and reveal [the truth];[114] these I shall pardon. I am the Pardoner, the Merciful.

161. Upon those who disbelieve and die as unbelievers is the Curse of Allah, the angels, and the whole of mankind.

162. They abide forever in it;[115] their punishment will not be reduced, nor will they be given any respite.

163. Your God is One God. There is no God but He, the Compassionate, the Merciful.

164. In the creation of the heavens and the earth; in the alternation of night and day; in the ships which sail in the sea with what profits mankind; in the water which Allah sends down from the sky in order to bring the earth back to life after its death and disperses over it every type of beast; in the continuous changing of winds; and in clouds which are driven between heaven and earth - surely in these are signs for people who understand.

165. Yet, there are people who set up equals to Allah, whom they love as they love Allah. Those who believe, however, have greater love for Allah. If only the evil-doers could understand, upon seeing the punishment, that all power is Allah's and that Allah is Stern in punishment.

166. Those who were followed will disown those who followed them[116] when they will

---

113. The Torah.
114. Which they had concealed.
115. The curse or, according to some classical commentaries on the Qur'an, Hell.
116. They will deny that they had misled them.

see the punishment and their relations with each other will be severed.

ٱلۡعَذَابَ وَتَقَطَّعَتۡ بِهِمُ ٱلۡأَسۡبَابُ ﴿١٦٦﴾

167. Those who followed will say: "If only we could go back[117] we would disown them as they disowned us." Thus Allah will show them their works as sources of deep regret. And they will never come out of the Fire.

وَقَالَ ٱلَّذِينَ ٱتَّبَعُوا۟ لَوۡ أَنَّ لَنَا كَرَّةً فَنَتَبَرَّأَ مِنۡهُمۡ كَمَا تَبَرَّءُوا۟ مِنَّا كَذَٰلِكَ يُرِيهِمُ ٱللَّهُ أَعۡمَٰلَهُمۡ حَسَرَٰتٍ عَلَيۡهِمۡ وَمَا هُم بِخَٰرِجِينَ مِنَ ٱلنَّارِ ﴿١٦٧﴾

168. O people eat from the earth's lawful and pleasant produce, and do not follow in Satan's footsteps; for he is a manifest enemy of yours.

يَٰٓأَيُّهَا ٱلنَّاسُ كُلُوا۟ مِمَّا فِى ٱلۡأَرۡضِ حَلَٰلًا طَيِّبًا وَلَا تَتَّبِعُوا۟ خُطُوَٰتِ ٱلشَّيۡطَٰنِ إِنَّهُۥ لَكُمۡ عَدُوٌّ مُّبِينٌ ﴿١٦٨﴾

169. He[118] commands you to do evil and indecency and to impute to Allah what you do not know.

إِنَّمَا يَأۡمُرُكُم بِٱلسُّوٓءِ وَٱلۡفَحۡشَآءِ وَأَن تَقُولُوا۟ عَلَى ٱللَّهِ مَا لَا تَعۡلَمُونَ ﴿١٦٩﴾

170. When it is said to them: "Follow what Allah has revealed", they say: "We would rather follow that which we found our fathers doing." What, even though their fathers understood nothing and were not rightly guided!

وَإِذَا قِيلَ لَهُمُ ٱتَّبِعُوا۟ مَآ أَنزَلَ ٱللَّهُ قَالُوا۟ بَلۡ نَتَّبِعُ مَآ أَلۡفَيۡنَا عَلَيۡهِ ءَابَآءَنَآ أَوَلَوۡ كَانَ ءَابَآؤُهُمۡ لَا يَعۡقِلُونَ شَيۡـًٔا وَلَا يَهۡتَدُونَ ﴿١٧٠﴾

171. Those who disbelieve are like one who screams but is heard by one who hears only calling and shouting. They are deaf, dumb and blind, and so they do not understand.

وَمَثَلُ ٱلَّذِينَ كَفَرُوا۟ كَمَثَلِ ٱلَّذِى يَنۡعِقُ بِمَا لَا يَسۡمَعُ إِلَّا دُعَآءً وَنِدَآءً صُمٌّۢ بُكۡمٌ عُمۡىٌ فَهُمۡ لَا يَعۡقِلُونَ ﴿١٧١﴾

172. O believers, eat of the good things which We have provided for you and give thanks to Allah, if He is the One Whom you worship.

يَٰٓأَيُّهَا ٱلَّذِينَ ءَامَنُوا۟ كُلُوا۟ مِن طَيِّبَٰتِ مَا رَزَقۡنَٰكُمۡ وَٱشۡكُرُوا۟ لِلَّهِ إِن كُنتُمۡ إِيَّاهُ تَعۡبُدُونَ ﴿١٧٢﴾

173. He has only forbidden you [to eat] carrion, blood, pork and that over which[119] any name other than that of Allah is invoked.[120] But he who is constrained,[121] without intending to disobey or transgress,

إِنَّمَا حَرَّمَ عَلَيۡكُمُ ٱلۡمَيۡتَةَ وَٱلدَّمَ وَلَحۡمَ ٱلۡخِنزِيرِ وَمَآ أُهِلَّ بِهِۦ لِغَيۡرِ ٱللَّهِ فَمَنِ ٱضۡطُرَّ غَيۡرَ بَاغٍ وَلَا عَادٍ

---

117. To life on earth.
118. Satan.
119. When slaughtered.
120. Because the pre-Islamic Arabs used to invoke the names of their gods.
121. Constrained to eat those forbidden things.

فَلَا إِثْمَ عَلَيْهِ إِنَّ ٱللَّهَ غَفُورٌ رَحِيمٌ ﴿١٧٣﴾

will commit no sin. Allah is Forgiving, Merciful.

174. Those who conceal anything from the Book which Allah has revealed and sell it for a small price will swallow nothing but fire in their bellies.[122] Allah will not speak to them on the Day of Resurrection, nor will He purify them,[123] and their punishment is very painful.

إِنَّ ٱلَّذِينَ يَكْتُمُونَ مَا أَنزَلَ ٱللَّهُ مِنَ ٱلْكِتَٰبِ وَيَشْتَرُونَ بِهِۦ ثَمَنًا قَلِيلًا أُوْلَٰٓئِكَ مَا يَأْكُلُونَ فِي بُطُونِهِمْ إِلَّا ٱلنَّارَ وَلَا يُكَلِّمُهُمُ ٱللَّهُ يَوْمَ ٱلْقِيَٰمَةِ وَلَا يُزَكِّيهِمْ وَلَهُمْ عَذَابٌ أَلِيمٌ ﴿١٧٤﴾

175. It is those who prefer to commit error rather than seek guidance, and incur punishment in place of forgiveness. How bold they are in the face of the Fire!

أُوْلَٰٓئِكَ ٱلَّذِينَ ٱشْتَرَوُا ٱلضَّلَٰلَةَ بِٱلْهُدَىٰ وَٱلْعَذَابَ بِٱلْمَغْفِرَةِ فَمَآ أَصْبَرَهُمْ عَلَى ٱلنَّارِ ﴿١٧٥﴾

176. That is because Allah has revealed the Book with the truth; and those who disagree about the Book are in great dissent.

ذَٰلِكَ بِأَنَّ ٱللَّهَ نَزَّلَ ٱلْكِتَٰبَ بِٱلْحَقِّ وَإِنَّ ٱلَّذِينَ ٱخْتَلَفُوا۟ فِي ٱلْكِتَٰبِ لَفِي شِقَاقٍ بَعِيدٍ ﴿١٧٦﴾

177. Righteousness is not to turn your faces towards the East and the West; the righteous is he who believes in Allah, the Last Day, the angels, the Book and the Prophets; who gives of his money, in spite of loving it, to the near of kin, the orphans, the needy, the wayfarers and the beggars, and for the freeing of slaves; who performs the prayers and pays the alms-tax. Such are also those who keep their pledges once they have made them, and endure patiently privation,[124] affliction[125] and in times of fighting.[126] Those are the truthful and the God-fearing.

لَّيْسَ ٱلْبِرَّ أَن تُوَلُّوا۟ وُجُوهَكُمْ قِبَلَ ٱلْمَشْرِقِ وَٱلْمَغْرِبِ وَلَٰكِنَّ ٱلْبِرَّ مَنْ ءَامَنَ بِٱللَّهِ وَٱلْيَوْمِ ٱلْأَخِرِ وَٱلْمَلَٰٓئِكَةِ وَٱلْكِتَٰبِ وَٱلنَّبِيِّۧنَ وَءَاتَى ٱلْمَالَ عَلَىٰ حُبِّهِۦ ذَوِي ٱلْقُرْبَىٰ وَٱلْيَتَٰمَىٰ وَٱلْمَسَٰكِينَ وَٱبْنَ ٱلسَّبِيلِ وَٱلسَّآئِلِينَ وَفِي ٱلرِّقَابِ وَأَقَامَ ٱلصَّلَوٰةَ وَءَاتَى ٱلزَّكَوٰةَ وَٱلْمُوفُونَ بِعَهْدِهِمْ إِذَا عَٰهَدُوا۟ وَٱلصَّٰبِرِينَ فِي ٱلْبَأْسَآءِ وَٱلضَّرَّآءِ وَحِينَ ٱلْبَأْسِ أُوْلَٰٓئِكَ ٱلَّذِينَ صَدَقُوا۟ وَأُوْلَٰٓئِكَ هُمُ ٱلْمُتَّقُونَ ﴿١٧٧﴾

178. O believers, retaliation for the slain is prescribed for you: a free [man] for a free [man], a slave for a slave and a female for a female. But if he is pardoned by his

يَٰٓأَيُّهَا ٱلَّذِينَ ءَامَنُوا۟ كُتِبَ عَلَيْكُمُ ٱلْقِصَاصُ فِي ٱلْقَتْلَى ٱلْحُرُّ بِٱلْحُرِّ وَٱلْعَبْدُ بِٱلْعَبْدِ وَٱلْأُنثَىٰ بِٱلْأُنثَىٰ فَمَنْ عُفِيَ لَهُۥ مِنْ أَخِيهِ شَىْءٌ فَٱتِّبَاعٌ بِٱلْمَعْرُوفِ وَأَدَآءٌ إِلَيْهِ بِإِحْسَٰنٍ ذَٰلِكَ

---

122. Because they will end in the Fire.
123. From their sins.
124. Particularly with regard to money.
125. Particularly with regard to illness.
126. In the way of Allah.

brother,[127] usage[128] should be followed and he should pay[129] him liberally and kindly. This is remission and mercy from your Lord. He who transgresses after that will have a painful punishment.

تَخْفِيفٌ مِّن رَّبِّكُمْ وَرَحْمَةٌ فَمَنِ ٱعْتَدَىٰ بَعْدَ ذَٰلِكَ فَلَهُ عَذَابٌ أَلِيمٌ ۝

179. In retaliation there is life for you, O people of understanding, that you may be God-fearing.

وَلَكُمْ فِى ٱلْقِصَاصِ حَيَوٰةٌ يَٰٓأُوْلِى ٱلْأَلْبَٰبِ لَعَلَّكُمْ تَتَّقُونَ ۝

180. It is prescribed for you that when death is imminent for one of you and he leaves wealth, he should equitably make a testament in favour of the parents and the near of kin.[130] This is incumbent upon the righteous.

كُتِبَ عَلَيْكُمْ إِذَا حَضَرَ أَحَدَكُمُ ٱلْمَوْتُ إِن تَرَكَ خَيْرًا ٱلْوَصِيَّةُ لِلْوَٰلِدَيْنِ وَٱلْأَقْرَبِينَ بِٱلْمَعْرُوفِ حَقًّا عَلَى ٱلْمُتَّقِينَ ۝

181. Whoever then changes it after he had heard it, the sin committed is that of those who change it. Allah is All-Hearing, All-Knowing.

فَمَنۢ بَدَّلَهُۥ بَعْدَمَا سَمِعَهُۥ فَإِنَّمَآ إِثْمُهُۥ عَلَى ٱلَّذِينَ يُبَدِّلُونَهُۥٓ إِنَّ ٱللَّهَ سَمِيعٌ عَلِيمٌ ۝

182. Should anyone, however, fear any iniquity or offence from a testator and reconciles them,[131] he shall incur no sin. Allah is Forgiving, Merciful.

فَمَنْ خَافَ مِن مُّوصٍ جَنَفًا أَوْ إِثْمًا فَأَصْلَحَ بَيْنَهُمْ فَلَآ إِثْمَ عَلَيْهِ إِنَّ ٱللَّهَ غَفُورٌ رَّحِيمٌ ۝

183. O you who believe, fasting is prescribed for you as it was prescribed for those before you, so that you may be God-fearing;

يَٰٓأَيُّهَا ٱلَّذِينَ ءَامَنُوا۟ كُتِبَ عَلَيْكُمُ ٱلصِّيَامُ كَمَا كُتِبَ عَلَى ٱلَّذِينَ مِن قَبْلِكُمْ لَعَلَّكُمْ تَتَّقُونَ ۝

184. For a fixed number of days. If any of you is sick or on a journey, then [an equal] number of other days. And those who find it extremely difficult[132] should, as a penance, feed a poor man. He who spontaneously does more good,[133] it is for his own good. To fast is better for you, if only you knew.

أَيَّامًا مَّعْدُودَٰتٍ فَمَن كَانَ مِنكُم مَّرِيضًا أَوْ عَلَىٰ سَفَرٍ فَعِدَّةٌ مِّنْ أَيَّامٍ أُخَرَ وَعَلَى ٱلَّذِينَ يُطِيقُونَهُۥ فِدْيَةٌ طَعَامُ مِسْكِينٍ فَمَن تَطَوَّعَ خَيْرًا فَهُوَ خَيْرٌ لَّهُۥ وَأَن تَصُومُوا۟ خَيْرٌ لَّكُمْ إِن كُنتُمْ تَعْلَمُونَ ۝

---

127. The aggrieved.
128. According to usage, capital punishment would be replaced by blood-money.
129. The aggrieved.
130. According to some classical commentators this verse was later abrogated by the law of inheritance.
131. The testator and the beneficiary.
132. That is, extremely difficult to fast.
133. If he increases the penance.

185. The month of Ramadan is the month in which the Qur'an was revealed, providing guidance for mankind, with clear verses to guide and to distinguish right from wrong. He who witnesses that month should fast it. But if anyone is sick or on a journey, [he ought to fast] a number of other days. Allah desires ease and does not desire hardship for you, that you may complete the total number;[134] glorify Allah for His Guidance, and that you may be thankful.

186. And when My servants ask you about Me, say: "I am near; I answer the prayer of the supplicant when he calls; so they should answer My Call[135] and believe in Me, that they may be rightly guided."

187. It has been made lawful to you on the night of fasting to approach your wives; they are a raiment for you, and you are a raiment for them.[136] Allah knows that you used to betray yourselves, but He accepted your repentance and pardoned you. So now get to them[137] and seek what Allah has ordained for you. Eat and drink until you can discern the white thread from the black thread of dawn. Then complete the fast till nightfall. But do not approach them[138] while you are in devotion at the mosque. Those are the bounds of Allah; do not approach them. Thus Allah makes clear his revelations to mankind, that they may fear Him.

188. Do not devour each other's money unjustly or offer it to the judges in order to devour a part of other people's money sinfully and knowingly.

شَهْرُ رَمَضَانَ ٱلَّذِىٓ أُنزِلَ فِيهِ ٱلْقُرْءَانُ هُدًى لِّلنَّاسِ وَبَيِّنَتٍ مِّنَ ٱلْهُدَىٰ وَٱلْفُرْقَانِ فَمَن شَهِدَ مِنكُمُ ٱلشَّهْرَ فَلْيَصُمْهُ وَمَن كَانَ مَرِيضًا أَوْ عَلَىٰ سَفَرٍ فَعِدَّةٌ مِّنْ أَيَّامٍ أُخَرَ يُرِيدُ ٱللَّهُ بِكُمُ ٱلْيُسْرَ وَلَا يُرِيدُ بِكُمُ ٱلْعُسْرَ وَلِتُكْمِلُوا۟ ٱلْعِدَّةَ وَلِتُكَبِّرُوا۟ ٱللَّهَ عَلَىٰ مَا هَدَىٰكُمْ وَلَعَلَّكُمْ تَشْكُرُونَ ۝

وَإِذَا سَأَلَكَ عِبَادِى عَنِّى فَإِنِّى قَرِيبٌ أُجِيبُ دَعْوَةَ ٱلدَّاعِ إِذَا دَعَانِ فَلْيَسْتَجِيبُوا۟ لِى وَلْيُؤْمِنُوا۟ بِى لَعَلَّهُمْ يَرْشُدُونَ ۝

أُحِلَّ لَكُمْ لَيْلَةَ ٱلصِّيَامِ ٱلرَّفَثُ إِلَىٰ نِسَآئِكُمْ هُنَّ لِبَاسٌ لَّكُمْ وَأَنتُمْ لِبَاسٌ لَّهُنَّ عَلِمَ ٱللَّهُ أَنَّكُمْ كُنتُمْ تَخْتَانُونَ أَنفُسَكُمْ فَتَابَ عَلَيْكُمْ وَعَفَا عَنكُمْ فَٱلْـَٰٔنَ بَٰشِرُوهُنَّ وَٱبْتَغُوا۟ مَا كَتَبَ ٱللَّهُ لَكُمْ وَكُلُوا۟ وَٱشْرَبُوا۟ حَتَّىٰ يَتَبَيَّنَ لَكُمُ ٱلْخَيْطُ ٱلْأَبْيَضُ مِنَ ٱلْخَيْطِ ٱلْأَسْوَدِ مِنَ ٱلْفَجْرِ ثُمَّ أَتِمُّوا۟ ٱلصِّيَامَ إِلَى ٱلَّيْلِ وَلَا تُبَٰشِرُوهُنَّ وَأَنتُمْ عَٰكِفُونَ فِى ٱلْمَسَٰجِدِ تِلْكَ حُدُودُ ٱللَّهِ فَلَا تَقْرَبُوهَا كَذَٰلِكَ يُبَيِّنُ ٱللَّهُ ءَايَٰتِهِ لِلنَّاسِ لَعَلَّهُمْ يَتَّقُونَ ۝

وَلَا تَأْكُلُوٓا۟ أَمْوَٰلَكُم بَيْنَكُم بِٱلْبَٰطِلِ وَتُدْلُوا۟ بِهَآ إِلَى ٱلْحُكَّامِ لِتَأْكُلُوا۟ فَرِيقًا مِّنْ أَمْوَٰلِ ٱلنَّاسِ بِٱلْإِثْمِ وَأَنتُمْ تَعْلَمُونَ ۝

---

134. The total number of fasting days.
135. By obeying Me.
136. That is, you need each other.
137. The wives.
138. The wives.

189. They ask you about the crescents,[139] say: "They are times fixed for mankind and for the pilgrimage." It is not righteousness to enter houses from the back; but the righteous is he who fears Allah. Enter then the houses by their front doors;[140] and fear Allah that you may prosper.

يَسْـَٔلُونَكَ عَنِ ٱلْأَهِلَّةِ قُلْ هِىَ مَوَٰقِيتُ لِلنَّاسِ وَٱلْحَجِّ وَلَيْسَ ٱلْبِرُّ بِأَن تَأْتُوا۟ ٱلْبُيُوتَ مِن ظُهُورِهَا وَلَٰكِنَّ ٱلْبِرَّ مَنِ ٱتَّقَىٰ وَأْتُوا۟ ٱلْبُيُوتَ مِنْ أَبْوَٰبِهَا وَٱتَّقُوا۟ ٱللَّهَ لَعَلَّكُمْ تُفْلِحُونَ ﴿١٨٩﴾

190. And fight for the Cause of Allah those who fight you, but do not be aggressive. Surely Allah does not like the aggressors.

وَقَٰتِلُوا۟ فِى سَبِيلِ ٱللَّهِ ٱلَّذِينَ يُقَٰتِلُونَكُمْ وَلَا تَعْتَدُوٓا۟ إِنَّ ٱللَّهَ لَا يُحِبُّ ٱلْمُعْتَدِينَ ﴿١٩٠﴾

191. Kill them wherever you find them and drive them out from wherever they drove you out.[141] Sedition is worse than slaughter. Do not fight them at the Sacred Mosque until they fight you at it. If they fight you there, kill them. Such is the reward of the unbelievers.

وَٱقْتُلُوهُمْ حَيْثُ ثَقِفْتُمُوهُمْ وَأَخْرِجُوهُم مِّنْ حَيْثُ أَخْرَجُوكُمْ وَٱلْفِتْنَةُ أَشَدُّ مِنَ ٱلْقَتْلِ وَلَا تُقَٰتِلُوهُمْ عِندَ ٱلْمَسْجِدِ ٱلْحَرَامِ حَتَّىٰ يُقَٰتِلُوكُمْ فِيهِ فَإِن قَٰتَلُوكُمْ فَٱقْتُلُوهُمْ كَذَٰلِكَ جَزَآءُ ٱلْكَٰفِرِينَ ﴿١٩١﴾

192. But if they desist, Allah is truly All-forgiving, Merciful.

فَإِنِ ٱنتَهَوْا۟ فَإِنَّ ٱللَّهَ غَفُورٌ رَّحِيمٌ ﴿١٩٢﴾

193. Fight them until there is no sedition and the religion becomes that of Allah. But if they desist, there will be no aggression except against the evil-doers.

وَقَٰتِلُوهُمْ حَتَّىٰ لَا تَكُونَ فِتْنَةٌ وَيَكُونَ ٱلدِّينُ لِلَّهِ فَإِنِ ٱنتَهَوْا۟ فَلَا عُدْوَٰنَ إِلَّا عَلَى ٱلظَّٰلِمِينَ ﴿١٩٣﴾

194. A sacred month for a sacred month; and retaliation [is allowed] when sacred things [are violated]. Thus, whoever commits aggression against you, retaliate against him in the same way. Fear Allah and know that Allah is with those who fear Him.

ٱلشَّهْرُ ٱلْحَرَامُ بِٱلشَّهْرِ ٱلْحَرَامِ وَٱلْحُرُمَٰتُ قِصَاصٌ فَمَنِ ٱعْتَدَىٰ عَلَيْكُمْ فَٱعْتَدُوا۟ عَلَيْهِ بِمِثْلِ مَا ٱعْتَدَىٰ عَلَيْكُمْ وَٱتَّقُوا۟ ٱللَّهَ وَٱعْلَمُوٓا۟ أَنَّ ٱللَّهَ مَعَ ٱلْمُتَّقِينَ ﴿١٩٤﴾

195. Spend [money] for the Cause of Allah and do not cast yourselves with your own hands into destruction,[142] and be charitable. Surely Allah loves the charitable.

وَأَنفِقُوا۟ فِى سَبِيلِ ٱللَّهِ وَلَا تُلْقُوا۟ بِأَيْدِيكُمْ إِلَى ٱلتَّهْلُكَةِ وَأَحْسِنُوٓا۟ إِنَّ ٱللَّهَ يُحِبُّ ٱلْمُحْسِنِينَ ﴿١٩٥﴾

---

139. The new moons.
140. The reference here may be to a pre-Islamic practice by which the Arabs, upon beginning the rituals of pilgrimage, used to enter a house from the back door.
141. From Mecca.
142. By withholding money or giving up fighting for the Cause of Allah.

196. Perform the proper pilgrimage and the lesser pilgrimage for the sake of Allah. But if you are prevented, then make whatever offering[143] is available; then do not shave your heads until the offering reaches its destination.[144] Whoever of you is sick or has an injury in the head can atone for it by fasting, giving alms or sacrificing. When you are secure, whoever combines the lesser pilgrimage and the proper pilgrimage, should make whatever offering is available. But if he cannot, then let him fast for three days during the pilgrimage and seven days when he returns. That is a total of ten full days. This is incumbent on him whose family is not present at the Sacred Mosque. Fear Allah and know that His retribution is severe.

وَأَتِمُّوا۟ ٱلْحَجَّ وَٱلْعُمْرَةَ لِلَّهِ فَإِنْ أُحْصِرْتُمْ فَمَا ٱسْتَيْسَرَ مِنَ ٱلْهَدْىِ وَلَا تَحْلِقُوا۟ رُءُوسَكُمْ حَتَّىٰ يَبْلُغَ ٱلْهَدْىُ مَحِلَّهُ فَمَن كَانَ مِنكُم مَّرِيضًا أَوْ بِهِۦٓ أَذًى مِّن رَّأْسِهِۦ فَفِدْيَةٌ مِّن صِيَامٍ أَوْ صَدَقَةٍ أَوْ نُسُكٍ فَإِذَآ أَمِنتُمْ فَمَن تَمَتَّعَ بِٱلْعُمْرَةِ إِلَى ٱلْحَجِّ فَمَا ٱسْتَيْسَرَ مِنَ ٱلْهَدْىِ فَمَن لَّمْ يَجِدْ فَصِيَامُ ثَلَٰثَةِ أَيَّامٍ فِى ٱلْحَجِّ وَسَبْعَةٍ إِذَا رَجَعْتُمْ تِلْكَ عَشَرَةٌ كَامِلَةٌ ذَٰلِكَ لِمَن لَّمْ يَكُنْ أَهْلُهُۥ حَاضِرِى ٱلْمَسْجِدِ ٱلْحَرَامِ وَٱتَّقُوا۟ ٱللَّهَ وَٱعْلَمُوٓا۟ أَنَّ ٱللَّهَ شَدِيدُ ٱلْعِقَابِ ﴿١٩٦﴾

197. Pilgrimage is [during] the appointed months.[145] He who determines to perform the pilgrimage during them, shall abstain from intercourse, debauchery and acrimonious quarrel. And whatever good you do, Allah knows it. Make provision.[146] The best provision, however, is the fear of Allah. So fear Me, O people of understanding.

ٱلْحَجُّ أَشْهُرٌ مَّعْلُومَٰتٌ فَمَن فَرَضَ فِيهِنَّ ٱلْحَجَّ فَلَا رَفَثَ وَلَا فُسُوقَ وَلَا جِدَالَ فِى ٱلْحَجِّ وَمَا تَفْعَلُوا۟ مِنْ خَيْرٍ يَعْلَمْهُ ٱللَّهُ وَتَزَوَّدُوا۟ فَإِنَّ خَيْرَ ٱلزَّادِ ٱلتَّقْوَىٰ وَٱتَّقُونِ يَٰٓأُو۟لِى ٱلْأَلْبَٰبِ ﴿١٩٧﴾

198. It is no offence to seek a bounty from your Lord. So when you take off from 'Arafat, remember[147] Allah at the sacred monument.[148] Remember Him as He guided you, although you were, before that, among those in error.

لَيْسَ عَلَيْكُمْ جُنَاحٌ أَن تَبْتَغُوا۟ فَضْلًا مِّن رَّبِّكُمْ فَإِذَآ أَفَضْتُم مِّنْ عَرَفَٰتٍ فَٱذْكُرُوا۟ ٱللَّهَ عِندَ ٱلْمَشْعَرِ ٱلْحَرَامِ وَٱذْكُرُوهُ كَمَا هَدَىٰكُمْ وَإِن كُنتُم مِّن قَبْلِهِۦ لَمِنَ ٱلضَّآلِّينَ ﴿١٩٨﴾

---

143. A sheep.
144. Where it can be slaughtered.
145. These are the months of Shawwal, Dhul-Qa'da and the first ten days of Dhul-Hijjah.
146. For your journey.
147. Pray to Him.
148. A mountain near Muzdalafa, where pilgrims stop for the night on their journey back from 'Arafat.

199. Then take off from where people take off and ask Allah's forgiveness. Surely Allah is All-Forgiving, Merciful.

200. Once you have performed your rites, remember Allah as you remember your fathers, or even with greater glorification. Some people say: "Our Lord, give us [a share] in this world." And yet they have no share in the Hereafter.

201. Others say: "Our Lord, give us a bounty in this world and a bounty in the Hereafter, and protect us from the torment of the Fire."

202. Those have a share[149] of what they have earned.[150] Allah is quick in retribution.

203. And remember Allah during appointed days;[151] but he who hastens [making] them two[152] incurs no sin. And he who stays behind[153] incurs no sin, if he fears Allah. So fear Allah and know that you will surely be gathered together before Him.

204. [You will find] among the people a person whose discourse about life in this world pleases you, and who calls Allah to vouch for what is in his heart, although he is your worst enemy.[154]

205. And when he departs,[155] he roams the land sowing corruption therein and destroying crops and livestock; but Allah does not like corruption.

206. And if it is said to him: "Fear Allah", he is seized with pride in sin. Hell shall be sufficient for him and what a miserable resting-place!

---

149. Reward.
150. The good they did.
151. The three days following the day of sacrifice.
152. The reference is to him who departs on the second day.
153. After the three days.
154. This verse refers to al-Akhnas Ibn Shurayq.
155. This may mean, according to some commentaries: when he is in authority or assumes power.

207. And some people sell themselves for the sake of Allah's Favour. Allah is kind to [His] servants.

208. O believers, enter into complete peace[156] and do not follow in the footsteps of Satan; for he is truly your manifest enemy.

209. If however you slip after the clear proofs have come to you, know that Allah is Mighty, Wise.

210. Do they wait until Allah comes to them[157] in canopies of clouds with the angels, and thus the matter is settled? Unto Allah all matters shall be referred.

211. Ask the Children of Israel how many clear signs did We bring them. He who changes Allah's Grace[158] after it has come to him [will find] Allah to be Severe in retribution.

212. Life in this world has been made alluring for those who disbelieve. They mock those who believe; but those who fear Allah will be above them on the Day of Resurrection. Allah provides for those whom He wills without measure.

213. Mankind was one nation.[159] Then Allah sent forth the Prophets as bearers of good news and as warners. He sent with them the Book[160] in truth, to judge between people regarding what[161] they differed on. And none differed on it[162] except those to whom it[163]

وَمِنَ ٱلنَّاسِ مَن يَشۡرِى نَفۡسَهُ ٱبۡتِغَآءَ مَرۡضَاتِ ٱللَّهِۚ وَٱللَّهُ رَءُوفُۢ بِٱلۡعِبَادِ ۝

يَٰٓأَيُّهَا ٱلَّذِينَ ءَامَنُوا۟ ٱدۡخُلُوا۟ فِى ٱلسِّلۡمِ كَآفَّةً وَلَا تَتَّبِعُوا۟ خُطُوَٰتِ ٱلشَّيۡطَٰنِۚ إِنَّهُۥ لَكُمۡ عَدُوٌّ مُّبِينٌ ۝

فَإِن زَلَلۡتُم مِّنۢ بَعۡدِ مَا جَآءَتۡكُمُ ٱلۡبَيِّنَٰتُ فَٱعۡلَمُوٓا۟ أَنَّ ٱللَّهَ عَزِيزٌ حَكِيمٌ ۝

هَلۡ يَنظُرُونَ إِلَّآ أَن يَأۡتِيَهُمُ ٱللَّهُ فِى ظُلَلٍ مِّنَ ٱلۡغَمَامِ وَٱلۡمَلَٰٓئِكَةُ وَقُضِىَ ٱلۡأَمۡرُۚ وَإِلَى ٱللَّهِ تُرۡجَعُ ٱلۡأُمُورُ ۝

سَلۡ بَنِىٓ إِسۡرَٰٓءِيلَ كَمۡ ءَاتَيۡنَٰهُم مِّنۡ ءَايَةٍۭ بَيِّنَةٍۢۗ وَمَن يُبَدِّلۡ نِعۡمَةَ ٱللَّهِ مِنۢ بَعۡدِ مَا جَآءَتۡهُ فَإِنَّ ٱللَّهَ شَدِيدُ ٱلۡعِقَابِ ۝

زُيِّنَ لِلَّذِينَ كَفَرُوا۟ ٱلۡحَيَوٰةُ ٱلدُّنۡيَا وَيَسۡخَرُونَ مِنَ ٱلَّذِينَ ءَامَنُوا۟ۘ وَٱلَّذِينَ ٱتَّقَوۡا۟ فَوۡقَهُمۡ يَوۡمَ ٱلۡقِيَٰمَةِۗ وَٱللَّهُ يَرۡزُقُ مَن يَشَآءُ بِغَيۡرِ حِسَابٍ ۝

كَانَ ٱلنَّاسُ أُمَّةً وَٰحِدَةً فَبَعَثَ ٱللَّهُ ٱلنَّبِيِّۧنَ مُبَشِّرِينَ وَمُنذِرِينَ وَأَنزَلَ مَعَهُمُ ٱلۡكِتَٰبَ بِٱلۡحَقِّ لِيَحۡكُمَ بَيۡنَ ٱلنَّاسِ فِيمَا ٱخۡتَلَفُوا۟ فِيهِۚ وَمَا ٱخۡتَلَفَ فِيهِ إِلَّا ٱلَّذِينَ أُوتُوهُ مِنۢ بَعۡدِ مَا جَآءَتۡهُمُ ٱلۡبَيِّنَٰتُ بَغۡيَۢا بَيۡنَهُمۡۖ فَهَدَى ٱللَّهُ ٱلَّذِينَ

---

156. The Arabic equivalent for "complete peace" can also be rendered as "complete submission" or "true religion".
157. The coming of Allah stands for "the execution of His Decrees".
158. This refers to those who turn from Allah's clear signs to disbelief.
159. "One nation" may stand for common disbelief.
160. The reference is to all Books or Scriptures.
161. This stands for religion.
162. Religion.
163. The Book.

was given after clear proofs had reached them, out of envy for one another. Allah, by His Will, guided those who believed to the truth on which they had differed. Allah guides whom He wills to the Right Path.

214. Or do you suppose that you will enter Paradise before the example of those who came before you had reached you? They were stricken by privation and affliction and were so shaken that the Messenger and those who believed along with him said: "When is Allah's Support coming?" Surely Allah's Support is close at hand.

215. They ask you[164] what they should spend. Say: "Whatever bounty you give is for the parents, the near of kin, the orphans, the needy and the wayfarer." And whatever good you do, Allah is fully cognizant of it."

216. You are enjoined to fight, though it is something you dislike. For it may well be that you dislike a thing, although it is good for you; or like something although it is bad for you. Allah knows and you do not.

217. They ask you about the sacred month: "Is there fighting in it?" Say: "Fighting in it is a great sin; but to debar people from Allah's Way and to deny Him and the Sacred Mosque, and to drive its people out of it is a greater sin in Allah's Sight. Sedition is worse than murder." Nor will they cease to fight you until they make you, if they can, renounce your religion. Those of you who renounce their religion and die, while they are unbelievers, are those whose works come to grief, [both] in this world and in the Hereafter. And they are the people of the Fire, abiding in it forever.

ءَامَنُوا لِمَا اخْتَلَفُوا فِيهِ مِنَ الْحَقِّ بِإِذْنِهِ وَاللَّهُ يَهْدِي مَن يَشَاءُ إِلَىٰ صِرَاطٍ مُّسْتَقِيمٍ ﴿٢١٣﴾

أَمْ حَسِبْتُمْ أَن تَدْخُلُوا الْجَنَّةَ وَلَمَّا يَأْتِكُم مَّثَلُ الَّذِينَ خَلَوْا مِن قَبْلِكُم مَّسَّتْهُمُ الْبَأْسَاءُ وَالضَّرَّاءُ وَزُلْزِلُوا حَتَّىٰ يَقُولَ الرَّسُولُ وَالَّذِينَ ءَامَنُوا مَعَهُ مَتَىٰ نَصْرُ اللَّهِ أَلَا إِنَّ نَصْرَ اللَّهِ قَرِيبٌ ﴿٢١٤﴾

يَسْأَلُونَكَ مَاذَا يُنفِقُونَ قُلْ مَا أَنفَقْتُم مِّنْ خَيْرٍ فَلِلْوَالِدَيْنِ وَالْأَقْرَبِينَ وَالْيَتَامَىٰ وَالْمَسَاكِينِ وَابْنِ السَّبِيلِ وَمَا تَفْعَلُوا مِنْ خَيْرٍ فَإِنَّ اللَّهَ بِهِ عَلِيمٌ ﴿٢١٥﴾

كُتِبَ عَلَيْكُمُ الْقِتَالُ وَهُوَ كُرْهٌ لَّكُمْ وَعَسَىٰ أَن تَكْرَهُوا شَيْئًا وَهُوَ خَيْرٌ لَّكُمْ وَعَسَىٰ أَن تُحِبُّوا شَيْئًا وَهُوَ شَرٌّ لَّكُمْ وَاللَّهُ يَعْلَمُ وَأَنتُمْ لَا تَعْلَمُونَ ﴿٢١٦﴾

يَسْأَلُونَكَ عَنِ الشَّهْرِ الْحَرَامِ قِتَالٍ فِيهِ قُلْ قِتَالٌ فِيهِ كَبِيرٌ وَصَدٌّ عَن سَبِيلِ اللَّهِ وَكُفْرٌ بِهِ وَالْمَسْجِدِ الْحَرَامِ وَإِخْرَاجُ أَهْلِهِ مِنْهُ أَكْبَرُ عِندَ اللَّهِ وَالْفِتْنَةُ أَكْبَرُ مِنَ الْقَتْلِ وَلَا يَزَالُونَ يُقَاتِلُونَكُمْ حَتَّىٰ يَرُدُّوكُمْ عَن دِينِكُمْ إِنِ اسْتَطَاعُوا وَمَن يَرْتَدِدْ مِنكُمْ عَن دِينِهِ فَيَمُتْ وَهُوَ كَافِرٌ فَأُولَٰئِكَ حَبِطَتْ أَعْمَالُهُمْ فِي الدُّنْيَا وَالْآخِرَةِ وَأُولَٰئِكَ أَصْحَابُ النَّارِ هُمْ فِيهَا خَالِدُونَ ﴿٢١٧﴾

---

164. This question was put to the Messenger by a wealthy old man.

218. Those who believed and those who emigrated and strove for the Cause of Allah are those who may surely hope for Allah's Mercy. Allah is Forgiving, Merciful.

219. They ask you about wine and gambling, say: "In both there is great sin and some benefit for people. But the sin is greater than the benefit." And they ask you about what they should spend, say: "What you can spare." Thus Allah makes clear to you His Revelations so that you may reflect,

220. Upon this world and the Hereafter. And they ask you about orphans, say: "To improve their condition is better for them. And if you associate with them, they are your brethren." Allah knows the dishonest and the honest. And if Allah wills, He would over-burden you with restrictions. Allah is Mighty, Wise.

221. Do not marry unbelieving women [polytheists] until they believe. A believing slave-girl is certainly better than an unbelieving woman, even if the latter pleases you. And do not give your women[165] in marriage to polytheists until they believe. A believing slave is certainly better than a polytheist, even if the latter pleases you. Those[166] call to the Fire and Allah calls to Paradise and Forgiveness by His Leave; and He makes clear His Revelations to mankind so that they may be mindful.

222. And they ask you about menstruation, say: "It is an impurity." So keep away from women during their menstruation and do not approach them[167] until they are clean. Once

---

165. Believing women.
166. The polytheists.
167. That is, do not have sexual relations with them.

39

they get clean get to them as Allah commanded you.[168] Allah loves the repentant and loves those who purify themselves.

فَأْتُوهُنَّ مِنْ حَيْثُ أَمَرَكُمُ اللَّهُ إِنَّ اللَّهَ يُحِبُّ التَّوَّابِينَ وَيُحِبُّ الْمُتَطَهِّرِينَ ۝

223. Your women are a tillage for you. So get to your tillage whenever you like. Do good for yourselves, fear Allah and know that you shall meet Him. And give good news to the believers.

نِسَاؤُكُمْ حَرْثٌ لَّكُمْ فَأْتُوا حَرْثَكُمْ أَنَّىٰ شِئْتُمْ وَقَدِّمُوا لِأَنفُسِكُمْ وَاتَّقُوا اللَّهَ وَاعْلَمُوا أَنَّكُم مُّلَاقُوهُ وَبَشِّرِ الْمُؤْمِنِينَ ۝

224. Do not make Allah in your oaths[169] a hindrance to doing good, to fearing Allah and to making peace between people. Allah is All-Hearing, All-Knowing.

وَلَا تَجْعَلُوا اللَّهَ عُرْضَةً لِّأَيْمَانِكُمْ أَن تَبَرُّوا وَتَتَّقُوا وَتُصْلِحُوا بَيْنَ النَّاسِ وَاللَّهُ سَمِيعٌ عَلِيمٌ ۝

225. Allah will not take you to task for what is not meant [to be said] in your oaths; but He will take you to task for what you mean in your hearts. Allah is Forgiving, Clement.

لَّا يُؤَاخِذُكُمُ اللَّهُ بِاللَّغْوِ فِي أَيْمَانِكُمْ وَلَٰكِن يُؤَاخِذُكُم بِمَا كَسَبَتْ قُلُوبُكُمْ وَاللَّهُ غَفُورٌ حَلِيمٌ ۝

226. Those who swear not to approach their wives should wait for four months; then if they change their minds, Allah is Forgiving, Merciful.

لِّلَّذِينَ يُؤْلُونَ مِن نِّسَائِهِمْ تَرَبُّصُ أَرْبَعَةِ أَشْهُرٍ فَإِن فَاءُو فَإِنَّ اللَّهَ غَفُورٌ رَّحِيمٌ ۝

227. If they resolve on divorce, Allah is All-Hearing, All-Knowing.

وَإِنْ عَزَمُوا الطَّلَاقَ فَإِنَّ اللَّهَ سَمِيعٌ عَلِيمٌ ۝

228. Divorced women should keep away from men for three menstrual periods. And it is not lawful for them to conceal that which Allah has created in their wombs, if they truly believe in Allah and the Last Day. Their husbands have the right in the meantime to take them back, should they seek reconciliation; and women have rights equal to what is incumbent upon them according to what is just, although men are one degree above them.[170] Allah is Mighty, Wise.

وَالْمُطَلَّقَاتُ يَتَرَبَّصْنَ بِأَنفُسِهِنَّ ثَلَاثَةَ قُرُوءٍ وَلَا يَحِلُّ لَهُنَّ أَن يَكْتُمْنَ مَا خَلَقَ اللَّهُ فِي أَرْحَامِهِنَّ إِن كُنَّ يُؤْمِنَّ بِاللَّهِ وَالْيَوْمِ الْآخِرِ وَبُعُولَتُهُنَّ أَحَقُّ بِرَدِّهِنَّ فِي ذَٰلِكَ إِنْ أَرَادُوا إِصْلَاحًا وَلَهُنَّ مِثْلُ الَّذِي عَلَيْهِنَّ بِالْمَعْرُوفِ وَلِلرِّجَالِ عَلَيْهِنَّ دَرَجَةٌ وَاللَّهُ عَزِيزٌ حَكِيمٌ ۝

---

168. The believers are commanded to approach in the proper way.
169. When you swear by Allah.
170. What is meant here is that men have a superior authority. But this does not prejudice their rights which are stated above.

229. Divorce may be pronounced twice. Then they [women] are to be retained in a rightful manner or released with kindness. And it is unlawful for you [men] to take back anything of what you have given them, unless both parties fear that they cannot comply with Allah's Bounds.[171] If you fear that they cannot do that, then it is no offence if the woman ransoms herself.[172] Those are the bounds set by Allah. Do not transgress them. Those who transgress the bounds set by Allah are the wrongdoers.

ٱلطَّلَـٰقُ مَرَّتَانِ فَإِمْسَاكُۢ بِمَعْرُوفٍ أَوْ تَسْرِيحُۢ بِإِحْسَـٰنٍ وَلَا يَحِلُّ لَكُمْ أَن تَأْخُذُوا۟ مِمَّآ ءَاتَيْتُمُوهُنَّ شَيْـًٔا إِلَّآ أَن يَخَافَآ أَلَّا يُقِيمَا حُدُودَ ٱللَّهِ فَإِنْ خِفْتُمْ أَلَّا يُقِيمَا حُدُودَ ٱللَّهِ فَلَا جُنَاحَ عَلَيْهِمَا فِيمَا ٱفْتَدَتْ بِهِۦ تِلْكَ حُدُودُ ٱللَّهِ فَلَا تَعْتَدُوهَا وَمَن يَتَعَدَّ حُدُودَ ٱللَّهِ فَأُو۟لَـٰٓئِكَ هُمُ ٱلظَّـٰلِمُونَ ۝

230. If he divorces her, she shall not be lawful to him again until she has married another husband. If the latter divorces her, then it is no offence if they go back to each other, if they both think that they shall keep within Allah's Bounds. Those are Allah's Bounds which He makes clear to men who have knowledge.

فَإِن طَلَّقَهَا فَلَا تَحِلُّ لَهُۥ مِنۢ بَعْدُ حَتَّىٰ تَنكِحَ زَوْجًا غَيْرَهُۥ فَإِن طَلَّقَهَا فَلَا جُنَاحَ عَلَيْهِمَآ أَن يَتَرَاجَعَآ إِن ظَنَّآ أَن يُقِيمَا حُدُودَ ٱللَّهِ وَتِلْكَ حُدُودُ ٱللَّهِ يُبَيِّنُهَا لِقَوْمٍ يَعْلَمُونَ ۝

231. If you divorce [your] women and they reach the end of their [waiting] period, retain them in an honourable manner or release them in an honourable manner. Do not, however, retain them for the sake of causing them harm and in order to commit aggression.[173] Whoever does that shall do wrong to himself. Do not make a mockery of Allah's Revelations; and remember the Grace Allah has bestowed upon you, and the Book[174] and the wisdom He has revealed to you in order to admonish you. Fear Allah and know that He knows everything.

وَإِذَا طَلَّقْتُمُ ٱلنِّسَآءَ فَبَلَغْنَ أَجَلَهُنَّ فَأَمْسِكُوهُنَّ بِمَعْرُوفٍ أَوْ سَرِّحُوهُنَّ بِمَعْرُوفٍ وَلَا تُمْسِكُوهُنَّ ضِرَارًا لِّتَعْتَدُوا۟ وَمَن يَفْعَلْ ذَٰلِكَ فَقَدْ ظَلَمَ نَفْسَهُۥ وَلَا تَتَّخِذُوٓا۟ ءَايَـٰتِ ٱللَّهِ هُزُوًا وَٱذْكُرُوا۟ نِعْمَتَ ٱللَّهِ عَلَيْكُمْ وَمَآ أَنزَلَ عَلَيْكُم مِّنَ ٱلْكِتَـٰبِ وَٱلْحِكْمَةِ يَعِظُكُم بِهِۦ وَٱتَّقُوا۟ ٱللَّهَ وَٱعْلَمُوٓا۟ أَنَّ ٱللَّهَ بِكُلِّ شَىْءٍ عَلِيمٌ ۝

232. If you divorce your women and they reach the end of their [waiting] period, do not

وَإِذَا طَلَّقْتُمُ ٱلنِّسَآءَ فَبَلَغْنَ أَجَلَهُنَّ فَلَا تَعْضُلُوهُنَّ أَن

---

171. By obeying his commands.
172. Pays money to be set free.
173. By forcing them to ransom themselves, or by retaining them for a longer period.
174. The Qur'an.

prevent them from marrying their [former] husbands if they agree among themselves in a rightful manner. With this are admonished those who believe in Allah and the Last Day; it is better and more decent for you. Allah knows and you do not.

يَنكِحْنَ أَزْوَٰجَهُنَّ إِذَا تَرَٰضَوْا بَيْنَهُم بِٱلْمَعْرُوفِ ذَٰلِكَ يُوعَظُ بِهِۦ مَن كَانَ مِنكُمْ يُؤْمِنُ بِٱللَّهِ وَٱلْيَوْمِ ٱلْءَاخِرِ ذَٰلِكُمْ أَزْكَىٰ لَكُمْ وَأَطْهَرُ وَٱللَّهُ يَعْلَمُ وَأَنتُمْ لَا تَعْلَمُونَ ۝

233. Mothers shall suckle their children for two whole years; [that is] for those who wish to complete the suckling. Those to whom the children are born[175] shall maintain and clothe them kindly. No soul is charged beyond its capacity. No mother should suffer on account of her child and he to whom a child is born should not suffer on account of his child. The same [duties][176] devolve upon the [father's] heir.[177] But they commit no offence if by mutual agreement and following consultation they choose to wean the child. You also commit no offence if you engage wet-nurses, provided that you give them what you promised to give kindly. Fear Allah and know that Allah has knowledge of what you do.

وَٱلْوَٰلِدَٰتُ يُرْضِعْنَ أَوْلَٰدَهُنَّ حَوْلَيْنِ كَامِلَيْنِ لِمَنْ أَرَادَ أَن يُتِمَّ ٱلرَّضَاعَةَ وَعَلَى ٱلْمَوْلُودِ لَهُۥ رِزْقُهُنَّ وَكِسْوَتُهُنَّ بِٱلْمَعْرُوفِ لَا تُكَلَّفُ نَفْسٌ إِلَّا وُسْعَهَا لَا تُضَآرَّ وَٰلِدَةٌ بِوَلَدِهَا وَلَا مَوْلُودٌ لَّهُۥ بِوَلَدِهِۦ وَعَلَى ٱلْوَارِثِ مِثْلُ ذَٰلِكَ فَإِنْ أَرَادَا فِصَالًا عَن تَرَاضٍ مِّنْهُمَا وَتَشَاوُرٍ فَلَا جُنَاحَ عَلَيْهِمَا وَإِنْ أَرَدتُّمْ أَن تَسْتَرْضِعُوٓا أَوْلَٰدَكُمْ فَلَا جُنَاحَ عَلَيْكُمْ إِذَا سَلَّمْتُم مَّآ ءَاتَيْتُم بِٱلْمَعْرُوفِ وَٱتَّقُوا ٱللَّهَ وَٱعْلَمُوٓا أَنَّ ٱللَّهَ بِمَا تَعْمَلُونَ بَصِيرٌ ۝

234. As for those of you who die leaving wives behind, their wives should observe a waiting period[178] of four months and ten days. When they have completed that period you incur no offence on account of what they may do with themselves[179] in a lawful manner. Allah has knowledge of what you do.

وَٱلَّذِينَ يُتَوَفَّوْنَ مِنكُمْ وَيَذَرُونَ أَزْوَٰجًا يَتَرَبَّصْنَ بِأَنفُسِهِنَّ أَرْبَعَةَ أَشْهُرٍ وَعَشْرًا فَإِذَا بَلَغْنَ أَجَلَهُنَّ فَلَا جُنَاحَ عَلَيْكُمْ فِيمَا فَعَلْنَ فِىٓ أَنفُسِهِنَّ بِٱلْمَعْرُوفِ وَٱللَّهُ بِمَا تَعْمَلُونَ خَبِيرٌ ۝

235. You incur no offence by disclosing your marriage proposals to women or by concealing them; Allah knows that you will

وَلَا جُنَاحَ عَلَيْكُمْ فِيمَا عَرَّضْتُم بِهِۦ مِنْ خِطْبَةِ ٱلنِّسَآءِ أَوْ أَكْنَنتُمْ فِىٓ أَنفُسِكُمْ عَلِمَ ٱللَّهُ أَنَّكُمْ سَتَذْكُرُونَهُنَّ

---

175. The fathers.
176. The maintenance and clothing of divorced women.
177. If the heir is a child and has a guardian the latter would be charged with those duties.
178. During this period, they should keep away from men.
179. Such as adorning themselves or looking out for suitors.

remember them. And do not arrange anything secretly with them unless you speak
what is recognized as true; and do not
resolve on contracting the marriage until the
prescribed period[180] ends. And know that
Allah knows what you have in mind, and that
Allah is Forgiving, Clement.

236. You incur no offence if you divorce
women before the consummation of marriage or fixing the dowry. And provide for
them in the rightful way: the wealthy
according to his means, and the less
fortunate according to his means. This is
incumbent on the righteous.

237. If, however, you divorce them before
the consummation of marriage, but after
fixing a dowry, then [give them] half of the
fixed dowry, unless they forgo that, or the
man in whose hand is the marriage tie[181]
forgoes his half. To forgo it is more righteous.
And do not forget to be bountiful to each
other. Allah sees what you do.

238. Attend regularly to the prayers including
the middle prayer,[182] standing up in devotion
to Allah.

239. If you are in danger, then[183] on foot or
on horseback, when you feel secure remember Allah, just as He has taught you
what you did not know.

240. Those of you who die leaving wives
behind should bequeath to them a year's
provision without turning [them] out.[184] If,
however, they leave [their homes], then

وَلَٰكِن لَّا تُوَاعِدُوهُنَّ سِرًّا إِلَّآ أَن تَقُولُوا۟ قَوْلًا مَّعْرُوفًا ۚ
وَلَا تَعْزِمُوا۟ عُقْدَةَ ٱلنِّكَاحِ حَتَّىٰ يَبْلُغَ ٱلْكِتَٰبُ أَجَلَهُۥ ۚ
وَٱعْلَمُوٓا۟ أَنَّ ٱللَّهَ يَعْلَمُ مَا فِىٓ أَنفُسِكُمْ فَٱحْذَرُوهُ ۚ
وَٱعْلَمُوٓا۟ أَنَّ ٱللَّهَ غَفُورٌ حَلِيمٌ ﴿٢٣٥﴾

لَّا جُنَاحَ عَلَيْكُمْ إِن طَلَّقْتُمُ ٱلنِّسَآءَ مَا لَمْ تَمَسُّوهُنَّ أَوْ
تَفْرِضُوا۟ لَهُنَّ فَرِيضَةً ۚ وَمَتِّعُوهُنَّ عَلَى ٱلْمُوسِعِ قَدَرُهُۥ وَعَلَى
ٱلْمُقْتِرِ قَدَرُهُۥ مَتَٰعًۢا بِٱلْمَعْرُوفِ ۖ حَقًّا عَلَى ٱلْمُحْسِنِينَ ﴿٢٣٦﴾

وَإِن طَلَّقْتُمُوهُنَّ مِن قَبْلِ أَن تَمَسُّوهُنَّ وَقَدْ فَرَضْتُمْ
لَهُنَّ فَرِيضَةً فَنِصْفُ مَا فَرَضْتُمْ إِلَّآ أَن يَعْفُونَ أَوْ
يَعْفُوَا۟ ٱلَّذِى بِيَدِهِۦ عُقْدَةُ ٱلنِّكَاحِ ۚ وَأَن تَعْفُوٓا۟ أَقْرَبُ
لِلتَّقْوَىٰ ۚ وَلَا تَنسَوُا۟ ٱلْفَضْلَ بَيْنَكُمْ ۚ إِنَّ ٱللَّهَ بِمَا
تَعْمَلُونَ بَصِيرٌ ﴿٢٣٧﴾

حَٰفِظُوا۟ عَلَى ٱلصَّلَوَٰتِ وَٱلصَّلَوٰةِ ٱلْوُسْطَىٰ وَقُومُوا۟ لِلَّهِ
قَٰنِتِينَ ﴿٢٣٨﴾

فَإِنْ خِفْتُمْ فَرِجَالًا أَوْ رُكْبَانًا ۖ فَإِذَآ أَمِنتُمْ فَٱذْكُرُوا۟
ٱللَّهَ كَمَا عَلَّمَكُم مَّا لَمْ تَكُونُوا۟ تَعْلَمُونَ ﴿٢٣٩﴾

وَٱلَّذِينَ يُتَوَفَّوْنَ مِنكُمْ وَيَذَرُونَ أَزْوَٰجًا وَصِيَّةً
لِّأَزْوَٰجِهِم مَّتَٰعًا إِلَى ٱلْحَوْلِ غَيْرَ إِخْرَاجٍ ۚ فَإِنْ
خَرَجْنَ فَلَا جُنَاحَ عَلَيْكُمْ فِى مَا فَعَلْنَ فِىٓ

---

180. The waiting period.
181. The husband.
182. Probably the afternoon prayer.
183. Perform the prayers.
184. From their homes.

you[185] incur no offence for what they do in a rightful way to themselves. Allah is Mighty, Wise.

241. Divorced women should be provided with an affordable provision. This is incumbent on the righteous.

242. Thus Allah makes clear to you His Revelations, so that you may understand.

243. Have you not considered those[186] who fled their homes in thousands for fear of death? Allah said to them: "Die." Then He brought them back to life. Surely Allah is gracious to mankind, but most people do not give thanks.

244. Fight for the Cause of Allah and know that Allah is All-Hearing, All-Knowing.

245. Who is it that will lend Allah a generous loan,[187] so that He might multiply it for him manifold? Allah provides sparingly and generously, and to Him you shall be returned.

246. Have you not considered the leaders of the Children of Israel who after Moses said to one of their Prophets: "Set up a king for us and we will fight in the Way of Allah."
He replied: "What if you refuse to fight when you are ordered to fight?"
They said: "How could we refuse to fight when we have been driven, along with our children, from our homes?"
But when they were ordered to fight, they turned away except for a few of them. And Allah knows the wrongdoers.

---

185. The relatives of the dead.
186. The Israelites.
187. Spends money in His way.

247. Then their Prophet said to them: "Allah has set up Saul to be your King." They replied: "How can he be given the kingship over us when we have a better right to it, and when he is not rich enough?" He said to them: "Allah has chosen him [to rule] over you and caused him to have greater knowledge and better stature. Allah bestows His Sovereignty on whom He wills. He is Munificent and All-Knowing."

248. Their Prophet also said to them: "The proof of his kingship is that there shall come to you the Ark in which there is tranquillity from your Lord and the relics of Moses and the family of Aaron borne by the angels. In this there is a proof for you if you are real believers."

249. And when Saul set out with [his] troops he said: "Allah will test you with a river. He who drinks from it is no part of me,[188] but he who does not drink from it is part of me, except for him[189] who scoops up with his hand a handful from it." They drank from it except for a few of them; but when he, along with those who believed, crossed it, they said: "Today we are unable to face Goliath and his troops." But those of them who believed that they would meet Allah said: "How many a small band has defeated a large one by Allah's Leave." Allah is with the steadfast.

250. And when they confronted Goliath and his troops, they said: "Lord, fill us with forbearance, enable us to stand fast, and help us against the unbelievers."

وَقَالَ لَهُمْ نَبِيُّهُمْ إِنَّ ٱللَّهَ قَدْ بَعَثَ لَكُمْ طَالُوتَ مَلِكًا قَالُوٓا۟ أَنَّىٰ يَكُونُ لَهُ ٱلْمُلْكُ عَلَيْنَا وَنَحْنُ أَحَقُّ بِٱلْمُلْكِ مِنْهُ وَلَمْ يُؤْتَ سَعَةً مِّنَ ٱلْمَالِ قَالَ إِنَّ ٱللَّهَ ٱصْطَفَىٰهُ عَلَيْكُمْ وَزَادَهُ بَسْطَةً فِى ٱلْعِلْمِ وَٱلْجِسْمِ وَٱللَّهُ يُؤْتِى مُلْكَهُ مَن يَشَآءُ وَٱللَّهُ وَٰسِعٌ عَلِيمٌ ۝

وَقَالَ لَهُمْ نَبِيُّهُمْ إِنَّ ءَايَةَ مُلْكِهِۦٓ أَن يَأْتِيَكُمُ ٱلتَّابُوتُ فِيهِ سَكِينَةٌ مِّن رَّبِّكُمْ وَبَقِيَّةٌ مِّمَّا تَرَكَ ءَالُ مُوسَىٰ وَءَالُ هَٰرُونَ تَحْمِلُهُ ٱلْمَلَٰٓئِكَةُ إِنَّ فِى ذَٰلِكَ لَءَايَةً لَّكُمْ إِن كُنتُم مُّؤْمِنِينَ ۝

فَلَمَّا فَصَلَ طَالُوتُ بِٱلْجُنُودِ قَالَ إِنَّ ٱللَّهَ مُبْتَلِيكُم بِنَهَرٍ فَمَن شَرِبَ مِنْهُ فَلَيْسَ مِنِّى وَمَن لَّمْ يَطْعَمْهُ فَإِنَّهُۥ مِنِّىٓ إِلَّا مَنِ ٱغْتَرَفَ غُرْفَةً بِيَدِهِۦ فَشَرِبُوا۟ مِنْهُ إِلَّا قَلِيلًا مِّنْهُمْ فَلَمَّا جَاوَزَهُ هُوَ وَٱلَّذِينَ ءَامَنُوا۟ مَعَهُۥ قَالُوا۟ لَا طَاقَةَ لَنَا ٱلْيَوْمَ بِجَالُوتَ وَجُنُودِهِۦ قَالَ ٱلَّذِينَ يَظُنُّونَ أَنَّهُم مُّلَٰقُوا۟ ٱللَّهِ كَم مِّن فِئَةٍ قَلِيلَةٍ غَلَبَتْ فِئَةً كَثِيرَةً بِإِذْنِ ٱللَّهِ وَٱللَّهُ مَعَ ٱلصَّٰبِرِينَ ۝

وَلَمَّا بَرَزُوا۟ لِجَالُوتَ وَجُنُودِهِۦ قَالُوا۟ رَبَّنَآ أَفْرِغْ عَلَيْنَا صَبْرًا وَثَبِّتْ أَقْدَامَنَا وَٱنصُرْنَا عَلَى ٱلْقَوْمِ ٱلْكَٰفِرِينَ ۝

---

188. Stands for: "Is not one of my followers".
189. Means that such a person is one of my followers.

251. And so they defeated them by Allah's Leave. David killed Goliath and Allah bestowed on him the kingship and the wisdom, and taught him what He pleased. Had Allah not caused some people to repel others, the earth would have been corrupted. But Allah bestows his Favours on all mankind.

فَهَزَمُوهُم بِإِذْنِ ٱللَّهِ وَقَتَلَ دَاوُۥدُ جَالُوتَ وَءَاتَىٰهُ ٱللَّهُ ٱلْمُلْكَ وَٱلْحِكْمَةَ وَعَلَّمَهُ مِمَّا يَشَآءُ وَلَوْلَا دَفْعُ ٱللَّهِ ٱلنَّاسَ بَعْضَهُم بِبَعْضٍ لَّفَسَدَتِ ٱلْأَرْضُ وَلَٰكِنَّ ٱللَّهَ ذُو فَضْلٍ عَلَى ٱلْعَٰلَمِينَ ﴿٢٥١﴾

252. These are Allah's Revelations. We recite them to you in all truth, and surely you are one of the Messengers.

تِلْكَ ءَايَٰتُ ٱللَّهِ نَتْلُوهَا عَلَيْكَ بِٱلْحَقِّ وَإِنَّكَ لَمِنَ ٱلْمُرْسَلِينَ ﴿٢٥٢﴾

253. [Of] those Messengers, We have made some excel the others; to some of them Allah spoke[190] and He exalted some many degrees [above the others].[191] We gave Jesus, son of Mary, clear signs and strengthened him with the Holy Spirit. Had Allah so willed, those who succeeded them would not have fought one another after they had received the clear signs. But they disagreed [among themselves]; some of them believed and some did not. Had Allah pleased they would not have fought each other, but Allah does what He wills.

تِلْكَ ٱلرُّسُلُ فَضَّلْنَا بَعْضَهُمْ عَلَىٰ بَعْضٍ مِّنْهُم مَّن كَلَّمَ ٱللَّهُ وَرَفَعَ بَعْضَهُمْ دَرَجَٰتٍ وَءَاتَيْنَا عِيسَى ٱبْنَ مَرْيَمَ ٱلْبَيِّنَٰتِ وَأَيَّدْنَٰهُ بِرُوحِ ٱلْقُدُسِ وَلَوْ شَآءَ ٱللَّهُ مَا ٱقْتَتَلَ ٱلَّذِينَ مِنۢ بَعْدِهِم مِّنۢ بَعْدِ مَا جَآءَتْهُمُ ٱلْبَيِّنَٰتُ وَلَٰكِنِ ٱخْتَلَفُوا۟ فَمِنْهُم مَّنْ ءَامَنَ وَمِنْهُم مَّن كَفَرَ وَلَوْ شَآءَ ٱللَّهُ مَا ٱقْتَتَلُوا۟ وَلَٰكِنَّ ٱللَّهَ يَفْعَلُ مَا يُرِيدُ ﴿٢٥٣﴾

254. O believers, spend of what We have provided for you before a Day comes[192] in which there is neither trading, nor friendship, nor intercession. The unbelievers are the wrongdoers.

يَٰٓأَيُّهَا ٱلَّذِينَ ءَامَنُوٓا۟ أَنفِقُوا۟ مِمَّا رَزَقْنَٰكُم مِّن قَبْلِ أَن يَأْتِىَ يَوْمٌ لَّا بَيْعٌ فِيهِ وَلَا خُلَّةٌ وَلَا شَفَٰعَةٌ وَٱلْكَٰفِرُونَ هُمُ ٱلظَّٰلِمُونَ ﴿٢٥٤﴾

255. Allah! There is no God but He, the Living, the Everlasting. Neither slumber nor sleep overtakes Him. His is what is in the heavens and on the earth. Who shall intercede with Him except with His Leave?

ٱللَّهُ لَآ إِلَٰهَ إِلَّا هُوَ ٱلْحَىُّ ٱلْقَيُّومُ لَا تَأْخُذُهُۥ سِنَةٌ وَلَا نَوْمٌ لَّهُۥ مَا فِى ٱلسَّمَٰوَٰتِ وَمَا فِى ٱلْأَرْضِ مَن ذَا ٱلَّذِى يَشْفَعُ عِندَهُۥٓ إِلَّا بِإِذْنِهِۦ يَعْلَمُ مَا بَيْنَ أَيْدِيهِمْ وَمَا

---

190. The reference here is to Moses, or to both Moses and Muhammad.
191. The reference here is to Muhammad.
192. The Day of Judgement.

He knows what is before them[193] and what is behind them.[194] And they do not comprehend of His Knowledge except what He wills. His Throne encompasses the heavens and the earth, and their preservation does not burden Him. He is the Exalted, the Great.

256. There is no compulsion in religion; true guidance has become distinct from error. Thus he who disbelieves in the Devil and believes in Allah grasps the firmest handle that will never break. Allah is All-Hearing, All-Knowing.

257. Allah is the Supporter of the believers. He brings them out of darkness into light. As for those who disbelieve, their supporters are the devils who bring them out of light into darkness. Those are the people of the Fire in which they shall abide forever.

258. Have you not considered him who disputed with Abraham regarding his Lord, because He had given him the kingdom? When Abraham said: "My Lord is He Who gives life and causes death", the other said: "I give life and cause death." Abraham [then] said: "Allah brings the sun from the East, bring it up from the West." Thereupon the unbeliever was confounded. Allah does not guide the wrongdoers.

259. Or [consider] him who, passing by a ruined city[195] said: "How will God bring this to life after its death?" Thereupon Allah caused him to die for a hundred years, then brought him back to life.

خَلْفَهُمْ وَلَا يُحِيطُونَ بِشَيْءٍ مِّنْ عِلْمِهِ إِلَّا بِمَا شَاءَ وَسِعَ كُرْسِيُّهُ السَّمَٰوَٰتِ وَالْأَرْضَ وَلَا يَـُٔودُهُ حِفْظُهُمَا وَهُوَ الْعَلِيُّ الْعَظِيمُ ﴿٢٥٥﴾

لَا إِكْرَاهَ فِي الدِّينِ قَد تَّبَيَّنَ الرُّشْدُ مِنَ الْغَيِّ فَمَن يَكْفُرْ بِالطَّٰغُوتِ وَيُؤْمِنۢ بِاللَّهِ فَقَدِ اسْتَمْسَكَ بِالْعُرْوَةِ الْوُثْقَىٰ لَا انفِصَامَ لَهَا وَاللَّهُ سَمِيعٌ عَلِيمٌ ﴿٢٥٦﴾

اللَّهُ وَلِيُّ الَّذِينَ ءَامَنُوا يُخْرِجُهُم مِّنَ الظُّلُمَٰتِ إِلَى النُّورِ وَالَّذِينَ كَفَرُوا أَوْلِيَآؤُهُمُ الطَّٰغُوتُ يُخْرِجُونَهُم مِّنَ النُّورِ إِلَى الظُّلُمَٰتِ أُولَٰٓئِكَ أَصْحَٰبُ النَّارِ هُمْ فِيهَا خَٰلِدُونَ ﴿٢٥٧﴾

أَلَمْ تَرَ إِلَى الَّذِي حَآجَّ إِبْرَٰهِـۧمَ فِي رَبِّهِ أَنْ ءَاتَىٰهُ اللَّهُ الْمُلْكَ إِذْ قَالَ إِبْرَٰهِـۧمُ رَبِّيَ الَّذِي يُحْيِۦ وَيُمِيتُ قَالَ أَنَا أُحْيِۦ وَأُمِيتُ قَالَ إِبْرَٰهِـۧمُ فَإِنَّ اللَّهَ يَأْتِي بِالشَّمْسِ مِنَ الْمَشْرِقِ فَأْتِ بِهَا مِنَ الْمَغْرِبِ فَبُهِتَ الَّذِي كَفَرَ وَاللَّهُ لَا يَهْدِي الْقَوْمَ الظَّٰلِمِينَ ﴿٢٥٨﴾

أَوْ كَالَّذِي مَرَّ عَلَىٰ قَرْيَةٍ وَهِيَ خَاوِيَةٌ عَلَىٰ عُرُوشِهَا قَالَ أَنَّىٰ يُحْيِۦ هَٰذِهِ اللَّهُ بَعْدَ مَوْتِهَا فَأَمَاتَهُ اللَّهُ مِائَةَ عَامٍ

---

193. In this world.
194. In the Hereafter.
195. Jerusalem.

Allah asked him: "For how long have you tarried?" He said: "I tarried for a day or part of a day."

Allah said: "No, you have tarried for a hundred years. Look at your food and drink; the years have not changed them. Look at your ass. With this We make of you a sign for mankind. Look also at the bones [and see] how We have restored them, then clothed them with flesh."

When [all] this became clear to him, he said: "[Now] I know that Allah has power over all things."

260. And when Abraham said: "My Lord, show me how You raise the dead", He replied: "Have you not embraced the faith?" Abraham said: "Yes, but so that my heart be reassured." Allah then said: "Take four birds, draw them to you, then [cut them to pieces] and place a part thereof on each mountain. If you then call them, they will come rushing to you. And know that Allah is Mighty, Wise."

261. Those who spend their wealth in the Way of Allah are like a grain [of wheat] which grows seven ears, each carrying one hundred grains. Allah multiplies [further] to whom He wills. Allah is Munificent, All-Knowing.

262. Those who spend their wealth in the Way of Allah, and then do not follow what they spend with taunts and injury, their reward is with their Lord. They shall have nothing to fear and shall not grieve.

263. A kind word and forgiveness are better than charity followed by injury. Allah is Self-Sufficient and Forbearing.

ثُمَّ بَعَثَهُ قَالَ كَمْ لَبِثْتَ قَالَ لَبِثْتُ يَوْمًا أَوْ بَعْضَ يَوْمٍ قَالَ بَل لَّبِثْتَ مِائَةَ عَامٍ فَٱنظُرْ إِلَىٰ طَعَامِكَ وَشَرَابِكَ لَمْ يَتَسَنَّهْ وَٱنظُرْ إِلَىٰ حِمَارِكَ وَلِنَجْعَلَكَ ءَايَةً لِّلنَّاسِ وَٱنظُرْ إِلَى ٱلْعِظَامِ كَيْفَ نُنشِزُهَا ثُمَّ نَكْسُوهَا لَحْمًا فَلَمَّا تَبَيَّنَ لَهُ قَالَ أَعْلَمُ أَنَّ ٱللَّهَ عَلَىٰ كُلِّ شَىْءٍ قَدِيرٌ ﴿٢٥٩﴾

وَإِذْ قَالَ إِبْرَٰهِۦمُ رَبِّ أَرِنِى كَيْفَ تُحْىِ ٱلْمَوْتَىٰ قَالَ أَوَلَمْ تُؤْمِن قَالَ بَلَىٰ وَلَٰكِن لِّيَطْمَئِنَّ قَلْبِى قَالَ فَخُذْ أَرْبَعَةً مِّنَ ٱلطَّيْرِ فَصُرْهُنَّ إِلَيْكَ ثُمَّ ٱجْعَلْ عَلَىٰ كُلِّ جَبَلٍ مِّنْهُنَّ جُزْءًا ثُمَّ ٱدْعُهُنَّ يَأْتِينَكَ سَعْيًا وَٱعْلَمْ أَنَّ ٱللَّهَ عَزِيزٌ حَكِيمٌ ﴿٢٦٠﴾

مَّثَلُ ٱلَّذِينَ يُنفِقُونَ أَمْوَٰلَهُمْ فِى سَبِيلِ ٱللَّهِ كَمَثَلِ حَبَّةٍ أَنۢبَتَتْ سَبْعَ سَنَابِلَ فِى كُلِّ سُنۢبُلَةٍ مِّائَةُ حَبَّةٍ وَٱللَّهُ يُضَٰعِفُ لِمَن يَشَآءُ وَٱللَّهُ وَٰسِعٌ عَلِيمٌ ﴿٢٦١﴾

ٱلَّذِينَ يُنفِقُونَ أَمْوَٰلَهُمْ فِى سَبِيلِ ٱللَّهِ ثُمَّ لَا يُتْبِعُونَ مَآ أَنفَقُوا مَنًّا وَلَآ أَذًى لَّهُمْ أَجْرُهُمْ عِندَ رَبِّهِمْ وَلَا خَوْفٌ عَلَيْهِمْ وَلَا هُمْ يَحْزَنُونَ ﴿٢٦٢﴾

قَوْلٌ مَّعْرُوفٌ وَمَغْفِرَةٌ خَيْرٌ مِّن صَدَقَةٍ يَتْبَعُهَآ أَذًى وَٱللَّهُ غَنِىٌّ حَلِيمٌ ﴿٢٦٣﴾

264. O believers, do not render vain your charities by taunts and injury, like him who spends his wealth for the sake of ostentation and does not believe in Allah and the Last Day. He is like a smooth rock covered by earth; when heavy rain falls on it, it leaves it completely bare. Such people get no reward for their works. Allah does not guide the unbelievers.

265. But those who spend their money in order to please Allah and to strengthen their souls[196] are like a garden on a hill which, when heavy rain falls on it, its produce is doubled; and if no heavy rain falls on it, then a shower [suffices]. Allah is aware of what you do.

266. Does any one of you wish to have a garden of palms and vines, under which rivers flow and from which he gets all kinds of fruits; and when he gets old and has weak offspring a whirlwind with fire hits the garden and burns it down? Thus Allah makes clear to you His Revelations so that you may reflect.

267. O believers, spend[197] of the good things you have earned and from what We bring out of the earth for you. Do not turn to the vile and spend from it. For you, yourselves, would not accept it except indulgently. Know that Allah is Self-Sufficient, Praise-worthy.

268. Satan induces you to expect poverty and orders you to be niggardly, and Allah promises you His Forgiveness and His Bounty. Allah is Munificent, All-Knowing.

يَـٰٓأَيُّهَا ٱلَّذِينَ ءَامَنُوا۟ لَا تُبْطِلُوا۟ صَدَقَـٰتِكُم بِٱلْمَنِّ وَٱلْأَذَىٰ كَٱلَّذِى يُنفِقُ مَالَهُۥ رِئَآءَ ٱلنَّاسِ وَلَا يُؤْمِنُ بِٱللَّهِ وَٱلْيَوْمِ ٱلْءَاخِرِ ۖ فَمَثَلُهُۥ كَمَثَلِ صَفْوَانٍ عَلَيْهِ تُرَابٌ فَأَصَابَهُۥ وَابِلٌ فَتَرَكَهُۥ صَلْدًا ۖ لَّا يَقْدِرُونَ عَلَىٰ شَىْءٍ مِّمَّا كَسَبُوا۟ ۗ وَٱللَّهُ لَا يَهْدِى ٱلْقَوْمَ ٱلْكَـٰفِرِينَ ﴿٢٦٤﴾

وَمَثَلُ ٱلَّذِينَ يُنفِقُونَ أَمْوَٰلَهُمُ ٱبْتِغَآءَ مَرْضَاتِ ٱللَّهِ وَتَثْبِيتًا مِّنْ أَنفُسِهِمْ كَمَثَلِ جَنَّةٍ بِرَبْوَةٍ أَصَابَهَا وَابِلٌ فَـَٔاتَتْ أُكُلَهَا ضِعْفَيْنِ فَإِن لَّمْ يُصِبْهَا وَابِلٌ فَطَلٌّ ۗ وَٱللَّهُ بِمَا تَعْمَلُونَ بَصِيرٌ ﴿٢٦٥﴾

أَيَوَدُّ أَحَدُكُمْ أَن تَكُونَ لَهُۥ جَنَّةٌ مِّن نَّخِيلٍ وَأَعْنَابٍ تَجْرِى مِن تَحْتِهَا ٱلْأَنْهَـٰرُ لَهُۥ فِيهَا مِن كُلِّ ٱلثَّمَرَٰتِ وَأَصَابَهُ ٱلْكِبَرُ وَلَهُۥ ذُرِّيَّةٌ ضُعَفَآءُ فَأَصَابَهَآ إِعْصَارٌ فِيهِ نَارٌ فَٱحْتَرَقَتْ ۗ كَذَٰلِكَ يُبَيِّنُ ٱللَّهُ لَكُمُ ٱلْءَايَـٰتِ لَعَلَّكُمْ تَتَفَكَّرُونَ ﴿٢٦٦﴾

يَـٰٓأَيُّهَا ٱلَّذِينَ ءَامَنُوٓا۟ أَنفِقُوا۟ مِن طَيِّبَـٰتِ مَا كَسَبْتُمْ وَمِمَّآ أَخْرَجْنَا لَكُم مِّنَ ٱلْأَرْضِ ۖ وَلَا تَيَمَّمُوا۟ ٱلْخَبِيثَ مِنْهُ تُنفِقُونَ وَلَسْتُم بِـَٔاخِذِيهِ إِلَّآ أَن تُغْمِضُوا۟ فِيهِ ۚ وَٱعْلَمُوٓا۟ أَنَّ ٱللَّهَ غَنِىٌّ حَمِيدٌ ﴿٢٦٧﴾

ٱلشَّيْطَـٰنُ يَعِدُكُمُ ٱلْفَقْرَ وَيَأْمُرُكُم بِٱلْفَحْشَآءِ ۖ وَٱللَّهُ يَعِدُكُم مَّغْفِرَةً مِّنْهُ وَفَضْلًا ۗ وَٱللَّهُ وَٰسِعٌ عَلِيمٌ ﴿٢٦٨﴾

---

196. By having a stronger grasp of the faith.
197. Spend as charity.

269. He gives wisdom to whom He wills. And he who receives wisdom has received an abundant good. But none takes heed except people of understanding.

270. And whatever expense you spend and whatever vow you vow are known to Allah. The evil-doers shall have no supporters.

271. To give alms publicly is commendable; but to keep it secret and give it to the poor is better for you, and will atone for some of your sins. Allah has knowledge of what you do.

272. You are not responsible for guiding them. Allah guides whom He wills. And whatever good you spend is for yourselves; for you do not spend except for Allah's Sake. And whatever you spend will yield good returns.[198] And you shall not be wronged.

273. [Alms is] for the poor who are held up [fighting] in the Way of Allah, and thus cannot travel in the land. The ignorant think they are rich because they are too proud [to beg]. But you can recognize them by their mark. They do not importune people for alms. Whatever good you spend is known to Allah.

274. Those who spend their wealth day and night, in private and in public, will be rewarded by their Lord. They have nothing to fear and they shall not grieve.

275. Those who take usury will not rise up[199] except like those maddened by Satan's touch. For they claim that trading is like

يُؤْتِي الْحِكْمَةَ مَن يَشَآءُ وَمَن يُؤْتَ الْحِكْمَةَ فَقَدْ أُوتِىَ خَيْرًا كَثِيرًا وَمَا يَذَّكَّرُ إِلَّآ أُوْلُوا الْأَلْبَبِ ﴿٢٦٩﴾

وَمَآ أَنفَقْتُم مِّن نَّفَقَةٍ أَوْ نَذَرْتُم مِّن نَّذْرٍ فَإِنَّ اللَّهَ يَعْلَمُهُۥ وَمَا لِلظَّٰلِمِينَ مِنْ أَنصَارٍ ﴿٢٧٠﴾

إِن تُبْدُوا الصَّدَقَٰتِ فَنِعِمَّا هِىَ وَإِن تُخْفُوهَا وَتُؤْتُوهَا الْفُقَرَآءَ فَهُوَ خَيْرٌ لَّكُمْ وَيُكَفِّرُ عَنكُم مِّن سَيِّئَاتِكُمْ وَاللَّهُ بِمَا تَعْمَلُونَ خَبِيرٌ ﴿٢٧١﴾

لَّيْسَ عَلَيْكَ هُدَىٰهُمْ وَلَٰكِنَّ اللَّهَ يَهْدِى مَن يَشَآءُ وَمَا تُنفِقُوا مِنْ خَيْرٍ فَلِأَنفُسِكُمْ وَمَا تُنفِقُونَ إِلَّا ابْتِغَآءَ وَجْهِ اللَّهِ وَمَا تُنفِقُوا مِنْ خَيْرٍ يُوَفَّ إِلَيْكُمْ وَأَنتُمْ لَا تُظْلَمُونَ ﴿٢٧٢﴾

لِلْفُقَرَآءِ الَّذِينَ أُحْصِرُوا فِى سَبِيلِ اللَّهِ لَا يَسْتَطِيعُونَ ضَرْبًا فِى الْأَرْضِ يَحْسَبُهُمُ الْجَاهِلُ أَغْنِيَآءَ مِنَ التَّعَفُّفِ تَعْرِفُهُم بِسِيمَٰهُمْ لَا يَسْـَٔلُونَ النَّاسَ إِلْحَافًا وَمَا تُنفِقُوا مِنْ خَيْرٍ فَإِنَّ اللَّهَ بِهِۦ عَلِيمٌ ﴿٢٧٣﴾

الَّذِينَ يُنفِقُونَ أَمْوَٰلَهُم بِالَّيْلِ وَالنَّهَارِ سِرًّا وَعَلَانِيَةً فَلَهُمْ أَجْرُهُمْ عِندَ رَبِّهِمْ وَلَا خَوْفٌ عَلَيْهِمْ وَلَا هُمْ يَحْزَنُونَ ﴿٢٧٤﴾

الَّذِينَ يَأْكُلُونَ الرِّبَوٰا لَا يَقُومُونَ إِلَّا كَمَا يَقُومُ الَّذِى يَتَخَبَّطُهُ الشَّيْطَٰنُ مِنَ الْمَسِّ ذَٰلِكَ بِأَنَّهُمْ قَالُوٓا

---

198. That is, it will be fully rewarded.
199. On the Day of Resurrection.

usury, whereas Allah has made trading lawful and prohibited usury. Hence, he who has received an admonition from his Lord and desisted can keep what he has taken[200] and his fate is to be left to Allah. But those who revert [to it][201] - those are the people of the Fire in which they shall abide forever.

276. Allah prohibits usury and does not bless it; but He compounds alms. And Allah does not like a vicious unbeliever.

277. Verily, those who believe, do good works, perform the prayers and give the alms-tax, shall find their reward with their Lord. They have nothing to fear, and they shall not grieve.

278. O believers, fear Allah and forgo what is still due from usury, if you are [true] believers.

279. But if you fail to do that, take note of a war [waged] by Allah and His Messenger. But if you repent you will have your capital, neither wronging nor being wronged.

280. If he [the debtor] is in straits, then allow days of grace until he is at ease. But to remit [the debt] as alms is better for you, if you only knew.

281. Fear a Day when you will return to Allah; then each soul will be rewarded fully for what it has earned;[202] and none shall be wronged.

إِنَّمَا الْبَيْعُ مِثْلُ الرِّبَوٰا وَأَحَلَّ اللَّهُ الْبَيْعَ وَحَرَّمَ الرِّبَوٰا فَمَن جَآءَهُ مَوْعِظَةٌ مِّن رَّبِّهِۦ فَٱنتَهَىٰ فَلَهُۥ مَا سَلَفَ وَأَمْرُهُۥٓ إِلَى اللَّهِ وَمَنْ عَادَ فَأُوْلَٰٓئِكَ أَصْحَٰبُ النَّارِ هُمْ فِيهَا خَٰلِدُونَ ﴿٢٧٥﴾

يَمْحَقُ اللَّهُ الرِّبَوٰا وَيُرْبِي الصَّدَقَٰتِ وَاللَّهُ لَا يُحِبُّ كُلَّ كَفَّارٍ أَثِيمٍ ﴿٢٧٦﴾

إِنَّ الَّذِينَ ءَامَنُوا وَعَمِلُوا الصَّٰلِحَٰتِ وَأَقَامُوا الصَّلَوٰةَ وَءَاتَوُا الزَّكَوٰةَ لَهُمْ أَجْرُهُمْ عِندَ رَبِّهِمْ وَلَا خَوْفٌ عَلَيْهِمْ وَلَا هُمْ يَحْزَنُونَ ﴿٢٧٧﴾

يَٰٓأَيُّهَا الَّذِينَ ءَامَنُوا اتَّقُوا اللَّهَ وَذَرُوا مَا بَقِيَ مِنَ الرِّبَوٰٓا إِن كُنتُم مُّؤْمِنِينَ ﴿٢٧٨﴾

فَإِن لَّمْ تَفْعَلُوا فَأْذَنُوا بِحَرْبٍ مِّنَ اللَّهِ وَرَسُولِهِۦ وَإِن تُبْتُمْ فَلَكُمْ رُءُوسُ أَمْوَٰلِكُمْ لَا تَظْلِمُونَ وَلَا تُظْلَمُونَ ﴿٢٧٩﴾

وَإِن كَانَ ذُو عُسْرَةٍ فَنَظِرَةٌ إِلَىٰ مَيْسَرَةٍ وَأَن تَصَدَّقُوا خَيْرٌ لَّكُمْ إِن كُنتُمْ تَعْلَمُونَ ﴿٢٨٠﴾

وَاتَّقُوا يَوْمًا تُرْجَعُونَ فِيهِ إِلَى اللَّهِ ثُمَّ تُوَفَّىٰ كُلُّ نَفْسٍ مَّا كَسَبَتْ وَهُمْ لَا يُظْلَمُونَ ﴿٢٨١﴾

---

200. As usury, prior to the prohibition.
201. Taking usury.
202. For the good works it has done.

282. O believers, when you contract a debt for a fixed period, write it down. Let a scribe write it for you with fairness. No scribe should decline to write as Allah has taught him. So let him then write and let the debtor dictate. He should fear his Lord and not diminish the debt in the least. If the debtor is feeble-minded or weak or ignorant, then let his guardian dictate with fairness. And call to witness two witnesses of your men; if not two men, then one man and two women from such witnesses you approve of, so that if one of them[203] fails to remember, the other would remind her. The witnesses should not decline [to testify] when they are called upon [to do so]. So do not be averse to writing down the debt, be it small or large, as well as when it is due. This is more equitable in Allah's sight, more suitable for testimony and less likely to rouse your doubts. If it is an instant transaction among yourselves;[204] then it is no offence if you do not write it down. And let there be witnesses when you sell one to another; but neither the scribe nor the witness should be harmed, because if you do that, it is an act of transgression. Fear Allah; Allah teaches you. He has knowledge of everything.

283. If you are travelling and cannot find a scribe, a security should be taken. But if you trust one another, then let him who is entrusted deliver the security and fear Allah his Lord. Do not withhold the testimony. He

يَٰٓأَيُّهَا ٱلَّذِينَ ءَامَنُوٓا۟ إِذَا تَدَايَنتُم بِدَيْنٍ إِلَىٰٓ أَجَلٍ مُّسَمًّى فَٱكْتُبُوهُ ۚ وَلْيَكْتُب بَّيْنَكُمْ كَاتِبٌۢ بِٱلْعَدْلِ ۚ وَلَا يَأْبَ كَاتِبٌ أَن يَكْتُبَ كَمَا عَلَّمَهُ ٱللَّهُ ۚ فَلْيَكْتُبْ وَلْيُمْلِلِ ٱلَّذِى عَلَيْهِ ٱلْحَقُّ وَلْيَتَّقِ ٱللَّهَ رَبَّهُۥ وَلَا يَبْخَسْ مِنْهُ شَيْـًٔا ۚ فَإِن كَانَ ٱلَّذِى عَلَيْهِ ٱلْحَقُّ سَفِيهًا أَوْ ضَعِيفًا أَوْ لَا يَسْتَطِيعُ أَن يُمِلَّ هُوَ فَلْيُمْلِلْ وَلِيُّهُۥ بِٱلْعَدْلِ ۚ وَٱسْتَشْهِدُوا۟ شَهِيدَيْنِ مِن رِّجَالِكُمْ ۖ فَإِن لَّمْ يَكُونَا رَجُلَيْنِ فَرَجُلٌ وَٱمْرَأَتَانِ مِمَّن تَرْضَوْنَ مِنَ ٱلشُّهَدَآءِ أَن تَضِلَّ إِحْدَىٰهُمَا فَتُذَكِّرَ إِحْدَىٰهُمَا ٱلْأُخْرَىٰ ۚ وَلَا يَأْبَ ٱلشُّهَدَآءُ إِذَا مَا دُعُوا۟ ۚ وَلَا تَسْـَٔمُوٓا۟ أَن تَكْتُبُوهُ صَغِيرًا أَوْ كَبِيرًا إِلَىٰٓ أَجَلِهِ ۚ ذَٰلِكُمْ أَقْسَطُ عِندَ ٱللَّهِ وَأَقْوَمُ لِلشَّهَٰدَةِ وَأَدْنَىٰٓ أَلَّا تَرْتَابُوٓا۟ ۖ إِلَّآ أَن تَكُونَ تِجَٰرَةً حَاضِرَةً تُدِيرُونَهَا بَيْنَكُمْ فَلَيْسَ عَلَيْكُمْ جُنَاحٌ أَلَّا تَكْتُبُوهَا ۗ وَأَشْهِدُوٓا۟ إِذَا تَبَايَعْتُمْ ۚ وَلَا يُضَآرَّ كَاتِبٌ وَلَا شَهِيدٌ ۚ وَإِن تَفْعَلُوا۟ فَإِنَّهُۥ فُسُوقٌۢ بِكُمْ ۗ وَٱتَّقُوا۟ ٱللَّهَ ۖ وَيُعَلِّمُكُمُ ٱللَّهُ ۗ وَٱللَّهُ بِكُلِّ شَىْءٍ عَلِيمٌ ۝

وَإِن كُنتُمْ عَلَىٰ سَفَرٍ وَلَمْ تَجِدُوا۟ كَاتِبًا فَرِهَٰنٌ مَّقْبُوضَةٌ ۖ فَإِنْ أَمِنَ بَعْضُكُم بَعْضًا فَلْيُؤَدِّ ٱلَّذِى ٱؤْتُمِنَ أَمَٰنَتَهُۥ وَلْيَتَّقِ ٱللَّهَ رَبَّهُۥ ۗ وَلَا تَكْتُمُوا۟ ٱلشَّهَٰدَةَ ۚ وَمَن

---

203. The two women.
204. Involving no debt.

who withholds it has a sinful heart. Allah has knowledge of what you do.

284. To Allah belongs whatever is in the heavens and on the earth. And whether you reveal or conceal what is in your hearts, Allah will call you to account for it. He will then forgive whom He wills, and punish whom He wills. He is Able to do everything.

285. The Messenger[205] believes in what has been revealed to him by his Lord, and so do the believers too. All believe in Allah, His Angels, His Books and His Messengers. We make no distinction between any of His Messengers. And they[206] say: "We hear and obey. Grant us Your Forgiveness, our Lord. And to You is our return."

286. Allah does not charge any soul beyond its capacity. It gets [rewarded for] what [good] it has earned, and is called to account for what [evil] it has committed. Lord, forgive us if we have forgotten or erred. Lord, do not lay on us a burden like that You laid on those before us, and do not burden us with what we cannot bear. Pardon us, forgive us and have mercy on us. You are our Protector. Give us victory over the unbelieving people.

يَكْتُمْهَا فَإِنَّهُۥ ءَاثِمٌ قَلْبُهُۥ وَٱللَّهُ بِمَا تَعْمَلُونَ عَلِيمٌ ۝

لِّلَّهِ مَا فِى ٱلسَّمَٰوَٰتِ وَمَا فِى ٱلْأَرْضِ وَإِن تُبْدُوا۟ مَا فِىٓ أَنفُسِكُمْ أَوْ تُخْفُوهُ يُحَاسِبْكُم بِهِ ٱللَّهُ فَيَغْفِرُ لِمَن يَشَآءُ وَيُعَذِّبُ مَن يَشَآءُ وَٱللَّهُ عَلَىٰ كُلِّ شَىْءٍ قَدِيرٌ ۝

ءَامَنَ ٱلرَّسُولُ بِمَآ أُنزِلَ إِلَيْهِ مِن رَّبِّهِۦ وَٱلْمُؤْمِنُونَ كُلٌّ ءَامَنَ بِٱللَّهِ وَمَلَٰٓئِكَتِهِۦ وَكُتُبِهِۦ وَرُسُلِهِۦ لَا نُفَرِّقُ بَيْنَ أَحَدٍ مِّن رُّسُلِهِۦ وَقَالُوا۟ سَمِعْنَا وَأَطَعْنَا غُفْرَانَكَ رَبَّنَا وَإِلَيْكَ ٱلْمَصِيرُ ۝

لَا يُكَلِّفُ ٱللَّهُ نَفْسًا إِلَّا وُسْعَهَا لَهَا مَا كَسَبَتْ وَعَلَيْهَا مَا ٱكْتَسَبَتْ رَبَّنَا لَا تُؤَاخِذْنَآ إِن نَّسِينَآ أَوْ أَخْطَأْنَا رَبَّنَا وَلَا تَحْمِلْ عَلَيْنَآ إِصْرًا كَمَا حَمَلْتَهُۥ عَلَى ٱلَّذِينَ مِن قَبْلِنَا رَبَّنَا وَلَا تُحَمِّلْنَا مَا لَا طَاقَةَ لَنَا بِهِۦ وَٱعْفُ عَنَّا وَٱغْفِرْ لَنَا وَٱرْحَمْنَآ أَنتَ مَوْلَىٰنَا فَٱنصُرْنَا عَلَى ٱلْقَوْمِ ٱلْكَٰفِرِينَ ۝

---

205. Muhmmad.
206. The believers.

Sûrat Âl-'Imrân, **(The Family of 'Imran) 3**	

In the Name of Allah,
the Compassionate, the Merciful

1. Alif, Lam, Mim.

2. Allah, there is no God but He, the Living,
the Everlasting.

3. He has revealed the Book[207] to you in
truth, confirming what came before it; and
He has revealed the Torah and the Gospel,

4. Aforetime, as a guidance to mankind. And
He has also revealed the Criterion.[208] Verily,
those who have disbelieved in Allah's Signs,
a terrible punishment awaits them; Allah is
Mighty and Stern in retribution.

5. Indeed, nothing is hidden from Allah
whether on earth or in the heavens.

6. It is He Who forms you in the wombs as
He pleases; there is no God but He, the
Mighty, the Wise.

7. It is He Who has revealed to you the Book,
with verses which are precise in meaning
and which are the Mother of the Book, and
others which are ambiguous. As to those in
whose hearts there is vacillation, they follow
what is ambiguous in it, seeking sedition and
intending to interpret it. However, no one
except Allah knows its interpretation. Those
well-grounded in knowledge say: "We
believe in it; all is from our Lord"; yet none
remembers save those possessed of understanding!

---

207. The Qur'an.
208. Of right and wrong, Arabic: *Al-Furqan;* that is, the Qur'an itself.

8. Lord, do not cause our hearts to vacillate after You have guided us and grant us Your Mercy. You are indeed the Munificent Giver.

9. Lord, You will surely gather mankind for a Day[209] which is undoubted. Allah will never fail to keep the appointed time!

10. As to the unbelievers, neither their riches nor their children will avail them anything against Allah; in fact, they shall be the fuel of the Fire.

11. Like Pharaoh's people and those before them who denounced Our Revelations. Allah smote them on account of their sins. Allah is Stern in retribution!

12. Say to those who disbelieved:[210] "You shall be defeated and driven together into Hell; and what an awful resting-place."

13. There surely was a sign for you in the two armies that confronted each other;[211] the one side fighting for the Cause of Allah, and the other consisting of unbelievers. The believers saw them with their very eyes to be twice their actual number. God will strengthen with His Might whomever He pleases. Surely, there is in this a lesson for those who are possessed of vision.

14. Attractive to mankind is made the love of the pleasures of women, children, heaps upon heaps of gold and silver, thoroughbred horses, cattle and cultivable land. Such is the pleasure of this worldly life, but unto Allah is the fairest return.

15. Say: "Shall I tell you about something better than all that?" For those who are God-fearing, from their Lord are gardens beneath

---

209. Day of Resurrection.
210. The Jews.
211. In the Battle of Badr, 2 AH/624 AD.

which rivers flow, and in which they abide forever [along with] purified spouses and Allah's good pleasure. Allah sees His servants well!

16. Those who say: "Our Lord, we have believed, so forgive us our sins and guard us against the torments of Hell."

17. They are the patient, the truthful, the devout, the charitable and the seekers of forgiveness at daybreak.

18. Allah bears witness that there is no God but He, and so do the angels and men of learning. He upholds justice. There is no God but He, the Mighty and Wise One.

19. The [true] religion with Allah is Islam. Those who were given the Book[212] did not disagree among themselves, except after certain knowledge came to them, out of envy among themselves. Whoever disbelieves in Allah's Revelations will find Allah Swift in retribution!

20. So, if they dispute with you, say: "I have submitted myself to Allah and so have those who followed me"; and say also to those who have received the Book and to the unlearned:[213] "Have you submitted?" If they have submitted, then they are rightly guided; but if they have turned their backs, then your duty is simply to deliver the Message. Allah perceives His servants well.

21. Those who disbelieve in Allah's Revelations and kill the Prophets unjustly, and kill those people who enjoin fair dealing, announce to them a painful punishment.

---

212. The Jews and the Christians.
213. The Arab idolaters of Mecca.

أُوْلَـٰٓئِكَ ٱلَّذِينَ حَبِطَتْ أَعْمَٰلُهُمْ فِى ٱلدُّنْيَا

وَٱلْءَاخِرَةِ وَمَا لَهُم مِّن نَّـٰصِرِينَ ﴿٢٢﴾

22. Those are the people whose works have come to naught in this world and the next, and they will have no supporters whatsoever!

أَلَمْ تَرَ إِلَى ٱلَّذِينَ أُوتُوا۟ نَصِيبًا مِّنَ ٱلْكِتَٰبِ يُدْعَوْنَ إِلَىٰ

كِتَٰبِ ٱللَّهِ لِيَحْكُمَ بَيْنَهُمْ ثُمَّ يَتَوَلَّىٰ فَرِيقٌ مِّنْهُمْ وَهُم

مُّعْرِضُونَ ﴿٢٣﴾

23. Have you not considered those who have received a portion of the Book? Upon being called to let the Book of Allah decide between them, some of them turn their backs, refusing to pay attention.

ذَٰلِكَ بِأَنَّهُمْ قَالُوا۟ لَن تَمَسَّنَا ٱلنَّارُ إِلَّا أَيَّامًا مَّعْدُودَٰتٍ

وَغَرَّهُمْ فِى دِينِهِم مَّا كَانُوا۟ يَفْتَرُونَ ﴿٢٤﴾

24. That is because they say: "The Fire will only touch us for a few days." They have been deluded in their religion by their lies.

فَكَيْفَ إِذَا جَمَعْنَٰهُمْ لِيَوْمٍ لَّا رَيْبَ فِيهِ وَوُفِّيَتْ كُلُّ

نَفْسٍ مَّا كَسَبَتْ وَهُمْ لَا يُظْلَمُونَ ﴿٢٥﴾

25. But how will they fare when We gather them together on a Day which is undoubted, and each soul shall be paid in full for whatever it has earned, and they shall not be dealt with unjustly?

قُلِ ٱللَّهُمَّ مَٰلِكَ ٱلْمُلْكِ تُؤْتِى ٱلْمُلْكَ مَن تَشَآءُ وَتَنزِعُ

ٱلْمُلْكَ مِمَّن تَشَآءُ وَتُعِزُّ مَن تَشَآءُ وَتُذِلُّ مَن تَشَآءُ

بِيَدِكَ ٱلْخَيْرُ إِنَّكَ عَلَىٰ كُلِّ شَىْءٍ قَدِيرٌ ﴿٢٦﴾

26. Say: "O Allah, Master of the Kingdom, You give the kingship to whom You please and take away the kingship from whom You please. You exalt whom You please and humble whom You please. In Your Hand is all the good, and You have power over everything!

تُولِجُ ٱلَّيْلَ فِى ٱلنَّهَارِ وَتُولِجُ ٱلنَّهَارَ فِى ٱلَّيْلِ وَتُخْرِجُ

ٱلْحَىَّ مِنَ ٱلْمَيِّتِ وَتُخْرِجُ ٱلْمَيِّتَ مِنَ ٱلْحَىِّ وَتَرْزُقُ مَن

تَشَآءُ بِغَيْرِ حِسَابٍ ﴿٢٧﴾

27. "You cause the night to pass into the day, and the day to pass into the night. You bring forth the living from the dead and You bring forth the dead from the living, and You provide for whomever You please without measure."

لَّا يَتَّخِذِ ٱلْمُؤْمِنُونَ ٱلْكَٰفِرِينَ أَوْلِيَآءَ مِن دُونِ ٱلْمُؤْمِنِينَ

وَمَن يَفْعَلْ ذَٰلِكَ فَلَيْسَ مِنَ ٱللَّهِ فِى شَىْءٍ إِلَّآ أَن

تَتَّقُوا۟ مِنْهُمْ تُقَىٰةً وَيُحَذِّرُكُمُ ٱللَّهُ نَفْسَهُ وَإِلَى ٱللَّهِ

ٱلْمَصِيرُ ﴿٢٨﴾

28. Let not the believers take the unbelievers for friends, rather than the believers. Who-ever does that has nothing to do with Allah, unless you guard against them fully! Allah warns you to beware of Him;[214] and unto Him is the ultimate return!

---

214. Warns you of His anger.

29. Say: "Whether you conceal what is in your hearts or you reveal it, Allah knows it; and He knows what is in the heavens or on the earth, and He has power over everything!"

قُلْ إِن تُخْفُوا۟ مَا فِى صُدُورِكُمْ أَوْ تُبْدُوهُ يَعْلَمْهُ ٱللَّهُ ۗ وَيَعْلَمُ مَا فِى ٱلسَّمَٰوَٰتِ وَمَا فِى ٱلْأَرْضِ ۗ وَٱللَّهُ عَلَىٰ كُلِّ شَىْءٍ قَدِيرٌ ۝

30. The Day [will come] when every soul shall find every good it has done set before it; and whatever evil it did, it wishes that it was far away from it. Allah warns you to be wary of Him, and Allah is Compassionate towards His servants!

يَوْمَ تَجِدُ كُلُّ نَفْسٍ مَّا عَمِلَتْ مِنْ خَيْرٍ مُّحْضَرًا وَمَا عَمِلَتْ مِن سُوٓءٍ تَوَدُّ لَوْ أَنَّ بَيْنَهَا وَبَيْنَهُۥٓ أَمَدًۢا بَعِيدًا ۗ وَيُحَذِّرُكُمُ ٱللَّهُ نَفْسَهُۥ ۗ وَٱللَّهُ رَءُوفٌۢ بِٱلْعِبَادِ ۝

31. Say: "If you love Allah, follow me; then Allah will love you and forgive your sins." Allah is Forgiving, Merciful.

قُلْ إِن كُنتُمْ تُحِبُّونَ ٱللَّهَ فَٱتَّبِعُونِى يُحْبِبْكُمُ ٱللَّهُ وَيَغْفِرْ لَكُمْ ذُنُوبَكُمْ ۗ وَٱللَّهُ غَفُورٌ رَّحِيمٌ ۝

32. Say: "Obey Allah and the Messenger." Should they turn their backs, surely Allah does not love the unbelievers.

قُلْ أَطِيعُوا۟ ٱللَّهَ وَٱلرَّسُولَ ۖ فَإِن تَوَلَّوْا۟ فَإِنَّ ٱللَّهَ لَا يُحِبُّ ٱلْكَٰفِرِينَ ۝

33. Allah chose Adam, Noah, the family of Abraham and the family of 'Imran above all mankind;

۞ إِنَّ ٱللَّهَ ٱصْطَفَىٰٓ ءَادَمَ وَنُوحًا وَءَالَ إِبْرَٰهِيمَ وَءَالَ عِمْرَٰنَ عَلَى ٱلْعَٰلَمِينَ ۝

34. Descending one from another; and Allah is All-Hearing, All-Knowing!

ذُرِّيَّةًۢ بَعْضُهَا مِنۢ بَعْضٍ ۗ وَٱللَّهُ سَمِيعٌ عَلِيمٌ ۝

35. [Remember] when the wife of 'Imran said: "Lord, I have vowed to You what is in my womb to be devoted [to Your service]. Accept it from me, for You are the All-Hearing, the All-Knowing."

إِذْ قَالَتِ ٱمْرَأَتُ عِمْرَٰنَ رَبِّ إِنِّى نَذَرْتُ لَكَ مَا فِى بَطْنِى مُحَرَّرًا فَتَقَبَّلْ مِنِّىٓ ۖ إِنَّكَ أَنتَ ٱلسَّمِيعُ ٱلْعَلِيمُ ۝

36. And when she delivered her, she said: "Lord, I have given birth to a female", - and Allah knew best what she gave birth to; the male is not the same as the female - "I have named her Mary and I commend her and her descendants to You to protect her from the accursed Devil."

فَلَمَّا وَضَعَتْهَا قَالَتْ رَبِّ إِنِّى وَضَعْتُهَآ أُنثَىٰ وَٱللَّهُ أَعْلَمُ بِمَا وَضَعَتْ وَلَيْسَ ٱلذَّكَرُ كَٱلْأُنثَىٰ ۖ وَإِنِّى سَمَّيْتُهَا مَرْيَمَ وَإِنِّىٓ أُعِيذُهَا بِكَ وَذُرِّيَّتَهَا مِنَ ٱلشَّيْطَٰنِ ٱلرَّجِيمِ ۝

37. Then her Lord accepted her graciously and made her to grow into a fine child, entrusting her to Zachariah. Whenever Zachariah went in to see her in the sanctuary,

فَتَقَبَّلَهَا رَبُّهَا بِقَبُولٍ حَسَنٍ وَأَنۢبَتَهَا نَبَاتًا حَسَنًا وَكَفَّلَهَا زَكَرِيَّا ۖ كُلَّمَا دَخَلَ عَلَيْهَا زَكَرِيَّا ٱلْمِحْرَابَ وَجَدَ عِندَهَا رِزْقًا ۖ قَالَ يَٰمَرْيَمُ أَنَّىٰ

he found that she had some provision. "Mary," he asked, "where did you get this?" She replied: "It is from Allah, and Allah provides for whom He wishes without measure."

38. Thereupon, Zachariah prayed to his Lord saying: "Lord, grant me from Your Bounty fine descendants. Indeed You hear every prayer!"

39. Then the angels called him while he was at prayer in the sanctuary, saying: "Allah bids you rejoice in John, confirming a word[215] from Allah, a master, chaste and a Prophet and one of the righteous."

40. He said: "Lord, how will I have a son, seeing I have been overtaken by old age and my wife is barren?" "This is how Allah does whatever He pleases," He replied.

41. He said: "Lord, give me a sign." Allah said: "Your sign is that you will not speak to anybody for three days, except by signs; and remember your Lord often and give praise evening and morning."

42. And when the angels said: "O Mary, Allah has chosen you and purified you, preferring you to all womankind."

43. "O Mary, be obedient to your Lord, prostrate yourself and bow down with those who bow down."

44. This is part of the tidings of the Unseen which We reveal to you. You were not in their midst when they cast their pens[216] to see who will take charge of Mary, and you were not in their midst when they were disputing.

---

215. Jesus.
216. They were casting lots.

45. When the angels said: "O Mary, Allah bids you rejoice in a word from Him, whose name is the Messiah, Jesus, son of Mary. He shall be prominent in this world[217] and the next[218] and shall be near to God."

إِذْ قَالَتِ ٱلْمَلَـٰٓئِكَةُ يَـٰمَرْيَمُ إِنَّ ٱللَّهَ يُبَشِّرُكِ بِكَلِمَةٍ مِّنْهُ ٱسْمُهُ ٱلْمَسِيحُ عِيسَى ٱبْنُ مَرْيَمَ وَجِيهًا فِى ٱلدُّنْيَا وَٱلْأَخِرَةِ وَمِنَ ٱلْمُقَرَّبِينَ ﴿٤٥﴾

46. "He shall speak to people from the cradle and while an old man and will be one of the righteous."

وَيُكَلِّمُ ٱلنَّاسَ فِى ٱلْمَهْدِ وَكَهْلًا وَمِنَ ٱلصَّـٰلِحِينَ ﴿٤٦﴾

47. She said: "Lord, how can I have a child when I have not been touched by any man?" Allah said: "Thus Allah creates whatever He pleases. When He decrees a matter, He simply says to it: 'Be', and it comes to be."

قَالَتْ رَبِّ أَنَّىٰ يَكُونُ لِى وَلَدٌ وَلَمْ يَمْسَسْنِى بَشَرٌ قَالَ كَذَٰلِكِ ٱللَّهُ يَخْلُقُ مَا يَشَآءُ إِذَا قَضَىٰٓ أَمْرًا فَإِنَّمَا يَقُولُ لَهُ كُن فَيَكُونُ ﴿٤٧﴾

48. And He will teach him the Book, the Wisdom, the Torah and the Gospel.

وَيُعَلِّمُهُ ٱلْكِتَـٰبَ وَٱلْحِكْمَةَ وَٱلتَّوْرَىٰةَ وَٱلْإِنجِيلَ ﴿٤٨﴾

49. And [send him forth as a] Messenger to the Children of Israel [saying]: "I bring you a sign from your Lord. I will create for you out of clay the likeness of a bird; then I will breathe into it and it will become a bird, by Allah's Leave. And I will heal the blind and the leper and will raise the dead, by Allah's Leave. And I will inform you concerning what you eat and what you hoard in your homes. In all this there is surely a sign for you, if you are believers!"

وَرَسُولًا إِلَىٰ بَنِىٓ إِسْرَٰٓءِيلَ أَنِّى قَدْ جِئْتُكُم بِـَٔايَةٍ مِّن رَّبِّكُمْ أَنِّىٓ أَخْلُقُ لَكُم مِّنَ ٱلطِّينِ كَهَيْـَٔةِ ٱلطَّيْرِ فَأَنفُخُ فِيهِ فَيَكُونُ طَيْرًۢا بِإِذْنِ ٱللَّهِ وَأُبْرِئُ ٱلْأَكْمَهَ وَٱلْأَبْرَصَ وَأُحْىِ ٱلْمَوْتَىٰ بِإِذْنِ ٱللَّهِ وَأُنَبِّئُكُم بِمَا تَأْكُلُونَ وَمَا تَدَّخِرُونَ فِى بُيُوتِكُمْ إِنَّ فِى ذَٰلِكَ لَـَٔايَةً لَّكُمْ إِن كُنتُم مُّؤْمِنِينَ ﴿٤٩﴾

50. "I have come to confirm what came before me of the Torah and make lawful to you some of the things that were forbidden to you. I have come to you with a sign from your Lord; so fear Allah and obey me."

وَمُصَدِّقًا لِّمَا بَيْنَ يَدَىَّ مِنَ ٱلتَّوْرَىٰةِ وَلِأُحِلَّ لَكُم بَعْضَ ٱلَّذِى حُرِّمَ عَلَيْكُمْ وَجِئْتُكُم بِـَٔايَةٍ مِّن رَّبِّكُمْ فَٱتَّقُوا۟ ٱللَّهَ وَأَطِيعُونِ ﴿٥٠﴾

51. "Allah is indeed your Lord and my Lord; so worship Him. This is the Straight Path!"

إِنَّ ٱللَّهَ رَبِّى وَرَبُّكُمْ فَٱعْبُدُوهُ هَـٰذَا صِرَٰطٌ مُّسْتَقِيمٌ ﴿٥١﴾

52. When Jesus sensed their disbelief, he said: "Who are my supporters in Allah's

فَلَمَّآ أَحَسَّ عِيسَىٰ مِنْهُمُ ٱلْكُفْرَ قَالَ مَنْ أَنصَارِىٓ إِلَى

---

217. Through prophethood.
218. Through intercession.

Way?" The disciples said: "We are Allah's supporters; we believe in Allah, so bear witness that we submit."

53. "Lord, we believe in what You have revealed, and we have followed the Messenger; write us down with those who bear witness."

54. And they[219] contrived and Allah contrived; Allah is the Best of the contrivers.

55. When Allah said: "O Jesus, I will cause you to die, will lift you up to Me, purify you from those who have disbelieved and place those who followed you above those who have disbelieved, till the Day of Resurrection. Then unto Me is your return, so that I may judge between you regarding what you were disputing."

56. "But as for those who disbelieved, I will sternly punish them in this world and the Hereafter, and they shall have no supporters."[220]

57. And as for those who have believed and done the good deeds, He will pay them their rewards in full. Allah does not love the evildoers.

58. This is what We recite[221] to you[222] of the Revelations and Wise Reminder.[223]

59. Jesus in Allah's Sight is like Adam; He created him from dust, then He said to him: "Be", and there he was.

60. [This is] the truth from your Lord; so do not be one of the doubters.

---

219. The Jews.
220. No protectors.
221. Reveal.
222. Muhammad.
223. The Qur'an.

61. To those who dispute with it[224] after the knowledge which has come to you, say [to them]: "Come now; let us call our sons and your sons, our wives and your wives, ourselves and yourselves. Then let us pray to Allah and so call down Allah's curse upon the liars."

فَمَنْ حَاجَّكَ فِيهِ مِنْ بَعْدِ مَا جَاءَكَ مِنَ ٱلْعِلْمِ فَقُلْ تَعَالَوْا نَدْعُ أَبْنَاءَنَا وَأَبْنَاءَكُمْ وَنِسَاءَنَا وَنِسَاءَكُمْ وَأَنْفُسَنَا وَأَنْفُسَكُمْ ثُمَّ نَبْتَهِلْ فَنَجْعَل لَّعْنَتَ ٱللَّهِ عَلَى ٱلْكَٰذِبِينَ ۝

62. This indeed is the true story, and there is no God but Allah, and Allah is truly the Mighty, the Wise!

إِنَّ هَٰذَا لَهُوَ ٱلْقَصَصُ ٱلْحَقُّ وَمَا مِنْ إِلَٰهٍ إِلَّا ٱللَّهُ وَإِنَّ ٱللَّهَ لَهُوَ ٱلْعَزِيزُ ٱلْحَكِيمُ ۝

63. And if they turn their backs, then Allah certainly knows the mischief-makers.

فَإِن تَوَلَّوْا فَإِنَّ ٱللَّهَ عَلِيمٌ بِٱلْمُفْسِدِينَ ۝

64. Say: 'O People of the Book, come to an equitable word between you and us, that we worship none but Allah, do not associate anything with Him and do not set up each other as lords besides Allah." If they turn their backs, say: 'Bear witness that we are Muslims."

قُلْ يَٰأَهْلَ ٱلْكِتَٰبِ تَعَالَوْا إِلَىٰ كَلِمَةٍ سَوَاءٍ بَيْنَنَا وَبَيْنَكُمْ أَلَّا نَعْبُدَ إِلَّا ٱللَّهَ وَلَا نُشْرِكَ بِهِ شَيْئًا وَلَا يَتَّخِذَ بَعْضُنَا بَعْضًا أَرْبَابًا مِّن دُونِ ٱللَّهِ فَإِن تَوَلَّوْا فَقُولُوا ٱشْهَدُوا بِأَنَّا مُسْلِمُونَ ۝

65. O People of the Book, why do you dispute concerning Abraham, when the Torah and the Gospel were only revealed after him. Do you have no sense?

يَٰأَهْلَ ٱلْكِتَٰبِ لِمَ تُحَاجُّونَ فِي إِبْرَٰهِيمَ وَمَا أُنزِلَتِ ٱلتَّوْرَىٰةُ وَٱلْإِنجِيلُ إِلَّا مِنْ بَعْدِهِ أَفَلَا تَعْقِلُونَ ۝

66. There, you have disputed concerning what you know; so why do you dispute concerning what you do not know? Allah knows and you do not know.

هَٰأَنتُمْ هَٰؤُلَاءِ حَاجَجْتُمْ فِيمَا لَكُم بِهِ عِلْمٌ فَلِمَ تُحَاجُّونَ فِيمَا لَيْسَ لَكُم بِهِ عِلْمٌ وَٱللَّهُ يَعْلَمُ وَأَنتُمْ لَا تَعْلَمُونَ ۝

67. Abraham was neither a Jew nor a Christian, but a hanif[225] and a Muslim.[226] And he was not one of the polytheists.

مَا كَانَ إِبْرَٰهِيمُ يَهُودِيًّا وَلَا نَصْرَانِيًّا وَلَٰكِن كَانَ حَنِيفًا مُّسْلِمًا وَمَا كَانَ مِنَ ٱلْمُشْرِكِينَ ۝

68. Surely, the people who are worthiest of Abraham are those who followed him, together with this Prophet[227] and the believers. Allah is the Guardian of the believers!

إِنَّ أَوْلَى ٱلنَّاسِ بِإِبْرَٰهِيمَ لَلَّذِينَ ٱتَّبَعُوهُ وَهَٰذَا ٱلنَّبِيُّ وَٱلَّذِينَ ءَامَنُوا وَٱللَّهُ وَلِيُّ ٱلْمُؤْمِنِينَ ۝

---

224. The truth regarding Jesus.
225. This Arabic word means "one who turned away from paganism."
226. "Muslim" here stands for one who believes in the unity of Allah.
227. Muhammad.

69. A party of the People of the Book[228] wished that they would lead you astray; they only lead themselves astray without perceiving it.

وَدَّت طَّآئِفَةٌ مِّنْ أَهْلِ ٱلْكِتَٰبِ لَوْ يُضِلُّونَكُمْ وَمَا يُضِلُّونَ إِلَّآ أَنفُسَهُمْ وَمَا يَشْعُرُونَ ﴿٦٩﴾

70. O People of the Book, why do you disbelieve in Allah's Revelations while you yourselves know that they are true?

يَٰٓأَهْلَ ٱلْكِتَٰبِ لِمَ تَكْفُرُونَ بِـَٔايَٰتِ ٱللَّهِ وَأَنتُمْ تَشْهَدُونَ ﴿٧٠﴾

71. People of the Book, why do you confound truth with error and knowingly conceal the truth?

يَٰٓأَهْلَ ٱلْكِتَٰبِ لِمَ تَلْبِسُونَ ٱلْحَقَّ بِٱلْبَٰطِلِ وَتَكْتُمُونَ ٱلْحَقَّ وَأَنتُمْ تَعْلَمُونَ ﴿٧١﴾

72. Some of the People of the Book say: "Believe in what has been revealed to the believers at the beginning of the day, and disbelieve in it at its end; perchance they[229] will turn back!"

وَقَالَت طَّآئِفَةٌ مِّنْ أَهْلِ ٱلْكِتَٰبِ ءَامِنُوا۟ بِٱلَّذِىٓ أُنزِلَ عَلَى ٱلَّذِينَ ءَامَنُوا۟ وَجْهَ ٱلنَّهَارِ وَٱكْفُرُوٓا۟ ءَاخِرَهُۥ لَعَلَّهُمْ يَرْجِعُونَ ﴿٧٢﴾

73. "And do not believe except in him who follows your religion." Say: "True guidance is Allah's Guidance. [Do not believe] that anyone would be given what you have been given, or that they will dispute with you before your Lord." Say: "Bounty is in Allah's Hands; He gives to whom He pleases, and Allah is All-Embracing, All-Knowing."

وَلَا تُؤْمِنُوٓا۟ إِلَّا لِمَن تَبِعَ دِينَكُمْ قُلْ إِنَّ ٱلْهُدَىٰ هُدَى ٱللَّهِ أَن يُؤْتَىٰٓ أَحَدٌ مِّثْلَ مَآ أُوتِيتُمْ أَوْ يُحَآجُّوكُمْ عِندَ رَبِّكُمْ قُلْ إِنَّ ٱلْفَضْلَ بِيَدِ ٱللَّهِ يُؤْتِيهِ مَن يَشَآءُ وَٱللَّهُ وَٰسِعٌ عَلِيمٌ ﴿٧٣﴾

74. He favours with His Mercy whomever He pleases. Allah's Bounty is unlimited!

يَخْتَصُّ بِرَحْمَتِهِۦ مَن يَشَآءُ وَٱللَّهُ ذُو ٱلْفَضْلِ ٱلْعَظِيمِ ﴿٧٤﴾

75. And among the People of the Book there are those who, if you entrust them with a heap of gold will return it to you; and there are those who, if you entrust them with one dinar, will not return it to you, unless you keep on demanding it. That is because they say: "We have no obligation towards the Gentiles";[230] and they knowingly speak falsehood against Allah.

وَمِنْ أَهْلِ ٱلْكِتَٰبِ مَنْ إِن تَأْمَنْهُ بِقِنطَارٍ يُؤَدِّهِۦٓ إِلَيْكَ وَمِنْهُم مَّنْ إِن تَأْمَنْهُ بِدِينَارٍ لَّا يُؤَدِّهِۦٓ إِلَيْكَ إِلَّا مَا دُمْتَ عَلَيْهِ قَآئِمًا ذَٰلِكَ بِأَنَّهُمْ قَالُوا۟ لَيْسَ عَلَيْنَا فِى ٱلْأُمِّيِّۧنَ سَبِيلٌ وَيَقُولُونَ عَلَى ٱللَّهِ ٱلْكَذِبَ وَهُمْ يَعْلَمُونَ ﴿٧٥﴾

---

228. The Jews.
229. The believers.
230. *Al-Ummiyun.*

63

76. Yea, whoever fulfils his pledge and is pious - truly Allah loves the pious!

77. Those who sell the Covenant of Allah and their own oaths for a small price will have no share in the life to come; Allah will neither speak to them nor look at them nor purify them on the Day of Resurrection. A painful punishment is in store for them!

78. And there is a group of them who twist their tongues while reading the Book, so that you may suppose it is part of the Book; whereas it is not part of the Book. They also say: "It is from Allah", whereas it is not from Allah; they only speak falsehood against Allah knowingly.

79. It is not given to any mortal that Allah should give him the Book, the judgement and the Prophethood and then he should say to the people: "Be servants to me, rather than to Allah"; but rather: "Be learned men, by virtue of what you used to teach of the Book and what you used to study."

80. Nor would he enjoin you to take the angels and the Prophets as lords. Would he enjoin you to be unbelievers after you have become Muslims?

81. And when Allah made His Covenant with the Prophets, [He said]: "I gave you the Book and the Wisdom. Then a Messenger[231] came to you confirming what you already possessed; so you must believe in him and give him support." He said: "Do you affirm this and accept my covenant in this matter?" They said: "We do affirm it." He said: "Bear witness and I will be with you one of the witnesses."

---

231. Muhammad.

82. "Whoever turns his back thereafter; such are the true sinners."

83. Do they desire a religion other than Allah's, after everyone in the heavens and on earth has submitted to Him willingly or unwillingly; and unto Him they shall all be brought back!

فَمَن تَوَلَّىٰ بَعْدَ ذَٰلِكَ فَأُوْلَٰٓئِكَ هُمُ ٱلْفَٰسِقُونَ ﴿٨٢﴾

أَفَغَيْرَ دِينِ ٱللَّهِ يَبْغُونَ وَلَهُۥٓ أَسْلَمَ مَن فِى ٱلسَّمَٰوَٰتِ وَٱلْأَرْضِ طَوْعًا وَكَرْهًا وَإِلَيْهِ يُرْجَعُونَ ﴿٨٣﴾

84. Say: "We believe in Allah and in what has been revealed to us and has been revealed to Abraham, Isma'il, Isaac, Jacob and the Tribes; and in what Moses, Jesus and the Prophets have received from their Lord. We do not discriminate between any of them, and to Him we submit."

قُلْ ءَامَنَّا بِٱللَّهِ وَمَآ أُنزِلَ عَلَيْنَا وَمَآ أُنزِلَ عَلَىٰٓ إِبْرَٰهِيمَ وَإِسْمَٰعِيلَ وَإِسْحَٰقَ وَيَعْقُوبَ وَٱلْأَسْبَاطِ وَمَآ أُوتِىَ مُوسَىٰ وَعِيسَىٰ وَٱلنَّبِيُّونَ مِن رَّبِّهِمْ لَا نُفَرِّقُ بَيْنَ أَحَدٍ مِّنْهُمْ وَنَحْنُ لَهُۥ مُسْلِمُونَ ﴿٨٤﴾

85. Whoever seeks a religion other than Islam, it will never be accepted from him, and in the Hereafter he will be one of the losers.

وَمَن يَبْتَغِ غَيْرَ ٱلْإِسْلَٰمِ دِينًا فَلَن يُقْبَلَ مِنْهُ وَهُوَ فِى ٱلْأَخِرَةِ مِنَ ٱلْخَٰسِرِينَ ﴿٨٥﴾

86. How will Allah guide a people who disbelieved after they had believed and bore witness that the Messenger is true, and after the clear proofs had come to them? Allah will not guide the unjust people.

كَيْفَ يَهْدِى ٱللَّهُ قَوْمًا كَفَرُوا۟ بَعْدَ إِيمَٰنِهِمْ وَشَهِدُوٓا۟ أَنَّ ٱلرَّسُولَ حَقٌّ وَجَآءَهُمُ ٱلْبَيِّنَٰتُ وَٱللَّهُ لَا يَهْدِى ٱلْقَوْمَ ٱلظَّٰلِمِينَ ﴿٨٦﴾

87. The reward of those people shall be that the curse of Allah, the angels and mankind as a whole shall be upon them.

أُوْلَٰٓئِكَ جَزَآؤُهُمْ أَنَّ عَلَيْهِمْ لَعْنَةَ ٱللَّهِ وَٱلْمَلَٰٓئِكَةِ وَٱلنَّاسِ أَجْمَعِينَ ﴿٨٧﴾

88. They will abide therein forever; their punishment shall not be lightened and they shall have no respite.

خَٰلِدِينَ فِيهَا لَا يُخَفَّفُ عَنْهُمُ ٱلْعَذَابُ وَلَا هُمْ يُنظَرُونَ ﴿٨٨﴾

89. Except for those who repent afterwards and mend their ways; for Allah is Forgiving and Merciful.

إِلَّا ٱلَّذِينَ تَابُوا۟ مِنۢ بَعْدِ ذَٰلِكَ وَأَصْلَحُوا۟ فَإِنَّ ٱللَّهَ غَفُورٌ رَّحِيمٌ ﴿٨٩﴾

90. Surely those who disbelieve after believing, and then grow in disbelief, their repentance shall not be accepted. Those are the ones who have gone astray!

إِنَّ ٱلَّذِينَ كَفَرُوا۟ بَعْدَ إِيمَٰنِهِمْ ثُمَّ ٱزْدَادُوا۟ كُفْرًا لَّن تُقْبَلَ تَوْبَتُهُمْ وَأُوْلَٰٓئِكَ هُمُ ٱلضَّآلُّونَ ﴿٩٠﴾

91. As for those who disbelieve and die as unbelievers, the earth's fill of gold will not be

إِنَّ ٱلَّذِينَ كَفَرُوا۟ وَمَاتُوا۟ وَهُمْ كُفَّارٌ فَلَن يُقْبَلَ مِن

accepted from any of them, even if it is offered as ransom. For those, a painful punishment is reserved and they will have no supporters!

أَحَدِهِم مِّلْءُ ٱلْأَرْضِ ذَهَبًا وَلَوِ ٱفْتَدَىٰ بِهِۦٓ أُوْلَٰٓئِكَ لَهُمْ عَذَابٌ أَلِيمٌ وَمَا لَهُم مِّن نَّٰصِرِينَ ﴿٩١﴾

92. You will not achieve piety until you spend part of what you cherish; and whatever you spend, Allah knows it very well.

لَن تَنَالُوا۟ ٱلْبِرَّ حَتَّىٰ تُنفِقُوا۟ مِمَّا تُحِبُّونَ وَمَا تُنفِقُوا۟ مِن شَىْءٍ فَإِنَّ ٱللَّهَ بِهِۦ عَلِيمٌ ﴿٩٢﴾

93. All food was lawful to the Children of Israel, save what Israel forbade itself before the Torah was revealed. Say: "Bring then the Torah and recite it, if you are truthful."

كُلُّ ٱلطَّعَامِ كَانَ حِلًّا لِّبَنِىٓ إِسْرَٰٓءِيلَ إِلَّا مَا حَرَّمَ إِسْرَٰٓءِيلُ عَلَىٰ نَفْسِهِۦ مِن قَبْلِ أَن تُنَزَّلَ ٱلتَّوْرَىٰةُ قُلْ فَأْتُوا۟ بِٱلتَّوْرَىٰةِ فَٱتْلُوهَآ إِن كُنتُمْ صَٰدِقِينَ ﴿٩٣﴾

94. Whoever, afterwards, fabricates false-hood against Allah, those are truly the evil-doers.

فَمَنِ ٱفْتَرَىٰ عَلَى ٱللَّهِ ٱلْكَذِبَ مِنۢ بَعْدِ ذَٰلِكَ فَأُوْلَٰٓئِكَ هُمُ ٱلظَّٰلِمُونَ ﴿٩٤﴾

95. Say: "Allah has spoken the truth. Follow then the religion of Abraham, the upright; he was not one of the polytheists."

قُلْ صَدَقَ ٱللَّهُ فَٱتَّبِعُوا۟ مِلَّةَ إِبْرَٰهِيمَ حَنِيفًا وَمَا كَانَ مِنَ ٱلْمُشْرِكِينَ ﴿٩٥﴾

96. The first House founded for mankind is truly that at Bakka,[232] blessed and a guidance to all the nations.

إِنَّ أَوَّلَ بَيْتٍ وُضِعَ لِلنَّاسِ لَلَّذِى بِبَكَّةَ مُبَارَكًا وَهُدًى لِّلْعَٰلَمِينَ ﴿٩٦﴾

97. Therein are clear signs and the sacred site of Abraham. Whoever enters it will be secure. It is the duty to Allah incumbent on those who can, to make the pilgrimage to the House. But with respect to those who disbelieve, Allah has no need of all mankind.

فِيهِ ءَايَٰتٌۢ بَيِّنَٰتٌ مَّقَامُ إِبْرَٰهِيمَ وَمَن دَخَلَهُۥ كَانَ ءَامِنًا وَلِلَّهِ عَلَى ٱلنَّاسِ حِجُّ ٱلْبَيْتِ مَنِ ٱسْتَطَاعَ إِلَيْهِ سَبِيلًا وَمَن كَفَرَ فَإِنَّ ٱللَّهَ غَنِىٌّ عَنِ ٱلْعَٰلَمِينَ ﴿٩٧﴾

98. Say: "O People of the Book, why do you disbelieve in the Revelations of Allah, when Allah witnesses whatever you do?"

قُلْ يَٰٓأَهْلَ ٱلْكِتَٰبِ لِمَ تَكْفُرُونَ بِـَٔايَٰتِ ٱللَّهِ وَٱللَّهُ شَهِيدٌ عَلَىٰ مَا تَعْمَلُونَ ﴿٩٨﴾

99. Say: "O People of the Book, why do you debar those who have believed from the Path[233] of Allah, seeking to make it crooked, while you are witnesses?[234] Allah is not unaware of what you do!"

قُلْ يَٰٓأَهْلَ ٱلْكِتَٰبِ لِمَ تَصُدُّونَ عَن سَبِيلِ ٱللَّهِ مَنْ ءَامَنَ تَبْغُونَهَا عِوَجًا وَأَنتُمْ شُهَدَآءُ وَمَا ٱللَّهُ بِغَٰفِلٍ عَمَّا تَعْمَلُونَ ﴿٩٩﴾

---

232. Mecca.
233. The religion.
234. While you know it is the right religion.

100. O believers, if you obey a group of those who have received the Book, they will turn you, after you have believed, into unbelievers.

101. How could you disbelieve, while God's Revelations are recited to you, and His Messenger is in your midst? He who holds fast to Allah has been guided to a straight path.

102. O believers, fear Allah as He should be feared, and do not die except as Muslims.

103. And hold fast to Allah's Bond,[235] all of you, and do not fall apart. And remember Allah's Grace upon you; how you were enemies, then He united your hearts[236] so that you have become, by His Grace, brethren. You were on the brink of the pit of Fire, but He saved you from it. Thus Allah manifests to you His Revelations so that perchance you might be rightly guided!

104. And let there be among you a nation calling to goodness, bidding the right and forbidding the wrong. Those are the prosperous.

105. And do not be like those who fell apart and quarrelled, after the clear proofs came to them. For those a terrible punishment is in store.

106. On the Day when some faces will turn white and others will turn black. As to those whose faces turn black [it will be said]: "Did you disbelieve after you had believed? Then taste the punishment because you have disbelieved."

107. But as for those whose faces turned white, they will dwell in Allah's Mercy[237] forever.

يَـٰٓأَيُّهَا ٱلَّذِينَ ءَامَنُوٓاْ إِن تُطِيعُواْ فَرِيقًا مِّنَ ٱلَّذِينَ أُوتُواْ ٱلْكِتَـٰبَ يَرُدُّوكُم بَعْدَ إِيمَـٰنِكُمْ كَـٰفِرِينَ ﴿١٠٠﴾

وَكَيْفَ تَكْفُرُونَ وَأَنتُمْ تُتْلَىٰ عَلَيْكُمْ ءَايَـٰتُ ٱللَّهِ وَفِيكُمْ رَسُولُهُۥ وَمَن يَعْتَصِم بِٱللَّهِ فَقَدْ هُدِىَ إِلَىٰ صِرَٰطٍ مُّسْتَقِيمٍ ﴿١٠١﴾

يَـٰٓأَيُّهَا ٱلَّذِينَ ءَامَنُواْ ٱتَّقُواْ ٱللَّهَ حَقَّ تُقَاتِهِۦ وَلَا تَمُوتُنَّ إِلَّا وَأَنتُم مُّسْلِمُونَ ﴿١٠٢﴾

وَٱعْتَصِمُواْ بِحَبْلِ ٱللَّهِ جَمِيعًا وَلَا تَفَرَّقُواْ وَٱذْكُرُواْ نِعْمَتَ ٱللَّهِ عَلَيْكُمْ إِذْ كُنتُمْ أَعْدَآءً فَأَلَّفَ بَيْنَ قُلُوبِكُمْ فَأَصْبَحْتُم بِنِعْمَتِهِۦٓ إِخْوَٰنًا وَكُنتُمْ عَلَىٰ شَفَا حُفْرَةٍ مِّنَ ٱلنَّارِ فَأَنقَذَكُم مِّنْهَا كَذَٰلِكَ يُبَيِّنُ ٱللَّهُ لَكُمْ ءَايَـٰتِهِۦ لَعَلَّكُمْ تَهْتَدُونَ ﴿١٠٣﴾

وَلْتَكُن مِّنكُمْ أُمَّةٌ يَدْعُونَ إِلَى ٱلْخَيْرِ وَيَأْمُرُونَ بِٱلْمَعْرُوفِ وَيَنْهَوْنَ عَنِ ٱلْمُنكَرِ وَأُوْلَـٰٓئِكَ هُمُ ٱلْمُفْلِحُونَ ﴿١٠٤﴾

وَلَا تَكُونُواْ كَٱلَّذِينَ تَفَرَّقُواْ وَٱخْتَلَفُواْ مِنۢ بَعْدِ مَا جَآءَهُمُ ٱلْبَيِّنَـٰتُ وَأُوْلَـٰٓئِكَ لَهُمْ عَذَابٌ عَظِيمٌ ﴿١٠٥﴾

يَوْمَ تَبْيَضُّ وُجُوهٌ وَتَسْوَدُّ وُجُوهٌ فَأَمَّا ٱلَّذِينَ ٱسْوَدَّتْ وُجُوهُهُمْ أَكَفَرْتُم بَعْدَ إِيمَـٰنِكُمْ فَذُوقُواْ ٱلْعَذَابَ بِمَا كُنتُمْ تَكْفُرُونَ ﴿١٠٦﴾

وَأَمَّا ٱلَّذِينَ ٱبْيَضَّتْ وُجُوهُهُمْ فَفِى رَحْمَةِ ٱللَّهِ هُمْ فِيهَا خَـٰلِدُونَ ﴿١٠٧﴾

---

235. His religion.
236. By becoming Muslims.
237. In Paradise.

108. These are the Revelations of Allah. We recite them to you in truth, and Allah does not desire any injustice for mankind.

تِلْكَ ءَايَتُ ٱللَّهِ نَتْلُوهَا عَلَيْكَ بِٱلْحَقِّ وَمَا ٱللَّهُ يُرِيدُ ظُلْمًا لِلْعَٰلَمِينَ ۝

109. And to Allah belongs what is in the heavens and on earth, and unto Him all matters shall be referred.

وَلِلَّهِ مَا فِى ٱلسَّمَٰوَٰتِ وَمَا فِى ٱلْأَرْضِ وَإِلَى ٱللَّهِ تُرْجَعُ ٱلْأُمُورُ ۝

110. You were the best nation brought forth to mankind, bidding the right and forbidding the wrong, and believing in Allah. Had the People of the Book believed, it would have been far better for them; some of them are believers, but most of them are sinners.

كُنتُمْ خَيْرَ أُمَّةٍ أُخْرِجَتْ لِلنَّاسِ تَأْمُرُونَ بِٱلْمَعْرُوفِ وَتَنْهَوْنَ عَنِ ٱلْمُنكَرِ وَتُؤْمِنُونَ بِٱللَّهِ وَلَوْ ءَامَنَ أَهْلُ ٱلْكِتَٰبِ لَكَانَ خَيْرًا لَّهُم مِّنْهُمُ ٱلْمُؤْمِنُونَ وَأَكْثَرُهُمُ ٱلْفَٰسِقُونَ ۝

111. They will only cause you a little harm; and if they fight you, they will turn their backs on you,[238] and will have no support.

لَن يَضُرُّوكُمْ إِلَّا أَذًى وَإِن يُقَٰتِلُوكُمْ يُوَلُّوكُمُ ٱلْأَدْبَارَ ثُمَّ لَا يُنصَرُونَ ۝

112. Ignominy shall attend them wherever they are found, unless [they are bound] by a covenant from Allah and a covenant from the people. They will incur Allah's anger, and wretchedness shall be stamped on them, because they disbelieved in Allah's Revelations and killed Prophets unjustly. That is because they disobeyed and exceeded the limits.[239]

ضُرِبَتْ عَلَيْهِمُ ٱلذِّلَّةُ أَيْنَ مَا ثُقِفُوٓا۟ إِلَّا بِحَبْلٍ مِّنَ ٱللَّهِ وَحَبْلٍ مِّنَ ٱلنَّاسِ وَبَآءُو بِغَضَبٍ مِّنَ ٱللَّهِ وَضُرِبَتْ عَلَيْهِمُ ٱلْمَسْكَنَةُ ذَٰلِكَ بِأَنَّهُمْ كَانُوا۟ يَكْفُرُونَ بِـَٔايَٰتِ ٱللَّهِ وَيَقْتُلُونَ ٱلْأَنۢبِيَآءَ بِغَيْرِ حَقٍّ ذَٰلِكَ بِمَا عَصَوا۟ وَّكَانُوا۟ يَعْتَدُونَ ۝

113. They are not all alike. For of the People of the Book, there is an upright nation[240] who recite Allah's Revelations, throughout the night, while prostrating themselves.

لَيْسُوا۟ سَوَآءً مِّنْ أَهْلِ ٱلْكِتَٰبِ أُمَّةٌ قَآئِمَةٌ يَتْلُونَ ءَايَٰتِ ٱللَّهِ ءَانَآءَ ٱلَّيْلِ وَهُمْ يَسْجُدُونَ ۝

114. They believe in Allah and the Last Day, bid the right and forbid the wrong and hasten to do the good deeds. Those are among the righteous people!

يُؤْمِنُونَ بِٱللَّهِ وَٱلْيَوْمِ ٱلْأَخِرِ وَيَأْمُرُونَ بِٱلْمَعْرُوفِ وَيَنْهَوْنَ عَنِ ٱلْمُنكَرِ وَيُسَٰرِعُونَ فِى ٱلْخَيْرَٰتِ وَأُو۟لَٰٓئِكَ مِنَ ٱلصَّٰلِحِينَ ۝

115. And whatever good they do, they will not be denied it. Allah knows well the God-fearing!

وَمَا يَفْعَلُوا۟ مِنْ خَيْرٍ فَلَن يُكْفَرُوهُ وَٱللَّهُ عَلِيمٌۢ بِٱلْمُتَّقِينَ ۝

---

238. In defeat.
239. By doing what is unlawful.
240. Group.

116. As for the unbelievers, neither their riches nor their children will avail them anything against Allah. Those are the people of Hell, abiding therein forever!

إِنَّ ٱلَّذِينَ كَفَرُوا لَن تُغْنِىَ عَنْهُمْ أَمْوَٰلُهُمْ وَلَآ أَوْلَٰدُهُم مِّنَ ٱللَّهِ شَيْئًا وَأُوْلَٰٓئِكَ أَصْحَٰبُ ٱلنَّارِ هُمْ فِيهَا خَٰلِدُونَ ۝

117. That which they spend in this present life is similar to a frosty wind which smote the harvest of a people who had wronged themselves, and so destroyed it. Allah did not wrong them, but they wronged themselves!

مَثَلُ مَا يُنفِقُونَ فِى هَٰذِهِ ٱلْحَيَوٰةِ ٱلدُّنْيَا كَمَثَلِ رِيحٍ فِيهَا صِرٌّ أَصَابَتْ حَرْثَ قَوْمٍ ظَلَمُوٓا أَنفُسَهُمْ فَأَهْلَكَتْهُ وَمَا ظَلَمَهُمُ ٱللَّهُ وَلَٰكِنْ أَنفُسَهُمْ يَظْلِمُونَ ۝

118. O believers, do not take as close friends other than your own people;[241] they will spare no effort to corrupt you and wish to see you suffer. Hatred has already been manifested in what they utter, but what their hearts conceal is greater still. We have made clear Our Signs to you if only you understand.

يَٰٓأَيُّهَا ٱلَّذِينَ ءَامَنُوا لَا تَتَّخِذُوا بِطَانَةً مِّن دُونِكُمْ لَا يَأْلُونَكُمْ خَبَالًا وَدُّوا مَا عَنِتُّمْ قَدْ بَدَتِ ٱلْبَغْضَآءُ مِنْ أَفْوَٰهِهِمْ وَمَا تُخْفِى صُدُورُهُمْ أَكْبَرُ قَدْ بَيَّنَّا لَكُمُ ٱلْءَايَٰتِ إِن كُنتُمْ تَعْقِلُونَ ۝

119. There you are, you love them, but they do not love you, and you believe in the entire Book.[242] When they meet you, they say: "We believe", but when they are alone they bite their fingertips with rage. Say: "Die of your fury. Allah knows what is hidden in the hearts!"

هَٰٓأَنتُمْ أُوْلَآءِ تُحِبُّونَهُمْ وَلَا يُحِبُّونَكُمْ وَتُؤْمِنُونَ بِٱلْكِتَٰبِ كُلِّهِ وَإِذَا لَقُوكُمْ قَالُوٓا ءَامَنَّا وَإِذَا خَلَوْا عَضُّوا عَلَيْكُمُ ٱلْأَنَامِلَ مِنَ ٱلْغَيْظِ قُلْ مُوتُوا بِغَيْظِكُمْ إِنَّ ٱللَّهَ عَلِيمٌ بِذَاتِ ٱلصُّدُورِ ۝

120. If you are visited by some good fortune, it vexes them; and if you are visited by some misfortune, they rejoice at it; but if you forbear and fear Allah, their wiles will not hurt you at all. Allah knows fully what they do!

إِن تَمْسَسْكُمْ حَسَنَةٌ تَسُؤْهُمْ وَإِن تُصِبْكُمْ سَيِّئَةٌ يَفْرَحُوا بِهَا وَإِن تَصْبِرُوا وَتَتَّقُوا لَا يَضُرُّكُمْ كَيْدُهُمْ شَيْئًا إِنَّ ٱللَّهَ بِمَا يَعْمَلُونَ مُحِيطٌ ۝

121. [And remember] when you[243] went at daybreak, away from your family, in order to lead the believers to their battle-stations;[244] Allah is All-Hearing, All-Knowing!

وَإِذْ غَدَوْتَ مِنْ أَهْلِكَ تُبَوِّئُ ٱلْمُؤْمِنِينَ مَقَٰعِدَ لِلْقِتَالِ وَٱللَّهُ سَمِيعٌ عَلِيمٌ ۝

---

241. Other than your co-religionists.
242. In all Scriptures.
243. Muhammad.
244. The Prophet led them to the Battle of Uhud, 2 AH/625 AD to fight Abu Sufyan who had led his troops to attack Medina.

122. Two of your battalions[245] were about to lose heart, and Allah was their Protector. In Allah let the believers put their trust!

إِذْ هَمَّت طَّآئِفَتَانِ مِنكُمْ أَن تَفْشَلَا وَٱللَّهُ وَلِيُّهُمَا ۗ وَعَلَى ٱللَّهِ فَلْيَتَوَكَّلِ ٱلْمُؤْمِنُونَ ﴿١٢٢﴾

123. Allah had already given you victory at Badr, at a time when you were still power-less; so fear Allah that perchance you might be thankful!

وَلَقَدْ نَصَرَكُمُ ٱللَّهُ بِبَدْرٍ وَأَنتُمْ أَذِلَّةٌ ۖ فَٱتَّقُوا۟ ٱللَّهَ لَعَلَّكُمْ تَشْكُرُونَ ﴿١٢٣﴾

124. When you were telling the believers: "Is it not enough that your Lord should reinforce you with three thousand angels sent down?"

إِذْ تَقُولُ لِلْمُؤْمِنِينَ أَلَن يَكْفِيَكُمْ أَن يُمِدَّكُمْ رَبُّكُم بِثَلَٰثَةِ ءَالَٰفٍ مِّنَ ٱلْمَلَٰٓئِكَةِ مُنزَلِينَ ﴿١٢٤﴾

125. Yes, if you forbear and fear Allah and the enemy attack you at once, your Lord will reinforce you with five thousand marked angels.

بَلَىٰٓ ۚ إِن تَصْبِرُوا۟ وَتَتَّقُوا۟ وَيَأْتُوكُم مِّن فَوْرِهِمْ هَٰذَا يُمْدِدْكُمْ رَبُّكُم بِخَمْسَةِ ءَالَٰفٍ مِّنَ ٱلْمَلَٰٓئِكَةِ مُسَوِّمِينَ ﴿١٢٥﴾

126. Allah has not intended this except as good news to you and that your hearts might be reassured thereby. Victory comes only from Allah, the Mighty, the Wise!

وَمَا جَعَلَهُ ٱللَّهُ إِلَّا بُشْرَىٰ لَكُمْ وَلِتَطْمَئِنَّ قُلُوبُكُم بِهِ ۗ وَمَا ٱلنَّصْرُ إِلَّا مِنْ عِندِ ٱللَّهِ ٱلْعَزِيزِ ٱلْحَكِيمِ ﴿١٢٦﴾

127. That He may cut off a group of the unbelievers or humiliate them,[246] so that they may turn away completely baffled.

لِيَقْطَعَ طَرَفًا مِّنَ ٱلَّذِينَ كَفَرُوٓا۟ أَوْ يَكْبِتَهُمْ فَيَنقَلِبُوا۟ خَآئِبِينَ ﴿١٢٧﴾

128. It is no business of yours whether Allah forgives them or punishes them; for they are indeed evil-doers!

لَيْسَ لَكَ مِنَ ٱلْأَمْرِ شَىْءٌ أَوْ يَتُوبَ عَلَيْهِمْ أَوْ يُعَذِّبَهُمْ فَإِنَّهُمْ ظَٰلِمُونَ ﴿١٢٨﴾

129. And to Allah belongs what is in the heavens and on earth; He forgives whom He pleases and punishes whom He pleases. Allah is All-Forgiving and Merciful!

وَلِلَّهِ مَا فِى ٱلسَّمَٰوَٰتِ وَمَا فِى ٱلْأَرْضِ ۚ يَغْفِرُ لِمَن يَشَآءُ وَيُعَذِّبُ مَن يَشَآءُ ۚ وَٱللَّهُ غَفُورٌ رَّحِيمٌ ﴿١٢٩﴾

130. O believers, do not devour usury, doubled and redoubled, and fear Allah that you may prosper!

يَٰٓأَيُّهَا ٱلَّذِينَ ءَامَنُوا۟ لَا تَأْكُلُوا۟ ٱلرِّبَوٰٓا۟ أَضْعَٰفًا مُّضَٰعَفَةً ۖ وَٱتَّقُوا۟ ٱللَّهَ لَعَلَّكُمْ تُفْلِحُونَ ﴿١٣٠﴾

131. And guard yourselves against the Fire which has been prepared for the unbelievers.

وَٱتَّقُوا۟ ٱلنَّارَ ٱلَّتِىٓ أُعِدَّتْ لِلْكَٰفِرِينَ ﴿١٣١﴾

---

245. They belonged to Banu Salamah and Banu Harithah who formed the two wings of the Muslim army which was led by the Prophet.
246. Humiliate them by their defeat.

132. And obey Allah and the Messenger, that perchance you may find mercy.

133. And hasten to forgiveness from your Lord and a Paradise as wide as the heavens and the earth, prepared for the God-fearing;

134. Those who spend freely in prosperity and in adversity, those who curb their anger and those who pardon their fellow men. Allah loves the beneficent!

135. And those who, when they commit an indecency or wrong themselves, remember Allah and ask forgiveness for their sins. For who but Allah forgives sins? And they will not persist in what they do knowingly.

136. The reward of these is Forgiveness from their Lord and Gardens beneath which rivers flow, abiding therein forever. Blessed is the reward of the workers!

137. There have been examples[247] before you; so travel in the land and behold the fate of those who disbelieved.[248]

138. This is a declaration for mankind, a guidance and admonition for the God-fearing.

139. Do not be faint-hearted and do not grieve; you will have the upper hand, if you are true believers.

140. If you have been afflicted by a wound, a similar wound has afflicted the others.[249] Such are the times; We alternate them among the people, so that Allah may know who are the believers and choose martyrs from among you. Allah does not like the evildoers!

141. And that Allah might purify the believers and annihilate the unbelievers.

وَأَطِيعُوا۟ ٱللَّهَ وَٱلرَّسُولَ لَعَلَّكُمْ تُرْحَمُونَ ﴿١٣٢﴾

وَسَارِعُوٓا۟ إِلَىٰ مَغْفِرَةٍ مِّن رَّبِّكُمْ وَجَنَّةٍ عَرْضُهَا ٱلسَّمَـٰوَٰتُ وَٱلْأَرْضُ أُعِدَّتْ لِلْمُتَّقِينَ ﴿١٣٣﴾

ٱلَّذِينَ يُنفِقُونَ فِى ٱلسَّرَّآءِ وَٱلضَّرَّآءِ وَٱلْكَـٰظِمِينَ ٱلْغَيْظَ وَٱلْعَافِينَ عَنِ ٱلنَّاسِ وَٱللَّهُ يُحِبُّ ٱلْمُحْسِنِينَ ﴿١٣٤﴾

وَٱلَّذِينَ إِذَا فَعَلُوا۟ فَـٰحِشَةً أَوْ ظَلَمُوٓا۟ أَنفُسَهُمْ ذَكَرُوا۟ ٱللَّهَ فَٱسْتَغْفَرُوا۟ لِذُنُوبِهِمْ وَمَن يَغْفِرُ ٱلذُّنُوبَ إِلَّا ٱللَّهُ وَلَمْ يُصِرُّوا۟ عَلَىٰ مَا فَعَلُوا۟ وَهُمْ يَعْلَمُونَ ﴿١٣٥﴾

أُو۟لَـٰٓئِكَ جَزَآؤُهُم مَّغْفِرَةٌ مِّن رَّبِّهِمْ وَجَنَّـٰتٌ تَجْرِى مِن تَحْتِهَا ٱلْأَنْهَـٰرُ خَـٰلِدِينَ فِيهَا وَنِعْمَ أَجْرُ ٱلْعَـٰمِلِينَ ﴿١٣٦﴾

قَدْ خَلَتْ مِن قَبْلِكُمْ سُنَنٌ فَسِيرُوا۟ فِى ٱلْأَرْضِ فَٱنظُرُوا۟ كَيْفَ كَانَ عَـٰقِبَةُ ٱلْمُكَذِّبِينَ ﴿١٣٧﴾

هَـٰذَا بَيَانٌ لِّلنَّاسِ وَهُدًى وَمَوْعِظَةٌ لِّلْمُتَّقِينَ ﴿١٣٨﴾

وَلَا تَهِنُوا۟ وَلَا تَحْزَنُوا۟ وَأَنتُمُ ٱلْأَعْلَوْنَ إِن كُنتُم مُّؤْمِنِينَ ﴿١٣٩﴾

إِن يَمْسَسْكُمْ قَرْحٌ فَقَدْ مَسَّ ٱلْقَوْمَ قَرْحٌ مِّثْلُهُۥ وَتِلْكَ ٱلْأَيَّامُ نُدَاوِلُهَا بَيْنَ ٱلنَّاسِ وَلِيَعْلَمَ ٱللَّهُ ٱلَّذِينَ ءَامَنُوا۟ وَيَتَّخِذَ مِنكُمْ شُهَدَآءَ وَٱللَّهُ لَا يُحِبُّ ٱلظَّـٰلِمِينَ ﴿١٤٠﴾

وَلِيُمَحِّصَ ٱللَّهُ ٱلَّذِينَ ءَامَنُوا۟ وَيَمْحَقَ ٱلْكَـٰفِرِينَ ﴿١٤١﴾

---

247. Examples of how Allah dealt with the unbelievers.
248. Who disbelieved the Messengers.
249. The unbelievers.

142. Or did you suppose that you will enter Paradise, before Allah has known who were those of you who have struggled, and those who are steadfast.

أَمْ حَسِبْتُمْ أَن تَدْخُلُوا الْجَنَّةَ وَلَمَّا يَعْلَمِ اللَّهُ الَّذِينَ جَهَدُوا مِنكُمْ وَيَعْلَمَ الصَّبِرِينَ ﴿١٤٢﴾

143. You were yearning for death before you actually met it. Now you have seen it and you are beholding it.

وَلَقَدْ كُنتُمْ تَمَنَّوْنَ الْمَوْتَ مِن قَبْلِ أَن تَلْقَوْهُ فَقَدْ رَأَيْتُمُوهُ وَأَنتُمْ تَنظُرُونَ ﴿١٤٣﴾

144. Muhammad is merely a Messenger, before whom many Messengers have come and gone. If then he dies or gets killed, you will turn on your heels? Should any man turn on his heels, he will not cause Allah any harm; and Allah will reward the thankful.

وَمَا مُحَمَّدٌ إِلَّا رَسُولٌ قَدْ خَلَتْ مِن قَبْلِهِ الرُّسُلُ أَفَإِن مَّاتَ أَوْ قُتِلَ انقَلَبْتُمْ عَلَى أَعْقَبِكُمْ وَمَن يَنقَلِبْ عَلَى عَقِبَيْهِ فَلَن يَضُرَّ اللَّهَ شَيْئًا وَسَيَجْزِي اللَّهُ الشَّكِرِينَ ﴿١٤٤﴾

145. It is not given to any soul to die, except with Allah's Leave, at a fixed time. He who desires the reward of this world, We will give him [part] of it, and he who desires the reward of the life to come, We will give him [part] of it; and We shall reward the thankful.

وَمَا كَانَ لِنَفْسٍ أَن تَمُوتَ إِلَّا بِإِذْنِ اللَّهِ كِتَبًا مُّؤَجَّلًا وَمَن يُرِدْ ثَوَابَ الدُّنْيَا نُؤْتِهِ مِنْهَا وَمَن يُرِدْ ثَوَابَ الْآخِرَةِ نُؤْتِهِ مِنْهَا وَسَنَجْزِي الشَّكِرِينَ ﴿١٤٥﴾

146. How many Prophets with whom large multitudes have fought; they were not daunted on account of what befell them in the Cause of Allah. They did not weaken or cringe; and Allah loves the steadfast!

وَكَأَيِّن مِّن نَّبِيٍّ قَتَلَ مَعَهُ رِبِّيُّونَ كَثِيرٌ فَمَا وَهَنُوا لِمَا أَصَابَهُمْ فِي سَبِيلِ اللَّهِ وَمَا ضَعُفُوا وَمَا اسْتَكَانُوا وَاللَّهُ يُحِبُّ الصَّبِرِينَ ﴿١٤٦﴾

147. Their only words were: "Lord, forgive us our sins and our excess in our affairs. Make firm our feet and grant us victory over the unbelieving people."

وَمَا كَانَ قَوْلَهُمْ إِلَّا أَن قَالُوا رَبَّنَا اغْفِرْ لَنَا ذُنُوبَنَا وَإِسْرَافَنَا فِي أَمْرِنَا وَثَبِّتْ أَقْدَامَنَا وَانصُرْنَا عَلَى الْقَوْمِ الْكَفِرِينَ ﴿١٤٧﴾

148. Therefore Allah granted them the reward of this life and the excellent reward[250] of the life to come, and Allah loves the beneficent!

فَآتَاهُمُ اللَّهُ ثَوَابَ الدُّنْيَا وَحُسْنَ ثَوَابِ الْآخِرَةِ وَاللَّهُ يُحِبُّ الْمُحْسِنِينَ ﴿١٤٨﴾

149. O believers, if you obey the unbelievers, they will turn you upon your heels,[251] and thus you will become complete losers.

يَأَيُّهَا الَّذِينَ ءَامَنُوا إِن تُطِيعُوا الَّذِينَ كَفَرُوا يَرُدُّوكُمْ عَلَى أَعْقَبِكُمْ فَتَنقَلِبُوا خَسِرِينَ ﴿١٤٩﴾

---

250. Paradise.
251. Thus turning you back from your true religion.

150. Rather, Allah is your Protector, and He is the Best Supporter!

151. We will cast terror into the hearts of the unbelievers on account of their associating with Allah that for which He sent down no authority. Their abode is the Fire and wretched is the dwelling-place of the evildoers!

152. Allah fulfilled His Promise to you when, by His Leave, you went on killing them; until you lost heart and dissented about the affair and disobeyed,[252] after He had shown you what you cherished. Some of you desired this world,[253] others the Hereafter. Then, He turned you away from them[254] in order to test you, and He has forgiven you. Allah is Gracious to the believers!

153. [Remember] how you fled and paid heed to no one, while the Messenger was calling you from the rear. Thus He rewarded you with grief upon grief, lest you should not be sorry for what you missed or what befell you. Allah is Aware of what you do!

154. Then He sent down upon you, after the grief, as a security, slumber overcoming a group of you, whereas another group were only concerned about themselves, entertaining untrue thoughts about Allah, like the thoughts of the pagans. They say: "Do we have any part in the affair?" Say: "The whole affair is Allah's." They conceal in their hearts what they do not reveal to you.
They say: "Had we had any part in the affair, we would not have been killed here." Say: "Had you been in your homes, those who

بَلِ ٱللَّهُ مَوْلَىٰكُمْ وَهُوَ خَيْرُ ٱلنَّٰصِرِينَ ۝

سَنُلْقِى فِى قُلُوبِ ٱلَّذِينَ كَفَرُوا ٱلرُّعْبَ بِمَآ أَشْرَكُوا بِٱللَّهِ مَا لَمْ يُنَزِّلْ بِهِۦ سُلْطَٰنًا وَمَأْوَىٰهُمُ ٱلنَّارُ وَبِئْسَ مَثْوَى ٱلظَّٰلِمِينَ ۝

وَلَقَدْ صَدَقَكُمُ ٱللَّهُ وَعْدَهُۥٓ إِذْ تَحُسُّونَهُم بِإِذْنِهِۦ حَتَّىٰ إِذَا فَشِلْتُمْ وَتَنَٰزَعْتُمْ فِى ٱلْأَمْرِ وَعَصَيْتُم مِّنۢ بَعْدِ مَآ أَرَىٰكُم مَّا تُحِبُّونَ مِنكُم مَّن يُرِيدُ ٱلدُّنْيَا وَمِنكُم مَّن يُرِيدُ ٱلْءَاخِرَةَ ثُمَّ صَرَفَكُمْ عَنْهُمْ لِيَبْتَلِيَكُمْ وَلَقَدْ عَفَا عَنكُمْ وَٱللَّهُ ذُو فَضْلٍ عَلَى ٱلْمُؤْمِنِينَ ۝

إِذْ تُصْعِدُونَ وَلَا تَلْوُۥنَ عَلَىٰٓ أَحَدٍ وَٱلرَّسُولُ يَدْعُوكُمْ فِىٓ أُخْرَىٰكُمْ فَأَثَٰبَكُمْ غَمًّۢا بِغَمٍّ لِّكَيْلَا تَحْزَنُوا عَلَىٰ مَا فَاتَكُمْ وَلَا مَآ أَصَٰبَكُمْ وَٱللَّهُ خَبِيرٌۢ بِمَا تَعْمَلُونَ ۝

ثُمَّ أَنزَلَ عَلَيْكُم مِّنۢ بَعْدِ ٱلْغَمِّ أَمَنَةً نُّعَاسًا يَغْشَىٰ طَآئِفَةً مِّنكُمْ وَطَآئِفَةٌ قَدْ أَهَمَّتْهُمْ أَنفُسُهُمْ يَظُنُّونَ بِٱللَّهِ غَيْرَ ٱلْحَقِّ ظَنَّ ٱلْجَٰهِلِيَّةِ يَقُولُونَ هَل لَّنَا مِنَ ٱلْأَمْرِ مِن شَىْءٍ قُلْ إِنَّ ٱلْأَمْرَ كُلَّهُۥ لِلَّهِ يُخْفُونَ فِىٓ أَنفُسِهِم مَّا لَا يُبْدُونَ لَكَ يَقُولُونَ لَوْ كَانَ لَنَا مِنَ ٱلْأَمْرِ شَىْءٌ مَّا قُتِلْنَا هَٰهُنَا قُل لَّوْ كُنتُمْ فِى بُيُوتِكُمْ

---

252. This part refers to the Battle of Uhud. The Muslims were victorious until the archers disobeyed the Prophet's orders.
253. They left their position to get a share of the booty.
254. The Qurashite foes of the Muslims.

were destined to be killed would have sallied forth to the places where they would be slain; so that Allah might purify what is in your hearts. Allah knows well what is hidden in the breasts."

155. Those of you, who fled on the day the two armies met, were made to slip by the Devil, on account of something they had done. However, Allah has forgiven them; Allah is indeed Forgiving and Merciful.

156. O believers, do not be like the unbelievers, who say about their brethren when they [die] while travelling abroad or fighting: "Had they stayed with us, they would not have died or been killed." Allah wished to make that a cause of anguish in their hearts. It is Allah Who causes men to live and die, and Allah has knowledge of what you do!

157. And were you to be killed or to die in the Way of Allah, forgiveness and mercy from Allah are far better than what they amass.

158. And were you to die or to be killed, it is unto Allah that you will be gathered.

159. It was by a mercy from Allah that you dealt leniently with them;[255] for had you been cruel and hard-hearted, they would have dispersed from around you. So, pardon them, ask Allah's Forgiveness for them and consult them in the conduct of affairs. Then, when you are resolved, trust in Allah; Allah indeed loves those who trust [in Him].

160. If Allah supports you, no one will overcome you; but if He forsakes you, then who will be able to support you after Him? And in Allah let the believers put their trust!

---

255. Those Muslim fighters who flinched in the midst of the battle.

161. It does not benefit any Prophet to cheat;[256] for whoever cheats will bring the fruit of his dishonesty with him on the Day of Resurrection. Then, each soul shall be paid in full for what it earned;[257] and they will not be wronged.

وَمَا كَانَ لِنَبِيٍّ أَن يَغُلَّ وَمَن يَغْلُلْ يَأْتِ بِمَا غَلَّ يَوْمَ الْقِيَٰمَةِ ثُمَّ تُوَفَّىٰ كُلُّ نَفْسٍ مَّا كَسَبَتْ وَهُمْ لَا يُظْلَمُونَ ﴿١٦١﴾

162. What, is he who follows Allah's good Pleasure like him who brings upon himself God's Wrath? Hell is his refuge, and what a wretched destiny!

أَفَمَنِ اتَّبَعَ رِضْوَٰنَ اللَّهِ كَمَنْ بَآءَ بِسَخَطٍ مِّنَ اللَّهِ وَمَأْوَىٰهُ جَهَنَّمُ وَبِئْسَ الْمَصِيرُ ﴿١٦٢﴾

163. They[258] have different grades in Allah's Sight; and Allah has knowledge of what they do!

هُمْ دَرَجَٰتٌ عِندَ اللَّهِ وَاللَّهُ بَصِيرٌ بِمَا يَعْمَلُونَ ﴿١٦٣﴾

164. Allah has been gracious to the believers, sending them a Messenger from among themselves to recite to them His Revelations, to purify them and to teach them the Book and the Wisdom, though they had been in manifest error before that.

لَقَدْ مَنَّ اللَّهُ عَلَى الْمُؤْمِنِينَ إِذْ بَعَثَ فِيهِمْ رَسُولًا مِّنْ أَنفُسِهِمْ يَتْلُوا عَلَيْهِمْ ءَايَٰتِهِ وَيُزَكِّيهِمْ وَيُعَلِّمُهُمُ الْكِتَٰبَ وَالْحِكْمَةَ وَإِن كَانُوا مِن قَبْلُ لَفِى ضَلَٰلٍ مُّبِينٍ ﴿١٦٤﴾

165. And when a misfortune befell you[259] after you had inflicted twice as much,[260] you said: "Whence is this?"; say: 'It is from yourselves." Surely Allah has power over everything!

أَوَلَمَّا أَصَٰبَتْكُم مُّصِيبَةٌ قَدْ أَصَبْتُم مِّثْلَيْهَا قُلْتُمْ أَنَّىٰ هَٰذَا قُلْ هُوَ مِنْ عِندِ أَنفُسِكُمْ إِنَّ اللَّهَ عَلَىٰ كُلِّ شَىْءٍ قَدِيرٌ ﴿١٦٥﴾

166. And what befell you on the day the two armies met[261] was by Allah's Leave, that He might know the true believers;

وَمَا أَصَٰبَكُمْ يَوْمَ الْتَقَى الْجَمْعَانِ فَبِإِذْنِ اللَّهِ وَلِيَعْلَمَ الْمُؤْمِنِينَ ﴿١٦٦﴾

167. And that he might know the hypocrites. When it was said to them: "Come, fight in the Way of Allah or defend yourselves", they replied: "If only we knew how to fight, we would have followed you." On that day, they were closer to disbelief than to belief.

وَلِيَعْلَمَ الَّذِينَ نَافَقُوا وَقِيلَ لَهُمْ تَعَالَوْا قَٰتِلُوا فِى سَبِيلِ اللَّهِ أَوِ ادْفَعُوا قَالُوا لَوْ نَعْلَمُ قِتَالًا لَّاتَّبَعْنَٰكُمْ هُمْ لِلْكُفْرِ يَوْمَئِذٍ أَقْرَبُ مِنْهُمْ لِلْإِيمَٰنِ يَقُولُونَ

---

256. To cheat in handling the booty.
257. For its works.
258. The believers.
259. In the Battle of Uhud.
260. In the Battle of Badr.
261. In the Battle of Uhud.

They say with their tongues what is not in their hearts; and Allah knows best what they conceal!

يَقُولُونَ بِأَفْوَاهِهِم مَّا لَيْسَ فِي قُلُوبِهِمْ وَاللَّهُ أَعْلَمُ بِمَا يَكْتُمُونَ ۝

168. Those who said to their brethren, while they themselves stayed at home: "Had they obeyed us they would not have been killed?" Say: "Then ward off death from yourselves, if you are truthful."

ٱلَّذِينَ قَالُوا لِإِخْوَانِهِمْ وَقَعَدُوا لَوْ أَطَاعُونَا مَا قُتِلُوا ۗ قُلْ فَٱدْرَءُوا عَنْ أَنفُسِكُمُ ٱلْمَوْتَ إِن كُنتُمْ صَادِقِينَ ۝

169. And do not think those who have been killed in the Way of Allah as dead; they are rather living with their Lord, well-provided for.

وَلَا تَحْسَبَنَّ ٱلَّذِينَ قُتِلُوا فِي سَبِيلِ ٱللَّهِ أَمْوَاتًۢا ۚ بَلْ أَحْيَآءٌ عِندَ رَبِّهِمْ يُرْزَقُونَ ۝

170. Rejoicing in what their Lord has given them of His Bounty, and they rejoice for those who stayed behind and did not join them; knowing that they have nothing to fear and that they shall not grieve.

فَرِحِينَ بِمَآ ءَاتَىٰهُمُ ٱللَّهُ مِن فَضْلِهِۦ وَيَسْتَبْشِرُونَ بِٱلَّذِينَ لَمْ يَلْحَقُوا بِهِم مِّنْ خَلْفِهِمْ أَلَّا خَوْفٌ عَلَيْهِمْ وَلَا هُمْ يَحْزَنُونَ ۝

171. They rejoice in the Grace of Allah and His Favour, and that Allah will not withhold the reward of the faithful;

يَسْتَبْشِرُونَ بِنِعْمَةٍ مِّنَ ٱللَّهِ وَفَضْلٍ وَأَنَّ ٱللَّهَ لَا يُضِيعُ أَجْرَ ٱلْمُؤْمِنِينَ ۝

172. Those who responded to Allah's Call and the Messenger's after they had incurred many wounds. To those of them who do what is right and fear Allah, a great reward is in store.

ٱلَّذِينَ ٱسْتَجَابُوا لِلَّهِ وَٱلرَّسُولِ مِنۢ بَعْدِ مَآ أَصَابَهُمُ ٱلْقَرْحُ ۚ لِلَّذِينَ أَحْسَنُوا مِنْهُمْ وَٱتَّقَوْا أَجْرٌ عَظِيمٌ ۝

173. Those to whom the people said: "The people have been arrayed against you; so fear them." But this increased their faith and so they said: "Allah is Sufficient for us. He is the Best Guardian!"

ٱلَّذِينَ قَالَ لَهُمُ ٱلنَّاسُ إِنَّ ٱلنَّاسَ قَدْ جَمَعُوا لَكُمْ فَٱخْشَوْهُمْ فَزَادَهُمْ إِيمَانًا وَقَالُوا حَسْبُنَا ٱللَّهُ وَنِعْمَ ٱلْوَكِيلُ ۝

174. Thus they came back with a Grace and Bounty from Allah. No harm touched them; and they complied with Allah's good Pleasure. Allah's Bounty is great!

فَٱنقَلَبُوا بِنِعْمَةٍ مِّنَ ٱللَّهِ وَفَضْلٍ لَّمْ يَمْسَسْهُمْ سُوٓءٌ وَٱتَّبَعُوا رِضْوَٰنَ ٱللَّهِ ۗ وَٱللَّهُ ذُو فَضْلٍ عَظِيمٍ ۝

175. That indeed is the Devil frightening his followers; but do not fear them and fear Me, if you are true believers!

إِنَّمَا ذَٰلِكُمُ ٱلشَّيْطَٰنُ يُخَوِّفُ أَوْلِيَآءَهُۥ فَلَا تَخَافُوهُمْ وَخَافُونِ إِن كُنتُم مُّؤْمِنِينَ ۝

176. And do not let those who hasten to disbelieve make you grieve. They will certainly not cause Allah any harm. Allah wishes not to give them any share in the Hereafter, and a terrible punishment awaits them!

وَلَا يَحْزُنكَ ٱلَّذِينَ يُسَٰرِعُونَ فِى ٱلْكُفْرِ إِنَّهُمْ لَن يَضُرُّوا۟ ٱللَّهَ شَيْـًٔا يُرِيدُ ٱللَّهُ أَلَّا يَجْعَلَ لَهُمْ حَظًّا فِى ٱلْءَاخِرَةِ وَلَهُمْ عَذَابٌ عَظِيمٌ ۝

177. Those who trade belief for disbelief will not cause Allah any harm, and a painful punishment awaits them!

إِنَّ ٱلَّذِينَ ٱشْتَرَوُا۟ ٱلْكُفْرَ بِٱلْإِيمَٰنِ لَن يَضُرُّوا۟ ٱللَّهَ شَيْـًٔا وَلَهُمْ عَذَابٌ أَلِيمٌ ۝

178. Let the unbelievers not suppose that Our prolonging their days is better for them. We only prolong their days so that they may grow in sin, and a humbling punishment awaits them.

وَلَا يَحْسَبَنَّ ٱلَّذِينَ كَفَرُوٓا۟ أَنَّمَا نُمْلِى لَهُمْ خَيْرٌ لِّأَنفُسِهِمْ إِنَّمَا نُمْلِى لَهُمْ لِيَزْدَادُوٓا۟ إِثْمًا وَلَهُمْ عَذَابٌ مُّهِينٌ ۝

179. Allah will not leave the faithful in the state in which you are, until He separates the vile from the decent. Nor will Allah make known to you the unseen; but Allah chooses of His Messengers whomever He pleases. Believe then in Allah and His Messengers; and if you believe and fear Allah, you will have a great reward.

مَّا كَانَ ٱللَّهُ لِيَذَرَ ٱلْمُؤْمِنِينَ عَلَىٰ مَآ أَنتُمْ عَلَيْهِ حَتَّىٰ يَمِيزَ ٱلْخَبِيثَ مِنَ ٱلطَّيِّبِ وَمَا كَانَ ٱللَّهُ لِيُطْلِعَكُمْ عَلَى ٱلْغَيْبِ وَلَٰكِنَّ ٱللَّهَ يَجْتَبِى مِن رُّسُلِهِۦ مَن يَشَآءُ فَـَٔامِنُوا۟ بِٱللَّهِ وَرُسُلِهِۦ وَإِن تُؤْمِنُوا۟ وَتَتَّقُوا۟ فَلَكُمْ أَجْرٌ عَظِيمٌ ۝

180. And let not those who are niggardly in spending what God has given them of His Bounty suppose that it is good for them. No, it is evil; they shall carry what they stinted around their necks on the Day of Resurrection. And to Allah belongs the inheritance of the heavens and the earth. Allah is Aware of what you do!

وَلَا يَحْسَبَنَّ ٱلَّذِينَ يَبْخَلُونَ بِمَآ ءَاتَىٰهُمُ ٱللَّهُ مِن فَضْلِهِۦ هُوَ خَيْرًا لَّهُم بَلْ هُوَ شَرٌّ لَّهُمْ سَيُطَوَّقُونَ مَا بَخِلُوا۟ بِهِۦ يَوْمَ ٱلْقِيَٰمَةِ وَلِلَّهِ مِيرَٰثُ ٱلسَّمَٰوَٰتِ وَٱلْأَرْضِ وَٱللَّهُ بِمَا تَعْمَلُونَ خَبِيرٌ ۝

181. Allah has heard the words of those who said: "Allah is poor, and we are rich." We shall write down what they said, together with their killing of the Prophets unjustly, and We shall say: "Taste the torment of burning [in the Fire]!"

لَّقَدْ سَمِعَ ٱللَّهُ قَوْلَ ٱلَّذِينَ قَالُوٓا۟ إِنَّ ٱللَّهَ فَقِيرٌ وَنَحْنُ أَغْنِيَآءُ سَنَكْتُبُ مَا قَالُوا۟ وَقَتْلَهُمُ ٱلْأَنۢبِيَآءَ بِغَيْرِ حَقٍّ وَنَقُولُ ذُوقُوا۟ عَذَابَ ٱلْحَرِيقِ ۝

182. That is, on account of what your hands did earlier, and that Allah is not unjust to His servants;

ذَٰلِكَ بِمَا قَدَّمَتْ أَيْدِيكُمْ وَأَنَّ ٱللَّهَ لَيْسَ بِظَلَّٰمٍ لِّلْعَبِيدِ ۝

183. Those who say: "Allah has actually commanded us not to trust a messenger until he brings us an offering consumed by the Fire." Say [to them]: "Messengers have already come to you with clear proofs[262] before me, together with what you asked for. Why then did you kill them, if you are truthful?"

184. If, however, they accuse you of lying, Messengers who before you brought clear proofs,[263] the Scriptures and the illuminating Book were also accused of lying.

185. Every soul shall taste death; and you shall receive your rewards in full on the Day of Resurrection. Whoever is removed from Hell and is admitted to Paradise wins. Life in this world is nothing but an illusory pleasure.

186. You shall be tried in your possessions and yourselves, and shall hear from those who received the Book before you,[264] and from the idolaters, a lot of abuse; but if you forbear and guard against evil, that indeed is a mark of great determination.

187. And when Allah made a covenant with those who were given the Book: "You shall reveal it to mankind and not conceal it", they simply cast it behind their backs, and sold it for a small price. Evil then is their deal.

188. Do not think those who are pleased with what they have done and love to be praised for what they have not done, immune from punishment; a painful punishment is in store for them.

189. And to Allah belongs the kingdom of the heavens and the earth, and Allah has power over everything!

---

262. Miracles.
263. Miracles.
264. The Jews and the Christians.

190. There are in the creation of the heavens and the earth and the alternation of night and day real signs for people of understanding.

إِنَّ فِى خَلْقِ ٱلسَّمَوَٰتِ وَٱلْأَرْضِ وَٱخْتِلَٰفِ ٱلَّيْلِ وَٱلنَّهَارِ لَآيَٰتٍ لِّأُوْلِى ٱلْأَلْبَٰبِ ﴿١٩٠﴾

191. Those who remember Allah while standing, sitting or lying on their sides, reflecting upon the creation of the heavens and the earth [saying]: "Our Lord You did not create this in vain. Glory be to You! Save us from the torment of the Fire.

ٱلَّذِينَ يَذْكُرُونَ ٱللَّهَ قِيَٰمًا وَقُعُودًا وَعَلَىٰ جُنُوبِهِمْ وَيَتَفَكَّرُونَ فِى خَلْقِ ٱلسَّمَوَٰتِ وَٱلْأَرْضِ رَبَّنَا مَا خَلَقْتَ هَٰذَا بَٰطِلًا سُبْحَٰنَكَ فَقِنَا عَذَابَ ٱلنَّارِ ﴿١٩١﴾

192. "Our Lord, he whom You throw into the Fire will be disgraced by You". The evildoers shall have no supporters.

رَبَّنَا إِنَّكَ مَن تُدْخِلِ ٱلنَّارَ فَقَدْ أَخْزَيْتَهُ وَمَا لِلظَّٰلِمِينَ مِنْ أَنصَارٍ ﴿١٩٢﴾

193. "Our Lord, we have heard a caller summoning to belief, saying: 'Believe in your Lord'; and so we have believed. Lord, forgive us our sins and acquit us of our evil deeds and cause us to die with the pious.

رَبَّنَا إِنَّنَا سَمِعْنَا مُنَادِيًا يُنَادِى لِلْإِيمَٰنِ أَنْ ءَامِنُوا بِرَبِّكُمْ فَـَٔامَنَّا رَبَّنَا فَٱغْفِرْ لَنَا ذُنُوبَنَا وَكَفِّرْ عَنَّا سَيِّـَٔاتِنَا وَتَوَفَّنَا مَعَ ٱلْأَبْرَارِ ﴿١٩٣﴾

194. "Lord, and give us what You promised us through Your Messengers, and do not disgrace us on the Day of Resurrection. Surely You will never break a Promise."

رَبَّنَا وَءَاتِنَا مَا وَعَدتَّنَا عَلَىٰ رُسُلِكَ وَلَا تُخْزِنَا يَوْمَ ٱلْقِيَٰمَةِ إِنَّكَ لَا تُخْلِفُ ٱلْمِيعَادَ ﴿١٩٤﴾

195. And so their Lord answered them saying: "Indeed, I will not cause the loss of the work of any worker among you, whether male or female; you come one from the other." Those who have emigrated[265] and were driven out of their homes, were persecuted for My Sake, fought and were killed, I will forgive their sins and will admit them into Gardens, beneath which rivers flow, as a reward from Allah. With Allah is the best reward!

فَٱسْتَجَابَ لَهُمْ رَبُّهُمْ أَنِّى لَا أُضِيعُ عَمَلَ عَٰمِلٍ مِّنكُم مِّن ذَكَرٍ أَوْ أُنثَىٰ بَعْضُكُم مِّنۢ بَعْضٍ فَٱلَّذِينَ هَاجَرُوا وَأُخْرِجُوا مِن دِيَٰرِهِمْ وَأُوذُوا فِى سَبِيلِى وَقَٰتَلُوا وَقُتِلُوا لَأُكَفِّرَنَّ عَنْهُمْ سَيِّـَٔاتِهِمْ وَلَأُدْخِلَنَّهُمْ جَنَّٰتٍ تَجْرِى مِن تَحْتِهَا ٱلْأَنْهَٰرُ ثَوَابًا مِّنْ عِندِ ٱللَّهِ وَٱللَّهُ عِندَهُ حُسْنُ ٱلثَّوَابِ ﴿١٩٥﴾

196. Do not be deceived by the wanderings[266] of those who disbelieved in the land;

لَا يَغُرَّنَّكَ تَقَلُّبُ ٱلَّذِينَ كَفَرُوا فِى ٱلْبِلَٰدِ ﴿١٩٦﴾

---

265. The Meccan Muslims who, because of persecution, emigrated to Medina.
266. For business purposes.

197. A little enjoyment, and then their abode is Hell; and what a wretched resting-place!

مَتَٰعٌ قَلِيلٌ ثُمَّ مَأْوَىٰهُمْ جَهَنَّمُ وَبِئْسَ ٱلْمِهَادُ ۝

198. However, those who fear their Lord will have Gardens, beneath which rivers flow, abiding therein forever, as a bounty from Allah. What Allah has is far better for the righteous.

لَٰكِنِ ٱلَّذِينَ ٱتَّقَوْا۟ رَبَّهُمْ لَهُمْ جَنَّٰتٌ تَجْرِى مِن تَحْتِهَا ٱلْأَنْهَٰرُ خَٰلِدِينَ فِيهَا نُزُلًا مِّنْ عِندِ ٱللَّهِ وَمَا عِندَ ٱللَّهِ خَيْرٌ لِّلْأَبْرَارِ ۝

199. Of the People of the Book, there are some who indeed believe in Allah and in what has been revealed to you[267] or has been revealed to them, humbling themselves before Allah and not selling Allah's Revelations for a small price. Those will have their reward with their Lord; indeed Allah's Reckoning is swift.

وَإِنَّ مِنْ أَهْلِ ٱلْكِتَٰبِ لَمَن يُؤْمِنُ بِٱللَّهِ وَمَا أُنزِلَ إِلَيْكُمْ وَمَا أُنزِلَ إِلَيْهِمْ خَٰشِعِينَ لِلَّهِ لَا يَشْتَرُونَ بِـَٔايَٰتِ ٱللَّهِ ثَمَنًا قَلِيلًا أُو۟لَٰئِكَ لَهُمْ أَجْرُهُمْ عِندَ رَبِّهِمْ إِنَّ ٱللَّهَ سَرِيعُ ٱلْحِسَابِ ۝

200. O believers, forbear and vie in forbearance and steadfastness; and fear Allah so that you may prosper!

يَٰٓأَيُّهَا ٱلَّذِينَ ءَامَنُوا۟ ٱصْبِرُوا۟ وَصَابِرُوا۟ وَرَابِطُوا۟ وَٱتَّقُوا۟ ٱللَّهَ لَعَلَّكُمْ تُفْلِحُونَ ۝

Sûrat An-Nisa', (Women) 4

سُورَةُ النِّسَاءِ

In the Name of Allah, the Compassionate, the Merciful

بِسْمِ ٱللَّهِ ٱلرَّحْمَٰنِ ٱلرَّحِيمِ

1. O people, fear your Lord Who created you from a single soul,[268] and from it He created its mate,[269] and from both He scattered abroad many men and women; and fear Allah in Whose Name you appeal to one another, and invoke family relationships. Surely Allah is a Watcher over you.

يَٰٓأَيُّهَا ٱلنَّاسُ ٱتَّقُوا۟ رَبَّكُمُ ٱلَّذِى خَلَقَكُم مِّن نَّفْسٍ وَٰحِدَةٍ وَخَلَقَ مِنْهَا زَوْجَهَا وَبَثَّ مِنْهُمَا رِجَالًا كَثِيرًا وَنِسَآءً وَٱتَّقُوا۟ ٱللَّهَ ٱلَّذِى تَسَآءَلُونَ بِهِۦ وَٱلْأَرْحَامَ إِنَّ ٱللَّهَ كَانَ عَلَيْكُمْ رَقِيبًا ۝

2. Render unto the orphans their property and do not exchange worthless things for good ones, and do not devour their property together with your property. That indeed is a great sin!

وَءَاتُوا۟ ٱلْيَتَٰمَىٰٓ أَمْوَٰلَهُمْ وَلَا تَتَبَدَّلُوا۟ ٱلْخَبِيثَ بِٱلطَّيِّبِ وَلَا تَأْكُلُوٓا۟ أَمْوَٰلَهُمْ إِلَىٰٓ أَمْوَٰلِكُمْ إِنَّهُۥ كَانَ حُوبًا كَبِيرًا ۝

---

267. The Qur'an.
268. Adam.
269. Eve.

3. If you fear that you cannot deal justly with the orphans, then marry such of the women as appeal to you, two, three or four; but if you fear that you cannot be equitable, then only one, or what your right hands own.[270] That is more likely to enable you to avoid unfairness.[271]

وَإِنْ خِفْتُمْ أَلَّا تُقْسِطُوا۟ فِى ٱلْيَتَـٰمَىٰ فَٱنكِحُوا۟ مَا طَابَ لَكُم مِّنَ ٱلنِّسَآءِ مَثْنَىٰ وَثُلَـٰثَ وَرُبَـٰعَ فَإِنْ خِفْتُمْ أَلَّا تَعْدِلُوا۟ فَوَٰحِدَةً أَوْ مَا مَلَكَتْ أَيْمَـٰنُكُمْ ذَٰلِكَ أَدْنَىٰٓ أَلَّا تَعُولُوا۟ ۞

4. And give women their dowries as a free gift, but if they choose to give you anything of it, then consume it with enjoyment and pleasure.

وَءَاتُوا۟ ٱلنِّسَآءَ صَدُقَـٰتِهِنَّ نِحْلَةً فَإِن طِبْنَ لَكُمْ عَن شَىْءٍ مِّنْهُ نَفْسًا فَكُلُوهُ هَنِيٓـًٔا مَّرِيٓـًٔا ۞

5. But do not give the feeble-minded the property that Allah assigned to you as a means of livelihood. Provide for them therefrom, clothe them and speak kindly to them.

وَلَا تُؤْتُوا۟ ٱلسُّفَهَآءَ أَمْوَٰلَكُمُ ٱلَّتِى جَعَلَ ٱللَّهُ لَكُمْ قِيَـٰمًا وَٱرْزُقُوهُمْ فِيهَا وَٱكْسُوهُمْ وَقُولُوا۟ لَهُمْ قَوْلًا مَّعْرُوفًا ۞

6. Test the orphans until they reach the age of marriage; then, if you discern in them sound judgement, deliver to them their property; and do not consume it extravagantly and hastily before they come of age. He who is rich should be abstinent, and he who is poor should consume fairly. And when you deliver to them their property, call in witnesses thereon. God suffices as a Reckoner!

وَٱبْتَلُوا۟ ٱلْيَتَـٰمَىٰ حَتَّىٰٓ إِذَا بَلَغُوا۟ ٱلنِّكَاحَ فَإِنْ ءَانَسْتُم مِّنْهُمْ رُشْدًا فَٱدْفَعُوٓا۟ إِلَيْهِمْ أَمْوَٰلَهُمْ وَلَا تَأْكُلُوهَآ إِسْرَافًا وَبِدَارًا أَن يَكْبَرُوا۟ وَمَن كَانَ غَنِيًّا فَلْيَسْتَعْفِفْ وَمَن كَانَ فَقِيرًا فَلْيَأْكُلْ بِٱلْمَعْرُوفِ فَإِذَا دَفَعْتُمْ إِلَيْهِمْ أَمْوَٰلَهُمْ فَأَشْهِدُوا۟ عَلَيْهِمْ وَكَفَىٰ بِٱللَّهِ حَسِيبًا ۞

7. Men should have a share of what parents and kinsmen leave behind; and women a share of what parents and kinsmen leave, whether small or large, as an obligatory portion.

لِّلرِّجَالِ نَصِيبٌ مِّمَّا تَرَكَ ٱلْوَٰلِدَانِ وَٱلْأَقْرَبُونَ وَلِلنِّسَآءِ نَصِيبٌ مِّمَّا تَرَكَ ٱلْوَٰلِدَانِ وَٱلْأَقْرَبُونَ مِمَّا قَلَّ مِنْهُ أَوْ كَثُرَ نَصِيبًا مَّفْرُوضًا ۞

8. And if the division is attended by kinsmen, orphans or poor men, then give them a share of it and speak to them kindly.

وَإِذَا حَضَرَ ٱلْقِسْمَةَ أُو۟لُوا۟ ٱلْقُرْبَىٰ وَٱلْيَتَـٰمَىٰ وَٱلْمَسَـٰكِينُ فَٱرْزُقُوهُم مِّنْهُ وَقُولُوا۟ لَهُمْ قَوْلًا مَّعْرُوفًا ۞

---

270. Captives of war or slave-girls.

271. It should be noted that this verse permits polygamy under special circumstances, but does not enjoin it. No less important is the fact that this verse was revealed following the Battle of Uhud in which seventy Muslim fighters were killed, leaving many widows and other dependants without a provider for them. Hence most commentators regard the permission as an exception and not a rule.

9. And let those who worry about the weak offspring they may leave behind them[272] be mindful [of the orphans]. Let them fear Allah and speak justly.

10. Those who devour the property of orphans unjustly, devour fire in their bellies, and they will burn in a blazing fire.

11. Allah commands you, with respect to your children, that the male shall inherit the equivalent of the share of two females. If there be more than two females, then they should receive two-thirds of what he[273] leaves; but if there is only one female, she is entitled to one-half. To each of his parents, one-sixth of what he leaves, if he has any children; but if he has no children, then his parents will inherit him, the mother receiving one-third. But if he has any brothers, then his mother receives one-sixth, after any will he had made or any debt he had incurred [is taken care of]. Your fathers and sons - you know not who of them is of greater advantage to you. This is a law from Allah; Allah surely is All-Knowing, Forbearing.

12. You are entitled to half of what your wives leave, if they have no children; but if they have any children, then you are entitled to one-quarter of what they leave, after any will they had made or any loan they had incurred [is taken care of]. And they are entitled to one-quarter of what you leave, if you have no children; but if you have any children, then they are entitled to one-eighth of what you leave, after any will you had made or loan you had incurred [is taken care of]. And if a man or a woman dies having no

---

272. That is, after their death.
273. the deceased father.

children or parents, but has a brother or a sister, then each shall have one-sixth; if they are more than that, then they shall share one-third, after any will made or debt incurred [is taken care of] without prejudice. This is a Commandment from Allah, and Allah is All-Knowing, Forbearing.

كَانُوٓا۟ أَكْثَرَ مِن ذَٰلِكَ فَهُمْ شُرَكَآءُ فِى ٱلثُّلُثِ مِنۢ بَعْدِ وَصِيَّةٍ يُوصَىٰ بِهَآ أَوْ دَيْنٍ غَيْرَ مُضَآرٍّ وَصِيَّةً مِّنَ ٱللَّهِ وَٱللَّهُ عَلِيمٌ حَلِيمٌ ﴿١٢﴾

13. These are the Ordinances of Allah, and whoever obeys Allah and His Messenger, He will admit him into Gardens beneath which rivers flow, abiding therein forever. That is the great victory!

تِلْكَ حُدُودُ ٱللَّهِ وَمَن يُطِعِ ٱللَّهَ وَرَسُولَهُ يُدْخِلْهُ جَنَّٰتٍ تَجْرِى مِن تَحْتِهَا ٱلْأَنْهَٰرُ خَٰلِدِينَ فِيهَا وَذَٰلِكَ ٱلْفَوْزُ ٱلْعَظِيمُ ﴿١٣﴾

14. But whoever disobeys Allah and His Messenger and transgresses His bounds, He will admit him into the Fire, wherein he shall abide forever, and his will be a demeaning punishment!

وَمَن يَعْصِ ٱللَّهَ وَرَسُولَهُ وَيَتَعَدَّ حُدُودَهُ يُدْخِلْهُ نَارًا خَٰلِدًا فِيهَا وَلَهُ عَذَابٌ مُّهِينٌ ﴿١٤﴾

15. As for those of your women who commit adultery, call four witnesses from your own against them; and if they testify, then detain them in the houses till death overtakes them or Allah opens another way for them.[274]

وَٱلَّٰتِى يَأْتِينَ ٱلْفَٰحِشَةَ مِن نِّسَآئِكُمْ فَٱسْتَشْهِدُوا۟ عَلَيْهِنَّ أَرْبَعَةً مِّنكُمْ فَإِن شَهِدُوا۟ فَأَمْسِكُوهُنَّ فِى ٱلْبُيُوتِ حَتَّىٰ يَتَوَفَّىٰهُنَّ ٱلْمَوْتُ أَوْ يَجْعَلَ ٱللَّهُ لَهُنَّ سَبِيلًا ﴿١٥﴾

16. If two [men] of you commit it, punish them both. If they repent and mend their ways, then leave them alone. Allah is truly All-Forgiving, Merciful.

وَٱلَّذَانِ يَأْتِيَٰنِهَا مِنكُمْ فَـَٔاذُوهُمَا فَإِن تَابَا وَأَصْلَحَا فَأَعْرِضُوا۟ عَنْهُمَآ إِنَّ ٱللَّهَ كَانَ تَوَّابًا رَّحِيمًا ﴿١٦﴾

17. Allah has taken upon Himself to accept the repentance of those who commit evil in ignorance and then repent immediately after that. Those, He will forgive and Allah is All-Knowing, Wise.

إِنَّمَا ٱلتَّوْبَةُ عَلَى ٱللَّهِ لِلَّذِينَ يَعْمَلُونَ ٱلسُّوٓءَ بِجَهَٰلَةٍ ثُمَّ يَتُوبُونَ مِن قَرِيبٍ فَأُو۟لَٰٓئِكَ يَتُوبُ ٱللَّهُ عَلَيْهِمْ وَكَانَ ٱللَّهُ عَلِيمًا حَكِيمًا ﴿١٧﴾

18. But not the repentance of those who commit evil deeds, and when one of them is faced with death, he says: "Now I repent"; nor the repentance of those who die as unbelievers. For these, we have prepared a very painful punishment!

وَلَيْسَتِ ٱلتَّوْبَةُ لِلَّذِينَ يَعْمَلُونَ ٱلسَّيِّئَاتِ حَتَّىٰٓ إِذَا حَضَرَ أَحَدَهُمُ ٱلْمَوْتُ قَالَ إِنِّى تُبْتُ ٱلْـَٰٔنَ وَلَا ٱلَّذِينَ يَمُوتُونَ وَهُمْ كُفَّارٌ أُو۟لَٰٓئِكَ أَعْتَدْنَا لَهُمْ عَذَابًا أَلِيمًا ﴿١٨﴾

---

274. This verse was later abrogated and replaced by a hundred lashes for the unmarried and stoning for the married. See Surah 24, verse 2.

19. O believers, it is not lawful for you to inherit the women [of deceased kinsmen] against their will;[275] nor restrain them in order to take away part of what you had given them, unless they commit flagrant adultery. Associate with them kindly; and if you feel aversion towards them, it may well be that you will be averse to something, from which Allah brings out a lot of good.

20. If you wish to have one wife in the place of another and you have given either of them a heap of gold, do not take any of it back. Would you take it by recourse to injustice and manifest sin?

21. For how can you take it back, when you have been intimate one with the other, and they had taken from you a solemn pledge?

22. And do not marry women that your fathers had married, unless it has already happened. Surely it is indecent and hateful, and it is an evil course!

23. Unlawful to you are your mothers, your daughters, your sisters, your paternal and maternal aunts, your brother's daughters and sister's daughters, your foster-mothers who gave you suck, your foster-sisters, your wives' mothers, your step-daughters who are in your custody, born to your wives whom you have lain with. But if you have not lain with them, then you are not at fault. [It is also not lawful to marry] the wives of your sons who are of your own loins, or to take in two sisters together, unless this has already happened. Allah is truly All-Forgiving and Merciful!

---

275. The women of deceased relatives. Among the pre-Islamic Arabs, it was the custom that when a man died, his elder son or other relatives had the right to "own" his widow or widows. Then they either married them, themselves, without giving a dowry, or married them to others, or prohibited them from marriage.

24. Or married women, except those your right hands possess.[276] This is Allah's Decree for you. Beyond these it is lawful for you to seek, by means of your wealth, any women, to marry and not to debauch. Those of them you have enjoyed, you should give them their dowries as a matter of obligation; but you are not liable to reproach for whatever you mutually agree upon, apart from the obligatory payment.[277] Allah is indeed All-Knowing, Wise!

25. Whoever of you cannot afford to marry a free, believing woman, let him choose from whatever your right hands possess[278] of believing girls. Allah knows best your faith; you come one from the other. So marry them with their parents' leave and give them their dowry honourably, as chaste women, neither committing adultery nor taking lovers. If they are legally married and commit adultery, their punishment shall be half that of a free woman. Such is the law for those of you who fear committing sin; but to abstain is better for you. Allah is All-Forgiving and Merciful!

26. Allah wants to explain to you [His laws] and to guide you along the paths of those who preceded you, and to be Merciful to you. Allah is All-Knowing, Wise!

27. Allah also wants to be Merciful to you, but those who follow their lusts want you to deviate greatly from the right course.

28. Allah wishes to lighten your burden; for man was created weak.

---

276. The captives of war or slave-girls.
277. The dowry.
278. The captives of war or slave-girls.

29. O believers, do not consume your wealth illegally, unless there be trading by mutual agreement among you; and do not kill yourselves. Allah is indeed Merciful to you!

يَـٰٓأَيُّهَا ٱلَّذِينَ ءَامَنُوا لَا تَأْكُلُوٓا أَمْوَٰلَكُم بَيْنَكُم بِٱلْبَـٰطِلِ إِلَّآ أَن تَكُونَ تِجَـٰرَةً عَن تَرَاضٍ مِّنكُمْ وَلَا تَقْتُلُوٓا أَنفُسَكُمْ إِنَّ ٱللَّهَ كَانَ بِكُمْ رَحِيمًا ۝

30. And whoever acts aggressively and wrongfully, We shall cast him in the Fire; this being an easy matter for Allah.

وَمَن يَفْعَلْ ذَٰلِكَ عُدْوَٰنًا وَظُلْمًا فَسَوْفَ نُصْلِيهِ نَارًا وَكَانَ ذَٰلِكَ عَلَى ٱللَّهِ يَسِيرًا ۝

31. If you avoid the grave sins you are forbidden, We will remit your evil deeds and let you enter into an honourable place.[279]

إِن تَجْتَنِبُوا كَبَآئِرَ مَا تُنْهَوْنَ عَنْهُ نُكَفِّرْ عَنكُمْ سَيِّـَٔاتِكُمْ وَنُدْخِلْكُم مُّدْخَلًا كَرِيمًا ۝

32. Do not covet that with which Allah has favoured some of you over the others. Men have a share of what they earned, and women a share of what they earned. And ask Allah to give you of His Bounty. Allah indeed has knowledge of everything!

وَلَا تَتَمَنَّوْا مَا فَضَّلَ ٱللَّهُ بِهِۦ بَعْضَكُمْ عَلَىٰ بَعْضٍ لِّلرِّجَالِ نَصِيبٌ مِّمَّا ٱكْتَسَبُوا وَلِلنِّسَآءِ نَصِيبٌ مِّمَّا ٱكْتَسَبْنَ وَسْـَٔلُوا ٱللَّهَ مِن فَضْلِهِۦٓ إِنَّ ٱللَّهَ كَانَ بِكُلِّ شَىْءٍ عَلِيمًا ۝

33. To every one We have appointed heirs to inherit part of what the parents or the kinsmen bequeath. Those with whom you made a compact, give them their share. Surely Allah is witness to everything.

وَلِكُلٍّ جَعَلْنَا مَوَٰلِىَ مِمَّا تَرَكَ ٱلْوَٰلِدَانِ وَٱلْأَقْرَبُونَ وَٱلَّذِينَ عَقَدَتْ أَيْمَـٰنُكُمْ فَـَٔاتُوهُمْ نَصِيبَهُمْ إِنَّ ٱللَّهَ كَانَ عَلَىٰ كُلِّ شَىْءٍ شَهِيدًا ۝

34. Men are in charge of women, because Allah has made some of them excel the others, and because they spend some of their wealth. Hence righteous women are obedient, guarding the unseen which Allah has guarded. And those of them that you fear might rebel, admonish them and abandon them in their beds and beat them. Should they obey you, do not seek a way of harming them; for Allah is Sublime and Great!

ٱلرِّجَالُ قَوَّٰمُونَ عَلَى ٱلنِّسَآءِ بِمَا فَضَّلَ ٱللَّهُ بَعْضَهُمْ عَلَىٰ بَعْضٍ وَبِمَآ أَنفَقُوا مِنْ أَمْوَٰلِهِمْ فَٱلصَّـٰلِحَـٰتُ قَـٰنِتَـٰتٌ حَـٰفِظَـٰتٌ لِّلْغَيْبِ بِمَا حَفِظَ ٱللَّهُ وَٱلَّـٰتِى تَخَافُونَ نُشُوزَهُنَّ فَعِظُوهُنَّ وَٱهْجُرُوهُنَّ فِى ٱلْمَضَاجِعِ وَٱضْرِبُوهُنَّ فَإِنْ أَطَعْنَكُمْ فَلَا تَبْغُوا عَلَيْهِنَّ سَبِيلًا إِنَّ ٱللَّهَ كَانَ عَلِيًّا كَبِيرًا ۝

35. And if you fear a breach between the two,[280] then send forth an arbiter from his relatives and another arbiter from her relatives. If they both desire reconciliation, Allah will bring them together. Allah is indeed All-Knowing, Well-Informed.

وَإِنْ خِفْتُمْ شِقَاقَ بَيْنِهِمَا فَٱبْعَثُوا حَكَمًا مِّنْ أَهْلِهِۦ وَحَكَمًا مِّنْ أَهْلِهَآ إِن يُرِيدَآ إِصْلَـٰحًا يُوَفِّقِ ٱللَّهُ بَيْنَهُمَآ إِنَّ ٱللَّهَ كَانَ عَلِيمًا خَبِيرًا ۝

---

279. That is, into Paradise.
280. The husband and wife.

36. Worship Allah and do not associate with Him anything. Show kindness to the parents, to kinsmen, to orphans, the destitute, the close and distant neighbour, the companion by your side, the wayfarer and those whom your right hands possess. Allah does not love the arrogant and boastful,

37. Those who are niggardly, and order people to be niggardly, and conceal what Allah has given them of His Bounty, We have prepared for the unbelievers a demeaning punishment;

38. And for those who spend their wealth in order to show off, and do not believe in Allah and the Last Day. He who has the Devil as a companion, an evil companion has he!

39. And what would it cost them were they to believe in Allah and the Last Day and spend part of what Allah has provided for them? Allah knows them very well!

40. Surely Allah will not wrong anyone an atom's weight; and if it is a good deed, He will multiply it and give from Himself in addition a great reward.

41. How then will it be, when We bring forward from each nation a witness[281] and We bring you[282] forth as a witness against them?

42. On that Day, those who disbelieved and disobeyed the Messenger will wish that the earth were levelled upon them, and they will conceal nothing from Allah.

43. O believers, do not approach prayer while you are drunk, until you know what you say; nor when you are unclean - unless

وَٱعْبُدُوا۟ ٱللَّهَ وَلَا تُشْرِكُوا۟ بِهِۦ شَيْـًٔا وَبِٱلْوَٰلِدَيْنِ إِحْسَٰنًا وَبِذِى ٱلْقُرْبَىٰ وَٱلْيَتَٰمَىٰ وَٱلْمَسَٰكِينِ وَٱلْجَارِ ذِى ٱلْقُرْبَىٰ وَٱلْجَارِ ٱلْجُنُبِ وَٱلصَّاحِبِ بِٱلْجَنۢبِ وَٱبْنِ ٱلسَّبِيلِ وَمَا مَلَكَتْ أَيْمَٰنُكُمْ إِنَّ ٱللَّهَ لَا يُحِبُّ مَن كَانَ مُخْتَالًا فَخُورًا ﴿٣٦﴾

ٱلَّذِينَ يَبْخَلُونَ وَيَأْمُرُونَ ٱلنَّاسَ بِٱلْبُخْلِ وَيَكْتُمُونَ مَآ ءَاتَىٰهُمُ ٱللَّهُ مِن فَضْلِهِۦ وَأَعْتَدْنَا لِلْكَٰفِرِينَ عَذَابًا مُّهِينًا ﴿٣٧﴾

وَٱلَّذِينَ يُنفِقُونَ أَمْوَٰلَهُمْ رِئَآءَ ٱلنَّاسِ وَلَا يُؤْمِنُونَ بِٱللَّهِ وَلَا بِٱلْيَوْمِ ٱلْءَاخِرِ وَمَن يَكُنِ ٱلشَّيْطَٰنُ لَهُۥ قَرِينًا فَسَآءَ قَرِينًا ﴿٣٨﴾

وَمَاذَا عَلَيْهِمْ لَوْ ءَامَنُوا۟ بِٱللَّهِ وَٱلْيَوْمِ ٱلْءَاخِرِ وَأَنفَقُوا۟ مِمَّا رَزَقَهُمُ ٱللَّهُ وَكَانَ ٱللَّهُ بِهِمْ عَلِيمًا ﴿٣٩﴾

إِنَّ ٱللَّهَ لَا يَظْلِمُ مِثْقَالَ ذَرَّةٍ وَإِن تَكُ حَسَنَةً يُضَٰعِفْهَا وَيُؤْتِ مِن لَّدُنْهُ أَجْرًا عَظِيمًا ﴿٤٠﴾

فَكَيْفَ إِذَا جِئْنَا مِن كُلِّ أُمَّةٍۭ بِشَهِيدٍ وَجِئْنَا بِكَ عَلَىٰ هَٰٓؤُلَآءِ شَهِيدًا ﴿٤١﴾

يَوْمَئِذٍ يَوَدُّ ٱلَّذِينَ كَفَرُوا۟ وَعَصَوُا۟ ٱلرَّسُولَ لَوْ تُسَوَّىٰ بِهِمُ ٱلْأَرْضُ وَلَا يَكْتُمُونَ ٱللَّهَ حَدِيثًا ﴿٤٢﴾

يَٰٓأَيُّهَا ٱلَّذِينَ ءَامَنُوا۟ لَا تَقْرَبُوا۟ ٱلصَّلَوٰةَ وَأَنتُمْ سُكَٰرَىٰ حَتَّىٰ تَعْلَمُوا۟ مَا تَقُولُونَ وَلَا جُنُبًا إِلَّا عَابِرِى سَبِيلٍ حَتَّىٰ

---

281. Its Prophet.
282. Muhammad.

you are on a journey - until you have washed yourselves. And if you are sick or on a journey, or if any one of you has relieved himself, or you have touched women and could not find water, you might rub yourselves with clean earth, wiping your faces and hands with it. Allah indeed is Pardoning, All-Forgiving!

44. Have you not considered those who have received a portion of the Book, procuring error and wanting you to go astray?

45. Allah knows best your enemies; Allah suffices as Protector, Allah suffices as Supporter!

46. Some of the Jews take words out of their context and say: "We have heard, but disobey; and hear as though you hear not." And [they] say: "ra'ina",[283] twisting their tongues and slandering religion. Had they said: "We have heard and we obey: hear and look at us", it would have been better for them and more upright; but Allah has cursed them on account of their disbelief, so they - except for a few - do not believe.

47. O People of the Book, believe in what We have revealed confirming what you already possess, before We obliterate faces, turning them on their backs, or curse them as We have cursed the Sabbath-breakers, and Allah's Command was accomplished!

48. Allah will not forgive associating [other gods] with Him, but will forgive anything less than that to whom He pleases. And he who associates other gods with Allah has committed a very grave sin.

تَغْتَسِلُواْ وَإِن كُنتُم مَّرْضَىٰٓ أَوْ عَلَىٰ سَفَرٍ أَوْ جَآءَ أَحَدٌ مِّنكُم مِّنَ ٱلْغَآئِطِ أَوْ لَٰمَسْتُمُ ٱلنِّسَآءَ فَلَمْ تَجِدُواْ مَآءً فَتَيَمَّمُواْ صَعِيدًا طَيِّبًا فَٱمْسَحُواْ بِوُجُوهِكُمْ وَأَيْدِيكُمْ إِنَّ ٱللَّهَ كَانَ عَفُوًّا غَفُورًا ﴿٤٣﴾

أَلَمْ تَرَ إِلَى ٱلَّذِينَ أُوتُواْ نَصِيبًا مِّنَ ٱلْكِتَٰبِ يَشْتَرُونَ ٱلضَّلَٰلَةَ وَيُرِيدُونَ أَن تَضِلُّواْ ٱلسَّبِيلَ ﴿٤٤﴾

وَٱللَّهُ أَعْلَمُ بِأَعْدَآئِكُمْ وَكَفَىٰ بِٱللَّهِ وَلِيًّا وَكَفَىٰ بِٱللَّهِ نَصِيرًا ﴿٤٥﴾

مِّنَ ٱلَّذِينَ هَادُواْ يُحَرِّفُونَ ٱلْكَلِمَ عَن مَّوَاضِعِهِۦ وَيَقُولُونَ سَمِعْنَا وَعَصَيْنَا وَٱسْمَعْ غَيْرَ مُسْمَعٍ وَرَٰعِنَا لَيًّۢا بِأَلْسِنَتِهِمْ وَطَعْنًا فِى ٱلدِّينِ وَلَوْ أَنَّهُمْ قَالُواْ سَمِعْنَا وَأَطَعْنَا وَٱسْمَعْ وَٱنظُرْنَا لَكَانَ خَيْرًا لَّهُمْ وَأَقْوَمَ وَلَٰكِن لَّعَنَهُمُ ٱللَّهُ بِكُفْرِهِمْ فَلَا يُؤْمِنُونَ إِلَّا قَلِيلًا ﴿٤٦﴾

يَٰٓأَيُّهَا ٱلَّذِينَ أُوتُواْ ٱلْكِتَٰبَ ءَامِنُواْ بِمَا نَزَّلْنَا مُصَدِّقًا لِّمَا مَعَكُم مِّن قَبْلِ أَن نَّطْمِسَ وُجُوهًا فَنَرُدَّهَا عَلَىٰٓ أَدْبَارِهَآ أَوْ نَلْعَنَهُمْ كَمَا لَعَنَّآ أَصْحَٰبَ ٱلسَّبْتِ وَكَانَ أَمْرُ ٱللَّهِ مَفْعُولًا ﴿٤٧﴾

إِنَّ ٱللَّهَ لَا يَغْفِرُ أَن يُشْرَكَ بِهِۦ وَيَغْفِرُ مَا دُونَ ذَٰلِكَ لِمَن يَشَآءُ وَمَن يُشْرِكْ بِٱللَّهِ فَقَدِ ٱفْتَرَىٰٓ إِثْمًا عَظِيمًا ﴿٤٨﴾

---

283. A word of abuse.

49. Have you considered those who regard themselves as pure? Rather, only Allah will purify those whom He pleases, and they will not be wronged a whit.

أَلَمْ تَرَ إِلَى ٱلَّذِينَ يُزَكُّونَ أَنفُسَهُمْ بَلِ ٱللَّهُ يُزَكِّى مَن يَشَآءُ وَلَا يُظْلَمُونَ فَتِيلًا ﴿٤٩﴾

50. Behold, how they invent falsehood about Allah; and that in itself is a manifest sin!

ٱنظُرْ كَيْفَ يَفْتَرُونَ عَلَى ٱللَّهِ ٱلْكَذِبَ وَكَفَىٰ بِهِۦٓ إِثْمًا مُّبِينًا ﴿٥٠﴾

51. Have you not considered those who received a portion of the Book? They believe in idols and demons, and they say to the unbelievers: "Those are more rightly guided than those who believe."

أَلَمْ تَرَ إِلَى ٱلَّذِينَ أُوتُوا۟ نَصِيبًا مِّنَ ٱلْكِتَٰبِ يُؤْمِنُونَ بِٱلْجِبْتِ وَٱلطَّٰغُوتِ وَيَقُولُونَ لِلَّذِينَ كَفَرُوا۟ هَٰٓؤُلَآءِ أَهْدَىٰ مِنَ ٱلَّذِينَ ءَامَنُوا۟ سَبِيلًا ﴿٥١﴾

52. Those are the ones whom Allah has cursed; and whomever Allah curses will have no supporter.

أُو۟لَٰٓئِكَ ٱلَّذِينَ لَعَنَهُمُ ٱللَّهُ وَمَن يَلْعَنِ ٱللَّهُ فَلَن تَجِدَ لَهُۥ نَصِيرًا ﴿٥٢﴾

53. Or do they have a share in the kingdom? If so, they will not give the people a speck on a date-stone.

أَمْ لَهُمْ نَصِيبٌ مِّنَ ٱلْمُلْكِ فَإِذًا لَّا يُؤْتُونَ ٱلنَّاسَ نَقِيرًا ﴿٥٣﴾

54. Or do they envy the people[284] for what Allah has given them of His Bounty? For We have given Abraham's family the Book and the Wisdom and bestowed on them a great kingdom.

أَمْ يَحْسُدُونَ ٱلنَّاسَ عَلَىٰ مَآ ءَاتَىٰهُمُ ٱللَّهُ مِن فَضْلِهِۦ فَقَدْ ءَاتَيْنَآ ءَالَ إِبْرَٰهِيمَ ٱلْكِتَٰبَ وَٱلْحِكْمَةَ وَءَاتَيْنَٰهُم مُّلْكًا عَظِيمًا ﴿٥٤﴾

55. Some of them believed in him, others rejected him. Sufficient is the scourge of Hell.

فَمِنْهُم مَّنْ ءَامَنَ بِهِۦ وَمِنْهُم مَّن صَدَّ عَنْهُ وَكَفَىٰ بِجَهَنَّمَ سَعِيرًا ﴿٥٥﴾

56. Those who have disbelieved Our Signs, We shall surely cast them into the Fire; every time their skins are burnt, We will replace them by other skins, so that they might taste the punishment. Allah indeed is Mighty and Wise!

إِنَّ ٱلَّذِينَ كَفَرُوا۟ بِـَٔايَٰتِنَا سَوْفَ نُصْلِيهِمْ نَارًا كُلَّمَا نَضِجَتْ جُلُودُهُم بَدَّلْنَٰهُمْ جُلُودًا غَيْرَهَا لِيَذُوقُوا۟ ٱلْعَذَابَ إِنَّ ٱللَّهَ كَانَ عَزِيزًا حَكِيمًا ﴿٥٦﴾

57. As to those who have believed and do the good works, We shall admit them into Gardens, beneath which rivers flow, abiding therein forever. They have therein purified spouses, and We will admit them to a very shady place.

وَٱلَّذِينَ ءَامَنُوا۟ وَعَمِلُوا۟ ٱلصَّٰلِحَٰتِ سَنُدْخِلُهُمْ جَنَّٰتٍ تَجْرِى مِن تَحْتِهَا ٱلْأَنْهَٰرُ خَٰلِدِينَ فِيهَآ أَبَدًا لَّهُمْ فِيهَآ أَزْوَٰجٌ مُّطَهَّرَةٌ وَنُدْخِلُهُمْ ظِلًّا ظَلِيلًا ﴿٥٧﴾

---

284. The reference here, according to some commentaries, is to the Arabs.

58. God commands you to deliver trusts to their owners and, if you judge between people, to judge justly. Splendid is Allah's exhortation to you. Allah is indeed All-Hearing, All-Seeing.

59. O believers, obey Allah and obey the Messenger and those in authority among you. Should you quarrel over any matter, then refer it to Allah and the Messenger, if you really believe in Allah and the Last Day. That is far better for you and fairer in interpretation.

60. Have you not seen those who pretend that they believe in what has been revealed to you and what was revealed before you? They wish to submit their disputes to the Devil,[285] although they have been commanded to denounce him; but the Devil wishes to lead them far astray!

61. And if it is said to them: "Turn now to what Allah has revealed and to the Messenger", you will find the hypocrites turning away from you with aversion.

62. How then if they are afflicted with a disaster on account of what their own hands perpetrated, they come to you swearing by Allah: "We only sought kindness and conciliation"?

63. Allah knows what is in the hearts of those ones; so leave them alone, admonish them and say to them effective words about themselves.

64. We have not sent forth a Messenger, but that he may be obeyed by Allah's Leave. And had they, having wronged themselves, come to you and asked for Allah's Forgiveness and the Messenger had asked forgiveness for them, then they would have found Allah All-Forgiving, Merciful.

---

285. The reference here is said to be to a Jew called Ka'b Ibn al-Ashraf, who was a bitter enemy of the Muslims.

65. But no, by your Lord, they will not believe until they call you to arbitrate in their dispute; then they will not be embarrassed regarding your verdict and will submit fully.

66. And had We commanded them: "Slay yourselves or go forth from your homes", they would not have done it, except for a few of them; but had they done what they were exhorted to do,[286] it would have been far better for them and more reinforcing.

67. And then We would surely have bestowed on them a great reward from Ourselves.

68. And We would have guided them to a straight path.

69. Those who obey Allah and the Messenger will be in the company of those whom God has favoured of the Prophets, the saints, the martyrs and the righteous people. What excellent companions they are!

70. Such is the Bounty of Allah; Allah suffices as Knower.

71. O believers, be on your guard; so march in detachments or march all together.

72. Indeed, among you is the one who will stay behind, so that if a disaster befalls you, he will say: "Allah has favoured me, since I have not been a martyr with them."

73. If, however, a bounty from God comes to you, he will say, as though there was no friendship between you and him: "Would that I had been with them; then I would have won a great victory."

فَلَا وَرَبِّكَ لَا يُؤْمِنُونَ حَتَّىٰ يُحَكِّمُوكَ فِيمَا شَجَرَ بَيْنَهُمْ ثُمَّ لَا يَجِدُوا۟ فِىٓ أَنفُسِهِمْ حَرَجًا مِّمَّا قَضَيْتَ وَيُسَلِّمُوا۟ تَسْلِيمًا ۝

وَلَوْ أَنَّا كَتَبْنَا عَلَيْهِمْ أَنِ ٱقْتُلُوٓا۟ أَنفُسَكُمْ أَوِ ٱخْرُجُوا۟ مِن دِيَٰرِكُم مَّا فَعَلُوهُ إِلَّا قَلِيلٌ مِّنْهُمْ وَلَوْ أَنَّهُمْ فَعَلُوا۟ مَا يُوعَظُونَ بِهِۦ لَكَانَ خَيْرًا لَّهُمْ وَأَشَدَّ تَثْبِيتًا ۝

وَإِذًا لَّءَاتَيْنَٰهُم مِّن لَّدُنَّآ أَجْرًا عَظِيمًا ۝

وَلَهَدَيْنَٰهُمْ صِرَٰطًا مُّسْتَقِيمًا ۝

وَمَن يُطِعِ ٱللَّهَ وَٱلرَّسُولَ فَأُو۟لَٰٓئِكَ مَعَ ٱلَّذِينَ أَنْعَمَ ٱللَّهُ عَلَيْهِم مِّنَ ٱلنَّبِيِّۦنَ وَٱلصِّدِّيقِينَ وَٱلشُّهَدَآءِ وَٱلصَّٰلِحِينَ وَحَسُنَ أُو۟لَٰٓئِكَ رَفِيقًا ۝

ذَٰلِكَ ٱلْفَضْلُ مِنَ ٱللَّهِ وَكَفَىٰ بِٱللَّهِ عَلِيمًا ۝

يَٰٓأَيُّهَا ٱلَّذِينَ ءَامَنُوا۟ خُذُوا۟ حِذْرَكُمْ فَٱنفِرُوا۟ ثُبَاتٍ أَوِ ٱنفِرُوا۟ جَمِيعًا ۝

وَإِنَّ مِنكُمْ لَمَن لَّيُبَطِّئَنَّ فَإِنْ أَصَٰبَتْكُم مُّصِيبَةٌ قَالَ قَدْ أَنْعَمَ ٱللَّهُ عَلَىَّ إِذْ لَمْ أَكُن مَّعَهُمْ شَهِيدًا ۝

وَلَئِنْ أَصَٰبَكُمْ فَضْلٌ مِّنَ ٱللَّهِ لَيَقُولَنَّ كَأَن لَّمْ تَكُنۢ بَيْنَكُمْ وَبَيْنَهُۥ مَوَدَّةٌ يَٰلَيْتَنِى كُنتُ مَعَهُمْ فَأَفُوزَ فَوْزًا عَظِيمًا ۝

---

286. That is, to obey the Prophet.

74. So let those who sell the present life for the life to come fight in the Way of Allah. Whoever fights in the Way of Allah and is killed or conquers, We shall accord him a great reward.

75. And why don't you fight for the Cause of God and for the down-trodden, men, women and children, who say: "Lord, bring us out of this city[287] whose inhabitants are unjust and grant us, from You, a protector, and grant us, from You, a supporter."

76. Those who believe fight for the Cause of Allah, and those who disbelieve fight on behalf of the Devil. Fight then the followers of the Devil. Surely the guile of the Devil is weak.

77. Have you not seen those to whom it was said: "Hold back your hands, perform the prayer and give the alms-tax"; but when they were ordered to fight, a group of them appeared to fear men just as they fear Allah, or even more. They said: "Lord, why have You ordered us to fight? If only You would grant us respite for a short period." Say: "The pleasure of this world is small and the Hereafter is far better for the God-fearing; and you will not be wronged a whit."

78. Wherever you may be, death will overtake you, even if you are in high towers. And if a good fortune befalls them[288] they say: "This is from Allah." But when misfortune befalls them, they say: "It is from you."[289] Say: "All is from Allah." What is the matter with those people who barely understand any discourse!

---

287. Mecca.
288. The Jews.
289. That is, Muhammad.

92

79. Whatever good visits you, it is from Allah; and whatever evil befalls you, it is from yourself; and We have sent you[290] forth to mankind as a Messenger. Allah is the All-Sufficient Witness!

80. Whoever obeys the Messenger actually obeys Allah. As for those who turn away, We have not sent you to be their keeper.

81. They say: "Obedience"; but when they leave you, a group of them secretly plan something other than what you say. Allah writes down what they have in mind. So, shun them and put your trust in Allah; Allah is the All-Sufficient Guardian.

82. Do they not, then, ponder over the Qur'an? Had it been from someone other than Allah, they would have found in it many inconsistencies.

83. And when a matter of security or fear reaches them, they broadcast it; but had they referred it to the Messenger or the people in authority among them,[291] those of them who investigate it would comprehend it. Had it not been for Allah's Bounty to you and His Mercy, you would all surely have followed the Devil, except for a few.

84. So, fight for the Cause of Allah; you are charged only of yourself. Urge the believers on that Allah may perchance restrain the unbelievers' might. Allah's Might is greater, and greater is His Retribution!

85. He who offers a good intercession[292] shall have a share[293] of it; and he who offers a bad intercession shall suffer from its consequences. Allah has power over every-thing!

مَّآ أَصَابَكَ مِنْ حَسَنَةٍ فَمِنَ ٱللَّهِ وَمَآ أَصَابَكَ مِن سَيِّئَةٍ فَمِن نَّفْسِكَ وَأَرْسَلْنَاكَ لِلنَّاسِ رَسُولًا وَكَفَىٰ بِٱللَّهِ شَهِيدًا ﴿٧٩﴾

مَّن يُطِعِ ٱلرَّسُولَ فَقَدْ أَطَاعَ ٱللَّهَ وَمَن تَوَلَّىٰ فَمَآ أَرْسَلْنَاكَ عَلَيْهِمْ حَفِيظًا ﴿٨٠﴾

وَيَقُولُونَ طَاعَةٌ فَإِذَا بَرَزُوا۟ مِنْ عِندِكَ بَيَّتَ طَآئِفَةٌ مِّنْهُمْ غَيْرَ ٱلَّذِى تَقُولُ وَٱللَّهُ يَكْتُبُ مَا يُبَيِّتُونَ فَأَعْرِضْ عَنْهُمْ وَتَوَكَّلْ عَلَى ٱللَّهِ وَكَفَىٰ بِٱللَّهِ وَكِيلًا ﴿٨١﴾

أَفَلَا يَتَدَبَّرُونَ ٱلْقُرْءَانَ وَلَوْ كَانَ مِنْ عِندِ غَيْرِ ٱللَّهِ لَوَجَدُوا۟ فِيهِ ٱخْتِلَٰفًا كَثِيرًا ﴿٨٢﴾

وَإِذَا جَآءَهُمْ أَمْرٌ مِّنَ ٱلْأَمْنِ أَوِ ٱلْخَوْفِ أَذَاعُوا۟ بِهِ وَلَوْ رَدُّوهُ إِلَى ٱلرَّسُولِ وَإِلَىٰٓ أُو۟لِى ٱلْأَمْرِ مِنْهُمْ لَعَلِمَهُ ٱلَّذِينَ يَسْتَنۢبِطُونَهُۥ مِنْهُمْ وَلَوْلَا فَضْلُ ٱللَّهِ عَلَيْكُمْ وَرَحْمَتُهُۥ لَٱتَّبَعْتُمُ ٱلشَّيْطَٰنَ إِلَّا قَلِيلًا ﴿٨٣﴾

فَقَٰتِلْ فِى سَبِيلِ ٱللَّهِ لَا تُكَلَّفُ إِلَّا نَفْسَكَ وَحَرِّضِ ٱلْمُؤْمِنِينَ عَسَى ٱللَّهُ أَن يَكُفَّ بَأْسَ ٱلَّذِينَ كَفَرُوا۟ وَٱللَّهُ أَشَدُّ بَأْسًا وَأَشَدُّ تَنكِيلًا ﴿٨٤﴾

مَّن يَشْفَعْ شَفَٰعَةً حَسَنَةً يَكُن لَّهُۥ نَصِيبٌ مِّنْهَا وَمَن يَشْفَعْ شَفَٰعَةً سَيِّئَةً يَكُن لَّهُۥ كِفْلٌ مِّنْهَا وَكَانَ ٱللَّهُ عَلَىٰ كُلِّ شَىْءٍ مُّقِيتًا ﴿٨٥﴾

---

290. Muhammad.
291. That is, to the Companions of the Prophet.
292. That is, he who intercedes for people in accordance with Muslim law.
293. That is, he shall have a part of the reward.

86. And when you are greeted with a certain greeting, greet back with a better one or return it; for Allah keeps count of everything!

87. Allah, there is no God but He. He will gather you all together on the Day of Resurrection; there is no doubt about it. And who is more truthful than Allah?

88. How is it that you are divided into two parties regarding the hypocrites, when Allah turned them back[294] on account of what they earned?[295] Do you wish to guide those whom Allah leads astray? He whom Allah leads astray, you will not find a way out for him.

89. They wish that you disbelieve, as they have disbelieved, so that you will all be alike. Do not, then, take any companions from them, until they emigrate in the Way of Allah. Then should they turn back, seize them and kill them wherever you find them; and do not take from them any companion or supporter;

90. Except for those who seek refuge with a people with whom you are bound by a compact, or come to you because their hearts forbid them to fight you or fight their own people. Had Allah wished, He would have made them dominate you; and then they would have certainly fought you. If, however, they leave you alone and do not fight you and offer you peace, then Allah allows you no way against them.

91. You shall find others who wish to be secure from you and secure from their own people; yet, whenever they are called back to sedition[296] they plunge into it. If these do not keep away from you, nor offer you peace,

وَإِذَا حُيِّيتُم بِتَحِيَّةٍ فَحَيُّوا بِأَحْسَنَ مِنْهَا أَوْ رُدُّوهَا إِنَّ اللَّهَ كَانَ عَلَىٰ كُلِّ شَىْءٍ حَسِيبًا ﴿٨٦﴾

اللَّهُ لَا إِلَٰهَ إِلَّا هُوَ لَيَجْمَعَنَّكُمْ إِلَىٰ يَوْمِ الْقِيَامَةِ لَا رَيْبَ فِيهِ وَمَنْ أَصْدَقُ مِنَ اللَّهِ حَدِيثًا ﴿٨٧﴾

۞ فَمَا لَكُمْ فِى الْمُنَافِقِينَ فِئَتَيْنِ وَاللَّهُ أَرْكَسَهُم بِمَا كَسَبُوا أَتُرِيدُونَ أَن تَهْدُوا مَنْ أَضَلَّ اللَّهُ وَمَن يُضْلِلِ اللَّهُ فَلَن تَجِدَ لَهُ سَبِيلًا ﴿٨٨﴾

وَدُّوا لَوْ تَكْفُرُونَ كَمَا كَفَرُوا فَتَكُونُونَ سَوَاءً فَلَا تَتَّخِذُوا مِنْهُمْ أَوْلِيَاءَ حَتَّىٰ يُهَاجِرُوا فِى سَبِيلِ اللَّهِ فَإِن تَوَلَّوْا فَخُذُوهُمْ وَاقْتُلُوهُمْ حَيْثُ وَجَدتُّمُوهُمْ وَلَا تَتَّخِذُوا مِنْهُمْ وَلِيًّا وَلَا نَصِيرًا ﴿٨٩﴾

إِلَّا الَّذِينَ يَصِلُونَ إِلَىٰ قَوْمٍ بَيْنَكُمْ وَبَيْنَهُم مِّيثَٰقٌ أَوْ جَاءُوكُمْ حَصِرَتْ صُدُورُهُمْ أَن يُقَاتِلُوكُمْ أَوْ يُقَاتِلُوا قَوْمَهُمْ وَلَوْ شَاءَ اللَّهُ لَسَلَّطَهُمْ عَلَيْكُمْ فَلَقَاتَلُوكُمْ فَإِنِ اعْتَزَلُوكُمْ فَلَمْ يُقَاتِلُوكُمْ وَأَلْقَوْا إِلَيْكُمُ السَّلَمَ فَمَا جَعَلَ اللَّهُ لَكُمْ عَلَيْهِمْ سَبِيلًا ﴿٩٠﴾

سَتَجِدُونَ ءَاخَرِينَ يُرِيدُونَ أَن يَأْمَنُوكُمْ وَيَأْمَنُوا قَوْمَهُمْ كُلَّ مَا رُدُّوا إِلَى الْفِتْنَةِ أُرْكِسُوا فِيهَا فَإِن لَّمْ يَعْتَزِلُوكُمْ وَيُلْقُوا إِلَيْكُمُ السَّلَمَ وَيَكُفُّوا أَيْدِيَهُمْ فَخُذُوهُمْ

---

294. Turned them back to disbelief.
295. That is, on account of their sins and disbelief.
296. That is, to polytheism.

nor hold their hands back, then seize them and kill them wherever you find them. Those, We have given you clear authority over them.

92. It is not given to a believer to kill another believer except by mistake; and he who kills a believer by mistake should free a slave who is a believer and pay blood-money to his relatives, unless they remit it as alms. If he happens to belong to a people who are your enemies, but he is a believer, then you should free a believing slave. If he belongs to a people bound with you by a compact, then blood-money should be paid to his relatives and a believing slave should be freed. As for him who has not the means, he should fast for two consecutive months, as a penance from Allah. Allah is All-Knowing, Wise!

93. And he who kills a believer intentionally will, as punishment, be thrown into Hell, dwelling in it forever; and Allah will be angry with him, curse him and prepare for him a dreadful punishment.

94. O believers, if you journey in the Way of Allah, be discerning and do not say to him who greets you: "You are not a believer", seeking the fleeting goods of the present life. For with Allah are abundant gains. This is how you were before and Allah has been gracious to you; so discern well. Allah is indeed Fully Aware of what you do!

95. Those of the believers who stay at home while suffering from no injury are not equal to those who fight for the Cause of Allah with their possessions and persons. Allah has raised those who fight with their possessions

وَٱقْتُلُوهُمْ حَيْثُ ثَقِفْتُمُوهُمْ وَأُوْلَٰٓئِكُمْ جَعَلْنَا لَكُمْ عَلَيْهِمْ سُلْطَٰنًا مُّبِينًا ۝

وَمَا كَانَ لِمُؤْمِنٍ أَن يَقْتُلَ مُؤْمِنًا إِلَّا خَطَـًٔا وَمَن قَتَلَ مُؤْمِنًا خَطَـًٔا فَتَحْرِيرُ رَقَبَةٍ مُّؤْمِنَةٍ وَدِيَةٌ مُّسَلَّمَةٌ إِلَىٰٓ أَهْلِهِۦٓ إِلَّآ أَن يَصَّدَّقُوا۟ فَإِن كَانَ مِن قَوْمٍ عَدُوٍّ لَّكُمْ وَهُوَ مُؤْمِنٌ فَتَحْرِيرُ رَقَبَةٍ مُّؤْمِنَةٍ وَإِن كَانَ مِن قَوْمٍ بَيْنَكُمْ وَبَيْنَهُم مِّيثَٰقٌ فَدِيَةٌ مُّسَلَّمَةٌ إِلَىٰٓ أَهْلِهِۦ وَتَحْرِيرُ رَقَبَةٍ مُّؤْمِنَةٍ فَمَن لَّمْ يَجِدْ فَصِيَامُ شَهْرَيْنِ مُتَتَابِعَيْنِ تَوْبَةً مِّنَ ٱللَّهِ وَكَانَ ٱللَّهُ عَلِيمًا حَكِيمًا ۝

وَمَن يَقْتُلْ مُؤْمِنًا مُّتَعَمِّدًا فَجَزَآؤُهُۥ جَهَنَّمُ خَٰلِدًا فِيهَا وَغَضِبَ ٱللَّهُ عَلَيْهِ وَلَعَنَهُۥ وَأَعَدَّ لَهُۥ عَذَابًا عَظِيمًا ۝

يَٰٓأَيُّهَا ٱلَّذِينَ ءَامَنُوٓا۟ إِذَا ضَرَبْتُمْ فِى سَبِيلِ ٱللَّهِ فَتَبَيَّنُوا۟ وَلَا تَقُولُوا۟ لِمَنْ أَلْقَىٰٓ إِلَيْكُمُ ٱلسَّلَٰمَ لَسْتَ مُؤْمِنًا تَبْتَغُونَ عَرَضَ ٱلْحَيَوٰةِ ٱلدُّنْيَا فَعِندَ ٱللَّهِ مَغَانِمُ كَثِيرَةٌ كَذَٰلِكَ كُنتُم مِّن قَبْلُ فَمَنَّ ٱللَّهُ عَلَيْكُمْ فَتَبَيَّنُوٓا۟ إِنَّ ٱللَّهَ كَانَ بِمَا تَعْمَلُونَ خَبِيرًا ۝

لَّا يَسْتَوِى ٱلْقَٰعِدُونَ مِنَ ٱلْمُؤْمِنِينَ غَيْرُ أُو۟لِى ٱلضَّرَرِ وَٱلْمُجَٰهِدُونَ فِى سَبِيلِ ٱللَّهِ بِأَمْوَٰلِهِمْ وَأَنفُسِهِمْ فَضَّلَ ٱللَّهُ ٱلْمُجَٰهِدِينَ بِأَمْوَٰلِهِمْ وَأَنفُسِهِمْ عَلَى ٱلْقَٰعِدِينَ دَرَجَةً وَكُلًّا وَعَدَ

and persons one degree over those who stay at home; and to each Allah has promised the fairest good. Yet Allah has granted a great reward to those who fight and not to those who stay behind.

96. Degrees of honour from Him, Forgiveness and Mercy. Allah is All-Forgiving, Merciful.

97. Those whom the angels cause to die while they are unjust to themselves[297] will be asked [by the angels]: "What were you doing?" They will say: "We were oppressed in the land." They [the angels] will add saying: "Was not Allah's Land spacious enough for you to emigrate to some other part?" Those people - their refuge is Hell, and what a wretched destiny!

98. Except the oppressed men, women and children who have no recourse and cannot find a way out.[298]

99. Those, Allah may pardon them; Allah is All-Pardoning, All-Forgiving.

100. He who emigrates for the Cause of Allah will find on earth many a place of refuge and abundance; and he who leaves his home as an emigrant to Allah and His Messenger and is then overtaken by death, has already earned his reward from Allah. Allah is All-Forgiving, Merciful!

101. And when you journey in the land, you are not at fault if you shorten the prayer for fear that the unbelievers will harm you. The unbelievers are your manifest enemies.

ٱللَّهُ ٱلْحُسْنَىٰ وَفَضَّلَ ٱللَّهُ ٱلْمُجَٰهِدِينَ عَلَى ٱلْقَٰعِدِينَ أَجْرًا عَظِيمًا ﴿٩٥﴾

دَرَجَٰتٍ مِّنْهُ وَمَغْفِرَةً وَرَحْمَةً وَكَانَ ٱللَّهُ غَفُورًا رَّحِيمًا ﴿٩٦﴾

إِنَّ ٱلَّذِينَ تَوَفَّىٰهُمُ ٱلْمَلَٰئِكَةُ ظَالِمِىٓ أَنفُسِهِمْ قَالُوا۟ فِيمَ كُنتُمْ قَالُوا۟ كُنَّا مُسْتَضْعَفِينَ فِى ٱلْأَرْضِ قَالُوٓا۟ أَلَمْ تَكُنْ أَرْضُ ٱللَّهِ وَٰسِعَةً فَتُهَاجِرُوا۟ فِيهَا فَأُو۟لَٰٓئِكَ مَأْوَىٰهُمْ جَهَنَّمُ وَسَآءَتْ مَصِيرًا ﴿٩٧﴾

إِلَّا ٱلْمُسْتَضْعَفِينَ مِنَ ٱلرِّجَالِ وَٱلنِّسَآءِ وَٱلْوِلْدَٰنِ لَا يَسْتَطِيعُونَ حِيلَةً وَلَا يَهْتَدُونَ سَبِيلًا ﴿٩٨﴾

فَأُو۟لَٰٓئِكَ عَسَى ٱللَّهُ أَن يَعْفُوَ عَنْهُمْ وَكَانَ ٱللَّهُ عَفُوًّا غَفُورًا ﴿٩٩﴾

۞ وَمَن يُهَاجِرْ فِى سَبِيلِ ٱللَّهِ يَجِدْ فِى ٱلْأَرْضِ مُرَٰغَمًا كَثِيرًا وَسَعَةً وَمَن يَخْرُجْ مِنۢ بَيْتِهِۦ مُهَاجِرًا إِلَى ٱللَّهِ وَرَسُولِهِۦ ثُمَّ يُدْرِكْهُ ٱلْمَوْتُ فَقَدْ وَقَعَ أَجْرُهُۥ عَلَى ٱللَّهِ وَكَانَ ٱللَّهُ غَفُورًا رَّحِيمًا ﴿١٠٠﴾

وَإِذَا ضَرَبْتُمْ فِى ٱلْأَرْضِ فَلَيْسَ عَلَيْكُمْ جُنَاحٌ أَن تَقْصُرُوا۟ مِنَ ٱلصَّلَوٰةِ إِنْ خِفْتُمْ أَن يَفْتِنَكُمُ ٱلَّذِينَ كَفَرُوٓا۟ إِنَّ ٱلْكَٰفِرِينَ كَانُوا۟ لَكُمْ عَدُوًّا مُّبِينًا ﴿١٠١﴾

---

297. The reference is to those Meccans who could have accepted the faith and emigrated, but did not.
298. The reference here is to those Meccans who were weak and could not emigrate.

102. When you[299] are among them,[300] conducting the prayer for them, let a group of them rise with you and let them take their weapons; but when they have prostrated themselves, let them withdraw to the rear; and let another party who had not prayed come forward and pray with you, taking their precaution and carrying their weapons. The unbelievers wish that you would neglect your arms and your equipment, so that they may swoop down on you in a united attack. You are not at fault, however, if you lay aside your weapons in case you are hampered by rain or are sick; but take heed. Allah has prepared for the unbelievers a demeaning punishment.

وَإِذَا كُنتَ فِيهِمْ فَأَقَمْتَ لَهُمُ ٱلصَّلَوٰةَ فَلْتَقُمْ طَآئِفَةٌ مِّنْهُم مَّعَكَ وَلْيَأْخُذُوٓا۟ أَسْلِحَتَهُمْ فَإِذَا سَجَدُوا۟ فَلْيَكُونُوا۟ مِن وَرَآئِكُمْ وَلْتَأْتِ طَآئِفَةٌ أُخْرَىٰ لَمْ يُصَلُّوا۟ فَلْيُصَلُّوا۟ مَعَكَ وَلْيَأْخُذُوا۟ حِذْرَهُمْ وَأَسْلِحَتَهُمْ وَدَّ ٱلَّذِينَ كَفَرُوا۟ لَوْ تَغْفُلُونَ عَنْ أَسْلِحَتِكُمْ وَأَمْتِعَتِكُمْ فَيَمِيلُونَ عَلَيْكُم مَّيْلَةً وَٰحِدَةً وَلَا جُنَاحَ عَلَيْكُمْ إِن كَانَ بِكُمْ أَذًى مِّن مَّطَرٍ أَوْ كُنتُم مَّرْضَىٰٓ أَن تَضَعُوٓا۟ أَسْلِحَتَكُمْ وَخُذُوا۟ حِذْرَكُمْ إِنَّ ٱللَّهَ أَعَدَّ لِلْكَٰفِرِينَ عَذَابًا مُّهِينًا ۝

103. When you have completed the prayer, remember Allah standing, sitting and reclining. Once you feel secure, then perform the prayer; for prayer is enjoined on the believers at fixed times.

فَإِذَا قَضَيْتُمُ ٱلصَّلَوٰةَ فَٱذْكُرُوا۟ ٱللَّهَ قِيَٰمًا وَقُعُودًا وَعَلَىٰ جُنُوبِكُمْ فَإِذَا ٱطْمَأْنَنتُمْ فَأَقِيمُوا۟ ٱلصَّلَوٰةَ إِنَّ ٱلصَّلَوٰةَ كَانَتْ عَلَى ٱلْمُؤْمِنِينَ كِتَٰبًا مَّوْقُوتًا ۝

104. Do not be weak-hearted in pursuing the enemy. If you are suffering, they are suffering too; but you hope from Allah what they cannot hope. Allah is All-Knowing, Wise.

وَلَا تَهِنُوا۟ فِي ٱبْتِغَآءِ ٱلْقَوْمِ إِن تَكُونُوا۟ تَأْلَمُونَ فَإِنَّهُمْ يَأْلَمُونَ كَمَا تَأْلَمُونَ وَتَرْجُونَ مِنَ ٱللَّهِ مَا لَا يَرْجُونَ وَكَانَ ٱللَّهُ عَلِيمًا حَكِيمًا ۝

105. We have revealed the Book to you in truth, so as to judge between people in accordance with what Allah has shown you. And do not be an advocate of the treacherous!

إِنَّآ أَنزَلْنَآ إِلَيْكَ ٱلْكِتَٰبَ بِٱلْحَقِّ لِتَحْكُمَ بَيْنَ ٱلنَّاسِ بِمَآ أَرَىٰكَ ٱللَّهُ وَلَا تَكُن لِّلْخَآئِنِينَ خَصِيمًا ۝

106. And ask Allah's forgiveness; Allah is indeed All-Forgiving, Merciful!

وَٱسْتَغْفِرِ ٱللَّهَ إِنَّ ٱللَّهَ كَانَ غَفُورًا رَّحِيمًا ۝

107. And do not plead on behalf of those who betray themselves; for Allah does not like the treacherous or sinful.

وَلَا تُجَٰدِلْ عَنِ ٱلَّذِينَ يَخْتَانُونَ أَنفُسَهُمْ إِنَّ ٱللَّهَ لَا يُحِبُّ مَن كَانَ خَوَّانًا أَثِيمًا ۝

---

299. Muhammad.
300. The faithful.

108. They seek to hide themselves from men, but they cannot hide themselves from Allah; for He is with them while they secretly contemplate words that do not please Him. And Allah is fully aware of what they do!

يَسْتَخْفُونَ مِنَ ٱلنَّاسِ وَلَا يَسْتَخْفُونَ مِنَ ٱللَّهِ وَهُوَ مَعَهُمْ إِذْ يُبَيِّتُونَ مَا لَا يَرْضَىٰ مِنَ ٱلْقَوْلِ وَكَانَ ٱللَّهُ بِمَا يَعْمَلُونَ مُحِيطًا ۝

109. There you are, you have pleaded on their behalf in the present world; who then will plead with Allah on their behalf on the Day of Resurrection, or who will be their guardian?

هَٰٓأَنتُمْ هَٰٓؤُلَآءِ جَٰدَلْتُمْ عَنْهُمْ فِى ٱلْحَيَوٰةِ ٱلدُّنْيَا فَمَن يُجَٰدِلُ ٱللَّهَ عَنْهُمْ يَوْمَ ٱلْقِيَٰمَةِ أَم مَّن يَكُونُ عَلَيْهِمْ وَكِيلًا ۝

110. But he, who does evil or wrongs himself, then asks Allah's forgiveness, will find Allah All-Forgiving, Merciful.

وَمَن يَعْمَلْ سُوٓءًا أَوْ يَظْلِمْ نَفْسَهُۥ ثُمَّ يَسْتَغْفِرِ ٱللَّهَ يَجِدِ ٱللَّهَ غَفُورًا رَّحِيمًا ۝

111. And whoever commits a sin, will only commit it against himself. Allah is All-Knowing, Wise!

وَمَن يَكْسِبْ إِثْمًا فَإِنَّمَا يَكْسِبُهُۥ عَلَىٰ نَفْسِهِۦ وَكَانَ ٱللَّهُ عَلِيمًا حَكِيمًا ۝

112. And whoever commits an offence or a sin then charges an innocent man with it bears the burden of a falsehood and a manifest sin.

وَمَن يَكْسِبْ خَطِيٓئَةً أَوْ إِثْمًا ثُمَّ يَرْمِ بِهِۦ بَرِيٓئًا فَقَدِ ٱحْتَمَلَ بُهْتَٰنًا وَإِثْمًا مُّبِينًا ۝

113. And, but for Allah's Bounty and Mercy upon you,[301] a group of them would have tried to lead you astray; however, they only lead themselves astray. They do not cause you any harm. Allah has revealed to you the Book and the Wisdom and taught you what you did not know, and Allah's Goodness to you has been great.

وَلَوْلَا فَضْلُ ٱللَّهِ عَلَيْكَ وَرَحْمَتُهُۥ لَهَمَّت طَّآئِفَةٌ مِّنْهُمْ أَن يُضِلُّوكَ وَمَا يُضِلُّونَ إِلَّآ أَنفُسَهُمْ وَمَا يَضُرُّونَكَ مِن شَىْءٍ وَأَنزَلَ ٱللَّهُ عَلَيْكَ ٱلْكِتَٰبَ وَٱلْحِكْمَةَ وَعَلَّمَكَ مَا لَمْ تَكُن تَعْلَمُ وَكَانَ فَضْلُ ٱللَّهِ عَلَيْكَ عَظِيمًا ۝

114. There is no good in much of their secret talk, except for him who enjoins charity, kindness or conciliation between people. Whoever does that seeking God's good Pleasure, We will surely grant him a great reward.

۞ لَّا خَيْرَ فِى كَثِيرٍ مِّن نَّجْوَىٰهُمْ إِلَّا مَنْ أَمَرَ بِصَدَقَةٍ أَوْ مَعْرُوفٍ أَوْ إِصْلَٰحٍ بَيْنَ ٱلنَّاسِ وَمَن يَفْعَلْ ذَٰلِكَ ٱبْتِغَآءَ مَرْضَاتِ ٱللَّهِ فَسَوْفَ نُؤْتِيهِ أَجْرًا عَظِيمًا ۝

---

301. Muhammad.

115. But he who opposes the Messenger after the guidance has been manifested to him, and follows a path other than that of the believers, We will let him follow the way he has chosen for himself, and throw him into Hell; and what a wretched fate!

وَمَن يُشَاقِقِ ٱلرَّسُولَ مِنۢ بَعْدِ مَا تَبَيَّنَ لَهُ ٱلْهُدَىٰ وَيَتَّبِعْ غَيْرَ سَبِيلِ ٱلْمُؤْمِنِينَ نُوَلِّهِۦ مَا تَوَلَّىٰ وَنُصْلِهِۦ جَهَنَّمَ وَسَآءَتْ مَصِيرًا ﴿١١٥﴾

116. Allah will not forgive associating [any other god] with Him, but will forgive anything less than that, to whomever He wills. He who associates [any other god] with Allah, has really gone very far astray!

إِنَّ ٱللَّهَ لَا يَغْفِرُ أَن يُشْرَكَ بِهِۦ وَيَغْفِرُ مَا دُونَ ذَٰلِكَ لِمَن يَشَآءُ وَمَن يُشْرِكْ بِٱللَّهِ فَقَدْ ضَلَّ ضَلَٰلًۢا بَعِيدًا ﴿١١٦﴾

117. Apart from Him, they only invoke[302] the goddesses of Quraysh; they only invoke a rebellious devil,[303]

إِن يَدْعُونَ مِن دُونِهِۦٓ إِلَّآ إِنَٰثًا وَإِن يَدْعُونَ إِلَّا شَيْطَٰنًا مَّرِيدًا ﴿١١٧﴾

118. Cursed by Allah. For he[304] said: "I shall take from your servants for myself a fixed number,

لَّعَنَهُ ٱللَّهُ وَقَالَ لَأَتَّخِذَنَّ مِنْ عِبَادِكَ نَصِيبًا مَّفْرُوضًا ﴿١١٨﴾

119. "And I will lead them astray, will raise their expectations and order them to cut off the cattle's ears. I will order them to alter Allah's creation." Whoever takes the Devil for a companion, instead of Allah, has incurred a grave loss!

وَلَأُضِلَّنَّهُمْ وَلَأُمَنِّيَنَّهُمْ وَلَآمُرَنَّهُمْ فَلَيُبَتِّكُنَّ ءَاذَانَ ٱلْأَنْعَٰمِ وَلَآمُرَنَّهُمْ فَلَيُغَيِّرُنَّ خَلْقَ ٱللَّهِ وَمَن يَتَّخِذِ ٱلشَّيْطَٰنَ وَلِيًّا مِّن دُونِ ٱللَّهِ فَقَدْ خَسِرَ خُسْرَانًا مُّبِينًا ﴿١١٩﴾

120. He promises them and raises their expectations; but the Devil promises them nothing but illusion.

يَعِدُهُمْ وَيُمَنِّيهِمْ وَمَا يَعِدُهُمُ ٱلشَّيْطَٰنُ إِلَّا غُرُورًا ﴿١٢٠﴾

121. Those people, their shelter shall be Hell and they shall find no escape from it.

أُوْلَٰٓئِكَ مَأْوَىٰهُمْ جَهَنَّمُ وَلَا يَجِدُونَ عَنْهَا مَحِيصًا ﴿١٢١﴾

122. But those who have believed and done the good deeds, We shall admit them into Gardens beneath which rivers flow, dwelling therein forever. This is Allah's True Promise; and who is more truthful in speech than Allah?

وَٱلَّذِينَ ءَامَنُوا۟ وَعَمِلُوا۟ ٱلصَّٰلِحَٰتِ سَنُدْخِلُهُمْ جَنَّٰتٍ تَجْرِى مِن تَحْتِهَا ٱلْأَنْهَٰرُ خَٰلِدِينَ فِيهَآ أَبَدًا وَعْدَ ٱللَّهِ حَقًّا وَمَنْ أَصْدَقُ مِنَ ٱللَّهِ قِيلًا ﴿١٢٢﴾

---

302. What is meant here is worship.
303. Satan.
304. The Devil.

123. It will not be in accordance with your wishes or the wishes of the People of the Book. Whoever does evil shall be requited for it and will not find, apart from Allah, a friend or supporter

124. And whoever does some good deeds, whether male or female, and is a believer - those shall be admitted to Paradise and shall not be wronged a whit.

125. And who has a better religion than one who submits himself to Allah, does right and follows the true religion of Abraham the upright one? Allah has taken Abraham for a friend.

126. To Allah belongs what is in the heavens and on earth, and Allah encompasses everything!

127. They consult you concerning women. Say: "Allah has instructed you concerning them, and concerning what is recited to you in the Book regarding orphan women for whom you do not give what is prescribed for them, although you wish to marry them, and concerning the weak children, and your duty to deal justly with orphans.[305] For whatever good you do, Allah knows it very well."

128. And if a woman fears maltreatment or aversion from her husband, they[306] would not commit an offence if they are reconciled amicably; reconciliation is best. Souls are prone to avarice, and if you are charitable and if you ward off evil, He is surely Well Aware of what you do!

---

305. When considering the dowry and inheritance.
306. She and her husband.

129. You will never be able to treat wives equitably, even if you are bent on doing that. So do not turn away altogether [from any of them] leaving her, like one in suspense; and if you do justice [to her] and guard against evil, He[307] is surely All-Forgiving, Merciful!

130. And if they separate, Allah will give each one plenty of His Abundance; and Allah is Munificent, Wise.

131. And to Allah belongs what is in the heavens and on earth. We have enjoined those who received the Book before you, as well as yourselves: "Fear Allah, and if you disbelieve, surely to Allah belongs what is in the heavens and on earth. Allah is All-Sufficient, Praiseworthy."

132. To Allah belongs what is in the heavens and on earth, and Allah suffices as Guardian!

133. If Allah wants, O people, He would annihilate you and replace you by others. Allah has the power to do that.

134. Whoever desires the reward of this world, [let him know that] with Allah is the reward of this world and the next. Allah is All-Hearing, All-Seeing!

135. O believers, be upholders of justice, witnesses for Allah, even if it be against yourselves, your parents or kinsmen. Whether rich or poor, Allah takes better care of both. Do not follow your desire to refrain from justice. If you twist [your testimony] or turn away, Allah is Fully Aware of what you do.

---

307. Allah.

وَلَن تَسْتَطِيعُوٓا۟ أَن تَعْدِلُوا۟ بَيْنَ ٱلنِّسَآءِ وَلَوْ حَرَصْتُمْ فَلَا تَمِيلُوا۟ كُلَّ ٱلْمَيْلِ فَتَذَرُوهَا كَٱلْمُعَلَّقَةِ وَإِن تُصْلِحُوا۟ وَتَتَّقُوا۟ فَإِنَّ ٱللَّهَ كَانَ غَفُورًا رَّحِيمًا ﴿١٢٩﴾

وَإِن يَتَفَرَّقَا يُغْنِ ٱللَّهُ كُلًّا مِّن سَعَتِهِۦ وَكَانَ ٱللَّهُ وَٰسِعًا حَكِيمًا ﴿١٣٠﴾

وَلِلَّهِ مَا فِى ٱلسَّمَٰوَٰتِ وَمَا فِى ٱلْأَرْضِ وَلَقَدْ وَصَّيْنَا ٱلَّذِينَ أُوتُوا۟ ٱلْكِتَٰبَ مِن قَبْلِكُمْ وَإِيَّاكُمْ أَنِ ٱتَّقُوا۟ ٱللَّهَ وَإِن تَكْفُرُوا۟ فَإِنَّ لِلَّهِ مَا فِى ٱلسَّمَٰوَٰتِ وَمَا فِى ٱلْأَرْضِ وَكَانَ ٱللَّهُ غَنِيًّا حَمِيدًا ﴿١٣١﴾

وَلِلَّهِ مَا فِى ٱلسَّمَٰوَٰتِ وَمَا فِى ٱلْأَرْضِ وَكَفَىٰ بِٱللَّهِ وَكِيلًا ﴿١٣٢﴾

إِن يَشَأْ يُذْهِبْكُمْ أَيُّهَا ٱلنَّاسُ وَيَأْتِ بِـَٔاخَرِينَ وَكَانَ ٱللَّهُ عَلَىٰ ذَٰلِكَ قَدِيرًا ﴿١٣٣﴾

مَّن كَانَ يُرِيدُ ثَوَابَ ٱلدُّنْيَا فَعِندَ ٱللَّهِ ثَوَابُ ٱلدُّنْيَا وَٱلْءَاخِرَةِ وَكَانَ ٱللَّهُ سَمِيعًۢا بَصِيرًا ﴿١٣٤﴾

۞ يَٰٓأَيُّهَا ٱلَّذِينَ ءَامَنُوا۟ كُونُوا۟ قَوَّٰمِينَ بِٱلْقِسْطِ شُهَدَآءَ لِلَّهِ وَلَوْ عَلَىٰٓ أَنفُسِكُمْ أَوِ ٱلْوَٰلِدَيْنِ وَٱلْأَقْرَبِينَ إِن يَكُنْ غَنِيًّا أَوْ فَقِيرًا فَٱللَّهُ أَوْلَىٰ بِهِمَا فَلَا تَتَّبِعُوا۟ ٱلْهَوَىٰٓ أَن تَعْدِلُوا۟ وَإِن تَلْوُۥٓا۟ أَوْ تُعْرِضُوا۟ فَإِنَّ ٱللَّهَ كَانَ بِمَا تَعْمَلُونَ خَبِيرًا ﴿١٣٥﴾

136. O believers, believe in Allah and His Messenger and in the Book which He revealed to His Messenger, and the Book which He revealed before. Whoever disbelieves in Allah, His Angels, His Books, His Prophets and the Last Day has gone far astray.

يَٰٓأَيُّهَا ٱلَّذِينَ ءَامَنُوٓاْ ءَامِنُواْ بِٱللَّهِ وَرَسُولِهِۦ وَٱلْكِتَٰبِ ٱلَّذِى نَزَّلَ عَلَىٰ رَسُولِهِۦ وَٱلْكِتَٰبِ ٱلَّذِىٓ أَنزَلَ مِن قَبْلُ وَمَن يَكْفُرْ بِٱللَّهِ وَمَلَٰٓئِكَتِهِۦ وَكُتُبِهِۦ وَرُسُلِهِۦ وَٱلْيَوْمِ ٱلْأَخِرِ فَقَدْ ضَلَّ ضَلَٰلَۢا بَعِيدًا ۝

137. Those who believe, then disbelieve, then again believe, then disbelieve, then grow in disbelief, Allah shall not forgive them nor guide them to the Right Path.

إِنَّ ٱلَّذِينَ ءَامَنُواْ ثُمَّ كَفَرُواْ ثُمَّ ءَامَنُواْ ثُمَّ كَفَرُواْ ثُمَّ ٱزْدَادُواْ كُفْرًا لَّمْ يَكُنِ ٱللَّهُ لِيَغْفِرَ لَهُمْ وَلَا لِيَهْدِيَهُمْ سَبِيلَۢا ۝

138. Announce to the hypocrites that a very painful punishment is reserved for them.

بَشِّرِ ٱلْمُنَٰفِقِينَ بِأَنَّ لَهُمْ عَذَابًا أَلِيمًا ۝

139. Those who take the unbelievers as friends, instead of the believers - do they seek glory from them? For all glory belongs to Allah.

ٱلَّذِينَ يَتَّخِذُونَ ٱلْكَٰفِرِينَ أَوْلِيَآءَ مِن دُونِ ٱلْمُؤْمِنِينَ أَيَبْتَغُونَ عِندَهُمُ ٱلْعِزَّةَ فَإِنَّ ٱلْعِزَّةَ لِلَّهِ جَمِيعًا ۝

140. He has revealed to you in the Book that, should you hear the Revelations of Allah being denied or mocked, you should not sit with them until they engage in some other discussion. Otherwise, you are like them. Allah shall assemble all the hypocrites and the unbelievers in Hell;

وَقَدْ نَزَّلَ عَلَيْكُمْ فِى ٱلْكِتَٰبِ أَنْ إِذَا سَمِعْتُمْ ءَايَٰتِ ٱللَّهِ يُكْفَرُ بِهَا وَيُسْتَهْزَأُ بِهَا فَلَا تَقْعُدُواْ مَعَهُمْ حَتَّىٰ يَخُوضُواْ فِى حَدِيثٍ غَيْرِهِۦٓ إِنَّكُمْ إِذَا مِّثْلُهُمْ إِنَّ ٱللَّهَ جَامِعُ ٱلْمُنَٰفِقِينَ وَٱلْكَٰفِرِينَ فِى جَهَنَّمَ جَمِيعًا ۝

141. Those who wait for [misfortune to befall] you. And if a victory is accorded to you from Allah, they will say: "Were we not on your side?"; and if the unbelievers have a share [in victory], they will say: "Did we not subdue you, and thus protect you from the believers?" Allah shall judge between you on the Day of Resurrection; and Allah will not give the unbelievers the upper hand over the believers.

ٱلَّذِينَ يَتَرَبَّصُونَ بِكُمْ فَإِن كَانَ لَكُمْ فَتْحٌ مِّنَ ٱللَّهِ قَالُوٓاْ أَلَمْ نَكُن مَّعَكُمْ وَإِن كَانَ لِلْكَٰفِرِينَ نَصِيبٌ قَالُوٓاْ أَلَمْ نَسْتَحْوِذْ عَلَيْكُمْ وَنَمْنَعْكُم مِّنَ ٱلْمُؤْمِنِينَ فَٱللَّهُ يَحْكُمُ بَيْنَكُمْ يَوْمَ ٱلْقِيَٰمَةِ وَلَن يَجْعَلَ ٱللَّهُ لِلْكَٰفِرِينَ عَلَى ٱلْمُؤْمِنِينَ سَبِيلَۢا ۝

142. Surely, the hypocrites seek to deceive Allah, but Allah causes their deceit to backfire. And if they rise to perform the prayer, they rise lazily, trying to show off in public and they remember Allah but little.

إِنَّ ٱلْمُنَٰفِقِينَ يُخَٰدِعُونَ ٱللَّهَ وَهُوَ خَٰدِعُهُمْ وَإِذَا قَامُوٓاْ إِلَى ٱلصَّلَوٰةِ قَامُواْ كُسَالَىٰ يُرَآءُونَ ٱلنَّاسَ وَلَا يَذْكُرُونَ ٱللَّهَ إِلَّا قَلِيلًا ۝

143. Vacillating between the two,[308] inclining neither to these nor to those;[309] and whomever Allah leads astray, you will not find him a way out.

مُّذَبْذَبِينَ بَيْنَ ذَلِكَ لَا إِلَى هَؤُلَاءِ وَلَا إِلَى هَؤُلَاءِ وَمَن يُضْلِلِ اللَّهُ فَلَن تَجِدَ لَهُ سَبِيلًا ﴿١٤٣﴾

144. O believers, do not take the unbelievers for friends, instead of the believers. Do you wish to give Allah a clear proof against you?

يَٰٓأَيُّهَا ٱلَّذِينَ ءَامَنُوا۟ لَا تَتَّخِذُوا۟ ٱلْكَٰفِرِينَ أَوْلِيَآءَ مِن دُونِ ٱلْمُؤْمِنِينَ أَتُرِيدُونَ أَن تَجْعَلُوا۟ لِلَّهِ عَلَيْكُمْ سُلْطَٰنًا مُّبِينًا ﴿١٤٤﴾

145. Surely, the hypocrites will be in the lowest depths of the Fire, and you will not find any supporter for them.

إِنَّ ٱلْمُنَٰفِقِينَ فِى ٱلدَّرْكِ ٱلْأَسْفَلِ مِنَ ٱلنَّارِ وَلَن تَجِدَ لَهُمْ نَصِيرًا ﴿١٤٥﴾

146. Except for those who repent and mend their ways, hold fast to Allah and are sincere in their obedience to Allah - those will be among the believers; and Allah shall grant the believers a great reward.

إِلَّا ٱلَّذِينَ تَابُوا۟ وَأَصْلَحُوا۟ وَٱعْتَصَمُوا۟ بِٱللَّهِ وَأَخْلَصُوا۟ دِينَهُمْ لِلَّهِ فَأُو۟لَٰٓئِكَ مَعَ ٱلْمُؤْمِنِينَ وَسَوْفَ يُؤْتِ ٱللَّهُ ٱلْمُؤْمِنِينَ أَجْرًا عَظِيمًا ﴿١٤٦﴾

147. Why should Allah punish you, if you are thankful and faithful? Allah Himself is Thankful, All-Knowing.

مَّا يَفْعَلُ ٱللَّهُ بِعَذَابِكُمْ إِن شَكَرْتُمْ وَءَامَنتُمْ وَكَانَ ٱللَّهُ شَاكِرًا عَلِيمًا ﴿١٤٧﴾

148. Allah does not like the public uttering of foul words, except by one who has been wronged. Allah is All-Hearing, All-Knowing.

۞ لَّا يُحِبُّ ٱللَّهُ ٱلْجَهْرَ بِٱلسُّوٓءِ مِنَ ٱلْقَوْلِ إِلَّا مَن ظُلِمَ وَكَانَ ٱللَّهُ سَمِيعًا عَلِيمًا ﴿١٤٨﴾

149. Whether you do good openly or secretly, or pardon an evil deed, Allah is indeed All-Pardoning, All-Powerful.

إِن تُبْدُوا۟ خَيْرًا أَوْ تُخْفُوهُ أَوْ تَعْفُوا۟ عَن سُوٓءٍ فَإِنَّ ٱللَّهَ كَانَ عَفُوًّا قَدِيرًا ﴿١٤٩﴾

150. Those who disbelieve in Allah and His Messengers and want to make a distinction between Allah and His Messengers, and say: "We believe in some and disbelieve in the others", wanting to take a middle course in between,

إِنَّ ٱلَّذِينَ يَكْفُرُونَ بِٱللَّهِ وَرُسُلِهِۦ وَيُرِيدُونَ أَن يُفَرِّقُوا۟ بَيْنَ ٱللَّهِ وَرُسُلِهِۦ وَيَقُولُونَ نُؤْمِنُ بِبَعْضٍ وَنَكْفُرُ بِبَعْضٍ وَيُرِيدُونَ أَن يَتَّخِذُوا۟ بَيْنَ ذَلِكَ سَبِيلًا ﴿١٥٠﴾

151. Those are the true unbelievers, and We have prepared for the unbelievers a demeaning punishment.

أُو۟لَٰٓئِكَ هُمُ ٱلْكَٰفِرُونَ حَقًّا وَأَعْتَدْنَا لِلْكَٰفِرِينَ عَذَابًا مُّهِينًا ﴿١٥١﴾

---

308. Belief and disbelief.
309. That is, neither to the believers nor to the unbelievers.

152. But those who believe in Allah and His Messengers and do not discriminate between any of them those He will grant them their rewards. Allah is All-Forgiving, Merciful!

وَٱلَّذِينَ ءَامَنُوا۟ بِٱللَّهِ وَرُسُلِهِۦ وَلَمْ يُفَرِّقُوا۟ بَيْنَ أَحَدٍ مِّنْهُمْ أُو۟لَـٰٓئِكَ سَوْفَ يُؤْتِيهِمْ أُجُورَهُمْ وَكَانَ ٱللَّهُ غَفُورًا رَّحِيمًا ۝

153. The People of the Book ask you to bring down a book from heaven for them; indeed, they asked Moses for greater than that, saying: "Show us God face to face." Thereupon the thunderbolt struck them for their wickedness. Then, they worshipped the calf, after they had received the clear proofs. Yet We pardoned all that and We gave Moses clear authority.

يَسْـَٔلُكَ أَهْلُ ٱلْكِتَـٰبِ أَن تُنَزِّلَ عَلَيْهِمْ كِتَـٰبًا مِّنَ ٱلسَّمَآءِ فَقَدْ سَأَلُوا۟ مُوسَىٰٓ أَكْبَرَ مِن ذَٰلِكَ فَقَالُوٓا۟ أَرِنَا ٱللَّهَ جَهْرَةً فَأَخَذَتْهُمُ ٱلصَّـٰعِقَةُ بِظُلْمِهِمْ ثُمَّ ٱتَّخَذُوا۟ ٱلْعِجْلَ مِنۢ بَعْدِ مَا جَآءَتْهُمُ ٱلْبَيِّنَـٰتُ فَعَفَوْنَا عَن ذَٰلِكَ وَءَاتَيْنَا مُوسَىٰ سُلْطَـٰنًا مُّبِينًا ۝

154. And We raised the Mount [Sinai] over them, in view of their covenant, and We said to them: "Enter the door prostrate", and We also said: "Do not transgress on the Sabbath", taking from them a solemn pledge.

وَرَفَعْنَا فَوْقَهُمُ ٱلطُّورَ بِمِيثَـٰقِهِمْ وَقُلْنَا لَهُمُ ٱدْخُلُوا۟ ٱلْبَابَ سُجَّدًا وَقُلْنَا لَهُمْ لَا تَعْدُوا۟ فِى ٱلسَّبْتِ وَأَخَذْنَا مِنْهُم مِّيثَـٰقًا غَلِيظًا ۝

155. But because they broke their covenant, disbelieved in Allah's Revelations, killed the Prophets unjustly, and said: "Our hearts are sealed", Allah has sealed them on account of their disbelief. So they do not believe, except for a few!

فَبِمَا نَقْضِهِم مِّيثَـٰقَهُمْ وَكُفْرِهِم بِـَٔايَـٰتِ ٱللَّهِ وَقَتْلِهِمُ ٱلْأَنۢبِيَآءَ بِغَيْرِ حَقٍّ وَقَوْلِهِمْ قُلُوبُنَا غُلْفٌۢ بَلْ طَبَعَ ٱللَّهُ عَلَيْهَا بِكُفْرِهِمْ فَلَا يُؤْمِنُونَ إِلَّا قَلِيلًا ۝

156. And for their disbelief and their imputing to Mary a great falsehood;

وَبِكُفْرِهِمْ وَقَوْلِهِمْ عَلَىٰ مَرْيَمَ بُهْتَـٰنًا عَظِيمًا ۝

157. And their saying: "We have killed the Messiah, Jesus, son of Mary and the Messenger of Allah." They neither killed nor crucified him; but it was made to appear so unto them. Indeed, those who differ about him are in doubt about it. Their knowledge does not go beyond conjecture, and they did not kill him for certain;

وَقَوْلِهِمْ إِنَّا قَتَلْنَا ٱلْمَسِيحَ عِيسَى ٱبْنَ مَرْيَمَ رَسُولَ ٱللَّهِ وَمَا قَتَلُوهُ وَمَا صَلَبُوهُ وَلَـٰكِن شُبِّهَ لَهُمْ وَإِنَّ ٱلَّذِينَ ٱخْتَلَفُوا۟ فِيهِ لَفِى شَكٍّ مِّنْهُ مَا لَهُم بِهِۦ مِنْ عِلْمٍ إِلَّا ٱتِّبَاعَ ٱلظَّنِّ وَمَا قَتَلُوهُ يَقِينًۢا ۝

158. Rather Allah raised him unto Him. Allah is Mighty and Wise.

بَل رَّفَعَهُ ٱللَّهُ إِلَيْهِ وَكَانَ ٱللَّهُ عَزِيزًا حَكِيمًا ۝

159. None of the People of the Book will believe in him[310] before his death, and on the Day of Resurrection he[311] will be a witness against them.

وَإِن مِّنْ أَهْلِ ٱلْكِتَٰبِ إِلَّا لَيُؤْمِنَنَّ بِهِۦ قَبْلَ مَوْتِهِۦ وَيَوْمَ ٱلْقِيَٰمَةِ يَكُونُ عَلَيْهِمْ شَهِيدًا ۝

160. And it was on account of the wrong-doing of the Jews that We forbade them certain good things which had been lawful to them; as well as on account of their frequent debarring [of people] from Allah's Path;

فَبِظُلْمٍ مِّنَ ٱلَّذِينَ هَادُوا۟ حَرَّمْنَا عَلَيْهِمْ طَيِّبَٰتٍ أُحِلَّتْ لَهُمْ وَبِصَدِّهِمْ عَن سَبِيلِ ٱللَّهِ كَثِيرًا ۝

161. Their taking usury, although they had been forbidden from doing it and their devouring other people's wealth unjustly. We have prepared for the unbelievers among them a very painful punishment!

وَأَخْذِهِمُ ٱلرِّبَوٰا۟ وَقَدْ نُهُوا۟ عَنْهُ وَأَكْلِهِمْ أَمْوَٰلَ ٱلنَّاسِ بِٱلْبَٰطِلِ وَأَعْتَدْنَا لِلْكَٰفِرِينَ مِنْهُمْ عَذَابًا أَلِيمًا ۝

162. But those firmly rooted in knowledge among them and the believers do believe in what was revealed to you and what was revealed before you. Those who perform the prayers, give the alms and believe in Allah and the Last Day - to these We shall grant a great reward!

لَّٰكِنِ ٱلرَّٰسِخُونَ فِى ٱلْعِلْمِ مِنْهُمْ وَٱلْمُؤْمِنُونَ يُؤْمِنُونَ بِمَآ أُنزِلَ إِلَيْكَ وَمَآ أُنزِلَ مِن قَبْلِكَ وَٱلْمُقِيمِينَ ٱلصَّلَوٰةَ وَٱلْمُؤْتُونَ ٱلزَّكَوٰةَ وَٱلْمُؤْمِنُونَ بِٱللَّهِ وَٱلْيَوْمِ ٱلْءَاخِرِ أُو۟لَٰٓئِكَ سَنُؤْتِيهِمْ أَجْرًا عَظِيمًا ۝

163. We have revealed to you, as We revealed to Noah and the Prophets after him. And We revealed to Abraham, Isma'il, Isaac, Jacob and the Tribes; and to Jesus, Job, Jonah, Aaron and Solomon; and We gave David a Book.[312]

۞ إِنَّآ أَوْحَيْنَآ إِلَيْكَ كَمَآ أَوْحَيْنَآ إِلَىٰ نُوحٍ وَٱلنَّبِيِّۦنَ مِنۢ بَعْدِهِۦ وَأَوْحَيْنَآ إِلَىٰٓ إِبْرَٰهِيمَ وَإِسْمَٰعِيلَ وَإِسْحَٰقَ وَيَعْقُوبَ وَٱلْأَسْبَاطِ وَعِيسَىٰ وَأَيُّوبَ وَيُونُسَ وَهَٰرُونَ وَسُلَيْمَٰنَ وَءَاتَيْنَا دَاوُۥدَ زَبُورًا ۝

164. And [We sent forth] some Messengers We have already told you about, and some We have not told you about. And Allah spoke to Moses directly.

وَرُسُلًا قَدْ قَصَصْنَٰهُمْ عَلَيْكَ مِن قَبْلُ وَرُسُلًا لَّمْ نَقْصُصْهُمْ عَلَيْكَ وَكَلَّمَ ٱللَّهُ مُوسَىٰ تَكْلِيمًا ۝

165. Messengers, who were bearers of good news and warners,[313] so that mankind will have no plea against Allah, after the Messengers' coming. Allah is Mighty and Wise!

رُّسُلًا مُّبَشِّرِينَ وَمُنذِرِينَ لِئَلَّا يَكُونَ لِلنَّاسِ عَلَى ٱللَّهِ حُجَّةٌ بَعْدَ ٱلرُّسُلِ وَكَانَ ٱللَّهُ عَزِيزًا حَكِيمًا ۝

---

310. Jesus.
311. Jesus.
312. The zabûr, i.e. the psalms.
313. Bearers of good news to the believers and warners to the unbelievers.

166. But Allah bears witness[314] by what He has revealed to you, that He revealed it with His Knowledge. The angels bear witness too, and Allah suffices as a Witness!

167. Indeed, those who disbelieve and debar others from the Path of Allah have gone far astray!

168. Those who disbelieve and act unjustly, Allah will never forgive them nor lead them to any path,

169. Other than the path of Hell, abiding therein forever. That for Allah is an easy matter!

170. O mankind, the Messenger has come to you with the truth from your Lord. If you believe, it would be better for you; but if you disbelieve then surely to Allah belongs what is in the heavens and on the earth. Allah is All-Knowing, Wise.

171. O People of the Book, do not exceed the bounds of your religion, nor say about Allah except the truth. The Messiah, Jesus, son of Mary, is only Allah's Messenger and His Word, which He imparted to Mary, and is a spirit from Him! So believe in Allah and His Messengers and do not say "three" [gods]. Refrain; it is better for you. Allah is truly One God. How - glory be to Him - could He have a son? To Him belongs what is in the heavens and on earth. Allah suffices as a Guardian!

172. The Messiah does not disdain to be a servant of Allah, nor do the angels nearest to Him. And those who disdain to worship Him, and are arrogant, He shall gather all unto Himself!

لَّكِنِ ٱللَّهُ يَشْهَدُ بِمَآ أَنزَلَ إِلَيْكَ أَنزَلَهُۥ بِعِلْمِهِۦ وَٱلْمَلَـٰٓئِكَةُ يَشْهَدُونَ وَكَفَىٰ بِٱللَّهِ شَهِيدًا ﴿١٦٦﴾

إِنَّ ٱلَّذِينَ كَفَرُوا۟ وَصَدُّوا۟ عَن سَبِيلِ ٱللَّهِ قَدْ ضَلُّوا۟ ضَلَـٰلًۢا بَعِيدًا ﴿١٦٧﴾

إِنَّ ٱلَّذِينَ كَفَرُوا۟ وَظَلَمُوا۟ لَمْ يَكُنِ ٱللَّهُ لِيَغْفِرَ لَهُمْ وَلَا لِيَهْدِيَهُمْ طَرِيقًا ﴿١٦٨﴾

إِلَّا طَرِيقَ جَهَنَّمَ خَـٰلِدِينَ فِيهَآ أَبَدًا ۚ وَكَانَ ذَٰلِكَ عَلَى ٱللَّهِ يَسِيرًا ﴿١٦٩﴾

يَـٰٓأَيُّهَا ٱلنَّاسُ قَدْ جَآءَكُمُ ٱلرَّسُولُ بِٱلْحَقِّ مِن رَّبِّكُمْ فَـَٔامِنُوا۟ خَيْرًا لَّكُمْ ۚ وَإِن تَكْفُرُوا۟ فَإِنَّ لِلَّهِ مَا فِى ٱلسَّمَـٰوَٰتِ وَٱلْأَرْضِ ۚ وَكَانَ ٱللَّهُ عَلِيمًا حَكِيمًا ﴿١٧٠﴾

يَـٰٓأَهْلَ ٱلْكِتَـٰبِ لَا تَغْلُوا۟ فِى دِينِكُمْ وَلَا تَقُولُوا۟ عَلَى ٱللَّهِ إِلَّا ٱلْحَقَّ ۚ إِنَّمَا ٱلْمَسِيحُ عِيسَى ٱبْنُ مَرْيَمَ رَسُولُ ٱللَّهِ وَكَلِمَتُهُۥٓ أَلْقَىٰهَآ إِلَىٰ مَرْيَمَ وَرُوحٌ مِّنْهُ ۖ فَـَٔامِنُوا۟ بِٱللَّهِ وَرُسُلِهِۦ ۖ وَلَا تَقُولُوا۟ ثَلَـٰثَةٌ ۚ ٱنتَهُوا۟ خَيْرًا لَّكُمْ ۚ إِنَّمَا ٱللَّهُ إِلَـٰهٌ وَٰحِدٌ ۖ سُبْحَـٰنَهُۥٓ أَن يَكُونَ لَهُۥ وَلَدٌ ۘ لَّهُۥ مَا فِى ٱلسَّمَـٰوَٰتِ وَمَا فِى ٱلْأَرْضِ ۗ وَكَفَىٰ بِٱللَّهِ وَكِيلًا ﴿١٧١﴾

لَّن يَسْتَنكِفَ ٱلْمَسِيحُ أَن يَكُونَ عَبْدًا لِّلَّهِ وَلَا ٱلْمَلَـٰٓئِكَةُ ٱلْمُقَرَّبُونَ ۚ وَمَن يَسْتَنكِفْ عَنْ عِبَادَتِهِۦ وَيَسْتَكْبِرْ فَسَيَحْشُرُهُمْ إِلَيْهِ جَمِيعًا ﴿١٧٢﴾

---

314. Bears witness to your [Muhammad's] Prophethood.

173. But as for those who believe and do good deeds, He will give them their rewards in full and will increase them from His Bounty. And as for those who disdain and are arrogant, He will inflict on them a very painful punishment, and they will not find for themselves, apart from Allah, any friend or supporter.

174. O people, a proof from your Lord has come to you, and We sent down to you a clear light.[315]

175. As for those who believe in Allah and hold fast to Him, He will admit them into mercy and bounty from Him and guide them to Himself along a straight path.

176. [If] they consult you, say: "Allah enjoins you regarding him who dies leaving neither children nor parents. If he leaves a sister, she is entitled to half of what he leaves behind; and he inherits her if she has no children. If he leaves two sisters, they are entitled to two-thirds of what he leaves behind; but if they are brothers and sisters, the male will have the equivalent of the share of two females. Allah makes it clear to you lest you go astray. Allah has full knowledge of everything!"

Sûrat Al-Mâ'idah, (The Table) 5

In the Name of Allah, the Compassionate, the Merciful

1. O believers, fulfil your obligations. Lawful to you are the beasts of the flock, except what is being recited to you now: "Game is unlawful to you while you are on pilgrimage." Allah decrees whatever He pleases.

---

315. The Qur'an.

107

2. O believers, do not violate the Rites of Allah, or the Sacred Month, or the sacrificial offerings, or the animals with garlands, or those who repair to the Sacred House, seeking the bounty and pleasure of their Lord. When you are through with the rites of pilgrimage, you can go hunting. And let not the hatred of those who debar you from the Sacred Mosque prompt you to transgress. Help one another in righteousness and piety, but not in sin and aggression. Fear Allah; Allah is Severe in retribution.

3. You are forbidden the eating of carrion, blood, the flesh of swine as well as whatever is slaughtered in the name of any one other than Allah. [You are forbidden] also the animals strangled or beaten to death, those that fall and die, those killed by goring with the horn or mangled by wild beasts, except those which you slaughter and those sacrificed on stones set up [for idols]. [You are forbidden] to use divining arrows;[316] it is an evil practice. Today, those who disbelieve have despaired of your religion; so do not fear them, but fear Me. Today, I have perfected your religion for you, completed My Grace on you and approved Islam as a religion for you. Yet, whoever is compelled by reason of hunger,[317] but not intending to sin, then surely Allah is All-Forgiving, Merciful.

4. They ask you (O Muhammad) what is lawful to them. Say: "The good things are lawful; and such hunting birds or hounds that you have taught, as Allah has taught you. You may eat whatever they catch for you, mentioning Allah's Name over it. Fear Allah, for Allah is, indeed, Quick in reckoning!"

---

316. Arrows used by pre-Islamic Arabs to cast lots.
317. That is, compelled to eat what is forbidden.

5. This day the good things have been made lawful to you; the food of the People of the Book is lawful to you, and your food is lawful to them; and so are the believing women who are chaste, and the chaste women of those who were given the Book before you, provided you give them their dowries and take them in marriage, not in fornication or as mistresses. If any one denies the faith, his work shall be of no avail to him, and in the Hereafter he will rank with the losers.

6. O believers, if you rise to pray, wash your faces and your hands up to the elbows and wipe your heads and your feet up to the ankles. If you are unclean, then cleanse yourselves; and if you are sick or on a journey, and if one of you has come from the rest-room, or if you have touched women and cannot find any water, then take some clean earth and wipe your faces and hands with it. Allah does not wish to burden you, but to purify you and complete His Grace upon you, that you may be thankful.

7. And remember Allah's Grace upon you and His Covenant with which he bound you, when you said: "We hear and we obey." Fear Allah; Allah indeed knows well the thoughts in the hearts!

8. O believers, be dutiful to Allah and bearers of witness with justice; and do not let the hatred of a certain group drive you to be unequitable. Be equitable; that is nearer to piety, and fear Allah. Allah indeed is Fully Aware of what you do!

9. Allah has promised those who believe and do the good deeds they shall have forgiveness and a great reward.

10. But those who disbelieve and deny our Revelations those are the people of Hell.

ٱلْيَوْمَ أُحِلَّ لَكُمُ ٱلطَّيِّبَـٰتُ وَطَعَامُ ٱلَّذِينَ أُوتُوا۟ ٱلْكِتَـٰبَ حِلٌّ لَّكُمْ وَطَعَامُكُمْ حِلٌّ لَّهُمْ وَٱلْمُحْصَنَـٰتُ مِنَ ٱلْمُؤْمِنَـٰتِ وَٱلْمُحْصَنَـٰتُ مِنَ ٱلَّذِينَ أُوتُوا۟ ٱلْكِتَـٰبَ مِن قَبْلِكُمْ إِذَآ ءَاتَيْتُمُوهُنَّ أُجُورَهُنَّ مُحْصِنِينَ غَيْرَ مُسَـٰفِحِينَ وَلَا مُتَّخِذِىٓ أَخْدَانٍ وَمَن يَكْفُرْ بِٱلْإِيمَـٰنِ فَقَدْ حَبِطَ عَمَلُهُۥ وَهُوَ فِى ٱلْـَٔاخِرَةِ مِنَ ٱلْخَـٰسِرِينَ ۝

يَـٰٓأَيُّهَا ٱلَّذِينَ ءَامَنُوٓا۟ إِذَا قُمْتُمْ إِلَى ٱلصَّلَوٰةِ فَٱغْسِلُوا۟ وُجُوهَكُمْ وَأَيْدِيَكُمْ إِلَى ٱلْمَرَافِقِ وَٱمْسَحُوا۟ بِرُءُوسِكُمْ وَأَرْجُلَكُمْ إِلَى ٱلْكَعْبَيْنِ وَإِن كُنتُمْ جُنُبًا فَٱطَّهَّرُوا۟ وَإِن كُنتُم مَّرْضَىٰٓ أَوْ عَلَىٰ سَفَرٍ أَوْ جَآءَ أَحَدٌ مِّنكُم مِّنَ ٱلْغَآئِطِ أَوْ لَـٰمَسْتُمُ ٱلنِّسَآءَ فَلَمْ تَجِدُوا۟ مَآءً فَتَيَمَّمُوا۟ صَعِيدًا طَيِّبًا فَٱمْسَحُوا۟ بِوُجُوهِكُمْ وَأَيْدِيكُم مِّنْهُ مَا يُرِيدُ ٱللَّهُ لِيَجْعَلَ عَلَيْكُم مِّنْ حَرَجٍ وَلَـٰكِن يُرِيدُ لِيُطَهِّرَكُمْ وَلِيُتِمَّ نِعْمَتَهُۥ عَلَيْكُمْ لَعَلَّكُمْ تَشْكُرُونَ ۝

وَٱذْكُرُوا۟ نِعْمَةَ ٱللَّهِ عَلَيْكُمْ وَمِيثَـٰقَهُ ٱلَّذِى وَاثَقَكُم بِهِۦٓ إِذْ قُلْتُمْ سَمِعْنَا وَأَطَعْنَا وَٱتَّقُوا۟ ٱللَّهَ إِنَّ ٱللَّهَ عَلِيمٌۢ بِذَاتِ ٱلصُّدُورِ ۝

يَـٰٓأَيُّهَا ٱلَّذِينَ ءَامَنُوا۟ كُونُوا۟ قَوَّٰمِينَ لِلَّهِ شُهَدَآءَ بِٱلْقِسْطِ وَلَا يَجْرِمَنَّكُمْ شَنَـَٔانُ قَوْمٍ عَلَىٰٓ أَلَّا تَعْدِلُوا۟ ٱعْدِلُوا۟ هُوَ أَقْرَبُ لِلتَّقْوَىٰ وَٱتَّقُوا۟ ٱللَّهَ إِنَّ ٱللَّهَ خَبِيرٌۢ بِمَا تَعْمَلُونَ ۝

وَعَدَ ٱللَّهُ ٱلَّذِينَ ءَامَنُوا۟ وَعَمِلُوا۟ ٱلصَّـٰلِحَـٰتِ لَهُم مَّغْفِرَةٌ وَأَجْرٌ عَظِيمٌ ۝

وَٱلَّذِينَ كَفَرُوا۟ وَكَذَّبُوا۟ بِـَٔايَـٰتِنَآ أُو۟لَـٰٓئِكَ أَصْحَـٰبُ ٱلْجَحِيمِ ۝

11. O believers, remember Allah's Grace upon you, when certain people intended to reach out to you with their hands but Allah restrained them. Fear Allah, and in Allah let the believers put their trust.

12. Allah made a covenant with the Children of Israel, and We raised among them twelve chieftains. And Allah said: "I am with you. Surely, if you perform the prayer, give the alms, believe in My Messengers and support them and lend Allah a fair loan,[318] I will forgive you your sins and admit you into Gardens, beneath which rivers flow. But if any one of you disbelieves afterwards, he certainly strays from the Right Path.

13. And on account of their violating their covenant, We cursed them and caused their hearts to harden; they take the words[319] out of their context and forget part of what they were enjoined, and you do not cease to find them treacherous, except for a few of them. Yet, pardon them and forgive; Allah surely loves those who do good to others.

14. And with some of those who say: "We are Christians", we made a covenant; but they forgot part of what they were reminded of; so we stirred up enmity and hatred among them till the Day of Resurrection. Allah will let them know what they did.

15. O People of the Book,[320] Our Messenger came to you to show you much of what you used to conceal of the Book[321] and to pardon a great deal. Indeed, a light and a clear Book[322] has come to you from Allah.

---

318. That is, if you spend in the way ordered by Allah.
319. The words in the Torah.
320. The Jews and the Christians.
321. The Scriptures.
322. The Qur'an.

16. Allah guides with it those who seek His Good Pleasure to the paths of peace, brings them out of the shadows of darkness into the light, by His Leave, and guides them to a straight path.

17. Unbelievers are those who say: "Allah is the Messiah, son of Mary." Say: "Who could prevent Allah, if He wished, from destroying the Messiah, son of Mary, and his mother too, together with all those on the face of the earth?" To Allah belongs the kingdom of the heavens and the earth and what lies between them. He creates whatever He pleases, and Allah has power over everything!

18. The Jews and the Christians have said: "We are Allah's children and His beloved." Say: "Why then does He punish you for your sins? You are rather human beings, part of those whom He has created. He forgives whom He pleases and punishes whom He pleases." And to Allah belongs the kingdom of the heavens and the earth and what is in between, and unto Him is the final return!

19. O People of the Book, Our Messenger has come to you to make clear to you [the religious tenets] after a cessation of Messengers, lest you should say: "No bearer of good news or a warner has come to us." So now a bearer of good news and a warner has come to you; and Allah has power over everything!

20. And when Moses said to his people: "O my people, remember Allah's Grace upon you, how He raised up Prophets among you, made you kings and gave you what He has not given any other nation.

21. "My people, enter the Holy Land which Allah ordained for you,[323] and do not turn back, lest you become the losers."

يَهْدِى بِهِ ٱللَّهُ مَنِ ٱتَّبَعَ رِضْوَٰنَهُۥ سُبُلَ ٱلسَّلَٰمِ وَيُخْرِجُهُم مِّنَ ٱلظُّلُمَٰتِ إِلَى ٱلنُّورِ بِإِذْنِهِۦ وَيَهْدِيهِمْ إِلَىٰ صِرَٰطٍ مُّسْتَقِيمٍ ﴿١٦﴾

لَّقَدْ كَفَرَ ٱلَّذِينَ قَالُوٓا۟ إِنَّ ٱللَّهَ هُوَ ٱلْمَسِيحُ ٱبْنُ مَرْيَمَ قُلْ فَمَن يَمْلِكُ مِنَ ٱللَّهِ شَيْـًٔا إِنْ أَرَادَ أَن يُهْلِكَ ٱلْمَسِيحَ ٱبْنَ مَرْيَمَ وَأُمَّهُۥ وَمَن فِى ٱلْأَرْضِ جَمِيعًا وَلِلَّهِ مُلْكُ ٱلسَّمَٰوَٰتِ وَٱلْأَرْضِ وَمَا بَيْنَهُمَا يَخْلُقُ مَا يَشَآءُ وَٱللَّهُ عَلَىٰ كُلِّ شَىْءٍ قَدِيرٌ ﴿١٧﴾

وَقَالَتِ ٱلْيَهُودُ وَٱلنَّصَٰرَىٰ نَحْنُ أَبْنَٰٓؤُا۟ ٱللَّهِ وَأَحِبَّٰٓؤُهُۥ قُلْ فَلِمَ يُعَذِّبُكُم بِذُنُوبِكُم بَلْ أَنتُم بَشَرٌ مِّمَّنْ خَلَقَ يَغْفِرُ لِمَن يَشَآءُ وَيُعَذِّبُ مَن يَشَآءُ وَلِلَّهِ مُلْكُ ٱلسَّمَٰوَٰتِ وَٱلْأَرْضِ وَمَا بَيْنَهُمَا وَإِلَيْهِ ٱلْمَصِيرُ ﴿١٨﴾

يَٰٓأَهْلَ ٱلْكِتَٰبِ قَدْ جَآءَكُمْ رَسُولُنَا يُبَيِّنُ لَكُمْ عَلَىٰ فَتْرَةٍ مِّنَ ٱلرُّسُلِ أَن تَقُولُوا۟ مَا جَآءَنَا مِنۢ بَشِيرٍ وَلَا نَذِيرٍ فَقَدْ جَآءَكُم بَشِيرٌ وَنَذِيرٌ وَٱللَّهُ عَلَىٰ كُلِّ شَىْءٍ قَدِيرٌ ﴿١٩﴾

وَإِذْ قَالَ مُوسَىٰ لِقَوْمِهِۦ يَٰقَوْمِ ٱذْكُرُوا۟ نِعْمَةَ ٱللَّهِ عَلَيْكُمْ إِذْ جَعَلَ فِيكُمْ أَنۢبِيَآءَ وَجَعَلَكُم مُّلُوكًا وَءَاتَىٰكُم مَّا لَمْ يُؤْتِ أَحَدًا مِّنَ ٱلْعَٰلَمِينَ ﴿٢٠﴾

يَٰقَوْمِ ٱدْخُلُوا۟ ٱلْأَرْضَ ٱلْمُقَدَّسَةَ ٱلَّتِى كَتَبَ ٱللَّهُ لَكُمْ وَلَا تَرْتَدُّوا۟ عَلَىٰٓ أَدْبَارِكُمْ فَتَنقَلِبُوا۟ خَٰسِرِينَ ﴿٢١﴾

---

323. That is, ordained that you should enter.

22. They said: "O Moses, there is in it a mighty people; we shall not enter it until they leave it. If they leave it, then we shall enter."

قَالُوا يَٰمُوسَىٰٓ إِنَّ فِيهَا قَوۡمًا جَبَّارِينَ وَإِنَّا لَن نَّدۡخُلَهَا حَتَّىٰ يَخۡرُجُوا مِنۡهَا فَإِن يَخۡرُجُوا مِنۡهَا فَإِنَّا دَٰخِلُونَ ﴿٢٢﴾

23. Two men of those who feared [Allah] and whom Allah favoured said: "Enter the gate and [fall] upon them; if you enter it, you will be victorious. In Allah put your trust, if you are true believers."

قَالَ رَجُلَانِ مِنَ ٱلَّذِينَ يَخَافُونَ أَنۡعَمَ ٱللَّهُ عَلَيۡهِمَا ٱدۡخُلُوا عَلَيۡهِمُ ٱلۡبَابَ فَإِذَا دَخَلۡتُمُوهُ فَإِنَّكُمۡ غَٰلِبُونَ وَعَلَى ٱللَّهِ فَتَوَكَّلُوٓا إِن كُنتُم مُّؤۡمِنِينَ ﴿٢٣﴾

24. They said: "O Moses, we shall never enter it, so long as they are in it. So, go forth, you and your Lord, and fight; we are staying put here."

قَالُوا يَٰمُوسَىٰٓ إِنَّا لَن نَّدۡخُلَهَآ أَبَدًا مَّا دَامُوا فِيهَا فَٱذۡهَبۡ أَنتَ وَرَبُّكَ فَقَٰتِلَآ إِنَّا هَٰهُنَا قَٰعِدُونَ ﴿٢٤﴾

25. He said: "Lord, I have no power over anybody other than myself and my brother; so separate us from the ungodly people."

قَالَ رَبِّ إِنِّي لَآ أَمۡلِكُ إِلَّا نَفۡسِي وَأَخِي فَٱفۡرُقۡ بَيۡنَنَا وَبَيۡنَ ٱلۡقَوۡمِ ٱلۡفَٰسِقِينَ ﴿٢٥﴾

26. Allah said: "It shall be forbidden them for forty years, during which they shall wander aimlessly in the land; so do not grieve for the ungodly people!"

قَالَ فَإِنَّهَا مُحَرَّمَةٌ عَلَيۡهِمۡ أَرۡبَعِينَ سَنَةً يَتِيهُونَ فِي ٱلۡأَرۡضِ فَلَا تَأۡسَ عَلَى ٱلۡقَوۡمِ ٱلۡفَٰسِقِينَ ﴿٢٦﴾

27. And recite to them in all truth the tale of Adam's two sons, when they offered a sacrifice, which was accepted from one, but not accepted from the other. The latter said: "I will surely kill you", the other replied: "Allah accepts only from the God-fearing.

۞ وَٱتۡلُ عَلَيۡهِمۡ نَبَأَ ٱبۡنَيۡ ءَادَمَ بِٱلۡحَقِّ إِذۡ قَرَّبَا قُرۡبَانًا فَتُقُبِّلَ مِنۡ أَحَدِهِمَا وَلَمۡ يُتَقَبَّلۡ مِنَ ٱلۡأَخَرِ قَالَ لَأَقۡتُلَنَّكَ قَالَ إِنَّمَا يَتَقَبَّلُ ٱللَّهُ مِنَ ٱلۡمُتَّقِينَ ﴿٢٧﴾

28. "Should you stretch your hand out to kill me, I will not stretch my hand out to kill you; for I fear Allah, Lord of the Worlds.

لَئِنۢ بَسَطتَ إِلَيَّ يَدَكَ لِتَقۡتُلَنِي مَآ أَنَا۠ بِبَاسِطٍ يَدِيَ إِلَيۡكَ لِأَقۡتُلَكَ إِنِّيٓ أَخَافُ ٱللَّهَ رَبَّ ٱلۡعَٰلَمِينَ ﴿٢٨﴾

29. "I only wish that you be charged with my sin and yours and thus be one of the companions of the Fire; and that is the reward of the evildoers."

إِنِّيٓ أُرِيدُ أَن تَبُوٓأَ بِإِثۡمِي وَإِثۡمِكَ فَتَكُونَ مِنۡ أَصۡحَٰبِ ٱلنَّارِ وَذَٰلِكَ جَزَٰٓؤُا ٱلظَّٰلِمِينَ ﴿٢٩﴾

30. Then, his soul prompted him to kill his brother; and so he killed him and became one of the losers.

فَطَوَّعَتۡ لَهُۥ نَفۡسُهُۥ قَتۡلَ أَخِيهِ فَقَتَلَهُۥ فَأَصۡبَحَ مِنَ ٱلۡخَٰسِرِينَ ﴿٣٠﴾

31. Then, Allah sent forth a raven digging the earth to show him how to bury his brother's corpse. He said: "Woe is me, am I unable to

فَبَعَثَ ٱللَّهُ غُرَابًا يَبۡحَثُ فِي ٱلۡأَرۡضِ لِيُرِيَهُۥ كَيۡفَ يُوَٰرِي سَوۡءَةَ أَخِيهِ قَالَ يَٰوَيۡلَتَىٰٓ أَعَجَزۡتُ أَنۡ أَكُونَ

be like this raven and bury the corpse of my brother?" Thus he became one of the remorseful.

مِثْلَ هَـٰذَا ٱلْغُرَابِ فَأُوَٰرِىَ سَوْءَةَ أَخِى فَأَصْبَحَ مِنَ ٱلنَّـٰدِمِينَ ﴿٣١﴾

32. For that reason, We decreed for the Children of Israel that whoever kills a soul, not in retaliation for a soul or corruption in the land, is like one who has killed the whole of mankind; and whoever saves a life is like one who saves the lives of all mankind. Our Messengers came to them with the clear proofs; but afterwards many of them continued to commit excesses in the land.

مِنْ أَجْلِ ذَٰلِكَ كَتَبْنَا عَلَىٰ بَنِىٓ إِسْرَٰٓءِيلَ أَنَّهُۥ مَن قَتَلَ نَفْسًۢا بِغَيْرِ نَفْسٍ أَوْ فَسَادٍ فِى ٱلْأَرْضِ فَكَأَنَّمَا قَتَلَ ٱلنَّاسَ جَمِيعًا وَمَنْ أَحْيَاهَا فَكَأَنَّمَآ أَحْيَا ٱلنَّاسَ جَمِيعًا وَلَقَدْ جَآءَتْهُمْ رُسُلُنَا بِٱلْبَيِّنَٰتِ ثُمَّ إِنَّ كَثِيرًا مِّنْهُم بَعْدَ ذَٰلِكَ فِى ٱلْأَرْضِ لَمُسْرِفُونَ ﴿٣٢﴾

33. Indeed, the punishment of those who fight Allah and His Messenger and go around corrupting the land is to be killed, crucified, have their hands and feet cut off on opposite sides, or to be banished from the land. That is a disgrace for them in this life, and in the life to come theirs will be a terrible punishment.

إِنَّمَا جَزَٰٓؤُا۟ ٱلَّذِينَ يُحَارِبُونَ ٱللَّهَ وَرَسُولَهُۥ وَيَسْعَوْنَ فِى ٱلْأَرْضِ فَسَادًا أَن يُقَتَّلُوٓا۟ أَوْ يُصَلَّبُوٓا۟ أَوْ تُقَطَّعَ أَيْدِيهِمْ وَأَرْجُلُهُم مِّنْ خِلَٰفٍ أَوْ يُنفَوْا۟ مِنَ ٱلْأَرْضِ ذَٰلِكَ لَهُمْ خِزْىٌ فِى ٱلدُّنْيَا وَلَهُمْ فِى ٱلْءَاخِرَةِ عَذَابٌ عَظِيمٌ ﴿٣٣﴾

34. Except for those who repent before you overpower them. Know, then, that Allah is All-Forgiving, Merciful.

إِلَّا ٱلَّذِينَ تَابُوا۟ مِن قَبْلِ أَن تَقْدِرُوا۟ عَلَيْهِمْ فَٱعْلَمُوٓا۟ أَنَّ ٱللَّهَ غَفُورٌ رَّحِيمٌ ﴿٣٤﴾

35. O believers, fear Allah and seek the means to win His Favour. Fight in His Way so that you may prosper.

يَـٰٓأَيُّهَا ٱلَّذِينَ ءَامَنُوا۟ ٱتَّقُوا۟ ٱللَّهَ وَٱبْتَغُوٓا۟ إِلَيْهِ ٱلْوَسِيلَةَ وَجَٰهِدُوا۟ فِى سَبِيلِهِۦ لَعَلَّكُمْ تُفْلِحُونَ ﴿٣٥﴾

36. As to the unbelievers, even if they had all there is on earth and the like of it too, to redeem themselves from the punishment of the Day of Resurrection therewith, it will not be accepted from them, and a very painful punishment shall be in store for them.

إِنَّ ٱلَّذِينَ كَفَرُوا۟ لَوْ أَنَّ لَهُم مَّا فِى ٱلْأَرْضِ جَمِيعًا وَمِثْلَهُۥ مَعَهُۥ لِيَفْتَدُوا۟ بِهِۦ مِنْ عَذَابِ يَوْمِ ٱلْقِيَٰمَةِ مَا تُقُبِّلَ مِنْهُمْ وَلَهُمْ عَذَابٌ أَلِيمٌ ﴿٣٦﴾

37. They will then wish to come out of the Fire, but they will never come out, and theirs is an everlasting punishment!

يُرِيدُونَ أَن يَخْرُجُوا۟ مِنَ ٱلنَّارِ وَمَا هُم بِخَٰرِجِينَ مِنْهَا وَلَهُمْ عَذَابٌ مُّقِيمٌ ﴿٣٧﴾

38. As for the thieves, whether male or female, cut off their hands in punishment for what they did, as an exemplary punishment from Allah. Allah is Mighty and Wise.

وَٱلسَّارِقُ وَٱلسَّارِقَةُ فَٱقْطَعُوٓا۟ أَيْدِيَهُمَا جَزَآءًۢ بِمَا كَسَبَا نَكَٰلًا مِّنَ ٱللَّهِ وَٱللَّهُ عَزِيزٌ حَكِيمٌ ﴿٣٨﴾

39. But whoever repents after his wrong-doing and mends his ways, Allah will forgive him. Allah is indeed All-Forgiving, Merciful!

40. Did you not know that to Allah belongs the kingdom of the heavens and the earth? He punishes whom He wills and forgives whom He wills; and Allah has power over everything!

41. O Messenger, do not grieve on account of those who hasten to unbelief, from among those who say with their mouths: "We believe", while their hearts do not believe; or those Jews who listen to falsehood or listen to other people who did not come to you, and who alter the words.[324] They say: "If you are given this,[325] then take it, and if you are not given it, then beware!" Whoever Allah wishes to leave in error, you can do nothing to save him from Allah. Those whose hearts Allah does not wish to purify will have nothing but disgrace in this world, and a terrible punishment in the world to come.

42. They are consistent listeners to falsehood, devourers of unlawful gain. Should they come to you, either judge between them or turn away from them. If you turn away from them, they will not harm you in the least; but if you judge, judge between them justly. Allah loves those who act justly!

43. But how will they ask you to judge, when they are in possession of the Torah, which contains Allah's Judgement![326] Thus they soon turn away. Those people are not real believers!

---

324. The words in the Torah.
325. That is, if you are given by Muhammad something similar to what we say.
326. What is meant here is that they are not serious.

44. We have indeed revealed the Torah, wherein is guidance and light. By it the Prophets who submitted themselves [to Allah] did judge among the Jews, as did the rabbis and the masters, according to what they were made to guard of Allah's Book and were witnesses thereof. So fear not men, but fear Me and do not sell My Revelations for a small price. Whoever does not judge according to what Allah has revealed those are the unbelievers!

إِنَّا أَنزَلْنَا ٱلتَّوْرَىٰةَ فِيهَا هُدًى وَنُورٌ يَحْكُمُ بِهَا ٱلنَّبِيُّونَ ٱلَّذِينَ أَسْلَمُوا لِلَّذِينَ هَادُوا وَٱلرَّبَّٰنِيُّونَ وَٱلْأَحْبَارُ بِمَا ٱسْتُحْفِظُوا مِن كِتَٰبِ ٱللَّهِ وَكَانُوا عَلَيْهِ شُهَدَاءَ فَلَا تَخْشَوُا ٱلنَّاسَ وَٱخْشَوْنِ وَلَا تَشْتَرُوا بِـَٔايَٰتِي ثَمَنًا قَلِيلًا وَمَن لَّمْ يَحْكُم بِمَا أَنزَلَ ٱللَّهُ فَأُولَٰٓئِكَ هُمُ ٱلْكَٰفِرُونَ ۝

45. And We prescribed to them therein[327] that a life for a life, an eye for an eye, a nose for a nose, an ear for an ear, a tooth for a tooth, and for wounds retaliation; but whoever forgoes it charitably, it will be an atonement for him. Whoever does not judge according to what Allah has revealed, those are the evildoers!

وَكَتَبْنَا عَلَيْهِمْ فِيهَآ أَنَّ ٱلنَّفْسَ بِٱلنَّفْسِ وَٱلْعَيْنَ بِٱلْعَيْنِ وَٱلْأَنفَ بِٱلْأَنفِ وَٱلْأُذُنَ بِٱلْأُذُنِ وَٱلسِّنَّ بِٱلسِّنِّ وَٱلْجُرُوحَ قِصَاصٌ فَمَن تَصَدَّقَ بِهِۦ فَهُوَ كَفَّارَةٌ لَّهُۥ وَمَن لَّمْ يَحْكُم بِمَآ أَنزَلَ ٱللَّهُ فَأُولَٰٓئِكَ هُمُ ٱلظَّٰلِمُونَ ۝

46. After them[328] we sent Jesus, son of Mary, confirming what he had before him of the Torah, and We gave him the Gospel, wherein is guidance and light, confirming what he had before him of the Torah and a guidance and admonition to the God-fearing.

وَقَفَّيْنَا عَلَىٰٓ ءَاثَٰرِهِم بِعِيسَى ٱبْنِ مَرْيَمَ مُصَدِّقًا لِّمَا بَيْنَ يَدَيْهِ مِنَ ٱلتَّوْرَىٰةِ وَءَاتَيْنَٰهُ ٱلْإِنجِيلَ فِيهِ هُدًى وَنُورٌ وَمُصَدِّقًا لِّمَا بَيْنَ يَدَيْهِ مِنَ ٱلتَّوْرَىٰةِ وَهُدًى وَمَوْعِظَةً لِّلْمُتَّقِينَ ۝

47. And let the People of the Gospel judge in accordance with what Allah has revealed in it. He who does not judge according to what Allah has revealed those are the transgressors.

وَلْيَحْكُمْ أَهْلُ ٱلْإِنجِيلِ بِمَآ أَنزَلَ ٱللَّهُ فِيهِ وَمَن لَّمْ يَحْكُم بِمَآ أَنزَلَ ٱللَّهُ فَأُولَٰٓئِكَ هُمُ ٱلْفَٰسِقُونَ ۝

48. And We have revealed to you[329] the Book in truth, confirming the scriptures[330] that preceded it and superceding it. Judge between them, then, according to what Allah has revealed, and do not follow their illusory

وَأَنزَلْنَآ إِلَيْكَ ٱلْكِتَٰبَ بِٱلْحَقِّ مُصَدِّقًا لِّمَا بَيْنَ يَدَيْهِ مِنَ ٱلْكِتَٰبِ وَمُهَيْمِنًا عَلَيْهِ فَٱحْكُم بَيْنَهُم بِمَآ أَنزَلَ ٱللَّهُ وَلَا تَتَّبِعْ أَهْوَآءَهُمْ عَمَّا جَآءَكَ مِنَ ٱلْحَقِّ لِكُلٍّ

---

327. In the Torah.
328. The Prophets.
329. Muhammad.
330. That is, the Books preceding it.

جَعَلْنَا مِنكُمْ شِرْعَةً وَمِنْهَاجًا وَلَوْ شَاءَ ٱللَّهُ لَجَعَلَكُمْ أُمَّةً وَٰحِدَةً وَلَٰكِن لِّيَبْلُوَكُمْ فِى مَآ ءَاتَىٰكُمْ فَٱسْتَبِقُوا۟ ٱلْخَيْرَٰتِ إِلَى ٱللَّهِ مَرْجِعُكُمْ جَمِيعًا فَيُنَبِّئُكُم بِمَا كُنتُمْ فِيهِ تَخْتَلِفُونَ ﴿٤٨﴾

desires, diverging from what came to you of the Truth. To each of you, We have laid down an ordinance and a clear path; and had Allah pleased, He would have made you one nation, but [He wanted] to test you concerning what He gave to you. Be, then, forward in good deeds. To Allah is the ultimate return of all of you, that He may instruct you regarding that on which you differed.

49. And judge between them in accordance with what Allah has revealed, and do not follow their fancies. Beware of them lest they lure you away from part of what God has revealed to you. Should they turn away, know that Allah only wishes to afflict them for some of their sins, and that many people are indeed grave sinners!

وَأَنِ ٱحْكُم بَيْنَهُم بِمَآ أَنزَلَ ٱللَّهُ وَلَا تَتَّبِعْ أَهْوَآءَهُمْ وَٱحْذَرْهُمْ أَن يَفْتِنُوكَ عَن بَعْضِ مَآ أَنزَلَ ٱللَّهُ إِلَيْكَ فَإِن تَوَلَّوْا۟ فَٱعْلَمْ أَنَّمَا يُرِيدُ ٱللَّهُ أَن يُصِيبَهُم بِبَعْضِ ذُنُوبِهِمْ وَإِنَّ كَثِيرًا مِّنَ ٱلنَّاسِ لَفَٰسِقُونَ ﴿٤٩﴾

50. Now, is it the judgement of the "period of Ignorance"[331] that they[332] desire? Yet who is a better judge than Allah for a people who believe with certainty?

أَفَحُكْمَ ٱلْجَٰهِلِيَّةِ يَبْغُونَ وَمَنْ أَحْسَنُ مِنَ ٱللَّهِ حُكْمًا لِّقَوْمٍ يُوقِنُونَ ﴿٥٠﴾

51. O believers, do not take the Jews and the Christians as friends; some of them are friends of each other. Whoever of you takes them as friends is surely one of them. Allah indeed does not guide the wrongdoers.

۞ يَٰٓأَيُّهَا ٱلَّذِينَ ءَامَنُوا۟ لَا تَتَّخِذُوا۟ ٱلْيَهُودَ وَٱلنَّصَٰرَىٰٓ أَوْلِيَآءَ بَعْضُهُمْ أَوْلِيَآءُ بَعْضٍ وَمَن يَتَوَلَّهُم مِّنكُمْ فَإِنَّهُۥ مِنْهُمْ إِنَّ ٱللَّهَ لَا يَهْدِى ٱلْقَوْمَ ٱلظَّٰلِمِينَ ﴿٥١﴾

52. Yet, you will see those in whose hearts is a sickness hastening to woo them, saying: "We fear that a misfortune will befall us." However, it may be that Allah will bring victory or some other matter from Him; whereupon they will regret what they concealed within themselves.

فَتَرَى ٱلَّذِينَ فِى قُلُوبِهِم مَّرَضٌ يُسَٰرِعُونَ فِيهِمْ يَقُولُونَ نَخْشَىٰٓ أَن تُصِيبَنَا دَآئِرَةٌ فَعَسَى ٱللَّهُ أَن يَأْتِىَ بِٱلْفَتْحِ أَوْ أَمْرٍ مِّنْ عِندِهِۦ فَيُصْبِحُوا۟ عَلَىٰ مَآ أَسَرُّوا۟ فِىٓ أَنفُسِهِمْ نَٰدِمِينَ ﴿٥٢﴾

53. And the believers will then say: "Are those the ones who swore by Allah their most solemn oaths that they were indeed

وَيَقُولُ ٱلَّذِينَ ءَامَنُوٓا۟ أَهَٰٓؤُلَآءِ ٱلَّذِينَ أَقْسَمُوا۟ بِٱللَّهِ جَهْدَ أَيْمَٰنِهِمْ إِنَّهُمْ لَمَعَكُمْ حَبِطَتْ أَعْمَٰلُهُمْ

---

331. This period is known in Arabic as "Jahiliyah", which began about 500 AD and lasted until the rise of Islam in 610 AD.
332. The Jews.

with you?" Their works will come to nothing and thus they will be losers.

54. O believers, whoever of you renounces his religion, Allah will certainly bring forth[333] a people whom He loves and they love Him, humble towards the faithful, but mighty towards the unbelievers. They fight in the Way of Allah and do not fear anybody's reproach. That is a favour from Allah which He confers on whomever He pleases. Allah is Munificent, All-Knowing.

55. Your only friends are Allah, His Messenger and those who believe, performing the prayer and giving the alms, while they bow down.

56. Whoever takes Allah, His Messenger and those who believe as friends [must know] that Allah's party is indeed the triumphant.

57. O believers, do not take as friends those who take your religion as a mockery or a sport, be they from among those who received the Book before you, or the unbelievers. Fear Allah if you are true believers.

58. And when you call to prayer, they take it as a mockery and a sport; that is because they are a people who do not understand.

59. Say: "O People of the Book, do you resent anything we do other than that we believe in Allah and what has been revealed to us and what was revealed before, and that most of you are transgressors?"

60. Say: "Shall I tell you about those who will get a worse punishment from Allah? Those whom Allah cursed and on whom He poured forth His Wrath, transformed them into monkeys and swine, and worshippers of the Devil. They are worse off and farther astray."

---

333. That is, Allah will replace them by a people.

61. When they[334] come to you, they say: "We believe", although they come in as unbelievers and leave as unbelievers. Allah knows best what they conceal.

وَإِذَا جَآءُوكُمْ قَالُوٓا۟ ءَامَنَّا وَقَد دَّخَلُوا۟ بِٱلْكُفْرِ وَهُمْ قَدْ خَرَجُوا۟ بِهِۦ ۚ وَٱللَّهُ أَعْلَمُ بِمَا كَانُوا۟ يَكْتُمُونَ ﴿٦١﴾

62. And you will see many of them hastening to perpetrate sin and aggression and the devouring of unlawful gain. Evil is what they have been doing!

وَتَرَىٰ كَثِيرًا مِّنْهُمْ يُسَـٰرِعُونَ فِى ٱلْإِثْمِ وَٱلْعُدْوَٰنِ وَأَكْلِهِمُ ٱلسُّحْتَ ۚ لَبِئْسَ مَا كَانُوا۟ يَعْمَلُونَ ﴿٦٢﴾

63. Why do not the rabbis and masters forbid them from uttering sinful things and devouring unlawful gain? Evil indeed is what they used to do!

لَوْلَا يَنْهَىٰهُمُ ٱلرَّبَّـٰنِيُّونَ وَٱلْأَحْبَارُ عَن قَوْلِهِمُ ٱلْإِثْمَ وَأَكْلِهِمُ ٱلسُّحْتَ ۚ لَبِئْسَ مَا كَانُوا۟ يَصْنَعُونَ ﴿٦٣﴾

64. The Jews say: "Allah's Hand is tied";[335] may their own hands be tied and may they be damned for what they say. His Hands are rather outstretched; He grants freely as He pleases. And what has been sent down to you from your Lord will certainly increase many of them in arrogance and unbelief. And We have cast in their midst animosity and hatred till the Day of Resurrection. Whenever they kindle a fire for war, Allah extinguishes it; and they go about spreading mischief, but Allah does not like the mischief-makers.

وَقَالَتِ ٱلْيَهُودُ يَدُ ٱللَّهِ مَغْلُولَةٌ ۚ غُلَّتْ أَيْدِيهِمْ وَلُعِنُوا۟ بِمَا قَالُوا۟ ۘ بَلْ يَدَاهُ مَبْسُوطَتَانِ يُنفِقُ كَيْفَ يَشَآءُ ۚ وَلَيَزِيدَنَّ كَثِيرًا مِّنْهُم مَّآ أُنزِلَ إِلَيْكَ مِن رَّبِّكَ طُغْيَـٰنًا وَكُفْرًا ۚ وَأَلْقَيْنَا بَيْنَهُمُ ٱلْعَدَٰوَةَ وَٱلْبَغْضَآءَ إِلَىٰ يَوْمِ ٱلْقِيَـٰمَةِ ۚ كُلَّمَآ أَوْقَدُوا۟ نَارًا لِّلْحَرْبِ أَطْفَأَهَا ٱللَّهُ ۚ وَيَسْعَوْنَ فِى ٱلْأَرْضِ فَسَادًا ۚ وَٱللَّهُ لَا يُحِبُّ ٱلْمُفْسِدِينَ ﴿٦٤﴾

65. Had the People of the Book believed and warded off evil, We would have remitted their sins and admitted them into the Gardens of bliss.

وَلَوْ أَنَّ أَهْلَ ٱلْكِتَـٰبِ ءَامَنُوا۟ وَٱتَّقَوْا۟ لَكَفَّرْنَا عَنْهُمْ سَيِّـَٔاتِهِمْ وَلَأَدْخَلْنَـٰهُمْ جَنَّـٰتِ ٱلنَّعِيمِ ﴿٦٥﴾

66. And had they observed the Torah and the Gospel and what was revealed to them from their Lord, they would have eaten amply from above them and below their feet. Among them is a moderate group, but evil is what many of them are doing!

وَلَوْ أَنَّهُمْ أَقَامُوا۟ ٱلتَّوْرَىٰةَ وَٱلْإِنجِيلَ وَمَآ أُنزِلَ إِلَيْهِم مِّن رَّبِّهِمْ لَأَكَلُوا۟ مِن فَوْقِهِمْ وَمِن تَحْتِ أَرْجُلِهِم ۚ مِّنْهُمْ أُمَّةٌ مُّقْتَصِدَةٌ ۖ وَكَثِيرٌ مِّنْهُمْ سَآءَ مَا يَعْمَلُونَ ﴿٦٦﴾

---

334. The Jewish hypocrites.
335. That is, Allah is not generous in bestowing His Bounties upon them.

67. O Messenger, proclaim what has been revealed to you from your Lord; but if you do not, you would not have delivered His Message. Allah will protect you from mankind. Allah surely does not guide the unbelieving people!

68. Say: "O People of the Book, you have nothing [that counts] until you observe the Torah and the Gospel and what has been revealed to you from your Lord." Surely that which has been revealed to you[336] from your Lord will only make many of them increase in arrogance and unbelief; so do not be sorry for the unbelieving people.

69. Surely, the believers, the Jews, the Sabians and the Christians whoever believes in Allah and the Last Day and does good deeds shall all have nothing to fear and they shall not grieve.

70. We made the covenant with the Children of Israel and sent forth Messengers to them. Whenever a Messenger brought them what they did not like, they accused some of lying and killed some.

71. They supposed that there will be no punishment, so they became blind and deaf. Then Allah forgave them; but again many of them became blind and deaf. Allah is Fully Aware of what they do!

72. Those who say that Allah is the Messiah, son of Mary, are unbelievers. The Messiah said: "O Children of Israel, worship Allah, my Lord and your Lord. Surely, he who associates other gods with Allah, Allah forbids him access to Paradise and his dwelling is Hell. The evildoers have no supporters!"

---

336. The Prophet.

119

73. Unbelievers too are those who have said that Allah is the third of three. For there is no god except the One God; and if they will not refrain from what they say, those of them who have disbelieved will be severely punished.

لَّقَدْ كَفَرَ ٱلَّذِينَ قَالُوٓا۟ إِنَّ ٱللَّهَ ثَالِثُ ثَلَٰثَةٍ وَمَا مِنْ إِلَٰهٍ إِلَّآ إِلَٰهٌ وَٰحِدٌ وَإِن لَّمْ يَنتَهُوا۟ عَمَّا يَقُولُونَ لَيَمَسَّنَّ ٱلَّذِينَ كَفَرُوا۟ مِنْهُمْ عَذَابٌ أَلِيمٌ ﴿٧٣﴾

74. Will they not repent to Allah and ask His Forgiveness? For Allah is All-Forgiving, Merciful.

أَفَلَا يَتُوبُونَ إِلَى ٱللَّهِ وَيَسْتَغْفِرُونَهُۥ وَٱللَّهُ غَفُورٌ رَّحِيمٌ ﴿٧٤﴾

75. The Messiah, son of Mary, was only a Messenger before whom other Messengers had gone; and his mother was a godly woman. They both ate [earthly] food. Look how We make clear Our Revelations to them; then look how they are perverted!

مَّا ٱلْمَسِيحُ ٱبْنُ مَرْيَمَ إِلَّا رَسُولٌ قَدْ خَلَتْ مِن قَبْلِهِ ٱلرُّسُلُ وَأُمُّهُۥ صِدِّيقَةٌ كَانَا يَأْكُلَانِ ٱلطَّعَامَ ٱنظُرْ كَيْفَ نُبَيِّنُ لَهُمُ ٱلْءَايَٰتِ ثُمَّ ٱنظُرْ أَنَّىٰ يُؤْفَكُونَ ﴿٧٥﴾

76. Say: "Will you worship, instead of Allah, that which cannot hurt or profit you? Allah is All-Hearing, All-Knowing."

قُلْ أَتَعْبُدُونَ مِن دُونِ ٱللَّهِ مَا لَا يَمْلِكُ لَكُمْ ضَرًّا وَلَا نَفْعًا وَٱللَّهُ هُوَ ٱلسَّمِيعُ ٱلْعَلِيمُ ﴿٧٦﴾

77. Say: "O People of the Book, do not exceed the bounds in your religion unjustly, and do not follow the fancies of a people[337] who went astray in the past and led others astray and strayed from the Right Path."

قُلْ يَٰٓأَهْلَ ٱلْكِتَٰبِ لَا تَغْلُوا۟ فِى دِينِكُمْ غَيْرَ ٱلْحَقِّ وَلَا تَتَّبِعُوٓا۟ أَهْوَآءَ قَوْمٍ قَدْ ضَلُّوا۟ مِن قَبْلُ وَأَضَلُّوا۟ كَثِيرًا وَضَلُّوا۟ عَن سَوَآءِ ٱلسَّبِيلِ ﴿٧٧﴾

78. Those of the Children of Israel who disbelieved were cursed by David and Jesus, son of Mary; that, on account of their disobedience and their aggression.

لُعِنَ ٱلَّذِينَ كَفَرُوا۟ مِنۢ بَنِىٓ إِسْرَٰٓءِيلَ عَلَىٰ لِسَانِ دَاوُۥدَ وَعِيسَى ٱبْنِ مَرْيَمَ ذَٰلِكَ بِمَا عَصَوا۟ وَّكَانُوا۟ يَعْتَدُونَ ﴿٧٨﴾

79. They used not to forbid one another from committing any of the evils they were committing. Evil is what they did!

كَانُوا۟ لَا يَتَنَاهَوْنَ عَن مُّنكَرٍ فَعَلُوهُ لَبِئْسَ مَا كَانُوا۟ يَفْعَلُونَ ﴿٧٩﴾

80. You[338] see many of them befriending the unbelievers. Evil is what their souls prompt them to do. They have incurred Allah's Wrath and they will suffer torment forever.

تَرَىٰ كَثِيرًا مِّنْهُمْ يَتَوَلَّوْنَ ٱلَّذِينَ كَفَرُوا۟ لَبِئْسَ مَا قَدَّمَتْ لَهُمْ أَنفُسُهُمْ أَن سَخِطَ ٱللَّهُ عَلَيْهِمْ وَفِى ٱلْعَذَابِ هُمْ خَٰلِدُونَ ﴿٨٠﴾

---

337. The reference here is to their ancestors.
338. The Prophet.

81. Had they believed in Allah and the Prophet, and in what has been revealed to him, they would not have taken them as friends; but many of them are evildoers.

82. You shall find the most hostile people to the believers to be the Jews and the polytheists; and you shall find the closest in affection to the believers those who say: "We are Christians." For among them are priests and monks, and they are not arrogant.[339]

83. And when they hear what was revealed to the Messenger, you see their eyes overflow with tears on account of the truth they recognize. They say: "Our Lord, we believe, so write us down among the witnesses."

84. "And why should we not believe in Allah and in what has come to us of the truth, when we are eager that our Lord will let us enter along with the righteous people?"

85. Allah rewarded them for what they said with Gardens beneath which rivers flow, dwelling therein forever. Such is the reward of the righteous.

86. But those who disbelieve and denounce Our Revelations, such are the denizens of Hell.

87. O believers, do not forbid the good things that Allah has made lawful to you and do not transgress; for Allah does not like the transgressors.

88. Eat of the pleasant things which Allah has given you; and fear Allah in Whom you believe.

89. Allah will not take you to task for what is unintentional in your oaths, but will take you to task for the oaths you intentionally take.

وَلَوْ كَانُوا يُؤْمِنُونَ بِاللَّهِ وَالنَّبِيِّ وَمَا أُنزِلَ إِلَيْهِ مَا اتَّخَذُوهُمْ أَوْلِيَاءَ وَلَٰكِنَّ كَثِيرًا مِّنْهُمْ فَٰسِقُونَ ۝

۞ لَتَجِدَنَّ أَشَدَّ النَّاسِ عَدَاوَةً لِّلَّذِينَ آمَنُوا الْيَهُودَ وَالَّذِينَ أَشْرَكُوا وَلَتَجِدَنَّ أَقْرَبَهُم مَّوَدَّةً لِّلَّذِينَ آمَنُوا الَّذِينَ قَالُوا إِنَّا نَصَارَىٰ ذَٰلِكَ بِأَنَّ مِنْهُمْ قِسِّيسِينَ وَرُهْبَانًا وَأَنَّهُمْ لَا يَسْتَكْبِرُونَ ۝

وَإِذَا سَمِعُوا مَا أُنزِلَ إِلَى الرَّسُولِ تَرَىٰ أَعْيُنَهُمْ تَفِيضُ مِنَ الدَّمْعِ مِمَّا عَرَفُوا مِنَ الْحَقِّ يَقُولُونَ رَبَّنَا آمَنَّا فَاكْتُبْنَا مَعَ الشَّاهِدِينَ ۝

وَمَا لَنَا لَا نُؤْمِنُ بِاللَّهِ وَمَا جَاءَنَا مِنَ الْحَقِّ وَنَطْمَعُ أَن يُدْخِلَنَا رَبُّنَا مَعَ الْقَوْمِ الصَّالِحِينَ ۝

فَأَثَابَهُمُ اللَّهُ بِمَا قَالُوا جَنَّاتٍ تَجْرِي مِن تَحْتِهَا الْأَنْهَارُ خَالِدِينَ فِيهَا وَذَٰلِكَ جَزَاءُ الْمُحْسِنِينَ ۝

وَالَّذِينَ كَفَرُوا وَكَذَّبُوا بِآيَاتِنَا أُولَٰئِكَ أَصْحَابُ الْجَحِيمِ ۝

يَا أَيُّهَا الَّذِينَ آمَنُوا لَا تُحَرِّمُوا طَيِّبَاتِ مَا أَحَلَّ اللَّهُ لَكُمْ وَلَا تَعْتَدُوا إِنَّ اللَّهَ لَا يُحِبُّ الْمُعْتَدِينَ ۝

وَكُلُوا مِمَّا رَزَقَكُمُ اللَّهُ حَلَالًا طَيِّبًا وَاتَّقُوا اللَّهَ الَّذِي أَنتُم بِهِ مُؤْمِنُونَ ۝

لَا يُؤَاخِذُكُمُ اللَّهُ بِاللَّغْوِ فِي أَيْمَانِكُمْ وَلَٰكِن يُؤَاخِذُكُم بِمَا عَقَّدتُّمُ الْأَيْمَانَ فَكَفَّارَتُهُ إِطْعَامُ عَشَرَةِ مَسَاكِينَ مِنْ

---

339. That is, their pride does not prevent them from following what is right.

Expiation for it, is feeding ten poor people with such average food as you would feed your own families, clothing them or freeing one slave. But he who cannot find [the means] should fast three days. That is the expiation for your oaths when you have sworn.[340] Keep your oaths; that is how Allah makes clear His Revelations to you, that you may be thankful.

90. O believers, wine, gambling, idols and divining arrows are an abomination of the Devil's doing; so avoid them that perchance you may prosper!

91. The Devil only wishes to stir up enmity and hatred among you, through wine and gambling, and keep you away from remembering Allah and from prayer. Will you not desist, then?

92. Obey Allah and obey the Messenger and beware; but if you turn back, then know that it is the duty of Our Messenger to deliver the clear Message.

93. Those who believe and do the good deeds are not to blame for what they eat, if they are God-fearing, believe and do the good deeds, then fear God, and believe, then fear God and do good. Allah loves the charitable.

94. O believers, Allah will certainly test you with some game that your hands or lances may catch, so Allah may know who fears Him unseen. Whoever transgresses thereafter shall be painfully punished.

95. O believers, do not kill game while you are on pilgrimage. Whoever of you kills it wilfully will have to give the like of what he

---

340. The reference here is to those oaths which are not kept.

killed of cattle, as determined by two just men from yourselves, to reach the Ka'ba as an offering; or will have to feed as expiation a number of poor men, or the equivalent of that in fasting so that he may taste the evil consequences of his action. Allah will pardon what is past; but he who offends again, Allah will wreak vengeance upon him. Allah is Mighty, Capable of Retribution.

عَدْلٍ مِّنكُمْ هَدْيًا بَٰلِغَ ٱلْكَعْبَةِ أَوْ كَفَّٰرَةٌ طَعَامُ مَسَٰكِينَ أَوْ عَدْلُ ذَٰلِكَ صِيَامًا لِّيَذُوقَ وَبَالَ أَمْرِهِۦ عَفَا ٱللَّهُ عَمَّا سَلَفَ وَمَنْ عَادَ فَيَنتَقِمُ ٱللَّهُ مِنْهُ وَٱللَّهُ عَزِيزٌ ذُو ٱنتِقَامٍ ۝

96. Lawful to you is the catch of the sea and its food as an enjoyment for you and for travellers; but unlawful to you is the game of the land so long as you are on a pilgrimage. Fear Allah unto Whom you shall be gathered.

أُحِلَّ لَكُمْ صَيْدُ ٱلْبَحْرِ وَطَعَامُهُ مَتَٰعًا لَّكُمْ وَلِلسَّيَّارَةِ وَحُرِّمَ عَلَيْكُمْ صَيْدُ ٱلْبَرِّ مَا دُمْتُمْ حُرُمًا وَٱتَّقُوا۟ ٱللَّهَ ٱلَّذِىٓ إِلَيْهِ تُحْشَرُونَ ۝

97. Allah has made the Ka'ba, the Sacred House, a foundation of religion for all mankind, together with the Sacred Month and the sacrificial offerings and their garlands, so that you may know that Allah knows what is in the heavens and on the earth, and that Allah knows everything very well.

۞ جَعَلَ ٱللَّهُ ٱلْكَعْبَةَ ٱلْبَيْتَ ٱلْحَرَامَ قِيَٰمًا لِّلنَّاسِ وَٱلشَّهْرَ ٱلْحَرَامَ وَٱلْهَدْىَ وَٱلْقَلَٰئِدَ ذَٰلِكَ لِتَعْلَمُوٓا۟ أَنَّ ٱللَّهَ يَعْلَمُ مَا فِى ٱلسَّمَٰوَٰتِ وَمَا فِى ٱلْأَرْضِ وَأَنَّ ٱللَّهَ بِكُلِّ شَىْءٍ عَلِيمٌ ۝

98. Know that God is Severe in punishment and that Allah is All-Forgiving, Merciful.

ٱعْلَمُوٓا۟ أَنَّ ٱللَّهَ شَدِيدُ ٱلْعِقَابِ وَأَنَّ ٱللَّهَ غَفُورٌ رَّحِيمٌ ۝

99. The duty of the Messenger is only to deliver the Message, and Allah knows what you reveal and what you conceal.

مَّا عَلَى ٱلرَّسُولِ إِلَّا ٱلْبَلَٰغُ وَٱللَّهُ يَعْلَمُ مَا تُبْدُونَ وَمَا تَكْتُمُونَ ۝

100. Say: "The evil and the good are not equal, even if the abundance of the evil should appeal to you." Fear then Allah, O people of understanding, that perchance you may prosper.

قُل لَّا يَسْتَوِى ٱلْخَبِيثُ وَٱلطَّيِّبُ وَلَوْ أَعْجَبَكَ كَثْرَةُ ٱلْخَبِيثِ فَٱتَّقُوا۟ ٱللَّهَ يَٰٓأُو۟لِى ٱلْأَلْبَٰبِ لَعَلَّكُمْ تُفْلِحُونَ ۝

101. O believers, do not ask about things which, were they disclosed to you, would displease you; and which, should you ask about while the Qur'an is being revealed, will be disclosed to you. Allah has forgiven you for it; and Allah is All-Forgiving, Clement.

يَٰٓأَيُّهَا ٱلَّذِينَ ءَامَنُوا۟ لَا تَسْـَٔلُوا۟ عَنْ أَشْيَآءَ إِن تُبْدَ لَكُمْ تَسُؤْكُمْ وَإِن تَسْـَٔلُوا۟ عَنْهَا حِينَ يُنَزَّلُ ٱلْقُرْءَانُ تُبْدَ لَكُمْ عَفَا ٱللَّهُ عَنْهَا وَٱللَّهُ غَفُورٌ حَلِيمٌ ۝

123

102. A people preceding you asked about them, then disbelieved in them.

103. Allah has not prescribed the designation of Bahirah, Sa'ibah, Wasilah or Hami;[341] but the unbelievers impute falsehood to Allah, and most of them do not understand.

104. And if they are told: "Come now to what Allah has revealed and to the Messenger", they reply: "Sufficient unto us what we found our forefathers doing", even if their forefathers knew nothing and were not rightly guided!

105. O believers, take care of yourselves; you will not be harmed by him who has gone astray, if you are well-guided. To Allah you all will return; then He will tell you what you were doing.

106. O believers, when death approaches any of you, let two just men from among you act as witnesses at the time of testament; or two others from another folk, if you happen to be travelling abroad and are overtaken by the calamity of death. You will detain them[342] after the prayer and they will swear by Allah if you are in doubt: "We will not sell Him [Allah] for any price, even if a near kinsman is involved, and we will not keep secret the Testimony of Allah;[343] for then we would surely be sinners."

107. If, however, it is discovered that they have committed a sin, then two others shall take their places from among those against whom the first two had sinned. Whereupon they shall swear by Allah: "Our testimony is more truthful than their testimony and we have not transgressed, or else we would surely be evildoers."

قَدْ سَأَلَهَا قَوْمٌ مِّن قَبْلِكُمْ ثُمَّ أَصْبَحُوا بِهَا كَـٰفِرِينَ ۝

مَا جَعَلَ اللَّهُ مِنْ بَحِيرَةٍ وَلَا سَآئِبَةٍ وَلَا وَصِيلَةٍ وَلَا حَامٍ ۚ وَلَـٰكِنَّ الَّذِينَ كَفَرُوا يَفْتَرُونَ عَلَى اللَّهِ الْكَذِبَ ۖ وَأَكْثَرُهُمْ لَا يَعْقِلُونَ ۝

وَإِذَا قِيلَ لَهُمْ تَعَالَوْا إِلَىٰ مَا أَنزَلَ اللَّهُ وَإِلَى الرَّسُولِ قَالُوا حَسْبُنَا مَا وَجَدْنَا عَلَيْهِ ءَابَآءَنَآ ۚ أَوَلَوْ كَانَ ءَابَآؤُهُمْ لَا يَعْلَمُونَ شَيْئًا وَلَا يَهْتَدُونَ ۝

يَـٰٓأَيُّهَا الَّذِينَ ءَامَنُوا عَلَيْكُمْ أَنفُسَكُمْ ۖ لَا يَضُرُّكُم مَّن ضَلَّ إِذَا اهْتَدَيْتُمْ ۚ إِلَى اللَّهِ مَرْجِعُكُمْ جَمِيعًا فَيُنَبِّئُكُم بِمَا كُنتُمْ تَعْمَلُونَ ۝

يَـٰٓأَيُّهَا الَّذِينَ ءَامَنُوا شَهَـٰدَةُ بَيْنِكُمْ إِذَا حَضَرَ أَحَدَكُمُ الْمَوْتُ حِينَ الْوَصِيَّةِ اثْنَانِ ذَوَا عَدْلٍ مِّنكُمْ أَوْ ءَاخَرَانِ مِنْ غَيْرِكُمْ إِنْ أَنتُمْ ضَرَبْتُمْ فِى الْأَرْضِ فَأَصَـٰبَتْكُم مُّصِيبَةُ الْمَوْتِ ۚ تَحْبِسُونَهُمَا مِنْ بَعْدِ الصَّلَوٰةِ فَيُقْسِمَانِ بِاللَّهِ إِنِ ارْتَبْتُمْ لَا نَشْتَرِى بِهِ ثَمَنًا وَلَوْ كَانَ ذَا قُرْبَىٰ ۙ وَلَا نَكْتُمُ شَهَـٰدَةَ اللَّهِ إِنَّا إِذًا لَّمِنَ الْـَٔاثِمِينَ ۝

فَإِنْ عُثِرَ عَلَىٰٓ أَنَّهُمَا اسْتَحَقَّآ إِثْمًا فَـَٔاخَرَانِ يَقُومَانِ مَقَامَهُمَا مِنَ الَّذِينَ اسْتَحَقَّ عَلَيْهِمُ الْأَوْلَيَـٰنِ فَيُقْسِمَانِ بِاللَّهِ لَشَهَـٰدَتُنَآ أَحَقُّ مِن شَهَـٰدَتِهِمَا وَمَا اعْتَدَيْنَآ إِنَّآ إِذًا لَّمِنَ الظَّـٰلِمِينَ ۝

---

341. Cattle sacrificed to idols at the Ka'ba.
342. The two others.
343. That is, the testimony which Allah enjoins.

108. Thus, it is likelier that they will bear witness properly, or fear that other oaths will contradict their own oaths. Fear Allah and listen well; for Allah does not guide the wicked people.

ذَٰلِكَ أَدْنَىٰٓ أَن يَأْتُواْ بِٱلشَّهَٰدَةِ عَلَىٰ وَجْهِهَآ أَوْ يَخَافُوٓاْ أَن تُرَدَّ أَيْمَٰنٌۢ بَعْدَ أَيْمَٰنِهِمْ وَٱتَّقُواْ ٱللَّهَ وَٱسْمَعُواْ وَٱللَّهُ لَا يَهْدِى ٱلْقَوْمَ ٱلْفَٰسِقِينَ ﴿١٠٨﴾

109. The day when Allah shall assemble the Messengers, then say: "What response were you given?" They shall say: "We have no knowledge; You are indeed the Knower of the Unseen."

۞ يَوْمَ يَجْمَعُ ٱللَّهُ ٱلرُّسُلَ فَيَقُولُ مَاذَآ أُجِبْتُمْ قَالُواْ لَا عِلْمَ لَنَآ إِنَّكَ أَنتَ عَلَّٰمُ ٱلْغُيُوبِ ﴿١٠٩﴾

110. When Allah will say: "O Jesus, son of Mary, remember My Grace upon you and upon your mother, how I strengthened you with the Holy Spirit, so that you could speak to people in the cradle and as an old man; how I taught you the Book, the Wisdom, the Torah and the Gospel; and how, by My Leave, you created out of clay the likeness of a bird, and breathed into it, and then, by My Leave, it turned into a bird. And you could heal the blind and the leper by My Leave and you could raise the dead by My Leave. And [remember] how I restrained the Children of Israel from harming you, when you brought them the clear signs;[344] whereupon the unbelievers among them said: "That indeed is nothing but manifest sorcery."

إِذْ قَالَ ٱللَّهُ يَٰعِيسَى ٱبْنَ مَرْيَمَ ٱذْكُرْ نِعْمَتِى عَلَيْكَ وَعَلَىٰ وَٰلِدَتِكَ إِذْ أَيَّدتُّكَ بِرُوحِ ٱلْقُدُسِ تُكَلِّمُ ٱلنَّاسَ فِى ٱلْمَهْدِ وَكَهْلًا وَإِذْ عَلَّمْتُكَ ٱلْكِتَٰبَ وَٱلْحِكْمَةَ وَٱلتَّوْرَىٰةَ وَٱلْإِنجِيلَ وَإِذْ تَخْلُقُ مِنَ ٱلطِّينِ كَهَيْـَٔةِ ٱلطَّيْرِ بِإِذْنِى فَتَنفُخُ فِيهَا فَتَكُونُ طَيْرًۢا بِإِذْنِى وَتُبْرِئُ ٱلْأَكْمَهَ وَٱلْأَبْرَصَ بِإِذْنِى وَإِذْ تُخْرِجُ ٱلْمَوْتَىٰ بِإِذْنِى وَإِذْ كَفَفْتُ بَنِىٓ إِسْرَٰٓءِيلَ عَنكَ إِذْ جِئْتَهُم بِٱلْبَيِّنَٰتِ فَقَالَ ٱلَّذِينَ كَفَرُواْ مِنْهُمْ إِنْ هَٰذَآ إِلَّا سِحْرٌ مُّبِينٌ ﴿١١٠﴾

111. And when I revealed to the disciples:[345] "Believe in Me and My Messenger", they replied: "We believe, and You bear witness that we submit."

وَإِذْ أَوْحَيْتُ إِلَى ٱلْحَوَارِيِّۦنَ أَنْ ءَامِنُواْ بِى وَبِرَسُولِى قَالُوٓاْ ءَامَنَّا وَٱشْهَدْ بِأَنَّنَا مُسْلِمُونَ ﴿١١١﴾

112. When the disciples said: "Jesus, son of Mary, is your Lord able to bring down for us a table [spread with food] from heaven?"; he said: "Fear Allah, if you are true believers."

إِذْ قَالَ ٱلْحَوَارِيُّونَ يَٰعِيسَى ٱبْنَ مَرْيَمَ هَلْ يَسْتَطِيعُ رَبُّكَ أَن يُنَزِّلَ عَلَيْنَا مَآئِدَةً مِّنَ ٱلسَّمَآءِ قَالَ ٱتَّقُواْ ٱللَّهَ إِن كُنتُم مُّؤْمِنِينَ ﴿١١٢﴾

---

344. That is, miracles.
345. That is, ordered them through Jesus.

125

113. They said: "We would like to eat from it so that our hearts may be reassured and know that you have told us the truth and be witnesses thereof."

قَالُوا نُرِيدُ أَن نَّأْكُلَ مِنْهَا وَتَطْمَئِنَّ قُلُوبُنَا وَنَعْلَمَ أَن قَدْ صَدَقْتَنَا وَنَكُونَ عَلَيْهَا مِنَ الشَّٰهِدِينَ ﴿١١٣﴾

114. Jesus, son of Mary, then said: "O Allah, our Lord, send down to us a table spread with food from heaven that it may be a festival for the first and last of us and a sign from You; and provide for us, for You are the Best Provider."

قَالَ عِيسَى ابْنُ مَرْيَمَ اللَّهُمَّ رَبَّنَا أَنزِلْ عَلَيْنَا مَآئِدَةً مِّنَ السَّمَآءِ تَكُونُ لَنَا عِيدًا لِّأَوَّلِنَا وَءَاخِرِنَا وَءَايَةً مِّنكَ وَارْزُقْنَا وَأَنتَ خَيْرُ الرَّازِقِينَ ﴿١١٤﴾

115. Allah said: "I will send it down to you, so that whoever of you disbelieves thereafter I will inflict on him a punishment I do not inflict on any other being."

قَالَ اللَّهُ إِنِّي مُنَزِّلُهَا عَلَيْكُمْ فَمَن يَكْفُرْ بَعْدُ مِنكُمْ فَإِنِّي أُعَذِّبُهُ عَذَابًا لَّا أُعَذِّبُهُ أَحَدًا مِّنَ الْعَٰلَمِينَ ﴿١١٥﴾

116. And when Allah said: "O Jesus, son of Mary, did you say to the people: 'Take me and my mother as gods, apart from Allah?'" He said: "Glory be to You. It is not given me to say what is untrue. If I said it, You would have known it; You know what is in my soul, but I do not know what is in Thine. You are indeed the Knower of the Unseen.

وَإِذْ قَالَ اللَّهُ يَٰعِيسَى ابْنَ مَرْيَمَ ءَأَنتَ قُلْتَ لِلنَّاسِ اتَّخِذُونِي وَأُمِّيَ إِلَٰهَيْنِ مِن دُونِ اللَّهِ قَالَ سُبْحَٰنَكَ مَا يَكُونُ لِي أَنْ أَقُولَ مَا لَيْسَ لِي بِحَقٍّ إِن كُنتُ قُلْتُهُ فَقَدْ عَلِمْتَهُ تَعْلَمُ مَا فِي نَفْسِي وَلَا أَعْلَمُ مَا فِي نَفْسِكَ إِنَّكَ أَنتَ عَلَّٰمُ الْغُيُوبِ ﴿١١٦﴾

117. "I only told them what You commanded me: 'Worship Allah, your Lord and mine', and I was watcher over them while I was among them, but when You took me to Yourself, You became the Watcher over them; for You are the Witness of everything.

مَا قُلْتُ لَهُمْ إِلَّا مَا أَمَرْتَنِي بِهِ أَنِ اعْبُدُوا اللَّهَ رَبِّي وَرَبَّكُمْ وَكُنتُ عَلَيْهِمْ شَهِيدًا مَّا دُمْتُ فِيهِمْ فَلَمَّا تَوَفَّيْتَنِي كُنتَ أَنتَ الرَّقِيبَ عَلَيْهِمْ وَأَنتَ عَلَىٰ كُلِّ شَيْءٍ شَهِيدٌ ﴿١١٧﴾

118. "Should you punish them, they are surely Your servants; but should You forgive them, You are truly the Mighty, the Wise."

إِن تُعَذِّبْهُمْ فَإِنَّهُمْ عِبَادُكَ وَإِن تَغْفِرْ لَهُمْ فَإِنَّكَ أَنتَ الْعَزِيزُ الْحَكِيمُ ﴿١١٨﴾

119. Allah said: "This is a Day in which their truthfulness shall profit the truthful; they will have Gardens beneath which rivers flow, dwelling therein forever; Allah is pleased with them and they are pleased with Him. That is the great triumph."

قَالَ اللَّهُ هَٰذَا يَوْمُ يَنفَعُ الصَّٰدِقِينَ صِدْقُهُمْ لَهُمْ جَنَّٰتٌ تَجْرِي مِن تَحْتِهَا الْأَنْهَٰرُ خَٰلِدِينَ فِيهَا أَبَدًا رَّضِيَ اللَّهُ عَنْهُمْ وَرَضُوا عَنْهُ ذَٰلِكَ الْفَوْزُ الْعَظِيمُ ﴿١١٩﴾

120. To Allah belongs the dominion of the heavens and the earth and all there is in them, and He has power over everything.

لِلَّهِ مُلْكُ السَّمَٰوَٰتِ وَالْأَرْضِ وَمَا فِيهِنَّ وَهُوَ عَلَىٰ كُلِّ شَيْءٍ قَدِيرٌ ﴿١٢٠﴾

Sûrat Al-An'âm,
(The Cattle) 6

بِسْمِ ٱللَّهِ ٱلرَّحْمَٰنِ ٱلرَّحِيمِ

In the Name of Allah,
the Compassionate, the Merciful

1. Praise be to Allah, Who created the heavens and the earth and made the darkness and the light; yet the unbelievers set up equals to their Lord.

ٱلْحَمْدُ لِلَّهِ ٱلَّذِي خَلَقَ ٱلسَّمَٰوَٰتِ وَٱلْأَرْضَ وَجَعَلَ ٱلظُّلُمَٰتِ وَٱلنُّورَ ثُمَّ ٱلَّذِينَ كَفَرُوا بِرَبِّهِمْ يَعْدِلُونَ ۝

2. It is He Who created you from clay, then decreed a term [for you] and another set term with Him,[346] but still you doubt.

هُوَ ٱلَّذِي خَلَقَكُم مِّن طِينٍ ثُمَّ قَضَىٰ أَجَلًا وَأَجَلٌ مُّسَمًّى عِندَهُ ثُمَّ أَنتُمْ تَمْتَرُونَ ۝

3. He is Allah in the heavens and on earth. He knows your secrets and public utterances, and He knows what you earn.[347]

وَهُوَ ٱللَّهُ فِي ٱلسَّمَٰوَٰتِ وَفِي ٱلْأَرْضِ يَعْلَمُ سِرَّكُمْ وَجَهْرَكُمْ وَيَعْلَمُ مَا تَكْسِبُونَ ۝

4. And there comes not to them a revelation from Allah, but they turn away from it.

وَمَا تَأْتِيهِم مِّنْ ءَايَةٍ مِّنْ ءَايَٰتِ رَبِّهِمْ إِلَّا كَانُوا عَنْهَا مُعْرِضِينَ ۝

5. So, they denied the truth when it came to them; but surely the news of what they were mocking will come to them.

فَقَدْ كَذَّبُوا بِٱلْحَقِّ لَمَّا جَآءَهُمْ فَسَوْفَ يَأْتِيهِمْ أَنۢبَٰٓؤُا۟ مَا كَانُوا بِهِۦ يَسْتَهْزِءُونَ ۝

6. Do they not see how many generations before them We destroyed, after We had established them in the earth more firmly than We have established you, and how We let loose the sky upon them in torrents, and We made the rivers flow beneath them? Thus We destroyed them because of their sins. And after them We raised another generation.

أَلَمْ يَرَوْا كَمْ أَهْلَكْنَا مِن قَبْلِهِم مِّن قَرْنٍ مَّكَّنَّٰهُمْ فِي ٱلْأَرْضِ مَا لَمْ نُمَكِّن لَّكُمْ وَأَرْسَلْنَا ٱلسَّمَآءَ عَلَيْهِم مِّدْرَارًا وَجَعَلْنَا ٱلْأَنْهَٰرَ تَجْرِي مِن تَحْتِهِمْ فَأَهْلَكْنَٰهُم بِذُنُوبِهِمْ وَأَنشَأْنَا مِنۢ بَعْدِهِمْ قَرْنًا ءَاخَرِينَ ۝

7. Had We sent down upon you a Book on parchment so that they could touch it with their own hands, those who disbelieve would still have said: "This is nothing but manifest sorcery."

وَلَوْ نَزَّلْنَا عَلَيْكَ كِتَٰبًا فِي قِرْطَاسٍ فَلَمَسُوهُ بِأَيْدِيهِمْ لَقَالَ ٱلَّذِينَ كَفَرُوا إِنْ هَٰذَآ إِلَّا سِحْرٌ مُّبِينٌ ۝

---

346. Meaning a term in this world after which you die and another for resurrection.
347. Meaning the good and evil you do.

8. And they say: "Why has not an angel been sent down to him [the Prophet]?" But had We sent down an angel, their fate would have been sealed, and then they would not have been given any respite.

وَقَالُواْ لَوْلَآ أُنزِلَ عَلَيْهِ مَلَكٌ وَلَوْ أَنزَلْنَا مَلَكًا لَّقُضِىَ ٱلْأَمْرُ ثُمَّ لَا يُنظَرُونَ ﴿٨﴾

9. And had We made him an angel, We would have certainly made him [look like] a man and thus confounded them with what they are using to confound others.

وَلَوْ جَعَلْنَٰهُ مَلَكًا لَّجَعَلْنَٰهُ رَجُلًا وَلَلَبَسْنَا عَلَيْهِم مَّا يَلْبِسُونَ ﴿٩﴾

10. Other Messengers before you were mocked; but those who scoffed at them were stricken with that at which they scoffed.

وَلَقَدِ ٱسْتُهْزِئَ بِرُسُلٍ مِّن قَبْلِكَ فَحَاقَ بِٱلَّذِينَ سَخِرُواْ مِنْهُم مَّا كَانُواْ بِهِۦ يَسْتَهْزِءُونَ ﴿١٠﴾

11. Say: "Travel in the land and look what was the fate of those who disbelieved [the Messengers]."

قُلْ سِيرُواْ فِى ٱلْأَرْضِ ثُمَّ ٱنظُرُواْ كَيْفَ كَانَ عَٰقِبَةُ ٱلْمُكَذِّبِينَ ﴿١١﴾

12. Say: "To whom does that which exists in the heavens and on earth belong?" Say: "To Allah. He has prescribed to Himself Mercy. He will certainly gather you on the Day of Resurrection, which is undoubted. Those who lost their souls will not believe."

قُل لِّمَن مَّا فِى ٱلسَّمَٰوَٰتِ وَٱلْأَرْضِ قُل لِّلَّهِ كَتَبَ عَلَىٰ نَفْسِهِ ٱلرَّحْمَةَ لَيَجْمَعَنَّكُمْ إِلَىٰ يَوْمِ ٱلْقِيَٰمَةِ لَا رَيْبَ فِيهِ ٱلَّذِينَ خَسِرُوٓاْ أَنفُسَهُمْ فَهُمْ لَا يُؤْمِنُونَ ﴿١٢﴾

13. To Him belongs whatever comes to rest in the day and in the night; and He is the All-Hearing, the All-Knowing.

۞ وَلَهُۥ مَا سَكَنَ فِى ٱلَّيْلِ وَٱلنَّهَارِ وَهُوَ ٱلسَّمِيعُ ٱلْعَلِيمُ ﴿١٣﴾

14. Say: "Shall I take as guardian any one other than Allah, Who created the heavens and the earth, and Who feeds and is not fed?" Say: "I have been commanded to be the first to submit and not to be one of the polytheists."

قُلْ أَغَيْرَ ٱللَّهِ أَتَّخِذُ وَلِيًّا فَاطِرِ ٱلسَّمَٰوَٰتِ وَٱلْأَرْضِ وَهُوَ يُطْعِمُ وَلَا يُطْعَمُ قُلْ إِنِّىٓ أُمِرْتُ أَنْ أَكُونَ أَوَّلَ مَنْ أَسْلَمَ وَلَا تَكُونَنَّ مِنَ ٱلْمُشْرِكِينَ ﴿١٤﴾

15. Say: "Indeed, if I disobey my Lord, I fear the punishment of a Fateful Day."[348]

قُلْ إِنِّىٓ أَخَافُ إِنْ عَصَيْتُ رَبِّى عَذَابَ يَوْمٍ عَظِيمٍ ﴿١٥﴾

16. Whoever is spared on that Day has gained His Mercy, and that indeed is the manifest triumph!

مَّن يُصْرَفْ عَنْهُ يَوْمَئِذٍ فَقَدْ رَحِمَهُۥ وَذَٰلِكَ ٱلْفَوْزُ ٱلْمُبِينُ ﴿١٦﴾

---

348. The Day of Resurrection.

17. And if Allah lets you suffer an affliction, no one can lift it except He; and if He accords you any good, He surely has power over everything.

وَإِن يَمْسَسْكَ ٱللَّهُ بِضُرٍّ فَلَا كَاشِفَ لَهُۥٓ إِلَّا هُوَ ۖ وَإِن يَمْسَسْكَ بِخَيْرٍ فَهُوَ عَلَىٰ كُلِّ شَيْءٍ قَدِيرٌ ۝

18. And He is Sovereign over His servants and He is Wise, Well Acquainted with all things.

وَهُوَ ٱلْقَاهِرُ فَوْقَ عِبَادِهِۦ ۚ وَهُوَ ٱلْحَكِيمُ ٱلْخَبِيرُ ۝

19. Say: "What has the greatest testimony?" Say: "Allah is Witness between you and me, and He has revealed this Qur'an to me so that I may warn you and whomever it may reach. Do you indeed testify that there are gods besides Allah?" Say: "I do not testify." Say: "He is indeed One God and I am innocent of the association of idols [with Him]."

قُلْ أَىُّ شَىْءٍ أَكْبَرُ شَهَٰدَةً ۖ قُلِ ٱللَّهُ ۖ شَهِيدٌۢ بَيْنِى وَبَيْنَكُمْ ۚ وَأُوحِىَ إِلَىَّ هَٰذَا ٱلْقُرْءَانُ لِأُنذِرَكُم بِهِۦ وَمَنۢ بَلَغَ ۚ أَئِنَّكُمْ لَتَشْهَدُونَ أَنَّ مَعَ ٱللَّهِ ءَالِهَةً أُخْرَىٰ ۚ قُل لَّآ أَشْهَدُ ۚ قُلْ إِنَّمَا هُوَ إِلَٰهٌ وَٰحِدٌ وَإِنَّنِى بَرِىٓءٌ مِّمَّا تُشْرِكُونَ ۝

20. Those to whom We have given the Book know him,[349] as they know their own children; but those who have lost their souls will not believe.

ٱلَّذِينَ ءَاتَيْنَٰهُمُ ٱلْكِتَٰبَ يَعْرِفُونَهُۥ كَمَا يَعْرِفُونَ أَبْنَآءَهُمُ ۘ ٱلَّذِينَ خَسِرُوٓا۟ أَنفُسَهُمْ فَهُمْ لَا يُؤْمِنُونَ ۝

21. And who is more unjust than he who imputes falsehood to Allah or denies His Revelations? Indeed the unjust shall not prosper.

وَمَنْ أَظْلَمُ مِمَّنِ ٱفْتَرَىٰ عَلَى ٱللَّهِ كَذِبًا أَوْ كَذَّبَ بِـَٔايَٰتِهِۦٓ ۚ إِنَّهُۥ لَا يُفْلِحُ ٱلظَّٰلِمُونَ ۝

22. And on the Day that We shall gather them all together, then say to those who associated other gods [with Allah]: "Where are those whom you allege to have been your associate-gods?"

وَيَوْمَ نَحْشُرُهُمْ جَمِيعًا ثُمَّ نَقُولُ لِلَّذِينَ أَشْرَكُوٓا۟ أَيْنَ شُرَكَآؤُكُمُ ٱلَّذِينَ كُنتُمْ تَزْعُمُونَ ۝

23. Then their only excuse will be simply to say: "By Allah, our Lord, we have not been polytheists."

ثُمَّ لَمْ تَكُن فِتْنَتُهُمْ إِلَّآ أَن قَالُوا۟ وَٱللَّهِ رَبِّنَا مَا كُنَّا مُشْرِكِينَ ۝

24. Look,[350] how they will lie to themselves and how that which they fabricated will fail them.

ٱنظُرْ كَيْفَ كَذَبُوا۟ عَلَىٰٓ أَنفُسِهِمْ ۚ وَضَلَّ عَنْهُم مَّا كَانُوا۟ يَفْتَرُونَ ۝

25. And some of them listen to you, but We have cast veils over their hearts, lest they

وَمِنْهُم مَّن يَسْتَمِعُ إِلَيْكَ ۖ وَجَعَلْنَا عَلَىٰ قُلُوبِهِمْ أَكِنَّةً أَن

---

349. The Prophet.
350. Look, O Muhammad.

should understand it,[351] and a deafness in their ears. And even were they to see every sign, they will not believe in it; so that when they come to dispute with you, the unbelievers will say: "This is nothing but fables of the ancients."

26. And they forbid others from [following] him[352] and they keep away from him, but they only destroy themselves, without perceiving it.

27. And if only you could see when they are stationed before the Fire and thus they say: "Would that we could be brought back so that we would not denounce the Revelations of our Lord, but would be part of the believers."

28. Indeed, what they used to conceal before will become clear to them; and were they returned [to life], they would surely go back to that which they were forbidden from. They are indeed liars.

29. And they say: "There is only this life and we shall not be resurrected."

30. And if only you could see when they are made to stand before their Lord. He will say: "Is not this the truth?" They will say: "Yes, by our Lord." He will say: "Taste then the punishment, on account of your disbelief."

31. Those who deny the Encounter with Allah are losers. And when the Hour overtakes them suddenly, they will say: "Alas, We neglected much in it." For they carry their burdens on their backs. And evil is what they carry!

---

351. The Qur'an.
352. The Prophet.

32. The earthly life is nothing but sport and amusement, and the world to come is surely better for those who are God-fearing. Do you not understand?

33. We know that what they say grieves you. For they do not deny what you say; but the wrongdoers [continue to] deny Allah's Revelations.

34. Other Messengers were denounced before you, but they put up with the denunciation, and they were injured until Our Help came to them. None can change the Words[353] of Allah. Tidings have already been imparted about those Messengers.

35. And if you find their aversion unbearable, seek, if you can, a hole in the earth or a ladder to the sky in order to bring them a sign. Had Allah pleased, He would surely have led them all to guidance; so do not be one of the ignorant.

36. Only those who hear will respond, and the dead will be raised by Allah; and unto Him they shall be returned.

37. And they also say: "Why has no sign[354] come down to him from his Lord?" Say: "Allah is surely Able to send down a sign, but most of them do not know."

38. There is no animal [crawling] on land or a bird flying with its wings, but are communities like yourselves. We have not left anything out in the Book. Then unto their Lord they shall be gathered.

39. And those who deny Our Revelations are deaf and dumb in total darkness. Whoever Allah pleases, He will lead astray; and

وَمَا الْحَيَوٰةُ الدُّنْيَا إِلَّا لَعِبٌ وَلَهْوٌ وَلَلدَّارُ الْآخِرَةُ خَيْرٌ لِّلَّذِينَ يَتَّقُونَ أَفَلَا تَعْقِلُونَ ﴿٣٢﴾

قَدْ نَعْلَمُ إِنَّهُ لَيَحْزُنُكَ الَّذِي يَقُولُونَ فَإِنَّهُمْ لَا يُكَذِّبُونَكَ وَلَكِنَّ الظَّالِمِينَ بِآيَاتِ اللَّهِ يَجْحَدُونَ ﴿٣٣﴾

وَلَقَدْ كُذِّبَتْ رُسُلٌ مِّن قَبْلِكَ فَصَبَرُوا عَلَىٰ مَا كُذِّبُوا وَأُوذُوا حَتَّىٰ أَتَاهُمْ نَصْرُنَا وَلَا مُبَدِّلَ لِكَلِمَاتِ اللَّهِ وَلَقَدْ جَاءَكَ مِن نَّبَإِ الْمُرْسَلِينَ ﴿٣٤﴾

وَإِن كَانَ كَبُرَ عَلَيْكَ إِعْرَاضُهُمْ فَإِنِ اسْتَطَعْتَ أَن تَبْتَغِيَ نَفَقًا فِي الْأَرْضِ أَوْ سُلَّمًا فِي السَّمَاءِ فَتَأْتِيَهُم بِآيَةٍ وَلَوْ شَاءَ اللَّهُ لَجَمَعَهُمْ عَلَى الْهُدَىٰ فَلَا تَكُونَنَّ مِنَ الْجَاهِلِينَ ﴿٣٥﴾

۞ إِنَّمَا يَسْتَجِيبُ الَّذِينَ يَسْمَعُونَ وَالْمَوْتَىٰ يَبْعَثُهُمُ اللَّهُ ثُمَّ إِلَيْهِ يُرْجَعُونَ ﴿٣٦﴾

وَقَالُوا لَوْلَا نُزِّلَ عَلَيْهِ آيَةٌ مِّن رَّبِّهِ قُلْ إِنَّ اللَّهَ قَادِرٌ عَلَىٰ أَن يُنَزِّلَ آيَةً وَلَكِنَّ أَكْثَرَهُمْ لَا يَعْلَمُونَ ﴿٣٧﴾

وَمَا مِن دَابَّةٍ فِي الْأَرْضِ وَلَا طَائِرٍ يَطِيرُ بِجَنَاحَيْهِ إِلَّا أُمَمٌ أَمْثَالُكُم مَّا فَرَّطْنَا فِي الْكِتَابِ مِن شَيْءٍ ثُمَّ إِلَىٰ رَبِّهِمْ يُحْشَرُونَ ﴿٣٨﴾

وَالَّذِينَ كَذَّبُوا بِآيَاتِنَا صُمٌّ وَبُكْمٌ فِي الظُّلُمَاتِ مَن يَشَإِ

---

353. His Promises to support His Messengers.
354. That is, miracle.

whoever He pleases, He will lead onto a straight path.

40. Say: "Tell me, if Allah's Punishment overtakes you,[355] or the Hour[356] strikes, would you call upon any one other than Allah, if you are truthful?"

41. Nay, upon Him you will call and He will lighten that about which you call, if He pleases; and then you will forget what you used to associate [with Him].

42. We have indeed sent forth [Messengers] to other nations before you and We afflicted them with misery and hardship that per-chance they might humble themselves.

43. If only they humbled themselves when Our Punishment overtook them; but their hearts were hardened and the Devil made what they were doing seem fair to them.

44. Then, when they forgot what they were reminded of, We opened wide for them the gates of everything [good]; so that as soon as they rejoiced at what they were given, We struck them down suddenly, and they were driven to despair.

45. Thus the remnant of the wrongdoing people were rooted out, Praise be to Allah, the Lord of the Worlds!

46. Say: "Tell me! If Allah were to take away your hearing and sight and seal your hearts, what god other than Allah would give them back to you?" Behold, how we make plain Our Revelations, but they turn away.

47. Say: "Tell me! If Allah's Punishment should seize you suddenly or openly, will any be destroyed other than the wrongdoing people?"

اللَّهُ يُضْلِلْهُ وَمَن يَشَأْ يَجْعَلْهُ عَلَىٰ صِرَٰطٍ مُّسْتَقِيمٍ ﴿٣٩﴾

قُلْ أَرَءَيْتَكُمْ إِنْ أَتَىٰكُمْ عَذَابُ اللَّهِ أَوْ أَتَتْكُمُ السَّاعَةُ أَغَيْرَ اللَّهِ تَدْعُونَ إِن كُنتُمْ صَٰدِقِينَ ﴿٤٠﴾

بَلْ إِيَّاهُ تَدْعُونَ فَيَكْشِفُ مَا تَدْعُونَ إِلَيْهِ إِن شَآءَ وَتَنسَوْنَ مَا تُشْرِكُونَ ﴿٤١﴾

وَلَقَدْ أَرْسَلْنَآ إِلَىٰٓ أُمَمٍ مِّن قَبْلِكَ فَأَخَذْنَٰهُم بِٱلْبَأْسَآءِ وَٱلضَّرَّآءِ لَعَلَّهُمْ يَتَضَرَّعُونَ ﴿٤٢﴾

فَلَوْلَآ إِذْ جَآءَهُم بَأْسُنَا تَضَرَّعُوا۟ وَلَٰكِن قَسَتْ قُلُوبُهُمْ وَزَيَّنَ لَهُمُ ٱلشَّيْطَٰنُ مَا كَانُوا۟ يَعْمَلُونَ ﴿٤٣﴾

فَلَمَّا نَسُوا۟ مَا ذُكِّرُوا۟ بِهِ فَتَحْنَا عَلَيْهِمْ أَبْوَٰبَ كُلِّ شَىْءٍ حَتَّىٰٓ إِذَا فَرِحُوا۟ بِمَآ أُوتُوٓا۟ أَخَذْنَٰهُم بَغْتَةً فَإِذَا هُم مُّبْلِسُونَ ﴿٤٤﴾

فَقُطِعَ دَابِرُ ٱلْقَوْمِ ٱلَّذِينَ ظَلَمُوا۟ وَٱلْحَمْدُ لِلَّهِ رَبِّ ٱلْعَٰلَمِينَ ﴿٤٥﴾

قُلْ أَرَءَيْتُمْ إِنْ أَخَذَ ٱللَّهُ سَمْعَكُمْ وَأَبْصَٰرَكُمْ وَخَتَمَ عَلَىٰ قُلُوبِكُم مَّنْ إِلَٰهٌ غَيْرُ ٱللَّهِ يَأْتِيكُم بِهِ ٱنظُرْ كَيْفَ نُصَرِّفُ ٱلْآيَٰتِ ثُمَّ هُمْ يَصْدِفُونَ ﴿٤٦﴾

قُلْ أَرَءَيْتَكُمْ إِنْ أَتَىٰكُمْ عَذَابُ ٱللَّهِ بَغْتَةً أَوْ جَهْرَةً هَلْ يُهْلَكُ إِلَّا ٱلْقَوْمُ ٱلظَّٰلِمُونَ ﴿٤٧﴾

---

355. In this life.
356. Day of Resurrection.

48. And We only send forth the Messengers as bearers of good tidings and warners. Those who believe and mend their ways have nothing to fear and have no cause to grieve.

49. But those who deny Our Revelations will be punished for having been sinful.

50. Say: "I do not tell you that I have the treasures of Allah, and I do not know the Unseen; nor do I tell you that I am an angel. I only follow what is revealed to me." Say: "Are the blind man and the one who sees alike? Do you not reflect at all?"

51. And warn with it[357] those who fear that they will be gathered before their Lord, other than Whom they have neither a protector nor an intercessor, so that they may be God-fearing.

52. And do not drive away those who call upon their Lord morning and evening, seeking nothing but His Face. You are not in the least accountable for them, nor are they in the least accountable for you, so as to drive them away and become one of the wrongdoers.

53. Likewise, We test some of them through others so that they may say: "Are these the ones whom Allah has favoured among us?" Does not Allah know best the thankful?

54. And when those who believe in Our Revelations come to you, say: "Peace be upon you. Your Lord has prescribed Mercy upon Himself, that he who perpetrates evil in ignorance, repents afterwards and mends his ways [will find Him] All-Forgiving, Merciful.

55. And thus We expound the revelations so that the way of the criminals becomes clear.

---

357. The Qur'an.

56. Say: "I have been forbidden to worship those you call upon apart from Allah." Say: "I do not follow your fancies, or else I would have gone astray and would not be one of the well-guided."

57. Say: "I have clear proof from my Lord, and you deny Him. I do not possess that with which you seek to hasten [punishment]. Judgement is Allah's alone; He determines the right, and He is the Best Decision-maker."

58. Say: "If I possessed that which you seek to hasten, the matter between you and me would have been settled; and Allah knows best the wrongdoers."

59. With Him are the keys of the Unseen; only He knows them, and He knows what is on land and in the sea. Not a leaf falls but He knows it; and there is no grain in the dark bowels of the earth, nor anything green or dry, but is [recorded] in a Clear Book.

60. And it is He Who makes you die at night and knows what you do by day. He raises you up in it, until a fixed term is fulfilled; then unto Him is your ultimate return. He will declare to you what you used to do.

61. He is the Supreme Ruler over His servants, and He sends guardians[358] to watch over you, so that when death overtakes any one of you, Our Messengers[359] carry him off; and they do not fail [to perform their duty].

62. Then they are brought back to Allah, their true Master. Truly the judgement is His and He is the Fastest Reckoner.

---

358. Angels.
359. The angels.

134

63. Say: "Who will deliver you from the dark depths of the land and the sea? You call upon Him humbly and secretly saying: 'If He delivers us from this, we will certainly be thankful.' "

64. Say: "Allah delivers you from this and from every distress; yet you associate [other gods with Him]".

65. Say: "It is He Who has the power to inflict upon you punishment from above you or from under your feet; or to mix you up dividing you into factions, and make you taste the might of one another." See, how We make plain Our Revelations, that, perchance, they might understand.

66. And your people deny it,[360] whereas it is the truth. Say: "I am not your guardian."

67. For every event there is a fixed time, and you shall certainly know.

68. And when you see those who talk scornfully about Our Revelations, turn away from them, until they engage in another discourse. And should the devil cause you to forget, do not sit down after the reminder with the evil-doing people.

69. The righteous are in no way accountable for them; it is only a reminder so that they may fear [Allah].

70. And leave those who take their religion for sport and who are deluded by the life of this world, and remind by it,[361] lest any soul should perish on account of what it has earned.[362] Apart from Allah, it has no protector or intercessor; and if it offers any

---

360. The Qur'an.
361. The Qur'an.
362. That is, on account of the person's deeds.

135

ransom, it will not be accepted from it. Such are those who are turned over [to be punished] on account of what they have earned. They will have a drink of boiling water and a very painful punishment, because they disbelieved.

71. Say: "Shall we call, besides Allah, on what neither profits nor harms us, and turn on our heels after Allah has guided us?" [We shall then be] like one who, being tempted by the devils in the land, is bewildered though he has friends who call him to guidance [saying]: "Come to us." Say: "Guidance from Allah is the true guidance. And we are commanded to submit to the Lord of the Worlds;

72. "And perform the prayers and fear Him; for He is the One unto Whom you shall be gathered."

73. It is He Who created the heavens and the earth in truth, and the Day He says: "Be", it will come to be. His Word is the Truth, and His is the sovereignty on the Day the trumpet is blown. The Knower of the Unseen and the Seen, He is the Wise, the Well-Aware [of all things].

74. And when Abraham said to his father Azar, "Do you take idols for gods? I see you and your people are in manifest error."

75. Thus We show Abraham the kingdom of the heavens and the earth, that he might be one of those possessed of certainty.

76. And when night fell, he saw a star; so he said: "This is my Lord", but when it set, he said: "I do not like those that set."

77. Then, when he saw the moon rising, he said: "This is my Lord", but when it set, he said: "If my Lord does not guide me rightly, I will be one of the erring people."

بِمَا كَسَبُوا لَهُمْ شَرَابٌ مِّنْ حَمِيمٍ وَعَذَابٌ أَلِيمٌ بِمَا كَانُوا يَكْفُرُونَ ﴿٧٠﴾

قُلْ أَنَدْعُوا مِن دُونِ اللَّهِ مَا لَا يَنفَعُنَا وَلَا يَضُرُّنَا وَنُرَدُّ عَلَى أَعْقَابِنَا بَعْدَ إِذْ هَدَىٰنَا اللَّهُ كَالَّذِي اسْتَهْوَتْهُ الشَّيَاطِينُ فِي الْأَرْضِ حَيْرَانَ لَهُ أَصْحَابٌ يَدْعُونَهُ إِلَى الْهُدَى ائْتِنَا قُلْ إِنَّ هُدَى اللَّهِ هُوَ الْهُدَىٰ وَأُمِرْنَا لِنُسْلِمَ لِرَبِّ الْعَالَمِينَ ﴿٧١﴾

وَأَنْ أَقِيمُوا الصَّلَاةَ وَاتَّقُوهُ وَهُوَ الَّذِي إِلَيْهِ تُحْشَرُونَ ﴿٧٢﴾

وَهُوَ الَّذِي خَلَقَ السَّمَاوَاتِ وَالْأَرْضَ بِالْحَقِّ وَيَوْمَ يَقُولُ كُن فَيَكُونُ قَوْلُهُ الْحَقُّ وَلَهُ الْمُلْكُ يَوْمَ يُنفَخُ فِي الصُّورِ عَالِمُ الْغَيْبِ وَالشَّهَادَةِ وَهُوَ الْحَكِيمُ الْخَبِيرُ ﴿٧٣﴾

۞ وَإِذْ قَالَ إِبْرَاهِيمُ لِأَبِيهِ ءَازَرَ أَتَتَّخِذُ أَصْنَامًا ءَالِهَةً إِنِّي أَرَىٰكَ وَقَوْمَكَ فِي ضَلَالٍ مُّبِينٍ ﴿٧٤﴾

وَكَذَٰلِكَ نُرِي إِبْرَاهِيمَ مَلَكُوتَ السَّمَاوَاتِ وَالْأَرْضِ وَلِيَكُونَ مِنَ الْمُوقِنِينَ ﴿٧٥﴾

فَلَمَّا جَنَّ عَلَيْهِ الَّيْلُ رَءَا كَوْكَبًا قَالَ هَٰذَا رَبِّي فَلَمَّا أَفَلَ قَالَ لَا أُحِبُّ الْآفِلِينَ ﴿٧٦﴾

فَلَمَّا رَءَا الْقَمَرَ بَازِغًا قَالَ هَٰذَا رَبِّي فَلَمَّا أَفَلَ قَالَ لَئِن لَّمْ يَهْدِنِي رَبِّي لَأَكُونَنَّ مِنَ الْقَوْمِ الضَّالِّينَ ﴿٧٧﴾

136

78. Then, when he saw the sun rising, he said: "This is my Lord; this is larger", but when it set, he said: "O, my people, I am innocent of what you associate [with God].

79. "I turn my face towards Him Who fashioned the heavens and the earth, as an upright man, and I am not one of the polytheists."

80. His people disputed with him. He said: "Do you dispute with me regarding Allah Who has guided me? I do not fear what you associate with Him, unless my Lord wills anything. My Lord embraces everything in His Knowledge; do you not remember [this]?

81. "And how should I fear what you associate [with Him], while you do not fear the fact that you have associated with Allah that for which He has sent down upon you no authority? Which of the two parties, then, is more deserving of safety? [Tell me] if you know."

82. Those who believe and do not mix their faith up with injustice - to these belongs the safety, and they are the well-guided.

83. That is Our Argument which We imparted to Abraham against his people. We raise up in degrees whomever We please. Your Lord is indeed Wise, All-Knowing.

84. And We granted him Isaac and Jacob, and guided each of them; and Noah We guided before that, and of his progeny, [We guided] David, Solomon, Job, Joseph, Moses and Aaron. Thus We reward the beneficent.

85. And Zachariah, John, Jesus and Elias, each was one of the righteous.

86. And Isma'il, Elijah, Jonah and Lot; each We exalted above the whole world.

فَلَمَّا رَءَا ٱلشَّمْسَ بَازِغَةً قَالَ هَٰذَا رَبِّى هَٰذَآ أَكْبَرُ فَلَمَّآ أَفَلَتْ قَالَ يَٰقَوْمِ إِنِّى بَرِىٓءٌ مِّمَّا تُشْرِكُونَ ۝

إِنِّى وَجَّهْتُ وَجْهِىَ لِلَّذِى فَطَرَ ٱلسَّمَٰوَٰتِ وَٱلْأَرْضَ حَنِيفًا وَمَآ أَنَا۠ مِنَ ٱلْمُشْرِكِينَ ۝

وَحَآجَّهُۥ قَوْمُهُۥ قَالَ أَتُحَٰٓجُّوٓنِّى فِى ٱللَّهِ وَقَدْ هَدَٰنِ وَلَآ أَخَافُ مَا تُشْرِكُونَ بِهِۦٓ إِلَّآ أَن يَشَآءَ رَبِّى شَيْـًٔا وَسِعَ رَبِّى كُلَّ شَىْءٍ عِلْمًا أَفَلَا تَتَذَكَّرُونَ ۝

وَكَيْفَ أَخَافُ مَآ أَشْرَكْتُمْ وَلَا تَخَافُونَ أَنَّكُمْ أَشْرَكْتُم بِٱللَّهِ مَا لَمْ يُنَزِّلْ بِهِۦ عَلَيْكُمْ سُلْطَٰنًا فَأَىُّ ٱلْفَرِيقَيْنِ أَحَقُّ بِٱلْأَمْنِ إِن كُنتُمْ تَعْلَمُونَ ۝

ٱلَّذِينَ ءَامَنُوا۟ وَلَمْ يَلْبِسُوٓا۟ إِيمَٰنَهُم بِظُلْمٍ أُو۟لَٰٓئِكَ لَهُمُ ٱلْأَمْنُ وَهُم مُّهْتَدُونَ ۝

وَتِلْكَ حُجَّتُنَآ ءَاتَيْنَٰهَآ إِبْرَٰهِيمَ عَلَىٰ قَوْمِهِۦ نَرْفَعُ دَرَجَٰتٍ مَّن نَّشَآءُ إِنَّ رَبَّكَ حَكِيمٌ عَلِيمٌ ۝

وَوَهَبْنَا لَهُۥٓ إِسْحَٰقَ وَيَعْقُوبَ كُلًّا هَدَيْنَا وَنُوحًا هَدَيْنَا مِن قَبْلُ وَمِن ذُرِّيَّتِهِۦ دَاوُۥدَ وَسُلَيْمَٰنَ وَأَيُّوبَ وَيُوسُفَ وَمُوسَىٰ وَهَٰرُونَ وَكَذَٰلِكَ نَجْزِى ٱلْمُحْسِنِينَ ۝

وَزَكَرِيَّا وَيَحْيَىٰ وَعِيسَىٰ وَإِلْيَاسَ كُلٌّ مِّنَ ٱلصَّٰلِحِينَ ۝

وَإِسْمَٰعِيلَ وَٱلْيَسَعَ وَيُونُسَ وَلُوطًا وَكُلًّا فَضَّلْنَا عَلَى ٱلْعَٰلَمِينَ ۝

87. [We also exalted some] of their fathers, progeny and brethren. And We chose them and guided them to a straight path.

88. That is Allah's Guidance by which He guides whom He pleases of His servants. Had they associated [other gods with Allah], all that they did would have been nullified.

89. Those are the ones to whom We gave the Book, wisdom, authority and Prophethood. So if these[363] disbelieve in them,[364] We have entrusted them to a people who do not disbelieve in them.

90. Those are the ones whom Allah has guided; so follow their guidance. Say: "I ask you no reward for it; it is only a reminder to mankind."

91. They do not show proper regard for Allah's Greatness when they say: "Allah has not revealed anything to a mortal." Say: "Who revealed the Book which was brought by Moses as a light and guidance to mankind? You put it in scrolls which you reveal, while you conceal much. And [now] you are taught[365] what neither you nor your fathers knew." Say: "Allah [revealed it]. Then leave them to revel in their nonsense."

92. And this is a Book which We revealed. [It is] blessed and confirms what preceded it, that you may warn therewith the Mother of Cities[366] and those around it. Those who believe in the Hereafter believe in it and observe their prayers.

93. And who is more unjust than he who imputes falsehood to Allah, or says: "It has

---

363. The Meccan unbelievers.
364. The Book, wisdom and prophethood.
365. In the Qur'an.
366. Mecca.

been revealed to me", while nothing was revealed to him; or one who says: "I will reveal the like of what Allah has revealed?" If you could see the wrongdoers in the throes of death, and the angels, with arms out-stretched, saying: "Give us your souls. This day you receive the punishment of humilia-tion for what you used to say untruly about Allah, while scorning His Revelations."

94. You[367] have come to Us one by one, just as We created you initially, and you have left behind what We granted you. We do not see with you your intercessors whom you claimed were [Allah's] partners. Certainly what held you together is now cut off, and that which you claimed has failed you.

95. Allah is truly the Cleaver of the grain and the date-stone; He brings out the living from the dead and the dead from the living. That is Allah; how then were you perverted?

96. [He is] the Cleaver of the dawn; and He made the night a time of rest, and the sun and the moon a means of reckoning. Such is the ordering of Allah, the Mighty, the All-Knowing.

97. And it is He Who created the stars for you so as to be guided by them in the dark depths of the land and the sea. We have made plain the signs for a people who know.

98. And it is He Who created you from a single living soul; then [gave you] a resting-place and a repository. Indeed, We have made plain Our signs for a people who understand.

---

367. The following is said to them when they are resurrected.

99. And it is He Who sends down water from the sky. With it We bring forth all kinds of vegetation. From it We bring forth greenery, and clustered grain; and from the date-palm shoots come clusters of dates within reach. And [We bring forth] gardens of grapes, olives and pomegranates alike and unlike. Behold their fruits, when they bear fruit and their ripening, surely there are signs in that for a people who believe.

100. They set up the jinn as Allah's partners, although He created them; and they falsely ascribe to Him sons and daughters without any knowledge. Glory be to Him, and highly exalted is He above what they ascribe to Him!

101. [He is] the Creator of the heavens and the earth; how could He have a child when He has no consort, and has created every-thing and has knowledge of everything?

102. That is Allah, your Lord; there is no god but He, Creator of all things. Worship Him then; He is the Guardian of all things.

103. Vision does not attain Him, but He attains the vision, and He is the Kind, the All-Knowing.

104. Clear proofs have come to you from your Lord. Thus, he who perceives, perceives for his own advantage, and he who is blind, that is to his loss; and I am not your Keeper.

105. And thus We make clear the revelations so that they may say:[368] "You have studied",[369] and that We may make it clear to a people who know.

وَهُوَ ٱلَّذِىٓ أَنزَلَ مِنَ ٱلسَّمَآءِ مَآءً فَأَخْرَجْنَا بِهِۦ نَبَاتَ كُلِّ شَىْءٍ فَأَخْرَجْنَا مِنْهُ خَضِرًا نُّخْرِجُ مِنْهُ حَبًّا مُّتَرَاكِبًا وَمِنَ ٱلنَّخْلِ مِن طَلْعِهَا قِنْوَانٌ دَانِيَةٌ وَجَنَّٰتٍ مِّنْ أَعْنَابٍ وَٱلزَّيْتُونَ وَٱلرُّمَّانَ مُشْتَبِهًا وَغَيْرَ مُتَشَٰبِهٍ ٱنظُرُوٓا۟ إِلَىٰ ثَمَرِهِۦٓ إِذَآ أَثْمَرَ وَيَنْعِهِۦٓ إِنَّ فِى ذَٰلِكُمْ لَأٓيَٰتٍ لِّقَوْمٍ يُؤْمِنُونَ ﴿٩٩﴾

وَجَعَلُوا۟ لِلَّهِ شُرَكَآءَ ٱلْجِنَّ وَخَلَقَهُمْ وَخَرَقُوا۟ لَهُۥ بَنِينَ وَبَنَٰتٍ بِغَيْرِ عِلْمٍ سُبْحَٰنَهُۥ وَتَعَٰلَىٰ عَمَّا يَصِفُونَ ﴿١٠٠﴾

بَدِيعُ ٱلسَّمَٰوَٰتِ وَٱلْأَرْضِ أَنَّىٰ يَكُونُ لَهُۥ وَلَدٌ وَلَمْ تَكُن لَّهُۥ صَٰحِبَةٌ وَخَلَقَ كُلَّ شَىْءٍ وَهُوَ بِكُلِّ شَىْءٍ عَلِيمٌ ﴿١٠١﴾

ذَٰلِكُمُ ٱللَّهُ رَبُّكُمْ لَآ إِلَٰهَ إِلَّا هُوَ خَٰلِقُ كُلِّ شَىْءٍ فَٱعْبُدُوهُ وَهُوَ عَلَىٰ كُلِّ شَىْءٍ وَكِيلٌ ﴿١٠٢﴾

لَّا تُدْرِكُهُ ٱلْأَبْصَٰرُ وَهُوَ يُدْرِكُ ٱلْأَبْصَٰرَ وَهُوَ ٱللَّطِيفُ ٱلْخَبِيرُ ﴿١٠٣﴾

قَدْ جَآءَكُم بَصَآئِرُ مِن رَّبِّكُمْ فَمَنْ أَبْصَرَ فَلِنَفْسِهِۦ وَمَنْ عَمِىَ فَعَلَيْهَا وَمَآ أَنَا۠ عَلَيْكُم بِحَفِيظٍ ﴿١٠٤﴾

وَكَذَٰلِكَ نُصَرِّفُ ٱلْأٓيَٰتِ وَلِيَقُولُوا۟ دَرَسْتَ وَلِنُبَيِّنَهُۥ لِقَوْمٍ يَعْلَمُونَ ﴿١٠٥﴾

---

368. To Muhammad.
369. That is, discussed this with the People of the Book, or got it from the annals of the former peoples.

106. Follow what has been revealed to you from your Lord; for there is no god but He; and turn away from the polytheists.

107. Had Allah pleased, they would not have associated [other gods]; and We have not made you their keeper, and you are not their guardian.

108. Do not curse those [deities] whom they call upon besides Allah, lest they wrongfully curse Allah without knowledge. Thus We have made the deeds of every nation seem fair to them; then unto their Lord is their return, and He will tell them what they were doing.

109. They swear by Allah most solemnly that, were a sign to come to them, they would surely believe in it. Say: "Signs are only with Allah"; but how do you know that, if those signs come, they will still not believe?

110. And We will divert their hearts and their sights [from the truth], as they failed at first to believe in it; and We shall leave them dumbfounded in their wrongdoing.

111. Even if We send the angels to them and the dead speak to them, and if We bring everything before them, they would not believe, unless Allah wills; but most of them are ignorant.

112. Likewise, We have assigned to every Prophet an enemy, the devils of men and *jinn*, revealing one to the other tawdry speech in order to deceive; but had your Lord willed, they would not have done it. So leave them to what they invent;

113. So that the hearts of those who do not believe in the Hereafter may incline to it and accept it; as well as to perpetrate that which they themselves are perpetrating.

اتَّبِعْ مَا أُوحِيَ إِلَيْكَ مِن رَّبِّكَ لَا إِلَٰهَ إِلَّا هُوَ وَأَعْرِضْ عَنِ ٱلْمُشْرِكِينَ ﴿١٠٦﴾

وَلَوْ شَاءَ ٱللَّهُ مَا أَشْرَكُوا وَمَا جَعَلْنَاكَ عَلَيْهِمْ حَفِيظًا وَمَا أَنتَ عَلَيْهِم بِوَكِيلٍ ﴿١٠٧﴾

وَلَا تَسُبُّوا ٱلَّذِينَ يَدْعُونَ مِن دُونِ ٱللَّهِ فَيَسُبُّوا ٱللَّهَ عَدْوًا بِغَيْرِ عِلْمٍ كَذَٰلِكَ زَيَّنَّا لِكُلِّ أُمَّةٍ عَمَلَهُمْ ثُمَّ إِلَىٰ رَبِّهِم مَّرْجِعُهُمْ فَيُنَبِّئُهُم بِمَا كَانُوا يَعْمَلُونَ ﴿١٠٨﴾

وَأَقْسَمُوا بِٱللَّهِ جَهْدَ أَيْمَانِهِمْ لَئِن جَاءَتْهُمْ ءَايَةٌ لَّيُؤْمِنُنَّ بِهَا قُلْ إِنَّمَا ٱلْآيَاتُ عِندَ ٱللَّهِ وَمَا يُشْعِرُكُمْ أَنَّهَا إِذَا جَاءَتْ لَا يُؤْمِنُونَ ﴿١٠٩﴾

وَنُقَلِّبُ أَفْئِدَتَهُمْ وَأَبْصَارَهُمْ كَمَا لَمْ يُؤْمِنُوا بِهِ أَوَّلَ مَرَّةٍ وَنَذَرُهُمْ فِي طُغْيَانِهِمْ يَعْمَهُونَ ﴿١١٠﴾

۞ وَلَوْ أَنَّنَا نَزَّلْنَا إِلَيْهِمُ ٱلْمَلَائِكَةَ وَكَلَّمَهُمُ ٱلْمَوْتَىٰ وَحَشَرْنَا عَلَيْهِمْ كُلَّ شَيْءٍ قُبُلًا مَّا كَانُوا لِيُؤْمِنُوا إِلَّا أَن يَشَاءَ ٱللَّهُ وَلَٰكِنَّ أَكْثَرَهُمْ يَجْهَلُونَ ﴿١١١﴾

وَكَذَٰلِكَ جَعَلْنَا لِكُلِّ نَبِيٍّ عَدُوًّا شَيَاطِينَ ٱلْإِنسِ وَٱلْجِنِّ يُوحِي بَعْضُهُمْ إِلَىٰ بَعْضٍ زُخْرُفَ ٱلْقَوْلِ غُرُورًا وَلَوْ شَاءَ رَبُّكَ مَا فَعَلُوهُ فَذَرْهُمْ وَمَا يَفْتَرُونَ ﴿١١٢﴾

وَلِتَصْغَىٰ إِلَيْهِ أَفْئِدَةُ ٱلَّذِينَ لَا يُؤْمِنُونَ بِٱلْآخِرَةِ وَلِيَرْضَوْهُ وَلِيَقْتَرِفُوا مَا هُم مُّقْتَرِفُونَ ﴿١١٣﴾

114. Shall I seek a judge other than Allah, when He is the One Who sent down the Book to you fully expounded? Those to whom We have given the Book[370] know that it is revealed from your Lord in truth. Do not then be one of the doubters.

أَفَغَيْرَ ٱللَّهِ أَبْتَغِى حَكَمًا وَهُوَ ٱلَّذِىٓ أَنزَلَ إِلَيْكُمُ ٱلْكِتَـٰبَ مُفَصَّلًا وَٱلَّذِينَ ءَاتَيْنَـٰهُمُ ٱلْكِتَـٰبَ يَعْلَمُونَ أَنَّهُ مُنَزَّلٌ مِّن رَّبِّكَ بِٱلْحَقِّ فَلَا تَكُونَنَّ مِنَ ٱلْمُمْتَرِينَ ۝

115. The Word of your Lord has been completed in truth and justice; no one can change His Words. He is the All-Hearing, the All-Knowing.

وَتَمَّتْ كَلِمَتُ رَبِّكَ صِدْقًا وَعَدْلًا لَّا مُبَدِّلَ لِكَلِمَـٰتِهِ وَهُوَ ٱلسَّمِيعُ ٱلْعَلِيمُ ۝

116. And were you to obey most people on earth, they will lead you away from the Path of Allah. They follow nothing but conjecture, and they only lie.

وَإِن تُطِعْ أَكْثَرَ مَن فِى ٱلْأَرْضِ يُضِلُّوكَ عَن سَبِيلِ ٱللَّهِ إِن يَتَّبِعُونَ إِلَّا ٱلظَّنَّ وَإِنْ هُمْ إِلَّا يَخْرُصُونَ ۝

117. Your Lord knows best who strays from His Path, and He knows best who are the rightly guided.

إِنَّ رَبَّكَ هُوَ أَعْلَمُ مَن يَضِلُّ عَن سَبِيلِهِ وَهُوَ أَعْلَمُ بِٱلْمُهْتَدِينَ ۝

118. Eat, then, of that upon which the Name of Allah has been mentioned, if you really believe in His Revelations.

فَكُلُوا۟ مِمَّا ذُكِرَ ٱسْمُ ٱللَّهِ عَلَيْهِ إِن كُنتُم بِـَٔايَـٰتِهِ مُؤْمِنِينَ ۝

119. And why is it that you do not eat from that upon which Allah's Name is mentioned, when He has explained to you what is unlawful to you, except for what you are compelled to [eat]? Indeed many shall lead others astray by their fancies, without any knowledge. Surely, your Lord knows best the transgressors.

وَمَا لَكُمْ أَلَّا تَأْكُلُوا۟ مِمَّا ذُكِرَ ٱسْمُ ٱللَّهِ عَلَيْهِ وَقَدْ فَصَّلَ لَكُم مَّا حَرَّمَ عَلَيْكُمْ إِلَّا مَا ٱضْطُرِرْتُمْ إِلَيْهِ وَإِنَّ كَثِيرًا لَّيُضِلُّونَ بِأَهْوَآئِهِم بِغَيْرِ عِلْمٍ إِنَّ رَبَّكَ هُوَ أَعْلَمُ بِٱلْمُعْتَدِينَ ۝

120. Avoid open and secret sins. Surely those who commit sin shall be punished for what they have perpetrated.

وَذَرُوا۟ ظَـٰهِرَ ٱلْإِثْمِ وَبَاطِنَهُۥٓ إِنَّ ٱلَّذِينَ يَكْسِبُونَ ٱلْإِثْمَ سَيُجْزَوْنَ بِمَا كَانُوا۟ يَقْتَرِفُونَ ۝

121. And do not eat from that over which the Name of Allah has not been mentioned; it is indeed sinful. The devils shall insinuate to their followers to dispute with you; but if you obey them, then you will surely be poly-theists.

وَلَا تَأْكُلُوا۟ مِمَّا لَمْ يُذْكَرِ ٱسْمُ ٱللَّهِ عَلَيْهِ وَإِنَّهُۥ لَفِسْقٌ وَإِنَّ ٱلشَّيَـٰطِينَ لَيُوحُونَ إِلَىٰٓ أَوْلِيَآئِهِمْ لِيُجَـٰدِلُوكُمْ وَإِنْ أَطَعْتُمُوهُمْ إِنَّكُمْ لَمُشْرِكُونَ ۝

---

370. The Torah.

142

122. Is one who was dead, then We brought him back to life and gave him light to walk among the people, like one who is in total darkness and cannot get out of it? Thus the unbelievers' evil deeds are made attractive to them.

123. And thus We have set up in every city its leading wicked sinners so as to plot therein. However, they only plot against themselves, although they do not realize it.

124. And if a sign comes to them, they say: "We will not believe, until we are given the like of what Allah's Messengers have been given." Allah knows best where to place His Message. Those who commit sins will suffer humiliation and severe punishment from Allah on account of their plotting.

125. Whomever Allah wants to guide, He opens his heart up to Islam, and whomever He wants to lead astray, He makes his heart extremely constricted, as though he were ascending to heaven. Thus Allah inflicts His punishment upon those who do not believe.

126. This is the Path of your Lord, perfectly Straight. We have expounded the revelations to people who take heed.

127. Theirs is the abode of peace with their Lord and He is their Protector, for what they used to do.

128. And on the Day when He shall gather them all together [saying]: "O, company of jinn, you have misled a great many men." Their supporters among men will say: "Lord, we have profited much from each other and we have attained the term that you assigned for us." Then He will say: "The Fire is your resting-place, abiding therein forever, except as Allah wills. Your Lord is truly Wise, All-Knowing."

أَوَ مَن كَانَ مَيْتًا فَأَحْيَيْنَٰهُ وَجَعَلْنَا لَهُۥ نُورًا يَمْشِى بِهِۦ فِى ٱلنَّاسِ كَمَن مَّثَلُهُۥ فِى ٱلظُّلُمَٰتِ لَيْسَ بِخَارِجٍ مِّنْهَا ۚ كَذَٰلِكَ زُيِّنَ لِلْكَٰفِرِينَ مَا كَانُوا۟ يَعْمَلُونَ ﴿١٢٢﴾

وَكَذَٰلِكَ جَعَلْنَا فِى كُلِّ قَرْيَةٍ أَكَٰبِرَ مُجْرِمِيهَا لِيَمْكُرُوا۟ فِيهَا ۖ وَمَا يَمْكُرُونَ إِلَّا بِأَنفُسِهِمْ وَمَا يَشْعُرُونَ ﴿١٢٣﴾

وَإِذَا جَآءَتْهُمْ ءَايَةٌ قَالُوا۟ لَن نُّؤْمِنَ حَتَّىٰ نُؤْتَىٰ مِثْلَ مَآ أُوتِىَ رُسُلُ ٱللَّهِ ۘ ٱللَّهُ أَعْلَمُ حَيْثُ يَجْعَلُ رِسَالَتَهُۥ ۗ سَيُصِيبُ ٱلَّذِينَ أَجْرَمُوا۟ صَغَارٌ عِندَ ٱللَّهِ وَعَذَابٌ شَدِيدٌۢ بِمَا كَانُوا۟ يَمْكُرُونَ ﴿١٢٤﴾

فَمَن يُرِدِ ٱللَّهُ أَن يَهْدِيَهُۥ يَشْرَحْ صَدْرَهُۥ لِلْإِسْلَٰمِ ۖ وَمَن يُرِدْ أَن يُضِلَّهُۥ يَجْعَلْ صَدْرَهُۥ ضَيِّقًا حَرَجًا كَأَنَّمَا يَصَّعَّدُ فِى ٱلسَّمَآءِ ۚ كَذَٰلِكَ يَجْعَلُ ٱللَّهُ ٱلرِّجْسَ عَلَى ٱلَّذِينَ لَا يُؤْمِنُونَ ﴿١٢٥﴾

وَهَٰذَا صِرَٰطُ رَبِّكَ مُسْتَقِيمًا ۗ قَدْ فَصَّلْنَا ٱلْءَايَٰتِ لِقَوْمٍ يَذَّكَّرُونَ ﴿١٢٦﴾

۞ لَهُمْ دَارُ ٱلسَّلَٰمِ عِندَ رَبِّهِمْ ۖ وَهُوَ وَلِيُّهُم بِمَا كَانُوا۟ يَعْمَلُونَ ﴿١٢٧﴾

وَيَوْمَ يَحْشُرُهُمْ جَمِيعًا يَٰمَعْشَرَ ٱلْجِنِّ قَدِ ٱسْتَكْثَرْتُم مِّنَ ٱلْإِنسِ ۖ وَقَالَ أَوْلِيَآؤُهُم مِّنَ ٱلْإِنسِ رَبَّنَا ٱسْتَمْتَعَ بَعْضُنَا بِبَعْضٍ وَبَلَغْنَآ أَجَلَنَا ٱلَّذِىٓ أَجَّلْتَ لَنَا ۚ قَالَ ٱلنَّارُ مَثْوَىٰكُمْ خَٰلِدِينَ فِيهَآ إِلَّا مَا شَآءَ ٱللَّهُ ۗ إِنَّ رَبَّكَ حَكِيمٌ عَلِيمٌ ﴿١٢٨﴾

143

129. And thus We cause some of the evildoers to dominate the others, because of what they used to do.[371]

وَكَذَلِكَ نُوَلِّى بَعْضَ ٱلظَّٰلِمِينَ بَعْضًۢا بِمَا كَانُوا۟ يَكْسِبُونَ ﴿١٢٩﴾

130. O company of jinn and men, did there not come Messengers from among yourselves to you, reciting to you My Revelations and warning you of seeing this Day of yours? They will say: "We bear witness against ourselves." They were deluded by the earthly life and will bear witness against themselves that they were unbelievers.

يَٰمَعْشَرَ ٱلْجِنِّ وَٱلْإِنسِ أَلَمْ يَأْتِكُمْ رُسُلٌ مِّنكُمْ يَقُصُّونَ عَلَيْكُمْ ءَايَٰتِى وَيُنذِرُونَكُمْ لِقَآءَ يَوْمِكُمْ هَٰذَا قَالُوا۟ شَهِدْنَا عَلَىٰٓ أَنفُسِنَا وَغَرَّتْهُمُ ٱلْحَيَوٰةُ ٱلدُّنْيَا وَشَهِدُوا۟ عَلَىٰٓ أَنفُسِهِمْ أَنَّهُمْ كَانُوا۟ كَٰفِرِينَ ﴿١٣٠﴾

131. That is because your Lord would not destroy cities on account of their people's wrongdoing without warning them.[372]

ذَٰلِكَ أَن لَّمْ يَكُن رَّبُّكَ مُهْلِكَ ٱلْقُرَىٰ بِظُلْمٍ وَأَهْلُهَا غَٰفِلُونَ ﴿١٣١﴾

132. And to all are assigned ranks according to what they have done; and your Lord is not unaware of what they do.

وَلِكُلٍّ دَرَجَٰتٌ مِّمَّا عَمِلُوا۟ وَمَا رَبُّكَ بِغَٰفِلٍ عَمَّا يَعْمَلُونَ ﴿١٣٢﴾

133. Your Lord is the All-Sufficient, the Merciful. If He wishes, He will destroy you and bring out after you, as successors, whomever He wishes, as He had produced you from the seed of another people.

وَرَبُّكَ ٱلْغَنِىُّ ذُو ٱلرَّحْمَةِ إِن يَشَأْ يُذْهِبْكُمْ وَيَسْتَخْلِفْ مِنۢ بَعْدِكُم مَّا يَشَآءُ كَمَآ أَنشَأَكُم مِّن ذُرِّيَّةِ قَوْمٍ ءَاخَرِينَ ﴿١٣٣﴾

134. Indeed, whatever you are promised will surely come to pass, and you are not able to escape [it].

إِنَّ مَا تُوعَدُونَ لَءَاتٍ وَمَآ أَنتُم بِمُعْجِزِينَ ﴿١٣٤﴾

135. Say: "O my people, do whatever you can; and I shall do what I can. You shall surely know whose is the happy outcome in the Hereafter. Indeed, the wrongdoers shall not prosper."

قُلْ يَٰقَوْمِ ٱعْمَلُوا۟ عَلَىٰ مَكَانَتِكُمْ إِنِّى عَامِلٌ فَسَوْفَ تَعْلَمُونَ مَن تَكُونُ لَهُۥ عَٰقِبَةُ ٱلدَّارِ إِنَّهُۥ لَا يُفْلِحُ ٱلظَّٰلِمُونَ ﴿١٣٥﴾

136. They assigned to Allah a share of the tilth and cattle He created, saying: "This is for Allah," - as they declare - "and this is for our associate-gods." And while that which is assigned to their associate-gods does not

وَجَعَلُوا۟ لِلَّهِ مِمَّا ذَرَأَ مِنَ ٱلْحَرْثِ وَٱلْأَنْعَٰمِ نَصِيبًا فَقَالُوا۟ هَٰذَا لِلَّهِ بِزَعْمِهِمْ وَهَٰذَا لِشُرَكَآئِنَا فَمَا كَانَ لِشُرَكَآئِهِمْ فَلَا يَصِلُ إِلَى ٱللَّهِ وَمَا

---

371. That is, because of the evil they commit.
372. By sending a Messenger to them.

reach Allah, that which is set aside for Allah would reach their associate-gods. How evil is what they judge!

137. And likewise, their associate-gods have insinuated to them the killing of their children, so as to destroy them and confound them in their religion. Had Allah pleased, they would not have done it. So leave them to their fabrications.

138. And they say: "These cattle and tilth are taboo, and none shall eat them except those we wish," as they claim. And there are cattle whose backs are forbidden, and others over which they do not mention the Name of Allah. Such is their fabrication about Him. [But] He will punish them for their lies.

139. And they say: "What is in the bellies of these cattle is lawful to our males, but forbidden to our wives. If it is still-born both can share it." [Allah] will punish them for what they attribute [to Him]. He is surely Wise, All-Knowing.

140. Those who kill their children foolishly without knowledge are real losers; and they forbid what Allah has provided for them, thus fabricating lies against Allah. They go astray and they are not well-guided.

141. It is He Who created gardens, trellised and untrellised; palms and crops of diverse produce; and olives and pomegranates, both like and unlike. Eat of their fruits when they bear fruit, and pay their due on the day of harvesting them. And do not be prodigal; [for] He does not like the prodigals.

142. Of cattle there are some for burden and some for slaughter. Eat of what We provided for you and do not follow in the footsteps of the Devil. Surely he is a manifest enemy of yours.

كَانَ لِلّٰهِ فَهُوَ يَصِلُ إِلَىٰ شُرَكَآئِهِمْ سَآءَ مَا يَحْكُمُونَ ۝

وَكَذَٰلِكَ زَيَّنَ لِكَثِيرٍ مِّنَ ٱلْمُشْرِكِينَ قَتْلَ أَوْلَٰدِهِمْ شُرَكَآؤُهُمْ لِيُرْدُوهُمْ وَلِيَلْبِسُوا۟ عَلَيْهِمْ دِينَهُمْ وَلَوْ شَآءَ ٱللّٰهُ مَا فَعَلُوهُ فَذَرْهُمْ وَمَا يَفْتَرُونَ ۝

وَقَالُوا۟ هَٰذِهِۦ أَنْعَٰمٌ وَحَرْثٌ حِجْرٌ لَّا يَطْعَمُهَآ إِلَّا مَن نَّشَآءُ بِزَعْمِهِمْ وَأَنْعَٰمٌ حُرِّمَتْ ظُهُورُهَا وَأَنْعَٰمٌ لَّا يَذْكُرُونَ ٱسْمَ ٱللّٰهِ عَلَيْهَا ٱفْتِرَآءً عَلَيْهِ سَيَجْزِيهِم بِمَا كَانُوا۟ يَفْتَرُونَ ۝

وَقَالُوا۟ مَا فِى بُطُونِ هَٰذِهِ ٱلْأَنْعَٰمِ خَالِصَةٌ لِّذُكُورِنَا وَمُحَرَّمٌ عَلَىٰٓ أَزْوَٰجِنَا وَإِن يَكُن مَّيْتَةً فَهُمْ فِيهِ شُرَكَآءُ سَيَجْزِيهِمْ وَصْفَهُمْ إِنَّهُ حَكِيمٌ عَلِيمٌ ۝

قَدْ خَسِرَ ٱلَّذِينَ قَتَلُوٓا۟ أَوْلَٰدَهُمْ سَفَهًۢا بِغَيْرِ عِلْمٍ وَحَرَّمُوا۟ مَا رَزَقَهُمُ ٱللّٰهُ ٱفْتِرَآءً عَلَى ٱللّٰهِ قَدْ ضَلُّوا۟ وَمَا كَانُوا۟ مُهْتَدِينَ ۝

۞ وَهُوَ ٱلَّذِىٓ أَنشَأَ جَنَّٰتٍ مَّعْرُوشَٰتٍ وَغَيْرَ مَعْرُوشَٰتٍ وَٱلنَّخْلَ وَٱلزَّرْعَ مُخْتَلِفًا أُكُلُهُ وَٱلزَّيْتُونَ وَٱلرُّمَّانَ مُتَشَٰبِهًا وَغَيْرَ مُتَشَٰبِهٍ كُلُوا۟ مِن ثَمَرِهِۦٓ إِذَآ أَثْمَرَ وَءَاتُوا۟ حَقَّهُ يَوْمَ حَصَادِهِۦ وَلَا تُسْرِفُوٓا۟ إِنَّهُ لَا يُحِبُّ ٱلْمُسْرِفِينَ ۝

وَمِنَ ٱلْأَنْعَٰمِ حَمُولَةً وَفَرْشًا كُلُوا۟ مِمَّا رَزَقَكُمُ ٱللّٰهُ وَلَا تَتَّبِعُوا۟ خُطُوَٰتِ ٱلشَّيْطَٰنِ إِنَّهُ لَكُمْ عَدُوٌّ مُّبِينٌ ۝

143. [Take] eight in pairs: of sheep two and of goats two. Say: "Has He forbidden the two males, or the two females, or what the wombs of the two females contain? Tell me if you are truthful."

144. And [take] of camels two and of cows [and oxen] two. Say: "Has He forbidden the two males, the two females, or what the wombs of the females contain? Or have you been witnesses when Allah commanded you to do this?" Who then is more unjust than he who imputes falsehood to Allah, in order to lead people astray, without knowledge? Surely, Allah will not guide the wrongdoing people.

145. Say: "I do not find in what has been revealed to me anything forbidden to an eater to eat from, unless it is carrion, or running blood, or the flesh of swine - which are unclean. For it is profane and slaughtered to [gods] other than Allah. However, he who is constrained, intending neither to commit a sin nor to exceed the bounds, then surely your Lord is All-Forgiving, Merciful.

146. We have forbidden the Jews every [animal] with claws; and the fat of oxen and sheep except what their backs or entrails carry, or what is mixed with bones. This was the punishment We inflicted on them on account of their aggression. We are surely Truthful.

147. If they accuse you of lying, say: "Your Lord has an All-Encompassing Mercy and His Wrath cannot be prevented from afflicting the guilty people."

148. The polytheists will say: "If Allah pleased, we would not have associated [other gods with Him], nor would our fathers;

ثَمَـٰنِيَةَ أَزْوَٰجٍ مِّنَ ٱلضَّأْنِ ٱثْنَيْنِ وَمِنَ ٱلْمَعْزِ ٱثْنَيْنِ قُلْ ءَآلذَّكَرَيْنِ حَرَّمَ أَمِ ٱلْأُنثَيَيْنِ أَمَّا ٱشْتَمَلَتْ عَلَيْهِ أَرْحَامُ ٱلْأُنثَيَيْنِ نَبِّـُٔونِى بِعِلْمٍ إِن كُنتُمْ صَـٰدِقِينَ ﴿١٤٣﴾

وَمِنَ ٱلْإِبِلِ ٱثْنَيْنِ وَمِنَ ٱلْبَقَرِ ٱثْنَيْنِ قُلْ ءَآلذَّكَرَيْنِ حَرَّمَ أَمِ ٱلْأُنثَيَيْنِ أَمَّا ٱشْتَمَلَتْ عَلَيْهِ أَرْحَامُ ٱلْأُنثَيَيْنِ أَمْ كُنتُمْ شُهَدَآءَ إِذْ وَصَّىٰكُمُ ٱللَّهُ بِهَـٰذَا فَمَنْ أَظْلَمُ مِمَّنِ ٱفْتَرَىٰ عَلَى ٱللَّهِ كَذِبًا لِّيُضِلَّ ٱلنَّاسَ بِغَيْرِ عِلْمٍ إِنَّ ٱللَّهَ لَا يَهْدِى ٱلْقَوْمَ ٱلظَّـٰلِمِينَ ﴿١٤٤﴾

قُل لَّآ أَجِدُ فِى مَآ أُوحِىَ إِلَىَّ مُحَرَّمًا عَلَىٰ طَاعِمٍ يَطْعَمُهُۥٓ إِلَّآ أَن يَكُونَ مَيْتَةً أَوْ دَمًا مَّسْفُوحًا أَوْ لَحْمَ خِنزِيرٍ فَإِنَّهُۥ رِجْسٌ أَوْ فِسْقًا أُهِلَّ لِغَيْرِ ٱللَّهِ بِهِۦ فَمَنِ ٱضْطُرَّ غَيْرَ بَاغٍ وَلَا عَادٍ فَإِنَّ رَبَّكَ غَفُورٌ رَّحِيمٌ ﴿١٤٥﴾

وَعَلَى ٱلَّذِينَ هَادُوا۟ حَرَّمْنَا كُلَّ ذِى ظُفُرٍ وَمِنَ ٱلْبَقَرِ وَٱلْغَنَمِ حَرَّمْنَا عَلَيْهِمْ شُحُومَهُمَآ إِلَّا مَا حَمَلَتْ ظُهُورُهُمَآ أَوِ ٱلْحَوَايَآ أَوْ مَا ٱخْتَلَطَ بِعَظْمٍ ذَٰلِكَ جَزَيْنَـٰهُم بِبَغْيِهِمْ وَإِنَّا لَصَـٰدِقُونَ ﴿١٤٦﴾

فَإِن كَذَّبُوكَ فَقُل رَّبُّكُمْ ذُو رَحْمَةٍ وَٰسِعَةٍ وَلَا يُرَدُّ بَأْسُهُۥ عَنِ ٱلْقَوْمِ ٱلْمُجْرِمِينَ ﴿١٤٧﴾

سَيَقُولُ ٱلَّذِينَ أَشْرَكُوا۟ لَوْ شَآءَ ٱللَّهُ مَآ أَشْرَكْنَا وَلَآ ءَابَآؤُنَا وَلَا حَرَّمْنَا مِن شَىْءٍ كَذَٰلِكَ كَذَّبَ ٱلَّذِينَ

nor would we have forbidden anything." Thus those before them denied the truth until they tasted Our Wrath. Say: "Do you have any knowledge which you can produce for us? You only follow conjecture and you only tell lies."

149. Say: "To Allah belongs the decisive argument. Had He pleased He would have guided you all."

150. Say: "Produce your witnesses to testify that Allah has forbidden this." Then, if they testify, do not bear witness with them, and do not follow the fancies of those who deny Our Revelations and those who do not believe in the Hereafter and set up equals with their Lord."

151. Say: "Come, I will recite what your Lord has forbidden you: that you associate nothing with Him; that you show kindness to your parents; that you do not kill your children for fear of poverty; We will provide for you and for them; that you do not approach indecencies, whether open or secret; and that you do not kill the living soul which Allah has forbidden you to kill except for a just cause. This is what Allah commands you to do, so you may understand."

152. Do not approach the property of the orphan, except in the fairest manner, until he comes of age; and give full measure and weight equitably. We do not charge any soul except with what is within its power. And if you speak, be just even if it is against a relative, and fulfil Allah's Covenant. Thus He commands you, so that you may take heed.

153. This is indeed My Path, the straight path; follow it and do not follow the [other] paths, lest they divert you from His Path. Thus He commands you, that perchance you may fear God.

مِن قَبْلِهِمْ حَتَّىٰ ذَاقُوا بَأْسَنَا قُلْ هَلْ عِندَكُم مِّنْ عِلْمٍ فَتُخْرِجُوهُ لَنَا إِن تَتَّبِعُونَ إِلَّا ٱلظَّنَّ وَإِنْ أَنتُمْ إِلَّا تَخْرُصُونَ ۝

قُلْ فَلِلَّهِ ٱلْحُجَّةُ ٱلْبَٰلِغَةُ فَلَوْ شَآءَ لَهَدَىٰكُمْ أَجْمَعِينَ ۝

قُلْ هَلُمَّ شُهَدَآءَكُمُ ٱلَّذِينَ يَشْهَدُونَ أَنَّ ٱللَّهَ حَرَّمَ هَٰذَا فَإِن شَهِدُوا فَلَا تَشْهَدْ مَعَهُمْ وَلَا تَتَّبِعْ أَهْوَآءَ ٱلَّذِينَ كَذَّبُوا بِـَٔايَٰتِنَا وَٱلَّذِينَ لَا يُؤْمِنُونَ بِٱلْأَخِرَةِ وَهُم بِرَبِّهِمْ يَعْدِلُونَ ۝

۞ قُل تَعَالَوْا أَتْلُ مَا حَرَّمَ رَبُّكُمْ عَلَيْكُمْ أَلَّا تُشْرِكُوا بِهِ شَيْـًٔا وَبِٱلْوَٰلِدَيْنِ إِحْسَٰنًا وَلَا تَقْتُلُوا أَوْلَٰدَكُم مِّنْ إِمْلَٰقٍ نَّحْنُ نَرْزُقُكُمْ وَإِيَّاهُمْ وَلَا تَقْرَبُوا ٱلْفَوَٰحِشَ مَا ظَهَرَ مِنْهَا وَمَا بَطَنَ وَلَا تَقْتُلُوا ٱلنَّفْسَ ٱلَّتِي حَرَّمَ ٱللَّهُ إِلَّا بِٱلْحَقِّ ذَٰلِكُمْ وَصَّىٰكُم بِهِ لَعَلَّكُمْ تَعْقِلُونَ ۝

وَلَا تَقْرَبُوا مَالَ ٱلْيَتِيمِ إِلَّا بِٱلَّتِي هِيَ أَحْسَنُ حَتَّىٰ يَبْلُغَ أَشُدَّهُ وَأَوْفُوا ٱلْكَيْلَ وَٱلْمِيزَانَ بِٱلْقِسْطِ لَا نُكَلِّفُ نَفْسًا إِلَّا وُسْعَهَا وَإِذَا قُلْتُمْ فَٱعْدِلُوا وَلَوْ كَانَ ذَا قُرْبَىٰ وَبِعَهْدِ ٱللَّهِ أَوْفُوا ذَٰلِكُمْ وَصَّىٰكُم بِهِ لَعَلَّكُمْ تَذَكَّرُونَ ۝

وَأَنَّ هَٰذَا صِرَٰطِي مُسْتَقِيمًا فَٱتَّبِعُوهُ وَلَا تَتَّبِعُوا ٱلسُّبُلَ فَتَفَرَّقَ بِكُمْ عَن سَبِيلِهِ ذَٰلِكُمْ وَصَّىٰكُم بِهِ لَعَلَّكُمْ تَتَّقُونَ ۝

147

154. Then We gave Moses the Book, completing Our Grace on him who would do good, making plain everything and serving as a guidance and mercy, so that they[373] may believe in the encounter with their Lord.

155. This Book[374] which We sent down is blessed; so follow it and fear God, so that you may receive mercy.

156. Lest you should say: "The Book was revealed only to two sects[375] before us, and we were unaware of their reading."

157. Or lest you should say: "Had the Book been revealed to us, we would have been better guided than they." A clear proof has come to you from your Lord, and a guidance and mercy, too. Who, then, is more unjust than he who denies Allah's Revelations and turns away from them? We will surely inflict on those who turn away from Our Signs grievous punishment, because they turned away.

158. What! Do they expect the angels, or your Lord or some of your Lord's Signs to come to them? The day some of your Lord's Signs come, faith will not avail any soul which did not already accept it, nor earned some good through its faith. Say: "Wait, we too are awaiting."

159. Surely, you are not in any way part of those who have differentiated between parts of their religion and split into sects. Their fate is in Allah's Hands. He will inform them about what they have done.

ثُمَّ ءَاتَيْنَا مُوسَى ٱلْكِتَبَ تَمَامًا عَلَى ٱلَّذِى أَحْسَنَ وَتَفْصِيلًا لِّكُلِّ شَىْءٍ وَهُدًى وَرَحْمَةً لَّعَلَّهُم بِلِقَآءِ رَبِّهِمْ يُؤْمِنُونَ ۝

وَهَذَا كِتَبٌ أَنزَلْنَهُ مُبَارَكٌ فَٱتَّبِعُوهُ وَٱتَّقُوا لَعَلَّكُمْ تُرْحَمُونَ ۝

أَن تَقُولُوٓا إِنَّمَآ أُنزِلَ ٱلْكِتَبُ عَلَى طَآئِفَتَيْنِ مِن قَبْلِنَا وَإِن كُنَّا عَن دِرَاسَتِهِمْ لَغَفِلِينَ ۝

أَوْ تَقُولُوا لَوْ أَنَّا أُنزِلَ عَلَيْنَا ٱلْكِتَبُ لَكُنَّا أَهْدَى مِنْهُمْ فَقَدْ جَآءَكُم بَيِّنَةٌ مِّن رَّبِّكُمْ وَهُدًى وَرَحْمَةٌ فَمَنْ أَظْلَمُ مِمَّن كَذَّبَ بِـَٔايَتِ ٱللَّهِ وَصَدَفَ عَنْهَا سَنَجْزِى ٱلَّذِينَ يَصْدِفُونَ عَنْ ءَايَتِنَا سُوٓءَ ٱلْعَذَابِ بِمَا كَانُوا يَصْدِفُونَ ۝

هَلْ يَنظُرُونَ إِلَّآ أَن تَأْتِيَهُمُ ٱلْمَلَٰٓئِكَةُ أَوْ يَأْتِىَ رَبُّكَ أَوْ يَأْتِىَ بَعْضُ ءَايَتِ رَبِّكَ يَوْمَ يَأْتِى بَعْضُ ءَايَتِ رَبِّكَ لَا يَنفَعُ نَفْسًا إِيمَنُهَا لَمْ تَكُنْ ءَامَنَتْ مِن قَبْلُ أَوْ كَسَبَتْ فِىٓ إِيمَنِهَا خَيْرًا قُلِ ٱنتَظِرُوٓا إِنَّا مُنتَظِرُونَ ۝

إِنَّ ٱلَّذِينَ فَرَّقُوا دِينَهُمْ وَكَانُوا شِيَعًا لَّسْتَ مِنْهُمْ فِى شَىْءٍ إِنَّمَآ أَمْرُهُمْ إِلَى ٱللَّهِ ثُمَّ يُنَبِّئُهُم بِمَا كَانُوا يَفْعَلُونَ ۝

---

373. The Children of Israel.
374. The Qur'an.
375. The Jews and Christians.

160. He who comes up with a good deed shall have ten times its like; and he who comes up with an evil deed will only be requited for it once, and they shall not be wronged.

161. Say: "My Lord has guided me to a Straight Path, a right religion, the creed of Abraham, an upright man who was no polytheist."

162. Say: "My prayer and my sacrifice, my life and my death, are Allah's, the Lord of the Worlds.

163. "He has no associate, and thus I am commanded, and I am the first of those who submit."

164. Say: "Shall I seek a Lord other than Allah, Who is the Lord of all things? Every soul is accountable for what [evil] it commits, and no soul shall bear the burden of another soul. Then, unto your Lord is your return; and He will inform you about that over which you used to differ."

165. And it is He Who made you successors on earth, and raised some of you above the others in rank, so as to test you regarding what He has given you. Your Lord is indeed Quick in retribution, and He is indeed All-Forgiving, Merciful.

Sûrat Al-A'râf,
(The Ramparts) 7

In the Name of Allah,
the Compassionate, the Merciful

1. Alif - Lam - Mim - Sad.

2. [This is] a Book revealed to you;[376] let there be no gall in your heart because of it.

---

376. Muhammad.

[It is revealed] so that you may warn with it, and as a reminder to the believers.

لِتُنذِرَ بِهِۦ وَذِكْرَىٰ لِلْمُؤْمِنِينَ ﴿٢﴾

3. Follow what has been revealed to you from your Lord and do not follow other patrons besides Him. How little you heed the warning.

ٱتَّبِعُوا مَا أُنزِلَ إِلَيْكُم مِّن رَّبِّكُمْ وَلَا تَتَّبِعُوا مِن دُونِهِۦٓ أَوْلِيَآءَ قَلِيلًا مَّا تَذَكَّرُونَ ﴿٣﴾

4. How many a town We have destroyed; Our Might struck them at night or while they were napping.

وَكَم مِّن قَرْيَةٍ أَهْلَكْنَٰهَا فَجَآءَهَا بَأْسُنَا بَيَٰتًا أَوْ هُمْ قَآئِلُونَ ﴿٤﴾

5. Their only assertion when Our Might struck them was to say: "We have indeed been wrongdoers."

فَمَا كَانَ دَعْوَىٰهُمْ إِذْ جَآءَهُم بَأْسُنَآ إِلَّآ أَن قَالُوٓا إِنَّا كُنَّا ظَٰلِمِينَ ﴿٥﴾

6. So, We shall question those to whom Messengers were sent, and We shall question the Messengers.

فَلَنَسْـَٔلَنَّ ٱلَّذِينَ أُرْسِلَ إِلَيْهِمْ وَلَنَسْـَٔلَنَّ ٱلْمُرْسَلِينَ ﴿٦﴾

7. Then, We shall recount to them in full knowledge; for We are never absent.

فَلَنَقُصَّنَّ عَلَيْهِم بِعِلْمٍ وَمَا كُنَّا غَآئِبِينَ ﴿٧﴾

8. On that Day the weighing of deeds will be just; those whose scales are heavy will prosper;

وَٱلْوَزْنُ يَوْمَئِذٍ ٱلْحَقُّ فَمَن ثَقُلَتْ مَوَٰزِينُهُ فَأُو۟لَٰٓئِكَ هُمُ ٱلْمُفْلِحُونَ ﴿٨﴾

9. But those whose scales are light, are those who lost their souls on account of denying Our Revelations.

وَمَنْ خَفَّتْ مَوَٰزِينُهُ فَأُو۟لَٰٓئِكَ ٱلَّذِينَ خَسِرُوٓا أَنفُسَهُم بِمَا كَانُوا بِـَٔايَٰتِنَا يَظْلِمُونَ ﴿٩﴾

10. And We have established you firmly in the earth and provided you therein with means of livelihood. But seldom do you give thanks.

وَلَقَدْ مَكَّنَّٰكُمْ فِى ٱلْأَرْضِ وَجَعَلْنَا لَكُمْ فِيهَا مَعَٰيِشَ قَلِيلًا مَّا تَشْكُرُونَ ﴿١٠﴾

11. And We created you, then fashioned you, then said to the angels: "Prostrate yourselves to Adam"; so they prostrated themselves, except for Satan who was not one of those who prostrated themselves.

وَلَقَدْ خَلَقْنَٰكُمْ ثُمَّ صَوَّرْنَٰكُمْ ثُمَّ قُلْنَا لِلْمَلَٰٓئِكَةِ ٱسْجُدُوا لِـَٔادَمَ فَسَجَدُوٓا إِلَّآ إِبْلِيسَ لَمْ يَكُن مِّنَ ٱلسَّٰجِدِينَ ﴿١١﴾

12. He[377] said: "What prevented you from prostrating yourself when I commanded

قَالَ مَا مَنَعَكَ أَلَّا تَسْجُدَ إِذْ أَمَرْتُكَ قَالَ أَنَا۠ خَيْرٌ مِّنْهُ

---

377. That is, Allah.

you?" He[378] said: "I am better than he; You created me from fire, and You created him from clay."

خَلَقْتَنِي مِن نَّارٍ وَخَلَقْتَهُ مِن طِينٍ ۝

13. He said: "Get down from it,[379] then. It is not given you to be arrogant therein. Get out; you are indeed one of the lowly."

قَالَ فَاهْبِطْ مِنْهَا فَمَا يَكُونُ لَكَ أَن تَتَكَبَّرَ فِيهَا فَاخْرُجْ إِنَّكَ مِنَ الصَّاغِرِينَ ۝

14. Satan said: "Give me a respite, until the Day when they shall be resurrected."

قَالَ أَنظِرْنِي إِلَىٰ يَوْمِ يُبْعَثُونَ ۝

15. He (Allah) said: "You are one of those who are granted respite."

قَالَ إِنَّكَ مِنَ الْمُنظَرِينَ ۝

16. Satan said: "Because You have misled me, I will lie in wait for them on Your Straight Path.

قَالَ فَبِمَا أَغْوَيْتَنِي لَأَقْعُدَنَّ لَهُمْ صِرَاطَكَ الْمُسْتَقِيمَ ۝

17. "Then I will come upon them from before them and behind them, from their right and their left; and You will not find most of them thankful."

ثُمَّ لَآتِيَنَّهُم مِّن بَيْنِ أَيْدِيهِمْ وَمِنْ خَلْفِهِمْ وَعَنْ أَيْمَانِهِمْ وَعَن شَمَائِلِهِمْ وَلَا تَجِدُ أَكْثَرَهُمْ شَاكِرِينَ ۝

18. He (Allah) said: "Get out of it despised and vanquished. I will fill Hell with all who follow you!"

قَالَ اخْرُجْ مِنْهَا مَذْءُومًا مَّدْحُورًا لَّمَن تَبِعَكَ مِنْهُمْ لَأَمْلَأَنَّ جَهَنَّمَ مِنكُمْ أَجْمَعِينَ ۝

19. And [We said]: "Adam, dwell you and your wife in Paradise, and eat from wherever you wish; but do not come close to this tree, lest you both become wrongdoers."

وَيَا آدَمُ اسْكُنْ أَنتَ وَزَوْجُكَ الْجَنَّةَ فَكُلَا مِنْ حَيْثُ شِئْتُمَا وَلَا تَقْرَبَا هَذِهِ الشَّجَرَةَ فَتَكُونَا مِنَ الظَّالِمِينَ ۝

20. But Satan tempted them secretly in order to expose their nakedness to them saying: "Your Lord has forbidden you this tree, lest you become angels or become immortal."

فَوَسْوَسَ لَهُمَا الشَّيْطَانُ لِيُبْدِيَ لَهُمَا مَا وُورِيَ عَنْهُمَا مِن سَوْءَاتِهِمَا وَقَالَ مَا نَهَاكُمَا رَبُّكُمَا عَنْ هَذِهِ الشَّجَرَةِ إِلَّا أَن تَكُونَا مَلَكَيْنِ أَوْ تَكُونَا مِنَ الْخَالِدِينَ ۝

21. And he swore to them: "I am indeed a sincere advisor to you both."

وَقَاسَمَهُمَا إِنِّي لَكُمَا لَمِنَ النَّاصِحِينَ ۝

22. Then he brought about their downfall by deceit; so that when they tasted the tree, their private parts became visible to them, and they started to cover themselves with the leaves of Paradise. Then their Lord called out

فَدَلَّاهُمَا بِغُرُورٍ فَلَمَّا ذَاقَا الشَّجَرَةَ بَدَتْ لَهُمَا سَوْءَاتُهُمَا وَطَفِقَا يَخْصِفَانِ عَلَيْهِمَا مِن وَرَقِ الْجَنَّةِ وَنَادَاهُمَا رَبُّهُمَا أَلَمْ أَنْهَكُمَا عَن تِلْكُمَا الشَّجَرَةِ وَأَقُل لَّكُمَا

---

378. Satan.
379. Paradise.

to them: "Have I not forbidden you that tree and said to you: 'Indeed Satan is your sworn enemy'?"

23. They said: "Our Lord, we have wronged ourselves and if you do not forgive us and have mercy on us, we will surely be among the losers."

24. He said: "Go down, some of you as enemies of the others. On earth you will have a dwelling-place and a means of enjoyment for a while."

25. He said: "Therein you shall live and therein you shall die, and from it you will be brought out.

26. "O Children of Adam, We have provided you with clothing and finery to cover your private parts. But the attire of piety is the best." Such are Allah's Signs, that they may take heed.

27. "O Children of Adam, do not let Satan lead you astray as he drove your parents out of Paradise, stripping them of their clothes so as to show them their private parts. He and his host see you from a place where you cannot see them. We have made the devils the friends of those who do not believe."

28. When they commit an indecency, they say: "We have found our fathers doing it, and Allah commanded us to do it." Say: "Allah does not command indecencies. Do you impute to Allah what you do not know?"

29. Say: "My Lord commands justice. Set your faces straight at every place of prayer and call on Him in true devotion. As He originated you, you shall return.

إِنَّ ٱلشَّيْطَٰنَ لَكُمَا عَدُوٌّ مُّبِينٌ ۝

قَالَا رَبَّنَا ظَلَمْنَا أَنفُسَنَا وَإِن لَّمْ تَغْفِرْ لَنَا وَتَرْحَمْنَا لَنَكُونَنَّ مِنَ ٱلْخَٰسِرِينَ ۝

قَالَ ٱهْبِطُوا۟ بَعْضُكُمْ لِبَعْضٍ عَدُوٌّ وَلَكُمْ فِى ٱلْأَرْضِ مُسْتَقَرٌّ وَمَتَٰعٌ إِلَىٰ حِينٍ ۝

قَالَ فِيهَا تَحْيَوْنَ وَفِيهَا تَمُوتُونَ وَمِنْهَا تُخْرَجُونَ ۝

يَٰبَنِىٓ ءَادَمَ قَدْ أَنزَلْنَا عَلَيْكُمْ لِبَاسًا يُوَٰرِى سَوْءَٰتِكُمْ وَرِيشًا وَلِبَاسُ ٱلتَّقْوَىٰ ذَٰلِكَ خَيْرٌ ذَٰلِكَ مِنْ ءَايَٰتِ ٱللَّهِ لَعَلَّهُمْ يَذَّكَّرُونَ ۝

يَٰبَنِىٓ ءَادَمَ لَا يَفْتِنَنَّكُمُ ٱلشَّيْطَٰنُ كَمَآ أَخْرَجَ أَبَوَيْكُم مِّنَ ٱلْجَنَّةِ يَنزِعُ عَنْهُمَا لِبَاسَهُمَا لِيُرِيَهُمَا سَوْءَٰتِهِمَآ إِنَّهُ يَرَىٰكُمْ هُوَ وَقَبِيلُهُۥ مِنْ حَيْثُ لَا تَرَوْنَهُمْ إِنَّا جَعَلْنَا ٱلشَّيَٰطِينَ أَوْلِيَآءَ لِلَّذِينَ لَا يُؤْمِنُونَ ۝

وَإِذَا فَعَلُوا۟ فَٰحِشَةً قَالُوا۟ وَجَدْنَا عَلَيْهَآ ءَابَآءَنَا وَٱللَّهُ أَمَرَنَا بِهَا قُلْ إِنَّ ٱللَّهَ لَا يَأْمُرُ بِٱلْفَحْشَآءِ أَتَقُولُونَ عَلَى ٱللَّهِ مَا لَا تَعْلَمُونَ ۝

قُلْ أَمَرَ رَبِّى بِٱلْقِسْطِ وَأَقِيمُوا۟ وُجُوهَكُمْ عِندَ كُلِّ مَسْجِدٍ وَٱدْعُوهُ مُخْلِصِينَ لَهُ ٱلدِّينَ كَمَا بَدَأَكُمْ تَعُودُونَ ۝

30. "A group of you He has guided and another group was doomed to error; for they have taken the devils for patrons, apart from Allah, and they still think that they are rightly guided."

فَرِيقًا هَدَىٰ وَفَرِيقًا حَقَّ عَلَيْهِمُ الضَّلَٰلَةُ إِنَّهُمُ اتَّخَذُوا الشَّيَٰطِينَ أَوْلِيَآءَ مِن دُونِ اللَّهِ وَيَحْسَبُونَ أَنَّهُم مُّهْتَدُونَ ﴿٣٠﴾

31. O Children of Adam, put on your finery at every place of prayer. Eat and drink, but do not be prodigal, He does not like the prodigals.

۞ يَٰبَنِىٓ ءَادَمَ خُذُوا زِينَتَكُمْ عِندَ كُلِّ مَسْجِدٍ وَكُلُوا وَاشْرَبُوا وَلَا تُسْرِفُوٓا إِنَّهُ لَا يُحِبُّ الْمُسْرِفِينَ ﴿٣١﴾

32. Say: "Who has forbidden Allah's finery which He fashioned for His servants, or the good things He provided?" Say: "These are meant, in this present world, for those who believe, and exclusively for them on the Day of Resurrection." Thus We make clear Our Revelations for a people who know.

قُلْ مَنْ حَرَّمَ زِينَةَ اللَّهِ الَّتِىٓ أَخْرَجَ لِعِبَادِهِ وَالطَّيِّبَٰتِ مِنَ الرِّزْقِ قُلْ هِىَ لِلَّذِينَ ءَامَنُوا فِى الْحَيَوٰةِ الدُّنْيَا خَالِصَةً يَوْمَ الْقِيَٰمَةِ كَذَٰلِكَ نُفَصِّلُ الْءَايَٰتِ لِقَوْمٍ يَعْلَمُونَ ﴿٣٢﴾

33. Say: "My Lord has only forbidden open and secret indecencies, sin, unjust aggression, and your association with Allah that for which He sent down no authority, and your saying about Allah that which you do not know."

قُلْ إِنَّمَا حَرَّمَ رَبِّىَ الْفَوَٰحِشَ مَا ظَهَرَ مِنْهَا وَمَا بَطَنَ وَالْإِثْمَ وَالْبَغْىَ بِغَيْرِ الْحَقِّ وَأَن تُشْرِكُوا بِاللَّهِ مَا لَمْ يُنَزِّلْ بِهِۦ سُلْطَٰنًا وَأَن تَقُولُوا عَلَى اللَّهِ مَا لَا تَعْلَمُونَ ﴿٣٣﴾

34. For every nation there is a [fixed] term, so that when its term comes, they will not be able to put it back or bring it forward a single hour.

وَلِكُلِّ أُمَّةٍ أَجَلٌ فَإِذَا جَآءَ أَجَلُهُمْ لَا يَسْتَأْخِرُونَ سَاعَةً وَلَا يَسْتَقْدِمُونَ ﴿٣٤﴾

35. "O Children of Adam, when Messengers from your own people come to you reciting to you My Verses - then those who fear God and mend their ways have nothing to fear, and they will not grieve."

يَٰبَنِىٓ ءَادَمَ إِمَّا يَأْتِيَنَّكُمْ رُسُلٌ مِّنكُمْ يَقُصُّونَ عَلَيْكُمْ ءَايَٰتِى فَمَنِ اتَّقَىٰ وَأَصْلَحَ فَلَا خَوْفٌ عَلَيْهِمْ وَلَا هُمْ يَحْزَنُونَ ﴿٣٥﴾

36. But those who deny Our Revelations and reject them arrogantly - those are the people of the Fire; therein they shall abide forever.

وَالَّذِينَ كَذَّبُوا بِـَٔايَٰتِنَا وَاسْتَكْبَرُوا عَنْهَآ أُوْلَٰٓئِكَ أَصْحَٰبُ النَّارِ هُمْ فِيهَا خَٰلِدُونَ ﴿٣٦﴾

37. For who is more unjust than he who fabricates lies about Allah or denies His Revelations? Those will get their share of the

فَمَنْ أَظْلَمُ مِمَّنِ افْتَرَىٰ عَلَى اللَّهِ كَذِبًا أَوْ كَذَّبَ بِـَٔايَٰتِهِۦٓ أُوْلَٰٓئِكَ يَنَالُهُمْ نَصِيبُهُم مِّنَ الْكِتَٰبِ حَتَّىٰٓ إِذَا جَآءَتْهُمْ

punishment ordained for them. When Our Messengers[380] come to take their souls they will say: "Where are those upon whom you called besides Allah?" They will say: "They have left us", and they will bear witness against themselves that they were unbelievers.

38. Allah will say: "Enter together with nations who have gone before you, jinn and men, into the Fire. Every time a nation enters it, it curses its sister-nation; so that when they shall have followed each other into it, the last of them will say of the first: "Our Lord, these led us astray; inflict on them a double punishment in the Fire." He will say: "A double [punishment] to each, but you do not know."

39. And the first of them will say to the last: "In no way are you better than us; so taste the punishment for what you did."

40. Indeed, those who have denied Our Revelations and rejected them arrogantly - the gates of heaven shall not be opened for them and they shall not enter Paradise until the camel passes through the eye of the needle. Thus We punish the wicked sinners.

41. Hell shall be their couch and over them shall be canopies [of fire]. Thus We punish the wrongdoers.

42. As to those who believe and do the good deeds, We do not charge any soul except with what is within its power. Those are the people of Paradise, abiding therein forever.

43. And We shall remove all rancour from their hearts; and under them rivers will flow. They will say: "Praise be to Allah Who guided us to this; we would never have

رُسُلُنَا يَتَوَفَّوْنَهُمْ قَالُوٓاْ أَيْنَ مَا كُنتُمْ تَدْعُونَ مِن دُونِ ٱللَّهِ قَالُواْ ضَلُّواْ عَنَّا وَشَهِدُواْ عَلَىٰٓ أَنفُسِهِمْ أَنَّهُمْ كَانُواْ كَٰفِرِينَ ﴿٣٧﴾

قَالَ ٱدْخُلُواْ فِىٓ أُمَمٍ قَدْ خَلَتْ مِن قَبْلِكُم مِّنَ ٱلْجِنِّ وَٱلْإِنسِ فِى ٱلنَّارِ كُلَّمَا دَخَلَتْ أُمَّةٌ لَّعَنَتْ أُخْتَهَا حَتَّىٰٓ إِذَا ٱدَّارَكُواْ فِيهَا جَمِيعًا قَالَتْ أُخْرَىٰهُمْ لِأُولَىٰهُمْ رَبَّنَا هَٰٓؤُلَآءِ أَضَلُّونَا فَـَٔاتِهِمْ عَذَابًا ضِعْفًا مِّنَ ٱلنَّارِ قَالَ لِكُلٍّ ضِعْفٌ وَلَٰكِن لَّا تَعْلَمُونَ ﴿٣٨﴾

وَقَالَتْ أُولَىٰهُمْ لِأُخْرَىٰهُمْ فَمَا كَانَ لَكُمْ عَلَيْنَا مِن فَضْلٍ فَذُوقُواْ ٱلْعَذَابَ بِمَا كُنتُمْ تَكْسِبُونَ ﴿٣٩﴾

إِنَّ ٱلَّذِينَ كَذَّبُواْ بِـَٔايَٰتِنَا وَٱسْتَكْبَرُواْ عَنْهَا لَا تُفَتَّحُ لَهُمْ أَبْوَٰبُ ٱلسَّمَآءِ وَلَا يَدْخُلُونَ ٱلْجَنَّةَ حَتَّىٰ يَلِجَ ٱلْجَمَلُ فِى سَمِّ ٱلْخِيَاطِ وَكَذَٰلِكَ نَجْزِى ٱلْمُجْرِمِينَ ﴿٤٠﴾

لَهُم مِّن جَهَنَّمَ مِهَادٌ وَمِن فَوْقِهِمْ غَوَاشٍ وَكَذَٰلِكَ نَجْزِى ٱلظَّٰلِمِينَ ﴿٤١﴾

وَٱلَّذِينَ ءَامَنُواْ وَعَمِلُواْ ٱلصَّٰلِحَٰتِ لَا نُكَلِّفُ نَفْسًا إِلَّا وُسْعَهَآ أُوْلَٰٓئِكَ أَصْحَٰبُ ٱلْجَنَّةِ هُمْ فِيهَا خَٰلِدُونَ ﴿٤٢﴾

وَنَزَعْنَا مَا فِى صُدُورِهِم مِّنْ غِلٍّ تَجْرِى مِن تَحْتِهِمُ ٱلْأَنْهَٰرُ وَقَالُواْ ٱلْحَمْدُ لِلَّهِ ٱلَّذِى هَدَىٰنَا لِهَٰذَا وَمَا كُنَّا لِنَهْتَدِىَ

---

380. The Angels, messengers of death.

been guided, had not Allah guided us. The Messengers of our Lord came with the truth." Then a voice will cry out to them: "This is indeed the Paradise which you have been made to inherit for what [good] you used to do."

44. And the people of Paradise will call out to the people of the Fire: "We have found what our Lord promised us to be true; so have you found what your Lord promised to be true?" They will say: "Yes". Thereupon a caller from their midst shall call out: "May Allah's curse be upon the wrongdoers;

45. "Who bar [others] from Allah's Way and desire it to be crooked; and they disbelieve in the Hereafter."

46. Between them[381] is a veil, and on the Ramparts[382] are men who know everyone by his mark. And they will call out to the people of Paradise: "Peace be upon you." That is, before they[383] enter it, though they hope to do so.

47. And when their eyes are turned towards the people of the Fire, they will say: "Lord, do not place us among the wrongdoing people."

48. And the people of the Ramparts will cry out to some men whom they will recognize by their marks saying: "Your amassing [of wealth] and your arrogance are of no avail to you."

49. "Are those the people that you swore Allah will have no mercy on?" [To these people will be said]: "Enter Paradise, you have nothing to fear, and you shall not grieve."

---

381. The people of Paradise and the people of the Fire.
382. The walls separating Paradise from Hell.
383. Those on the Ramparts.

155

50. Then the people of the Fire will call out to the people of Paradise: "Pour out upon us some water or part of what Allah has provided you with." They will say: "Allah forbids them both unto the unbelievers,

51. "Who take their religion as an amusement and sport, and the present life deludes them." Today, We forget them as they forgot the encounter of this Day and used to deny Our Revelations."

52. And We have brought them a Book, which We have expounded with knowledge, as a guidance and mercy for a people who believe.

53. Do they only wait for its fulfilment? The Day its fulfilment comes, those who forgot it before will say: "The Messengers of our Lord brought the truth. Have we then any intercessors to intercede for us, or shall we be taken back, so as to do something other than what we used to do?" They have indeed lost their souls, and what they fabricated has failed them.

54. Your Lord is truly Allah, Who has created the heavens and the earth in six days, then He sat upon the Throne. He covers the day with the night, which pursues it relentlessly. The sun, the moon and the stars are made subservient by His Command. To Him belongs the Creation and the Command. Blessed is Allah the Lord of the Worlds.

55. Call on your Lord humbly and secretly. He certainly does not like the aggressors.

56. And do not sow corruption in the land after it has been put in order. Call on Him with fear and hope. Allah's Mercy is indeed close at hand for the beneficent.

وَنَادَىٰ أَصْحَٰبُ ٱلنَّارِ أَصْحَٰبَ ٱلْجَنَّةِ أَنْ أَفِيضُوا۟ عَلَيْنَا مِنَ ٱلْمَآءِ أَوْ مِمَّا رَزَقَكُمُ ٱللَّهُ قَالُوٓا۟ إِنَّ ٱللَّهَ حَرَّمَهُمَا عَلَى ٱلْكَٰفِرِينَ ﴿٥٠﴾

ٱلَّذِينَ ٱتَّخَذُوا۟ دِينَهُمْ لَهْوًا وَلَعِبًا وَغَرَّتْهُمُ ٱلْحَيَوٰةُ ٱلدُّنْيَا فَٱلْيَوْمَ نَنسَىٰهُمْ كَمَا نَسُوا۟ لِقَآءَ يَوْمِهِمْ هَٰذَا وَمَا كَانُوا۟ بِـَٔايَٰتِنَا يَجْحَدُونَ ﴿٥١﴾

وَلَقَدْ جِئْنَٰهُم بِكِتَٰبٍ فَصَّلْنَٰهُ عَلَىٰ عِلْمٍ هُدًى وَرَحْمَةً لِّقَوْمٍ يُؤْمِنُونَ ﴿٥٢﴾

هَلْ يَنظُرُونَ إِلَّا تَأْوِيلَهُۥ يَوْمَ يَأْتِى تَأْوِيلُهُۥ يَقُولُ ٱلَّذِينَ نَسُوهُ مِن قَبْلُ قَدْ جَآءَتْ رُسُلُ رَبِّنَا بِٱلْحَقِّ فَهَل لَّنَا مِن شُفَعَآءَ فَيَشْفَعُوا۟ لَنَآ أَوْ نُرَدُّ فَنَعْمَلَ غَيْرَ ٱلَّذِى كُنَّا نَعْمَلُ قَدْ خَسِرُوٓا۟ أَنفُسَهُمْ وَضَلَّ عَنْهُم مَّا كَانُوا۟ يَفْتَرُونَ ﴿٥٣﴾

إِنَّ رَبَّكُمُ ٱللَّهُ ٱلَّذِى خَلَقَ ٱلسَّمَٰوَٰتِ وَٱلْأَرْضَ فِى سِتَّةِ أَيَّامٍ ثُمَّ ٱسْتَوَىٰ عَلَى ٱلْعَرْشِ يُغْشِى ٱلَّيْلَ ٱلنَّهَارَ يَطْلُبُهُۥ حَثِيثًا وَٱلشَّمْسَ وَٱلْقَمَرَ وَٱلنُّجُومَ مُسَخَّرَٰتٍ بِأَمْرِهِۦٓ أَلَا لَهُ ٱلْخَلْقُ وَٱلْأَمْرُ تَبَارَكَ ٱللَّهُ رَبُّ ٱلْعَٰلَمِينَ ﴿٥٤﴾

ٱدْعُوا۟ رَبَّكُمْ تَضَرُّعًا وَخُفْيَةً إِنَّهُۥ لَا يُحِبُّ ٱلْمُعْتَدِينَ ﴿٥٥﴾

وَلَا تُفْسِدُوا۟ فِى ٱلْأَرْضِ بَعْدَ إِصْلَٰحِهَا وَٱدْعُوهُ خَوْفًا وَطَمَعًا إِنَّ رَحْمَتَ ٱللَّهِ قَرِيبٌ مِّنَ ٱلْمُحْسِنِينَ ﴿٥٦﴾

57. It is He Who sends forth the winds bearing good news of His Mercy; so that when they bear heavy clouds, We drive them towards some dead land upon which We send down water. With it We bring forth every variety of fruit. Thus We bring out the dead, so that you may take heed.

58. Good land[384] produces vegetation by the Will of its Lord; but that which has gone bad will not produce vegetation except with difficulty. Thus We make plain the revelations to a people who give thanks.

59. We sent Noah forth to his people, and he said: "O my people, worship Allah, you have no other god but Him. I fear for you the punishment of an Awful Day."

60. The dignitaries among his people said: "We see you, indeed, in manifest error."

61. He said: "O my people, I am not in any error, but am a Messenger from the Lord of the Worlds.

62. "I deliver to you the Messages of my Lord and give you good advice, and I know from Allah what you do not know.

63. "Do you wonder that a reminder from your Lord has come to you at the hands of a man from your own people to warn you, and to induce you to fear Allah so that mercy may be shown to you?"

64. However, they denounced him, and so We delivered him, together with those in the ark, and drowned those who denied Our Revelations. For they were indeed a blind people.

65. And to 'Ad,[385] [We sent] their brother Hud. He said: "O my people, worship Allah; you have no other god but He. Will you not fear [Allah]?"

وَهُوَ ٱلَّذِى يُرْسِلُ ٱلرِّيَٰحَ بُشْرًۢا بَيْنَ يَدَىْ رَحْمَتِهِۦ حَتَّىٰٓ إِذَآ أَقَلَّتْ سَحَابًا ثِقَالًا سُقْنَٰهُ لِبَلَدٍ مَّيِّتٍ فَأَنزَلْنَا بِهِ ٱلْمَآءَ فَأَخْرَجْنَا بِهِۦ مِن كُلِّ ٱلثَّمَرَٰتِ كَذَٰلِكَ نُخْرِجُ ٱلْمَوْتَىٰ لَعَلَّكُمْ تَذَكَّرُونَ ﴿٥٧﴾

وَٱلْبَلَدُ ٱلطَّيِّبُ يَخْرُجُ نَبَاتُهُۥ بِإِذْنِ رَبِّهِۦ وَٱلَّذِى خَبُثَ لَا يَخْرُجُ إِلَّا نَكِدًا كَذَٰلِكَ نُصَرِّفُ ٱلْءَايَٰتِ لِقَوْمٍ يَشْكُرُونَ ﴿٥٨﴾

لَقَدْ أَرْسَلْنَا نُوحًا إِلَىٰ قَوْمِهِۦ فَقَالَ يَٰقَوْمِ ٱعْبُدُوا۟ ٱللَّهَ مَا لَكُم مِّنْ إِلَٰهٍ غَيْرُهُۥٓ إِنِّىٓ أَخَافُ عَلَيْكُمْ عَذَابَ يَوْمٍ عَظِيمٍ ﴿٥٩﴾

قَالَ ٱلْمَلَأُ مِن قَوْمِهِۦٓ إِنَّا لَنَرَىٰكَ فِى ضَلَٰلٍ مُّبِينٍ ﴿٦٠﴾

قَالَ يَٰقَوْمِ لَيْسَ بِى ضَلَٰلَةٌ وَلَٰكِنِّى رَسُولٌ مِّن رَّبِّ ٱلْعَٰلَمِينَ ﴿٦١﴾

أُبَلِّغُكُمْ رِسَٰلَٰتِ رَبِّى وَأَنصَحُ لَكُمْ وَأَعْلَمُ مِنَ ٱللَّهِ مَا لَا تَعْلَمُونَ ﴿٦٢﴾

أَوَعَجِبْتُمْ أَن جَآءَكُمْ ذِكْرٌ مِّن رَّبِّكُمْ عَلَىٰ رَجُلٍ مِّنكُمْ لِيُنذِرَكُمْ وَلِتَتَّقُوا۟ وَلَعَلَّكُمْ تُرْحَمُونَ ﴿٦٣﴾

فَكَذَّبُوهُ فَأَنجَيْنَٰهُ وَٱلَّذِينَ مَعَهُۥ فِى ٱلْفُلْكِ وَأَغْرَقْنَا ٱلَّذِينَ كَذَّبُوا۟ بِـَٔايَٰتِنَآ إِنَّهُمْ كَانُوا۟ قَوْمًا عَمِينَ ﴿٦٤﴾

۞ وَإِلَىٰ عَادٍ أَخَاهُمْ هُودًا قَالَ يَٰقَوْمِ ٱعْبُدُوا۟ ٱللَّهَ مَا لَكُم مِّنْ إِلَٰهٍ غَيْرُهُۥٓ أَفَلَا تَتَّقُونَ ﴿٦٥﴾

---

384. That is, land with a good soil.
385. A pre-Islamic Arab tribe.

66. The dignitaries of his people, who were unbelievers, said: "We see that you are foolish and we believe that you are a liar."

67. He said: "O my people, I am not foolish but am a Messenger from the Lord of the Worlds;

68. "Delivering to you the Revelations of my Lord, and I am a sincere advisor of yours.

69. "Do you wonder that a Reminder from your Lord has come to you through a man of your own people, in order to warn you? Remember how He made you successors[386] after the people of Noah and increased you in physical stature. Remember then Allah's Bounties, that perchance you may prosper."

70. They said: "Have you come to us, so that we may worship Allah alone and forsake what our fathers used to worship? Bring us then what you promise us, if you are one of the truthful."

71. He said: "A scourge and wrath have descended on you from your Lord. Do you dispute with me over names[387] which you and your fathers have invented, and for which Allah has sent down no authority? Wait[388] then. Surely I shall be, along with you, among those who wait."

72. We delivered him thereupon, with those in his company, by a mercy from Us, and cut off the roots of those who denied Our Revelations and were no believers.

73. And to Thamud[389] [We sent] their brother Salih. He said: "O my people, worship Allah; you have no other god but He. A clear proof

قَالَ ٱلۡمَلَأُ ٱلَّذِينَ كَفَرُوا۟ مِن قَوۡمِهِۦٓ إِنَّا لَنَرَىٰكَ فِى سَفَاهَةٖ وَإِنَّا لَنَظُنُّكَ مِنَ ٱلۡكَٰذِبِينَ ٦٦

قَالَ يَٰقَوۡمِ لَيۡسَ بِى سَفَاهَةٞ وَلَٰكِنِّى رَسُولٞ مِّن رَّبِّ ٱلۡعَٰلَمِينَ ٦٧

أُبَلِّغُكُمۡ رِسَٰلَٰتِ رَبِّى وَأَنَا۠ لَكُمۡ نَاصِحٌ أَمِينٌ ٦٨

أَوَعَجِبۡتُمۡ أَن جَآءَكُمۡ ذِكۡرٞ مِّن رَّبِّكُمۡ عَلَىٰ رَجُلٖ مِّنكُمۡ لِيُنذِرَكُمۡ وَٱذۡكُرُوٓا۟ إِذۡ جَعَلَكُمۡ خُلَفَآءَ مِنۢ بَعۡدِ قَوۡمِ نُوحٖ وَزَادَكُمۡ فِى ٱلۡخَلۡقِ بَصۜۡطَةٗ فَٱذۡكُرُوٓا۟ ءَالَآءَ ٱللَّهِ لَعَلَّكُمۡ تُفۡلِحُونَ ٦٩

قَالُوٓا۟ أَجِئۡتَنَا لِنَعۡبُدَ ٱللَّهَ وَحۡدَهُۥ وَنَذَرَ مَا كَانَ يَعۡبُدُ ءَابَآؤُنَا فَأۡتِنَا بِمَا تَعِدُنَآ إِن كُنتَ مِنَ ٱلصَّٰدِقِينَ ٧٠

قَالَ قَدۡ وَقَعَ عَلَيۡكُم مِّن رَّبِّكُمۡ رِجۡسٞ وَغَضَبٌ أَتُجَٰدِلُونَنِى فِىٓ أَسۡمَآءٖ سَمَّيۡتُمُوهَآ أَنتُمۡ وَءَابَآؤُكُم مَّا نَزَّلَ ٱللَّهُ بِهَا مِن سُلۡطَٰنٖ فَٱنتَظِرُوٓا۟ إِنِّى مَعَكُم مِّنَ ٱلۡمُنتَظِرِينَ ٧١

فَأَنجَيۡنَٰهُ وَٱلَّذِينَ مَعَهُۥ بِرَحۡمَةٖ مِّنَّا وَقَطَعۡنَا دَابِرَ ٱلَّذِينَ كَذَّبُوا۟ بِـَٔايَٰتِنَا وَمَا كَانُوا۟ مُؤۡمِنِينَ ٧٢

وَإِلَىٰ ثَمُودَ أَخَاهُمۡ صَٰلِحٗا قَالَ يَٰقَوۡمِ ٱعۡبُدُوا۟ ٱللَّهَ مَا لَكُم مِّنۡ إِلَٰهٍ غَيۡرُهُۥ قَدۡ جَآءَتۡكُم بَيِّنَةٞ

---

386. That is, possessors of a vast kingdom.
387. Names of idols.
388. That is, wait for the punishment.
389. An Arab tribe.

from your Lord has now come to you. This is Allah's she-camel, to be a sign unto you; so let it graze in Allah's Land and do not cause her any harm; for you will then be seized by a very painful punishment.

74. "And remember how He made you as successors after 'Ad, and established you in the land, wherein you built yourselves castles on its plains and hewed the mountains into houses. Remember then Allah's Bounties and do not corrupt the earth with mischief."

75. The arrogant dignitaries among his people said to some of those who had believed and were deemed to be weak: "Do you know that Salih is sent forth from his Lord?" They said: "Indeed, we believe in what he has been sent with."

76. The arrogant dignitaries said: "In that which you have believed, we definitely disbelieve."

77. So they hamstrung the she-camel and defied their Lord's Command and said: "O Salih, bring upon us what you are promising us, if you are one of the Messengers."

78. Whereupon the earthquake overtook them, and so they lay prostrate in their own homes.

79. Then he turned his back on them and said: "O my people, I have delivered to you my Lord's Message and given you advice, but you do not like the givers of advice."

80. And [remember] Lot when he said to his people: "Do you commit indecencies which no one in the whole world committed before you?"

81. "You approach men instead of women lustfully; you are rather a people given to excess."

159

82. His people's response was simply to say: "Expel them[390] from your city; for they are men who wish to remain chaste."

وَمَا كَانَ جَوَابَ قَوْمِهِ إِلَّا أَن قَالُوٓا أَخْرِجُوهُم مِّن قَرْيَتِكُمْ إِنَّهُمْ أُنَاسٌ يَتَطَهَّرُونَ ۝

83. So We delivered him and his household, except for his wife who stayed behind.

فَأَنجَيْنَاهُ وَأَهْلَهُۥٓ إِلَّا ٱمْرَأَتَهُۥ كَانَتْ مِنَ ٱلْغَابِرِينَ ۝

84. And We rained a shower [of brimstone] upon them. See then what was the end of the sinners.

وَأَمْطَرْنَا عَلَيْهِم مَّطَرًا فَٱنظُرْ كَيْفَ كَانَ عَٰقِبَةُ ٱلْمُجْرِمِينَ ۝

85. And [to the people of] Midian We sent their brother Shu'ayb, who said: "O my people, worship Allah, you have no other god but He. A clear proof has now come to you from your Lord; so fulfil the measure and the weight; and do not withhold anything of what is due to people; and do not make mischief in the land after it has been put in order. That is better for you if you are true believers.

وَإِلَىٰ مَدْيَنَ أَخَاهُمْ شُعَيْبًا قَالَ يَٰقَوْمِ ٱعْبُدُوا۟ ٱللَّهَ مَا لَكُم مِّنْ إِلَٰهٍ غَيْرُهُۥ قَدْ جَآءَتْكُم بَيِّنَةٌ مِّن رَّبِّكُمْ فَأَوْفُوا۟ ٱلْكَيْلَ وَٱلْمِيزَانَ وَلَا تَبْخَسُوا۟ ٱلنَّاسَ أَشْيَآءَهُمْ وَلَا تُفْسِدُوا۟ فِى ٱلْأَرْضِ بَعْدَ إِصْلَٰحِهَا ذَٰلِكُمْ خَيْرٌ لَّكُمْ إِن كُنتُم مُّؤْمِنِينَ ۝

86. "And do not sit down at every roadside, threatening and barring from Allah's Path those who have believed, seeking to make it crooked. And remember when you were few in number and He multiplied you, and see what was the fate of those who sought to corrupt.

وَلَا تَقْعُدُوا۟ بِكُلِّ صِرَٰطٍ تُوعِدُونَ وَتَصُدُّونَ عَن سَبِيلِ ٱللَّهِ مَنْ ءَامَنَ بِهِۦ وَتَبْغُونَهَا عِوَجًا وَٱذْكُرُوٓا۟ إِذْ كُنتُمْ قَلِيلًا فَكَثَّرَكُمْ وَٱنظُرُوا۟ كَيْفَ كَانَ عَٰقِبَةُ ٱلْمُفْسِدِينَ ۝

87. "And if one group of you believes in the message I have been sent with, and another group does not believe, wait then until Allah judges between us; for He is the Best of judges."

وَإِن كَانَ طَآئِفَةٌ مِّنكُمْ ءَامَنُوا۟ بِٱلَّذِىٓ أُرْسِلْتُ بِهِۦ وَطَآئِفَةٌ لَّمْ يُؤْمِنُوا۟ فَٱصْبِرُوا۟ حَتَّىٰ يَحْكُمَ ٱللَّهُ بَيْنَنَا وَهُوَ خَيْرُ ٱلْحَٰكِمِينَ ۝

88. The arrogant dignitaries of his people said: "O Shu'ayb, we will surely drive you, together with those who believe, out of our city, unless you return to our religion." He said: "Even if we were unwilling?

۞ قَالَ ٱلْمَلَأُ ٱلَّذِينَ ٱسْتَكْبَرُوا۟ مِن قَوْمِهِۦ لَنُخْرِجَنَّكَ يَٰشُعَيْبُ وَٱلَّذِينَ ءَامَنُوا۟ مَعَكَ مِن قَرْيَتِنَآ أَوْ لَتَعُودُنَّ فِى مِلَّتِنَا قَالَ أَوَلَوْ كُنَّا كَٰرِهِينَ ۝

---

390. Lot and his followers.

89. "We would actually be fabricating lies about Allah, if we were to return to your religion, after Allah has delivered us from it. It is not given to us to return to it, unless Allah our Lord wills it. Our Lord embraces all things in knowledge. In Allah we have put our trust. Our Lord, judge between us and our people in truth, for You are the Best of judges."

قَدِ ٱفْتَرَيْنَا عَلَى ٱللَّهِ كَذِبًا إِنْ عُدْنَا فِى مِلَّتِكُم بَعْدَ إِذْ نَجَّىٰنَا ٱللَّهُ مِنْهَا وَمَا يَكُونُ لَنَا أَن نَّعُودَ فِيهَا إِلَّا أَن يَشَآءَ ٱللَّهُ رَبُّنَا وَسِعَ رَبُّنَا كُلَّ شَىْءٍ عِلْمًا عَلَى ٱللَّهِ تَوَكَّلْنَا رَبَّنَا ٱفْتَحْ بَيْنَنَا وَبَيْنَ قَوْمِنَا بِٱلْحَقِّ وَأَنتَ خَيْرُ ٱلْفَٰتِحِينَ ﴿٨٩﴾

90. The dignitaries of his people who disbelieved then said: "If you follow Shu'ayb, then you are the losers.'

وَقَالَ ٱلْمَلَأُ ٱلَّذِينَ كَفَرُوا۟ مِن قَوْمِهِۦ لَئِنِ ٱتَّبَعْتُمْ شُعَيْبًا إِنَّكُمْ إِذًا لَّخَٰسِرُونَ ﴿٩٠﴾

91. Thereupon, the earthquake overtook them, and so they lay prostrate in their own homes.

فَأَخَذَتْهُمُ ٱلرَّجْفَةُ فَأَصْبَحُوا۟ فِى دَارِهِمْ جَٰثِمِينَ ﴿٩١﴾

92. Those who denounced Shu'ayb were as though they had never dwelt there; those who denounced Shu'ayb were the losers.

ٱلَّذِينَ كَذَّبُوا۟ شُعَيْبًا كَأَن لَّمْ يَغْنَوْا۟ فِيهَا ٱلَّذِينَ كَذَّبُوا۟ شُعَيْبًا كَانُوا۟ هُمُ ٱلْخَٰسِرِينَ ﴿٩٢﴾

93. So he turned away from them and said: "O my people, I have delivered to you the revelations of my Lord and given you advice. How should I then grieve for an unbelieving people?"

فَتَوَلَّىٰ عَنْهُمْ وَقَالَ يَٰقَوْمِ لَقَدْ أَبْلَغْتُكُمْ رِسَٰلَٰتِ رَبِّى وَنَصَحْتُ لَكُمْ فَكَيْفَ ءَاسَىٰ عَلَىٰ قَوْمٍ كَٰفِرِينَ ﴿٩٣﴾

94. We did not send forth a Prophet to any city but afflicted its people with distress and suffering, that perchance they might humble themselves.

وَمَآ أَرْسَلْنَا فِى قَرْيَةٍ مِّن نَّبِىٍّ إِلَّا أَخَذْنَآ أَهْلَهَا بِٱلْبَأْسَآءِ وَٱلضَّرَّآءِ لَعَلَّهُمْ يَضَّرَّعُونَ ﴿٩٤﴾

95. Then We changed their adversity into well-being, till they multiplied. They said: "Hardship and prosperity did visit our fathers." Then, We seized them suddenly, while they were unaware.

ثُمَّ بَدَّلْنَا مَكَانَ ٱلسَّيِّئَةِ ٱلْحَسَنَةَ حَتَّىٰ عَفَوا۟ وَّقَالُوا۟ قَدْ مَسَّ ءَابَآءَنَا ٱلضَّرَّآءُ وَٱلسَّرَّآءُ فَأَخَذْنَٰهُم بَغْتَةً وَهُمْ لَا يَشْعُرُونَ ﴿٩٥﴾

96. Yet had the people of the cities believed and feared Allah, We would have opened upon them blessings from the sky and the earth;[391] but they denied [the Prophets], and so We destroyed them on account of their misdeeds.

وَلَوْ أَنَّ أَهْلَ ٱلْقُرَىٰٓ ءَامَنُوا۟ وَٱتَّقَوْا۟ لَفَتَحْنَا عَلَيْهِم بَرَكَٰتٍ مِّنَ ٱلسَّمَآءِ وَٱلْأَرْضِ وَلَٰكِن كَذَّبُوا۟ فَأَخَذْنَٰهُم بِمَا كَانُوا۟ يَكْسِبُونَ ﴿٩٦﴾

---

391. That is, rain from the sky and plants from the earth.

97. Did the people of the cities feel assured that Our punishment would not come upon them at night while they were sleeping?

98. Or did the people of the cities feel assured that Our punishment would not come upon them during the day while they were playing?

99. Or did they feel secure against Allah's Scheming? For none feels secure from Allah's Scheming save the losing people.

100. Is it not clear to those who inherit the earth after its people [are gone] that if We will, We can smite them for their sins and seal their hearts so that they cannot hear.

101. Those cities, We relate to you some of their tales; their Messengers came to them with clear signs, but they would not believe in what they had denied earlier. Thus Allah seals the hearts of the unbelievers.

102. And We have not found among most of them any who honours a covenant; but We found most of them evildoers.

103. Then after them, We sent Moses with Our Revelations to Pharaoh and his people, but they repudiated them. See then what was the fate of the mischief-makers.

104. Moses said: "O Pharaoh, I am a Messenger from the Lord of the Worlds.

105. "It is only proper that I should not say about Allah anything other than the truth. I have brought you a clear sign from your Lord; so send forth the Children of Israel with me."

106. He said: "If you have brought a sign, produce it if you are really truthful."

أَفَأَمِنَ أَهْلُ ٱلْقُرَىٰ أَن يَأْتِيَهُم بَأْسُنَا بَيَٰتًا وَهُمْ نَآئِمُونَ ۝

أَوَ أَمِنَ أَهْلُ ٱلْقُرَىٰ أَن يَأْتِيَهُم بَأْسُنَا ضُحًى وَهُمْ يَلْعَبُونَ ۝

أَفَأَمِنُوا۟ مَكْرَ ٱللَّهِ فَلَا يَأْمَنُ مَكْرَ ٱللَّهِ إِلَّا ٱلْقَوْمُ ٱلْخَٰسِرُونَ ۝

أَوَلَمْ يَهْدِ لِلَّذِينَ يَرِثُونَ ٱلْأَرْضَ مِنۢ بَعْدِ أَهْلِهَآ أَن لَّوْ نَشَآءُ أَصَبْنَٰهُم بِذُنُوبِهِمْ وَنَطْبَعُ عَلَىٰ قُلُوبِهِمْ فَهُمْ لَا يَسْمَعُونَ ۝

تِلْكَ ٱلْقُرَىٰ نَقُصُّ عَلَيْكَ مِنْ أَنۢبَآئِهَا وَلَقَدْ جَآءَتْهُمْ رُسُلُهُم بِٱلْبَيِّنَٰتِ فَمَا كَانُوا۟ لِيُؤْمِنُوا۟ بِمَا كَذَّبُوا۟ مِن قَبْلُ كَذَٰلِكَ يَطْبَعُ ٱللَّهُ عَلَىٰ قُلُوبِ ٱلْكَٰفِرِينَ ۝

وَمَا وَجَدْنَا لِأَكْثَرِهِم مِّنْ عَهْدٍ وَإِن وَجَدْنَآ أَكْثَرَهُمْ لَفَٰسِقِينَ ۝

ثُمَّ بَعَثْنَا مِنۢ بَعْدِهِم مُّوسَىٰ بِـَٔايَٰتِنَآ إِلَىٰ فِرْعَوْنَ وَمَلَإِي۟هِ فَظَلَمُوا۟ بِهَا فَٱنظُرْ كَيْفَ كَانَ عَٰقِبَةُ ٱلْمُفْسِدِينَ ۝

وَقَالَ مُوسَىٰ يَٰفِرْعَوْنُ إِنِّي رَسُولٌ مِّن رَّبِّ ٱلْعَٰلَمِينَ ۝

حَقِيقٌ عَلَىٰ أَن لَّآ أَقُولَ عَلَى ٱللَّهِ إِلَّا ٱلْحَقَّ قَدْ جِئْتُكُم بِبَيِّنَةٍ مِّن رَّبِّكُمْ فَأَرْسِلْ مَعِىَ بَنِىٓ إِسْرَٰٓءِيلَ ۝

قَالَ إِن كُنتَ جِئْتَ بِـَٔايَةٍ فَأْتِ بِهَآ إِن كُنتَ مِنَ ٱلصَّٰدِقِينَ ۝

107. So he cast his staff and, behold, it was a manifest serpent.

فَأَلْقَىٰ عَصَاهُ فَإِذَا هِىَ ثُعْبَانٌ مُّبِينٌ ۝

108. And he drew his hand; and, behold, it appeared white to the onlookers.

وَنَزَعَ يَدَهُ فَإِذَا هِىَ بَيْضَآءُ لِلنَّٰظِرِينَ ۝

109. The dignitaries among Pharaoh's people said: "This, indeed, is a shrewd magician.

قَالَ ٱلْمَلَأُ مِن قَوْمِ فِرْعَوْنَ إِنَّ هَٰذَا لَسَٰحِرٌ عَلِيمٌ ۝

110. "He wishes to drive you out of your land; so what do you advise?"

يُرِيدُ أَن يُخْرِجَكُم مِّنْ أَرْضِكُمْ فَمَاذَا تَأْمُرُونَ ۝

111. They said: "Leave him and his brother for a while, and send forth summoners to the cities;

قَالُوٓا۟ أَرْجِهْ وَأَخَاهُ وَأَرْسِلْ فِى ٱلْمَدَآئِنِ حَٰشِرِينَ ۝

112. "To bring you every shrewd magician."

يَأْتُوكَ بِكُلِّ سَٰحِرٍ عَلِيمٍ ۝

113. The magicians then came to Pharaoh and said: "We shall surely have a reward, if we are the winners."

وَجَآءَ ٱلسَّحَرَةُ فِرْعَوْنَ قَالُوٓا۟ إِنَّ لَنَا لَأَجْرًا إِن كُنَّا نَحْنُ ٱلْغَٰلِبِينَ ۝

114. He said: "Yes, and you will be, indeed, among those I favour."

قَالَ نَعَمْ وَإِنَّكُمْ لَمِنَ ٱلْمُقَرَّبِينَ ۝

115. They said: "O Moses, either you cast or we will be the first to cast."

قَالُوا۟ يَٰمُوسَىٰٓ إِمَّآ أَن تُلْقِىَ وَإِمَّآ أَن نَّكُونَ نَحْنُ ٱلْمُلْقِينَ ۝

116. He said: "You cast"; but when they cast, they put a spell upon the eyes of the people and frightened them, producing a mighty feat of magic.

قَالَ أَلْقُوا۟ فَلَمَّآ أَلْقَوْا۟ سَحَرُوٓا۟ أَعْيُنَ ٱلنَّاسِ وَٱسْتَرْهَبُوهُمْ وَجَآءُو بِسِحْرٍ عَظِيمٍ ۝

117. We revealed to Moses: "Cast your staff", and behold, it proceeded to devour what they faked.

۞ وَأَوْحَيْنَآ إِلَىٰ مُوسَىٰٓ أَنْ أَلْقِ عَصَاكَ فَإِذَا هِىَ تَلْقَفُ مَا يَأْفِكُونَ ۝

118. So the truth was vindicated and what they were doing was nullified.

فَوَقَعَ ٱلْحَقُّ وَبَطَلَ مَا كَانُوا۟ يَعْمَلُونَ ۝

119. And they were vanquished there and then, and they turned away humiliated.

فَغُلِبُوا۟ هُنَالِكَ وَٱنقَلَبُوا۟ صَٰغِرِينَ ۝

120. And the magicians fell down prostrate.

وَأُلْقِىَ ٱلسَّحَرَةُ سَٰجِدِينَ ۝

121. They said: "We believe now in the Lord of the Worlds;

قَالُوٓا۟ ءَامَنَّا بِرَبِّ ٱلْعَٰلَمِينَ ۝

122. "The Lord of Moses and Aaron."

رَبِّ مُوسَىٰ وَهَٰرُونَ ۝

123. Pharaoh then said: "Do you believe in Him before I give you leave? This is indeed a plot you contrived in the city, in order to drive its people out. Now you shall know.

124. "I will surely cut off your hands and your feet on opposite sides; then I will crucify you all together."

125. They said: "Unto our Lord we surely shall return.

126. "You only resent from us that we have believed in the Signs of our Lord when they came to us. Lord, grant us patience and let us die as men who submit to You."

127. And the dignitaries among Pharaoh's people said: "Will you leave Moses and his people to make mischief in the land and to abandon you and your gods?" He said: "We will massacre their sons, but spare their women, and over them we shall surely triumph."

128. Moses said to his people: "Seek Allah's assistance and be patient; the earth is Allah's and He gives it to whomever of His servants He pleases; and for the righteous is the happy end."

129. They said: "We were persecuted before you came to us and after you came to us." He said: "Perchance your Lord will destroy your enemy and make you successors in the land and, then, observe what you will do."

130. And We made Pharaoh and his people suffer from drought and shortage of fruits, that perchance they may take heed.

131. So, when a good fortune came to them they said: "This is ours", but if a misfortune befell them, they ascribed the evil omen to Moses and his companions. In fact, their omen is with Allah; but most of them do not know.

قَالَ فِرْعَوْنُ ءَامَنتُم بِهِ قَبْلَ أَنْ ءَاذَنَ لَكُمْ إِنَّ هَٰذَا لَمَكْرٌ مَّكَرْتُمُوهُ فِى الْمَدِينَةِ لِتُخْرِجُوا مِنْهَا أَهْلَهَا فَسَوْفَ تَعْلَمُونَ ۝

لَأُقَطِّعَنَّ أَيْدِيَكُمْ وَأَرْجُلَكُم مِّنْ خِلَٰفٍ ثُمَّ لَأُصَلِّبَنَّكُمْ أَجْمَعِينَ ۝

قَالُوٓا إِنَّآ إِلَىٰ رَبِّنَا مُنقَلِبُونَ ۝

وَمَا تَنقِمُ مِنَّآ إِلَّآ أَنْ ءَامَنَّا بِـَٔايَٰتِ رَبِّنَا لَمَّا جَآءَتْنَا رَبَّنَآ أَفْرِغْ عَلَيْنَا صَبْرًا وَتَوَفَّنَا مُسْلِمِينَ ۝

وَقَالَ الْمَلَأُ مِن قَوْمِ فِرْعَوْنَ أَتَذَرُ مُوسَىٰ وَقَوْمَهُۥ لِيُفْسِدُوا فِى الْأَرْضِ وَيَذَرَكَ وَءَالِهَتَكَ قَالَ سَنُقَتِّلُ أَبْنَآءَهُمْ وَنَسْتَحْىِۦ نِسَآءَهُمْ وَإِنَّا فَوْقَهُمْ قَٰهِرُونَ ۝

قَالَ مُوسَىٰ لِقَوْمِهِ اسْتَعِينُوا بِاللَّهِ وَاصْبِرُوٓا إِنَّ الْأَرْضَ لِلَّهِ يُورِثُهَا مَن يَشَآءُ مِنْ عِبَادِهِ وَالْعَٰقِبَةُ لِلْمُتَّقِينَ ۝

قَالُوٓا أُوذِينَا مِن قَبْلِ أَن تَأْتِيَنَا وَمِنۢ بَعْدِ مَا جِئْتَنَا قَالَ عَسَىٰ رَبُّكُمْ أَن يُهْلِكَ عَدُوَّكُمْ وَيَسْتَخْلِفَكُمْ فِى الْأَرْضِ فَيَنظُرَ كَيْفَ تَعْمَلُونَ ۝

وَلَقَدْ أَخَذْنَآ ءَالَ فِرْعَوْنَ بِالسِّنِينَ وَنَقْصٍ مِّنَ الثَّمَرَٰتِ لَعَلَّهُمْ يَذَّكَّرُونَ ۝

فَإِذَا جَآءَتْهُمُ الْحَسَنَةُ قَالُوا لَنَا هَٰذِهِ وَإِن تُصِبْهُمْ سَيِّئَةٌ يَطَّيَّرُوا بِمُوسَىٰ وَمَن مَّعَهُۥٓ أَلَآ إِنَّمَا طَٰٓئِرُهُمْ عِندَ اللَّهِ وَلَٰكِنَّ أَكْثَرَهُمْ لَا يَعْلَمُونَ ۝

132. And they said: "Whatever sign you may bring us in order to cast a spell upon us, we will not believe in you."

وَقَالُوا۟ مَهْمَا تَأْتِنَا بِهِۦ مِنْ ءَايَةٍ لِّتَسْحَرَنَا بِهَا فَمَا نَحْنُ لَكَ بِمُؤْمِنِينَ ﴿١٣٢﴾

133. So, We let loose upon them the deluge, locusts, lice, frogs and blood, as explicit signs; but they grew arrogant and were a sinful people.

فَأَرْسَلْنَا عَلَيْهِمُ ٱلطُّوفَانَ وَٱلْجَرَادَ وَٱلْقُمَّلَ وَٱلضَّفَادِعَ وَٱلدَّمَ ءَايَٰتٍ مُّفَصَّلَٰتٍ فَٱسْتَكْبَرُوا۟ وَكَانُوا۟ قَوْمًا مُّجْرِمِينَ ﴿١٣٣﴾

134. And when the scourge descended on them, they said: "O Moses, call upon your Lord for us in virtue of the covenant He made with you. If you lift the scourge from us, we will surely believe you and send forth the Children of Israel with you."

وَلَمَّا وَقَعَ عَلَيْهِمُ ٱلرِّجْزُ قَالُوا۟ يَٰمُوسَى ٱدْعُ لَنَا رَبَّكَ بِمَا عَهِدَ عِندَكَ لَئِن كَشَفْتَ عَنَّا ٱلرِّجْزَ لَنُؤْمِنَنَّ لَكَ وَلَنُرْسِلَنَّ مَعَكَ بَنِىٓ إِسْرَٰٓءِيلَ ﴿١٣٤﴾

135. But when We lifted the scourge from them for a period We accorded them, behold, they broke their pledge.

فَلَمَّا كَشَفْنَا عَنْهُمُ ٱلرِّجْزَ إِلَىٰٓ أَجَلٍ هُم بَٰلِغُوهُ إِذَا هُمْ يَنكُثُونَ ﴿١٣٥﴾

136. Then We exacted retribution from them and drowned them in the sea, because they denounced Our Signs and failed to pay heed to them.

فَٱنتَقَمْنَا مِنْهُمْ فَأَغْرَقْنَٰهُمْ فِى ٱلْيَمِّ بِأَنَّهُمْ كَذَّبُوا۟ بِـَٔايَٰتِنَا وَكَانُوا۟ عَنْهَا غَٰفِلِينَ ﴿١٣٦﴾

137. And We bequeathed to the people who were held to be weak[392] the eastern and western parts of the land which we had blessed;[393] and the fairest Word of your Lord in regard to the Children of Israel was fulfilled, because of their endurance; and We destroyed the houses and towers which Pharaoh and his people were building.

وَأَوْرَثْنَا ٱلْقَوْمَ ٱلَّذِينَ كَانُوا۟ يُسْتَضْعَفُونَ مَشَٰرِقَ ٱلْأَرْضِ وَمَغَٰرِبَهَا ٱلَّتِى بَٰرَكْنَا فِيهَا وَتَمَّتْ كَلِمَتُ رَبِّكَ ٱلْحُسْنَىٰ عَلَىٰ بَنِىٓ إِسْرَٰٓءِيلَ بِمَا صَبَرُوا۟ وَدَمَّرْنَا مَا كَانَ يَصْنَعُ فِرْعَوْنُ وَقَوْمُهُۥ وَمَا كَانُوا۟ يَعْرِشُونَ ﴿١٣٧﴾

138. And We caused the Children of Israel to cross the sea, and they came upon a people devoted to idols of their own. They said: "O Moses, make us a god as they have gods of their own." He said: "You are indeed an ignorant people.

وَجَٰوَزْنَا بِبَنِىٓ إِسْرَٰٓءِيلَ ٱلْبَحْرَ فَأَتَوْا۟ عَلَىٰ قَوْمٍ يَعْكُفُونَ عَلَىٰٓ أَصْنَامٍ لَّهُمْ قَالُوا۟ يَٰمُوسَى ٱجْعَل لَّنَآ إِلَٰهًا كَمَا لَهُمْ ءَالِهَةٌ قَالَ إِنَّكُمْ قَوْمٌ تَجْهَلُونَ ﴿١٣٨﴾

---

392. The Children of Israel.
393. The Holy Land.

139. "Surely what those [people] are engaged in is doomed to destruction, and what they are doing is a vanity."

إِنَّ هَؤُلَآءِ مُتَبَّرٌ مَّا هُمْ فِيهِ وَبَـٰطِلٌ مَّا كَانُوا۟ يَعْمَلُونَ ﴿١٣٩﴾

140. And he said: "Shall I seek for you a god other than Allah, Who has preferred you to all mankind?"

قَالَ أَغَيْرَ ٱللَّهِ أَبْغِيكُمْ إِلَـٰهًا وَهُوَ فَضَّلَكُمْ عَلَى ٱلْعَـٰلَمِينَ ﴿١٤٠﴾

141. And [remember] how We delivered you from Pharaoh's people who inflicted the worst punishment on you, killing your sons and sparing your women. In that was a grievous trial from your Lord.

وَإِذْ أَنجَيْنَـٰكُم مِّنْ ءَالِ فِرْعَوْنَ يَسُومُونَكُمْ سُوٓءَ ٱلْعَذَابِ يُقَتِّلُونَ أَبْنَآءَكُمْ وَيَسْتَحْيُونَ نِسَآءَكُمْ وَفِى ذَٰلِكُم بَلَآءٌ مِّن رَّبِّكُمْ عَظِيمٌ ﴿١٤١﴾

142. And We appointed to Moses thirty nights to which We added ten, and thus the term appointed by his Lord was forty nights. And Moses said to his brother Aaron: "Succeed me at the head of my people, set matters right and do not follow the path of the mischief-makers."

۞ وَوَٰعَدْنَا مُوسَىٰ ثَلَـٰثِينَ لَيْلَةً وَأَتْمَمْنَـٰهَا بِعَشْرٍ فَتَمَّ مِيقَـٰتُ رَبِّهِۦٓ أَرْبَعِينَ لَيْلَةً وَقَالَ مُوسَىٰ لِأَخِيهِ هَـٰرُونَ ٱخْلُفْنِى فِى قَوْمِى وَأَصْلِحْ وَلَا تَتَّبِعْ سَبِيلَ ٱلْمُفْسِدِينَ ﴿١٤٢﴾

143. And when Moses came on Our appointed time and his Lord spoke to him, he said: "Lord, show me [Yourself] so that I may look at You." He said: "You will not see Me; but look at the mountain. If it stays in its place, you shall see Me." But when his Lord revealed Himself to the mountain, He levelled it to the ground, and Moses fell down unconscious. When he woke up, he said: "Glory be to You, I repent unto You and I am the first of the believers."

وَلَمَّا جَآءَ مُوسَىٰ لِمِيقَـٰتِنَا وَكَلَّمَهُۥ رَبُّهُۥ قَالَ رَبِّ أَرِنِىٓ أَنظُرْ إِلَيْكَ قَالَ لَن تَرَىٰنِى وَلَـٰكِنِ ٱنظُرْ إِلَى ٱلْجَبَلِ فَإِنِ ٱسْتَقَرَّ مَكَانَهُۥ فَسَوْفَ تَرَىٰنِى فَلَمَّا تَجَلَّىٰ رَبُّهُۥ لِلْجَبَلِ جَعَلَهُۥ دَكًّا وَخَرَّ مُوسَىٰ صَعِقًا فَلَمَّآ أَفَاقَ قَالَ سُبْحَـٰنَكَ تُبْتُ إِلَيْكَ وَأَنَا۠ أَوَّلُ ٱلْمُؤْمِنِينَ ﴿١٤٣﴾

144. Then He said: "O Moses, I have chosen you above all men for My Messages and My words; so take what I have given you and be one of the thankful."

قَالَ يَـٰمُوسَىٰٓ إِنِّى ٱصْطَفَيْتُكَ عَلَى ٱلنَّاسِ بِرِسَـٰلَـٰتِى وَبِكَلَـٰمِى فَخُذْ مَآ ءَاتَيْتُكَ وَكُن مِّنَ ٱلشَّـٰكِرِينَ ﴿١٤٤﴾

145. And We wrote for him in the Tablets[394] about everything, providing exhortation and a clear exposition of everything: "So [We said]

وَكَتَبْنَا لَهُۥ فِى ٱلْأَلْوَاحِ مِن كُلِّ شَىْءٍ مَّوْعِظَةً وَتَفْصِيلًا لِّكُلِّ شَىْءٍ فَخُذْهَا بِقُوَّةٍ

---

394. The Tablets of the Torah.

take it resolutely and bid your people to take the best part of it. I will show you the abode of the wicked.

146. "I will turn away from My Signs those who are unjustifiably arrogant on earth, and who, if they see each sign, will not believe in it; and if they see the path of rectitude will not follow it, but if they see the path of error, will follow it as their path. That is because they denied the truth of Our Signs and failed to pay heed.

147. "Those who deny Our Signs and the Meeting of the Hereafter - their works are nullified. Will they be rewarded except according to what they do?"

148. And the people of Moses took, after he went away, a calf made of their jewellery - a mere body which lowed. Did they not see that it did not speak to them and could not guide them to any path? They took it [for worship] and were wrongdoers.

149. And when they felt deep regret, and saw that they had gone astray, they said: "If our Lord will not have mercy on us and will not forgive us, we will certainly be among the losers."

150. And when Moses returned to his people, angry and very sad, he said: "Evil is what you did following my departure. Were you in a hurry regarding your Lord's Commandment?" He cast the Tablets down and took hold of his brother's head, dragging him towards him. He[395] said: "Son of my mother, the people deemed me weak and were about to kill me, so do not let the enemies rejoice at my plight, and do not reckon me one of the unjust people."

---

395. Aaron.

وَأْمُرْ قَوْمَكَ يَأْخُذُوا بِأَحْسَنِهَا سَأُورِيكُمْ دَارَ الْفَاسِقِينَ ﴿١٤٥﴾

سَأَصْرِفُ عَنْ ءَايَـٰتِيَ الَّذِينَ يَتَكَبَّرُونَ فِى الْأَرْضِ بِغَيْرِ الْحَقِّ وَإِن يَرَوْا كُلَّ ءَايَةٍ لَّا يُؤْمِنُوا بِهَا وَإِن يَرَوْا سَبِيلَ الرُّشْدِ لَا يَتَّخِذُوهُ سَبِيلًا وَإِن يَرَوْا سَبِيلَ الْغَيِّ يَتَّخِذُوهُ سَبِيلًا ذَٰلِكَ بِأَنَّهُمْ كَذَّبُوا بِئَايَـٰتِنَا وَكَانُوا عَنْهَا غَـٰفِلِينَ ﴿١٤٦﴾

وَالَّذِينَ كَذَّبُوا بِئَايَـٰتِنَا وَلِقَاءِ الْآخِرَةِ حَبِطَتْ أَعْمَـٰلُهُمْ هَلْ يُجْزَوْنَ إِلَّا مَا كَانُوا يَعْمَلُونَ ﴿١٤٧﴾

وَاتَّخَذَ قَوْمُ مُوسَىٰ مِنۢ بَعْدِهِ مِنْ حُلِيِّهِمْ عِجْلًا جَسَدًا لَّهُ خُوَارٌ أَلَمْ يَرَوْا أَنَّهُ لَا يُكَلِّمُهُمْ وَلَا يَهْدِيهِمْ سَبِيلًا اتَّخَذُوهُ وَكَانُوا ظَـٰلِمِينَ ﴿١٤٨﴾

وَلَمَّا سُقِطَ فِىٓ أَيْدِيهِمْ وَرَأَوْا أَنَّهُمْ قَدْ ضَلُّوا قَالُوا لَئِن لَّمْ يَرْحَمْنَا رَبُّنَا وَيَغْفِرْ لَنَا لَنَكُونَنَّ مِنَ الْخَاسِرِينَ ﴿١٤٩﴾

وَلَمَّا رَجَعَ مُوسَىٰ إِلَىٰ قَوْمِهِ غَضْبَـٰنَ أَسِفًا قَالَ بِئْسَمَا خَلَفْتُمُونِى مِنۢ بَعْدِىٓ أَعَجِلْتُمْ أَمْرَ رَبِّكُمْ وَأَلْقَى الْأَلْوَاحَ وَأَخَذَ بِرَأْسِ أَخِيهِ يَجُرُّهُۥٓ إِلَيْهِ قَالَ ابْنَ أُمَّ إِنَّ الْقَوْمَ اسْتَضْعَفُونِى وَكَادُوا يَقْتُلُونَنِى فَلَا تُشْمِتْ بِىَ الْأَعْدَآءَ وَلَا تَجْعَلْنِى مَعَ الْقَوْمِ الظَّـٰلِمِينَ ﴿١٥٠﴾

167

قَالَ رَبِّ اغْفِرْ لِي وَلِأَخِي وَأَدْخِلْنَا فِي رَحْمَتِكَ وَأَنتَ أَرْحَمُ الرَّاحِمِينَ ﴿١٥١﴾

151. He[396] said: "Lord, forgive me and my brother and admit us into Your Mercy; for you are the Most Merciful of all."

إِنَّ الَّذِينَ اتَّخَذُوا الْعِجْلَ سَيَنَالُهُمْ غَضَبٌ مِّن رَّبِّهِمْ وَذِلَّةٌ فِي الْحَيَاةِ الدُّنْيَا وَكَذَلِكَ نَجْزِي الْمُفْتَرِينَ ﴿١٥٢﴾

152. Surely, those who worshipped the calf will be visited by wrath from their Lord and humiliation in the present life; and thus We recompense those who invent lies.

وَالَّذِينَ عَمِلُوا السَّيِّئَاتِ ثُمَّ تَابُوا مِنْ بَعْدِهَا وَآمَنُوا إِنَّ رَبَّكَ مِنْ بَعْدِهَا لَغَفُورٌ رَّحِيمٌ ﴿١٥٣﴾

153. And those who perpetrated the evil deeds and repented thereafter and believed - surely your Lord is thereafter All-Forgiving and Merciful.

وَلَمَّا سَكَتَ عَن مُّوسَى الْغَضَبُ أَخَذَ الْأَلْوَاحَ وَفِي نُسْخَتِهَا هُدًى وَرَحْمَةٌ لِّلَّذِينَ هُمْ لِرَبِّهِمْ يَرْهَبُونَ ﴿١٥٤﴾

154. And when the anger of Moses abated, he took up the Tablets, in the text of which are guidance and mercy for those who fear their Lord.

وَاخْتَارَ مُوسَى قَوْمَهُ سَبْعِينَ رَجُلًا لِّمِيقَاتِنَا فَلَمَّا أَخَذَتْهُمُ الرَّجْفَةُ قَالَ رَبِّ لَوْ شِئْتَ أَهْلَكْتَهُم مِّن قَبْلُ وَإِيَّايَ أَتُهْلِكُنَا بِمَا فَعَلَ السُّفَهَاءُ مِنَّا إِنْ هِيَ إِلَّا فِتْنَتُكَ تُضِلُّ بِهَا مَن تَشَاءُ وَتَهْدِي مَن تَشَاءُ أَنتَ وَلِيُّنَا فَاغْفِرْ لَنَا وَارْحَمْنَا وَأَنتَ خَيْرُ الْغَافِرِينَ ﴿١٥٥﴾

155. And Moses chose from his people seventy men for Our appointed time. When the earthquake overtook them, he said: "Lord, had You pleased, You would have destroyed them, together with me, before this time. Will You destroy us for what the fools among us have done? This is only Your Trial, with which You lead astray whomever You will and guide whomever You will. You are our Protector; so forgive us and have mercy on us. You are the Best Forgiver of all.

﴿ وَاكْتُبْ لَنَا فِي هَذِهِ الدُّنْيَا حَسَنَةً وَفِي الْآخِرَةِ إِنَّا هُدْنَا إِلَيْكَ قَالَ عَذَابِي أُصِيبُ بِهِ مَنْ أَشَاءُ وَرَحْمَتِي وَسِعَتْ كُلَّ شَيْءٍ فَسَأَكْتُبُهَا لِلَّذِينَ يَتَّقُونَ وَيُؤْتُونَ الزَّكَاةَ وَالَّذِينَ هُم بِآيَاتِنَا يُؤْمِنُونَ ﴿١٥٦﴾

156. "And ordain for us good in this world and in the Hereafter; we turn repentant to You." He said: "I smite with My punishment whomsoever I please, and My Mercy encompasses all things; and I will ordain it to those who are pious and give the alms, and to those who believe in Our Signs.

الَّذِينَ يَتَّبِعُونَ الرَّسُولَ النَّبِيَّ الْأُمِّيَّ الَّذِي يَجِدُونَهُ مَكْتُوبًا عِندَهُمْ فِي التَّوْرَاةِ وَالْإِنجِيلِ يَأْمُرُهُم

157. "And to those who follow the Messenger, the unlettered Prophet whom they find mentioned in their Torah and Gospel. He

---

396. Moses.

بِالْمَعْرُوفِ وَيَنْهَنهُمْ عَنِ الْمُنكَرِ وَيُحِلُّ لَهُمُ الطَّيِّبَتِ وَيُحَرِّمُ عَلَيْهِمُ الْخَبَئِثَ وَيَضَعُ عَنْهُمْ إِصْرَهُمْ وَالْأَغْلَلَ الَّتِى كَانَتْ عَلَيْهِمْ فَالَّذِينَ ءَامَنُوا بِهِ وَعَزَّرُوهُ وَنَصَرُوهُ وَاتَّبَعُوا النُّورَ الَّذِى أُنزِلَ مَعَهُ أُوْلَئِكَ هُمُ الْمُفْلِحُونَ ۝

enjoins them to do good and to forbid evil, and makes lawful to them the good things and unlawful the impure things. And He relieves them of their heavy burden and the shackles that were upon them. Thus those who believe in him and who honour and support him and follow the light which has been sent down with him - those are the prosperous."

قُلْ يَأَيُّهَا النَّاسُ إِنِّى رَسُولُ اللَّهِ إِلَيْكُمْ جَمِيعًا الَّذِى لَهُ مُلْكُ السَّمَوَتِ وَالْأَرْضِ لَا إِلَهَ إِلَّا هُوَ يُحْىِ وَيُمِيتُ فَـَامِنُوا بِاللَّهِ وَرَسُولِهِ النَّبِىِّ الْأُمِّىِّ الَّذِى يُؤْمِنُ بِاللَّهِ وَكَلِمَتِهِ وَاتَّبِعُوهُ لَعَلَّكُمْ تَهْتَدُونَ ۝

158. Say: "O people, I am Allah's Messenger to you all; He to Whom belongs the dominion of the heavens and the earth. There is no god but He. He gives life and causes to die; so believe in Allah and His Messenger, the unlettered Prophet who believes in Allah and His words; and follow him, that perchance you may be well-guided."

وَمِن قَوْمِ مُوسَى أُمَّةٌ يَهْدُونَ بِالْحَقِّ وَبِهِ يَعْدِلُونَ ۝

159. And of the people of Moses, there is a group who guide by the truth, and by it act justly.

وَقَطَّعْنَهُمُ اثْنَتَىْ عَشْرَةَ أَسْبَاطًا أُمَمًا وَأَوْحَيْنَا إِلَى مُوسَى إِذِ اسْتَسْقَهُ قَوْمُهُ أَنِ اضْرِب بِّعَصَاكَ الْحَجَرَ فَانبَجَسَتْ مِنْهُ اثْنَتَا عَشْرَةَ عَيْنًا قَدْ عَلِمَ كُلُّ أُنَاسٍ مَّشْرَبَهُمْ وَظَلَّلْنَا عَلَيْهِمُ الْغَمَمَ وَأَنزَلْنَا عَلَيْهِمُ الْمَنَّ وَالسَّلْوَى كُلُوا مِن طَيِّبَتِ مَا رَزَقْنَكُمْ وَمَا ظَلَمُونَا وَلَكِن كَانُوا أَنفُسَهُمْ يَظْلِمُونَ ۝

160. And We divided them into twelve nation-tribes; and We revealed to Moses, when his people asked him for water: "Strike the rock with your staff"; whereupon twelve springs gushed forth from it, with each tribe recognizing its drinking-place. And We spread the clouds over them to shade them and sent down upon them the manna and quails [saying to them]: "Eat from the good things We have provided for you." They did not wrong us, but they wronged themselves.

وَإِذْ قِيلَ لَهُمُ اسْكُنُوا هَذِهِ الْقَرْيَةَ وَكُلُوا مِنْهَا حَيْثُ شِئْتُمْ وَقُولُوا حِطَّةٌ وَادْخُلُوا الْبَابَ سُجَّدًا نَّغْفِرْ لَكُمْ خَطِيئَتِكُمْ سَنَزِيدُ الْمُحْسِنِينَ ۝

161. And it was said to them: "Dwell in this city and eat from it wherever you please. Seek forgiveness and enter the gate prostrate, so that We may forgive your sins. We shall give more to the beneficent."

فَبَدَّلَ الَّذِينَ ظَلَمُوا مِنْهُمْ قَوْلًا غَيْرَ الَّذِى قِيلَ لَهُمْ فَأَرْسَلْنَا عَلَيْهِمْ رِجْزًا مِّنَ السَّمَاءِ بِمَا كَانُوا يَظْلِمُونَ ۝

162. But the evildoers among them replaced what was said to them with other words; and so We sent upon them a punishment from heaven, on account of their wrongdoing.

163. And ask them about the city which stood close to the sea, when they violated the Sabbath. Their fish which used to come floating on the sea on the Sabbath did not appear when they violated the Sabbath. Thus We tried them because they transgressed.

164. And when one group of them said: "Why do you exhort a people whom Allah has doomed to destruction or to terrible punishment?", they replied: "As an excuse for your Lord, and that perchance they may fear God."

165. Then, when they neglected what they were reminded of, We saved those who were forbidding evil and inflicted upon the wrongdoers a terrible punishment, on account of their sinfulness.

166. Then, when they disdained arrogantly what they were forbidden, We said to them: "Be miserable monkeys."

167. Thereupon your Lord made it known that He would send against them one who would inflict on them the worst punishment until the Day of Resurrection. Your Lord is Quick in Retribution, and He is indeed All-Forgiving, Merciful.

168. And We split them up throughout the land into groups, some of them righteous and some otherwise. Then We tried them with prosperity and adversity, that perchance they might desist [from sinning].

169. Then there succeeded them [an evil] posterity who inherited the Book,[397] but chose the vanities of this world saying: "We shall be forgiven." And should similar vanities come their way, they would again seize them. Are they not bound by

وَسْـَٔلْهُمْ عَنِ ٱلْقَرْيَةِ ٱلَّتِى كَانَتْ حَاضِرَةَ ٱلْبَحْرِ إِذْ يَعْدُونَ فِى ٱلسَّبْتِ إِذْ تَأْتِيهِمْ حِيتَانُهُمْ يَوْمَ سَبْتِهِمْ شُرَّعًا وَيَوْمَ لَا يَسْبِتُونَ لَا تَأْتِيهِمْ كَذَٰلِكَ نَبْلُوهُم بِمَا كَانُوا۟ يَفْسُقُونَ ﴿١٦٣﴾

وَإِذْ قَالَتْ أُمَّةٌ مِّنْهُمْ لِمَ تَعِظُونَ قَوْمًا ٱللَّهُ مُهْلِكُهُمْ أَوْ مُعَذِّبُهُمْ عَذَابًا شَدِيدًا قَالُوا۟ مَعْذِرَةً إِلَىٰ رَبِّكُمْ وَلَعَلَّهُمْ يَتَّقُونَ ﴿١٦٤﴾

فَلَمَّا نَسُوا۟ مَا ذُكِّرُوا۟ بِهِۦٓ أَنجَيْنَا ٱلَّذِينَ يَنْهَوْنَ عَنِ ٱلسُّوٓءِ وَأَخَذْنَا ٱلَّذِينَ ظَلَمُوا۟ بِعَذَابٍۭ بَـِٔيسٍۭ بِمَا كَانُوا۟ يَفْسُقُونَ ﴿١٦٥﴾

فَلَمَّا عَتَوْا۟ عَن مَّا نُهُوا۟ عَنْهُ قُلْنَا لَهُمْ كُونُوا۟ قِرَدَةً خَـٰسِـِٔينَ ﴿١٦٦﴾

وَإِذْ تَأَذَّنَ رَبُّكَ لَيَبْعَثَنَّ عَلَيْهِمْ إِلَىٰ يَوْمِ ٱلْقِيَـٰمَةِ مَن يَسُومُهُمْ سُوٓءَ ٱلْعَذَابِ إِنَّ رَبَّكَ لَسَرِيعُ ٱلْعِقَابِ وَإِنَّهُۥ لَغَفُورٌ رَّحِيمٌ ﴿١٦٧﴾

وَقَطَّعْنَـٰهُمْ فِى ٱلْأَرْضِ أُمَمًا مِّنْهُمُ ٱلصَّـٰلِحُونَ وَمِنْهُمْ دُونَ ذَٰلِكَ وَبَلَوْنَـٰهُم بِٱلْحَسَنَـٰتِ وَٱلسَّيِّـَٔاتِ لَعَلَّهُمْ يَرْجِعُونَ ﴿١٦٨﴾

فَخَلَفَ مِنۢ بَعْدِهِمْ خَلْفٌ وَرِثُوا۟ ٱلْكِتَـٰبَ يَأْخُذُونَ عَرَضَ هَـٰذَا ٱلْأَدْنَىٰ وَيَقُولُونَ سَيُغْفَرُ لَنَا وَإِن يَأْتِهِمْ عَرَضٌ مِّثْلُهُۥ يَأْخُذُوهُ أَلَمْ يُؤْخَذْ عَلَيْهِم مِّيثَـٰقُ ٱلْكِتَـٰبِ أَن لَّا يَقُولُوا۟

---

397. The Torah.

على ٱللَّهِ إِلَّا ٱلْحَقَّ وَدَرَسُوا مَا فِيهِ وَٱلدَّارُ ٱلْءَاخِرَةُ خَيْرٌ لِلَّذِينَ يَتَّقُونَ أَفَلَا تَعْقِلُونَ ۝

them. Are they not bound by the covenant of the Book, that they should not say about Allah except the truth? They studied what is in it and the world to come is better for those who fear God. Do they not understand?

وَٱلَّذِينَ يُمَسِّكُونَ بِٱلْكِتَبِ وَأَقَامُوا ٱلصَّلَوٰةَ إِنَّا لَا نُضِيعُ أَجْرَ ٱلْمُصْلِحِينَ ۝

170. As for those who hold fast to the Book and perform the prayer - surely We do not dissipate the reward of the righteous.

۞ وَإِذْ نَتَقْنَا ٱلْجَبَلَ فَوْقَهُمْ كَأَنَّهُ ظُلَّةٌ وَظَنُّوا أَنَّهُ وَاقِعٌ بِهِمْ خُذُوا مَا ءَاتَيْنَٰكُم بِقُوَّةٍ وَٱذْكُرُوا مَا فِيهِ لَعَلَّكُمْ تَتَّقُونَ ۝

171. And [remember] when We raised the mountain over them, as though it was a canopy; and they thought that it was about to fall down on them. Hold on firmly to what We have given you, and remember what is in it, that perchance you may be God-fearing.

وَإِذْ أَخَذَ رَبُّكَ مِنۢ بَنِىٓ ءَادَمَ مِن ظُهُورِهِمْ ذُرِّيَّتَهُمْ وَأَشْهَدَهُمْ عَلَىٰٓ أَنفُسِهِمْ أَلَسْتُ بِرَبِّكُمْ قَالُوا بَلَىٰ شَهِدْنَآ أَن تَقُولُوا يَوْمَ ٱلْقِيَٰمَةِ إِنَّا كُنَّا عَنْ هَٰذَا غَٰفِلِينَ ۝

172. And [remember] when your Lord brought forth from the loins of the Children of Adam their posterity and made them testify against themselves. [He said]: "Am I not your Lord?" They said: "Yes, we testify." [This] lest you should say on the Day of Resurrection: "We were in fact unaware of this."

أَوْ تَقُولُوٓا إِنَّمَآ أَشْرَكَ ءَابَآؤُنَا مِن قَبْلُ وَكُنَّا ذُرِّيَّةً مِّنۢ بَعْدِهِمْ أَفَتُهْلِكُنَا بِمَا فَعَلَ ٱلْمُبْطِلُونَ ۝

173. Or lest you should say: "Our fathers associated [other gods with Allah] before [us] and we are their posterity. Will You destroy us for what the fabricators of falsehood did?"

وَكَذَٰلِكَ نُفَصِّلُ ٱلْءَايَٰتِ وَلَعَلَّهُمْ يَرْجِعُونَ ۝

174. And thus We expound the revelations so that they may return.[398]

وَٱتْلُ عَلَيْهِمْ نَبَأَ ٱلَّذِىٓ ءَاتَيْنَٰهُ ءَايَٰتِنَا فَٱنسَلَخَ مِنْهَا فَأَتْبَعَهُ ٱلشَّيْطَٰنُ فَكَانَ مِنَ ٱلْغَاوِينَ ۝

175. And tell them [O Muhammad] about the man[399] to whom We gave Our Revelations, but he renounced them and was followed by the Devil. Thus he became one of those condemned to perdition.

وَلَوْ شِئْنَا لَرَفَعْنَٰهُ بِهَا وَلَٰكِنَّهُۥٓ أَخْلَدَ إِلَى ٱلْأَرْضِ وَٱتَّبَعَ هَوَىٰهُ فَمَثَلُهُۥ كَمَثَلِ ٱلْكَلْبِ إِن تَحْمِلْ

176. And had We pleased, We would have elevated him through them,[400] but he clung to earth and followed his fancy. His case is

---

398. Return to the Truth.
399. The person intended here may be a Jewish rabbi called Balaam.
400. The revelations.

171

similar to that of a dog; if you attack it, it will pant, and if you leave it, it will pant too. Such are those who deny Our Revelations. So relate to them these narratives, that perchance they may reflect.

177. How evil is the example of the people who deny Our Revelations. They only wrong themselves.

178. Whomever Allah guides is well-guided; and whomever He leads astray - those are the losers.

179. And We have created for Hell multitudes of jinn and men. They have hearts, but do not understand; and they have eyes, but do not see; and they have ears, but do not hear. Those are like cattle, or rather are even more misguided. Those are the heedless ones.

180. And to Allah belong the Most Beautiful Names; so call Him by them and leave those who pervert His Names. They shall be punished for what they used to do.

181. And among those We have created is a nation that guides by the truth, and by it the nation acts justly.

182. And those who deny Our Revelations, We shall lure them step by step to destruction, whence they do not know.

183. And I will grant them respite. Surely My Scheme is very effective.

184. Do they not consider that their companion[401] is not mad. He is only a plain warner.

185. Have they not considered the kingdom of the heavens and the earth and all the

عَلَيْهِ يَلْهَثْ أَوْ تَتْرُكْهُ يَلْهَثْ ذَّٰلِكَ مَثَلُ ٱلْقَوْمِ ٱلَّذِينَ كَذَّبُوا۟ بِـَٔايَٰتِنَا ۚ فَٱقْصُصِ ٱلْقَصَصَ لَعَلَّهُمْ يَتَفَكَّرُونَ ۝

سَآءَ مَثَلًا ٱلْقَوْمُ ٱلَّذِينَ كَذَّبُوا۟ بِـَٔايَٰتِنَا وَأَنفُسَهُمْ كَانُوا۟ يَظْلِمُونَ ۝

مَن يَهْدِ ٱللَّهُ فَهُوَ ٱلْمُهْتَدِى ۖ وَمَن يُضْلِلْ فَأُو۟لَٰٓئِكَ هُمُ ٱلْخَٰسِرُونَ ۝

وَلَقَدْ ذَرَأْنَا لِجَهَنَّمَ كَثِيرًا مِّنَ ٱلْجِنِّ وَٱلْإِنسِ ۖ لَهُمْ قُلُوبٌ لَّا يَفْقَهُونَ بِهَا وَلَهُمْ أَعْيُنٌ لَّا يُبْصِرُونَ بِهَا وَلَهُمْ ءَاذَانٌ لَّا يَسْمَعُونَ بِهَآ ۚ أُو۟لَٰٓئِكَ كَٱلْأَنْعَٰمِ بَلْ هُمْ أَضَلُّ ۚ أُو۟لَٰٓئِكَ هُمُ ٱلْغَٰفِلُونَ ۝

وَلِلَّهِ ٱلْأَسْمَآءُ ٱلْحُسْنَىٰ فَٱدْعُوهُ بِهَا ۖ وَذَرُوا۟ ٱلَّذِينَ يُلْحِدُونَ فِىٓ أَسْمَٰٓئِهِ ۚ سَيُجْزَوْنَ مَا كَانُوا۟ يَعْمَلُونَ ۝

وَمِمَّنْ خَلَقْنَآ أُمَّةٌ يَهْدُونَ بِٱلْحَقِّ وَبِهِۦ يَعْدِلُونَ ۝

وَٱلَّذِينَ كَذَّبُوا۟ بِـَٔايَٰتِنَا سَنَسْتَدْرِجُهُم مِّنْ حَيْثُ لَا يَعْلَمُونَ ۝

وَأُمْلِى لَهُمْ ۚ إِنَّ كَيْدِى مَتِينٌ ۝

أَوَلَمْ يَتَفَكَّرُوا۟ ۗ مَا بِصَاحِبِهِم مِّن جِنَّةٍ ۚ إِنْ هُوَ إِلَّا نَذِيرٌ مُّبِينٌ ۝

أَوَلَمْ يَنظُرُوا۟ فِى مَلَكُوتِ ٱلسَّمَٰوَٰتِ وَٱلْأَرْضِ وَمَا خَلَقَ

---

401. Muhammad.

things Allah has created, and how perhaps their appointed term may have drawn near? In what other message after this[402] will they, then, believe?

186. Whomever Allah leads astray will have no guide; and He leaves them in their arrogance to wander aimlessly.

187. They ask you about the Hour, when it will strike. Say: "The knowledge thereof is with my Lord; none but He will disclose it at the right time. It will be fateful in the heavens and on earth, and will not come upon you except suddenly." They ask you, as though you know about it. Say: "The knowledge thereof is with Allah, but most people do not know."

188. Say: "I do not have the power to benefit or harm myself, except as Allah pleases. Had I the knowledge of the Unseen, I would have acquired much good, and misfortune would not have touched me. I am only a warner and a bearer of good news to a people who believe."

189. It is He Who created you from a single soul from which He created her mate to live in comfort with her. Then when he approached her she bore a light burden; and so she carried on easily. When she became heavy, they called upon Allah, their Lord, saying: "If You grant us a righteous child, we shall be thankful."

190. He then gave them a righteous child. But they considered it to be given not only by Him, but also by associates whom they set up with Him. But Allah is exalted above those associates.

---

402. The Qur'an.

191. Do they associate with Allah those who can create nothing, while they, themselves, are created?

192. And they can neither help them nor help themselves.

193. And if you call them to guidance, they do not follow you. It is the same, for you, whether you call them or you remain silent.

194. Indeed those you call, apart from Allah, are servants like you; so call them and let them answer you, if you are truthful.

195. Do they have feet to walk with; do they have hands to smite with; do they have eyes to see with; or do they have ears to hear with? Say:[403] "Call your associate-gods, then plot against me and give me no respite."

196. My protector is Allah who sent down the Book and He protects the righteous.

197. And those you call, apart from Him, are not able to help you or even to help themselves.

198. If you call them to the guidance they do not hear; and you see them look at you, but they do not see.

199. Hold to forgiveness, enjoin the good and turn away from the ignorant.

200. And if a temptation from the Devil troubles you, seek refuge in Allah; He is truly All-Hearing, All-Knowing.

201. Indeed, those who fear God, when a visitation from the Devil afflicts them, will remember [Allah's Commands], and behold they will see clearly.

202. But their brethren will plunge them further into error, and [then] they will not desist.

---

403. Say, O Muhammad.

203. And if you do not bring them a revelation, they say: "Why don't you yourself invent it?" Say: "I only follow what is revealed to me from my Lord. This[404] constitutes a clear proof from your Lord and a guidance and mercy to those people who believe."

وَإِذَا لَمْ تَأْتِهِم بِـَٔايَةٍ قَالُوا۟ لَوْلَا ٱجْتَبَيْتَهَا قُلْ إِنَّمَآ أَتَّبِعُ مَا يُوحَىٰٓ إِلَىَّ مِن رَّبِّى هَٰذَا بَصَآئِرُ مِن رَّبِّكُمْ وَهُدًى وَرَحْمَةٌ لِّقَوْمٍ يُؤْمِنُونَ ﴿٢٠٣﴾

204. When the Qur'an is recited, listen to it and pay attention, that perchance you may receive mercy.

وَإِذَا قُرِئَ ٱلْقُرْءَانُ فَٱسْتَمِعُوا۟ لَهُۥ وَأَنصِتُوا۟ لَعَلَّكُمْ تُرْحَمُونَ ﴿٢٠٤﴾

205. And remember your Lord within yourself, in humility and awe and without raising your voice in the morning and evening; and do not be one of the heedless.

وَٱذْكُر رَّبَّكَ فِى نَفْسِكَ تَضَرُّعًا وَخِيفَةً وَدُونَ ٱلْجَهْرِ مِنَ ٱلْقَوْلِ بِٱلْغُدُوِّ وَٱلْـَٔاصَالِ وَلَا تَكُن مِّنَ ٱلْغَٰفِلِينَ ﴿٢٠٥﴾

206. Indeed, those[405] who are with your Lord are not too proud to worship Him, and they glorify Him and prostrate themselves before Him.

إِنَّ ٱلَّذِينَ عِندَ رَبِّكَ لَا يَسْتَكْبِرُونَ عَنْ عِبَادَتِهِۦ وَيُسَبِّحُونَهُۥ وَلَهُۥ يَسْجُدُونَ ۩ ﴿٢٠٦﴾

Sûrat Al-Anfâl, (The Spoils) 8

In the Name of Allah, the Compassionate, the Merciful

بِسْمِ ٱللَّهِ ٱلرَّحْمَٰنِ ٱلرَّحِيمِ

1. They ask you about the spoils,[406] say: "The spoils belong to Allah and to the Messenger. So fear Allah and settle your differences." Obey Allah and His Messenger if you are true believers.

يَسْـَٔلُونَكَ عَنِ ٱلْأَنفَالِ قُلِ ٱلْأَنفَالُ لِلَّهِ وَٱلرَّسُولِ فَٱتَّقُوا۟ ٱللَّهَ وَأَصْلِحُوا۟ ذَاتَ بَيْنِكُمْ وَأَطِيعُوا۟ ٱللَّهَ وَرَسُولَهُۥٓ إِن كُنتُم مُّؤْمِنِينَ ﴿١﴾

2. The true believers are those whose hearts, upon mention of Allah, quiver with fear; and when His Revelations are recited to them, they strengthen their faith. They put their trust in their Lord.

إِنَّمَا ٱلْمُؤْمِنُونَ ٱلَّذِينَ إِذَا ذُكِرَ ٱللَّهُ وَجِلَتْ قُلُوبُهُمْ وَإِذَا تُلِيَتْ عَلَيْهِمْ ءَايَٰتُهُۥ زَادَتْهُمْ إِيمَٰنًا وَعَلَىٰ رَبِّهِمْ يَتَوَكَّلُونَ ﴿٢﴾

---

404. The Qur'an.
405. The angels.
406. The spoils taken by the Muslims following the Battle of Badr 2 AH/624 AD.

3. Those who perform the prayer, and spend of what We provided for them.

4. Those are in truth the believers; they shall enjoy with their Lord a high station and receive forgiveness and a generous provision.

5. Just as when your[407] Lord brought you out in truth from your house, though a group of the believers disliked it.

6. They disputed with you concerning the Truth after it had become manifest, as though they were being led to their deaths while looking on.

7. And [remember] how Allah promised you that one of the two [enemy] groups[408] would be yours, and you wanted the unarmed one[409] to be yours. Allah, however, willed the Truth to triumph in accordance with His Words and to cut off the remnants of the unbelievers.

8. So that He may cause the Truth to triumph and nullify falsehood, even though the wicked sinners dislike it.

9. And when you called upon your Lord for help, He answered you: "I will reinforce you with a thousand angels following one another."

10. Allah did this only as good tidings and that your hearts might be assured thereby. Victory comes only from Allah; Allah is indeed Mighty and Wise.

11. [Remember] when He allowed slumber to overcome you as an assurance from Him, and sent you water down from heaven so as

الَّذِينَ يُقِيمُونَ الصَّلَوٰةَ وَمِمَّا رَزَقْنَٰهُمْ يُنفِقُونَ ٣

أُوْلَٰٓئِكَ هُمُ الْمُؤْمِنُونَ حَقًّا ۚ لَّهُمْ دَرَجَٰتٌ عِندَ رَبِّهِمْ وَمَغْفِرَةٌ وَرِزْقٌ كَرِيمٌ ٤

كَمَآ أَخْرَجَكَ رَبُّكَ مِنۢ بَيْتِكَ بِالْحَقِّ وَإِنَّ فَرِيقًا مِّنَ الْمُؤْمِنِينَ لَكَٰرِهُونَ ٥

يُجَٰدِلُونَكَ فِى الْحَقِّ بَعْدَمَا تَبَيَّنَ كَأَنَّمَا يُسَاقُونَ إِلَى الْمَوْتِ وَهُمْ يَنظُرُونَ ٦

وَإِذْ يَعِدُكُمُ اللَّهُ إِحْدَى الطَّآئِفَتَيْنِ أَنَّهَا لَكُمْ وَتَوَدُّونَ أَنَّ غَيْرَ ذَاتِ الشَّوْكَةِ تَكُونُ لَكُمْ وَيُرِيدُ اللَّهُ أَن يُحِقَّ الْحَقَّ بِكَلِمَٰتِهِۦ وَيَقْطَعَ دَابِرَ الْكَٰفِرِينَ ٧

لِيُحِقَّ الْحَقَّ وَيُبْطِلَ الْبَٰطِلَ وَلَوْ كَرِهَ الْمُجْرِمُونَ ٨

إِذْ تَسْتَغِيثُونَ رَبَّكُمْ فَاسْتَجَابَ لَكُمْ أَنِّى مُمِدُّكُم بِأَلْفٍ مِّنَ الْمَلَٰٓئِكَةِ مُرْدِفِينَ ٩

وَمَا جَعَلَهُ اللَّهُ إِلَّا بُشْرَىٰ وَلِتَطْمَئِنَّ بِهِۦ قُلُوبُكُمْ ۚ وَمَا النَّصْرُ إِلَّا مِنْ عِندِ اللَّهِ ۚ إِنَّ اللَّهَ عَزِيزٌ حَكِيمٌ ١٠

إِذْ يُغَشِّيكُمُ النُّعَاسَ أَمَنَةً مِّنْهُ وَيُنَزِّلُ عَلَيْكُم مِّنَ السَّمَآءِ مَآءً لِّيُطَهِّرَكُم بِهِۦ وَيُذْهِبَ عَنكُمْ رِجْزَ

---

407. Meaning Muhammad.
408. The Meccan caravan of Quraysh and the army which was sent to defend it.
409. The caravan.

to purify you, relieve you of the Devil's temptation, fortify your hearts and steady your feet therewith.

12. And when your Lord revealed to the angels: "I am with you; so support those who believe. I will cast terror into the hearts of those who disbelieve; so strike upon the necks and strike every fingertip of theirs."

13. That is because they opposed Allah and His Messenger; and he who opposes Allah and His Messenger [will find] Allah's Punishment very severe.

14. This is how it will be; so taste it; the torture of the Fire is awaiting the unbelievers.

15. O believers, if you meet the unbelievers on the march, do not turn your backs upon them.

16. Whoever turns his back on that day, unless preparing to resume fighting, or joining another group, incurs Allah's Wrath and his refuge is Hell; and what an evil fate!

17. It was not you[410] who slew them, but Allah; and when you[411] threw[412] it was actually Allah Who threw, so that He might generously reward the believers. Allah is All-Hearing, All-Knowing.

18. That was done, so that Allah might foil the machinations of the unbelievers.

19. If you seek victory, the victory has been granted you; and if you desist, it will be better for you; but if you come back, We will come back,[413] and your forces will avail you nothing, however numerous they are. Allah is on the side of the believers.

---

410. Those addressed are the Muslims.
411. Muhammad is addressed here.
412. Threw the pebbles or a handful of dust at the enemy in retaliation.
413. That is, We will again support the believers.

20. O you who believe, obey Allah and His Messenger, and do not turn away from Him while you hear.

21. And do not be like those who say: "We hear", while they hear not.

22. The worst beasts in Allah's sight are the deaf and dumb who do not understand.

23. If Allah knew of any good in them, He would have made them hear; and had He made them hear, they would still have turned away defiantly.

24. O believers, respond to Allah and to the Messenger if he calls you to that which will give you life; and know that Allah stands between a man and his heart, and that unto Him you shall be gathered.

25. And fear a calamity which will not only afflict the wrongdoers among you; and know that Allah is Severe in retribution.

26. And remember when you were few and were deemed weak in the land, fearing that the people will snatch you away; but He gave you a shelter, strengthened you with His support and provided you with the good things, that perchance you may give thanks.

27. O you who believe, do not betray Allah and the Messenger, nor betray your trusts knowingly.

28. And know that your wealth and your children are a temptation, and with Allah is a great reward.

29. O you who believe, if you fear Allah, He will provide you with a criteria [to distinguish right from wrong], and absolve you from your sins and forgive you. Allah's Bounty is great.

يَـٰٓأَيُّهَا ٱلَّذِينَ ءَامَنُوٓا۟ أَطِيعُوا۟ ٱللَّهَ وَرَسُولَهُۥ وَلَا تَوَلَّوْا۟ عَنْهُ وَأَنتُمْ تَسْمَعُونَ ۝

وَلَا تَكُونُوا۟ كَٱلَّذِينَ قَالُوا۟ سَمِعْنَا وَهُمْ لَا يَسْمَعُونَ ۝

۞ إِنَّ شَرَّ ٱلدَّوَآبِّ عِندَ ٱللَّهِ ٱلصُّمُّ ٱلْبُكْمُ ٱلَّذِينَ لَا يَعْقِلُونَ ۝

وَلَوْ عَلِمَ ٱللَّهُ فِيهِمْ خَيْرًا لَّأَسْمَعَهُمْ وَلَوْ أَسْمَعَهُمْ لَتَوَلَّوا۟ وَّهُم مُّعْرِضُونَ ۝

يَـٰٓأَيُّهَا ٱلَّذِينَ ءَامَنُوا۟ ٱسْتَجِيبُوا۟ لِلَّهِ وَلِلرَّسُولِ إِذَا دَعَاكُمْ لِمَا يُحْيِيكُمْ وَٱعْلَمُوٓا۟ أَنَّ ٱللَّهَ يَحُولُ بَيْنَ ٱلْمَرْءِ وَقَلْبِهِۦ وَأَنَّهُۥٓ إِلَيْهِ تُحْشَرُونَ ۝

وَٱتَّقُوا۟ فِتْنَةً لَّا تُصِيبَنَّ ٱلَّذِينَ ظَلَمُوا۟ مِنكُمْ خَآصَّةً وَٱعْلَمُوٓا۟ أَنَّ ٱللَّهَ شَدِيدُ ٱلْعِقَابِ ۝

وَٱذْكُرُوٓا۟ إِذْ أَنتُمْ قَلِيلٌ مُّسْتَضْعَفُونَ فِى ٱلْأَرْضِ تَخَافُونَ أَن يَتَخَطَّفَكُمُ ٱلنَّاسُ فَـَٔاوَىٰكُمْ وَأَيَّدَكُم بِنَصْرِهِۦ وَرَزَقَكُم مِّنَ ٱلطَّيِّبَـٰتِ لَعَلَّكُمْ تَشْكُرُونَ ۝

يَـٰٓأَيُّهَا ٱلَّذِينَ ءَامَنُوا۟ لَا تَخُونُوا۟ ٱللَّهَ وَٱلرَّسُولَ وَتَخُونُوٓا۟ أَمَـٰنَـٰتِكُمْ وَأَنتُمْ تَعْلَمُونَ ۝

وَٱعْلَمُوٓا۟ أَنَّمَآ أَمْوَٰلُكُمْ وَأَوْلَـٰدُكُمْ فِتْنَةٌ وَأَنَّ ٱللَّهَ عِندَهُۥٓ أَجْرٌ عَظِيمٌ ۝

يَـٰٓأَيُّهَا ٱلَّذِينَ ءَامَنُوٓا۟ إِن تَتَّقُوا۟ ٱللَّهَ يَجْعَل لَّكُمْ فُرْقَانًا وَيُكَفِّرْ عَنكُمْ سَيِّـَٔاتِكُمْ وَيَغْفِرْ لَكُمْ وَٱللَّهُ ذُو ٱلْفَضْلِ ٱلْعَظِيمِ ۝

30. And [remember] when the unbelievers plotted against you, so as to confine you, kill you or expel you. They schemed and Allah schemed, but Allah is the Best of schemers.

31. And when Our Revelations are recited to them, they say: "We have heard. Had we wished, we would have uttered the like of this; this is nothing but the fables of the ancients."

32. And when they said: "O Allah, if this is indeed the truth from You, then rain down upon us brickstones from heaven, or inflict upon us a very painful punishment."

33. And Allah did not wish to punish them while you[414] were in their midst, and Allah was not going to punish them while they were asking for forgiveness.

34. And what excuse do they have that Allah should not punish them, when they bar people from the Sacred Mosque, although they were not its guardians? Its guardians are only those who fear Allah; but most of them do not know.

35. Their prayer at the House is nothing but whistling and clapping; so taste the punishment for your disbelief.

36. Indeed, the unbelievers spend their wealth to bar [people] from Allah's Path. They will continue to spend it, but it will become a source of anguish for them; then they will be vanquished. And those who disbelieve shall be gathered in Hell.

37. So that Allah might separate the foul from the fair and place the foul, one upon the other, piling them up all together and casting them into Hell. Those are truly the losers.

---

414. The Prophet.

38. Say to those who disbelieve:[415] "If they desist, He will forgive them what is already done; but if they go back, then [they should remember] what befell those before them."

39. And fight them, so that sedition might end and the only religion will be that of Allah. Then if they desist, Allah is Fully Aware of what they do.

40. But if they turn away, then know that Allah is your Protector; and what an Excellent Protector and Supporter He is!

41. And know that whatever booty you take, the fifth thereof is for Allah, the Messenger, the near of kin, the orphan, and the wayfarer, if you really believe in Allah and in what We revealed to Our servant on the day of decision,[416] the day when the two hosts met. Allah has power over everything.

42. While you were on the nearer side [of the valley] and they were on the farther side, with the cavalcade beneath you. Had you made an appointment, you would surely have failed to keep the appointment. But [this happened] so that Allah might bring about a matter already decreed, and that those who were to perish would perish after a clear proof [had been given], and those who were to survive would survive after a clear proof [had been given]. And surely Allah is All-Hearing, All-Knowing.

43. [Remember] when Allah showed them to you [O Muhammad] in your sleep as few. Had He showed them as many, you would have lost heart and you would have differed over the matter. But Allah saved you. He knows what is hidden in the hearts.

قُل لِّلَّذِينَ كَفَرُوٓا۟ إِن يَنتَهُوا۟ يُغْفَرْ لَهُم مَّا قَدْ سَلَفَ وَإِن يَعُودُوا۟ فَقَدْ مَضَتْ سُنَّتُ ٱلْأَوَّلِينَ ﴿٣٨﴾

وَقَٰتِلُوهُمْ حَتَّىٰ لَا تَكُونَ فِتْنَةٌ وَيَكُونَ ٱلدِّينُ كُلُّهُۥ لِلَّهِ فَإِنِ ٱنتَهَوْا۟ فَإِنَّ ٱللَّهَ بِمَا يَعْمَلُونَ بَصِيرٌ ﴿٣٩﴾

وَإِن تَوَلَّوْا۟ فَٱعْلَمُوٓا۟ أَنَّ ٱللَّهَ مَوْلَىٰكُمْ نِعْمَ ٱلْمَوْلَىٰ وَنِعْمَ ٱلنَّصِيرُ ﴿٤٠﴾

۞ وَٱعْلَمُوٓا۟ أَنَّمَا غَنِمْتُم مِّن شَىْءٍ فَأَنَّ لِلَّهِ خُمُسَهُۥ وَلِلرَّسُولِ وَلِذِى ٱلْقُرْبَىٰ وَٱلْيَتَٰمَىٰ وَٱلْمَسَٰكِينِ وَٱبْنِ ٱلسَّبِيلِ إِن كُنتُمْ ءَامَنتُم بِٱللَّهِ وَمَآ أَنزَلْنَا عَلَىٰ عَبْدِنَا يَوْمَ ٱلْفُرْقَانِ يَوْمَ ٱلْتَقَى ٱلْجَمْعَانِ وَٱللَّهُ عَلَىٰ كُلِّ شَىْءٍ قَدِيرٌ ﴿٤١﴾

إِذْ أَنتُم بِٱلْعُدْوَةِ ٱلدُّنْيَا وَهُم بِٱلْعُدْوَةِ ٱلْقُصْوَىٰ وَٱلرَّكْبُ أَسْفَلَ مِنكُمْ وَلَوْ تَوَاعَدتُّمْ لَٱخْتَلَفْتُمْ فِى ٱلْمِيعَٰدِ وَلَٰكِن لِّيَقْضِىَ ٱللَّهُ أَمْرًا كَانَ مَفْعُولًا لِّيَهْلِكَ مَنْ هَلَكَ عَنۢ بَيِّنَةٍ وَيَحْيَىٰ مَنْ حَىَّ عَنۢ بَيِّنَةٍ وَإِنَّ ٱللَّهَ لَسَمِيعٌ عَلِيمٌ ﴿٤٢﴾

إِذْ يُرِيكَهُمُ ٱللَّهُ فِى مَنَامِكَ قَلِيلًا وَلَوْ أَرَىٰكَهُمْ كَثِيرًا لَّفَشِلْتُمْ وَلَتَنَٰزَعْتُمْ فِى ٱلْأَمْرِ وَلَٰكِنَّ ٱللَّهَ سَلَّمَ إِنَّهُۥ عَلِيمٌۢ بِذَاتِ ٱلصُّدُورِ ﴿٤٣﴾

---

415. Those included Abu Sufyan, the Meccan leader, and his companions.
416. The reference here is to the Battle of Badr.

44. And [remember] when He showed them to you, as you met, few in your eyes, and made you few in their eyes; so that Allah might bring about a matter already decreed. And unto Allah shall all matters return.

45. O believers, if you encounter an enemy host, stand fast and remember Allah frequently, that perchance you may prosper.

46. And obey Allah and His Messenger and do not quarrel among yourselves lest you lose heart and your strength dissipates. And stand fast, for Allah is on the side of those who stand fast.

47. And do not be like those who went out of their homes boastfully showing off in front of the people, while they barred others from the Path of Allah. Allah is Fully Aware of what they do.

48. And the Devil made their [foul] deeds look fair to them saying: "No man shall overcome you today; and I am indeed by your side." But when the two hosts sighted each other, he turned on his heels saying: "I am quit of you; I see what you do not see; I fear Allah, and Allah is Stern in retribution."

49. And the hypocrites and those in whose hearts is a sickness said: "Their religion has misled those people."[417] But he who trusts in Allah will find Allah is Mighty and Wise.

50. And if you could only see when the angels carry off the unbelievers, striking their faces and their rears [saying]: "Taste the punishment of the Fire."

51. That is on account of what you have done, and Allah is not unjust to His servants.

---

417. The Muslims.

181

كَدَأْبِ ءَالِ فِرْعَوْنَ وَالَّذِينَ مِن قَبْلِهِمْ كَفَرُواْ بِـَٔايَٰتِ

52. Just like the wont of Pharaoh's people and those who preceded them; they disbelieved their Lord's Revelations; so Allah punished them for their sins. Allah is Strong and Stern in retribution.

اللَّهِ فَأَخَذَهُمُ اللَّهُ بِذُنُوبِهِمْ إِنَّ اللَّهَ قَوِيٌّ شَدِيدُ ٱلْعِقَابِ ۝

53. That is because Allah never changes a favour He confers on a people unless they change what is in their hearts, and because Allah is All-Hearing, All-Knowing.

ذَٰلِكَ بِأَنَّ اللَّهَ لَمْ يَكُ مُغَيِّرًا نِّعْمَةً أَنْعَمَهَا عَلَىٰ قَوْمٍ حَتَّىٰ يُغَيِّرُواْ مَا بِأَنفُسِهِمْ وَأَنَّ اللَّهَ سَمِيعٌ عَلِيمٌ ۝

54. Just like the wont of Pharaoh's people and those who preceded them; they denied Allah's Revelations, so We destroyed them because of their sins and We drowned Pharaoh's people. They were all wrongdoers.

كَدَأْبِ ءَالِ فِرْعَوْنَ وَالَّذِينَ مِن قَبْلِهِمْ كَذَّبُواْ بِـَٔايَٰتِ رَبِّهِمْ فَأَهْلَكْنَٰهُم بِذُنُوبِهِمْ وَأَغْرَقْنَا ءَالَ فِرْعَوْنَ وَكُلٌّ كَانُواْ ظَٰلِمِينَ ۝

55. The worst beasts in the Sight of Allah are those who disbelieve, because they will never believe.

إِنَّ شَرَّ ٱلدَّوَآبِّ عِندَ اللَّهِ ٱلَّذِينَ كَفَرُواْ فَهُمْ لَا يُؤْمِنُونَ ۝

56. Those, who each time you make a covenant with them, break it, and do not fear God.

ٱلَّذِينَ عَٰهَدتَّ مِنْهُمْ ثُمَّ يَنقُضُونَ عَهْدَهُمْ فِى كُلِّ مَرَّةٍ وَهُمْ لَا يَتَّقُونَ ۝

57. So, if you should come upon them in the war, scatter[418] them with those behind them, that perchance they may pay heed.

فَإِمَّا تَثْقَفَنَّهُمْ فِى ٱلْحَرْبِ فَشَرِّدْ بِهِم مَّنْ خَلْفَهُمْ لَعَلَّهُمْ يَذَّكَّرُونَ ۝

58. And should you fear treachery from any people, throw back their treaty to them in like manner. Allah does not like the treacherous.

وَإِمَّا تَخَافَنَّ مِن قَوْمٍ خِيَانَةً فَٱنبِذْ إِلَيْهِمْ عَلَىٰ سَوَآءٍ إِنَّ اللَّهَ لَا يُحِبُّ ٱلْخَآئِنِينَ ۝

59. Let not the unbelievers think that they can escape [Us]. They will never be able to escape.

وَلَا يَحْسَبَنَّ ٱلَّذِينَ كَفَرُواْ سَبَقُواْ إِنَّهُمْ لَا يُعْجِزُونَ ۝

60. And make ready for them whatever you can of fighting men and horses, to terrify thereby the enemies of Allah and your enemy, as well as others besides them whom you do not know, but Allah knows well. Everything you spend in the Path of Allah will be repaid in full, and you will never be wronged.

وَأَعِدُّواْ لَهُم مَّا ٱسْتَطَعْتُم مِّن قُوَّةٍ وَمِن رِّبَاطِ ٱلْخَيْلِ تُرْهِبُونَ بِهِۦ عَدُوَّ اللَّهِ وَعَدُوَّكُمْ وَءَاخَرِينَ مِن دُونِهِمْ لَا تَعْلَمُونَهُمُ اللَّهُ يَعْلَمُهُمْ وَمَا تُنفِقُواْ مِن شَىْءٍ فِى سَبِيلِ اللَّهِ يُوَفَّ إِلَيْكُمْ وَأَنتُمْ لَا تُظْلَمُونَ ۝

---

418. That is, by punishing them severely.

61. And if they incline to peace, incline to it too, and put your trust in Allah. He is truly the Hearer, the Knower.

62. And if they wish to deceive you, then Allah is Sufficient for you and so are the believers, it is He Who has strengthened you with His Support and with the believers;

63. He brought their hearts together. Had you spent all there is on earth, you could not have brought their hearts together, but Allah has brought them together. He is Mighty and Wise.

64. O Prophet, Allah is Sufficient for you and so are the believers who follow you.

65. O Prophet, urge the believers to fight. If there are twenty steadfast men among you, they will defeat two hundred; and if there are a hundred, they will defeat a thousand of the unbelievers, because they are a people who do not understand.

66. Now Allah has lightened your burden; He knows that there is a weakness in you. So, if there are a hundred steadfast men among you, they will overcome two hundred; and if there are a thousand men among you, they will overcome two thousand, by Allah's Leave. Allah is with the steadfast.

67. It is not up to any Prophet to take captives except after too much blood is shed in the land.[419] You desire the fleeting goods of this world, but Allah desires the Hereafter, and Allah is Mighty, Wise.

68. But for a prior ordinance of Allah, you would have been afflicted on account of what you have taken[420] by a terrible punishment.

---

419. What is meant here is the Prophet should not allow the taking of captives for the sake of ransom. He may, however, allow taking captives after the enemy is hard hit and subdued.

420. An ordinance which made it lawful for the Muslims to take spoils and captives.

69. So eat of the lawful and good things you have taken as booty. Fear Allah; Allah is truly All-Forgiving, Merciful.

70. O Prophet, tell those captives in your keeping: "If Allah knows of any good in your hearts, He will give you in return better than what has been taken from you and forgive you." Allah is All-Forgiving, Merciful.

71. But if they wish to betray you, they have previously betrayed Allah, and so He subdued them. Allah is All-Knowing, Wise.

72. Those who have believed and emigrated and struggled with their wealth and their lives in the Path of Allah, and those who gave refuge and support - those are friends of one another; but those who have believed, yet did not emigrate, you will not be responsible for their protection until they emigrate. Should they seek your support for religion's sake, you ought to support them, but not against a people with whom you have a compact. Allah is Fully Aware of what you do.

73. As to the unbelievers, they are friends of one another. If you do not do this,[421] there will be great sedition and corruption in the land.

74. And those who believed, emigrated and struggled in the Path of Allah, and those who have given refuge and support - those are the true believers. They will have forgiveness and bountiful provision.

75. And those who believed afterwards, emigrated and struggled with you - those are part of you. And the blood relatives are closer to one another in Allah's Book. Allah is truly Cognizant of everything.

---

421. That is, if you do not support the Muslims and subdue the unbelievers.

184

Sûrat At-Tawbah, (Repentance) 9

1. This is an immunity from Allah and His Messenger to those idolaters with whom you made compacts.

2. Travel, then, in the land freely for four months, and know that you will never be able to thwart Allah, and that Allah shall disgrace the unbelievers.

3. This is a proclamation from Allah and His Messenger to mankind on the day of the great pilgrimage,[422] that Allah is absolved of the idolaters, as is His Messenger. If you repent, it will be better for you; but if you turn away, know that you shall never thwart Allah. Proclaim to those who disbelieve a grievous punishment.

4. Except for those idolaters with whom you made a compact, then they did not fail you in anything and did not lend support to anybody against you. Honour your compact with them until the end of its term. Allah loves the righteous.

5. Then, when the Sacred Months[423] are over, kill the idolaters wherever you find them, take them [as captives], besiege them, and lie in wait for them at every point of observation. If they repent afterwards, perform the prayer and pay the alms, then release them. Allah is truly All-Forgiving, Merciful.

6. And if any one of the idolaters should seek refuge with you, give him refuge, so that he may hear the Word of Allah; then convey him to his place of security. That is because they are a people who do not know.

---

422. On the 10th of Dhul Hijjah.
423. These are the four months during which war was prohibited in pre-Islamic times.

7. How can the idolaters have a compact with Allah and His Messenger, except for those you made a compact with at the Sacred Mosque? So long as these honour their obligations to you, honour yours to them. Allah loves the righteous.

8. How [can that be]? If they overcome you, they will observe neither kinship nor compact with you. They only give you satisfaction with their mouths, while their hearts refuse, and most of them are sinners.

9. They have sold Allah's Revelations for a small price, and have barred [others] from His Path. Evil indeed is what they do!

10. They observe with the believers neither kinship nor compact. Those are the real transgressors.

11. Yet, if they repent, perform the prayer and pay the alms, they will be your brethren in religion. We expound the revelations to a people who know.

12. But if they break their oaths after their pledge [is made] and abuse your religion, then fight the leaders of unbelief; for they have no regard for oaths, and that perchance they may desist.

13. Will you not fight a people who broke their oaths and intended to drive the Messenger out, seeing that they attacked you first? Do you fear them? Surely, you ought to fear Allah more, if you are real believers.

14. Fight them, Allah will punish them at your hands, will disgrace them, give you victory over them, and heal the hearts of a believing people.

15. And He will remove the rage from their hearts. Allah shows mercy to whomever He pleases, and Allah is All-Knowing, Wise.

كَيْفَ يَكُونُ لِلْمُشْرِكِينَ عَهْدٌ عِندَ ٱللَّهِ وَعِندَ رَسُولِهِ إِلَّا ٱلَّذِينَ عَٰهَدتُّمْ عِندَ ٱلْمَسْجِدِ ٱلْحَرَامِ فَمَا ٱسْتَقَٰمُوا۟ لَكُمْ فَٱسْتَقِيمُوا۟ لَهُمْ إِنَّ ٱللَّهَ يُحِبُّ ٱلْمُتَّقِينَ ۝

كَيْفَ وَإِن يَظْهَرُوا۟ عَلَيْكُمْ لَا يَرْقُبُوا۟ فِيكُمْ إِلًّا وَلَا ذِمَّةً يُرْضُونَكُم بِأَفْوَٰهِهِمْ وَتَأْبَىٰ قُلُوبُهُمْ وَأَكْثَرُهُمْ فَٰسِقُونَ ۝

ٱشْتَرَوْا۟ بِـَٔايَٰتِ ٱللَّهِ ثَمَنًا قَلِيلًا فَصَدُّوا۟ عَن سَبِيلِهِ إِنَّهُمْ سَآءَ مَا كَانُوا۟ يَعْمَلُونَ ۝

لَا يَرْقُبُونَ فِى مُؤْمِنٍ إِلًّا وَلَا ذِمَّةً وَأُو۟لَٰٓئِكَ هُمُ ٱلْمُعْتَدُونَ ۝

فَإِن تَابُوا۟ وَأَقَامُوا۟ ٱلصَّلَوٰةَ وَءَاتَوُا۟ ٱلزَّكَوٰةَ فَإِخْوَٰنُكُمْ فِى ٱلدِّينِ وَنُفَصِّلُ ٱلْءَايَٰتِ لِقَوْمٍ يَعْلَمُونَ ۝

وَإِن نَّكَثُوٓا۟ أَيْمَٰنَهُم مِّنۢ بَعْدِ عَهْدِهِمْ وَطَعَنُوا۟ فِى دِينِكُمْ فَقَٰتِلُوٓا۟ أَئِمَّةَ ٱلْكُفْرِ إِنَّهُمْ لَآ أَيْمَٰنَ لَهُمْ لَعَلَّهُمْ يَنتَهُونَ ۝

أَلَا تُقَٰتِلُونَ قَوْمًا نَّكَثُوٓا۟ أَيْمَٰنَهُمْ وَهَمُّوا۟ بِإِخْرَاجِ ٱلرَّسُولِ وَهُم بَدَءُوكُمْ أَوَّلَ مَرَّةٍ أَتَخْشَوْنَهُمْ فَٱللَّهُ أَحَقُّ أَن تَخْشَوْهُ إِن كُنتُم مُّؤْمِنِينَ ۝

قَٰتِلُوهُمْ يُعَذِّبْهُمُ ٱللَّهُ بِأَيْدِيكُمْ وَيُخْزِهِمْ وَيَنصُرْكُمْ عَلَيْهِمْ وَيَشْفِ صُدُورَ قَوْمٍ مُّؤْمِنِينَ ۝

وَيُذْهِبْ غَيْظَ قُلُوبِهِمْ وَيَتُوبُ ٱللَّهُ عَلَىٰ مَن يَشَآءُ وَٱللَّهُ عَلِيمٌ حَكِيمٌ ۝

16. Do you imagine that Allah would leave you alone before knowing who of you fight [in the way of Allah] and do not seek supporters besides Allah and His Messenger? Allah is Fully Aware of what you do.

17. The unbelievers should not enter Allah's Mosques bearing witness thereby against themselves that they are unbelievers. The works of those are vain and in the Fire they will abide forever.

18. Only he who believes in Allah and the Hereafter, performs the prayers, gives the alms and fears no one but Allah, shall visit Allah's Mosques. Those shall be reckoned among the rightly guided.

19. Do you consider those, who give the pilgrims water to drink and maintain the Sacred Mosque, like those who believe in Allah and the Hereafter and fight in Allah's Way? They are not alike in Allah's Sight, and Allah will not guide the wrongdoing people.

20. Those who have believed, emigrated and fought in the Path of Allah with their lives are higher in rank in Allah's Sight; and those are the winners.

21. Their Lord announces to them the good news of mercy from Him, good pleasure and Gardens wherein they have everlasting bliss;

22. Abiding therein forever. With Allah is a great reward.

23. O believers, do not take your fathers and brothers as friends, if they prefer disbelief to belief. Those who take them as friends are the wrongdoers.

24. Say: "If your fathers, your sons, your brothers, your spouses, your relatives, the wealth you have gained, a trade you fear might slacken, and dwellings you love are

أَمْ حَسِبْتُمْ أَن تُتْرَكُوا۟ وَلَمَّا يَعْلَمِ ٱللَّهُ ٱلَّذِينَ جَهَدُوا۟ مِنكُمْ وَلَمْ يَتَّخِذُوا۟ مِن دُونِ ٱللَّهِ وَلَا رَسُولِهِ وَلَا ٱلْمُؤْمِنِينَ وَلِيجَةً وَٱللَّهُ خَبِيرٌۢ بِمَا تَعْمَلُونَ ﴿١٦﴾

مَا كَانَ لِلْمُشْرِكِينَ أَن يَعْمُرُوا۟ مَسَٰجِدَ ٱللَّهِ شَٰهِدِينَ عَلَىٰٓ أَنفُسِهِم بِٱلْكُفْرِ أُو۟لَٰٓئِكَ حَبِطَتْ أَعْمَٰلُهُمْ وَفِى ٱلنَّارِ هُمْ خَٰلِدُونَ ﴿١٧﴾

إِنَّمَا يَعْمُرُ مَسَٰجِدَ ٱللَّهِ مَنْ ءَامَنَ بِٱللَّهِ وَٱلْيَوْمِ ٱلْءَاخِرِ وَأَقَامَ ٱلصَّلَوٰةَ وَءَاتَى ٱلزَّكَوٰةَ وَلَمْ يَخْشَ إِلَّا ٱللَّهَ فَعَسَىٰٓ أُو۟لَٰٓئِكَ أَن يَكُونُوا۟ مِنَ ٱلْمُهْتَدِينَ ﴿١٨﴾

۞ أَجَعَلْتُمْ سِقَايَةَ ٱلْحَآجِّ وَعِمَارَةَ ٱلْمَسْجِدِ ٱلْحَرَامِ كَمَنْ ءَامَنَ بِٱللَّهِ وَٱلْيَوْمِ ٱلْءَاخِرِ وَجَٰهَدَ فِى سَبِيلِ ٱللَّهِ لَا يَسْتَوُۥنَ عِندَ ٱللَّهِ وَٱللَّهُ لَا يَهْدِى ٱلْقَوْمَ ٱلظَّٰلِمِينَ ﴿١٩﴾

ٱلَّذِينَ ءَامَنُوا۟ وَهَاجَرُوا۟ وَجَٰهَدُوا۟ فِى سَبِيلِ ٱللَّهِ بِأَمْوَٰلِهِمْ وَأَنفُسِهِمْ أَعْظَمُ دَرَجَةً عِندَ ٱللَّهِ وَأُو۟لَٰٓئِكَ هُمُ ٱلْفَآئِزُونَ ﴿٢٠﴾

يُبَشِّرُهُمْ رَبُّهُم بِرَحْمَةٍ مِّنْهُ وَرِضْوَٰنٍ وَجَنَّٰتٍ لَّهُمْ فِيهَا نَعِيمٌ مُّقِيمٌ ﴿٢١﴾

خَٰلِدِينَ فِيهَآ أَبَدًا إِنَّ ٱللَّهَ عِندَهُۥٓ أَجْرٌ عَظِيمٌ ﴿٢٢﴾

يَٰٓأَيُّهَا ٱلَّذِينَ ءَامَنُوا۟ لَا تَتَّخِذُوٓا۟ ءَابَآءَكُمْ وَإِخْوَٰنَكُمْ أَوْلِيَآءَ إِنِ ٱسْتَحَبُّوا۟ ٱلْكُفْرَ عَلَى ٱلْإِيمَٰنِ وَمَن يَتَوَلَّهُم مِّنكُمْ فَأُو۟لَٰٓئِكَ هُمُ ٱلظَّٰلِمُونَ ﴿٢٣﴾

قُلْ إِن كَانَ ءَابَآؤُكُمْ وَأَبْنَآؤُكُمْ وَإِخْوَٰنُكُمْ وَأَزْوَٰجُكُمْ وَعَشِيرَتُكُمْ وَأَمْوَٰلٌ ٱقْتَرَفْتُمُوهَا وَتِجَٰرَةٌ تَخْشَوْنَ كَسَادَهَا وَمَسَٰكِنُ تَرْضَوْنَهَآ أَحَبَّ إِلَيْكُم مِّنَ ٱللَّهِ وَرَسُولِهِۦ

dearer to you than Allah and His Messenger or than fighting in His Way, then wait until Allah fulfils His Decree. Allah does not guide the sinful people.

25. Allah gave you victory in numerous places and on the day of Hunayn[424] when you were pleased with your large number; but it availed you nothing and the land became too strait for you, despite its breadth, whereupon you turned back and fled.

26. Then Allah sent down His Tranquillity upon His Messenger and upon the believers, and He sent down soldiers you did not see, and punished the unbelievers. That is the reward of the unbelievers.

27. Then, Allah will pardon thereafter whom He pleases. Allah is All-Forgiving, Merciful.

28. O believers, the polytheists are truly unclean; so let them not come near the Sacred Mosque after this year of theirs; and if you fear poverty, Allah shall enrich you from His Bounty, if He pleases. Allah is truly All-Knowing, Wise.

29. Fight those among the People of the Book who do not believe in Allah and the Last Day, do not forbid what Allah and His Messenger have forbidden and do not profess the true religion, till they pay the poll-tax out of hand and submissively.

30. The Jews say: "Ezra is the son of Allah", and the Christians say: "The Messiah is the son of Allah." That is their statement, by their mouths; they emulate the statement of the unbelievers of yore. May Allah damn them; how they are perverted!

---

424. A valley between Mecca and Ta'if.

31. They take their rabbis and monks as lords besides Allah, as well as the Messiah, son of Mary, although they are commanded to worship none but One God. There is no god but He; exalted He is above what they associate with Him.

32. They wish to put out Allah's Light with their mouths, and Allah allows nothing less than perfecting His Light, even if the unbelievers should resent it.

33. It is He Who sent His Messenger with the guidance and the true religion, in order to make it triumph over every religion, even if the polytheists should resent it.

34. O believers, many of the rabbis and monks devour the property of the people unjustly and bar others from the Path of Allah. Those who hoard gold and silver and do not spend them in Allah's Path, announce to them a very painful punishment.

35. On the Day when all that will be heated in the Fire of Hell, and their foreheads, sides and backs will be branded with it. This is what you hoarded for yourselves; taste now what you used to hoard.

36. The number of months, with Allah, is twelve months by Allah's Ordinance from the day He created the heavens and the earth. Four of these are Sacred. This is the right religion, so do not wrong yourselves during them; but fight the polytheists all together just as they fight you all together; and know that Allah is on the side of the righteous.

37. Postponing the [Sacred Month] is an added disbelief by which the unbelievers seek to mislead, allowing it one year and prohibiting it another year, so as to equal the number [of months] Allah has made sacred. Their evil deeds are made attractive to them; and Allah does not guide the unbelieving people.

ٱتَّخَذُوٓاْ أَحْبَارَهُمْ وَرُهْبَٰنَهُمْ أَرْبَابًا مِّن دُونِ ٱللَّهِ وَٱلْمَسِيحَ ٱبْنَ مَرْيَمَ وَمَآ أُمِرُوٓاْ إِلَّا لِيَعْبُدُوٓاْ إِلَٰهًا وَٰحِدًا لَّآ إِلَٰهَ إِلَّا هُوَ سُبْحَٰنَهُۥ عَمَّا يُشْرِكُونَ ﴿٣١﴾

يُرِيدُونَ أَن يُطْفِـُٔواْ نُورَ ٱللَّهِ بِأَفْوَٰهِهِمْ وَيَأْبَى ٱللَّهُ إِلَّآ أَن يُتِمَّ نُورَهُۥ وَلَوْ كَرِهَ ٱلْكَٰفِرُونَ ﴿٣٢﴾

هُوَ ٱلَّذِىٓ أَرْسَلَ رَسُولَهُۥ بِٱلْهُدَىٰ وَدِينِ ٱلْحَقِّ لِيُظْهِرَهُۥ عَلَى ٱلدِّينِ كُلِّهِۦ وَلَوْ كَرِهَ ٱلْمُشْرِكُونَ ﴿٣٣﴾

يَٰٓأَيُّهَا ٱلَّذِينَ ءَامَنُوٓاْ إِنَّ كَثِيرًا مِّنَ ٱلْأَحْبَارِ وَٱلرُّهْبَانِ لَيَأْكُلُونَ أَمْوَٰلَ ٱلنَّاسِ بِٱلْبَٰطِلِ وَيَصُدُّونَ عَن سَبِيلِ ٱللَّهِ وَٱلَّذِينَ يَكْنِزُونَ ٱلذَّهَبَ وَٱلْفِضَّةَ وَلَا يُنفِقُونَهَا فِى سَبِيلِ ٱللَّهِ فَبَشِّرْهُم بِعَذَابٍ أَلِيمٍ ﴿٣٤﴾

يَوْمَ يُحْمَىٰ عَلَيْهَا فِى نَارِ جَهَنَّمَ فَتُكْوَىٰ بِهَا جِبَاهُهُمْ وَجُنُوبُهُمْ وَظُهُورُهُمْ هَٰذَا مَا كَنَزْتُمْ لِأَنفُسِكُمْ فَذُوقُواْ مَا كُنتُمْ تَكْنِزُونَ ﴿٣٥﴾

إِنَّ عِدَّةَ ٱلشُّهُورِ عِندَ ٱللَّهِ ٱثْنَا عَشَرَ شَهْرًا فِى كِتَٰبِ ٱللَّهِ يَوْمَ خَلَقَ ٱلسَّمَٰوَٰتِ وَٱلْأَرْضَ مِنْهَآ أَرْبَعَةٌ حُرُمٌ ذَٰلِكَ ٱلدِّينُ ٱلْقَيِّمُ فَلَا تَظْلِمُواْ فِيهِنَّ أَنفُسَكُمْ وَقَٰتِلُواْ ٱلْمُشْرِكِينَ كَآفَّةً كَمَا يُقَٰتِلُونَكُمْ كَآفَّةً وَٱعْلَمُوٓاْ أَنَّ ٱللَّهَ مَعَ ٱلْمُتَّقِينَ ﴿٣٦﴾

إِنَّمَا ٱلنَّسِىٓءُ زِيَادَةٌ فِى ٱلْكُفْرِ يُضَلُّ بِهِ ٱلَّذِينَ كَفَرُواْ يُحِلُّونَهُۥ عَامًا وَيُحَرِّمُونَهُۥ عَامًا لِّيُوَاطِـُٔواْ عِدَّةَ مَا حَرَّمَ ٱللَّهُ فَيُحِلُّواْ مَا حَرَّمَ ٱللَّهُ زُيِّنَ لَهُمْ سُوٓءُ أَعْمَٰلِهِمْ وَٱللَّهُ لَا يَهْدِى ٱلْقَوْمَ ٱلْكَٰفِرِينَ ﴿٣٧﴾

38. O believers, what is the matter with you? If you are told: "March forth in the Way of Allah", you simply cling heavily to the ground. Are you satisfied with the present life rather than the Hereafter? Yet the pleasures of the present life are very small compared with those of the Hereafter.

39. If you do not march forth, He will inflict a very painful punishment on you and replace you by another people, and you will not harm Him[425] in the least; for Allah has power over everything.

40. If you do not support him, Allah did support him, when the unbelievers drove him out - he being the second of two,[426] while they were both in the cave. He said to his companion: "Do not grieve; Allah is with us." Whereupon, Allah sent down His Tranquillity upon him and assisted him with soldiers you did not see, and made the word of the unbelievers the lowest. The Word of Allah is indeed the highest and Allah is Mighty and Wise.

41. Charge forth, on foot or mounted, and struggle with your possessions and yourselves in the Way of Allah. That is far better for you, if only you knew.

42. Had it been a gain near at hand and a short journey, they would surely have followed you. But the distance seemed too long to them. Still they will swear by Allah: "Had we been able, we would have marched forth with you." They damn themselves, and Allah knows that they are liars.

---

425. Allah.
426. The Prophet and Abu Bakr.

190

43. May Allah pardon you! Why did you allow them[427] before it became clear to you who were the truthful ones, and you knew who were the liars?

عَفَا ٱللَّهُ عَنكَ لِمَ أَذِنتَ لَهُمْ حَتَّىٰ يَتَبَيَّنَ لَكَ ٱلَّذِينَ صَدَقُوا۟ وَتَعْلَمَ ٱلْكَـٰذِبِينَ ﴿٤٣﴾

44. Those who believe in Allah and the Last Day do not ask you for [exemption from] fighting in the Way of Allah with their wealth and lives. Allah knows well the righteous.

لَا يَسْتَـْٔذِنُكَ ٱلَّذِينَ يُؤْمِنُونَ بِٱللَّهِ وَٱلْيَوْمِ ٱلْـَٔاخِرِ أَن يُجَـٰهِدُوا۟ بِأَمْوَٰلِهِمْ وَأَنفُسِهِمْ وَٱللَّهُ عَلِيمٌۢ بِٱلْمُتَّقِينَ ﴿٤٤﴾

45. Only those who do not believe in Allah and the Last Day will ask you [for exemption] and their hearts are in doubt. Thus they vacillate in their state of doubt.

إِنَّمَا يَسْتَـْٔذِنُكَ ٱلَّذِينَ لَا يُؤْمِنُونَ بِٱللَّهِ وَٱلْيَوْمِ ٱلْـَٔاخِرِ وَٱرْتَابَتْ قُلُوبُهُمْ فَهُمْ فِى رَيْبِهِمْ يَتَرَدَّدُونَ ﴿٤٥﴾

46. Had they wanted to go forth, they would have made preparations for that; but Allah was averse to their going forth, and so He held them back, and it was said to them: "Sit back with those who sit back."

۞ وَلَوْ أَرَادُوا۟ ٱلْخُرُوجَ لَأَعَدُّوا۟ لَهُۥ عُدَّةً وَلَـٰكِن كَرِهَ ٱللَّهُ ٱنۢبِعَاثَهُمْ فَثَبَّطَهُمْ وَقِيلَ ٱقْعُدُوا۟ مَعَ ٱلْقَـٰعِدِينَ ﴿٤٦﴾

47. Had they gone out with you, they would have only increased your confusion, and would have kept moving among you sowing sedition. And some of you would have listened to them. Allah knows well the wrongdoers.

لَوْ خَرَجُوا۟ فِيكُم مَّا زَادُوكُمْ إِلَّا خَبَالًا وَلَأَوْضَعُوا۟ خِلَـٰلَكُمْ يَبْغُونَكُمُ ٱلْفِتْنَةَ وَفِيكُمْ سَمَّـٰعُونَ لَهُمْ وَٱللَّهُ عَلِيمٌۢ بِٱلظَّـٰلِمِينَ ﴿٤٧﴾

48. They have sought to sow sedition before and turned things around for you, until the truth came out and Allah's Command was manifested, although they were averse [to it].

لَقَدِ ٱبْتَغَوُا۟ ٱلْفِتْنَةَ مِن قَبْلُ وَقَلَّبُوا۟ لَكَ ٱلْأُمُورَ حَتَّىٰ جَآءَ ٱلْحَقُّ وَظَهَرَ أَمْرُ ٱللَّهِ وَهُمْ كَـٰرِهُونَ ﴿٤٨﴾

49. Some of them say: "Allow me and do not tempt me." Indeed they have already fallen into temptation and Hell shall encompass the unbelievers.

وَمِنْهُم مَّن يَقُولُ ٱئْذَن لِّى وَلَا تَفْتِنِّىٓ أَلَا فِى ٱلْفِتْنَةِ سَقَطُوا۟ وَإِنَّ جَهَنَّمَ لَمُحِيطَةٌۢ بِٱلْكَـٰفِرِينَ ﴿٤٩﴾

50. If a good fortune befalls you, they are displeased, and if a disaster befalls you they say: "We took our precaution before." Then, they turn away rejoicing.

إِن تُصِبْكَ حَسَنَةٌ تَسُؤْهُمْ وَإِن تُصِبْكَ مُصِيبَةٌ يَقُولُوا۟ قَدْ أَخَذْنَا أَمْرَنَا مِن قَبْلُ وَيَتَوَلَّوا۟ وَّهُمْ فَرِحُونَ ﴿٥٠﴾

---

427. The reference is to those whom the Prophet allowed to stay behind.

51. Say: "Nothing will befall us except what Allah has decreed for us. He is our Lord, and in Allah let the believers put their trust."

52. Say: "Do you expect for us anything other than one of the two fairest outcomes;[428] while we await for you that Allah will smite you with a punishment, either from Himself, or at our hands?" So wait and watch, we are waiting and watching with you.

53. Say: "Spend willingly or unwillingly; it shall not be accepted from you. You are truly a sinful people."

54. And nothing prevents what they spend from being accepted but that they disbelieve in Allah and His Messenger and that they do not perform the prayer except lazily, and do not spend [anything] except grudgingly.

55. So do not let their wealth and their children win your approval, Allah only wishes to torture them therewith in the present life, so that their souls might depart while they are still unbelievers.

56. They swear by Allah that they [are believers] like you, but they are not; they are a people who fear [you].

57. If they could find a shelter or dens or any place to crawl into, they would make for it in great haste.

58. And some of them disparage your handling of the alms. If they are given part of it they are satisfied, but if they are not given any, they turn away angrily.

59. And would that they were satisfied with what Allah and His Messenger gave them and said: "Allah suffices us; Allah will give us of His Bounty, as will His Messenger. We turn humbly to Him."

---

428. Martyrdom and victory.

قُل لَّن يُصِيبَنَآ إِلَّا مَا كَتَبَ ٱللَّهُ لَنَا هُوَ مَوْلَىٰنَا وَعَلَى ٱللَّهِ فَلْيَتَوَكَّلِ ٱلْمُؤْمِنُونَ ﴿٥١﴾

قُلْ هَلْ تَرَبَّصُونَ بِنَآ إِلَّا إِحْدَى ٱلْحُسْنَيَيْنِ وَنَحْنُ نَتَرَبَّصُ بِكُمْ أَن يُصِيبَكُمُ ٱللَّهُ بِعَذَابٍ مِّنْ عِندِهِۦٓ أَوْ بِأَيْدِينَا فَتَرَبَّصُوٓا إِنَّا مَعَكُم مُّتَرَبِّصُونَ ﴿٥٢﴾

قُلْ أَنفِقُوا طَوْعًا أَوْ كَرْهًا لَّن يُتَقَبَّلَ مِنكُمْ إِنَّكُمْ كُنتُمْ قَوْمًا فَٰسِقِينَ ﴿٥٣﴾

وَمَا مَنَعَهُمْ أَن تُقْبَلَ مِنْهُمْ نَفَقَٰتُهُمْ إِلَّآ أَنَّهُمْ كَفَرُوا بِٱللَّهِ وَبِرَسُولِهِۦ وَلَا يَأْتُونَ ٱلصَّلَوٰةَ إِلَّا وَهُمْ كُسَالَىٰ وَلَا يُنفِقُونَ إِلَّا وَهُمْ كَٰرِهُونَ ﴿٥٤﴾

فَلَا تُعْجِبْكَ أَمْوَٰلُهُمْ وَلَآ أَوْلَٰدُهُمْ إِنَّمَا يُرِيدُ ٱللَّهُ لِيُعَذِّبَهُم بِهَا فِى ٱلْحَيَوٰةِ ٱلدُّنْيَا وَتَزْهَقَ أَنفُسُهُمْ وَهُمْ كَٰفِرُونَ ﴿٥٥﴾

وَيَحْلِفُونَ بِٱللَّهِ إِنَّهُمْ لَمِنكُمْ وَمَا هُم مِّنكُمْ وَلَٰكِنَّهُمْ قَوْمٌ يَفْرَقُونَ ﴿٥٦﴾

لَوْ يَجِدُونَ مَلْجَـًٔا أَوْ مَغَٰرَٰتٍ أَوْ مُدَّخَلًا لَّوَلَّوْا إِلَيْهِ وَهُمْ يَجْمَحُونَ ﴿٥٧﴾

وَمِنْهُم مَّن يَلْمِزُكَ فِى ٱلصَّدَقَٰتِ فَإِنْ أُعْطُوا مِنْهَا رَضُوا وَإِن لَّمْ يُعْطَوْا مِنْهَآ إِذَا هُمْ يَسْخَطُونَ ﴿٥٨﴾

وَلَوْ أَنَّهُمْ رَضُوا مَآ ءَاتَىٰهُمُ ٱللَّهُ وَرَسُولُهُۥ وَقَالُوا حَسْبُنَا ٱللَّهُ سَيُؤْتِينَا ٱللَّهُ مِن فَضْلِهِۦ وَرَسُولُهُۥٓ إِنَّآ إِلَى ٱللَّهِ رَٰغِبُونَ ﴿٥٩﴾

60. The alms are for the poor, the needy, their collectors and those whose hearts are bound together, as well as for the freeing of slaves, [repaying] the debtors, spending in Allah's Path, and for the wayfarer. Thus Allah commands. Allah is All-Knowing, Wise.

61. And some of them molest the Prophet saying: "He hears [all what is said and believes what he hears]." Say: "He hears what is good for you. He believes in Allah and believes what he hears from the believers; and he is a mercy for those who believe." Those who hurt the Messenger of Allah will have a very painful punishment.

62. They swear to you by Allah to please you; but Allah and His Messenger they should rather please first, if they are true believers.

63. Do they not know that whoever opposes Allah and His Messenger, the Fire of Hell is reserved for them, abiding in it forever. That indeed is the great disgrace.

64. The hypocrites fear that a Surah will be revealed informing them of what is in their hearts. Say: "Go on mocking, Allah will surely bring into the open what you fear."

65. And should you ask them, they would surely say: "We were only talking idly and playing." Say: "Were you then mocking Allah, His Revelations and His Messenger?"

66. Make no excuses; you have disbelieved after believing. If We pardon a group of you, We shall punish another group, because they were wicked sinners.

67. The hypocrites, males and females, are all alike. They enjoin evil and forbid what is good and close their fists.[429] They have

---

429. That is, they do not spend in Allah's way.

forgotten Allah,[430] and so He has forgotten them.[431] The hypocrites are the wicked sinners.

68. Allah has promised the hypocrites, males and females, and the unbelievers, the Fire of Hell, abiding in it forever. It is sufficient unto them. He has also cursed them, and a lasting punishment awaits them.

69. Like those who came before you;[432] they were mightier than you and had more wealth and children. So they enjoyed their share;[433] then you enjoyed your share as did those before you, and you engaged in idle talk as they did. Those, their works in this world and in the Hereafter are vain; they are the losers.

70. Have you not heard about those who came before them, the people of Noah, of 'Ad, of Thamud, the people of Abraham, the people of Madyan (Midian), and the over-turned towns?[434] Their Messengers came to them with clear proofs; Allah never wronged them, but they wronged themselves.

71. As to the believers, males and females, they are friends of one another. They enjoin what is good and forbid what is evil, perform the prayers, give the alms and obey Allah and His Messenger. It is those on whom Allah will have mercy. Allah is Mighty, Wise.

72. Allah has promised the believers, males and females, Gardens beneath which rivers flow, abiding therein forever, and fair dwellings in the Gardens of Eden. However, Allah's Good Pleasure is greater. That is the great triumph.

نَسُوا اللَّهَ فَنَسِيَهُمْ إِنَّ الْمُنَٰفِقِينَ هُمُ الْفَٰسِقُونَ ﴿٦٧﴾

وَعَدَ اللَّهُ الْمُنَٰفِقِينَ وَالْمُنَٰفِقَٰتِ وَالْكُفَّارَ نَارَ جَهَنَّمَ خَٰلِدِينَ فِيهَا هِىَ حَسْبُهُمْ وَلَعَنَهُمُ اللَّهُ وَلَهُمْ عَذَابٌ مُّقِيمٌ ﴿٦٨﴾

كَالَّذِينَ مِن قَبْلِكُمْ كَانُوٓا أَشَدَّ مِنكُمْ قُوَّةً وَأَكْثَرَ أَمْوَٰلًا وَأَوْلَٰدًا فَاسْتَمْتَعُوا بِخَلَٰقِهِمْ فَاسْتَمْتَعْتُم بِخَلَٰقِكُمْ كَمَا اسْتَمْتَعَ الَّذِينَ مِن قَبْلِكُم بِخَلَٰقِهِمْ وَخُضْتُمْ كَالَّذِى خَاضُوٓا أُو۟لَٰٓئِكَ حَبِطَتْ أَعْمَٰلُهُمْ فِى الدُّنْيَا وَالْءَاخِرَةِ وَأُو۟لَٰٓئِكَ هُمُ الْخَٰسِرُونَ ﴿٦٩﴾

أَلَمْ يَأْتِهِمْ نَبَأُ الَّذِينَ مِن قَبْلِهِمْ قَوْمِ نُوحٍ وَعَادٍ وَثَمُودَ وَقَوْمِ إِبْرَٰهِيمَ وَأَصْحَٰبِ مَدْيَنَ وَالْمُؤْتَفِكَٰتِ أَتَتْهُمْ رُسُلُهُم بِالْبَيِّنَٰتِ فَمَا كَانَ اللَّهُ لِيَظْلِمَهُمْ وَلَٰكِن كَانُوٓا أَنفُسَهُمْ يَظْلِمُونَ ﴿٧٠﴾

وَالْمُؤْمِنُونَ وَالْمُؤْمِنَٰتُ بَعْضُهُمْ أَوْلِيَآءُ بَعْضٍ يَأْمُرُونَ بِالْمَعْرُوفِ وَيَنْهَوْنَ عَنِ الْمُنكَرِ وَيُقِيمُونَ الصَّلَوٰةَ وَيُؤْتُونَ الزَّكَوٰةَ وَيُطِيعُونَ اللَّهَ وَرَسُولَهُ أُو۟لَٰٓئِكَ سَيَرْحَمُهُمُ اللَّهُ إِنَّ اللَّهَ عَزِيزٌ حَكِيمٌ ﴿٧١﴾

وَعَدَ اللَّهُ الْمُؤْمِنِينَ وَالْمُؤْمِنَٰتِ جَنَّٰتٍ تَجْرِى مِن تَحْتِهَا الْأَنْهَٰرُ خَٰلِدِينَ فِيهَا وَمَسَٰكِنَ طَيِّبَةً فِى جَنَّٰتِ عَدْنٍ وَرِضْوَٰنٌ مِّنَ اللَّهِ أَكْبَرُ ذَٰلِكَ هُوَ الْفَوْزُ الْعَظِيمُ ﴿٧٢﴾

---

430. That is, they have been disobedient.
431. That is, He has deprived them of His mercy.
432. The hypocrites.
433. Share of earthly life.
434. The towns of Lot's people.

73. O Prophet, fight the unbelievers and the hypocrites and be stern with them. Their abode is Hell, and what a terrible fate!

74. They swear by Allah that they said nothing [evil], but they said the word of disbelief and disbelieved after professing Islam, and they aimed at[435] what they could not attain. They only resented that Allah and His Messenger have enriched them from His Bounty. If they repent, it will be better for them; but if they turn away, Allah will inflict a very painful punishment on them in this world and the Hereafter, and they will have on earth no friend or supporter.

75. And some of them make a compact with Allah: "If He gives us of His Bounty, we shall give in charity and be among the righteous."

76. But when He gave them of His Bounty, they grew mean and turned away disobediently.

77. So he caused hypocrisy to cling to their hearts until the day they meet Him, on account of revoking what they promised Allah and on account of lying.

78. Do they not know that Allah knows their hidden thoughts and private talk, and that Allah knows fully the things unseen?

79. Those disparage the believers who give voluntary alms and those who find nothing to offer but their utmost endeavour, and they scoff at them. May Allah mock them. There is a painful punishment [in store] for them.

80. Ask forgiveness for them or do not ask forgiveness for them. If you ask forgiveness for them seventy times, Allah will not forgive them; because they disbelieve in Allah and His Messenger. Allah does not guide the sinful people.

يَٰٓأَيُّهَا ٱلنَّبِيُّ جَٰهِدِ ٱلۡكُفَّارَ وَٱلۡمُنَٰفِقِينَ وَٱغۡلُظۡ عَلَيۡهِمۡۚ وَمَأۡوَىٰهُمۡ جَهَنَّمُۖ وَبِئۡسَ ٱلۡمَصِيرُ ﴿٧٣﴾

يَحۡلِفُونَ بِٱللَّهِ مَا قَالُواْ وَلَقَدۡ قَالُواْ كَلِمَةَ ٱلۡكُفۡرِ وَكَفَرُواْ بَعۡدَ إِسۡلَٰمِهِمۡ وَهَمُّواْ بِمَا لَمۡ يَنَالُواْۚ وَمَا نَقَمُوٓاْ إِلَّآ أَنۡ أَغۡنَىٰهُمُ ٱللَّهُ وَرَسُولُهُۥ مِن فَضۡلِهِۦۚ فَإِن يَتُوبُواْ يَكُ خَيۡرٗا لَّهُمۡۖ وَإِن يَتَوَلَّوۡاْ يُعَذِّبۡهُمُ ٱللَّهُ عَذَابًا أَلِيمٗا فِي ٱلدُّنۡيَا وَٱلۡأٓخِرَةِۚ وَمَا لَهُمۡ فِي ٱلۡأَرۡضِ مِن وَلِيّٖ وَلَا نَصِيرٖ ﴿٧٤﴾

۞ وَمِنۡهُم مَّنۡ عَٰهَدَ ٱللَّهَ لَئِنۡ ءَاتَىٰنَا مِن فَضۡلِهِۦ لَنَصَّدَّقَنَّ وَلَنَكُونَنَّ مِنَ ٱلصَّٰلِحِينَ ﴿٧٥﴾

فَلَمَّآ ءَاتَىٰهُم مِّن فَضۡلِهِۦ بَخِلُواْ بِهِۦ وَتَوَلَّواْ وَّهُم مُّعۡرِضُونَ ﴿٧٦﴾

فَأَعۡقَبَهُمۡ نِفَاقٗا فِي قُلُوبِهِمۡ إِلَىٰ يَوۡمِ يَلۡقَوۡنَهُۥ بِمَآ أَخۡلَفُواْ ٱللَّهَ مَا وَعَدُوهُ وَبِمَا كَانُواْ يَكۡذِبُونَ ﴿٧٧﴾

أَلَمۡ يَعۡلَمُوٓاْ أَنَّ ٱللَّهَ يَعۡلَمُ سِرَّهُمۡ وَنَجۡوَىٰهُمۡ وَأَنَّ ٱللَّهَ عَلَّٰمُ ٱلۡغُيُوبِ ﴿٧٨﴾

ٱلَّذِينَ يَلۡمِزُونَ ٱلۡمُطَّوِّعِينَ مِنَ ٱلۡمُؤۡمِنِينَ فِي ٱلصَّدَقَٰتِ وَٱلَّذِينَ لَا يَجِدُونَ إِلَّا جُهۡدَهُمۡ فَيَسۡخَرُونَ مِنۡهُمۡ سَخِرَ ٱللَّهُ مِنۡهُمۡ وَلَهُمۡ عَذَابٌ أَلِيمٌ ﴿٧٩﴾

ٱسۡتَغۡفِرۡ لَهُمۡ أَوۡ لَا تَسۡتَغۡفِرۡ لَهُمۡ إِن تَسۡتَغۡفِرۡ لَهُمۡ سَبۡعِينَ مَرَّةٗ فَلَن يَغۡفِرَ ٱللَّهُ لَهُمۡۚ ذَٰلِكَ بِأَنَّهُمۡ كَفَرُواْ بِٱللَّهِ وَرَسُولِهِۦۗ وَٱللَّهُ لَا يَهۡدِي ٱلۡقَوۡمَ ٱلۡفَٰسِقِينَ ﴿٨٠﴾

---

435. According to some commentators they aimed at killing the Prophet, while he was returning from Tabuk.

81. Those who stayed behind[436] rejoiced at tarrying behind the Messenger of Allah and hated to struggle with their wealth and their lives in Allah's Path, saying: "Do not march forth in the heat." Say: "The Fire of Hell is hotter, if only they could understand."

فَرِحَ الْمُخَلَّفُونَ بِمَقْعَدِهِمْ خِلَافَ رَسُولِ اللَّهِ وَكَرِهُوٓا أَن يُجَٰهِدُوا۟ بِأَمْوَٰلِهِمْ وَأَنفُسِهِمْ فِى سَبِيلِ اللَّهِ وَقَالُوا۟ لَا تَنفِرُوا۟ فِى الْحَرِّ قُلْ نَارُ جَهَنَّمَ أَشَدُّ حَرًّا لَّوْ كَانُوا۟ يَفْقَهُونَ ۝

82. Let them laugh a little and cry a lot, as a reward for what they used to do.

فَلْيَضْحَكُوا۟ قَلِيلًا وَلْيَبْكُوا۟ كَثِيرًا جَزَآءًۢ بِمَا كَانُوا۟ يَكْسِبُونَ ۝

83. Then, if Allah brings you back to a party of them and they ask your permission to go forth with you, say: "You will never go forth with me, and you will never fight with me against any enemy. You were content to sit back the first time; so sit back with those who stay behind."

فَإِن رَّجَعَكَ اللَّهُ إِلَىٰ طَآئِفَةٍ مِّنْهُمْ فَاسْتَـٔذَنُوكَ لِلْخُرُوجِ فَقُل لَّن تَخْرُجُوا۟ مَعِىَ أَبَدًا وَلَن تُقَٰتِلُوا۟ مَعِىَ عَدُوًّا إِنَّكُمْ رَضِيتُم بِالْقُعُودِ أَوَّلَ مَرَّةٍ فَاقْعُدُوا۟ مَعَ الْخَٰلِفِينَ ۝

84. And do not ever pray over any one of them who dies, or be present at his grave; indeed they disbelieve in Allah and His Messenger, and died while still ungodly.

وَلَا تُصَلِّ عَلَىٰٓ أَحَدٍ مِّنْهُم مَّاتَ أَبَدًا وَلَا تَقُمْ عَلَىٰ قَبْرِهِۦٓ إِنَّهُمْ كَفَرُوا۟ بِاللَّهِ وَرَسُولِهِۦ وَمَاتُوا۟ وَهُمْ فَٰسِقُونَ ۝

85. And do not let their wealth or children win your admiration. Allah only wishes to punish them therewith in the present life, so that their souls may depart while they are still unbelievers.

وَلَا تُعْجِبْكَ أَمْوَٰلُهُمْ وَأَوْلَٰدُهُمْ إِنَّمَا يُرِيدُ اللَّهُ أَن يُعَذِّبَهُم بِهَا فِى الدُّنْيَا وَتَزْهَقَ أَنفُسُهُمْ وَهُمْ كَٰفِرُونَ ۝

86. And if a Surah is revealed stating: "Believe in Allah and fight along with His Messenger", the affluent among them will ask your permission and say: "Let us be with those who stay behind."

وَإِذَآ أُنزِلَتْ سُورَةٌ أَنْ ءَامِنُوا۟ بِاللَّهِ وَجَٰهِدُوا۟ مَعَ رَسُولِهِ اسْتَـٔذَنَكَ أُو۟لُوا۟ الطَّوْلِ مِنْهُمْ وَقَالُوا۟ ذَرْنَا نَكُن مَّعَ الْقَٰعِدِينَ ۝

87. They are content to be among the women who stay behind, and a seal is set upon their hearts, and thus they do not understand.

رَضُوا۟ بِأَن يَكُونُوا۟ مَعَ الْخَوَالِفِ وَطُبِعَ عَلَىٰ قُلُوبِهِمْ فَهُمْ لَا يَفْقَهُونَ ۝

88. But the Messenger and those who believe with him struggle with their wealth and their lives. To those are the good things reserved, and those are the prosperous.

لَٰكِنِ الرَّسُولُ وَالَّذِينَ ءَامَنُوا۟ مَعَهُ جَٰهَدُوا۟ بِأَمْوَٰلِهِمْ وَأَنفُسِهِمْ وَأُو۟لَٰٓئِكَ لَهُمُ الْخَيْرَٰتُ وَأُو۟لَٰٓئِكَ هُمُ الْمُفْلِحُونَ ۝

---

436. Those who failed to join the Tabuk expedition.

89. Allah has prepared for them Gardens beneath which rivers flow, abiding therein forever. That is the great triumph!

أَعَدَّ ٱللَّهُ لَهُم جَنَّٰتٍ تَجْرِى مِن تَحْتِهَا ٱلْأَنْهَٰرُ خَٰلِدِينَ فِيهَا ذَٰلِكَ ٱلْفَوْزُ ٱلْعَظِيمُ ﴿٨٩﴾

90. Some of the desert Arabs who gave excuses came to seek permission, whereas those who lied to Allah and His Messenger stayed behind. Those of them who disbelieved shall be afflicted with a very painful punishment.

وَجَآءَ ٱلْمُعَذِّرُونَ مِنَ ٱلْأَعْرَابِ لِيُؤْذَنَ لَهُمْ وَقَعَدَ ٱلَّذِينَ كَذَبُوا۟ ٱللَّهَ وَرَسُولَهُۥ سَيُصِيبُ ٱلَّذِينَ كَفَرُوا۟ مِنْهُمْ عَذَابٌ أَلِيمٌ ﴿٩٠﴾

91. The weak, the sick, and those who have nothing to spend are not at fault, if they are true to Allah and His Messenger. There can be no blame on the beneficent; and Allah is All-Forgiving, Merciful.

لَّيْسَ عَلَى ٱلضُّعَفَآءِ وَلَا عَلَى ٱلْمَرْضَىٰ وَلَا عَلَى ٱلَّذِينَ لَا يَجِدُونَ مَا يُنفِقُونَ حَرَجٌ إِذَا نَصَحُوا۟ لِلَّهِ وَرَسُولِهِۦ مَا عَلَى ٱلْمُحْسِنِينَ مِن سَبِيلٍ وَٱللَّهُ غَفُورٌ رَّحِيمٌ ﴿٩١﴾

92. Nor on those who, when they came to you asking you for mounts, you said: "I do not find that whereon I can mount you." Thereupon they went back, their eyes overflowing with tears, sorrowing for not finding the means to spend.[437]

وَلَا عَلَى ٱلَّذِينَ إِذَا مَآ أَتَوْكَ لِتَحْمِلَهُمْ قُلْتَ لَآ أَجِدُ مَآ أَحْمِلُكُمْ عَلَيْهِ تَوَلَّوا۟ وَّأَعْيُنُهُمْ تَفِيضُ مِنَ ٱلدَّمْعِ حَزَنًا أَلَّا يَجِدُوا۟ مَا يُنفِقُونَ ﴿٩٢﴾

93. The blame is on those who ask your permission, although they are rich. They are content to join those women who stay behind. Allah has placed a seal upon their hearts and so they do not know.

۞ إِنَّمَا ٱلسَّبِيلُ عَلَى ٱلَّذِينَ يَسْتَـْٔذِنُونَكَ وَهُم أَغْنِيَآءُ رَضُوا۟ بِأَن يَكُونُوا۟ مَعَ ٱلْخَوَالِفِ وَطَبَعَ ٱللَّهُ عَلَىٰ قُلُوبِهِمْ فَهُمْ لَا يَعْلَمُونَ ﴿٩٣﴾

94. They present to you [false] excuses when you return to them. Say: "Do not offer excuses; we will not believe you. Allah has told us [all] about you. Allah shall see your work, and His Messenger too. Then you will be turned over to Him Who knows the unseen and the seen, and He will apprise you of what you used to do."

يَعْتَذِرُونَ إِلَيْكُمْ إِذَا رَجَعْتُمْ إِلَيْهِمْ قُل لَّا تَعْتَذِرُوا۟ لَن نُّؤْمِنَ لَكُمْ قَدْ نَبَّأَنَا ٱللَّهُ مِنْ أَخْبَارِكُمْ وَسَيَرَى ٱللَّهُ عَمَلَكُمْ وَرَسُولُهُۥ ثُمَّ تُرَدُّونَ إِلَىٰ عَٰلِمِ ٱلْغَيْبِ وَٱلشَّهَٰدَةِ فَيُنَبِّئُكُم بِمَا كُنتُمْ تَعْمَلُونَ ﴿٩٤﴾

95. They will swear by Allah to you, when you return to them, that you may leave them alone. So leave them alone; they are an abomination and their abode is Hell, as a reward for what they used to do.

سَيَحْلِفُونَ بِٱللَّهِ لَكُمْ إِذَا ٱنقَلَبْتُمْ إِلَيْهِمْ لِتُعْرِضُوا۟ عَنْهُمْ فَأَعْرِضُوا۟ عَنْهُمْ إِنَّهُمْ رِجْسٌ وَمَأْوَىٰهُمْ جَهَنَّمُ جَزَآءً بِمَا كَانُوا۟ يَكْسِبُونَ ﴿٩٥﴾

---

437. That is, to provide the expenses of war.

96. They swear to you that you may be well-pleased with them; but should you be well-pleased with them, Allah will not be well-pleased with the sinful people.

يَحْلِفُونَ لَكُمْ لِتَرْضَوْا عَنْهُمْ فَإِن تَرْضَوْا عَنْهُمْ فَإِنَّ اللَّهَ لَا يَرْضَى عَنِ الْقَوْمِ الْفَسِقِينَ ﴿٩٦﴾

97. The desert Arabs are more steeped in unbelief and hypocrisy and are more likely not to know the bounds of what Allah has revealed to His Messenger. Allah is All-Knowing, Wise.

الْأَعْرَابُ أَشَدُّ كُفْرًا وَنِفَاقًا وَأَجْدَرُ أَلَّا يَعْلَمُوا حُدُودَ مَا أَنزَلَ اللَّهُ عَلَى رَسُولِهِ وَاللَّهُ عَلِيمٌ حَكِيمٌ ﴿٩٧﴾

98. And some of the desert Arabs regard what they spend as a fine, and await the turns of fortune to go against you. May the evil turn go against them! Allah is All-Hearing, All-Knowing.

وَمِنَ الْأَعْرَابِ مَن يَتَّخِذُ مَا يُنفِقُ مَغْرَمًا وَيَتَرَبَّصُ بِكُمُ الدَّوَائِرَ عَلَيْهِمْ دَائِرَةُ السَّوْءِ وَاللَّهُ سَمِيعٌ عَلِيمٌ ﴿٩٨﴾

99. And some of the desert Arabs believe in Allah and the Last Day and regard what they spend [in the Way of Allah] as a means to get closer to Allah and to earn the prayers of the Messenger. Indeed, that will bring them closer [to Allah]. He will admit them into His Mercy. Allah is truly All-Forgiving, Merciful.

وَمِنَ الْأَعْرَابِ مَن يُؤْمِنُ بِاللَّهِ وَالْيَوْمِ الْآخِرِ وَيَتَّخِذُ مَا يُنفِقُ قُرُبَاتٍ عِندَ اللَّهِ وَصَلَوَاتِ الرَّسُولِ أَلَا إِنَّهَا قُرْبَةٌ لَهُمْ سَيُدْخِلُهُمُ اللَّهُ فِي رَحْمَتِهِ إِنَّ اللَّهَ غَفُورٌ رَحِيمٌ ﴿٩٩﴾

100. The early Emigrants[438] and the Helpers[439] and those who followed them up in beneficence - Allah is well-pleased with them, and they are well-pleased with Him, and He has prepared for them Gardens beneath which rivers flow, abiding therein forever. That is the great triumph!

وَالسَّابِقُونَ الْأَوَّلُونَ مِنَ الْمُهَاجِرِينَ وَالْأَنصَارِ وَالَّذِينَ اتَّبَعُوهُم بِإِحْسَانٍ رَّضِيَ اللَّهُ عَنْهُمْ وَرَضُوا عَنْهُ وَأَعَدَّ لَهُمْ جَنَّاتٍ تَجْرِي تَحْتَهَا الْأَنْهَارُ خَالِدِينَ فِيهَا أَبَدًا ذَلِكَ الْفَوْزُ الْعَظِيمُ ﴿١٠٠﴾

101. And some of the desert Arabs around you are hypocrites, and some of the people of Medina persist in hypocrisy. You do not know them, but We know them. We shall punish them twice, then they will be afflicted with a terrible punishment.[440]

وَمِمَّنْ حَوْلَكُم مِّنَ الْأَعْرَابِ مُنَافِقُونَ وَمِنْ أَهْلِ الْمَدِينَةِ مَرَدُوا عَلَى النِّفَاقِ لَا تَعْلَمُهُمْ نَحْنُ نَعْلَمُهُمْ سَنُعَذِّبُهُم مَّرَّتَيْنِ ثُمَّ يُرَدُّونَ إِلَى عَذَابٍ عَظِيمٍ ﴿١٠١﴾

---

438. The early Muslims who emigrated to Medina.
439. The early Muslims of Medina who supported the Emigrants.
440. That is, before they are thrown into the Fire.

102. Others have confessed their sins; they mixed a good deed with a bad one.[441] Perhaps Allah will pardon them. Allah is truly All-Forgiving, Merciful.

103. Take of their wealth voluntary alms to purify and cleanse them therewith; and pray for them, for your prayers are a source of tranquillity for them. Allah is All-Hearing, All-Knowing.

104. Do they not know that Allah is He Who accepts the repentance from His servants, and accepts voluntary alms, and that Allah is All-Forgiving, Merciful?

105. And say: "Work, for Allah shall see your work, and His Messenger and the believers too. And you shall be brought back[442] to Him Who knows the unseen and the seen, and He will apprise you of what you used to do."

106. And others are deferred to Allah's Decree; He will either punish them or pardon them. And Allah is All-Knowing, Wise.

107. And those who built a mosque[443] or hurt [the Muslims], to spread unbelief, to disunite [the believers] and to await him[444] who had fought Allah and His Messenger - they will certainly swear that they meant nothing but good. Allah bears witness that they are liars.

108. Do not stand up there [for prayer]; for a mosque founded on piety from the first day is worthier of your standing in it. Therein are men who love to be purified; and Allah loves those who purify themselves.

وَءَاخَرُونَ ٱعْتَرَفُواْ بِذُنُوبِهِمْ خَلَطُواْ عَمَلًا صَٰلِحًا وَءَاخَرَ سَيِّئًا عَسَى ٱللَّهُ أَن يَتُوبَ عَلَيْهِمْ إِنَّ ٱللَّهَ غَفُورٌ رَّحِيمٌ ۝

خُذْ مِنْ أَمْوَٰلِهِمْ صَدَقَةً تُطَهِّرُهُمْ وَتُزَكِّيهِم بِهَا وَصَلِّ عَلَيْهِمْ إِنَّ صَلَوٰتَكَ سَكَنٌ لَّهُمْ وَٱللَّهُ سَمِيعٌ عَلِيمٌ ۝

أَلَمْ يَعْلَمُوٓاْ أَنَّ ٱللَّهَ هُوَ يَقْبَلُ ٱلتَّوْبَةَ عَنْ عِبَادِهِ وَيَأْخُذُ ٱلصَّدَقَٰتِ وَأَنَّ ٱللَّهَ هُوَ ٱلتَّوَّابُ ٱلرَّحِيمُ ۝

وَقُلِ ٱعْمَلُواْ فَسَيَرَى ٱللَّهُ عَمَلَكُمْ وَرَسُولُهُۥ وَٱلْمُؤْمِنُونَ وَسَتُرَدُّونَ إِلَىٰ عَٰلِمِ ٱلْغَيْبِ وَٱلشَّهَٰدَةِ فَيُنَبِّئُكُم بِمَا كُنتُمْ تَعْمَلُونَ ۝

وَءَاخَرُونَ مُرْجَوْنَ لِأَمْرِ ٱللَّهِ إِمَّا يُعَذِّبُهُمْ وَإِمَّا يَتُوبُ عَلَيْهِمْ وَٱللَّهُ عَلِيمٌ حَكِيمٌ ۝

وَٱلَّذِينَ ٱتَّخَذُواْ مَسْجِدًا ضِرَارًا وَكُفْرًا وَتَفْرِيقًا بَيْنَ ٱلْمُؤْمِنِينَ وَإِرْصَادًا لِّمَنْ حَارَبَ ٱللَّهَ وَرَسُولَهُۥ مِن قَبْلُ وَلَيَحْلِفُنَّ إِنْ أَرَدْنَآ إِلَّا ٱلْحُسْنَىٰ وَٱللَّهُ يَشْهَدُ إِنَّهُمْ لَكَٰذِبُونَ ۝

لَا تَقُمْ فِيهِ أَبَدًا لَّمَسْجِدٌ أُسِّسَ عَلَى ٱلتَّقْوَىٰ مِنْ أَوَّلِ يَوْمٍ أَحَقُّ أَن تَقُومَ فِيهِ فِيهِ رِجَالٌ يُحِبُّونَ أَن يَتَطَهَّرُواْ وَٱللَّهُ يُحِبُّ ٱلْمُطَّهِّرِينَ ۝

---

441. The good deed is confessing sins and the bad one is that they stayed behind when the Muslims marched against the enemy.

442. On the Day of Resurrection.

443. The reference is to the mosque which the hypocrites built in the neighbourhood of the mosque of Quba', the first mosque to be built by the Muslims.

444. He is said to be Abu 'Amir surnamed al-Rahib [the Monk].

109. Is one who founds his edifice upon the fear and Good Pleasure of Allah better, or one who founds his edifice upon the brink of a crumbling precipice that will tumble down with him into the Fire of Hell? Allah does not guide the unjust people.

110. The edifice which they have built will continue to be a source of doubt in their hearts, unless their hearts are cut up into pieces. Allah is All-Knowing, Wise.

111. Allah has bought from the believers their lives and their wealth in return for Paradise; they fight in the Way of Allah, kill and get killed. That is a true promise from Him in the Torah, the Gospel and the Qur'an; and who fulfils his promise better than Allah? Rejoice then at the bargain you have made with Him; for that is the great triumph.

112. Those who repent, worship, praise, fast, kneel down, prostrate themselves, enjoin what is good and forbid what is evil and observe the ordinances of Allah - to [such] believers give the good tidings.[445]

113. It is not for the Prophet and those who believe to ask forgiveness for the polytheists even if they are near relatives, after it becomes clear to [the believers] that they are the people of the Fire.

114. Abraham asked forgiveness for his father, only because of a promise he had made to him; but when it became clear to him that he was an enemy of Allah, he disowned him. Indeed Abraham was compassionate, forbearing.

115. Allah would not lead any people astray after He has guided them, until He makes clear to them what they should fear. Allah, indeed, has knowledge of everything.

---

445. That they shall be pardoned.

إِنَّ اللَّهَ لَهُ مُلْكُ السَّمَوَاتِ وَالْأَرْضِ يُحْيِ وَيُمِيتُ وَمَا لَكُم مِّن دُونِ اللَّهِ مِن وَلِيٍّ وَلَا نَصِيرٍ ﴿١١٦﴾

116. To Allah belongs the dominion of the heavens and the earth; He gives life and causes death and, apart from Allah, you have no friend or supporter.

لَقَد تَّابَ اللَّهُ عَلَى النَّبِيِّ وَالْمُهَاجِرِينَ وَالْأَنصَارِ الَّذِينَ اتَّبَعُوهُ فِي سَاعَةِ الْعُسْرَةِ مِن بَعْدِ مَا كَادَ يَزِيغُ قُلُوبُ فَرِيقٍ مِّنْهُمْ ثُمَّ تَابَ عَلَيْهِمْ إِنَّهُ بِهِمْ رَءُوفٌ رَّحِيمٌ ﴿١١٧﴾

117. Allah has forgiven the Prophet, the Emigrants and the Helpers who followed him in the hour of distress, after the hearts of a group of them had almost deviated. Then He forgave them; for He is, indeed, Most Kind and Most Merciful towards them.

وَعَلَى الثَّلَاثَةِ الَّذِينَ خُلِّفُوا حَتَّى إِذَا ضَاقَتْ عَلَيْهِمُ الْأَرْضُ بِمَا رَحُبَتْ وَضَاقَتْ عَلَيْهِمْ أَنفُسُهُمْ وَظَنُّوا أَن لَّا مَلْجَأَ مِنَ اللَّهِ إِلَّا إِلَيْهِ ثُمَّ تَابَ عَلَيْهِمْ لِيَتُوبُوا إِنَّ اللَّهَ هُوَ التَّوَّابُ الرَّحِيمُ ﴿١١٨﴾

118. And [He also forgave] the three[446] who were left behind till the earth, for all its vastness, became too small for them,[447] and their souls were distressed, and they realized that there was no refuge from Allah except with Him. Allah then forgave them so that they might repent. Allah is the All-Forgiving, the Merciful.

يَا أَيُّهَا الَّذِينَ آمَنُوا اتَّقُوا اللَّهَ وَكُونُوا مَعَ الصَّادِقِينَ ﴿١١٩﴾

119. O you who believe, fear Allah and side with the truthful.

مَا كَانَ لِأَهْلِ الْمَدِينَةِ وَمَنْ حَوْلَهُم مِّنَ الْأَعْرَابِ أَن يَتَخَلَّفُوا عَن رَّسُولِ اللَّهِ وَلَا يَرْغَبُوا بِأَنفُسِهِمْ عَن نَّفْسِهِ ذَلِكَ بِأَنَّهُمْ لَا يُصِيبُهُمْ ظَمَأٌ وَلَا نَصَبٌ وَلَا مَخْمَصَةٌ فِي سَبِيلِ اللَّهِ وَلَا يَطَئُونَ مَوْطِئًا يَغِيظُ الْكُفَّارَ وَلَا يَنَالُونَ مِنْ عَدُوٍّ نَّيْلًا إِلَّا كُتِبَ لَهُم بِهِ عَمَلٌ صَالِحٌ إِنَّ اللَّهَ لَا يُضِيعُ أَجْرَ الْمُحْسِنِينَ ﴿١٢٠﴾

120. It is not given to the people of Medina and the desert Arabs around them to stay behind the Messenger of Allah, nor to prefer their own lives to his life for they are afflicted neither by thirst nor fatigue nor hunger in Allah's Way, nor do they take a step that upsets the unbelievers, nor inflict a blow on the enemy but a good deed is recorded for them on account of it. Allah does not allow the beneficent to lose their reward.

وَلَا يُنفِقُونَ نَفَقَةً صَغِيرَةً وَلَا كَبِيرَةً وَلَا يَقْطَعُونَ وَادِيًا إِلَّا كُتِبَ لَهُمْ لِيَجْزِيَهُمُ اللَّهُ أَحْسَنَ مَا كَانُوا يَعْمَلُونَ ﴿١٢١﴾

121. Nor do they spend anything whether small or large, nor cross a valley but it is recorded for them, so that Allah may reward them for the best of their deeds.

---

446. Three of the Helpers of Medina.
447. Meaning that they could not find refuge.

122. The believers should not all go to war. Why doesn't a company from each group go forth to instruct themselves in religion and admonish their people[448] when they return, that perchance, they may beware.

123. O you who believe, fight those of the unbelievers who are near to you and let them see how harsh you can be. Know that Allah is with the righteous.

124. Whenever a Surah is revealed, some of them would say: "Who of you has this one increased in faith?" It has increased the faith of those who believe, and they rejoice.

125. But for those in whose hearts there is a sickness, it will add disbelief to their disbelief, and they will die while they are unbelievers.

126. Do they not see that they are tried once or twice every year? Yet they neither repent nor take heed.

127. And whenever a Surah is revealed, they look at each other [saying]: "Does anyone see you?" Then they turn away. Allah has turned away their hearts, because they are a people who do not understand.

128. There has come to you a Messenger from among yourselves. It grieves him to see you suffer, he cares much for you, and is kind and merciful towards the believers.

129. But if they turn away, say: "Sufficient for me is Allah; there is no God but He; in Him I put my trust. He is the Lord of the Glorious Throne."

---

448. Those who go to war.

Sûrat Yûnus,
(Jonah) 10

In the Name of Allah,
the Compassionate, the Merciful

1. Alif - Lam - Ra.
Those are the verses of the sound Book.[449]

2. Is it a wonder to the people that We have revealed to one of them: "Warn the people and announce to the believers the good news that they have a sure footing with their Lord?" The unbelievers say: "This indeed is a manifest sorcerer."

3. Truly, your Lord is Allah Who created the heavens and the earth in six days, then He sat on the Throne controlling all things. There is no intercessor without His Leave. That is Allah, your Lord; so worship Him. Do you not pay heed?

4. Unto Him you shall all return; it is Allah's Promise in truth. He originates the creation, then He brings it back to reward equitably those who believe and do the good deeds. But those who disbelieve shall drink boiling water and shall be severely punished on account of their disbelief.

5. It is He Who made the sun a bright radiance and the moon a light, and determined phases for it[450] so that you may know the number of years and the reckoning. Allah did not create that except in truth, expounding the Signs to a people who know.

6. Indeed, in the alternation of night and day and in what Allah has created in the heavens and the earth are real signs for a people who are God-fearing.

---

449. The Qur'an.
450. The moon.

7. Those who do not hope to meet Us and are content with the present life and are at ease in it, and those who pay no heed to Our signs;

إِنَّ ٱلَّذِينَ لَا يَرْجُونَ لِقَآءَنَا وَرَضُوا۟ بِٱلْحَيَوٰةِ ٱلدُّنْيَا وَٱطْمَأَنُّوا۟ بِهَا وَٱلَّذِينَ هُمْ عَنْ ءَايَٰتِنَا غَٰفِلُونَ ٧

8. Their refuge is the Fire, on account of [what] they used to do.

أُو۟لَٰٓئِكَ مَأْوَىٰهُمُ ٱلنَّارُ بِمَا كَانُوا۟ يَكْسِبُونَ ٨

9. Surely, those who believe and do the good, their Lord shall guide them for their belief; beneath them rivers will flow in the Gardens of Bliss.

إِنَّ ٱلَّذِينَ ءَامَنُوا۟ وَعَمِلُوا۟ ٱلصَّٰلِحَٰتِ يَهْدِيهِمْ رَبُّهُم بِإِيمَٰنِهِمْ تَجْرِى مِن تَحْتِهِمُ ٱلْأَنْهَٰرُ فِى جَنَّٰتِ ٱلنَّعِيمِ ٩

10. Their prayer therein shall be: "Glory be to You, O Allah"; and their greeting in it shall be: "Peace!" and they conclude their prayer by saying: "Praise belongs to Allah, the Lord of the Worlds."

دَعْوَىٰهُمْ فِيهَا سُبْحَٰنَكَ ٱللَّهُمَّ وَتَحِيَّتُهُمْ فِيهَا سَلَٰمٌ وَءَاخِرُ دَعْوَىٰهُمْ أَنِ ٱلْحَمْدُ لِلَّهِ رَبِّ ٱلْعَٰلَمِينَ ١٠

11. And were Allah to hasten the evil for mankind[451] just as they would hasten the good for themselves,[452] their term would have been fulfilled. Then We would leave those who do not hope to meet Us in their arrogance wandering aimlessly.

۞ وَلَوْ يُعَجِّلُ ٱللَّهُ لِلنَّاسِ ٱلشَّرَّ ٱسْتِعْجَالَهُم بِٱلْخَيْرِ لَقُضِىَ إِلَيْهِمْ أَجَلُهُمْ فَنَذَرُ ٱلَّذِينَ لَا يَرْجُونَ لِقَآءَنَا فِى طُغْيَٰنِهِمْ يَعْمَهُونَ ١١

12. And if hardship afflicts man, he calls Us lying down, sitting or standing; but when We lift his hardship, he passes on, as though he never called Us to [lift] a hardship that afflicted him. Thus what the transgressors do seems fair to them.

وَإِذَا مَسَّ ٱلْإِنسَٰنَ ٱلضُّرُّ دَعَانَا لِجَنۢبِهِۦٓ أَوْ قَاعِدًا أَوْ قَآئِمًا فَلَمَّا كَشَفْنَا عَنْهُ ضُرَّهُۥ مَرَّ كَأَن لَّمْ يَدْعُنَآ إِلَىٰ ضُرٍّ مَّسَّهُۥ كَذَٰلِكَ زُيِّنَ لِلْمُسْرِفِينَ مَا كَانُوا۟ يَعْمَلُونَ ١٢

13. And We have destroyed generations before you, when they did wrong and their Messengers brought them the clear proofs, but they would not believe. Thus We reward the wicked sinners.

وَلَقَدْ أَهْلَكْنَا ٱلْقُرُونَ مِن قَبْلِكُمْ لَمَّا ظَلَمُوا۟ وَجَآءَتْهُمْ رُسُلُهُم بِٱلْبَيِّنَٰتِ وَمَا كَانُوا۟ لِيُؤْمِنُوا۟ كَذَٰلِكَ نَجْزِى ٱلْقَوْمَ ٱلْمُجْرِمِينَ ١٣

14. Then We made you successors on earth, after them, to see how you would behave.

ثُمَّ جَعَلْنَٰكُمْ خَلَٰٓئِفَ فِى ٱلْأَرْضِ مِنۢ بَعْدِهِمْ لِنَنظُرَ كَيْفَ تَعْمَلُونَ ١٤

---

451. That is, hasten their punishment.
452. From God.

وَإِذَا تُتْلَىٰ عَلَيْهِمْ ءَايَاتُنَا بَيِّنَٰتٍ قَالَ ٱلَّذِينَ لَا

15. And if Our revelations are clearly recited to them, those who do not hope to meet Us say: "Bring a Qur'an other than this one or alter it." Say: "It is not for me to alter it of my own accord. I only follow what is revealed to me. Indeed, I fear, if I disobey my Lord, the punishment of a Fateful Day."[453]

يَرْجُونَ لِقَآءَنَا ٱئْتِ بِقُرْءَانٍ غَيْرِ هَٰذَآ أَوْ بَدِّلْهُ قُلْ مَا يَكُونُ لِيٓ أَنْ أُبَدِّلَهُۥ مِن تِلْقَآئِ نَفْسِيٓ إِنْ أَتَّبِعُ إِلَّا مَا يُوحَىٰٓ إِلَيَّ إِنِّيٓ أَخَافُ إِنْ عَصَيْتُ رَبِّي عَذَابَ يَوْمٍ عَظِيمٍ ۝

16. Say: "If Allah had willed, I would not have recited it to you, and He would not have told you about it. I have dwelt in your midst a lifetime before it. Do you not understand?"

قُل لَّوْ شَآءَ ٱللَّهُ مَا تَلَوْتُهُۥ عَلَيْكُمْ وَلَآ أَدْرَىٰكُم بِهِۦ فَقَدْ لَبِثْتُ فِيكُمْ عُمُرًا مِّن قَبْلِهِۦٓ أَفَلَا تَعْقِلُونَ ۝

17. For, who is more wicked than one who forges lies about Allah or denies His Revelations? Indeed, the wicked sinners shall never prosper.

فَمَنْ أَظْلَمُ مِمَّنِ ٱفْتَرَىٰ عَلَى ٱللَّهِ كَذِبًا أَوْ كَذَّبَ بِـَٔايَٰتِهِۦٓ إِنَّهُۥ لَا يُفْلِحُ ٱلْمُجْرِمُونَ ۝

18. They worship, apart from Allah, what neither harms nor benefits them, and say: "These are our intercessors with Allah." Say: "Do you inform Allah about what he does not know in the heavens or on earth?" Glory be to Him, and may He be exalted above what they associate [with Him]!

وَيَعْبُدُونَ مِن دُونِ ٱللَّهِ مَا لَا يَضُرُّهُمْ وَلَا يَنفَعُهُمْ وَيَقُولُونَ هَٰٓؤُلَآءِ شُفَعَٰٓؤُنَا عِندَ ٱللَّهِ قُلْ أَتُنَبِّـُٔونَ ٱللَّهَ بِمَا لَا يَعْلَمُ فِي ٱلسَّمَٰوَٰتِ وَلَا فِي ٱلْأَرْضِ سُبْحَٰنَهُۥ وَتَعَٰلَىٰ عَمَّا يُشْرِكُونَ ۝

19. Mankind were a single nation; then they differed. Had it not been for a prior order of your Lord, the matter over which they had differed would have been settled.

وَمَا كَانَ ٱلنَّاسُ إِلَّآ أُمَّةً وَٰحِدَةً فَٱخْتَلَفُوا۟ وَلَوْلَا كَلِمَةٌ سَبَقَتْ مِن رَّبِّكَ لَقُضِيَ بَيْنَهُمْ فِيمَا فِيهِ يَخْتَلِفُونَ ۝

20. And they say: "If only a sign is sent to him from his Lord." Say then: "The Unseen belongs to Allah; so wait, and I will be waiting with you."

وَيَقُولُونَ لَوْلَآ أُنزِلَ عَلَيْهِ ءَايَةٌ مِّن رَّبِّهِۦ فَقُلْ إِنَّمَا ٱلْغَيْبُ لِلَّهِ فَٱنتَظِرُوٓا۟ إِنِّي مَعَكُم مِّنَ ٱلْمُنتَظِرِينَ ۝

21. And if We let people taste a mercy after an affliction touches them, they begin to scheme against Our Revelations. Say: "Allah is Quicker at scheming."[454] Surely Our Messengers write down what you scheme.

وَإِذَآ أَذَقْنَا ٱلنَّاسَ رَحْمَةً مِّنۢ بَعْدِ ضَرَّآءَ مَسَّتْهُمْ إِذَا لَهُم مَّكْرٌ فِيٓ ءَايَاتِنَا قُلِ ٱللَّهُ أَسْرَعُ مَكْرًا إِنَّ رُسُلَنَا يَكْتُبُونَ مَا تَمْكُرُونَ ۝

---

453. That is, the Day of Resurrection.
454. What is meant is quick retribution.

22. It is He Who makes your journey on land and on sea; so that when you are in the ships and they sail with them driven by a fair wind, and they rejoice in it, a stormy wind comes upon them and waves surge over them from every side, and they think that they are being overwhelmed. Then they call upon Allah, professing submission to Him sincerely: "If You save us from this, we shall be truly thankful."

هُوَ ٱلَّذِى يُسَيِّرُكُمْ فِى ٱلْبَرِّ وَٱلْبَحْرِ حَتَّىٰ إِذَا كُنتُمْ فِى ٱلْفُلْكِ وَجَرَيْنَ بِهِم بِرِيحٍ طَيِّبَةٍ وَفَرِحُوا۟ بِهَا جَآءَتْهَا رِيحٌ عَاصِفٌ وَجَآءَهُمُ ٱلْمَوْجُ مِن كُلِّ مَكَانٍ وَظَنُّوٓا۟ أَنَّهُمْ أُحِيطَ بِهِمْ دَعَوُا۟ ٱللَّهَ مُخْلِصِينَ لَهُ ٱلدِّينَ لَئِنْ أَنجَيْتَنَا مِنْ هَٰذِهِۦ لَنَكُونَنَّ مِنَ ٱلشَّٰكِرِينَ ۝

23. But when He saves them, they resort to aggression in the land wrongfully. O people, your aggression shall recoil upon yourselves. It is what you enjoy in the present life; then unto Us shall be your return; whereupon We will inform you about what you were doing.

فَلَمَّآ أَنجَىٰهُمْ إِذَا هُمْ يَبْغُونَ فِى ٱلْأَرْضِ بِغَيْرِ ٱلْحَقِّ يَٰٓأَيُّهَا ٱلنَّاسُ إِنَّمَا بَغْيُكُمْ عَلَىٰٓ أَنفُسِكُم مَّتَٰعَ ٱلْحَيَوٰةِ ٱلدُّنْيَا ثُمَّ إِلَيْنَا مَرْجِعُكُمْ فَنُنَبِّئُكُم بِمَا كُنتُمْ تَعْمَلُونَ ۝

24. The present life is like water We send down from the sky, causing the vegetation of the earth, from which people and cattle eat, to grow luxuriant. But when the earth puts on its ornamental garb and is adorned, and its people think they are able to get what they want from it, Our Retribution comes upon it day or night, making its produce like a cropped harvest, as if it had never flourished before. Thus We expound Our Revelations to people who reflect.

إِنَّمَا مَثَلُ ٱلْحَيَوٰةِ ٱلدُّنْيَا كَمَآءٍ أَنزَلْنَٰهُ مِنَ ٱلسَّمَآءِ فَٱخْتَلَطَ بِهِۦ نَبَاتُ ٱلْأَرْضِ مِمَّا يَأْكُلُ ٱلنَّاسُ وَٱلْأَنْعَٰمُ حَتَّىٰٓ إِذَآ أَخَذَتِ ٱلْأَرْضُ زُخْرُفَهَا وَٱزَّيَّنَتْ وَظَنَّ أَهْلُهَآ أَنَّهُمْ قَٰدِرُونَ عَلَيْهَآ أَتَىٰهَآ أَمْرُنَا لَيْلًا أَوْ نَهَارًا فَجَعَلْنَٰهَا حَصِيدًا كَأَن لَّمْ تَغْنَ بِٱلْأَمْسِ كَذَٰلِكَ نُفَصِّلُ ٱلْءَايَٰتِ لِقَوْمٍ يَتَفَكَّرُونَ ۝

25. And Allah summons to the Abode of Peace and leads whomever He pleases to a straight path.

وَٱللَّهُ يَدْعُوٓا۟ إِلَىٰ دَارِ ٱلسَّلَٰمِ وَيَهْدِى مَن يَشَآءُ إِلَىٰ صِرَٰطٍ مُّسْتَقِيمٍ ۝

26. To those who do the good is the best reward[455] and more;[456] and their faces shall not be covered with blackness or misery. Those are the people of Paradise, wherein they will abide forever.

۞ لِّلَّذِينَ أَحْسَنُوا۟ ٱلْحُسْنَىٰ وَزِيَادَةٌ وَلَا يَرْهَقُ وُجُوهَهُمْ قَتَرٌ وَلَا ذِلَّةٌ أُو۟لَٰٓئِكَ أَصْحَٰبُ ٱلْجَنَّةِ هُمْ فِيهَا خَٰلِدُونَ ۝

---

455. That is, Paradise.
456. •More• refers to their ability to look at Allah.

27. But for those who do the evil deeds, the reward for an evil deed shall be its like, and humiliation shall overtake them. Against Allah they will have no defender; it is as though their faces have been covered with dark patches of the night. Those are the people of the Fire, abiding therein forever.

28. On the Day We will muster them all together; then We will say to those who set up associates with Allah: "Stay in your places, you and your associates." Then We shall separate them, and their associates will say: "You were not worshipping us.

29. "Allah is a sufficient witness between us and you; for we were unaware of your worshipping us."

30. There, each soul shall know what it had done in advance; and they will be turned over to Allah, their true Master; and what [falsehood] they invented will stray away from them.

31. Say (O Mohammad): "Who provides for you from heaven and earth? Who controls the hearing and sight? Who brings forth the living from the dead and brings forth the dead from the living? And who is in control of all things?" They will surely say: "Allah." Then say: "Will you not fear God?

32. "That indeed is Allah, your true Lord. What is there, after truth, except error? How can you then be turned away [from the Truth]?"

33. Thus, your Lord's Word against those who have sinned has been accomplished, that they shall not believe.

34. Say: "Is there among your associates one who originates creation, then brings it

وَٱلَّذِينَ كَسَبُوا۟ ٱلسَّيِّـَٔاتِ جَزَآءُ سَيِّئَةٍۭ بِمِثْلِهَا وَتَرْهَقُهُمْ ذِلَّةٌ مَّا لَهُم مِّنَ ٱللَّهِ مِنْ عَاصِمٍ كَأَنَّمَآ أُغْشِيَتْ وُجُوهُهُمْ قِطَعًا مِّنَ ٱلَّيْلِ مُظْلِمًا أُو۟لَٰٓئِكَ أَصْحَٰبُ ٱلنَّارِ هُمْ فِيهَا خَٰلِدُونَ ﴿٢٧﴾

وَيَوْمَ نَحْشُرُهُمْ جَمِيعًا ثُمَّ نَقُولُ لِلَّذِينَ أَشْرَكُوا۟ مَكَانَكُمْ أَنتُمْ وَشُرَكَآؤُكُمْ فَزَيَّلْنَا بَيْنَهُمْ وَقَالَ شُرَكَآؤُهُم مَّا كُنتُمْ إِيَّانَا تَعْبُدُونَ ﴿٢٨﴾

فَكَفَىٰ بِٱللَّهِ شَهِيدًۢا بَيْنَنَا وَبَيْنَكُمْ إِن كُنَّا عَنْ عِبَادَتِكُمْ لَغَٰفِلِينَ ﴿٢٩﴾

هُنَالِكَ تَبْلُوا۟ كُلُّ نَفْسٍ مَّآ أَسْلَفَتْ وَرُدُّوٓا۟ إِلَى ٱللَّهِ مَوْلَىٰهُمُ ٱلْحَقِّ وَضَلَّ عَنْهُم مَّا كَانُوا۟ يَفْتَرُونَ ﴿٣٠﴾

قُلْ مَن يَرْزُقُكُم مِّنَ ٱلسَّمَآءِ وَٱلْأَرْضِ أَمَّن يَمْلِكُ ٱلسَّمْعَ وَٱلْأَبْصَٰرَ وَمَن يُخْرِجُ ٱلْحَىَّ مِنَ ٱلْمَيِّتِ وَيُخْرِجُ ٱلْمَيِّتَ مِنَ ٱلْحَىِّ وَمَن يُدَبِّرُ ٱلْأَمْرَ فَسَيَقُولُونَ ٱللَّهُ فَقُلْ أَفَلَا تَتَّقُونَ ﴿٣١﴾

فَذَٰلِكُمُ ٱللَّهُ رَبُّكُمُ ٱلْحَقُّ فَمَاذَا بَعْدَ ٱلْحَقِّ إِلَّا ٱلضَّلَٰلُ فَأَنَّىٰ تُصْرَفُونَ ﴿٣٢﴾

كَذَٰلِكَ حَقَّتْ كَلِمَتُ رَبِّكَ عَلَى ٱلَّذِينَ فَسَقُوٓا۟ أَنَّهُمْ لَا يُؤْمِنُونَ ﴿٣٣﴾

قُلْ هَلْ مِن شُرَكَآئِكُم مَّن يَبْدَؤُا۟ ٱلْخَلْقَ ثُمَّ يُعِيدُهُۥ قُلِ ٱللَّهُ

back?"[457] Say: "Allah originates creation, then brings it back. How then are you perverted?"

35. Say: "Is there any of your associates who guides to the truth?" Say: "Allah guides to the truth. Who is, then, more worthy of being followed, He Who guides to the truth or he who does not guide, unless he is guided? What is the matter with you? How do you judge?"

36. Most of them follow nothing but conjecture. Surely conjecture avails nothing against the truth. Allah knows well what they do.

37. This Qur'an could never have been produced except by Allah. It is a confirmation of that [which was revealed] before it and an exposition of the Book. There is no doubt about it. It is from the Lord of the Worlds.

38. Or do they say: "He[458] has forged it." Say: "Come up, then, with a single Surah like it, and call upon whomever you can, apart from Allah, if you are truthful."

39. No, they deny that[459] whereof they have no knowledge, and whose interpretation has not yet come to them. That is how those who came before them denied [it]. Look, then, what was the fate of the wrongdoers.

40. Some of them believe in it, and some do not; but your Lord knows best the mischief-makers.

41. If they deny what you say, then say: "What I do is mine, and what you do is yours. You are quit of what I do, and I am quit of what you do."

---

457. Brings it back to life after death.
458. The Prophet.
459. The Qur'an.

208

42. And some of them listen to you; but can you make the deaf hear, even if they do not understand?

43. And some of them look at you; but can you guide the blind, even if they do not see?

44. Surely, Allah does not wrong people at all; but people wrong themselves.

45. And on the Day He musters them, it is as though they have only tarried for one hour of the day, recognizing each other. Those who have disbelieved in meeting Allah are the real losers, and are not well-guided.

46. And whether We show you[460] part of what We promise them or cause you to die, surely unto Us is their return; and then Allah is Witness of what they do.

47. Every nation has its Messenger; and when their Messenger comes, they will be justly judged, and they will not be wronged.

48. And they say: "When is this promise, if you are truthful?"

49. Say: "I have no power to harm or to profit myself, except as Allah wills. To every nation is a term;[461] when its term comes, it will not put it back a single hour, nor will it put it forward."

50. Say: "Tell me, if His punishment over-takes you by night or day, what part of it will the wicked sinners seek to hasten?"[462]

51. Is it then, when it has overtaken you, that you will believe in Him? Now [you believe] while you were seeking to hasten it!

---

460. That is, during your lifetime.
461. A term of life.
462. That is, will the wicked sinners after seeing how terrible the punishment is, still be seeking to hasten it through mockery and disbelief?

52. Then it will be said to the wrongdoers: "Taste the everlasting punishment. Will you be rewarded except for what you did?"

ثُمَّ قِيلَ لِلَّذِينَ ظَلَمُوا ذُوقُوا عَذَابَ الْخُلْدِ هَلْ تُجْزَوْنَ إِلَّا بِمَا كُنتُمْ تَكْسِبُونَ ۝

53. And they ask you to tell them: "Is it true?" Say: "Yes, by my Lord, it is the truth, and you cannot escape [punishment]."

۞ وَيَسْتَنْبِئُونَكَ أَحَقٌّ هُوَ قُلْ إِى وَرَبِّى إِنَّهُ لَحَقٌّ وَمَا أَنتُم بِمُعْجِزِينَ ۝

54. Had every soul which did wrong possessed whatever is on earth, it would offer it as ransom, and they will feel remorseful when they see the punishment; but they will be justly judged, and they will not be wronged.

وَلَوْ أَنَّ لِكُلِّ نَفْسٍ ظَلَمَتْ مَا فِى الْأَرْضِ لَافْتَدَتْ بِهِ وَأَسَرُّوا النَّدَامَةَ لَمَّا رَأَوُا الْعَذَابَ وَقُضِىَ بَيْنَهُم بِالْقِسْطِ وَهُمْ لَا يُظْلَمُونَ ۝

55. Indeed, to Allah belongs what is in the heavens and the earth. Indeed, Allah's Promise is true, but most of them do not know.

أَلَا إِنَّ لِلَّهِ مَا فِى السَّمَوَاتِ وَالْأَرْضِ أَلَا إِنَّ وَعْدَ اللَّهِ حَقٌّ وَلَكِنَّ أَكْثَرَهُمْ لَا يَعْلَمُونَ ۝

56. He gives life and causes death, and unto Him you shall be returned.

هُوَ يُحْيِ وَيُمِيتُ وَإِلَيْهِ تُرْجَعُونَ ۝

57. O mankind, there has come to you from your Lord an admonition,[463] a healing for what is in the hearts, and a guidance and mercy for the believers.

يَٰأَيُّهَا النَّاسُ قَدْ جَاءَتْكُم مَّوْعِظَةٌ مِّن رَّبِّكُمْ وَشِفَاءٌ لِّمَا فِى الصُّدُورِ وَهُدًى وَرَحْمَةٌ لِّلْمُؤْمِنِينَ ۝

58. Say: "In Allah's Bounty and Mercy - in those let them rejoice. It is better than that which they amass."

قُلْ بِفَضْلِ اللَّهِ وَبِرَحْمَتِهِ فَبِذَلِكَ فَلْيَفْرَحُوا هُوَ خَيْرٌ مِّمَّا يَجْمَعُونَ ۝

59. Say: "Have you considered the provision Allah has sent down for you, and how then you made some of it unlawful and some lawful?" Say: "Has Allah allowed you or are you lying about Allah?"

قُلْ أَرَءَيْتُم مَّا أَنزَلَ اللَّهُ لَكُم مِّن رِّزْقٍ فَجَعَلْتُم مِّنْهُ حَرَامًا وَحَلَالًا قُلْ ءَاللَّهُ أَذِنَ لَكُمْ أَمْ عَلَى اللَّهِ تَفْتَرُونَ ۝

60. And what will those who impute lies to Allah think on the Day of Resurrection? Allah is Bountiful to mankind, but most of them are not thankful.

وَمَا ظَنُّ الَّذِينَ يَفْتَرُونَ عَلَى اللَّهِ الْكَذِبَ يَوْمَ الْقِيَٰمَةِ إِنَّ اللَّهَ لَذُو فَضْلٍ عَلَى النَّاسِ وَلَكِنَّ أَكْثَرَهُمْ لَا يَشْكُرُونَ ۝

---

463. The Qur'an.

61. You[464] do not go about any affair, nor do you recite any portion of the Qur'an, nor do you[465] do anything, but We are witnesses thereof, as you press on with it. And not a speck's weight in the earth or in the heavens escapes Allah; and nothing smaller or bigger than that, but is in a Manifest Book.

62. Indeed, the friends of Allah have nothing to fear, nor will they grieve.

63. Those who believe and are righteous;

64. Theirs is the good news in the present life and the Hereafter. And there will be no alteration of the Words of Allah. That is the great triumph.

65. And let not what they say grieve you. All power is Allah's; He is the All-Hearing, the All-Knowing.

66. Indeed, to Allah belongs whoever is in the heavens or the earth. Those who call upon others, apart from Allah, do not follow any associate. They only follow conjecture and they are only lying.

67. It is He Who created the night for you to rest therein and the day to see. Surely, in this are signs for a people who listen.

68. They say: "Allah has taken a child." Glory be to Him! He is the Self-Sufficient; His is everything in the heavens and on earth. You have no authority for this. Do you attribute to Allah what you do not know?

69. Say: "Those who invent lies about Allah will not prosper."

70. [It is only] a little enjoyment in this life; then unto Us is their return; then We will make them taste the terrible punishment, on account of their disbelief.

---

464. The Prophet.
465. The Prophet and the Muslims.

وَمَا تَكُونُ فِي شَأْنٍ وَمَا تَتْلُواْ مِنْهُ مِن قُرْآنٍ وَلَا تَعْمَلُونَ مِنْ عَمَلٍ إِلَّا كُنَّا عَلَيْكُمْ شُهُودًا إِذْ تُفِيضُونَ فِيهِ وَمَا يَعْزُبُ عَن رَّبِّكَ مِن مِّثْقَالِ ذَرَّةٍ فِي ٱلْأَرْضِ وَلَا فِي ٱلسَّمَاءِ وَلَا أَصْغَرَ مِن ذَٰلِكَ وَلَا أَكْبَرَ إِلَّا فِي كِتَٰبٍ مُّبِينٍ ﴿٦١﴾

أَلَا إِنَّ أَوْلِيَاءَ ٱللَّهِ لَا خَوْفٌ عَلَيْهِمْ وَلَا هُمْ يَحْزَنُونَ ﴿٦٢﴾

ٱلَّذِينَ ءَامَنُواْ وَكَانُواْ يَتَّقُونَ ﴿٦٣﴾

لَهُمُ ٱلْبُشْرَىٰ فِي ٱلْحَيَوٰةِ ٱلدُّنْيَا وَفِي ٱلْأَخِرَةِ لَا تَبْدِيلَ لِكَلِمَٰتِ ٱللَّهِ ذَٰلِكَ هُوَ ٱلْفَوْزُ ٱلْعَظِيمُ ﴿٦٤﴾

وَلَا يَحْزُنكَ قَوْلُهُمْ إِنَّ ٱلْعِزَّةَ لِلَّهِ جَمِيعًا هُوَ ٱلسَّمِيعُ ٱلْعَلِيمُ ﴿٦٥﴾

أَلَا إِنَّ لِلَّهِ مَن فِي ٱلسَّمَٰوَٰتِ وَمَن فِي ٱلْأَرْضِ وَمَا يَتَّبِعُ ٱلَّذِينَ يَدْعُونَ مِن دُونِ ٱللَّهِ شُرَكَاءَ إِن يَتَّبِعُونَ إِلَّا ٱلظَّنَّ وَإِنْ هُمْ إِلَّا يَخْرُصُونَ ﴿٦٦﴾

هُوَ ٱلَّذِي جَعَلَ لَكُمُ ٱلَّيْلَ لِتَسْكُنُواْ فِيهِ وَٱلنَّهَارَ مُبْصِرًا إِنَّ فِي ذَٰلِكَ لَآيَٰتٍ لِّقَوْمٍ يَسْمَعُونَ ﴿٦٧﴾

قَالُواْ ٱتَّخَذَ ٱللَّهُ وَلَدًا سُبْحَٰنَهُ هُوَ ٱلْغَنِيُّ لَهُ مَا فِي ٱلسَّمَٰوَٰتِ وَمَا فِي ٱلْأَرْضِ إِنْ عِندَكُم مِّن سُلْطَٰنٍ بِهَٰذَآ أَتَقُولُونَ عَلَى ٱللَّهِ مَا لَا تَعْلَمُونَ ﴿٦٨﴾

قُلْ إِنَّ ٱلَّذِينَ يَفْتَرُونَ عَلَى ٱللَّهِ ٱلْكَذِبَ لَا يُفْلِحُونَ ﴿٦٩﴾

مَتَٰعٌ فِي ٱلدُّنْيَا ثُمَّ إِلَيْنَا مَرْجِعُهُمْ ثُمَّ نُذِيقُهُمُ ٱلْعَذَابَ ٱلشَّدِيدَ بِمَا كَانُواْ يَكْفُرُونَ ﴿٧٠﴾

71. And relate to them the story of Noah, when he said to his people: "O my people, if my dwelling [among you] and my reminding you of the Revelations of Allah, is too much for you, then in Allah I have put my trust. Agree upon a course of action with your associates; then let not that course of action be a burden to you; then pass to me [your decision] and give me no respite.

72. "If you turn away, I have asked for no reward from you. My reward is only with Allah. I have been ordered to be one of those who submit."

73. But they denounced him; so We delivered him and those with him in the Ark and made them successors, while drowning those who denied Our Signs. See then what was the fate of those who were warned!

74. Then We sent after him Messengers to their people. They brought them clear proofs; but they would not believe in what they had denied earlier. Thus do We seal the hearts of the aggressors.

75. Then We sent forth after them Moses and Aaron to Pharaoh and his dignitaries, with Our Signs; but they were arrogant; they were sinful people.

76. Then when the truth came to them from Us, they said: "This indeed is manifest sorcery."

77. Moses said: "Do you say to the truth, when it has come to you: 'Is this sorcery?' Sorcerers will never prosper."

78. They said: "Have you come to us to turn us away from that[466] in which we found our fathers so that sovereignty may be yours,[467] in the land? We shall not believe in you both."

---

466. That faith.
467. Moses and his brother.

79. Then Pharaoh said: "Bring me every skilful magician."

80. Then, when the magicians came, Moses said to them: "Cast down what you intend to cast down."

81. Then, when they cast down, Moses said: "What you brought forward is real sorcery. Allah will bring it to naught. Allah indeed does not uphold the work of the mischief-makers.

82. "Allah vindicates the truth by His Words, even if the wicked sinners dislike it."

83. And so only a handful of his people believed in Moses for fear that Pharaoh and his dignitaries would persecute them. Pharaoh was truly a tyrant in the land and one of the transgressors.

84. And Moses said: "O my people, if you believe in Allah, then in Him put your trust, if you submit [to Him]."

85. Whereupon they said: "In Allah we have put our trust. Our Lord, do not let us be tried by the wrongdoing people.

86. "And deliver us by Your Mercy from the unbelieving people."

87. And We revealed to Moses and his brother: "Take for your people dwellings in Egypt and make your dwellings places of worship, perform the prayer and announce the good news to the believers."

88. Moses then said: "Lord, you have given Pharaoh and his dignitaries adornment and wealth in the present life, with which they lead people away from Your Path. O Lord, obliterate their wealth and harden their hearts so that they will not believe, till they see the very painful punishment."

وَقَالَ فِرْعَوْنُ ٱئْتُونِى بِكُلِّ سَٰحِرٍ عَلِيمٍ ۝

فَلَمَّا جَآءَ ٱلسَّحَرَةُ قَالَ لَهُم مُّوسَىٰٓ أَلْقُوا۟ مَآ أَنتُم مُّلْقُونَ ۝

فَلَمَّآ أَلْقَوْا۟ قَالَ مُوسَىٰ مَا جِئْتُم بِهِ ٱلسِّحْرُ إِنَّ ٱللَّهَ سَيُبْطِلُهُۥٓ إِنَّ ٱللَّهَ لَا يُصْلِحُ عَمَلَ ٱلْمُفْسِدِينَ ۝

وَيُحِقُّ ٱللَّهُ ٱلْحَقَّ بِكَلِمَٰتِهِۦ وَلَوْ كَرِهَ ٱلْمُجْرِمُونَ ۝

فَمَآ ءَامَنَ لِمُوسَىٰٓ إِلَّا ذُرِّيَّةٌ مِّن قَوْمِهِۦ عَلَىٰ خَوْفٍ مِّن فِرْعَوْنَ وَمَلَإِي۟هِمْ أَن يَفْتِنَهُمْ وَإِنَّ فِرْعَوْنَ لَعَالٍ فِى ٱلْأَرْضِ وَإِنَّهُۥ لَمِنَ ٱلْمُسْرِفِينَ ۝

وَقَالَ مُوسَىٰ يَٰقَوْمِ إِن كُنتُمْ ءَامَنتُم بِٱللَّهِ فَعَلَيْهِ تَوَكَّلُوٓا۟ إِن كُنتُم مُّسْلِمِينَ ۝

فَقَالُوا۟ عَلَى ٱللَّهِ تَوَكَّلْنَا رَبَّنَا لَا تَجْعَلْنَا فِتْنَةً لِّلْقَوْمِ ٱلظَّٰلِمِينَ ۝

وَنَجِّنَا بِرَحْمَتِكَ مِنَ ٱلْقَوْمِ ٱلْكَٰفِرِينَ ۝

وَأَوْحَيْنَآ إِلَىٰ مُوسَىٰ وَأَخِيهِ أَن تَبَوَّءَا لِقَوْمِكُمَا بِمِصْرَ بُيُوتًا وَٱجْعَلُوا۟ بُيُوتَكُمْ قِبْلَةً وَأَقِيمُوا۟ ٱلصَّلَوٰةَ وَبَشِّرِ ٱلْمُؤْمِنِينَ ۝

وَقَالَ مُوسَىٰ رَبَّنَآ إِنَّكَ ءَاتَيْتَ فِرْعَوْنَ وَمَلَأَهُۥ زِينَةً وَأَمْوَٰلًا فِى ٱلْحَيَوٰةِ ٱلدُّنْيَا رَبَّنَا لِيُضِلُّوا۟ عَن سَبِيلِكَ رَبَّنَا ٱطْمِسْ عَلَىٰٓ أَمْوَٰلِهِمْ وَٱشْدُدْ عَلَىٰ قُلُوبِهِمْ فَلَا يُؤْمِنُوا۟ حَتَّىٰ يَرَوُا۟ ٱلْعَذَابَ ٱلْأَلِيمَ ۝

89. He said: "Your prayer is answered; carry on both with your call and go straight, and do not follow the path of those who do not know."

قَالَ قَدْ أُجِيبَت دَّعْوَتُكُمَا فَٱسْتَقِيمَا وَلَا تَتَّبِعَآنِّ سَبِيلَ ٱلَّذِينَ لَا يَعْلَمُونَ ﴿٨٩﴾

90. And We brought the Children of Israel across the sea. Pharaoh and his troops followed them insolently and aggressively; but when he was about to drown, he said: "I believe that there is no god but He in Whom the Children of Israel believe, and I am one of those who submit [to Allah]."

۞ وَجَٰوَزْنَا بِبَنِىٓ إِسْرَٰٓءِيلَ ٱلْبَحْرَ فَأَتْبَعَهُمْ فِرْعَوْنُ وَجُنُودُهُ بَغْيًا وَعَدْوًا حَتَّىٰٓ إِذَآ أَدْرَكَهُ ٱلْغَرَقُ قَالَ ءَامَنتُ أَنَّهُۥ لَآ إِلَٰهَ إِلَّا ٱلَّذِىٓ ءَامَنَتْ بِهِۦ بَنُوٓا۟ إِسْرَٰٓءِيلَ وَأَنَا۠ مِنَ ٱلْمُسْلِمِينَ ﴿٩٠﴾

91. [It was said to him]: "Now [you believe]! But you disobeyed earlier and you were one of the mischief-makers.

ءَآلْـَٰٔنَ وَقَدْ عَصَيْتَ قَبْلُ وَكُنتَ مِنَ ٱلْمُفْسِدِينَ ﴿٩١﴾

92. "Today, then, We shall save you bodily, so that you may become a sign to those who come after you. Indeed, many people are heedless of Our Signs."

فَٱلْيَوْمَ نُنَجِّيكَ بِبَدَنِكَ لِتَكُونَ لِمَنْ خَلْفَكَ ءَايَةً وَإِنَّ كَثِيرًا مِّنَ ٱلنَّاسِ عَنْ ءَايَٰتِنَا لَغَٰفِلُونَ ﴿٩٢﴾

93. And We have established the Children of Israel in a dignified domain and provided them with good things. Thus they did not differ among themselves until the certain knowledge came to them. Surely, your Lord shall judge between them on the Day of Resurrection regarding that about which they differed.

وَلَقَدْ بَوَّأْنَا بَنِىٓ إِسْرَٰٓءِيلَ مُبَوَّأَ صِدْقٍ وَرَزَقْنَٰهُم مِّنَ ٱلطَّيِّبَٰتِ فَمَا ٱخْتَلَفُوا۟ حَتَّىٰ جَآءَهُمُ ٱلْعِلْمُ إِنَّ رَبَّكَ يَقْضِى بَيْنَهُمْ يَوْمَ ٱلْقِيَٰمَةِ فِيمَا كَانُوا۟ فِيهِ يَخْتَلِفُونَ ﴿٩٣﴾

94. So, if you[468] are in doubt concerning what We have revealed to you, then ask those who have been reading the Book[469] before you. Indeed, the truth has come to you from your Lord; so do not be one of the doubters.

فَإِن كُنتَ فِى شَكٍّ مِّمَّآ أَنزَلْنَآ إِلَيْكَ فَسْـَٔلِ ٱلَّذِينَ يَقْرَءُونَ ٱلْكِتَٰبَ مِن قَبْلِكَ لَقَدْ جَآءَكَ ٱلْحَقُّ مِن رَّبِّكَ فَلَا تَكُونَنَّ مِنَ ٱلْمُمْتَرِينَ ﴿٩٤﴾

95. And do not be one of those who deny Allah's Revelations and thus become one of the losers.

وَلَا تَكُونَنَّ مِنَ ٱلَّذِينَ كَذَّبُوا۟ بِـَٔايَٰتِ ٱللَّهِ فَتَكُونَ مِنَ ٱلْخَٰسِرِينَ ﴿٩٥﴾

---

468. The person addressed here, according to some commentators, is Muhammad.
469. The Torah.

96. Surely, those against whom the Word of your Lord will be fulfilled are not going to believe;

إِنَّ ٱلَّذِينَ حَقَّتْ عَلَيْهِمْ كَلِمَتُ رَبِّكَ لَا يُؤْمِنُونَ ۝

97. Even if every sign comes to them, till they see the very painful punishment.

وَلَوْ جَآءَتْهُمْ كُلُّ ءَايَةٍ حَتَّىٰ يَرَوُاْ ٱلْعَذَابَ ٱلْأَلِيمَ ۝

98. How is it, then, that no town believed so that its belief would profit it, except the people of Jonah? When they believed, We removed from them the punishment of disgrace in the present life and allowed them to enjoy life for a while.

فَلَوْلَا كَانَتْ قَرْيَةٌ ءَامَنَتْ فَنَفَعَهَآ إِيمَانُهَآ إِلَّا قَوْمَ يُونُسَ لَمَّآ ءَامَنُواْ كَشَفْنَا عَنْهُمْ عَذَابَ ٱلْخِزْيِ فِى ٱلْحَيَوٰةِ ٱلدُّنْيَا وَمَتَّعْنَٰهُمْ إِلَىٰ حِينٍ ۝

99. Had your Lord willed, everybody on earth would have believed. Will you then compel people to become believers?

وَلَوْ شَآءَ رَبُّكَ لَآمَنَ مَن فِى ٱلْأَرْضِ كُلُّهُمْ جَمِيعًا أَفَأَنتَ تُكْرِهُ ٱلنَّاسَ حَتَّىٰ يَكُونُواْ مُؤْمِنِينَ ۝

100. It is not given to any soul to believe, except by Allah's Leave. And He lays the scourge on those who do not understand.

وَمَا كَانَ لِنَفْسٍ أَن تُؤْمِنَ إِلَّا بِإِذْنِ ٱللَّهِ وَيَجْعَلُ ٱلرِّجْسَ عَلَى ٱلَّذِينَ لَا يَعْقِلُونَ ۝

101. Say: "Behold what is in the heavens and the earth." But neither the signs nor the warnings will avail a people who do not believe.

قُلِ ٱنظُرُواْ مَاذَا فِى ٱلسَّمَٰوَٰتِ وَٱلْأَرْضِ وَمَا تُغْنِى ٱلْءَايَٰتُ وَٱلنُّذُرُ عَن قَوْمٍ لَّا يُؤْمِنُونَ ۝

102. Do they, then, expect anything other than the like of the days of those who passed away before them? Say: "Wait on, I am with you one of those who wait."

فَهَلْ يَنتَظِرُونَ إِلَّا مِثْلَ أَيَّامِ ٱلَّذِينَ خَلَوْاْ مِن قَبْلِهِمْ قُلْ فَٱنتَظِرُوٓاْ إِنِّى مَعَكُم مِّنَ ٱلْمُنتَظِرِينَ ۝

103. Then, We shall deliver Our Messengers and the believers; it is only right that We should deliver the believers.

ثُمَّ نُنَجِّى رُسُلَنَا وَٱلَّذِينَ ءَامَنُواْ كَذَٰلِكَ حَقًّا عَلَيْنَا نُنجِ ٱلْمُؤْمِنِينَ ۝

104. Say: "O people, if you are in doubt regarding my religion, [know that] I worship not those you worship, apart from Allah; but I worship Allah who causes you to die, and I have been commanded to be one of the believers."

قُلْ يَٰٓأَيُّهَا ٱلنَّاسُ إِن كُنتُمْ فِى شَكٍّ مِّن دِينِى فَلَآ أَعْبُدُ ٱلَّذِينَ تَعْبُدُونَ مِن دُونِ ٱللَّهِ وَلَٰكِنْ أَعْبُدُ ٱللَّهَ ٱلَّذِى يَتَوَفَّىٰكُمْ وَأُمِرْتُ أَنْ أَكُونَ مِنَ ٱلْمُؤْمِنِينَ ۝

105. And [it was said to me]: "Set your face towards religion, in an upright way, and do not be one of the polytheists."

وَأَنْ أَقِمْ وَجْهَكَ لِلدِّينِ حَنِيفًا وَلَا تَكُونَنَّ مِنَ ٱلْمُشْرِكِينَ ۝

106. "And do not call, apart from Allah, on anything which neither profits nor harms you. If you do, you are then one of the wrongdoers."

وَلَا تَدْعُ مِن دُونِ ٱللَّهِ مَا لَا يَنفَعُكَ وَلَا يَضُرُّكَ فَإِن فَعَلْتَ فَإِنَّكَ إِذًا مِّنَ ٱلظَّٰلِمِينَ ﴿١٠٦﴾

107. And if Allah afflicts you with adversity, none can lift it other than He; and if He wills any good for you, none can bar His Bounty. He will accord it to whomever He pleases of His servants and He is the All-Forgiving, the Merciful.

وَإِن يَمْسَسْكَ ٱللَّهُ بِضُرٍّ فَلَا كَاشِفَ لَهُۥ إِلَّا هُوَ وَإِن يُرِدْكَ بِخَيْرٍ فَلَا رَآدَّ لِفَضْلِهِۦ يُصِيبُ بِهِۦ مَن يَشَآءُ مِنْ عِبَادِهِۦ وَهُوَ ٱلْغَفُورُ ٱلرَّحِيمُ ﴿١٠٧﴾

108. Say: "O people, the truth has come to you from your Lord; whoever is well-guided is well-guided only to his own advantage, and whoever goes astray goes astray only to his disadvantage, and I am not a guardian over you."

قُلْ يَٰٓأَيُّهَا ٱلنَّاسُ قَدْ جَآءَكُمُ ٱلْحَقُّ مِن رَّبِّكُمْ فَمَنِ ٱهْتَدَىٰ فَإِنَّمَا يَهْتَدِى لِنَفْسِهِۦ وَمَن ضَلَّ فَإِنَّمَا يَضِلُّ عَلَيْهَا وَمَآ أَنَا۠ عَلَيْكُم بِوَكِيلٍ ﴿١٠٨﴾

109. And (O Mohammad) follow what is revealed to you and be patient and steadfast, until Allah judges; for He is the Best of judges.

وَٱتَّبِعْ مَا يُوحَىٰٓ إِلَيْكَ وَٱصْبِرْ حَتَّىٰ يَحْكُمَ ٱللَّهُ وَهُوَ خَيْرُ ٱلْحَٰكِمِينَ ﴿١٠٩﴾

Sûrat Hud,
(The Prophet Hud) 11

سُورَةُ هُودٍ

In the Name of Allah,
the Compassionate, the Merciful

بِسْمِ ٱللَّهِ ٱلرَّحْمَٰنِ ٱلرَّحِيمِ

1. Alif - Lam - Ra.
[This is] a Book with Verses which are elaborately formulated and clearly expounded from the Wise, the All-Aware.

الٓر كِتَٰبٌ أُحْكِمَتْ ءَايَٰتُهُۥ ثُمَّ فُصِّلَتْ مِن لَّدُنْ حَكِيمٍ خَبِيرٍ ﴿١﴾

2. That you should worship none other than Allah; I am truly a warner and a bearer of good news to you from Him;

أَلَّا تَعْبُدُوٓا۟ إِلَّا ٱللَّهَ إِنَّنِى لَكُم مِّنْهُ نَذِيرٌ وَبَشِيرٌ ﴿٢﴾

3. And ask forgiveness of your Lord; then turn to him in repentance, that He may allow you a fair enjoyment [in this life] for a fixed term, and may bestow His Bounty on every worthy one; but if you turn away I fear for you the punishment of a Great Day.

وَأَنِ ٱسْتَغْفِرُوا۟ رَبَّكُمْ ثُمَّ تُوبُوٓا۟ إِلَيْهِ يُمَتِّعْكُم مَّتَٰعًا حَسَنًا إِلَىٰٓ أَجَلٍ مُّسَمًّى وَيُؤْتِ كُلَّ ذِى فَضْلٍ فَضْلَهُۥ وَإِن تَوَلَّوْا۟ فَإِنِّىٓ أَخَافُ عَلَيْكُمْ عَذَابَ يَوْمٍ كَبِيرٍ ﴿٣﴾

4. Unto Allah is your return, and He has power over everything.

5. Behold, they turn their breasts sideways so as to hide [what they harbour] from Him. Indeed, when they wrap themselves in their clothes He knows what they conceal and what they reveal. He knows the secrets of the hearts.

6. There is no beast on earth but its sustenance is [provided] by Allah; and He knows its resting-place and its repository. All is in a Manifest Book.

7. And it is He Who created the heavens and the earth in six days, and His Throne was upon the water, that He might try you [and see] which one of you does the best work. And if you[470] say: "You will surely be raised up after death", the unbelievers will say: "This is nothing but manifest sorcery."

8. And if We hold punishment back from them for a fixed period, they will say: "What holds it back?" Surely, the day it will overtake them will not be turned away from them, and they shall be afflicted by what they used to mock.

9. And if We let man have a taste of mercy from Us, then wrest it from him, he yields to despair and becomes ungrateful.

10. And if We let him taste prosperity after an adversity has afflicted him, he will say: "Misfortunes have gone away from me", and becomes joyful and proud.

11. Except for those who are patient and do the good deeds; for those are forgiveness and a great reward.

إِلَى ٱللَّهِ مَرْجِعُكُمْ وَهُوَ عَلَىٰ كُلِّ شَىْءٍ قَدِيرٌ ﴿٤﴾

أَلَا إِنَّهُمْ يَثْنُونَ صُدُورَهُمْ لِيَسْتَخْفُوا مِنْهُ أَلَا حِينَ يَسْتَغْشُونَ ثِيَابَهُمْ يَعْلَمُ مَا يُسِرُّونَ وَمَا يُعْلِنُونَ إِنَّهُ عَلِيمٌ بِذَاتِ ٱلصُّدُورِ ﴿٥﴾

۞ وَمَا مِن دَآبَّةٍ فِى ٱلْأَرْضِ إِلَّا عَلَى ٱللَّهِ رِزْقُهَا وَيَعْلَمُ مُسْتَقَرَّهَا وَمُسْتَوْدَعَهَا كُلٌّ فِى كِتَابٍ مُّبِينٍ ﴿٦﴾

وَهُوَ ٱلَّذِى خَلَقَ ٱلسَّمَاوَاتِ وَٱلْأَرْضَ فِى سِتَّةِ أَيَّامٍ وَكَانَ عَرْشُهُ عَلَى ٱلْمَآءِ لِيَبْلُوَكُمْ أَيُّكُمْ أَحْسَنُ عَمَلًا وَلَئِن قُلْتَ إِنَّكُم مَّبْعُوثُونَ مِنۢ بَعْدِ ٱلْمَوْتِ لَيَقُولَنَّ ٱلَّذِينَ كَفَرُوا إِنْ هَٰذَا إِلَّا سِحْرٌ مُّبِينٌ ﴿٧﴾

وَلَئِنْ أَخَّرْنَا عَنْهُمُ ٱلْعَذَابَ إِلَىٰ أُمَّةٍ مَّعْدُودَةٍ لَّيَقُولُنَّ مَا يَحْبِسُهُ أَلَا يَوْمَ يَأْتِيهِمْ لَيْسَ مَصْرُوفًا عَنْهُمْ وَحَاقَ بِهِم مَّا كَانُوا بِهِۦ يَسْتَهْزِءُونَ ﴿٨﴾

وَلَئِنْ أَذَقْنَا ٱلْإِنسَانَ مِنَّا رَحْمَةً ثُمَّ نَزَعْنَاهَا مِنْهُ إِنَّهُ لَيَئُوسٌ كَفُورٌ ﴿٩﴾

وَلَئِنْ أَذَقْنَاهُ نَعْمَآءَ بَعْدَ ضَرَّآءَ مَسَّتْهُ لَيَقُولَنَّ ذَهَبَ ٱلسَّيِّئَاتُ عَنِّى إِنَّهُ لَفَرِحٌ فَخُورٌ ﴿١٠﴾

إِلَّا ٱلَّذِينَ صَبَرُوا وَعَمِلُوا ٱلصَّالِحَاتِ أُولَٰئِكَ لَهُم مَّغْفِرَةٌ وَأَجْرٌ كَبِيرٌ ﴿١١﴾

---

470. The Prophet.

12. Perhaps you are passing over[471] a part of what is revealed to you, and your heart is distressed lest they should say: "If only a treasure was sent down upon him or an angel accompanied him!" You are only a warner, and Allah is in charge of everything.

فَلَعَلَّكَ تَارِكٌ بَعْضَ مَا يُوحَىٰ إِلَيْكَ وَضَائِقٌ بِهِ صَدْرُكَ أَن يَقُولُوا لَوْلَا أُنزِلَ عَلَيْهِ كَنزٌ أَوْ جَاءَ مَعَهُ مَلَكٌ إِنَّمَا أَنتَ نَذِيرٌ وَاللَّهُ عَلَىٰ كُلِّ شَيْءٍ وَكِيلٌ ۝

13. Or will they say: "He has forged it."[472] Say: "Come up then with ten forged surahs like it, and call upon whomever you can, apart from Allah, if you are truthful."

أَمْ يَقُولُونَ افْتَرَاهُ قُلْ فَأْتُوا بِعَشْرِ سُوَرٍ مِّثْلِهِ مُفْتَرَيَاتٍ وَادْعُوا مَنِ اسْتَطَعْتُم مِّن دُونِ اللَّهِ إِن كُنتُمْ صَادِقِينَ ۝

14. But if they[473] do not answer you, then know that it[474] was revealed with Allah's Knowledge and that there is no god but He. Will you then submit?

فَإِلَّمْ يَسْتَجِيبُوا لَكُمْ فَاعْلَمُوا أَنَّمَا أُنزِلَ بِعِلْمِ اللَّهِ وَأَن لَّا إِلَٰهَ إِلَّا هُوَ فَهَلْ أَنتُم مُّسْلِمُونَ ۝

15. Whoever desires the life of this world and its finery, We will reward them [during it] for their [good] works, and they will not be given less than their due.

مَن كَانَ يُرِيدُ الْحَيَاةَ الدُّنْيَا وَزِينَتَهَا نُوَفِّ إِلَيْهِمْ أَعْمَالَهُمْ فِيهَا وَهُمْ فِيهَا لَا يُبْخَسُونَ ۝

16. [Yet] those [are the people] who shall have nothing in the Hereafter except the Fire, and what they did [here] will go there to waste, and their works will be in vain.

أُولَٰئِكَ الَّذِينَ لَيْسَ لَهُمْ فِي الْآخِرَةِ إِلَّا النَّارُ وَحَبِطَ مَا صَنَعُوا فِيهَا وَبَاطِلٌ مَّا كَانُوا يَعْمَلُونَ ۝

17. Are those then [like these] who have a clear proof[475] from their Lord recited by a witness from Him, and preceded by the Book of Moses as a guide and mercy? Those believe in it; but those who disbelieve in it from among the parties[476] - their appointed place is the Fire. So do not be in doubt about it. It is indeed the truth from your Lord; but most people do not believe.

أَفَمَن كَانَ عَلَىٰ بَيِّنَةٍ مِّن رَّبِّهِ وَيَتْلُوهُ شَاهِدٌ مِّنْهُ وَمِن قَبْلِهِ كِتَابُ مُوسَىٰ إِمَامًا وَرَحْمَةً أُولَٰئِكَ يُؤْمِنُونَ بِهِ وَمَن يَكْفُرْ بِهِ مِنَ الْأَحْزَابِ فَالنَّارُ مَوْعِدُهُ فَلَا تَكُ فِي مِرْيَةٍ مِّنْهُ إِنَّهُ الْحَقُّ مِن رَّبِّكَ وَلَٰكِنَّ أَكْثَرَ النَّاسِ لَا يُؤْمِنُونَ ۝

---

471. That is, you are not reciting.
472. The Qur'an.
473. Those gods set up besides Allah.
474. The Qur'an.
475. The Qur'an.
476. The Meccans and neighbouring tribes who opposed the Prophet.

18. And who is more perverse than he who invents lies about Allah? Those shall be brought before their Lord and the witnesses[477] shall say: "These are the ones who lied about their Lord. May Allah's curse be upon the wrongdoers!"

19. Those who bar people from the Path of Allah, and wish it to be crooked; they truly disbelieve in the Hereafter.

20. Those will not escape on earth and they have, apart from Allah, no protectors. Their punishment will be doubled; they were unable to hear, nor did they perceive.

21. Those are the ones who lost their souls and that which they invented[478] strayed away from them.

22. Without doubt, they will be, in the Hereafter, the greatest losers.

23. As to those who believe and do the good deeds and turn humbly to their Lord, they shall be the people of Paradise, dwelling therein forever.

24. The case of the two parties[479] is like the blind and the deaf compared with the man who sees and hears. Are they both alike? Do you not pay heed?

25. And We have sent Noah forth to his people; [he said]: "I am a plain warner to you;

26. "That you worship none but Allah. I fear for you the punishment of a very painful Day."

27. Thereupon the unbelieving dignitaries among his people said to him: "We do not see in you except a mortal like ourselves; nor

وَمَنْ أَظْلَمُ مِمَّنِ ٱفْتَرَىٰ عَلَى ٱللَّهِ كَذِبًا أُوْلَـٰٓئِكَ يُعْرَضُونَ عَلَىٰ رَبِّهِمْ وَيَقُولُ ٱلْأَشْهَادُ هَـٰٓؤُلَآءِ ٱلَّذِينَ كَذَبُوا۟ عَلَىٰ رَبِّهِمْ أَلَا لَعْنَةُ ٱللَّهِ عَلَى ٱلظَّـٰلِمِينَ ﴿١٨﴾

ٱلَّذِينَ يَصُدُّونَ عَن سَبِيلِ ٱللَّهِ وَيَبْغُونَهَا عِوَجًا وَهُم بِٱلْأَخِرَةِ هُمْ كَـٰفِرُونَ ﴿١٩﴾

أُوْلَـٰٓئِكَ لَمْ يَكُونُوا۟ مُعْجِزِينَ فِى ٱلْأَرْضِ وَمَا كَانَ لَهُم مِّن دُونِ ٱللَّهِ مِنْ أَوْلِيَآءَ يُضَـٰعَفُ لَهُمُ ٱلْعَذَابُ مَا كَانُوا۟ يَسْتَطِيعُونَ ٱلسَّمْعَ وَمَا كَانُوا۟ يُبْصِرُونَ ﴿٢٠﴾

أُوْلَـٰٓئِكَ ٱلَّذِينَ خَسِرُوٓا۟ أَنفُسَهُمْ وَضَلَّ عَنْهُم مَّا كَانُوا۟ يَفْتَرُونَ ﴿٢١﴾

لَا جَرَمَ أَنَّهُمْ فِى ٱلْأَخِرَةِ هُمُ ٱلْأَخْسَرُونَ ﴿٢٢﴾

إِنَّ ٱلَّذِينَ ءَامَنُوا۟ وَعَمِلُوا۟ ٱلصَّـٰلِحَـٰتِ وَأَخْبَتُوٓا۟ إِلَىٰ رَبِّهِمْ أُوْلَـٰٓئِكَ أَصْحَـٰبُ ٱلْجَنَّةِ هُمْ فِيهَا خَـٰلِدُونَ ﴿٢٣﴾

۞ مَثَلُ ٱلْفَرِيقَيْنِ كَٱلْأَعْمَىٰ وَٱلْأَصَمِّ وَٱلْبَصِيرِ وَٱلسَّمِيعِ هَلْ يَسْتَوِيَانِ مَثَلًا أَفَلَا تَذَكَّرُونَ ﴿٢٤﴾

وَلَقَدْ أَرْسَلْنَا نُوحًا إِلَىٰ قَوْمِهِۦٓ إِنِّى لَكُمْ نَذِيرٌ مُّبِينٌ ﴿٢٥﴾

أَن لَّا تَعْبُدُوٓا۟ إِلَّا ٱللَّهَ إِنِّىٓ أَخَافُ عَلَيْكُمْ عَذَابَ يَوْمٍ أَلِيمٍ ﴿٢٦﴾

فَقَالَ ٱلْمَلَأُ ٱلَّذِينَ كَفَرُوا۟ مِن قَوْمِهِۦ مَا نَرَىٰكَ إِلَّا بَشَرًا مِّثْلَنَا وَمَا نَرَىٰكَ ٱتَّبَعَكَ إِلَّا ٱلَّذِينَ هُمْ أَرَاذِلُنَا

---

477. The angels.
478. The associates they assign to Allah.
479. The believers and the unbelievers.

do we see in those who hastily followed you except the scum of our people. We do not see that you[480] have any merit over us, but rather think that you are liars."

28. He said: "O my people, do you think that if I have a clear proof from my Lord and He has granted me a mercy from Him but it has been hidden from your sight, we would force it on you while you are averse to it?

29. "And O my people, I do not ask you money for it; my reward is with Allah; and I will not drive away those who believe, for they will surely meet their Lord, but I see that you are an ignorant people.

30. "O my people, who will save me from Allah if I drive [the believers] away? Will you pay heed?

31. "I do not say to you that I possess Allah's Treasures; and I do not know the Unseen. I do not claim to be an angel; nor do I say to those at whom you look with disdain that Allah will not accord them any good; Allah knows best what is in their hearts. For I would be, then, one of the wrongdoers."

32. They said: "O Noah, you have disputed and disputed much with us. Bring us, then, what you promise us, if you are truthful."

33. He said: "It is Allah who will bring it to you, if He wills, and you will not be able to escape.

34. "My advice will not profit you, should I wish to give you advice, if Allah wills to lead you astray. He is your Lord and unto Him you shall be brought back."

35. Or will they (the pagans of Mecca) say: "He has forged it." Say: "If I have forged it, my guilt is upon me and I am innocent of the evil you commit."

---

480. The addressed here are Noah and the believers.

36. And it was revealed to Noah: "None of your people will believe except those who have already believed, so do not grieve at what they do;

37. "And make the Ark under Our Eyes and with Our Revelation, and do not plead with Me regarding the wrongdoers; they shall be drowned."

38. So he started making the Ark, and whenever a group of his people passed by him, they mocked him. [But] he would say: "If you mock us, we will mock you, as you are mocking.

39. "You shall surely learn who will be afflicted by a degrading chastisement, and will undergo a lasting punishment."

40. And when Our Command came, and the water gushed forth from the earth, We said: "Carry in it[481] two of every kind, together with your family, except for those who have been doomed, and [take] those who believe." However only a few believers besides him were there.

41. And he said: "Embark on it. In the name of Allah will be its sailing and anchor. My Lord is indeed All-Forgiving, Merciful."

42. And as it[482] sailed along with them amid waves like mountains, Noah called out to his son, who stood apart: "My son, embark with us, and do not remain with the unbelievers."

43. He[483] said: "I will seek refuge in a mountain that will protect me from water." He[484] said: "Today, there is no protector from Allah's Decree, except for him on whom He has mercy." Then the waves came between them and so he was one of those who were drowned.

---

481. The Ark.
482. The Ark.
483. Noah's son.
484. Noah.

44. And it was said:[485] "O earth, swallow your waters, and O heaven, desist." The water then subsided and the Decree [of Allah] was accomplished; and it[486] settled upon al-Judi mountain; and it was said: "Away with the wrongdoing people."

45. Noah then called out to his Lord saying: "My Lord, my son is of my family; and Your Promise is surely the truth and you are the Best of judges."

46. He said: "O Noah, he is not of your family. It is an act which is not righteous, so do not ask Me about that of which you have no knowledge. I admonish you not to be one of the ignorant."

47. He said: "Lord, I seek refuge with You, lest I should ask You that of which I have no knowledge. For unless You forgive me and have mercy on me I will be one of the losers."

48. It was said to Noah: "Come down [from the Ark] in peace from Us and blessings on you and on [some] nations [descending] from those with you, and We shall provide for others [in this life]. Then they will be afflicted by severe punishment from Us."

49. That is part of the tidings of the Unseen which We are revealing to you. Neither you, nor your people knew it before this. Forbear, then, the [good] outcome belongs to the righteous.

50. And [We sent] to 'Ad their brother Hud. He said: "O my people, worship Allah; you have no other god but He. You are only lying [about Allah].

---

485. By Allah.
486. The Ark.

51. "O my people, I ask you no reward for it; my reward is only with Him Who created me. Do you not understand?

52. "O my people, ask forgiveness from your Lord, then repent unto Him, for He will send you torrents of rain from the sky and add strength to your strength. And do not turn away guilty."

53. They said: "O Hud, you have not brought us any clear proof, and we will not abandon our gods because of what you say, and we will not believe in you.

54. "We only say that some of our gods have smitten you with some evil." He said: "I call Allah to witness and call you to witness that I am innocent of what you associate,

55. "With Him. So try your guile on me, all of you; then do not give me any respite.

56. "I have put my trust in Allah, my Lord and your Lord. There is no creature which crawls, but He takes it by the forelock.[487] My Lord is truly on a Straight Path.

57. "Then, if you turn away, I have actually delivered to you what I was sent forth to you with, and my Lord will raise up as successors a people other than you, and you will not cause Him any harm. My Lord watches over all things."

58. And when Our Decree came, We saved Hud and those who believed with him, by a mercy of Ours, and delivered them from a harsh punishment.

59. Such were the [people of] 'Ad; they denied the signs of their Lord and disobeyed His Messengers and followed the command of every obstinate tyrant.

يَٰقَوْمِ لَآ أَسْـَٔلُكُمْ عَلَيْهِ أَجْرًا إِنْ أَجْرِىَ إِلَّا عَلَى ٱلَّذِى فَطَرَنِىٓ أَفَلَا تَعْقِلُونَ ﴿٥١﴾

وَيَٰقَوْمِ ٱسْتَغْفِرُوا۟ رَبَّكُمْ ثُمَّ تُوبُوٓا۟ إِلَيْهِ يُرْسِلِ ٱلسَّمَآءَ عَلَيْكُم مِّدْرَارًا وَيَزِدْكُمْ قُوَّةً إِلَىٰ قُوَّتِكُمْ وَلَا تَتَوَلَّوْا۟ مُجْرِمِينَ ﴿٥٢﴾

قَالُوا۟ يَٰهُودُ مَا جِئْتَنَا بِبَيِّنَةٍ وَمَا نَحْنُ بِتَارِكِىٓ ءَالِهَتِنَا عَن قَوْلِكَ وَمَا نَحْنُ لَكَ بِمُؤْمِنِينَ ﴿٥٣﴾

إِن نَّقُولُ إِلَّا ٱعْتَرَىٰكَ بَعْضُ ءَالِهَتِنَا بِسُوٓءٍ قَالَ إِنِّىٓ أُشْهِدُ ٱللَّهَ وَٱشْهَدُوٓا۟ أَنِّى بَرِىٓءٌ مِّمَّا تُشْرِكُونَ ﴿٥٤﴾

مِن دُونِهِۦ فَكِيدُونِى جَمِيعًا ثُمَّ لَا تُنظِرُونِ ﴿٥٥﴾

إِنِّى تَوَكَّلْتُ عَلَى ٱللَّهِ رَبِّى وَرَبِّكُم مَّا مِن دَآبَّةٍ إِلَّا هُوَ ءَاخِذٌۢ بِنَاصِيَتِهَآ إِنَّ رَبِّى عَلَىٰ صِرَٰطٍ مُّسْتَقِيمٍ ﴿٥٦﴾

فَإِن تَوَلَّوْا۟ فَقَدْ أَبْلَغْتُكُم مَّآ أُرْسِلْتُ بِهِۦٓ إِلَيْكُمْ وَيَسْتَخْلِفُ رَبِّى قَوْمًا غَيْرَكُمْ وَلَا تَضُرُّونَهُۥ شَيْـًٔا إِنَّ رَبِّى عَلَىٰ كُلِّ شَىْءٍ حَفِيظٌ ﴿٥٧﴾

وَلَمَّا جَآءَ أَمْرُنَا نَجَّيْنَا هُودًا وَٱلَّذِينَ ءَامَنُوا۟ مَعَهُۥ بِرَحْمَةٍ مِّنَّا وَنَجَّيْنَٰهُم مِّنْ عَذَابٍ غَلِيظٍ ﴿٥٨﴾

وَتِلْكَ عَادٌ جَحَدُوا۟ بِـَٔايَٰتِ رَبِّهِمْ وَعَصَوْا۟ رُسُلَهُۥ وَٱتَّبَعُوٓا۟ أَمْرَ كُلِّ جَبَّارٍ عَنِيدٍ ﴿٥٩﴾

---

487. That is, he controls it.

60. And they were pursued by a curse in this world and [shall be cursed] on the Day of Resurrection. Surely, 'Ad disbelieved their Lord. Away with 'Ad, the people of Hud.

61. And to Thamud [We sent] their brother Salih. He said: "O my people, worship Allah; you have no other god but Him. He brought you out from the earth and made you inhabit it; so ask His forgiveness and repent unto Him. My Lord is indeed close at hand and answers [the prayer]."

62. They said: "O Salih, we set our hopes on you before this. Do you forbid us to worship what our fathers worshipped? We are indeed in grave doubt regarding what you are calling us to."

63. He said: "O my people, what if I am in possession of a clear proof from my Lord, and He has accorded me a mercy of His Own? Who then will protect me from Allah if I disobey Him? Surely, you will only compound my perdition.

64. "O my people, here is the she-camel of Allah, a sign unto you. Let her graze in Allah's land and do not do her any harm, lest a swift punishment should overtake you."

65. However, they hamstrung her, and so he said: "[You can] stay in your houses [only] for three days. This is a promise which will not be belied."

66. Then, when Our Command came, We saved Salih and those who believed with him, by a mercy of Our Own, from the disgrace of that day. Your Lord is truly the Strong, and Mighty.

67. And the evildoers were overtaken by the [thundering] cry and they lay prostrate in their own homes,

وَأُتْبِعُواْ فِى هَٰذِهِ ٱلدُّنْيَا لَعْنَةً وَيَوْمَ ٱلْقِيَٰمَةِ أَلَآ إِنَّ عَادًا كَفَرُواْ رَبَّهُمْ أَلَا بُعْدًا لِّعَادٍ قَوْمِ هُودٍ ﴿٦٠﴾

۞ وَإِلَىٰ ثَمُودَ أَخَاهُمْ صَٰلِحًا قَالَ يَٰقَوْمِ ٱعْبُدُواْ ٱللَّهَ مَا لَكُم مِّنْ إِلَٰهٍ غَيْرُهُۥ هُوَ أَنشَأَكُم مِّنَ ٱلْأَرْضِ وَٱسْتَعْمَرَكُمْ فِيهَا فَٱسْتَغْفِرُوهُ ثُمَّ تُوبُوٓاْ إِلَيْهِ إِنَّ رَبِّى قَرِيبٌ مُّجِيبٌ ﴿٦١﴾

قَالُواْ يَٰصَٰلِحُ قَدْ كُنتَ فِينَا مَرْجُوًّا قَبْلَ هَٰذَآ أَتَنْهَىٰنَآ أَن نَّعْبُدَ مَا يَعْبُدُ ءَابَآؤُنَا وَإِنَّنَا لَفِى شَكٍّ مِّمَّا تَدْعُونَآ إِلَيْهِ مُرِيبٍ ﴿٦٢﴾

قَالَ يَٰقَوْمِ أَرَءَيْتُمْ إِن كُنتُ عَلَىٰ بَيِّنَةٍ مِّن رَّبِّى وَءَاتَىٰنِى مِنْهُ رَحْمَةً فَمَن يَنصُرُنِى مِنَ ٱللَّهِ إِنْ عَصَيْتُهُۥ فَمَا تَزِيدُونَنِى غَيْرَ تَخْسِيرٍ ﴿٦٣﴾

وَيَٰقَوْمِ هَٰذِهِۦ نَاقَةُ ٱللَّهِ لَكُمْ ءَايَةً فَذَرُوهَا تَأْكُلْ فِىٓ أَرْضِ ٱللَّهِ وَلَا تَمَسُّوهَا بِسُوٓءٍ فَيَأْخُذَكُمْ عَذَابٌ قَرِيبٌ ﴿٦٤﴾

فَعَقَرُوهَا فَقَالَ تَمَتَّعُواْ فِى دَارِكُمْ ثَلَٰثَةَ أَيَّامٍ ذَٰلِكَ وَعْدٌ غَيْرُ مَكْذُوبٍ ﴿٦٥﴾

فَلَمَّا جَآءَ أَمْرُنَا نَجَّيْنَا صَٰلِحًا وَٱلَّذِينَ ءَامَنُواْ مَعَهُۥ بِرَحْمَةٍ مِّنَّا وَمِنْ خِزْىِ يَوْمِئِذٍ إِنَّ رَبَّكَ هُوَ ٱلْقَوِىُّ ٱلْعَزِيزُ ﴿٦٦﴾

وَأَخَذَ ٱلَّذِينَ ظَلَمُواْ ٱلصَّيْحَةُ فَأَصْبَحُواْ فِى دِيَٰرِهِمْ جَٰثِمِينَ ﴿٦٧﴾

224

68. As if they never dwelt therein. Truly, Thamud disbelieved their Lord. Away with Thamud!

كَأَن لَّمْ يَغْنَوْا فِيهَآ أَلَآ إِنَّ ثَمُودَا۟ كَفَرُوا۟ رَبَّهُمْ أَلَا بُعْدًا لِّثَمُودَ ۝

69. Our messengers[488] indeed came to Abraham bearing good news. They said: "Peace", he said: "Peace." Then he brought a roasted calf at once.

وَلَقَدْ جَآءَتْ رُسُلُنَآ إِبْرَٰهِيمَ بِٱلْبُشْرَىٰ قَالُوا۟ سَلَٰمًا قَالَ سَلَٰمٌ فَمَا لَبِثَ أَن جَآءَ بِعِجْلٍ حَنِيذٍ ۝

70. But when he saw that their hands did not reach out to it, he became suspicious of them and conceived a fear of them. They said: "Fear not, we have been sent to the people of Lot."

فَلَمَّا رَءَآ أَيْدِيَهُمْ لَا تَصِلُ إِلَيْهِ نَكِرَهُمْ وَأَوْجَسَ مِنْهُمْ خِيفَةً قَالُوا۟ لَا تَخَفْ إِنَّآ أُرْسِلْنَآ إِلَىٰ قَوْمِ لُوطٍ ۝

71. His wife was standing by, so she laughed. Thereupon We announced to her the good news of Isaac, and after Isaac, of Jacob.

وَٱمْرَأَتُهُۥ قَآئِمَةٌ فَضَحِكَتْ فَبَشَّرْنَٰهَا بِإِسْحَٰقَ وَمِن وَرَآءِ إِسْحَٰقَ يَعْقُوبَ ۝

72. She said: "Woe is me, shall I bear a child while I am an old woman, and this, my husband, is an old man too? This is truly a very strange thing."

قَالَتْ يَٰوَيْلَتَىٰٓ ءَأَلِدُ وَأَنَا۠ عَجُوزٌ وَهَٰذَا بَعْلِي شَيْخًا إِنَّ هَٰذَا لَشَىْءٌ عَجِيبٌ ۝

73. They said: "Do you wonder at Allah's Command? May the Mercy and Blessings of Allah be upon you, O people of the House.[489] Surely He is Praiseworthy and Glorious."

قَالُوٓا۟ أَتَعْجَبِينَ مِنْ أَمْرِ ٱللَّهِ رَحْمَتُ ٱللَّهِ وَبَرَكَٰتُهُۥ عَلَيْكُمْ أَهْلَ ٱلْبَيْتِ إِنَّهُۥ حَمِيدٌ مَّجِيدٌ ۝

74. Then when fear left Abraham and the good news came to him, he started pleading with Us concerning the people of Lot.

فَلَمَّا ذَهَبَ عَنْ إِبْرَٰهِيمَ ٱلرَّوْعُ وَجَآءَتْهُ ٱلْبُشْرَىٰ يُجَٰدِلُنَا فِى قَوْمِ لُوطٍ ۝

75. Abraham is truly clement, contrite, penitent.

إِنَّ إِبْرَٰهِيمَ لَحَلِيمٌ أَوَّٰهٌ مُّنِيبٌ ۝

76. "O Abraham, desist from this; the Command of your Lord has come and an irreversible punishment shall surely smite them."

يَٰٓإِبْرَٰهِيمُ أَعْرِضْ عَنْ هَٰذَآ إِنَّهُۥ قَدْ جَآءَ أَمْرُ رَبِّكَ وَإِنَّهُمْ ءَاتِيهِمْ عَذَابٌ غَيْرُ مَرْدُودٍ ۝

77. And when Our messengers came to Lot, he was grieved by them and felt unable to protect them. He said: "This is a dreadful day."

وَلَمَّا جَآءَتْ رُسُلُنَا لُوطًا سِيٓءَ بِهِمْ وَضَاقَ بِهِمْ ذَرْعًا وَقَالَ هَٰذَا يَوْمٌ عَصِيبٌ ۝

---

488. They are generally believed to be angels who looked like men.
489. The House of Abraham.

225

78. And his people came rushing towards him; and before that time they used to perpetrate evil deeds.[490] He said: "O my people, these are my daughters; they are purer for you. So fear Allah and do not disgrace me by [wronging] my guests. Is there not one right-minded man among you?"

79. They said: "You know that we have no right to your daughters, and you know well what we want."

80. He said: "Would that I had the power to stand against you, or could seek refuge with a strong supporter."

81. They[491] said: "O Lot, we are your Lord's messengers to you; they will not reach you. So set out with your family in watch of the night and let no one look back, except for your wife.[492] She will be afflicted with what they have been afflicted with. Their appointed time is the morning. Is not the morning close enough?"

82. And when Our Decree came, We turned [the town][493] upside down and rained down upon it stones of clay in clusters;

83. Marked from your Lord; and they were never far off from the wrongdoers.

84. And to Midian [We sent] their brother Shu'ayb. He said: "O my people, worship Allah; you have no other god but Him. Do not skimp the measure and the weight. I see that you are prospering, but I fear for you the punishment of an encompassing Day.

وَجَآءَهُۥ قَوۡمُهُۥ يُهۡرَعُونَ إِلَيۡهِ وَمِن قَبۡلُ كَانُواْ يَعۡمَلُونَ ٱلسَّيِّـَٔاتِ قَالَ يَٰقَوۡمِ هَٰٓؤُلَآءِ بَنَاتِي هُنَّ أَطۡهَرُ لَكُمۡ فَٱتَّقُواْ ٱللَّهَ وَلَا تُخۡزُونِ فِي ضَيۡفِيٓ أَلَيۡسَ مِنكُمۡ رَجُلٌ رَّشِيدٌ ۝

قَالُواْ لَقَدۡ عَلِمۡتَ مَا لَنَا فِي بَنَاتِكَ مِنۡ حَقٍّ وَإِنَّكَ لَتَعۡلَمُ مَا نُرِيدُ ۝

قَالَ لَوۡ أَنَّ لِي بِكُمۡ قُوَّةً أَوۡ ءَاوِيٓ إِلَىٰ رُكۡنٍ شَدِيدٍ ۝

قَالُواْ يَٰلُوطُ إِنَّا رُسُلُ رَبِّكَ لَن يَصِلُوٓاْ إِلَيۡكَ فَأَسۡرِ بِأَهۡلِكَ بِقِطۡعٍ مِّنَ ٱلَّيۡلِ وَلَا يَلۡتَفِتۡ مِنكُمۡ أَحَدٌ إِلَّا ٱمۡرَأَتَكَ إِنَّهُۥ مُصِيبُهَا مَآ أَصَابَهُمۡ إِنَّ مَوۡعِدَهُمُ ٱلصُّبۡحُ أَلَيۡسَ ٱلصُّبۡحُ بِقَرِيبٍ ۝

فَلَمَّا جَآءَ أَمۡرُنَا جَعَلۡنَا عَٰلِيَهَا سَافِلَهَا وَأَمۡطَرۡنَا عَلَيۡهَا حِجَارَةً مِّن سِجِّيلٍ مَّنضُودٍ ۝

مُّسَوَّمَةً عِندَ رَبِّكَ وَمَا هِيَ مِنَ ٱلظَّٰلِمِينَ بِبَعِيدٍ ۝

۞ وَإِلَىٰ مَدۡيَنَ أَخَاهُمۡ شُعَيۡبًا قَالَ يَٰقَوۡمِ ٱعۡبُدُواْ ٱللَّهَ مَا لَكُم مِّنۡ إِلَٰهٍ غَيۡرُهُۥ وَلَا تَنقُصُواْ ٱلۡمِكۡيَالَ وَٱلۡمِيزَانَ إِنِّيٓ أَرَىٰكُم بِخَيۡرٍ وَإِنِّيٓ أَخَافُ عَلَيۡكُمۡ عَذَابَ يَوۡمٍ مُّحِيطٍ ۝

---

490. That is, practise sodomy.
491. The angels who were Lot's guests.
492. She was disobedient to her husband.
493. The town of Sodom.

85. "And my people, be just and give full measure and full weight, and do not cheat people out of things due to them, and do not sow corruption in the land by committing evil.

86. "What remains for you from Allah's provision is better for you if you are true believers; and I am not a watcher over you."

87. They said: "O Shu'ayb, does your prayer[494] command you that we should abandon what our fathers worshipped and that we should not do with our wealth what we wish? You are indeed the clement and right-minded one."[495]

88. He said: "O my people, do you think that if I have a clear proof from my Lord and He has granted me a fair provision from Him [I would commit any of those evils]? I do not want to do what I forbid you to do. I only want to do what I can to set things right. My success comes only from Allah. In Him I have put my trust and to Him I turn.

89. "O my people, let not my disagreement with you bring upon you what the people of Noah, the people of Hud or the people of Salih brought upon themselves.[496] The people of Lot are not far away from you.

90. "And ask forgiveness from your Lord; then repent upon Him. My Lord is truly Merciful, Kind."

91. They said: "O Shu'ayb, we do not understand much of what you say; and surely we see you weak in our midst. Were it not for your family, we would have stoned you; for you are not too dear [to be stoned]."

---

494. That is, religion.
495. They said this mockingly.
496. That is, destruction.

92. He said: "O my people, is my family dearer to you than Allah? You have turned your backs on Him. My Lord knows what you do.

93. "O my people, continue to do what you can, and I shall continue too. You will surely learn who will be seized by a punishment disgracing him, and who is a liar. Wait and see, and I shall be waiting with you."

94. And when Our Decree came, We delivered Shu'ayb and those who believed with him by a mercy of Ours, and the wrongdoers were overtaken by the [thundering] Cry, and they lay prostrate in their own homes,

95. As if they never dwelt therein. Away with Midian. [It perished] as did Thamud before.

96. And We have indeed sent Moses with Our Signs and a manifest authority,

97. To Pharaoh and his dignitaries; but they followed Pharaoh's command, and Pharaoh's command was not sound.

98. He shall be at the head of his people on the Day of Resurrection; thus he shall lead them into the Fire. How wretched is the place to which they will be led!

99. And they are followed in this life with a curse and on the Day of Resurrection too. Wretched is the support they shall be given!

100. That is part of the tidings of the towns We recount to you; some of them are still standing and some have been reduced to rubble.

101. And We have not wronged them, but they have wronged themselves. Their deities, upon whom they called, apart from Allah, did not avail them anything when the Decree of your Lord came; but they only added to their destruction.

قَالَ يَـٰقَوْمِ أَرَهْطِىٓ أَعَزُّ عَلَيْكُم مِّنَ ٱللَّهِ وَٱتَّخَذْتُمُوهُ وَرَآءَكُمْ ظِهْرِيًّا إِنَّ رَبِّى بِمَا تَعْمَلُونَ مُحِيطٌ ۝

وَيَـٰقَوْمِ ٱعْمَلُوا۟ عَلَىٰ مَكَانَتِكُمْ إِنِّى عَـٰمِلٌ سَوْفَ تَعْلَمُونَ مَن يَأْتِيهِ عَذَابٌ يُخْزِيهِ وَمَنْ هُوَ كَـٰذِبٌ وَٱرْتَقِبُوٓا۟ إِنِّى مَعَكُمْ رَقِيبٌ ۝

وَلَمَّا جَآءَ أَمْرُنَا نَجَّيْنَا شُعَيْبًا وَٱلَّذِينَ ءَامَنُوا۟ مَعَهُۥ بِرَحْمَةٍ مِّنَّا وَأَخَذَتِ ٱلَّذِينَ ظَلَمُوا۟ ٱلصَّيْحَةُ فَأَصْبَحُوا۟ فِى دِيَـٰرِهِمْ جَـٰثِمِينَ ۝

كَأَن لَّمْ يَغْنَوْا۟ فِيهَآ أَلَا بُعْدًا لِّمَدْيَنَ كَمَا بَعِدَتْ ثَمُودُ ۝

وَلَقَدْ أَرْسَلْنَا مُوسَىٰ بِـَٔايَـٰتِنَا وَسُلْطَـٰنٍ مُّبِينٍ ۝

إِلَىٰ فِرْعَوْنَ وَمَلَإِي۟هِۦ فَٱتَّبَعُوٓا۟ أَمْرَ فِرْعَوْنَ وَمَآ أَمْرُ فِرْعَوْنَ بِرَشِيدٍ ۝

يَقْدُمُ قَوْمَهُۥ يَوْمَ ٱلْقِيَـٰمَةِ فَأَوْرَدَهُمُ ٱلنَّارَ وَبِئْسَ ٱلْوِرْدُ ٱلْمَوْرُودُ ۝

وَأُتْبِعُوا۟ فِى هَـٰذِهِۦ لَعْنَةً وَيَوْمَ ٱلْقِيَـٰمَةِ بِئْسَ ٱلرِّفْدُ ٱلْمَرْفُودُ ۝

ذَٰلِكَ مِنْ أَنۢبَآءِ ٱلْقُرَىٰ نَقُصُّهُۥ عَلَيْكَ مِنْهَا قَآئِمٌ وَحَصِيدٌ ۝

وَمَا ظَلَمْنَـٰهُمْ وَلَـٰكِن ظَلَمُوٓا۟ أَنفُسَهُمْ فَمَآ أَغْنَتْ عَنْهُمْ ءَالِهَتُهُمُ ٱلَّتِى يَدْعُونَ مِن دُونِ ٱللَّهِ مِن شَىْءٍ لَّمَّا جَآءَ أَمْرُ رَبِّكَ وَمَا زَادُوهُمْ غَيْرَ تَتْبِيبٍ ۝

102. And such is your Lord's punishment when He punishes the cities which are unjust. His punishment is indeed very painful, very hard.

103. There is surely in this a sign for him who fears the punishment of the Hereafter. That is a Day on which men will be gathered together, and that is a Day to be witnessed.

104. And we shall not delay it, but for an appointed term.

105. The day it comes, no soul shall speak without His Leave. Some of them[497] shall be wretched, some happy.

106. As for the wretched, they shall be in the Fire; they shall have therein groaning and moaning;

107. Abiding therein forever, so long as the heavens and the earth shall endure, except as your Lord pleases. Your Lord does indeed what He wants.

108. But as for the blessed, they shall be in Paradise abiding therein as long as the heavens and the earth shall endure; except as your Lord pleases, a gift, uninterrupted.

109. So do not be in doubt as to what these [people] worship; they only worship as their fathers worshipped before them, and We shall accord them their share[498] undiminished.

110. And We have given Moses the Book, but discord broke out around it; and but for a Word that preceded from your Lord, the matter would have been decided between them. They are indeed in disturbing doubt with respect to it.

وَكَذَٰلِكَ أَخْذُ رَبِّكَ إِذَآ أَخَذَ ٱلْقُرَىٰ وَهِيَ ظَٰلِمَةٌ إِنَّ أَخْذَهُۥ أَلِيمٌ شَدِيدٌ ۝

إِنَّ فِى ذَٰلِكَ لَآيَةً لِّمَنْ خَافَ عَذَابَ ٱلْأَخِرَةِ ذَٰلِكَ يَوْمٌ مَّجْمُوعٌ لَّهُ ٱلنَّاسُ وَذَٰلِكَ يَوْمٌ مَّشْهُودٌ ۝

وَمَا نُؤَخِّرُهُۥٓ إِلَّا لِأَجَلٍ مَّعْدُودٍ ۝

يَوْمَ يَأْتِ لَا تَكَلَّمُ نَفْسٌ إِلَّا بِإِذْنِهِۦ فَمِنْهُمْ شَقِىٌّ وَسَعِيدٌ ۝

فَأَمَّا ٱلَّذِينَ شَقُوا۟ فَفِى ٱلنَّارِ لَهُمْ فِيهَا زَفِيرٌ وَشَهِيقٌ ۝

خَٰلِدِينَ فِيهَا مَا دَامَتِ ٱلسَّمَٰوَٰتُ وَٱلْأَرْضُ إِلَّا مَا شَآءَ رَبُّكَ إِنَّ رَبَّكَ فَعَّالٌ لِّمَا يُرِيدُ ۝

۞ وَأَمَّا ٱلَّذِينَ سُعِدُوا۟ فَفِى ٱلْجَنَّةِ خَٰلِدِينَ فِيهَا مَا دَامَتِ ٱلسَّمَٰوَٰتُ وَٱلْأَرْضُ إِلَّا مَا شَآءَ رَبُّكَ عَطَآءً غَيْرَ مَجْذُوذٍ ۝

فَلَا تَكُ فِى مِرْيَةٍ مِّمَّا يَعْبُدُ هَٰٓؤُلَآءِ مَا يَعْبُدُونَ إِلَّا كَمَا يَعْبُدُ ءَابَآؤُهُم مِّن قَبْلُ وَإِنَّا لَمُوَفُّوهُمْ نَصِيبَهُمْ غَيْرَ مَنقُوصٍ ۝

وَلَقَدْ ءَاتَيْنَا مُوسَى ٱلْكِتَٰبَ فَٱخْتُلِفَ فِيهِ وَلَوْلَا كَلِمَةٌ سَبَقَتْ مِن رَّبِّكَ لَقُضِىَ بَيْنَهُمْ وَإِنَّهُمْ لَفِى شَكٍّ مِّنْهُ مُرِيبٍ ۝

---

497. Those gathered.
498. Their share of the punishment.

111. And your Lord will surely pay them all in full for their works. He is truly Aware of what they do.

وَإِنَّ كُلًّا لَّمَّا لَيُوَفِّيَنَّهُمْ رَبُّكَ أَعْمَالَهُمْ إِنَّهُ بِمَا يَعْمَلُونَ خَبِيرٌ ﴿١١١﴾

112. Be then upright as you have been commanded, together with those who repented with you, and do not be unjust; for He sees whatever you do.

فَاسْتَقِمْ كَمَا أُمِرْتَ وَمَن تَابَ مَعَكَ وَلَا تَطْغَوْا إِنَّهُ بِمَا تَعْمَلُونَ بَصِيرٌ ﴿١١٢﴾

113. And do not incline towards the wrongdoers, lest the Fire should touch you. You have no supporters apart from Allah, and you will not be helped.

وَلَا تَرْكَنُوا إِلَى الَّذِينَ ظَلَمُوا فَتَمَسَّكُمُ النَّارُ وَمَا لَكُم مِّن دُونِ اللَّهِ مِنْ أَوْلِيَاءَ ثُمَّ لَا تُنصَرُونَ ﴿١١٣﴾

114. And perform the prayer at the two ends of the day and [the first] watches of the night. Surely the good deeds will wipe out the evil deeds; that is a reminder for those who remember.

وَأَقِمِ الصَّلَاةَ طَرَفَيِ النَّهَارِ وَزُلَفًا مِّنَ اللَّيْلِ إِنَّ الْحَسَنَاتِ يُذْهِبْنَ السَّيِّئَاتِ ذَلِكَ ذِكْرَى لِلذَّاكِرِينَ ﴿١١٤﴾

115. And be patient; for Allah does not waste the reward of the righteous.

وَاصْبِرْ فَإِنَّ اللَّهَ لَا يُضِيعُ أَجْرَ الْمُحْسِنِينَ ﴿١١٥﴾

116. If only there had been among the generations who preceded you men possessing understanding and forbidding corruption in the earth, except for a few of them whom We saved! The wrongdoers continued to indulge in what they used to enjoy and, in fact, were wicked sinners.

فَلَوْلَا كَانَ مِنَ الْقُرُونِ مِن قَبْلِكُمْ أُولُوا بَقِيَّةٍ يَنْهَوْنَ عَنِ الْفَسَادِ فِي الْأَرْضِ إِلَّا قَلِيلًا مِّمَّنْ أَنجَيْنَا مِنْهُمْ وَاتَّبَعَ الَّذِينَ ظَلَمُوا مَا أُتْرِفُوا فِيهِ وَكَانُوا مُجْرِمِينَ ﴿١١٦﴾

117. And your Lord would not have destroyed the cities unjustly, had their inhabitants been righteous.

وَمَا كَانَ رَبُّكَ لِيُهْلِكَ الْقُرَى بِظُلْمٍ وَأَهْلُهَا مُصْلِحُونَ ﴿١١٧﴾

118. And had your Lord willed, He would have made mankind a single nation; but they will continue to differ among themselves,

وَلَوْ شَاءَ رَبُّكَ لَجَعَلَ النَّاسَ أُمَّةً وَاحِدَةً وَلَا يَزَالُونَ مُخْتَلِفِينَ ﴿١١٨﴾

119. Except for those on whom your Lord has mercy. To that end He created them, and the Word of your Lord has been accomplished: "I will surely fill up Hell with jinn and humans, all together."

إِلَّا مَن رَّحِمَ رَبُّكَ وَلِذَلِكَ خَلَقَهُمْ وَتَمَّتْ كَلِمَةُ رَبِّكَ لَأَمْلَأَنَّ جَهَنَّمَ مِنَ الْجِنَّةِ وَالنَّاسِ أَجْمَعِينَ ﴿١١٩﴾

120. And all We relate to you of the tidings of the Messengers is to strengthen your heart; and you have received in these the truth, admonition and a reminder for the believers.

وَكُلًّا نَّقُصُّ عَلَيْكَ مِنْ أَنۢبَآءِ ٱلرُّسُلِ مَا نُثَبِّتُ بِهِۦ فُؤَادَكَ ۚ وَجَآءَكَ فِى هَٰذِهِ ٱلْحَقُّ وَمَوْعِظَةٌ وَذِكْرَىٰ لِلْمُؤْمِنِينَ ﴿١٢٠﴾

121. And say to the unbelievers: "Continue with what you are doing, and we shall continue with ours.

وَقُل لِّلَّذِينَ لَا يُؤْمِنُونَ ٱعْمَلُوا۟ عَلَىٰ مَكَانَتِكُمْ إِنَّا عَٰمِلُونَ ﴿١٢١﴾

122. "And wait; we too are waiting."

وَٱنتَظِرُوٓا۟ إِنَّا مُنتَظِرُونَ ﴿١٢٢﴾

123. To Allah belongs the Unseen in the heavens and on earth, and to Him the whole affair shall be referred. So worship Him and put your trust in Him; your Lord is not unaware of the things you do.

وَلِلَّهِ غَيْبُ ٱلسَّمَٰوَٰتِ وَٱلْأَرْضِ وَإِلَيْهِ يُرْجَعُ ٱلْأَمْرُ كُلُّهُۥ فَٱعْبُدْهُ وَتَوَكَّلْ عَلَيْهِ ۚ وَمَا رَبُّكَ بِغَٰفِلٍ عَمَّا تَعْمَلُونَ ﴿١٢٣﴾

Sûrat Yûsuf, (The Prophet Joseph) 12

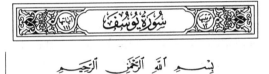

In the Name of Allah, the Compassionate, the Merciful

بِسْمِ ٱللَّهِ ٱلرَّحْمَٰنِ ٱلرَّحِيمِ

1. Alif - Lam - Ra.
These are the verses of the clear Book.

الٓر ۚ تِلْكَ ءَايَٰتُ ٱلْكِتَٰبِ ٱلْمُبِينِ ﴿١﴾

2. We have revealed it as an Arabic Qur'an, that perchance you may understand.

إِنَّآ أَنزَلْنَٰهُ قُرْءَٰنًا عَرَبِيًّا لَّعَلَّكُمْ تَعْقِلُونَ ﴿٢﴾

3. We narrate to you the fairest narratives in revealing to you this Qur'an, although you were, prior to it, one of the heedless.

نَحْنُ نَقُصُّ عَلَيْكَ أَحْسَنَ ٱلْقَصَصِ بِمَآ أَوْحَيْنَآ إِلَيْكَ هَٰذَا ٱلْقُرْءَانَ وَإِن كُنتَ مِن قَبْلِهِۦ لَمِنَ ٱلْغَٰفِلِينَ ﴿٣﴾

4. When Joseph said to his father: "O my father, I saw [in my dream] eleven planets and the sun and the moon, I saw them prostrating themselves before me."

إِذْ قَالَ يُوسُفُ لِأَبِيهِ يَٰٓأَبَتِ إِنِّى رَأَيْتُ أَحَدَ عَشَرَ كَوْكَبًا وَٱلشَّمْسَ وَٱلْقَمَرَ رَأَيْتُهُمْ لِى سَٰجِدِينَ ﴿٤﴾

5. He said: "My son, do not relate your dream to your brothers, lest they plot evil against you. Surely, the Devil is the sworn enemy of man."

قَالَ يَٰبُنَىَّ لَا تَقْصُصْ رُءْيَاكَ عَلَىٰٓ إِخْوَتِكَ فَيَكِيدُوا۟ لَكَ كَيْدًا ۖ إِنَّ ٱلشَّيْطَٰنَ لِلْإِنسَٰنِ عَدُوٌّ مُّبِينٌ ﴿٥﴾

6. And thus your Lord will choose you and teach you the interpretation of dreams[499] and

وَكَذَٰلِكَ يَجْتَبِيكَ رَبُّكَ وَيُعَلِّمُكَ مِن تَأْوِيلِ ٱلْأَحَادِيثِ

---

499. Dreams or, according to some commentators, events and signs.

will perfect His Grace upon you and upon the family of Jacob, as He has perfected it formerly upon your two fathers, Abraham and Isaac. Surely your Lord is All-Knowing, Wise.

7. There are indeed in Joseph and his brothers signs for the inquiring.

8. When they said: "Joseph and his brother are dearer to our father than the rest of us, although we are a large group. Our father is truly in manifest error."

9. "Kill Joseph or cast him away in some land that your father's love may be wholly yours, and you may become after him a righteous people."

10. One of them said: "Do not kill Joseph, but rather throw him in the bottom of the pit, so that some traveller may pick him up, if you must do anything."

11. They said: "Our father, why do you not trust us with Joseph? We certainly wish him well.

12. "Send him forth with us tomorrow that he may frolic and play, and we will surely take care of him."

13. He said: "It grieves me to let you take him away; and I fear that the wolf may devour him while you are not watching him."

14. They said: "If the wolf should devour him while we are a large group, we should then be the real losers."

15. But when they took him away and decided to cast him in the bottom of the pit, We revealed to him: "You should tell them about their intention while they are unaware."

16. And they came to their father in the evening weeping.

وَيُتِمُّ نِعْمَتَهُ عَلَيْكَ وَعَلَىٰٓ ءَالِ يَعْقُوبَ كَمَآ أَتَمَّهَا عَلَىٰٓ أَبَوَيْكَ مِن قَبْلُ إِبْرَٰهِيمَ وَإِسْحَٰقَ إِنَّ رَبَّكَ عَلِيمٌ حَكِيمٌ ۝

۞ لَّقَدْ كَانَ فِى يُوسُفَ وَإِخْوَتِهِۦٓ ءَايَٰتٌ لِّلسَّآئِلِينَ ۝

إِذْ قَالُوا۟ لَيُوسُفُ وَأَخُوهُ أَحَبُّ إِلَىٰٓ أَبِينَا مِنَّا وَنَحْنُ عُصْبَةٌ إِنَّ أَبَانَا لَفِى ضَلَٰلٍ مُّبِينٍ ۝

ٱقْتُلُوا۟ يُوسُفَ أَوِ ٱطْرَحُوهُ أَرْضًا يَخْلُ لَكُمْ وَجْهُ أَبِيكُمْ وَتَكُونُوا۟ مِنۢ بَعْدِهِۦ قَوْمًا صَٰلِحِينَ ۝

قَالَ قَآئِلٌ مِّنْهُمْ لَا تَقْتُلُوا۟ يُوسُفَ وَأَلْقُوهُ فِى غَيَٰبَتِ ٱلْجُبِّ يَلْتَقِطْهُ بَعْضُ ٱلسَّيَّارَةِ إِن كُنتُمْ فَٰعِلِينَ ۝

قَالُوا۟ يَٰٓأَبَانَا مَا لَكَ لَا تَأْمَنَّا عَلَىٰ يُوسُفَ وَإِنَّا لَهُۥ لَنَٰصِحُونَ ۝

أَرْسِلْهُ مَعَنَا غَدًا يَرْتَعْ وَيَلْعَبْ وَإِنَّا لَهُۥ لَحَٰفِظُونَ ۝

قَالَ إِنِّى لَيَحْزُنُنِىٓ أَن تَذْهَبُوا۟ بِهِۦ وَأَخَافُ أَن يَأْكُلَهُ ٱلذِّئْبُ وَأَنتُمْ عَنْهُ غَٰفِلُونَ ۝

قَالُوا۟ لَئِنْ أَكَلَهُ ٱلذِّئْبُ وَنَحْنُ عُصْبَةٌ إِنَّآ إِذًا لَّخَٰسِرُونَ ۝

فَلَمَّا ذَهَبُوا۟ بِهِۦ وَأَجْمَعُوٓا۟ أَن يَجْعَلُوهُ فِى غَيَٰبَتِ ٱلْجُبِّ وَأَوْحَيْنَآ إِلَيْهِ لَتُنَبِّئَنَّهُم بِأَمْرِهِمْ هَٰذَا وَهُمْ لَا يَشْعُرُونَ ۝

وَجَآءُوٓ أَبَاهُمْ عِشَآءً يَبْكُونَ ۝

232

17. They said: "Our father, we went away racing and left Joseph by our baggage; and so the wolf devoured him. You will not believe us, even if we are truthful."

قَالُوا۟ يَـٰٓأَبَانَآ إِنَّا ذَهَبْنَا نَسْتَبِقُ وَتَرَكْنَا يُوسُفَ عِندَ مَتَـٰعِنَا فَأَكَلَهُ ٱلذِّئْبُ وَمَآ أَنتَ بِمُؤْمِنٍ لَّنَا وَلَوْ كُنَّا صَـٰدِقِينَ ۝

18. And they stained his shirt with false blood. He said: "Rather, your souls tempted you to do something. So come gentle patience! To Allah I turn for help against what you say."

وَجَآءُو عَلَىٰ قَمِيصِهِۦ بِدَمٍ كَذِبٍ قَالَ بَلْ سَوَّلَتْ لَكُمْ أَنفُسُكُمْ أَمْرًا فَصَبْرٌ جَمِيلٌ وَٱللَّهُ ٱلْمُسْتَعَانُ عَلَىٰ مَا تَصِفُونَ ۝

19. And some travellers came, and they sent their water-drawer, who let down his bucket. He said: "Good news! Here is a boy." And they hid him as merchandise, Allah being Fully Aware of what they were doing.

وَجَآءَتْ سَيَّارَةٌ فَأَرْسَلُوا۟ وَارِدَهُمْ فَأَدْلَىٰ دَلْوَهُۥ قَالَ يَـٰبُشْرَىٰ هَـٰذَا غُلَـٰمٌ وَأَسَرُّوهُ بِضَـٰعَةً وَٱللَّهُ عَلِيمٌ بِمَا يَعْمَلُونَ ۝

20. And they sold him for a cheap price, a number of dirhams, since they were not interested in him.

وَشَرَوْهُ بِثَمَنٍۭ بَخْسٍ دَرَٰهِمَ مَعْدُودَةٍ وَكَانُوا۟ فِيهِ مِنَ ٱلزَّٰهِدِينَ ۝

21. And the Egyptian who bought him said to his wife: "Make his stay honourable; perhaps he will profit us or we may take him for a son." Thus We established Joseph in the land and taught him the interpretation of dreams. Allah has control over His Affairs though most people do not know.

وَقَالَ ٱلَّذِى ٱشْتَرَىٰهُ مِن مِّصْرَ لِٱمْرَأَتِهِۦٓ أَكْرِمِى مَثْوَىٰهُ عَسَىٰٓ أَن يَنفَعَنَآ أَوْ نَتَّخِذَهُۥ وَلَدًا وَكَذَٰلِكَ مَكَّنَّا لِيُوسُفَ فِى ٱلْأَرْضِ وَلِنُعَلِّمَهُۥ مِن تَأْوِيلِ ٱلْأَحَادِيثِ وَٱللَّهُ غَالِبٌ عَلَىٰٓ أَمْرِهِۦ وَلَـٰكِنَّ أَكْثَرَ ٱلنَّاسِ لَا يَعْلَمُونَ ۝

22. When he was fully grown, We gave him judgement and knowledge, and thus We reward the beneficent.

وَلَمَّا بَلَغَ أَشُدَّهُۥٓ ءَاتَيْنَـٰهُ حُكْمًا وَعِلْمًا وَكَذَٰلِكَ نَجْزِى ٱلْمُحْسِنِينَ ۝

23. And the woman, in whose house he was, sought to seduce him. She closed the doors firmly and said: "Come." He said: "Allah forbid. It is my Lord who gave me a good abode. Surely, the wrongdoers do not prosper."

وَرَٰوَدَتْهُ ٱلَّتِى هُوَ فِى بَيْتِهَا عَن نَّفْسِهِۦ وَغَلَّقَتِ ٱلْأَبْوَٰبَ وَقَالَتْ هَيْتَ لَكَ قَالَ مَعَاذَ ٱللَّهِ إِنَّهُۥ رَبِّىٓ أَحْسَنَ مَثْوَاىَ إِنَّهُۥ لَا يُفْلِحُ ٱلظَّـٰلِمُونَ ۝

24. Certainly she made for him and he would have made for her if it were not for a sign from his Lord. And that was to divert him from evil and indecency. He was indeed one of Our sincere servants.

وَلَقَدْ هَمَّتْ بِهِۦ وَهَمَّ بِهَا لَوْلَآ أَن رَّءَا بُرْهَـٰنَ رَبِّهِۦ كَذَٰلِكَ لِنَصْرِفَ عَنْهُ ٱلسُّوٓءَ وَٱلْفَحْشَآءَ إِنَّهُۥ مِنْ عِبَادِنَا ٱلْمُخْلَصِينَ ۝

وَٱسۡتَبَقَا ٱلۡبَابَ وَقَدَّتۡ قَمِيصَهُۥ مِن دُبُرٖ وَأَلۡفَيَا سَيِّدَهَا لَدَا ٱلۡبَابِ قَالَتۡ مَا جَزَآءُ مَنۡ أَرَادَ بِأَهۡلِكَ سُوٓءًا إِلَّآ أَن يُسۡجَنَ أَوۡ عَذَابٌ أَلِيمٞ ﴿٢٥﴾

25. They raced to the door, and she ripped his shirt from behind. When they met her husband at the door, she said: "What is the penalty of one who intended evil for your wife except imprisonment or severe punishment?"

قَالَ هِيَ رَٰوَدَتۡنِي عَن نَّفۡسِيۚ وَشَهِدَ شَاهِدٞ مِّنۡ أَهۡلِهَآ إِن كَانَ قَمِيصُهُۥ قُدَّ مِن قُبُلٖ فَصَدَقَتۡ وَهُوَ مِنَ ٱلۡكَٰذِبِينَ ﴿٢٦﴾

26. He[500] said: "She sought to seduce me." And a member of her household bore witness: "If his shirt was torn from the front, then she is telling the truth and he is a liar.

وَإِن كَانَ قَمِيصُهُۥ قُدَّ مِن دُبُرٖ فَكَذَبَتۡ وَهُوَ مِنَ ٱلصَّٰدِقِينَ ﴿٢٧﴾

27. "But if his shirt is torn from behind, then she lies and he is one of the truthful."

فَلَمَّا رَءَا قَمِيصَهُۥ قُدَّ مِن دُبُرٖ قَالَ إِنَّهُۥ مِن كَيۡدِكُنَّۖ إِنَّ كَيۡدَكُنَّ عَظِيمٞ ﴿٢٨﴾

28. When he[501] saw that his shirt was torn from behind, he said: "This is part of your guile, you women. Your guile is indeed very great.

يُوسُفُ أَعۡرِضۡ عَنۡ هَٰذَاۚ وَٱسۡتَغۡفِرِي لِذَنۢبِكِۖ إِنَّكِ كُنتِ مِنَ ٱلۡخَاطِئِينَ ﴿٢٩﴾

29. "Joseph, overlook this matter; and you, woman, ask forgiveness for your sin. You are indeed one of the sinners."

۞ وَقَالَ نِسۡوَةٞ فِي ٱلۡمَدِينَةِ ٱمۡرَأَتُ ٱلۡعَزِيزِ تُرَٰوِدُ فَتَىٰهَا عَن نَّفۡسِهِۦۖ قَدۡ شَغَفَهَا حُبًّاۖ إِنَّا لَنَرَىٰهَا فِي ضَلَٰلٖ مُّبِينٖ ﴿٣٠﴾

30. And some women in the city said: "The wife of the governor has been seeking to seduce her slave; he has infatuated her with his love. We see her in manifest error."

فَلَمَّا سَمِعَتۡ بِمَكۡرِهِنَّ أَرۡسَلَتۡ إِلَيۡهِنَّ وَأَعۡتَدَتۡ لَهُنَّ مُتَّكَـٔٗا وَءَاتَتۡ كُلَّ وَٰحِدَةٖ مِّنۡهُنَّ سِكِّينٗا وَقَالَتِ ٱخۡرُجۡ عَلَيۡهِنَّۖ فَلَمَّا رَأَيۡنَهُۥٓ أَكۡبَرۡنَهُۥ وَقَطَّعۡنَ أَيۡدِيَهُنَّ وَقُلۡنَ حَٰشَ لِلَّهِ مَا هَٰذَا بَشَرًا إِنۡ هَٰذَآ إِلَّا مَلَكٞ كَرِيمٞ ﴿٣١﴾

31. When she heard about their wiles, she sent after them and prepared for each of them a dining couch. Then she gave each one of them a knife and said to him:[502] "Come out unto them." But when they saw him, they admired him and cut their hands and said: "Allah forbid! This is no mortal, he is but a noble angel."

قَالَتۡ فَذَٰلِكُنَّ ٱلَّذِي لُمۡتُنَّنِي فِيهِۖ وَلَقَدۡ رَٰوَدتُّهُۥ عَن نَّفۡسِهِۦ فَٱسۡتَعۡصَمَۖ وَلَئِن لَّمۡ يَفۡعَلۡ مَآ ءَامُرُهُۥ لَيُسۡجَنَنَّ وَلَيَكُونٗا مِّنَ ٱلصَّٰغِرِينَ ﴿٣٢﴾

32. She said: "This is the one you reproached me for. I have in fact sought to seduce him, but he held back. If he will not do what I command him, he will surely be imprisoned and will be one of the humbled."

---

500. Joseph.
501. The husband.
502. That is, Joseph.

33. He said: "My Lord, prison is dearer to me than that which they call me to. If you do not rid me of their guile, I will be inclined towards them and will be one of the ignorant."

قَالَ رَبِّ ٱلسِّجْنُ أَحَبُّ إِلَىَّ مِمَّا يَدْعُونَنِىٓ إِلَيْهِ وَإِلَّا تَصْرِفْ عَنِّى كَيْدَهُنَّ أَصْبُ إِلَيْهِنَّ وَأَكُن مِّنَ ٱلْجَٰهِلِينَ ﴿٣٣﴾

34. Thereupon his Lord answered his prayer and so rid him of their guile. He is indeed the Hearer, the Knower.

فَٱسْتَجَابَ لَهُۥ رَبُّهُۥ فَصَرَفَ عَنْهُ كَيْدَهُنَّ إِنَّهُۥ هُوَ ٱلسَّمِيعُ ٱلْعَلِيمُ ﴿٣٤﴾

35. Then it occurred to them after they had seen the signs[503] to imprison him for some time.

ثُمَّ بَدَا لَهُم مِّنۢ بَعْدِ مَا رَأَوُا۟ ٱلْءَايَٰتِ لَيَسْجُنُنَّهُۥ حَتَّىٰ حِينٍ ﴿٣٥﴾

36. And there entered the prison with him two youths. One of them said: "I saw in my dream that I am pressing grapes." And the other said: "I saw in my dream that I am carrying on my head bread from which the birds were eating. Tell us their interpretation; we see that you are one of the righteous."

وَدَخَلَ مَعَهُ ٱلسِّجْنَ فَتَيَانِ قَالَ أَحَدُهُمَآ إِنِّىٓ أَرَىٰنِىٓ أَعْصِرُ خَمْرًا وَقَالَ ٱلْءَاخَرُ إِنِّىٓ أَرَىٰنِىٓ أَحْمِلُ فَوْقَ رَأْسِى خُبْزًا تَأْكُلُ ٱلطَّيْرُ مِنْهُ نَبِّئْنَا بِتَأْوِيلِهِۦٓ إِنَّا نَرَىٰكَ مِنَ ٱلْمُحْسِنِينَ ﴿٣٦﴾

37. He said: "No food with which you are provided will be given to you but I will tell you its interpretation before it arrives. This is part of what my Lord has taught me. I have forsaken the religion of a people who do not believe in Allah, and disbelieve in the Hereafter.

قَالَ لَا يَأْتِيكُمَا طَعَامٌ تُرْزَقَانِهِۦٓ إِلَّا نَبَّأْتُكُمَا بِتَأْوِيلِهِۦ قَبْلَ أَن يَأْتِيَكُمَا ذَٰلِكُمَا مِمَّا عَلَّمَنِى رَبِّىٓ إِنِّى تَرَكْتُ مِلَّةَ قَوْمٍ لَّا يُؤْمِنُونَ بِٱللَّهِ وَهُم بِٱلْءَاخِرَةِ هُمْ كَٰفِرُونَ ﴿٣٧﴾

38. "And I have followed the religion of my fathers, Abraham, Isaac and Jacob. It was not for us to associate anything with Allah. That is part of Allah's Favour upon us and upon mankind; but most men do not give thanks.

وَٱتَّبَعْتُ مِلَّةَ ءَابَآءِى إِبْرَٰهِيمَ وَإِسْحَٰقَ وَيَعْقُوبَ مَا كَانَ لَنَآ أَن نُّشْرِكَ بِٱللَّهِ مِن شَىْءٍ ذَٰلِكَ مِن فَضْلِ ٱللَّهِ عَلَيْنَا وَعَلَى ٱلنَّاسِ وَلَٰكِنَّ أَكْثَرَ ٱلنَّاسِ لَا يَشْكُرُونَ ﴿٣٨﴾

39. "O my two fellow-prisoners, are diverse lords better, or the One, the Omnipotent?

يَٰصَٰحِبَىِ ٱلسِّجْنِ ءَأَرْبَابٌ مُّتَفَرِّقُونَ خَيْرٌ أَمِ ٱللَّهُ ٱلْوَٰحِدُ ٱلْقَهَّارُ ﴿٣٩﴾

40. "You do not worship, besides Him, except names you have named, you and your fathers, for which Allah has not sent down any authority. Judgement belongs only

مَا تَعْبُدُونَ مِن دُونِهِۦٓ إِلَّآ أَسْمَآءً سَمَّيْتُمُوهَآ أَنتُمْ وَءَابَآؤُكُم مَّآ أَنزَلَ ٱللَّهُ بِهَا مِن سُلْطَٰنٍ إِنِ ٱلْحُكْمُ

---

503. Signs of Joseph's innocence.

to Allah; He has commanded that you worship none but Him. That is the right religion, but most men do not know.

41. "O my two fellow-prisoners, one of you shall give his Lord wine to drink; whereas the other will be crucified, then the birds shall eat from his head. Thus the matter you are inquiring about is settled."

42. And he said to the one of the two whom he thought would be saved: "Mention me to your Lord." However, the Devil caused him to forget to mention him to his Lord and so he[504] remained in prison a number of years.

43. And the King[505] said: "I saw in my dream seven fat cows devoured by seven lean cows, and seven green ears of corn together with seven other withered ones. O my dignitaries, explain to me my dream, if you are able to interpret dreams."

44. They said: "Confused dreams, and we know nothing about the interpretation of dreams."

45. And the one of the two[506] who had been released remembered after a while and said: "I will tell you its interpretation, so let me go."

46. "Joseph, O truthful one, enlighten us concerning seven fat cows devoured by seven lean ones, and concerning seven green ears of corn and seven withered ones, so that I might go back to the people, that perchance they might learn."

47. He said: "You shall sow for seven consecutive years, but what you harvest, you should leave in its ears, except for the little whereof you need to eat.

---

504. Joseph.
505. The King of Egypt.
506. Fellow-prisoners.

48. "Then, afterwards seven hard years will consume what you laid up for them, except for a little of what you have stored.

49. "Then there will come after that a year in which the people will receive help and will be able to press grapes in it."

50. The King said: "Bring him[507] to me." Then when the messenger came to him, he said: "Go back to your lord and ask him about the women who cut their own hands. My Lord knows well their guile."

51. He[508] said: "What was the matter with you, women, when you sought to seduce Joseph?" They said: "Allah forbid! We learnt nothing evil about him." The governor's wife then said: "Now the truth has come out, I was the one who sought to seduce him, and he is indeed one of the truthful."

52. [Joseph said]: "That was said so that [my Lord] may know that I did not betray him in secret, and that Allah will not guide the guile of the treacherous.

53. "I do not exonerate myself from sin. Surely the [human] soul commands evil, except for those on whom my Lord has Mercy. My Lord is truly All-Forgiving, Merciful.

54. The King said: "Bring him to me; I will attach him to my person alone." And when he spoke to him, he said: "Today you are firmly established and secure with us."

55. He[509] said: "Put me in charge of the treasures of the land; I am a keeper who knows."

---

507. Joseph.
508. The King.
509. Joseph.

56. And thus We established Joseph firmly in the land, dwelling wherever he wished. We bestow Our Mercy on whom We will, and We do not waste the reward of the righteous.

57. And the reward of the Hereafter is surely better for those who believe and fear Allah.

58. Then Joseph's brothers came and went in to him. He recognized them while they did not know him.

59. When he provided them with their supplies, he said: "Bring me a brother of yours from your father. Do you not see that I fill up the measure and am the best of hosts?

60. "But, if you do not bring him to me, you shall have no measure from me and you will not come near me."

61. They said: "We will solicit him from his father. Surely we shall do that."

62. He said to his servants: "Put their merchandise in their saddlebags, that perchance they may recognize it when they return to their people, and perchance they will come back."

63. When they returned to their father, they said: "Our father, we have been denied the full measure; so send forth our brother with us that we may receive the measure; we will surely guard him."

64. He said: "Can I entrust him to you except as I had entrusted his brother to you before? Allah is the Best Guardian, and He is the Most Merciful of those who show mercy."

65. And when they opened their bags, they found that their merchandise was returned to them. They said: "Father, what more do we desire? This is our merchandise; it has been returned to us. We shall get food for our family, guard our brother and receive an added camel's load. That is an easy measure."

وَكَذَلِكَ مَكَّنَّا لِيُوسُفَ فِى ٱلْأَرْضِ يَتَبَوَّأُ مِنْهَا حَيْثُ يَشَآءُ نُصِيبُ بِرَحْمَتِنَا مَن نَّشَآءُ وَلَا نُضِيعُ أَجْرَ ٱلْمُحْسِنِينَ ۝

وَلَأَجْرُ ٱلْآخِرَةِ خَيْرٌ لِّلَّذِينَ ءَامَنُوا۟ وَكَانُوا۟ يَتَّقُونَ ۝

وَجَآءَ إِخْوَةُ يُوسُفَ فَدَخَلُوا۟ عَلَيْهِ فَعَرَفَهُمْ وَهُمْ لَهُۥ مُنكِرُونَ ۝

وَلَمَّا جَهَّزَهُم بِجَهَازِهِمْ قَالَ ٱئْتُونِى بِأَخٍ لَّكُم مِّنْ أَبِيكُمْ أَلَا تَرَوْنَ أَنِّى أُوفِى ٱلْكَيْلَ وَأَنَا۠ خَيْرُ ٱلْمُنزِلِينَ ۝

فَإِن لَّمْ تَأْتُونِى بِهِۦ فَلَا كَيْلَ لَكُمْ عِندِى وَلَا تَقْرَبُونِ ۝

قَالُوا۟ سَنُرَٰوِدُ عَنْهُ أَبَاهُ وَإِنَّا لَفَاعِلُونَ ۝

وَقَالَ لِفِتْيَٰنِهِ ٱجْعَلُوا۟ بِضَٰعَتَهُمْ فِى رِحَالِهِمْ لَعَلَّهُمْ يَعْرِفُونَهَآ إِذَا ٱنقَلَبُوٓا۟ إِلَىٰٓ أَهْلِهِمْ لَعَلَّهُمْ يَرْجِعُونَ ۝

فَلَمَّا رَجَعُوٓا۟ إِلَىٰٓ أَبِيهِمْ قَالُوا۟ يَٰٓأَبَانَا مُنِعَ مِنَّا ٱلْكَيْلُ فَأَرْسِلْ مَعَنَآ أَخَانَا نَكْتَلْ وَإِنَّا لَهُۥ لَحَٰفِظُونَ ۝

قَالَ هَلْ ءَامَنُكُمْ عَلَيْهِ إِلَّا كَمَآ أَمِنتُكُمْ عَلَىٰٓ أَخِيهِ مِن قَبْلُ فَٱللَّهُ خَيْرٌ حَٰفِظًا وَهُوَ أَرْحَمُ ٱلرَّٰحِمِينَ ۝

وَلَمَّا فَتَحُوا۟ مَتَٰعَهُمْ وَجَدُوا۟ بِضَٰعَتَهُمْ رُدَّتْ إِلَيْهِمْ قَالُوا۟ يَٰٓأَبَانَا مَا نَبْغِى هَٰذِهِۦ بِضَٰعَتُنَا رُدَّتْ إِلَيْنَا وَنَمِيرُ أَهْلَنَا وَنَحْفَظُ أَخَانَا وَنَزْدَادُ كَيْلَ بَعِيرٍ ذَٰلِكَ كَيْلٌ يَسِيرٌ ۝

66. He said: "I will not send him with you until you swear in Allah's Name that you will bring him back to me, unless you are constrained." So when they brought him their pledge he said: "Allah is Witness of what we say."

قَالَ لَنْ أُرْسِلَهُ مَعَكُمْ حَتَّىٰ تُؤْتُونِ مَوْثِقًا مِّنَ اللَّهِ لَتَأْتُنَّنِي بِهِ إِلَّا أَن يُحَاطَ بِكُمْ فَلَمَّا آتَوْهُ مَوْثِقَهُمْ قَالَ اللَّهُ عَلَىٰ مَا نَقُولُ وَكِيلٌ ﴿٦٦﴾

67. And he said: "My sons, do not enter by one door, but enter by separate doors. I cannot avail you anything against Allah; the judgement is truly Allah's; in Him I put my trust, and in Him let all who trust put their trust."

وَقَالَ يَٰبَنِيَّ لَا تَدْخُلُوا مِنۢ بَابٍ وَٰحِدٍ وَٱدْخُلُوا مِنْ أَبْوَٰبٍ مُّتَفَرِّقَةٍ وَمَا أُغْنِي عَنكُم مِّنَ اللَّهِ مِن شَيْءٍ إِنِ ٱلْحُكْمُ إِلَّا لِلَّهِ عَلَيْهِ تَوَكَّلْتُ وَعَلَيْهِ فَلْيَتَوَكَّلِ ٱلْمُتَوَكِّلُونَ ﴿٦٧﴾

68. And when they entered wherefrom their father commanded them, nothing could avail them against Allah. It was only a desire in Jacob's breast which he satisfied. He was indeed in possession of knowledge, because We taught him. But most people do not know.

وَلَمَّا دَخَلُوا مِنْ حَيْثُ أَمَرَهُمْ أَبُوهُم مَّا كَانَ يُغْنِي عَنْهُم مِّنَ اللَّهِ مِن شَيْءٍ إِلَّا حَاجَةً فِي نَفْسِ يَعْقُوبَ قَضَىٰهَا وَإِنَّهُ لَذُو عِلْمٍ لِّمَا عَلَّمْنَٰهُ وَلَٰكِنَّ أَكْثَرَ ٱلنَّاسِ لَا يَعْلَمُونَ ﴿٦٨﴾

69. And when they came into Joseph's presence, he took his brother into his arms saying: "I am your own brother; so do not grieve at what they were doing."

وَلَمَّا دَخَلُوا عَلَىٰ يُوسُفَ آوَىٰ إِلَيْهِ أَخَاهُ قَالَ إِنِّي أَنَا أَخُوكَ فَلَا تَبْتَئِسْ بِمَا كَانُوا يَعْمَلُونَ ﴿٦٩﴾

70. Then, when he provided them with their supplies, he put the drinking-vessel in his brother's bag. Then a crier shouted: "O men of the caravan, you are thieves."

فَلَمَّا جَهَّزَهُم بِجَهَازِهِمْ جَعَلَ ٱلسِّقَايَةَ فِي رَحْلِ أَخِيهِ ثُمَّ أَذَّنَ مُؤَذِّنٌ أَيَّتُهَا ٱلْعِيرُ إِنَّكُمْ لَسَٰرِقُونَ ﴿٧٠﴾

71. They said, as they approached them: "What is it that you miss?"

قَالُوا وَأَقْبَلُوا عَلَيْهِم مَّاذَا تَفْقِدُونَ ﴿٧١﴾

72. They said: "We miss the King's drinking-cup; and to him who brings it a camel's load will be given, and I am the guarantor thereof."

قَالُوا نَفْقِدُ صُوَاعَ ٱلْمَلِكِ وَلِمَن جَآءَ بِهِ حِمْلُ بَعِيرٍ وَأَنَا بِهِ زَعِيمٌ ﴿٧٢﴾

73. They said: "By Allah, you know well that we have not come to spread corruption in the land, and we are no thieves."

قَالُوا تَٱللَّهِ لَقَدْ عَلِمْتُم مَّا جِئْنَا لِنُفْسِدَ فِي ٱلْأَرْضِ وَمَا كُنَّا سَٰرِقِينَ ﴿٧٣﴾

74. They said: "What is the penalty thereof, if you are liars?"

قَالُوا فَمَا جَزَٰٓؤُهُۥ إِن كُنتُمْ كَٰذِبِينَ ﴿٧٤﴾

75. They said: "The penalty thereof is that whoever it is found in his bag shall himself be the penalty.[510] This is how we punish the wrongdoers."

76. And so he[511] began with their bags before the bag of his brother. Then he took it out from his brother's bag. This is how We contrived for Joseph's sake; for he could not take his brother in accordance with the King's law, except if Allah pleased. We raise by degrees whom We will, and above every man of learning, there is one more learned.

77. They said: "If he has stolen, a brother of his has stolen before." Joseph kept that to himself and did not reveal it to them. He said: "You are in a worse position, and Allah knows best [the truth of] what you say."

78. They said: "O mighty one, he has a very old father; so take one of us in his place. We see that you are one of those who are beneficent."

79. He said: "Allah forbid that we take any one other than the one with whom we found our property. For then we will be wrong-doers."

80. Then when they despaired of him, they conferred privately. Their eldest said: "Did you not know that your father took a solemn pledge in the Name of Allah from you, and before that you failed to perform your duty in the case of Joseph. I will not leave this land until my father permits me or Allah decides for me; for He is the Best of judges."

---

510. That is, he shall be enslaved.
511. Joseph.

81. "Go back to your father and say: 'Our father, your son has stolen. We bear witness only to what we know, and we could not keep watch over the Unseen.'

82. "'Ask the town where we were and the caravan which we came along with. Surely we are truthful.'"

83. He[512] said: "Rather, your souls made some matter look fair to you. Come gentle patience! Maybe Allah will bring them all back to me. He is indeed the All-Knowing, the Wise."

84. And he turned away from them and said: "Alas for Joseph!" and his eyes turned white, because of the grief which he repressed.

85. They said: "By Allah, you shall continue to remember Joseph until you are about to perish or even when you do perish."

86. He said: "I only complain of my sorrow and grief to Allah and I know, from Allah, what you know not.

87. "O my sons, go forth and inquire about Joseph and his brother and do not despair of Allah's Mercy. Surely no one despairs of Allah's Mercy, except the unbelieving people."

88. When they went to him, they said: "O mighty one, we and our people have been visited by affliction and we have brought scant merchandise. So fill up the measure for us and be charitable to us; Allah will surely reward the charitable."

89. He said: "Do you know what you did with Joseph and his brother, in your dire ignorance?"

أَرْجِعُوٓاْ إِلَىٰٓ أَبِيكُمْ فَقُولُواْ يَٰٓأَبَانَآ إِنَّ ٱبْنَكَ سَرَقَ وَمَا شَهِدْنَآ إِلَّا بِمَا عَلِمْنَا وَمَا كُنَّا لِلْغَيْبِ حَٰفِظِينَ ۝

وَسْـَٔلِ ٱلْقَرْيَةَ ٱلَّتِى كُنَّا فِيهَا وَٱلْعِيرَ ٱلَّتِىٓ أَقْبَلْنَا فِيهَا وَإِنَّا لَصَٰدِقُونَ ۝

قَالَ بَلْ سَوَّلَتْ لَكُمْ أَنفُسُكُمْ أَمْرًا فَصَبْرٌ جَمِيلٌ عَسَى ٱللَّهُ أَن يَأْتِيَنِى بِهِمْ جَمِيعًا إِنَّهُۥ هُوَ ٱلْعَلِيمُ ٱلْحَكِيمُ ۝

وَتَوَلَّىٰ عَنْهُمْ وَقَالَ يَٰٓأَسَفَىٰ عَلَىٰ يُوسُفَ وَٱبْيَضَّتْ عَيْنَاهُ مِنَ ٱلْحُزْنِ فَهُوَ كَظِيمٌ ۝

قَالُواْ تَٱللَّهِ تَفْتَؤُاْ تَذْكُرُ يُوسُفَ حَتَّىٰ تَكُونَ حَرَضًا أَوْ تَكُونَ مِنَ ٱلْهَٰلِكِينَ ۝

قَالَ إِنَّمَآ أَشْكُواْ بَثِّى وَحُزْنِىٓ إِلَى ٱللَّهِ وَأَعْلَمُ مِنَ ٱللَّهِ مَا لَا تَعْلَمُونَ ۝

يَٰبَنِىَّ ٱذْهَبُواْ فَتَحَسَّسُواْ مِن يُوسُفَ وَأَخِيهِ وَلَا تَا۟يْـَٔسُواْ مِن رَّوْحِ ٱللَّهِ إِنَّهُۥ لَا يَا۟يْـَٔسُ مِن رَّوْحِ ٱللَّهِ إِلَّا ٱلْقَوْمُ ٱلْكَٰفِرُونَ ۝

فَلَمَّا دَخَلُواْ عَلَيْهِ قَالُواْ يَٰٓأَيُّهَا ٱلْعَزِيزُ مَسَّنَا وَأَهْلَنَا ٱلضُّرُّ وَجِئْنَا بِبِضَٰعَةٍ مُّزْجَىٰةٍ فَأَوْفِ لَنَا ٱلْكَيْلَ وَتَصَدَّقْ عَلَيْنَآ إِنَّ ٱللَّهَ يَجْزِى ٱلْمُتَصَدِّقِينَ ۝

قَالَ هَلْ عَلِمْتُم مَّا فَعَلْتُم بِيُوسُفَ وَأَخِيهِ إِذْ أَنتُمْ جَٰهِلُونَ ۝

---

512. Jacob.

90. They said: "Are you truly Joseph?" He said: "Yes, I am Joseph and this is my brother. Allah has been gracious to us. Surely, whoever fears God and forbears will find that Allah will never deprive those who do the good of their reward."

91. They said: "By Allah, Allah has exalted you above us, and we have only been sinful."

92. He said: "Let there be no reproach against you today. Allah will forgive you and He is the Most Merciful of those who have mercy.

93. "Take this shirt of mine and lay it on my father's face, and he will regain his sight; then come to me with all your family."

94. And when the caravan set out, their father said: "I find Joseph's scent, though you may deny it."

95. They said: "By Allah, you persist in your old error."

96. Then when the bearer of good news came, he placed it[513] on his face and so he regained his sight. He said: "Did I not tell you that I know from Allah what you know not?"

97. They said: "Father, ask forgiveness for our sins; we have indeed been sinful."

98. He said: "I shall ask my Lord to forgive you. He is indeed the All-Forgiving, the Merciful."

99. Then, when they went in to Joseph, he lodged his parents with him and said: "Enter Egypt, Allah willing, in security."

100. And he raised both his parents to the high seat, and they fell prostrate before him. He said: "Father, this is the interpretation of my old dream; my Lord has made it come

قَالُوٓاْ أَءِنَّكَ لَأَنتَ يُوسُفُ قَالَ أَنَا۠ يُوسُفُ وَهَٰذَآ أَخِى قَدۡ مَنَّ ٱللَّهُ عَلَيۡنَآ إِنَّهُۥ مَن يَتَّقِ وَيَصۡبِرۡ فَإِنَّ ٱللَّهَ لَا يُضِيعُ أَجۡرَ ٱلۡمُحۡسِنِينَ ﴿٩٠﴾

قَالُواْ تَٱللَّهِ لَقَدۡ ءَاثَرَكَ ٱللَّهُ عَلَيۡنَا وَإِن كُنَّا لَخَٰطِـِٔينَ ﴿٩١﴾

قَالَ لَا تَثۡرِيبَ عَلَيۡكُمُ ٱلۡيَوۡمَ يَغۡفِرُ ٱللَّهُ لَكُمۡ وَهُوَ أَرۡحَمُ ٱلرَّٰحِمِينَ ﴿٩٢﴾

ٱذۡهَبُواْ بِقَمِيصِى هَٰذَا فَأَلۡقُوهُ عَلَىٰ وَجۡهِ أَبِى يَأۡتِ بَصِيرٗا وَأۡتُونِى بِأَهۡلِكُمۡ أَجۡمَعِينَ ﴿٩٣﴾

وَلَمَّا فَصَلَتِ ٱلۡعِيرُ قَالَ أَبُوهُمۡ إِنِّى لَأَجِدُ رِيحَ يُوسُفَ لَوۡلَآ أَن تُفَنِّدُونِ ﴿٩٤﴾

قَالُواْ تَٱللَّهِ إِنَّكَ لَفِى ضَلَٰلِكَ ٱلۡقَدِيمِ ﴿٩٥﴾

فَلَمَّآ أَن جَآءَ ٱلۡبَشِيرُ أَلۡقَىٰهُ عَلَىٰ وَجۡهِهِۦ فَٱرۡتَدَّ بَصِيرٗا قَالَ أَلَمۡ أَقُل لَّكُمۡ إِنِّىٓ أَعۡلَمُ مِنَ ٱللَّهِ مَا لَا تَعۡلَمُونَ ﴿٩٦﴾

قَالُواْ يَٰٓأَبَانَا ٱسۡتَغۡفِرۡ لَنَا ذُنُوبَنَآ إِنَّا كُنَّا خَٰطِـِٔينَ ﴿٩٧﴾

قَالَ سَوۡفَ أَسۡتَغۡفِرُ لَكُمۡ رَبِّىٓ إِنَّهُۥ هُوَ ٱلۡغَفُورُ ٱلرَّحِيمُ ﴿٩٨﴾

فَلَمَّا دَخَلُواْ عَلَىٰ يُوسُفَ ءَاوَىٰٓ إِلَيۡهِ أَبَوَيۡهِ وَقَالَ ٱدۡخُلُواْ مِصۡرَ إِن شَآءَ ٱللَّهُ ءَامِنِينَ ﴿٩٩﴾

وَرَفَعَ أَبَوَيۡهِ عَلَى ٱلۡعَرۡشِ وَخَرُّواْ لَهُۥ سُجَّدٗا وَقَالَ يَٰٓأَبَتِ هَٰذَا تَأۡوِيلُ رُءۡيَٰىَ مِن قَبۡلُ قَدۡ جَعَلَهَا رَبِّى حَقّٗا وَقَدۡ أَحۡسَنَ بِىٓ إِذۡ أَخۡرَجَنِى مِنَ ٱلسِّجۡنِ وَجَآءَ بِكُم مِّنَ

---

513. The shirt.

242

true. He was kind to me when He brought me out of prison and brought you out of the desert, after the Devil had sown mischief between me and my brothers. My Lord is truly Subtle in bringing about what He wills. He is indeed the All-Knowing, the Wise.

ٱلْبَدْوِ مِنۢ بَعْدِ أَن نَّزَغَ ٱلشَّيْطَٰنُ بَيْنِى وَبَيْنَ إِخْوَتِىٓ ۚ إِنَّ رَبِّى لَطِيفٌ لِّمَا يَشَآءُ ۚ إِنَّهُۥ هُوَ ٱلْعَلِيمُ ٱلْحَكِيمُ ۝

101. "Lord, you have given me power and taught me the interpretation of dreams. O Creator of the heavens and the earth; you are my Protector in this world and in the Hereafter; receive my soul as a submissive one, and let me join the ranks of the righteous."

۞ رَبِّ قَدْ ءَاتَيْتَنِى مِنَ ٱلْمُلْكِ وَعَلَّمْتَنِى مِن تَأْوِيلِ ٱلْأَحَادِيثِ ۚ فَاطِرَ ٱلسَّمَٰوَٰتِ وَٱلْأَرْضِ أَنتَ وَلِىِّۦ فِى ٱلدُّنْيَا وَٱلْءَاخِرَةِ ۖ تَوَفَّنِى مُسْلِمًا وَأَلْحِقْنِى بِٱلصَّٰلِحِينَ ۝

102. That is part of the news of the Unseen [which] We reveal to you; for you were not with them when they concurred in their affair, while they plotted.

ذَٰلِكَ مِنْ أَنۢبَآءِ ٱلْغَيْبِ نُوحِيهِ إِلَيْكَ ۖ وَمَا كُنتَ لَدَيْهِمْ إِذْ أَجْمَعُوٓا۟ أَمْرَهُمْ وَهُمْ يَمْكُرُونَ ۝

103. And even if you desire it, most people[514] are not believers.

وَمَآ أَكْثَرُ ٱلنَّاسِ وَلَوْ حَرَصْتَ بِمُؤْمِنِينَ ۝

104. And you do not ask them for a reward for it;[515] it is nothing but a reminder for all mankind.

وَمَا تَسْـَٔلُهُمْ عَلَيْهِ مِنْ أَجْرٍ ۚ إِنْ هُوَ إِلَّا ذِكْرٌ لِّلْعَٰلَمِينَ ۝

105. How many a sign in the heavens and on earth by which they pass while they turn their faces away from it!

وَكَأَيِّن مِّنْ ءَايَةٍ فِى ٱلسَّمَٰوَٰتِ وَٱلْأَرْضِ يَمُرُّونَ عَلَيْهَا وَهُمْ عَنْهَا مُعْرِضُونَ ۝

106. And most of them do not believe in Allah, unless they continue to associate others [with Him].

وَمَا يُؤْمِنُ أَكْثَرُهُم بِٱللَّهِ إِلَّا وَهُم مُّشْرِكُونَ ۝

107. Do they guard against a crushing strike of Allah's Punishment or the sudden coming of the Hour while they are unaware?

أَفَأَمِنُوٓا۟ أَن تَأْتِيَهُمْ غَٰشِيَةٌ مِّنْ عَذَابِ ٱللَّهِ أَوْ تَأْتِيَهُمُ ٱلسَّاعَةُ بَغْتَةً وَهُمْ لَا يَشْعُرُونَ ۝

108. Say: "This is my way; I call to Allah with knowledge, I and those who follow me. Glory be to Allah; and I am not one of the polytheists."

قُلْ هَٰذِهِۦ سَبِيلِىٓ أَدْعُوٓا۟ إِلَى ٱللَّهِ ۚ عَلَىٰ بَصِيرَةٍ أَنَا۠ وَمَنِ ٱتَّبَعَنِى ۖ وَسُبْحَٰنَ ٱللَّهِ وَمَآ أَنَا۠ مِنَ ٱلْمُشْرِكِينَ ۝

---

514. The Meccans.
515. The Qur'an.

109. We did not send forth [as Messengers] before you except men from the people of the cities who received Our Revelations. Have they[516] not travelled in the land and seen what was the end of those who came before them? The abode of the Hereafter is surely better for those who fear God. Do you not understand?

110. And when the Messengers despaired and thought they would be regarded as liars, Our help came to them and We delivered whom We pleased. The sinners could not escape Our punishment.

111. In these narratives about them, there is a lesson for people of understanding. It is not an invented tale, but a confirmation of what came before it, and a clear exposition of all things, and a guidance and mercy for people who believe.

Sûrat Ar-Ra'd, (Thunder) 13

In the Name of Allah, the Compassionate, the Merciful

1. Alif - Lam - Mim - Ra.

Those are the verses of the Book; and that which has been revealed to you by your Lord is the truth, but most people do not believe.

2. Allah is He Who raised the heavens without pillars that you can see; there He sat upright on the Throne and made the sun and the moon subservient, each running for an appointed term. He manages the [whole] affair and makes clear the Revelations so that you may be certain of meeting your Lord.

---

516. The Meccans.

244

3. And it is He Who spread out the earth and placed therein firm mountains and rivers; and of each kind of fruit He created two pairs.[517] He causes the night to cover the day. Surely in that are signs for people who reflect.

وَهُوَ ٱلَّذِى مَدَّ ٱلْأَرْضَ وَجَعَلَ فِيهَا رَوَٰسِىَ وَأَنْهَٰرًا وَمِن كُلِّ ٱلثَّمَرَٰتِ جَعَلَ فِيهَا زَوْجَيْنِ ٱثْنَيْنِ يُغْشِى ٱلَّيْلَ ٱلنَّهَارَ إِنَّ فِى ذَٰلِكَ لَءَايَٰتٍ لِّقَوْمٍ يَتَفَكَّرُونَ ۝

4. And in the earth are plots adjoining each other and gardens of vines, tillage and palm-trees, from one or different roots, which are irrigated by the same water; yet, We prefer some of them over the others in produce. Surely in that are signs for a people who understand.

وَفِى ٱلْأَرْضِ قِطَعٌ مُّتَجَٰوِرَٰتٌ وَجَنَّٰتٌ مِّنْ أَعْنَٰبٍ وَزَرْعٌ وَنَخِيلٌ صِنْوَانٌ وَغَيْرُ صِنْوَانٍ يُسْقَىٰ بِمَآءٍ وَٰحِدٍ وَنُفَضِّلُ بَعْضَهَا عَلَىٰ بَعْضٍ فِى ٱلْأُكُلِ إِنَّ فِى ذَٰلِكَ لَءَايَٰتٍ لِّقَوْمٍ يَعْقِلُونَ ۝

5. Should you[518] wonder, the wonder is their saying: "What, if we turn into dust, will we be created anew?" Those are the ones who disbelieve in their Lord, and those are the ones round whose necks are chains, and those are the people of the Fire, abiding therein forever.

۞ وَإِن تَعْجَبْ فَعَجَبٌ قَوْلُهُمْ أَءِذَا كُنَّا تُرَٰبًا أَءِنَّا لَفِى خَلْقٍ جَدِيدٍ أُو۟لَٰٓئِكَ ٱلَّذِينَ كَفَرُوا۟ بِرَبِّهِمْ وَأُو۟لَٰٓئِكَ ٱلْأَغْلَٰلُ فِىٓ أَعْنَاقِهِمْ وَأُو۟لَٰٓئِكَ أَصْحَٰبُ ٱلنَّارِ هُمْ فِيهَا خَٰلِدُونَ ۝

6. And they ask you to hasten the evil before the good; yet there were punishments before them. Your Lord forgives people notwithstanding their wrongdoing, but your Lord is truly Severe in retribution.

وَيَسْتَعْجِلُونَكَ بِٱلسَّيِّئَةِ قَبْلَ ٱلْحَسَنَةِ وَقَدْ خَلَتْ مِن قَبْلِهِمُ ٱلْمَثُلَٰتُ وَإِنَّ رَبَّكَ لَذُو مَغْفِرَةٍ لِّلنَّاسِ عَلَىٰ ظُلْمِهِمْ وَإِنَّ رَبَّكَ لَشَدِيدُ ٱلْعِقَابِ ۝

7. Those who disbelieve say: "Why has no sign been sent down to him from his Lord?" You are only a warner; and for each people there is a guide.

وَيَقُولُ ٱلَّذِينَ كَفَرُوا۟ لَوْلَآ أُنزِلَ عَلَيْهِ ءَايَةٌ مِّن رَّبِّهِۦٓ إِنَّمَآ أَنتَ مُنذِرٌ وَلِكُلِّ قَوْمٍ هَادٍ ۝

8. Allah knows what every female bears and what the wombs carry for a shorter or a longer term; and everything with Him is by measure.

ٱللَّهُ يَعْلَمُ مَا تَحْمِلُ كُلُّ أُنثَىٰ وَمَا تَغِيضُ ٱلْأَرْحَامُ وَمَا تَزْدَادُ وَكُلُّ شَىْءٍ عِندَهُۥ بِمِقْدَارٍ ۝

9. [He is] the Knower of the Unseen and the Seen, the Great, the Most High.

عَٰلِمُ ٱلْغَيْبِ وَٱلشَّهَٰدَةِ ٱلْكَبِيرُ ٱلْمُتَعَالِ ۝

---

517. That is, males and females.
518. Muhammad.

10. It is the same whether any of you conceals his words or utters them, and whether he hides by night or goes forth by day.

سَوَآءٌ مِّنكُم مَّنْ أَسَرَّ ٱلْقَوْلَ وَمَن جَهَرَ بِهِۦ وَمَنْ هُوَ مُسْتَخْفٍ بِٱلَّيْلِ وَسَارِبٌ بِٱلنَّهَارِ ﴿١٠﴾

11. There are guardian [angels] before him and behind him, guarding him by Allah's Command. Allah does not change the condition of a people until they change what is in their hearts. And if Allah wills to afflict a people with a misfortune, it cannot be turned away, and they have, apart from Allah, no protector.

لَهُۥ مُعَقِّبَٰتٌ مِّنۢ بَيْنِ يَدَيْهِ وَمِنْ خَلْفِهِۦ يَحْفَظُونَهُۥ مِنْ أَمْرِ ٱللَّهِ إِنَّ ٱللَّهَ لَا يُغَيِّرُ مَا بِقَوْمٍ حَتَّىٰ يُغَيِّرُوا۟ مَا بِأَنفُسِهِمْ وَإِذَآ أَرَادَ ٱللَّهُ بِقَوْمٍ سُوٓءًا فَلَا مَرَدَّ لَهُۥ وَمَا لَهُم مِّن دُونِهِۦ مِن وَالٍ ﴿١١﴾

12. It is He Who shows you the lightning, inspiring fear and hope, and originates the laden clouds.

هُوَ ٱلَّذِى يُرِيكُمُ ٱلْبَرْقَ خَوْفًا وَطَمَعًا وَيُنشِئُ ٱلسَّحَابَ ٱلثِّقَالَ ﴿١٢﴾

13. And the thunder sounds His praise and the angels, too, in awe of Him. And He sends forth the thunderbolts smiting with them whomever He pleases. Nevertheless, they dispute about Allah, but He is Mighty in prowess.

وَيُسَبِّحُ ٱلرَّعْدُ بِحَمْدِهِۦ وَٱلْمَلَٰٓئِكَةُ مِنْ خِيفَتِهِۦ وَيُرْسِلُ ٱلصَّوَٰعِقَ فَيُصِيبُ بِهَا مَن يَشَآءُ وَهُمْ يُجَٰدِلُونَ فِى ٱللَّهِ وَهُوَ شَدِيدُ ٱلْمِحَالِ ﴿١٣﴾

14. To Him is the Call of Truth; and those on whom they call besides Him will not answer any of their prayers. They are like one who stretches out his hand to the water so that it might reach his mouth, but it will not reach it. The call of the unbelievers is only wasted.

لَهُۥ دَعْوَةُ ٱلْحَقِّ وَٱلَّذِينَ يَدْعُونَ مِن دُونِهِۦ لَا يَسْتَجِيبُونَ لَهُم بِشَىْءٍ إِلَّا كَبَٰسِطِ كَفَّيْهِ إِلَى ٱلْمَآءِ لِيَبْلُغَ فَاهُ وَمَا هُوَ بِبَٰلِغِهِۦ وَمَا دُعَآءُ ٱلْكَٰفِرِينَ إِلَّا فِى ضَلَٰلٍ ﴿١٤﴾

15. Those in the heavens and on earth prostrate themselves to Allah willingly or unwillingly, and so do their shadows mornings and evenings.

وَلِلَّهِ يَسْجُدُ مَن فِى ٱلسَّمَٰوَٰتِ وَٱلْأَرْضِ طَوْعًا وَكَرْهًا وَظِلَٰلُهُم بِٱلْغُدُوِّ وَٱلْءَاصَالِ ۩ ﴿١٥﴾

16. Say: "Who is the Lord of the heavens and the earth?" Say: "Allah." Say: "Have you then taken, besides Him, protectors who have no power to profit or harm even themselves?" Say: "Are the blind and the man who sees alike; or are the darkness and the light alike? Or have they assigned to Allah associates

قُل مَّن رَّبُّ ٱلسَّمَٰوَٰتِ وَٱلْأَرْضِ قُلِ ٱللَّهُ قُلْ أَفَٱتَّخَذْتُم مِّن دُونِهِۦٓ أَوْلِيَآءَ لَا يَمْلِكُونَ لِأَنفُسِهِمْ نَفْعًا وَلَا ضَرًّا قُلْ هَلْ يَسْتَوِى ٱلْأَعْمَىٰ وَٱلْبَصِيرُ أَمْ هَلْ تَسْتَوِى ٱلظُّلُمَٰتُ وَٱلنُّورُ أَمْ جَعَلُوا۟ لِلَّهِ شُرَكَآءَ خَلَقُوا۟ كَخَلْقِهِۦ فَتَشَٰبَهَ ٱلْخَلْقُ عَلَيْهِمْ قُلِ

ٱللَّهُ خَلِقُ كُلِّ شَيْءٍ وَهُوَ ٱلْوَٰحِدُ ٱلْقَهَّـٰرُ ﴿١٦﴾

who created the likeness of His creation, so that both creations seemed to them alike?" Say: "Allah is the Creator of everything and He is the One, the Almighty."

17. He sends water from the sky making riverbeds flow, each according to its measure. Then the torrent carries along swelling foam; similar to it is the scum that comes out from that which they smelt on the fire for making ornaments or tools. Thus Allah illustrates truth and falsehood. The scum is cast away, but what profits mankind remains in the earth. Thus Allah sets forth the parables.

أَنزَلَ مِنَ ٱلسَّمَاءِ مَاءً فَسَالَتْ أَوْدِيَةٌ بِقَدَرِهَا فَٱحْتَمَلَ ٱلسَّيْلُ زَبَدًا رَّابِيًا وَمِمَّا يُوقِدُونَ عَلَيْهِ فِى ٱلنَّارِ ٱبْتِغَاءَ حِلْيَةٍ أَوْ مَتَٰعٍ زَبَدٌ مِّثْلُهُ كَذَٰلِكَ يَضْرِبُ ٱللَّهُ ٱلْحَقَّ وَٱلْبَٰطِلَ فَأَمَّا ٱلزَّبَدُ فَيَذْهَبُ جُفَاءً وَأَمَّا مَا يَنفَعُ ٱلنَّاسَ فَيَمْكُثُ فِى ٱلْأَرْضِ كَذَٰلِكَ يَضْرِبُ ٱللَّهُ ٱلْأَمْثَالَ ﴿١٧﴾

18. To those who obey their Lord belongs the best [reward],[519] but those who disobey Him, were they to have all that is on earth plus its equal, would offer it as ransom. To those a bad reckoning is reserved, and their abode will be Hell, and what a miserable resting-place!

لِلَّذِينَ ٱسْتَجَابُوا لِرَبِّهِمُ ٱلْحُسْنَىٰ وَٱلَّذِينَ لَمْ يَسْتَجِيبُوا لَهُ لَوْ أَنَّ لَهُم مَّا فِى ٱلْأَرْضِ جَمِيعًا وَمِثْلَهُ مَعَهُ لَٱفْتَدَوْا بِهِ أُوْلَٰئِكَ لَهُمْ سُوءُ ٱلْحِسَابِ وَمَأْوَىٰهُمْ جَهَنَّمُ وَبِئْسَ ٱلْمِهَادُ ﴿١٨﴾

19. Is he who knows that what is revealed to you from your Lord is the truth, like he who is blind? Indeed, only the people of understanding take heed.

أَفَمَن يَعْلَمُ أَنَّمَا أُنزِلَ إِلَيْكَ مِن رَّبِّكَ ٱلْحَقُّ كَمَنْ هُوَ أَعْمَىٰ إِنَّمَا يَتَذَكَّرُ أُوْلُوا ٱلْأَلْبَٰبِ ﴿١٩﴾

20. Those who fulfil their pledge to Allah and do not violate the Covenant;

ٱلَّذِينَ يُوفُونَ بِعَهْدِ ٱللَّهِ وَلَا يَنقُضُونَ ٱلْمِيثَٰقَ ﴿٢٠﴾

21. And those who join together what Allah has commanded to be joined, fear their Lord and dread the terror of reckoning;

وَٱلَّذِينَ يَصِلُونَ مَا أَمَرَ ٱللَّهُ بِهِ أَن يُوصَلَ وَيَخْشَوْنَ رَبَّهُمْ وَيَخَافُونَ سُوءَ ٱلْحِسَابِ ﴿٢١﴾

22. And those who forbear, seeking the face of their Lord, perform the prayer, spend freely of what We have provided them with, secretly and in public, and counter evil with good - to those belongs the blissful end of the Hereafter.

وَٱلَّذِينَ صَبَرُوا ٱبْتِغَاءَ وَجْهِ رَبِّهِمْ وَأَقَامُوا ٱلصَّلَوٰةَ وَأَنفَقُوا مِمَّا رَزَقْنَٰهُمْ سِرًّا وَعَلَانِيَةً وَيَدْرَءُونَ بِٱلْحَسَنَةِ ٱلسَّيِّئَةَ أُوْلَٰئِكَ لَهُمْ عُقْبَى ٱلدَّارِ ﴿٢٢﴾

---

519. That is, Paradise.

23. They shall enter the Gardens of Eden, together with the righteous among their fathers, their spouses and their posterity; and the angels shall enter upon them from every gate [saying]:

24. "Peace be upon you for your forbearance and blessed is the final Abode!"

25. As to those who break Allah's Covenant once it is contracted, sever what Allah commanded to be joined and spread corruption in the land, upon them shall be the curse and theirs is the evil abode.[520]

26. Allah enlarges and restricts the provision to whom He pleases. They rejoice at this worldly life, but worldly life is nothing but a fleeting pleasure compared with the life to come.

27. And the unbelievers say: "If only a sign were sent down to him by his Lord!" Say: "Allah leads astray whomever He pleases and guides to Himself those who repent,

28. Those who believe and whose hearts find comfort in remembering Allah." Indeed, in remembering Allah the hearts find comfort.

29. May those who believe and do the good works be blessed and have a happy homecoming!

30. Thus We have sent you forth to a nation before which other nations had passed away, so as to recite to them what We revealed to you; and yet they deny the Compassionate. Say: "He is my Lord; there is no God but He. In Him I have put my trust and unto Him is my return."

جَنَّتُ عَدْنٍ يَدْخُلُونَهَا وَمَن صَلَحَ مِنْ ءَابَآبِهِمْ وَأَزْوَجِهِمْ وَذُرِّيَّتِهِمْ وَٱلْمَلَٰٓئِكَةُ يَدْخُلُونَ عَلَيْهِم مِّن كُلِّ بَابٍ ۝

سَلَٰمٌ عَلَيْكُم بِمَا صَبَرْتُمْ فَنِعْمَ عُقْبَى ٱلدَّارِ ۝

وَٱلَّذِينَ يَنقُضُونَ عَهْدَ ٱللَّهِ مِنۢ بَعْدِ مِيثَٰقِهِ وَيَقْطَعُونَ مَآ أَمَرَ ٱللَّهُ بِهِۦٓ أَن يُوصَلَ وَيُفْسِدُونَ فِى ٱلْأَرْضِ أُو۟لَٰٓئِكَ لَهُمُ ٱللَّعْنَةُ وَلَهُمْ سُوٓءُ ٱلدَّارِ ۝

ٱللَّهُ يَبْسُطُ ٱلرِّزْقَ لِمَن يَشَآءُ وَيَقْدِرُ وَفَرِحُوا۟ بِٱلْحَيَوٰةِ ٱلدُّنْيَا وَمَا ٱلْحَيَوٰةُ ٱلدُّنْيَا فِى ٱلْءَاخِرَةِ إِلَّا مَتَٰعٌ ۝

وَيَقُولُ ٱلَّذِينَ كَفَرُوا۟ لَوْلَآ أُنزِلَ عَلَيْهِ ءَايَةٌ مِّن رَّبِّهِۦ قُلْ إِنَّ ٱللَّهَ يُضِلُّ مَن يَشَآءُ وَيَهْدِىٓ إِلَيْهِ مَنْ أَنَابَ ۝

ٱلَّذِينَ ءَامَنُوا۟ وَتَطْمَئِنُّ قُلُوبُهُم بِذِكْرِ ٱللَّهِ أَلَا بِذِكْرِ ٱللَّهِ تَطْمَئِنُّ ٱلْقُلُوبُ ۝

ٱلَّذِينَ ءَامَنُوا۟ وَعَمِلُوا۟ ٱلصَّٰلِحَٰتِ طُوبَىٰ لَهُمْ وَحُسْنُ مَـَٔابٍ ۝

كَذَٰلِكَ أَرْسَلْنَٰكَ فِىٓ أُمَّةٍ قَدْ خَلَتْ مِن قَبْلِهَآ أُمَمٌ لِّتَتْلُوَا۟ عَلَيْهِمُ ٱلَّذِىٓ أَوْحَيْنَآ إِلَيْكَ وَهُمْ يَكْفُرُونَ بِٱلرَّحْمَٰنِ قُلْ هُوَ رَبِّى لَآ إِلَٰهَ إِلَّا هُوَ عَلَيْهِ تَوَكَّلْتُ وَإِلَيْهِ مَتَابِ ۝

---

520. Hell.

31. Had there been a Qur'an by which the mountains are made to move, or the land cleft asunder, or the dead spoken to [they would not believe]. No, the whole affair is Allah's. Do not the believers know that had Allah pleased, He would have guided all mankind? As for those who disbelieve, disaster will not cease to afflict them because of what they did or will settle near their homes until Allah's Promise is fulfilled. Surely Allah does not break His Promise.

32. Many Messengers before you were mocked; so I gave the unbelievers a respite; then I seized them. How then was My retribution!

33. Is he, then, Who watches every soul, noting what it earns [like one who does not]? Yet they set up associates with Allah. Say: "Name them. Are you informing Him about what He does not know on earth, or is it an outward speech only." Rather, the cunning of the unbelievers is embellished to them and they are kept away from the Path.[521] Those whom Allah leads astray will have no one to guide them.

34. Theirs is punishment in the present life, but the punishment of the Hereafter is much harder; and they will have no one to protect them from Allah.

35. The likeness of Paradise, which the righteous have been promised is this: rivers flow beneath it, its produce and shade are permanent. That is the ultimate fate of those who guard against evil; but the fate of the unbelievers is the Fire.

وَلَوْ أَنَّ قُرْآنًا سُيِّرَتْ بِهِ ٱلْجِبَالُ أَوْ قُطِّعَتْ بِهِ ٱلْأَرْضُ أَوْ كُلِّمَ بِهِ ٱلْمَوْتَىٰ بَل لِّلَّهِ ٱلْأَمْرُ جَمِيعًا أَفَلَمْ يَاْيْـَٔسِ ٱلَّذِينَ ءَامَنُوٓاْ أَن لَّوْ يَشَآءُ ٱللَّهُ لَهَدَى ٱلنَّاسَ جَمِيعًا وَلَا يَزَالُ ٱلَّذِينَ كَفَرُواْ تُصِيبُهُم بِمَا صَنَعُواْ قَارِعَةٌ أَوْ تَحُلُّ قَرِيبًا مِّن دَارِهِمْ حَتَّىٰ يَأْتِيَ وَعْدُ ٱللَّهِ إِنَّ ٱللَّهَ لَا يُخْلِفُ ٱلْمِيعَادَ ﴿٣١﴾

وَلَقَدِ ٱسْتُهْزِئَ بِرُسُلٍ مِّن قَبْلِكَ فَأَمْلَيْتُ لِلَّذِينَ كَفَرُواْ ثُمَّ أَخَذْتُهُمْ فَكَيْفَ كَانَ عِقَابِ ﴿٣٢﴾

أَفَمَنْ هُوَ قَآئِمٌ عَلَىٰ كُلِّ نَفْسٍ بِمَا كَسَبَتْ وَجَعَلُواْ لِلَّهِ شُرَكَآءَ قُلْ سَمُّوهُمْ أَمْ تُنَبِّئُونَهُ بِمَا لَا يَعْلَمُ فِى ٱلْأَرْضِ أَم بِظَـٰهِرٍ مِّنَ ٱلْقَوْلِ بَلْ زُيِّنَ لِلَّذِينَ كَفَرُواْ مَكْرُهُمْ وَصُدُّواْ عَنِ ٱلسَّبِيلِ وَمَن يُضْلِلِ ٱللَّهُ فَمَا لَهُۥ مِنْ هَادٍ ﴿٣٣﴾

لَّهُمْ عَذَابٌ فِى ٱلْحَيَوٰةِ ٱلدُّنْيَا وَلَعَذَابُ ٱلْأَخِرَةِ أَشَقُّ وَمَا لَهُم مِّنَ ٱللَّهِ مِن وَاقٍ ﴿٣٤﴾

۞ مَّثَلُ ٱلْجَنَّةِ ٱلَّتِى وُعِدَ ٱلْمُتَّقُونَ تَجْرِى مِن تَحْتِهَا ٱلْأَنْهَـٰرُ أُكُلُهَا دَآئِمٌ وَظِلُّهَا تِلْكَ عُقْبَى ٱلَّذِينَ ٱتَّقَواْ وَّعُقْبَى ٱلْكَـٰفِرِينَ ٱلنَّارُ ﴿٣٥﴾

---

521. That is, guidance.

36. And those to whom We have given the Book rejoice in what was revealed to you, but some of the factions deny a part of it. Say: "I have only been commanded to worship Allah and not to associate any one with Him; Him I call, and unto Him is my return."

وَٱلَّذِينَ ءَاتَيْنَٰهُمُ ٱلْكِتَٰبَ يَفْرَحُونَ بِمَآ أُنزِلَ إِلَيْكَ وَمِنَ ٱلْأَحْزَابِ مَن يُنكِرُ بَعْضَهُۥ قُلْ إِنَّمَآ أُمِرْتُ أَنْ أَعْبُدَ ٱللَّهَ وَلَآ أُشْرِكَ بِهِۦٓ إِلَيْهِ أَدْعُوا۟ وَإِلَيْهِ مَتَابِ ۞

37. And thus We revealed it [to be a Book of] judgement in Arabic; and were you to follow their desires after the knowledge which came to you, you would have neither a guardian nor a protector [to save you] from Allah.

وَكَذَٰلِكَ أَنزَلْنَٰهُ حُكْمًا عَرَبِيًّا وَلَئِنِ ٱتَّبَعْتَ أَهْوَآءَهُم بَعْدَ مَا جَآءَكَ مِنَ ٱلْعِلْمِ مَا لَكَ مِنَ ٱللَّهِ مِن وَلِيٍّ وَلَا وَاقٍ ۞

38. And We have sent forth Messengers before you and given them wives and progeny; but no Messenger had the power to come up with a sign except with Allah's Permission. Every age has its own Book.

وَلَقَدْ أَرْسَلْنَا رُسُلًا مِّن قَبْلِكَ وَجَعَلْنَا لَهُمْ أَزْوَٰجًا وَذُرِّيَّةً وَمَا كَانَ لِرَسُولٍ أَن يَأْتِيَ بِآيَةٍ إِلَّا بِإِذْنِ ٱللَّهِ لِكُلِّ أَجَلٍ كِتَابٌ ۞

39. Allah blots out and confirms what He pleases; and with Him is the Mother of the Book.[522]

يَمْحُوا۟ ٱللَّهُ مَا يَشَآءُ وَيُثْبِتُ وَعِندَهُۥٓ أُمُّ ٱلْكِتَٰبِ ۞

40. And whether We show you a part of what We promise them or cause you to die, your duty is to deliver the Message and it is for Us to do the reckoning.

وَإِن مَّا نُرِيَنَّكَ بَعْضَ ٱلَّذِى نَعِدُهُمْ أَوْ نَتَوَفَّيَنَّكَ فَإِنَّمَا عَلَيْكَ ٱلْبَلَٰغُ وَعَلَيْنَا ٱلْحِسَابُ ۞

41. Do they not see how We tackle the earth, causing it to shrink from its extremities? When Allah judges no one can reverse His Judgement. And He is Quick in calling to account.

أَوَلَمْ يَرَوْا۟ أَنَّا نَأْتِى ٱلْأَرْضَ نَنقُصُهَا مِنْ أَطْرَافِهَا وَٱللَّهُ يَحْكُمُ لَا مُعَقِّبَ لِحُكْمِهِۦ وَهُوَ سَرِيعُ ٱلْحِسَابِ ۞

42. Those who came before them did scheme, but Allah is Master of all scheming. He knows what each soul earns, and the unbelievers shall know to whom is the happy end in the Hereafter.

وَقَدْ مَكَرَ ٱلَّذِينَ مِن قَبْلِهِمْ فَلِلَّهِ ٱلْمَكْرُ جَمِيعًا يَعْلَمُ مَا تَكْسِبُ كُلُّ نَفْسٍ وَسَيَعْلَمُ ٱلْكُفَّٰرُ لِمَنْ عُقْبَى ٱلدَّارِ ۞

43. The unbelievers say: "You are not a Messenger." Say: "Allah suffices as a witness between me and you, as well as those who have a knowledge of the Book."[523]

وَيَقُولُ ٱلَّذِينَ كَفَرُوا۟ لَسْتَ مُرْسَلًا قُلْ كَفَىٰ بِٱللَّهِ شَهِيدًۢا بَيْنِى وَبَيْنَكُمْ وَمَنْ عِندَهُۥ عِلْمُ ٱلْكِتَٰبِ ۞

---

522. That is, the original codex of the Qur'an, i.e. heaven.
523. The Book here stands for previous revelations from Allah.

سُورَةُ إِبْرَاهِيمَ

بِسْمِ ٱللَّهِ ٱلرَّحْمَٰنِ ٱلرَّحِيمِ

In the Name of Allah,
the Compassionate, the Merciful

1. Alif - Lam - Ra.
A Book which We have revealed to you so that you may, with the will of their Lord, bring mankind from darkness to light, to the Path of the Mighty, the Praiseworthy One.

2. Allah to whom belongs what is in the heavens and on earth. And woe betide the unbelievers, for a terrible punishment!

3. Those who prefer the present life to the Hereafter and bar others from Allah's Path and seek to make it crooked, are far astray.

4. And We have sent forth no Messenger except in the tongue of his own people so that he may expound to them clearly. Then Allah leads astray whom He pleases and guides whom He pleases. He is the Mighty, the Wise.

5. We have, indeed, sent Moses with Our Signs [saying]: "Bring your people out of the darkness into the light and remind them of Allah's Days."[524] Surely in those are signs for every steadfast and thankful person.

6. And when Moses said to his people: "Remember Allah's Favour to you, when He delivered you from Pharaoh's people who were inflicting upon you the worst punishment, slaughtering your sons and sparing your women. In that, there truly was a great trial from your Lord."

7. [Remember] when your Lord proclaimed: "If you give thanks, I will increase you; but if you disbelieve, My punishment is certainly severe."

الٓرۚ كِتَٰبٌ أَنزَلْنَٰهُ إِلَيْكَ لِتُخْرِجَ ٱلنَّاسَ مِنَ ٱلظُّلُمَٰتِ إِلَى ٱلنُّورِ بِإِذْنِ رَبِّهِمْ إِلَىٰ صِرَٰطِ ٱلْعَزِيزِ ٱلْحَمِيدِ ۞

ٱللَّهِ ٱلَّذِى لَهُۥ مَا فِى ٱلسَّمَٰوَٰتِ وَمَا فِى ٱلْأَرْضِ وَوَيْلٌ لِّلْكَٰفِرِينَ مِنْ عَذَابٍ شَدِيدٍ ۞

ٱلَّذِينَ يَسْتَحِبُّونَ ٱلْحَيَوٰةَ ٱلدُّنْيَا عَلَى ٱلْءَاخِرَةِ وَيَصُدُّونَ عَن سَبِيلِ ٱللَّهِ وَيَبْغُونَهَا عِوَجًا أُو۟لَٰٓئِكَ فِى ضَلَٰلٍۭ بَعِيدٍ ۞

وَمَآ أَرْسَلْنَا مِن رَّسُولٍ إِلَّا بِلِسَانِ قَوْمِهِۦ لِيُبَيِّنَ لَهُمْ فَيُضِلُّ ٱللَّهُ مَن يَشَآءُ وَيَهْدِى مَن يَشَآءُ وَهُوَ ٱلْعَزِيزُ ٱلْحَكِيمُ ۞

وَلَقَدْ أَرْسَلْنَا مُوسَىٰ بِـَٔايَٰتِنَآ أَنْ أَخْرِجْ قَوْمَكَ مِنَ ٱلظُّلُمَٰتِ إِلَى ٱلنُّورِ وَذَكِّرْهُم بِأَيَّىٰمِ ٱللَّهِ إِنَّ فِى ذَٰلِكَ لَءَايَٰتٍ لِّكُلِّ صَبَّارٍ شَكُورٍ ۞

وَإِذْ قَالَ مُوسَىٰ لِقَوْمِهِ ٱذْكُرُوا۟ نِعْمَةَ ٱللَّهِ عَلَيْكُمْ إِذْ أَنجَىٰكُم مِّنْ ءَالِ فِرْعَوْنَ يَسُومُونَكُمْ سُوٓءَ ٱلْعَذَابِ وَيُذَبِّحُونَ أَبْنَآءَكُمْ وَيَسْتَحْيُونَ نِسَآءَكُمْ وَفِى ذَٰلِكُم بَلَآءٌ مِّن رَّبِّكُمْ عَظِيمٌ ۞

وَإِذْ تَأَذَّنَ رَبُّكُمْ لَئِن شَكَرْتُمْ لَأَزِيدَنَّكُمْ وَلَئِن كَفَرْتُمْ إِنَّ عَذَابِى لَشَدِيدٌ ۞

---

524. What is meant by •Days• is major events or calamities.

8. And Moses said: "If you are thankless, together with everyone on earth, surely Allah is All-Sufficient, Praiseworthy.

وَقَالَ مُوسَىٰٓ إِن تَكْفُرُوٓاْ أَنتُمْ وَمَن فِى ٱلْأَرْضِ جَمِيعًا فَإِنَّ ٱللَّهَ لَغَنِىٌّ حَمِيدٌ ۝

9. "Have you not heard the story of those who preceded you - the people of Noah, of 'Ad and Thamud, and those who came after them, whom none but Allah knows? Their Messengers came to them with the clear proofs, but they put their hands in their mouths saying: "We disbelieve in what you have been sent forth with, and we are certainly in disturbing doubt regarding what you are calling us to."

أَلَمْ يَأْتِكُمْ نَبَؤُاْ ٱلَّذِينَ مِن قَبْلِكُمْ قَوْمِ نُوحٍ وَعَادٍ وَثَمُودَ وَٱلَّذِينَ مِنۢ بَعْدِهِمْ لَا يَعْلَمُهُمْ إِلَّا ٱللَّهُ جَآءَتْهُمْ رُسُلُهُم بِٱلْبَيِّنَٰتِ فَرَدُّوٓاْ أَيْدِيَهُمْ فِىٓ أَفْوَٰهِهِمْ وَقَالُوٓاْ إِنَّا كَفَرْنَا بِمَآ أُرْسِلْتُم بِهِۦ وَإِنَّا لَفِى شَكٍّ مِّمَّا تَدْعُونَنَآ إِلَيْهِ مُرِيبٍ ۝

10. Their Messengers said: "Is there any doubt about Allah, Maker of the heavens and the earth? He calls you that He may forgive you some of your sins and reprieve you until an appointed term." They said: "You are only humans like ourselves; you want to turn us away from what our fathers worshipped. Bring us then a manifest authority."

۞ قَالَتْ رُسُلُهُمْ أَفِى ٱللَّهِ شَكٌّ فَاطِرِ ٱلسَّمَٰوَٰتِ وَٱلْأَرْضِ يَدْعُوكُمْ لِيَغْفِرَ لَكُم مِّن ذُنُوبِكُمْ وَيُؤَخِّرَكُمْ إِلَىٰٓ أَجَلٍ مُّسَمًّى قَالُوٓاْ إِنْ أَنتُمْ إِلَّا بَشَرٌ مِّثْلُنَا تُرِيدُونَ أَن تَصُدُّونَا عَمَّا كَانَ يَعْبُدُ ءَابَآؤُنَا فَأْتُونَا بِسُلْطَٰنٍ مُّبِينٍ ۝

11. Their Messengers said to them: "We are only humans like yourselves. However, Allah bestows His Grace on whom He pleases of His servants. It is not in our power to bring you an authority, save by Allah's Leave; and in Allah let the believers put their trust.

قَالَتْ لَهُمْ رُسُلُهُمْ إِن نَّحْنُ إِلَّا بَشَرٌ مِّثْلُكُمْ وَلَٰكِنَّ ٱللَّهَ يَمُنُّ عَلَىٰ مَن يَشَآءُ مِنْ عِبَادِهِۦ وَمَا كَانَ لَنَآ أَن نَّأْتِيَكُم بِسُلْطَٰنٍ إِلَّا بِإِذْنِ ٱللَّهِ وَعَلَى ٱللَّهِ فَلْيَتَوَكَّلِ ٱلْمُؤْمِنُونَ ۝

12. "And why should we not put our trust in Allah, when He has guided us on our ways? We will surely endure patiently the harm you cause us; and in Allah let those who trust put their trust."

وَمَا لَنَآ أَلَّا نَتَوَكَّلَ عَلَى ٱللَّهِ وَقَدْ هَدَىٰنَا سُبُلَنَا وَلَنَصْبِرَنَّ عَلَىٰ مَآ ءَاذَيْتُمُونَا وَعَلَى ٱللَّهِ فَلْيَتَوَكَّلِ ٱلْمُتَوَكِّلُونَ ۝

13. The unbelievers said to their Messengers: "We will certainly expel you from our land, unless you return to our religion." Then their Lord revealed to them: "We shall destroy the wrongdoers.

وَقَالَ ٱلَّذِينَ كَفَرُواْ لِرُسُلِهِمْ لَنُخْرِجَنَّكُم مِّنْ أَرْضِنَآ أَوْ لَتَعُودُنَّ فِى مِلَّتِنَا فَأَوْحَىٰٓ إِلَيْهِمْ رَبُّهُمْ لَنُهْلِكَنَّ ٱلظَّٰلِمِينَ ۝

14. "And We will make you dwell in the land after them. That is for him who fears My presence and fears My threats."

وَلَنُسْكِنَنَّكُمُ ٱلْأَرْضَ مِنۢ بَعْدِهِمْ ذَٰلِكَ لِمَنْ خَافَ مَقَامِى وَخَافَ وَعِيدِ ۝

15. And they called [on their Lord] for help, and every stubborn tyrant was disappointed.

16. Behind him is Hell, and He is given stinking water to drink.

17. He sips it but can hardly swallow it, and death surrounds him from every side, but he will not die; and beyond this is still a terrible punishment.

18. The likeness of those who disbelieve in their Lord is this: their works are like ashes scattered by the wind on a stormy day, and they have no power over anything they have earned. That is truly the great perdition.

19. Do you not see that Allah created the heavens and the earth in truth? If He pleases He will destroy you and bring forth a new creation.

20. And that is not a difficult matter for Allah.

21. And when they all appear before Allah, the weak will say to the overbearing: "We were indeed your followers; can you, then, do anything to save us from Allah's Punishment?" They will say: •Had Allah guided us, we would have guided you. Whether we fear or forbear, we have no escape."

22. And the Devil said when the issue was settled: "Allah has surely given you a true promise; and I made you a promise but did not keep it. I had no authority over you, except that I called you and you answered me. Do not blame me then, but blame yourselves; I cannot help you and you cannot help me. I deny your associating me [with Allah] before. The wrongdoers will have a very painful punishment."

23. And those who believe and do good works shall be admitted to Gardens beneath which rivers flow, abiding therein forever, by their Lord's Leave; their greeting therein shall be: "Peace."

وَٱسْتَفْتَحُوا۟ وَخَابَ كُلُّ جَبَّارٍ عَنِيدٍ ﴿١٥﴾

مِّن وَرَآئِهِۦ جَهَنَّمُ وَيُسْقَىٰ مِن مَّآءٍ صَدِيدٍ ﴿١٦﴾

يَتَجَرَّعُهُۥ وَلَا يَكَادُ يُسِيغُهُۥ وَيَأْتِيهِ ٱلْمَوْتُ مِن كُلِّ مَكَانٍ وَمَا هُوَ بِمَيِّتٍ وَمِن وَرَآئِهِۦ عَذَابٌ غَلِيظٌ ﴿١٧﴾

مَّثَلُ ٱلَّذِينَ كَفَرُوا۟ بِرَبِّهِمْ أَعْمَٰلُهُمْ كَرَمَادٍ ٱشْتَدَّتْ بِهِ ٱلرِّيحُ فِى يَوْمٍ عَاصِفٍ لَّا يَقْدِرُونَ مِمَّا كَسَبُوا۟ عَلَىٰ شَىْءٍ ذَٰلِكَ هُوَ ٱلضَّلَٰلُ ٱلْبَعِيدُ ﴿١٨﴾

أَلَمْ تَرَ أَنَّ ٱللَّهَ خَلَقَ ٱلسَّمَٰوَٰتِ وَٱلْأَرْضَ بِٱلْحَقِّ إِن يَشَأْ يُذْهِبْكُمْ وَيَأْتِ بِخَلْقٍ جَدِيدٍ ﴿١٩﴾

وَمَا ذَٰلِكَ عَلَى ٱللَّهِ بِعَزِيزٍ ﴿٢٠﴾

وَبَرَزُوا۟ لِلَّهِ جَمِيعًا فَقَالَ ٱلضُّعَفَٰٓؤُا۟ لِلَّذِينَ ٱسْتَكْبَرُوٓا۟ إِنَّا كُنَّا لَكُمْ تَبَعًا فَهَلْ أَنتُم مُّغْنُونَ عَنَّا مِنْ عَذَابِ ٱللَّهِ مِن شَىْءٍ قَالُوا۟ لَوْ هَدَىٰنَا ٱللَّهُ لَهَدَيْنَٰكُمْ سَوَآءٌ عَلَيْنَآ أَجَزِعْنَآ أَمْ صَبَرْنَا مَا لَنَا مِن مَّحِيصٍ ﴿٢١﴾

وَقَالَ ٱلشَّيْطَٰنُ لَمَّا قُضِىَ ٱلْأَمْرُ إِنَّ ٱللَّهَ وَعَدَكُمْ وَعْدَ ٱلْحَقِّ وَوَعَدتُّكُمْ فَأَخْلَفْتُكُمْ وَمَا كَانَ لِىَ عَلَيْكُم مِّن سُلْطَٰنٍ إِلَّآ أَن دَعَوْتُكُمْ فَٱسْتَجَبْتُمْ لِى فَلَا تَلُومُونِى وَلُومُوٓا۟ أَنفُسَكُم مَّآ أَنَا۠ بِمُصْرِخِكُمْ وَمَآ أَنتُم بِمُصْرِخِىَّ إِنِّى كَفَرْتُ بِمَآ أَشْرَكْتُمُونِ مِن قَبْلُ إِنَّ ٱلظَّٰلِمِينَ لَهُمْ عَذَابٌ أَلِيمٌ ﴿٢٢﴾

وَأُدْخِلَ ٱلَّذِينَ ءَامَنُوا۟ وَعَمِلُوا۟ ٱلصَّٰلِحَٰتِ جَنَّٰتٍ تَجْرِى مِن تَحْتِهَا ٱلْأَنْهَٰرُ خَٰلِدِينَ فِيهَا بِإِذْنِ رَبِّهِمْ تَحِيَّتُهُمْ فِيهَا سَلَٰمٌ ﴿٢٣﴾

24. Do you not see how Allah sets forth as a parable that a good word is like a good tree, whose root is firm and its branches are in the sky.

أَلَمْ تَرَ كَيْفَ ضَرَبَ اللَّهُ مَثَلًا كَلِمَةً طَيِّبَةً كَشَجَرَةٍ طَيِّبَةٍ أَصْلُهَا ثَابِتٌ وَفَرْعُهَا فِى السَّمَاءِ ﴿٢٤﴾

25. It brings forth its fruit all the time, by its Lord's Leave. Allah gives parables to mankind that perchance they may be mindful.

تُؤْتِى أُكُلَهَا كُلَّ حِينٍ بِإِذْنِ رَبِّهَا وَيَضْرِبُ اللَّهُ الْأَمْثَالَ لِلنَّاسِ لَعَلَّهُمْ يَتَذَكَّرُونَ ﴿٢٥﴾

26. And a foul word is like a foul tree which has been uprooted from the surface of the earth, having no stable base.

وَمَثَلُ كَلِمَةٍ خَبِيثَةٍ كَشَجَرَةٍ خَبِيثَةٍ اجْتُثَّتْ مِن فَوْقِ الْأَرْضِ مَا لَهَا مِن قَرَارٍ ﴿٢٦﴾

27. Allah confirms those who believe with the firm word in the present life, and in the life to come; but He leads the wrongdoers astray. Allah does whatever He pleases.

يُثَبِّتُ اللَّهُ الَّذِينَ ءَامَنُوا بِالْقَوْلِ الثَّابِتِ فِى الْحَيَوةِ الدُّنْيَا وَفِى الْآخِرَةِ وَيُضِلُّ اللَّهُ الظَّالِمِينَ وَيَفْعَلُ اللَّهُ مَا يَشَاءُ ﴿٢٧﴾

28. Have you not seen those who turn Allah's Grace into disbelief and lead their people to the abode of ruin?[525]

أَلَمْ تَرَ إِلَى الَّذِينَ بَدَّلُوا نِعْمَتَ اللَّهِ كُفْرًا وَأَحَلُّوا قَوْمَهُمْ دَارَ الْبَوَارِ ﴿٢٨﴾

29. In Hell they will burn, and what a wretched abode!

جَهَنَّمَ يَصْلَوْنَهَا وَبِئْسَ الْقَرَارُ ﴿٢٩﴾

30. And they set up equals to Allah in order to lead people away from His Path. Say: "Take your pleasure; for your fate is the Fire."

وَجَعَلُوا لِلَّهِ أَندَادًا لِّيُضِلُّوا عَن سَبِيلِهِ قُلْ تَمَتَّعُوا فَإِنَّ مَصِيرَكُمْ إِلَى النَّارِ ﴿٣٠﴾

31. Tell My servants who believe, to perform the prayer and give freely of what We have provided them with, secretly and in public, before a Day comes wherein there is no trade or friendship.

قُل لِّعِبَادِىَ الَّذِينَ ءَامَنُوا يُقِيمُوا الصَّلَوةَ وَيُنفِقُوا مِمَّا رَزَقْنَاهُمْ سِرًّا وَعَلَانِيَةً مِّن قَبْلِ أَن يَأْتِىَ يَوْمٌ لَّا بَيْعٌ فِيهِ وَلَا خِلَالٌ ﴿٣١﴾

32. [It is] Allah Who created the heavens and the earth and sends down water from the sky, bringing forth fruits for your sustenance. He has made the ships subservient to you so as to sail in the sea at His Behest and He has subjected to you the rivers.

اللَّهُ الَّذِى خَلَقَ السَّمَوَاتِ وَالْأَرْضَ وَأَنزَلَ مِنَ السَّمَاءِ مَاءً فَأَخْرَجَ بِهِ مِنَ الثَّمَرَاتِ رِزْقًا لَّكُمْ وَسَخَّرَ لَكُمُ الْفُلْكَ لِتَجْرِىَ فِى الْبَحْرِ بِأَمْرِهِ وَسَخَّرَ لَكُمُ الْأَنْهَارَ ﴿٣٢﴾

33. And He has made subservient to you the sun and the moon pursuing their courses, and subjected also the night and the day.

وَسَخَّرَ لَكُمُ الشَّمْسَ وَالْقَمَرَ دَائِبَيْنِ وَسَخَّرَ لَكُمُ الَّيْلَ وَالنَّهَارَ ﴿٣٣﴾

---

525. That is, Hell.

34. He gives you of all you ask Him for. And were you to count Allah's Favours you will never be able to exhaust them. Man is truly unjust and ungrateful.

وَءَاتَىٰكُم مِّن كُلِّ مَا سَأَلْتُمُوهُ وَإِن تَعُدُّوا نِعْمَتَ ٱللَّهِ لَا تُحْصُوهَآ إِنَّ ٱلْإِنسَٰنَ لَظَلُومٌ كَفَّارٌ ﴿٣٤﴾

35. And [remember] when Abraham said: "Lord, make this town secure, and keep me and my sons away from worshipping the idols.

وَإِذْ قَالَ إِبْرَٰهِيمُ رَبِّ ٱجْعَلْ هَٰذَا ٱلْبَلَدَ ءَامِنًا وَٱجْنُبْنِي وَبَنِيَّ أَن نَّعْبُدَ ٱلْأَصْنَامَ ﴿٣٥﴾

36. "Lord, they have led many people astray; therefore he who follows me, shall belong to me, and he who disobeys me, surely You are All-Forgiving, Merciful.

رَبِّ إِنَّهُنَّ أَضْلَلْنَ كَثِيرًا مِّنَ ٱلنَّاسِ فَمَن تَبِعَنِي فَإِنَّهُ مِنِّي وَمَنْ عَصَانِي فَإِنَّكَ غَفُورٌ رَّحِيمٌ ﴿٣٦﴾

37. "Our Lord, I have settled some of my offspring in a valley which has no tillage, by Your Sacred House, so that, Lord, they may perform the prayer. Make, then, the hearts of some people incline towards them, and provide them with some fruits, that perchance they may give thanks.

رَّبَّنَآ إِنِّي أَسْكَنتُ مِن ذُرِّيَّتِي بِوَادٍ غَيْرِ ذِي زَرْعٍ عِندَ بَيْتِكَ ٱلْمُحَرَّمِ رَبَّنَا لِيُقِيمُوا ٱلصَّلَوٰةَ فَٱجْعَلْ أَفْـِٔدَةً مِّنَ ٱلنَّاسِ تَهْوِىٓ إِلَيْهِمْ وَٱرْزُقْهُم مِّنَ ٱلثَّمَرَٰتِ لَعَلَّهُمْ يَشْكُرُونَ ﴿٣٧﴾

38. "Our Lord, You know what we conceal and what we reveal, and nothing on earth or in heaven is concealed from Allah.

رَبَّنَآ إِنَّكَ تَعْلَمُ مَا نُخْفِي وَمَا نُعْلِنُ وَمَا يَخْفَىٰ عَلَى ٱللَّهِ مِن شَيْءٍ فِي ٱلْأَرْضِ وَلَا فِي ٱلسَّمَآءِ ﴿٣٨﴾

39. "Praise be to Allah, who has given me, in old age, Isma'il and Isaac. Surely my Lord is the Hearer of Prayer.

ٱلْحَمْدُ لِلَّهِ ٱلَّذِي وَهَبَ لِي عَلَى ٱلْكِبَرِ إِسْمَٰعِيلَ وَإِسْحَٰقَ إِنَّ رَبِّي لَسَمِيعُ ٱلدُّعَآءِ ﴿٣٩﴾

40. "Lord, make me and my posterity keep up the prayers; and, our Lord, accept my supplication.

رَبِّ ٱجْعَلْنِي مُقِيمَ ٱلصَّلَوٰةِ وَمِن ذُرِّيَّتِي رَبَّنَا وَتَقَبَّلْ دُعَآءِ ﴿٤٠﴾

41. "Our Lord, forgive me, my parents and the believers, on the Day when the reckoning shall come to pass."

رَبَّنَا ٱغْفِرْ لِي وَلِوَٰلِدَيَّ وَلِلْمُؤْمِنِينَ يَوْمَ يَقُومُ ٱلْحِسَابُ ﴿٤١﴾

42. And do not think that Allah is unaware of what the wrongdoers do. He only gives them respite until the Day in which eyes shall stare blankly;

وَلَا تَحْسَبَنَّ ٱللَّهَ غَٰفِلًا عَمَّا يَعْمَلُ ٱلظَّٰلِمُونَ إِنَّمَا يُؤَخِّرُهُمْ لِيَوْمٍ تَشْخَصُ فِيهِ ٱلْأَبْصَٰرُ ﴿٤٢﴾

43. Hastening forward, their heads upraised, their gaze not returning to them, and their hearts vacant.

مُهْطِعِينَ مُقْنِعِى رُءُوسِهِمْ لَا يَرْتَدُّ إِلَيْهِمْ طَرْفُهُمْ وَأَفْئِدَتُهُمْ هَوَاءٌ ۝

44. And warn mankind of the Day when the punishment shall overtake them. Whereupon the wrongdoers will say: "Our Lord, give us respite for a near period and we will answer Your Call and follow the Messengers." [It will be said to them]: "Did you not swear before, that you will never cease to exist?"

وَأَنذِرِ ٱلنَّاسَ يَوْمَ يَأْتِيهِمُ ٱلْعَذَابُ فَيَقُولُ ٱلَّذِينَ ظَلَمُوا رَبَّنَا أَخِّرْنَا إِلَى أَجَلٍ قَرِيبٍ نُّجِبْ دَعْوَتَكَ وَنَتَّبِعِ ٱلرُّسُلَ أَوَلَمْ تَكُونُوا أَقْسَمْتُم مِّن قَبْلُ مَا لَكُم مِّن زَوَالٍ ۝

45. You lived in the dwellings of those who wronged themselves, and thus you saw clearly how We dealt with them, and We made [them] examples to you.

وَسَكَنتُمْ فِى مَسَاكِنِ ٱلَّذِينَ ظَلَمُوا أَنفُسَهُمْ وَتَبَيَّنَ لَكُمْ كَيْفَ فَعَلْنَا بِهِمْ وَضَرَبْنَا لَكُمُ ٱلْأَمْثَالَ ۝

46. And they hatched their plots, and Allah knew their plotting although their plotting was such as to move the mountains.

وَقَدْ مَكَرُوا مَكْرَهُمْ وَعِندَ ٱللَّهِ مَكْرُهُمْ وَإِن كَانَ مَكْرُهُمْ لِتَزُولَ مِنْهُ ٱلْجِبَالُ ۝

47. Do not think, then, that Allah will break His Promise to His messengers. Allah is truly Mighty and Capable of Retribution.

فَلَا تَحْسَبَنَّ ٱللَّهَ مُخْلِفَ وَعْدِهِ رُسُلَهُ إِنَّ ٱللَّهَ عَزِيزٌ ذُو ٱنتِقَامٍ ۝

48. On the Day the earth shall change into another earth, and the heavens too; and they shall appear before Allah, the One, the Conqueror.

يَوْمَ تُبَدَّلُ ٱلْأَرْضُ غَيْرَ ٱلْأَرْضِ وَٱلسَّمَٰوَٰتُ وَبَرَزُوا لِلَّهِ ٱلْوَٰحِدِ ٱلْقَهَّارِ ۝

49. And you will see the wicked sinners on that Day bound together in chains.

وَتَرَى ٱلْمُجْرِمِينَ يَوْمَئِذٍ مُّقَرَّنِينَ فِى ٱلْأَصْفَادِ ۝

50. Their garments made of pitch, and their faces covered with fire.

سَرَابِيلُهُم مِّن قَطِرَانٍ وَتَغْشَىٰ وُجُوهَهُمُ ٱلنَّارُ ۝

51. That Allah may reward every soul according to what it has earned. Surely Allah is Quick at reckoning.

لِيَجْزِىَ ٱللَّهُ كُلَّ نَفْسٍ مَّا كَسَبَتْ إِنَّ ٱللَّهَ سَرِيعُ ٱلْحِسَابِ ۝

52. This is a proclamation to mankind that they may be warned thereby, and know that He is One God, and that men of under-standing may remember well.

هَٰذَا بَلَٰغٌ لِّلنَّاسِ وَلِيُنذَرُوا بِهِ وَلِيَعْلَمُوا أَنَّمَا هُوَ إِلَٰهٌ وَٰحِدٌ وَلِيَذَّكَّرَ أُولُوا ٱلْأَلْبَٰبِ ۝

Sûrat Al-Hijr, (The Rock[526]) 15

بِسۡمِ ٱللَّهِ ٱلرَّحۡمَٰنِ ٱلرَّحِيمِ

In the Name of Allah,
the Compassionate, the Merciful

الٓرۚ تِلۡكَ ءَايَٰتُ ٱلۡكِتَٰبِ وَقُرۡءَانٖ مُّبِينٖ ١

1. Alif - Lam - Ra.
These are the Verses of the Book and a manifest Qur'an.

رُّبَمَا يَوَدُّ ٱلَّذِينَ كَفَرُواْ لَوۡ كَانُواْ مُسۡلِمِينَ ٢

2. Perhaps, those who disbelieve wish they were Muslims.

ذَرۡهُمۡ يَأۡكُلُواْ وَيَتَمَتَّعُواْ وَيُلۡهِهِمُ ٱلۡأَمَلُۖ فَسَوۡفَ يَعۡلَمُونَ ٣

3. Leave them to eat, enjoy themselves and let [false] hopes beguile them; for they will soon know.

وَمَآ أَهۡلَكۡنَا مِن قَرۡيَةٍ إِلَّا وَلَهَا كِتَابٞ مَّعۡلُومٞ ٤

4. We have never destroyed a town but it had a fixed decree.

مَّا تَسۡبِقُ مِنۡ أُمَّةٍ أَجَلَهَا وَمَا يَسۡتَـٔۡخِرُونَ ٥

5. No nation can hasten its term, nor defer it.

وَقَالُواْ يَٰٓأَيُّهَا ٱلَّذِي نُزِّلَ عَلَيۡهِ ٱلذِّكۡرُ إِنَّكَ لَمَجۡنُونٞ ٦

6. They say: "O you, to whom the Reminder[527] is revealed, you are indeed a madman.

لَّوۡ مَا تَأۡتِينَا بِٱلۡمَلَٰٓئِكَةِ إِن كُنتَ مِنَ ٱلصَّٰدِقِينَ ٧

7. "Why do you not bring us the angels, if you are truthful?"

مَا نُنَزِّلُ ٱلۡمَلَٰٓئِكَةَ إِلَّا بِٱلۡحَقِّ وَمَا كَانُوٓاْ إِذٗا مُّنظَرِينَ ٨

8. We do not send the angels down except with the Truth; and then they will have no respite.

إِنَّا نَحۡنُ نَزَّلۡنَا ٱلذِّكۡرَ وَإِنَّا لَهُۥ لَحَٰفِظُونَ ٩

9. It is truly We Who have revealed the Reminder, and We are truly its guardians.

وَلَقَدۡ أَرۡسَلۡنَا مِن قَبۡلِكَ فِي شِيَعِ ٱلۡأَوَّلِينَ ١٠

10. And We have sent forth Messengers before you to the sects of old.

وَمَا يَأۡتِيهِم مِّن رَّسُولٍ إِلَّا كَانُواْ بِهِۦ يَسۡتَهۡزِءُونَ ١١

11. And no Messenger came to them but they mocked him.

كَذَٰلِكَ نَسۡلُكُهُۥ فِي قُلُوبِ ٱلۡمُجۡرِمِينَ ١٢

12. That is how We instil it into the hearts of the sinners.

لَا يُؤۡمِنُونَ بِهِۦۖ وَقَدۡ خَلَتۡ سُنَّةُ ٱلۡأَوَّلِينَ ١٣

13. They do not believe in him despite the example of the ancients.

---

526. The land of Thamud, north of Medina.
527. The Qur'an.

14. And if We open for them a gate of heaven, so that they could continue to ascend through it;

وَلَوْ فَتَحْنَا عَلَيْهِم بَابًا مِّنَ ٱلسَّمَآءِ فَظَلُّواْ فِيهِ يَعْرُجُونَ ۝

15. They would simply say: "Our eyes have been covered over, or rather we are a people bewitched."

لَقَالُوٓاْ إِنَّمَا سُكِّرَتْ أَبْصَٰرُنَا بَلْ نَحْنُ قَوْمٌ مَّسْحُورُونَ ۝

16. We have indeed set up constellations in the heavens and made them attractive to the beholders;

وَلَقَدْ جَعَلْنَا فِى ٱلسَّمَآءِ بُرُوجًا وَزَيَّنَّٰهَا لِلنَّٰظِرِينَ ۝

17. And guarded them against every ac-cursed devil;

وَحَفِظْنَٰهَا مِن كُلِّ شَيْطَٰنٍ رَّجِيمٍ ۝

18. Except for him who eavesdrops stealthily and was pursued by a visible flame.

إِلَّا مَنِ ٱسْتَرَقَ ٱلسَّمْعَ فَأَتْبَعَهُۥ شِهَابٌ مُّبِينٌ ۝

19. As for the earth, We have spread it out, laid down upon it firm mountains and caused to grow therein all sorts of fair.

وَٱلْأَرْضَ مَدَدْنَٰهَا وَأَلْقَيْنَا فِيهَا رَوَٰسِىَ وَأَنۢبَتْنَا فِيهَا مِن كُلِّ شَىْءٍ مَّوْزُونٍ ۝

20. And We have made in it provisions for you and for those whom you do not provide for.

وَجَعَلْنَا لَكُمْ فِيهَا مَعَٰيِشَ وَمَن لَّسْتُمْ لَهُۥ بِرَٰزِقِينَ ۝

21. There is nothing for which We do not have the store-houses and sources, and We send it down only in a well-known measure.

وَإِن مِّن شَىْءٍ إِلَّا عِندَنَا خَزَآئِنُهُۥ وَمَا نُنَزِّلُهُۥٓ إِلَّا بِقَدَرٍ مَّعْلُومٍ ۝

22. And We send forth the winds as fertilizers; and then We send down water from the sky and give it to you to drink. But you do not store it up.

وَأَرْسَلْنَا ٱلرِّيَٰحَ لَوَٰقِحَ فَأَنزَلْنَا مِنَ ٱلسَّمَآءِ مَآءً فَأَسْقَيْنَٰكُمُوهُ وَمَآ أَنتُمْ لَهُۥ بِخَٰزِنِينَ ۝

23. It is We Who give life and cause to die, and We are the Inheritors.

وَإِنَّا لَنَحْنُ نُحْىِۦ وَنُمِيتُ وَنَحْنُ ٱلْوَٰرِثُونَ ۝

24. And We know those of you who came before and those who will come later.

وَلَقَدْ عَلِمْنَا ٱلْمُسْتَقْدِمِينَ مِنكُمْ وَلَقَدْ عَلِمْنَا ٱلْمُسْتَأْخِرِينَ ۝

25. And surely your Lord shall gather them. He is truly Wise, All-Knowing.

وَإِنَّ رَبَّكَ هُوَ يَحْشُرُهُمْ إِنَّهُۥ حَكِيمٌ عَلِيمٌ ۝

26. And We have created man from potter's clay, moulded out of slime.

وَلَقَدْ خَلَقْنَا ٱلْإِنسَٰنَ مِن صَلْصَٰلٍ مِّنْ حَمَإٍ مَّسْنُونٍ ۝

27. And the jinn We created before that from blazing fire.

وَٱلْجَآنَّ خَلَقْنَٰهُ مِن قَبْلُ مِن نَّارِ ٱلسَّمُومِ ۝

28. When your Lord said to the angels: "Behold, I have created a man from potter's clay, out of moulded slime.

وَإِذْ قَالَ رَبُّكَ لِلْمَلَٰٓئِكَةِ إِنِّى خَٰلِقٌۢ بَشَرًا مِّن صَلْصَٰلٍ مِّنْ حَمَإٍ مَّسْنُونٍ ﴿٢٨﴾

29. "When I have fashioned him and breathed into him of My Spirit, fall down prostrating yourselves to him."

فَإِذَا سَوَّيْتُهُۥ وَنَفَخْتُ فِيهِ مِن رُّوحِى فَقَعُوا۟ لَهُۥ سَٰجِدِينَ ﴿٢٩﴾

30. The angels prostrated themselves, all together;

فَسَجَدَ ٱلْمَلَٰٓئِكَةُ كُلُّهُمْ أَجْمَعُونَ ﴿٣٠﴾

31. Except Satan who refused to be one of those who prostrated themselves.

إِلَّآ إِبْلِيسَ أَبَىٰٓ أَن يَكُونَ مَعَ ٱلسَّٰجِدِينَ ﴿٣١﴾

32. He said: "O Satan, what keeps you from being one of those who prostrate themselves?"

قَالَ يَٰٓإِبْلِيسُ مَا لَكَ أَلَّا تَكُونَ مَعَ ٱلسَّٰجِدِينَ ﴿٣٢﴾

33. He said: "I refuse to prostrate myself before a mortal You created from potter's clay out of moulded slime."

قَالَ لَمْ أَكُن لِّأَسْجُدَ لِبَشَرٍ خَلَقْتَهُۥ مِن صَلْصَٰلٍ مِّنْ حَمَإٍ مَّسْنُونٍ ﴿٣٣﴾

34. He said: "Get out of here,[528] then, for you are surely accursed.

قَالَ فَٱخْرُجْ مِنْهَا فَإِنَّكَ رَجِيمٌ ﴿٣٤﴾

35. "And the curse shall be upon you till the Day of Judgement."

وَإِنَّ عَلَيْكَ ٱللَّعْنَةَ إِلَىٰ يَوْمِ ٱلدِّينِ ﴿٣٥﴾

36. He said: "My Lord, reprieve me till the Day of Resurrection."

قَالَ رَبِّ فَأَنظِرْنِىٓ إِلَىٰ يَوْمِ يُبْعَثُونَ ﴿٣٦﴾

37. He said: "You are indeed one of those reprieved,

قَالَ فَإِنَّكَ مِنَ ٱلْمُنظَرِينَ ﴿٣٧﴾

38. "Till the Appointed Day."

إِلَىٰ يَوْمِ ٱلْوَقْتِ ٱلْمَعْلُومِ ﴿٣٨﴾

39. [Satan said]: "My Lord, since you misguided me, I will make what is foul on earth seem fair to them, and I shall mislead them all,

قَالَ رَبِّ بِمَآ أَغْوَيْتَنِى لَأُزَيِّنَنَّ لَهُمْ فِى ٱلْأَرْضِ وَلَأُغْوِيَنَّهُمْ أَجْمَعِينَ ﴿٣٩﴾

40. "Except for Your sincere servants among them."

إِلَّا عِبَادَكَ مِنْهُمُ ٱلْمُخْلَصِينَ ﴿٤٠﴾

41. He[529] said: "This is My Straight Path.

قَالَ هَٰذَا صِرَٰطٌ عَلَىَّ مُسْتَقِيمٌ ﴿٤١﴾

42. "Over My servants you have no authority, except for those sinners who follow you.

إِنَّ عِبَادِى لَيْسَ لَكَ عَلَيْهِمْ سُلْطَٰنٌ إِلَّا مَنِ ٱتَّبَعَكَ مِنَ ٱلْغَاوِينَ ﴿٤٢﴾

---

528. That is, Paradise or the Garden of Eden.
529. Allah.

43. "Hell shall be the appointed place for them all.

وَإِنَّ جَهَنَّمَ لَمَوْعِدُهُمْ أَجْمَعِينَ ﴿٤٣﴾

44. "Seven gates it has; and to each gate a part of them is assigned.

لَهَا سَبْعَةُ أَبْوَابٍ لِّكُلِّ بَابٍ مِّنْهُمْ جُزْءٌ مَّقْسُومٌ ﴿٤٤﴾

45. "The righteous will surely be amidst gardens and fountains.

إِنَّ الْمُتَّقِينَ فِي جَنَّاتٍ وَعُيُونٍ ﴿٤٥﴾

46. [It will be said to them]: "Enter therein in peace and security."

ادْخُلُوهَا بِسَلَامٍ آمِنِينَ ﴿٤٦﴾

47. We shall remove all hatred from their hearts, and as brethren they shall recline, facing each other, upon couches.

وَنَزَعْنَا مَا فِي صُدُورِهِم مِّنْ غِلٍّ إِخْوَانًا عَلَى سُرُرٍ مُّتَقَابِلِينَ ﴿٤٧﴾

48. They shall not be touched by fatigue therein, nor will they be driven out.

لَا يَمَسُّهُمْ فِيهَا نَصَبٌ وَمَا هُم مِّنْهَا بِمُخْرَجِينَ ﴿٤٨﴾

49. Tell My servants that I am truly the All-Forgiving, the Merciful.

۞ نَبِّئْ عِبَادِي أَنِّي أَنَا الْغَفُورُ الرَّحِيمُ ﴿٤٩﴾

50. And that My Punishment is truly the painful punishment.

وَأَنَّ عَذَابِي هُوَ الْعَذَابُ الْأَلِيمُ ﴿٥٠﴾

51. And tell them about the guests (the angels) of Abraham.

وَنَبِّئْهُمْ عَن ضَيْفِ إِبْرَاهِيمَ ﴿٥١﴾

52. When they entered unto him saying: "Peace"; he said: "We are afraid of you."

إِذْ دَخَلُوا عَلَيْهِ فَقَالُوا سَلَامًا قَالَ إِنَّا مِنكُمْ وَجِلُونَ ﴿٥٢﴾

53. They said: "Do not be afraid; we bring you the good news of a boy possessing knowledge."

قَالُوا لَا تَوْجَلْ إِنَّا نُبَشِّرُكَ بِغُلَامٍ عَلِيمٍ ﴿٥٣﴾

54. He said: "Do you bring me good news, when old age has overtaken me? What good news do you bring, then?"

قَالَ أَبَشَّرْتُمُونِي عَلَى أَن مَّسَّنِيَ الْكِبَرُ فَبِمَ تُبَشِّرُونَ ﴿٥٤﴾

55. They said: "We bring you good news in truth, so do not be one of those who despair."

قَالُوا بَشَّرْنَاكَ بِالْحَقِّ فَلَا تَكُن مِّنَ الْقَانِطِينَ ﴿٥٥﴾

56. He said: "Who despairs of his Lord's Mercy, except those who have gone astray."

قَالَ وَمَن يَقْنَطُ مِن رَّحْمَةِ رَبِّهِ إِلَّا الضَّالُّونَ ﴿٥٦﴾

57. He said: "What is your errand, O messengers?"

قَالَ فَمَا خَطْبُكُمْ أَيُّهَا الْمُرْسَلُونَ ﴿٥٧﴾

58. They said: "We have been sent forth to [destroy] a sinful people.

قَالُوا إِنَّا أُرْسِلْنَا إِلَى قَوْمٍ مُّجْرِمِينَ ﴿٥٨﴾

59. "Except for the family of Lot; we shall deliver them all,

إِلَّا آلَ لُوطٍ إِنَّا لَمُنَجُّوهُمْ أَجْمَعِينَ ﴿٥٩﴾

60. "Except for his wife; We have decreed that she will remain behind [to perish]."

إِلَّا ٱمْرَأَتَهُۥ قَدَّرْنَآ إِنَّهَا لَمِنَ ٱلْغَـٰبِرِينَ ۝

61. And when the messengers (the angels) came to the family of Lot;

فَلَمَّا جَآءَ ءَالَ لُوطٍ ٱلْمُرْسَلُونَ ۝

62. He said: "You are surely a people unknown [to us]."

قَالَ إِنَّكُمْ قَوْمٌ مُّنكَرُونَ ۝

63. They said: "No; we bring you that whereof they were in doubt.

قَالُوا بَلْ جِئْنَـٰكَ بِمَا كَانُوا فِيهِ يَمْتَرُونَ ۝

64. "And we bring you the truth, and we are truthful, indeed.

وَأَتَيْنَـٰكَ بِٱلْحَقِّ وَإِنَّا لَصَـٰدِقُونَ ۝

65. "Set out, then, with your family in a watch of the night, and follow in their rear; and let no one of you look back, and go forth wherever you are ordered."

فَأَسْرِ بِأَهْلِكَ بِقِطْعٍ مِّنَ ٱلَّيْلِ وَٱتَّبِعْ أَدْبَـٰرَهُمْ وَلَا يَلْتَفِتْ مِنكُمْ أَحَدٌ وَٱمْضُوا حَيْثُ تُؤْمَرُونَ ۝

66. And We conveyed to him this decree that these [sinners] will be rooted out in the morning.

وَقَضَيْنَآ إِلَيْهِ ذَٰلِكَ ٱلْأَمْرَ أَنَّ دَابِرَ هَـٰٓؤُلَآءِ مَقْطُوعٌ مُّصْبِحِينَ ۝

67. And the people of the town came rejoicing.

وَجَآءَ أَهْلُ ٱلْمَدِينَةِ يَسْتَبْشِرُونَ ۝

68. He said: "These are my guests, so do not disgrace me.

قَالَ إِنَّ هَـٰٓؤُلَآءِ ضَيْفِي فَلَا تَفْضَحُونِ ۝

69. "And fear Allah and do not shame me."

وَٱتَّقُوا ٱللَّهَ وَلَا تُخْزُونِ ۝

70. They said: "Did we not forbid you [to approach] strangers?"

قَالُوٓا أَوَلَمْ نَنْهَكَ عَنِ ٱلْعَـٰلَمِينَ ۝

71. He said: "These are my daughters, if you are intent on doing anything."

قَالَ هَـٰٓؤُلَآءِ بَنَاتِي إِن كُنتُمْ فَـٰعِلِينَ ۝

72. By your life [O Muhammad] they wandered blindly in their folly.

لَعَمْرُكَ إِنَّهُمْ لَفِي سَكْرَتِهِمْ يَعْمَهُونَ ۝

73. Thereupon, the dreadful Cry overtook them at sunrise.

فَأَخَذَتْهُمُ ٱلصَّيْحَةُ مُشْرِقِينَ ۝

74. And so We turned their towns upside down, and We rained upon them stones of baked clay.

فَجَعَلْنَا عَـٰلِيَهَا سَافِلَهَا وَأَمْطَرْنَا عَلَيْهِمْ حِجَارَةً مِّن سِجِّيلٍ ۝

75. In this, there are truly signs for those who ponder.

إِنَّ فِي ذَٰلِكَ لَءَايَـٰتٍ لِّلْمُتَوَسِّمِينَ ۝

76. And they[530] lie along an existing road.

وَإِنَّهَا لَبِسَبِيلٍ مُّقِيمٍ ۝

77. In that, there is indeed a sign for the believers.

إِنَّ فِى ذَٰلِكَ لَآيَةً لِّلْمُؤْمِنِينَ ۝

78. Surely, the People of the Thicket[531] were also wrongdoers.

وَإِن كَانَ أَصْحَابُ ٱلْأَيْكَةِ لَظَالِمِينَ ۝

79. So We punished them. And they[532] lie along a plain road.

فَٱنتَقَمْنَا مِنْهُمْ وَإِنَّهُمَا لَبِإِمَامٍ مُّبِينٍ ۝

80. And the people of al-Hijr[533] denounced the Messengers.

وَلَقَدْ كَذَّبَ أَصْحَابُ ٱلْحِجْرِ ٱلْمُرْسَلِينَ ۝

81. We brought them Our Signs, but they turned away from them.

وَءَاتَيْنَٰهُمْ ءَايَٰتِنَا فَكَانُوا۟ عَنْهَا مُعْرِضِينَ ۝

82. They hewed their houses in the mountains in security.

وَكَانُوا۟ يَنْحِتُونَ مِنَ ٱلْجِبَالِ بُيُوتًا ءَامِنِينَ ۝

83. The Cry overtook them in the morning.

فَأَخَذَتْهُمُ ٱلصَّيْحَةُ مُصْبِحِينَ ۝

84. Thus, what they did availed them nothing.

فَمَآ أَغْنَىٰ عَنْهُم مَّا كَانُوا۟ يَكْسِبُونَ ۝

85. We have not created the heavens and the earth and what lies between them save in truth; and the Hour is surely coming. So forgive them magnanimously.

وَمَا خَلَقْنَا ٱلسَّمَٰوَٰتِ وَٱلْأَرْضَ وَمَا بَيْنَهُمَآ إِلَّا بِٱلْحَقِّ وَإِنَّ ٱلسَّاعَةَ لَآتِيَةٌ فَٱصْفَحِ ٱلصَّفْحَ ٱلْجَمِيلَ ۝

86. Your Lord is indeed the Creator, the Knower.

إِنَّ رَبَّكَ هُوَ ٱلْخَلَّٰقُ ٱلْعَلِيمُ ۝

87. And We have given you seven oft-repeated[534] [Verses] and the great Qur'an.

وَلَقَدْ ءَاتَيْنَٰكَ سَبْعًا مِّنَ ٱلْمَثَانِى وَٱلْقُرْءَانَ ٱلْعَظِيمَ ۝

88. Do not strain your gaze towards what We gave certain groups of them to enjoy, and do not grieve for them, and lower your wing[535] to the believers.

لَا تَمُدَّنَّ عَيْنَيْكَ إِلَىٰ مَا مَتَّعْنَا بِهِۦٓ أَزْوَٰجًا مِّنْهُمْ وَلَا تَحْزَنْ عَلَيْهِمْ وَٱخْفِضْ جَنَاحَكَ لِلْمُؤْمِنِينَ ۝

89. And say: "I am truly the plain warner."

وَقُلْ إِنِّىٓ أَنَا ٱلنَّذِيرُ ٱلْمُبِينُ ۝

90. Just as We sent down [punishment] upon the dividers,[536]

كَمَآ أَنزَلْنَا عَلَى ٱلْمُقْتَسِمِينَ ۝

---

530. The towns.
531. Near Midian.
532. Lot's towns and the Thicket.
533. The dwellers in Hijr, north of Medina, were Thamud.
534. The seven oft-repeated verses of the Opening Surah of the Qur'an.
535. That is, be modest.
536. The Jews and Christians.

91. Who divided the Qur'an into parts.[537]

92. By your Lord, We shall question them all,

93. Regarding what they used to do.

94. So proclaim what you are commanded and turn away from the polytheists.

95. Our support to you against the scoffers will be sufficient;

96. Those who set up another god with Allah. They will surely come to know.

97. And We know well that your heart is distressed at what they say.

98. So, celebrate the praise of your Lord and be one of those who prostrate themselves.

99. And worship your Lord, till the certain[538] [Hour] overtakes you!

Sûrat An-Nahl,
(The Bees) 16

In the Name of Allah,
the Compassionate, the Merciful

1. Allah's Decree will be fulfilled; so do not hasten it. Glory be to Him and may He be exalted above what they associate [with Him]!

2. He sends down the angels with the Spirit by His Command upon whom He pleases of His servants [saying]: "Warn that there is no god but I; so fear Me."

3. He created the heavens and the earth in truth; may He be exalted above what they associate [with Him].

4. He created man from a sperm-drop and, behold, he is a professed disputant.

---

537. That is, they accepted a part of it and rejected the rest.
538. That is, certain death.

263

5. And the cattle He created for you. Therein are warmth and other advantages, and from them you eat.

وَالْأَنْعَمَ خَلَقَهَا لَكُمْ فِيهَا دِفْءٌ وَمَنَفِعُ وَمِنْهَا تَأْكُلُونَ ﴿٥﴾

6. And in them you witness beauty, when you bring them back [home], and when you drive them out for pasture.

وَلَكُمْ فِيهَا جَمَالٌ حِينَ تُرِيحُونَ وَحِينَ تَسْرَحُونَ ﴿٦﴾

7. And they carry your burdens to a distant land which you could only reach with great hardship. Surely your Lord is Clement and Merciful.

وَتَحْمِلُ أَثْقَالَكُمْ إِلَىٰ بَلَدٍ لَّمْ تَكُونُوا بَلِغِيهِ إِلَّا بِشِقِّ الْأَنفُسِ إِنَّ رَبَّكُمْ لَرَءُوفٌ رَّحِيمٌ ﴿٧﴾

8. And horses, mules and asses [He created] for you to mount, and as an adornment; and He creates what you do not know.

وَالْخَيْلَ وَالْبِغَالَ وَالْحَمِيرَ لِتَرْكَبُوهَا وَزِينَةً وَيَخْلُقُ مَا لَا تَعْلَمُونَ ﴿٨﴾

9. It belongs to Allah to show the Straight Path; some, however, deviate from it. Had Allah pleased He would have guided you all.

وَعَلَى اللَّهِ قَصْدُ السَّبِيلِ وَمِنْهَا جَائِرٌ وَلَوْ شَاءَ لَهَدَىٰكُمْ أَجْمَعِينَ ﴿٩﴾

10. It is He who sends down water from the sky; from it you drink, and through it grow the plants on which you feed your cattle.

هُوَ الَّذِي أَنزَلَ مِنَ السَّمَاءِ مَاءً لَّكُم مِّنْهُ شَرَابٌ وَمِنْهُ شَجَرٌ فِيهِ تُسِيمُونَ ﴿١٠﴾

11. From it He brings forth for you vegetation, olives, palms, vines and all kinds of fruit. In that, surely, there is a sign for a people who reflect.

يُنبِتُ لَكُم بِهِ الزَّرْعَ وَالزَّيْتُونَ وَالنَّخِيلَ وَالْأَعْنَبَ وَمِن كُلِّ الثَّمَرَٰتِ إِنَّ فِي ذَٰلِكَ لَآيَةً لِّقَوْمٍ يَتَفَكَّرُونَ ﴿١١﴾

12. And He has subjected to you the night and the day, the sun and the moon; and the stars are subjected by His Command. In that there are signs for a people who understand.

وَسَخَّرَ لَكُمُ الَّيْلَ وَالنَّهَارَ وَالشَّمْسَ وَالْقَمَرَ وَالنُّجُومُ مُسَخَّرَٰتٌ بِأَمْرِهِ إِنَّ فِي ذَٰلِكَ لَآيَٰتٍ لِّقَوْمٍ يَعْقِلُونَ ﴿١٢﴾

13. And what He created for you in the earth is of multifarious colours; in that there is, surely, a sign for a people who are mindful.

وَمَا ذَرَأَ لَكُمْ فِي الْأَرْضِ مُخْتَلِفًا أَلْوَٰنُهُ إِنَّ فِي ذَٰلِكَ لَآيَةً لِّقَوْمٍ يَذَّكَّرُونَ ﴿١٣﴾

14. And it is He Who subjected the sea, so that you may eat from it tender meat and bring out from it jewellery for you to wear; and you see the ships cruising therein. [He subjected it for you] so that you may also seek His Bounty and give thanks.

وَهُوَ الَّذِي سَخَّرَ الْبَحْرَ لِتَأْكُلُوا مِنْهُ لَحْمًا طَرِيًّا وَتَسْتَخْرِجُوا مِنْهُ حِلْيَةً تَلْبَسُونَهَا وَتَرَى الْفُلْكَ مَوَاخِرَ فِيهِ وَلِتَبْتَغُوا مِن فَضْلِهِ وَلَعَلَّكُمْ تَشْكُرُونَ ﴿١٤﴾

15. And He laid up in the earth firm mountains, lest it shake under you; as well as rivers and pathways that, perchance, you may be guided.

16. And He [laid] landmarks; and by the stars they are guided.

17. Now, is He Who creates like him who does not create? Do you not take heed?

18. Were you to count Allah's Blessings, you will not exhaust them. Allah is truly All-Forgiving, Merciful.

19. And Allah knows what you conceal and what you reveal.

20. Those they call upon, apart from Allah, do not create anything, but are themselves created.

21. [They are] dead, not alive, and they do not know when they will be raised from the dead.

22. Your God is One God; those, then, who do not believe in the Hereafter, their hearts deny and they are arrogant.

23. Undoubtedly, Allah knows what they conceal and what they reveal. Indeed, He does not like the arrogant.

24. And if it is said to them: "What has your Lord revealed?" they say: "Fables of the ancients."

25. So let them on the Day of Resurrection bear in full their burdens and some of the burdens of the ignorant whom they lead astray. How evil is that which they shall bear!

26. Those who came before them schemed and Allah razed their building from the foundations and the roof fell upon them from above them, and punishment came upon them from whence they did not know.

وَأَلْقَىٰ فِى ٱلْأَرْضِ رَوَٰسِىَ أَن تَمِيدَ بِكُمْ وَأَنْهَٰرًا وَسُبُلًا لَّعَلَّكُمْ تَهْتَدُونَ ﴿١٥﴾

وَعَلَٰمَٰتٍ وَبِٱلنَّجْمِ هُمْ يَهْتَدُونَ ﴿١٦﴾

أَفَمَن يَخْلُقُ كَمَن لَّا يَخْلُقُ أَفَلَا تَذَكَّرُونَ ﴿١٧﴾

وَإِن تَعُدُّوا۟ نِعْمَةَ ٱللَّهِ لَا تُحْصُوهَآ إِنَّ ٱللَّهَ لَغَفُورٌ رَّحِيمٌ ﴿١٨﴾

وَٱللَّهُ يَعْلَمُ مَا تُسِرُّونَ وَمَا تُعْلِنُونَ ﴿١٩﴾

وَٱلَّذِينَ يَدْعُونَ مِن دُونِ ٱللَّهِ لَا يَخْلُقُونَ شَيْئًا وَهُمْ يُخْلَقُونَ ﴿٢٠﴾

أَمْوَٰتٌ غَيْرُ أَحْيَآءٍ وَمَا يَشْعُرُونَ أَيَّانَ يُبْعَثُونَ ﴿٢١﴾

إِلَٰهُكُمْ إِلَٰهٌ وَٰحِدٌ فَٱلَّذِينَ لَا يُؤْمِنُونَ بِٱلْأَخِرَةِ قُلُوبُهُم مُّنكِرَةٌ وَهُم مُّسْتَكْبِرُونَ ﴿٢٢﴾

لَا جَرَمَ أَنَّ ٱللَّهَ يَعْلَمُ مَا يُسِرُّونَ وَمَا يُعْلِنُونَ إِنَّهُ لَا يُحِبُّ ٱلْمُسْتَكْبِرِينَ ﴿٢٣﴾

وَإِذَا قِيلَ لَهُم مَّاذَآ أَنزَلَ رَبُّكُمْ قَالُوٓا۟ أَسَٰطِيرُ ٱلْأَوَّلِينَ ﴿٢٤﴾

لِيَحْمِلُوٓا۟ أَوْزَارَهُمْ كَامِلَةً يَوْمَ ٱلْقِيَٰمَةِ وَمِنْ أَوْزَارِ ٱلَّذِينَ يُضِلُّونَهُم بِغَيْرِ عِلْمٍ أَلَا سَآءَ مَا يَزِرُونَ ﴿٢٥﴾

قَدْ مَكَرَ ٱلَّذِينَ مِن قَبْلِهِمْ فَأَتَى ٱللَّهُ بُنْيَٰنَهُم مِّنَ ٱلْقَوَاعِدِ فَخَرَّ عَلَيْهِمُ ٱلسَّقْفُ مِن فَوْقِهِمْ وَأَتَىٰهُمُ ٱلْعَذَابُ مِنْ حَيْثُ لَا يَشْعُرُونَ ﴿٢٦﴾

27. Then, on the Day of Resurrection, He will disgrace them and will say: "Where are My associates about whom you used to argue?" Those who are given knowledge will say: "Disgrace and evil will this day be upon the unbelievers;

ثُمَّ يَوْمَ ٱلْقِيَٰمَةِ يُخْزِيهِمْ وَيَقُولُ أَيْنَ شُرَكَآءِىَ ٱلَّذِينَ كُنتُمْ تُشَٰٓقُّونَ فِيهِمْ قَالَ ٱلَّذِينَ أُوتُوا۟ ٱلْعِلْمَ إِنَّ ٱلْخِزْىَ ٱلْيَوْمَ وَٱلسُّوٓءَ عَلَى ٱلْكَٰفِرِينَ ﴿٢٧﴾

28. "Who are carried off by the angels while still wronging themselves." Then, they will offer submission saying: "We did not do any evil." Surely, Allah knows well what you were doing.

ٱلَّذِينَ تَتَوَفَّىٰهُمُ ٱلْمَلَٰٓئِكَةُ ظَالِمِىٓ أَنفُسِهِمْ فَأَلْقَوُا۟ ٱلسَّلَمَ مَا كُنَّا نَعْمَلُ مِن سُوٓءٍ بَلَىٰٓ إِنَّ ٱللَّهَ عَلِيمٌۢ بِمَا كُنتُمْ تَعْمَلُونَ ﴿٢٨﴾

29. Enter, then, the gates of Hell, abiding therein forever. Wretched indeed is the abode of the arrogant!

فَٱدْخُلُوٓا۟ أَبْوَٰبَ جَهَنَّمَ خَٰلِدِينَ فِيهَا فَلَبِئْسَ مَثْوَى ٱلْمُتَكَبِّرِينَ ﴿٢٩﴾

30. And it is said to those who fear God: "What has your Lord revealed?" They say: "Something good." To those who do good in this world is the good reward; and the Hereafter is surely much better. Blessed indeed is the abode of the God-fearing!

۞ وَقِيلَ لِلَّذِينَ ٱتَّقَوْا۟ مَاذَآ أَنزَلَ رَبُّكُمْ قَالُوا۟ خَيْرًا لِّلَّذِينَ أَحْسَنُوا۟ فِى هَٰذِهِ ٱلدُّنْيَا حَسَنَةٌ وَلَدَارُ ٱلْءَاخِرَةِ خَيْرٌ وَلَنِعْمَ دَارُ ٱلْمُتَّقِينَ ﴿٣٠﴾

31. Gardens of Eden they shall enter, beneath which rivers flow. They will have therein whatever they desire. Thus Allah rewards the God-fearing.

جَنَّٰتُ عَدْنٍ يَدْخُلُونَهَا تَجْرِى مِن تَحْتِهَا ٱلْأَنْهَٰرُ لَهُمْ فِيهَا مَا يَشَآءُونَ كَذَٰلِكَ يَجْزِى ٱللَّهُ ٱلْمُتَّقِينَ ﴿٣١﴾

32. Those whom the angels will carry off while in a state of grace, saying: "Peace upon you; enter Paradise for what you did."

ٱلَّذِينَ تَتَوَفَّىٰهُمُ ٱلْمَلَٰٓئِكَةُ طَيِّبِينَ يَقُولُونَ سَلَٰمٌ عَلَيْكُمُ ٱدْخُلُوا۟ ٱلْجَنَّةَ بِمَا كُنتُمْ تَعْمَلُونَ ﴿٣٢﴾

33. Do they only expect that the angels should come to them, or that your Lord's Command should come? This is what those who came before them did. Allah did not wrong them, but they wronged themselves.

هَلْ يَنظُرُونَ إِلَّآ أَن تَأْتِيَهُمُ ٱلْمَلَٰٓئِكَةُ أَوْ يَأْتِىَ أَمْرُ رَبِّكَ كَذَٰلِكَ فَعَلَ ٱلَّذِينَ مِن قَبْلِهِمْ وَمَا ظَلَمَهُمُ ٱللَّهُ وَلَٰكِن كَانُوٓا۟ أَنفُسَهُمْ يَظْلِمُونَ ﴿٣٣﴾

34. They were afflicted by the evil consequences of their actions, and were overtaken by what they mocked.

فَأَصَابَهُمْ سَيِّئَاتُ مَا عَمِلُوا۟ وَحَاقَ بِهِم مَّا كَانُوا۟ بِهِۦ يَسْتَهْزِءُونَ ﴿٣٤﴾

35. The idolaters say: "Had Allah pleased, neither we nor our fathers would have worshipped any [gods] besides Him; nor

وَقَالَ ٱلَّذِينَ أَشْرَكُوا۟ لَوْ شَآءَ ٱللَّهُ مَا عَبَدْنَا مِن دُونِهِۦ مِن شَىْءٍ نَّحْنُ وَلَآ ءَابَآؤُنَا وَلَا حَرَّمْنَا مِن دُونِهِۦ مِن

would we have forbidden anything against His will." [But] thus did those who came before them. What should the Messengers do except to deliver the plain Message?

36. We have sent forth to every nation a Messenger saying: "Worship Allah and avoid the idols. Some of them Allah guided and others were justly left in error. Travel, then, in the land and see what was the end of the denyers."

37. If you[539] are eager to guide them, Allah surely will not guide those whom He leads astray, and they will have no supporters.

38. And they solemnly swear by Allah that Allah will not raise from the dead anyone who dies. Surely, His is a true promise, but most people do not know.

39. [They shall be raised up] so as to make clear to them that whereof they differ, and that the unbelievers may know that they were lying.

40. Indeed, when We want a thing to be, We just say to it: "Be", and it comes to be.

41. To those who emigrated for Allah's Sake, after they had been oppressed, We shall provide a good life in this world; but the reward of the Hereafter is greater, if only they knew.

42. [They are] those who are patient, and in their Lord they put their trust.

43. We have sent forth, before you, none but men to whom We have revealed. So ask those who have knowledge[540] if you do not know.

---

539. Muhammad.
540. The Christians and Jews who have knowledge of their scriptures.

44. [We sent them] with clear proofs and scriptures. And We revealed to you the Reminder, so that you may make clear to mankind what has been revealed to them, and that, perchance, they may reflect.

بِٱلْبَيِّنَٰتِ وَٱلزُّبُرِ وَأَنزَلْنَآ إِلَيْكَ ٱلذِّكْرَ لِتُبَيِّنَ لِلنَّاسِ مَا نُزِّلَ إِلَيْهِمْ وَلَعَلَّهُمْ يَتَفَكَّرُونَ ﴿٤٤﴾

45. Do those who devise evil feel assured that Allah will not cause the earth to swallow them up, or that punishment will not overtake them from whence they do not expect?

أَفَأَمِنَ ٱلَّذِينَ مَكَرُوا۟ ٱلسَّيِّـَٔاتِ أَن يَخْسِفَ ٱللَّهُ بِهِمُ ٱلْأَرْضَ أَوْ يَأْتِيَهُمُ ٱلْعَذَابُ مِنْ حَيْثُ لَا يَشْعُرُونَ ﴿٤٥﴾

46. Or that He will not seize them in the course of their journeys, when they will not be able to escape?

أَوْ يَأْخُذَهُمْ فِى تَقَلُّبِهِمْ فَمَا هُم بِمُعْجِزِينَ ﴿٤٦﴾

47. Or that He will not seize them while in dread? Surely your Lord is Clement, Merciful.

أَوْ يَأْخُذَهُمْ عَلَىٰ تَخَوُّفٍ فَإِنَّ رَبَّكُمْ لَرَءُوفٌ رَّحِيمٌ ﴿٤٧﴾

48. Have they not considered all the things Allah has created, casting their shades right and left, and prostrating themselves before Allah in all humility?

أَوَلَمْ يَرَوْا۟ إِلَىٰ مَا خَلَقَ ٱللَّهُ مِن شَىْءٍ يَتَفَيَّؤُا۟ ظِلَٰلُهُۥ عَنِ ٱلْيَمِينِ وَٱلشَّمَآئِلِ سُجَّدًا لِّلَّهِ وَهُمْ دَٰخِرُونَ ﴿٤٨﴾

49. And before Allah all creatures in the heavens and on the earth, together with the angels, prostrate themselves, and they are not proud.

وَلِلَّهِ يَسْجُدُ مَا فِى ٱلسَّمَٰوَٰتِ وَمَا فِى ٱلْأَرْضِ مِن دَآبَّةٍ وَٱلْمَلَٰئِكَةُ وَهُمْ لَا يَسْتَكْبِرُونَ ﴿٤٩﴾

50. They fear their Lord, high above them, and they do what they are commanded.

يَخَافُونَ رَبَّهُم مِّن فَوْقِهِمْ وَيَفْعَلُونَ مَا يُؤْمَرُونَ ۩ ﴿٥٠﴾

51. Allah has said: "Do not take two gods; He is only One God. So fear Me Alone."

۞ وَقَالَ ٱللَّهُ لَا تَتَّخِذُوٓا۟ إِلَٰهَيْنِ ٱثْنَيْنِ إِنَّمَا هُوَ إِلَٰهٌ وَٰحِدٌ فَإِيَّٰىَ فَٱرْهَبُونِ ﴿٥١﴾

52. To Him belongs what is in the heavens and on earth, and to Him obedience is due always. Do you, then, fear anyone other than Allah?

وَلَهُۥ مَا فِى ٱلسَّمَٰوَٰتِ وَٱلْأَرْضِ وَلَهُ ٱلدِّينُ وَاصِبًا أَفَغَيْرَ ٱللَّهِ تَتَّقُونَ ﴿٥٢﴾

53. Whatever blessing you have is from Allah. Then, if adversity touches you, unto Him you turn for help.

وَمَا بِكُم مِّن نِّعْمَةٍ فَمِنَ ٱللَّهِ ثُمَّ إِذَا مَسَّكُمُ ٱلضُّرُّ فَإِلَيْهِ تَجْـَٔرُونَ ﴿٥٣﴾

54. Then, once He lifts the adversity from you, behold, some of you associate [other gods] with their Lord;

ثُمَّ إِذَا كَشَفَ ٱلضُّرَّ عَنكُمْ إِذَا فَرِيقٌ مِّنكُم بِرَبِّهِمْ يُشْرِكُونَ ﴿٥٤﴾

55. So as to deny what We gave them. Enjoy yourselves then, for soon you shall know.

لِيَكْفُرُوا۟ بِمَآ ءَاتَيْنَٰهُمْ فَتَمَتَّعُوا۟ فَسَوْفَ تَعْلَمُونَ ﴿٥٥﴾

56. And they set apart, for what they know not,[541] a portion of what We have provided for them. By Allah, you will be questioned about what you fabricated.

وَيَجْعَلُونَ لِمَا لَا يَعْلَمُونَ نَصِيبًا مِّمَّا رَزَقْنَاهُمْ تَاللَّهِ لَتُسْأَلُنَّ عَمَّا كُنتُمْ تَفْتَرُونَ ۝

57. And they ascribe to Allah daughters [glory be to Him!], but to themselves what they desire.[542]

وَيَجْعَلُونَ لِلَّهِ الْبَنَاتِ سُبْحَانَهُ وَلَهُم مَّا يَشْتَهُونَ ۝

58. And if the birth of a daughter is announced to any of them, his face turns black, and he is enraged.

وَإِذَا بُشِّرَ أَحَدُهُم بِالْأُنثَىٰ ظَلَّ وَجْهُهُ مُسْوَدًّا وَهُوَ كَظِيمٌ ۝

59. He hides from the people on account of the evil news broken to him; should he keep it in humiliation or bury it in the ground? Evil is what they judge!

يَتَوَارَىٰ مِنَ الْقَوْمِ مِن سُوءِ مَا بُشِّرَ بِهِ أَيُمْسِكُهُ عَلَىٰ هُونٍ أَمْ يَدُسُّهُ فِي التُّرَابِ أَلَا سَاءَ مَا يَحْكُمُونَ ۝

60. As for those who do not believe in the Hereafter, theirs is the evil exemplar; but Allah's is the sublime exemplar. He is the Almighty, the Wise.

لِلَّذِينَ لَا يُؤْمِنُونَ بِالْآخِرَةِ مَثَلُ السَّوْءِ وَلِلَّهِ الْمَثَلُ الْأَعْلَىٰ وَهُوَ الْعَزِيزُ الْحَكِيمُ ۝

61. Were Allah to take mankind to task for their wrongdoing, He would not leave upon it[543] a single creature; but He reprieves them until an appointed term. Then, when their term comes, they will not delay nor advance it a single hour.

وَلَوْ يُؤَاخِذُ اللَّهُ النَّاسَ بِظُلْمِهِم مَّا تَرَكَ عَلَيْهَا مِن دَابَّةٍ وَلَٰكِن يُؤَخِّرُهُمْ إِلَىٰ أَجَلٍ مُّسَمًّى فَإِذَا جَاءَ أَجَلُهُمْ لَا يَسْتَأْخِرُونَ سَاعَةً وَلَا يَسْتَقْدِمُونَ ۝

62. And they ascribe to Allah what they themselves dislike.[544] Their tongues utter the lie that theirs will be the best reward. There is no doubt that the Fire awaits them, and that they will be left [there].

وَيَجْعَلُونَ لِلَّهِ مَا يَكْرَهُونَ وَتَصِفُ أَلْسِنَتُهُمُ الْكَذِبَ أَنَّ لَهُمُ الْحُسْنَىٰ لَا جَرَمَ أَنَّ لَهُمُ النَّارَ وَأَنَّهُم مُّفْرَطُونَ ۝

63. By Allah, We sent forth [Messengers] to nations before you. But the Devil made their foul deeds seem fair to them. He is their patron, and they shall have a very painful punishment.

تَاللَّهِ لَقَدْ أَرْسَلْنَا إِلَىٰ أُمَمٍ مِّن قَبْلِكَ فَزَيَّنَ لَهُمُ الشَّيْطَانُ أَعْمَالَهُمْ فَهُوَ وَلِيُّهُمُ الْيَوْمَ وَلَهُمْ عَذَابٌ أَلِيمٌ ۝

---

541. Their idols.
542. That is, whereas they ascribe daughters to Allah, they ascribe sons to themselves.
543. The earth.
544. That is, they ascribe daughters to Him.

64. We have not revealed to you the Book but that you may make clear to them that wherein they differ, and as a guidance and a mercy to a people who believe.

65. It is Allah who sends down water from the sky reviving thereby the earth after its death. Surely, there is in that a sign to a people who listen.

66. And there is, surely, a lesson for you in the cattle. We give you to drink of what is in their bellies, between the bowels and blood, pure milk which is palatable to the drinkers.

67. And from the fruits of palms and vines, you get wine and fair provision. Surely, there is in that a sign to a people who understand.

68. And your Lord revealed to the bees: "Build homes in the mountains, the trees and in what men construct for you.

69. "Then eat from all the fruits and follow your Lord's smoothed paths." From their bellies comes out a syrup of different hues, wherein is healing for mankind. Surely, in that there is a sign for a people who reflect.

70. Allah created you, then He will cause you to die. For some of you will be brought back to the worst age, so that they will no longer know anything, after having acquired knowledge. Surely, Allah is All-Knowing, All-Powerful.

71. Allah has favoured some of you over the others in provision; but those favoured will not give their provision to those [slaves] whom their right hands possess so as to be equal therein. Will they then deny Allah's Blessings?

72. Allah has given you wives from among yourselves, and from your wives, sons and grandsons, and has provided you with all the good things. Will they believe in falsehood, then, and deny Allah's Blessings?

وَمَآ أَنزَلۡنَا عَلَيۡكَ ٱلۡكِتَٰبَ إِلَّا لِتُبَيِّنَ لَهُمُ ٱلَّذِى ٱخۡتَلَفُوا۟ فِيهِ وَهُدًى وَرَحۡمَةً لِّقَوۡمٍ يُؤۡمِنُونَ ۝٦٤

وَٱللَّهُ أَنزَلَ مِنَ ٱلسَّمَآءِ مَآءً فَأَحۡيَا بِهِ ٱلۡأَرۡضَ بَعۡدَ مَوۡتِهَآ إِنَّ فِى ذَٰلِكَ لَءَايَةً لِّقَوۡمٍ يَسۡمَعُونَ ۝٦٥

وَإِنَّ لَكُمۡ فِى ٱلۡأَنۡعَٰمِ لَعِبۡرَةً نُّسۡقِيكُم مِّمَّا فِى بُطُونِهِ مِنۢ بَيۡنِ فَرۡثٍ وَدَمٍ لَّبَنًا خَالِصًا سَآئِغًا لِّلشَّٰرِبِينَ ۝٦٦

وَمِن ثَمَرَٰتِ ٱلنَّخِيلِ وَٱلۡأَعۡنَٰبِ تَتَّخِذُونَ مِنۡهُ سَكَرًا وَرِزۡقًا حَسَنًا إِنَّ فِى ذَٰلِكَ لَءَايَةً لِّقَوۡمٍ يَعۡقِلُونَ ۝٦٧

وَأَوۡحَىٰ رَبُّكَ إِلَى ٱلنَّحۡلِ أَنِ ٱتَّخِذِى مِنَ ٱلۡجِبَالِ بُيُوتًا وَمِنَ ٱلشَّجَرِ وَمِمَّا يَعۡرِشُونَ ۝٦٨

ثُمَّ كُلِى مِن كُلِّ ٱلثَّمَرَٰتِ فَٱسۡلُكِى سُبُلَ رَبِّكِ ذُلُلًا يَخۡرُجُ مِنۢ بُطُونِهَا شَرَابٌ مُّخۡتَلِفٌ أَلۡوَٰنُهُ فِيهِ شِفَآءٌ لِّلنَّاسِ إِنَّ فِى ذَٰلِكَ لَءَايَةً لِّقَوۡمٍ يَتَفَكَّرُونَ ۝٦٩

وَٱللَّهُ خَلَقَكُمۡ ثُمَّ يَتَوَفَّىٰكُمۡ وَمِنكُم مَّن يُرَدُّ إِلَىٰٓ أَرۡذَلِ ٱلۡعُمُرِ لِكَىۡ لَا يَعۡلَمَ بَعۡدَ عِلۡمٍ شَيۡـًٔا إِنَّ ٱللَّهَ عَلِيمٌ قَدِيرٌ ۝٧٠

وَٱللَّهُ فَضَّلَ بَعۡضَكُمۡ عَلَىٰ بَعۡضٍ فِى ٱلرِّزۡقِ فَمَا ٱلَّذِينَ فُضِّلُوا۟ بِرَآدِّى رِزۡقِهِمۡ عَلَىٰ مَا مَلَكَتۡ أَيۡمَٰنُهُمۡ فَهُمۡ فِيهِ سَوَآءٌ أَفَبِنِعۡمَةِ ٱللَّهِ يَجۡحَدُونَ ۝٧١

وَٱللَّهُ جَعَلَ لَكُم مِّنۡ أَنفُسِكُمۡ أَزۡوَٰجًا وَجَعَلَ لَكُم مِّنۡ أَزۡوَٰجِكُم بَنِينَ وَحَفَدَةً وَرَزَقَكُم مِّنَ ٱلطَّيِّبَٰتِ أَفَبِٱلۡبَٰطِلِ يُؤۡمِنُونَ وَبِنِعۡمَتِ ٱللَّهِ هُمۡ يَكۡفُرُونَ ۝٧٢

73. And they worship, besides Allah, what cannot provide anything for them from the heavens or the earth and can do nothing.

74. Do not set forth parables for Allah. Surely Allah knows and you do not know.

75. Allah sets forth this parable. Consider an owned slave who is unable to do anything; and one for whom We have provided from Our Bounty a fair provision, and he spends from it secretly and publicly. Are they, then, alike? Praise be to Allah; but most of them do not know.

76. And Allah sets forth the parable of two men. One of them is dumb, unable to do anything and is a burden on his master; wherever he directs him, he brings no good. Is he equal to him who enjoins justice and is upon a straight path?

77. To Allah belongs the Unseen of the heavens and the earth. The coming of the Hour is only like the twinkling of the eye, or even nearer. Surely, Allah has power over everything.

78. And Allah brought you out of your mothers' bellies knowing nothing; and gave you hearing, sight and hearts, that perchance you may give thanks.

79. Do they not see the birds subservient in the vault of the sky, nothing holding them aloft but Allah? Surely, there is in that signs for a people who believe.

80. Allah has made of your homes places for you to dwell in, and has made for you from the hides of cattle light houses to carry on the day of moving and on the day of settling down. And from their wools and their furs and their hair He [has made for you] furnishings and means of enjoyment for a while.

وَيَعْبُدُونَ مِن دُونِ ٱللَّهِ مَا لَا يَمْلِكُ لَهُمْ رِزْقًا مِّنَ ٱلسَّمَٰوَٰتِ وَٱلْأَرْضِ شَيْئًا وَلَا يَسْتَطِيعُونَ ۝

فَلَا تَضْرِبُوا لِلَّهِ ٱلْأَمْثَالَ إِنَّ ٱللَّهَ يَعْلَمُ وَأَنتُمْ لَا تَعْلَمُونَ ۝

۞ ضَرَبَ ٱللَّهُ مَثَلًا عَبْدًا مَّمْلُوكًا لَّا يَقْدِرُ عَلَىٰ شَيْءٍ وَمَن رَّزَقْنَٰهُ مِنَّا رِزْقًا حَسَنًا فَهُوَ يُنفِقُ مِنْهُ سِرًّا وَجَهْرًا هَلْ يَسْتَوُۥنَ ٱلْحَمْدُ لِلَّهِ بَلْ أَكْثَرُهُمْ لَا يَعْلَمُونَ ۝

وَضَرَبَ ٱللَّهُ مَثَلًا رَّجُلَيْنِ أَحَدُهُمَآ أَبْكَمُ لَا يَقْدِرُ عَلَىٰ شَيْءٍ وَهُوَ كَلٌّ عَلَىٰ مَوْلَىٰهُ أَيْنَمَا يُوَجِّههُّ لَا يَأْتِ بِخَيْرٍ هَلْ يَسْتَوِى هُوَ وَمَن يَأْمُرُ بِٱلْعَدْلِ وَهُوَ عَلَىٰ صِرَٰطٍ مُّسْتَقِيمٍ ۝

وَلِلَّهِ غَيْبُ ٱلسَّمَٰوَٰتِ وَٱلْأَرْضِ وَمَآ أَمْرُ ٱلسَّاعَةِ إِلَّا كَلَمْحِ ٱلْبَصَرِ أَوْ هُوَ أَقْرَبُ إِنَّ ٱللَّهَ عَلَىٰ كُلِّ شَيْءٍ قَدِيرٌ ۝

وَٱللَّهُ أَخْرَجَكُم مِّنۢ بُطُونِ أُمَّهَٰتِكُمْ لَا تَعْلَمُونَ شَيْئًا وَجَعَلَ لَكُمُ ٱلسَّمْعَ وَٱلْأَبْصَٰرَ وَٱلْأَفْـِٔدَةَ لَعَلَّكُمْ تَشْكُرُونَ ۝

أَلَمْ يَرَوْا إِلَى ٱلطَّيْرِ مُسَخَّرَٰتٍ فِى جَوِّ ٱلسَّمَآءِ مَا يُمْسِكُهُنَّ إِلَّا ٱللَّهُ إِنَّ فِى ذَٰلِكَ لَءَايَٰتٍ لِّقَوْمٍ يُؤْمِنُونَ ۝

وَٱللَّهُ جَعَلَ لَكُم مِّنۢ بُيُوتِكُمْ سَكَنًا وَجَعَلَ لَكُم مِّن جُلُودِ ٱلْأَنْعَٰمِ بُيُوتًا تَسْتَخِفُّونَهَا يَوْمَ ظَعْنِكُمْ وَيَوْمَ إِقَامَتِكُمْ وَمِنْ أَصْوَافِهَا وَأَوْبَارِهَا وَأَشْعَارِهَآ أَثَٰثًا وَمَتَٰعًا إِلَىٰ حِينٍ ۝

81. Allah has made for you from what He created, sunshades, and from the mountains, places of retreat, and has given you garments to protect you from the heat and coats of mail to protect you while fighting. Thus He perfects His Blessing to you so that you may submit.

82. Then, if they turn away, your duty is only to deliver the clear Message.

83. They know Allah's Blessing, then they deny it; and most of them are ungrateful.

84. And on the Day when We raise from every nation a witness, the unbelievers shall not be given leave or allowed to repent.

85. And when the wrongdoers behold the punishment, it shall not be lightened for them and they shall not be reprieved.

86. And when those who associated other gods with Allah see their associates they shall say: "Our Lord, these are our associates whom we used to call upon besides you." But their associates will retort: "Surely you are liars."

87. And they shall offer Allah submission on that Day; and what they used to fabricate shall stray away from them.

88. [As for] those who disbelieve and debar people from the Path of Allah, We will add punishment to their punishment on account of the mischief they used to make.

89. On the Day when We shall raise up in each nation a witness against them from among themselves, We will bring you[545] as a witness against them. We have revealed to you the Book[546] which explains everything, as a guide, a mercy and good news to those who submit.

وَٱللَّهُ جَعَلَ لَكُم مِّمَّا خَلَقَ ظِلَـٰلًا وَجَعَلَ لَكُم مِّنَ ٱلْجِبَالِ أَكْنَـٰنًا وَجَعَلَ لَكُمْ سَرَٰبِيلَ تَقِيكُمُ ٱلْحَرَّ وَسَرَٰبِيلَ تَقِيكُم بَأْسَكُمْ كَذَٰلِكَ يُتِمُّ نِعْمَتَهُۥ عَلَيْكُمْ لَعَلَّكُمْ تُسْلِمُونَ ۝

فَإِن تَوَلَّوْا۟ فَإِنَّمَا عَلَيْكَ ٱلْبَلَـٰغُ ٱلْمُبِينُ ۝

يَعْرِفُونَ نِعْمَتَ ٱللَّهِ ثُمَّ يُنكِرُونَهَا وَأَكْثَرُهُمُ ٱلْكَـٰفِرُونَ ۝

وَيَوْمَ نَبْعَثُ مِن كُلِّ أُمَّةٍ شَهِيدًا ثُمَّ لَا يُؤْذَنُ لِلَّذِينَ كَفَرُوا۟ وَلَا هُمْ يُسْتَعْتَبُونَ ۝

وَإِذَا رَءَا ٱلَّذِينَ ظَلَمُوا۟ ٱلْعَذَابَ فَلَا يُخَفَّفُ عَنْهُمْ وَلَا هُمْ يُنظَرُونَ ۝

وَإِذَا رَءَا ٱلَّذِينَ أَشْرَكُوا۟ شُرَكَآءَهُمْ قَالُوا۟ رَبَّنَا هَـٰٓؤُلَآءِ شُرَكَآؤُنَا ٱلَّذِينَ كُنَّا نَدْعُوا۟ مِن دُونِكَ فَأَلْقَوْا۟ إِلَيْهِمُ ٱلْقَوْلَ إِنَّكُمْ لَكَـٰذِبُونَ ۝

وَأَلْقَوْا۟ إِلَى ٱللَّهِ يَوْمَئِذٍ ٱلسَّلَمَ وَضَلَّ عَنْهُم مَّا كَانُوا۟ يَفْتَرُونَ ۝

ٱلَّذِينَ كَفَرُوا۟ وَصَدُّوا۟ عَن سَبِيلِ ٱللَّهِ زِدْنَـٰهُمْ عَذَابًا فَوْقَ ٱلْعَذَابِ بِمَا كَانُوا۟ يُفْسِدُونَ ۝

وَيَوْمَ نَبْعَثُ فِى كُلِّ أُمَّةٍ شَهِيدًا عَلَيْهِم مِّنْ أَنفُسِهِمْ وَجِئْنَا بِكَ شَهِيدًا عَلَىٰ هَـٰٓؤُلَآءِ وَنَزَّلْنَا عَلَيْكَ ٱلْكِتَـٰبَ تِبْيَـٰنًا لِّكُلِّ شَىْءٍ وَهُدًى وَرَحْمَةً وَبُشْرَىٰ لِلْمُسْلِمِينَ ۝

---

545. Muhammad.
546. The Qur'an.

90. Allah enjoins justice, charity and the giving to kindred; He forbids indecency, evil and aggression. He admonishes you that you may take heed.

91. Fulfil the Covenant of Allah when you make a covenant [with Him], and do not break the oaths after you solemnly affirm them, taking Allah as Witness. Surely Allah knows what you do.

92. And do not be like her who unravels her yarn after she has spun it first; taking your oaths as means of deception among you, because one party is more numerous than another. Allah only tries you by this, and He will certainly make clear to you on the Day of Resurrection that whereon you differ.

93. Had Allah pleased, He would have made you a single nation, but He leads whom He pleases astray and guides whom He pleases. And you will surely be questioned about what you did.

94. And do not make your oaths as means of deception among you, lest a foot should slip[547] after being firm, and lest you should taste evil on account of debarring others from Allah's Path. Grievous will be your punishment!

95. Do not sell Allah's Covenant for a small price. Surely what is with Allah is better for you, if only you knew.

96. What you have will be exhausted, and what is with Allah remains [undiminished]. And We will give the steadfast a better reward than the best of their actions [deserved].

---

547. That is, lest your faith be shaken.

97. Whoever does a good deed, whether male or female, while a believer, We shall make him live a good life; and We will give them a better reward than what they have done.

98. When you recite the Qur'an, seek refuge with Allah from the accursed Devil.

99. He has no authority over those who believe and have put their trust in their Lord.

100. His authority is only over those who befriend him and who associate others with Him.[548]

101. And if We replace a verse by another - and Allah knows best what He reveals - they say: "You are only a forger." Surely, most of them do not know.

102. Say: "The Holy Spirit[549] has brought it down from your Lord in truth, in order to reassure the believers, and as a guidance and good news to those who submit.

103. And We surely know that they say: "Surely a mortal teaches him." The tongue of him to whom they allude is foreign, whereas this is a clear Arabic tongue.

104. Those who do not believe in Allah's Revelations shall not be guided by Allah, and a very painful punishment awaits them.

105. It is those who do not believe in Allah's Revelations that fabricate falsehood. It is they who lie.

106. He who disbelieves in Allah after he has believed, except him who is compelled, but his heart remains firm in belief;[550] but those whose hearts rejoice in disbelief shall incur Allah's Wrath and a grievous punishment awaits them.

مَنْ عَمِلَ صَٰلِحًا مِّن ذَكَرٍ أَوْ أُنثَىٰ وَهُوَ مُؤْمِنٌ فَلَنُحْيِيَنَّهُ حَيَوٰةً طَيِّبَةً وَلَنَجْزِيَنَّهُمْ أَجْرَهُم بِأَحْسَنِ مَا كَانُوا۟ يَعْمَلُونَ ﴿٩٧﴾

فَإِذَا قَرَأْتَ ٱلْقُرْءَانَ فَٱسْتَعِذْ بِٱللَّهِ مِنَ ٱلشَّيْطَٰنِ ٱلرَّجِيمِ ﴿٩٨﴾

إِنَّهُۥ لَيْسَ لَهُۥ سُلْطَٰنٌ عَلَى ٱلَّذِينَ ءَامَنُوا۟ وَعَلَىٰ رَبِّهِمْ يَتَوَكَّلُونَ ﴿٩٩﴾

إِنَّمَا سُلْطَٰنُهُۥ عَلَى ٱلَّذِينَ يَتَوَلَّوْنَهُۥ وَٱلَّذِينَ هُم بِهِۦ مُشْرِكُونَ ﴿١٠٠﴾

وَإِذَا بَدَّلْنَآ ءَايَةً مَّكَانَ ءَايَةٍ وَٱللَّهُ أَعْلَمُ بِمَا يُنَزِّلُ قَالُوٓا۟ إِنَّمَآ أَنتَ مُفْتَرٍ بَلْ أَكْثَرُهُمْ لَا يَعْلَمُونَ ﴿١٠١﴾

قُلْ نَزَّلَهُۥ رُوحُ ٱلْقُدُسِ مِن رَّبِّكَ بِٱلْحَقِّ لِيُثَبِّتَ ٱلَّذِينَ ءَامَنُوا۟ وَهُدًى وَبُشْرَىٰ لِلْمُسْلِمِينَ ﴿١٠٢﴾

وَلَقَدْ نَعْلَمُ أَنَّهُمْ يَقُولُونَ إِنَّمَا يُعَلِّمُهُۥ بَشَرٌ لِّسَانُ ٱلَّذِى يُلْحِدُونَ إِلَيْهِ أَعْجَمِىٌّ وَهَٰذَا لِسَانٌ عَرَبِىٌّ مُّبِينٌ ﴿١٠٣﴾

إِنَّ ٱلَّذِينَ لَا يُؤْمِنُونَ بِـَٔايَٰتِ ٱللَّهِ لَا يَهْدِيهِمُ ٱللَّهُ وَلَهُمْ عَذَابٌ أَلِيمٌ ﴿١٠٤﴾

إِنَّمَا يَفْتَرِى ٱلْكَذِبَ ٱلَّذِينَ لَا يُؤْمِنُونَ بِـَٔايَٰتِ ٱللَّهِ وَأُو۟لَٰٓئِكَ هُمُ ٱلْكَٰذِبُونَ ﴿١٠٥﴾

مَن كَفَرَ بِٱللَّهِ مِنۢ بَعْدِ إِيمَٰنِهِۦٓ إِلَّا مَنْ أُكْرِهَ وَقَلْبُهُۥ مُطْمَئِنٌّۢ بِٱلْإِيمَٰنِ وَلَٰكِن مَّن شَرَحَ بِٱلْكُفْرِ صَدْرًا فَعَلَيْهِمْ غَضَبٌ مِّنَ ٱللَّهِ وَلَهُمْ عَذَابٌ عَظِيمٌ ﴿١٠٦﴾

---

548. Allah.
549. Gabriel.
550. Will be forgiven.

107. That is because they love the present life more than the Hereafter, and because Allah does not guide the unbelievers.

108. They are those whose hearts, ears and eyes Allah has sealed; and those are the heedless.

109. There is no doubt that in the Hereafter they shall be the losers.

110. As for those who emigrated after they had been persecuted, then fought in the Way of Allah and stood fast, your Lord is Forgiving, Merciful.

111. The Day every soul shall come pleading for itself, and every soul shall be paid in full for what it did, they shall not be dealt with unjustly.

112. Allah has given as a parable a town which was safe and secure, and its provision came in abundance from every side; then it denied Allah's Blessings, and so Allah made it taste the engulfing hunger and fear on account of what they[551] used to do.

113. A Messenger from among them came to them, but they denounced him, and so they were smitten by Our punishment for being wrongdoers.

114. Eat then from the lawful and good things which Allah provided for you, and give thanks for Allah's Blessing, if you truly worship Him.

115. He has forbidden you carrion, blood, the flesh of swine and that over which any name other than that of Allah is invoked. But whoever is compelled while neither transgressing nor exceeding the bounds, Allah is All-Forgiving, Merciful.

---

551. Its people.

116. And when you speak do not lie by saying: "This is lawful and this is unlawful", in order to impute lies to Allah. Surely those who impute lies to Allah will not prosper.

117. A little enjoyment and then a great punishment is in store for them.

118. We forbade the Jews what We have related to you earlier. And We did not wrong them, but they wronged themselves.

119. Surely, with respect to those who commit evil in ignorance, and later repent and make amends, your Lord thereafter is All-Forgiving, Merciful.

120. Indeed, Abraham was a model [of virtue], obedient to Allah and upright; and he was not one of the polytheists.

121. [He was] thankful for His Blessings, and Allah elected and guided him to a Straight Path.

122. We made him praiseworthy in this world, and in the Hereafter he will be one of the righteous.

123. Then We revealed to you:[552] "Follow the religion of Abraham, the upright; for he was not one of the polytheists."

124. The Sabbath was ordained only for those who differed with respect to it.[553] Your Lord shall decide between them on the Day of Resurrection, regarding that wherein they differed.

125. Call to the Way of your Lord with wisdom and mild exhortation, and argue with them in the best manner. Your Lord surely knows best those who stray from His Path, and He knows well those who are rightly guided.

وَلَا تَقُولُوا لِمَا تَصِفُ أَلْسِنَتُكُمُ ٱلْكَذِبَ هَٰذَا حَلَٰلٌ وَهَٰذَا حَرَامٌ لِّتَفْتَرُوا عَلَى ٱللَّهِ ٱلْكَذِبَ إِنَّ ٱلَّذِينَ يَفْتَرُونَ عَلَى ٱللَّهِ ٱلْكَذِبَ لَا يُفْلِحُونَ ﴿١١٦﴾

مَتَٰعٌ قَلِيلٌ وَلَهُمْ عَذَابٌ أَلِيمٌ ﴿١١٧﴾

وَعَلَى ٱلَّذِينَ هَادُوا حَرَّمْنَا مَا قَصَصْنَا عَلَيْكَ مِن قَبْلُ وَمَا ظَلَمْنَٰهُمْ وَلَٰكِن كَانُوا أَنفُسَهُمْ يَظْلِمُونَ ﴿١١٨﴾

ثُمَّ إِنَّ رَبَّكَ لِلَّذِينَ عَمِلُوا ٱلسُّوٓءَ بِجَهَٰلَةٍ ثُمَّ تَابُوا مِنۢ بَعْدِ ذَٰلِكَ وَأَصْلَحُوٓا إِنَّ رَبَّكَ مِنۢ بَعْدِهَا لَغَفُورٌ رَّحِيمٌ ﴿١١٩﴾

إِنَّ إِبْرَٰهِيمَ كَانَ أُمَّةً قَانِتًا لِّلَّهِ حَنِيفًا وَلَمْ يَكُ مِنَ ٱلْمُشْرِكِينَ ﴿١٢٠﴾

شَاكِرًا لِّأَنْعُمِهِ ٱجْتَبَٰهُ وَهَدَىٰهُ إِلَىٰ صِرَٰطٍ مُّسْتَقِيمٍ ﴿١٢١﴾

وَءَاتَيْنَٰهُ فِى ٱلدُّنْيَا حَسَنَةً وَإِنَّهُ فِى ٱلْءَاخِرَةِ لَمِنَ ٱلصَّٰلِحِينَ ﴿١٢٢﴾

ثُمَّ أَوْحَيْنَآ إِلَيْكَ أَنِ ٱتَّبِعْ مِلَّةَ إِبْرَٰهِيمَ حَنِيفًا وَمَا كَانَ مِنَ ٱلْمُشْرِكِينَ ﴿١٢٣﴾

إِنَّمَا جُعِلَ ٱلسَّبْتُ عَلَى ٱلَّذِينَ ٱخْتَلَفُوا فِيهِ وَإِنَّ رَبَّكَ لَيَحْكُمُ بَيْنَهُمْ يَوْمَ ٱلْقِيَٰمَةِ فِيمَا كَانُوا فِيهِ يَخْتَلِفُونَ ﴿١٢٤﴾

ٱدْعُ إِلَىٰ سَبِيلِ رَبِّكَ بِٱلْحِكْمَةِ وَٱلْمَوْعِظَةِ ٱلْحَسَنَةِ وَجَٰدِلْهُم بِٱلَّتِى هِىَ أَحْسَنُ إِنَّ رَبَّكَ هُوَ أَعْلَمُ بِمَن ضَلَّ عَن سَبِيلِهِۦ وَهُوَ أَعْلَمُ بِٱلْمُهْتَدِينَ ﴿١٢٥﴾

---

552. Muhammad.
553. The Jews.

126. If you punish, then let your punishment be proportionate to the wrong done to you. Yet should you forbear, that is truly better for those who forbear.

وَإِنْ عَاقَبْتُمْ فَعَاقِبُوا بِمِثْلِ مَا عُوقِبْتُم بِهِ وَلَئِن صَبَرْتُمْ لَهُوَ خَيْرٌ لِّلصَّابِرِينَ ﴿١٢٦﴾

127. Be patient; yet your patience is only through Allah. Do not grieve for them,[554] and do not be distressed on account of what they devise.

وَاصْبِرْ وَمَا صَبْرُكَ إِلَّا بِاللَّهِ وَلَا تَحْزَنْ عَلَيْهِمْ وَلَا تَكُ فِي ضَيْقٍ مِّمَّا يَمْكُرُونَ ﴿١٢٧﴾

128. Allah is with those who are God-fearing and those who are beneficent.

إِنَّ اللَّهَ مَعَ الَّذِينَ اتَّقَوا وَّالَّذِينَ هُم مُّحْسِنُونَ ﴿١٢٨﴾

Sûrat Al-Isrâ', (The Night Journey) 17

سُورَةُ الإسراء

In the Name of Allah, the Compassionate, the Merciful

بِسْمِ اللَّهِ الرَّحْمَنِ الرَّحِيمِ

1. Glory be to Him Who caused His servant to travel by night from the Sacred Mosque to the Farthest Mosque, whose precincts We have blessed, in order to show him some of Our Signs. He is indeed the All-Hearing, the All-Seeing.

سُبْحَانَ الَّذِي أَسْرَىٰ بِعَبْدِهِ لَيْلًا مِّنَ الْمَسْجِدِ الْحَرَامِ إِلَى الْمَسْجِدِ الْأَقْصَى الَّذِي بَارَكْنَا حَوْلَهُ لِنُرِيَهُ مِنْ آيَاتِنَا إِنَّهُ هُوَ السَّمِيعُ الْبَصِيرُ ﴿١﴾

2. We gave Moses the Book and made it a guidance to the Children of Israel [saying]: "Do not take besides Me any other guardian."

وَآتَيْنَا مُوسَى الْكِتَابَ وَجَعَلْنَاهُ هُدًى لِّبَنِي إِسْرَائِيلَ أَلَّا تَتَّخِذُوا مِن دُونِي وَكِيلًا ﴿٢﴾

3. O progeny of those whom We caused to be carried along with Noah; He was truly a very thankful servant.

ذُرِّيَّةَ مَنْ حَمَلْنَا مَعَ نُوحٍ إِنَّهُ كَانَ عَبْدًا شَكُورًا ﴿٣﴾

4. And We decreed for the Children of Israel in the Book: "You shall make mischief in the land twice, and you shall become very haughty."

وَقَضَيْنَا إِلَىٰ بَنِي إِسْرَائِيلَ فِي الْكِتَابِ لَتُفْسِدُنَّ فِي الْأَرْضِ مَرَّتَيْنِ وَلَتَعْلُنَّ عُلُوًّا كَبِيرًا ﴿٤﴾

5. And when the punishment for the first [making of mischief] became due, We sent forth against you servants of Ours possessing great might who went after you in your country. Thus Our threat was accomplished.

فَإِذَا جَاءَ وَعْدُ أُولَاهُمَا بَعَثْنَا عَلَيْكُمْ عِبَادًا لَّنَا أُولِي بَأْسٍ شَدِيدٍ فَجَاسُوا خِلَالَ الدِّيَارِ وَكَانَ وَعْدًا مَّفْعُولًا ﴿٥﴾

---

554. The evildoers or unbelievers.

6. Then, We gave you back your turn against them and aided you with wealth and children and increased you in number.

ثُمَّ رَدَدْنَا لَكُمُ ٱلْكَرَّةَ عَلَيْهِمْ وَأَمْدَدْنَكُم بِأَمْوَلٍ وَبَنِينَ وَجَعَلْنَكُمْ أَكْثَرَ نَفِيرًا ﴿٦﴾

7. [And We said]: "If you do good, you do good for yourselves, and if you do evil, you do it for yourselves too. And when the punishment for the second [making of mischief] became due, [We sent Our men again] to afflict you, and to enter the Mosque as they entered it the first time and to utterly destroy what they conquered.

إِنْ أَحْسَنتُمْ أَحْسَنتُمْ لِأَنفُسِكُمْ وَإِنْ أَسَأْتُمْ فَلَهَا فَإِذَا جَاءَ وَعْدُ ٱلْأَخِرَةِ لِيَسُوءُوا وُجُوهَكُمْ وَلِيَدْخُلُوا ٱلْمَسْجِدَ كَمَا دَخَلُوهُ أَوَّلَ مَرَّةٍ وَلِيُتَبِّرُوا مَا عَلَوْا تَتْبِيرًا ﴿٧﴾

8. It may be that your Lord will have mercy on you; but if you go back [to mischief], We shall come back and make Hell a prison for the unbelievers.

عَسَىٰ رَبُّكُمْ أَن يَرْحَمَكُمْ وَإِنْ عُدتُّمْ عُدْنَا وَجَعَلْنَا جَهَنَّمَ لِلْكَفِرِينَ حَصِيرًا ﴿٨﴾

9. Surely, this Qur'an guides to that which is most upright and announces to the believers who do good works the good news that they shall have a great reward.

إِنَّ هَذَا ٱلْقُرْءَانَ يَهْدِى لِلَّتِى هِىَ أَقْوَمُ وَيُبَشِّرُ ٱلْمُؤْمِنِينَ ٱلَّذِينَ يَعْمَلُونَ ٱلصَّلِحَتِ أَنَّ لَهُمْ أَجْرًا كَبِيرًا ﴿٩﴾

10. And those who do not believe in the Hereafter, We have prepared for them a very painful punishment.

وَأَنَّ ٱلَّذِينَ لَا يُؤْمِنُونَ بِٱلْأَخِرَةِ أَعْتَدْنَا لَهُمْ عَذَابًا أَلِيمًا ﴿١٠﴾

11. Man prays for evil, just as he prays for good; and man is very hasty.

وَيَدْعُ ٱلْإِنسَنُ بِٱلشَّرِّ دُعَاءَهُ بِٱلْخَيْرِ وَكَانَ ٱلْإِنسَنُ عَجُولًا ﴿١١﴾

12. We have made the night and the day two signs; then We blotted out the sign of the night and made the sign of the day luminous, that you may seek bounty from your Lord, and learn the number of years and the reckoning, and everything We have expounded clearly.

وَجَعَلْنَا ٱلَّيْلَ وَٱلنَّهَارَ ءَايَتَيْنِ فَمَحَوْنَا ءَايَةَ ٱلَّيْلِ وَجَعَلْنَا ءَايَةَ ٱلنَّهَارِ مُبْصِرَةً لِّتَبْتَغُوا فَضْلًا مِّن رَّبِّكُمْ وَلِتَعْلَمُوا عَدَدَ ٱلسِّنِينَ وَٱلْحِسَابَ وَكُلَّ شَىْءٍ فَصَّلْنَهُ تَفْصِيلًا ﴿١٢﴾

13. And every man's omen We have fastened to his neck; and on the Day of Resurrection, We shall bring out for him a book which he will find spread wide open, [saying to him]:

وَكُلَّ إِنسَنٍ أَلْزَمْنَهُ طَئِرَهُ فِى عُنُقِهِ وَنُخْرِجُ لَهُ يَوْمَ ٱلْقِيَمَةِ كِتَبًا يَلْقَىٰهُ مَنشُورًا ﴿١٣﴾

14. "Read your book; your own soul shall suffice today as a reckoner against you."

ٱقْرَأْ كِتَبَكَ كَفَىٰ بِنَفْسِكَ ٱلْيَوْمَ عَلَيْكَ حَسِيبًا ﴿١٤﴾

15. He who is well-guided is well-guided for himself, and he who goes astray, goes astray to his own loss. No soul shall bear the burden of another soul, and We do not punish until We have sent a Messenger.

مَّنِ اهْتَدَىٰ فَإِنَّمَا يَهْتَدِى لِنَفْسِهِ وَمَن ضَلَّ فَإِنَّمَا يَضِلُّ عَلَيْهَا وَلَا تَزِرُ وَازِرَةٌ وِزْرَ أُخْرَىٰ وَمَا كُنَّا مُعَذِّبِينَ حَتَّىٰ نَبْعَثَ رَسُولًا ۝

16. And when We want to destroy a city, We command those of its people who are given to luxury; but as they transgress therein Our sentence against it is pronounced and We utterly destroy it.

وَإِذَآ أَرَدْنَآ أَن نُّهْلِكَ قَرْيَةً أَمَرْنَا مُتْرَفِيهَا فَفَسَقُوا فِيهَا فَحَقَّ عَلَيْهَا الْقَوْلُ فَدَمَّرْنَاهَا تَدْمِيرًا ۝

17. How many generations We have destroyed since Noah! It suffices that your Lord knows and sees the sins of His servants.

وَكَمْ أَهْلَكْنَا مِنَ الْقُرُونِ مِنۢ بَعْدِ نُوحٍ وَكَفَىٰ بِرَبِّكَ بِذُنُوبِ عِبَادِهِ خَبِيرًۢا بَصِيرًا ۝

18. He who desires the transitory life, We hasten to him and to whomsoever We desire whatever We please. Later We consign him to Hell in which he will burn despised and rejected.

مَّن كَانَ يُرِيدُ الْعَاجِلَةَ عَجَّلْنَا لَهُۥ فِيهَا مَا نَشَآءُ لِمَن نُّرِيدُ ثُمَّ جَعَلْنَا لَهُۥ جَهَنَّمَ يَصْلَاهَا مَذْمُومًا مَّدْحُورًا ۝

19. But as for those who desire the Hereafter and strive for it, as they should, while they are believers, their effort will be appreciated.

وَمَنْ أَرَادَ الْءَاخِرَةَ وَسَعَىٰ لَهَا سَعْيَهَا وَهُوَ مُؤْمِنٌ فَأُو۟لَٰٓئِكَ كَانَ سَعْيُهُم مَّشْكُورًا ۝

20. For them all - these and those - We shall provide from Allah's Bounty; and the Bounty of your Lord will not be denied to anyone.

كُلًّا نُّمِدُّ هَٰٓؤُلَآءِ وَهَٰٓؤُلَآءِ مِنْ عَطَآءِ رَبِّكَ وَمَا كَانَ عَطَآءُ رَبِّكَ مَحْظُورًا ۝

21. Behold how We have made some of them surpass the others, although the Hereafter is far higher in rank and more preferable.

انظُرْ كَيْفَ فَضَّلْنَا بَعْضَهُمْ عَلَىٰ بَعْضٍ وَلَلْءَاخِرَةُ أَكْبَرُ دَرَجَٰتٍ وَأَكْبَرُ تَفْضِيلًا ۝

22. Do not set up another god with Allah, lest you be despised and forsaken.

لَّا تَجْعَلْ مَعَ اللَّهِ إِلَٰهًا ءَاخَرَ فَتَقْعُدَ مَذْمُومًا مَّخْذُولًا ۝

23. Your Lord has decreed that you worship none but Him and to be kind to your parents. If either of them or both reach old age with you, do not say to them "Fie", nor tell them off, but say to them kind words.

۞ وَقَضَىٰ رَبُّكَ أَلَّا تَعْبُدُوٓا۟ إِلَّآ إِيَّاهُ وَبِالْوَٰلِدَيْنِ إِحْسَٰنًا إِمَّا يَبْلُغَنَّ عِندَكَ الْكِبَرَ أَحَدُهُمَآ أَوْ كِلَاهُمَا فَلَا تَقُل لَّهُمَآ أُفٍّ وَلَا تَنْهَرْهُمَا وَقُل لَّهُمَا قَوْلًا كَرِيمًا ۝

24. And lower to them the wing of humility out of mercy and say: "Lord, have mercy on them, as they took care of me when I was a child."

وَاخْفِضْ لَهُمَا جَنَاحَ الذُّلِّ مِنَ الرَّحْمَةِ وَقُل رَّبِّ ارْحَمْهُمَا كَمَا رَبَّيَانِى صَغِيرًا ۝

25. Your Lord knows best what is in your hearts. If you are righteous, He is All-Forgiving to those who repent.

وَرَبُّكُمْ أَعْلَمُ بِمَا فِي نُفُوسِكُمْ إِن تَكُونُوا صَلِحِينَ فَإِنَّهُ كَانَ لِلْأَوَّبِينَ غَفُورًا ﴿٢٥﴾

26. And give the kinsman his due, and to the destitute and the wayfarer, and do not squander your wealth wastefully.

وَءَاتِ ذَا الْقُرْبَى حَقَّهُ وَالْمِسْكِينَ وَابْنَ السَّبِيلِ وَلَا تُبَذِّرْ تَبْذِيرًا ﴿٢٦﴾

27. Surely the spendthrifts are the brothers of the devils; and the Devil is ever ungrateful to his Lord.

إِنَّ الْمُبَذِّرِينَ كَانُوا إِخْوَانَ الشَّيَطِينِ وَكَانَ الشَّيْطَنُ لِرَبِّهِ كَفُورًا ﴿٢٧﴾

28. But if you turn away from them,[555] seeking a mercy[556] you expect from your Lord, then speak to them kindly.

وَإِمَّا تُعْرِضَنَّ عَنْهُمُ ابْتِغَاءَ رَحْمَةٍ مِّن رَّبِّكَ تَرْجُوهَا فَقُل لَّهُمْ قَوْلًا مَّيْسُورًا ﴿٢٨﴾

29. Do not keep your hand chained to your neck, nor spread it out fully, lest you sit around condemned and reduced to poverty.

وَلَا تَجْعَلْ يَدَكَ مَغْلُولَةً إِلَى عُنُقِكَ وَلَا تَبْسُطْهَا كُلَّ الْبَسْطِ فَتَقْعُدَ مَلُومًا مَّحْسُورًا ﴿٢٩﴾

30. Surely your Lord gives generously to whom He pleases, and He gives sparingly [to whom He pleases]. He knows and observes His servants well.

إِنَّ رَبَّكَ يَبْسُطُ الرِّزْقَ لِمَن يَشَاءُ وَيَقْدِرُ إِنَّهُ كَانَ بِعِبَادِهِ خَبِيرًا بَصِيرًا ﴿٣٠﴾

31. Do not kill your children for fear of poverty. We will provide for you and for them. To kill them is a great sin.

وَلَا تَقْتُلُوا أَوْلَدَكُمْ خَشْيَةَ إِمْلَقٍ نَّحْنُ نَرْزُقُهُمْ وَإِيَّاكُمْ إِنَّ قَتْلَهُمْ كَانَ خِطْئًا كَبِيرًا ﴿٣١﴾

32. Do not draw near adultery; it is an abomination and an evil way.

وَلَا تَقْرَبُوا الزِّنَى إِنَّهُ كَانَ فَحِشَةً وَسَاءَ سَبِيلًا ﴿٣٢﴾

33. Do not kill the soul which Allah has forbidden except for a just cause. Whoever is killed unjustly, We have given his heir the power [to demand satisfaction]; but let him not exceed the limit in slaying, for he will be the victor.

وَلَا تَقْتُلُوا النَّفْسَ الَّتِي حَرَّمَ اللَّهُ إِلَّا بِالْحَقِّ وَمَن قُتِلَ مَظْلُومًا فَقَدْ جَعَلْنَا لِوَلِيِّهِ سُلْطَنًا فَلَا يُسْرِف فِي الْقَتْلِ إِنَّهُ كَانَ مَنْصُورًا ﴿٣٣﴾

34. Do not go near the orphan's property except in the fairest way until he comes of age; and honour your pledge, because the pledge involves responsibility.

وَلَا تَقْرَبُوا مَالَ الْيَتِيمِ إِلَّا بِالَّتِي هِيَ أَحْسَنُ حَتَّى يَبْلُغَ أَشُدَّهُ وَأَوْفُوا بِالْعَهْدِ إِنَّ الْعَهْدَ كَانَ مَسْئُولًا ﴿٣٤﴾

---

555. The kinsman, the destitute and the wayfarer.
556. That is, because you have nothing to give and you seek the bounty of your Lord.

35. And give full measure when you measure, and weigh with a just balance. That is fair and better in the end.

وَأَوْفُوا۟ ٱلْكَيْلَ إِذَا كِلْتُمْ وَزِنُوا۟ بِٱلْقِسْطَاسِ ٱلْمُسْتَقِيمِ ذَٰلِكَ خَيْرٌ وَأَحْسَنُ تَأْوِيلًا ﴿٣٥﴾

36. Do not pursue what you have no knowledge of. Hearing, sight and the heart - all these (you) shall be questioned about.

وَلَا تَقْفُ مَا لَيْسَ لَكَ بِهِۦ عِلْمٌ إِنَّ ٱلسَّمْعَ وَٱلْبَصَرَ وَٱلْفُؤَادَ كُلُّ أُو۟لَٰٓئِكَ كَانَ عَنْهُ مَسْـُٔولًا ﴿٣٦﴾

37. And do not walk in the land haughtily; for you certainly will not pierce the earth, nor equal the mountains in height.

وَلَا تَمْشِ فِى ٱلْأَرْضِ مَرَحًا إِنَّكَ لَن تَخْرِقَ ٱلْأَرْضَ وَلَن تَبْلُغَ ٱلْجِبَالَ طُولًا ﴿٣٧﴾

38. The evil of all this is hateful in the sight of your Lord.

كُلُّ ذَٰلِكَ كَانَ سَيِّئُهُۥ عِندَ رَبِّكَ مَكْرُوهًا ﴿٣٨﴾

39. That is part of what your Lord has revealed to you of wisdom. Do not set up with Allah another god, or else you will be cast in Hell, despised and rejected.

ذَٰلِكَ مِمَّآ أَوْحَىٰٓ إِلَيْكَ رَبُّكَ مِنَ ٱلْحِكْمَةِ وَلَا تَجْعَلْ مَعَ ٱللَّهِ إِلَٰهًا ءَاخَرَ فَتُلْقَىٰ فِى جَهَنَّمَ مَلُومًا مَّدْحُورًا ﴿٣٩﴾

40. Has your Lord, then, favoured you with sons and taken to Himself females from among the angels? Surely, you are uttering a monstrous thing.

أَفَأَصْفَىٰكُمْ رَبُّكُم بِٱلْبَنِينَ وَٱتَّخَذَ مِنَ ٱلْمَلَٰٓئِكَةِ إِنَٰثًا إِنَّكُمْ لَتَقُولُونَ قَوْلًا عَظِيمًا ﴿٤٠﴾

41. We have expatiated in this Qur'an so that they may be mindful, but it only increases their aversion.

وَلَقَدْ صَرَّفْنَا فِى هَٰذَا ٱلْقُرْءَانِ لِيَذَّكَّرُوا۟ وَمَا يَزِيدُهُمْ إِلَّا نُفُورًا ﴿٤١﴾

42. Say: "If there were other gods with Him, as they say, then surely they would have sought access to the Lord of the Throne."

قُل لَّوْ كَانَ مَعَهُۥٓ ءَالِهَةٌ كَمَا يَقُولُونَ إِذًا لَّٱبْتَغَوْا۟ إِلَىٰ ذِى ٱلْعَرْشِ سَبِيلًا ﴿٤٢﴾

43. Glory be to Him and may He be greatly exalted above what they say.

سُبْحَٰنَهُۥ وَتَعَٰلَىٰ عَمَّا يَقُولُونَ عُلُوًّا كَبِيرًا ﴿٤٣﴾

44. The seven heavens, the earth and what is in them praise Him, and there is nothing which does not celebrate His Praise; but you do not understand their praise. He is indeed Clement, All-Forgiving.

تُسَبِّحُ لَهُ ٱلسَّمَٰوَٰتُ ٱلسَّبْعُ وَٱلْأَرْضُ وَمَن فِيهِنَّ وَإِن مِّن شَىْءٍ إِلَّا يُسَبِّحُ بِحَمْدِهِۦ وَلَٰكِن لَّا تَفْقَهُونَ تَسْبِيحَهُمْ إِنَّهُۥ كَانَ حَلِيمًا غَفُورًا ﴿٤٤﴾

45. When you recite the Qur'an, We will place between you and those who do not believe in the Hereafter a hidden curtain.

وَإِذَا قَرَأْتَ ٱلْقُرْءَانَ جَعَلْنَا بَيْنَكَ وَبَيْنَ ٱلَّذِينَ لَا يُؤْمِنُونَ بِٱلْءَاخِرَةِ حِجَابًا مَّسْتُورًا ﴿٤٥﴾

46. And We have placed veils upon their hearts and deafness in their ears lest they understand it. And if you mention your Lord alone in the Qur'an, they turn their backs in aversion.

47. We know best what they listen to when they listen to you, as they confer secretly, when the wrongdoers say: "You only follow a man bewitched."

48. See how they coin similes for you and so go astray and are unable to find their way.

49. And they say: "What, when we have become bones and mortal remains, shall we really be raised up as a new creation?"

50. Say: "[Even if you] be stones or iron;

51. "Or some creation magnified in your minds." They will say: "Who will bring us back?" Say: "He Who created you the first time." Then they will shake their heads at you and say: "When will that be?" Say: "Perhaps, it will be soon.

52. "The Day He will summon you and you will respond with His Praise, and you will imagine that you have tarried but for a short while."

53. And tell My servants to say that which is best. Surely the Devil sows dissension among them; the Devil is surely a sworn enemy of man.

54. Your Lord knows you best. If He pleases, He will have mercy on you, and if He pleases He will torture you. We have not sent you to be their guardian.

55. And your Lord knows best what is in the heavens and on earth. We bestowed on some of the Prophets more gifts than on the others, and We gave David the Psalms.

56. Say: "Call on those whom you claim to be His associates. They will not be able to lift adversity from you nor divert it."

57. Those they call upon are themselves seeking means of access to their Lord, to show who is closer to Him. They hope for His Mercy and fear His Torment. Indeed, the Torment of your Lord should be feared.

58. There is no city but We will destroy before the Day of Resurrection, or will punish terribly. That is written in the Book.

59. Nothing prevents Us from sending the signs except that the ancients denied them. We gave to Thamud the she-camel as a manifest sign, but they maltreated her. We do not send the signs except to warn.

60. [Remember] when We said to you: "Your Lord encompasses mankind. We did not make the vision We showed you except as a trial to mankind, and likewise the tree cursed in the Qur'an. We warn them, but that only increases their tyranny."

61. And when We said to the angels: "Prostrate yourselves before Adam", they all prostrated themselves, except Satan, who said: "Shall I prostrate myself before one You have created from clay?"

62. He[557] said: "Do you see this one whom you honoured more than me? If you would reprieve me until the Day of Resurrection, I will certainly destroy his progeny except for a few."

63. He[558] said: "Begone! Whoever of them follows you, Hell is surely your reward, an ample reward.

قُلِ ٱدْعُوا۟ ٱلَّذِينَ زَعَمْتُم مِّن دُونِهِۦ فَلَا يَمْلِكُونَ كَشْفَ ٱلضُّرِّ عَنكُمْ وَلَا تَحْوِيلًا ۝

أُو۟لَٰٓئِكَ ٱلَّذِينَ يَدْعُونَ يَبْتَغُونَ إِلَىٰ رَبِّهِمُ ٱلْوَسِيلَةَ أَيُّهُمْ أَقْرَبُ وَيَرْجُونَ رَحْمَتَهُۥ وَيَخَافُونَ عَذَابَهُۥٓ إِنَّ عَذَابَ رَبِّكَ كَانَ مَحْذُورًا ۝

وَإِن مِّن قَرْيَةٍ إِلَّا نَحْنُ مُهْلِكُوهَا قَبْلَ يَوْمِ ٱلْقِيَٰمَةِ أَوْ مُعَذِّبُوهَا عَذَابًا شَدِيدًا كَانَ ذَٰلِكَ فِى ٱلْكِتَٰبِ مَسْطُورًا ۝

وَمَا مَنَعَنَآ أَن نُّرْسِلَ بِٱلْءَايَٰتِ إِلَّآ أَن كَذَّبَ بِهَا ٱلْأَوَّلُونَ وَءَاتَيْنَا ثَمُودَ ٱلنَّاقَةَ مُبْصِرَةً فَظَلَمُوا۟ بِهَا وَمَا نُرْسِلُ بِٱلْءَايَٰتِ إِلَّا تَخْوِيفًا ۝

وَإِذْ قُلْنَا لَكَ إِنَّ رَبَّكَ أَحَاطَ بِٱلنَّاسِ وَمَا جَعَلْنَا ٱلرُّءْيَا ٱلَّتِىٓ أَرَيْنَٰكَ إِلَّا فِتْنَةً لِّلنَّاسِ وَٱلشَّجَرَةَ ٱلْمَلْعُونَةَ فِى ٱلْقُرْءَانِ وَنُخَوِّفُهُمْ فَمَا يَزِيدُهُمْ إِلَّا طُغْيَٰنًا كَبِيرًا ۝

وَإِذْ قُلْنَا لِلْمَلَٰٓئِكَةِ ٱسْجُدُوا۟ لِءَادَمَ فَسَجَدُوٓا۟ إِلَّآ إِبْلِيسَ قَالَ ءَأَسْجُدُ لِمَنْ خَلَقْتَ طِينًا ۝

قَالَ أَرَءَيْتَكَ هَٰذَا ٱلَّذِى كَرَّمْتَ عَلَىَّ لَئِنْ أَخَّرْتَنِ إِلَىٰ يَوْمِ ٱلْقِيَٰمَةِ لَأَحْتَنِكَنَّ ذُرِّيَّتَهُۥٓ إِلَّا قَلِيلًا ۝

قَالَ ٱذْهَبْ فَمَن تَبِعَكَ مِنْهُمْ فَإِنَّ جَهَنَّمَ جَزَآؤُكُمْ جَزَآءً مَّوْفُورًا ۝

---

557. Satan.
558. Allah.

64. "Stir up those of them you can with your voice, rally against them your horsemen and your infantry, share with them their wealth and children and promise them." But Satan makes them only deceitful promises.

وَٱسْتَفْزِزْ مَنِ ٱسْتَطَعْتَ مِنْهُم بِصَوْتِكَ وَأَجْلِبْ عَلَيْهِم بِخَيْلِكَ وَرَجِلِكَ وَشَارِكْهُمْ فِى ٱلْأَمْوَٰلِ وَٱلْأَوْلَٰدِ وَعِدْهُمْ وَمَا يَعِدُهُمُ ٱلشَّيْطَٰنُ إِلَّا غُرُورًا ﴿٦٤﴾

65. "Surely, over My servants you have no authority. Your Lord suffices as a Guardian".

إِنَّ عِبَادِى لَيْسَ لَكَ عَلَيْهِمْ سُلْطَٰنٌ وَكَفَىٰ بِرَبِّكَ وَكِيلًا ﴿٦٥﴾

66. Your Lord Who drives for you the ships at sea, that you may seek His Bounty. He is indeed Merciful to you.

رَّبُّكُمُ ٱلَّذِى يُزْجِى لَكُمُ ٱلْفُلْكَ فِى ٱلْبَحْرِ لِتَبْتَغُوا۟ مِن فَضْلِهِ إِنَّهُ كَانَ بِكُمْ رَحِيمًا ﴿٦٦﴾

67. And if you are touched by adversity at sea, those you call upon other than He will wander away; but when He delivers you to land safely, you turn away. Man is ever thankless.

وَإِذَا مَسَّكُمُ ٱلضُّرُّ فِى ٱلْبَحْرِ ضَلَّ مَن تَدْعُونَ إِلَّا إِيَّاهُ فَلَمَّا نَجَّىٰكُمْ إِلَى ٱلْبَرِّ أَعْرَضْتُمْ وَكَانَ ٱلْإِنسَٰنُ كَفُورًا ﴿٦٧﴾

68. Are you, then, assured that He will not cause the land to cave in under you, or release a sandstorm upon you, and then you will find no one to protect you?

أَفَأَمِنتُمْ أَن يَخْسِفَ بِكُمْ جَانِبَ ٱلْبَرِّ أَوْ يُرْسِلَ عَلَيْكُمْ حَاصِبًا ثُمَّ لَا تَجِدُوا۟ لَكُمْ وَكِيلًا ﴿٦٨﴾

69. Or are you assured that He will not return you to it a second time, releasing upon you a roaring wind and drowning you, on account of your disbelief. Then you will find no one to defend you against Us.

أَمْ أَمِنتُمْ أَن يُعِيدَكُمْ فِيهِ تَارَةً أُخْرَىٰ فَيُرْسِلَ عَلَيْكُمْ قَاصِفًا مِّنَ ٱلرِّيحِ فَيُغْرِقَكُم بِمَا كَفَرْتُمْ ثُمَّ لَا تَجِدُوا۟ لَكُمْ عَلَيْنَا بِهِۦ تَبِيعًا ﴿٦٩﴾

70. We have honoured the Children of Adam and carried them on land and sea, provided them with good things and preferred them greatly over many of those We have created.

وَلَقَدْ كَرَّمْنَا بَنِى ءَادَمَ وَحَمَلْنَٰهُمْ فِى ٱلْبَرِّ وَٱلْبَحْرِ وَرَزَقْنَٰهُم مِّنَ ٱلطَّيِّبَٰتِ وَفَضَّلْنَٰهُمْ عَلَىٰ كَثِيرٍ مِّمَّنْ خَلَقْنَا تَفْضِيلًا ﴿٧٠﴾

71. The Day [will come] when We will call every people with their leader. Then they who are given their book in their right hand - those will read their book and will not be wronged a whit.

يَوْمَ نَدْعُوا۟ كُلَّ أُنَاسٍ بِإِمَٰمِهِمْ فَمَنْ أُوتِىَ كِتَٰبَهُ بِيَمِينِهِ فَأُو۟لَٰٓئِكَ يَقْرَءُونَ كِتَٰبَهُمْ وَلَا يُظْلَمُونَ فَتِيلًا ﴿٧١﴾

72. And he who is blind in this world will be blind in the Hereafter and will stray even more from the right Way.

وَمَن كَانَ فِى هَٰذِهِۦٓ أَعْمَىٰ فَهُوَ فِى ٱلْءَاخِرَةِ أَعْمَىٰ وَأَضَلُّ سَبِيلًا ﴿٧٢﴾

73. They were about to lure you away from what We have revealed to you, so that you might replace it with false inventions against Us. Then they would have taken you for a friend.

وَإِن كَادُوا لَيَفْتِنُونَكَ عَنِ ٱلَّذِى أَوْحَيْنَا إِلَيْكَ لِتَفْتَرِىَ عَلَيْنَا غَيْرَهُۥ وَإِذًا لَّٱتَّخَذُوكَ خَلِيلًا ٧٣

74. Had We not enabled you to stand firm, you might have inclined towards them a little.

وَلَوْلَا أَن ثَبَّتْنَٰكَ لَقَدْ كِدتَّ تَرْكَنُ إِلَيْهِمْ شَيْـًٔا قَلِيلًا ٧٤

75. Then, We would have made you taste double [the punishment in life] and double the punishment after death, and then you would not have found any supporter against Us.

إِذًا لَّأَذَقْنَٰكَ ضِعْفَ ٱلْحَيَوٰةِ وَضِعْفَ ٱلْمَمَاتِ ثُمَّ لَا تَجِدُ لَكَ عَلَيْنَا نَصِيرًا ٧٥

76. They were about to provoke you so as to expel you from the land. Then they would not stay after you except a little while.

وَإِن كَادُوا لَيَسْتَفِزُّونَكَ مِنَ ٱلْأَرْضِ لِيُخْرِجُوكَ مِنْهَا وَإِذًا لَّا يَلْبَثُونَ خِلَٰفَكَ إِلَّا قَلِيلًا ٧٦

77. This was Our Way with those Messengers We sent before you, and you will not find any change in Our Way.

سُنَّةَ مَن قَدْ أَرْسَلْنَا قَبْلَكَ مِن رُّسُلِنَا وَلَا تَجِدُ لِسُنَّتِنَا تَحْوِيلًا ٧٧

78. Perform the prayer at the declining of the sun till the darkness of the night and recite the Qur'an at dawn. Surely the recital of the Qur'an at dawn is memorable.

أَقِمِ ٱلصَّلَوٰةَ لِدُلُوكِ ٱلشَّمْسِ إِلَىٰ غَسَقِ ٱلَّيْلِ وَقُرْءَانَ ٱلْفَجْرِ إِنَّ قُرْءَانَ ٱلْفَجْرِ كَانَ مَشْهُودًا ٧٨

79. And during the latter part of the night, pray as an additional observance. For your Lord may raise you to a praiseworthy position.

وَمِنَ ٱلَّيْلِ فَتَهَجَّدْ بِهِۦ نَافِلَةً لَّكَ عَسَىٰ أَن يَبْعَثَكَ رَبُّكَ مَقَامًا مَّحْمُودًا ٧٩

80. Say: "My Lord, make my entry a truthful one and my going out a truthful one, and grant me from You a supporting power."

وَقُل رَّبِّ أَدْخِلْنِى مُدْخَلَ صِدْقٍ وَأَخْرِجْنِى مُخْرَجَ صِدْقٍ وَٱجْعَل لِّى مِن لَّدُنكَ سُلْطَٰنًا نَّصِيرًا ٨٠

81. And say: "The truth has come and falsehood has perished. Falsehood is ever perishing."

وَقُلْ جَآءَ ٱلْحَقُّ وَزَهَقَ ٱلْبَٰطِلُ إِنَّ ٱلْبَٰطِلَ كَانَ زَهُوقًا ٨١

82. And We reveal of the Qur'an that which is healing and merciful for the believers, and it yields nothing but perdition to the wrongdoers.

وَنُنَزِّلُ مِنَ ٱلْقُرْءَانِ مَا هُوَ شِفَآءٌ وَرَحْمَةٌ لِّلْمُؤْمِنِينَ وَلَا يَزِيدُ ٱلظَّٰلِمِينَ إِلَّا خَسَارًا ٨٢

83. And when We are gracious to man, he turns away and withdraws haughtily; and if adversity touches him, he is in despair.[559]

84. Say: "Everyone acts according to his own manner, but your Lord knows well who is best guided on his way."

85. And they ask you about the Spirit. Say: "The Spirit is of my Lord's Command, and you have not been given except a little knowledge."

86. If We please, We certainly can blot out that which We have revealed to you; then you would find no guardian to assist you against Us.

87. [But it was left] as a Mercy from your Lord. His Favours upon you have surely been great.

88. Say: "Were men and jinn to band together in order to come up with the like of this Qur'an, they will never come up with the like of it, even if they back up one another."

89. We have indeed given mankind in this Qur'an every kind of example, but most people insist on being ungrateful.

90. And they say: "We will not believe you until you cause a spring to gush out from the ground for us.

91. "Or have a garden of palms and vines; then cause the rivers therein to gush out abundantly;

92. "Or cause heaven to fall upon us in fragments, as you claim; or bring Allah and the angels down, so that we can see them face to face.

---

559. That is, he loses hope in Allah's mercy.

93. "Or possess a house of gold, or ascend to heaven. Yet, we will not believe in your ascension, until you send down to us a book we can read." Say: "Glory be to my Lord; am I anything other than a human Messenger?"

أَوْ يَكُونَ لَكَ بَيْتٌ مِّن زُخْرُفٍ أَوْ تَرْقَىٰ فِى ٱلسَّمَآءِ وَلَن نُّؤْمِنَ لِرُقِيِّكَ حَتَّىٰ تُنَزِّلَ عَلَيْنَا كِتَٰبًا نَّقْرَؤُهُ قُلْ سُبْحَانَ رَبِّى هَلْ كُنتُ إِلَّا بَشَرًا رَّسُولًا ۝

94. Men are not prevented from believing, once the guidance has come to them, except that they say: "Has Allah sent forth a human messenger?"

وَمَا مَنَعَ ٱلنَّاسَ أَن يُؤْمِنُوٓا۟ إِذْ جَآءَهُمُ ٱلْهُدَىٰٓ إِلَّآ أَن قَالُوٓا۟ أَبَعَثَ ٱللَّهُ بَشَرًا رَّسُولًا ۝

95. Say: "Were there on earth angels strolling in peace, We would have sent down upon them from heaven an angel as a Messenger."

قُل لَّوْ كَانَ فِى ٱلْأَرْضِ مَلَٰٓئِكَةٌ يَمْشُونَ مُطْمَئِنِّينَ لَنَزَّلْنَا عَلَيْهِم مِّنَ ٱلسَّمَآءِ مَلَكًا رَّسُولًا ۝

96. Say: "Allah suffices as a witness between me and you. He is, indeed, fully Apprised and Observant of His servants."

قُلْ كَفَىٰ بِٱللَّهِ شَهِيدًۢا بَيْنِى وَبَيْنَكُمْ إِنَّهُۥ كَانَ بِعِبَادِهِۦ خَبِيرًۢا بَصِيرًا ۝

97. Whoever Allah guides is certainly well-guided, and those whom He leaves in error you shall not find for them, besides Allah, any protectors. We shall gather them on the Day of Resurrection, falling on their faces, blind, dumb and deaf. Their dwelling shall be Hell, and whenever it abates, We shall rekindle its flames.

وَمَن يَهْدِ ٱللَّهُ فَهُوَ ٱلْمُهْتَدِ وَمَن يُضْلِلْ فَلَن تَجِدَ لَهُمْ أَوْلِيَآءَ مِن دُونِهِۦ وَنَحْشُرُهُمْ يَوْمَ ٱلْقِيَٰمَةِ عَلَىٰ وُجُوهِهِمْ عُمْيًا وَبُكْمًا وَصُمًّا مَّأْوَىٰهُمْ جَهَنَّمُ كُلَّمَا خَبَتْ زِدْنَٰهُمْ سَعِيرًا ۝

98. That is their punishment because they disbelieve in Our Signs and say: "Shall we, after we have become bones and dust, be raised up as a new creation?"

ذَٰلِكَ جَزَآؤُهُم بِأَنَّهُمْ كَفَرُوا۟ بِـَٔايَٰتِنَا وَقَالُوٓا۟ أَءِذَا كُنَّا عِظَٰمًا وَرُفَٰتًا أَءِنَّا لَمَبْعُوثُونَ خَلْقًا جَدِيدًا ۝

99. Have they not considered that Allah, Who created the heavens and the earth, is able to create the like of them? He has appointed for them a term which is un-doubted; yet the wrongdoers insist on being ungrateful.

۞ أَوَلَمْ يَرَوْا۟ أَنَّ ٱللَّهَ ٱلَّذِى خَلَقَ ٱلسَّمَٰوَٰتِ وَٱلْأَرْضَ قَادِرٌ عَلَىٰٓ أَن يَخْلُقَ مِثْلَهُمْ وَجَعَلَ لَهُمْ أَجَلًا لَّا رَيْبَ فِيهِ فَأَبَى ٱلظَّٰلِمُونَ إِلَّا كُفُورًا ۝

100. Say: "Even if you possess the treasures of my Lord's Mercy, you would still withhold them for fear of spending." Man has ever been niggardly.

قُل لَّوْ أَنتُمْ تَمْلِكُونَ خَزَآئِنَ رَحْمَةِ رَبِّىٓ إِذًا لَّأَمْسَكْتُمْ خَشْيَةَ ٱلْإِنفَاقِ وَكَانَ ٱلْإِنسَٰنُ قَتُورًا ۝

101. And We gave Moses nine clear signs. Ask the Children of Israel, then, how, when he came to them and Pharaoh said to him: "I really think you are bewitched, O Moses."

102. He (Moses) said: "You know that these [signs] have not been sent down by any one other than the Lord of the heavens and the earth as clear proofs, and I think that you, Pharaoh, are doomed."

103. So, he wanted to scare them out of the land, but We drowned him, together with all those who were with him.

104. And after him, We said to the Children of Israel: "Dwell in the land, and when the promise of the Hereafter comes, We shall bring you all together."

105. We have revealed it in truth, and in truth it came down; and We have sent you only as a bearer of good news and a warner.

106. It is a Qur'an which We have divided into parts that you may recite it with deliberation, and We revealed it piecemeal.

107. Say: "Believe or do not believe in it. Surely when it is recited those, who were given the knowledge[560] before it, fall down prostrate on their faces."

108. And they say: "Glory be to our Lord. Certainly the Promise of our Lord is fulfilled."

109. And they fall down upon their faces weeping, and it adds to their humility.

110. Say: "Call on Allah or the Compassionate. By whatever name you call [Him], His are the Most Beautiful Names." And pray neither with a loud nor with a low voice, but follow a middle course.

وَلَقَدْ ءَاتَيْنَا مُوسَىٰ تِسْعَ ءَايَٰتٍ بَيِّنَٰتٍ فَسْـَٔلْ بَنِىٓ إِسْرَٰٓءِيلَ إِذْ جَآءَهُمْ فَقَالَ لَهُۥ فِرْعَوْنُ إِنِّى لَأَظُنُّكَ يَٰمُوسَىٰ مَسْحُورًا ﴿١٠١﴾

قَالَ لَقَدْ عَلِمْتَ مَآ أَنزَلَ هَٰٓؤُلَآءِ إِلَّا رَبُّ ٱلسَّمَٰوَٰتِ وَٱلْأَرْضِ بَصَآئِرَ وَإِنِّى لَأَظُنُّكَ يَٰفِرْعَوْنُ مَثْبُورًا ﴿١٠٢﴾

فَأَرَادَ أَن يَسْتَفِزَّهُم مِّنَ ٱلْأَرْضِ فَأَغْرَقْنَٰهُ وَمَن مَّعَهُۥ جَمِيعًا ﴿١٠٣﴾

وَقُلْنَا مِنۢ بَعْدِهِۦ لِبَنِىٓ إِسْرَٰٓءِيلَ ٱسْكُنُوا۟ ٱلْأَرْضَ فَإِذَا جَآءَ وَعْدُ ٱلْءَاخِرَةِ جِئْنَا بِكُمْ لَفِيفًا ﴿١٠٤﴾

وَبِٱلْحَقِّ أَنزَلْنَٰهُ وَبِٱلْحَقِّ نَزَلَ وَمَآ أَرْسَلْنَٰكَ إِلَّا مُبَشِّرًا وَنَذِيرًا ﴿١٠٥﴾

وَقُرْءَانًا فَرَقْنَٰهُ لِتَقْرَأَهُۥ عَلَى ٱلنَّاسِ عَلَىٰ مُكْثٍ وَنَزَّلْنَٰهُ تَنزِيلًا ﴿١٠٦﴾

قُلْ ءَامِنُوا۟ بِهِۦٓ أَوْ لَا تُؤْمِنُوٓا۟ إِنَّ ٱلَّذِينَ أُوتُوا۟ ٱلْعِلْمَ مِن قَبْلِهِۦٓ إِذَا يُتْلَىٰ عَلَيْهِمْ يَخِرُّونَ لِلْأَذْقَانِ سُجَّدًا ﴿١٠٧﴾

وَيَقُولُونَ سُبْحَٰنَ رَبِّنَآ إِن كَانَ وَعْدُ رَبِّنَا لَمَفْعُولًا ﴿١٠٨﴾

وَيَخِرُّونَ لِلْأَذْقَانِ يَبْكُونَ وَيَزِيدُهُمْ خُشُوعًا ۩ ﴿١٠٩﴾

قُلِ ٱدْعُوا۟ ٱللَّهَ أَوِ ٱدْعُوا۟ ٱلرَّحْمَٰنَ أَيًّا مَّا تَدْعُوا۟ فَلَهُ ٱلْأَسْمَآءُ ٱلْحُسْنَىٰ وَلَا تَجْهَرْ بِصَلَاتِكَ وَلَا تُخَافِتْ بِهَا وَٱبْتَغِ بَيْنَ ذَٰلِكَ سَبِيلًا ﴿١١٠﴾

---

560. The People of the Book.

111. And say: "Praise be to Allah Who has not taken a son to Himself, and Who has no partner in sovereignty and no supporter to protect Him from humiliation. And proclaim His greatness."

وَقُلِ ٱلْحَمْدُ لِلَّهِ ٱلَّذِى لَمْ يَتَّخِذْ وَلَدًا وَلَمْ يَكُن لَّهُ شَرِيكٌ فِى ٱلْمُلْكِ وَلَمْ يَكُن لَّهُ وَلِىٌّ مِّنَ ٱلذُّلِّ وَكَبِّرْهُ تَكْبِيرًا ﴿١١١﴾

Sûrat Al-Kahf,
(The Cave) 18

سُورَةُ ٱلْكَهْفِ

In the Name of Allah,
the Compassionate, the Merciful

بِسْمِ ٱللَّهِ ٱلرَّحْمَٰنِ ٱلرَّحِيمِ

1. Praise be to Allah, Who revealed the Book to His servant and did not leave in it any crookedness.

ٱلْحَمْدُ لِلَّهِ ٱلَّذِى أَنزَلَ عَلَىٰ عَبْدِهِ ٱلْكِتَٰبَ وَلَمْ يَجْعَل لَّهُ عِوَجًا ﴿١﴾

2. He has made it straight to warn of severe punishment from Himself and announce the good news to the believers, who do righteous deeds, that they shall have a good reward.[561]

قَيِّمًا لِّيُنذِرَ بَأْسًا شَدِيدًا مِّن لَّدُنْهُ وَيُبَشِّرَ ٱلْمُؤْمِنِينَ ٱلَّذِينَ يَعْمَلُونَ ٱلصَّٰلِحَٰتِ أَنَّ لَهُمْ أَجْرًا حَسَنًا ﴿٢﴾

3. Abiding therein forever.

مَّٰكِثِينَ فِيهِ أَبَدًا ﴿٣﴾

4. And to warn those who say: "Allah has taken a son."

وَيُنذِرَ ٱلَّذِينَ قَالُوا ٱتَّخَذَ ٱللَّهُ وَلَدًا ﴿٤﴾

5. They have no knowledge thereof, nor do their fathers. What a dreadful word that comes out of their mouths! They only utter a lie.

مَّا لَهُم بِهِ مِنْ عِلْمٍ وَلَا لِءَابَآئِهِمْ كَبُرَتْ كَلِمَةً تَخْرُجُ مِنْ أَفْوَٰهِهِمْ إِن يَقُولُونَ إِلَّا كَذِبًا ﴿٥﴾

6. You may destroy yourself with grief, sorrowing after them,[562] if they do not believe in this revelation.

فَلَعَلَّكَ بَٰخِعٌ نَّفْسَكَ عَلَىٰٓ ءَاثَٰرِهِمْ إِن لَّمْ يُؤْمِنُوا بِهَٰذَا ٱلْحَدِيثِ أَسَفًا ﴿٦﴾

7. We have made everything on earth an adornment, in order to test them [and see] who of them is best in work.

إِنَّا جَعَلْنَا مَا عَلَى ٱلْأَرْضِ زِينَةً لَّهَا لِنَبْلُوَهُمْ أَيُّهُمْ أَحْسَنُ عَمَلًا ﴿٧﴾

8. And we shall reduce what is on it to barren dry soil.

وَإِنَّا لَجَٰعِلُونَ مَا عَلَيْهَا صَعِيدًا جُرُزًا ﴿٨﴾

---

561. Paradise.
562. Literally following after them in their wake.

9. Or did you think that the people of the Cave and al-Raqim[563] were the wonders of Our Signs?

أَمْ حَسِبْتَ أَنَّ أَصْحَٰبَ ٱلْكَهْفِ وَٱلرَّقِيمِ كَانُوا۟ مِنْ ءَايَٰتِنَا عَجَبًا ۝

10. When the youths took refuge in the Cave saying: "Our Lord, accord us from Yourself mercy, and guide us well in our affair."

إِذْ أَوَى ٱلْفِتْيَةُ إِلَى ٱلْكَهْفِ فَقَالُوا۟ رَبَّنَا ءَاتِنَا مِن لَّدُنكَ رَحْمَةً وَهَيِّئْ لَنَا مِنْ أَمْرِنَا رَشَدًا ۝

11. Then We sealed their hearing in the cave for many years.

فَضَرَبْنَا عَلَىٰٓ ءَاذَانِهِمْ فِى ٱلْكَهْفِ سِنِينَ عَدَدًا ۝

12. Then We roused them to learn who of the two parties[564] was able to calculate the time they had lingered.

ثُمَّ بَعَثْنَٰهُمْ لِنَعْلَمَ أَىُّ ٱلْحِزْبَيْنِ أَحْصَىٰ لِمَا لَبِثُوٓا۟ أَمَدًا ۝

13. We relate to you their story in truth. They were youths who believed in their Lord and We increased them in guidance.

نَّحْنُ نَقُصُّ عَلَيْكَ نَبَأَهُم بِٱلْحَقِّ إِنَّهُمْ فِتْيَةٌ ءَامَنُوا۟ بِرَبِّهِمْ وَزِدْنَٰهُمْ هُدًى ۝

14. And We strengthened their hearts when they arose saying: "Our Lord is the Lord of the heavens and the earth. We will not call on any god besides Him. For then we would be uttering an enormity.

وَرَبَطْنَا عَلَىٰ قُلُوبِهِمْ إِذْ قَامُوا۟ فَقَالُوا۟ رَبُّنَا رَبُّ ٱلسَّمَٰوَٰتِ وَٱلْأَرْضِ لَن نَّدْعُوَا۟ مِن دُونِهِۦٓ إِلَٰهًا لَّقَدْ قُلْنَآ إِذًا شَطَطًا ۝

15. "These our people have taken other gods besides Him. Why do they not bring a clear authority for them? Who is, then, more unjust than he who invents lies about Allah?"

هَٰٓؤُلَآءِ قَوْمُنَا ٱتَّخَذُوا۟ مِن دُونِهِۦٓ ءَالِهَةً لَّوْلَا يَأْتُونَ عَلَيْهِم بِسُلْطَٰنٍۭ بَيِّنٍ فَمَنْ أَظْلَمُ مِمَّنِ ٱفْتَرَىٰ عَلَى ٱللَّهِ كَذِبًا ۝

16. When you withdraw from them and what they worship, apart from Allah, take refuge in the Cave, and your Lord will extend to you some of His Mercy and prepare for you a suitable course in your affair.

وَإِذِ ٱعْتَزَلْتُمُوهُمْ وَمَا يَعْبُدُونَ إِلَّا ٱللَّهَ فَأْوُۥٓا۟ إِلَى ٱلْكَهْفِ يَنشُرْ لَكُمْ رَبُّكُم مِّن رَّحْمَتِهِۦ وَيُهَيِّئْ لَكُم مِّنْ أَمْرِكُم مِّرْفَقًا ۝

17. And you might have seen the sun, when it rose, inclining from their Cave towards the right, and when it set, inclining to the left, while they were in an open space inside it.[565] That was one of Allah's Signs. He whom Allah guides is well-guided; and he whom Allah leads astray, you will not find a friend to direct him.

۞ وَتَرَى ٱلشَّمْسَ إِذَا طَلَعَت تَّزَٰوَرُ عَن كَهْفِهِمْ ذَاتَ ٱلْيَمِينِ وَإِذَا غَرَبَت تَّقْرِضُهُمْ ذَاتَ ٱلشِّمَالِ وَهُمْ فِى فَجْوَةٍ مِّنْهُ ذَٰلِكَ مِنْ ءَايَٰتِ ٱللَّهِ مَن يَهْدِ ٱللَّهُ فَهُوَ ٱلْمُهْتَدِ وَمَن يُضْلِلْ فَلَن تَجِدَ لَهُۥ وَلِيًّا مُّرْشِدًا ۝

---

563. The name of the mountain where the Cave was.

564. The two parties of the Sleepers of Ephesus, who, according to tradition, were not aware of the time they had spent in the cave.

565. The Cave.

18. You would think them awake, whereas they were sleeping. We turned them over to the right, then to the left, while their dog was stretching its paws in the yard. If you looked at them, you would have turned away from them in flight, and would have been filled with fear.

19. Thus We roused them, that they might question each other. One of them said: "How long have you lingered?" They said: "A day or part of a day." They said: "Your Lord knows best how long you have lingered. So send someone with this silver [coin] of yours to the city, and let him see what food is purest. Then let him bring you some provision thereof, and let him be gentle and let him apprise no one about you.

20. "Surely, if they learn about you, they will stone you or force you back into their religion; and then you will never prosper."

21. That is how We made them known [to people] so as to know that Allah's Promise is true and that the Hour is undoubted. As they were arguing among themselves concerning their affair, they said: "Build over them an edifice; their Lord knows best their condition." Then those who prevailed over them said: "Let us build over them a mosque."

22. Some say: "[The sleepers were] three; their dog was the fourth of them"; and [others] say: "Five; their dog was the sixth of them", interpreting the unseen. And they say: "Seven; their dog being the eighth of them." Say (O Mohammad): "My Lord knows best their number; none knows them, save a few." Do not, then, dispute concerning them, except with reference to that which is clear to you, and do not question, concerning them, any of them."

وَتَحْسَبُهُمْ أَيْقَاظًا وَهُمْ رُقُودٌ وَنُقَلِّبُهُمْ ذَاتَ ٱلْيَمِينِ وَذَاتَ ٱلشِّمَالِ وَكَلْبُهُم بَٰسِطٌ ذِرَاعَيْهِ بِٱلْوَصِيدِ لَوِ ٱطَّلَعْتَ عَلَيْهِمْ لَوَلَّيْتَ مِنْهُمْ فِرَارًا وَلَمُلِئْتَ مِنْهُمْ رُعْبًا ۝

وَكَذَٰلِكَ بَعَثْنَٰهُمْ لِيَتَسَآءَلُوا۟ بَيْنَهُمْ قَالَ قَآئِلٌ مِّنْهُمْ كَمْ لَبِثْتُمْ قَالُوا۟ لَبِثْنَا يَوْمًا أَوْ بَعْضَ يَوْمٍ قَالُوا۟ رَبُّكُمْ أَعْلَمُ بِمَا لَبِثْتُمْ فَٱبْعَثُوٓا۟ أَحَدَكُم بِوَرِقِكُمْ هَٰذِهِۦٓ إِلَى ٱلْمَدِينَةِ فَلْيَنظُرْ أَيُّهَآ أَزْكَىٰ طَعَامًا فَلْيَأْتِكُم بِرِزْقٍ مِّنْهُ وَلْيَتَلَطَّفْ وَلَا يُشْعِرَنَّ بِكُمْ أَحَدًا ۝

إِنَّهُمْ إِن يَظْهَرُوا۟ عَلَيْكُمْ يَرْجُمُوكُمْ أَوْ يُعِيدُوكُمْ فِى مِلَّتِهِمْ وَلَن تُفْلِحُوٓا۟ إِذًا أَبَدًا ۝

وَكَذَٰلِكَ أَعْثَرْنَا عَلَيْهِمْ لِيَعْلَمُوٓا۟ أَنَّ وَعْدَ ٱللَّهِ حَقٌّ وَأَنَّ ٱلسَّاعَةَ لَا رَيْبَ فِيهَآ إِذْ يَتَنَٰزَعُونَ بَيْنَهُمْ أَمْرَهُمْ فَقَالُوا۟ ٱبْنُوا۟ عَلَيْهِم بُنْيَٰنًا رَّبُّهُمْ أَعْلَمُ بِهِمْ قَالَ ٱلَّذِينَ غَلَبُوا۟ عَلَىٰٓ أَمْرِهِمْ لَنَتَّخِذَنَّ عَلَيْهِم مَّسْجِدًا ۝

سَيَقُولُونَ ثَلَٰثَةٌ رَّابِعُهُمْ كَلْبُهُمْ وَيَقُولُونَ خَمْسَةٌ سَادِسُهُمْ كَلْبُهُمْ رَجْمًۢا بِٱلْغَيْبِ وَيَقُولُونَ سَبْعَةٌ وَثَامِنُهُمْ كَلْبُهُمْ قُل رَّبِّىٓ أَعْلَمُ بِعِدَّتِهِم مَّا يَعْلَمُهُمْ إِلَّا قَلِيلٌ فَلَا تُمَارِ فِيهِمْ إِلَّا مِرَآءً ظَٰهِرًا وَلَا تَسْتَفْتِ فِيهِم مِّنْهُمْ أَحَدًا ۝

23. And do not say of anything: "I will do that tomorrow," [unless you add]:

وَلَا تَقُولَنَّ لِشَا۟ىۢءٍ إِنِّى فَاعِلٌ ذَٰلِكَ غَدًا ﴿٢٣﴾

24. "If Allah wills." Remember your Lord, if you forget, and say: "Perhaps, my Lord will guide me to something closer to this in rectitude?"

إِلَّآ أَن يَشَآءَ ٱللَّهُ وَٱذْكُر رَّبَّكَ إِذَا نَسِيتَ وَقُلْ عَسَىٰٓ أَن يَهْدِيَنِ رَبِّى لِأَقْرَبَ مِنْ هَٰذَا رَشَدًا ﴿٢٤﴾

25. And they lingered in their Cave three hundred years, and [some] add nine.

وَلَبِثُوا۟ فِى كَهْفِهِمْ ثَلَٰثَ مِا۟ئَةٍ سِنِينَ وَٱزْدَادُوا۟ تِسْعًا ﴿٢٥﴾

26. Say: "Allah knows best how long they lingered. His is the Unseen of the heavens and the earth. How clear is His Sight and His Hearing! Apart from Him, they have no protector, and He has no associates in His Sovereignty."

قُلِ ٱللَّهُ أَعْلَمُ بِمَا لَبِثُوا۟ لَهُۥ غَيْبُ ٱلسَّمَٰوَٰتِ وَٱلْأَرْضِ أَبْصِرْ بِهِۦ وَأَسْمِعْ مَا لَهُم مِّن دُونِهِۦ مِن وَلِىٍّ وَلَا يُشْرِكُ فِى حُكْمِهِۦٓ أَحَدًا ﴿٢٦﴾

27. Recite what was revealed to you from your Lord's Book; no one can alter His Words, and from Him, you will find no refuge.

وَٱتْلُ مَآ أُوحِىَ إِلَيْكَ مِن كِتَابِ رَبِّكَ لَا مُبَدِّلَ لِكَلِمَٰتِهِۦ وَلَن تَجِدَ مِن دُونِهِۦ مُلْتَحَدًا ﴿٢٧﴾

28. And confine yourself to those who call upon their Lord, morning and evening, desiring His Face. And let not your eyes wander away from them, desiring the finery of the present life. And do not obey him whose heart We have made heedless of Our Remembrance, he has followed his own desires, and his case has become hopeless.

وَٱصْبِرْ نَفْسَكَ مَعَ ٱلَّذِينَ يَدْعُونَ رَبَّهُم بِٱلْغَدَوٰةِ وَٱلْعَشِىِّ يُرِيدُونَ وَجْهَهُۥ وَلَا تَعْدُ عَيْنَاكَ عَنْهُمْ تُرِيدُ زِينَةَ ٱلْحَيَوٰةِ ٱلدُّنْيَا وَلَا تُطِعْ مَنْ أَغْفَلْنَا قَلْبَهُۥ عَن ذِكْرِنَا وَٱتَّبَعَ هَوَىٰهُ وَكَانَ أَمْرُهُۥ فُرُطًا ﴿٢٨﴾

29. And say: "The Truth is from your Lord. Whoever wishes, let him believe; and whoever wishes, let him disbelieve." We have prepared for the wrongdoers a Fire whose canopy encompasses them all. If they call for relief, they will be relieved with water like molten brass which scalds the faces. Wretched is that drink and wretched is the resting-place!

وَقُلِ ٱلْحَقُّ مِن رَّبِّكُمْ فَمَن شَآءَ فَلْيُؤْمِن وَمَن شَآءَ فَلْيَكْفُرْ إِنَّآ أَعْتَدْنَا لِلظَّٰلِمِينَ نَارًا أَحَاطَ بِهِمْ سُرَادِقُهَا وَإِن يَسْتَغِيثُوا۟ يُغَاثُوا۟ بِمَآءٍ كَٱلْمُهْلِ يَشْوِى ٱلْوُجُوهَ بِئْسَ ٱلشَّرَابُ وَسَآءَتْ مُرْتَفَقًا ﴿٢٩﴾

30. As for those who believe and do the good deeds, surely, We will not waste the reward of him who does the good work.

إِنَّ ٱلَّذِينَ ءَامَنُوا۟ وَعَمِلُوا۟ ٱلصَّٰلِحَٰتِ إِنَّا لَا نُضِيعُ أَجْرَ مَنْ أَحْسَنَ عَمَلًا ﴿٣٠﴾

31. Those shall have Gardens of Eden, beneath which rivers flow, bejewelled therein with bracelets of gold, and wearing green clothes of silk and brocade, reclining therein on couches. Blessed is their reward and fair is the resting-place!

أُوْلَـٰٓئِكَ لَهُمْ جَنَّـٰتُ عَدْنٍ تَجْرِى مِن تَحْتِهِمُ ٱلْأَنْهَـٰرُ يُحَلَّوْنَ فِيهَا مِنْ أَسَاوِرَ مِن ذَهَبٍ وَيَلْبَسُونَ ثِيَابًا خُضْرًا مِّن سُندُسٍ وَإِسْتَبْرَقٍ مُّتَّكِئِينَ فِيهَا عَلَى ٱلْأَرَآئِكِ نِعْمَ ٱلثَّوَابُ وَحَسُنَتْ مُرْتَفَقًا ۝

32. And relate to them as a parable the case of two men. To one of them, We gave two gardens of vine, which We surrounded with palm trees and placed between them a cornfield.

۞ وَٱضْرِبْ لَهُم مَّثَلًا رَّجُلَيْنِ جَعَلْنَا لِأَحَدِهِمَا جَنَّتَيْنِ مِنْ أَعْنَـٰبٍ وَحَفَفْنَـٰهُمَا بِنَخْلٍ وَجَعَلْنَا بَيْنَهُمَا زَرْعًا ۝

33. Both gardens yielded their produce and did not waste any of it, and We caused a river to flow through them both.

كِلْتَا ٱلْجَنَّتَيْنِ ءَاتَتْ أُكُلَهَا وَلَمْ تَظْلِم مِّنْهُ شَيْئًا وَفَجَّرْنَا خِلَـٰلَهُمَا نَهَرًا ۝

34. And he had some fruit. So he said to his companion, while conversing with him: "I have greater wealth than you and a mightier following."

وَكَانَ لَهُ ثَمَرٌ فَقَالَ لِصَـٰحِبِهِ وَهُوَ يُحَاوِرُهُ أَنَا۠ أَكْثَرُ مِنكَ مَالًا وَأَعَزُّ نَفَرًا ۝

35. Then he entered his garden, wronging himself. He said: "I do not think this will ever perish.

وَدَخَلَ جَنَّتَهُ وَهُوَ ظَالِمٌ لِّنَفْسِهِ قَالَ مَآ أَظُنُّ أَن تَبِيدَ هَـٰذِهِۦٓ أَبَدًا ۝

36. "And I do not think the Hour is coming. If I am returned to my Lord, I will surely find a better place than this."

وَمَآ أَظُنُّ ٱلسَّاعَةَ قَآئِمَةً وَلَئِن رُّدِدتُّ إِلَىٰ رَبِّى لَأَجِدَنَّ خَيْرًا مِّنْهَا مُنقَلَبًا ۝

37. His companion said to him, while conversing with him: "Do you disbelieve in Him Who created you from dust, then from a sperm, then fashioned you into a man?

قَالَ لَهُ صَاحِبُهُ وَهُوَ يُحَاوِرُهُۥٓ أَكَفَرْتَ بِٱلَّذِى خَلَقَكَ مِن تُرَابٍ ثُمَّ مِن نُّطْفَةٍ ثُمَّ سَوَّىٰكَ رَجُلًا ۝

38. "But as for me, Allah is my Lord and I do not associate anyone with my Lord.

لَّـٰكِنَّا۠ هُوَ ٱللَّهُ رَبِّى وَلَآ أُشْرِكُ بِرَبِّىٓ أَحَدًا ۝

39. "If only you were to say, upon entering your garden: 'What Allah pleases [shall come to be]; there is no power save in Allah'. If you see me possessing less wealth and children than you;

وَلَوْلَآ إِذْ دَخَلْتَ جَنَّتَكَ قُلْتَ مَا شَآءَ ٱللَّهُ لَا قُوَّةَ إِلَّا بِٱللَّهِ إِن تَرَنِ أَنَا۠ أَقَلَّ مِنكَ مَالًا وَوَلَدًا ۝

40. "Perhaps, my Lord will give me a better garden than yours and will release upon yours a thunderbolt from the sky, so that it will turn into a barren wasteland.

فَعَسَىٰ رَبِّىٓ أَن يُؤْتِيَنِ خَيْرًا مِّن جَنَّتِكَ وَيُرْسِلَ عَلَيْهَا حُسْبَانًا مِّنَ ٱلسَّمَآءِ فَتُصْبِحَ صَعِيدًا زَلَقًا ۝

41. "Or its water will sink into the ground, so that you will not be able to draw it."

أَوْ يُصْبِحَ مَاؤُهَا غَوْرًا فَلَن تَسْتَطِيعَ لَهُ طَلَبًا ۝

42. Then, his fruit was destroyed, and so he began to wring his hands at what he had spent on it, while it had fallen down upon its trellises, and he was saying: "I wish I had not associated anyone with my Lord."

وَأُحِيطَ بِثَمَرِهِ فَأَصْبَحَ يُقَلِّبُ كَفَّيْهِ عَلَى مَا أَنفَقَ فِيهَا وَهِيَ خَاوِيَةٌ عَلَى عُرُوشِهَا وَيَقُولُ يَٰلَيْتَنِى لَمْ أُشْرِكْ بِرَبِّى أَحَدًا ۝

43. And he did not have a faction to help him besides Allah, nor was he able to defend himself.

وَلَمْ تَكُن لَّهُۥ فِئَةٌ يَنصُرُونَهُۥ مِن دُونِ ٱللَّهِ وَمَا كَانَ مُنتَصِرًا ۝

44. There, protection is from Allah, the True God. He is Best in rewarding and Best in requiting.

هُنَالِكَ ٱلْوَلَٰيَةُ لِلَّهِ ٱلْحَقِّ هُوَ خَيْرٌ ثَوَابًا وَخَيْرٌ عُقْبًا ۝

45. And give them the simile of the present life; it is like the water We send down from the sky; then the vegetation of the earth is mixed with it, and so it becomes straw which the wind scatters. Allah has power over everything.

وَٱضْرِبْ لَهُم مَّثَلَ ٱلْحَيَوٰةِ ٱلدُّنْيَا كَمَآءٍ أَنزَلْنَٰهُ مِنَ ٱلسَّمَآءِ فَٱخْتَلَطَ بِهِۦ نَبَاتُ ٱلْأَرْضِ فَأَصْبَحَ هَشِيمًا تَذْرُوهُ ٱلرِّيَٰحُ وَكَانَ ٱللَّهُ عَلَىٰ كُلِّ شَىْءٍ مُّقْتَدِرًا ۝

46. Wealth and children are the adornment of the present life, but the everlasting good works are better in your Lord's Sight in reward and better in expectation.

ٱلْمَالُ وَٱلْبَنُونَ زِينَةُ ٱلْحَيَوٰةِ ٱلدُّنْيَا وَٱلْبَٰقِيَٰتُ ٱلصَّٰلِحَٰتُ خَيْرٌ عِندَ رَبِّكَ ثَوَابًا وَخَيْرٌ أَمَلًا ۝

47. And on the Day We shall cause the mountains to move and you see the earth uncovered, and we gather them all, having left no one behind.

وَيَوْمَ نُسَيِّرُ ٱلْجِبَالَ وَتَرَى ٱلْأَرْضَ بَارِزَةً وَحَشَرْنَٰهُمْ فَلَمْ نُغَادِرْ مِنْهُمْ أَحَدًا ۝

48. And they will be brought before your Lord in rows: "Now you come to Us as We created you the first time. Nay, you claimed that We would not fix for you an appointed time."

وَعُرِضُوا۟ عَلَىٰ رَبِّكَ صَفًّا لَّقَدْ جِئْتُمُونَا كَمَا خَلَقْنَٰكُمْ أَوَّلَ مَرَّةٍ بَلْ زَعَمْتُمْ أَلَّن نَّجْعَلَ لَكُم مَّوْعِدًا ۝

49. And the book will be set down, and you will see the wicked apprehensive at what is in it, and they will say: "Woe betide us. What book is this? It does not leave out anything, small or big, but enumerates it." And they will find what they did in front of them; and your Lord will not wrong any one.

وَوُضِعَ ٱلْكِتَٰبُ فَتَرَى ٱلْمُجْرِمِينَ مُشْفِقِينَ مِمَّا فِيهِ وَيَقُولُونَ يَٰوَيْلَتَنَا مَالِ هَٰذَا ٱلْكِتَٰبِ لَا يُغَادِرُ صَغِيرَةً وَلَا كَبِيرَةً إِلَّآ أَحْصَىٰهَا وَوَجَدُوا۟ مَا عَمِلُوا۟ حَاضِرًا وَلَا يَظْلِمُ رَبُّكَ أَحَدًا ۝

50. And [remember] when We said to the angels: "Prostrate yourselves to Adam", and they all did except Satan; he was one of the jinn, then he disobeyed the Command of his Lord. Will you, then, take him and his progeny as protectors, besides Me, while they are all your enemies? Evil is the exchange for the wrongdoers!"

51. I (Allah) did not call them to witness the creation of the heavens and the earth, nor their own creation; and I did not take those who lead astray as supporters.

52. And on the day He will say: "Call on whom you claimed to be My associates." They will call on them, but they will not answer them, and We will set a valley of destruction between them.

53. The wicked will see the Fire and will think that they will fall in it, and will find no escape from it.

54. We have set out, in this Qur'an for the people, every manner of example; but man is the most contentious being.

55. Nothing prevents men from believing when the guidance comes to them, or from seeking forgiveness from their Lord; but they wait for the fate of the ancients to overtake them, or to be confronted with the punishment.

56. We do not send Messengers except as bearers of good news and warners; yet the unbelievers dispute with falsehood, to refute the truth thereby; and they take My Revelations and what they were warned about as an object of mockery.

57. And who is more unjust than one who, upon being reminded of his Lord's Revelations, turns away from them, and forgets

وَإِذْ قُلْنَا لِلْمَلَٰٓئِكَةِ ٱسْجُدُوا۟ لِءَادَمَ فَسَجَدُوٓا۟ إِلَّآ إِبْلِيسَ كَانَ مِنَ ٱلْجِنِّ فَفَسَقَ عَنْ أَمْرِ رَبِّهِۦٓ أَفَتَتَّخِذُونَهُۥ وَذُرِّيَّتَهُۥٓ أَوْلِيَآءَ مِن دُونِى وَهُمْ لَكُمْ عَدُوٌّۢ بِئْسَ لِلظَّٰلِمِينَ بَدَلًا ۝

۞ مَّآ أَشْهَدتُّهُمْ خَلْقَ ٱلسَّمَٰوَٰتِ وَٱلْأَرْضِ وَلَا خَلْقَ أَنفُسِهِمْ وَمَا كُنتُ مُتَّخِذَ ٱلْمُضِلِّينَ عَضُدًا ۝

وَيَوْمَ يَقُولُ نَادُوا۟ شُرَكَآءِىَ ٱلَّذِينَ زَعَمْتُمْ فَدَعَوْهُمْ فَلَمْ يَسْتَجِيبُوا۟ لَهُمْ وَجَعَلْنَا بَيْنَهُم مَّوْبِقًا ۝

وَرَءَا ٱلْمُجْرِمُونَ ٱلنَّارَ فَظَنُّوٓا۟ أَنَّهُم مُّوَاقِعُوهَا وَلَمْ يَجِدُوا۟ عَنْهَا مَصْرِفًا ۝

وَلَقَدْ صَرَّفْنَا فِى هَٰذَا ٱلْقُرْءَانِ لِلنَّاسِ مِن كُلِّ مَثَلٍ وَكَانَ ٱلْإِنسَٰنُ أَكْثَرَ شَىْءٍ جَدَلًا ۝

وَمَا مَنَعَ ٱلنَّاسَ أَن يُؤْمِنُوٓا۟ إِذْ جَآءَهُمُ ٱلْهُدَىٰ وَيَسْتَغْفِرُوا۟ رَبَّهُمْ إِلَّآ أَن تَأْتِيَهُمْ سُنَّةُ ٱلْأَوَّلِينَ أَوْ يَأْتِيَهُمُ ٱلْعَذَابُ قُبُلًا ۝

وَمَا نُرْسِلُ ٱلْمُرْسَلِينَ إِلَّا مُبَشِّرِينَ وَمُنذِرِينَ وَيُجَٰدِلُ ٱلَّذِينَ كَفَرُوا۟ بِٱلْبَٰطِلِ لِيُدْحِضُوا۟ بِهِ ٱلْحَقَّ وَٱتَّخَذُوٓا۟ ءَايَٰتِى وَمَآ أُنذِرُوا۟ هُزُوًا ۝

وَمَنْ أَظْلَمُ مِمَّن ذُكِّرَ بِـَٔايَٰتِ رَبِّهِۦ فَأَعْرَضَ عَنْهَا وَنَسِىَ مَا قَدَّمَتْ يَدَاهُ إِنَّا جَعَلْنَا عَلَىٰ قُلُوبِهِمْ أَكِنَّةً أَن يَفْقَهُوهُ

what his hands have done? We have placed coverings upon their hearts lest they understand it,[566] and put a deafness in their ears. If you call them to the guidance, they will never be guided.

وَفِى ءَاذَانِهِمْ وَقْرًا وَإِن تَدْعُهُمْ إِلَى ٱلْهُدَىٰ فَلَن يَهْتَدُوٓا۟ إِذًا أَبَدًا ﴿٥٧﴾

58. And your Lord is All-Forgiving and Merciful. Were He to call them to account for what they have earned, He would have hastened their punishment. However, they have an appointment from which they will find no escape.

وَرَبُّكَ ٱلْغَفُورُ ذُو ٱلرَّحْمَةِ لَوْ يُؤَاخِذُهُم بِمَا كَسَبُوا۟ لَعَجَّلَ لَهُمُ ٱلْعَذَابَ بَل لَّهُم مَّوْعِدٌ لَّن يَجِدُوا۟ مِن دُونِهِۦ مَوْئِلًا ﴿٥٨﴾

59. And those towns, We have destroyed them when they did wrong, and we set for their destruction an appointed time.

وَتِلْكَ ٱلْقُرَىٰٓ أَهْلَكْنَٰهُمْ لَمَّا ظَلَمُوا۟ وَجَعَلْنَا لِمَهْلِكِهِم مَّوْعِدًا ﴿٥٩﴾

60. And [remember] when Moses said to his servant:[567] "I will not give up until I reach the confluence of the two seas,[568] or else walk on for years."

وَإِذْ قَالَ مُوسَىٰ لِفَتَىٰهُ لَآ أَبْرَحُ حَتَّىٰٓ أَبْلُغَ مَجْمَعَ ٱلْبَحْرَيْنِ أَوْ أَمْضِىَ حُقُبًا ﴿٦٠﴾

61. Then, when they reached their confluence, they forgot their fish, and thus it slipped away into the sea unhindered.

فَلَمَّا بَلَغَا مَجْمَعَ بَيْنِهِمَا نَسِيَا حُوتَهُمَا فَٱتَّخَذَ سَبِيلَهُۥ فِى ٱلْبَحْرِ سَرَبًا ﴿٦١﴾

62. But when they had passed on, he said to his servant: "Bring us our food; we have been exposed in our travels to a lot of fatigue."

فَلَمَّا جَاوَزَا قَالَ لِفَتَىٰهُ ءَاتِنَا غَدَآءَنَا لَقَدْ لَقِينَا مِن سَفَرِنَا هَٰذَا نَصَبًا ﴿٦٢﴾

63. He[569] said: "Do you see; when we repaired to the rock, I forgot the fish. It was only the Devil who made me forget to mention it; and so it slipped away into the sea in a strange way."

قَالَ أَرَءَيْتَ إِذْ أَوَيْنَآ إِلَى ٱلصَّخْرَةِ فَإِنِّى نَسِيتُ ٱلْحُوتَ وَمَآ أَنسَىٰنِيهُ إِلَّا ٱلشَّيْطَٰنُ أَنْ أَذْكُرَهُۥ وَٱتَّخَذَ سَبِيلَهُۥ فِى ٱلْبَحْرِ عَجَبًا ﴿٦٣﴾

64. He[570] said: "This is what we were seeking"; and so they turned back retracing their steps.

قَالَ ذَٰلِكَ مَا كُنَّا نَبْغِ فَٱرْتَدَّا عَلَىٰٓ ءَاثَارِهِمَا قَصَصًا ﴿٦٤﴾

---

566. The Qur'an.
567. He is believed to be Joshua.
568. The Gulf of 'Aqaba and the Gulf of Suez in the Red Sea.
569. The servant.
570. Moses.

65. And so, they found one of Our servants whom We had accorded a mercy of Our own and had imparted to him knowledge from Ourselves.

فَوَجَدَا عَبْدًا مِّنْ عِبَادِنَا ءَاتَيْنَهُ رَحْمَةً مِّنْ عِندِنَا وَعَلَّمْنَهُ مِن لَّدُنَّا عِلْمًا ﴿٦٥﴾

66. Moses said to him (Khidr): "Shall I follow you so that you may teach me of the good you have been taught."

قَالَ لَهُ مُوسَىٰ هَلْ أَتَّبِعُكَ عَلَىٰ أَن تُعَلِّمَنِ مِمَّا عُلِّمْتَ رُشْدًا ﴿٦٦﴾

67. He (Khidr) said: "You will not be able to bear with me.

قَالَ إِنَّكَ لَن تَسْتَطِيعَ مَعِيَ صَبْرًا ﴿٦٧﴾

68. "And how will you bear with what you have no knowledge of?"

وَكَيْفَ تَصْبِرُ عَلَىٰ مَا لَمْ تُحِطْ بِهِ خُبْرًا ﴿٦٨﴾

69. He[571] said: "You will find me, Allah willing, patient and I will not disobey any order of yours."

قَالَ سَتَجِدُنِي إِن شَآءَ ٱللَّهُ صَابِرًا وَلَآ أَعْصِي لَكَ أَمْرًا ﴿٦٩﴾

70. He said: "If you follow me, do not ask me about anything, until I make mention of it."

قَالَ فَإِنِ ٱتَّبَعْتَنِي فَلَا تَسْـَٔلْنِي عَن شَيْءٍ حَتَّىٰ أُحْدِثَ لَكَ مِنْهُ ذِكْرًا ﴿٧٠﴾

71. So, they set out; but no sooner had they boarded the ship than he made a hole in it. He [Moses] said: "Have you made a hole in it so as to drown its passengers? You have indeed done a grievous thing."

فَٱنطَلَقَا حَتَّىٰ إِذَا رَكِبَا فِي ٱلسَّفِينَةِ خَرَقَهَا قَالَ أَخَرَقْتَهَا لِتُغْرِقَ أَهْلَهَا لَقَدْ جِئْتَ شَيْئًا إِمْرًا ﴿٧١﴾

72. He (Khidr) said: "Did I not tell you that you will not be able to bear with me?"

قَالَ أَلَمْ أَقُلْ إِنَّكَ لَن تَسْتَطِيعَ مَعِيَ صَبْرًا ﴿٧٢﴾

73. He[572] said: "Do not reproach me for what I have forgotten, and do not overburden me with hardship."

قَالَ لَا تُؤَاخِذْنِي بِمَا نَسِيتُ وَلَا تُرْهِقْنِي مِنْ أَمْرِي عُسْرًا ﴿٧٣﴾

74. Then they departed; but when they met a boy, he (Khidr) killed him. Moses said: "Have you killed an innocent person who has not killed another? You have surely committed a horrible deed."

فَٱنطَلَقَا حَتَّىٰ إِذَا لَقِيَا غُلَٰمًا فَقَتَلَهُ قَالَ أَقَتَلْتَ نَفْسًا زَكِيَّةً بِغَيْرِ نَفْسٍ لَقَدْ جِئْتَ شَيْئًا نُّكْرًا ﴿٧٤﴾

75. He (Khidr) said: "Did I not tell you that you will not be able to bear with me?"

۞ قَالَ أَلَمْ أَقُل لَّكَ إِنَّكَ لَن تَسْتَطِيعَ مَعِيَ صَبْرًا ﴿٧٥﴾

---

571. Moses.
572. Moses.

76. He (Moses) said: "If I ask you about anything after this, do not keep company with me. You have received an excuse from me."

قَالَ إِن سَأَلْتُكَ عَن شَيْءٍ بَعْدَهَا فَلَا تُصَٰحِبْنِي قَدْ بَلَغْتَ مِن لَّدُنِّي عُذْرًا ۝

77. So, they went on, until they reached the inhabitants of a town. Whereupon they asked its inhabitants for food, but they refused to offer them hospitality. Then, they found in it a wall about to fall down, and so he (Khidr) straightened it. He[573] said: "Had you wished, you could have been paid for that."

فَانطَلَقَا حَتَّىٰٓ إِذَآ أَتَيَآ أَهْلَ قَرْيَةٍ ٱسْتَطْعَمَآ أَهْلَهَا فَأَبَوْا أَن يُضَيِّفُوهُمَا فَوَجَدَا فِيهَا جِدَارًا يُرِيدُ أَن يَنقَضَّ فَأَقَامَهُ قَالَ لَوْ شِئْتَ لَتَّخَذْتَ عَلَيْهِ أَجْرًا ۝

78. He (Khidr) said: "This is where we part company. [Now] I will tell you the interpretation of that which you could not bear patiently with.

قَالَ هَٰذَا فِرَاقُ بَيْنِي وَبَيْنِكَ سَأُنَبِّئُكَ بِتَأْوِيلِ مَا لَمْ تَسْتَطِع عَّلَيْهِ صَبْرًا ۝

79. "As for the ship, it belonged to some poor fellows who worked upon the sea. I wanted to damage it, because, on their trail, there was a king, who was seizing every ship by force.

أَمَّا ٱلسَّفِينَةُ فَكَانَتْ لِمَسَٰكِينَ يَعْمَلُونَ فِي ٱلْبَحْرِ فَأَرَدتُّ أَنْ أَعِيبَهَا وَكَانَ وَرَآءَهُم مَّلِكٌ يَأْخُذُ كُلَّ سَفِينَةٍ غَصْبًا ۝

80. "As for the boy, his parents were believers; so we feared that he might overwhelm them with oppression and unbelief.

وَأَمَّا ٱلْغُلَٰمُ فَكَانَ أَبَوَاهُ مُؤْمِنَيْنِ فَخَشِينَآ أَن يُرْهِقَهُمَا طُغْيَٰنًا وَكُفْرًا ۝

81. "So we wanted that their Lord might replace him with someone better in purity and closer to mercy.

فَأَرَدْنَآ أَن يُبْدِلَهُمَا رَبُّهُمَا خَيْرًا مِّنْهُ زَكَوٰةً وَأَقْرَبَ رُحْمًا ۝

82. "And as for the wall, it belonged to two orphan boys in the town; and beneath it there was a treasure for both of them. Their father was a righteous man; so your Lord wanted them to come of age and dig up the treasure, as a mercy from your Lord. What I did was not of my own will. This is the interpretation of what you could not bear with patiently."

وَأَمَّا ٱلْجِدَارُ فَكَانَ لِغُلَٰمَيْنِ يَتِيمَيْنِ فِي ٱلْمَدِينَةِ وَكَانَ تَحْتَهُ كَنزٌ لَّهُمَا وَكَانَ أَبُوهُمَا صَٰلِحًا فَأَرَادَ رَبُّكَ أَن يَبْلُغَآ أَشُدَّهُمَا وَيَسْتَخْرِجَا كَنزَهُمَا رَحْمَةً مِّن رَّبِّكَ وَمَا فَعَلْتُهُ عَنْ أَمْرِي ذَٰلِكَ تَأْوِيلُ مَا لَمْ تَسْطِع عَّلَيْهِ صَبْرًا ۝

---

573. Moses.

83. And they ask you about Dhul-Qar-nayn.[574] Say: "I will give you this account of him."

وَيَسْـَٔلُونَكَ عَن ذِى ٱلْقَرْنَيْنِ قُلْ سَأَتْلُوا۟ عَلَيْكُم مِّنْهُ ذِكْرًا ﴿٨٣﴾

84. We established him firmly in the land and We gave him access to everything.

إِنَّا مَكَّنَّا لَهُۥ فِى ٱلْأَرْضِ وَءَاتَيْنَـٰهُ مِن كُلِّ شَىْءٍ سَبَبًا ﴿٨٤﴾

85. And so he followed a course;

فَأَتْبَعَ سَبَبًا ﴿٨٥﴾

86. Then, when he reached the setting-place of the sun, he found that it sets in a spring of black mud and found, by it, a people. We said: "O Dhul-Qarnayn, either you punish them or show them kindness."

حَتَّىٰٓ إِذَا بَلَغَ مَغْرِبَ ٱلشَّمْسِ وَجَدَهَا تَغْرُبُ فِى عَيْنٍ حَمِئَةٍ وَوَجَدَ عِندَهَا قَوْمًا قُلْنَا يَـٰذَا ٱلْقَرْنَيْنِ إِمَّآ أَن تُعَذِّبَ وَإِمَّآ أَن تَتَّخِذَ فِيهِمْ حُسْنًا ﴿٨٦﴾

87. He said: "As to the wrongdoer, we shall torture him; then he will be returned over to his Lord, Who will punish him a terrible punishment.

قَالَ أَمَّا مَن ظَلَمَ فَسَوْفَ نُعَذِّبُهُۥ ثُمَّ يُرَدُّ إِلَىٰ رَبِّهِۦ فَيُعَذِّبُهُۥ عَذَابًا نُّكْرًا ﴿٨٧﴾

88. "But he who believes and does good deeds, he will have the fairest reward,[575] and we will command him to do what is easy for him."

وَأَمَّا مَنْ ءَامَنَ وَعَمِلَ صَـٰلِحًا فَلَهُۥ جَزَآءً ٱلْحُسْنَىٰ وَسَنَقُولُ لَهُۥ مِنْ أَمْرِنَا يُسْرًا ﴿٨٨﴾

89. Then he[576] followed [another] course.

ثُمَّ أَتْبَعَ سَبَبًا ﴿٨٩﴾

90. But when he reached the rising-place of the sun, he found it rising on a people whom We have not provided with any screen against it.

حَتَّىٰٓ إِذَا بَلَغَ مَطْلِعَ ٱلشَّمْسِ وَجَدَهَا تَطْلُعُ عَلَىٰ قَوْمٍ لَّمْ نَجْعَل لَّهُم مِّن دُونِهَا سِتْرًا ﴿٩٠﴾

91. So it was. We had full knowledge of what he had.

كَذَٰلِكَ وَقَدْ أَحَطْنَا بِمَا لَدَيْهِ خُبْرًا ﴿٩١﴾

92. Then he followed another course.

ثُمَّ أَتْبَعَ سَبَبًا ﴿٩٢﴾

93. But when he reached the point separating the two barriers, he found beside them a people who could barely understand what is said.

حَتَّىٰٓ إِذَا بَلَغَ بَيْنَ ٱلسَّدَّيْنِ وَجَدَ مِن دُونِهِمَا قَوْمًا لَّا يَكَادُونَ يَفْقَهُونَ قَوْلًا ﴿٩٣﴾

94. They said: "O Dhul-Qarnayn, surely Gog and Magog[577] are making mischief in the land. Shall we pay you a tribute so that you may build a barrier between us and them?"

قَالُوا۟ يَـٰذَا ٱلْقَرْنَيْنِ إِنَّ يَأْجُوجَ وَمَأْجُوجَ مُفْسِدُونَ فِى ٱلْأَرْضِ فَهَلْ نَجْعَلُ لَكَ خَرْجًا عَلَىٰٓ أَن تَجْعَلَ بَيْنَنَا وَبَيْنَهُمْ سَدًّا ﴿٩٤﴾

---

574. He is believed to be Alexander the Great.
575. That is, Paradise.
576. Dhul-Qarnayn.
577. Gog and Magog are the names of two tribes.

95. He said: "What my Lord has empowered me to do is better. So help me forcefully and I will build a barrier between you and them.

96. "Bring me large pieces of iron." So that when he had levelled up [the gap] between the two sides, he said: "Blow." And having turned it[578] into fire, he said: "Bring me molten brass to pour on it."

97. Then, they[579] could neither scale it nor make a hole through it.

98. He said: "This is a mercy from my Lord; but when my Lord's Promise comes to pass, He will turn it into rubble, and the Promise of my Lord is ever true."

99. And on that Day We shall make them surge upon one another, and the trumpet shall be blown, and We shall gather them together.

100. On that Day We shall boldly set Hell before the unbelievers.

101. Those whose eyes were closed to My Reminder[580] and they could not hear [it].

102. Have the unbelievers, then, supposed that they can take My servants besides Me, as protectors? We have indeed prepared Hell for the unbelievers as an abode.

103. Say: "Shall We inform you about the greatest losers of their works?

104. "Those whose endeavour in the present life has gone astray and they still believe that they are doing well.

105. "Those who disbelieve in the Revelations of their Lord and in meeting Him. Their works are in vain and We will not take any account of them on the Day of Resurrection.

قَالَ مَا مَكَّنِّي فِيهِ رَبِّي خَيْرٌ فَأَعِينُونِي بِقُوَّةٍ أَجْعَلْ بَيْنَكُمْ وَبَيْنَهُمْ رَدْمًا ﴿٩٥﴾

ءَاتُونِي زُبَرَ ٱلْحَدِيدِ حَتَّىٰ إِذَا سَاوَىٰ بَيْنَ ٱلصَّدَفَيْنِ قَالَ ٱنفُخُواْ حَتَّىٰ إِذَا جَعَلَهُ نَارًا قَالَ ءَاتُونِي أُفْرِغْ عَلَيْهِ قِطْرًا ﴿٩٦﴾

فَمَا ٱسْطَٰعُواْ أَن يَظْهَرُوهُ وَمَا ٱسْتَطَٰعُواْ لَهُ نَقْبًا ﴿٩٧﴾

قَالَ هَٰذَا رَحْمَةٌ مِّن رَّبِّي فَإِذَا جَآءَ وَعْدُ رَبِّي جَعَلَهُ دَكَّآءَ وَكَانَ وَعْدُ رَبِّي حَقًّا ﴿٩٨﴾

۞ وَتَرَكْنَا بَعْضَهُمْ يَوْمَئِذٍ يَمُوجُ فِي بَعْضٍ وَنُفِخَ فِي ٱلصُّورِ فَجَمَعْنَٰهُمْ جَمْعًا ﴿٩٩﴾

وَعَرَضْنَا جَهَنَّمَ يَوْمَئِذٍ لِّلْكَٰفِرِينَ عَرْضًا ﴿١٠٠﴾

ٱلَّذِينَ كَانَتْ أَعْيُنُهُمْ فِي غِطَآءٍ عَن ذِكْرِي وَكَانُواْ لَا يَسْتَطِيعُونَ سَمْعًا ﴿١٠١﴾

أَفَحَسِبَ ٱلَّذِينَ كَفَرُوٓاْ أَن يَتَّخِذُواْ عِبَادِي مِن دُونِيٓ أَوْلِيَآءَ إِنَّآ أَعْتَدْنَا جَهَنَّمَ لِلْكَٰفِرِينَ نُزُلًا ﴿١٠٢﴾

قُلْ هَلْ نُنَبِّئُكُم بِٱلْأَخْسَرِينَ أَعْمَٰلًا ﴿١٠٣﴾

ٱلَّذِينَ ضَلَّ سَعْيُهُمْ فِي ٱلْحَيَوٰةِ ٱلدُّنْيَا وَهُمْ يَحْسَبُونَ أَنَّهُمْ يُحْسِنُونَ صُنْعًا ﴿١٠٤﴾

أُوْلَٰٓئِكَ ٱلَّذِينَ كَفَرُواْ بِـَٔايَٰتِ رَبِّهِمْ وَلِقَآئِهِ فَحَبِطَتْ أَعْمَٰلُهُمْ فَلَا نُقِيمُ لَهُمْ يَوْمَ ٱلْقِيَٰمَةِ وَزْنًا ﴿١٠٥﴾

---

578. The iron.
579. Gog and Magog.
580. The Qur'an.

106. "That is their reward - Hell, on account of their disbelief and their taking My Revelations and My Messengers as objects of scorn.

107. "Indeed, those who believe and do the good works, the Gardens of Paradise shall be their dwelling.

108. "Abiding therein forever and not desiring to be ever removed therefrom."

109. Say: "Were the sea to become ink for my Lord's Words, the sea would be exhausted before the Words of my Lord are exhausted, even if We were to bring its like to replenish it."

110. Say: "I am only a mortal like you. It has been revealed to me that your God is One God. Let him who hopes to meet his Lord, do what is good and associate none in the worship of his Lord."

Sûrat Maryam, (Mary) 19

In the Name of Allah, the Compassionate, the Merciful

1. Kaf - Ha - Ya - 'Ain - Sâd.

2. This is the story of your Lord's Mercy unto His servant Zacharia;

3. When he called upon his Lord secretly.

4. He said: "Lord, my bones have weakened and my head is aflame with grey hair, and I have not, Lord, in vain called upon You.

5. "In truth, I fear my kinsmen, after I am gone, as my wife is barren. Grant me, then, from Your Bounty, a successor.

6. "To inherit me and inherit the house of Jacob, and make him, Lord, well-pleasing to You."

ذَٰلِكَ جَزَاؤُهُمْ جَهَنَّمُ بِمَا كَفَرُوا وَاتَّخَذُوا ءَايَٰتِي وَرُسُلِي هُزُوًا ﴿١٠٦﴾

إِنَّ الَّذِينَ ءَامَنُوا وَعَمِلُوا الصَّٰلِحَٰتِ كَانَتْ لَهُمْ جَنَّٰتُ الْفِرْدَوْسِ نُزُلًا ﴿١٠٧﴾

خَٰلِدِينَ فِيهَا لَا يَبْغُونَ عَنْهَا حِوَلًا ﴿١٠٨﴾

قُل لَّوْ كَانَ الْبَحْرُ مِدَادًا لِّكَلِمَٰتِ رَبِّي لَنَفِدَ الْبَحْرُ قَبْلَ أَن تَنفَدَ كَلِمَٰتُ رَبِّي وَلَوْ جِئْنَا بِمِثْلِهِۦ مَدَدًا ﴿١٠٩﴾

قُلْ إِنَّمَا أَنَا بَشَرٌ مِّثْلُكُمْ يُوحَىٰ إِلَيَّ أَنَّمَا إِلَٰهُكُمْ إِلَٰهٌ وَٰحِدٌ فَمَن كَانَ يَرْجُوا لِقَاءَ رَبِّهِۦ فَلْيَعْمَلْ عَمَلًا صَٰلِحًا وَلَا يُشْرِكْ بِعِبَادَةِ رَبِّهِۦٓ أَحَدًا ﴿١١٠﴾

سُورَةُ مَرْيَمَ

بِسْمِ اللَّهِ الرَّحْمَٰنِ الرَّحِيمِ

كٓهيعٓصٓ ﴿١﴾

ذِكْرُ رَحْمَتِ رَبِّكَ عَبْدَهُ زَكَرِيَّا ﴿٢﴾

إِذْ نَادَىٰ رَبَّهُۥ نِدَاءً خَفِيًّا ﴿٣﴾

قَالَ رَبِّ إِنِّي وَهَنَ الْعَظْمُ مِنِّي وَاشْتَعَلَ الرَّأْسُ شَيْبًا وَلَمْ أَكُن بِدُعَائِكَ رَبِّ شَقِيًّا ﴿٤﴾

وَإِنِّي خِفْتُ الْمَوَٰلِيَ مِن وَرَاءِي وَكَانَتِ امْرَأَتِي عَاقِرًا فَهَبْ لِي مِن لَّدُنكَ وَلِيًّا ﴿٥﴾

يَرِثُنِي وَيَرِثُ مِنْ ءَالِ يَعْقُوبَ وَاجْعَلْهُ رَبِّ رَضِيًّا ﴿٦﴾

7. [It was said to him]: "O Zacharia, We announce to you the good news of a boy whose name is John; We have not hitherto given the same name to anyone else."

8. He said: "Lord, how shall I have a boy, seeing that my wife is barren and I have reached an advanced old age?"

9. He said: "That is what your Lord says. It is easy for Me. Indeed I created you formerly, when you were nothing."

10. He said: "Lord, give me a sign." He said: "Your sign is that you will not talk to anybody for three nights, although you are sound of body."

11. He came out to his people from the sanctuary and told them by signs: "Pray and glorify morning and evening."

12. It was then said to John: "O John, hold fast to the Book." And We granted him wisdom when he was still a child;

13. And tenderness from Us and purity. He was devout;

14. And devoted to his parents; and he was not arrogant and disobedient.

15. Peace be upon him the day he was born, the day he dies and the day he is raised from the dead.

16. And remember [the account] of Mary in the Book when she withdrew from her people to an eastern place.

17. She screened herself away from them, and We sent to her Our Spirit and it appeared to her in the form of a well-shaped human being.

18. She said: "I seek refuge with Allah from you, if you do fear Allah."

19. He said: "I am only the messenger of your Lord to grant you a boy most pure."

يَٰزَكَرِيَّآ إِنَّا نُبَشِّرُكَ بِغُلَٰمٍ ٱسْمُهُۥ يَحْيَىٰ لَمْ نَجْعَل لَّهُۥ مِن قَبْلُ سَمِيًّا ٧

قَالَ رَبِّ أَنَّىٰ يَكُونُ لِي غُلَٰمٌ وَكَانَتِ ٱمْرَأَتِي عَاقِرًا وَقَدْ بَلَغْتُ مِنَ ٱلْكِبَرِ عِتِيًّا ٨

قَالَ كَذَٰلِكَ قَالَ رَبُّكَ هُوَ عَلَىَّ هَيِّنٌ وَقَدْ خَلَقْتُكَ مِن قَبْلُ وَلَمْ تَكُ شَيْـًٔا ٩

قَالَ رَبِّ ٱجْعَل لِّيٓ ءَايَةً قَالَ ءَايَتُكَ أَلَّا تُكَلِّمَ ٱلنَّاسَ ثَلَٰثَ لَيَالٍ سَوِيًّا ١٠

فَخَرَجَ عَلَىٰ قَوْمِهِۦ مِنَ ٱلْمِحْرَابِ فَأَوْحَىٰٓ إِلَيْهِمْ أَن سَبِّحُوا بُكْرَةً وَعَشِيًّا ١١

يَٰيَحْيَىٰ خُذِ ٱلْكِتَٰبَ بِقُوَّةٍ وَءَاتَيْنَٰهُ ٱلْحُكْمَ صَبِيًّا ١٢

وَحَنَانًا مِّن لَّدُنَّا وَزَكَوٰةً وَكَانَ تَقِيًّا ١٣

وَبَرًّۢا بِوَٰلِدَيْهِ وَلَمْ يَكُن جَبَّارًا عَصِيًّا ١٤

وَسَلَٰمٌ عَلَيْهِ يَوْمَ وُلِدَ وَيَوْمَ يَمُوتُ وَيَوْمَ يُبْعَثُ حَيًّا ١٥

وَٱذْكُرْ فِي ٱلْكِتَٰبِ مَرْيَمَ إِذِ ٱنتَبَذَتْ مِنْ أَهْلِهَا مَكَانًا شَرْقِيًّا ١٦

فَٱتَّخَذَتْ مِن دُونِهِمْ حِجَابًا فَأَرْسَلْنَآ إِلَيْهَا رُوحَنَا فَتَمَثَّلَ لَهَا بَشَرًا سَوِيًّا ١٧

قَالَتْ إِنِّيٓ أَعُوذُ بِٱلرَّحْمَٰنِ مِنكَ إِن كُنتَ تَقِيًّا ١٨

قَالَ إِنَّمَآ أَنَا۠ رَسُولُ رَبِّكِ لِأَهَبَ لَكِ غُلَٰمًا زَكِيًّا ١٩

20. She said: "Shall I have a boy, when no man has touched me and I have not been an unchaste woman?"

قَالَتْ أَنَّىٰ يَكُونُ لِي غُلَٰمٌ وَلَمْ يَمْسَسْنِي بَشَرٌ وَلَمْ أَكُ بَغِيًّا ﴿٢٠﴾

21. He[581] said: "Thus [it will be], your Lord has said: 'This is an easy matter for Me; that We may make him[582] a sign unto mankind and a Mercy from Us.' " And thus it was decreed.

قَالَ كَذَٰلِكِ قَالَ رَبُّكِ هُوَ عَلَىَّ هَيِّنٌ وَلِنَجْعَلَهُ ءَايَةً لِّلنَّاسِ وَرَحْمَةً مِّنَّا وَكَانَ أَمْرًا مَّقْضِيًّا ﴿٢١﴾

22. So, she conceived him and she withdrew with him to a distant place.

﴿ فَحَمَلَتْهُ فَٱنتَبَذَتْ بِهِۦ مَكَانًا قَصِيًّا ﴿٢٢﴾

23. Then labour pangs drove her towards the trunk of a palm tree. She said: "I wish I had died before this and had become completely forgotten."

فَأَجَآءَهَا ٱلْمَخَاضُ إِلَىٰ جِذْعِ ٱلنَّخْلَةِ قَالَتْ يَٰلَيْتَنِي مِتُّ قَبْلَ هَٰذَا وَكُنتُ نَسْيًا مَّنسِيًّا ﴿٢٣﴾

24. Whereupon [the babe (Jesus) or (Gabriel)] called her from beneath her: "Do not grieve. Your Lord has created below you a stream.

فَنَادَىٰهَا مِن تَحْتِهَآ أَلَّا تَحْزَنِي قَدْ جَعَلَ رَبُّكِ تَحْتَكِ سَرِيًّا ﴿٢٤﴾

25. "Shake the trunk of the palm tree towards you and it will drop upon you fresh ripe dates."

وَهُزِّي إِلَيْكِ بِجِذْعِ ٱلنَّخْلَةِ تُسَٰقِطْ عَلَيْكِ رُطَبًا جَنِيًّا ﴿٢٥﴾

26. "Eat, drink and rejoice. Then if you see any human say: 'I have vowed to the Compassionate to fast, and so I shall not talk today to any human being.' "

فَكُلِي وَٱشْرَبِي وَقَرِّي عَيْنًا فَإِمَّا تَرَيِنَّ مِنَ ٱلْبَشَرِ أَحَدًا فَقُولِي إِنِّي نَذَرْتُ لِلرَّحْمَٰنِ صَوْمًا فَلَنْ أُكَلِّمَ ٱلْيَوْمَ إِنسِيًّا ﴿٢٦﴾

27. Then she brought him[583] to her people, carrying him. They said: "O Mary, you have surely committed a strange thing.

فَأَتَتْ بِهِۦ قَوْمَهَا تَحْمِلُهُۥ قَالُوا۟ يَٰمَرْيَمُ لَقَدْ جِئْتِ شَيْئًا فَرِيًّا ﴿٢٧﴾

28. "Sister of Aaron, your father was not an evil man and your mother was not unchaste."

يَٰٓأُخْتَ هَٰرُونَ مَا كَانَ أَبُوكِ ٱمْرَأَ سَوْءٍ وَمَا كَانَتْ أُمُّكِ بَغِيًّا ﴿٢٨﴾

29. Whereupon she pointed to him. They said: "How will we talk to one who is still an infant in the cradle?"

فَأَشَارَتْ إِلَيْهِ قَالُوا۟ كَيْفَ نُكَلِّمُ مَن كَانَ فِي ٱلْمَهْدِ صَبِيًّا ﴿٢٩﴾

30. He (Jesus) said "Indeed, I am the servant of Allah, Who gave me the Book and made me a Prophet.

قَالَ إِنِّي عَبْدُ ٱللَّهِ ءَاتَٰنِيَ ٱلْكِتَٰبَ وَجَعَلَنِي نَبِيًّا ﴿٣٠﴾

---

581. The angel.
582. The boy, Jesus.
583. The child.

31. "And He made me blessed wherever I am, and has commanded me to pray and to give the alms, so long as I live;

32. "And be devoted to my mother; and He did not make me arrogant and mischievous.

33. "Peace be upon me the day I was born, the day I die and the day I rise from the dead."

34. Such was Jesus, son of Mary; it is the truth which they[584] dispute.

35. It is not fitting for Allah to have a son. Glory be to Him; when He decrees a thing, He simply says: "Be", and it comes to be.

36. Allah is truly your Lord and my Lord; so worship Him. That is a straight path.

37. Yet, the sects among them differed. Woe to those who have disbelieved from the spectacle of a great Day!

38. How well they will hear and how well they will see, on the Day they will come unto Us; but the wrongdoers today are in manifest error.

39. And warn them of the Day of sorrow, when the issue is decided, while they are heedless and do not believe.

40. It is We Who shall inherit the earth and whomever is on it, and to Us they shall be returned.

41. And remember in the Book Abraham. He was a truthful man, a Prophet.

42. He said to his father: "Father, why do you worship that which neither sees nor hears, and can do nothing to help you?

43. "To me has come knowledge which has not come to you; so follow me and I will guide you to a straight path.

---

584. The Christians.

44. "Father, do not worship the Devil; for the Devil has been rebelling against the Compassionate.

45. "Father, I fear that a punishment from the Compassionate shall afflict you, and so you will become a friend of the Devil."

46. He (the father) said: "Are you forsaking my gods, O Abraham? If you will not desist, I will certainly stone you. So leave me alone for a while."

47. (Abraham) said: "Peace be upon you. I will seek forgiveness for you from my Lord. He has, indeed, been gracious to me.

48. "And I will draw away from you and from those you call upon besides Allah, and I will pray to my Lord. Perhaps I may not be unfortunate in praying to my Lord."

49. Then, when he drew away from them and what they worshipped besides Allah, We granted him Isaac and Jacob and each We made a Prophet.

50. And We gave them freely of Our Mercy and We accorded them an honourable and true renown.

51. And [remember] in the Book Moses; he was sincere, a Messenger and a Prophet.

52. We called him from the right side of the Mount, and brought him closer in communion.

53. And We granted him, out of Our Mercy, his brother Aaron, a Prophet.

54. And mention in the Book Isma'il; he was true to his promises and was a Messenger and a Prophet.

55. He enjoined on his people prayer and almsgiving and was well-pleasing to his Lord.

56. And mention in the Book Idris; he was truthful and a Prophet.

يَٰٓأَبَتِ لَا تَعْبُدِ ٱلشَّيْطَٰنَ إِنَّ ٱلشَّيْطَٰنَ كَانَ لِلرَّحْمَٰنِ عَصِيًّا ﴿٤٤﴾

يَٰٓأَبَتِ إِنِّىٓ أَخَافُ أَن يَمَسَّكَ عَذَابٌ مِّنَ ٱلرَّحْمَٰنِ فَتَكُونَ لِلشَّيْطَٰنِ وَلِيًّا ﴿٤٥﴾

قَالَ أَرَاغِبٌ أَنتَ عَنْ ءَالِهَتِى يَٰٓإِبْرَٰهِيمُ لَئِن لَّمْ تَنتَهِ لَأَرْجُمَنَّكَ وَٱهْجُرْنِى مَلِيًّا ﴿٤٦﴾

قَالَ سَلَٰمٌ عَلَيْكَ سَأَسْتَغْفِرُ لَكَ رَبِّىٓ إِنَّهُۥ كَانَ بِى حَفِيًّا ﴿٤٧﴾

وَأَعْتَزِلُكُمْ وَمَا تَدْعُونَ مِن دُونِ ٱللَّهِ وَأَدْعُوا۟ رَبِّى عَسَىٰٓ أَلَّآ أَكُونَ بِدُعَآءِ رَبِّى شَقِيًّا ﴿٤٨﴾

فَلَمَّا ٱعْتَزَلَهُمْ وَمَا يَعْبُدُونَ مِن دُونِ ٱللَّهِ وَهَبْنَا لَهُۥٓ إِسْحَٰقَ وَيَعْقُوبَ وَكُلًّا جَعَلْنَا نَبِيًّا ﴿٤٩﴾

وَوَهَبْنَا لَهُم مِّن رَّحْمَتِنَا وَجَعَلْنَا لَهُمْ لِسَانَ صِدْقٍ عَلِيًّا ﴿٥٠﴾

وَٱذْكُرْ فِى ٱلْكِتَٰبِ مُوسَىٰٓ إِنَّهُۥ كَانَ مُخْلَصًا وَكَانَ رَسُولًا نَّبِيًّا ﴿٥١﴾

وَنَٰدَيْنَٰهُ مِن جَانِبِ ٱلطُّورِ ٱلْأَيْمَنِ وَقَرَّبْنَٰهُ نَجِيًّا ﴿٥٢﴾

وَوَهَبْنَا لَهُۥ مِن رَّحْمَتِنَآ أَخَاهُ هَٰرُونَ نَبِيًّا ﴿٥٣﴾

وَٱذْكُرْ فِى ٱلْكِتَٰبِ إِسْمَٰعِيلَ إِنَّهُۥ كَانَ صَادِقَ ٱلْوَعْدِ وَكَانَ رَسُولًا نَّبِيًّا ﴿٥٤﴾

وَكَانَ يَأْمُرُ أَهْلَهُۥ بِٱلصَّلَوٰةِ وَٱلزَّكَوٰةِ وَكَانَ عِندَ رَبِّهِۦ مَرْضِيًّا ﴿٥٥﴾

وَٱذْكُرْ فِى ٱلْكِتَٰبِ إِدْرِيسَ إِنَّهُۥ كَانَ صِدِّيقًا نَّبِيًّا ﴿٥٦﴾

57. And We raised him to a high place.

58. Those are the ones whom Allah favoured from among the Prophets of the progeny of Adam, of those We carried with Noah, of the progeny of Abraham and Israel and of those We have guided and elected. When the Revelations of the Compassionate were recited to them, they fell down prostrate and weeping.

59. Then there came after them a posterity who forgot all about prayer and followed their lusts. They shall face perdition.

60. Except for those who repent, believe and do what is right. Those shall enter Paradise and will not be wronged at all,

61. Gardens of Eden that the Compassionate has promised His servants in the Unseen. His Promise will certainly be accomplished.

62. They hear therein no idle talk, but only: "Peace"; and they receive their provision therein morning and evening.

63. Such is the Paradise which We shall give as inheritance to those of Our servants who are God-fearing.

64. We[585] do not come down except at the Command of your Lord. His is what is before us, what is behind us and what is in between. Your Lord is never forgetful.

65. Lord of the heavens and the earth and what is between them. So worship Him and be steadfast in His worship; do you know anyone who is worthy of the same name?

66. Man says: "If I die, shall I be raised from the dead?"

67. Does not man remember that We created him before, when he was nothing?

---

585. That is, the angels.

68. By your Lord, then, We shall certainly gather them together with the devils, then We will lead them around Hell on their knees.

69. Then We shall seize from each group the most rebellious against the Compassionate.

70. And We certainly know best who among them deserves most to be burned therein.

71. There is not one of you but will go down to it.[586] That is for your Lord a Decree which must be accomplished.

72. Then, We shall deliver the righteous and leave the wrongdoers therein on their knees.

73. And when Our Revelations are clearly recited to them, the unbelievers will say to the believers: "Which of the two parties is better in position and fairer in company?"

74. How many generations before them We have destroyed, who had better furnishings and appearance?

75. Say: "Whoever is in error, let the Compassionate prolong his term; so that when they see what they are threatened with, whether it be the punishment or the Hour, they will know who is worse in position and weaker in supporters."

76. Allah increases in guidance those who are rightly guided; and the good works which last will receive a better reward from Allah and better returns.

77. Have you seen him who disbelieves in Our Revelations and [yet] says: "I shall certainly be given wealth and children."

78. Does he have knowledge of the Unseen, or did he take a pledge from the Compassionate?

---

586. That is, Hell.

307

79. No, We shall write down what he says and shall add punishment to his punishment.

كَلَّا سَنَكْتُبُ مَا يَقُولُ وَنَمُدُّ لَهُ مِنَ ٱلْعَذَابِ مَدًّا ﴿٧٩﴾

80. And We will inherit from him what he says and he will come to Us alone.

وَنَرِثُهُ مَا يَقُولُ وَيَأْتِينَا فَرْدًا ﴿٨٠﴾

81. And they took, besides Allah, other gods, to be for them a source of strength.

وَٱتَّخَذُوا۟ مِن دُونِ ٱللَّهِ ءَالِهَةً لِّيَكُونُوا۟ لَهُمْ عِزًّا ﴿٨١﴾

82. No, they shall repudiate their worship and turn against them.

كَلَّا سَيَكْفُرُونَ بِعِبَادَتِهِمْ وَيَكُونُونَ عَلَيْهِمْ ضِدًّا ﴿٨٢﴾

83. Have you not seen how We sent the devils against the unbelievers to keep inciting them [to sin].

أَلَمْ تَرَ أَنَّا أَرْسَلْنَا ٱلشَّيَٰطِينَ عَلَى ٱلْكَٰفِرِينَ تَؤُزُّهُمْ أَزًّا ﴿٨٣﴾

84. So do not hasten [their punishment]. We are indeed counting for them the days.

فَلَا تَعْجَلْ عَلَيْهِمْ إِنَّمَا نَعُدُّ لَهُمْ عَدًّا ﴿٨٤﴾

85. The day We shall gather the God-fearing before the Compassionate as one party.

يَوْمَ نَحْشُرُ ٱلْمُتَّقِينَ إِلَى ٱلرَّحْمَٰنِ وَفْدًا ﴿٨٥﴾

86. And drive the wicked into Hell as one thirsty herd.

وَنَسُوقُ ٱلْمُجْرِمِينَ إِلَىٰ جَهَنَّمَ وِرْدًا ﴿٨٦﴾

87. They have no power of intercession, except for him who has taken a pledge from the Compassionate.

لَّا يَمْلِكُونَ ٱلشَّفَٰعَةَ إِلَّا مَنِ ٱتَّخَذَ عِندَ ٱلرَّحْمَٰنِ عَهْدًا ﴿٨٧﴾

88. And they say: "The Compassionate has taken to Himself a son."

وَقَالُوا۟ ٱتَّخَذَ ٱلرَّحْمَٰنُ وَلَدًا ﴿٨٨﴾

89. You have, indeed, made a shocking assertion,

لَّقَدْ جِئْتُمْ شَيْئًا إِدًّا ﴿٨٩﴾

90. From which the heavens are almost rent asunder, the earth is split and the mountains fall to pieces.

تَكَادُ ٱلسَّمَٰوَٰتُ يَتَفَطَّرْنَ مِنْهُ وَتَنشَقُّ ٱلْأَرْضُ وَتَخِرُّ ٱلْجِبَالُ هَدًّا ﴿٩٠﴾

91. For they ascribe a son to the Compassionate.

أَن دَعَوْا۟ لِلرَّحْمَٰنِ وَلَدًا ﴿٩١﴾

92. Whereas, it is not fitting that the Compassionate should have a son.

وَمَا يَنۢبَغِى لِلرَّحْمَٰنِ أَن يَتَّخِذَ وَلَدًا ﴿٩٢﴾

93. Everyone in the heavens and on earth will surely come to the Compassionate as a servant.

إِن كُلُّ مَن فِى ٱلسَّمَٰوَٰتِ وَٱلْأَرْضِ إِلَّآ ءَاتِى ٱلرَّحْمَٰنِ عَبْدًا ﴿٩٣﴾

94. He keeps count of them and has numbered them.

لَّقَدْ أَحْصَىٰهُمْ وَعَدَّهُمْ عَدًّا ﴿٩٤﴾

وَكُلُّهُمْ ءَاتِيهِ يَوْمَ ٱلْقِيَمَةِ فَرْدًا ﴿٩٥﴾

95. And every one of them will come to Him on the Day of Resurrection alone.

إِنَّ ٱلَّذِينَ ءَامَنُوا وَعَمِلُوا ٱلصَّلِحَتِ سَيَجْعَلُ لَهُمُ ٱلرَّحْمَنُ وُدًّا ﴿٩٦﴾

96. Those who believe and do what is right, the Compassionate will favour with love.[587]

فَإِنَّمَا يَسَّرْنَهُ بِلِسَانِكَ لِتُبَشِّرَ بِهِ ٱلْمُتَّقِينَ وَتُنذِرَ بِهِ قَوْمًا لُّدًّا ﴿٩٧﴾

97. For We made it easy[588] [to understand] in your own tongue, so as to announce the good news to the God-fearing and warn through it.[589]

وَكَمْ أَهْلَكْنَا قَبْلَهُم مِّن قَرْنٍ هَلْ تُحِسُّ مِنْهُم مِّنْ أَحَدٍ أَوْ تَسْمَعُ لَهُمْ رِكْزًا ﴿٩٨﴾

98. And how many a generation before them We have destroyed! Do you perceive any one of them or hear any sound of theirs?

Sûrat Tâ Hâ, (Taha) 20

In the Name of Allah, the Compassionate, the Merciful

بِسْمِ ٱللَّهِ ٱلرَّحْمَنِ ٱلرَّحِيمِ

1. Ta Ha.[590]

طه ﴿١﴾

2. We have not revealed the Qur'an to you so as to make you unhappy.

مَا أَنزَلْنَا عَلَيْكَ ٱلْقُرْءَانَ لِتَشْقَى ﴿٢﴾

3. But only as a reminder to him who fears.

إِلَّا تَذْكِرَةً لِّمَن يَخْشَى ﴿٣﴾

4. A revelation from Him Who created the earth and the high heavens.

تَنزِيلًا مِّمَّنْ خَلَقَ ٱلْأَرْضَ وَٱلسَّمَوَتِ ٱلْعُلَى ﴿٤﴾

5. The Compassionate has sat upon the Throne.

ٱلرَّحْمَنُ عَلَى ٱلْعَرْشِ ٱسْتَوَى ﴿٥﴾

6. To Him belongs what is in the heavens, and what is in the earth, and what is in between them, as well as what is beneath the ground.

لَهُ مَا فِي ٱلسَّمَوَتِ وَمَا فِي ٱلْأَرْضِ وَمَا بَيْنَهُمَا وَمَا تَحْتَ ٱلثَّرَى ﴿٦﴾

7. If you speak aloud, He surely knows the secret and what is even more hidden.

وَإِن تَجْهَرْ بِٱلْقَوْلِ فَإِنَّهُ يَعْلَمُ ٱلسِّرَّ وَأَخْفَى ﴿٧﴾

8. Allah, there is no god but He. His are the Most Beautiful Names.

ٱللَّهُ لَا إِلَهَ إِلَّا هُوَ لَهُ ٱلْأَسْمَاءُ ٱلْحُسْنَى ﴿٨﴾

---

587. His love and that of their fellow creatures.
588. The Qur'an.
589. The Meccan unbelievers.
590. These two Arabic letters mean, according to some commentators, •O man•.

9. Has the story of Moses reached you?

10. When he saw a fire, he said to his people: "Stay. I see a fire. Perhaps I can bring you a lighted torch therefrom or find guidance by the fire."

11. Then, when he came to it, a voice called out: "O Moses,

12. "I am truly your Lord; so take off your shoes, you are in the holy valley, Tuwa.

13. "And I have chosen you; so listen to what is being revealed.

14. "I am truly Allah; there is no god but I; so worship Me and perform the prayer for My Remembrance.

15. "Surely, the Hour is coming - but I keep it almost hidden - so that each soul may be rewarded for its work.

16. "Let no one who does not believe and follows his own desires, bar you from it lest you perish.

17. "And what is that in your right hand, O Moses?"

18. He said: "It is my staff. I lean on it and I beat leaves for my sheep with it and I have other uses for it."

19. He (Allah) said: "Cast it down, O Moses."

20. So he cast it down, and lo and behold, it was a serpent, sliding.

21. He (Allah) said: "Pick it up and do not fear; We shall restore it to its original condition.

22. "And press your hand to your side; it will come out white, without blemish, as another sign,

23. "That We may show you some of Our Greatest Signs.

24. "Go to Pharaoh; for he has transgressed."

وَهَلْ أَتَىٰكَ حَدِيثُ مُوسَىٰ ﴿٩﴾

إِذْ رَءَا نَارًا فَقَالَ لِأَهْلِهِ ٱمْكُثُوٓا۟ إِنِّىٓ ءَانَسْتُ نَارًا لَّعَلِّىٓ ءَاتِيكُم مِّنْهَا بِقَبَسٍ أَوْ أَجِدُ عَلَى ٱلنَّارِ هُدًى ﴿١٠﴾

فَلَمَّآ أَتَىٰهَا نُودِىَ يَٰمُوسَىٰٓ ﴿١١﴾

إِنِّىٓ أَنَا۠ رَبُّكَ فَٱخْلَعْ نَعْلَيْكَ إِنَّكَ بِٱلْوَادِ ٱلْمُقَدَّسِ طُوًى ﴿١٢﴾

وَأَنَا ٱخْتَرْتُكَ فَٱسْتَمِعْ لِمَا يُوحَىٰٓ ﴿١٣﴾

إِنَّنِىٓ أَنَا ٱللَّهُ لَآ إِلَٰهَ إِلَّآ أَنَا۠ فَٱعْبُدْنِى وَأَقِمِ ٱلصَّلَوٰةَ لِذِكْرِىٓ ﴿١٤﴾

إِنَّ ٱلسَّاعَةَ ءَاتِيَةٌ أَكَادُ أُخْفِيهَا لِتُجْزَىٰ كُلُّ نَفْسٍ بِمَا تَسْعَىٰ ﴿١٥﴾

فَلَا يَصُدَّنَّكَ عَنْهَا مَن لَّا يُؤْمِنُ بِهَا وَٱتَّبَعَ هَوَىٰهُ فَتَرْدَىٰ ﴿١٦﴾

وَمَا تِلْكَ بِيَمِينِكَ يَٰمُوسَىٰ ﴿١٧﴾

قَالَ هِىَ عَصَاىَ أَتَوَكَّؤُا۟ عَلَيْهَا وَأَهُشُّ بِهَا عَلَىٰ غَنَمِى وَلِىَ فِيهَا مَـَٔارِبُ أُخْرَىٰ ﴿١٨﴾

قَالَ أَلْقِهَا يَٰمُوسَىٰ ﴿١٩﴾

فَأَلْقَىٰهَا فَإِذَا هِىَ حَيَّةٌ تَسْعَىٰ ﴿٢٠﴾

قَالَ خُذْهَا وَلَا تَخَفْ سَنُعِيدُهَا سِيرَتَهَا ٱلْأُولَىٰ ﴿٢١﴾

وَٱضْمُمْ يَدَكَ إِلَىٰ جَنَاحِكَ تَخْرُجْ بَيْضَآءَ مِنْ غَيْرِ سُوٓءٍ ءَايَةً أُخْرَىٰ ﴿٢٢﴾

لِنُرِيَكَ مِنْ ءَايَٰتِنَا ٱلْكُبْرَى ﴿٢٣﴾

ٱذْهَبْ إِلَىٰ فِرْعَوْنَ إِنَّهُ طَغَىٰ ﴿٢٤﴾

310

25. He said: "Lord, open[591] my breast for me,

قَالَ رَبِّ ٱشۡرَحۡ لِي صَدۡرِي ﴿٢٥﴾

26. "And make my task easy for me.

وَيَسِّرۡ لِيٓ أَمۡرِي ﴿٢٦﴾

27. "And unravel the knot of my tongue.

وَٱحۡلُلۡ عُقۡدَةً مِّن لِّسَانِي ﴿٢٧﴾

28. "That they may understand my words.

يَفۡقَهُواْ قَوۡلِي ﴿٢٨﴾

29. "And give me, from my own family, a supporter,[592]

وَٱجۡعَل لِّي وَزِيرًا مِّنۡ أَهۡلِي ﴿٢٩﴾

30. "Aaron, my brother.

هَٰرُونَ أَخِي ﴿٣٠﴾

31. "And increase through him my strength.

ٱشۡدُدۡ بِهِۦٓ أَزۡرِي ﴿٣١﴾

32. "And associate him with me in my task.

وَأَشۡرِكۡهُ فِيٓ أَمۡرِي ﴿٣٢﴾

33. "So that we may glorify You;

كَيۡ نُسَبِّحَكَ كَثِيرًا ﴿٣٣﴾

34. "And remember You often.

وَنَذۡكُرَكَ كَثِيرًا ﴿٣٤﴾

35. "You have surely been observant of us."

إِنَّكَ كُنتَ بِنَا بَصِيرًا ﴿٣٥﴾

36. He[593] said: "You have been granted your request, O Moses.

قَالَ قَدۡ أُوتِيتَ سُؤۡلَكَ يَٰمُوسَىٰ ﴿٣٦﴾

37. "And We have favoured you another time.

وَلَقَدۡ مَنَنَّا عَلَيۡكَ مَرَّةً أُخۡرَىٰٓ ﴿٣٧﴾

38. "When We revealed to your mother a revelation [saying]:

إِذۡ أَوۡحَيۡنَآ إِلَىٰٓ أُمِّكَ مَا يُوحَىٰٓ ﴿٣٨﴾

39. "'Put him in a chest and cast him into the river. The river will then cast him off on the shore, and he will be taken by an enemy of Mine and an enemy of his. And I bestowed upon you a love from Me, so that you may be reared before My Eyes.'

أَنِ ٱقۡذِفِيهِ فِي ٱلتَّابُوتِ فَٱقۡذِفِيهِ فِي ٱلۡيَمِّ فَلۡيُلۡقِهِ ٱلۡيَمُّ بِٱلسَّاحِلِ يَأۡخُذۡهُ عَدُوٌّ لِّي وَعَدُوٌّ لَّهُۥۚ وَأَلۡقَيۡتُ عَلَيۡكَ مَحَبَّةً مِّنِّي وَلِتُصۡنَعَ عَلَىٰ عَيۡنِيٓ ﴿٣٩﴾

40. "When your sister went and said: 'Shall I tell you about one who will take charge of him?'[594] So We turned you over to your mother, that she may rejoice and not grieve. Then you killed a living soul, but We delivered you from anguish; and We tried you repeatedly, so you stayed years among the people of Midian. Then you came, as decreed, O Moses.

إِذۡ تَمۡشِيٓ أُخۡتُكَ فَتَقُولُ هَلۡ أَدُلُّكُمۡ عَلَىٰ مَن يَكۡفُلُهُۥۖ فَرَجَعۡنَٰكَ إِلَىٰٓ أُمِّكَ كَيۡ تَقَرَّ عَيۡنُهَا وَلَا تَحۡزَنَۚ وَقَتَلۡتَ نَفۡسًا فَنَجَّيۡنَٰكَ مِنَ ٱلۡغَمِّ وَفَتَنَّٰكَ فُتُونًاۚ فَلَبِثۡتَ سِنِينَ فِيٓ أَهۡلِ مَدۡيَنَ ثُمَّ جِئۡتَ عَلَىٰ قَدَرٍ يَٰمُوسَىٰ ﴿٤٠﴾

---

591. Literally, expand.
592. Literally, a minister.
593. Allah.
594. That is, will nurse him.

41. "And I chose you for Myself.

وَٱصْطَنَعْتُكَ لِنَفْسِى ﴿٤١﴾

42. "Go, then, you and your brother, with My Signs, and do not tire of remembering Me.

ٱذْهَبْ أَنتَ وَأَخُوكَ بِـَٔايَٰتِى وَلَا تَنِيَا فِى ذِكْرِى ﴿٤٢﴾

43. "Go forth to Pharaoh; for he has surely transgressed.

ٱذْهَبَآ إِلَىٰ فِرْعَوْنَ إِنَّهُۥ طَغَىٰ ﴿٤٣﴾

44. "Speak to him gently, that perchance he may take heed or fear."

فَقُولَا لَهُۥ قَوْلًا لَّيِّنًا لَّعَلَّهُۥ يَتَذَكَّرُ أَوْ يَخْشَىٰ ﴿٤٤﴾

45. They said: "Our Lord, we fear that he may hasten to do us harm, or transgress."

قَالَا رَبَّنَآ إِنَّنَا نَخَافُ أَن يَفْرُطَ عَلَيْنَآ أَوْ أَن يَطْغَىٰ ﴿٤٥﴾

46. He (Allah) said: "Do not fear. Surely I am with you hearing and seeing.

قَالَ لَا تَخَافَآ إِنَّنِى مَعَكُمَآ أَسْمَعُ وَأَرَىٰ ﴿٤٦﴾

47. "So go forth to him and say: 'We are your Lord's Messengers; so send the Children of Israel along with us and do not torture them. We have brought you a sign from your Lord. Peace be upon him who follows the guidance.' "

فَأْتِيَاهُ فَقُولَآ إِنَّا رَسُولَا رَبِّكَ فَأَرْسِلْ مَعَنَا بَنِىٓ إِسْرَٰٓئِيلَ وَلَا تُعَذِّبْهُمْ قَدْ جِئْنَٰكَ بِـَٔايَةٍ مِّن رَّبِّكَ وَٱلسَّلَٰمُ عَلَىٰ مَنِ ٱتَّبَعَ ٱلْهُدَىٰٓ ﴿٤٧﴾

48. "It has been revealed to us [Moses and Aaron] that punishment shall afflict him who disbelieves and turns his back."

إِنَّا قَدْ أُوحِىَ إِلَيْنَآ أَنَّ ٱلْعَذَابَ عَلَىٰ مَن كَذَّبَ وَتَوَلَّىٰ ﴿٤٨﴾

49. He[595] said: "Who, then, is your Lord, O Moses?"

قَالَ فَمَن رَّبُّكُمَا يَٰمُوسَىٰ ﴿٤٩﴾

50. He (Moses) said: "Our Lord is He Who gave everything its nature, then guided it."

قَالَ رَبُّنَا ٱلَّذِىٓ أَعْطَىٰ كُلَّ شَىْءٍ خَلْقَهُۥ ثُمَّ هَدَىٰ ﴿٥٠﴾

51. (Paraoh) said: "What about the former generations?"

قَالَ فَمَا بَالُ ٱلْقُرُونِ ٱلْأُولَىٰ ﴿٥١﴾

52. (Moses) said: "The knowledge thereof is with my Lord in a Book. My Lord neither errs nor forgets."

قَالَ عِلْمُهَا عِندَ رَبِّى فِى كِتَٰبٍ لَّا يَضِلُّ رَبِّى وَلَا يَنسَى ﴿٥٢﴾

53. He Who made the earth a bed for you, and opened routes for you in it, and sent down water from the sky; from it We bring forth diverse pairs of plants.

ٱلَّذِى جَعَلَ لَكُمُ ٱلْأَرْضَ مَهْدًا وَسَلَكَ لَكُمْ فِيهَا سُبُلًا وَأَنزَلَ مِنَ ٱلسَّمَآءِ مَآءً فَأَخْرَجْنَا بِهِۦٓ أَزْوَٰجًا مِّن نَّبَاتٍ شَتَّىٰ ﴿٥٣﴾

54. Eat and pasture your cattle. In that there are signs for people of understanding.

كُلُوا۟ وَٱرْعَوْا۟ أَنْعَٰمَكُمْ إِنَّ فِى ذَٰلِكَ لَءَايَٰتٍ لِّأُو۟لِى ٱلنُّهَىٰ ﴿٥٤﴾

---

595. Pharaoh.

55. From it We have created you, and into it We shall return you, and from it We shall raise you a second time.

56. And We have shown him[596] all Our Signs, but he denied them and refused [to believe].

57. He (Paraoh) said: "Have you come, Moses, to drive us out of our land by means of your sorcery?

58. "We shall bring you similar sorcery; so make an appointment between us and you, which neither we nor you shall break, in a central place."

59. He (Moses) said: "Your appointment is set for the day of the Feast, so let the people be gathered together before noon."

60. Pharaoh turned away and gathered [his men] of guile, then came along.

61. Moses said to them: "Woe to you. Do not lie about Allah lest He should destroy you with punishment. Indeed, he who lies shall fail."

62. So, they disagreed among themselves with respect to their affair and conferred secretly.

63. They said: "Those are two sorcerers who want to drive you out of your land with their sorcery and put an end to your ideal tradition.

64. "So gather your guile and then come forward in battle array; for today he who has the upper hand shall prosper."

65. They said: "O Moses, either you cast down, or we will be the first to cast down."

---

596. Pharaoh.

66. He said: "You had better cast down"; and behold, their ropes and staffs appeared to him, by reason of their sorcery, to glide.

قَالَ بَلْ أَلْقُوا فَإِذَا حِبَالُهُمْ وَعِصِيُّهُمْ يُخَيَّلُ إِلَيْهِ مِن سِحْرِهِمْ أَنَّهَا تَسْعَىٰ ٦٦

67. So, Moses felt apprehensive within himself.

فَأَوْجَسَ فِي نَفْسِهِ خِيفَةً مُّوسَىٰ ٦٧

68. We (Allah) said: "Do not be afraid, you certainly have the upper hand.

قُلْنَا لَا تَخَفْ إِنَّكَ أَنتَ الْأَعْلَىٰ ٦٨

69. "Cast down what is in your right hand and it will swallow what they have faked. They have only faked the guile of a magician, and the magician will never prosper wherever he goes."

وَأَلْقِ مَا فِي يَمِينِكَ تَلْقَفْ مَا صَنَعُوا إِنَّمَا صَنَعُوا كَيْدُ سَاحِرٍ وَلَا يُفْلِحُ السَّاحِرُ حَيْثُ أَتَىٰ ٦٩

70. Then the magicians fell down prostrate. They said: "We believe [now] in the Lord of Aaron and Moses."

فَأُلْقِيَ السَّحَرَةُ سُجَّدًا قَالُوا آمَنَّا بِرَبِّ هَارُونَ وَمُوسَىٰ ٧٠

71. He[597] said: "Do you believe in him before I give you leave? It must be your chief who has taught you magic. I shall then cut your hands and feet on alternate sides, and I will crucify you upon the trunks of palm trees, and you will certainly know whose punishment is sterner and more lasting."

قَالَ آمَنتُمْ لَهُ قَبْلَ أَنْ آذَنَ لَكُمْ إِنَّهُ لَكَبِيرُكُمُ الَّذِي عَلَّمَكُمُ السِّحْرَ فَلَأُقَطِّعَنَّ أَيْدِيَكُمْ وَأَرْجُلَكُم مِّنْ خِلَافٍ وَلَأُصَلِّبَنَّكُمْ فِي جُذُوعِ النَّخْلِ وَلَتَعْلَمُنَّ أَيُّنَا أَشَدُّ عَذَابًا وَأَبْقَىٰ ٧١

72. They said: "We cannot prefer you to what came to us of clear proofs and to Him Who created us. So, decide what you will decide; you only decide regarding this present life.

قَالُوا لَن نُّؤْثِرَكَ عَلَىٰ مَا جَاءَنَا مِنَ الْبَيِّنَاتِ وَالَّذِي فَطَرَنَا فَاقْضِ مَا أَنتَ قَاضٍ إِنَّمَا تَقْضِي هَٰذِهِ الْحَيَاةَ الدُّنْيَا ٧٢

73. "We have believed in our Lord, that He may forgive us our sins and what you forced us to practise of magic. Allah is best and most abiding."

إِنَّا آمَنَّا بِرَبِّنَا لِيَغْفِرَ لَنَا خَطَايَانَا وَمَا أَكْرَهْتَنَا عَلَيْهِ مِنَ السِّحْرِ وَاللَّهُ خَيْرٌ وَأَبْقَىٰ ٧٣

74. For him who comes to his Lord, as a wicked sinner, is Hell, where he neither dies nor lives.

إِنَّهُ مَن يَأْتِ رَبَّهُ مُجْرِمًا فَإِنَّ لَهُ جَهَنَّمَ لَا يَمُوتُ فِيهَا وَلَا يَحْيَىٰ ٧٤

75. But those who come to Him as believers, who have done good works will have the highest ranks;

وَمَن يَأْتِهِ مُؤْمِنًا قَدْ عَمِلَ الصَّالِحَاتِ فَأُولَٰئِكَ لَهُمُ الدَّرَجَاتُ الْعُلَىٰ ٧٥

---

597. Pharaoh.

76. Gardens of Eden, beneath which rivers flow, dwelling therein forever. That is the reward of him who purifies himself.

جَنَّـٰتُ عَدۡنٖ تَجۡرِى مِن تَحۡتِهَا ٱلۡأَنۡهَـٰرُ خَـٰلِدِينَ فِيهَاۚ وَذَٰلِكَ جَزَآءُ مَن تَزَكَّىٰ ﴿٧٦﴾

77. And We revealed to Moses (saying): "Set out at night with My servants and strike for them a dry path in the sea, not fearing to be overtaken nor dreading anything."

وَلَقَدۡ أَوۡحَيۡنَآ إِلَىٰ مُوسَىٰٓ أَنۡ أَسۡرِ بِعِبَادِى فَٱضۡرِبۡ لَهُمۡ طَرِيقٗا فِى ٱلۡبَحۡرِ يَبَسٗا لَّا تَخَـٰفُ دَرَكٗا وَلَا تَخۡشَىٰ ﴿٧٧﴾

78. Then Pharaoh pursued them with his troops and so they[598] were overwhelmed by the water.

فَأَتۡبَعَهُمۡ فِرۡعَوۡنُ بِجُنُودِهِۦ فَغَشِيَهُم مِّنَ ٱلۡيَمِّ مَا غَشِيَهُمۡ ﴿٧٨﴾

79. Pharaoh thus led his people astray and did not guide them rightly.

وَأَضَلَّ فِرۡعَوۡنُ قَوۡمَهُۥ وَمَا هَدَىٰ ﴿٧٩﴾

80. O Children of Israel, We have delivered you from your enemy and We made a covenant with you on the right side of the Mount, and sent down to you the manna and quails.

يَـٰبَنِىٓ إِسۡرَٰٓءِيلَ قَدۡ أَنجَيۡنَـٰكُم مِّنۡ عَدُوِّكُمۡ وَوَٰعَدۡنَـٰكُمۡ جَانِبَ ٱلطُّورِ ٱلۡأَيۡمَنَ وَنَزَّلۡنَا عَلَيۡكُمُ ٱلۡمَنَّ وَٱلسَّلۡوَىٰ ﴿٨٠﴾

81. Eat of the good things We have provided you with, but do not be excessive therein, lest My Wrath descend upon you. Those upon whom My Wrath descends shall be ruined.

كُلُوا۟ مِن طَيِّبَـٰتِ مَا رَزَقۡنَـٰكُمۡ وَلَا تَطۡغَوۡا۟ فِيهِ فَيَحِلَّ عَلَيۡكُمۡ غَضَبِىۖ وَمَن يَحۡلِلۡ عَلَيۡهِ غَضَبِى فَقَدۡ هَوَىٰ ﴿٨١﴾

82. I am, indeed, All-Forgiving unto him who repents, does the righteous deed and is well-guided.

وَإِنِّى لَغَفَّارٌ لِّمَن تَابَ وَءَامَنَ وَعَمِلَ صَـٰلِحٗا ثُمَّ ٱهۡتَدَىٰ ﴿٨٢﴾

83. "What has led you to go ahead of your people, O Moses?"

۞ وَمَآ أَعۡجَلَكَ عَن قَوۡمِكَ يَـٰمُوسَىٰ ﴿٨٣﴾

84. He said: "Those people are on my tracks, so I have hastened towards You, O Lord, that You may be well-pleased."

قَالَ هُمۡ أُو۟لَآءِ عَلَىٰٓ أَثَرِى وَعَجِلۡتُ إِلَيۡكَ رَبِّ لِتَرۡضَىٰ ﴿٨٤﴾

85. He (Allah) said: "We have tried your people after you left and the Samaritan[599] has led them astray."

قَالَ فَإِنَّا قَدۡ فَتَنَّا قَوۡمَكَ مِنۢ بَعۡدِكَ وَأَضَلَّهُمُ ٱلسَّامِرِىُّ ﴿٨٥﴾

---

598. Pharaoh's troops.
599. A Samaritan Jew.

86. So, Moses went back to his people furious and sorrowful. He said: "O my people, has not your Lord made a fair promise to you? Has the promise, then, been protracted for you? Or did you want your Lord's anger to overtake you, and so you broke your promise to me?"

فَرَجَعَ مُوسَىٰ إِلَىٰ قَوْمِهِ غَضْبَٰنَ أَسِفًا قَالَ أَلَمْ يَعِدْكُمْ رَبُّكُمْ وَعْدًا حَسَنًا أَفَطَالَ عَلَيْكُمُ ٱلْعَهْدُ أَمْ أَرَدتُّمْ أَن يَحِلَّ عَلَيْكُمْ غَضَبٌ مِّن رَّبِّكُمْ فَأَخْلَفْتُم مَّوْعِدِى ۝

87. They said: "We have not broken the promise to you by our choice, but we have been forced to carry loads of the people's finery and so we threw them away, as the Samaritan also did."

قَالُوا مَا أَخْلَفْنَا مَوْعِدَكَ بِمَلْكِنَا وَلَٰكِنَّا حُمِّلْنَا أَوْزَارًا مِّن زِينَةِ ٱلْقَوْمِ فَقَذَفْنَٰهَا فَكَذَٰلِكَ أَلْقَى ٱلسَّامِرِىُّ ۝

88. Then he produced for them a calf - a mere body which lowed; and so they said: "This is your god and the god of Moses, but he has forgotten."

فَأَخْرَجَ لَهُمْ عِجْلًا جَسَدًا لَّهُ خُوَارٌ فَقَالُوا هَٰذَا إِلَٰهُكُمْ وَإِلَٰهُ مُوسَىٰ فَنَسِىَ ۝

89. Do they not see that it does not return any reply to them and does not have the power to harm or profit them?

أَفَلَا يَرَوْنَ أَلَّا يَرْجِعُ إِلَيْهِمْ قَوْلًا وَلَا يَمْلِكُ لَهُمْ ضَرًّا وَلَا نَفْعًا ۝

90. Aaron had said to them before: "O my people, you have been tried by it and your Lord is truly the Compassionate. Follow me, then, and obey my order."

وَلَقَدْ قَالَ لَهُمْ هَٰرُونُ مِن قَبْلُ يَٰقَوْمِ إِنَّمَا فُتِنتُم بِهِ وَإِنَّ رَبَّكُمُ ٱلرَّحْمَٰنُ فَٱتَّبِعُونِى وَأَطِيعُوا أَمْرِى ۝

91. They said: "We will not stop worshipping it, till Moses comes back to us."

قَالُوا لَن نَّبْرَحَ عَلَيْهِ عَٰكِفِينَ حَتَّىٰ يَرْجِعَ إِلَيْنَا مُوسَىٰ ۝

92. He[600] said: "O Aaron, what prevented you, when you saw them going astray,

قَالَ يَٰهَٰرُونُ مَا مَنَعَكَ إِذْ رَأَيْتَهُمْ ضَلُّوا ۝

93. "From following me. Have you, then, disobeyed my order?"

أَلَّا تَتَّبِعَنِ أَفَعَصَيْتَ أَمْرِى ۝

94. He (Aaron) said: "Son of my mother, do not seize me by the beard or the head, I feared that you would say: 'You have caused division among the Children of Israel and did not observe my words.' "

قَالَ يَبْنَؤُمَّ لَا تَأْخُذْ بِلِحْيَتِى وَلَا بِرَأْسِى إِنِّى خَشِيتُ أَن تَقُولَ فَرَّقْتَ بَيْنَ بَنِى إِسْرَٰءِيلَ وَلَمْ تَرْقُبْ قَوْلِى ۝

---

600. Moses.

قَالَ فَمَا خَطْبُكَ يَسَـٰمِرِىُّ ۝

95. He[601] said: "What is the matter with you, O Samaritan?"

قَالَ بَصُرْتُ بِمَا لَمْ يَبْصُرُوا بِهِ فَقَبَضْتُ قَبْضَةً مِّنْ أَثَرِ ٱلرَّسُولِ فَنَبَذْتُهَا وَكَذَٰلِكَ سَوَّلَتْ لِى نَفْسِى ۝

96. He said: "I perceived what they did not perceive, and so I grasped a handful of dust from the messenger's[602] trail and threw it down. That is what my soul prompted me to do."

قَالَ فَٱذْهَبْ فَإِنَّ لَكَ فِى ٱلْحَيَوٰةِ أَن تَقُولَ لَا مِسَاسَ وَإِنَّ لَكَ مَوْعِدًا لَّن تُخْلَفَهُ وَٱنظُرْ إِلَىٰ إِلَـٰهِكَ ٱلَّذِى ظَلْتَ عَلَيْهِ عَاكِفًا لَّنُحَرِّقَنَّهُ ثُمَّ لَنَنسِفَنَّهُ فِى ٱلْيَمِّ نَسْفًا ۝

97. He (Moses) said: "Begone; it shall be given you in your lifetime to say: 'Do not touch' and you shall be given a promise which you will not break. Look then at your god, whom you continued to worship. We shall burn him; then We shall scatter his ashes in the sea."

إِنَّمَا إِلَـٰهُكُمُ ٱللَّهُ ٱلَّذِى لَا إِلَـٰهَ إِلَّا هُوَ وَسِعَ كُلَّ شَىْءٍ عِلْمًا ۝

98. Surely, your God is only Allah; there is no god but He. He has knowledge of all things.

كَذَٰلِكَ نَقُصُّ عَلَيْكَ مِنْ أَنۢبَآءِ مَا قَدْ سَبَقَ وَقَدْ ءَاتَيْنَـٰكَ مِن لَّدُنَّا ذِكْرًا ۝

99. That is how We relate to you some of the stories of things past; and We have imparted to you a reminder from Us (this Qur'an).

مَّنْ أَعْرَضَ عَنْهُ فَإِنَّهُ يَحْمِلُ يَوْمَ ٱلْقِيَـٰمَةِ وِزْرًا ۝

100. Whoever turns away from it will bear a heavy burden on the Day of Resurrection;

خَـٰلِدِينَ فِيهِ وَسَآءَ لَهُمْ يَوْمَ ٱلْقِيَـٰمَةِ حِمْلًا ۝

101. Abiding therein[603] forever. And what a wretched burden they will bear on the Day of Resurrection!

يَوْمَ يُنفَخُ فِى ٱلصُّورِ وَنَحْشُرُ ٱلْمُجْرِمِينَ يَوْمَئِذٍ زُرْقًا ۝

102. On the Day when the trumpet shall be blown and We will gather the wicked sinners blue-eyed [with terror];

يَتَخَـٰفَتُونَ بَيْنَهُمْ إِن لَّبِثْتُمْ إِلَّا عَشْرًا ۝

103. Whispering to each other: "You have only lingered for ten [days]."

نَّحْنُ أَعْلَمُ بِمَا يَقُولُونَ إِذْ يَقُولُ أَمْثَلُهُمْ طَرِيقَةً إِن لَّبِثْتُمْ إِلَّا يَوْمًا ۝

104. We know better what they say; for the straightest of them in direction will say: "You have only lingered a single day."

وَيَسْـَٔلُونَكَ عَنِ ٱلْجِبَالِ فَقُلْ يَنسِفُهَا رَبِّى نَسْفًا ۝

105. And they will ask you about the mountains, say: "My Lord will reduce them to dust,

---

601. Moses.
602. Gabriel.
603. In this state.

106. "And leave them as bare flatland,

فَيَذَرُهَا قَاعًا صَفْصَفًا ۝

107. "In which you see no ups and downs."

لَّا تَرَىٰ فِيهَا عِوَجًا وَلَا أَمْتًا ۝

108. On that Day, they will have to follow the caller who is not crooked, and the voices shall be hushed unto the Compassionate, so that you will hear nothing but whispering.

يَوْمَئِذٍ يَتَّبِعُونَ ٱلدَّاعِىَ لَا عِوَجَ لَهُۥ وَخَشَعَتِ ٱلْأَصْوَاتُ لِلرَّحْمَٰنِ فَلَا تَسْمَعُ إِلَّا هَمْسًا ۝

109. On that Day, intercession will not avail, except him to whom the Compassionate gives leave and He is pleased with his words.

يَوْمَئِذٍ لَّا تَنفَعُ ٱلشَّفَٰعَةُ إِلَّا مَنْ أَذِنَ لَهُ ٱلرَّحْمَٰنُ وَرَضِىَ لَهُۥ قَوْلًا ۝

110. He (Allah) knows what is before them and what is behind them; but they have no knowledge of that.

يَعْلَمُ مَا بَيْنَ أَيْدِيهِمْ وَمَا خَلْفَهُمْ وَلَا يُحِيطُونَ بِهِۦ عِلْمًا ۝

111. And they shall submit to the Living and Self-Subsisting One, and he who carries [a burden of] wrongdoing shall lose hope.

۞ وَعَنَتِ ٱلْوُجُوهُ لِلْحَىِّ ٱلْقَيُّومِ وَقَدْ خَابَ مَنْ حَمَلَ ظُلْمًا ۝

112. And he who does the righteous deeds, while a believer, will fear neither injustice nor inequity.

وَمَن يَعْمَلْ مِنَ ٱلصَّٰلِحَٰتِ وَهُوَ مُؤْمِنٌ فَلَا يَخَافُ ظُلْمًا وَلَا هَضْمًا ۝

113. Thus We have revealed it as an Arabic Qur'an and expounded therein in detail some of our warnings, so that they may fear God, and so that it may be a reminder for them.

وَكَذَٰلِكَ أَنزَلْنَٰهُ قُرْءَانًا عَرَبِيًّا وَصَرَّفْنَا فِيهِ مِنَ ٱلْوَعِيدِ لَعَلَّهُمْ يَتَّقُونَ أَوْ يُحْدِثُ لَهُمْ ذِكْرًا ۝

114. Exalted be Allah, the True King. Do not hasten [to discuss] the Qur'an before its revelation to you is complete, and say: "Lord, increase me in knowledge."

فَتَعَٰلَى ٱللَّهُ ٱلْمَلِكُ ٱلْحَقُّ وَلَا تَعْجَلْ بِٱلْقُرْءَانِ مِن قَبْلِ أَن يُقْضَىٰٓ إِلَيْكَ وَحْيُهُۥ وَقُل رَّبِّ زِدْنِى عِلْمًا ۝

115. And We commanded Adam before, but he forgot, and We found in him no firm resolve.

وَلَقَدْ عَهِدْنَآ إِلَىٰٓ ءَادَمَ مِن قَبْلُ فَنَسِىَ وَلَمْ نَجِدْ لَهُۥ عَزْمًا ۝

116. And when We said to the angels: "Prostrate yourselves to Adam", they prostrated themselves, except for Satan who refused.

وَإِذْ قُلْنَا لِلْمَلَٰٓئِكَةِ ٱسْجُدُوا۟ لِءَادَمَ فَسَجَدُوٓا۟ إِلَّآ إِبْلِيسَ أَبَىٰ ۝

117. So We said: "O Adam, this is surely an enemy to you and to your wife; so do not let him drive you out of Paradise; for then, you will be miserable.

فَقُلْنَا يَٰٓـَٔادَمُ إِنَّ هَٰذَا عَدُوٌّ لَّكَ وَلِزَوْجِكَ فَلَا يُخْرِجَنَّكُمَا مِنَ ٱلْجَنَّةِ فَتَشْقَىٰٓ ۝

118. "You will certainly not be hungry therein, nor be naked.

119. "And you will not thirst therein, nor be exposed to the heat of the sun."

120. But the Devil whispered to him, saying: "O Adam, shall I show you the Tree of Immortality and a kingdom which will never perish?"

121. And so they both[604] ate from it; whereupon their shameful parts were revealed to them and they started fastening upon themselves leaves of Paradise. Adam thus disobeyed his Lord and so went astray.

122. Then, his Lord favoured him, and so He relented towards him, and guided him.

123. He (Allah) said: "Go down from it both of you, as enemies of one another; but should guidance from Me come to you, he who follows My Guidance will not go astray or suffer.

124. "But he who shuns My Reminder will have a life of hardship, and We shall raise him up a blind man, on the Day of Resurrection."

125. He will say: "Lord, why did you raise me up a blind man, while I was originally capable of seeing?"

126. He (Allah) will say: "That is how Our Revelations came to you, but you forgot them; and that is how, today, you shall be forgotten."

127. And that is how We reward the extravagant who would not believe in the Revelations of his Lord. The punishment of the Hereafter is surely more terrible and more lasting.

إِنَّ لَكَ أَلَّا تَجُوعَ فِيهَا وَلَا تَعْرَىٰ ﴿١١٨﴾

وَأَنَّكَ لَا تَظْمَؤُا۟ فِيهَا وَلَا تَضْحَىٰ ﴿١١٩﴾

فَوَسْوَسَ إِلَيْهِ ٱلشَّيْطَٰنُ قَالَ يَٰٓـَٔادَمُ هَلْ أَدُلُّكَ عَلَىٰ شَجَرَةِ ٱلْخُلْدِ وَمُلْكٍ لَّا يَبْلَىٰ ﴿١٢٠﴾

فَأَكَلَا مِنْهَا فَبَدَتْ لَهُمَا سَوْءَٰتُهُمَا وَطَفِقَا يَخْصِفَانِ عَلَيْهِمَا مِن وَرَقِ ٱلْجَنَّةِ وَعَصَىٰٓ ءَادَمُ رَبَّهُۥ فَغَوَىٰ ﴿١٢١﴾

ثُمَّ ٱجْتَبَٰهُ رَبُّهُۥ فَتَابَ عَلَيْهِ وَهَدَىٰ ﴿١٢٢﴾

قَالَ ٱهْبِطَا مِنْهَا جَمِيعًۢا بَعْضُكُمْ لِبَعْضٍ عَدُوٌّ فَإِمَّا يَأْتِيَنَّكُم مِّنِّى هُدًى فَمَنِ ٱتَّبَعَ هُدَايَ فَلَا يَضِلُّ وَلَا يَشْقَىٰ ﴿١٢٣﴾

وَمَنْ أَعْرَضَ عَن ذِكْرِى فَإِنَّ لَهُۥ مَعِيشَةً ضَنكًا وَنَحْشُرُهُۥ يَوْمَ ٱلْقِيَٰمَةِ أَعْمَىٰ ﴿١٢٤﴾

قَالَ رَبِّ لِمَ حَشَرْتَنِىٓ أَعْمَىٰ وَقَدْ كُنتُ بَصِيرًا ﴿١٢٥﴾

قَالَ كَذَٰلِكَ أَتَتْكَ ءَايَٰتُنَا فَنَسِيتَهَا وَكَذَٰلِكَ ٱلْيَوْمَ تُنسَىٰ ﴿١٢٦﴾

وَكَذَٰلِكَ نَجْزِى مَنْ أَسْرَفَ وَلَمْ يُؤْمِنۢ بِـَٔايَٰتِ رَبِّهِۦ وَلَعَذَابُ ٱلْءَاخِرَةِ أَشَدُّ وَأَبْقَىٰ ﴿١٢٧﴾

---

604. Adam and Eve.

128. Did He not reveal to them, as a guidance, how many generations before them We destroyed as they were walking inside their dwellings? Surely, in that are signs for people of understanding.

129. And but for a Word which preceded from your Lord and an appointed term, it[605] would have been inexorable.

130. So bear[606] patiently what they say, and celebrate the praise of your Lord before the rising of the sun and before its setting; and glorify Him during the hours of the night and at the two ends[607] of the day, that you may be well-pleased.

131. And do not allow your eyes to reach out to what We allowed some to enjoy of the flowers of the present life, so as to try them thereby. Your Lord's provision is better and more lasting.

132. And enjoin your family to pray and be constant therein. We do not ask you for any provision; We rather provide for you. The happy ending is reserved for righteousness.

133. They say: "If only he would bring us a sign from his Lord." Has not a clear proof come to them in the previous scriptures?

134. And had We destroyed them with a punishment before him,[608] they would have said: "Lord, if only you had sent us a messenger, we would have followed your Revelations before we were humiliated and disgraced."

135. Say: "Everybody is waiting, so wait; and then you will know who are the people of the Straight Path and who are the well-guided."

---

605. The punishment.
606. This is addressed to Muhammad.
607. According to some commentators, the prayers at the two ends of the day are the evening and morning prayers.
608. The Prophet Muhammad.

**Sûrat Al-Anbiyâ',
(The Prophets) 21**

سُورَةُ الأَنبِيَاءِ

*In the Name of Allah,
the Compassionate, the Merciful*

بِسْمِ اللَّهِ الرَّحْمَٰنِ الرَّحِيمِ

1. Mankind's reckoning is drawing near, but they are turning away heedlessly.

ٱقْتَرَبَ لِلنَّاسِ حِسَابُهُمْ وَهُمْ فِي غَفْلَةٍ مُّعْرِضُونَ ۝

2. No new reminder comes to them from their Lord but they listen to it while they are at play.

مَا يَأْتِيهِم مِّن ذِكْرٍ مِّن رَّبِّهِم مُّحْدَثٍ إِلَّا ٱسْتَمَعُوهُ وَهُمْ يَلْعَبُونَ ۝

3. Their hearts are distracted. The wrong-doers say in secret: "Is this not a mortal like you? Will you then take to sorcery, with your eyes wide open?"

لَاهِيَةً قُلُوبُهُمْ وَأَسَرُّوا ٱلنَّجْوَى ٱلَّذِينَ ظَلَمُوا هَلْ هَٰذَا إِلَّا بَشَرٌ مِّثْلُكُمْ أَفَتَأْتُونَ ٱلسِّحْرَ وَأَنتُمْ تُبْصِرُونَ ۝

4. He (Mohammad) said: "My Lord knows what is said in the heavens and the earth, and He is the All-Hearing, the All-Knowing."

قَالَ رَبِّي يَعْلَمُ ٱلْقَوْلَ فِي ٱلسَّمَاءِ وَٱلْأَرْضِ وَهُوَ ٱلسَّمِيعُ ٱلْعَلِيمُ ۝

5. "No", they say: "It is just a load of dreams. He has rather forged it; he is rather a poet. Let him bring us a sign, just as the former [Prophets] were sent [with]."

بَلْ قَالُوا أَضْغَٰثُ أَحْلَٰمٍ بَلِ ٱفْتَرَىٰهُ بَلْ هُوَ شَاعِرٌ فَلْيَأْتِنَا بِـَٔايَةٍ كَمَا أُرْسِلَ ٱلْأَوَّلُونَ ۝

6. No city We destroyed, before them, actually believed. Will they, then, believe?

مَا ءَامَنَتْ قَبْلَهُم مِّن قَرْيَةٍ أَهْلَكْنَٰهَا أَفَهُمْ يُؤْمِنُونَ ۝

7. And we did not send before you but men to whom We revealed. So ask those acquainted [with the Scriptures] if you do not know.

وَمَا أَرْسَلْنَا قَبْلَكَ إِلَّا رِجَالًا نُّوحِي إِلَيْهِمْ فَسْـَٔلُوا أَهْلَ ٱلذِّكْرِ إِن كُنتُمْ لَا تَعْلَمُونَ ۝

8. And We did not make them (the Massengers) as mere bodies that did not eat food; nor were they immortal.

وَمَا جَعَلْنَٰهُمْ جَسَدًا لَّا يَأْكُلُونَ ٱلطَّعَامَ وَمَا كَانُوا خَٰلِدِينَ ۝

9. Then We fulfilled the promise, and so We delivered them together with whomever We pleased, and We destroyed the extravagant.

ثُمَّ صَدَقْنَٰهُمُ ٱلْوَعْدَ فَأَنجَيْنَٰهُمْ وَمَن نَّشَاءُ وَأَهْلَكْنَا ٱلْمُسْرِفِينَ ۝

10. We have indeed sent down to you a Book (the Qur'an) in which there is admonition for you. Do you not understand, then?

لَقَدْ أَنزَلْنَا إِلَيْكُمْ كِتَٰبًا فِيهِ ذِكْرُكُمْ أَفَلَا تَعْقِلُونَ ۝

11. How many an unjust town We have levelled down and created in its wake another people.

وَكَمْ قَصَمْنَا مِن قَرْيَةٍ كَانَتْ ظَالِمَةً وَأَنشَأْنَا بَعْدَهَا قَوْمًا ءَاخَرِينَ ﴿١١﴾

12. Then, when they sensed Our Might, behold, they started running away from it.

فَلَمَّا أَحَسُّوا بَأْسَنَا إِذَا هُم مِّنْهَا يَرْكُضُونَ ﴿١٢﴾

13. "Do not run. Return to what you enjoyed of luxury, and to your dwellings, that perchance you may be questioned."

لَا تَرْكُضُوا وَارْجِعُوا إِلَىٰ مَا أُتْرِفْتُمْ فِيهِ وَمَسَاكِنِكُمْ لَعَلَّكُمْ تُسْأَلُونَ ﴿١٣﴾

14. They said: "Woe to us! We have indeed been wrongdoers."

قَالُوا يَٰوَيْلَنَا إِنَّا كُنَّا ظَٰلِمِينَ ﴿١٤﴾

15. This continued to be their lament, until We [cut them down] to stubble, senseless.

فَمَا زَالَت تِّلْكَ دَعْوَىٰهُمْ حَتَّىٰ جَعَلْنَٰهُمْ حَصِيدًا خَٰمِدِينَ ﴿١٥﴾

16. We did not create the heavens and the earth and what is in between them in sport.

وَمَا خَلَقْنَا ٱلسَّمَآءَ وَٱلْأَرْضَ وَمَا بَيْنَهُمَا لَٰعِبِينَ ﴿١٦﴾

17. Had We wished to take to Ourselves a means of sport, We would have found it within Us, if We wanted to do it.

لَوْ أَرَدْنَا أَن نَّتَّخِذَ لَهْوًا لَّٱتَّخَذْنَٰهُ مِن لَّدُنَّا إِن كُنَّا فَٰعِلِينَ ﴿١٧﴾

18. No, We hurl the truth against falsehood and it overcomes it; and, behold, it has vanished. Woe unto you,[609] for what you describe.[610]

بَلْ نَقْذِفُ بِٱلْحَقِّ عَلَى ٱلْبَٰطِلِ فَيَدْمَغُهُ فَإِذَا هُوَ زَاهِقٌ وَلَكُمُ ٱلْوَيْلُ مِمَّا تَصِفُونَ ﴿١٨﴾

19. To Him belongs what is in the heavens and on earth; and those with Him[611] are not too proud to worship Him, nor do they tire;

وَلَهُۥ مَن فِى ٱلسَّمَٰوَٰتِ وَٱلْأَرْضِ وَمَنْ عِندَهُۥ لَا يَسْتَكْبِرُونَ عَنْ عِبَادَتِهِۦ وَلَا يَسْتَحْسِرُونَ ﴿١٩﴾

20. Glorifying Him night and day without growing weary.

يُسَبِّحُونَ ٱلَّيْلَ وَٱلنَّهَارَ لَا يَفْتُرُونَ ﴿٢٠﴾

21. Or have they taken to themselves gods out of the earth, able to raise the dead?

أَمِ ٱتَّخَذُوا ءَالِهَةً مِّنَ ٱلْأَرْضِ هُمْ يُنشِرُونَ ﴿٢١﴾

22. Were there in them both[612] other gods than Allah, they would surely have been ruined. Allah be exalted, the Lord of the Throne, above what they describe.

لَوْ كَانَ فِيهِمَآ ءَالِهَةٌ إِلَّا ٱللَّهُ لَفَسَدَتَا فَسُبْحَٰنَ ٱللَّهِ رَبِّ ٱلْعَرْشِ عَمَّا يَصِفُونَ ﴿٢٢﴾

---

609. The Meccans.
610. The way you describe Allah.
611. The angels.
612. Heaven and earth.

لَا يُسْتَلُ عَمَّا يَفْعَلُ وَهُمْ يُسْتَلُونَ ﴿٢٣﴾

23. He is not questioned about what He does, but they are questioned.

أَمِ اتَّخَذُوا مِن دُونِهِ ءَالِهَةً قُلْ هَاتُوا بُرْهَانَكُمْ هَذَا ذِكْرُ مَن مَّعِيَ وَذِكْرُ مَن قَبْلِي بَلْ أَكْثَرُهُمْ لَا يَعْلَمُونَ الْحَقَّ فَهُم مُّعْرِضُونَ ﴿٢٤﴾

24. Or, have they taken, besides Him, other gods? Say: "Bring your proof." This is the Reminder[613] of those with me and the Reminder of those before me. However, most of them do not know the Truth, so they turn away.

وَمَا أَرْسَلْنَا مِن قَبْلِكَ مِن رَّسُولٍ إِلَّا نُوحِي إِلَيْهِ أَنَّهُ لَا إِلَهَ إِلَّا أَنَا فَاعْبُدُونِ ﴿٢٥﴾

25. We have not sent before you any Messenger, but We revealed to him that there is no god but I; so worship Me.

وَقَالُوا اتَّخَذَ الرَّحْمَنُ وَلَدًا سُبْحَانَهُ بَلْ عِبَادٌ مُّكْرَمُونَ ﴿٢٦﴾

26. They say: "The Compassionate has taken to Himself a son." Glory be to Him; they[614] are [merely] honoured servants.

لَا يَسْبِقُونَهُ بِالْقَوْلِ وَهُم بِأَمْرِهِ يَعْمَلُونَ ﴿٢٧﴾

27. They never speak until He has spoken; they only act on His Command.

يَعْلَمُ مَا بَيْنَ أَيْدِيهِمْ وَمَا خَلْفَهُمْ وَلَا يَشْفَعُونَ إِلَّا لِمَنِ ارْتَضَى وَهُم مِّنْ خَشْيَتِهِ مُشْفِقُونَ ﴿٢٨﴾

28. He knows what is before them and what is behind them, and they do not intercede except for him whom He approves; and they tremble for fear of Him.

وَمَن يَقُلْ مِنْهُمْ إِنِّي إِلَهٌ مِّن دُونِهِ فَذَلِكَ نَجْزِيهِ جَهَنَّمَ كَذَلِكَ نَجْزِي الظَّالِمِينَ ﴿٢٩﴾

29. And whoever of them says: "I am a god besides Him" - that one We shall reward with Hell. That is how We reward the wrongdoers.

أَوَلَمْ يَرَ الَّذِينَ كَفَرُوا أَنَّ السَّمَوَاتِ وَالْأَرْضَ كَانَتَا رَتْقًا فَفَتَقْنَاهُمَا وَجَعَلْنَا مِنَ الْمَاءِ كُلَّ شَيْءٍ حَيٍّ أَفَلَا يُؤْمِنُونَ ﴿٣٠﴾

30. Have the unbelievers not beheld that the heavens and the earth were a solid mass, then We separated them; and of water We produced every living thing. Will they not believe, then?

وَجَعَلْنَا فِي الْأَرْضِ رَوَاسِيَ أَن تَمِيدَ بِهِمْ وَجَعَلْنَا فِيهَا فِجَاجًا سُبُلًا لَّعَلَّهُمْ يَهْتَدُونَ ﴿٣١﴾

31. And We set up in the earth immovable mountains lest it should shake with them; and We created therein wide roads, that perchance they may be guided.

وَجَعَلْنَا السَّمَاءَ سَقْفًا مَّحْفُوظًا وَهُمْ عَنْ ءَايَاتِهَا مُعْرِضُونَ ﴿٣٢﴾

32. And We made the sky a well-guarded canopy; and they still turn away from its signs.

---

613. The Qur'an.
614. The angels.

33. It is He Who created the night and the day, the sun and the moon, each floating in its orbit.

وَهُوَ ٱلَّذِى خَلَقَ ٱلَّيْلَ وَٱلنَّهَارَ وَٱلشَّمْسَ وَٱلْقَمَرَ كُلٌّ فِى فَلَكٍ يَسْبَحُونَ ۝

34. And We did not grant immortality to any human before you. If you die, are they then immortal?

وَمَا جَعَلْنَا لِبَشَرٍ مِّن قَبْلِكَ ٱلْخُلْدَ أَفَإِيْن مِّتَّ فَهُمُ ٱلْخَٰلِدُونَ ۝

35. Every living soul shall taste death, and We test you by evil and good as a temptation and unto Us you shall be returned.

كُلُّ نَفْسٍ ذَآئِقَةُ ٱلْمَوْتِ وَنَبْلُوكُم بِٱلشَّرِّ وَٱلْخَيْرِ فِتْنَةً وَإِلَيْنَا تُرْجَعُونَ ۝

36. And if the unbelievers see you, they only take you as an object of mockery [saying]: "Is this the one who talks about your gods?" And they disbelieve in the mention of the Compassionate.

وَإِذَا رَءَاكَ ٱلَّذِينَ كَفَرُوٓاْ إِن يَتَّخِذُونَكَ إِلَّا هُزُوًا أَهَٰذَا ٱلَّذِى يَذْكُرُ ءَالِهَتَكُمْ وَهُم بِذِكْرِ ٱلرَّحْمَٰنِ هُمْ كَٰفِرُونَ ۝

37. Man is created in haste. I will bring you My Signs; so do not hasten them.

خُلِقَ ٱلْإِنسَٰنُ مِنْ عَجَلٍ سَأُوْرِيكُمْ ءَايَٰتِى فَلَا تَسْتَعْجِلُونِ ۝

38. And they say: "When will this threat come to pass if you are truthful?"

وَيَقُولُونَ مَتَىٰ هَٰذَا ٱلْوَعْدُ إِن كُنتُمْ صَٰدِقِينَ ۝

39. If only the unbelievers knew the time when they will not be able to ward off the Fire from their faces or their backs, and they will not be helped!

لَوْ يَعْلَمُ ٱلَّذِينَ كَفَرُواْ حِينَ لَا يَكُفُّونَ عَن وُجُوهِهِمُ ٱلنَّارَ وَلَا عَن ظُهُورِهِمْ وَلَا هُمْ يُنصَرُونَ ۝

40. But it will come upon them suddenly confounding them, and so they will not be able to repel it, nor will they be respited.

بَلْ تَأْتِيهِم بَغْتَةً فَتَبْهَتُهُمْ فَلَا يَسْتَطِيعُونَ رَدَّهَا وَلَا هُمْ يُنظَرُونَ ۝

41. Many Messengers before you were mocked; then those who scoffed at them were afflicted by that which they used to mock.

وَلَقَدِ ٱسْتُهْزِئَ بِرُسُلٍ مِّن قَبْلِكَ فَحَاقَ بِٱلَّذِينَ سَخِرُواْ مِنْهُم مَّا كَانُواْ بِهِ يَسْتَهْزِءُونَ ۝

42. Say: "Who guards you night and day against the Compassionate?" Yet they turn away from the mention of their Lord.

قُلْ مَن يَكْلَؤُكُم بِٱلَّيْلِ وَٱلنَّهَارِ مِنَ ٱلرَّحْمَٰنِ بَلْ هُمْ عَن ذِكْرِ رَبِّهِم مُّعْرِضُونَ ۝

43. Or do they have gods who will defend them against Us? They cannot help themselves and they will not be protected from Us.

أَمْ لَهُمْ ءَالِهَةٌ تَمْنَعُهُم مِّن دُونِنَا لَا يَسْتَطِيعُونَ نَصْرَ أَنفُسِهِمْ وَلَا هُم مِّنَّا يُصْحَبُونَ ۝

44. No, We gave ease to those people and their fathers until they became advanced in age. Do they not see that We come upon the land [under their control] reducing it from its extremities? Are they then the victors?

45. Say: "I only warn you through the Revelation; but the deaf people do not hear the call, when they are warned."

46. And if the least hint of your Lord's punishment touches them, they will surely say: "Woe to us; we have been truly wrongdoers."

47. We set up the just scales for the Day of Resurrection, so that no soul shall be wronged a whit; and even if it be the weight of a mustard seed, We shall produce it. We suffice as reckoners.

48. And We gave Moses and Aaron the criterion[615] and a light, and a Reminder for the righteous,

49. Who fear their Lord Unseen and are apprehensive of the Hour.

50. This is a blessed Reminder[616] We have revealed. Are you, then, going to deny it?

51. And We gave Abraham his right judgement formerly; for We knew him well.

52. When he said to his father and his people: "What are these statues to which you are devoted?"

53. They said: "We found our fathers worshipping them."

54. He said: "Indeed, you and your fathers have been in manifest error."

55. They said: "Have you brought us the truth, or are you one of those who jest?"

---

615. The Torah.
616. The Qur'an.

56. He said: "No, your Lord is the Lord of the heavens and the earth, Who created them both; and I bear witness to that.

قَالَ بَل رَّبُّكُمْ رَبُّ ٱلسَّمَـٰوَٰتِ وَٱلْأَرْضِ ٱلَّذِي فَطَرَهُنَّ وَأَنَا۠ عَلَىٰ ذَٰلِكُم مِّنَ ٱلشَّـٰهِدِينَ ۝

57. "And by Allah, I will show your idols my guile, after you turn your backs."

وَتَٱللَّهِ لَأَكِيدَنَّ أَصْنَـٰمَكُم بَعْدَ أَن تُوَلُّوا۟ مُدْبِرِينَ ۝

58. Then he reduced them to pieces except for their chief, so that they might turn to him.

فَجَعَلَهُمْ جُذَٰذًا إِلَّا كَبِيرًا لَّهُمْ لَعَلَّهُمْ إِلَيْهِ يَرْجِعُونَ ۝

59. They said: "He who did this to our gods is certainly one of the wrongdoers."

قَالُوا۟ مَن فَعَلَ هَـٰذَا بِـَٔالِهَتِنَا إِنَّهُۥ لَمِنَ ٱلظَّـٰلِمِينَ ۝

60. They said: "We heard a youth called Abraham mentioning them."

قَالُوا۟ سَمِعْنَا فَتًى يَذْكُرُهُمْ يُقَالُ لَهُۥٓ إِبْرَٰهِيمُ ۝

61. They said: "Bring him along in full view of the people, so that they may bear witness."

قَالُوا۟ فَأْتُوا۟ بِهِۦ عَلَىٰٓ أَعْيُنِ ٱلنَّاسِ لَعَلَّهُمْ يَشْهَدُونَ ۝

62. They said: "Are you the one who did this to our gods, O Abraham?"

قَالُوٓا۟ ءَأَنتَ فَعَلْتَ هَـٰذَا بِـَٔالِهَتِنَا يَـٰٓإِبْرَٰهِيمُ ۝

63. He said: "No, but their chief did this; so ask them if they can speak."

قَالَ بَلْ فَعَلَهُۥ كَبِيرُهُمْ هَـٰذَا فَسْـَٔلُوهُمْ إِن كَانُوا۟ يَنطِقُونَ ۝

64. Then, they turned to themselves and said: "Surely, you are the wrongdoers."

فَرَجَعُوٓا۟ إِلَىٰٓ أَنفُسِهِمْ فَقَالُوٓا۟ إِنَّكُمْ أَنتُمُ ٱلظَّـٰلِمُونَ ۝

65. And so they were utterly confounded and [they said]: "You know that these [idols] do not speak."

ثُمَّ نُكِسُوا۟ عَلَىٰ رُءُوسِهِمْ لَقَدْ عَلِمْتَ مَا هَـٰٓؤُلَآءِ يَنطِقُونَ ۝

66. He (Abraham) said: "Do you, then, worship, besides Allah, what does not profit or harm you a whit?

قَالَ أَفَتَعْبُدُونَ مِن دُونِ ٱللَّهِ مَا لَا يَنفَعُكُمْ شَيْـًٔا وَلَا يَضُرُّكُمْ ۝

67. "Fie on you and on what you worship besides Allah. Do you not understand?"

أُفٍّ لَّكُمْ وَلِمَا تَعْبُدُونَ مِن دُونِ ٱللَّهِ أَفَلَا تَعْقِلُونَ ۝

68. They said: "Burn him and support your gods, if you are going to do anything."

قَالُوا۟ حَرِّقُوهُ وَٱنصُرُوٓا۟ ءَالِهَتَكُمْ إِن كُنتُمْ فَـٰعِلِينَ ۝

69. We (Allah) said: "O fire, be coolness and peace upon Abraham."

قُلْنَا يَـٰنَارُ كُونِى بَرْدًا وَسَلَـٰمًا عَلَىٰٓ إِبْرَٰهِيمَ ۝

70. They wanted to plot against him, but We made them the worst losers.

وَأَرَادُوا۟ بِهِۦ كَيْدًا فَجَعَلْنَـٰهُمُ ٱلْأَخْسَرِينَ ۝

71. And We delivered him and Lot unto the land which We have blessed for all mankind.

وَنَجَّيْنَـٰهُ وَلُوطًا إِلَى ٱلْأَرْضِ ٱلَّتِى بَـٰرَكْنَا فِيهَا لِلْعَـٰلَمِينَ ۝

72. And We granted him Isaac, and Jacob, his son's son, as a bounty and each We made to be righteous.

وَوَهَبْنَا لَهُ إِسْحَٰقَ وَيَعْقُوبَ نَافِلَةً وَكُلًّا جَعَلْنَا صَٰلِحِينَ ۝

73. And We made them leaders, guiding others at Our Behest; and We revealed to them to do good, perform the prayer and give the alms, and they have worshipped Us.

وَجَعَلْنَٰهُمْ أَئِمَّةً يَهْدُونَ بِأَمْرِنَا وَأَوْحَيْنَا إِلَيْهِمْ فِعْلَ الْخَيْرَٰتِ وَإِقَامَ الصَّلَوٰةِ وَإِيتَآءَ الزَّكَوٰةِ وَكَانُوا لَنَا عَٰبِدِينَ ۝

74. And Lot, We gave him good judgement and knowledge, and We delivered him from the city which practised foul deeds.[617] They were indeed an evil and sinful people.

وَلُوطًا ءَاتَيْنَٰهُ حُكْمًا وَعِلْمًا وَنَجَّيْنَٰهُ مِنَ الْقَرْيَةِ الَّتِي كَانَت تَّعْمَلُ الْخَبَٰئِثَ إِنَّهُمْ كَانُوا قَوْمَ سَوْءٍ فَٰسِقِينَ ۝

75. And We admitted him into Our Mercy; for he was one of the righteous.

وَأَدْخَلْنَٰهُ فِي رَحْمَتِنَآ إِنَّهُ مِنَ الصَّٰلِحِينَ ۝

76. And Noah, when he called before, and so We answered him and delivered him and his people from the great calamity.

وَنُوحًا إِذْ نَادَىٰ مِن قَبْلُ فَٱسْتَجَبْنَا لَهُ فَنَجَّيْنَٰهُ وَأَهْلَهُ مِنَ الْكَرْبِ الْعَظِيمِ ۝

77. And supported him against the people who had denied Our Signs. They were an evil people, and so We drowned them all.

وَنَصَرْنَٰهُ مِنَ الْقَوْمِ الَّذِينَ كَذَّبُوا بِـَٔايَٰتِنَآ إِنَّهُمْ كَانُوا قَوْمَ سَوْءٍ فَأَغْرَقْنَٰهُمْ أَجْمَعِينَ ۝

78. And David and Solomon, when they gave judgement, regarding the tillage, when the people's sheep wandered therein by night; and We bore witness to their judgement.

وَدَاوُۥدَ وَسُلَيْمَٰنَ إِذْ يَحْكُمَانِ فِي الْحَرْثِ إِذْ نَفَشَتْ فِيهِ غَنَمُ الْقَوْمِ وَكُنَّا لِحُكْمِهِمْ شَٰهِدِينَ ۝

79. And so We made Solomon understand it, and to each We gave judgement and knowledge. And with David, We subjected the mountains and the birds so as to glorify God; and that We accomplished.

فَفَهَّمْنَٰهَا سُلَيْمَٰنَ وَكُلًّا ءَاتَيْنَا حُكْمًا وَعِلْمًا وَسَخَّرْنَا مَعَ دَاوُۥدَ الْجِبَالَ يُسَبِّحْنَ وَالطَّيْرَ وَكُنَّا فَٰعِلِينَ ۝

80. And We taught him the craft of making coats of mail for you, so as to protect you from your own might. Are you, then, thankful?

وَعَلَّمْنَٰهُ صَنْعَةَ لَبُوسٍ لَّكُمْ لِتُحْصِنَكُم مِّن بَأْسِكُمْ فَهَلْ أَنتُمْ شَٰكِرُونَ ۝

81. And to Solomon We subjected the stormy wind blowing at his command towards the land which We have blessed, and We have knowledge of everything.

وَلِسُلَيْمَٰنَ الرِّيحَ عَاصِفَةً تَجْرِي بِأَمْرِهِ إِلَى الْأَرْضِ الَّتِي بَٰرَكْنَا فِيهَا وَكُنَّا بِكُلِّ شَيْءٍ عَٰلِمِينَ ۝

---

617. Sodom.

82. And some of the devils dived for him and did other work besides that and We were watching them.

وَمِنَ ٱلشَّيَـٰطِينِ مَن يَغُوصُونَ لَهُۥ وَيَعْمَلُونَ عَمَلًا دُونَ ذَٰلِكَ وَكُنَّا لَهُمْ حَـٰفِظِينَ ۝

83. And [remember] Job, when he called upon his Lord saying: "Affliction has touched me and you are the Most Merciful of the Merciful."

۞ وَأَيُّوبَ إِذْ نَادَىٰ رَبَّهُۥٓ أَنِّي مَسَّنِيَ ٱلضُّرُّ وَأَنتَ أَرْحَمُ ٱلرَّٰحِمِينَ ۝

84. And so, We answered him and lifted the affliction which he suffered; and We gave him his people and the like thereof along with them, as a mercy from Us and a Reminder to the worshippers.

فَٱسْتَجَبْنَا لَهُۥ فَكَشَفْنَا مَا بِهِۦ مِن ضُرٍّ وَءَاتَيْنَـٰهُ أَهْلَهُۥ وَمِثْلَهُم مَّعَهُمْ رَحْمَةً مِّنْ عِندِنَا وَذِكْرَىٰ لِلْعَـٰبِدِينَ ۝

85. And Isma'il and Idris and Dhul-Kifl; each was one of the steadfast.

وَإِسْمَـٰعِيلَ وَإِدْرِيسَ وَذَا ٱلْكِفْلِ كُلٌّ مِّنَ ٱلصَّـٰبِرِينَ ۝

86. And We admitted them into Our Mercy; they were all truly righteous.

وَأَدْخَلْنَـٰهُمْ فِي رَحْمَتِنَآ إِنَّهُم مِّنَ ٱلصَّـٰلِحِينَ ۝

87. And Dhun-Nun,[618] when he went out enraged, and he thought that We will have no power over him. So he called out in the darkness: "There is no god but You; glory be to You; I have certainly been one of the wrongdoers."

وَذَا ٱلنُّونِ إِذ ذَّهَبَ مُغَـٰضِبًا فَظَنَّ أَن لَّن نَّقْدِرَ عَلَيْهِ فَنَادَىٰ فِي ٱلظُّلُمَـٰتِ أَن لَّآ إِلَـٰهَ إِلَّآ أَنتَ سُبْحَـٰنَكَ إِنِّي كُنتُ مِنَ ٱلظَّـٰلِمِينَ ۝

88. So, We answered him and delivered him from distress; and thus We deliver the believers.

فَٱسْتَجَبْنَا لَهُۥ وَنَجَّيْنَـٰهُ مِنَ ٱلْغَمِّ وَكَذَٰلِكَ نُـۨجِى ٱلْمُؤْمِنِينَ ۝

89. And Zacharia, when he called upon his Lord [said]: "Lord, do not leave me alone; for You are the Best of the inheritors."

وَزَكَرِيَّآ إِذْ نَادَىٰ رَبَّهُۥ رَبِّ لَا تَذَرْنِي فَرْدًا وَأَنتَ خَيْرُ ٱلْوَٰرِثِينَ ۝

90. So, We answered him and gave him John and set his wife right for him. Indeed, they vied with each other in good deeds, and they called upon Us out of affection and out of fear; and they were submissive to Us.

فَٱسْتَجَبْنَا لَهُۥ وَوَهَبْنَا لَهُۥ يَحْيَىٰ وَأَصْلَحْنَا لَهُۥ زَوْجَهُۥٓ إِنَّهُمْ كَانُوا۟ يُسَـٰرِعُونَ فِي ٱلْخَيْرَٰتِ وَيَدْعُونَنَا رَغَبًا وَرَهَبًا وَكَانُوا۟ لَنَا خَـٰشِعِينَ ۝

---

618. Another name for Jonah, the Arabic equivalent of which is Yunus.

91. And she who guarded her chastity,[619] and so We breathed into her of Our Spirit and made her and her son (Jesus) a sign unto the world.

وَٱلَّتِىٓ أَحْصَنَتْ فَرْجَهَا فَنَفَخْنَا فِيهَا مِن رُّوحِنَا وَجَعَلْنَـٰهَا وَٱبْنَهَآ ءَايَةً لِّلْعَـٰلَمِينَ ﴿٩١﴾

92. This, your community is indeed a single community and I am your Lord; so worship Me.

إِنَّ هَـٰذِهِۦٓ أُمَّتُكُمْ أُمَّةً وَٰحِدَةً وَأَنَا۠ رَبُّكُمْ فَٱعْبُدُونِ ﴿٩٢﴾

93. They fell apart into factions; but they will all return unto Us.

وَتَقَطَّعُوٓا۟ أَمْرَهُم بَيْنَهُمْ كُلٌّ إِلَيْنَا رَٰجِعُونَ ﴿٩٣﴾

94. Whoever does what is good, while a believer, his endeavour will not be denied, and We are indeed writing it down for him.

فَمَن يَعْمَلْ مِنَ ٱلصَّـٰلِحَـٰتِ وَهُوَ مُؤْمِنٌ فَلَا كُفْرَانَ لِسَعْيِهِۦ وَإِنَّا لَهُۥ كَـٰتِبُونَ ﴿٩٤﴾

95. And it is forbidden that any city We have destroyed should come back.

وَحَرَٰمٌ عَلَىٰ قَرْيَةٍ أَهْلَكْنَـٰهَآ أَنَّهُمْ لَا يَرْجِعُونَ ﴿٩٥﴾

96. Until Gog and Magog are let loose, and they slink away from every quarter.

حَتَّىٰٓ إِذَا فُتِحَتْ يَأْجُوجُ وَمَأْجُوجُ وَهُم مِّن كُلِّ حَدَبٍ يَنسِلُونَ ﴿٩٦﴾

97. Then the true promise will draw near; and, behold, the eyes of the unbelievers are staring [and they will say]: "Woe to us! We were heedless of this; no, we were wrong-doers."

وَٱقْتَرَبَ ٱلْوَعْدُ ٱلْحَقُّ فَإِذَا هِىَ شَـٰخِصَةٌ أَبْصَـٰرُ ٱلَّذِينَ كَفَرُوا۟ يَـٰوَيْلَنَا قَدْ كُنَّا فِى غَفْلَةٍ مِّنْ هَـٰذَا بَلْ كُنَّا ظَـٰلِمِينَ ﴿٩٧﴾

98. You and what you worship, besides Allah, are the fuel of Hell, and into it you shall all descend.

إِنَّكُمْ وَمَا تَعْبُدُونَ مِن دُونِ ٱللَّهِ حَصَبُ جَهَنَّمَ أَنتُمْ لَهَا وَٰرِدُونَ ﴿٩٨﴾

99. Had those been real gods, they would not have gone down into it; yet they will all dwell in it forever.

لَوْ كَانَ هَـٰٓؤُلَآءِ ءَالِهَةً مَّا وَرَدُوهَا وَكُلٌّ فِيهَا خَـٰلِدُونَ ﴿٩٩﴾

100. They groan with pain therein and they do not hear.

لَهُمْ فِيهَا زَفِيرٌ وَهُمْ فِيهَا لَا يَسْمَعُونَ ﴿١٠٠﴾

101. Those to whom We had given the fairest reward are kept away from it.

إِنَّ ٱلَّذِينَ سَبَقَتْ لَهُم مِّنَّا ٱلْحُسْنَىٰٓ أُو۟لَـٰٓئِكَ عَنْهَا مُبْعَدُونَ ﴿١٠١﴾

102. They do not hear its hissing, and they abide forever in what their hearts desire.

لَا يَسْمَعُونَ حَسِيسَهَا وَهُمْ فِى مَا ٱشْتَهَتْ أَنفُسُهُمْ خَـٰلِدُونَ ﴿١٠٢﴾

---

619. Mary.

103. The greatest terror shall not cause them to grieve and the angels shall receive them saying: "This is your day that you were promised";

104. The day when We will fold heaven like a scroll of writing, just as We began Our first creation, We shall bring it back - a promise [binding] on Us that We shall fulfil.

105. We have written in the Psalms that, after the Reminder, My righteous servants shall inherit the earth.

106. Surely, there is in this (the Qur'an) a Message to a worshipping people.

107. And We have only sent you,[620] as a mercy to the whole of mankind.

108. Say: "It is revealed to me that truly your God is One God; will you then submit?"

109. If they turn away, then say: "I have warned you all equally, but I do not know whether what you are promised is near or far."

110. He (Allah) knows what you say openly, and He knows what you conceal.

111. I do not know whether it is perhaps a trial for you, and an enjoyment for a while.

112. He (Muhammad) said: "Lord, judge rightly. Our Lord is the Compassionate Whose Help is sought to counter what you allege."

لَا يَحْزُنُهُمُ ٱلْفَزَعُ ٱلْأَكْبَرُ وَتَتَلَقَّىٰهُمُ ٱلْمَلَٰٓئِكَةُ هَٰذَا يَوْمُكُمُ ٱلَّذِى كُنتُمْ تُوعَدُونَ ۝

يَوْمَ نَطْوِى ٱلسَّمَآءَ كَطَىِّ ٱلسِّجِلِّ لِلْكُتُبِ كَمَا بَدَأْنَآ أَوَّلَ خَلْقٍ نُّعِيدُهُۥ وَعْدًا عَلَيْنَآ إِنَّا كُنَّا فَٰعِلِينَ ۝

وَلَقَدْ كَتَبْنَا فِى ٱلزَّبُورِ مِنۢ بَعْدِ ٱلذِّكْرِ أَنَّ ٱلْأَرْضَ يَرِثُهَا عِبَادِىَ ٱلصَّٰلِحُونَ ۝

إِنَّ فِى هَٰذَا لَبَلَٰغًا لِّقَوْمٍ عَٰبِدِينَ ۝

وَمَآ أَرْسَلْنَٰكَ إِلَّا رَحْمَةً لِّلْعَٰلَمِينَ ۝

قُلْ إِنَّمَا يُوحَىٰٓ إِلَىَّ أَنَّمَآ إِلَٰهُكُمْ إِلَٰهٌ وَٰحِدٌ فَهَلْ أَنتُم مُّسْلِمُونَ ۝

فَإِن تَوَلَّوْا۟ فَقُلْ ءَاذَنتُكُمْ عَلَىٰ سَوَآءٍ وَإِنْ أَدْرِىٓ أَقَرِيبٌ أَم بَعِيدٌ مَّا تُوعَدُونَ ۝

إِنَّهُۥ يَعْلَمُ ٱلْجَهْرَ مِنَ ٱلْقَوْلِ وَيَعْلَمُ مَا تَكْتُمُونَ ۝

وَإِنْ أَدْرِى لَعَلَّهُۥ فِتْنَةٌ لَّكُمْ وَمَتَٰعٌ إِلَىٰ حِينٍ ۝

قَٰلَ رَبِّ ٱحْكُم بِٱلْحَقِّ وَرَبُّنَا ٱلرَّحْمَٰنُ ٱلْمُسْتَعَانُ عَلَىٰ مَا تَصِفُونَ ۝

---

620. Muhammad.

Sûrat Al-Hajj,
(The Pilgrimage) 22

بِسۡمِ ٱللَّهِ ٱلرَّحۡمَٰنِ ٱلرَّحِيمِ

In the Name of Allah,
the Compassionate, the Merciful

1. O people, fear your Lord. Surely the clamour of the Hour is a terrible thing.

يَٰٓأَيُّهَا ٱلنَّاسُ ٱتَّقُوا۟ رَبَّكُمۡ إِنَّ زَلۡزَلَةَ ٱلسَّاعَةِ شَىۡءٌ عَظِيمٌ ١

2. The Day you will witness it, every suckling mother will be distracted from the child she is suckling, and every pregnant woman will deliver her burden, and you will see people drunk, whereas they are not drunk; but the punishment of Allah is terrible.

يَوۡمَ تَرَوۡنَهَا تَذۡهَلُ كُلُّ مُرۡضِعَةٍ عَمَّآ أَرۡضَعَتۡ وَتَضَعُ كُلُّ ذَاتِ حَمۡلٍ حَمۡلَهَا وَتَرَى ٱلنَّاسَ سُكَٰرَىٰ وَمَا هُم بِسُكَٰرَىٰ وَلَٰكِنَّ عَذَابَ ٱللَّهِ شَدِيدٌ ٢

3. And there are some people who dispute regarding Allah without any knowledge, and follow every rebellious devil.

وَمِنَ ٱلنَّاسِ مَن يُجَٰدِلُ فِى ٱللَّهِ بِغَيۡرِ عِلۡمٍ وَيَتَّبِعُ كُلَّ شَيۡطَٰنٍ مَّرِيدٍ ٣

4. It has been written against him (the Devil) that whoever takes him for a friend, he will lead astray and guide him to the punishment of Hell.

كُتِبَ عَلَيۡهِ أَنَّهُۥ مَن تَوَلَّاهُ فَأَنَّهُۥ يُضِلُّهُۥ وَيَهۡدِيهِ إِلَىٰ عَذَابِ ٱلسَّعِيرِ ٤

5. O people, if you are in doubt regarding the Resurrection, We have indeed created you from dust, then from a sperm, then from a clot, then from a little lump of flesh, partly formed and partly unformed, in order to show you. We deposit in the wombs whatever We please, for an appointed term; then We bring you out as infants, till you attain full strength. Some of you are made to die, and some are returned to the vilest age, so that they may not know, after having acquired some knowledge, anything. And you see the earth barren, but when We send down water upon it, it stirs and swells and produces vegetation of every pleasing variety.

يَٰٓأَيُّهَا ٱلنَّاسُ إِن كُنتُمۡ فِى رَيۡبٍ مِّنَ ٱلۡبَعۡثِ فَإِنَّا خَلَقۡنَٰكُم مِّن تُرَابٍ ثُمَّ مِن نُّطۡفَةٍ ثُمَّ مِنۡ عَلَقَةٍ ثُمَّ مِن مُّضۡغَةٍ مُّخَلَّقَةٍ وَغَيۡرِ مُخَلَّقَةٍ لِّنُبَيِّنَ لَكُمۡ وَنُقِرُّ فِى ٱلۡأَرۡحَامِ مَا نَشَآءُ إِلَىٰٓ أَجَلٍ مُّسَمًّى ثُمَّ نُخۡرِجُكُمۡ طِفۡلًا ثُمَّ لِتَبۡلُغُوٓا۟ أَشُدَّكُمۡ وَمِنكُم مَّن يُتَوَفَّىٰ وَمِنكُم مَّن يُرَدُّ إِلَىٰٓ أَرۡذَلِ ٱلۡعُمُرِ لِكَيۡلَا يَعۡلَمَ مِنۢ بَعۡدِ عِلۡمٍ شَيۡـًٔا وَتَرَى ٱلۡأَرۡضَ هَامِدَةً فَإِذَآ أَنزَلۡنَا عَلَيۡهَا ٱلۡمَآءَ ٱهۡتَزَّتۡ وَرَبَتۡ وَأَنۢبَتَتۡ مِن كُلِّ زَوۡجٍ بَهِيجٍ ٥

6. That is because Allah is the Truth, and He brings the dead to life and He has power over everything.

ذَٰلِكَ بِأَنَّ ٱللَّهَ هُوَ ٱلۡحَقُّ وَأَنَّهُۥ يُحۡيِ ٱلۡمَوۡتَىٰ وَأَنَّهُۥ عَلَىٰ كُلِّ شَىۡءٍ قَدِيرٌ ٦

7. And that the Hour is coming, no doubt about it; and that Allah raises up those who are in their graves.

8. And of the people, there is one who disputes concerning Allah without any knowledge, or guidance, or an illuminating Book.

9. Bearing himself proudly so as to lead people away from Allah's Path. His is disgrace in the present world and, on the Day of Resurrection, We shall make him taste the agony of burning:

10. That is what your hands have advanced in deeds and Allah is never unjust to His servants.

11. And of the people, there are some who worship Allah tepidly.[621] When good fortune comes his way, he is pleased with it, but if an ordeal befalls him, he turns around,[622] losing both this world and the world to come. That is the manifest loss.

12. He calls, besides Allah, on that which neither harms nor profits him. That is the worst[623] error.

13. He calls upon him whose harm is likelier than his profit. Wretched is the master and wretched is the ally!

14. Allah shall admit those who believe and do the righteous deeds into Gardens underneath which rivers flow. Allah surely does whatever He pleases.

15. He who thinks that Allah will not give him support in this world or the next, let him stretch a rope to the sky then cut it up. Let him then see if his guile will remove what angers him.

---

621. Literally, they worship on the brink of faith.
622. That is, goes back to disbelief.
623. Literally, the farthest from the way.

16. That is how We revealed it (the Qur'an) as clear revelations, and Allah guides whomever He pleases.

17. Indeed, the believers, the Jews, the Sabians, the Christians, the Magians and the idolaters - Allah shall decide between them on the Day of Resurrection. Surely, Allah is a witness of everything.

18. Have you not seen that to Allah bows down whoever is in the heavens and whoever is on earth, as well as the sun, the moon, the stars, the mountains, the trees, the beasts and many of the people? And for many the punishment has been decreed. And he whom Allah humiliates, will have no one to honour him. Allah does whatever He pleases.

19. Here are two adversaries who dispute about their Lord. To the unbelievers, garments of fire shall be cut up and over their heads boiling water shall be poured;

20. Whereby whatever is in their bellies and in their skins shall be melted.

21. And for them are iron rods.[624]

22. Every time they want, in their gloom, to get out of it,[625] they are brought back into it. [And it is said to them]: "Taste the agony of burning."

23. Allah shall admit those who believe and do the righteous deeds into Gardens, beneath which rivers flow. Therein they shall be adorned with gold bracelets and pearls, and their raiment there shall be of silk.

24. They had been guided to the fair words and guided to the Path of the Praiseworthy.

وَكَذَٰلِكَ أَنزَلْنَٰهُ ءَايَٰتٍ بَيِّنَٰتٍ وَأَنَّ ٱللَّهَ يَهْدِى مَن يُرِيدُ ﴿١٦﴾

إِنَّ ٱلَّذِينَ ءَامَنُواْ وَٱلَّذِينَ هَادُواْ وَٱلصَّٰبِئِينَ وَٱلنَّصَٰرَىٰ وَٱلْمَجُوسَ وَٱلَّذِينَ أَشْرَكُوٓاْ إِنَّ ٱللَّهَ يَفْصِلُ بَيْنَهُمْ يَوْمَ ٱلْقِيَٰمَةِ إِنَّ ٱللَّهَ عَلَىٰ كُلِّ شَىْءٍ شَهِيدٌ ﴿١٧﴾

أَلَمْ تَرَ أَنَّ ٱللَّهَ يَسْجُدُ لَهُۥ مَن فِى ٱلسَّمَٰوَٰتِ وَمَن فِى ٱلْأَرْضِ وَٱلشَّمْسُ وَٱلْقَمَرُ وَٱلنُّجُومُ وَٱلْجِبَالُ وَٱلشَّجَرُ وَٱلدَّوَآبُّ وَكَثِيرٌ مِّنَ ٱلنَّاسِ وَكَثِيرٌ حَقَّ عَلَيْهِ ٱلْعَذَابُ وَمَن يُهِنِ ٱللَّهُ فَمَا لَهُۥ مِن مُّكْرِمٍ إِنَّ ٱللَّهَ يَفْعَلُ مَا يَشَآءُ ۩ ﴿١٨﴾

۞ هَٰذَانِ خَصْمَانِ ٱخْتَصَمُواْ فِى رَبِّهِمْ فَٱلَّذِينَ كَفَرُواْ قُطِّعَتْ لَهُمْ ثِيَابٌ مِّن نَّارٍ يُصَبُّ مِن فَوْقِ رُءُوسِهِمُ ٱلْحَمِيمُ ﴿١٩﴾

يُصْهَرُ بِهِۦ مَا فِى بُطُونِهِمْ وَٱلْجُلُودُ ﴿٢٠﴾

وَلَهُم مَّقَٰمِعُ مِنْ حَدِيدٍ ﴿٢١﴾ كُلَّمَآ أَرَادُوٓاْ أَن يَخْرُجُواْ مِنْهَا مِنْ غَمٍّ أُعِيدُواْ فِيهَا وَذُوقُواْ عَذَابَ ٱلْحَرِيقِ ﴿٢٢﴾

إِنَّ ٱللَّهَ يُدْخِلُ ٱلَّذِينَ ءَامَنُواْ وَعَمِلُواْ ٱلصَّٰلِحَٰتِ جَنَّٰتٍ تَجْرِى مِن تَحْتِهَا ٱلْأَنْهَٰرُ يُحَلَّوْنَ فِيهَا مِنْ أَسَاوِرَ مِن ذَهَبٍ وَلُؤْلُؤًا وَلِبَاسُهُمْ فِيهَا حَرِيرٌ ﴿٢٣﴾

وَهُدُوٓاْ إِلَى ٱلطَّيِّبِ مِنَ ٱلْقَوْلِ وَهُدُوٓاْ إِلَىٰ صِرَٰطِ ٱلْحَمِيدِ ﴿٢٤﴾

---

624. To beat their heads with.
625. The Fire.

25. But those who disbelieve and bar others from the Path of Allah and the Sacred Mosque, which We have made open to all people equally - both those who dwell in it and those who visit it. He who wishes to incline in it towards wrongdoing, We shall make him taste a very painful punishment.

26. And [remember] when We appointed for Abraham the site of the (Sacred) House [saying]: "You shall not associate with Me anything and purify My House for those who circle round, those who stand up, those who kneel and those who prostrate themselves;"

27. And proclaim the pilgrimage to the people, and then they will come on foot or on every lean mount, coming from every deep ravine,

28. To witness benefits of theirs, and mention Allah's Name, during certain numbered days, over such beasts of the flocks as He has provided them with. Eat, then, from them and feed the wretched poor.

29. Then, let them complete their self-cleansing and fulfil their vows and circle round the Ancient House (the Ka'bah).

30. All that; and whoever venerates the sacred things of Allah, it shall be well for him with his Lord. Cattle have been made lawful to you, except what is recited to you [to avoid]: so shun the abomination of idols, and shun false testimony.

31. Remain true to Allah, associating no gods with Him. He who associates anything with Allah is like one who has fallen from the sky and is snatched by the birds, or the wind hurls him down a very steep place.

إِنَّ ٱلَّذِينَ كَفَرُوا۟ وَيَصُدُّونَ عَن سَبِيلِ ٱللَّهِ وَٱلْمَسْجِدِ ٱلْحَرَامِ ٱلَّذِى جَعَلْنَٰهُ لِلنَّاسِ سَوَآءً ٱلْعَٰكِفُ فِيهِ وَٱلْبَادِ وَمَن يُرِدْ فِيهِ بِإِلْحَادٍ بِظُلْمٍ نُّذِقْهُ مِنْ عَذَابٍ أَلِيمٍ ۝

وَإِذْ بَوَّأْنَا لِإِبْرَٰهِيمَ مَكَانَ ٱلْبَيْتِ أَن لَّا تُشْرِكْ بِى شَيْئًا وَطَهِّرْ بَيْتِىَ لِلطَّآئِفِينَ وَٱلْقَآئِمِينَ وَٱلرُّكَّعِ ٱلسُّجُودِ ۝

وَأَذِّن فِى ٱلنَّاسِ بِٱلْحَجِّ يَأْتُوكَ رِجَالًا وَعَلَىٰ كُلِّ ضَامِرٍ يَأْتِينَ مِن كُلِّ فَجٍّ عَمِيقٍ ۝

لِّيَشْهَدُوا۟ مَنَٰفِعَ لَهُمْ وَيَذْكُرُوا۟ ٱسْمَ ٱللَّهِ فِى أَيَّامٍ مَّعْلُومَٰتٍ عَلَىٰ مَا رَزَقَهُم مِّنۢ بَهِيمَةِ ٱلْأَنْعَٰمِ فَكُلُوا۟ مِنْهَا وَأَطْعِمُوا۟ ٱلْبَآئِسَ ٱلْفَقِيرَ ۝

ثُمَّ لْيَقْضُوا۟ تَفَثَهُمْ وَلْيُوفُوا۟ نُذُورَهُمْ وَلْيَطَّوَّفُوا۟ بِٱلْبَيْتِ ٱلْعَتِيقِ ۝

ذَٰلِكَ وَمَن يُعَظِّمْ حُرُمَٰتِ ٱللَّهِ فَهُوَ خَيْرٌ لَّهُ عِندَ رَبِّهِ وَأُحِلَّتْ لَكُمُ ٱلْأَنْعَٰمُ إِلَّا مَا يُتْلَىٰ عَلَيْكُمْ فَٱجْتَنِبُوا۟ ٱلرِّجْسَ مِنَ ٱلْأَوْثَٰنِ وَٱجْتَنِبُوا۟ قَوْلَ ٱلزُّورِ ۝

حُنَفَآءَ لِلَّهِ غَيْرَ مُشْرِكِينَ بِهِۦ وَمَن يُشْرِكْ بِٱللَّهِ فَكَأَنَّمَا خَرَّ مِنَ ٱلسَّمَآءِ فَتَخْطَفُهُ ٱلطَّيْرُ أَوْ تَهْوِى بِهِ ٱلرِّيحُ فِى مَكَانٍ سَحِيقٍ ۝

32. All that; and he who venerates the sacred rites of Allah - it is the fruit of the piety of the hearts.

ذَٰلِكَ وَمَن يُعَظِّمْ شَعَـٰٓئِرَ ٱللَّهِ فَإِنَّهَا مِن تَقْوَى ٱلْقُلُوبِ ﴿٣٢﴾

33. You have some benefits therefrom, for an appointed term; then their place of sacrifice is the Ancient House.

لَكُمْ فِيهَا مَنَـٰفِعُ إِلَىٰٓ أَجَلٍ مُّسَمًّى ثُمَّ مَحِلُّهَآ إِلَى ٱلْبَيْتِ ٱلْعَتِيقِ ﴿٣٣﴾

34. And to every nation, We have appointed a holy rite, so that they might mention Allah's Name over whatever He has provided them with of the beasts of the flock. For your God is One God. Submit to Him and announce the good news to the humble;

وَلِكُلِّ أُمَّةٍ جَعَلْنَا مَنسَكًا لِّيَذْكُرُوا۟ ٱسْمَ ٱللَّهِ عَلَىٰ مَا رَزَقَهُم مِّنۢ بَهِيمَةِ ٱلْأَنْعَـٰمِ فَإِلَـٰهُكُمْ إِلَـٰهٌ وَٰحِدٌ فَلَهُۥٓ أَسْلِمُوا۟ وَبَشِّرِ ٱلْمُخْبِتِينَ ﴿٣٤﴾

35. Those who, when Allah is mentioned, their hearts tremble, and those who endure what befalls them, and those who perform the prayer and spend from what We have provided them with.

ٱلَّذِينَ إِذَا ذُكِرَ ٱللَّهُ وَجِلَتْ قُلُوبُهُمْ وَٱلصَّـٰبِرِينَ عَلَىٰ مَآ أَصَابَهُمْ وَٱلْمُقِيمِى ٱلصَّلَوٰةِ وَمِمَّا رَزَقْنَـٰهُمْ يُنفِقُونَ ﴿٣٥﴾

36. And the camels We have made for you as parts of the sacred rites of Allah. You have some good therein; so mention Allah's Name over them as they stand in line. When their sides fall to the ground, eat of them and feed the contented and the beggar. That is how We subjected them to you, that perchance you may be thankful.

وَٱلْبُدْنَ جَعَلْنَـٰهَا لَكُم مِّن شَعَـٰٓئِرِ ٱللَّهِ لَكُمْ فِيهَا خَيْرٌ فَٱذْكُرُوا۟ ٱسْمَ ٱللَّهِ عَلَيْهَا صَوَآفَّ فَإِذَا وَجَبَتْ جُنُوبُهَا فَكُلُوا۟ مِنْهَا وَأَطْعِمُوا۟ ٱلْقَانِعَ وَٱلْمُعْتَرَّ كَذَٰلِكَ سَخَّرْنَـٰهَا لَكُمْ لَعَلَّكُمْ تَشْكُرُونَ ﴿٣٦﴾

37. Their flesh and blood will not reach Allah, but your piety will reach Him. Thus He subjected them to you, so that you may glorify Allah for guiding you. And announce the good news to the beneficent.

لَن يَنَالَ ٱللَّهَ لُحُومُهَا وَلَا دِمَآؤُهَا وَلَـٰكِن يَنَالُهُ ٱلتَّقْوَىٰ مِنكُمْ كَذَٰلِكَ سَخَّرَهَا لَكُمْ لِتُكَبِّرُوا۟ ٱللَّهَ عَلَىٰ مَا هَدَىٰكُمْ وَبَشِّرِ ٱلْمُحْسِنِينَ ﴿٣٧﴾

38. Allah will defend the believers; Allah surely does not like any thankless traitor.

۞ إِنَّ ٱللَّهَ يُدَٰفِعُ عَنِ ٱلَّذِينَ ءَامَنُوٓا۟ إِنَّ ٱللَّهَ لَا يُحِبُّ كُلَّ خَوَّانٍ كَفُورٍ ﴿٣٨﴾

39. Permission is given to those who fight because they are wronged. Surely Allah is Capable of giving them victory.

أُذِنَ لِلَّذِينَ يُقَـٰتَلُونَ بِأَنَّهُمْ ظُلِمُوا۟ وَإِنَّ ٱللَّهَ عَلَىٰ نَصْرِهِمْ لَقَدِيرٌ ﴿٣٩﴾

40. Those who were driven out of their homes unjustly, merely for their saying: "Our Lord is Allah." Had Allah not repelled some people by others, surely monasteries, churches, synagogues and mosques, wherein the Name of Allah is mentioned frequently, would have been demolished. Indeed, Allah will support whoever supports Him. Allah is surely Strong and Mighty.

41. Those who, if We establish them firmly in the land, will perform the prayer, give the alms, command the good and prohibit evil. To Allah belongs the outcome of all affairs.

42. If they denounce you as a liar, then the people of Noah, 'Ad and Thamud have denounced before them;

43. And the people of Abraham and the people of Lot, too;

44. And the people of Midian. And Moses was denounced. Then I reprieved the unbelievers; then I struck them down. How, then, was my punishment?

45. How many a city We destroyed when it was doing wrong; and now it is fallen down upon its turrets; and how many a deserted well, and lofty palace?

46. Have they not travelled in the land, so as to acquire hearts to reason with, or ears to hear by? For it is not the eyes which are blind, but the hearts within the breasts.

47. They ask you to hasten the punishment. Allah will never break His Promise; but a day for your Lord is like a thousand years of what you reckon.

48. And how many a city have I reprieved, although it was unjust? Then I struck it down, and unto Me is the ultimate return.

ٱلَّذِينَ أُخْرِجُوا۟ مِن دِيَٰرِهِم بِغَيْرِ حَقٍّ إِلَّآ أَن يَقُولُوا۟ رَبُّنَا ٱللَّهُ وَلَوْلَا دَفْعُ ٱللَّهِ ٱلنَّاسَ بَعْضَهُم بِبَعْضٍ لَّهُدِّمَتْ صَوَٰمِعُ وَبِيَعٌ وَصَلَوَٰتٌ وَمَسَٰجِدُ يُذْكَرُ فِيهَا ٱسْمُ ٱللَّهِ كَثِيرًا وَلَيَنصُرَنَّ ٱللَّهُ مَن يَنصُرُهُۥٓ إِنَّ ٱللَّهَ لَقَوِىٌّ عَزِيزٌ ﴿٤٠﴾

ٱلَّذِينَ إِن مَّكَّنَّٰهُمْ فِى ٱلْأَرْضِ أَقَامُوا۟ ٱلصَّلَوٰةَ وَءَاتَوُا۟ ٱلزَّكَوٰةَ وَأَمَرُوا۟ بِٱلْمَعْرُوفِ وَنَهَوْا۟ عَنِ ٱلْمُنكَرِ وَلِلَّهِ عَٰقِبَةُ ٱلْأُمُورِ ﴿٤١﴾

وَإِن يُكَذِّبُوكَ فَقَدْ كَذَّبَتْ قَبْلَهُمْ قَوْمُ نُوحٍ وَعَادٌ وَثَمُودُ ﴿٤٢﴾

وَقَوْمُ إِبْرَٰهِيمَ وَقَوْمُ لُوطٍ ﴿٤٣﴾

وَأَصْحَٰبُ مَدْيَنَ وَكُذِّبَ مُوسَىٰ فَأَمْلَيْتُ لِلْكَٰفِرِينَ ثُمَّ أَخَذْتُهُمْ فَكَيْفَ كَانَ نَكِيرِ ﴿٤٤﴾

فَكَأَيِّن مِّن قَرْيَةٍ أَهْلَكْنَٰهَا وَهِىَ ظَالِمَةٌ فَهِىَ خَاوِيَةٌ عَلَىٰ عُرُوشِهَا وَبِئْرٍ مُّعَطَّلَةٍ وَقَصْرٍ مَّشِيدٍ ﴿٤٥﴾

أَفَلَمْ يَسِيرُوا۟ فِى ٱلْأَرْضِ فَتَكُونَ لَهُمْ قُلُوبٌ يَعْقِلُونَ بِهَآ أَوْ ءَاذَانٌ يَسْمَعُونَ بِهَا فَإِنَّهَا لَا تَعْمَى ٱلْأَبْصَٰرُ وَلَٰكِن تَعْمَى ٱلْقُلُوبُ ٱلَّتِى فِى ٱلصُّدُورِ ﴿٤٦﴾

وَيَسْتَعْجِلُونَكَ بِٱلْعَذَابِ وَلَن يُخْلِفَ ٱللَّهُ وَعْدَهُۥ وَإِنَّ يَوْمًا عِندَ رَبِّكَ كَأَلْفِ سَنَةٍ مِّمَّا تَعُدُّونَ ﴿٤٧﴾

وَكَأَيِّن مِّن قَرْيَةٍ أَمْلَيْتُ لَهَا وَهِىَ ظَالِمَةٌ ثُمَّ أَخَذْتُهَا وَإِلَىَّ ٱلْمَصِيرُ ﴿٤٨﴾

49. Say: "O people,[626] I am only a plain warner to you."

50. Those who believe and do the righteous deeds will receive forgiveness and a bountiful provision,

51. But those who strive against Our Revelations defying Us - those are the people of Hell.

52. We have not sent a Messenger or Prophet before you but when he recited the Devil would intrude into his recitation. Yet Allah annuls what the Devil had cast. Then Allah establishes His Revelations. Allah is All-Knowing, Wise.

53. So as to make what Satan casts a temptation to those in whose hearts there is a sickness, and to those whose hearts are hard. The wrongdoers are indeed in profound discord!

54. And so that those who have been given the knowledge might understand that it is the truth from your Lord and so believe in it. Then their hearts will submit to it. Allah will certainly guide the believers to a straight path.

55. The unbelievers will continue to be in doubt concerning it, until the Hour comes upon them suddenly, or the punishment of a disastrous day seizes them.

56. Dominion on that Day shall be Allah's and He will judge between them. Then, those who believe and do the righteous deeds shall be in the Gardens of Bliss.

57. But those who disbelieve and deny Our Revelations, to those a demeaning punishment is in store.

قُل يَٰٓأَيُّهَا ٱلنَّاسُ إِنَّمَآ أَنَا۠ لَكُمۡ نَذِيرٌ مُّبِينٌ ﴿٤٩﴾

فَٱلَّذِينَ ءَامَنُوا۟ وَعَمِلُوا۟ ٱلصَّٰلِحَٰتِ لَهُم مَّغۡفِرَةٌ وَرِزۡقٌ كَرِيمٌ ﴿٥٠﴾

وَٱلَّذِينَ سَعَوۡا۟ فِىٓ ءَايَٰتِنَا مُعَٰجِزِينَ أُو۟لَٰٓئِكَ أَصۡحَٰبُ ٱلۡجَحِيمِ ﴿٥١﴾

وَمَآ أَرۡسَلۡنَا مِن قَبۡلِكَ مِن رَّسُولٍ وَلَا نَبِىٍّ إِلَّآ إِذَا تَمَنَّىٰٓ أَلۡقَى ٱلشَّيۡطَٰنُ فِىٓ أُمۡنِيَّتِهِۦ فَيَنسَخُ ٱللَّهُ مَا يُلۡقِى ٱلشَّيۡطَٰنُ ثُمَّ يُحۡكِمُ ٱللَّهُ ءَايَٰتِهِۦ وَٱللَّهُ عَلِيمٌ حَكِيمٌ ﴿٥٢﴾

لِّيَجۡعَلَ مَا يُلۡقِى ٱلشَّيۡطَٰنُ فِتۡنَةً لِّلَّذِينَ فِى قُلُوبِهِم مَّرَضٌ وَٱلۡقَاسِيَةِ قُلُوبُهُمۡ وَإِنَّ ٱلظَّٰلِمِينَ لَفِى شِقَاقٍ بَعِيدٍ ﴿٥٣﴾

وَلِيَعۡلَمَ ٱلَّذِينَ أُوتُوا۟ ٱلۡعِلۡمَ أَنَّهُ ٱلۡحَقُّ مِن رَّبِّكَ فَيُؤۡمِنُوا۟ بِهِۦ فَتُخۡبِتَ لَهُۥ قُلُوبُهُمۡ وَإِنَّ ٱللَّهَ لَهَادِ ٱلَّذِينَ ءَامَنُوٓا۟ إِلَىٰ صِرَٰطٍ مُّسۡتَقِيمٍ ﴿٥٤﴾

وَلَا يَزَالُ ٱلَّذِينَ كَفَرُوا۟ فِى مِرۡيَةٍ مِّنۡهُ حَتَّىٰ تَأۡتِيَهُمُ ٱلسَّاعَةُ بَغۡتَةً أَوۡ يَأۡتِيَهُمۡ عَذَابُ يَوۡمٍ عَقِيمٍ ﴿٥٥﴾

ٱلۡمُلۡكُ يَوۡمَئِذٍ لِّلَّهِ يَحۡكُمُ بَيۡنَهُمۡ فَٱلَّذِينَ ءَامَنُوا۟ وَعَمِلُوا۟ ٱلصَّٰلِحَٰتِ فِى جَنَّٰتِ ٱلنَّعِيمِ ﴿٥٦﴾

وَٱلَّذِينَ كَفَرُوا۟ وَكَذَّبُوا۟ بِـَٔايَٰتِنَا فَأُو۟لَٰٓئِكَ لَهُمۡ عَذَابٌ مُّهِينٌ ﴿٥٧﴾

---

626. The Meccans.

58. And those who emigrated in the Path of Allah, then were killed or died, Allah shall provide them with a fair provision. Allah is surely the Best Provider.

59. He will admit them into a place with which they will be well-pleased. Surely, Allah is All-Knowing, Clement.

60. All that; and he who chastises in the same way he was chastised, then he is wronged, Allah shall support him. Allah is surely a Pardoner, All-Forgiver.

61. That is because Allah causes the night to pass into the day and the day to pass into the night, and that Allah is All-Hearing, All-Seeing.

62. That is because Allah is the Truth and what they call upon besides Him is the falsehood; and that Allah is the Exalted, the Great One.

63. Do you not see that Allah sends down water from the sky, whereupon the earth turns green. Allah is Gracious, Well-Informed.

64. To Him belongs what is in the heavens and the earth and it is Allah Who is the Self-Sufficient and the Praiseworthy.

65. Do you not see that Allah has subjected to you what is on earth and the ships which sail in the sea at His Command? And He keeps the sky from falling to the ground, save by His Leave. Allah is Gracious and Merciful to mankind.

66. And it is He Who gives you life, then He causes you to die, then He will bring you back to life. Man, however, is truly thankless.

67. To every nation, We have given a sacred rite which they observe. So do not let them dispute with you in this matter. Call them to your Lord, for you are on a straight course.

وَالَّذِينَ هَاجَرُوا فِى سَبِيلِ اللَّهِ ثُمَّ قُتِلُوا أَوْ مَاتُوا لَيَرْزُقَنَّهُمُ اللَّهُ رِزْقًا حَسَنًا وَإِنَّ اللَّهَ لَهُوَ خَيْرُ الرَّازِقِينَ ۝

لَيُدْخِلَنَّهُم مُّدْخَلًا يَرْضَوْنَهُ وَإِنَّ اللَّهَ لَعَلِيمٌ حَلِيمٌ ۝

۞ ذَلِكَ وَمَنْ عَاقَبَ بِمِثْلِ مَا عُوقِبَ بِهِ ثُمَّ بُغِيَ عَلَيْهِ لَيَنصُرَنَّهُ اللَّهُ إِنَّ اللَّهَ لَعَفُوٌّ غَفُورٌ ۝

ذَلِكَ بِأَنَّ اللَّهَ يُولِجُ الَّيْلَ فِى النَّهَارِ وَيُولِجُ النَّهَارَ فِى الَّيْلِ وَأَنَّ اللَّهَ سَمِيعٌ بَصِيرٌ ۝

ذَلِكَ بِأَنَّ اللَّهَ هُوَ الْحَقُّ وَأَنَّ مَا يَدْعُونَ مِن دُونِهِ هُوَ الْبَاطِلُ وَأَنَّ اللَّهَ هُوَ الْعَلِيُّ الْكَبِيرُ ۝

أَلَمْ تَرَ أَنَّ اللَّهَ أَنزَلَ مِنَ السَّمَاءِ مَاءً فَتُصْبِحُ الْأَرْضُ مُخْضَرَّةً إِنَّ اللَّهَ لَطِيفٌ خَبِيرٌ ۝

لَهُ مَا فِى السَّمَوَاتِ وَمَا فِى الْأَرْضِ وَإِنَّ اللَّهَ لَهُوَ الْغَنِىُّ الْحَمِيدُ ۝

أَلَمْ تَرَ أَنَّ اللَّهَ سَخَّرَ لَكُم مَّا فِى الْأَرْضِ وَالْفُلْكَ تَجْرِى فِى الْبَحْرِ بِأَمْرِهِ وَيُمْسِكُ السَّمَاءَ أَن تَقَعَ عَلَى الْأَرْضِ إِلَّا بِإِذْنِهِ إِنَّ اللَّهَ بِالنَّاسِ لَرَءُوفٌ رَّحِيمٌ ۝

وَهُوَ الَّذِى أَحْيَاكُمْ ثُمَّ يُمِيتُكُمْ ثُمَّ يُحْيِيكُمْ إِنَّ الْإِنسَانَ لَكَفُورٌ ۝

لِكُلِّ أُمَّةٍ جَعَلْنَا مَنسَكًا هُمْ نَاسِكُوهُ فَلَا يُنَازِعُنَّكَ فِى الْأَمْرِ وَادْعُ إِلَى رَبِّكَ إِنَّكَ لَعَلَى هُدًى مُّسْتَقِيمٍ ۝

68. And if they dispute with you, say: "Allah knows best what you are doing."

69. Allah will judge between you on the Day of Resurrection, regarding what you disagree about.

70. Do you not know that Allah knows what is in the heavens and on earth. All that is in a Book; and that is an easy matter for Allah.

71. And they worship, besides Allah, that concerning which He did not send down any authority, and of which they have no knowledge. The wrongdoers shall have no supporter.

72. And when Our Clear Revelations are recited to them, you will recognize in the faces of the unbelievers the denial. They will almost fall upon those who recite to them Our Revelations. Say: "Shall I tell you about what is worse than that? It is the Fire which Allah has promised the unbelievers; and what a wretched fate!"

73. O people, an example has been given; so listen to it. Surely, those whom you call upon, besides Allah, will never create a fly, even if they band together. And if a fly should rob them of something, they cannot retrieve it from it. How weak is the invoker and the invoked!

74. They do not give Allah His True Measure. Surely, Allah is Strong and Mighty.

75. Allah chooses from angels and men Messengers; Allah is All-Hearing, All-Seeing.

76. He knows what is before them and what is behind them, and to Allah are all things returned.

وَإِن جَٰدَلُوكَ فَقُلِ ٱللَّهُ أَعْلَمُ بِمَا تَعْمَلُونَ ۝

ٱللَّهُ يَحْكُمُ بَيْنَكُمْ يَوْمَ ٱلْقِيَٰمَةِ فِيمَا كُنتُمْ فِيهِ تَخْتَلِفُونَ ۝

أَلَمْ تَعْلَمْ أَنَّ ٱللَّهَ يَعْلَمُ مَا فِى ٱلسَّمَآءِ وَٱلْأَرْضِ إِنَّ ذَٰلِكَ فِى كِتَٰبٍ إِنَّ ذَٰلِكَ عَلَى ٱللَّهِ يَسِيرٌ ۝

وَيَعْبُدُونَ مِن دُونِ ٱللَّهِ مَا لَمْ يُنَزِّلْ بِهِۦ سُلْطَٰنًا وَمَا لَيْسَ لَهُم بِهِۦ عِلْمٌ وَمَا لِلظَّٰلِمِينَ مِن نَّصِيرٍ ۝

وَإِذَا تُتْلَىٰ عَلَيْهِمْ ءَايَٰتُنَا بَيِّنَٰتٍ تَعْرِفُ فِى وُجُوهِ ٱلَّذِينَ كَفَرُوا ٱلْمُنكَرَ يَكَادُونَ يَسْطُونَ بِٱلَّذِينَ يَتْلُونَ عَلَيْهِمْ ءَايَٰتِنَا قُلْ أَفَأُنَبِّئُكُم بِشَرٍّ مِّن ذَٰلِكُمُ ٱلنَّارُ وَعَدَهَا ٱللَّهُ ٱلَّذِينَ كَفَرُوا وَبِئْسَ ٱلْمَصِيرُ ۝

يَٰٓأَيُّهَا ٱلنَّاسُ ضُرِبَ مَثَلٌ فَٱسْتَمِعُوا لَهُۥ إِنَّ ٱلَّذِينَ تَدْعُونَ مِن دُونِ ٱللَّهِ لَن يَخْلُقُوا ذُبَابًا وَلَوِ ٱجْتَمَعُوا لَهُۥ وَإِن يَسْلُبْهُمُ ٱلذُّبَابُ شَيْئًا لَّا يَسْتَنقِذُوهُ مِنْهُ ضَعُفَ ٱلطَّالِبُ وَٱلْمَطْلُوبُ ۝

مَا قَدَرُوا ٱللَّهَ حَقَّ قَدْرِهِۦٓ إِنَّ ٱللَّهَ لَقَوِىٌّ عَزِيزٌ ۝

ٱللَّهُ يَصْطَفِى مِنَ ٱلْمَلَٰٓئِكَةِ رُسُلًا وَمِنَ ٱلنَّاسِ إِنَّ ٱللَّهَ سَمِيعٌ بَصِيرٌ ۝

يَعْلَمُ مَا بَيْنَ أَيْدِيهِمْ وَمَا خَلْفَهُمْ وَإِلَى ٱللَّهِ تُرْجَعُ ٱلْأُمُورُ ۝

77. O believers, kneel down, prostrate yourselves and worship your Lord and do good, that you may perchance prosper.

78. And strive for Allah as you ought to strive. He elected you, and did not impose on you any hardship in religion - the faith of your father Abraham. He called you Muslims before and in this,[627] that the Messenger may bear witness against you and you may be witnesses against mankind. So, perform the prayer, give the alms and hold fast to Allah. He is your Master; and what a Blessed Master and a Blessed Supporter!

يَتَأَيُّهَا ٱلَّذِينَ ءَامَنُوا ٱرْكَعُوا وَٱسْجُدُوا وَٱعْبُدُوا رَبَّكُمْ وَٱفْعَلُوا ٱلْخَيْرَ لَعَلَّكُمْ تُفْلِحُونَ ۩ ٧٧

وَجَٰهِدُوا فِى ٱللَّهِ حَقَّ جِهَادِهِۦ هُوَ ٱجْتَبَىٰكُمْ وَمَا جَعَلَ عَلَيْكُمْ فِى ٱلدِّينِ مِنْ حَرَجٍ مِّلَّةَ أَبِيكُمْ إِبْرَٰهِيمَ هُوَ سَمَّىٰكُمُ ٱلْمُسْلِمِينَ مِن قَبْلُ وَفِى هَٰذَا لِيَكُونَ ٱلرَّسُولُ شَهِيدًا عَلَيْكُمْ وَتَكُونُوا شُهَدَآءَ عَلَى ٱلنَّاسِ فَأَقِيمُوا ٱلصَّلَوٰةَ وَءَاتُوا ٱلزَّكَوٰةَ وَٱعْتَصِمُوا بِٱللَّهِ هُوَ مَوْلَىٰكُمْ فَنِعْمَ ٱلْمَوْلَىٰ وَنِعْمَ ٱلنَّصِيرُ ٧٨

Sûrat Al-Mu'minûn, (The Believers) 23

سورة المؤمنون

In the Name of Allah, the Compassionate, the Merciful

بِسْمِ ٱللَّهِ ٱلرَّحْمَٰنِ ٱلرَّحِيمِ

1. The believers have prospered;

قَدْ أَفْلَحَ ٱلْمُؤْمِنُونَ ١

2. Those who are submissive in their prayers,

ٱلَّذِينَ هُمْ فِى صَلَاتِهِمْ خَٰشِعُونَ ٢

3. And those who turn away from idle talk,

وَٱلَّذِينَ هُمْ عَنِ ٱللَّغْوِ مُعْرِضُونَ ٣

4. And those who give the alms.

وَٱلَّذِينَ هُمْ لِلزَّكَوٰةِ فَٰعِلُونَ ٤

5. And those who guard their private parts.

وَٱلَّذِينَ هُمْ لِفُرُوجِهِمْ حَٰفِظُونَ ٥

6. Except from their wives and what their right hands possess.[628] [For these] they are not blameworthy.

إِلَّا عَلَىٰ أَزْوَٰجِهِمْ أَوْ مَا مَلَكَتْ أَيْمَٰنُهُمْ فَإِنَّهُمْ غَيْرُ مَلُومِينَ ٦

7. Whoever seeks anything beyond that - those are the transgressors.

فَمَنِ ٱبْتَغَىٰ وَرَآءَ ذَٰلِكَ فَأُوْلَٰئِكَ هُمُ ٱلْعَادُونَ ٧

8. Those who honour their trusts and promises;

وَٱلَّذِينَ هُمْ لِأَمَٰنَٰتِهِمْ وَعَهْدِهِمْ رَٰعُونَ ٨

9. And observe their prayers;

وَٱلَّذِينَ هُمْ عَلَىٰ صَلَوَٰتِهِمْ يُحَافِظُونَ ٩

10. Those are the inheritors,

أُوْلَٰئِكَ هُمُ ٱلْوَٰرِثُونَ ١٠

---

627. The Qur'an.
628. Slave-girls.

11. Who will inherit Paradise wherein they will dwell forever.

ٱلَّذِينَ يَرِثُونَ ٱلْفِرْدَوْسَ هُمْ فِيهَا خَٰلِدُونَ ۝

12. We have created man from an extract of clay;

وَلَقَدْ خَلَقْنَا ٱلْإِنسَٰنَ مِن سُلَٰلَةٍ مِّن طِينٍ ۝

13. Then We placed him as a sperm in a secure place;

ثُمَّ جَعَلْنَٰهُ نُطْفَةً فِى قَرَارٍ مَّكِينٍ ۝

14. Then We created out of the sperm a clot; then made from the clot a lump of flesh, then made the lump of flesh into bones; and then covered the bones with flesh; then fashioned him into another creation. So Blessed be Allah, the Best of Creators.

ثُمَّ خَلَقْنَا ٱلنُّطْفَةَ عَلَقَةً فَخَلَقْنَا ٱلْعَلَقَةَ مُضْغَةً فَخَلَقْنَا ٱلْمُضْغَةَ عِظَٰمًا فَكَسَوْنَا ٱلْعِظَٰمَ لَحْمًا ثُمَّ أَنشَأْنَٰهُ خَلْقًا ءَاخَرَ فَتَبَارَكَ ٱللَّهُ أَحْسَنُ ٱلْخَٰلِقِينَ ۝

15. Then after that you will surely die.

ثُمَّ إِنَّكُم بَعْدَ ذَٰلِكَ لَمَيِّتُونَ ۝

16. Then on the Day of Resurrection you will surely be raised from the dead.

ثُمَّ إِنَّكُمْ يَوْمَ ٱلْقِيَٰمَةِ تُبْعَثُونَ ۝

17. We have created above you seven spheres, and We were not oblivious of the creation.

وَلَقَدْ خَلَقْنَا فَوْقَكُمْ سَبْعَ طَرَآئِقَ وَمَا كُنَّا عَنِ ٱلْخَلْقِ غَٰفِلِينَ ۝

18. And We send down water from heaven in measure, then lodge it in the ground, although We are Able to allow it to drain away.

وَأَنزَلْنَا مِنَ ٱلسَّمَآءِ مَآءً بِقَدَرٍ فَأَسْكَنَّٰهُ فِى ٱلْأَرْضِ وَإِنَّا عَلَىٰ ذَهَابٍ بِهِ لَقَٰدِرُونَ ۝

19. Then through it We produce for you gardens of palm trees and vines, from which you get many fruits whereof you eat.

فَأَنشَأْنَا لَكُم بِهِ جَنَّٰتٍ مِّن نَّخِيلٍ وَأَعْنَٰبٍ لَّكُمْ فِيهَا فَوَٰكِهُ كَثِيرَةٌ وَمِنْهَا تَأْكُلُونَ ۝

20. And a tree[629] growing out of Mount Sinai that produces oil and condiment for eaters.

وَشَجَرَةً تَخْرُجُ مِن طُورِ سَيْنَآءَ تَنۢبُتُ بِٱلدُّهْنِ وَصِبْغٍ لِّلْءَاكِلِينَ ۝

21. And surely in the cattle you have a lesson. We give you to drink from what is in their bellies, and you have therein many uses, and from them you eat.

وَإِنَّ لَكُمْ فِى ٱلْأَنْعَٰمِ لَعِبْرَةً نُّسْقِيكُم مِّمَّا فِى بُطُونِهَا وَلَكُمْ فِيهَا مَنَٰفِعُ كَثِيرَةٌ وَمِنْهَا تَأْكُلُونَ ۝

22. And on them and on the ships you are borne.

وَعَلَيْهَا وَعَلَى ٱلْفُلْكِ تُحْمَلُونَ ۝

---

629. The olive tree.

23. And We sent Noah forth to his people, and he said: "O my people, worship Allah; you have no god other than He. Do you not fear [Allah]?"

وَلَقَدْ أَرْسَلْنَا نُوحًا إِلَىٰ قَوْمِهِ فَقَالَ يَـٰقَوْمِ ٱعْبُدُوا۟ ٱللَّهَ مَا لَكُم مِّنْ إِلَـٰهٍ غَيْرُهُۥٓ أَفَلَا تَتَّقُونَ ۝

24. Then, the dignitaries of his people who had disbelieved said: "This is only a mortal like you, who wishes to show you favours. Had Allah willed, He would have sent down angels. We never heard of this from our forefathers.

فَقَالَ ٱلْمَلَؤُا۟ ٱلَّذِينَ كَفَرُوا۟ مِن قَوْمِهِ مَا هَـٰذَآ إِلَّا بَشَرٌ مِّثْلُكُمْ يُرِيدُ أَن يَتَفَضَّلَ عَلَيْكُمْ وَلَوْ شَآءَ ٱللَّهُ لَأَنزَلَ مَلَـٰٓئِكَةً مَّا سَمِعْنَا بِهَـٰذَا فِىٓ ءَابَآئِنَا ٱلْأَوَّلِينَ ۝

25. "He is a man possessed; so watch him for a while."

إِنْ هُوَ إِلَّا رَجُلٌۢ بِهِۦ جِنَّةٌ فَتَرَبَّصُوا۟ بِهِۦ حَتَّىٰ حِينٍ ۝

26. He (Noah) said: "Lord, help me, for they deny me."

قَالَ رَبِّ ٱنصُرْنِى بِمَا كَذَّبُونِ ۝

27. We revealed to him, then: "Make the Ark under Our Very Eyes and according to Our Revelation. Then when Our Command comes and the oven boils over, take into it a couple of every kind, together with your family, except for him against whom the Decree has already been pronounced. Do not speak to Me concerning those who are wrongdoers; for they will certainly be drowned.

فَأَوْحَيْنَآ إِلَيْهِ أَنِ ٱصْنَعِ ٱلْفُلْكَ بِأَعْيُنِنَا وَوَحْيِنَا فَإِذَا جَآءَ أَمْرُنَا وَفَارَ ٱلتَّنُّورُ فَٱسْلُكْ فِيهَا مِن كُلٍّ زَوْجَيْنِ ٱثْنَيْنِ وَأَهْلَكَ إِلَّا مَن سَبَقَ عَلَيْهِ ٱلْقَوْلُ مِنْهُمْ وَلَا تُخَـٰطِبْنِى فِى ٱلَّذِينَ ظَلَمُوٓا۟ إِنَّهُم مُّغْرَقُونَ ۝

28. "Then, when you are seated, you and your company, upon the Ark, say: 'Praise be to Allah Who delivered us from the wrong-doing people.' "

فَإِذَا ٱسْتَوَيْتَ أَنتَ وَمَن مَّعَكَ عَلَى ٱلْفُلْكِ فَقُلِ ٱلْحَمْدُ لِلَّهِ ٱلَّذِى نَجَّىٰنَا مِنَ ٱلْقَوْمِ ٱلظَّـٰلِمِينَ ۝

29. And say: "Lord, let me land in a blessed way; for you are the Best of those who make people land."

وَقُل رَّبِّ أَنزِلْنِى مُنزَلًا مُّبَارَكًا وَأَنتَ خَيْرُ ٱلْمُنزِلِينَ ۝

30. Surely in that are signs. Thus We put them to the test.

إِنَّ فِى ذَٰلِكَ لَءَايَـٰتٍ وَإِن كُنَّا لَمُبْتَلِينَ ۝

31. Then, We brought out after them another generation.

ثُمَّ أَنشَأْنَا مِنۢ بَعْدِهِمْ قَرْنًا ءَاخَرِينَ ۝

32. So, We sent to them a Messenger of their own, saying: "Worship Allah, you have no other god than Him. Do you not fear [Allah]?"

فَأَرْسَلْنَا فِيهِمْ رَسُولًا مِّنْهُمْ أَنِ ٱعْبُدُوا۟ ٱللَّهَ مَا لَكُم مِّنْ إِلَـٰهٍ غَيْرُهُۥٓ أَفَلَا تَتَّقُونَ ۝

33. Then the dignitaries of his people, who had disbelieved and denied the meeting of the Hereafter and whom We had accorded ease in the present life, said: "This is, indeed, merely a mortal like you; he eats from what you eat and drinks from what you drink.

وَقَالَ ٱلْمَلَأُ مِن قَوْمِهِ ٱلَّذِينَ كَفَرُوا۟ وَكَذَّبُوا۟ بِلِقَآءِ ٱلْأَخِرَةِ وَأَتْرَفْنَٰهُمْ فِى ٱلْحَيَوٰةِ ٱلدُّنْيَا مَا هَٰذَآ إِلَّا بَشَرٌ مِّثْلُكُمْ يَأْكُلُ مِمَّا تَأْكُلُونَ مِنْهُ وَيَشْرَبُ مِمَّا تَشْرَبُونَ ۝

34. "If you obey a mortal like yourselves, you are surely the losers.

وَلَئِنْ أَطَعْتُم بَشَرًا مِّثْلَكُمْ إِنَّكُمْ إِذًا لَّخَٰسِرُونَ ۝

35. "Does he promise you that once you die and turn into dust and bones, you will be brought back?

أَيَعِدُكُمْ أَنَّكُمْ إِذَا مِتُّمْ وَكُنتُمْ تُرَابًا وَعِظَٰمًا أَنَّكُم مُّخْرَجُونَ ۝

36. "Far, far away is what you are promised!

۞ هَيْهَاتَ هَيْهَاتَ لِمَا تُوعَدُونَ ۝

37. "There is only this our earthly life; we die and we live, but we shall not be raised from the dead.

إِنْ هِىَ إِلَّا حَيَاتُنَا ٱلدُّنْيَا نَمُوتُ وَنَحْيَا وَمَا نَحْنُ بِمَبْعُوثِينَ ۝

38. "He is only a man who fabricates lies about Allah and we will not believe in him."

إِنْ هُوَ إِلَّا رَجُلٌ ٱفْتَرَىٰ عَلَى ٱللَّهِ كَذِبًا وَمَا نَحْنُ لَهُ بِمُؤْمِنِينَ ۝

39. He said: "Lord, support me against their calling me a liar."

قَالَ رَبِّ ٱنصُرْنِى بِمَا كَذَّبُونِ ۝

40. He (Allah) said: "In a little while they will regret."

قَالَ عَمَّا قَلِيلٍ لَّيُصْبِحُنَّ نَٰدِمِينَ ۝

41. Then the Cry seized them justly, and so We turned them into scum. Away then with the wrongdoing people!

فَأَخَذَتْهُمُ ٱلصَّيْحَةُ بِٱلْحَقِّ فَجَعَلْنَٰهُمْ غُثَآءً فَبُعْدًا لِّلْقَوْمِ ٱلظَّٰلِمِينَ ۝

42. Then We raised up after them other generations.

ثُمَّ أَنشَأْنَا مِنۢ بَعْدِهِمْ قُرُونًا ءَاخَرِينَ ۝

43. No nation hastens its term; nor will they put it back.

مَا تَسْبِقُ مِنْ أُمَّةٍ أَجَلَهَا وَمَا يَسْتَـْٔخِرُونَ ۝

44. Then We sent Our Messengers one after the other. Every time a Messenger came to his nation, they denied him. So We made them succeed one another and reduced them to mere tales. Away with a people who do not believe.

ثُمَّ أَرْسَلْنَا رُسُلَنَا تَتْرَا كُلَّ مَا جَآءَ أُمَّةً رَّسُولُهَا كَذَّبُوهُ فَأَتْبَعْنَا بَعْضَهُم بَعْضًا وَجَعَلْنَٰهُمْ أَحَادِيثَ فَبُعْدًا لِّقَوْمٍ لَّا يُؤْمِنُونَ ۝

45. Then We sent Moses and his brother Aaron with Our Signs and a decisive authority;

ثُمَّ أَرْسَلْنَا مُوسَىٰ وَأَخَاهُ هَٰرُونَ بِـَٔايَٰتِنَا وَسُلْطَٰنٍ مُّبِينٍ ۝

46. To Pharaoh and his dignitaries, but they were an arrogant people.

إِلَىٰ فِرْعَوْنَ وَمَلَإِيْهِۦ فَٱسْتَكْبَرُوا۟ وَكَانُوا۟ قَوْمًا عَالِينَ ﴿٤٦﴾

47. And so they said: "Shall we believe in two mortals like ourselves, while their own people are serving us?"

فَقَالُوٓا۟ أَنُؤْمِنُ لِبَشَرَيْنِ مِثْلِنَا وَقَوْمُهُمَا لَنَا عَٰبِدُونَ ﴿٤٧﴾

48. Then they denounced them both as liars, and so they were destroyed.

فَكَذَّبُوهُمَا فَكَانُوا۟ مِنَ ٱلْمُهْلَكِينَ ﴿٤٨﴾

49. And We gave Moses the Book, that perchance they may be guided.

وَلَقَدْ ءَاتَيْنَا مُوسَى ٱلْكِتَٰبَ لَعَلَّهُمْ يَهْتَدُونَ ﴿٤٩﴾

50. And We made Mary's son and his mother a sign, and We sheltered them on a lofty ground which had [settled] meadows and a spring.

وَجَعَلْنَا ٱبْنَ مَرْيَمَ وَأُمَّهُۥٓ ءَايَةً وَءَاوَيْنَٰهُمَآ إِلَىٰ رَبْوَةٍ ذَاتِ قَرَارٍ وَمَعِينٍ ﴿٥٠﴾

51. O Messengers, eat from the good things and do what is right. Surely, I am aware of what you do.

يَٰٓأَيُّهَا ٱلرُّسُلُ كُلُوا۟ مِنَ ٱلطَّيِّبَٰتِ وَٱعْمَلُوا۟ صَٰلِحًا إِنِّى بِمَا تَعْمَلُونَ عَلِيمٌ ﴿٥١﴾

52. And this your nation is a single nation and I am your Lord; so fear Me.

وَإِنَّ هَٰذِهِۦٓ أُمَّتُكُمْ أُمَّةً وَٰحِدَةً وَأَنَا۠ رَبُّكُمْ فَٱتَّقُونِ ﴿٥٢﴾

53. But they broke up, regarding their affairs, into factions, each party rejoicing in what they had.

فَتَقَطَّعُوٓا۟ أَمْرَهُم بَيْنَهُمْ زُبُرًا كُلُّ حِزْبٍۭ بِمَا لَدَيْهِمْ فَرِحُونَ ﴿٥٣﴾

54. So, leave them in their error for a while.

فَذَرْهُمْ فِى غَمْرَتِهِمْ حَتَّىٰ حِينٍ ﴿٥٤﴾

55. What? Do you think that in what We provide them with of money and children,

أَيَحْسَبُونَ أَنَّمَا نُمِدُّهُم بِهِۦ مِن مَّالٍ وَبَنِينَ ﴿٥٥﴾

56. We are hastening to them Our Bounties? No, they do not understand.

نُسَارِعُ لَهُمْ فِى ٱلْخَيْرَٰتِ بَل لَّا يَشْعُرُونَ ﴿٥٦﴾

57. Those who are awed by the fear of their Lord,

إِنَّ ٱلَّذِينَ هُم مِّنْ خَشْيَةِ رَبِّهِم مُّشْفِقُونَ ﴿٥٧﴾

58. And those who believe in the Revelations of their Lord,

وَٱلَّذِينَ هُم بِـَٔايَٰتِ رَبِّهِمْ يُؤْمِنُونَ ﴿٥٨﴾

59. And those who do not associate anything with their Lord,

وَٱلَّذِينَ هُم بِرَبِّهِمْ لَا يُشْرِكُونَ ﴿٥٩﴾

60. And those who give what they give while their hearts tremble for fear that they are returning to their Lord;

وَٱلَّذِينَ يُؤْتُونَ مَآ ءَاتَوا۟ وَّقُلُوبُهُمْ وَجِلَةٌ أَنَّهُمْ إِلَىٰ رَبِّهِمْ رَٰجِعُونَ ﴿٦٠﴾

61. All those shall hasten to do the right deeds and they are the first to attain them.

62. We do not charge any soul beyond its capacity; and We have a Book which utters the truth, and they shall not be wronged.

63. But their hearts are in confusion with respect to this;[630] and they have works, other than that, which they continue to do.

64. Until We seize those who live in luxury among them, and then they groan.

65. Do not groan today; you shall not be supported against Us.

66. My Revelations were recited to you, but you were turning upon your heels in flight;

67. In arrogance, talking nonsense about it by night.

68. Have they not pondered the Word;[631] or have they received what was not given to their forefathers?

69. Or have they not recognized their Messenger, and so they are denying him?

70. Or do they say: "He is possessed"? Rather, he brought them the Truth, but most of them hate the Truth.

71. If the Truth followed their whims, the heavens and the earth would be corrupted, together with everything therein; but We have brought them their reminder, yet from their reminder they turn away.

72. Or are you asking them for a reward? But, the reward of your Lord is better, and He is the Best Provider.

73. And you are surely calling them to a straight path.

---

630. The Qur'an.
631. The Qur'an.

74. Those who do not believe in the Hereafter are deviating from the Path.

75. If We show them mercy and lift their affliction, they would persist in their arrogance, wandering aimlessly.

76. We seized them with the punishment; but they would not submit to their Lord and they would not supplicate.

77. Until We opened up against them a gate of terrible punishment and, behold, they were in utter despair.

78. It is He Who created for you ears, eyes and hearts; but how little you give thanks.

79. And it is He Who created and multiplied you in the land, and unto Him you will be gathered.

80. And it is He Who gives life and causes death, and His is the alternation of night and day. Do you not understand?

81. No, they said just what the ancients said.

82. They said: "What, when we are dead and become dust and bones, will we be brought back to life?

83. "We have been promised this, we and our fathers before. This is merely legends of the ancients."

84. Say: "Whose is the earth and all those in it, if you really know?"

85. They will say: "Allah's"; say: "Do you not reflect, then?"

86. Say: "Who is the Lord of the seven heavens and the Lord of the Mighty Throne?"

87. They will say: "They are Allah's." Say: "Do you not fear God, then?"

88. Say: "In whose hand is the dominion of everything, protecting and is not protected, if you really know?"

وَإِنَّ ٱلَّذِينَ لَا يُؤْمِنُونَ بِٱلْأَخِرَةِ عَنِ ٱلصِّرَٰطِ لَنَٰكِبُونَ ۝

۞ وَلَوْ رَحِمْنَٰهُمْ وَكَشَفْنَا مَا بِهِم مِّن ضُرٍّ لَّلَجُّوا۟ فِى طُغْيَٰنِهِمْ يَعْمَهُونَ ۝

وَلَقَدْ أَخَذْنَٰهُم بِٱلْعَذَابِ فَمَا ٱسْتَكَانُوا۟ لِرَبِّهِمْ وَمَا يَتَضَرَّعُونَ ۝

حَتَّىٰٓ إِذَا فَتَحْنَا عَلَيْهِم بَابًا ذَا عَذَابٍ شَدِيدٍ إِذَا هُمْ فِيهِ مُبْلِسُونَ ۝

وَهُوَ ٱلَّذِىٓ أَنشَأَ لَكُمُ ٱلسَّمْعَ وَٱلْأَبْصَٰرَ وَٱلْأَفْـِٔدَةَ قَلِيلًا مَّا تَشْكُرُونَ ۝

وَهُوَ ٱلَّذِى ذَرَأَكُمْ فِى ٱلْأَرْضِ وَإِلَيْهِ تُحْشَرُونَ ۝

وَهُوَ ٱلَّذِى يُحْىِۦ وَيُمِيتُ وَلَهُ ٱخْتِلَٰفُ ٱلَّيْلِ وَٱلنَّهَارِ أَفَلَا تَعْقِلُونَ ۝

بَلْ قَالُوا۟ مِثْلَ مَا قَالَ ٱلْأَوَّلُونَ ۝

قَالُوٓا۟ أَءِذَا مِتْنَا وَكُنَّا تُرَابًا وَعِظَٰمًا أَءِنَّا لَمَبْعُوثُونَ ۝

لَقَدْ وُعِدْنَا نَحْنُ وَءَابَآؤُنَا هَٰذَا مِن قَبْلُ إِنْ هَٰذَآ إِلَّآ أَسَٰطِيرُ ٱلْأَوَّلِينَ ۝

قُل لِّمَنِ ٱلْأَرْضُ وَمَن فِيهَآ إِن كُنتُمْ تَعْلَمُونَ ۝

سَيَقُولُونَ لِلَّهِ قُلْ أَفَلَا تَذَكَّرُونَ ۝

قُلْ مَن رَّبُّ ٱلسَّمَٰوَٰتِ ٱلسَّبْعِ وَرَبُّ ٱلْعَرْشِ ٱلْعَظِيمِ ۝

سَيَقُولُونَ لِلَّهِ قُلْ أَفَلَا تَتَّقُونَ ۝

قُلْ مَنۢ بِيَدِهِۦ مَلَكُوتُ كُلِّ شَىْءٍ وَهُوَ يُجِيرُ وَلَا يُجَارُ عَلَيْهِ إِن كُنتُمْ تَعْلَمُونَ ۝

89. They will say: "[In] Allah's." Say: "How, then, are you bewitched?"

سَيَقُولُونَ لِلَّهِ قُلْ فَأَنَّىٰ تُسْحَرُونَ ﴿٨٩﴾

90. Nay, We brought them the truth, but they are liars.

بَلْ أَتَيْنَـٰهُم بِٱلْحَقِّ وَإِنَّهُمْ لَكَـٰذِبُونَ ﴿٩٠﴾

91. Allah did not take to Himself a child and there was never another god with Him; or else each god would have carried off what he has created, and some of them would have risen against the others. Exalted be Allah above what they describe!

مَا ٱتَّخَذَ ٱللَّهُ مِن وَلَدٍ وَمَا كَانَ مَعَهُ مِنْ إِلَـٰهٍ إِذًا لَّذَهَبَ كُلُّ إِلَـٰهٍ بِمَا خَلَقَ وَلَعَلَا بَعْضُهُمْ عَلَىٰ بَعْضٍ سُبْحَـٰنَ ٱللَّهِ عَمَّا يَصِفُونَ ﴿٩١﴾

92. Knower of the Unseen and the Seen; He is exalted above what they associate.

عَـٰلِمِ ٱلْغَيْبِ وَٱلشَّهَـٰدَةِ فَتَعَـٰلَىٰ عَمَّا يُشْرِكُونَ ﴿٩٢﴾

93. Say: "Lord, if you would show me what they are promised.

قُل رَّبِّ إِمَّا تُرِيَنِّي مَا يُوعَدُونَ ﴿٩٣﴾

94. "Lord, do not reckon me among the wrongdoing people".

رَبِّ فَلَا تَجْعَلْنِي فِي ٱلْقَوْمِ ٱلظَّـٰلِمِينَ ﴿٩٤﴾

95. And We are surely Able to show you what We promise them.

وَإِنَّا عَلَىٰ أَن نُّرِيَكَ مَا نَعِدُهُمْ لَقَـٰدِرُونَ ﴿٩٥﴾

96. Ward off evil with that which is fairer. We know best what they describe.

ٱدْفَعْ بِٱلَّتِي هِيَ أَحْسَنُ ٱلسَّيِّئَةَ نَحْنُ أَعْلَمُ بِمَا يَصِفُونَ ﴿٩٦﴾

97. And say: "Lord, I seek refuge with You from the goadings of the devils.

وَقُل رَّبِّ أَعُوذُ بِكَ مِنْ هَمَزَٰتِ ٱلشَّيَـٰطِينِ ﴿٩٧﴾

98. "And I seek refuge with You lest they join me".

وَأَعُوذُ بِكَ رَبِّ أَن يَحْضُرُونِ ﴿٩٨﴾

99. Yet, when death visits one of them, he says: "Lord, bring me back;[632]

حَتَّىٰ إِذَا جَآءَ أَحَدَهُمُ ٱلْمَوْتُ قَالَ رَبِّ ٱرْجِعُونِ ﴿٩٩﴾

100. "That perchance I might act rightly with respect to what I have omitted." No, it is just a word he is uttering; and behind them is a barrier till the day they are raised from the dead.

لَعَلِّي أَعْمَلُ صَـٰلِحًا فِيمَا تَرَكْتُ كَلَّا إِنَّهَا كَلِمَةٌ هُوَ قَآئِلُهَا وَمِن وَرَآئِهِم بَرْزَخٌ إِلَىٰ يَوْمِ يُبْعَثُونَ ﴿١٠٠﴾

101. And when the Trumpet is blown, they will have no kinship to bind them on that Day, and they will not question one another.

فَإِذَا نُفِخَ فِي ٱلصُّورِ فَلَآ أَنسَابَ بَيْنَهُمْ يَوْمَئِذٍ وَلَا يَتَسَآءَلُونَ ﴿١٠١﴾

102. Then, those whose scales are heavy - those are the prosperous.

فَمَن ثَقُلَتْ مَوَٰزِينُهُ فَأُوْلَـٰئِكَ هُمُ ٱلْمُفْلِحُونَ ﴿١٠٢﴾

---

632. To the world.

103. But those whose scales are light - those are the ones who have lost their souls. In Hell, they will dwell forever.

104. The Fire lashes their faces, and therein they shrivel.

105. "Were not My Signs (this Qur'an) recited to you, but you used to denouce them as lies?"

106. They will say: "Lord, our misery overcame us and we were an erring people.

107. "Lord, bring us out of it;[633] then, if we revert we are indeed wrongoers."

108. He (Allah) said: "Rot in it and do not talk to Me.

109. "There was a group of My servants who used to say: 'Lord, we believe, so forgive us and have mercy on us; You are the Best of the merciful.'

110. "But you took them for a laughing-stock, till they made you forget My Name, while you were mocking them.

111. "I have rewarded them this Day for their forbearance, making them the winners."

112. He (Allah) will say: "How long did you linger on earth, in terms of years?"

113. The will say: "We lingered a day or a part of a day; so ask those who count."

114. He (Allah) will say: "You only lingered for a little while, if only you knew.

115. "Did you, then, think that We created you in vain and that unto Us you will not be returned?"

116. Glory be to Allah, the True King; there is no god but He. He is indeed the Lord of the Noble Throne.

---

633. Hell.

117. He who calls, along with Allah, upon another god of whom he has no proof, his reckoning is with his Lord. Surely, the unbelievers will never prosper.

118. Say: "Lord forgive and have mercy; for You are the Best of the merciful."

Sûrat An-Nûr, (The Light) 24

In the Name of Allah, the Compassionate, the Merciful

1. A Surah that We have sent down and stipulated, and We have sent down in it clear revelations, that perchance you might re- member.

2. The adulteress and the adulterer, whip each one of them a hundred lashes; and let no pity move you in Allah's religion, regarding them; if you believe in Allah and the Hereafter. And let a group of believers witness their punishment.

3. The adulterer shall marry none but an adulteress or an idolatress; and the adulteress none shall marry her but an adulterer or idolater. That has been forbidden the believers.

4. Those who accuse chaste women, then cannot bring four witnesses, whip them eighty lashes, and do not ever accept their testimony. For those are the wicked sinners.

5. Except for those who repent afterwards and mend their ways. For Allah is surely All-Forgiving, Merciful.

6. And those who accuse their wives and have no witnesses except themselves, the testimony of one of them shall be to swear by Allah four times that he is truthful.

7. The fifth time shall be Allah's Curse on him, if he is a liar.

8. And her swearing four times by Allah that he is a liar will ward off punishment from her.

9. And the fifth time will be that Allah's Wrath be upon her, if he (her husband) is truthful.

10. And, but for Allah's Bounty towards you and His Mercy and that Allah is a remitter of sins and is All-Wise;

11. Those who spread the slander[634] are a band of you. Do not reckon it an evil for you; rather it is a good thing for you. Everyone of them will be credited with the sin he has earned, and he who bore the brunt of it shall have a terrible punishment.

12. Would that the believers, men and women, when you heard it,[635] had thought well of themselves saying: "This is a manifest slander!"

13. And would that they had brought forth four witnesses [to vouch for it]! But since they did not bring any witnesses, those are, in Allah's sight, the real liars.

14. And but for Allah's Bounty to you and His Mercy, in this world and the next, you would have been visited, due to your chatter, by a terrible punishment.

15. Since you received it on your tongues and you uttered with your mouths what you had no knowledge of, deeming it a simple matter; whereas in Allah's Sight it was very grave.

16. And would that, upon hearing it, you were to say: "It is not for us to speak about this. Glory be to You; this is truly a great calumny."

---

634. Against 'Aisha, wife of the Prophet, according to the commentators.
635. The slander.

17. Allah admonishes you never to return to the like of this, if you are real believers.

يَعِظُكُمُ ٱللَّهُ أَن تَعُودُوا لِمِثْلِهِ أَبَدًا إِن كُنتُم مُّؤْمِنِينَ ﴿١٧﴾

18. And Allah expounds clearly for you the Signs. Allah is All-Knowing, Wise.

وَيُبَيِّنُ ٱللَّهُ لَكُمُ ٱلْآيَاتِ وَٱللَّهُ عَلِيمٌ حَكِيمٌ ﴿١٨﴾

19. Indeed, those who love to see indecency spread among the believers will have in this world and the next a very painful punishment. Allah knows, but you do not know.

إِنَّ ٱلَّذِينَ يُحِبُّونَ أَن تَشِيعَ ٱلْفَاحِشَةُ فِي ٱلَّذِينَ ءَامَنُوا لَهُمْ عَذَابٌ أَلِيمٌ فِي ٱلدُّنْيَا وَٱلْآخِرَةِ وَٱللَّهُ يَعْلَمُ وَأَنتُمْ لَا تَعْلَمُونَ ﴿١٩﴾

20. And but for Allah's Bounty to you and His Mercy and that Allah is truly Clement and Merciful;

وَلَوْلَا فَضْلُ ٱللَّهِ عَلَيْكُمْ وَرَحْمَتُهُ وَأَنَّ ٱللَّهَ رَءُوفٌ رَّحِيمٌ ﴿٢٠﴾

21. O believers, do not follow in the footsteps of Satan; for he who follows in the footsteps of Satan, simply bids to indecency and disrepute. But for Allah's Bounty to you and His Mercy, not one of you would have ever been pure; but Allah purifies whomever He pleases. Allah is All-Hearing, All-Knowing.

۞ يَٰٓأَيُّهَا ٱلَّذِينَ ءَامَنُوا لَا تَتَّبِعُوا خُطُوَٰتِ ٱلشَّيْطَٰنِ وَمَن يَتَّبِعْ خُطُوَٰتِ ٱلشَّيْطَٰنِ فَإِنَّهُ يَأْمُرُ بِٱلْفَحْشَاءِ وَٱلْمُنكَرِ وَلَوْلَا فَضْلُ ٱللَّهِ عَلَيْكُمْ وَرَحْمَتُهُ مَا زَكَىٰ مِنكُم مِّنْ أَحَدٍ أَبَدًا وَلَٰكِنَّ ٱللَّهَ يُزَكِّي مَن يَشَاءُ وَٱللَّهُ سَمِيعٌ عَلِيمٌ ﴿٢١﴾

22. Let not the bounteous and wealthy among you swear off giving freely to kinsmen, the destitute and the Emigrants in the Path of Allah. Let them pardon and forgive. Do you not wish that Allah should forgive you? Allah is All-Forgiving, Merciful.

وَلَا يَأْتَلِ أُو۟لُوا ٱلْفَضْلِ مِنكُمْ وَٱلسَّعَةِ أَن يُؤْتُوا أُو۟لِي ٱلْقُرْبَىٰ وَٱلْمَسَٰكِينَ وَٱلْمُهَٰجِرِينَ فِي سَبِيلِ ٱللَّهِ وَلْيَعْفُوا وَلْيَصْفَحُوا أَلَا تُحِبُّونَ أَن يَغْفِرَ ٱللَّهُ لَكُمْ وَٱللَّهُ غَفُورٌ رَّحِيمٌ ﴿٢٢﴾

23. Surely those who slander married women, who are heedless and believing, are accursed in this world and the next, and they shall have a terrible punishment;

إِنَّ ٱلَّذِينَ يَرْمُونَ ٱلْمُحْصَنَٰتِ ٱلْغَٰفِلَٰتِ ٱلْمُؤْمِنَٰتِ لُعِنُوا فِي ٱلدُّنْيَا وَٱلْآخِرَةِ وَلَهُمْ عَذَابٌ عَظِيمٌ ﴿٢٣﴾

24. On the Day when their tongues, their hands and their feet shall bear witness against them, regarding what they used to do.

يَوْمَ تَشْهَدُ عَلَيْهِمْ أَلْسِنَتُهُمْ وَأَيْدِيهِمْ وَأَرْجُلُهُم بِمَا كَانُوا يَعْمَلُونَ ﴿٢٤﴾

25. On that Day Allah will pay them their just dues and they will know that Allah is the Manifest Truth.

يَوْمَئِذٍ يُوَفِّيهِمُ ٱللَّهُ دِينَهُمُ ٱلْحَقَّ وَيَعْلَمُونَ أَنَّ ٱللَّهَ هُوَ ٱلْحَقُّ ٱلْمُبِينُ ﴿٢٥﴾

26. Foul women for foul men, and foul men for foul women; and good women for good men, and good men for good women. Those are acquitted of the burden of what they say; they will have forgiveness and a generous provision.

27. O believers, do not enter houses other than your own before you ask leave and greet their occupants. That is better for you, that perchance you may remember well.

28. If you find no one in them, do not enter until you are given permission; and if it is said to you: "Go back", then go back. That is purer for you, and Allah knows well what you do.

29. It is no offence for you to enter uninhabited houses in which you have some means of enjoyment. Allah knows what you reveal and what you conceal.

30. Tell the believers to cast down their eyes and guard their private parts. That is purer for them. Allah is conversant with what they do.

31. And tell believing women to cast down their eyes and guard their private parts and not show their finery, except the outward part of it. And let them drape their bossoms with their veils and not show their finery except to their husbands, their fathers, their husbands' fathers, their sons, the sons of their husbands, their brothers, the sons of their brothers, the sons of their sisters, their women, their maid-servants, the men-followers who have no sexual desire, or infants who have no knowledge of women's sexual parts yet. Let them, also, not stamp their feet, so that what they have concealed of their finery might be known. Repent to Allah, all of you, O believers, that perchance you may prosper.

32. Encourage the unmarried among you and the righteous among your servants and maids to marry. If they are poor, Allah will enrich them from His Bounty. Allah is All-Embracing, All-Knowing.

وَأَنكِحُوا الْأَيَامَىٰ مِنكُمْ وَالصَّالِحِينَ مِنْ عِبَادِكُمْ وَإِمَآئِكُمْ إِن يَكُونُوا فُقَرَآءَ يُغْنِهِمُ اللَّهُ مِن فَضْلِهِ وَاللَّهُ وَاسِعٌ عَلِيمٌ ﴿٣٢﴾

33. Let those who do not find the means to marry be abstinent, till Allah enriches them from His Bounty. Those whom your right hands own and who wish to pay for their emancipation, conclude a contract with them, if you know that there is some good in them, and give them of Allah's wealth which He gave you. Do not force your slave-girls into prostitution, if they wish to be chaste, in order to seek the fleeting goods of this life. Whoever forces them, surely Allah, after their being forced, is Forgiving, Merciful.

وَلْيَسْتَعْفِفِ الَّذِينَ لَا يَجِدُونَ نِكَاحًا حَتَّىٰ يُغْنِيَهُمُ اللَّهُ مِن فَضْلِهِ وَالَّذِينَ يَبْتَغُونَ الْكِتَابَ مِمَّا مَلَكَتْ أَيْمَانُكُمْ فَكَاتِبُوهُمْ إِنْ عَلِمْتُمْ فِيهِمْ خَيْرًا وَآتُوهُم مِّن مَّالِ اللَّهِ الَّذِي آتَاكُمْ وَلَا تُكْرِهُوا فَتَيَاتِكُمْ عَلَى الْبِغَاءِ إِنْ أَرَدْنَ تَحَصُّنًا لِّتَبْتَغُوا عَرَضَ الْحَيَاةِ الدُّنْيَا وَمَن يُكْرِههُّنَّ فَإِنَّ اللَّهَ مِنْ بَعْدِ إِكْرَاهِهِنَّ غَفُورٌ رَّحِيمٌ ﴿٣٣﴾

34. And We have sent down to you signs making everything clear, and an example of those who have gone before you, and an exhortation to the God-fearing.

وَلَقَدْ أَنزَلْنَا إِلَيْكُمْ آيَاتٍ مُّبَيِّنَاتٍ وَمَثَلًا مِّنَ الَّذِينَ خَلَوْا مِن قَبْلِكُمْ وَمَوْعِظَةً لِّلْمُتَّقِينَ ﴿٣٤﴾

35. Allah is the Light of the heavens and the earth. His Light is like a niche in which there is a lamp, the lamp is in a glass, the glass is like a glittering star. It is kindled from a blessed olive tree, neither of the East nor the West. Its oil will almost shine, even if no fire has touched it. Light upon light, Allah guides to His Light whomever He pleases and gives the examples to mankind. Allah has knowledge of everything.

۞ اللَّهُ نُورُ السَّمَاوَاتِ وَالْأَرْضِ مَثَلُ نُورِهِ كَمِشْكَاةٍ فِيهَا مِصْبَاحٌ الْمِصْبَاحُ فِي زُجَاجَةٍ الزُّجَاجَةُ كَأَنَّهَا كَوْكَبٌ دُرِّيٌّ يُوقَدُ مِن شَجَرَةٍ مُّبَارَكَةٍ زَيْتُونَةٍ لَّا شَرْقِيَّةٍ وَلَا غَرْبِيَّةٍ يَكَادُ زَيْتُهَا يُضِيءُ وَلَوْ لَمْ تَمْسَسْهُ نَارٌ نُّورٌ عَلَىٰ نُورٍ يَهْدِي اللَّهُ لِنُورِهِ مَن يَشَآءُ وَيَضْرِبُ اللَّهُ الْأَمْثَالَ لِلنَّاسِ وَاللَّهُ بِكُلِّ شَيْءٍ عَلِيمٌ ﴿٣٥﴾

36. In houses Allah allowed to be raised and His Name to be mentioned therein, He is glorified therein, mornings and evenings,

فِي بُيُوتٍ أَذِنَ اللَّهُ أَن تُرْفَعَ وَيُذْكَرَ فِيهَا اسْمُهُ يُسَبِّحُ لَهُ فِيهَا بِالْغُدُوِّ وَالْآصَالِ ﴿٣٦﴾

37. By men who are not distracted, by trading or trafficking, from mentioning Allah's Name, performing the prayer and giving the alms. They fear a Day whereon the hearts and eyesights shall be turned around;

رِجَالٌ لَّا تُلْهِيهِمْ تِجَارَةٌ وَلَا بَيْعٌ عَن ذِكْرِ اللَّهِ وَإِقَامِ الصَّلَوٰةِ وَإِيتَآءِ الزَّكَوٰةِ يَخَافُونَ يَوْمًا تَتَقَلَّبُ فِيهِ الْقُلُوبُ وَالْأَبْصَارُ ﴿٣٧﴾

353

38. So that Allah may reward them for their fairest works and increase them from His Bounty. Allah provides for whomever He pleases without reckoning.

39. As to the unbelievers, their works are like a mirage in level ground, which the thirsty supposes to be water; but when he comes close to it, he finds that it is nothing. Instead, he finds Allah there and so He pays him his account in full. Allah is Quick in reckoning.

40. Or like dark shadows in a turbulent sea, covered by waves upon waves, above which are clouds. Dark shadows above which are dark shadows; if he brings his hand out, he will hardly see it. He to whom Allah has not granted a light will have no light.

41. Have you not seen that Allah is glorified by whatever is in the heavens or the earth, and by the birds in flight. He knows the prayer of each and its glorification. Allah knows well what they do.

42. To Allah belongs the dominion of the heavens and the earth and unto Allah is the ultimate return.

43. Have you not seen that Allah drives the clouds, then brings them together, then piles them into a heap, from which you can see rain coming. He brings mountains of hail from the sky, with which He smites whomever He pleases and diverts it from whomever He pleases. The gleam of its lightning almost blinds the eyes.

44. He alternates the night and day. In that there is a lesson for those who have eyes to see.

45. Allah created every beast from water. Some of them crawl on their bellies, some walk on two feet and others walk on four. Allah creates whatever He pleases. Allah, indeed, has power over everything.

لِيَجْزِيَهُمُ اللَّهُ أَحْسَنَ مَا عَمِلُوا وَيَزِيدَهُم مِّن فَضْلِهِ وَاللَّهُ يَرْزُقُ مَن يَشَاءُ بِغَيْرِ حِسَابٍ ﴿٣٨﴾

وَالَّذِينَ كَفَرُوا أَعْمَالُهُمْ كَسَرَابٍ بِقِيعَةٍ يَحْسَبُهُ الظَّمْآنُ مَاءً حَتَّىٰ إِذَا جَاءَهُ لَمْ يَجِدْهُ شَيْئًا وَوَجَدَ اللَّهَ عِندَهُ فَوَفَّاهُ حِسَابَهُ وَاللَّهُ سَرِيعُ الْحِسَابِ ﴿٣٩﴾

أَوْ كَظُلُمَاتٍ فِي بَحْرٍ لُّجِّيٍّ يَغْشَاهُ مَوْجٌ مِّن فَوْقِهِ مَوْجٌ مِّن فَوْقِهِ سَحَابٌ ظُلُمَاتٌ بَعْضُهَا فَوْقَ بَعْضٍ إِذَا أَخْرَجَ يَدَهُ لَمْ يَكَدْ يَرَاهَا وَمَن لَّمْ يَجْعَلِ اللَّهُ لَهُ نُورًا فَمَا لَهُ مِن نُّورٍ ﴿٤٠﴾

أَلَمْ تَرَ أَنَّ اللَّهَ يُسَبِّحُ لَهُ مَن فِي السَّمَاوَاتِ وَالْأَرْضِ وَالطَّيْرُ صَافَّاتٍ كُلٌّ قَدْ عَلِمَ صَلَاتَهُ وَتَسْبِيحَهُ وَاللَّهُ عَلِيمٌ بِمَا يَفْعَلُونَ ﴿٤١﴾

وَلِلَّهِ مُلْكُ السَّمَاوَاتِ وَالْأَرْضِ وَإِلَى اللَّهِ الْمَصِيرُ ﴿٤٢﴾

أَلَمْ تَرَ أَنَّ اللَّهَ يُزْجِي سَحَابًا ثُمَّ يُؤَلِّفُ بَيْنَهُ ثُمَّ يَجْعَلُهُ رُكَامًا فَتَرَى الْوَدْقَ يَخْرُجُ مِنْ خِلَالِهِ وَيُنَزِّلُ مِنَ السَّمَاءِ مِن جِبَالٍ فِيهَا مِن بَرَدٍ فَيُصِيبُ بِهِ مَن يَشَاءُ وَيَصْرِفُهُ عَن مَّن يَشَاءُ يَكَادُ سَنَا بَرْقِهِ يَذْهَبُ بِالْأَبْصَارِ ﴿٤٣﴾

يُقَلِّبُ اللَّهُ اللَّيْلَ وَالنَّهَارَ إِنَّ فِي ذَٰلِكَ لَعِبْرَةً لِّأُولِي الْأَبْصَارِ ﴿٤٤﴾

وَاللَّهُ خَلَقَ كُلَّ دَابَّةٍ مِّن مَّاءٍ فَمِنْهُم مَّن يَمْشِي عَلَىٰ بَطْنِهِ وَمِنْهُم مَّن يَمْشِي عَلَىٰ رِجْلَيْنِ وَمِنْهُم مَّن يَمْشِي عَلَىٰ أَرْبَعٍ يَخْلُقُ اللَّهُ مَا يَشَاءُ إِنَّ اللَّهَ عَلَىٰ كُلِّ شَيْءٍ قَدِيرٌ ﴿٤٥﴾

46. We have sent down (in this Qur'an) signs making everything clear, and Allah guides whomever He pleases to a straight path.

47. They say: "We believe in Allah and the Messenger and we obey." Then a group of them turn away, afterwards. Those are not real believers.

48. And if they are called unto Allah and His Messenger to judge between them, behold, a group of them turns away.

49. But if they have the right, they come to him[636] submissively.

50. Is there a sickness in their hearts, or are they in doubt, or do they fear that Allah and His Messenger might deal with them unjustly? No, those are the wrongdoers.

51. As to the believers, if they are called unto Allah and His Messenger to judge between them, they only say: "We hear and obey." Those are the prosperous.

52. Those who obey Allah and His Messenger and fear Allah and beware Him; those are the real winners.

53. They swear their most solemn oaths that, should you order them, they will go forth. Say: "Do not swear; it is a well-known obedience. Allah is fully conversant with what you do."

54. Say: "Obey Allah and obey the Messenger; but if you turn away, then upon him (Messenger Muhammad) rests what he was charged with, and upon you what you were charged with. However, if you obey him, you will be well-guided. It is only incumbent on the Messenger to deliver the manifest message."

لَقَدْ أَنزَلْنَآ ءَايَتٍ مُّبَيِّنَتٍ وَٱللَّهُ يَهْدِى مَن يَشَآءُ إِلَىٰ صِرَٰطٍ مُّسْتَقِيمٍ ٤٦

وَيَقُولُونَ ءَامَنَّا بِٱللَّهِ وَبِٱلرَّسُولِ وَأَطَعْنَا ثُمَّ يَتَوَلَّىٰ فَرِيقٌ مِّنْهُم مِّنۢ بَعْدِ ذَٰلِكَ وَمَآ أُوْلَٰٓئِكَ بِٱلْمُؤْمِنِينَ ٤٧

وَإِذَا دُعُوٓاْ إِلَى ٱللَّهِ وَرَسُولِهِۦ لِيَحْكُمَ بَيْنَهُمْ إِذَا فَرِيقٌ مِّنْهُم مُّعْرِضُونَ ٤٨

وَإِن يَكُن لَّهُمُ ٱلْحَقُّ يَأْتُوٓاْ إِلَيْهِ مُذْعِنِينَ ٤٩

أَفِى قُلُوبِهِم مَّرَضٌ أَمِ ٱرْتَابُوٓاْ أَمْ يَخَافُونَ أَن يَحِيفَ ٱللَّهُ عَلَيْهِمْ وَرَسُولُهُۥ بَلْ أُوْلَٰٓئِكَ هُمُ ٱلظَّٰلِمُونَ ٥٠

إِنَّمَا كَانَ قَوْلَ ٱلْمُؤْمِنِينَ إِذَا دُعُوٓاْ إِلَى ٱللَّهِ وَرَسُولِهِۦ لِيَحْكُمَ بَيْنَهُمْ أَن يَقُولُواْ سَمِعْنَا وَأَطَعْنَا وَأُوْلَٰٓئِكَ هُمُ ٱلْمُفْلِحُونَ ٥١

وَمَن يُطِعِ ٱللَّهَ وَرَسُولَهُۥ وَيَخْشَ ٱللَّهَ وَيَتَّقْهِ فَأُوْلَٰٓئِكَ هُمُ ٱلْفَآئِزُونَ ٥٢

۞ وَأَقْسَمُواْ بِٱللَّهِ جَهْدَ أَيْمَٰنِهِمْ لَئِنْ أَمَرْتَهُمْ لَيَخْرُجُنَّ قُل لَّا تُقْسِمُواْ طَاعَةٌ مَّعْرُوفَةٌ إِنَّ ٱللَّهَ خَبِيرٌۢ بِمَا تَعْمَلُونَ ٥٣

قُلْ أَطِيعُواْ ٱللَّهَ وَأَطِيعُواْ ٱلرَّسُولَ فَإِن تَوَلَّوْاْ فَإِنَّمَا عَلَيْهِ مَا حُمِّلَ وَعَلَيْكُم مَّا حُمِّلْتُمْ وَإِن تُطِيعُوهُ تَهْتَدُواْ وَمَا عَلَى ٱلرَّسُولِ إِلَّا ٱلْبَلَٰغُ ٱلْمُبِينُ ٥٤

---

636. The Prophet.

55. Allah promised those of you who have believed and done the righteous deeds that He will surely make them successors in the land, and He made those who came before them successors, and that He will establish firmly for them their religion, which He chose for them, and that He will give them, as a substitute for their fear, security. "They worship Me and do not associate anything with Me. He who disbelieves afterwards - those are the real sinners."

56. Perform the prayer, give the alms and obey the Messenger, that perchance you might receive mercy.

57. Do not suppose that the unbelievers are able to thwart Allah on earth. Their refuge shall be the Fire, and what a wretched fate!

58. O believers, let those your right hands possess[637] and those who have not reached the age of puberty ask your leave three times:[638] before the dawn prayer, when you put off your clothes at noon and after the evening prayer. These are three occasions of nudity for you; after which you or they are not at fault, if you approach each other. That is how Allah makes clear His Signs to you. Allah is All-Knowing, Wise.

59. And when your children reach puberty, let them ask leave, as those who came before them asked leave. That is how Allah makes clear His Signs to you. Allah is All-Knowing, Wise.

60. Those women who are past child-bearing and have no hope of marriage are not at fault if they take off their outer garments, not exhibiting any finery; but to refrain is better for them. Allah is All-Hearing, All-Knowing.

وَعَدَ ٱللَّهُ ٱلَّذِينَ ءَامَنُوا۟ مِنكُمْ وَعَمِلُوا۟ ٱلصَّٰلِحَٰتِ لَيَسْتَخْلِفَنَّهُمْ فِى ٱلْأَرْضِ كَمَا ٱسْتَخْلَفَ ٱلَّذِينَ مِن قَبْلِهِمْ وَلَيُمَكِّنَنَّ لَهُمْ دِينَهُمُ ٱلَّذِى ٱرْتَضَىٰ لَهُمْ وَلَيُبَدِّلَنَّهُم مِّنۢ بَعْدِ خَوْفِهِمْ أَمْنًا يَعْبُدُونَنِى لَا يُشْرِكُونَ بِى شَيْـًٔا وَمَن كَفَرَ بَعْدَ ذَٰلِكَ فَأُو۟لَٰٓئِكَ هُمُ ٱلْفَٰسِقُونَ ۝

وَأَقِيمُوا۟ ٱلصَّلَوٰةَ وَءَاتُوا۟ ٱلزَّكَوٰةَ وَأَطِيعُوا۟ ٱلرَّسُولَ لَعَلَّكُمْ تُرْحَمُونَ ۝

لَا تَحْسَبَنَّ ٱلَّذِينَ كَفَرُوا۟ مُعْجِزِينَ فِى ٱلْأَرْضِ وَمَأْوَىٰهُمُ ٱلنَّارُ وَلَبِئْسَ ٱلْمَصِيرُ ۝

يَٰٓأَيُّهَا ٱلَّذِينَ ءَامَنُوا۟ لِيَسْتَـْٔذِنكُمُ ٱلَّذِينَ مَلَكَتْ أَيْمَٰنُكُمْ وَٱلَّذِينَ لَمْ يَبْلُغُوا۟ ٱلْحُلُمَ مِنكُمْ ثَلَٰثَ مَرَّٰتٍ مِّن قَبْلِ صَلَوٰةِ ٱلْفَجْرِ وَحِينَ تَضَعُونَ ثِيَابَكُم مِّنَ ٱلظَّهِيرَةِ وَمِنۢ بَعْدِ صَلَوٰةِ ٱلْعِشَآءِ ثَلَٰثُ عَوْرَٰتٍ لَّكُمْ لَيْسَ عَلَيْكُمْ وَلَا عَلَيْهِمْ جُنَاحٌۢ بَعْدَهُنَّ طَوَّٰفُونَ عَلَيْكُم بَعْضُكُمْ عَلَىٰ بَعْضٍ كَذَٰلِكَ يُبَيِّنُ ٱللَّهُ لَكُمُ ٱلْءَايَٰتِ وَٱللَّهُ عَلِيمٌ حَكِيمٌ ۝

وَإِذَا بَلَغَ ٱلْأَطْفَٰلُ مِنكُمُ ٱلْحُلُمَ فَلْيَسْتَـْٔذِنُوا۟ كَمَا ٱسْتَـْٔذَنَ ٱلَّذِينَ مِن قَبْلِهِمْ كَذَٰلِكَ يُبَيِّنُ ٱللَّهُ لَكُمْ ءَايَٰتِهِۦ وَٱللَّهُ عَلِيمٌ حَكِيمٌ ۝

وَٱلْقَوَٰعِدُ مِنَ ٱلنِّسَآءِ ٱلَّٰتِى لَا يَرْجُونَ نِكَاحًا فَلَيْسَ عَلَيْهِنَّ جُنَاحٌ أَن يَضَعْنَ ثِيَابَهُنَّ غَيْرَ مُتَبَرِّجَٰتٍۭ بِزِينَةٍ وَأَن يَسْتَعْفِفْنَ خَيْرٌ لَّهُنَّ وَٱللَّهُ سَمِيعٌ عَلِيمٌ ۝

---

637. Slaves and maid-servants.
638. To attend to you or approach you.

61. The blind are not at fault, the lame are not at fault, the sick are not at fault, nor are you if you eat in your houses, the houses of your fathers, the houses of your mothers, the houses of your brothers, the houses of your sisters, the houses of your paternal uncles, the houses of your paternal aunts, the houses of your maternal uncles, the houses of your maternal aunts, those of which you are in possession of the keys or those of your friend. You are not at fault if you eat all together or separately, but if you enter any houses, greet each other with a blessed and good greeting from Allah. That is how Allah makes clear to you the Signs, that perchance you may understand.

62. The true believers, who believe in Allah and His Messenger , if they are with him for some common affair, will not depart till they take their leave. Indeed, those who ask leave from you are those who believe in Allah and His Messenger. If they ask leave from you for some affair of theirs, give leave to whom you wish and ask Allah's forgiveness for them. Allah is surely All-Forgiving, Merciful.

63. Do not make calling the Messenger out among you like your calling one another out. Allah knows those of you who slip away stealthily. So, let those who disobey His command beware of an ordeal that might befall them, or a very painful punishment that might befall them.

64. Surely, to Allah belongs what is in the heavens and on earth. He knows what you are about and the Day they will be returned to Him. Then He will tell them about what they did. Allah knows everything.

Sûrat Al-Furqân,
(The Criterion) 25

*In the Name of Allah,
the Compassionate, the Merciful*

1. Blessed is He Who sent down the Criterion[639] upon His servant,[640] so as to be a warner to all mankind.

2. To Whom belongs the dominion of the heavens and the earth and He has not taken to Himself a child, and has no associate in this dominion, and He created everything, preordaining it fully.

3. Yet they have taken, apart from Him, other gods who do not create anything, but are themselves created. They do not have the power to harm or profit themselves, nor the power over death, life or resurrection.

4. The unbelievers say: "This (the Qur'an) is nothing but deceit, which he (Muhammad) has invented and was assisted therein by other people."[641] They have simply come up with wrongdoing and falsehood.

5. And they say: "Legends of the ancients which he solicited their writing down. Hence they are dictated to him morning and evening."

6. Say: "He Who knows the secret in the heavens and the earth has sent it down; He is indeed All-Forgiving, Merciful."

7. And they say: "What is the matter with the Messenger? He eats food and strolls in the markets. If only an angel had been sent to him to be a warner with him;

---

639. Arabic *al-Furqân*, or Criterion, distinguishing right from wrong.
640. Muhammad.
641. That is, the Jews.

8. "Or a treasure had been cast upon him, or he was given a garden from which he could eat." And the wrongdoers say: "You only follow a man bewitched."

9. See how they invent the parables for you, and so they err, and then cannot find their way.

10. Blessed is He Who, if He wishes, will accord you better than that - Gardens underneath which rivers flow, and will build palaces for you.

11. No, they deny the Hour; yet We have prepared for those who deny the Hour a blazing Fire.

12. When it (Hell) sights them from a distance, they hear its raging and exhalation.

13. And if they are hurled in a narrow space therein, tied up in fetters, they would call out there for ruination.

14. Call not out today for one ruination, but call out for many ruinations.

15. Say: "Is that better or the Garden of Eternity which the God-fearing have been promised, as a reward and ultimate resort?"

16. They have therein what they desire, abiding forever, as a promise binding upon your Lord.

17. And the Day He shall muster them and what they worship, apart from Allah, then He says: "Was it you, then, who misled these My servants, or did they stray from the Path themselves?"

18. They will say: "Glory be to You; we should never have taken, apart from You, any protectors; but You accorded them and their fathers momentary enjoyment, until they forgot the Reminder and became a lost people."

أَوْ يُلْقَىٰ إِلَيْهِ كَنزٌ أَوْ تَكُونُ لَهُ جَنَّةٌ يَأْكُلُ مِنْهَا ۚ وَقَالَ ٱلظَّٰلِمُونَ إِن تَتَّبِعُونَ إِلَّا رَجُلًا مَّسْحُورًا ۝

ٱنظُرْ كَيْفَ ضَرَبُوا لَكَ ٱلْأَمْثَٰلَ فَضَلُّوا فَلَا يَسْتَطِيعُونَ سَبِيلًا ۝

تَبَارَكَ ٱلَّذِى إِن شَآءَ جَعَلَ لَكَ خَيْرًا مِّن ذَٰلِكَ جَنَّٰتٍ تَجْرِى مِن تَحْتِهَا ٱلْأَنْهَٰرُ وَيَجْعَل لَّكَ قُصُورًا ۝

بَلْ كَذَّبُوا بِٱلسَّاعَةِ ۖ وَأَعْتَدْنَا لِمَن كَذَّبَ بِٱلسَّاعَةِ سَعِيرًا ۝

إِذَا رَأَتْهُم مِّن مَّكَانٍ بَعِيدٍ سَمِعُوا لَهَا تَغَيُّظًا وَزَفِيرًا ۝

وَإِذَآ أُلْقُوا مِنْهَا مَكَانًا ضَيِّقًا مُّقَرَّنِينَ دَعَوْا هُنَالِكَ ثُبُورًا ۝

لَّا تَدْعُوا ٱلْيَوْمَ ثُبُورًا وَٰحِدًا وَٱدْعُوا ثُبُورًا كَثِيرًا ۝

قُلْ أَذَٰلِكَ خَيْرٌ أَمْ جَنَّةُ ٱلْخُلْدِ ٱلَّتِى وُعِدَ ٱلْمُتَّقُونَ ۚ كَانَتْ لَهُمْ جَزَآءً وَمَصِيرًا ۝

لَّهُمْ فِيهَا مَا يَشَآءُونَ خَٰلِدِينَ ۚ كَانَ عَلَىٰ رَبِّكَ وَعْدًا مَّسْـُٔولًا ۝

وَيَوْمَ يَحْشُرُهُمْ وَمَا يَعْبُدُونَ مِن دُونِ ٱللَّهِ فَيَقُولُ ءَأَنتُمْ أَضْلَلْتُمْ عِبَادِى هَٰٓؤُلَآءِ أَمْ هُمْ ضَلُّوا ٱلسَّبِيلَ ۝

قَالُوا سُبْحَٰنَكَ مَا كَانَ يَنۢبَغِى لَنَآ أَن نَّتَّخِذَ مِن دُونِكَ مِنْ أَوْلِيَآءَ وَلَٰكِن مَّتَّعْتَهُمْ وَءَابَآءَهُمْ حَتَّىٰ نَسُوا ٱلذِّكْرَ وَكَانُوا قَوْمًۢا بُورًا ۝

19. They have denounced you as liars, regarding what you say; and so you are not able to divert punishment or give support. He who does wrong among you, We shall make him taste a grievous punishment.

20. We never sent any Messengers before you but they ate food and strolled in the markets; and We made some of you tempters of each other. Will you stand fast? Your Lord is All-Seeing.

21. And those who do not hope for Our Encounter, say: "If only the angels were sent down to us, or we were made to see our Lord." They have grown arrogant within themselves and became most overbearing.

22. The Day they see the angels, there is no longer any cause for rejoicing for the criminals; and they[642] will say: "A firm prohibition [upon you]."

23. And We shall proceed to the work they did and turn it into scattered dust.

24. The companions of Paradise on that Day shall be better lodged and more fairly accommodated.

25. The Day heaven shall be parted by clouds and the angels are sent down in throngs.

26. The true dominion on that Day shall be the Compassionate's, and it shall be a strenuous Day for the unbelievers.

27. The Day the wrongdoer shall bite his hands and say: "Would that I had taken with the Messenger a common path.

28. "Woe betide me, would that I had not taken so-and-so as a friend.

---

642. The angels.

29. "He led me away from the Reminder after it had reached me. Satan has always been a betrayer of man."

لَّقَدْ أَضَلَّنِى عَنِ ٱلذِّكْرِ بَعْدَ إِذْ جَآءَنِى وَكَانَ ٱلشَّيْطَنُ لِلْإِنسَنِ خَذُولًا ﴿٢٩﴾

30. The Messenger says: "Lord, my people have taken this Qur'an as a thing to be shunned."

وَقَالَ ٱلرَّسُولُ يَرَبِّ إِنَّ قَوْمِى ٱتَّخَذُوا هَذَا ٱلْقُرْءَانَ مَهْجُورًا ﴿٣٠﴾

31. And that is how We appointed to every Prophet an enemy from the criminals. Your Lord suffices as a Guide and a Supporter.

وَكَذَلِكَ جَعَلْنَا لِكُلِّ نَبِىٍّ عَدُوًّا مِّنَ ٱلْمُجْرِمِينَ وَكَفَى بِرَبِّكَ هَادِيًا وَنَصِيرًا ﴿٣١﴾

32. The unbelievers say: "If only the Qur'an had been sent down on him all at once." That is how We wanted to strengthen your heart with it and We have revealed it in stages.

وَقَالَ ٱلَّذِينَ كَفَرُوا لَوْلَا نُزِّلَ عَلَيْهِ ٱلْقُرْءَانُ جُمْلَةً وَحِدَةً كَذَلِكَ لِنُثَبِّتَ بِهِ فُؤَادَكَ وَرَتَّلْنَهُ تَرْتِيلًا ﴿٣٢﴾

33. They never bring you any simile but We bring you the truth and a better exposition.

وَلَا يَأْتُونَكَ بِمَثَلٍ إِلَّا جِئْنَكَ بِٱلْحَقِّ وَأَحْسَنَ تَفْسِيرًا ﴿٣٣﴾

34. Those who are mustered on their faces in Hell; those are in a worse position and are more wayward.

ٱلَّذِينَ يُحْشَرُونَ عَلَى وُجُوهِهِمْ إِلَى جَهَنَّمَ أُوْلَئِكَ شَرٌّ مَّكَانًا وَأَضَلُّ سَبِيلًا ﴿٣٤﴾

35. We have indeed brought Moses the Book and appointed his brother Aaron with him as minister.

وَلَقَدْ ءَاتَيْنَا مُوسَى ٱلْكِتَبَ وَجَعَلْنَا مَعَهُ أَخَاهُ هَرُونَ وَزِيرًا ﴿٣٥﴾

36. Then We said: "Go forth to the people who denounced Our Signs as lies"; and so We destroyed them fully.

فَقُلْنَا ٱذْهَبَا إِلَى ٱلْقَوْمِ ٱلَّذِينَ كَذَّبُوا بِـَٔايَتِنَا فَدَمَّرْنَهُمْ تَدْمِيرًا ﴿٣٦﴾

37. And the people of Noah, when they denounced the Messengers, We drowned them and made them a sign unto mankind. We have prepared for the wrongdoers a very painful punishment.

وَقَوْمَ نُوحٍ لَّمَّا كَذَّبُوا ٱلرُّسُلَ أَغْرَقْنَهُمْ وَجَعَلْنَهُمْ لِلنَّاسِ ءَايَةً وَأَعْتَدْنَا لِلظَّلِمِينَ عَذَابًا أَلِيمًا ﴿٣٧﴾

38. And 'Ad, Thamud, the companions of al-Rass and many generations in between;

وَعَادًا وَثَمُودَا۟ وَأَصْحَبَ ٱلرَّسِّ وَقُرُونًا بَيْنَ ذَلِكَ كَثِيرًا ﴿٣٨﴾

39. To each, We proposed similes and each We ruined utterly.

وَكُلًّا ضَرَبْنَا لَهُ ٱلْأَمْثَلَ وَكُلًّا تَبَّرْنَا تَتْبِيرًا ﴿٣٩﴾

40. And they came upon the city (of Lot) which was drenched by an evil rain. Did they not see it? No, they did not hope to be raised from the dead.

وَلَقَدْ أَتَوْا عَلَى ٱلْقَرْيَةِ ٱلَّتِى أُمْطِرَتْ مَطَرَ ٱلسَّوْءِ أَفَلَمْ يَكُونُوا يَرَوْنَهَا بَلْ كَانُوا لَا يَرْجُونَ نُشُورًا ﴿٤٠﴾

41. And when they see you, they only take you for a laughing stock: "Is this the one Allah sent as a Messenger?

42. "He almost led us away from our gods, had we not stood fast by them." They will certainly know, when they see the punishment, who is more wayward.

43. Do you see him who has taken his fancy as his god? Will you, then, have to be his guardian?

44. Or do you suppose that most of them hear or understand? Indeed, they are merely like cattle; no, even more wayward.

45. Have you not considered your Lord, how He has stretched out the shadow? Had He willed, He would have made it still, then made the sun a signal thereof.

46. Then, We would have drawn it towards Us slowly.

47. It is He Who made the night a raiment for you, and sleep a period of rest, and made the day a rising up.

48. And it is He Who sent the wind as good news before His Mercy; and We have sent down from heaven pure water,

49. To bring to life thereby a dead town, and give it to drink to such numerous cattle and humans as We have created.

50. And We have alternated it among them, so that they may remember. However, most men have refused all but thanklessness.

51. Had We wished, We would have sent forth to every city a warner.

52. So, do not obey the unbelievers and strive against them with it[643] mightily.

---

643. The Qur'an.

362

53. And it is He Who mixed the two seas, this one sweet and pure and that one salty and bitter; and He set up between them a barrier and a firm prohibition.

54. And it is He Who created from water a human being; then He made him a kin by blood or marriage. Your Lord is All-Powerful.

55. They worship, apart from Allah, what neither profits nor harms them; and the unbeliever has always been a partisan[644] against his Lord.

56. We have only sent you forth as a bearer of good news and a warner.

57. Say: "I do not ask you for any wages for this, except for him who wishes to follow a path leading to his Lord."

58. Put your trust in the Living God Who does not die and sing His Praise. He suffices as the All-Informed Knower of the sins of His servants,

59. Who created the heavens and the earth and what lies between them in six days. Then the Compassionate sat upon the Throne. So ask about Him, the Well-Informed.

60. And if it is said to them: "Prostrate yourselves before the Compassionate"; they reply: "But who is the Compassionate? Shall we prostrate ourselves to what you order us?" This only increases their aversion.

61. Blessed is He Who placed in the heaven constellations and placed in it a lamp and an illuminating moon.

62. And it is He Who made the night and the day to succeed each other, for him who wants to remember or wants to give thanks.

---

644. Of Satan.

63. And the servants of the Compassionate who walk in the land gently and, if the ignorant address them, they say: "Peace."

وَعِبَادُ ٱلرَّحْمَٰنِ ٱلَّذِينَ يَمْشُونَ عَلَى ٱلْأَرْضِ هَوْنًا وَإِذَا خَاطَبَهُمُ ٱلْجَٰهِلُونَ قَالُوا۟ سَلَٰمًا ﴿٦٣﴾

64. And those who pass the night prostrating themselves to their Lord or standing up.

وَٱلَّذِينَ يَبِيتُونَ لِرَبِّهِمْ سُجَّدًا وَقِيَٰمًا ﴿٦٤﴾

65. And those who say: "Lord, divert from us the agony of Hell"; but its agony is unavoidable punishment.

وَٱلَّذِينَ يَقُولُونَ رَبَّنَا ٱصْرِفْ عَنَّا عَذَابَ جَهَنَّمَ إِنَّ عَذَابَهَا كَانَ غَرَامًا ﴿٦٥﴾

66. Wretched it is as a final resort and a resting-place!

إِنَّهَا سَآءَتْ مُسْتَقَرًّا وَمُقَامًا ﴿٦٦﴾

67. And those who, when they spend, do not squander or stint, but choose a middle course between that.

وَٱلَّذِينَ إِذَآ أَنفَقُوا۟ لَمْ يُسْرِفُوا۟ وَلَمْ يَقْتُرُوا۟ وَكَانَ بَيْنَ ذَٰلِكَ قَوَامًا ﴿٦٧﴾

68. And those who do not call upon any other god than Allah, and do not kill the soul which Allah forbade, except justly; and they do not commit adultery. He who does that shall meet with retribution.

وَٱلَّذِينَ لَا يَدْعُونَ مَعَ ٱللَّهِ إِلَٰهًا ءَاخَرَ وَلَا يَقْتُلُونَ ٱلنَّفْسَ ٱلَّتِى حَرَّمَ ٱللَّهُ إِلَّا بِٱلْحَقِّ وَلَا يَزْنُونَ وَمَن يَفْعَلْ ذَٰلِكَ يَلْقَ أَثَامًا ﴿٦٨﴾

69. Punishment shall be doubled for him on the Day of Resurrection and he will dwell forever in it down-trodden;

يُضَٰعَفْ لَهُ ٱلْعَذَابُ يَوْمَ ٱلْقِيَٰمَةِ وَيَخْلُدْ فِيهِ مُهَانًا ﴿٦٩﴾

70. Except for him who repents, believes and does the righteous deed. Those Allah will change their evil deeds into good deeds. Allah is ever All-Forgiving, Merciful.

إِلَّا مَن تَابَ وَءَامَنَ وَعَمِلَ عَمَلًا صَٰلِحًا فَأُو۟لَٰٓئِكَ يُبَدِّلُ ٱللَّهُ سَيِّـَٔاتِهِمْ حَسَنَٰتٍ وَكَانَ ٱللَّهُ غَفُورًا رَّحِيمًا ﴿٧٠﴾

71. He who repents and does the righteous deed returns to Allah unhampered.

وَمَن تَابَ وَعَمِلَ صَٰلِحًا فَإِنَّهُۥ يَتُوبُ إِلَى ٱللَّهِ مَتَابًا ﴿٧١﴾

72. Those who do not bear false witness; and when they pass by idle talk, pass by with dignity;

وَٱلَّذِينَ لَا يَشْهَدُونَ ٱلزُّورَ وَإِذَا مَرُّوا۟ بِٱللَّغْوِ مَرُّوا۟ كِرَامًا ﴿٧٢﴾

73. And those who, when reminded of the Signs of their Lord, do not fall down upon them deaf and blind;

وَٱلَّذِينَ إِذَا ذُكِّرُوا۟ بِـَٔايَٰتِ رَبِّهِمْ لَمْ يَخِرُّوا۟ عَلَيْهَا صُمًّا وَعُمْيَانًا ﴿٧٣﴾

74. And those who say: "Our Lord, grant us, through our wives and progeny, beloved offspring, and make us a model for the God-fearing."

وَٱلَّذِينَ يَقُولُونَ رَبَّنَا هَبْ لَنَا مِنْ أَزْوَٰجِنَا وَذُرِّيَّٰتِنَا قُرَّةَ أَعْيُنٍ وَٱجْعَلْنَا لِلْمُتَّقِينَ إِمَامًا ﴿٧٤﴾

75. Those shall be rewarded with a high chamber[645] for their steadfastness, and will be received therein with greeting and peace.

76. Dwelling therein forever. What a delightful resort and lodging!

77. Say: "My Lord will take no notice of your supplication. For you have disbelieved and that shall be your inevitable perdition."

أُوْلَٰٓئِكَ يُجْزَوْنَ ٱلْغُرْفَةَ بِمَا صَبَرُواْ وَيُلَقَّوْنَ فِيهَا تَحِيَّةً وَسَلَٰمًا ۝

خَٰلِدِينَ فِيهَا حَسُنَتْ مُسْتَقَرًّا وَمُقَامًا ۝

قُلْ مَا يَعْبَؤُاْ بِكُمْ رَبِّي لَوْلَا دُعَآؤُكُمْ فَقَدْ كَذَّبْتُمْ فَسَوْفَ يَكُونُ لِزَامًا ۝

**Sûrat Ash-Shu'ara',
(The Poets) 26**

*In the Name of Allah,
the Compassionate, the Merciful*

1. Tah - Sin - Mim.[646]

2. Those are the Signs of the Manifest Book.

3. Perhaps, you are exhausting yourself, because they will not believe.

4. If We will, We would send down on them from heaven a sign, so their necks will stay subjugated thereto.

5. No new reminder from the Compassionate ever comes to them but they will turn away from it.

6. They have indeed disbelieved; therefore, there will come to them the news of what they used to mock at.

7. Have they not considered the earth, how much We have caused to grow therein of every noble pair?

8. There is surely in that a sign; but most of them will not believe.

9. Your Lord, indeed, is the All-Mighty, the Merciful.

بِسْمِ ٱللَّهِ ٱلرَّحْمَٰنِ ٱلرَّحِيمِ

طسٓمٓ ۝

تِلْكَ ءَايَٰتُ ٱلْكِتَٰبِ ٱلْمُبِينِ ۝

لَعَلَّكَ بَٰخِعٌ نَّفْسَكَ أَلَّا يَكُونُواْ مُؤْمِنِينَ ۝

إِن نَّشَأْ نُنَزِّلْ عَلَيْهِم مِّنَ ٱلسَّمَآءِ ءَايَةً فَظَلَّتْ أَعْنَٰقُهُمْ لَهَا خَٰضِعِينَ ۝

وَمَا يَأْتِيهِم مِّن ذِكْرٍ مِّنَ ٱلرَّحْمَٰنِ مُحْدَثٍ إِلَّا كَانُواْ عَنْهُ مُعْرِضِينَ ۝

فَقَدْ كَذَّبُواْ فَسَيَأْتِيهِمْ أَنۢبَٰٓؤُاْ مَا كَانُواْ بِهِۦ يَسْتَهْزِءُونَ ۝

أَوَلَمْ يَرَوْاْ إِلَى ٱلْأَرْضِ كَمْ أَنۢبَتْنَا فِيهَا مِن كُلِّ زَوْجٍ كَرِيمٍ ۝

إِنَّ فِي ذَٰلِكَ لَأٓيَةً وَمَا كَانَ أَكْثَرُهُم مُّؤْمِنِينَ ۝

وَإِنَّ رَبَّكَ لَهُوَ ٱلْعَزِيزُ ٱلرَّحِيمُ ۝

---

645. In Paradise.
646. The same letters occur at the beginning of Surah 28; the significance of this is not clear.

10. When Your Lord called Moses: "Go forth to the wrongdoing people;

11. "The people of Pharaoh; will they not fear God?"

12. He said: "Lord, I fear that they will denounce me as a liar;

13. "And my chest would be constricted and my tongue will not be loosed. So, send for Aaron.

14. "And they accuse me of a guilt;[647] so I fear they might kill me."

15. He said: "Never; so go both of you with Our Signs; We are with you listening.

16. "So go both of you to Pharaoh and tell him; 'We are the Messengers of the Lord of the Worlds';

17. "So send with us the Children of Israel.' "

18. He (Pharaoh) said: "Did we not raise you[648] among us as a child, and you lingered among us for many years of your life?

19. "And you committed the crime you committed, being one of the thankless?"

20. He said: "Indeed, I did it then while I was one of the perverse.

21. "So I fled from you when I feared you. Then my Lord granted me wisdom and made me one of the Messengers.

22. "And this is a grace you reproach me with, having enslaved the Children of Israel."

23. Pharaoh said: "And what is the Lord of the Worlds?"

24. He (Moses) said: "The Lord of the heavens and the earth and what lies between them, if you have any kind of certainty."

وَإِذْ نَادَىٰ رَبُّكَ مُوسَىٰٓ أَنِ ٱئْتِ ٱلْقَوْمَ ٱلظَّٰلِمِينَ ۝

قَوْمَ فِرْعَوْنَ أَلَا يَتَّقُونَ ۝

قَالَ رَبِّ إِنِّىٓ أَخَافُ أَن يُكَذِّبُونِ ۝

وَيَضِيقُ صَدْرِى وَلَا يَنطَلِقُ لِسَانِى فَأَرْسِلْ إِلَىٰ هَٰرُونَ ۝

وَلَهُمْ عَلَىَّ ذَنۢبٌ فَأَخَافُ أَن يَقْتُلُونِ ۝

قَالَ كَلَّا فَٱذْهَبَا بِـَٔايَٰتِنَآ إِنَّا مَعَكُم مُّسْتَمِعُونَ ۝

فَأْتِيَا فِرْعَوْنَ فَقُولَآ إِنَّا رَسُولُ رَبِّ ٱلْعَٰلَمِينَ ۝

أَنْ أَرْسِلْ مَعَنَا بَنِىٓ إِسْرَٰٓءِيلَ ۝

قَالَ أَلَمْ نُرَبِّكَ فِينَا وَلِيدًا وَلَبِثْتَ فِينَا مِنْ عُمُرِكَ سِنِينَ ۝

وَفَعَلْتَ فَعْلَتَكَ ٱلَّتِى فَعَلْتَ وَأَنتَ مِنَ ٱلْكَٰفِرِينَ ۝

قَالَ فَعَلْتُهَآ إِذًا وَأَنَا۠ مِنَ ٱلضَّآلِّينَ ۝

فَفَرَرْتُ مِنكُمْ لَمَّا خِفْتُكُمْ فَوَهَبَ لِى رَبِّى حُكْمًا وَجَعَلَنِى مِنَ ٱلْمُرْسَلِينَ ۝

وَتِلْكَ نِعْمَةٌ تَمُنُّهَا عَلَىَّ أَنْ عَبَّدتَّ بَنِىٓ إِسْرَٰٓءِيلَ ۝

قَالَ فِرْعَوْنُ وَمَا رَبُّ ٱلْعَٰلَمِينَ ۝

قَالَ رَبُّ ٱلسَّمَٰوَٰتِ وَٱلْأَرْضِ وَمَا بَيْنَهُمَآ إِن كُنتُم مُّوقِنِينَ ۝

---

647. Slaying the Egyptian, whom Moses saw smite an Israelite.
648. Moses.

25. He[649] said to those around him: "Do you not hear?"

قَالَ لِمَنْ حَوْلَهُ أَلَا تَسْتَمِعُونَ ٢٥

26. He[650] said: "Your Lord and the Lord of your fathers."

قَالَ رَبُّكُمْ وَرَبُّ ءَابَآئِكُمُ ٱلْأَوَّلِينَ ٢٦

27. He[651] said: "Surely your Messenger who has been sent forth to you is truly mad."

قَالَ إِنَّ رَسُولَكُمُ ٱلَّذِي أُرْسِلَ إِلَيْكُمْ لَمَجْنُونٌ ٢٧

28. He[652] said: "The Lord of the East and the West and what is between them, if only you understand."

قَالَ رَبُّ ٱلْمَشْرِقِ وَٱلْمَغْرِبِ وَمَا بَيْنَهُمَآ إِن كُنتُمْ تَعْقِلُونَ ٢٨

29. He said: "If you take a god other than me,[653] I will certainly make you a prisoner."

قَالَ لَئِنِ ٱتَّخَذْتَ إِلَٰهًا غَيْرِي لَأَجْعَلَنَّكَ مِنَ ٱلْمَسْجُونِينَ ٢٩

30. He (Moses) said: "Even if I should bring you something manifest?"

قَالَ أَوَلَوْ جِئْتُكَ بِشَيْءٍ مُّبِينٍ ٣٠

31. He (Pharaoh) said: "Bring it, then, if you are truthful."

قَالَ فَأْتِ بِهِ إِن كُنتَ مِنَ ٱلصَّٰدِقِينَ ٣١

32. Then he cast his staff down, and behold, it was a manifest serpent.

فَأَلْقَىٰ عَصَاهُ فَإِذَا هِيَ ثُعْبَانٌ مُّبِينٌ ٣٢

33. And he held out his hand, and, behold, it appeared white to the onlookers.

وَنَزَعَ يَدَهُ فَإِذَا هِيَ بَيْضَآءُ لِلنَّٰظِرِينَ ٣٣

34. He[654] said to the dignitaries around him: "This man is, indeed, a cunning sorcerer.

قَالَ لِلْمَلَإِ حَوْلَهُ إِنَّ هَٰذَا لَسَٰحِرٌ عَلِيمٌ ٣٤

35. "He wants to drive you out of your land by his sorcery; so what do you command?"

يُرِيدُ أَن يُخْرِجَكُم مِّنْ أَرْضِكُم بِسِحْرِهِ فَمَاذَا تَأْمُرُونَ ٣٥

36. They said: "Leave him and his brother alone for a while and send out to the cities summoning agents,

قَالُوٓا أَرْجِهْ وَأَخَاهُ وَٱبْعَثْ فِي ٱلْمَدَآئِنِ حَٰشِرِينَ ٣٦

37. "To bring you every cunning sorcerer."

يَأْتُوكَ بِكُلِّ سَحَّارٍ عَلِيمٍ ٣٧

38. And so the sorcerers were gathered together for an appointment on a fixed day.

فَجُمِعَ ٱلسَّحَرَةُ لِمِيقَٰتِ يَوْمٍ مَّعْلُومٍ ٣٨

39. And it was said to the people: "Will you come together?

وَقِيلَ لِلنَّاسِ هَلْ أَنتُم مُّجْتَمِعُونَ ٣٩

---

649. Pharaoh.
650. Moses.
651. Pharaoh.
652. Moses.
653. Pharaoh.
654. Pharaoh.

40. "So that we might watch the sorcerers, if they should be the winners."

لَعَلَّنَا نَتَّبِعُ ٱلسَّحَرَةَ إِن كَانُوا۟ هُمُ ٱلْغَٰلِبِينَ ۝

41. So when the sorcerers came they said to Pharaoh: "Will we have a wage, if we are the winners?"

فَلَمَّا جَآءَ ٱلسَّحَرَةُ قَالُوا۟ لِفِرْعَوْنَ أَئِنَّ لَنَا لَأَجْرًا إِن كُنَّا نَحْنُ ٱلْغَٰلِبِينَ ۝

42. He said: "Yes, and you shall be, then, among those favoured."

قَالَ نَعَمْ وَإِنَّكُمْ إِذًا لَّمِنَ ٱلْمُقَرَّبِينَ ۝

43. Moses said to them: "Cast down what you wish to cast down."

قَالَ لَهُم مُّوسَىٰٓ أَلْقُوا۟ مَآ أَنتُم مُّلْقُونَ ۝

44. So, they cast their ropes and staffs and said: "By the might of Pharaoh, we shall be the winners."

فَأَلْقَوْا۟ حِبَالَهُمْ وَعِصِيَّهُمْ وَقَالُوا۟ بِعِزَّةِ فِرْعَوْنَ إِنَّا لَنَحْنُ ٱلْغَٰلِبُونَ ۝

45. Then, Moses cast down his staff, and, behold, it swallowed forthwith what they had simulated.

فَأَلْقَىٰ مُوسَىٰ عَصَاهُ فَإِذَا هِىَ تَلْقَفُ مَا يَأْفِكُونَ ۝

46. Then the sorcerers fell on their faces prostrate.

فَأُلْقِىَ ٱلسَّحَرَةُ سَٰجِدِينَ ۝

47. They said: "We believe now in the Lord of the Worlds;

قَالُوٓا۟ ءَامَنَّا بِرَبِّ ٱلْعَٰلَمِينَ ۝

48. "The Lord of Moses and Aaron."

رَبِّ مُوسَىٰ وَهَٰرُونَ ۝

49. He[655] said: "You have believed before I gave you leave. He[656] is indeed your chief, who taught you sorcery, and so you will learn. I shall cut off your hands and feet alternately and will crucify you all."

قَالَ ءَامَنتُمْ لَهُۥ قَبْلَ أَنْ ءَاذَنَ لَكُمْ إِنَّهُۥ لَكَبِيرُكُمُ ٱلَّذِى عَلَّمَكُمُ ٱلسِّحْرَ فَلَسَوْفَ تَعْلَمُونَ لَأُقَطِّعَنَّ أَيْدِيَكُمْ وَأَرْجُلَكُم مِّنْ خِلَٰفٍ وَلَأُصَلِّبَنَّكُمْ أَجْمَعِينَ ۝

50. They said: "No harm; we are returning unto our Lord.

قَالُوا۟ لَا ضَيْرَ إِنَّآ إِلَىٰ رَبِّنَا مُنقَلِبُونَ ۝

51. "We hope that our Lord will forgive our sins, as we are the first believers."

إِنَّا نَطْمَعُ أَن يَغْفِرَ لَنَا رَبُّنَا خَطَٰيَٰنَآ أَن كُنَّآ أَوَّلَ ٱلْمُؤْمِنِينَ ۝

52. And We revealed to Moses: "Go forth with My servants at night; for you are being followed."

۞ وَأَوْحَيْنَآ إِلَىٰ مُوسَىٰٓ أَنْ أَسْرِ بِعِبَادِىٓ إِنَّكُم مُّتَّبَعُونَ ۝

53. Then Pharaoh sent out summoning agents to all the cities:

فَأَرْسَلَ فِرْعَوْنُ فِى ٱلْمَدَآئِنِ حَٰشِرِينَ ۝

54. "These, indeed, are a small band;

إِنَّ هَٰٓؤُلَآءِ لَشِرْذِمَةٌ قَلِيلُونَ ۝

---

655. Pharaoh.
656. Moses.

55. "And they are enraging us;

وَإِنَّهُمْ لَنَا لَغَائِظُونَ ﴿٥٥﴾

56. "And we are all on our guard."

وَإِنَّا لَجَمِيعٌ حَذِرُونَ ﴿٥٦﴾

57. Then, We drove them out of gardens and springs;

فَأَخْرَجْنَاهُم مِّن جَنَّاتٍ وَعُيُونٍ ﴿٥٧﴾

58. And treasures and a noble abode.

وَكُنُوزٍ وَمَقَامٍ كَرِيمٍ ﴿٥٨﴾

59. That is how We bequeathed them to the Children of Israel.

كَذَلِكَ وَأَوْرَثْنَاهَا بَنِي إِسْرَائِيلَ ﴿٥٩﴾

60. So they followed them at sunrise.

فَأَتْبَعُوهُم مُّشْرِقِينَ ﴿٦٠﴾

61. Then when the two hosts sighted each other, the companions of Moses said: "We shall be overtaken."

فَلَمَّا تَرَاءَا الْجَمْعَانِ قَالَ أَصْحَابُ مُوسَى إِنَّا لَمُدْرَكُونَ ﴿٦١﴾

62. He said: "Never; my Lord is with me, He will guide me."

قَالَ كَلَّا إِنَّ مَعِيَ رَبِّي سَيَهْدِينِ ﴿٦٢﴾

63. So, We revealed to Moses: "Strike the sea with your staff;" whereupon it split, so that each part was like a huge mountain.

فَأَوْحَيْنَا إِلَى مُوسَى أَنِ اضْرِب بِّعَصَاكَ الْبَحْرَ فَانفَلَقَ فَكَانَ كُلُّ فِرْقٍ كَالطَّوْدِ الْعَظِيمِ ﴿٦٣﴾

64. And there We brought the others closer.

وَأَزْلَفْنَا ثَمَّ الْآخَرِينَ ﴿٦٤﴾

65. And We delivered Moses and those with him, all together.

وَأَنجَيْنَا مُوسَى وَمَن مَّعَهُ أَجْمَعِينَ ﴿٦٥﴾

66. Then, We drowned the others.

ثُمَّ أَغْرَقْنَا الْآخَرِينَ ﴿٦٦﴾

67. Surely, in that is a sign; yet most of them were not believers.

إِنَّ فِي ذَلِكَ لَآيَةً وَمَا كَانَ أَكْثَرُهُم مُّؤْمِنِينَ ﴿٦٧﴾

68. Your Lord is surely the All-Mighty, the Merciful.

وَإِنَّ رَبَّكَ لَهُوَ الْعَزِيزُ الرَّحِيمُ ﴿٦٨﴾

69. And relate to them the tale of Abraham;

وَاتْلُ عَلَيْهِمْ نَبَأَ إِبْرَاهِيمَ ﴿٦٩﴾

70. When he said to his father and his people: "What do you worship?"

إِذْ قَالَ لِأَبِيهِ وَقَوْمِهِ مَا تَعْبُدُونَ ﴿٧٠﴾

71. They said: "We worship idols, to which we continue to be devoted."

قَالُوا نَعْبُدُ أَصْنَامًا فَنَظَلُّ لَهَا عَاكِفِينَ ﴿٧١﴾

72. He said: "Do they hear when you call upon them?

قَالَ هَلْ يَسْمَعُونَكُمْ إِذْ تَدْعُونَ ﴿٧٢﴾

73. "Or profit or harm you?"

أَوْ يَنفَعُونَكُمْ أَوْ يَضُرُّونَ ﴿٧٣﴾

74. They said: "No, but we found our fathers doing that."

قَالُوا بَلْ وَجَدْنَا آبَاءَنَا كَذَلِكَ يَفْعَلُونَ ﴿٧٤﴾

75. He said: "Have you considered what you have been worshipping,

قَالَ أَفَرَأَيْتُم مَّا كُنتُمْ تَعْبُدُونَ ﴿٧٥﴾

76. "You and your forefathers?

أَنتُمْ وَآبَاؤُكُمُ الْأَقْدَمُونَ ﴿٧٦﴾

77. "They are surely an enemy of mine, except for the Lord of the Worlds;

فَإِنَّهُمْ عَدُوٌّ لِّي إِلَّا رَبَّ ٱلْعَٰلَمِينَ ۝

78. "Who created me, and He guides me;

ٱلَّذِى خَلَقَنِى فَهُوَ يَهْدِينِ ۝

79. "And He is the One Who feeds me and gives me to drink;

وَٱلَّذِى هُوَ يُطْعِمُنِى وَيَسْقِينِ ۝

80. "And if I am sick, it is He Who heals me;

وَإِذَا مَرِضْتُ فَهُوَ يَشْفِينِ ۝

81. "And He is the One Who causes me to die, then brings me back to life.

وَٱلَّذِى يُمِيتُنِى ثُمَّ يُحْيِينِ ۝

82. "And He is the One Whom I hope will forgive me my sins on the Day of Judgement.

وَٱلَّذِىٓ أَطْمَعُ أَن يَغْفِرَ لِى خَطِيٓـَٔتِى يَوْمَ ٱلدِّينِ ۝

83. "Lord, grant me sound judgement and make me join the righteous;

رَبِّ هَبْ لِى حُكْمًا وَأَلْحِقْنِى بِٱلصَّٰلِحِينَ ۝

84. "And give me a truthful tongue among the others;

وَٱجْعَل لِّى لِسَانَ صِدْقٍ فِى ٱلْءَاخِرِينَ ۝

85. "And make me one of the heirs of the Garden of Bliss.

وَٱجْعَلْنِى مِن وَرَثَةِ جَنَّةِ ٱلنَّعِيمِ ۝

86. "And forgive my father; for he was one of the wayward.

وَٱغْفِرْ لِأَبِىٓ إِنَّهُۥ كَانَ مِنَ ٱلضَّآلِّينَ ۝

87. "And do not disgrace me on the day they will be raised from the dead,

وَلَا تُخْزِنِى يَوْمَ يُبْعَثُونَ ۝

88. "The day when neither wealth nor children will avail one;

يَوْمَ لَا يَنفَعُ مَالٌ وَلَا بَنُونَ ۝

89. "Except for him who comes to Allah with a pure heart.

إِلَّا مَنْ أَتَى ٱللَّهَ بِقَلْبٍ سَلِيمٍ ۝

90. "And Paradise shall be brought closer to the God-fearing.

وَأُزْلِفَتِ ٱلْجَنَّةُ لِلْمُتَّقِينَ ۝

91. "And Hell shall be exhibited to the perverse."

وَبُرِّزَتِ ٱلْجَحِيمُ لِلْغَاوِينَ ۝

92. And it will be said to them: "Where are those you used to worship;

وَقِيلَ لَهُمْ أَيْنَ مَا كُنتُمْ تَعْبُدُونَ ۝

93. "Apart from Allah? Will they support you or support themselves?"

مِن دُونِ ٱللَّهِ هَلْ يَنصُرُونَكُمْ أَوْ يَنتَصِرُونَ ۝

94. Then they will be cast down, together with the perverse ones;

فَكُبْكِبُوا۟ فِيهَا هُمْ وَٱلْغَاوُۥنَ ۝

95. And the hosts of Iblis, all together.

وَجُنُودُ إِبْلِيسَ أَجْمَعُونَ ۝

96. They will say, while they disputed there with each other:

قَالُوا۟ وَهُمْ فِيهَا يَخْتَصِمُونَ ۝

97. "By Allah, we were indeed in manifest error,

تَٱللَّهِ إِن كُنَّا لَفِى ضَلَٰلٍ مُّبِينٍ ۝

98. "When we made you (false gods) equal to the Lord of the Worlds.

إِذْ نُسَوِّيكُم بِرَبِّ ٱلْعَٰلَمِينَ ۝

99. "We were only misled by the criminals;

وَمَآ أَضَلَّنَآ إِلَّا ٱلْمُجْرِمُونَ ۝

100. "So, we have no intercessors;

فَمَا لَنَا مِن شَٰفِعِينَ ۝

101. "Nor, an intimate friend.

وَلَا صَدِيقٍ حَمِيمٍ ۝

102. "If only we could have another chance; then we will be among the believers."

فَلَوْ أَنَّ لَنَا كَرَّةً فَنَكُونَ مِنَ ٱلْمُؤْمِنِينَ ۝

103. Surely in that is a sign; but most of them are not believers.

إِنَّ فِى ذَٰلِكَ لَءَايَةً وَمَا كَانَ أَكْثَرُهُم مُّؤْمِنِينَ ۝

104. Your Lord is surely the All-Mighty, the Merciful.

وَإِنَّ رَبَّكَ لَهُوَ ٱلْعَزِيزُ ٱلرَّحِيمُ ۝

105. The people of Noah have denounced the Messengers as liars;

كَذَّبَتْ قَوْمُ نُوحٍ ٱلْمُرْسَلِينَ ۝

106. When their brother Noah said to them: "Do you not fear God?

إِذْ قَالَ لَهُمْ أَخُوهُمْ نُوحٌ أَلَا تَتَّقُونَ ۝

107. "I am to you a faithful Messenger.

إِنِّى لَكُمْ رَسُولٌ أَمِينٌ ۝

108. "So, fear Allah and obey me.

فَٱتَّقُوا۟ ٱللَّهَ وَأَطِيعُونِ ۝

109. "I ask you no wage for this; my wage is with the Lord of the Worlds.

وَمَآ أَسْـَٔلُكُمْ عَلَيْهِ مِنْ أَجْرٍ إِنْ أَجْرِىَ إِلَّا عَلَىٰ رَبِّ ٱلْعَٰلَمِينَ ۝

110. "So, fear Allah and obey me."

فَٱتَّقُوا۟ ٱللَّهَ وَأَطِيعُونِ ۝

111. They said: "Shall we believe in you, when the lowliest crowd has followed you?"

قَالُوٓا۟ أَنُؤْمِنُ لَكَ وَٱتَّبَعَكَ ٱلْأَرْذَلُونَ ۝

112. He said: "How could I know what they used to do?

قَالَ وَمَا عِلْمِى بِمَا كَانُوا۟ يَعْمَلُونَ ۝

113. "They will only be called to account by my Lord; if only you had any sense.

إِنْ حِسَابُهُمْ إِلَّا عَلَىٰ رَبِّى لَوْ تَشْعُرُونَ ۝

114. "And it is not for me to drive away the believers.

وَمَآ أَنَا۠ بِطَارِدِ ٱلْمُؤْمِنِينَ ۝

115. "I am only a manifest warner."

إِنْ أَنَا۠ إِلَّا نَذِيرٌ مُّبِينٌ ۝

116. They said: "If you will not desist, O Noah, you will surely be stoned."

قَالُوا۟ لَئِن لَّمْ تَنتَهِ يَٰنُوحُ لَتَكُونَنَّ مِنَ ٱلْمَرْجُومِينَ ۝

117. He said: "Lord, my people have called me a liar.

قَالَ رَبِّ إِنَّ قَوْمِى كَذَّبُونِ ۝

118. "So, judge between me and them decisively and deliver me and the believers who have joined me."

فَٱفْتَحْ بَيْنِي وَبَيْنَهُمْ فَتْحًا وَنَجِّنِي وَمَن مَّعِيَ مِنَ ٱلْمُؤْمِنِينَ ﴿١١٨﴾

119. And so, We delivered him and those who joined him in the laden Ark.

فَأَنجَيْنَٰهُ وَمَن مَّعَهُ فِي ٱلْفُلْكِ ٱلْمَشْحُونِ ﴿١١٩﴾

120. Then We drowned all the rest.

ثُمَّ أَغْرَقْنَا بَعْدُ ٱلْبَاقِينَ ﴿١٢٠﴾

121. There is in that a sign, but most of them would not believe.

إِنَّ فِي ذَٰلِكَ لَآيَةً وَمَا كَانَ أَكْثَرُهُم مُّؤْمِنِينَ ﴿١٢١﴾

122. And your Lord is the All-Mighty, the Merciful.

وَإِنَّ رَبَّكَ لَهُوَ ٱلْعَزِيزُ ٱلرَّحِيمُ ﴿١٢٢﴾

123. 'Ad called the Messengers liars,

كَذَّبَتْ عَادٌ ٱلْمُرْسَلِينَ ﴿١٢٣﴾

124. When their brother Hud said to them: "Do you not fear God?

إِذْ قَالَ لَهُمْ أَخُوهُمْ هُودٌ أَلَا تَتَّقُونَ ﴿١٢٤﴾

125. "I am truly a faithful Messenger to you.

إِنِّي لَكُمْ رَسُولٌ أَمِينٌ ﴿١٢٥﴾

126. "So, fear Allah and obey me.

فَٱتَّقُوا ٱللَّهَ وَأَطِيعُونِ ﴿١٢٦﴾

127. "I do not ask you for it (my Message) any wage; my wage is with the Lord of the Worlds.

وَمَا أَسْـَٔلُكُمْ عَلَيْهِ مِنْ أَجْرٍ إِنْ أَجْرِيَ إِلَّا عَلَىٰ رَبِّ ٱلْعَٰلَمِينَ ﴿١٢٧﴾

128. "Do you build upon every elevation an edifice for amusement?

أَتَبْنُونَ بِكُلِّ رِيعٍ ءَايَةً تَعْبَثُونَ ﴿١٢٨﴾

129. "And acquire castles, that perchance you may live forever?

وَتَتَّخِذُونَ مَصَانِعَ لَعَلَّكُمْ تَخْلُدُونَ ﴿١٢٩﴾

130. "And when you attack, you attack like giants?

وَإِذَا بَطَشْتُم بَطَشْتُمْ جَبَّارِينَ ﴿١٣٠﴾

131. "So fear Allah and obey me;

فَٱتَّقُوا ٱللَّهَ وَأَطِيعُونِ ﴿١٣١﴾

132. "And fear Him, Who imparted to you whatever knowledge you have.

وَٱتَّقُوا ٱلَّذِيٓ أَمَدَّكُم بِمَا تَعْلَمُونَ ﴿١٣٢﴾

133. "He granted you cattle and children;

أَمَدَّكُم بِأَنْعَٰمٍ وَبَنِينَ ﴿١٣٣﴾

134. "And gardens and springs.

وَجَنَّٰتٍ وَعُيُونٍ ﴿١٣٤﴾

135. "I certainly fear for you the punishment of a Great Day."

إِنِّيٓ أَخَافُ عَلَيْكُمْ عَذَابَ يَوْمٍ عَظِيمٍ ﴿١٣٥﴾

136. They said: "It is the same to us whether you exhort or are not one of those who exhort.

قَالُوا سَوَآءٌ عَلَيْنَآ أَوَعَظْتَ أَمْ لَمْ تَكُن مِّنَ ٱلْوَٰعِظِينَ ﴿١٣٦﴾

137. "This is only the manner of the ancients.

إِنْ هَٰذَآ إِلَّا خُلُقُ ٱلْأَوَّلِينَ ﴿١٣٧﴾

138. "And we shall not be punished."

وَمَا نَحْنُ بِمُعَذَّبِينَ ﴿١٣٨﴾

139. They denounced him as a liar, and so We destroyed them. There is in that a sign, but most of them would not believe.

فَكَذَّبُوهُ فَأَهْلَكْنَٰهُمْ إِنَّ فِي ذَٰلِكَ لَآيَةً وَمَا كَانَ أَكْثَرُهُم مُّؤْمِنِينَ ﴿١٣٩﴾

140. Your Lord is surely the All-Mighty, the Merciful.

وَإِنَّ رَبَّكَ لَهُوَ ٱلْعَزِيزُ ٱلرَّحِيمُ ﴿١٤٠﴾

141. Thamud denounced the Messengers as liars.

كَذَّبَتْ ثَمُودُ ٱلْمُرْسَلِينَ ﴿١٤١﴾

142. When their brother Salih said to them: "Do you not fear God?

إِذْ قَالَ لَهُمْ أَخُوهُمْ صَٰلِحٌ أَلَا تَتَّقُونَ ﴿١٤٢﴾

143. "I am a faithful Messenger to you.

إِنِّي لَكُمْ رَسُولٌ أَمِينٌ ﴿١٤٣﴾

144. "So fear Allah and obey me.

فَٱتَّقُوا ٱللَّهَ وَأَطِيعُونِ ﴿١٤٤﴾

145. "I do not ask you any wage for this; my wage is with the Lord of the Worlds.

وَمَا أَسْـَٔلُكُمْ عَلَيْهِ مِنْ أَجْرٍ إِنْ أَجْرِيَ إِلَّا عَلَىٰ رَبِّ ٱلْعَٰلَمِينَ ﴿١٤٥﴾

146. "Will you be left herebelow in peace?

أَتُتْرَكُونَ فِي مَا هَٰهُنَآ ءَامِنِينَ ﴿١٤٦﴾

147. "In gardens and springs;

فِي جَنَّٰتٍ وَعُيُونٍ ﴿١٤٧﴾

148. "And plantations and palm trees, whose shoots are tender?

وَزُرُوعٍ وَنَخْلٍ طَلْعُهَا هَضِيمٌ ﴿١٤٨﴾

149. "And will you hew skilfully houses in the mountains?

وَتَنْحِتُونَ مِنَ ٱلْجِبَالِ بُيُوتًا فَٰرِهِينَ ﴿١٤٩﴾

150. "So fear Allah and obey me.

فَٱتَّقُوا ٱللَّهَ وَأَطِيعُونِ ﴿١٥٠﴾

151. "And do not obey the orders of the extravagant;

وَلَا تُطِيعُوٓا أَمْرَ ٱلْمُسْرِفِينَ ﴿١٥١﴾

152. "Who work corruption in the land and do not make amends."

ٱلَّذِينَ يُفْسِدُونَ فِي ٱلْأَرْضِ وَلَا يُصْلِحُونَ ﴿١٥٢﴾

153. They said: "You are certainly a man bewitched.

قَالُوٓا إِنَّمَآ أَنتَ مِنَ ٱلْمُسَحَّرِينَ ﴿١٥٣﴾

154. "You are only a mortal like us. Produce, then, a sign, if you are truthful."

مَآ أَنتَ إِلَّا بَشَرٌ مِّثْلُنَا فَأْتِ بِـَٔايَةٍ إِن كُنتَ مِنَ ٱلصَّٰدِقِينَ ﴿١٥٤﴾

155. He said: "This is a she-camel; this has a drinking day, and you have a fixed drinking day.

قَالَ هَٰذِهِ نَاقَةٌ لَّهَا شِرْبٌ وَلَكُمْ شِرْبُ يَوْمٍ مَّعْلُومٍ ﴿١٥٥﴾

156. "Do not cause her any harm, or else the punishment of a Great Day will smite you."

وَلَا تَمَسُّوهَا بِسُوٓءٍ فَيَأْخُذَكُمْ عَذَابُ يَوْمٍ عَظِيمٍ ﴿١٥٦﴾

157. However, they hamstrung her, and became full of remorse.

فَعَقَرُوهَا فَأَصْبَحُوا نَدِمِينَ ﴿١٥٧﴾

158. Then, punishment smote them. There is surely in that a sign; and most of them were not believers.

فَأَخَذَهُمُ ٱلْعَذَابُ إِنَّ فِى ذَٰلِكَ لَآيَةً وَمَا كَانَ أَكْثَرُهُم مُّؤْمِنِينَ ﴿١٥٨﴾

159. Your Lord is truly the All-Mighty, the Merciful.

وَإِنَّ رَبَّكَ لَهُوَ ٱلْعَزِيزُ ٱلرَّحِيمُ ﴿١٥٩﴾

160. The people of Lot denounced the Messengers as liars.

كَذَّبَتْ قَوْمُ لُوطٍ ٱلْمُرْسَلِينَ ﴿١٦٠﴾

161. When their brother Lot said to them: "Do you not fear God?

إِذْ قَالَ لَهُمْ أَخُوهُمْ لُوطٌ أَلَا تَتَّقُونَ ﴿١٦١﴾

162. "I am a faithful Messenger to you;

إِنِّى لَكُمْ رَسُولٌ أَمِينٌ ﴿١٦٢﴾

163. "So, fear Allah and obey me.

فَٱتَّقُوا ٱللَّهَ وَأَطِيعُونِ ﴿١٦٣﴾

164. "I do not ask you any wage for this; my wage is with the Lord of the Worlds.

وَمَا أَسْأَلُكُمْ عَلَيْهِ مِنْ أَجْرٍ إِنْ أَجْرِىَ إِلَّا عَلَىٰ رَبِّ ٱلْعَٰلَمِينَ ﴿١٦٤﴾

165. "Do you approach the males from all mankind;

أَتَأْتُونَ ٱلذُّكْرَانَ مِنَ ٱلْعَٰلَمِينَ ﴿١٦٥﴾

166. "And leave the wives that your Lord created for you? No, you are a transgressing people."

وَتَذَرُونَ مَا خَلَقَ لَكُمْ رَبُّكُم مِّنْ أَزْوَٰجِكُم بَلْ أَنتُمْ قَوْمٌ عَادُونَ ﴿١٦٦﴾

167. They said: "If you will not desist, O Lot, you will certainly be one of those expelled."

قَالُوا لَئِن لَّمْ تَنتَهِ يَٰلُوطُ لَتَكُونَنَّ مِنَ ٱلْمُخْرَجِينَ ﴿١٦٧﴾

168. He said: "I am a detester of your deed.

قَالَ إِنِّى لِعَمَلِكُم مِّنَ ٱلْقَالِينَ ﴿١٦٨﴾

169. "Lord, save me and my family from what they do."

رَبِّ نَجِّنِى وَأَهْلِى مِمَّا يَعْمَلُونَ ﴿١٦٩﴾

170. So, We delivered him and his family, all together.

فَنَجَّيْنَٰهُ وَأَهْلَهُ أَجْمَعِينَ ﴿١٧٠﴾

171. Except for an old woman who was one of those who lingered behind.

إِلَّا عَجُوزًا فِى ٱلْغَٰبِرِينَ ﴿١٧١﴾

172. Then, We destroyed the others.

ثُمَّ دَمَّرْنَا ٱلْآخَرِينَ ﴿١٧٢﴾

173. And We loosed on them a rain. Wretched is the rain of those forewarned!

وَأَمْطَرْنَا عَلَيْهِم مَّطَرًا فَسَآءَ مَطَرُ ٱلْمُنذَرِينَ ﴿١٧٣﴾

174. There is in that a sign, but most of them were not believers.

إِنَّ فِى ذَٰلِكَ لَآيَةً وَمَا كَانَ أَكْثَرُهُم مُّؤْمِنِينَ ﴿١٧٤﴾

175. Truly, your Lord is the All-Mighty, the Merciful.

وَإِنَّ رَبَّكَ لَهُوَ ٱلْعَزِيزُ ٱلرَّحِيمُ ﴿١٧٥﴾

176. The companions of the Thicket denounced the Messengers as liars.

كَذَّبَ أَصْحَبُ لَيْكَةِ الْمُرْسَلِينَ ۝

177. When Shu'aib said to them: "Do you not fear God?

إِذْ قَالَ لَهُمْ شُعَيْبٌ أَلَا تَتَّقُونَ ۝

178. "I am a faithful Messenger to you.

إِنِّى لَكُمْ رَسُولٌ أَمِينٌ ۝

179. "So fear Allah and obey me.

فَاتَّقُوا اللَّهَ وَأَطِيعُونِ ۝

180. "I do not ask you for any wage. My wage is with the Lord of the Worlds.

وَمَا أَسْتَلُكُمْ عَلَيْهِ مِنْ أَجْرٍ إِنْ أَجْرِىَ إِلَّا عَلَى رَبِّ الْعَلَمِينَ ۝

181. "Fill up the measure and do not be swindlers.

۞ أَوْفُوا الْكَيْلَ وَلَا تَكُونُوا مِنَ الْمُخْسِرِينَ ۝

182. "And weigh with the just scales,

وَزِنُوا بِالْقِسْطَاسِ الْمُسْتَقِيمِ ۝

183. "Do not stint people their things and do not work corruption in the land.

وَلَا تَبْخَسُوا النَّاسَ أَشْيَاءَهُمْ وَلَا تَعْثَوْا فِى الْأَرْضِ مُفْسِدِينَ ۝

184. "Fear Him Who created you and the generations of old."

وَاتَّقُوا الَّذِى خَلَقَكُمْ وَالْجِبِلَّةَ الْأَوَّلِينَ ۝

185. They said: "Surely, you are one of those bewitched.

قَالُوا إِنَّمَا أَنْتَ مِنَ الْمُسَحَّرِينَ ۝

186. "And you are only a mortal like us, and we think you are simply a liar.

وَمَا أَنْتَ إِلَّا بَشَرٌ مِثْلُنَا وَإِن نَّظُنُّكَ لَمِنَ الْكَذِبِينَ ۝

187. "Do, then, bring down upon us chips from heaven, if you are truthful."

فَأَسْقِطْ عَلَيْنَا كِسَفًا مِنَ السَّمَاءِ إِن كُنتَ مِنَ الصَّدِقِينَ ۝

188. He said: "My Lord knows best what you do."

قَالَ رَبِّى أَعْلَمُ بِمَا تَعْمَلُونَ ۝

189. They denounced him as a liar, and so the punishment of the Day of the Parasol seized them. It was, indeed, the punishment of a Great Day.

فَكَذَّبُوهُ فَأَخَذَهُمْ عَذَابُ يَوْمِ الظُّلَّةِ إِنَّهُ كَانَ عَذَابَ يَوْمٍ عَظِيمٍ ۝

190. In that, there is a sign, but most of them were not believers.

إِنَّ فِى ذَلِكَ لَآيَةً وَمَا كَانَ أَكْثَرُهُم مُؤْمِنِينَ ۝

191. And your Lord is truly the All-Mighty, the Merciful.

وَإِنَّ رَبَّكَ لَهُوَ الْعَزِيزُ الرَّحِيمُ ۝

192. And this (the Qur'an) is the revelation of the Lord of the Worlds;

وَإِنَّهُ لَتَنزِيلُ رَبِّ الْعَلَمِينَ ۝

193. Brought down by the Faithful Spirit,[657]

نَزَلَ بِهِ ٱلرُّوحُ ٱلْأَمِينُ ﴿١٩٣﴾

194. Upon your heart, so that you might be one of the warners;

عَلَىٰ قَلْبِكَ لِتَكُونَ مِنَ ٱلْمُنذِرِينَ ﴿١٩٤﴾

195. In manifest Arabic tongue.

بِلِسَانٍ عَرَبِيٍّ مُّبِينٍ ﴿١٩٥﴾

196. And it is, indeed, in the Scriptures of the ancients.

وَإِنَّهُ لَفِى زُبُرِ ٱلْأَوَّلِينَ ﴿١٩٦﴾

197. Is it not a sign for them that the scholars of the Children of Israel recognized it?

أَوَلَمْ يَكُن لَّهُمْ ءَايَةً أَن يَعْلَمَهُ عُلَمَٰٓؤُاْ بَنِىٓ إِسْرَٰٓءِيلَ ﴿١٩٧﴾

198. Had We sent it down on some foreigner;

وَلَوْ نَزَّلْنَٰهُ عَلَىٰ بَعْضِ ٱلْأَعْجَمِينَ ﴿١٩٨﴾

199. And he had read it to them; they would still not have believed in it.

فَقَرَأَهُۥ عَلَيْهِم مَّا كَانُواْ بِهِۦ مُؤْمِنِينَ ﴿١٩٩﴾

200. Thus We have insinuated it into the hearts of the criminals.

كَذَٰلِكَ سَلَكْنَٰهُ فِى قُلُوبِ ٱلْمُجْرِمِينَ ﴿٢٠٠﴾

201. They will not believe in it until they witness the very painful punishment.

لَا يُؤْمِنُونَ بِهِۦ حَتَّىٰ يَرَوُاْ ٱلْعَذَابَ ٱلْأَلِيمَ ﴿٢٠١﴾

202. It will come upon them suddenly, while they are unaware.

فَيَأْتِيَهُم بَغْتَةً وَهُمْ لَا يَشْعُرُونَ ﴿٢٠٢﴾

203. Then, they will say: "Are we given any respite?"

فَيَقُولُواْ هَلْ نَحْنُ مُنظَرُونَ ﴿٢٠٣﴾

204. Do they, then, seek to hasten Our Punishment?

أَفَبِعَذَابِنَا يَسْتَعْجِلُونَ ﴿٢٠٤﴾

205. Do you see, if we were to allow them some enjoyment for some years?

أَفَرَءَيْتَ إِن مَّتَّعْنَٰهُمْ سِنِينَ ﴿٢٠٥﴾

206. Then, they are visited by what they were promised.

ثُمَّ جَآءَهُم مَّا كَانُواْ يُوعَدُونَ ﴿٢٠٦﴾

207. What would that whereof they derived enjoyment avail them?

مَآ أَغْنَىٰ عَنْهُم مَّا كَانُواْ يُمَتَّعُونَ ﴿٢٠٧﴾

208. We have never destroyed a city, but it had prior warners,

وَمَآ أَهْلَكْنَا مِن قَرْيَةٍ إِلَّا لَهَا مُنذِرُونَ ﴿٢٠٨﴾

209. As a reminder; and We have never been unjust.

ذِكْرَىٰ وَمَا كُنَّا ظَٰلِمِينَ ﴿٢٠٩﴾

---

657. Gabriel.

210. And this (the Qur'an) was not brought down by demons.

وَمَا نَزَّلَتْ بِهِ الشَّيَطِينُ ۝

211. They should not and could not.

وَمَا يَنۢبَغِى لَهُمْ وَمَا يَسْتَطِيعُونَ ۝

212. For they are barred from hearing.

إِنَّهُمْ عَنِ السَّمْعِ لَمَعْزُولُونَ ۝

213. So do not call, with Allah, upon another god. For then you will be one of those chastized.

فَلَا تَدْعُ مَعَ اللَّهِ إِلَهًا ءَاخَرَ فَتَكُونَ مِنَ الْمُعَذَّبِينَ ۝

214. And warn your closest clan members.

وَأَنذِرْ عَشِيرَتَكَ الْأَقْرَبِينَ ۝

215. And lower your wing humbly to those of the believers who follow you.

وَاخْفِضْ جَنَاحَكَ لِمَنِ اتَّبَعَكَ مِنَ الْمُؤْمِنِينَ ۝

216. Should they disobey you, then say: "I am quit of what you are doing."

فَإِنْ عَصَوْكَ فَقُلْ إِنِّى بَرِىٓءٌ مِّمَّا تَعْمَلُونَ ۝

217. And put your trust in the All-Mighty, the Merciful;

وَتَوَكَّلْ عَلَى الْعَزِيزِ الرَّحِيمِ ۝

218. Who sees you when you stand up;

الَّذِى يَرَىٰكَ حِينَ تَقُومُ ۝

219. And when you go around those who prostrate themselves.

وَتَقَلُّبَكَ فِى السَّاجِدِينَ ۝

220. He is indeed the All-Seeing, the All-Knowing.

إِنَّهُ هُوَ السَّمِيعُ الْعَلِيمُ ۝

221. Shall I tell you upon whom do the demons descend?

هَلْ أُنَبِّئُكُمْ عَلَىٰ مَن تَنَزَّلُ الشَّيَطِينُ ۝

222. They descend upon every vicious impostor.

تَنَزَّلُ عَلَىٰ كُلِّ أَفَّاكٍ أَثِيمٍ ۝

223. They listen, but most of them are liars.

يُلْقُونَ السَّمْعَ وَأَكْثَرُهُمْ كَٰذِبُونَ ۝

224. And as to the poets, the perverse follow them.

وَالشُّعَرَآءُ يَتَّبِعُهُمُ الْغَاوُۥنَ ۝

225. Do you not see that they wander aimlessly in every glen?

أَلَمْ تَرَ أَنَّهُمْ فِى كُلِّ وَادٍ يَهِيمُونَ ۝

226. And that they say what they do not do?

وَأَنَّهُمْ يَقُولُونَ مَا لَا يَفْعَلُونَ ۝

227. Except for those who believe and do the righteous deeds, mention Allah frequently, and are victorious after they were wronged. Surely, the wrongdoers shall know what outcome is ultimately theirs.

إِلَّا الَّذِينَ ءَامَنُوا وَعَمِلُوا الصَّٰلِحَٰتِ وَذَكَرُوا اللَّهَ كَثِيرًا وَانتَصَرُوا مِنۢ بَعْدِ مَا ظُلِمُوا ۗ وَسَيَعْلَمُ الَّذِينَ ظَلَمُوٓا أَىَّ مُنقَلَبٍ يَنقَلِبُونَ ۝

Sûrat An-Naml,
(The Ants) 27

In the Name of Allah,
the Compassionate, the Merciful

1. Tah - Sin.[658]
Those are the verses of the Qur'an and a
Manifest Book,

2. A guidance and good tidings to the
believers,

3. Who perform the prayer, give the alms and
are certain of the Hereafter.

4. Those who do not believe in the Hereafter,
We have embellished for them their actions,
and thus they wander aimlessly.

5. Those are the ones who will receive the
grievous punishment and will be, in the
Hereafter, the greatest losers.

6. You certainly receive the Qur'an from an
All-Wise, All-Knowing One.

7. When Moses said to his family: "I have
sighted a fire and will bring you news of it, or
bring you a flaming spark that you might
warm yourselves."

8. Then, when he approached it, he was told
loudly: "Blessed is he who is in the fire and
those around it,[659] and glory be to the Lord of
the Worlds.

9. "O Moses, I am truly Allah, the All-Mighty,
Wise;

10. "Cast your staff"; but when he saw it
shaking, as though it was a serpent, he
turned around not looking back. "O Moses,
do not fear; the Messengers do not fear in My
Presence;

---

658. The same letters occur at the beginning of Surahs 26 and 28, with Mim added; the significance of this is not clear.
659. Moses and the other Prophets.

11. "Except for him who has done wrong, then changed, doing good after evil. For I am indeed All-Forgiving, Merciful.

إِلَّا مَن ظَلَمَ ثُمَّ بَدَّلَ حُسْنًۢا بَعْدَ سُوٓءٍ فَإِنِّى غَفُورٌ رَّحِيمٌ ﴿١١﴾

12. "Introduce your hand into your bosom and it will come out white, without blemish, as one of nine signs to Pharaoh and his people. They are, indeed, a wicked people."

وَأَدْخِلْ يَدَكَ فِى جَيْبِكَ تَخْرُجْ بَيْضَآءَ مِنْ غَيْرِ سُوٓءٍ فِى تِسْعِ ءَايَٰتٍ إِلَىٰ فِرْعَوْنَ وَقَوْمِهِۦٓ إِنَّهُمْ كَانُوا۟ قَوْمًا فَٰسِقِينَ ﴿١٢﴾

13. Then, when Our Signs came to them fully visible, they said: "This is manifest sorcery."

فَلَمَّا جَآءَتْهُمْ ءَايَٰتُنَا مُبْصِرَةً قَالُوا۟ هَٰذَا سِحْرٌ مُّبِينٌ ﴿١٣﴾

14. And they repudiated them, although their souls acknowledged them as certain, wrongfully and arrogantly. Behold, then what was the fate of the workers of corruption.

وَجَحَدُوا۟ بِهَا وَٱسْتَيْقَنَتْهَآ أَنفُسُهُمْ ظُلْمًا وَعُلُوًّا فَٱنظُرْ كَيْفَ كَانَ عَٰقِبَةُ ٱلْمُفْسِدِينَ ﴿١٤﴾

15. And We gave David and Solomon knowledge. They said: "Praise be to Allah Who preferred us over many of His believing servants."

وَلَقَدْ ءَاتَيْنَا دَاوُۥدَ وَسُلَيْمَٰنَ عِلْمًا وَقَالَا ٱلْحَمْدُ لِلَّهِ ٱلَّذِى فَضَّلَنَا عَلَىٰ كَثِيرٍ مِّنْ عِبَادِهِ ٱلْمُؤْمِنِينَ ﴿١٥﴾

16. Solomon inherited David, and he said: "O people, we have been taught the speech of birds and have been given part of everything. This is indeed the manifest bounty."

وَوَرِثَ سُلَيْمَٰنُ دَاوُۥدَ وَقَالَ يَٰٓأَيُّهَا ٱلنَّاسُ عُلِّمْنَا مَنطِقَ ٱلطَّيْرِ وَأُوتِينَا مِن كُلِّ شَىْءٍ إِنَّ هَٰذَا لَهُوَ ٱلْفَضْلُ ٱلْمُبِينُ ﴿١٦﴾

17. And Solomon's troops, jinn, men and birds, were mustered and duly held in check.

وَحُشِرَ لِسُلَيْمَٰنَ جُنُودُهُۥ مِنَ ٱلْجِنِّ وَٱلْإِنسِ وَٱلطَّيْرِ فَهُمْ يُوزَعُونَ ﴿١٧﴾

18. Until they reached an ants' hill; when an ant said: "O ants, enter your dwellings, lest Solomon and his troops crush you, without noticing it."

حَتَّىٰٓ إِذَآ أَتَوْا۟ عَلَىٰ وَادِ ٱلنَّمْلِ قَالَتْ نَمْلَةٌ يَٰٓأَيُّهَا ٱلنَّمْلُ ٱدْخُلُوا۟ مَسَٰكِنَكُمْ لَا يَحْطِمَنَّكُمْ سُلَيْمَٰنُ وَجُنُودُهُۥ وَهُمْ لَا يَشْعُرُونَ ﴿١٨﴾

19. Then he (Solomon) smiled, laughing at its words, and said: "Lord, inspire me to be thankful for Your Blessing, with which You blessed me and my parents, and to do the right pleasing to You. Admit me, by Your Mercy, into the company of Your righteous servants."

فَتَبَسَّمَ ضَاحِكًا مِّن قَوْلِهَا وَقَالَ رَبِّ أَوْزِعْنِىٓ أَنْ أَشْكُرَ نِعْمَتَكَ ٱلَّتِىٓ أَنْعَمْتَ عَلَىَّ وَعَلَىٰ وَٰلِدَىَّ وَأَنْ أَعْمَلَ صَٰلِحًا تَرْضَىٰهُ وَأَدْخِلْنِى بِرَحْمَتِكَ فِى عِبَادِكَ ٱلصَّٰلِحِينَ ﴿١٩﴾

20. He inspected the birds, then said: "Why do I not see the hoopoe?[660] Or is it gone away with the absent ones?

21. "I will punish it grievously or slaughter it, unless it brings me a manifest authority."

22. He lingered not for long, and so it[661] said: "I have learnt what you have not learnt and have brought from Sheba news which is certain.

23. "I have found a woman ruling over them and she has been given a share of everything and she has a great throne.

24. "I found her and her people prostrating themselves to the sun, instead of Allah, and Satan has embellished their actions, barring them from the Path. Therefore they are not well-guided;

25. "So that they may not prostrate themselves to Allah, Who brings out what is hidden in the heavens and the earth and knows what you conceal and what you reveal."

26. Allah, there is no god but He, the Lord of the Great Throne.

27. He[662] said: "We will see if you are telling the truth or are a liar.

28. "Take this letter of mine and deliver it to them; then turn away from them and see what they will give back in response."

29. She said:[663] "O my dignitaries, a gracious letter has been delivered to me.

30. "It is from Solomon and it says: 'In the Name of Allah, the Compassionate, the Merciful,

---

660. The hoopoe served Solomon as a carrier-pigeon would.
661. The hoopoe.
662. Solomon.
663. The Queen of Sheba in South Arabia.

31. "'Do not rise against me, and come to me submissively.'.[664]

32. She said: "O my dignitaries, give me your counsel in this, my affair. I will make no decision until you bear witness to me."

33. They said: "We are endowed with force and great might, but the command is yours; so see what you will command."

34. She said: "When kings enter a city, they ruin it and reduce its proud inhabitants to subjection. Thus they will always do.

35. "I am sending them a gift and will see what the envoys will bring back."

36. When [the emissary] came to Solomon, he said: "Are you supplying me with money? What Allah has given me is better than what He gave you. You are rather rejoicing in your gift.

37. "Go back to them;[665] for we shall array against them troops which they cannot resist and we shall drive them out of it degraded and abased."

38. He said: "O dignitaries, which one of you will bring me her throne, before they come forward submitting?"

39. A 'Ifreet of the jinn said: "I will bring it to you, before you rise from your seat, and I am indeed capable of it and faithful."

40. He who had knowledge of the Book said: "I will bring it to you, before your glance returns to you." So when he (Solomon) saw it ensconced before him, he said: "This is a bounty from my Lord, to test me, whether I am grateful or ungrateful. He who gives thanks, only gives thanks to his own credit, and he who is ungrateful will find my Lord All-Sufficient and Generous."

أَلَّا تَعْلُوا عَلَيَّ وَأْتُونِي مُسْلِمِينَ ۝

قَالَتْ يَـٰٓأَيُّهَا ٱلْمَلَؤُا۟ أَفْتُونِي فِي أَمْرِي مَا كُنتُ قَاطِعَةً أَمْرًا حَتَّىٰ تَشْهَدُونِ ۝

قَالُوا۟ نَحْنُ أُو۟لُوا۟ قُوَّةٍ وَأُو۟لُوا۟ بَأْسٍ شَدِيدٍ وَٱلْأَمْرُ إِلَيْكِ فَٱنظُرِي مَاذَا تَأْمُرِينَ ۝

قَالَتْ إِنَّ ٱلْمُلُوكَ إِذَا دَخَلُوا۟ قَرْيَةً أَفْسَدُوهَا وَجَعَلُوٓا۟ أَعِزَّةَ أَهْلِهَآ أَذِلَّةً وَكَذَٰلِكَ يَفْعَلُونَ ۝

وَإِنِّي مُرْسِلَةٌ إِلَيْهِم بِهَدِيَّةٍ فَنَاظِرَةٌۢ بِمَ يَرْجِعُ ٱلْمُرْسَلُونَ ۝

فَلَمَّا جَآءَ سُلَيْمَـٰنَ قَالَ أَتُمِدُّونَنِ بِمَالٍ فَمَآ ءَاتَـٰنِۦَ ٱللَّهُ خَيْرٌ مِّمَّآ ءَاتَـٰكُم بَلْ أَنتُم بِهَدِيَّتِكُمْ تَفْرَحُونَ ۝

ٱرْجِعْ إِلَيْهِمْ فَلَنَأْتِيَنَّهُم بِجُنُودٍ لَّا قِبَلَ لَهُم بِهَا وَلَنُخْرِجَنَّهُم مِّنْهَآ أَذِلَّةً وَهُمْ صَـٰغِرُونَ ۝

قَالَ يَـٰٓأَيُّهَا ٱلْمَلَؤُا۟ أَيُّكُمْ يَأْتِينِي بِعَرْشِهَا قَبْلَ أَن يَأْتُونِي مُسْلِمِينَ ۝

قَالَ عِفْرِيتٌ مِّنَ ٱلْجِنِّ أَنَا۠ ءَاتِيكَ بِهِۦ قَبْلَ أَن تَقُومَ مِن مَّقَامِكَ وَإِنِّي عَلَيْهِ لَقَوِيٌّ أَمِينٌ ۝

قَالَ ٱلَّذِي عِندَهُۥ عِلْمٌ مِّنَ ٱلْكِتَـٰبِ أَنَا۠ ءَاتِيكَ بِهِۦ قَبْلَ أَن يَرْتَدَّ إِلَيْكَ طَرْفُكَ فَلَمَّا رَءَاهُ مُسْتَقِرًّا عِندَهُۥ قَالَ هَـٰذَا مِن فَضْلِ رَبِّي لِيَبْلُوَنِۦٓ ءَأَشْكُرُ أَمْ أَكْفُرُ وَمَن شَكَرَ فَإِنَّمَا يَشْكُرُ لِنَفْسِهِۦ وَمَن كَفَرَ فَإِنَّ رَبِّي غَنِيٌّ كَرِيمٌ ۝

---

664. Arabic *Muslimin*, which became the attribute Muslims.
665. The people of Sheba.

41. He said: "Disguise her throne for her, so that we might see whether she will be well-guided or will be one of those who are not well-guided."

قَالَ نَكِّرُوا لَهَا عَرْشَهَا نَنظُرْ أَتَهْتَدِىٓ أَمْ تَكُونُ مِنَ ٱلَّذِينَ لَا يَهْتَدُونَ ٤١

42. When she arrived, it was said (to her): "Is your throne like this one?" She said: "It looks like it." "We[666] were given the knowledge before her and were submissive."

فَلَمَّا جَآءَتْ قِيلَ أَهَٰكَذَا عَرْشُكِ قَالَتْ كَأَنَّهُۥ هُوَ وَأُوتِينَا ٱلْعِلْمَ مِن قَبْلِهَا وَكُنَّا مُسْلِمِينَ ٤٢

43. However, what she worshipped, apart from Allah, barred her; she was indeed one of the unbelieving people.

وَصَدَّهَا مَا كَانَت تَّعْبُدُ مِن دُونِ ٱللَّهِ إِنَّهَا كَانَتْ مِن قَوْمٍ كَٰفِرِينَ ٤٣

44. It was said to her: "Enter the mansion"; but when she saw it, she thought it was a deep pond, and she bared her legs. He[667] said: "This is actually a mansion made of glass." She said: "Lord, I have wronged myself and have submitted, along with Solomon, to Allah the Lord of the Worlds."

قِيلَ لَهَا ٱدْخُلِى ٱلصَّرْحَ فَلَمَّا رَأَتْهُ حَسِبَتْهُ لُجَّةً وَكَشَفَتْ عَن سَاقَيْهَا قَالَ إِنَّهُۥ صَرْحٌ مُّمَرَّدٌ مِّن قَوَارِيرَ قَالَتْ رَبِّ إِنِّى ظَلَمْتُ نَفْسِى وَأَسْلَمْتُ مَعَ سُلَيْمَٰنَ لِلَّهِ رَبِّ ٱلْعَٰلَمِينَ ٤٤

45. And We have sent to Thamud their brother Salih, saying: "Worship Allah"; and lo and behold, they split into two groups fighting each other.

وَلَقَدْ أَرْسَلْنَآ إِلَىٰ ثَمُودَ أَخَاهُمْ صَٰلِحًا أَنِ ٱعْبُدُوا ٱللَّهَ فَإِذَا هُمْ فَرِيقَانِ يَخْتَصِمُونَ ٤٥

46. He said: "O my people, why do you hasten the evil course before the fair? If only you would seek Allah's Forgiveness, that perchance you may receive mercy!"

قَالَ يَٰقَوْمِ لِمَ تَسْتَعْجِلُونَ بِٱلسَّيِّئَةِ قَبْلَ ٱلْحَسَنَةِ لَوْلَا تَسْتَغْفِرُونَ ٱللَّهَ لَعَلَّكُمْ تُرْحَمُونَ ٤٦

47. They said: "We augured ill of you and your companions." He said: "Your bird of omen is with Allah, but you are a people who are being tested."

قَالُوا ٱطَّيَّرْنَا بِكَ وَبِمَن مَّعَكَ قَالَ طَٰٓئِرُكُمْ عِندَ ٱللَّهِ بَلْ أَنتُمْ قَوْمٌ تُفْتَنُونَ ٤٧

48. And there were in the city nine individuals, who worked corruption in the land and did not set things right.

وَكَانَ فِى ٱلْمَدِينَةِ تِسْعَةُ رَهْطٍ يُفْسِدُونَ فِى ٱلْأَرْضِ وَلَا يُصْلِحُونَ ٤٨

---

666. The reference is to Solomon.
667. Solomon.

49. They said: "Swear one to the other by Allah: We will attack him and his family at night; then we will tell his guardian: 'We did not witness the slaying of his family, and we are indeed truthful.'"

قَالُوا تَقَاسَمُوا بِاللَّهِ لَنُبَيِّتَنَّهُ وَأَهْلَهُ ثُمَّ لَنَقُولَنَّ لِوَلِيِّهِ مَا شَهِدْنَا مَهْلِكَ أَهْلِهِ وَإِنَّا لَصَادِقُونَ ﴿٤٩﴾

50. They schemed a scheme and We schemed a scheme, while they were unaware.

وَمَكَرُوا مَكْرًا وَمَكَرْنَا مَكْرًا وَهُمْ لَا يَشْعُرُونَ ﴿٥٠﴾

51. See, then, what was the outcome of their scheming; We destroyed them together with all their people.

فَانظُرْ كَيْفَ كَانَ عَاقِبَةُ مَكْرِهِمْ أَنَّا دَمَّرْنَاهُمْ وَقَوْمَهُمْ أَجْمَعِينَ ﴿٥١﴾

52. Their houses are in ruin, on account of their wrongdoing. There is in that a sign for a people who know.

فَتِلْكَ بُيُوتُهُمْ خَاوِيَةً بِمَا ظَلَمُوا إِنَّ فِي ذَلِكَ لَآيَةً لِقَوْمٍ يَعْلَمُونَ ﴿٥٢﴾

53. And We delivered those who believed and were God-fearing.

وَأَنجَيْنَا الَّذِينَ آمَنُوا وَكَانُوا يَتَّقُونَ ﴿٥٣﴾

54. And Lot, when he said to his people: "Do you commit the foul act, while you perceive?

وَلُوطًا إِذْ قَالَ لِقَوْمِهِ أَتَأْتُونَ الْفَاحِشَةَ وَأَنتُمْ تُبْصِرُونَ ﴿٥٤﴾

55. "What then, do you approach men lustfully, instead of women? No, you are an ignorant people."

أَئِنَّكُمْ لَتَأْتُونَ الرِّجَالَ شَهْوَةً مِّن دُونِ النِّسَاءِ بَلْ أَنتُمْ قَوْمٌ تَجْهَلُونَ ﴿٥٥﴾

56. The only response of his people was to say: "Drive the family of Lot out of your city. They are a people who keep themselves clean."

فَمَا كَانَ جَوَابَ قَوْمِهِ إِلَّا أَن قَالُوا أَخْرِجُوا آلَ لُوطٍ مِّن قَرْيَتِكُمْ إِنَّهُمْ أُنَاسٌ يَتَطَهَّرُونَ ﴿٥٦﴾

57. We delivered him and his family, except for his wife; We decreed that she should stay behind.

فَأَنجَيْنَاهُ وَأَهْلَهُ إِلَّا امْرَأَتَهُ قَدَّرْنَاهَا مِنَ الْغَابِرِينَ ﴿٥٧﴾

58. And We sent down upon them a torrent of rain. Wretched is the rain of those who have been forewarned!

وَأَمْطَرْنَا عَلَيْهِم مَّطَرًا فَسَاءَ مَطَرُ الْمُنذَرِينَ ﴿٥٨﴾

59. Say: "Praise be to Allah and peace upon those of His servants whom He has chosen. Is Allah better or those they associate with Him?"

قُلِ الْحَمْدُ لِلَّهِ وَسَلَامٌ عَلَى عِبَادِهِ الَّذِينَ اصْطَفَى آللَّهُ خَيْرٌ أَمَّا يُشْرِكُونَ ﴿٥٩﴾

60. Is He not the One Who created the heavens and the earth and sent down upon you water from the sky; and so We caused to grow thereby delightful gardens. It was not in your power to cause their trees to grow. Is there, then, another god with Allah? Yet, they are a people who assign to Him an equal.

61. Is He not the One Who made the earth a stable abode and created rivers flowing through it, created immovable mountains therein and created a barrier between the two seas. Is there, then, another god with Allah? Yet, most of them do not know.

62. It is He Who answers the one in trouble when he calls upon Him and lifts the adversity and appoints you as successors on earth. Is there then another god with Allah? Little do you recollect.

63. He Who guides you through the dark shadows of land and sea, and sends forth the wind as good news ahead of His Mercy. Is there then another god with Allah? No, He is exalted above what they associate!

64. He Who originates the creation, then brings it back, and Who provides for you from the heavens and the earth. Is there, then, another god with Allah. Say: "Produce your proof, if you are truthful."

65. Say: "No one in the heavens or on earth knows the Unseen, except Allah; and they will have no inkling when they shall be resuscitated.

66. Has their knowledge of the Hereafter continued? Nay, they are in doubt regarding it, or rather, they are blind to it.

67. The unbelievers say: "What then, will we and our fathers be raised up, once we have turned into dust?

أَمَّنْ خَلَقَ ٱلسَّمَٰوَٰتِ وَٱلْأَرْضَ وَأَنزَلَ لَكُم مِّنَ ٱلسَّمَآءِ مَآءً فَأَنۢبَتْنَا بِهِۦ حَدَآئِقَ ذَاتَ بَهْجَةٍ مَّا كَانَ لَكُمْ أَن تُنۢبِتُوا۟ شَجَرَهَآ أَءِلَٰهٌ مَّعَ ٱللَّهِ بَلْ هُمْ قَوْمٌ يَعْدِلُونَ ﴿٦٠﴾

أَمَّن جَعَلَ ٱلْأَرْضَ قَرَارًا وَجَعَلَ خِلَٰلَهَآ أَنْهَٰرًا وَجَعَلَ لَهَا رَوَٰسِيَ وَجَعَلَ بَيْنَ ٱلْبَحْرَيْنِ حَاجِزًا أَءِلَٰهٌ مَّعَ ٱللَّهِ بَلْ أَكْثَرُهُمْ لَا يَعْلَمُونَ ﴿٦١﴾

أَمَّن يُجِيبُ ٱلْمُضْطَرَّ إِذَا دَعَاهُ وَيَكْشِفُ ٱلسُّوٓءَ وَيَجْعَلُكُمْ خُلَفَآءَ ٱلْأَرْضِ أَءِلَٰهٌ مَّعَ ٱللَّهِ قَلِيلًا مَّا تَذَكَّرُونَ ﴿٦٢﴾

أَمَّن يَهْدِيكُمْ فِى ظُلُمَٰتِ ٱلْبَرِّ وَٱلْبَحْرِ وَمَن يُرْسِلُ ٱلرِّيَٰحَ بُشْرًۢا بَيْنَ يَدَىْ رَحْمَتِهِۦ أَءِلَٰهٌ مَّعَ ٱللَّهِ تَعَٰلَى ٱللَّهُ عَمَّا يُشْرِكُونَ ﴿٦٣﴾

أَمَّن يَبْدَؤُا۟ ٱلْخَلْقَ ثُمَّ يُعِيدُهُۥ وَمَن يَرْزُقُكُم مِّنَ ٱلسَّمَآءِ وَٱلْأَرْضِ أَءِلَٰهٌ مَّعَ ٱللَّهِ قُلْ هَاتُوا۟ بُرْهَٰنَكُمْ إِن كُنتُمْ صَٰدِقِينَ ﴿٦٤﴾

قُل لَّا يَعْلَمُ مَن فِى ٱلسَّمَٰوَٰتِ وَٱلْأَرْضِ ٱلْغَيْبَ إِلَّا ٱللَّهُ وَمَا يَشْعُرُونَ أَيَّانَ يُبْعَثُونَ ﴿٦٥﴾

بَلِ ٱدَّٰرَكَ عِلْمُهُمْ فِى ٱلْءَاخِرَةِ بَلْ هُمْ فِى شَكٍّ مِّنْهَا بَلْ هُم مِّنْهَا عَمُونَ ﴿٦٦﴾

وَقَالَ ٱلَّذِينَ كَفَرُوٓا۟ أَءِذَا كُنَّا تُرَٰبًا وَءَابَآؤُنَآ أَئِنَّا لَمُخْرَجُونَ ﴿٦٧﴾

68. "We have been promised that, we and our fathers before. These are only the legends of the ancients."

لَقَدْ وُعِدْنَا هَٰذَا نَحْنُ وَءَابَآؤُنَا مِن قَبْلُ إِنْ هَٰذَآ إِلَّآ أَسَٰطِيرُ ٱلْأَوَّلِينَ ﴿٦٨﴾

69. Say: "Travel in the land and see what was the end of the criminals."

قُلْ سِيرُوا۟ فِى ٱلْأَرْضِ فَٱنظُرُوا۟ كَيْفَ كَانَ عَٰقِبَةُ ٱلْمُجْرِمِينَ ﴿٦٩﴾

70. Do not grieve for them and do not be distressed on account of what they contrive.

وَلَا تَحْزَنْ عَلَيْهِمْ وَلَا تَكُن فِى ضَيْقٍ مِّمَّا يَمْكُرُونَ ﴿٧٠﴾

71. And they say: "When is this promise to be fulfilled, if you are truthful?"

وَيَقُولُونَ مَتَىٰ هَٰذَا ٱلْوَعْدُ إِن كُنتُمْ صَٰدِقِينَ ﴿٧١﴾

72. Say: "Perhaps some of what you seek to hasten is drawing near."

قُلْ عَسَىٰ أَن يَكُونَ رَدِفَ لَكُم بَعْضُ ٱلَّذِى تَسْتَعْجِلُونَ ﴿٧٢﴾

73. Your Lord, indeed, is Bountiful to mankind, but most of them do not give thanks.

وَإِنَّ رَبَّكَ لَذُو فَضْلٍ عَلَى ٱلنَّاسِ وَلَٰكِنَّ أَكْثَرَهُمْ لَا يَشْكُرُونَ ﴿٧٣﴾

74. And your Lord knows what their breasts conceal and what they reveal.

وَإِنَّ رَبَّكَ لَيَعْلَمُ مَا تُكِنُّ صُدُورُهُمْ وَمَا يُعْلِنُونَ ﴿٧٤﴾

75. There is no hidden secret in heaven or on earth, but is in a Manifest Book.

وَمَا مِنْ غَآئِبَةٍ فِى ٱلسَّمَآءِ وَٱلْأَرْضِ إِلَّا فِى كِتَٰبٍ مُّبِينٍ ﴿٧٥﴾

76. This Qur'an relates to the Children of Israel most of what they differ on.

إِنَّ هَٰذَا ٱلْقُرْءَانَ يَقُصُّ عَلَىٰ بَنِىٓ إِسْرَٰٓءِيلَ أَكْثَرَ ٱلَّذِى هُمْ فِيهِ يَخْتَلِفُونَ ﴿٧٦﴾

77. And it is, indeed, a guidance and mercy to the believers.

وَإِنَّهُۥ لَهُدًى وَرَحْمَةٌ لِّلْمُؤْمِنِينَ ﴿٧٧﴾

78. Your Lord will decide between them according to His Judgement. He is the All-Mighty, the All-Knowing.

إِنَّ رَبَّكَ يَقْضِى بَيْنَهُم بِحُكْمِهِۦ وَهُوَ ٱلْعَزِيزُ ٱلْعَلِيمُ ﴿٧٨﴾

79. So put your trust in Allah; you are on the manifest and true [path].

فَتَوَكَّلْ عَلَى ٱللَّهِ إِنَّكَ عَلَى ٱلْحَقِّ ٱلْمُبِينِ ﴿٧٩﴾

80. You will certainly not cause the dead to hear or the deaf to hear the call, if they turn away in flight.

إِنَّكَ لَا تُسْمِعُ ٱلْمَوْتَىٰ وَلَا تُسْمِعُ ٱلصُّمَّ ٱلدُّعَآءَ إِذَا وَلَّوْا۟ مُدْبِرِينَ ﴿٨٠﴾

81. And you will not deflect the blind from their error. You will only cause those who believe in Our Signs to hear; for they have submitted.

وَمَآ أَنتَ بِهَٰدِى ٱلْعُمْىِ عَن ضَلَٰلَتِهِمْ إِن تُسْمِعُ إِلَّا مَن يُؤْمِنُ بِـَٔايَٰتِنَا فَهُم مُّسْلِمُونَ ﴿٨١﴾

82. And when the Word[668] is fulfilled against them, We shall bring out of the earth for them a beast which shall address them thus: "Mankind has not believed with certainty in Our Signs."

83. On the Day when We shall muster from each nation a throng of those who denied Our Signs; then they will be held in check.

84. Until they come forward and He says: "Have you denied My Signs, and did not comprehend them? Otherwise, what were you doing?"

85. And the Word shall come down upon them for their wrongdoing and so they will not speak.

86. Do they not see that We made the night, so that they might rest in it, and the day so that they might see? Surely in that are signs for a believing people.

87. And on the Day the Trumpet is blown, those in the heavens and on earth are terrified, except for whomever Allah wills; and everyone will come to Him humbly.

88. And you will see the mountains and suppose them immobile, whereas they are passing quickly like clouds - the Handiwork of Allah Who perfected everything. He is truly conversant with what you do.

89. Whoever performs a good deed will receive a reward better than it, and they are secure on that day against terror.

90. And those who perpetrate an evil deed, their faces will be cast into the Fire. Will you be rewarded except for what you used to do?

---

668. Divine Decree.

91. I was only ordered to worship the Lord of this city[669] which He has sanctified. His is everything, and I was ordered to be one of those who submit [to Allah];[670]

إِنَّمَا أُمِرْتُ أَنْ أَعْبُدَ رَبَّ هَذِهِ ٱلْبَلْدَةِ ٱلَّذِى حَرَّمَهَا وَلَهُ كُلُّ شَىْءٍ وَأُمِرْتُ أَنْ أَكُونَ مِنَ ٱلْمُسْلِمِينَ ﴿٩١﴾

92. And to recite the Qur'an. He who is well-guided is only well-guided to his own advantage, and to him who goes astray, say: "I am only one of the warners."

وَأَنْ أَتْلُوَا۟ ٱلْقُرْءَانَ فَمَنِ ٱهْتَدَى فَإِنَّمَا يَهْتَدِى لِنَفْسِهِ وَمَن ضَلَّ فَقُلْ إِنَّمَا أَنَا۠ مِنَ ٱلْمُنذِرِينَ ﴿٩٢﴾

93. And say: "Praise be to Allah. He will show you His Signs and then you will recognize them. Your Lord is not heedless of what you do."

وَقُلِ ٱلْحَمْدُ لِلَّهِ سَيُرِيكُمْ ءَايَتِهِ فَتَعْرِفُونَهَا وَمَا رَبُّكَ بِغَفِلٍ عَمَّا تَعْمَلُونَ ﴿٩٣﴾

**Sûrat Al-Qasas,
(Storytelling) 28**

سُورَةُ القَصَص

*In the Name of Allah,
the Compassionate, the Merciful*

بِسْمِ ٱللَّهِ ٱلرَّحْمَنِ ٱلرَّحِيمِ

1. Tah - Sin - Mim.[671]

طسم ﴿١﴾

2. Those are the verses of the Manifest Book,

تِلْكَ ءَايَتُ ٱلْكِتَبِ ٱلْمُبِينِ ﴿٢﴾

3. We recite to you part of the news of Moses and Pharaoh truthfully, for a people who believe.

نَتْلُوا۟ عَلَيْكَ مِن نَّبَإِ مُوسَى وَفِرْعَوْنَ بِٱلْحَقِّ لِقَوْمٍ يُؤْمِنُونَ ﴿٣﴾

4. Pharaoh waxed proud in the land and reduced its inhabitants into factions, subduing a group of them, slaughtering their sons and sparing their women. He was truly a corruption-worker.

إِنَّ فِرْعَوْنَ عَلَا فِى ٱلْأَرْضِ وَجَعَلَ أَهْلَهَا شِيَعًا يَسْتَضْعِفُ طَآئِفَةً مِّنْهُمْ يُذَبِّحُ أَبْنَآءَهُمْ وَيَسْتَحْىِۦ نِسَآءَهُمْ إِنَّهُۥ كَانَ مِنَ ٱلْمُفْسِدِينَ ﴿٤﴾

5. We wish to favour the downtrodden in the land and make them leaders and make them the inheritors;

وَنُرِيدُ أَن نَّمُنَّ عَلَى ٱلَّذِينَ ٱسْتُضْعِفُوا۟ فِى ٱلْأَرْضِ وَنَجْعَلَهُمْ أَئِمَّةً وَنَجْعَلَهُمُ ٱلْوَرِثِينَ ﴿٥﴾

6. And establish them firmly in the land and show Pharaoh and Haman and their troops what they used to fear.

وَنُمَكِّنَ لَهُمْ فِى ٱلْأَرْضِ وَنُرِىَ فِرْعَوْنَ وَهَمَنَ وَجُنُودَهُمَا مِنْهُم مَّا كَانُوا۟ يَحْذَرُونَ ﴿٦﴾

---

669. That is, Mecca.
670. i.e. *Al-Muslimin*.
671. The same letters occur at the beginning of Surah 26; the significance of this is not clear.

7. We revealed to Moses' mother: "Suckle him; but if you fear for him, cast him into the water and do not fear or grieve. We shall return him to you and make him one of the Messengers."

8. Then the folk of Pharaoh picked him up, to become an enemy and a source of sorrow for them. Pharaoh, Haman,[672] and their troops were surely sinful.

9. Pharaoh's wife said: "He is a comfort to you and me. Do not kill him; perhaps he will profit us or we will take him for a son." Yet they were not well aware.

10. The heart of Moses' mother became vacant; she almost exposed him, but for Our fortifying her heart, so that she might be one of the believers.

11. She said to his sister: "Follow his tracks", and so she observed him from a distance, while they were unaware.

12. And We forbade him earlier from being nursed by foster-mothers; so she[673] said: "Shall I lead you to a household who will take charge of him for you and will take good care of him?"

13. Then We returned him to his mother, so that she might be comforted and not grieve, and that she might know that Allah's Promise is true; but most of them do not know.

14. When he was fully grown, and became an adult, We conferred on him judgement and knowledge. That is how We reward the beneficent.

وَأَوْحَيْنَا إِلَىٰ أُمِّ مُوسَىٰ أَنْ أَرْضِعِيهِ فَإِذَا خِفْتِ عَلَيْهِ فَأَلْقِيهِ فِي الْيَمِّ وَلَا تَخَافِي وَلَا تَحْزَنِي إِنَّا رَادُّوهُ إِلَيْكِ وَجَاعِلُوهُ مِنَ الْمُرْسَلِينَ ﴿٧﴾

فَالْتَقَطَهُ آلُ فِرْعَوْنَ لِيَكُونَ لَهُمْ عَدُوًّا وَحَزَنًا إِنَّ فِرْعَوْنَ وَهَامَٰنَ وَجُنُودَهُمَا كَانُوا خَاطِئِينَ ﴿٨﴾

وَقَالَتِ امْرَأَتُ فِرْعَوْنَ قُرَّتُ عَيْنٍ لِّي وَلَكَ لَا تَقْتُلُوهُ عَسَىٰ أَن يَنفَعَنَا أَوْ نَتَّخِذَهُ وَلَدًا وَهُمْ لَا يَشْعُرُونَ ﴿٩﴾

وَأَصْبَحَ فُؤَادُ أُمِّ مُوسَىٰ فَارِغًا إِن كَادَتْ لَتُبْدِي بِهِ لَوْلَا أَن رَّبَطْنَا عَلَىٰ قَلْبِهَا لِتَكُونَ مِنَ الْمُؤْمِنِينَ ﴿١٠﴾

وَقَالَتْ لِأُخْتِهِ قُصِّيهِ فَبَصُرَتْ بِهِ عَن جُنُبٍ وَهُمْ لَا يَشْعُرُونَ ﴿١١﴾

۞ وَحَرَّمْنَا عَلَيْهِ الْمَرَاضِعَ مِن قَبْلُ فَقَالَتْ هَلْ أَدُلُّكُمْ عَلَىٰ أَهْلِ بَيْتٍ يَكْفُلُونَهُ لَكُمْ وَهُمْ لَهُ نَاصِحُونَ ﴿١٢﴾

فَرَدَدْنَاهُ إِلَىٰ أُمِّهِ كَيْ تَقَرَّ عَيْنُهَا وَلَا تَحْزَنَ وَلِتَعْلَمَ أَنَّ وَعْدَ اللَّهِ حَقٌّ وَلَٰكِنَّ أَكْثَرَهُمْ لَا يَعْلَمُونَ ﴿١٣﴾

وَلَمَّا بَلَغَ أَشُدَّهُ وَاسْتَوَىٰ آتَيْنَاهُ حُكْمًا وَعِلْمًا وَكَذَٰلِكَ نَجْزِي الْمُحْسِنِينَ ﴿١٤﴾

---

672. The minister of Pharaoh.
673. Moses' sister.

388

15. And he entered the city at a time when its inhabitants were unheeding; and so he found in it two men fighting, one of his own sect, the other from his enemies. Whereupon the one of his sect solicited his assistance against the one from his enemies; so Moses struck him and killed him. He said: "This is the work of Satan; he is a manifestly misleading enemy."

16. He said: "Lord, I have wronged myself, so forgive me." Then He forgave him. He is indeed the All-Forgiving, the Merciful.

17. He said: "Lord, in as much as you have favoured me, I will not be a supporter of the criminals."

18. The next morning, He became fearful and vigilant; and lo and behold, the man who had sought his assistance on the previous day was calling out to him. Moses said to him: "You are clearly in error."

19. So, when he[674] was about to kill the one who was their enemy, he said: "O Moses, do you wish to kill me, as you killed another living soul yesterday? Do you only wish to become a tyrant in the land and do not wish to be one of the righteous?"

20. And a man came from the farthest part of the city running. He said: "O Moses, the dignitaries are conspiring to kill you. Depart then, I am one of your sincere advisors."

21. So, he departed from it fearful and vigilant. He said: "Lord, deliver me from the wrongdoing people."

22. And when he headed towards Midian, he said: "Perhaps, my Lord will guide me unto the Right Path."

---

674. Moses.

وَدَخَلَ ٱلْمَدِينَةَ عَلَىٰ حِينِ غَفْلَةٍ مِّنْ أَهْلِهَا فَوَجَدَ فِيهَا رَجُلَيْنِ يَقْتَتِلَانِ هَٰذَا مِن شِيعَتِهِ وَهَٰذَا مِنْ عَدُوِّهِ فَٱسْتَغَٰثَهُ ٱلَّذِي مِن شِيعَتِهِ عَلَى ٱلَّذِي مِنْ عَدُوِّهِ فَوَكَزَهُۥ مُوسَىٰ فَقَضَىٰ عَلَيْهِ قَالَ هَٰذَا مِنْ عَمَلِ ٱلشَّيْطَٰنِ إِنَّهُۥ عَدُوٌّ مُّضِلٌّ مُّبِينٌ ﴿١٥﴾

قَالَ رَبِّ إِنِّي ظَلَمْتُ نَفْسِي فَٱغْفِرْ لِي فَغَفَرَ لَهُۥ إِنَّهُۥ هُوَ ٱلْغَفُورُ ٱلرَّحِيمُ ﴿١٦﴾

قَالَ رَبِّ بِمَآ أَنْعَمْتَ عَلَيَّ فَلَنْ أَكُونَ ظَهِيرًا لِّلْمُجْرِمِينَ ﴿١٧﴾

فَأَصْبَحَ فِي ٱلْمَدِينَةِ خَآئِفًا يَتَرَقَّبُ فَإِذَا ٱلَّذِي ٱسْتَنصَرَهُۥ بِٱلْأَمْسِ يَسْتَصْرِخُهُ قَالَ لَهُۥ مُوسَىٰٓ إِنَّكَ لَغَوِيٌّ مُّبِينٌ ﴿١٨﴾

فَلَمَّآ أَنْ أَرَادَ أَن يَبْطِشَ بِٱلَّذِي هُوَ عَدُوٌّ لَّهُمَا قَالَ يَٰمُوسَىٰٓ أَتُرِيدُ أَن تَقْتُلَنِي كَمَا قَتَلْتَ نَفْسًا بِٱلْأَمْسِ إِن تُرِيدُ إِلَّآ أَن تَكُونَ جَبَّارًا فِي ٱلْأَرْضِ وَمَا تُرِيدُ أَن تَكُونَ مِنَ ٱلْمُصْلِحِينَ ﴿١٩﴾

وَجَآءَ رَجُلٌ مِّنْ أَقْصَا ٱلْمَدِينَةِ يَسْعَىٰ قَالَ يَٰمُوسَىٰٓ إِنَّ ٱلْمَلَأَ يَأْتَمِرُونَ بِكَ لِيَقْتُلُوكَ فَٱخْرُجْ إِنِّي لَكَ مِنَ ٱلنَّٰصِحِينَ ﴿٢٠﴾

فَخَرَجَ مِنْهَا خَآئِفًا يَتَرَقَّبُ قَالَ رَبِّ نَجِّنِي مِنَ ٱلْقَوْمِ ٱلظَّٰلِمِينَ ﴿٢١﴾

وَلَمَّا تَوَجَّهَ تِلْقَآءَ مَدْيَنَ قَالَ عَسَىٰ رَبِّي أَن يَهْدِيَنِي سَوَآءَ ٱلسَّبِيلِ ﴿٢٢﴾

23. And when he arrived at the water of Midian, he found there a company of men watering their cattle, and he found, apart from them, two women holding back. He said: "What is the matter with you both?" They said: "We will not water our flock until the cattle-herders leave off, and our father is a very old man."

24. So, he watered their flock for them, and then moved towards the shade and said: "Lord, I am in dire need of whatever good You might send down to me."

25. Then, one of the two women came to him walking coyly. She said: "My father is calling you in order to reward you for watering our flock." So, when he came to him and told him the story, he said: "Do not fear, you have escaped from the wrongdoing people."

26. One of the two women said: "Father, hire him. Surely, the best one you can hire is the strong and faithful one."

27. He said: "I want to marry you to one of these two daughters of mine, provided you serve me for eight years. If you complete ten years, that will be of your own accord; and I do not wish to make things hard for you. You will find me, if Allah wishes, one of the righteous."

28. He said: "This is a compact between you and me; whichever term I complete, my action will not be impugned, and Allah shall vouchsafe what we are saying."

29. So, when Moses completed the term and set out with his family, he observed a fire on the side of the Tur Mountain.[675] He said to

وَلَمَّا وَرَدَ مَآءَ مَدْيَنَ وَجَدَ عَلَيْهِ أُمَّةً مِّنَ ٱلنَّاسِ يَسْقُونَ وَوَجَدَ مِن دُونِهِمُ ٱمْرَأَتَيْنِ تَذُودَانِ قَالَ مَا خَطْبُكُمَا قَالَتَا لَا نَسْقِى حَتَّىٰ يُصْدِرَ ٱلرِّعَآءُ وَأَبُونَا شَيْخٌ كَبِيرٌ ﴿٢٣﴾

فَسَقَىٰ لَهُمَا ثُمَّ تَوَلَّىٰٓ إِلَى ٱلظِّلِّ فَقَالَ رَبِّ إِنِّى لِمَآ أَنزَلْتَ إِلَىَّ مِنْ خَيْرٍ فَقِيرٌ ﴿٢٤﴾

فَجَآءَتْهُ إِحْدَىٰهُمَا تَمْشِى عَلَى ٱسْتِحْيَآءٍ قَالَتْ إِنَّ أَبِى يَدْعُوكَ لِيَجْزِيَكَ أَجْرَ مَا سَقَيْتَ لَنَا فَلَمَّا جَآءَهُ وَقَصَّ عَلَيْهِ ٱلْقَصَصَ قَالَ لَا تَخَفْ نَجَوْتَ مِنَ ٱلْقَوْمِ ٱلظَّٰلِمِينَ ﴿٢٥﴾

قَالَتْ إِحْدَىٰهُمَا يَـٰٓأَبَتِ ٱسْتَـٔجِرْهُ إِنَّ خَيْرَ مَنِ ٱسْتَـٔجَرْتَ ٱلْقَوِىُّ ٱلْأَمِينُ ﴿٢٦﴾

قَالَ إِنِّىٓ أُرِيدُ أَنْ أُنكِحَكَ إِحْدَى ٱبْنَتَىَّ هَـٰتَيْنِ عَلَىٰٓ أَن تَأْجُرَنِى ثَمَـٰنِىَ حِجَجٍ فَإِنْ أَتْمَمْتَ عَشْرًا فَمِنْ عِندِكَ وَمَآ أُرِيدُ أَنْ أَشُقَّ عَلَيْكَ سَتَجِدُنِىٓ إِن شَآءَ ٱللَّهُ مِنَ ٱلصَّـٰلِحِينَ ﴿٢٧﴾

قَالَ ذَٰلِكَ بَيْنِى وَبَيْنَكَ أَيَّمَا ٱلْأَجَلَيْنِ قَضَيْتُ فَلَا عُدْوَٰنَ عَلَىَّ وَٱللَّهُ عَلَىٰ مَا نَقُولُ وَكِيلٌ ﴿٢٨﴾

۞ فَلَمَّا قَضَىٰ مُوسَى ٱلْأَجَلَ وَسَارَ بِأَهْلِهِ ءَانَسَ مِن جَانِبِ ٱلطُّورِ نَارًا قَالَ لِأَهْلِهِ ٱمْكُثُوٓا إِنِّىٓ ءَانَسْتُ نَارًا

---

675. Sinai Mountain.

390

his family: "Stay here, I have observed a fire. Perhaps, I can bring you some news of it or a brand of fire that you might warm yourselves."

30. When he approached it, he was summoned from the right side of the valley, on the sacred spot by the tree: "O Moses, it is I, Allah, the Lord of the Worlds;

31. "Cast your staff', but when he saw it shaking like a snake, he turned away running, not looking back. "O Moses, come forward and do not fear; you are certainly safe.

32. "Slip your hand into your bosom and it will come out white, without blemish; then press [your arm] to your side so as not to fear. Those, then, are two proofs to Pharaoh and his dignitaries from your Lord. Indeed, they have been a sinful people."

33. He said: "Lord, I have killed from them a living soul, and I fear that they might kill me.

34. "My brother Aaron is more eloquent than I; so send him with me as a supporter to vouch for me. I fear that they will denounce me as a liar."

35. He[676] said: "We will strengthen your arm with your brother and We will give you authority; so that they will not touch you. By Our Signs, you and those who follow you will be the victors."

36. But when Moses came to them with Our Clear Signs, they said: "This is only faked sorcery and we never heard of this among our forefathers."

لَعَلِّى ءَاتِيكُم مِّنْهَا بِخَبَرٍ أَوْ جَذْوَةٍ مِّنَ ٱلنَّارِ لَعَلَّكُمْ تَصْطَلُونَ ﴿٢٩﴾

فَلَمَّآ أَتَىٰهَا نُودِيَ مِن شَٰطِئِ ٱلْوَادِ ٱلْأَيْمَنِ فِى ٱلْبُقْعَةِ ٱلْمُبَٰرَكَةِ مِنَ ٱلشَّجَرَةِ أَن يَٰمُوسَىٰٓ إِنِّىٓ أَنَا ٱللَّهُ رَبُّ ٱلْعَٰلَمِينَ ﴿٣٠﴾

وَأَنْ أَلْقِ عَصَاكَ فَلَمَّا رَءَاهَا تَهْتَزُّ كَأَنَّهَا جَآنٌّ وَلَّىٰ مُدْبِرًا وَلَمْ يُعَقِّبْ يَٰمُوسَىٰٓ أَقْبِلْ وَلَا تَخَفْ إِنَّكَ مِنَ ٱلْءَامِنِينَ ﴿٣١﴾

ٱسْلُكْ يَدَكَ فِى جَيْبِكَ تَخْرُجْ بَيْضَآءَ مِنْ غَيْرِ سُوٓءٍ وَٱضْمُمْ إِلَيْكَ جَنَاحَكَ مِنَ ٱلرَّهْبِ فَذَٰنِكَ بُرْهَٰنَانِ مِن رَّبِّكَ إِلَىٰ فِرْعَوْنَ وَمَلَإِيْهِۦٓ إِنَّهُمْ كَانُوا۟ قَوْمًا فَٰسِقِينَ ﴿٣٣﴾

قَالَ رَبِّ إِنِّى قَتَلْتُ مِنْهُمْ نَفْسًا فَأَخَافُ أَن يَقْتُلُونِ ﴿٣٣﴾

وَأَخِى هَٰرُونُ هُوَ أَفْصَحُ مِنِّى لِسَانًا فَأَرْسِلْهُ مَعِىَ رِدْءًا يُصَدِّقُنِىٓ إِنِّىٓ أَخَافُ أَن يُكَذِّبُونِ ﴿٣٤﴾

قَالَ سَنَشُدُّ عَضُدَكَ بِأَخِيكَ وَنَجْعَلُ لَكُمَا سُلْطَٰنًا فَلَا يَصِلُونَ إِلَيْكُمَا بِـَٔايَٰتِنَآ أَنتُمَا وَمَنِ ٱتَّبَعَكُمَا ٱلْغَٰلِبُونَ ﴿٣٥﴾

فَلَمَّا جَآءَهُم مُّوسَىٰ بِـَٔايَٰتِنَا بَيِّنَٰتٍ قَالُوا۟ مَا هَٰذَآ إِلَّا سِحْرٌ مُّفْتَرًى وَمَا سَمِعْنَا بِهَٰذَا فِىٓ ءَابَآئِنَا ٱلْأَوَّلِينَ ﴿٣٦﴾

---

676. Allah.

37. Moses then said: "My Lord knows better him who brings the guidance from Him, and him who will have the reward of the ultimate abode. The wrongdoers shall never prosper."

38. Pharaoh then said: "O my dignitaries, I did not know that you had any god but me. So kindle for me, O Haman, a fire upon the clay and build me a tower that I might behold the God of Moses. I really think he is a liar."

39. And he and his troops waxed proud in the land unjustly, and thought that they will not be returned to Us.

40. Then We seized him and his troops and cast them into the sea; so behold what was the end of the wrongdoers!

41. And We made them leaders calling to the Fire; and on the Day of Resurrection, they will not be supported.

42. And We pursued them in this world with a curse, and on the Day of Resurrection they will be among the despised.

43. We have given Moses the Book, after We had destroyed the former generations, to serve as examples to mankind and as guidance and mercy, in order that they may remember well.

44. You were not on the western side [of the Mountain], when We decreed the commandment to Moses, and you were not one of the witnesses.

45. But We created other generations whose ages lasted for too long, and you were not dwelling among the inhabitants of Midian reciting Our Verses to them, but We were sending other Messengers.

وَقَالَ مُوسَىٰ رَبِّي أَعْلَمُ بِمَن جَآءَ بِٱلْهُدَىٰ مِنْ عِندِهِۦ وَمَن تَكُونُ لَهُۥ عَٰقِبَةُ ٱلدَّارِ إِنَّهُۥ لَا يُفْلِحُ ٱلظَّٰلِمُونَ ﴿٣٧﴾

وَقَالَ فِرْعَوْنُ يَٰٓأَيُّهَا ٱلْمَلَأُ مَا عَلِمْتُ لَكُم مِّنْ إِلَٰهٍ غَيْرِى فَأَوْقِدْ لِى يَٰهَٰمَٰنُ عَلَى ٱلطِّينِ فَٱجْعَل لِّى صَرْحًا لَّعَلِّىٓ أَطَّلِعُ إِلَىٰٓ إِلَٰهِ مُوسَىٰ وَإِنِّى لَأَظُنُّهُۥ مِنَ ٱلْكَٰذِبِينَ ﴿٣٨﴾

وَٱسْتَكْبَرَ هُوَ وَجُنُودُهُۥ فِى ٱلْأَرْضِ بِغَيْرِ ٱلْحَقِّ وَظَنُّوٓا۟ أَنَّهُمْ إِلَيْنَا لَا يُرْجَعُونَ ﴿٣٩﴾

فَأَخَذْنَٰهُ وَجُنُودَهُۥ فَنَبَذْنَٰهُمْ فِى ٱلْيَمِّ فَٱنظُرْ كَيْفَ كَانَ عَٰقِبَةُ ٱلظَّٰلِمِينَ ﴿٤٠﴾

وَجَعَلْنَٰهُمْ أَئِمَّةً يَدْعُونَ إِلَى ٱلنَّارِ وَيَوْمَ ٱلْقِيَٰمَةِ لَا يُنصَرُونَ ﴿٤١﴾

وَأَتْبَعْنَٰهُمْ فِى هَٰذِهِ ٱلدُّنْيَا لَعْنَةً وَيَوْمَ ٱلْقِيَٰمَةِ هُم مِّنَ ٱلْمَقْبُوحِينَ ﴿٤٢﴾

وَلَقَدْ ءَاتَيْنَا مُوسَى ٱلْكِتَٰبَ مِنۢ بَعْدِ مَآ أَهْلَكْنَا ٱلْقُرُونَ ٱلْأُولَىٰ بَصَآئِرَ لِلنَّاسِ وَهُدًى وَرَحْمَةً لَّعَلَّهُمْ يَتَذَكَّرُونَ ﴿٤٣﴾

وَمَا كُنتَ بِجَانِبِ ٱلْغَرْبِىِّ إِذْ قَضَيْنَآ إِلَىٰ مُوسَى ٱلْأَمْرَ وَمَا كُنتَ مِنَ ٱلشَّٰهِدِينَ ﴿٤٤﴾

وَلَٰكِنَّآ أَنشَأْنَا قُرُونًا فَتَطَاوَلَ عَلَيْهِمُ ٱلْعُمُرُ وَمَا كُنتَ ثَاوِيًا فِىٓ أَهْلِ مَدْيَنَ تَتْلُوا۟ عَلَيْهِمْ ءَايَٰتِنَا وَلَٰكِنَّا كُنَّا مُرْسِلِينَ ﴿٤٥﴾

46. You were not by the side of the Mountain when We called, but [We are sending you][677] as a mercy from your Lord, to warn a people who had no warner prior to you, that perchance they might remember.

47. And lest an adversity befall them, on account of what their hands have perpetrated, so that they could say: "Our Lord, if only You had sent us a Messenger, that we might follow Your Signs and be among the believers."

48. But, when the Truth came to them from Us, they said: "If only he[678] had been given the like of what Moses had received?" Had they not disbelieved in what Moses received formerly? They said: "Two sorceries backing each other up", and they said: "We are disbelieving in both."

49. Say: "Bring, then, a Book from Allah giving better guidance than both,[679] and I will follow it, if you are truthful."

50. If, however, they do not answer you, then know that they only follow their fancies; and who is more in error than he who follows his own fancy without guidance from Allah. Allah, surely, does not guide the wrongdoing people.

51. And now, We have communicated the Word to them, that perchance they may remember.

52. Those, to whom we have given the Book before it,[680] do believe in it.

وَمَا كُنتَ بِجَانِبِ ٱلطُّورِ إِذْ نَادَيْنَا وَلَٰكِن رَّحْمَةً مِّن رَّبِّكَ لِتُنذِرَ قَوْمًا مَّآ أَتَىٰهُم مِّن نَّذِيرٍ مِّن قَبْلِكَ لَعَلَّهُمْ يَتَذَكَّرُونَ ۝

وَلَوْلَآ أَن تُصِيبَهُم مُّصِيبَةٌ بِمَا قَدَّمَتْ أَيْدِيهِمْ فَيَقُولُوا۟ رَبَّنَا لَوْلَآ أَرْسَلْتَ إِلَيْنَا رَسُولًا فَنَتَّبِعَ ءَايَٰتِكَ وَنَكُونَ مِنَ ٱلْمُؤْمِنِينَ ۝

فَلَمَّا جَآءَهُمُ ٱلْحَقُّ مِنْ عِندِنَا قَالُوا۟ لَوْلَآ أُوتِىَ مِثْلَ مَآ أُوتِىَ مُوسَىٰٓ أَوَلَمْ يَكْفُرُوا۟ بِمَآ أُوتِىَ مُوسَىٰ مِن قَبْلُ قَالُوا۟ سِحْرَانِ تَظَٰهَرَا وَقَالُوٓا۟ إِنَّا بِكُلٍّ كَٰفِرُونَ ۝

قُلْ فَأْتُوا۟ بِكِتَٰبٍ مِّنْ عِندِ ٱللَّهِ هُوَ أَهْدَىٰ مِنْهُمَآ أَتَّبِعْهُ إِن كُنتُمْ صَٰدِقِينَ ۝

فَإِن لَّمْ يَسْتَجِيبُوا۟ لَكَ فَٱعْلَمْ أَنَّمَا يَتَّبِعُونَ أَهْوَآءَهُمْ وَمَنْ أَضَلُّ مِمَّنِ ٱتَّبَعَ هَوَىٰهُ بِغَيْرِ هُدًى مِّنَ ٱللَّهِ إِنَّ ٱللَّهَ لَا يَهْدِى ٱلْقَوْمَ ٱلظَّٰلِمِينَ ۝

۞ وَلَقَدْ وَصَّلْنَا لَهُمُ ٱلْقَوْلَ لَعَلَّهُمْ يَتَذَكَّرُونَ ۝

ٱلَّذِينَ ءَاتَيْنَٰهُمُ ٱلْكِتَٰبَ مِن قَبْلِهِ هُم بِهِۦ يُؤْمِنُونَ ۝

---

677. Muhammad.
678. Muhammad.
679. The Qur'an and the Torah.
680. The Qur'an.

53. When it is recited to them, they say: "We believe in it; it is the truth from our Lord. We were, even prior to it, submissive [to Allah]."[681]

وَإِذَا يُتْلَىٰ عَلَيْهِمْ قَالُوٓا۟ ءَامَنَّا بِهِۦٓ إِنَّهُ ٱلْحَقُّ مِن رَّبِّنَآ إِنَّا كُنَّا مِن قَبْلِهِۦ مُسْلِمِينَ ۞

54. Those shall be given their wages twice, because they stood fast, and will ward off the evil deed with the good one, and out of what We provided them with will spend freely.

أُو۟لَٰٓئِكَ يُؤْتَوْنَ أَجْرَهُم مَّرَّتَيْنِ بِمَا صَبَرُوا۟ وَيَدْرَءُونَ بِٱلْحَسَنَةِ ٱلسَّيِّئَةَ وَمِمَّا رَزَقْنَٰهُمْ يُنفِقُونَ ۞

55. And when they hear idle talk, they turn away from it and say: "We have our works and you have your works. Peace be upon you; we do not desire the company of the ignorant."

وَإِذَا سَمِعُوا۟ ٱللَّغْوَ أَعْرَضُوا۟ عَنْهُ وَقَالُوا۟ لَنَآ أَعْمَٰلُنَا وَلَكُمْ أَعْمَٰلُكُمْ سَلَٰمٌ عَلَيْكُمْ لَا نَبْتَغِى ٱلْجَٰهِلِينَ ۞

56. You do not guide whom you wish, but Allah guides whom He wishes, and He knows better the well-guided.

إِنَّكَ لَا تَهْدِى مَنْ أَحْبَبْتَ وَلَٰكِنَّ ٱللَّهَ يَهْدِى مَن يَشَآءُ وَهُوَ أَعْلَمُ بِٱلْمُهْتَدِينَ ۞

57. And they said: "If we follow the guidance with you, we will be snatched from our land." Have We not established a safe sanctuary for them, to which are brought all kinds of fruit, as provision, from Ourselves? However, most of them do not know.

وَقَالُوٓا۟ إِن نَّتَّبِعِ ٱلْهُدَىٰ مَعَكَ نُتَخَطَّفْ مِنْ أَرْضِنَآ أَوَلَمْ نُمَكِّن لَّهُمْ حَرَمًا ءَامِنًا يُجْبَىٰٓ إِلَيْهِ ثَمَرَٰتُ كُلِّ شَىْءٍ رِّزْقًا مِّن لَّدُنَّا وَلَٰكِنَّ أَكْثَرَهُمْ لَا يَعْلَمُونَ ۞

58. And how many a city We have destroyed that had grown prodigal in its living. There are its dwellings, left uninhabited after they were gone, except for a few. We became the inheritors.

وَكَمْ أَهْلَكْنَا مِن قَرْيَةٍ بَطِرَتْ مَعِيشَتَهَا فَتِلْكَ مَسَٰكِنُهُمْ لَمْ تُسْكَن مِّنۢ بَعْدِهِمْ إِلَّا قَلِيلًا وَكُنَّا نَحْنُ ٱلْوَٰرِثِينَ ۞

59. Your Lord, however, never destroys the cities, unless He first sends to their mother-city a Messenger, to recite to them Our Revelations. And We never destroy any cities, unless their inhabitants are wrongdoers.

وَمَا كَانَ رَبُّكَ مُهْلِكَ ٱلْقُرَىٰ حَتَّىٰ يَبْعَثَ فِىٓ أُمِّهَا رَسُولًا يَتْلُوا۟ عَلَيْهِمْ ءَايَٰتِنَا وَمَا كُنَّا مُهْلِكِى ٱلْقُرَىٰٓ إِلَّا وَأَهْلُهَا ظَٰلِمُونَ ۞

60. Whatever you have been given is merely the pleasure of this life and its finery; but what Allah has in His possession is better and more lasting. Do you not understand?

وَمَآ أُوتِيتُم مِّن شَىْءٍ فَمَتَٰعُ ٱلْحَيَوٰةِ ٱلدُّنْيَا وَزِينَتُهَا وَمَا عِندَ ٱللَّهِ خَيْرٌ وَأَبْقَىٰٓ أَفَلَا تَعْقِلُونَ ۞

---

681. That is, Muslims.

أَفَمَن وَعَدْنَـٰهُ وَعْدًا حَسَنًا فَهُوَ لَـٰقِيهِ كَمَن مَّتَّعْنَـٰهُ مَتَـٰعَ ٱلْحَيَوٰةِ ٱلدُّنْيَا ثُمَّ هُوَ يَوْمَ ٱلْقِيَـٰمَةِ مِنَ ٱلْمُحْضَرِينَ ۝

61. Is he, then, to whom We have promised a fair promise then bestowed it, like one to whom We granted enjoyment in the present life and shall summon on the Day of Resurrection?

وَيَوْمَ يُنَادِيهِمْ فَيَقُولُ أَيْنَ شُرَكَآءِىَ ٱلَّذِينَ كُنتُمْ تَزْعُمُونَ ۝

62. On the Day that He shall call them saying: "Where are My associates that you used to allege?"

قَالَ ٱلَّذِينَ حَقَّ عَلَيْهِمُ ٱلْقَوْلُ رَبَّنَا هَـٰٓؤُلَآءِ ٱلَّذِينَ أَغْوَيْنَآ أَغْوَيْنَـٰهُمْ كَمَا غَوَيْنَا تَبَرَّأْنَآ إِلَيْكَ مَا كَانُوٓا۟ إِيَّانَا يَعْبُدُونَ ۝

63. Those upon whom the sentence will be passed shall say: "Lord, those whom we induced into error, we induced into error just as we were induced. We proclaim our innocence to You. It was not us they were worshipping."

وَقِيلَ ٱدْعُوا۟ شُرَكَآءَكُمْ فَدَعَوْهُمْ فَلَمْ يَسْتَجِيبُوا۟ لَهُمْ وَرَأَوُا۟ ٱلْعَذَابَ لَوْ أَنَّهُمْ كَانُوا۟ يَهْتَدُونَ ۝

64. And it will be said to them: "Call your associates"; and so they call them, but the associates will not answer. They saw the punishment and they wished they had been well-guided.

وَيَوْمَ يُنَادِيهِمْ فَيَقُولُ مَاذَآ أَجَبْتُمُ ٱلْمُرْسَلِينَ ۝

65. On the Day He will call them, saying: "What did you answer the Messengers?"

فَعَمِيَتْ عَلَيْهِمُ ٱلْأَنۢبَآءُ يَوْمَئِذٍ فَهُمْ لَا يَتَسَآءَلُونَ ۝

66. On that day, the tidings will be obscured for them, and so they will not question each other.

فَأَمَّا مَن تَابَ وَءَامَنَ وَعَمِلَ صَـٰلِحًا فَعَسَىٰٓ أَن يَكُونَ مِنَ ٱلْمُفْلِحِينَ ۝

67. But he who repents, believes and does the righteous deed, perchance he will be among the prosperous.

وَرَبُّكَ يَخْلُقُ مَا يَشَآءُ وَيَخْتَارُ مَا كَانَ لَهُمُ ٱلْخِيَرَةُ سُبْحَـٰنَ ٱللَّهِ وَتَعَـٰلَىٰ عَمَّا يُشْرِكُونَ ۝

68. Your Lord creates and chooses whatever He wills; they have no choice. Glory be to Allah and may He be exalted above what they associate!

وَرَبُّكَ يَعْلَمُ مَا تُكِنُّ صُدُورُهُمْ وَمَا يُعْلِنُونَ ۝

69. And Your Lord knows what their breasts conceal and what they reveal.

وَهُوَ ٱللَّهُ لَآ إِلَـٰهَ إِلَّا هُوَ لَهُ ٱلْحَمْدُ فِى ٱلْأُولَىٰ وَٱلْءَاخِرَةِ وَلَهُ ٱلْحُكْمُ وَإِلَيْهِ تُرْجَعُونَ ۝

70. He is Allah; there is no god but He. His is the praise in the herebelow and the Hereafter and His is the judgement, and unto Him you will be returned.

71. Say: "Have you considered, what if Allah had made the night to last for you continuously till the Day of Resurrection? What other god than Allah will bring you light? Do you not hear?"

72. Say: "Have you considered, what if Allah had made the day to last for you continuously till the Day of Resurrection? What other god than Allah will bring you the night to rest in? Do you not see?"

73. It was out of His Mercy that He created the day and the night, so that you may rest in it and to seek some of His Bounty, that perchance you may give thanks.

74. On the Day He will call them saying: "Where are My associates which you used to allege?"

75. And We picked from every nation a witness and said: "Produce your proof." Then they knew that the truth is Allah's and those they used to invent[682] strayed away from them.

76. Now Karoon[683] belonged to the clan of Moses, then he lorded it over them. We had given him treasures, the keys of which would weigh down the mighty band. When his people said to him: "Do not exult; Allah does not like the exultant;

77. "But seek, thanks to what Allah gave you, the Hereafter, and do not forget your portion of the herebelow. Be charitable, as Allah has been charitable to you, and do not seek corruption in the land; for Allah does not like the seekers of corruption."

---

682. Their idols.
683. That is, Korah son of Izhar, who rebelled against Moses and Aaron and challenged their authority. *Numbers* 16, 1-35.

78. He said: "What I have been given is due to knowledge I possess." Did he not know that Allah has destroyed, before him, generations of men stronger than he and richer? However, the criminals shall not be questioned regarding their sins.

قَالَ إِنَّمَا أُوتِيتُهُ عَلَىٰ عِلْمٍ عِندِى أَوَلَمْ يَعْلَمْ أَنَّ ٱللَّهَ قَدْ أَهْلَكَ مِن قَبْلِهِ مِنَ ٱلْقُرُونِ مَنْ هُوَ أَشَدُّ مِنْهُ قُوَّةً وَأَكْثَرُ جَمْعاً وَلَا يُسْـَٔلُ عَن ذُنُوبِهِمُ ٱلْمُجْرِمُونَ ۝

79. And so he went out unto his people in his finery. Those who desire the present life said: "Would that we possessed the like of what Karoon has been given. He is indeed a very fortunate man."

فَخَرَجَ عَلَىٰ قَوْمِهِ فِى زِينَتِهِ قَالَ ٱلَّذِينَ يُرِيدُونَ ٱلْحَيَوٰةَ ٱلدُّنْيَا يَٰلَيْتَ لَنَا مِثْلَ مَا أُوتِىَ قَٰرُونُ إِنَّهُ لَذُو حَظٍّ عَظِيمٍ ۝

80. But those possessed of knowledge said: "Woe betide you; the Reward of Allah is better for him who believes and acts righteously, and that is not accorded except to the steadfast."

وَقَالَ ٱلَّذِينَ أُوتُوا۟ ٱلْعِلْمَ وَيْلَكُمْ ثَوَابُ ٱللَّهِ خَيْرٌ لِمَنْ ءَامَنَ وَعَمِلَ صَٰلِحاً وَلَا يُلَقَّىٰهَآ إِلَّا ٱلصَّٰبِرُونَ ۝

81. Then, We caused the earth to cave in on him and his household; and so he had no company to support him against Allah; and he was not one of the winners.

فَخَسَفْنَا بِهِ وَبِدَارِهِ ٱلْأَرْضَ فَمَا كَانَ لَهُ مِن فِئَةٍ يَنصُرُونَهُ مِن دُونِ ٱللَّهِ وَمَا كَانَ مِنَ ٱلْمُنتَصِرِينَ ۝

82. And those who had wished they were in his place yesterday were saying: "No wonder that Allah increases the provision to whomever He wishes of His servants and restricts it. Had Allah not been Gracious to us, He would have caused the earth to cave in on us. No wonder that the unbelievers will never prosper."

وَأَصْبَحَ ٱلَّذِينَ تَمَنَّوْا۟ مَكَانَهُ بِٱلْأَمْسِ يَقُولُونَ وَيْكَأَنَّ ٱللَّهَ يَبْسُطُ ٱلرِّزْقَ لِمَن يَشَآءُ مِنْ عِبَادِهِ وَيَقْدِرُ لَوْلَآ أَن مَّنَّ ٱللَّهُ عَلَيْنَا لَخَسَفَ بِنَا وَيْكَأَنَّهُ لَا يُفْلِحُ ٱلْكَٰفِرُونَ ۝

83. That is the Last Abode; We assign it to those who do not desire exaltation on earth or corruption; and the happy outcome belongs to the God-fearing.

تِلْكَ ٱلدَّارُ ٱلْءَاخِرَةُ نَجْعَلُهَا لِلَّذِينَ لَا يُرِيدُونَ عُلُوّاً فِى ٱلْأَرْضِ وَلَا فَسَاداً وَٱلْعَٰقِبَةُ لِلْمُتَّقِينَ ۝

84. Whoever comes up with a good deed will receive a reward better than it, but whoever comes up with an evil deed [should know] that the evildoers will not be rewarded except for what they have done.

مَن جَآءَ بِٱلْحَسَنَةِ فَلَهُ خَيْرٌ مِّنْهَا وَمَن جَآءَ بِٱلسَّيِّئَةِ فَلَا يُجْزَى ٱلَّذِينَ عَمِلُوا۟ ٱلسَّيِّـَٔاتِ إِلَّا مَا كَانُوا۟ يَعْمَلُونَ ۝

85. He Who imparted the Qur'an to you will surely return you to a safe resort. Say: "My Lord knows best who has brought the guidance and who is in manifest error."

86. You did not expect that the Book will be transmitted to you, except as a mercy from your Lord. So, do not be a partisan of the unbelievers.

87. And let them not divert you from the Revelations of Allah after they have been sent down to you. Call upon your Lord, and do not be one of the idolaters.

88. Do not call, besides Allah, upon any other god. There is no god but He. Everything will perish save His Face. His is the Judgement, and unto Him you shall all be returned.

Sûrat Al-'Ankabut, (The Spider) 29

In the Name of Allah,
the Compassionate, the Merciful

1. Alif - Lam - Mim.[684]

2. Have the people supposed that they will be left alone to say: "We believe", and then they will not be tested?

3. We have indeed tested those who preceded them; and Allah shall certainly know those who speak the truth and shall know those who lie.

4. Or have those who do the evil deeds 'supposed that they will outstrip Us? Wretched is what they judge!

---

684. The same letters occur at the beginning of Surahs 30, 31 and 32; the significance of this is not clear.

مَن كَانَ يَرْجُواْ لِقَآءَ ٱللَّهِ فَإِنَّ أَجَلَ ٱللَّهِ لَآتٍ وَهُوَ ٱلسَّمِيعُ ٱلْعَلِيمُ ۝

5. He who expects to encounter Allah, surely Allah's Term shall come; and He is the All-Hearing, the All-Knowing.

وَمَن جَهَدَ فَإِنَّمَا يُجَهِدُ لِنَفْسِهِۦٓ إِنَّ ٱللَّهَ لَغَنِيٌّ عَنِ ٱلْعَٰلَمِينَ ۝

6. He who strives only strives for himself. Allah is All-Sufficient, in need of no being.

وَٱلَّذِينَ ءَامَنُواْ وَعَمِلُواْ ٱلصَّٰلِحَٰتِ لَنُكَفِّرَنَّ عَنْهُمْ سَيِّـَٔاتِهِمْ وَلَنَجْزِيَنَّهُمْ أَحْسَنَ ٱلَّذِى كَانُواْ يَعْمَلُونَ ۝

7. And those who believe and do the righteous deeds, We shall remit their sins, and We shall reward them with the best of what they used to do.

وَوَصَّيْنَا ٱلْإِنسَٰنَ بِوَٰلِدَيْهِ حُسْنًا وَإِن جَٰهَدَاكَ لِتُشْرِكَ بِى مَا لَيْسَ لَكَ بِهِۦ عِلْمٌ فَلَا تُطِعْهُمَآ إِلَىَّ مَرْجِعُكُمْ فَأُنَبِّئُكُم بِمَا كُنتُمْ تَعْمَلُونَ ۝

8. We have commanded man to be kind to his parents; but if they strive with you to associate with Me that of which you have no knowledge, then do not obey them. Unto Me is your return and I will tell you what you used to do.

وَٱلَّذِينَ ءَامَنُواْ وَعَمِلُواْ ٱلصَّٰلِحَٰتِ لَنُدْخِلَنَّهُمْ فِى ٱلصَّٰلِحِينَ ۝

9. Those who believe and do the righteous deeds, We shall admit them into the company of the righteous.

وَمِنَ ٱلنَّاسِ مَن يَقُولُ ءَامَنَّا بِٱللَّهِ فَإِذَآ أُوذِىَ فِى ٱللَّهِ جَعَلَ فِتْنَةَ ٱلنَّاسِ كَعَذَابِ ٱللَّهِ وَلَئِن جَآءَ نَصْرٌ مِّن رَّبِّكَ لَيَقُولُنَّ إِنَّا كُنَّا مَعَكُمْ أَوَ لَيْسَ ٱللَّهُ بِأَعْلَمَ بِمَا فِى صُدُورِ ٱلْعَٰلَمِينَ ۝

10. There are some people who say: "We believe in Allah", but if one of them is injured on account of Allah, he reckons the persecution of men similar to Allah's punishment. If, however, victory comes from your Lord, they[685] will say: "We were with you." Does not Allah know better what is in the breasts of the whole of mankind?

وَلَيَعْلَمَنَّ ٱللَّهُ ٱلَّذِينَ ءَامَنُواْ وَلَيَعْلَمَنَّ ٱلْمُنَٰفِقِينَ ۝

11. And Allah certainly knows the believers and He knows the hypocrites.

وَقَالَ ٱلَّذِينَ كَفَرُواْ لِلَّذِينَ ءَامَنُواْ ٱتَّبِعُواْ سَبِيلَنَا وَلْنَحْمِلْ خَطَٰيَٰكُمْ وَمَا هُم بِحَٰمِلِينَ مِنْ خَطَٰيَٰهُم مِّن شَىْءٍ إِنَّهُمْ لَكَٰذِبُونَ ۝

12. The unbelievers said to the believers: "Follow our path and let us bear your sins"; but they will not bear any of their sins. Indeed they are liars.

وَلَيَحْمِلُنَّ أَثْقَالَهُمْ وَأَثْقَالًا مَّعَ أَثْقَالِهِمْ وَلَيُسْـَٔلُنَّ يَوْمَ ٱلْقِيَٰمَةِ عَمَّا كَانُواْ يَفْتَرُونَ ۝

13. They shall bear their own burdens, plus burdens upon burdens, and they will be questioned on the Day of Resurrection concerning what they used to fabricate.

---

685. The idolaters.

14. We sent Noah to his own people and he tarried among them a thousand years minus fifty years. Then the Deluge overtook them; for they were wrongdoers.

15. Yet We delivered him, together with the companions of the Ark, and We made it a Sign unto mankind.

16. And (remember) Abraham, when he said to his people: "Worship Allah and fear Him; that is far better for you, if only you knew.

17. "Indeed, you only worship, apart from Allah, mere idols, and you invent falsehood. Surely, those you worship, apart from Allah, have no power to provide for you. So, seek provision from Allah, worship Him and give Him thanks. You shall be returned unto Him.

18. "And if you denounce [the Prophets], other nations before you have denounced too. It is only incumbent on the Messenger to deliver the message plainly."

19. Have they not seen how Allah originates creation, then brings it back into being? That for Allah is an easy matter.

20. Say: "Travel in the land and see how Allah originated the creation; then Allah produces the other generation.[686] Allah truly has power over everything."

21. He punishes whom He pleases and has mercy on whom He pleases, and to Him you will be turned over.

22. You cannot thwart Him on earth or in heaven, and you have, apart from Allah, no friend or supporter.

23. Those who disbelieved in Allah's Signs and His Encounter are those who despaired of My Mercy. To those is reserved a very painful punishment.

686.That is, Resurrection.

24. His own people's only reply was their saying: "Kill him and burn him", but Allah delivered him from fire. Surely, in that are signs for a people who believe.

25. He (Abraham) said: "You only took, apart from Allah, idols, as a bond between you in the present life. Then on the Day of Resurrection you will disbelieve in each other and curse each other. Your refuge shall be the Fire and you will have no supporters."

26. Then Lot believed in him[687] and he said: "I will emigrate to my Lord; He is indeed the All-Mighty, the Wise."

27. And We granted him Isaac and Jacob and conferred on his progeny the Prophethood and the Book, and gave him his reward in this life; and in the Hereafter he shall be among the righteous.

28. And (remember) Lot, when he said to his people: "You are committing the foul act[688] which no one in the whole world ever committed before you."

29. "You approach men and waylay the traveller and commit in your gatherings reprehensible acts." To which the only reply of his people was: "Bring upon us Allah's punishment, if you are truthful."

30. He said: "Lord, support me against the workers of corruption."

31. When Our Emissaries[689] brought Abraham the good news, they said: "We are going to destroy the inhabitants of this city. Its inhabitants have indeed been wrongdoers."

فَمَا كَانَ جَوَابَ قَوْمِهِ إِلَّا أَن قَالُوا اقْتُلُوهُ أَوْ حَرِّقُوهُ فَأَنجَاهُ اللَّهُ مِنَ النَّارِ إِنَّ فِي ذَٰلِكَ لَآيَاتٍ لِّقَوْمٍ يُؤْمِنُونَ ۝

وَقَالَ إِنَّمَا اتَّخَذْتُم مِّن دُونِ اللَّهِ أَوْثَانًا مَّوَدَّةَ بَيْنِكُمْ فِي الْحَيَاةِ الدُّنْيَا ثُمَّ يَوْمَ الْقِيَامَةِ يَكْفُرُ بَعْضُكُم بِبَعْضٍ وَيَلْعَنُ بَعْضُكُم بَعْضًا وَمَأْوَاكُمُ النَّارُ وَمَا لَكُم مِّن نَّاصِرِينَ ۝

۞ فَآمَنَ لَهُ لُوطٌ وَقَالَ إِنِّي مُهَاجِرٌ إِلَىٰ رَبِّي إِنَّهُ هُوَ الْعَزِيزُ الْحَكِيمُ ۝

وَوَهَبْنَا لَهُ إِسْحَاقَ وَيَعْقُوبَ وَجَعَلْنَا فِي ذُرِّيَّتِهِ النُّبُوَّةَ وَالْكِتَابَ وَآتَيْنَاهُ أَجْرَهُ فِي الدُّنْيَا وَإِنَّهُ فِي الْآخِرَةِ لَمِنَ الصَّالِحِينَ ۝

وَلُوطًا إِذْ قَالَ لِقَوْمِهِ إِنَّكُمْ لَتَأْتُونَ الْفَاحِشَةَ مَا سَبَقَكُم بِهَا مِنْ أَحَدٍ مِّنَ الْعَالَمِينَ ۝

أَئِنَّكُمْ لَتَأْتُونَ الرِّجَالَ وَتَقْطَعُونَ السَّبِيلَ وَتَأْتُونَ فِي نَادِيكُمُ الْمُنكَرَ فَمَا كَانَ جَوَابَ قَوْمِهِ إِلَّا أَن قَالُوا ائْتِنَا بِعَذَابِ اللَّهِ إِن كُنتَ مِنَ الصَّادِقِينَ ۝

قَالَ رَبِّ انصُرْنِي عَلَى الْقَوْمِ الْمُفْسِدِينَ ۝

وَلَمَّا جَاءَتْ رُسُلُنَا إِبْرَاهِيمَ بِالْبُشْرَىٰ قَالُوا إِنَّا مُهْلِكُوا أَهْلِ هَٰذِهِ الْقَرْيَةِ إِنَّ أَهْلَهَا كَانُوا ظَالِمِينَ ۝

---

687. Abraham.
688. That is, Sodomy.
689. The angels.

32. He said: "Lot is in it"; they said: "We know better who is in it. We shall deliver him and his household, except for his wife; for she is one of those who will stay behind."

33. Then, when Our Emissaries came to Lot, he was troubled and distressed on their account, and they said: "Do not fear and do not grieve; we shall deliver you and your household, except for your wife; she is one of those who will stay behind."

34. We are sending down upon the inhabitants of this city a scourge from heaven, because of their sins.

35. And we have left as a vestige of it a clear sign to a people who understand.

36. And to Midian We sent their brother, Shu'ayb, who said: "O my people, worship Allah and hope for the Last Day, and do not spread corruption in the land."

37. They denounced him as a liar and so the tremor[690] overtook them, and they were left in their home prostrate.

38. And [remember] 'Ad and Thamud. It has become clear to you from their dwellings [what their fate was]. Satan embellished for them their deeds, barring them from the Path, while they were clear-sighted.

39. And [remember] Karoon, Pharaoh and Haman. Moses came to them with the clear proofs, but they waxed proud in the land and they did not outstrip Us.

40. Each, We seized for his sin. Upon some We loosed a squall of pebbles, some were overwhelmed with the Cry, some We caused the ground to cave in under and some We drowned. Allah did not wrong them, but they wronged themselves.

قَالَ إِنَّ فِيهَا لُوطًا قَالُوا نَحْنُ أَعْلَمُ بِمَن فِيهَا لَنُنَجِّيَنَّهُ وَأَهْلَهُ إِلَّا امْرَأَتَهُ كَانَتْ مِنَ الْغَابِرِينَ ۝

وَلَمَّا أَن جَاءَتْ رُسُلُنَا لُوطًا سِيءَ بِهِمْ وَضَاقَ بِهِمْ ذَرْعًا وَقَالُوا لَا تَخَفْ وَلَا تَحْزَنْ إِنَّا مُنَجُّوكَ وَأَهْلَكَ إِلَّا امْرَأَتَكَ كَانَتْ مِنَ الْغَابِرِينَ ۝

إِنَّا مُنزِلُونَ عَلَى أَهْلِ هَذِهِ الْقَرْيَةِ رِجْزًا مِّنَ السَّمَاءِ بِمَا كَانُوا يَفْسُقُونَ ۝

وَلَقَد تَّرَكْنَا مِنْهَا آيَةً بَيِّنَةً لِّقَوْمٍ يَعْقِلُونَ ۝

وَإِلَى مَدْيَنَ أَخَاهُمْ شُعَيْبًا فَقَالَ يَقَوْمِ اعْبُدُوا اللَّهَ وَارْجُوا الْيَوْمَ الْآخِرَ وَلَا تَعْثَوْا فِي الْأَرْضِ مُفْسِدِينَ ۝

فَكَذَّبُوهُ فَأَخَذَتْهُمُ الرَّجْفَةُ فَأَصْبَحُوا فِي دَارِهِمْ جَاثِمِينَ ۝

وَعَادًا وَثَمُودَا وَقَد تَّبَيَّنَ لَكُم مِّن مَّسَاكِنِهِمْ وَزَيَّنَ لَهُمُ الشَّيْطَانُ أَعْمَالَهُمْ فَصَدَّهُمْ عَنِ السَّبِيلِ وَكَانُوا مُسْتَبْصِرِينَ ۝

وَقَارُونَ وَفِرْعَوْنَ وَهَامَانَ وَلَقَدْ جَاءَهُم مُّوسَى بِالْبَيِّنَاتِ فَاسْتَكْبَرُوا فِي الْأَرْضِ وَمَا كَانُوا سَابِقِينَ ۝

فَكُلًّا أَخَذْنَا بِذَنبِهِ فَمِنْهُم مَّنْ أَرْسَلْنَا عَلَيْهِ حَاصِبًا وَمِنْهُم مَّنْ أَخَذَتْهُ الصَّيْحَةُ وَمِنْهُم مَّنْ خَسَفْنَا بِهِ الْأَرْضَ وَمِنْهُم مَّنْ أَغْرَقْنَا وَمَا كَانَ اللَّهُ لِيَظْلِمَهُمْ وَلَكِن كَانُوا أَنفُسَهُمْ يَظْلِمُونَ ۝

---

690. Of punishment (al Tabari).

41. The case of those who took up other protectors, apart from Allah, is like that of the spider who built a house. Truly, the most brittle of houses is the house of the spider, if only they knew.

مَثَلُ ٱلَّذِينَ ٱتَّخَذُوا۟ مِن دُونِ ٱللَّهِ أَوْلِيَآءَ كَمَثَلِ ٱلْعَنكَبُوتِ ٱتَّخَذَتْ بَيْتًا وَإِنَّ أَوْهَنَ ٱلْبُيُوتِ لَبَيْتُ ٱلْعَنكَبُوتِ لَوْ كَانُوا۟ يَعْلَمُونَ ﴿٤١﴾

42. Allah knows what they call upon, apart from Him, and He is the All-Mighty, the Wise.

إِنَّ ٱللَّهَ يَعْلَمُ مَا يَدْعُونَ مِن دُونِهِۦ مِن شَىْءٍ وَهُوَ ٱلْعَزِيزُ ٱلْحَكِيمُ ﴿٤٢﴾

43. Those are the parables We devise for mankind, and only the learned will grasp them.

وَتِلْكَ ٱلْأَمْثَٰلُ نَضْرِبُهَا لِلنَّاسِ وَمَا يَعْقِلُهَآ إِلَّا ٱلْعَٰلِمُونَ ﴿٤٣﴾

44. Allah created the heavens and the earth in truth. Surely there is in that a sign for those who believe.

خَلَقَ ٱللَّهُ ٱلسَّمَٰوَٰتِ وَٱلْأَرْضَ بِٱلْحَقِّ إِنَّ فِى ذَٰلِكَ لَءَايَةً لِّلْمُؤْمِنِينَ ﴿٤٤﴾

45. Recite what has been revealed to you of the Book and perform the prayer. Prayer surely forbids the foul act and abomination. Allah's remembrance is greater and Allah knows what you do.

ٱتْلُ مَآ أُوحِىَ إِلَيْكَ مِنَ ٱلْكِتَٰبِ وَأَقِمِ ٱلصَّلَوٰةَ إِنَّ ٱلصَّلَوٰةَ تَنْهَىٰ عَنِ ٱلْفَحْشَآءِ وَٱلْمُنكَرِ وَلَذِكْرُ ٱللَّهِ أَكْبَرُ وَٱللَّهُ يَعْلَمُ مَا تَصْنَعُونَ ﴿٤٥﴾

46. Do not dispute with the people of the Book save in the fairest way; except for those of them who are evildoers. And say: "We believe in what has been sent down to us and what has been sent down to you. Our God and your God are one and to Him we are submissive."

۞ وَلَا تُجَٰدِلُوٓا۟ أَهْلَ ٱلْكِتَٰبِ إِلَّا بِٱلَّتِى هِىَ أَحْسَنُ إِلَّا ٱلَّذِينَ ظَلَمُوا۟ مِنْهُمْ وَقُولُوٓا۟ ءَامَنَّا بِٱلَّذِىٓ أُنزِلَ إِلَيْنَا وَأُنزِلَ إِلَيْكُمْ وَإِلَٰهُنَا وَإِلَٰهُكُمْ وَٰحِدٌ وَنَحْنُ لَهُۥ مُسْلِمُونَ ﴿٤٦﴾

47. And thus We have sent down to you the Book. Those to whom We gave the Book[691] believe in it, and of these[692] some believe in it. Our Signs are only denied by the unbelievers.

وَكَذَٰلِكَ أَنزَلْنَآ إِلَيْكَ ٱلْكِتَٰبَ فَٱلَّذِينَ ءَاتَيْنَٰهُمُ ٱلْكِتَٰبَ يُؤْمِنُونَ بِهِۦ وَمِنْ هَٰٓؤُلَآءِ مَن يُؤْمِنُ بِهِۦ وَمَا يَجْحَدُ بِـَٔايَٰتِنَآ إِلَّا ٱلْكَٰفِرُونَ ﴿٤٧﴾

48. You did not recite before it any book or write it down with your right hand. Then the negators would have been in doubt.

وَمَا كُنتَ تَتْلُوا۟ مِن قَبْلِهِۦ مِن كِتَٰبٍ وَلَا تَخُطُّهُۥ بِيَمِينِكَ إِذًا لَّٱرْتَابَ ٱلْمُبْطِلُونَ ﴿٤٨﴾

49. It is rather clear signs in the breasts of those who have been granted knowledge. Only the wrongdoers will deny Our Signs.

بَلْ هُوَ ءَايَٰتٌۢ بَيِّنَٰتٌ فِى صُدُورِ ٱلَّذِينَ أُوتُوا۟ ٱلْعِلْمَ وَمَا يَجْحَدُ بِـَٔايَٰتِنَآ إِلَّا ٱلظَّٰلِمُونَ ﴿٤٩﴾

---

691. The People of the Book, Jews and Christians.
692. Muhammad's contemporaries, or the Meccans.

50. They said: "If only signs from his Lord were sent down on him."[693] Say: "Signs are only with Allah, and I am only a manifest warner."

51. Does it not suffice them that We have sent down on you the Book which is recited to them? There is, indeed, in that a mercy and a reminder to a believing people.

52. Say: "Allah suffices as a witness between you and me. He knows what is in the heavens and on the earth; and those who have believed in falsehood and disbelieved in Allah - those are the losers."

53. And they urge you to hasten the punishment; but had it not been for an appointed term, the punishment would have certainly smitten them. In fact, it will smite them suddenly, while they are unaware.

54. They urge you to hasten the punishment. Hell shall surely encompass the unbelievers.

55. Upon the Day the punishment shall overwhelm them from above them and from under their feet and He says: "Taste now what you used to do."

56. O My servants who believe and do the righteous deeds, My earth is vast, so worship Me alone.

57. Every living soul shall taste death; then unto Us you shall be returned.

58. Those who have believed and done the righteous deeds, We shall install them in chambers in Paradise, beneath which rivers flow, dwelling therein forever. Blessed is the wage of those who labour!

59. Those who stood fast and in their Lord they trust.

---

693. Muhammad.

‎وَقَالُوا۟ لَوْلَآ أُنزِلَ عَلَيْهِ ءَايَـٰتٌ مِّن رَّبِّهِۦ ۖ قُلْ إِنَّمَا ٱلْـَٔايَـٰتُ عِندَ ٱللَّهِ وَإِنَّمَآ أَنَا۠ نَذِيرٌ مُّبِينٌ ﴿٥٠﴾

‎أَوَلَمْ يَكْفِهِمْ أَنَّآ أَنزَلْنَا عَلَيْكَ ٱلْكِتَـٰبَ يُتْلَىٰ عَلَيْهِمْ ۚ إِنَّ فِى ذَٰلِكَ لَرَحْمَةً وَذِكْرَىٰ لِقَوْمٍ يُؤْمِنُونَ ﴿٥١﴾

‎قُلْ كَفَىٰ بِٱللَّهِ بَيْنِى وَبَيْنَكُمْ شَهِيدًا ۖ يَعْلَمُ مَا فِى ٱلسَّمَـٰوَٰتِ وَٱلْأَرْضِ ۗ وَٱلَّذِينَ ءَامَنُوا۟ بِٱلْبَـٰطِلِ وَكَفَرُوا۟ بِٱللَّهِ أُو۟لَـٰٓئِكَ هُمُ ٱلْخَـٰسِرُونَ ﴿٥٢﴾

‎وَيَسْتَعْجِلُونَكَ بِٱلْعَذَابِ ۚ وَلَوْلَآ أَجَلٌ مُّسَمًّى لَّجَآءَهُمُ ٱلْعَذَابُ وَلَيَأْتِيَنَّهُم بَغْتَةً وَهُمْ لَا يَشْعُرُونَ ﴿٥٣﴾

‎يَسْتَعْجِلُونَكَ بِٱلْعَذَابِ وَإِنَّ جَهَنَّمَ لَمُحِيطَةٌۢ بِٱلْكَـٰفِرِينَ ﴿٥٤﴾

‎يَوْمَ يَغْشَىٰهُمُ ٱلْعَذَابُ مِن فَوْقِهِمْ وَمِن تَحْتِ أَرْجُلِهِمْ وَيَقُولُ ذُوقُوا۟ مَا كُنتُمْ تَعْمَلُونَ ﴿٥٥﴾

‎يَـٰعِبَادِىَ ٱلَّذِينَ ءَامَنُوٓا۟ إِنَّ أَرْضِى وَٰسِعَةٌ فَإِيَّـٰىَ فَٱعْبُدُونِ ﴿٥٦﴾

‎كُلُّ نَفْسٍ ذَآئِقَةُ ٱلْمَوْتِ ۖ ثُمَّ إِلَيْنَا تُرْجَعُونَ ﴿٥٧﴾

‎وَٱلَّذِينَ ءَامَنُوا۟ وَعَمِلُوا۟ ٱلصَّـٰلِحَـٰتِ لَنُبَوِّئَنَّهُم مِّنَ ٱلْجَنَّةِ غُرَفًا تَجْرِى مِن تَحْتِهَا ٱلْأَنْهَـٰرُ خَـٰلِدِينَ فِيهَا ۚ نِعْمَ أَجْرُ ٱلْعَـٰمِلِينَ ﴿٥٨﴾

‎ٱلَّذِينَ صَبَرُوا۟ وَعَلَىٰ رَبِّهِمْ يَتَوَكَّلُونَ ﴿٥٩﴾

60. How many a beast does not bear its provision, yet Allah provides for it and for you. He is All-Hearing, All-Knowing.

وَكَأَيِّن مِّن دَآبَّةٖ لَّا تَحْمِلُ رِزْقَهَا ٱللَّهُ يَرْزُقُهَا وَإِيَّاكُمْ وَهُوَ ٱلسَّمِيعُ ٱلْعَلِيمُ ٦٠

61. And if you ask them: "Who created the heavens and the earth and subdued the sun and the moon?", they will say: "Allah." Why then do they vacillate?

وَلَئِن سَأَلْتَهُم مَّنْ خَلَقَ ٱلسَّمَـٰوَٰتِ وَٱلْأَرْضَ وَسَخَّرَ ٱلشَّمْسَ وَٱلْقَمَرَ لَيَقُولُنَّ ٱللَّهُ فَأَنَّىٰ يُؤْفَكُونَ ٦١

62. Allah expands the provision for whomever He wishes of His servants or restricts it. Surely, Allah has knowledge of all things.

ٱللَّهُ يَبْسُطُ ٱلرِّزْقَ لِمَن يَشَآءُ مِنْ عِبَادِهِۦ وَيَقْدِرُ لَهُۥٓ إِنَّ ٱللَّهَ بِكُلِّ شَىْءٍ عَلِيمٌ ٦٢

63. And if you ask them: "Who sends from heaven water [with which] He revives the earth after it was dead?", they will say: "Allah." Say: "Praise be to Allah." Yet most of them do not understand.

وَلَئِن سَأَلْتَهُم مَّن نَّزَّلَ مِنَ ٱلسَّمَآءِ مَآءٗ فَأَحْيَا بِهِ ٱلْأَرْضَ مِنۢ بَعْدِ مَوْتِهَا لَيَقُولُنَّ ٱللَّهُ قُلِ ٱلْحَمْدُ لِلَّهِ بَلْ أَكْثَرُهُمْ لَا يَعْقِلُونَ ٦٣

64. This present life is nothing but amusement and sport, but the Hereafter is real life, if only they knew.

وَمَا هَـٰذِهِ ٱلْحَيَوٰةُ ٱلدُّنْيَآ إِلَّا لَهْوٌ وَلَعِبٌ وَإِنَّ ٱلدَّارَ ٱلْـَٔاخِرَةَ لَهِىَ ٱلْحَيَوَانُ لَوْ كَانُوا۟ يَعْلَمُونَ ٦٤

65. When they embark in the ships, they will call on Allah, professing religion sincerely to Him. Yet when He delivers them safely to land, behold they associate.[694]

فَإِذَا رَكِبُوا۟ فِى ٱلْفُلْكِ دَعَوُا۟ ٱللَّهَ مُخْلِصِينَ لَهُ ٱلدِّينَ فَلَمَّا نَجَّىٰهُمْ إِلَى ٱلْبَرِّ إِذَا هُمْ يُشْرِكُونَ ٦٥

66. To disbelieve in what We have imparted to them and enjoy themselves. They will surely come to know.

لِيَكْفُرُوا۟ بِمَآ ءَاتَيْنَـٰهُمْ وَلِيَتَمَتَّعُوا۟ فَسَوْفَ يَعْلَمُونَ ٦٦

67. Do they not see that We have set up a safe sanctuary for them, while all around them people are being snatched away? Do they, then, believe in falsehood and repudiate Allah's Bounty?

أَوَلَمْ يَرَوْا۟ أَنَّا جَعَلْنَا حَرَمًا ءَامِنًا وَيُتَخَطَّفُ ٱلنَّاسُ مِنْ حَوْلِهِمْ أَفَبِٱلْبَـٰطِلِ يُؤْمِنُونَ وَبِنِعْمَةِ ٱللَّهِ يَكْفُرُونَ ٦٧

68. Who, then, is more unjust than one who imputes falsehood to Allah or denies the truth when it comes to him. Is there not in Hell a dwelling for the unbelievers?

وَمَنْ أَظْلَمُ مِمَّنِ ٱفْتَرَىٰ عَلَى ٱللَّهِ كَذِبًا أَوْ كَذَّبَ بِٱلْحَقِّ لَمَّا جَآءَهُۥٓ أَلَيْسَ فِى جَهَنَّمَ مَثْوٗى لِّلْكَـٰفِرِينَ ٦٨

69. And those who strive in Our Cause We shall guide in Our Ways, and Allah is with the beneficent.

وَٱلَّذِينَ جَـٰهَدُوا۟ فِينَا لَنَهْدِيَنَّهُمْ سُبُلَنَا وَإِنَّ ٱللَّهَ لَمَعَ ٱلْمُحْسِنِينَ ٦٩

---

694. Other gods with Him.

Sûrat Ar-Rum,
(The Greeks [or Byzantines]) 30

In the Name of Allah,
the Compassionate, the Merciful

1. Alif - Lam - Mim.

2. The Greeks have been vanquished

3. In the nearest part of the land; but after being vanquished, they shall vanquish,

4. In a few years. Allah's is the command before and after; and on that day the believers shall rejoice,

5. In Allah's support. He supports whom He wills; and He is the All-Mighty, the Merciful.

6. It is Allah's Promise. Allah does not break His Promise, although most people do not know.

7. They know the outward aspect of the present life, but they are heedless of the Hereafter.

8. Have they not considered within themselves that Allah did not create the heavens and the earth and what is between them except in truth and at an appointed time? Yet many people disbelieve in the Encounter of their Lord.

9. Have they not travelled in the land to see what was the fate of those who preceded them? They were stauncher than them in strength, and they ploughed the earth and built it up better than they themselves built it up, and their Messengers came to them with the clear proofs. Allah would never wrong them, but they wronged themselves.

10. Then, evil was the end of those who committed the gravest sin; for they have denounced Allah's Signs and used to scoff at them.

11. Allah originates creation and then brings it back into being. Then unto Him you shall be returned.

اللَّهُ يَبْدَؤُاْ الْخَلْقَ ثُمَّ يُعِيدُهُ ثُمَّ إِلَيْهِ تُرْجَعُونَ ﴿١١﴾

12. And on the Day that the Hour comes, the criminals will be confounded.

وَيَوْمَ تَقُومُ السَّاعَةُ يُبْلِسُ الْمُجْرِمُونَ ﴿١٢﴾

13. And they will have no intercessors among their associates and they will repudiate their associates.

وَلَمْ يَكُن لَّهُم مِّن شُرَكَآئِهِمْ شُفَعَـٰٓؤُاْ وَكَانُواْ بِشُرَكَآئِهِمْ كَـٰفِرِينَ ﴿١٣﴾

14. And on the Day that the Hour comes, they shall be divided.

وَيَوْمَ تَقُومُ السَّاعَةُ يَوْمَئِذٍ يَتَفَرَّقُونَ ﴿١٤﴾

15. As for those who have believed and done the righteous deeds, they will be in a garden, fully joyful.

فَأَمَّا الَّذِينَ ءَامَنُواْ وَعَمِلُواْ الصَّـٰلِحَـٰتِ فَهُمْ فِى رَوْضَةٍ يُحْبَرُونَ ﴿١٥﴾

16. But as for those who have disbelieved and denounced Our Signs and the Encounter of the Hereafter as lies, those shall be summoned to suffer the punishment.

وَأَمَّا الَّذِينَ كَفَرُواْ وَكَذَّبُواْ بِـَٔايَـٰتِنَا وَلِقَآئِ الْأَخِرَةِ فَأُوْلَـٰٓئِكَ فِى الْعَذَابِ مُحْضَرُونَ ﴿١٦﴾

17. So, glorify Allah in the evening and in the morning.

فَسُبْحَـٰنَ اللَّهِ حِينَ تُمْسُونَ وَحِينَ تُصْبِحُونَ ﴿١٧﴾

18. His is the praise in the heavens and on earth at sunset and at noontide.

وَلَهُ الْحَمْدُ فِى السَّمَـٰوَٰتِ وَالْأَرْضِ وَعَشِيًّا وَحِينَ تُظْهِرُونَ ﴿١٨﴾

19. He brings the living out of the dead and He brings the dead out of the living. He brings the earth to life after it was dead, and you shall be brought out likewise.

يُخْرِجُ الْحَىَّ مِنَ الْمَيِّتِ وَيُخْرِجُ الْمَيِّتَ مِنَ الْحَىِّ وَيُحْىِ الْأَرْضَ بَعْدَ مَوْتِهَا وَكَذَٰلِكَ تُخْرَجُونَ ﴿١٩﴾

20. And of His Signs is that He created you from dust; and behold, you are mortals scattered all round.

وَمِنْ ءَايَـٰتِهِ أَنْ خَلَقَكُم مِّن تُرَابٍ ثُمَّ إِذَآ أَنتُم بَشَرٌ تَنتَشِرُونَ ﴿٢٠﴾

21. And of His Signs is that He created for you, from yourselves, spouses to settle down with and He established friendship and mercy between you. There are in all that signs for a people who reflect.

وَمِنْ ءَايَـٰتِهِ أَنْ خَلَقَ لَكُم مِّنْ أَنفُسِكُمْ أَزْوَٰجًا لِّتَسْكُنُوٓاْ إِلَيْهَا وَجَعَلَ بَيْنَكُم مَّوَدَّةً وَرَحْمَةً إِنَّ فِى ذَٰلِكَ لَـَٔايَـٰتٍ لِّقَوْمٍ يَتَفَكَّرُونَ ﴿٢١﴾

22. And of His Signs is the creation of the heavens and the earth and the diversity of your tongues and colours. Indeed, there are in that signs for those who know.

وَمِنْ ءَايَـٰتِهِ خَلْقُ السَّمَـٰوَٰتِ وَالْأَرْضِ وَاخْتِلَـٰفُ أَلْسِنَتِكُمْ وَأَلْوَٰنِكُمْ إِنَّ فِى ذَٰلِكَ لَـَٔايَـٰتٍ لِّلْعَـٰلِمِينَ ﴿٢٢﴾

23. And of His Signs is your sleeping by night and day and your seeking some of His Bounty. There are in that signs for a people who hear.

24. And of His Signs is showing you the lightning, to fear and to hope; and He brings down from the sky water with which He revives the earth after it was dead. There are in that signs for people who understand.

25. And of His Signs is that the heavens and the earth shall arise at His Command. Then, if He summons you once, behold, you shall be brought out of the earth.

26. And to Him belongs whoever is in the heavens or on earth. They are all submitting to Him.

27. It is He Who originates the creation, then brings it back again; and that is easier for Him. His is the loftiest exemplar in the heavens and on earth, and He is the All-Mighty, the Wise.

28. He gave you a parable from your own selves. Do you have among what your hands own[695] partners in what We provided for you, so that you are equal therein? Do you fear them as you fear each other? Thus We expound the revelations to a people who understand.

29. Yet, the wrongdoers have followed their fancies without knowledge. Who, then, will guide those whom Allah has led astray and who have no supporters?

30. So, set your face towards religion uprightly. It is the original nature according to which Allah fashioned mankind. There is no altering Allah's Creation. That is the true religion; but most men do not know.

---

695. Your slaves.

31. Returning unto Him. Fear Him, perform the prayer and do not be like the idolaters;

32. Those who have rent their religion asunder and split into factions, each party rejoicing in what they had.

33. When people are visited by some adversity, they call upon their Lord, turning to Him; but when He lets them taste a mercy from Him, behold, a group of them associate [other gods] with their Lord;

34. So as to be ungrateful for what We have given them. Indulge yourselves, then. For you shall certainly know!

35. Or have We sent down to them an authority, and he speaks about that which they were associating with Him?

36. If We let people taste a certain mercy, they rejoice at it; but if a misfortune befalls them, on account of what their hands have perpetrated, behold, they are in despair.

37. Have they not seen that Allah expands and restricts the provision for whomever He wishes? Surely, there are in that signs for a people who believe.

38. So, give the kinsman his due, as well as the destitute and the wayfarer. That is better for those who desire the Face of Allah. Those are the prosperous.

39. And what you give in usury, so as to multiply people's wealth, will not multiply in Allah's Sight; but what you give in alms, desiring thereby Allah's Face. Such are the real multipliers.[696]

---

696. Of their wealth.

40. It is Allah Who created you, then provided for you and Who will cause you to die, then bring you back to life. Is there among your associates any one who does any of all this? Glory be to Him and may He be exalted above what they associate with Him!

اللَّهُ الَّذِى خَلَقَكُمْ ثُمَّ رَزَقَكُمْ ثُمَّ يُمِيتُكُمْ ثُمَّ يُحْيِيكُمْ هَلْ مِن شُرَكَائِكُم مَّن يَفْعَلُ مِن ذَلِكُم مِّن شَىْءٍ سُبْحَانَهُ وَتَعَالَى عَمَّا يُشْرِكُونَ ۝

41. Corruption has appeared in the land and the sea, on account of what men's hands have earned; so that He may let them taste the reward of some of their deeds, that perchance they may return.

ظَهَرَ الْفَسَادُ فِى الْبَرِّ وَالْبَحْرِ بِمَا كَسَبَتْ أَيْدِى النَّاسِ لِيُذِيقَهُم بَعْضَ الَّذِى عَمِلُوا لَعَلَّهُمْ يَرْجِعُونَ ۝

42. Say: "Travel in the land and behold what was the fate of those who came before; most of them were idolaters."

قُلْ سِيرُوا فِى الْأَرْضِ فَانظُرُوا كَيْفَ كَانَ عَاقِبَةُ الَّذِينَ مِن قَبْلُ كَانَ أَكْثَرُهُم مُّشْرِكِينَ ۝

43. So, set your face towards the true religion, before a Day from Allah comes, which cannot be turned back. On that Day they will be rent asunder.

فَأَقِمْ وَجْهَكَ لِلدِّينِ الْقَيِّمِ مِن قَبْلِ أَن يَأْتِىَ يَوْمٌ لَّا مَرَدَّ لَهُ مِنَ اللَّهِ يَوْمَئِذٍ يَصَّدَّعُونَ ۝

44. Whoever disbelieves, upon him shall recoil his unbelief and whoever does a righteous deed, it is for themselves that they will be preparing a comfortable abode.

مَن كَفَرَ فَعَلَيْهِ كُفْرُهُ وَمَنْ عَمِلَ صَلِحًا فَلِأَنفُسِهِمْ يَمْهَدُونَ ۝

45. That He may reward those who have believed and done the righteous deeds out of His Bounty. Indeed, He does not love the unbelievers.

لِيَجْزِىَ الَّذِينَ ءَامَنُوا وَعَمِلُوا الصَّلِحَاتِ مِن فَضْلِهِ إِنَّهُ لَا يُحِبُّ الْكَفِرِينَ ۝

46. And of His Signs is sending forth the winds bearing good news and to let you taste part of His Mercy, and that the ships may sail at His Command, and that you might seek part of His Bounty; that perchance you may give thanks.

وَمِنْ ءَايَتِهِ أَن يُرْسِلَ الرِّيَاحَ مُبَشِّرَتٍ وَلِيُذِيقَكُم مِّن رَّحْمَتِهِ وَلِتَجْرِىَ الْفُلْكُ بِأَمْرِهِ وَلِتَبْتَغُوا مِن فَضْلِهِ وَلَعَلَّكُمْ تَشْكُرُونَ ۝

47. We have, indeed, sent Messengers to their own people, before you, and they brought them clear proofs. Then We revenged upon those who sinned, and it was incumbent on Us to give the believers support.

وَلَقَدْ أَرْسَلْنَا مِن قَبْلِكَ رُسُلًا إِلَى قَوْمِهِمْ فَجَآءُوهُم بِالْبَيِّنَتِ فَانتَقَمْنَا مِنَ الَّذِينَ أَجْرَمُوا وَكَانَ حَقًّا عَلَيْنَا نَصْرُ الْمُؤْمِنِينَ ۝

48. It is Allah Who sends forth the winds, which stir up clouds. Then He spreads them out in the sky, as He pleases, and causes them to break up into pieces; and you see the rain issuing from their midst. Then, when He allows the rain to reach whomever He wishes of His servants, behold, they rejoice.

49. Whereas they were, before that, despondent.

50. Behold, then, the marks of Allah's Mercy, how He revives the earth after it was dead. He, indeed, is the One Who revives the dead and He has power over everything.

51. And were We to send forth a wind and they saw it turning yellow, they would continue thereafter to disbelieve.

52. For you cannot make the dead hear and you cannot make the deaf hear the call, if they flee turning their back.

53. And you shall not lead the blind away from their error. You will only make those who believe in Our Signs hear. For they are submitting.

54. It is Allah Who created you from a weak substance, then gave you strength after weakness, then after strength weakness and grey hair. He creates what He pleases and He is the All-Knowing, All-Powerful.

55. And the day the Hour comes, the criminals shall swear that they did not linger more than an hour. Thus they had been perverted.

56. But those who have been given knowledge and faith will say: "You have lingered in Allah's Book till the Day of Resurrection. This is the Day of Resurrection, but you did not know."

اللَّهُ الَّذِي يُرْسِلُ الرِّيَاحَ فَتُثِيرُ سَحَابًا فَيَبْسُطُهُ فِي السَّمَاءِ كَيْفَ يَشَاءُ وَيَجْعَلُهُ كِسَفًا فَتَرَى الْوَدْقَ يَخْرُجُ مِنْ خِلَالِهِ فَإِذَا أَصَابَ بِهِ مَن يَشَاءُ مِنْ عِبَادِهِ إِذَا هُمْ يَسْتَبْشِرُونَ ﴿٤٨﴾

وَإِن كَانُوا مِن قَبْلِ أَن يُنَزَّلَ عَلَيْهِم مِّن قَبْلِهِ لَمُبْلِسِينَ ﴿٤٩﴾

فَانظُرْ إِلَىٰ آثَارِ رَحْمَتِ اللَّهِ كَيْفَ يُحْيِ الْأَرْضَ بَعْدَ مَوْتِهَا إِنَّ ذَٰلِكَ لَمُحْيِ الْمَوْتَىٰ وَهُوَ عَلَىٰ كُلِّ شَيْءٍ قَدِيرٌ ﴿٥٠﴾

وَلَئِنْ أَرْسَلْنَا رِيحًا فَرَأَوْهُ مُصْفَرًّا لَّظَلُّوا مِنْ بَعْدِهِ يَكْفُرُونَ ﴿٥١﴾

فَإِنَّكَ لَا تُسْمِعُ الْمَوْتَىٰ وَلَا تُسْمِعُ الصُّمَّ الدُّعَاءَ إِذَا وَلَّوْا مُدْبِرِينَ ﴿٥٢﴾

وَمَا أَنتَ بِهَادِ الْعُمْيِ عَن ضَلَالَتِهِمْ إِن تُسْمِعُ إِلَّا مَن يُؤْمِنُ بِآيَاتِنَا فَهُم مُّسْلِمُونَ ﴿٥٣﴾

۞ اللَّهُ الَّذِي خَلَقَكُم مِّن ضَعْفٍ ثُمَّ جَعَلَ مِن بَعْدِ ضَعْفٍ قُوَّةً ثُمَّ جَعَلَ مِنْ بَعْدِ قُوَّةٍ ضَعْفًا وَشَيْبَةً يَخْلُقُ مَا يَشَاءُ وَهُوَ الْعَلِيمُ الْقَدِيرُ ﴿٥٤﴾

وَيَوْمَ تَقُومُ السَّاعَةُ يُقْسِمُ الْمُجْرِمُونَ مَا لَبِثُوا غَيْرَ سَاعَةٍ كَذَٰلِكَ كَانُوا يُؤْفَكُونَ ﴿٥٥﴾

وَقَالَ الَّذِينَ أُوتُوا الْعِلْمَ وَالْإِيمَانَ لَقَدْ لَبِثْتُمْ فِي كِتَابِ اللَّهِ إِلَىٰ يَوْمِ الْبَعْثِ فَهَٰذَا يَوْمُ الْبَعْثِ وَلَٰكِنَّكُمْ كُنتُمْ لَا تَعْلَمُونَ ﴿٥٦﴾

57. On that Day, the excuses of the wrongdoers will not avail them and they will not be allowed to plead for pardon.

58. We have cited in this Qur'an every manner of parable; indeed were you to bring the unbelievers a sign, they would only say: "You are purveyors of falsehood."

59. Thus Allah places a seal upon the hearts of those who do not know.

60. Be patient then, for Allah's Promise is true; and do not be disheartened by those who lack the certitude of faith.

Sûrat Luqmân,
(The Wise) 31

In the Name of Allah,
the Compassionate, the Merciful

1. Alif - Lam - Mim.

2. Those are the Signs of the wise Book;

3. A guidance and mercy to the beneficent,

4. Those who perform the prayer, give the alms and are certain of the Hereafter.

5. Those are accorded guidance from their Lord and those are the prosperous.

6. There are some people who purchase idle talk in order to lead away from Allah's Path without any knowledge; and take it in jest. Those will have a demeaning punishment.

7. And if Our Revelations are recited to him, he turns away arrogantly, as though he did not hear them, or as though there is a heaviness in his ears. Announce to him, then, the news of a very painful punishment.

8. Those who have believed and do the righteous deeds will inherit the Gardens of Bliss.

9. Dwelling therein forever, having been given Allah's True Promise. He is the All-Mighty the All-Wise.

خَٰلِدِينَ فِيهَا ۖ وَعْدَ ٱللَّهِ حَقًّا ۚ وَهُوَ ٱلْعَزِيزُ ٱلْحَكِيمُ ﴿٩﴾

10. He created the heavens without pillars that you can see and laid down in the earth immovable mountains, lest it shake with you, and scattered throughout it every variety of beast. And We have sent down water from heaven, thereby causing to grow in it every noble kind [of plant].

خَلَقَ ٱلسَّمَٰوَٰتِ بِغَيْرِ عَمَدٍ تَرَوْنَهَا ۖ وَأَلْقَىٰ فِى ٱلْأَرْضِ رَوَٰسِىَ أَن تَمِيدَ بِكُمْ وَبَثَّ فِيهَا مِن كُلِّ دَآبَّةٍ ۚ وَأَنزَلْنَا مِنَ ٱلسَّمَآءِ مَآءً فَأَنۢبَتْنَا فِيهَا مِن كُلِّ زَوْجٍ كَرِيمٍ ﴿١٠﴾

11. This is Allah's Creation; so show Me what those apart from Him have created. Indeed, the wrongdoers are in manifest error.

هَٰذَا خَلْقُ ٱللَّهِ فَأَرُونِى مَاذَا خَلَقَ ٱلَّذِينَ مِن دُونِهِۦ ۚ بَلِ ٱلظَّٰلِمُونَ فِى ضَلَٰلٍ مُّبِينٍ ﴿١١﴾

12. We have, indeed, imparted wisdom to Luqmân:[697] "Give thanks to Allah." Whoever gives thanks, gives thanks only for his own good and whoever disbelieves will find Allah All-Sufficient, Praiseworthy."

وَلَقَدْ ءَاتَيْنَا لُقْمَٰنَ ٱلْحِكْمَةَ أَنِ ٱشْكُرْ لِلَّهِ ۚ وَمَن يَشْكُرْ فَإِنَّمَا يَشْكُرُ لِنَفْسِهِۦ ۖ وَمَن كَفَرَ فَإِنَّ ٱللَّهَ غَنِىٌّ حَمِيدٌ ﴿١٢﴾

13. And when Luqmân said to his son, exhorting him: "My son, do not associate others with Allah; associating others [with Allah] is a mighty evil."

وَإِذْ قَالَ لُقْمَٰنُ لِٱبْنِهِۦ وَهُوَ يَعِظُهُۥ يَٰبُنَىَّ لَا تُشْرِكْ بِٱللَّهِ ۖ إِنَّ ٱلشِّرْكَ لَظُلْمٌ عَظِيمٌ ﴿١٣﴾

14. We have admonished man regarding his parents; as his mother bore him in weakness upon weakness, weaning him in two years: "Give thanks to Me and to your parents. Unto Me is the ultimate return.

وَوَصَّيْنَا ٱلْإِنسَٰنَ بِوَٰلِدَيْهِ حَمَلَتْهُ أُمُّهُۥ وَهْنًا عَلَىٰ وَهْنٍ وَفِصَٰلُهُۥ فِى عَامَيْنِ أَنِ ٱشْكُرْ لِى وَلِوَٰلِدَيْكَ إِلَىَّ ٱلْمَصِيرُ ﴿١٤﴾

15. "If they strive with you so as to associate with Me that of which you have no knowledge, do not obey them; but keep them company in the present world honourably. Follow the path of those who turn to Me. Then unto Me is your return, whereupon I will tell you what you used to do.

وَإِن جَٰهَدَاكَ عَلَىٰٓ أَن تُشْرِكَ بِى مَا لَيْسَ لَكَ بِهِۦ عِلْمٌ فَلَا تُطِعْهُمَا ۖ وَصَاحِبْهُمَا فِى ٱلدُّنْيَا مَعْرُوفًا ۖ وَٱتَّبِعْ سَبِيلَ مَنْ أَنَابَ إِلَىَّ ۚ ثُمَّ إِلَىَّ مَرْجِعُكُمْ فَأُنَبِّئُكُم بِمَا كُنتُمْ تَعْمَلُونَ ﴿١٥﴾

---

697. Luqman is a legendary figure in Islamic lore, regarded as a paragon of wisdom.

16. "O my son, if there be the weight of a mustard seed, whether in a rock, in the heavens or in the earth, Allah will bring it forth. Surely, Allah is Subtle, Well-Informed.

17. "O my son, perform the prayer, command the honourable and forbid the dishonourable and bear patiently what has befallen you. That is an instance of constancy in one's affairs.

18. "Do not turn your face away from people and do not walk in the land haughtily. Allah does not love any arrogant or boastful person.

19. "Be modest in your stride and lower your voice; for the most hideous voice is that of asses."

20. Have you not seen how Allah has subjected to you whatever is in the heavens and on earth and granted you His Blessings, both outward and inward? Some people, however, continue to dispute regarding Allah, without any knowledge or guidance or an illuminating Book.

21. If it is said to them: "Follow what Allah has sent down", they say: "Rather, we will follow what we found our fathers doing." It is as though Satan was summoning them to the punishment of Hell.

22. Whoever surrenders his will to Allah, while doing the right, has surely grasped the firmest handle. Unto Allah is the ultimate issue of all affairs.

23. Whoever disbelieves, let not his disbelief sadden you. Unto Us is their return and then We will tell them what they did. Allah knows well the secrets of the breasts.

24. We allow them to indulge themselves a little, then We will compel them to taste a harsh punishment.

يَٰبُنَىَّ إِنَّهَآ إِن تَكُ مِثْقَالَ حَبَّةٍ مِّنْ خَرْدَلٍ فَتَكُن فِى صَخْرَةٍ أَوْ فِى ٱلسَّمَٰوَٰتِ أَوْ فِى ٱلْأَرْضِ يَأْتِ بِهَا ٱللَّهُ إِنَّ ٱللَّهَ لَطِيفٌ خَبِيرٌ ۝

يَٰبُنَىَّ أَقِمِ ٱلصَّلَوٰةَ وَأْمُرْ بِٱلْمَعْرُوفِ وَٱنْهَ عَنِ ٱلْمُنكَرِ وَٱصْبِرْ عَلَىٰ مَآ أَصَابَكَ إِنَّ ذَٰلِكَ مِنْ عَزْمِ ٱلْأُمُورِ ۝

وَلَا تُصَعِّرْ خَدَّكَ لِلنَّاسِ وَلَا تَمْشِ فِى ٱلْأَرْضِ مَرَحًا إِنَّ ٱللَّهَ لَا يُحِبُّ كُلَّ مُخْتَالٍ فَخُورٍ ۝

وَٱقْصِدْ فِى مَشْيِكَ وَٱغْضُضْ مِن صَوْتِكَ إِنَّ أَنكَرَ ٱلْأَصْوَٰتِ لَصَوْتُ ٱلْحَمِيرِ ۝

أَلَمْ تَرَوْا۟ أَنَّ ٱللَّهَ سَخَّرَ لَكُم مَّا فِى ٱلسَّمَٰوَٰتِ وَمَا فِى ٱلْأَرْضِ وَأَسْبَغَ عَلَيْكُمْ نِعَمَهُۥ ظَٰهِرَةً وَبَاطِنَةً وَمِنَ ٱلنَّاسِ مَن يُجَٰدِلُ فِى ٱللَّهِ بِغَيْرِ عِلْمٍ وَلَا هُدًى وَلَا كِتَٰبٍ مُّنِيرٍ ۝

وَإِذَا قِيلَ لَهُمُ ٱتَّبِعُوا۟ مَآ أَنزَلَ ٱللَّهُ قَالُوا۟ بَلْ نَتَّبِعُ مَا وَجَدْنَا عَلَيْهِ ءَابَآءَنَآ أَوَلَوْ كَانَ ٱلشَّيْطَٰنُ يَدْعُوهُمْ إِلَىٰ عَذَابِ ٱلسَّعِيرِ ۝

۞ وَمَن يُسْلِمْ وَجْهَهُۥٓ إِلَى ٱللَّهِ وَهُوَ مُحْسِنٌ فَقَدِ ٱسْتَمْسَكَ بِٱلْعُرْوَةِ ٱلْوُثْقَىٰ وَإِلَى ٱللَّهِ عَٰقِبَةُ ٱلْأُمُورِ ۝

وَمَن كَفَرَ فَلَا يَحْزُنكَ كُفْرُهُۥٓ إِلَيْنَا مَرْجِعُهُمْ فَنُنَبِّئُهُم بِمَا عَمِلُوٓا۟ إِنَّ ٱللَّهَ عَلِيمٌۢ بِذَاتِ ٱلصُّدُورِ ۝

نُمَتِّعُهُمْ قَلِيلًا ثُمَّ نَضْطَرُّهُمْ إِلَىٰ عَذَابٍ غَلِيظٍ ۝

25. And if you ask them: "Who created the heavens and the earth", they will certainly say: "Allah." Say: "Praise be to Allah." However, most of them do not know.

26. To Allah belongs what is in the heavens and the earth. Allah is, indeed, the All-Sufficient, the Praiseworthy.

27. Were all trees on earth so many pens and the sea, coupled by seven other seas, supplying them with ink, Allah's Words would not be exhausted. Allah is, indeed, All-Mighty and Wise.

28. He did not create you or resuscitate you but as a single soul. Indeed, Allah is All-Hearing, All-Seeing.

29. Have you not seen how Allah causes the night to phase into the day, and the day to phase into the night; and He has subjected the sun and the moon, each of them running to an appointed term, and that Allah is Well-Aware of what you do?

30. That is because Allah is the Truth and what they call upon, apart from Him, is the falsehood and that Allah is the All-High, the Great.

31. Have you not seen that ships cruise upon the sea by Allah's Grace, to show you some of His Signs. There are in that signs for every steadfast, thankful one.

32. And if waves cover them like a canopy, they call upon Allah, professing religion sincerely to Him; but when He delivers them to the dry land, some of them are lukewarm. Yet none repudiate Our Signs except every ungrateful traitor.

33. O people, fear your Lord and beware of a Day when no father shall stand for his child and no infant shall stand for his father in the

وَلَئِن سَأَلْتَهُم مَّنْ خَلَقَ ٱلسَّمَٰوَٰتِ وَٱلْأَرْضَ لَيَقُولُنَّ ٱللَّهُ قُلِ ٱلْحَمْدُ لِلَّهِ بَلْ أَكْثَرُهُمْ لَا يَعْلَمُونَ ﴿٢٥﴾

لِلَّهِ مَا فِى ٱلسَّمَٰوَٰتِ وَٱلْأَرْضِ إِنَّ ٱللَّهَ هُوَ ٱلْغَنِىُّ ٱلْحَمِيدُ ﴿٢٦﴾

وَلَوْ أَنَّمَا فِى ٱلْأَرْضِ مِن شَجَرَةٍ أَقْلَٰمٌ وَٱلْبَحْرُ يَمُدُّهُ مِنۢ بَعْدِهِ سَبْعَةُ أَبْحُرٍ مَّا نَفِدَتْ كَلِمَٰتُ ٱللَّهِ إِنَّ ٱللَّهَ عَزِيزٌ حَكِيمٌ ﴿٢٧﴾

مَّا خَلْقُكُمْ وَلَا بَعْثُكُمْ إِلَّا كَنَفْسٍ وَٰحِدَةٍ إِنَّ ٱللَّهَ سَمِيعٌ بَصِيرٌ ﴿٢٨﴾

أَلَمْ تَرَ أَنَّ ٱللَّهَ يُولِجُ ٱلَّيْلَ فِى ٱلنَّهَارِ وَيُولِجُ ٱلنَّهَارَ فِى ٱلَّيْلِ وَسَخَّرَ ٱلشَّمْسَ وَٱلْقَمَرَ كُلٌّ يَجْرِى إِلَىٰٓ أَجَلٍ مُّسَمًّى وَأَنَّ ٱللَّهَ بِمَا تَعْمَلُونَ خَبِيرٌ ﴿٢٩﴾

ذَٰلِكَ بِأَنَّ ٱللَّهَ هُوَ ٱلْحَقُّ وَأَنَّ مَا يَدْعُونَ مِن دُونِهِ ٱلْبَٰطِلُ وَأَنَّ ٱللَّهَ هُوَ ٱلْعَلِىُّ ٱلْكَبِيرُ ﴿٣٠﴾

أَلَمْ تَرَ أَنَّ ٱلْفُلْكَ تَجْرِى فِى ٱلْبَحْرِ بِنِعْمَتِ ٱللَّهِ لِيُرِيَكُم مِّنْ ءَايَٰتِهِۦٓ إِنَّ فِى ذَٰلِكَ لَءَايَٰتٍ لِّكُلِّ صَبَّارٍ شَكُورٍ ﴿٣١﴾

وَإِذَا غَشِيَهُم مَّوْجٌ كَٱلظُّلَلِ دَعَوُا۟ ٱللَّهَ مُخْلِصِينَ لَهُ ٱلدِّينَ فَلَمَّا نَجَّىٰهُمْ إِلَى ٱلْبَرِّ فَمِنْهُم مُّقْتَصِدٌ وَمَا يَجْحَدُ بِـَٔايَٰتِنَآ إِلَّا كُلُّ خَتَّارٍ كَفُورٍ ﴿٣٢﴾

يَٰٓأَيُّهَا ٱلنَّاسُ ٱتَّقُوا۟ رَبَّكُمْ وَٱخْشَوْا۟ يَوْمًا لَّا يَجْزِى وَالِدٌ عَن وَلَدِهِ وَلَا مَوْلُودٌ هُوَ جَازٍ عَن وَالِدِهِ شَيْـًٔا إِنَّ

least. Allah's Promise is true, so let not the present life delude you or let any deceiver delude you regarding Allah.

وَعَدَ ٱللَّهِ حَقٌّ فَلَا تَغُرَّنَّكُمُ ٱلۡحَيَوٰةُ ٱلدُّنۡيَا وَلَا يَغُرَّنَّكُم بِٱللَّهِ ٱلۡغَرُورُ ٣٣

34. Allah surely has the knowledge of the Hour and He sends down the rain. He knows what is in the wombs, whereas no soul knows what it shall earn tomorrow; nor does any living soul know in what land it shall die. Allah is All-Knowing, Well-Informed.

إِنَّ ٱللَّهَ عِندَهُۥ عِلۡمُ ٱلسَّاعَةِ وَيُنَزِّلُ ٱلۡغَيۡثَ وَيَعۡلَمُ مَا فِي ٱلۡأَرۡحَامِ وَمَا تَدۡرِي نَفۡسٌ مَّاذَا تَكۡسِبُ غَدًا وَمَا تَدۡرِي نَفۡسُۢ بِأَيِّ أَرۡضٍ تَمُوتُ إِنَّ ٱللَّهَ عَلِيمٌ خَبِيرٌ ٣٤

Sûrat As-Sajdah, (The Prostration) 32

In the Name of Allah, the Compassionate, the Merciful

بِسۡمِ ٱللَّهِ ٱلرَّحۡمَٰنِ ٱلرَّحِيمِ

1. Alif - Lam - Mim.

الٓمٓ ١

2. The revelation of the Book from the Lord of the Worlds, wherein there is no doubt.

تَنزِيلُ ٱلۡكِتَٰبِ لَا رَيۡبَ فِيهِ مِن رَّبِّ ٱلۡعَٰلَمِينَ ٢

3. Or do they say: "He invented it?" Rather, it is the truth from your Lord, so as to warn a people to whom no warner came before you, that perchance they might be well-guided.

أَمۡ يَقُولُونَ ٱفۡتَرَىٰهُ بَلۡ هُوَ ٱلۡحَقُّ مِن رَّبِّكَ لِتُنذِرَ قَوۡمًا مَّآ أَتَىٰهُم مِّن نَّذِيرٍ مِّن قَبۡلِكَ لَعَلَّهُمۡ يَهۡتَدُونَ ٣

4. Allah, Who created the heavens and the earth in six days, sat upon the Throne. You have no guardian or intercessor, apart from Him. Do you not recollect?

ٱللَّهُ ٱلَّذِي خَلَقَ ٱلسَّمَٰوَٰتِ وَٱلۡأَرۡضَ وَمَا بَيۡنَهُمَا فِي سِتَّةِ أَيَّامٍ ثُمَّ ٱسۡتَوَىٰ عَلَى ٱلۡعَرۡشِ مَا لَكُم مِّن دُونِهِۦ مِن وَلِيٍّ وَلَا شَفِيعٍ أَفَلَا تَتَذَكَّرُونَ ٤

5. He manages the affair from the heaven to the earth; then, it ascends to Him in one day whose measure is a thousand years of what you reckon.

يُدَبِّرُ ٱلۡأَمۡرَ مِنَ ٱلسَّمَآءِ إِلَى ٱلۡأَرۡضِ ثُمَّ يَعۡرُجُ إِلَيۡهِ فِي يَوۡمٍ كَانَ مِقۡدَارُهُۥٓ أَلۡفَ سَنَةٍ مِّمَّا تَعُدُّونَ ٥

6. That is the Knower of the Unseen and the Seen, the All-Mighty, the Merciful.

ذَٰلِكَ عَٰلِمُ ٱلۡغَيۡبِ وَٱلشَّهَٰدَةِ ٱلۡعَزِيزُ ٱلرَّحِيمُ ٦

7. Who fashioned well everything He created, and originated the creation of man from clay.

ٱلَّذِيٓ أَحۡسَنَ كُلَّ شَيۡءٍ خَلَقَهُۥ وَبَدَأَ خَلۡقَ ٱلۡإِنسَٰنِ مِن طِينٍ ٧

8. Then He fashioned his progeny from an extract of fluid.

ثُمَّ جَعَلَ نَسۡلَهُۥ مِن سُلَٰلَةٍ مِّن مَّآءٍ مَّهِينٍ ٨

9. Then He shaped him well and breathed into him of His Spirit. He gave you hearing, sight and hearts. How little do you give thanks!

ثُمَّ سَوَّىٰهُ وَنَفَخَ فِيهِ مِن رُّوحِهِ وَجَعَلَ لَكُمُ ٱلسَّمْعَ وَٱلْأَبْصَٰرَ وَٱلْأَفْـِٔدَةَ قَلِيلًا مَّا تَشْكُرُونَ ﴿٩﴾

10. They say: "What, if we stray aimlessly in the land, shall we be created anew?" Indeed, they disbelieve in the Encounter of their Lord.

وَقَالُوٓا۟ أَءِذَا ضَلَلْنَا فِى ٱلْأَرْضِ أَءِنَّا لَفِى خَلْقٍ جَدِيدٍۭ بَلْ هُم بِلِقَآءِ رَبِّهِمْ كَٰفِرُونَ ﴿١٠﴾

11. Say: "The angel of death, who was charged with you, will carry you off; then you will be returned to your Lord."

۞ قُلْ يَتَوَفَّىٰكُم مَّلَكُ ٱلْمَوْتِ ٱلَّذِى وُكِّلَ بِكُمْ ثُمَّ إِلَىٰ رَبِّكُمْ تُرْجَعُونَ ﴿١١﴾

12. If only you could see how the criminals are hanging their heads down before their Lord, saying: "Our Lord, we have seen and heard; so send us back that we might do the righteous deed. Now we believe with certainty."

وَلَوْ تَرَىٰٓ إِذِ ٱلْمُجْرِمُونَ نَاكِسُوا۟ رُءُوسِهِمْ عِندَ رَبِّهِمْ رَبَّنَآ أَبْصَرْنَا وَسَمِعْنَا فَٱرْجِعْنَا نَعْمَلْ صَٰلِحًا إِنَّا مُوقِنُونَ ﴿١٢﴾

13. Had We wished, We would have granted every soul its guidance, but My Word is now fulfilled: "I shall fill Gehennam[698] with jinn and men, all together."

وَلَوْ شِئْنَا لَءَاتَيْنَا كُلَّ نَفْسٍ هُدَىٰهَا وَلَٰكِنْ حَقَّ ٱلْقَوْلُ مِنِّى لَأَمْلَأَنَّ جَهَنَّمَ مِنَ ٱلْجِنَّةِ وَٱلنَّاسِ أَجْمَعِينَ ﴿١٣﴾

14. So, taste, for forgetting the Encounter of this Day - We have forgotten you too, and taste the punishment of eternity, for what you used to do.

فَذُوقُوا۟ بِمَا نَسِيتُمْ لِقَآءَ يَوْمِكُمْ هَٰذَآ إِنَّا نَسِينَٰكُمْ وَذُوقُوا۟ عَذَابَ ٱلْخُلْدِ بِمَا كُنتُمْ تَعْمَلُونَ ﴿١٤﴾

15. Yet those believe in Our Signs who, when reminded of them, fall down prostrate and celebrate the praise of their Lord, and they are not overbearing.

إِنَّمَا يُؤْمِنُ بِـَٔايَٰتِنَا ٱلَّذِينَ إِذَا ذُكِّرُوا۟ بِهَا خَرُّوا۟ سُجَّدًا وَسَبَّحُوا۟ بِحَمْدِ رَبِّهِمْ وَهُمْ لَا يَسْتَكْبِرُونَ ۩ ﴿١٥﴾

16. Their sides shun their couches as they call on their Lord in fear and hope, and of what We have provided [them with, they give in charity].

تَتَجَافَىٰ جُنُوبُهُمْ عَنِ ٱلْمَضَاجِعِ يَدْعُونَ رَبَّهُمْ خَوْفًا وَطَمَعًا وَمِمَّا رَزَقْنَٰهُمْ يُنفِقُونَ ﴿١٦﴾

17. No soul knows what was laid up for them secretly of joyful relief, as a reward for what they used to do.

فَلَا تَعْلَمُ نَفْسٌ مَّآ أُخْفِىَ لَهُم مِّن قُرَّةِ أَعْيُنٍ جَزَآءًۢ بِمَا كَانُوا۟ يَعْمَلُونَ ﴿١٧﴾

---

698. Another word for Hell.

18. Is he who believes, then, like he who is a sinner? No, they are not equal.

19. As for those who believe and do the righteous deeds, they will have gardens of refuge to receive them, for what they used to do.

20. But, as for the sinners, their refuge is the Fire. Every time they want to get out of it, they are brought back and it will be said to them: "Taste the punishment of the Fire which you used to deny."

21. We shall surely let them taste the nearer punishment, prior to the greater punishment, that perchance they might repent.

22. Who is more unjust than he who is reminded of Our Signs, then he turns away from them? We will certainly wreak vengeance upon the criminals.

23. We have, indeed, given Moses the Book; so do not be in doubt concerning his encounter, and We made it a guidance to the Children of Israel.

24. And We appointed some of them as leaders, guiding by Our Command, when they stood fast and believed firmly in Our Signs.

25. It is your Lord Who will judge between them on the Day of Resurrection, regarding that whereof they used to differ.

26. Was it not shown to them how many generations We have destroyed before them, while they were strolling in their dwellings? Surely, there are signs in that; do they not hear?

27. Do they not see that We conduct the water onto the barren land, bringing forth thereby vegetation, from which their cattle and their own folk eat? Do they not see, then?

أَفَمَن كَانَ مُؤۡمِنًا كَمَن كَانَ فَاسِقًا لَّا يَسۡتَوُۥنَ ۝

أَمَّا ٱلَّذِينَ ءَامَنُوا۟ وَعَمِلُوا۟ ٱلصَّـٰلِحَـٰتِ فَلَهُمۡ جَنَّـٰتُ ٱلۡمَأۡوَىٰ نُزُلًۢا بِمَا كَانُوا۟ يَعۡمَلُونَ ۝

وَأَمَّا ٱلَّذِينَ فَسَقُوا۟ فَمَأۡوَىٰهُمُ ٱلنَّارُ كُلَّمَآ أَرَادُوٓا۟ أَن يَخۡرُجُوا۟ مِنۡهَآ أُعِيدُوا۟ فِيهَا وَقِيلَ لَهُمۡ ذُوقُوا۟ عَذَابَ ٱلنَّارِ ٱلَّذِى كُنتُم بِهِۦ تُكَذِّبُونَ ۝

وَلَنُذِيقَنَّهُم مِّنَ ٱلۡعَذَابِ ٱلۡأَدۡنَىٰ دُونَ ٱلۡعَذَابِ ٱلۡأَكۡبَرِ لَعَلَّهُمۡ يَرۡجِعُونَ ۝

وَمَنۡ أَظۡلَمُ مِمَّن ذُكِّرَ بِـَٔايَـٰتِ رَبِّهِۦ ثُمَّ أَعۡرَضَ عَنۡهَآ إِنَّا مِنَ ٱلۡمُجۡرِمِينَ مُنتَقِمُونَ ۝

وَلَقَدۡ ءَاتَيۡنَا مُوسَى ٱلۡكِتَـٰبَ فَلَا تَكُن فِى مِرۡيَةٍ مِّن لِّقَآئِهِۦ وَجَعَلۡنَـٰهُ هُدًى لِّبَنِىٓ إِسۡرَٰٓءِيلَ ۝

وَجَعَلۡنَا مِنۡهُمۡ أَئِمَّةً يَهۡدُونَ بِأَمۡرِنَا لَمَّا صَبَرُوا۟ وَكَانُوا۟ بِـَٔايَـٰتِنَا يُوقِنُونَ ۝

إِنَّ رَبَّكَ هُوَ يَفۡصِلُ بَيۡنَهُمۡ يَوۡمَ ٱلۡقِيَـٰمَةِ فِيمَا كَانُوا۟ فِيهِ يَخۡتَلِفُونَ ۝

أَوَلَمۡ يَهۡدِ لَهُمۡ كَمۡ أَهۡلَكۡنَا مِن قَبۡلِهِم مِّنَ ٱلۡقُرُونِ يَمۡشُونَ فِى مَسَـٰكِنِهِمۡ إِنَّ فِى ذَٰلِكَ لَءَايَـٰتٍ أَفَلَا يَسۡمَعُونَ ۝

أَوَلَمۡ يَرَوۡا۟ أَنَّا نَسُوقُ ٱلۡمَآءَ إِلَى ٱلۡأَرۡضِ ٱلۡجُرُزِ فَنُخۡرِجُ بِهِۦ زَرۡعًا تَأۡكُلُ مِنۡهُ أَنۡعَـٰمُهُمۡ وَأَنفُسُهُمۡ أَفَلَا يُبۡصِرُونَ ۝

28. And they say: "When will this victory come, if you are truthful?"

وَيَقُولُونَ مَتَىٰ هَٰذَا ٱلْفَتْحُ إِن كُنتُمْ صَٰدِقِينَ ﴿٢٨﴾

29. Say: "On the day of victory, their profession of faith will not avail the unbelievers and they will not be given respite."

قُلْ يَوْمَ ٱلْفَتْحِ لَا يَنفَعُ ٱلَّذِينَ كَفَرُوٓاْ إِيمَٰنُهُمْ وَلَا هُمْ يُنظَرُونَ ﴿٢٩﴾

30. So turn away from them and wait; they too shall be waiting.

فَأَعْرِضْ عَنْهُمْ وَٱنتَظِرْ إِنَّهُم مُّنتَظِرُونَ ﴿٣٠﴾

Sûrat Al-Ahzâb,
(The Confederates) 33

In the Name of Allah,
the Compassionate, the Merciful

1. O Prophet, fear Allah and do not obey the unbelievers and the hypocrites. Allah is All-Knowing, All-Wise.

يَٰٓأَيُّهَا ٱلنَّبِىُّ ٱتَّقِ ٱللَّهَ وَلَا تُطِعِ ٱلْكَٰفِرِينَ وَٱلْمُنَٰفِقِينَ إِنَّ ٱللَّهَ كَانَ عَلِيمًا حَكِيمًا ﴿١﴾

2. And follow what is revealed to you from your Lord. Indeed, Allah is Well-Informed about what you do.

وَٱتَّبِعْ مَا يُوحَىٰٓ إِلَيْكَ مِن رَّبِّكَ إِنَّ ٱللَّهَ كَانَ بِمَا تَعْمَلُونَ خَبِيرًا ﴿٢﴾

3. And trust in Allah; Allah suffices as a Guardian.

وَتَوَكَّلْ عَلَى ٱللَّهِ وَكَفَىٰ بِٱللَّهِ وَكِيلًا ﴿٣﴾

4. Allah did not create two hearts within the breast of any man; and He did not make your wives, whom you compare to your mothers' backs;[699] and He did not make your [adopted] sons your sons in fact. That is your own claim, by your words of mouth. Allah speaks the truth and He guides to the Right Path.

مَّا جَعَلَ ٱللَّهُ لِرَجُلٍ مِّن قَلْبَيْنِ فِى جَوْفِهِۦ وَمَا جَعَلَ أَزْوَٰجَكُمُ ٱلَّٰٓـِٔى تُظَٰهِرُونَ مِنْهُنَّ أُمَّهَٰتِكُمْ وَمَا جَعَلَ أَدْعِيَآءَكُمْ أَبْنَآءَكُمْ ذَٰلِكُمْ قَوْلُكُم بِأَفْوَٰهِكُمْ وَٱللَّهُ يَقُولُ ٱلْحَقَّ وَهُوَ يَهْدِى ٱلسَّبِيلَ ﴿٤﴾

5. Assign them to their own fathers. That is more equitable in the sight of Allah; but if you do not know their real fathers, then they are your brothers in religion, your adopted fellow-Muslims. You are not at fault if you err therein; but only in what your hearts intend. Allah is ever All-Forgiving, All-Merciful.

ٱدْعُوهُمْ لِءَابَآئِهِمْ هُوَ أَقْسَطُ عِندَ ٱللَّهِ فَإِن لَّمْ تَعْلَمُوٓاْ ءَابَآءَهُمْ فَإِخْوَٰنُكُمْ فِى ٱلدِّينِ وَمَوَٰلِيكُمْ وَلَيْسَ عَلَيْكُمْ جُنَاحٌ فِيمَآ أَخْطَأْتُم بِهِۦ وَلَٰكِن مَّا تَعَمَّدَتْ قُلُوبُكُمْ وَكَانَ ٱللَّهُ غَفُورًا رَّحِيمًا ﴿٥﴾

---

699. That is, you divorce them saying: ‹You are as our mothers' backs›.

6. The Prophet is closer to the believers than their own selves and his wives are like their mothers. The kinsmen are closer to each other, in Allah's Book, than the believers or the Emigrants; unless you are doing your friends an honourable deed, that has already been inscribed in the Book.

7. And [remember] when We took from the Prophets their covenant and from you and from Noah, Abraham, Moses and Jesus, son of Mary, too; and We took from them a solemn covenant;

8. So as to question the truthful about their truthfulness, and He has prepared for the unbelievers a very painful punishment.

9. O believers, remember Allah's Grace on you when enemy hosts[700] came upon you; then We sent against them a wind and hosts you did not actually see. Allah perceives well what you do.

10. When they came upon you from above you and from below you, and your eyes looked askew and your hearts reached your throats, while you entertained false thoughts about Allah.

11. There and then, the believers were sorely tried and shaken very violently.

12. And when the hypocrites and those in whose hearts is a sickness were saying: "Allah and His Messenger have only promised us vanity."

13. And when a group of them said: "O people of Yathrib,[701] there is no place for you to abide in, so turn back"; while another group of them were seeking the Prophet's permission, saying: "Our homes are exposed", whereas they were not exposed. They only wanted to flee.

---

700. Of confederates allied against Muslims in the Battle of the Ditch (khandaq) during the siege of Medina or Yathrib 5 AH.
701. The old name of Medina, the Prophet's City.

14. And were it[702] entered from its different quarters, and then they were asked to apostatise, they would certainly have done so, without lingering but a short while.

15. Although they had made a pledge to Allah, before, that they will not turn their backs. Pledges to Allah are always accountable.

16. Say: "Flight will not profit you, if you flee from death or murder; for then you will not partake of enjoying life except briefly."

17. Say: "Who will defend you against Allah, if He wishes you ill or if He wishes you well." They will find for themselves, apart from Allah, no protectors or supporters.

18. Allah would surely know those of you who hinder the others and those who say to their brothers: "Come over to us"; and they do not partake of fighting, except a little.

19. They are ever niggardly towards you, but if fear overtakes them, you will see them look at you, with their eyes rolling like one who is in the throes of death. But when fear subsides, they cut you with sharp tongues. They are niggardly in times of prosperity;[703] those are no believers. Thus Allah has frustrated their actions, that being for Allah an easy matter.

20. They think the Confederates have not departed, but were the Confederates to show up, they would wish that they were desert-dwellers with the Bedouins asking about your news. However, were they in your midst, they would fight but little.

---

702. The city of Yathrib.
703. As a result of the spoils of war.

21. You have had a good example in Allah's Messenger; surely for him who hopes for Allah and the Last Day and remembers Allah often.

22. When the believers saw the Confederates, they said: "This is what Allah and His Messenger have promised us, and Allah and His Messenger are truthful." And it only increased them in faith and submission.

23. Of the believers, there are men who fulfilled what they pledged to Allah; some of them have died, some are still waiting, without changing in the least.

24. So that Allah might reward the truthful for their truthfulness and punish the hypocrites, if He wishes, or forgive them. Surely Allah is All-Forgiving, All-Merciful.

25. Allah turned back the unbelievers in a state of rage, having not won any good,[704] and Allah spared the believers battle. Allah is, indeed, Strong and Mighty.

26. And He brought those of the People of the Book who supported them from their fortresses and cast terror into their hearts, some of them you slew and some you took captive.

27. And He bequeathed to you their lands, their homes and their possessions, together with land you have never trodden. Allah has power over everything.

28. O Prophet, say to your wives: "If you desire the present life and its finery, so come along that I might provide for you and set you free kindly.

لَّقَدْ كَانَ لَكُمْ فِى رَسُولِ ٱللَّهِ أُسْوَةٌ حَسَنَةٌ لِّمَن كَانَ يَرْجُوا۟ ٱللَّهَ وَٱلْيَوْمَ ٱلْآخِرَ وَذَكَرَ ٱللَّهَ كَثِيرًا ﴿٢١﴾

وَلَمَّا رَءَا ٱلْمُؤْمِنُونَ ٱلْأَحْزَابَ قَالُوا۟ هَٰذَا مَا وَعَدَنَا ٱللَّهُ وَرَسُولُهُۥ وَصَدَقَ ٱللَّهُ وَرَسُولُهُۥ وَمَا زَادَهُمْ إِلَّا إِيمَٰنًا وَتَسْلِيمًا ﴿٢٢﴾

مِّنَ ٱلْمُؤْمِنِينَ رِجَالٌ صَدَقُوا۟ مَا عَٰهَدُوا۟ ٱللَّهَ عَلَيْهِ فَمِنْهُم مَّن قَضَىٰ نَحْبَهُۥ وَمِنْهُم مَّن يَنتَظِرُ وَمَا بَدَّلُوا۟ تَبْدِيلًا ﴿٢٣﴾

لِّيَجْزِىَ ٱللَّهُ ٱلصَّٰدِقِينَ بِصِدْقِهِمْ وَيُعَذِّبَ ٱلْمُنَٰفِقِينَ إِن شَآءَ أَوْ يَتُوبَ عَلَيْهِمْ إِنَّ ٱللَّهَ كَانَ غَفُورًا رَّحِيمًا ﴿٢٤﴾

وَرَدَّ ٱللَّهُ ٱلَّذِينَ كَفَرُوا۟ بِغَيْظِهِمْ لَمْ يَنَالُوا۟ خَيْرًا وَكَفَى ٱللَّهُ ٱلْمُؤْمِنِينَ ٱلْقِتَالَ وَكَانَ ٱللَّهُ قَوِيًّا عَزِيزًا ﴿٢٥﴾

وَأَنزَلَ ٱلَّذِينَ ظَٰهَرُوهُم مِّنْ أَهْلِ ٱلْكِتَٰبِ مِن صَيَاصِيهِمْ وَقَذَفَ فِى قُلُوبِهِمُ ٱلرُّعْبَ فَرِيقًا تَقْتُلُونَ وَتَأْسِرُونَ فَرِيقًا ﴿٢٦﴾

وَأَوْرَثَكُمْ أَرْضَهُمْ وَدِيَٰرَهُمْ وَأَمْوَٰلَهُمْ وَأَرْضًا لَّمْ تَطَـُٔوهَا وَكَانَ ٱللَّهُ عَلَىٰ كُلِّ شَىْءٍ قَدِيرًا ﴿٢٧﴾

يَٰٓأَيُّهَا ٱلنَّبِىُّ قُل لِّأَزْوَٰجِكَ إِن كُنتُنَّ تُرِدْنَ ٱلْحَيَوٰةَ ٱلدُّنْيَا وَزِينَتَهَا فَتَعَالَيْنَ أُمَتِّعْكُنَّ وَأُسَرِّحْكُنَّ سَرَاحًا جَمِيلًا ﴿٢٨﴾

---

704. In the form of spoils.

29. "But if you desire Allah, His Messenger and the life to come, surely Allah has prepared for the beneficent among you a great wage."

30. O wives of the Prophet, whomever of you commits a flagrant foul act, her punishment will be doubled; and that for Allah is an easy matter.

31. Whoever of you obeys Allah and His Messenger and does the righteous deed, We shall pay her wage twice over, and We have prepared for her a generous provision.

32. O wives of the Prophet, you are not like any other women. If you are God-fearing, do not be abject in speech, so that he in whose heart is a sickness may covet you, but speak in an honourable way.

33. Stay in your homes and do not display your finery as the pagans of old did; perform the prayer, give the alms and obey Allah and His Messenger. Allah only wishes to turn away abomination from you and purify you fully, O People of the House.

34. And remember what is recited in your homes of Allah's Signs and of wisdom. Indeed, Allah is Subtle, Well-Informed.

35. Men and women who have submitted, believed, obeyed, are truthful, steadfast, reverent, giving in charity, fasting, guarding their private parts and remembering Allah often, Allah has prepared for them forgiveness and a great reward.

36. It is not up to any believer, man or woman, when Allah and His Messenger have passed a judgement, to have any choice in their affairs. Whoever disobeys Allah and His Messenger have gone astray in a manifest manner.

وَإِن كُنتُنَّ تُرِدْنَ ٱللَّهَ وَرَسُولَهُ وَٱلدَّارَ ٱلْآخِرَةَ فَإِنَّ ٱللَّهَ أَعَدَّ لِلْمُحْسِنَٰتِ مِنكُنَّ أَجْرًا عَظِيمًا ﴿٢٩﴾

يَٰنِسَاءَ ٱلنَّبِيِّ مَن يَأْتِ مِنكُنَّ بِفَٰحِشَةٍ مُّبَيِّنَةٍ يُضَٰعَفْ لَهَا ٱلْعَذَابُ ضِعْفَيْنِ وَكَانَ ذَٰلِكَ عَلَى ٱللَّهِ يَسِيرًا ﴿٣٠﴾

۞ وَمَن يَقْنُتْ مِنكُنَّ لِلَّهِ وَرَسُولِهِ وَتَعْمَلْ صَٰلِحًا نُّؤْتِهَا أَجْرَهَا مَرَّتَيْنِ وَأَعْتَدْنَا لَهَا رِزْقًا كَرِيمًا ﴿٣١﴾

يَٰنِسَاءَ ٱلنَّبِيِّ لَسْتُنَّ كَأَحَدٍ مِّنَ ٱلنِّسَاءِ إِنِ ٱتَّقَيْتُنَّ فَلَا تَخْضَعْنَ بِٱلْقَوْلِ فَيَطْمَعَ ٱلَّذِى فِى قَلْبِهِ مَرَضٌ وَقُلْنَ قَوْلًا مَّعْرُوفًا ﴿٣٢﴾

وَقَرْنَ فِى بُيُوتِكُنَّ وَلَا تَبَرَّجْنَ تَبَرُّجَ ٱلْجَٰهِلِيَّةِ ٱلْأُولَىٰ وَأَقِمْنَ ٱلصَّلَوٰةَ وَءَاتِينَ ٱلزَّكَوٰةَ وَأَطِعْنَ ٱللَّهَ وَرَسُولَهُ إِنَّمَا يُرِيدُ ٱللَّهُ لِيُذْهِبَ عَنكُمُ ٱلرِّجْسَ أَهْلَ ٱلْبَيْتِ وَيُطَهِّرَكُمْ تَطْهِيرًا ﴿٣٣﴾

وَٱذْكُرْنَ مَا يُتْلَىٰ فِى بُيُوتِكُنَّ مِنْ ءَايَٰتِ ٱللَّهِ وَٱلْحِكْمَةِ إِنَّ ٱللَّهَ كَانَ لَطِيفًا خَبِيرًا ﴿٣٤﴾

إِنَّ ٱلْمُسْلِمِينَ وَٱلْمُسْلِمَٰتِ وَٱلْمُؤْمِنِينَ وَٱلْمُؤْمِنَٰتِ وَٱلْقَٰنِتِينَ وَٱلْقَٰنِتَٰتِ وَٱلصَّٰدِقِينَ وَٱلصَّٰدِقَٰتِ وَٱلصَّٰبِرِينَ وَٱلصَّٰبِرَٰتِ وَٱلْخَٰشِعِينَ وَٱلْخَٰشِعَٰتِ وَٱلْمُتَصَدِّقِينَ وَٱلْمُتَصَدِّقَٰتِ وَٱلصَّٰئِمِينَ وَٱلصَّٰئِمَٰتِ وَٱلْحَٰفِظِينَ فُرُوجَهُمْ وَٱلْحَٰفِظَٰتِ وَٱلذَّٰكِرِينَ ٱللَّهَ كَثِيرًا وَٱلذَّٰكِرَٰتِ أَعَدَّ ٱللَّهُ لَهُم مَّغْفِرَةً وَأَجْرًا عَظِيمًا ﴿٣٥﴾

وَمَا كَانَ لِمُؤْمِنٍ وَلَا مُؤْمِنَةٍ إِذَا قَضَى ٱللَّهُ وَرَسُولُهُ أَمْرًا أَن يَكُونَ لَهُمُ ٱلْخِيَرَةُ مِنْ أَمْرِهِمْ وَمَن يَعْصِ ٱللَّهَ وَرَسُولَهُ فَقَدْ ضَلَّ ضَلَٰلًا مُّبِينًا ﴿٣٦﴾

37. And [remember] when you said to him whom Allah favoured and you favoured:[705] "Hold on to your wife and fear Allah", while you concealed within yourself what Allah would reveal and feared other men, whereas Allah had a better right to be feared by you. Then, when Zayd had satisfied his desire for her, We gave her to you in marriage; so that the believers should not be at fault, regarding the wives of their adopted sons, once they have satisfied their desire for them. For Allah's Command must be accomplished.

38. The Prophet was not at fault regarding what Allah prescribed for him as was His Way with those who were gone before. And Allah's Command is a pre-ordained decree.

39. Those who were delivering Allah's Messages and feared Him, fearing none other than Allah. Allah suffices as a Reckoner.

40. Muhammad is not the father of any of your men, but is the Messenger of Allah and the seal of the Prophets. Allah is Cognizant of everything.

41. O believers, remember Allah often;

42. And glorify Him morning and evening.

43. It is He Who blesses you, with His angels, that He may bring you out of the shadows of darkness into the light; and He is Ever Merciful towards the believers.

44. Their greeting, when they encounter Him is: "Peace", and He has prepared for them a generous reward.

45. O Prophet, We have sent you as a witness, a bearer of good news and a warner,

وَإِذْ تَقُولُ لِلَّذِى أَنْعَمَ اللَّهُ عَلَيْهِ وَأَنْعَمْتَ عَلَيْهِ أَمْسِكْ عَلَيْكَ زَوْجَكَ وَاتَّقِ اللَّهَ وَتُخْفِى فِى نَفْسِكَ مَا اللَّهُ مُبْدِيهِ وَتَخْشَى النَّاسَ وَاللَّهُ أَحَقُّ أَن تَخْشَىٰهُ فَلَمَّا قَضَىٰ زَيْدٌ مِّنْهَا وَطَرًا زَوَّجْنَٰكَهَا لِكَىْ لَا يَكُونَ عَلَى الْمُؤْمِنِينَ حَرَجٌ فِى أَزْوَٰجِ أَدْعِيَآئِهِمْ إِذَا قَضَوْا مِنْهُنَّ وَطَرًا وَكَانَ أَمْرُ اللَّهِ مَفْعُولًا ﴿٣٧﴾

مَّا كَانَ عَلَى النَّبِىِّ مِنْ حَرَجٍ فِيمَا فَرَضَ اللَّهُ لَهُ سُنَّةَ اللَّهِ فِى الَّذِينَ خَلَوْا مِن قَبْلُ وَكَانَ أَمْرُ اللَّهِ قَدَرًا مَّقْدُورًا ﴿٣٨﴾

الَّذِينَ يُبَلِّغُونَ رِسَٰلَٰتِ اللَّهِ وَيَخْشَوْنَهُ وَلَا يَخْشَوْنَ أَحَدًا إِلَّا اللَّهَ وَكَفَىٰ بِاللَّهِ حَسِيبًا ﴿٣٩﴾

مَّا كَانَ مُحَمَّدٌ أَبَآ أَحَدٍ مِّن رِّجَالِكُمْ وَلَٰكِن رَّسُولَ اللَّهِ وَخَاتَمَ النَّبِيِّۧنَ وَكَانَ اللَّهُ بِكُلِّ شَىْءٍ عَلِيمًا ﴿٤٠﴾

يَٰٓأَيُّهَا الَّذِينَ ءَامَنُوا اذْكُرُوا اللَّهَ ذِكْرًا كَثِيرًا ﴿٤١﴾ وَسَبِّحُوهُ بُكْرَةً وَأَصِيلًا ﴿٤٢﴾

هُوَ الَّذِى يُصَلِّى عَلَيْكُمْ وَمَلَٰٓئِكَتُهُ لِيُخْرِجَكُم مِّنَ الظُّلُمَٰتِ إِلَى النُّورِ وَكَانَ بِالْمُؤْمِنِينَ رَحِيمًا ﴿٤٣﴾

تَحِيَّتُهُمْ يَوْمَ يَلْقَوْنَهُ سَلَٰمٌ وَأَعَدَّ لَهُمْ أَجْرًا كَرِيمًا ﴿٤٤﴾

يَٰٓأَيُّهَا النَّبِىُّ إِنَّآ أَرْسَلْنَٰكَ شَٰهِدًا وَمُبَشِّرًا وَنَذِيرًا ﴿٤٥﴾

---

705. This is addressed to Zayd Ibn Harithah regarding his wife, Zaynab Bint Jahsh, whom the Prophet married upon her release from Zayd.

وَدَاعِيًا إِلَى اللَّهِ بِإِذْنِهِ وَسِرَاجًا مُّنِيرًا ۝

46. Calling to Allah by His Leave, and an illuminating beacon.

وَبَشِّرِ الْمُؤْمِنِينَ بِأَنَّ لَهُم مِّنَ اللَّهِ فَضْلًا كَبِيرًا ۝

47. Announce to the believers that they will have a generous bounty from Allah.

وَلَا تُطِعِ الْكَافِرِينَ وَالْمُنَافِقِينَ وَدَعْ أَذَاهُمْ وَتَوَكَّلْ عَلَى اللَّهِ وَكَفَى بِاللَّهِ وَكِيلًا ۝

48. And do not obey the unbelievers and the hypocrites, overlook their injury and trust in Allah. For Allah suffices as a Guardian.

يَا أَيُّهَا الَّذِينَ آمَنُوا إِذَا نَكَحْتُمُ الْمُؤْمِنَاتِ ثُمَّ طَلَّقْتُمُوهُنَّ مِن قَبْلِ أَن تَمَسُّوهُنَّ فَمَا لَكُمْ عَلَيْهِنَّ مِنْ عِدَّةٍ تَعْتَدُّونَهَا فَمَتِّعُوهُنَّ وَسَرِّحُوهُنَّ سَرَاحًا جَمِيلًا ۝

49. O believers, if you marry believing women then divorce them, before touching them, you owe them no fixed term to reckon. So make provision for them and set them free in an honourable way.

يَا أَيُّهَا النَّبِيُّ إِنَّا أَحْلَلْنَا لَكَ أَزْوَاجَكَ الَّتِي آتَيْتَ أُجُورَهُنَّ وَمَا مَلَكَتْ يَمِينُكَ مِمَّا أَفَاءَ اللَّهُ عَلَيْكَ وَبَنَاتِ عَمِّكَ وَبَنَاتِ عَمَّاتِكَ وَبَنَاتِ خَالِكَ وَبَنَاتِ خَالَاتِكَ اللَّاتِي هَاجَرْنَ مَعَكَ وَامْرَأَةً مُّؤْمِنَةً إِن وَهَبَتْ نَفْسَهَا لِلنَّبِيِّ إِنْ أَرَادَ النَّبِيُّ أَن يَسْتَنكِحَهَا خَالِصَةً لَّكَ مِن دُونِ الْمُؤْمِنِينَ قَدْ عَلِمْنَا مَا فَرَضْنَا عَلَيْهِمْ فِي أَزْوَاجِهِمْ وَمَا مَلَكَتْ أَيْمَانُهُمْ لِكَيْلَا يَكُونَ عَلَيْكَ حَرَجٌ وَكَانَ اللَّهُ غَفُورًا رَّحِيمًا ۝

50. O Prophet, We have made lawful, for you, your wives, whose dowry you have paid, what your right hand owns[706] out of the spoils of war that Allah gave you, the daughters of your paternal uncles, the daughters of your paternal aunts, the daughters of your maternal uncles, the daughters of your maternal aunts who emigrated with you, and any believing woman who gives herself freely to the Prophet, if the Prophet desires to marry her, granted exclusively to you, but not the believers. We know what We have pre-scribed for them, regarding their wives and what their right hands own, so that you may not be at fault. Allah is All-Forgiving, Merciful.

۞ تُرْجِي مَن تَشَاءُ مِنْهُنَّ وَتُؤْوِي إِلَيْكَ مَن تَشَاءُ وَمَنِ ابْتَغَيْتَ مِمَّنْ عَزَلْتَ فَلَا جُنَاحَ عَلَيْكَ ذَلِكَ أَدْنَى أَن تَقَرَّ أَعْيُنُهُنَّ وَلَا يَحْزَنَّ وَيَرْضَيْنَ بِمَا آتَيْتَهُنَّ كُلُّهُنَّ وَاللَّهُ يَعْلَمُ مَا فِي قُلُوبِكُمْ وَكَانَ اللَّهُ عَلِيمًا حَلِيمًا ۝

51. You may defer any of them you wish, and take in any of them that you wish, or any that you may have cut off. So you are not liable to reproach. For thus it is more likely that they will be delighted and will not grieve, but be content with what you have given each one of them. Allah knows what is within your hearts; and Allah is All-Knowing, Clement.

---

706. Slave-girls.

52. Thereafter, other women are not lawful to you, nor is substituting other wives for them, even if you admire their beauty, except for what your right hand owns. Allah is Watchful over everything.

53. O believers, do not enter the houses of the Prophet, unless you are invited to a meal, without awaiting the hour; but if you are invited, then enter; but when you have eaten, disperse, without lingering for idle talk. That is vexing to the Prophet who might be wary of you, but Allah is not wary of the truth. If you ask them[707] for an object, ask them from behind a curtain. That is purer for your hearts and theirs. You should never hurt the Messenger of Allah, nor take his wives in marriage after him. That is truly abominable in the Sight of Allah.

54. Whether you reveal a thing or conceal it, Allah has knowledge of everything.

55. They[708] are not at fault, regarding their fathers, their sons, their brothers, their brothers' sons, their sisters' sons or their wives and what their right hands possess; so fear Allah. Surely, Allah is Witness of everything.

56. Allah and His angels bless the Prophet. O believers, bless him and greet him graciously, too.

57. Those who cause Allah and His Messenger any injury, Allah has cursed them in this life and the life to come and has prepared for them a demeaning punishment.

58. And those who injure the believers, men and women, except for what they have incurred, have borne the burden of falsehood and manifest sin.

لَا يَحِلُّ لَكَ ٱلنِّسَآءُ مِنۢ بَعْدُ وَلَآ أَن تَبَدَّلَ بِهِنَّ مِنْ أَزْوَٰجٍ وَلَوْ أَعْجَبَكَ حُسْنُهُنَّ إِلَّا مَا مَلَكَتْ يَمِينُكَ وَكَانَ ٱللَّهُ عَلَىٰ كُلِّ شَىْءٍ رَّقِيبًا ٥٢

يَٰٓأَيُّهَا ٱلَّذِينَ ءَامَنُوا۟ لَا تَدْخُلُوا۟ بُيُوتَ ٱلنَّبِىِّ إِلَّآ أَن يُؤْذَنَ لَكُمْ إِلَىٰ طَعَامٍ غَيْرَ نَٰظِرِينَ إِنَىٰهُ وَلَٰكِنْ إِذَا دُعِيتُمْ فَٱدْخُلُوا۟ فَإِذَا طَعِمْتُمْ فَٱنتَشِرُوا۟ وَلَا مُسْتَـْٔنِسِينَ لِحَدِيثٍ إِنَّ ذَٰلِكُمْ كَانَ يُؤْذِى ٱلنَّبِىَّ فَيَسْتَحْىِۦ مِنكُمْ وَٱللَّهُ لَا يَسْتَحْىِۦ مِنَ ٱلْحَقِّ وَإِذَا سَأَلْتُمُوهُنَّ مَتَٰعًا فَسْـَٔلُوهُنَّ مِن وَرَآءِ حِجَابٍ ذَٰلِكُمْ أَطْهَرُ لِقُلُوبِكُمْ وَقُلُوبِهِنَّ وَمَا كَانَ لَكُمْ أَن تُؤْذُوا۟ رَسُولَ ٱللَّهِ وَلَآ أَن تَنكِحُوٓا۟ أَزْوَٰجَهُۥ مِنۢ بَعْدِهِۦٓ أَبَدًا إِنَّ ذَٰلِكُمْ كَانَ عِندَ ٱللَّهِ عَظِيمًا ٥٣

إِن تُبْدُوا۟ شَيْـًٔا أَوْ تُخْفُوهُ فَإِنَّ ٱللَّهَ كَانَ بِكُلِّ شَىْءٍ عَلِيمًا ٥٤

لَّا جُنَاحَ عَلَيْهِنَّ فِىٓ ءَابَآئِهِنَّ وَلَآ أَبْنَآئِهِنَّ وَلَآ إِخْوَٰنِهِنَّ وَلَآ أَبْنَآءِ إِخْوَٰنِهِنَّ وَلَآ أَبْنَآءِ أَخَوَٰتِهِنَّ وَلَا نِسَآئِهِنَّ وَلَا مَا مَلَكَتْ أَيْمَٰنُهُنَّ وَٱتَّقِينَ ٱللَّهَ إِنَّ ٱللَّهَ كَانَ عَلَىٰ كُلِّ شَىْءٍ شَهِيدًا ٥٥

إِنَّ ٱللَّهَ وَمَلَٰٓئِكَتَهُۥ يُصَلُّونَ عَلَى ٱلنَّبِىِّ يَٰٓأَيُّهَا ٱلَّذِينَ ءَامَنُوا۟ صَلُّوا۟ عَلَيْهِ وَسَلِّمُوا۟ تَسْلِيمًا ٥٦

إِنَّ ٱلَّذِينَ يُؤْذُونَ ٱللَّهَ وَرَسُولَهُۥ لَعَنَهُمُ ٱللَّهُ فِى ٱلدُّنْيَا وَٱلْءَاخِرَةِ وَأَعَدَّ لَهُمْ عَذَابًا مُّهِينًا ٥٧

وَٱلَّذِينَ يُؤْذُونَ ٱلْمُؤْمِنِينَ وَٱلْمُؤْمِنَٰتِ بِغَيْرِ مَا ٱكْتَسَبُوا۟ فَقَدِ ٱحْتَمَلُوا۟ بُهْتَٰنًا وَإِثْمًا مُّبِينًا ٥٨

---

707. The wives of the Prophet.
708. The wives of the Prophet, if they appear unveiled.

59. O Prophet, tell your wives and daughters and the wives of the believers, to draw their outer garments closer. That is more conducive to their being known, and not being injured. Allah is All-Forgiving, Merciful.

60. If the hypocrites, those in whose hearts is a sickness and those who spread lies in the city, do not desist, We will certainly urge you against them and then they will not dwell with you therein as neighbours but for a short time.

61. Accursed, wherever they are encountered they will be seized and slaughtered

62. That is Allah's Way of dealing with those who have gone before, and you will never find any alteration of Allah's Way.

63. People will ask you about the Hour. Say: "The knowledge thereof is with Allah." And what do you know? The Hour may be close at hand.

64. Allah has cursed the unbelievers and prepared for them a blazing fire;

65. Dwelling therein forever, not finding a protector or supporter.

66. The day their faces are turned around in the Fire, they will say: "If only we had obeyed Allah and the Messenger."

67. They will say: "Lord, we have obeyed our masters and our chiefs and so they have led us astray.

68. "Lord, give them the punishment twofold and curse them mightily."

69. O believers, do not be like those who injured Moses, but Allah exonerated him from what they said, and he was highly regarded in Allah's Sight.

427

70. O believers, fear Allah and speak in a straightforward way.

يَـٰٓأَيُّهَا ٱلَّذِينَ ءَامَنُوا۟ ٱتَّقُوا۟ ٱللَّهَ وَقُولُوا۟ قَوْلًا سَدِيدًا ۝

71. He will set right your deeds and forgive you your sins. Whoever obeys Allah and His Messenger has won a great victory.

يُصْلِحْ لَكُمْ أَعْمَـٰلَكُمْ وَيَغْفِرْ لَكُمْ ذُنُوبَكُمْ ۗ وَمَن يُطِعِ ٱللَّهَ وَرَسُولَهُۥ فَقَدْ فَازَ فَوْزًا عَظِيمًا ۝

72. We offered the Trust to the heavens, the earth, and the mountains, but they refused to carry it and were afraid of it, but man carried it. He has indeed been unjust and ignorant.

إِنَّا عَرَضْنَا ٱلْأَمَانَةَ عَلَى ٱلسَّمَـٰوَٰتِ وَٱلْأَرْضِ وَٱلْجِبَالِ فَأَبَيْنَ أَن يَحْمِلْنَهَا وَأَشْفَقْنَ مِنْهَا وَحَمَلَهَا ٱلْإِنسَـٰنُ ۖ إِنَّهُۥ كَانَ ظَلُومًا جَهُولًا ۝

73. That Allah might punish the hypocrites, men and women, the idolaters, men and women; and that Allah might pardon the believers, men and women.

لِّيُعَذِّبَ ٱللَّهُ ٱلْمُنَـٰفِقِينَ وَٱلْمُنَـٰفِقَـٰتِ وَٱلْمُشْرِكِينَ وَٱلْمُشْرِكَـٰتِ وَيَتُوبَ ٱللَّهُ عَلَى ٱلْمُؤْمِنِينَ وَٱلْمُؤْمِنَـٰتِ ۗ وَكَانَ ٱللَّهُ غَفُورًا رَّحِيمًا ۝

Sûrat Saba',
(The City of Sheba) 34

In the Name of Allah,
the Compassionate, the Merciful

بِسْمِ ٱللَّهِ ٱلرَّحْمَـٰنِ ٱلرَّحِيمِ

1. Praise be to Allah, to Whom belongs whatever is in the heavens and whatever is on earth, and praise be to Him in the Hereafter. He is the All-Wise, the All-Informed.

ٱلْحَمْدُ لِلَّهِ ٱلَّذِى لَهُۥ مَا فِى ٱلسَّمَـٰوَٰتِ وَمَا فِى ٱلْأَرْضِ وَلَهُ ٱلْحَمْدُ فِى ٱلْءَاخِرَةِ ۚ وَهُوَ ٱلْحَكِيمُ ٱلْخَبِيرُ ۝

2. He knows what penetrates into the earth and what goes out of it, what descends from heaven and what ascends to it. He is the All-Merciful, the All-Forgiving.

يَعْلَمُ مَا يَلِجُ فِى ٱلْأَرْضِ وَمَا يَخْرُجُ مِنْهَا وَمَا يَنزِلُ مِنَ ٱلسَّمَآءِ وَمَا يَعْرُجُ فِيهَا ۚ وَهُوَ ٱلرَّحِيمُ ٱلْغَفُورُ ۝

3. The unbelievers say: "The Hour will not come for us." Say: "Yes, indeed, it will come, by my Lord, Knower of the Unseen, from Whom not the weight of a speck of dust will escape in the heavens or on earth; nor is anything smaller or bigger than that but is in a Manifest Book."

وَقَالَ ٱلَّذِينَ كَفَرُوا۟ لَا تَأْتِينَا ٱلسَّاعَةُ ۖ قُلْ بَلَىٰ وَرَبِّى لَتَأْتِيَنَّكُمْ عَـٰلِمِ ٱلْغَيْبِ ۖ لَا يَعْزُبُ عَنْهُ مِثْقَالُ ذَرَّةٍ فِى ٱلسَّمَـٰوَٰتِ وَلَا فِى ٱلْأَرْضِ وَلَا أَصْغَرُ مِن ذَٰلِكَ وَلَا أَكْبَرُ إِلَّا فِى كِتَـٰبٍ مُّبِينٍ ۝

4. Those who have believed and did the righteous deeds those shall receive forgiveness and a generous provision.

لِّيَجْزِىَ ٱلَّذِينَ ءَامَنُوا۟ وَعَمِلُوا۟ ٱلصَّـٰلِحَـٰتِ ۚ أُو۟لَـٰٓئِكَ لَهُم مَّغْفِرَةٌ وَرِزْقٌ كَرِيمٌ ۝

5. But those who go around striving to rebut Our Signs those shall have the punishment of a very painful scourge.

6. And those who were given the knowledge,[709] which was sent down from your Lord, will see that it is the Truth and it guides onto the Path of the All-Mighty, the All-Praiseworthy.

7. The unbelievers say: "Shall we show you a man who will tell you that, once you have been torn to pieces, you shall become again a new creation?

8. "Does he impute falsehood to Allah or is he possessed?" No, those who do not believe in the Hereafter will undergo the punishment and are in grave error.

9. Have they not looked at what is in front of them and behind them of the heavens and the earth? Had We wished, We would have caused the earth to cave in under them, or dropped fragments from heaven upon them. Surely, in that is a sign to every repenting servant.

10. We have given David a bounty from Us: "O mountains, proclaim the praise with him, and you birds", and We softened the iron for him.

11. "Fashion ample coats of arms and measure well the links; and do you all the righteous deeds. I am fully observant of what you do."

12. And We subjected the wind to Solomon, blowing in the morning the space of a month and in the evening the space of a month; and We smelted for him the fount of brass. Of the jinn some worked before him, by the Leave

وَٱلَّذِينَ سَعَوْا فِىٓ ءَايَٰتِنَا مُعَٰجِزِينَ أُوْلَٰٓئِكَ لَهُمْ عَذَابٌ مِّن رِّجْزٍ أَلِيمٌ ۝

وَيَرَى ٱلَّذِينَ أُوتُوا ٱلْعِلْمَ ٱلَّذِىٓ أُنزِلَ إِلَيْكَ مِن رَّبِّكَ هُوَ ٱلْحَقَّ وَيَهْدِىٓ إِلَىٰ صِرَٰطِ ٱلْعَزِيزِ ٱلْحَمِيدِ ۝

وَقَالَ ٱلَّذِينَ كَفَرُوا هَلْ نَدُلُّكُمْ عَلَىٰ رَجُلٍ يُنَبِّئُكُمْ إِذَا مُزِّقْتُمْ كُلَّ مُمَزَّقٍ إِنَّكُمْ لَفِى خَلْقٍ جَدِيدٍ ۝

أَفْتَرَىٰ عَلَى ٱللَّهِ كَذِبًا أَم بِهِۦ جِنَّةٌۢ بَلِ ٱلَّذِينَ لَا يُؤْمِنُونَ بِٱلْءَاخِرَةِ فِى ٱلْعَذَابِ وَٱلضَّلَٰلِ ٱلْبَعِيدِ ۝

أَفَلَمْ يَرَوْا إِلَىٰ مَا بَيْنَ أَيْدِيهِمْ وَمَا خَلْفَهُم مِّنَ ٱلسَّمَآءِ وَٱلْأَرْضِ إِن نَّشَأْ نَخْسِفْ بِهِمُ ٱلْأَرْضَ أَوْ نُسْقِطْ عَلَيْهِمْ كِسَفًا مِّنَ ٱلسَّمَآءِ إِنَّ فِى ذَٰلِكَ لَءَايَةً لِّكُلِّ عَبْدٍ مُّنِيبٍ ۝

۞ وَلَقَدْ ءَاتَيْنَا دَاوُۥدَ مِنَّا فَضْلًا يَٰجِبَالُ أَوِّبِى مَعَهُۥ وَٱلطَّيْرَ وَأَلَنَّا لَهُ ٱلْحَدِيدَ ۝

أَنِ ٱعْمَلْ سَٰبِغَٰتٍ وَقَدِّرْ فِى ٱلسَّرْدِ وَٱعْمَلُوا صَٰلِحًا إِنِّى بِمَا تَعْمَلُونَ بَصِيرٌ ۝

وَلِسُلَيْمَٰنَ ٱلرِّيحَ غُدُوُّهَا شَهْرٌ وَرَوَاحُهَا شَهْرٌ وَأَسَلْنَا لَهُۥ عَيْنَ ٱلْقِطْرِ وَمِنَ ٱلْجِنِّ مَن يَعْمَلُ بَيْنَ يَدَيْهِ بِإِذْنِ رَبِّهِۦ وَمَن يَزِغْ مِنْهُمْ عَنْ

---

709. The People of the Book, or Jews and Christians.

of his Lord, and whoever of them swerved from Our Command, We shall make him taste the punishment of the blazing Fire.

13. To fashion for him whatever he wished of palaces, statues, basins like water-troughs and immovable cooking pots. "Work thankfully, O David's House; for few of My servants are truly thankful."

14. When We decreed his death, nothing indicated to them that he was dead except an earth-worm gnawing away at his staff. Then, when he fell down, the jinn realized that, had they known the Unseen, they would not have continued in the demeaning punishment.

15. For Sheba there also was a sign in their dwelling two gardens, to the right and the left: "Eat of your Lord's provision and give thanks to Him: a good land and an All-Forgiving Lord."

16. But they turned away; and so We loosed upon them the Overwhelming Flood,[710] and We substituted for their two gardens another two gardens bearing bitter fruit and having fir trees and a few lotus trees.

17. Thus We penalized them for their disbelief; and do We ever penalize any but the unbeliever?

18. We established between them and between the cities, which We blessed, other visible cities, and We determined the measure of travel therein: "Travel therein for nights and days in perfect security."

أَمْرِنَا نُذِقْهُ مِنْ عَذَابِ ٱلسَّعِيرِ ﴿١٢﴾

يَعْمَلُونَ لَهُۥ مَا يَشَآءُ مِن مَّحَٰرِيبَ وَتَمَٰثِيلَ وَجِفَانٍ كَٱلْجَوَابِ وَقُدُورٍ رَّاسِيَٰتٍ ٱعْمَلُوٓا۟ ءَالَ دَاوُۥدَ شُكْرًا وَقَلِيلٌ مِّنْ عِبَادِىَ ٱلشَّكُورُ ﴿١٣﴾

فَلَمَّا قَضَيْنَا عَلَيْهِ ٱلْمَوْتَ مَا دَلَّهُمْ عَلَىٰ مَوْتِهِۦٓ إِلَّا دَآبَّةُ ٱلْأَرْضِ تَأْكُلُ مِنسَأَتَهُۥ فَلَمَّا خَرَّ تَبَيَّنَتِ ٱلْجِنُّ أَن لَّوْ كَانُوا۟ يَعْلَمُونَ ٱلْغَيْبَ مَا لَبِثُوا۟ فِى ٱلْعَذَابِ ٱلْمُهِينِ ﴿١٤﴾

لَقَدْ كَانَ لِسَبَإٍ فِى مَسْكَنِهِمْ ءَايَةٌ جَنَّتَانِ عَن يَمِينٍ وَشِمَالٍ كُلُوا۟ مِن رِّزْقِ رَبِّكُمْ وَٱشْكُرُوا۟ لَهُۥ بَلْدَةٌ طَيِّبَةٌ وَرَبٌّ غَفُورٌ ﴿١٥﴾

فَأَعْرَضُوا۟ فَأَرْسَلْنَا عَلَيْهِمْ سَيْلَ ٱلْعَرِمِ وَبَدَّلْنَٰهُم بِجَنَّتَيْهِمْ جَنَّتَيْنِ ذَوَاتَىْ أُكُلٍ خَمْطٍ وَأَثْلٍ وَشَىْءٍ مِّن سِدْرٍ قَلِيلٍ ﴿١٦﴾

ذَٰلِكَ جَزَيْنَٰهُم بِمَا كَفَرُوا۟ وَهَلْ نُجَٰزِىٓ إِلَّا ٱلْكَفُورَ ﴿١٧﴾

وَجَعَلْنَا بَيْنَهُمْ وَبَيْنَ ٱلْقُرَى ٱلَّتِى بَٰرَكْنَا فِيهَا قُرًى ظَٰهِرَةً وَقَدَّرْنَا فِيهَا ٱلسَّيْرَ سِيرُوا۟ فِيهَا لَيَالِىَ وَأَيَّامًا ءَامِنِينَ ﴿١٨﴾

---

710. *Sadd al-'Arim* (following the break of the Ma'rib Dam in Yemen).

19. Then they said: "Lord, prolong the stages between our travels." They wronged themselves, so We reduced them to mere tales and tore them up utterly. Surely, there are in that signs for every steadfast and thankful man.

20. And Iblis definitely proved right his opinion of them, and so they followed him, except for a group of believers.

21. Yet he had no authority over them; but that We might distinguish him who believed in the Hereafter, from him who was in doubt regarding it. Your Lord is Watchful over everything.

22. Say: "Call upon those you allege, apart from Allah. They do not possess the weight of a speck of dust in the heavens or on earth, and they have no partnership in either of them; nor is any of them[711] a helper to Him."

23. Intercession will not avail with Him except for him whom He gave permission; until fear is lifted from their hearts, then they will say: "What has your Lord said?", they will say: "The truth, and He is the All-High, the Great One."

24. Say: "Who provides for you out of the heavens and the earth?", say: "Allah, and you or we are either rightly guided or in manifest error."

25. Say: "You will not be questioned about our misdeeds and we will not be questioned about what you do."

26. Say: "Our Lord shall bring us together and judge between us rightly. He is the All-Knowing Judge."

فَقَالُوا۟ رَبَّنَا بَـٰعِدْ بَيْنَ أَسْفَارِنَا وَظَلَمُوٓا۟ أَنفُسَهُمْ فَجَعَلْنَـٰهُمْ أَحَادِيثَ وَمَزَّقْنَـٰهُمْ كُلَّ مُمَزَّقٍ ۚ إِنَّ فِى ذَٰلِكَ لَـَٔايَـٰتٍ لِّكُلِّ صَبَّارٍ شَكُورٍ ﴿١٩﴾

وَلَقَدْ صَدَّقَ عَلَيْهِمْ إِبْلِيسُ ظَنَّهُۥ فَٱتَّبَعُوهُ إِلَّا فَرِيقًا مِّنَ ٱلْمُؤْمِنِينَ ﴿٢٠﴾

وَمَا كَانَ لَهُۥ عَلَيْهِم مِّن سُلْطَـٰنٍ إِلَّا لِنَعْلَمَ مَن يُؤْمِنُ بِٱلْـَٔاخِرَةِ مِمَّنْ هُوَ مِنْهَا فِى شَكٍّ ۗ وَرَبُّكَ عَلَىٰ كُلِّ شَىْءٍ حَفِيظٌ ﴿٢١﴾

قُلِ ٱدْعُوا۟ ٱلَّذِينَ زَعَمْتُم مِّن دُونِ ٱللَّهِ ۖ لَا يَمْلِكُونَ مِثْقَالَ ذَرَّةٍ فِى ٱلسَّمَـٰوَٰتِ وَلَا فِى ٱلْأَرْضِ وَمَا لَهُمْ فِيهِمَا مِن شِرْكٍ وَمَا لَهُۥ مِنْهُم مِّن ظَهِيرٍ ﴿٢٢﴾

وَلَا تَنفَعُ ٱلشَّفَـٰعَةُ عِندَهُۥٓ إِلَّا لِمَنْ أَذِنَ لَهُۥ ۚ حَتَّىٰٓ إِذَا فُزِّعَ عَن قُلُوبِهِمْ قَالُوا۟ مَاذَا قَالَ رَبُّكُمْ ۖ قَالُوا۟ ٱلْحَقَّ ۖ وَهُوَ ٱلْعَلِىُّ ٱلْكَبِيرُ ﴿٢٣﴾

۞ قُلْ مَن يَرْزُقُكُم مِّنَ ٱلسَّمَـٰوَٰتِ وَٱلْأَرْضِ ۖ قُلِ ٱللَّهُ ۖ وَإِنَّآ أَوْ إِيَّاكُمْ لَعَلَىٰ هُدًى أَوْ فِى ضَلَـٰلٍ مُّبِينٍ ﴿٢٤﴾

قُل لَّا تُسْـَٔلُونَ عَمَّآ أَجْرَمْنَا وَلَا نُسْـَٔلُ عَمَّا تَعْمَلُونَ ﴿٢٥﴾

قُلْ يَجْمَعُ بَيْنَنَا رَبُّنَا ثُمَّ يَفْتَحُ بَيْنَنَا بِٱلْحَقِّ وَهُوَ ٱلْفَتَّاحُ ٱلْعَلِيمُ ﴿٢٦﴾

---

711. The associates of the idolaters.

27. Say: "Show me those you have attached to Him as associates. Allah is rather the All-Mighty, the All-Wise."

قُلْ أَرُونِيَ الَّذِينَ أَلْحَقْتُم بِهِ شُرَكَآءَ كَلَّا بَلْ هُوَ اللَّهُ الْعَزِيزُ الْحَكِيمُ ۝

28. We have not sent you but to the whole of mankind, as a warner. Yet most people do not know.

وَمَا أَرْسَلْنَاكَ إِلَّا كَافَّةً لِّلنَّاسِ بَشِيرًا وَنَذِيرًا وَلَكِنَّ أَكْثَرَ النَّاسِ لَا يَعْلَمُونَ ۝

29. They say: "When will this promise be fulfilled, if you are truthful?"

وَيَقُولُونَ مَتَى هَذَا الْوَعْدُ إِن كُنتُمْ صَادِقِينَ ۝

30. Say: "You have the appointment of a Day from which you shall not be delayed nor advanced a single hour."

قُل لَّكُم مِّيعَادُ يَوْمٍ لَّا تَسْتَأْخِرُونَ عَنْهُ سَاعَةً وَلَا تَسْتَقْدِمُونَ ۝

31. The unbelievers say: "We will never believe in this Qur'an, nor in what came before it." If you could only see when the wrongdoers are arrayed before their Lord, each one reproaching the other, the down-trodden saying to the arrogant: "But for you, we would have been believers."

وَقَالَ الَّذِينَ كَفَرُوا لَن نُّؤْمِنَ بِهَذَا الْقُرْءَانِ وَلَا بِالَّذِي بَيْنَ يَدَيْهِ وَلَوْ تَرَىٰ إِذِ الظَّالِمُونَ مَوْقُوفُونَ عِندَ رَبِّهِمْ يَرْجِعُ بَعْضُهُمْ إِلَىٰ بَعْضٍ الْقَوْلَ يَقُولُ الَّذِينَ اسْتُضْعِفُوا لِلَّذِينَ اسْتَكْبَرُوا لَوْلَا أَنتُمْ لَكُنَّا مُؤْمِنِينَ ۝

32. The arrogant will say to the down-trodden: "Did we really bar you from the guidance after it came to you? No, you were rather ungodly."

قَالَ الَّذِينَ اسْتَكْبَرُوا لِلَّذِينَ اسْتُضْعِفُوا أَنَحْنُ صَدَدْنَاكُمْ عَنِ الْهُدَىٰ بَعْدَ إِذْ جَاءَكُم بَلْ كُنتُم مُّجْرِمِينَ ۝

33. Then the downtrodden will say to the arrogant: "It was rather your cunning night and day, when you commanded us to disbelieve in Allah and assign equals to Him." They will be secretly remorseful, when they see the punishment. We will put shackles round the necks of the unbelievers; will they be rewarded but for what they used to do?

وَقَالَ الَّذِينَ اسْتُضْعِفُوا لِلَّذِينَ اسْتَكْبَرُوا بَلْ مَكْرُ اللَّيْلِ وَالنَّهَارِ إِذْ تَأْمُرُونَنَا أَن نَّكْفُرَ بِاللَّهِ وَنَجْعَلَ لَهُ أَندَادًا وَأَسَرُّوا النَّدَامَةَ لَمَّا رَأَوُا الْعَذَابَ وَجَعَلْنَا الْأَغْلَالَ فِي أَعْنَاقِ الَّذِينَ كَفَرُوا هَلْ يُجْزَوْنَ إِلَّا مَا كَانُوا يَعْمَلُونَ ۝

34. We never sent forth a warner to a city but the extravagant in it said: "We disbelieve in the message you have been sent with."

وَمَا أَرْسَلْنَا فِي قَرْيَةٍ مِّن نَّذِيرٍ إِلَّا قَالَ مُتْرَفُوهَا إِنَّا بِمَا أُرْسِلْتُم بِهِ كَافِرُونَ ۝

35. They say: "We have more abundant wealth and children and we will not be punished."

وَقَالُوا نَحْنُ أَكْثَرُ أَمْوَالًا وَأَوْلَادًا وَمَا نَحْنُ بِمُعَذَّبِينَ ۝

36. Say: "Indeed, my Lord expands the provision to whomever He wishes and restricts it; but most people do not know."

37. It is not your wealth or your children that bring you closer to Us, but it is he who believes and does the righteous deed. To those will be meted out the double reward and in the lofty chambers they shall be secure.

38. But those who go around challenging Our Signs those will be summoned to the punishment.

39. Say: "It is my Lord Who expands the provision to whomever of His servants He wishes and restricts it. Anything you spend, He will replace it. He is the Best of providers."

40. On the Day that He will muster them, then say to the angels: "Are those the ones who used to worship you?"

41. They will say: "Glory be to You; You are our Protector, apart from them." No, rather, they used to worship the jinn, most of them believing in them.

42. Today, none of them has the power to profit or harm the other, and We will say to the wrongdoer: "Taste the punishment of the Fire which you used to question."

43. And when Our Signs are recited to them clearly, they say: "This is only a man who wishes to bar you from what your fathers used to worship." They also say: "This is nothing but a fabricated falsehood"; and the unbelievers say of the Truth when it comes to them: "This is nothing but manifest sorcery."

44. We did not bring them heretofore any Books to study and we did not send them before you[712] any warner.

---

712. Muhammad.

45. Those who preceded them denounced the Messengers, although they had not attained the tenth of what We gave them; yet they denounced My Messengers as liars. How, then, was My wrath?

46. Say: "I only give you one exhortation, that you arise for Allah in couples and singly, then to reflect that there is no madness in your companion.[713] He is merely a warner on the eve of a terrible punishment."

47. Say: "Whatever wage I asked you for is yours [to give]. My wage is with Allah and He is a Witness of everything."

48. Say: "My Lord hurls down the truth. He is the Knower of the Unseen."

49. Say: "The Truth has come. Falsehood neither originates nor brings back anything."

50. Say: "If I go astray, I only go astray to my loss; but if I am guided, it is merely by reason of what my Lord reveals to me. He is All-Hearing, All-Nigh."

51. If you could see how they were terrified. There was no escape, and they were seized from a near place.

52. And they say: "We believe in it", but whence can they attain it[714] from afar?

53. They have already disbelieved in Him and they speculate about the Unseen from a far-off place.

54. And they were barred from what they desired, as was done with their ilk before. Indeed, they were in disturbing doubt.

وَكَذَّبَ ٱلَّذِينَ مِن قَبْلِهِمْ وَمَا بَلَغُوا مِعْشَارَ مَآ ءَاتَيْنَهُمْ فَكَذَّبُوا رُسُلِى فَكَيْفَ كَانَ نَكِيرِ ۝

۞ قُلْ إِنَّمَآ أَعِظُكُم بِوَٰحِدَةٍ أَن تَقُومُوا لِلَّهِ مَثْنَىٰ وَفُرَٰدَىٰ ثُمَّ تَتَفَكَّرُوا مَا بِصَاحِبِكُم مِّن جِنَّةٍ إِنْ هُوَ إِلَّا نَذِيرٌ لَّكُم بَيْنَ يَدَىْ عَذَابٍ شَدِيدٍ ۝

قُلْ مَا سَأَلْتُكُم مِّنْ أَجْرٍ فَهُوَ لَكُمْ إِنْ أَجْرِىَ إِلَّا عَلَى ٱللَّهِ وَهُوَ عَلَىٰ كُلِّ شَىْءٍ شَهِيدٌ ۝

قُلْ إِنَّ رَبِّى يَقْذِفُ بِٱلْحَقِّ عَلَّٰمُ ٱلْغُيُوبِ ۝

قُلْ جَآءَ ٱلْحَقُّ وَمَا يُبْدِئُ ٱلْبَٰطِلُ وَمَا يُعِيدُ ۝

قُلْ إِن ضَلَلْتُ فَإِنَّمَآ أَضِلُّ عَلَىٰ نَفْسِى وَإِنِ ٱهْتَدَيْتُ فَبِمَا يُوحَىٰ إِلَىَّ رَبِّى إِنَّهُ سَمِيعٌ قَرِيبٌ ۝

وَلَوْ تَرَىٰ إِذْ فَزِعُوا فَلَا فَوْتَ وَأُخِذُوا مِن مَّكَانٍ قَرِيبٍ ۝

وَقَالُوٓا ءَامَنَّا بِهِۦ وَأَنَّىٰ لَهُمُ ٱلتَّنَاوُشُ مِن مَّكَانٍ بَعِيدٍ ۝

وَقَدْ كَفَرُوا بِهِۦ مِن قَبْلُ وَيَقْذِفُونَ بِٱلْغَيْبِ مِن مَّكَانٍ بَعِيدٍ ۝

وَحِيلَ بَيْنَهُمْ وَبَيْنَ مَا يَشْتَهُونَ كَمَا فُعِلَ بِأَشْيَاعِهِم مِّن قَبْلُ إِنَّهُمْ كَانُوا فِى شَكٍّ مُّرِيبٍ ۝

---

713. The Prophet.
714. The belief.

Sûrat Fâtir,
(The Originator of Creation) 35

بِسْمِ اللَّهِ الرَّحْمَٰنِ الرَّحِيمِ

In the Name of Allah,
the Compassionate, the Merciful

1. Praise be to Allah, Originator of the heavens and the earth, Who appointed the angels as messengers, having wings twofold, threefold and fourfold. He increases the creation, as He wills. Allah, indeed, has power over everything.

الْحَمْدُ لِلَّهِ فَاطِرِ السَّمَاوَاتِ وَالْأَرْضِ جَاعِلِ الْمَلَائِكَةِ رُسُلًا أُولِي أَجْنِحَةٍ مَّثْنَىٰ وَثُلَاثَ وَرُبَاعَ يَزِيدُ فِي الْخَلْقِ مَا يَشَاءُ إِنَّ اللَّهَ عَلَىٰ كُلِّ شَيْءٍ قَدِيرٌ ﴿١﴾

2. Whatever mercy Allah accords to mankind, none will be able to withhold; and whatever He withholds, none will be able to release thereafter. He is the All-Mighty, the All-Wise.

مَّا يَفْتَحِ اللَّهُ لِلنَّاسِ مِن رَّحْمَةٍ فَلَا مُمْسِكَ لَهَا وَمَا يُمْسِكْ فَلَا مُرْسِلَ لَهُ مِن بَعْدِهِ وَهُوَ الْعَزِيزُ الْحَكِيمُ ﴿٢﴾

3. O people, remember Allah's Grace upon you. Is there a creator other than Allah, providing for you from heaven and earth? There is no god but He; how then will you be diverted?

يَا أَيُّهَا النَّاسُ اذْكُرُوا نِعْمَتَ اللَّهِ عَلَيْكُمْ هَلْ مِنْ خَالِقٍ غَيْرُ اللَّهِ يَرْزُقُكُم مِّنَ السَّمَاءِ وَالْأَرْضِ لَا إِلَٰهَ إِلَّا هُوَ فَأَنَّىٰ تُؤْفَكُونَ ﴿٣﴾

4. If they denounce you as a liar, surely they have denounced other Messengers before you; and unto Allah all matters shall be returned.

وَإِن يُكَذِّبُوكَ فَقَدْ كُذِّبَتْ رُسُلٌ مِّن قَبْلِكَ وَإِلَى اللَّهِ تُرْجَعُ الْأُمُورُ ﴿٤﴾

5. O people, Allah's Promise is true, so do not let the present life delude you and do not let the Deceiver[715] delude you concerning Allah.

يَا أَيُّهَا النَّاسُ إِنَّ وَعْدَ اللَّهِ حَقٌّ فَلَا تَغُرَّنَّكُمُ الْحَيَاةُ الدُّنْيَا وَلَا يَغُرَّنَّكُم بِاللَّهِ الْغَرُورُ ﴿٥﴾

6. Satan is an enemy of yours, so regard him as an enemy. He only calls upon his partisans that they may be companions of the Blazing Fire.

إِنَّ الشَّيْطَانَ لَكُمْ عَدُوٌّ فَاتَّخِذُوهُ عَدُوًّا إِنَّمَا يَدْعُو حِزْبَهُ لِيَكُونُوا مِنْ أَصْحَابِ السَّعِيرِ ﴿٦﴾

7. Those who disbelieve will incur a terrible punishment and those who believe and do the righteous deeds will earn forgiveness and a great wage.

الَّذِينَ كَفَرُوا لَهُمْ عَذَابٌ شَدِيدٌ وَالَّذِينَ آمَنُوا وَعَمِلُوا الصَّالِحَاتِ لَهُم مَّغْفِرَةٌ وَأَجْرٌ كَبِيرٌ ﴿٧﴾

---

715. Satan.

8. What of him whose evil work was made attractive to him and so he regarded it as fair? Allah surely leads astray [whomever] He wishes and guides [whomever] He wishes; so do not let your soul waste away in regrets for them. Allah is Fully Aware of what they do.

9. It is Allah Who looses the wind, so as to stir up clouds; then We drive them towards a dead land, reviving the earth therewith after it was dead. Such is the Resurrection!

10. Whoever wishes glory, it is to Allah that the glory utterly belongs. Unto Him good words ascend and the righteous deed uplifts it. Those who contrive evil deeds will incur terrible punishment and the contriving of these will come to grief.

11. Allah created you from dust, then from a sperm, then made you into couples. No female bears or gives birth, save with His Knowledge, and no man advances in years or his life-span is diminished, except as ordained in a Book. That indeed is an easy matter for Allah.

12. The two seas are not the same; one is sweet, clear and delectable to drink and the other is salty and bitter. Yet from both you eat tender flesh and extract ornaments which you wear, and you see the ships cruising therein, that you may seek His Bounty, and that perchance you may be thankful.

13. He causes the night to phase into the day and the day to phase into the night and He has subjected the sun and the moon, each running for an appointed term. That is Allah, your Lord to Whom belongs the dominion, whereas those you call upon, apart from Him, do not possess a date's crust.

أَفَمَن زُيِّنَ لَهُ سُوءُ عَمَلِهِ فَرَآهُ حَسَنًا فَإِنَّ اللَّهَ يُضِلُّ مَن يَشَاءُ وَيَهْدِي مَن يَشَاءُ فَلَا تَذْهَبْ نَفْسُكَ عَلَيْهِمْ حَسَرَٰتٍ إِنَّ اللَّهَ عَلِيمٌ بِمَا يَصْنَعُونَ ۝

وَٱللَّهُ ٱلَّذِي أَرْسَلَ ٱلرِّيَٰحَ فَتُثِيرُ سَحَابًا فَسُقْنَٰهُ إِلَىٰ بَلَدٍ مَّيِّتٍ فَأَحْيَيْنَا بِهِ ٱلْأَرْضَ بَعْدَ مَوْتِهَا كَذَٰلِكَ ٱلنُّشُورُ ۝

مَن كَانَ يُرِيدُ ٱلْعِزَّةَ فَلِلَّهِ ٱلْعِزَّةُ جَمِيعًا إِلَيْهِ يَصْعَدُ ٱلْكَلِمُ ٱلطَّيِّبُ وَٱلْعَمَلُ ٱلصَّٰلِحُ يَرْفَعُهُ وَٱلَّذِينَ يَمْكُرُونَ ٱلسَّيِّئَاتِ لَهُمْ عَذَابٌ شَدِيدٌ وَمَكْرُ أُو۟لَٰئِكَ هُوَ يَبُورُ ۝

وَٱللَّهُ خَلَقَكُم مِّن تُرَابٍ ثُمَّ مِن نُّطْفَةٍ ثُمَّ جَعَلَكُمْ أَزْوَٰجًا وَمَا تَحْمِلُ مِنْ أُنثَىٰ وَلَا تَضَعُ إِلَّا بِعِلْمِهِ وَمَا يُعَمَّرُ مِن مُّعَمَّرٍ وَلَا يُنقَصُ مِنْ عُمُرِهِ إِلَّا فِي كِتَٰبٍ إِنَّ ذَٰلِكَ عَلَى ٱللَّهِ يَسِيرٌ ۝

وَمَا يَسْتَوِي ٱلْبَحْرَانِ هَٰذَا عَذْبٌ فُرَاتٌ سَآئِغٌ شَرَابُهُ وَهَٰذَا مِلْحٌ أُجَاجٌ وَمِن كُلٍّ تَأْكُلُونَ لَحْمًا طَرِيًّا وَتَسْتَخْرِجُونَ حِلْيَةً تَلْبَسُونَهَا وَتَرَى ٱلْفُلْكَ فِيهِ مَوَاخِرَ لِتَبْتَغُوا۟ مِن فَضْلِهِ وَلَعَلَّكُمْ تَشْكُرُونَ ۝

يُولِجُ ٱلَّيْلَ فِي ٱلنَّهَارِ وَيُولِجُ ٱلنَّهَارَ فِي ٱلَّيْلِ وَسَخَّرَ ٱلشَّمْسَ وَٱلْقَمَرَ كُلٌّ يَجْرِي لِأَجَلٍ مُّسَمًّى ذَٰلِكُمُ ٱللَّهُ رَبُّكُمْ لَهُ ٱلْمُلْكُ وَٱلَّذِينَ تَدْعُونَ مِن دُونِهِ مَا يَمْلِكُونَ مِن قِطْمِيرٍ ۝

14. If you call upon them, they do not hear your call; and were they to hear they will not answer you. On the Day of Resurrection they will repudiate your idolatry. None will inform you like the Well-Informed One.

15. O people, it is you who have need of Allah, whereas Allah is the All-Sufficient, Praiseworthy One.

16. If He wishes, He will annihilate you and bring forth a new creation.

17. That for Allah is not a grave matter.

18. No laden soul shall bear the burden of another; and if a heavy-burdened soul calls for its burden to be borne, not a whit of it will be borne, not even by one who is a kinsman. You[716] only warn those who fear their Lord although He is unseen, and who perform the prayer. He who purifies himself purifies himself for his own good, and unto Allah is the ultimate return.

19. The blind and the seeing man are not alike.

20. Nor dark shadows or light;

21. Nor shade and torrid heat.

22. Nor are the living and the dead alike. Allah makes whomever He wishes to hear, but you will not make those in their graves hear.

23. You are only a warner.

24. We have sent you forth in truth as a bearer of good news and a warner. There is no nation to whom a warner has not come and gone.

25. If they denounce you as a liar, those before them have also denounced; their Messengers came to them with clear proofs, with scriptures and the illuminating Book.

---

716. The reference is to the Prophet.

26. Then I seized the unbelievers; how then was My wrath!

ثُمَّ أَخَذْتُ الَّذِينَ كَفَرُوا فَكَيْفَ كَانَ نَكِيرِ ۝

27. Have you not seen how Allah sends water down from the sky, and then We bring forth thereby fruits of diverse hues. And of the mountains there are lanes, white and red, of diverse hues, and some pitch dark.

أَلَمْ تَرَ أَنَّ اللَّهَ أَنزَلَ مِنَ السَّمَاءِ مَاءً فَأَخْرَجْنَا بِهِ ثَمَرَاتٍ مُّخْتَلِفًا أَلْوَانُهَا وَمِنَ الْجِبَالِ جُدَدٌ بِيضٌ وَحُمْرٌ مُّخْتَلِفٌ أَلْوَانُهَا وَغَرَابِيبُ سُودٌ ۝

28. And of people, beasts and cattle, some are of diverse hues also. Indeed, of His servants, only the learned fear Allah. Allah is All-Mighty, All-Forgiving.

وَمِنَ النَّاسِ وَالدَّوَابِّ وَالْأَنْعَامِ مُخْتَلِفٌ أَلْوَانُهُ كَذَلِكَ إِنَّمَا يَخْشَى اللَّهَ مِنْ عِبَادِهِ الْعُلَمَاءُ إِنَّ اللَّهَ عَزِيزٌ غَفُورٌ ۝

29. Surely, those who recite the Book of Allah, perform the prayer and spend of what we provided for them, secretly and publicly, may hope for a trade which does not slacken.

إِنَّ الَّذِينَ يَتْلُونَ كِتَابَ اللَّهِ وَأَقَامُوا الصَّلَوٰةَ وَأَنفَقُوا مِمَّا رَزَقْنَاهُمْ سِرًّا وَعَلَانِيَةً يَرْجُونَ تِجَارَةً لَّن تَبُورَ ۝

30. That He might pay them their wages and increase them from His Bounty; He is indeed All-Forgiving, All-Thankful.

لِيُوَفِّيَهُمْ أُجُورَهُمْ وَيَزِيدَهُم مِّن فَضْلِهِ إِنَّهُ غَفُورٌ شَكُورٌ ۝

31. What We have revealed to you of the Book is the truth, confirming what preceded it. Allah is Well-Informed about His servants, All-Seeing.

وَالَّذِى أَوْحَيْنَا إِلَيْكَ مِنَ الْكِتَابِ هُوَ الْحَقُّ مُصَدِّقًا لِّمَا بَيْنَ يَدَيْهِ إِنَّ اللَّهَ بِعِبَادِهِ لَخَبِيرٌ بَصِيرٌ ۝

32. Then We bequeathed the Book upon those servants We chose; but some of them wrong themselves, some are lukewarm and some are forerunners in good deeds, by Allah's Leave. That truly is the great distinction.

ثُمَّ أَوْرَثْنَا الْكِتَابَ الَّذِينَ اصْطَفَيْنَا مِنْ عِبَادِنَا فَمِنْهُمْ ظَالِمٌ لِّنَفْسِهِ وَمِنْهُم مُّقْتَصِدٌ وَمِنْهُمْ سَابِقٌ بِالْخَيْرَاتِ بِإِذْنِ اللَّهِ ذَلِكَ هُوَ الْفَضْلُ الْكَبِيرُ ۝

33. Into Gardens of Eden they enter, wherein they are adorned with gold bracelets and pearls and their clothing therein will be silk.

جَنَّاتُ عَدْنٍ يَدْخُلُونَهَا يُحَلَّوْنَ فِيهَا مِنْ أَسَاوِرَ مِن ذَهَبٍ وَلُؤْلُؤًا وَلِبَاسُهُمْ فِيهَا حَرِيرٌ ۝

34. They say: "Praise be to Allah Who lifted off our sorrow. Our Lord is indeed All-Forgiving, All-Thankful.

وَقَالُوا الْحَمْدُ لِلَّهِ الَّذِى أَذْهَبَ عَنَّا الْحَزَنَ إِنَّ رَبَّنَا لَغَفُورٌ شَكُورٌ ۝

35. "He Who out of His Bounty has made us dwell in the Abode of Everlasting Life, where no fatigue will touch us, nor any weariness."

الَّذِى أَحَلَّنَا دَارَ الْمُقَامَةِ مِن فَضْلِهِ لَا يَمَسُّنَا فِيهَا نَصَبٌ وَلَا يَمَسُّنَا فِيهَا لُغُوبٌ ۝

36. But the unbelievers shall have the Fire of Hell, wherein they will not be finished off and die, nor will its punishment be lightened for them. Thus We will reward every thankless person.

37. Therein they will cry out: "Our Lord, bring us out and we will do the righteous deed, differently from what we used to do." Did we not prolong your life sufficiently for him to remember who is apt to remember? The warner came to you, so taste now. The wrongdoers shall have no supporter.

38. Surely, Allah knows the Unseen of the heavens and the earth. He knows fully the secrets within the breasts.

39. It is He Who made you successors in the lands. Then he who disbelieves, his unbelief will recoil upon him; and their unbelief will only increase the unbelievers in contempt in the sight of their Lord. No, their unbelief will only increase the unbelievers in perdition.

40. Say: "Have you seen your associates upon whom you call, apart from Allah? Show me what they have created on earth? Do they have any share in the heavens, or have We given them a Book, so that they are in possession of a clear proof therein? In fact, the wrongdoers only promise each other vanity."

41. Allah holds the heavens and the earth firmly lest they become displaced; were they displaced, none will hold them together after Him. He is indeed Clement, All-Forgiving.

42. They swore their most earnest oaths that if a warner came to them they would surely be more rightly guided than a certain nation.[717] But when a warner came to them, that only increased their aversion.

---

717. The Jewish or Christian nation.

43. Out of arrogance in the land and evil cunning. Yet the evil cunning will only recoil upon its perpetrators. Do they then look to anything other than the way of the ancients? For you will never find any alteration of Allah's Way, and you will never find any deflecting of Allah's Way.

44. Have they not travelled in the land to see what was the fate of those who came before them and were even mightier than they? Nothing in the heavens or the earth can thwart Allah; He is indeed All-Knowing, All-Powerful.

45. Were Allah to take men to task for what they have earned, He would not have left upon the face of the earth a single creature that crawls; but He defers them unto an appointed term. Then, when their term arrives, Allah is surely fully Conversant with His servants.

Sûrat Yâ Sîn, 36

In the Name of Allah,
the Compassionate, the Merciful

1. Yâ - Sîn.[718]

2. By the wise Qur'an.

3. You are truly one of the Messengers.

4. Upon a straight path.

5. It is the Revelation of the All-Mighty, the Merciful.

6. To warn a people, whose fathers were not warned and so they are heedless.

7. The sentence has been passed against most of them, for they do not believe.

أَسْتِكْبَارًا فِي ٱلْأَرْضِ وَمَكْرَ ٱلسَّيِّئِ وَلَا يَحِيقُ ٱلْمَكْرُ ٱلسَّيِّئُ إِلَّا بِأَهْلِهِ فَهَلْ يَنظُرُونَ إِلَّا سُنَّتَ ٱلْأَوَّلِينَ فَلَن تَجِدَ لِسُنَّتِ ٱللَّهِ تَبْدِيلًا وَلَن تَجِدَ لِسُنَّتِ ٱللَّهِ تَحْوِيلًا ﴿٤٣﴾

أَوَلَمْ يَسِيرُوا فِي ٱلْأَرْضِ فَيَنظُرُوا كَيْفَ كَانَ عَٰقِبَةُ ٱلَّذِينَ مِن قَبْلِهِمْ وَكَانُوٓا أَشَدَّ مِنْهُمْ قُوَّةً وَمَا كَانَ ٱللَّهُ لِيُعْجِزَهُ مِن شَيْءٍ فِي ٱلسَّمَٰوَٰتِ وَلَا فِي ٱلْأَرْضِ إِنَّهُ كَانَ عَلِيمًا قَدِيرًا ﴿٤٤﴾

وَلَوْ يُؤَاخِذُ ٱللَّهُ ٱلنَّاسَ بِمَا كَسَبُوا مَا تَرَكَ عَلَىٰ ظَهْرِهَا مِن دَآبَّةٍ وَلَٰكِن يُؤَخِّرُهُمْ إِلَىٰٓ أَجَلٍ مُّسَمًّى فَإِذَا جَآءَ أَجَلُهُمْ فَإِنَّ ٱللَّهَ كَانَ بِعِبَادِهِۦ بَصِيرًا ﴿٤٥﴾

بِسْمِ ٱللَّهِ ٱلرَّحْمَٰنِ ٱلرَّحِيمِ

يس ﴿١﴾

وَٱلْقُرْءَانِ ٱلْحَكِيمِ ﴿٢﴾

إِنَّكَ لَمِنَ ٱلْمُرْسَلِينَ ﴿٣﴾

عَلَىٰ صِرَٰطٍ مُّسْتَقِيمٍ ﴿٤﴾

تَنزِيلَ ٱلْعَزِيزِ ٱلرَّحِيمِ ﴿٥﴾

لِتُنذِرَ قَوْمًا مَّآ أُنذِرَ ءَابَآؤُهُمْ فَهُمْ غَٰفِلُونَ ﴿٦﴾

لَقَدْ حَقَّ ٱلْقَوْلُ عَلَىٰٓ أَكْثَرِهِمْ فَهُمْ لَا يُؤْمِنُونَ ﴿٧﴾

---

718. Yâ - Sîn came to be one of the Prophet's names.

8. We have placed shackles upon their necks down to their chins; and so their heads are held high.

إِنَّا جَعَلْنَا فِى أَعْنَـٰقِهِمْ أَغْلَـٰلًا فَهِىَ إِلَى ٱلْأَذْقَانِ فَهُم مُّقْمَحُونَ ۝

9. And We placed in front of them a barrier and behind them a barrier, and We have covered their eyes so they do not see.

وَجَعَلْنَا مِنۢ بَيْنِ أَيْدِيهِمْ سَدًّا وَمِنْ خَلْفِهِمْ سَدًّا فَأَغْشَيْنَـٰهُمْ فَهُمْ لَا يُبْصِرُونَ ۝

10. It is the same whether you warn them or do not warn them, they will not believe.

وَسَوَآءٌ عَلَيْهِمْ ءَأَنذَرْتَهُمْ أَمْ لَمْ تُنذِرْهُمْ لَا يُؤْمِنُونَ ۝

11. You only warn him who follows the Reminder and fears the All-Compassionate though unseen. Announce to him, then, the good news of forgiveness and a generous wage.

إِنَّمَا تُنذِرُ مَنِ ٱتَّبَعَ ٱلذِّكْرَ وَخَشِىَ ٱلرَّحْمَـٰنَ بِٱلْغَيْبِ فَبَشِّرْهُ بِمَغْفِرَةٍ وَأَجْرٍ كَرِيمٍ ۝

12. It is We Who bring the dead back to life and write down what they have advanced and their vestiges too. Everything We have enumerated in a clear Master Register.[719]

إِنَّا نَحْنُ نُحْىِ ٱلْمَوْتَىٰ وَنَكْتُبُ مَا قَدَّمُوا۟ وَءَاثَـٰرَهُمْ وَكُلَّ شَىْءٍ أَحْصَيْنَـٰهُ فِىٓ إِمَامٍ مُّبِينٍ ۝

13. And relate to them the case of the people of the city, when the Messengers came thereto.

وَٱضْرِبْ لَهُم مَّثَلًا أَصْحَـٰبَ ٱلْقَرْيَةِ إِذْ جَآءَهَا ٱلْمُرْسَلُونَ ۝

14. When We sent them two men, but they denounced them as liars, and so We reinforced them with a third. Then they said: "We are indeed Messengers unto you."

إِذْ أَرْسَلْنَآ إِلَيْهِمُ ٱثْنَيْنِ فَكَذَّبُوهُمَا فَعَزَّزْنَا بِثَالِثٍ فَقَالُوٓا۟ إِنَّآ إِلَيْكُم مُّرْسَلُونَ ۝

15. They said: "You are only mortals like ourselves and the All-Compassionate has not sent down anything. You are only lying."

قَالُوا۟ مَآ أَنتُمْ إِلَّا بَشَرٌ مِّثْلُنَا وَمَآ أَنزَلَ ٱلرَّحْمَـٰنُ مِن شَىْءٍ إِنْ أَنتُمْ إِلَّا تَكْذِبُونَ ۝

16. They (Messengers) said: "Our Lord knows that we are indeed Messengers unto you.

قَالُوا۟ رَبُّنَا يَعْلَمُ إِنَّآ إِلَيْكُمْ لَمُرْسَلُونَ ۝

17. "And it is up to us to deliver the Manifest Message."

وَمَا عَلَيْنَآ إِلَّا ٱلْبَلَـٰغُ ٱلْمُبِينُ ۝

18. They said: "We augur ill of you. If you will not desist, we will stone you and a very painful punishment from us will afflict you."

قَالُوٓا۟ إِنَّا تَطَيَّرْنَا بِكُمْ لَئِن لَّمْ تَنتَهُوا۟ لَنَرْجُمَنَّكُمْ وَلَيَمَسَّنَّكُم مِّنَّا عَذَابٌ أَلِيمٌ ۝

---

719. The reference is to *Umm al-Kitab* or *al-Lawh al-Mahfuz*, the original and eternal codex of the Qur'an in heaven.

19. They (the Messengers) said: "Your bird of omen is with you, if you are reminded, but you are an extravagant people."

قَالُوا طَـٰٓئِرُكُم مَّعَكُمْ أَإِن ذُكِّرْتُم بَلْ أَنتُمْ قَوْمٌ مُّسْرِفُونَ ﴿١٩﴾

20. Then a man came from the farthest point of the city. He said: "My people, follow the Messengers.

وَجَآءَ مِنْ أَقْصَا ٱلْمَدِينَةِ رَجُلٌ يَسْعَىٰ قَالَ يَـٰقَوْمِ ٱتَّبِعُوا ٱلْمُرْسَلِينَ ﴿٢٠﴾

21. "Follow those who do not ask you for a wage and are rightly guided.

ٱتَّبِعُوا مَن لَّا يَسْـَٔلُكُمْ أَجْرًا وَهُم مُّهْتَدُونَ ﴿٢١﴾

22. "And why should I not worship Him who created me and unto Him you shall be returned?

وَمَا لِيَ لَآ أَعْبُدُ ٱلَّذِى فَطَرَنِى وَإِلَيْهِ تُرْجَعُونَ ﴿٢٢﴾

23. "Shall I take, apart from Him, gods whose intercession, should the All-Compassionate wish me ill, will not avail me anything and they will not deliver me?

ءَأَتَّخِذُ مِن دُونِهِۦٓ ءَالِهَةً إِن يُرِدْنِ ٱلرَّحْمَـٰنُ بِضُرٍّ لَّا تُغْنِ عَنِّى شَفَـٰعَتُهُمْ شَيْـًٔا وَلَا يُنقِذُونِ ﴿٢٣﴾

24. "Then, I am truly in manifest error.

إِنِّىٓ إِذًا لَّفِى ضَلَـٰلٍ مُّبِينٍ ﴿٢٤﴾

25. "I have believed in your Lord, so listen to me."

إِنِّىٓ ءَامَنتُ بِرَبِّكُمْ فَٱسْمَعُونِ ﴿٢٥﴾

26. It was said: "Enter Paradise." He said: "I wished my own people knew;

قِيلَ ٱدْخُلِ ٱلْجَنَّةَ قَالَ يَـٰلَيْتَ قَوْمِى يَعْلَمُونَ ﴿٢٦﴾

27. "About my Lord's forgiving me and making me one of the favoured."

بِمَا غَفَرَ لِى رَبِّى وَجَعَلَنِى مِنَ ٱلْمُكْرَمِينَ ﴿٢٧﴾

28. After him, We sent down no troops from heaven; nor would We ever send any down.

۞ وَمَآ أَنزَلْنَا عَلَىٰ قَوْمِهِۦ مِنۢ بَعْدِهِۦ مِن جُندٍ مِّنَ ٱلسَّمَآءِ وَمَا كُنَّا مُنزِلِينَ ﴿٢٨﴾

29. It was only one cry; and behold they were silenced.

إِن كَانَتْ إِلَّا صَيْحَةً وَٰحِدَةً فَإِذَا هُمْ خَـٰمِدُونَ ﴿٢٩﴾

30. Woe betide the servants; no Messenger comes to them but they mock him.

يَـٰحَسْرَةً عَلَى ٱلْعِبَادِ مَا يَأْتِيهِم مِّن رَّسُولٍ إِلَّا كَانُوا بِهِۦ يَسْتَهْزِءُونَ ﴿٣٠﴾

31. Have they not seen how many generations before them We destroyed and that unto them they will not return?

أَلَمْ يَرَوْا كَمْ أَهْلَكْنَا قَبْلَهُم مِّنَ ٱلْقُرُونِ أَنَّهُمْ إِلَيْهِمْ لَا يَرْجِعُونَ ﴿٣١﴾

32. And all of them will be brought before Us?

وَإِن كُلٌّ لَّمَّا جَمِيعٌ لَّدَيْنَا مُحْضَرُونَ ﴿٣٢﴾

33. A sign unto them is the dead land, that We revived and brought out of it grain, from which they eat.

وَءَايَةٌ لَّهُمُ ٱلْأَرْضُ ٱلْمَيْتَةُ أَحْيَيْنَـٰهَا وَأَخْرَجْنَا مِنْهَا حَبًّا فَمِنْهُ يَأْكُلُونَ ﴿٣٣﴾

34. And We caused to grow in it gardens of palms and vines, and caused springs to gush forth therein.

وَجَعَلْنَا فِيهَا جَنَّتٍ مِّن نَّخِيلٍ وَأَعْنَبٍ وَفَجَّرْنَا فِيهَا مِنَ ٱلْعُيُونِ ﴿٣٤﴾

35. That they might eat from its fruit, although their hands brought it not out. Will they not, then, give thanks?

لِيَأْكُلُوا۟ مِن ثَمَرِهِۦ وَمَا عَمِلَتْهُ أَيْدِيهِمْ ۖ أَفَلَا يَشْكُرُونَ ﴿٣٥﴾

36. Glory be to Him Who created all the pairs of what the earth brings forth, of their own kinds and of what they know not.

سُبْحَٰنَ ٱلَّذِى خَلَقَ ٱلْأَزْوَٰجَ كُلَّهَا مِمَّا تُنۢبِتُ ٱلْأَرْضُ وَمِنْ أَنفُسِهِمْ وَمِمَّا لَا يَعْلَمُونَ ﴿٣٦﴾

37. And a sign unto them is the night, from which We strip off the day; and lo, they are in darkness.

وَءَايَةٌ لَّهُمُ ٱلَّيْلُ نَسْلَخُ مِنْهُ ٱلنَّهَارَ فَإِذَا هُم مُّظْلِمُونَ ﴿٣٧﴾

38. And the sun runs unto its fixed station. That is the Decree of the All-Mighty, the All-Knowing.

وَٱلشَّمْسُ تَجْرِى لِمُسْتَقَرٍّ لَّهَا ۚ ذَٰلِكَ تَقْدِيرُ ٱلْعَزِيزِ ٱلْعَلِيمِ ﴿٣٨﴾

39. And the moon, We have determined its phases, until it became like an old twig.

وَٱلْقَمَرَ قَدَّرْنَٰهُ مَنَازِلَ حَتَّىٰ عَادَ كَٱلْعُرْجُونِ ٱلْقَدِيمِ ﴿٣٩﴾

40. The sun ought not to overtake the moon, nor the night outstrip the day; and each in its orbit is floating.

لَا ٱلشَّمْسُ يَنۢبَغِى لَهَآ أَن تُدْرِكَ ٱلْقَمَرَ وَلَا ٱلَّيْلُ سَابِقُ ٱلنَّهَارِ ۚ وَكُلٌّ فِى فَلَكٍ يَسْبَحُونَ ﴿٤٠﴾

41. And a sign unto them is that We carried their progeny in the laden Ark.

وَءَايَةٌ لَّهُمْ أَنَّا حَمَلْنَا ذُرِّيَّتَهُمْ فِى ٱلْفُلْكِ ٱلْمَشْحُونِ ﴿٤١﴾

42. And We created for them the like of it that which they could board.

وَخَلَقْنَا لَهُم مِّن مِّثْلِهِۦ مَا يَرْكَبُونَ ﴿٤٢﴾

43. And if We wish, We would drown them; then there is none to deliver them, nor will they be rescued.

وَإِن نَّشَأْ نُغْرِقْهُمْ فَلَا صَرِيخَ لَهُمْ وَلَا هُمْ يُنقَذُونَ ﴿٤٣﴾

44. Except for a mercy from Us and enjoyment for a while.

إِلَّا رَحْمَةً مِّنَّا وَمَتَٰعًا إِلَىٰ حِينٍ ﴿٤٤﴾

45. If it is said to them: "Beware what came before you and what is behind you, that perchance you might receive mercy."

وَإِذَا قِيلَ لَهُمُ ٱتَّقُوا۟ مَا بَيْنَ أَيْدِيكُمْ وَمَا خَلْفَكُمْ لَعَلَّكُمْ تُرْحَمُونَ ﴿٤٥﴾

46. Yet, no Sign of their Lord's Signs comes to them but they turn away from it.

وَمَا تَأْتِيهِم مِّنْ ءَايَةٍ مِّنْ ءَايَٰتِ رَبِّهِمْ إِلَّا كَانُوا۟ عَنْهَا مُعْرِضِينَ ﴿٤٦﴾

47. And if it is said to them: "Spend freely from what Allah provided for you, the unbelievers say to the believers: 'Shall we feed him whom Allah would have fed, if He wished. You are only in manifest error?' "

وَإِذَا قِيلَ لَهُمْ أَنفِقُوا۟ مِمَّا رَزَقَكُمُ ٱللَّهُ قَالَ ٱلَّذِينَ كَفَرُوا۟ لِلَّذِينَ ءَامَنُوٓا۟ أَنُطْعِمُ مَن لَّوْ يَشَآءُ ٱللَّهُ أَطْعَمَهُۥٓ إِنْ أَنتُمْ إِلَّا فِى ضَلَٰلٍ مُّبِينٍ ﴿٤٧﴾

48. And they say: "When is this promise coming, if you are truthful?"

49. They are only awaiting a single cry to seize them, while they are feuding.

50. So they cannot make a testament nor return to their own people.

51. And the Trumpet is blown, then behold how from their graves, unto their Lord, they slink away.

52. They will say: "Woe betide us; whoever has roused us from our sleep? This is what the All-Compassionate has promised, and the Messengers have spoken the truth."

53. It was only a single cry, and behold they were all brought before Us.

54. So, today no soul shall be wronged a whit, and you will only be rewarded for what you used to do.

55. Today, the Companions of Paradise are busy enjoying themselves;

56. Together with their spouses they are reclining on couches in the shade.

57. Wherein they have fruit, and have all they call for.

58. "Peace", uttered by a Merciful Lord.

59. "Be singled out today, O criminals.

60. "Did I not exhort you, O Children of Adam, not to worship Satan? For he is a manifest enemy of yours.

61. "And worship Me; for this is a straight path.

62. "He has surely led astray numerous generations of you. Did you not understand, then?

63. "This, then, is Hell which you were promised.

وَيَقُولُونَ مَتَىٰ هَٰذَا ٱلْوَعْدُ إِن كُنتُمْ صَٰدِقِينَ ﴿٤٨﴾

مَا يَنظُرُونَ إِلَّا صَيْحَةً وَٰحِدَةً تَأْخُذُهُمْ وَهُمْ يَخِصِّمُونَ ﴿٤٩﴾

فَلَا يَسْتَطِيعُونَ تَوْصِيَةً وَلَآ إِلَىٰٓ أَهْلِهِمْ يَرْجِعُونَ ﴿٥٠﴾

وَنُفِخَ فِى ٱلصُّورِ فَإِذَا هُم مِّنَ ٱلْأَجْدَاثِ إِلَىٰ رَبِّهِمْ يَنسِلُونَ ﴿٥١﴾

قَالُوا۟ يَٰوَيْلَنَا مَنۢ بَعَثَنَا مِن مَّرْقَدِنَا ۜ هَٰذَا مَا وَعَدَ ٱلرَّحْمَٰنُ وَصَدَقَ ٱلْمُرْسَلُونَ ﴿٥٢﴾

إِن كَانَتْ إِلَّا صَيْحَةً وَٰحِدَةً فَإِذَا هُمْ جَمِيعٌ لَّدَيْنَا مُحْضَرُونَ ﴿٥٣﴾

فَٱلْيَوْمَ لَا تُظْلَمُ نَفْسٌ شَيْئًا وَلَا تُجْزَوْنَ إِلَّا مَا كُنتُمْ تَعْمَلُونَ ﴿٥٤﴾

إِنَّ أَصْحَٰبَ ٱلْجَنَّةِ ٱلْيَوْمَ فِى شُغُلٍ فَٰكِهُونَ ﴿٥٥﴾

هُمْ وَأَزْوَٰجُهُمْ فِى ظِلَٰلٍ عَلَى ٱلْأَرَآئِكِ مُتَّكِـُٔونَ ﴿٥٦﴾

لَهُمْ فِيهَا فَٰكِهَةٌ وَلَهُم مَّا يَدَّعُونَ ﴿٥٧﴾

سَلَٰمٌ قَوْلًا مِّن رَّبٍّ رَّحِيمٍ ﴿٥٨﴾

وَٱمْتَٰزُوا۟ ٱلْيَوْمَ أَيُّهَا ٱلْمُجْرِمُونَ ﴿٥٩﴾

أَلَمْ أَعْهَدْ إِلَيْكُمْ يَٰبَنِىٓ ءَادَمَ أَن لَّا تَعْبُدُوا۟ ٱلشَّيْطَٰنَ ۖ إِنَّهُۥ لَكُمْ عَدُوٌّ مُّبِينٌ ﴿٦٠﴾

وَأَنِ ٱعْبُدُونِى ۚ هَٰذَا صِرَٰطٌ مُّسْتَقِيمٌ ﴿٦١﴾

وَلَقَدْ أَضَلَّ مِنكُمْ جِبِلًّا كَثِيرًا ۖ أَفَلَمْ تَكُونُوا۟ تَعْقِلُونَ ﴿٦٢﴾

هَٰذِهِۦ جَهَنَّمُ ٱلَّتِى كُنتُمْ تُوعَدُونَ ﴿٦٣﴾

64. "Burn in it today for what you used to disbelieve."

اَصۡلَوۡهَا ٱلۡيَوۡمَ بِمَا كُنتُمۡ تَكۡفُرُونَ ۝

65. Today, We set a seal upon their mouths, and their hands will speak to Us and their feet will bear witness, regarding what they used to earn.

ٱلۡيَوۡمَ نَخۡتِمُ عَلَىٰٓ أَفۡوَٰهِهِمۡ وَتُكَلِّمُنَآ أَيۡدِيهِمۡ وَتَشۡهَدُ أَرۡجُلُهُم بِمَا كَانُوا۟ يَكۡسِبُونَ ۝

66. And had We wished, We would have blotted out their eyes. Then they would race upon the pathway but how will they see?

وَلَوۡ نَشَآءُ لَطَمَسۡنَا عَلَىٰٓ أَعۡيُنِهِمۡ فَٱسۡتَبَقُوا۟ ٱلصِّرَٰطَ فَأَنَّىٰ يُبۡصِرُونَ ۝

67. And had We wished, We would have deformed them upon their own seats, so that they could not take off or turn back.

وَلَوۡ نَشَآءُ لَمَسَخۡنَٰهُمۡ عَلَىٰ مَكَانَتِهِمۡ فَمَا ٱسۡتَطَٰعُوا۟ مُضِيًّا وَلَا يَرۡجِعُونَ ۝

68. Whoever We grant old age, We would cause to shrink in form. Do they not understand, then?

وَمَن نُّعَمِّرۡهُ نُنَكِّسۡهُ فِى ٱلۡخَلۡقِ أَفَلَا يَعۡقِلُونَ ۝

69. We did not teach him[720] poetry, nor did it become him. It is only a Reminder and a Manifest Qur'an;

وَمَا عَلَّمۡنَٰهُ ٱلشِّعۡرَ وَمَا يَنۢبَغِى لَهُۥٓ إِنۡ هُوَ إِلَّا ذِكۡرٌ وَقُرۡءَانٌ مُّبِينٌ ۝

70. So as to warn those who are alive and the word may be fulfilled against the unbelievers.

لِّيُنذِرَ مَن كَانَ حَيًّا وَيَحِقَّ ٱلۡقَوۡلُ عَلَى ٱلۡكَٰفِرِينَ ۝

71. Have they not seen that We have created for them, of Our Handiwork, cattle whereof they are now the owners?

أَوَلَمۡ يَرَوۡا۟ أَنَّا خَلَقۡنَا لَهُم مِّمَّا عَمِلَتۡ أَيۡدِينَآ أَنۡعَٰمًا فَهُمۡ لَهَا مَٰلِكُونَ ۝

72. And We subdued them to them, so that of some are their mounts and of some they eat.

وَذَلَّلۡنَٰهَا لَهُمۡ فَمِنۡهَا رَكُوبُهُمۡ وَمِنۡهَا يَأۡكُلُونَ ۝

73. And from them they have many benefits and beverages. Will they not, then, give thanks?

وَلَهُمۡ فِيهَا مَنَٰفِعُ وَمَشَارِبُ أَفَلَا يَشۡكُرُونَ ۝

74. Yet, they have taken, apart from Allah, other gods that they might receive support.

وَٱتَّخَذُوا۟ مِن دُونِ ٱللَّهِ ءَالِهَةً لَّعَلَّهُمۡ يُنصَرُونَ ۝

75. But they cannot support them, although they are arrayed as troops for them.

لَا يَسۡتَطِيعُونَ نَصۡرَهُمۡ وَهُمۡ لَهُمۡ جُندٌ مُّحۡضَرُونَ ۝

76. Do not let their words cause you grief; We know what they reveal and what they conceal.

فَلَا يَحۡزُنكَ قَوۡلُهُمۡ إِنَّا نَعۡلَمُ مَا يُسِرُّونَ وَمَا يُعۡلِنُونَ ۝

---

720. The Prophet.

77. Does not man see that We created him from a sperm; and behold he is a manifest trouble-maker?

أَوَلَمْ يَرَ ٱلْإِنسَٰنُ أَنَّا خَلَقْنَٰهُ مِن نُّطْفَةٍ فَإِذَا هُوَ خَصِيمٌ مُّبِينٌ ۝

78. And he produced an equal for Us, forgetting Our creating him. He said: "Who brings the bones back to life, once they are withered?"

وَضَرَبَ لَنَا مَثَلًا وَنَسِيَ خَلْقَهُۥ قَالَ مَن يُحْىِ ٱلْعِظَٰمَ وَهِىَ رَمِيمٌ ۝

79. Say: "He Who originated them the first time will bring them back to life and He has knowledge of every creation."

قُلْ يُحْيِيهَا ٱلَّذِىٓ أَنشَأَهَآ أَوَّلَ مَرَّةٍ وَهُوَ بِكُلِّ خَلْقٍ عَلِيمٌ ۝

80. It is He Who produces fire from green trees for you; and behold you are kindling flames from it.

ٱلَّذِى جَعَلَ لَكُم مِّنَ ٱلشَّجَرِ ٱلْأَخْضَرِ نَارًا فَإِذَآ أَنتُم مِّنْهُ تُوقِدُونَ ۝

81. Is not He Who created the heavens and the earth able, then, to create the like of them? Yes, indeed, and He is the All-Knowing Creator.

أَوَلَيْسَ ٱلَّذِى خَلَقَ ٱلسَّمَٰوَٰتِ وَٱلْأَرْضَ بِقَٰدِرٍ عَلَىٰٓ أَن يَخْلُقَ مِثْلَهُم بَلَىٰ وَهُوَ ٱلْخَلَّٰقُ ٱلْعَلِيمُ ۝

82. His Command is indeed such that if He wills a thing, He says to it: "Be", and it comes to be.

إِنَّمَآ أَمْرُهُۥٓ إِذَآ أَرَادَ شَيْـًٔا أَن يَقُولَ لَهُۥ كُن فَيَكُونُ ۝

83. Glory, then, to Him in Whose Hands is the dominion of everything and unto Whom you will be returned.

فَسُبْحَٰنَ ٱلَّذِى بِيَدِهِۦ مَلَكُوتُ كُلِّ شَىْءٍ وَإِلَيْهِ تُرْجَعُونَ ۝

Sûrat As-Sâffât, (The Rangers) 37

سُورَةُ الصَّافَات

In the Name of Allah, the Compassionate, the Merciful

بِسْمِ ٱللَّهِ ٱلرَّحْمَٰنِ ٱلرَّحِيمِ

1. By the rangers ranged in rows;

وَٱلصَّٰٓفَّٰتِ صَفًّا ۝

2. By the reprovers reproving;

فَٱلزَّٰجِرَٰتِ زَجْرًا ۝

3. By the reciters of a Reminder;

فَٱلتَّٰلِيَٰتِ ذِكْرًا ۝

4. Your God is surely One,

إِنَّ إِلَٰهَكُمْ لَوَٰحِدٌ ۝

5. The Lord of the heavens and the earth and what lies between them, Lord of the Orients.

رَّبُّ ٱلسَّمَٰوَٰتِ وَٱلْأَرْضِ وَمَا بَيْنَهُمَا وَرَبُّ ٱلْمَشَٰرِقِ ۝

6. We have adorned the lower sky with the ornament of the planets,

إِنَّا زَيَّنَّا ٱلسَّمَآءَ ٱلدُّنْيَا بِزِينَةٍ ٱلْكَوَاكِبِ ۝

7. To guard against every rebellious devil.

8. They do not listen to the Higher Assembly and are pelted from every side;

9. Expelled; and theirs is a lasting punishment.

10. Except for him who eavesdropped once; and so a shooting star followed him.

11. So ask them: "Are they mightier in constitution than those We have created?" We have actually created them from sticky clay.

12. You rather wonder, while they mock.

13. If they are reminded, they will not remember.

14. And if they see a sign, they simply scoff.

15. And they say: "This is only manifest sorcery.

16. "What! Once we are dead and turn into dust and bones, shall we be raised from the dead?

17. "Or our forefathers?"

18. Say: "Yes, and you will be totally subdued."

19. It is only one shout, and behold, they are watching.

20. And they say: "Woe betide us, this is the Day of Judgement.

21. "This is the Day of Decision which we used to question."

22. Gather together those who were wrong-doers, their spouses and what they used to worship;

23. Apart from Allah, and lead them to the path of Hell.

وَحِفْظًا مِّن كُلِّ شَيْطَانٍ مَّارِدٍ ۝

لَّا يَسَّمَّعُونَ إِلَى ٱلْمَلَإِ ٱلْأَعْلَىٰ وَيُقْذَفُونَ مِن كُلِّ جَانِبٍ ۝

دُحُورًا وَلَهُمْ عَذَابٌ وَاصِبٌ ۝

إِلَّا مَنْ خَطِفَ ٱلْخَطْفَةَ فَأَتْبَعَهُ شِهَابٌ ثَاقِبٌ ۝

فَٱسْتَفْتِهِمْ أَهُمْ أَشَدُّ خَلْقًا أَم مَّنْ خَلَقْنَا إِنَّا خَلَقْنَٰهُم مِّن طِينٍ لَّازِبٍ ۝

بَلْ عَجِبْتَ وَيَسْخَرُونَ ۝

وَإِذَا ذُكِّرُوا لَا يَذْكُرُونَ ۝

وَإِذَا رَأَوْا ءَايَةً يَسْتَسْخِرُونَ ۝

وَقَالُوا إِنْ هَٰذَا إِلَّا سِحْرٌ مُّبِينٌ ۝

أَءِذَا مِتْنَا وَكُنَّا تُرَابًا وَعِظَٰمًا أَءِنَّا لَمَبْعُوثُونَ ۝

أَوَ ءَابَاؤُنَا ٱلْأَوَّلُونَ ۝

قُلْ نَعَمْ وَأَنتُمْ دَٰخِرُونَ ۝

فَإِنَّمَا هِىَ زَجْرَةٌ وَٰحِدَةٌ فَإِذَا هُمْ يَنظُرُونَ ۝

وَقَالُوا يَٰوَيْلَنَا هَٰذَا يَوْمُ ٱلدِّينِ ۝

هَٰذَا يَوْمُ ٱلْفَصْلِ ٱلَّذِى كُنتُم بِهِ تُكَذِّبُونَ ۝

۞ ٱحْشُرُوا ٱلَّذِينَ ظَلَمُوا وَأَزْوَٰجَهُمْ وَمَا كَانُوا يَعْبُدُونَ ۝

مِن دُونِ ٱللَّهِ فَٱهْدُوهُمْ إِلَىٰ صِرَٰطِ ٱلْجَحِيمِ ۝

24. And arrest them for they are accountable.

وَقِفُوهُمْ إِنَّهُم مَّسْئُولُونَ ۝

25. Why is it you do not support each other?

مَا لَكُمْ لَا تَنَاصَرُونَ ۝

26. Instead, today they have surrendered.

بَلْ هُمُ ٱلْيَوْمَ مُسْتَسْلِمُونَ ۝

27. And some of them turned to one another asking.

وَأَقْبَلَ بَعْضُهُمْ عَلَىٰ بَعْضٍ يَتَسَآءَلُونَ ۝

28. They said: "You used to come to us from the right."

قَالُوٓا۟ إِنَّكُمْ كُنتُمْ تَأْتُونَنَا عَنِ ٱلْيَمِينِ ۝

29. They said: "No, you were no believers.

قَالُوا۟ بَل لَّمْ تَكُونُوا۟ مُؤْمِنِينَ ۝

30. "And we had no authority over you; for you were an aggressive people.

وَمَا كَانَ لَنَا عَلَيْكُم مِّن سُلْطَٰنٍۭ بَلْ كُنتُمْ قَوْمًا طَٰغِينَ ۝

31. "And thus the punishment of our Lord was meted out to us; therefore we are surely tasting it.

فَحَقَّ عَلَيْنَا قَوْلُ رَبِّنَآ إِنَّا لَذَآئِقُونَ ۝

32. "So, we misled you, being misled ourselves."

فَأَغْوَيْنَٰكُمْ إِنَّا كُنَّا غَٰوِينَ ۝

33. Therefore, they are on that Day partners in punishment.

فَإِنَّهُمْ يَوْمَئِذٍ فِى ٱلْعَذَابِ مُشْتَرِكُونَ ۝

34. This is how We treat the criminals.

إِنَّا كَذَٰلِكَ نَفْعَلُ بِٱلْمُجْرِمِينَ ۝

35. For when it used to be said to them: "There is no god but Allah", they would wax proud.

إِنَّهُمْ كَانُوٓا۟ إِذَا قِيلَ لَهُمْ لَآ إِلَٰهَ إِلَّا ٱللَّهُ يَسْتَكْبِرُونَ ۝

36. And they would say: "Are we going to forsake our gods for the sake of a poet possessed?"

وَيَقُولُونَ أَئِنَّا لَتَارِكُوٓا۟ ءَالِهَتِنَا لِشَاعِرٍ مَّجْنُونٍۭ ۝

37. Indeed, he brought the truth and confirmed the other Messengers.

بَلْ جَآءَ بِٱلْحَقِّ وَصَدَّقَ ٱلْمُرْسَلِينَ ۝

38. You shall indeed taste the painful punishment.

إِنَّكُمْ لَذَآئِقُوا۟ ٱلْعَذَابِ ٱلْأَلِيمِ ۝

39. And you shall only be rewarded for what you used to do.

وَمَا تُجْزَوْنَ إِلَّا مَا كُنتُمْ تَعْمَلُونَ ۝

40. Except for Allah's sincere servants.

إِلَّا عِبَادَ ٱللَّهِ ٱلْمُخْلَصِينَ ۝

41. To those is assigned a fixed provision,

أُو۟لَٰٓئِكَ لَهُمْ رِزْقٌ مَّعْلُومٌ ۝

42. Of fruits; and they shall be honoured;

فَوَٰكِهُ وَهُم مُّكْرَمُونَ ۝

43. In the Gardens of Bliss;

فِى جَنَّٰتِ ٱلنَّعِيمِ ۝

44. Upon couches, facing each other.

45. A cup of pure spring water shall be passed around them;

46. Snow-white, a delight to drinkers.

47. Wherein there is no gall and they are not intoxicated by it.

48. And they also shall have wide-eyed maidens averting their gaze.

49. They resemble hidden pearls.

50. Then, they will advance one towards the other asking each other.

51. One of them will say: "I had a comrade;

52. "Who used to say: 'Are you then one of the confirmed believers?'

53. "Will we, once we are dead and have become dust and bones, be really judged?"

54. He said:[721] "Are you looking down?"

55. He looked and saw him in the centre of Hell.

56. He said: "By Allah, you almost caused my perdition.

57. "But for my Lord's Grace, I would have been one of those brought forward."

58. "Are we not then going to die,

59. "Except for our first death? And will we not be punished?"

60. Surely, this is the great triumph.

61. For the like of this, let the workers work.

62. Is that a better outcome or the Tree of Bitterness?

63. We have made it a temptation for the wrongdoers.

64. It is a tree that grows out of the bottom of Hell;

عَلَىٰ سُرُرٍ مُّتَقَٰبِلِينَ ﴿٤٤﴾

يُطَافُ عَلَيْهِم بِكَأْسٍ مِّن مَّعِينٍ ﴿٤٥﴾

بَيْضَآءَ لَذَّةٍ لِّلشَّٰرِبِينَ ﴿٤٦﴾

لَا فِيهَا غَوْلٌ وَلَا هُمْ عَنْهَا يُنزَفُونَ ﴿٤٧﴾

وَعِندَهُمْ قَٰصِرَٰتُ ٱلطَّرْفِ عِينٌ ﴿٤٨﴾

كَأَنَّهُنَّ بَيْضٌ مَّكْنُونٌ ﴿٤٩﴾

فَأَقْبَلَ بَعْضُهُمْ عَلَىٰ بَعْضٍ يَتَسَآءَلُونَ ﴿٥٠﴾

قَالَ قَآئِلٌ مِّنْهُمْ إِنِّي كَانَ لِي قَرِينٌ ﴿٥١﴾

يَقُولُ أَءِنَّكَ لَمِنَ ٱلْمُصَدِّقِينَ ﴿٥٢﴾

أَءِذَا مِتْنَا وَكُنَّا تُرَابًا وَعِظَٰمًا أَءِنَّا لَمَدِينُونَ ﴿٥٣﴾

قَالَ هَلْ أَنتُم مُّطَّلِعُونَ ﴿٥٤﴾

فَٱطَّلَعَ فَرَءَاهُ فِي سَوَآءِ ٱلْجَحِيمِ ﴿٥٥﴾

قَالَ تَٱللَّهِ إِن كِدتَّ لَتُرْدِينِ ﴿٥٦﴾

وَلَوْلَا نِعْمَةُ رَبِّي لَكُنتُ مِنَ ٱلْمُحْضَرِينَ ﴿٥٧﴾

أَفَمَا نَحْنُ بِمَيِّتِينَ ﴿٥٨﴾

إِلَّا مَوْتَتَنَا ٱلْأُولَىٰ وَمَا نَحْنُ بِمُعَذَّبِينَ ﴿٥٩﴾

إِنَّ هَٰذَا لَهُوَ ٱلْفَوْزُ ٱلْعَظِيمُ ﴿٦٠﴾

لِمِثْلِ هَٰذَا فَلْيَعْمَلِ ٱلْعَٰمِلُونَ ﴿٦١﴾

أَذَٰلِكَ خَيْرٌ نُّزُلًا أَمْ شَجَرَةُ ٱلزَّقُّومِ ﴿٦٢﴾

إِنَّا جَعَلْنَٰهَا فِتْنَةً لِّلظَّٰلِمِينَ ﴿٦٣﴾

إِنَّهَا شَجَرَةٌ تَخْرُجُ فِي أَصْلِ ٱلْجَحِيمِ ﴿٦٤﴾

---

721. To his companions.

65. Its shoots are like the heads of devils.

طَلْعُهَا كَأَنَّهُ رُءُوسُ ٱلشَّيَٰطِينِ ﴿٦٥﴾

66. They shall eat from it till they fill their bellies.

فَإِنَّهُمْ لَأَكِلُونَ مِنْهَا فَمَالِـُٔونَ مِنْهَا ٱلْبُطُونَ ﴿٦٦﴾

67. In addition, they have with it a mixture of boiling water.

ثُمَّ إِنَّ لَهُمْ عَلَيْهَا لَشَوْبًا مِّنْ حَمِيمٍ ﴿٦٧﴾

68. Then, their return is unto Hell.

ثُمَّ إِنَّ مَرْجِعَهُمْ لَإِلَى ٱلْجَحِيمِ ﴿٦٨﴾

69. Indeed, they found their fathers steeped in error.

إِنَّهُمْ أَلْفَوْا۟ ءَابَآءَهُمْ ضَآلِّينَ ﴿٦٩﴾

70. And so they are fast following in their footsteps.

فَهُمْ عَلَىٰٓ ءَاثَٰرِهِمْ يُهْرَعُونَ ﴿٧٠﴾

71. And before them, most of the ancients were in error.

وَلَقَدْ ضَلَّ قَبْلَهُمْ أَكْثَرُ ٱلْأَوَّلِينَ ﴿٧١﴾

72. We had sent among them some warners.

وَلَقَدْ أَرْسَلْنَا فِيهِم مُّنذِرِينَ ﴿٧٢﴾

73. But behold what was the fate of those who were warned.

فَٱنظُرْ كَيْفَ كَانَ عَٰقِبَةُ ٱلْمُنذَرِينَ ﴿٧٣﴾

74. Except for Allah's sincere servants.

إِلَّا عِبَادَ ٱللَّهِ ٱلْمُخْلَصِينَ ﴿٧٤﴾

75. Noah called Us in times past; blessed then are the Answerers.

وَلَقَدْ نَادَىٰنَا نُوحٌ فَلَنِعْمَ ٱلْمُجِيبُونَ ﴿٧٥﴾

76. We delivered him and his people from the great calamity.

وَنَجَّيْنَٰهُ وَأَهْلَهُۥ مِنَ ٱلْكَرْبِ ٱلْعَظِيمِ ﴿٧٦﴾

77. And made his progeny the survivors.

وَجَعَلْنَا ذُرِّيَّتَهُۥ هُمُ ٱلْبَاقِينَ ﴿٧٧﴾

78. And We bequeathed to him, among those who succeeded:

وَتَرَكْنَا عَلَيْهِ فِى ٱلْءَاخِرِينَ ﴿٧٨﴾

79. "Peace upon Noah among all the nations."

سَلَٰمٌ عَلَىٰ نُوحٍ فِى ٱلْعَٰلَمِينَ ﴿٧٩﴾

80. Indeed, this is how We reward the beneficent.

إِنَّا كَذَٰلِكَ نَجْزِى ٱلْمُحْسِنِينَ ﴿٨٠﴾

81. He was truly one of Our believing servants.

إِنَّهُۥ مِنْ عِبَادِنَا ٱلْمُؤْمِنِينَ ﴿٨١﴾

82. Then, We drowned the others.

ثُمَّ أَغْرَقْنَا ٱلْءَاخَرِينَ ﴿٨٢﴾

83. And of his partisans was Abraham.

وَإِنَّ مِن شِيعَتِهِۦ لَإِبْرَٰهِيمَ ﴿٨٣﴾

84. When he came to his Lord with a sound heart.

إِذْ جَآءَ رَبَّهُۥ بِقَلْبٍ سَلِيمٍ ﴿٨٤﴾

85. He said to his father and his own people: "What are you worshipping?

إِذْ قَالَ لِأَبِيهِ وَقَوْمِهِۦ مَاذَا تَعْبُدُونَ ﴿٨٥﴾

86. "Do you desire, falsely, other gods, apart from Allah?

87. "What do you think, then, of the Lord of the Worlds?"

88. Then he cast a glance at the stars.

89. And said: "I am really sick."

90. Whereupon, they turned away from him in flight.

91. And he turned towards their gods, saying: "Will you not eat?"

92. "Why do you not speak?"

93. Then, he proceeded to hit them with his right hand.

94. Then, [his people] came towards him in haste.

95. He said: "Do you worship what you hew?

96. "When Allah created you and what you do?"

97. They said: "Build him a pyre"; and so they cast him into the furnace.

98. They wished him ill, but We reduced them to the lowest rung.

99. And he said: "I am going to my Lord; He will guide me.

100. "Lord, grant me a righteous child."

101. So, We announced to him the good news of a prudent boy.

102. Then, when he attained the age of consorting with him, he said: "My son, I have seen in sleep that I am slaughtering you. See what you think." He said: "My father, do what you are commanded; you will find me, Allah willing, one of the steadfast."

103. Then, when they both submitted and he flung him down upon his brow;

أَئِفْكًا ءَالِهَةً دُونَ ٱللَّهِ تُرِيدُونَ ۝

فَمَا ظَنُّكُم بِرَبِّ ٱلْعَٰلَمِينَ ۝

فَنَظَرَ نَظْرَةً فِى ٱلنُّجُومِ ۝

فَقَالَ إِنِّى سَقِيمٌ ۝

فَتَوَلَّوْا۟ عَنْهُ مُدْبِرِينَ ۝

فَرَاغَ إِلَىٰٓ ءَالِهَتِهِمْ فَقَالَ أَلَا تَأْكُلُونَ ۝

مَا لَكُمْ لَا تَنطِقُونَ ۝

فَرَاغَ عَلَيْهِمْ ضَرْبًۢا بِٱلْيَمِينِ ۝

فَأَقْبَلُوٓا۟ إِلَيْهِ يَزِفُّونَ ۝

قَالَ أَتَعْبُدُونَ مَا تَنْحِتُونَ ۝

وَٱللَّهُ خَلَقَكُمْ وَمَا تَعْمَلُونَ ۝

قَالُوا۟ ٱبْنُوا۟ لَهُۥ بُنْيَٰنًا فَأَلْقُوهُ فِى ٱلْجَحِيمِ ۝

فَأَرَادُوا۟ بِهِۦ كَيْدًا فَجَعَلْنَٰهُمُ ٱلْأَسْفَلِينَ ۝

وَقَالَ إِنِّى ذَاهِبٌ إِلَىٰ رَبِّى سَيَهْدِينِ ۝

رَبِّ هَبْ لِى مِنَ ٱلصَّٰلِحِينَ ۝

فَبَشَّرْنَٰهُ بِغُلَٰمٍ حَلِيمٍ ۝

فَلَمَّا بَلَغَ مَعَهُ ٱلسَّعْىَ قَالَ يَٰبُنَىَّ إِنِّىٓ أَرَىٰ فِى ٱلْمَنَامِ أَنِّىٓ أَذْبَحُكَ فَٱنظُرْ مَاذَا تَرَىٰ قَالَ يَٰٓأَبَتِ ٱفْعَلْ مَا تُؤْمَرُ سَتَجِدُنِىٓ إِن شَآءَ ٱللَّهُ مِنَ ٱلصَّٰبِرِينَ ۝

فَلَمَّآ أَسْلَمَا وَتَلَّهُۥ لِلْجَبِينِ ۝

104. And We called out to him: "O Abraham,

وَنَادَيْنَهُ أَن يَٰٓإِبْرَٰهِيمُ ۝

105. "You have believed the vision." Thus We reward the beneficent.

قَدْ صَدَّقْتَ ٱلرُّءْيَآ إِنَّا كَذَٰلِكَ نَجْزِى ٱلْمُحْسِنِينَ ۝

106. This, indeed, is the manifest trial.

إِنَّ هَٰذَا لَهُوَ ٱلْبَلَٰٓؤُا۟ ٱلْمُبِينُ ۝

107. And We ransomed him with a large sacrifice.

وَفَدَيْنَٰهُ بِذِبْحٍ عَظِيمٍ ۝

108. And We left with him for later generations:

وَتَرَكْنَا عَلَيْهِ فِى ٱلْءَاخِرِينَ ۝

109. "Peace be upon Abraham."

سَلَٰمٌ عَلَىٰٓ إِبْرَٰهِيمَ ۝

110. Thus, We reward the beneficent.

كَذَٰلِكَ نَجْزِى ٱلْمُحْسِنِينَ ۝

111. He is indeed one of Our believing servants.

إِنَّهُۥ مِنْ عِبَادِنَا ٱلْمُؤْمِنِينَ ۝

112. And We announced to him the good news of Isaac as a Prophet, one of the righteous.

وَبَشَّرْنَٰهُ بِإِسْحَٰقَ نَبِيًّا مِّنَ ٱلصَّٰلِحِينَ ۝

113. And We blessed him and blessed Isaac; and of their progeny some are beneficent and some are wronging themselves manifestly.

وَبَٰرَكْنَا عَلَيْهِ وَعَلَىٰٓ إِسْحَٰقَ وَمِن ذُرِّيَّتِهِمَا مُحْسِنٌ وَظَالِمٌ لِّنَفْسِهِۦ مُبِينٌ ۝

114. And We have favoured Moses and Aaron;

وَلَقَدْ مَنَنَّا عَلَىٰ مُوسَىٰ وَهَٰرُونَ ۝

115. And delivered them and their people from the great calamity.

وَنَجَّيْنَٰهُمَا وَقَوْمَهُمَا مِنَ ٱلْكَرْبِ ٱلْعَظِيمِ ۝

116. And We supported them, and so they were the victors.

وَنَصَرْنَٰهُمْ فَكَانُوا۟ هُمُ ٱلْغَٰلِبِينَ ۝

117. And We gave them both the clarifying Book.

وَءَاتَيْنَٰهُمَا ٱلْكِتَٰبَ ٱلْمُسْتَبِينَ ۝

118. And We guided them unto the Straight Path.

وَهَدَيْنَٰهُمَا ٱلصِّرَٰطَ ٱلْمُسْتَقِيمَ ۝

119. And We left with them both for later generations:

وَتَرَكْنَا عَلَيْهِمَا فِى ٱلْءَاخِرِينَ ۝

120. "Peace be upon Moses and Aaron."

سَلَٰمٌ عَلَىٰ مُوسَىٰ وَهَٰرُونَ ۝

121. Thus We reward the beneficent.

إِنَّا كَذَٰلِكَ نَجْزِى ٱلْمُحْسِنِينَ ۝

122. They are indeed among Our believing servants.

إِنَّهُمَا مِنْ عِبَادِنَا ٱلْمُؤْمِنِينَ ۝

123. And Elias[722] too was one of the Messengers.

وَإِنَّ إِلْيَاسَ لَمِنَ ٱلْمُرْسَلِينَ ۝

124. When he said to his people: "Do you not fear God?

إِذْ قَالَ لِقَوْمِهِۦٓ أَلَا تَتَّقُونَ ۝

125. "Do you call upon Baal,[723] forsaking the Best of Creators,

أَتَدْعُونَ بَعْلًا وَتَذَرُونَ أَحْسَنَ ٱلْخَٰلِقِينَ ۝

126. "Allah, your Lord and the Lord of your forefathers?"

ٱللَّهَ رَبَّكُمْ وَرَبَّ ءَابَآئِكُمُ ٱلْأَوَّلِينَ ۝

127. But they denounced him as a liar; and behold, they shall be brought forward.

فَكَذَّبُوهُ فَإِنَّهُمْ لَمُحْضَرُونَ ۝

128. Except for Our sincere servants.

إِلَّا عِبَادَ ٱللَّهِ ٱلْمُخْلَصِينَ ۝

129. And We left with him for the later generations:

وَتَرَكْنَا عَلَيْهِ فِي ٱلْءَاخِرِينَ ۝

130. "Peace be upon the family of Elias."

سَلَٰمٌ عَلَىٰٓ إِلْ يَاسِينَ ۝

131. Thus, We reward the beneficent.

إِنَّا كَذَٰلِكَ نَجْزِي ٱلْمُحْسِنِينَ ۝

132. He is one of Our believing servants.

إِنَّهُۥ مِنْ عِبَادِنَا ٱلْمُؤْمِنِينَ ۝

133. And Lot was one of the Messengers.

وَإِنَّ لُوطًا لَّمِنَ ٱلْمُرْسَلِينَ ۝

134. When We delivered him and his whole family,

إِذْ نَجَّيْنَٰهُ وَأَهْلَهُۥٓ أَجْمَعِينَ ۝

135. Except for an old woman who was among the lost.

إِلَّا عَجُوزًا فِي ٱلْغَٰبِرِينَ ۝

136. Then We destroyed the others.

ثُمَّ دَمَّرْنَا ٱلْءَاخَرِينَ ۝

137. And you pass by them in the morning,

وَإِنَّكُمْ لَتَمُرُّونَ عَلَيْهِم مُّصْبِحِينَ ۝

138. And at night. Do you not understand, then?

وَبِٱلَّيْلِ أَفَلَا تَعْقِلُونَ ۝

139. And Jonas was one of the Messengers.

وَإِنَّ يُونُسَ لَمِنَ ٱلْمُرْسَلِينَ ۝

140. When he fled towards the laden Ark.

إِذْ أَبَقَ إِلَى ٱلْفُلْكِ ٱلْمَشْحُونِ ۝

141. He cast lots, but was one of the losers.

فَسَاهَمَ فَكَانَ مِنَ ٱلْمُدْحَضِينَ ۝

142. Then the whale swallowed him, and he was to blame.

فَٱلْتَقَمَهُ ٱلْحُوتُ وَهُوَ مُلِيمٌ ۝

---

722. The biblical Prophet Elijah.
723. The Phoenician god of fertility.

143. Had he not been one of those who glorified [Allah];

فَلَوْلَا أَنَّهُ كَانَ مِنَ ٱلْمُسَبِّحِينَ ۝

144. He would have stayed in its belly until the Day they will be resuscitated.

لَلَبِثَ فِي بَطْنِهِ إِلَىٰ يَوْمِ يُبْعَثُونَ ۝

145. Then We cast him out in the wilderness while he was sick.

۞ فَنَبَذْنَاهُ بِٱلْعَرَاءِ وَهُوَ سَقِيمٌ ۝

146. And made to grow over him a gourd tree.

وَأَنبَتْنَا عَلَيْهِ شَجَرَةً مِّن يَقْطِينٍ ۝

147. And We sent him forth to a hundred thousand or more.

وَأَرْسَلْنَاهُ إِلَىٰ مِائَةِ أَلْفٍ أَوْ يَزِيدُونَ ۝

148. They believed, and so We accorded them enjoyment for a while.

فَآمَنُوا فَمَتَّعْنَاهُمْ إِلَىٰ حِينٍ ۝

149. Ask them: "Are the daughters your Lord's, and theirs the sons?

فَٱسْتَفْتِهِمْ أَلِرَبِّكَ ٱلْبَنَاتُ وَلَهُمُ ٱلْبَنُونَ ۝

150. "Or have We created the angels as females, while they were witnesses?"

أَمْ خَلَقْنَا ٱلْمَلَائِكَةَ إِنَاثًا وَهُمْ شَاهِدُونَ ۝

151. It is out of their perversion that they will say:

أَلَا إِنَّهُم مِّنْ إِفْكِهِمْ لَيَقُولُونَ ۝

152. "Allah has begotten", but they are liars.

وَلَدَ ٱللَّهُ وَإِنَّهُمْ لَكَاذِبُونَ ۝

153. Has He preferred daughters over sons?

أَصْطَفَى ٱلْبَنَاتِ عَلَى ٱلْبَنِينَ ۝

154. What is the matter with you; how do you judge?

مَا لَكُمْ كَيْفَ تَحْكُمُونَ ۝

155. Do you not remember?

أَفَلَا تَذَكَّرُونَ ۝

156. Or do you have manifest authority?

أَمْ لَكُمْ سُلْطَانٌ مُّبِينٌ ۝

157. Produce your Book, if you are truthful.

فَأْتُوا بِكِتَابِكُمْ إِن كُنتُمْ صَادِقِينَ ۝

158. And they alleged a kinship between Him and the jinn, whereas the jinn know very well that they will be summoned.

وَجَعَلُوا بَيْنَهُ وَبَيْنَ ٱلْجِنَّةِ نَسَبًا وَلَقَدْ عَلِمَتِ ٱلْجِنَّةُ إِنَّهُمْ لَمُحْضَرُونَ ۝

159. May Allah be exalted above their allegation.

سُبْحَانَ ٱللَّهِ عَمَّا يَصِفُونَ ۝

160. Except for Allah's sincere servants.

إِلَّا عِبَادَ ٱللَّهِ ٱلْمُخْلَصِينَ ۝

161. Surely, neither you nor what you worship,

فَإِنَّكُمْ وَمَا تَعْبُدُونَ ۝

162. Against Him can ever turn anyone;

163. Except he who will be roasting in Hell.

164. There is not one of us but has a well-known station.

165. And we are indeed the rangers.[724]

166. And we are those who glorify.

167. Even though they might say:

168. "If we had been given a Reminder from the ancients,

169. "We would have been among Allah's sincere servants."

170. Then, they disbelieved in it.[725] Surely, they will learn.

171. Our Word unto Our Messengers has already gone out.

172. They will surely be supported.

173. And Our hosts are the true victors.

174. So, turn away (O Muhammad) from them for a while.

175. And look at them; they shall soon be able to see.

176. Are they seeking to hasten Our punishment?

177. When it descends upon their backyard, wretched is the morning of those fore-warned!

178. And turn away from them for a while.

179. And look, for they shall soon be able to see.

180. Exulted be your Lord, the Lord of Glory, above their allegation.

181. And peace be upon the Messengers.

182. And praise to Allah, the Lord of the Worlds.

---

724. The reference in verses 164, 165 and 166, is to the angels.
725. The Qur'an.

455

Sûrat Sâd,
38

In the Name of Allah,
the Compassionate, the Merciful

1. Sâd.[726]
By the Qur'an which contains the Reminder.

2. But the unbelievers are steeped in arrogance and strife.

3. How many a generation We have destroyed before them? They called out, but time was past escaping.

4. They marvelled that a warner has come to them from their own, and the unbelievers said: "This is a lying sorcerer.

5. "What, has he made the gods one single God? This, indeed is a very strange thing."

6. And the dignitaries among them went forth saying: "Go on and be steadfast regarding your gods. This indeed is a matter premeditated.

7. "We have not heard about this in the latest religion.[727] This is only a mere invention.

8. "Has the Reminder been sent down upon him alone, apart from us all?" Indeed, they are in doubt regarding My Reminder. But, they have not yet tasted My Punishment.

9. Or, do they possess the treasuries of your Lord's Mercy, the All-Mighty, the All-Giving.

10. Or do they have the dominion of the heavens and the earth? Let them, then, ascend its rungs.

بِسْمِ اللَّهِ الرَّحْمَٰنِ الرَّحِيمِ

صٓ وَٱلْقُرْءَانِ ذِى ٱلذِّكْرِ ۝

بَلِ ٱلَّذِينَ كَفَرُوا۟ فِى عِزَّةٍ وَشِقَاقٍ ۝

كَمْ أَهْلَكْنَا مِن قَبْلِهِم مِّن قَرْنٍ فَنَادَوا۟ وَّلَاتَ حِينَ مَنَاصٍ ۝

وَعَجِبُوٓا۟ أَن جَآءَهُم مُّنذِرٌ مِّنْهُمْ وَقَالَ ٱلْكَٰفِرُونَ هَٰذَا سَٰحِرٌ كَذَّابٌ ۝

أَجَعَلَ ٱلْءَالِهَةَ إِلَٰهًا وَٰحِدًا إِنَّ هَٰذَا لَشَىْءٌ عُجَابٌ ۝

وَٱنطَلَقَ ٱلْمَلَأُ مِنْهُمْ أَنِ ٱمْشُوا۟ وَٱصْبِرُوا۟ عَلَىٰٓ ءَالِهَتِكُمْ إِنَّ هَٰذَا لَشَىْءٌ يُرَادُ ۝

مَا سَمِعْنَا بِهَٰذَا فِى ٱلْمِلَّةِ ٱلْءَاخِرَةِ إِنْ هَٰذَآ إِلَّا ٱخْتِلَٰقٌ ۝

أَءُنزِلَ عَلَيْهِ ٱلذِّكْرُ مِنۢ بَيْنِنَا بَلْ هُمْ فِى شَكٍّ مِّن ذِكْرِى بَل لَّمَّا يَذُوقُوا۟ عَذَابِ ۝

أَمْ عِندَهُمْ خَزَآئِنُ رَحْمَةِ رَبِّكَ ٱلْعَزِيزِ ٱلْوَهَّابِ ۝

أَمْ لَهُم مُّلْكُ ٱلسَّمَٰوَٰتِ وَٱلْأَرْضِ وَمَا بَيْنَهُمَا فَلْيَرْتَقُوا۟ فِى ٱلْأَسْبَٰبِ ۝

---

726. One of three Surahs which open with one symbolic letter only.
727. Christianity.

11. A host of the Confederates will be defeated there.

جُندٌ مَّا هُنَالِكَ مَهْزُومٌ مِّنَ ٱلْأَحْزَابِ ﴿١١﴾

12. Before them, the people of Noah, 'Ad, Pharaoh of the Pegs;[728]

كَذَّبَتْ قَبْلَهُمْ قَوْمُ نُوحٍ وَعَادٌ وَفِرْعَوْنُ ذُو ٱلْأَوْتَادِ ﴿١٢﴾

13. And Thamud and the people of Lot; as well as the Companions of the Thicket,[729] such were the Confederates.

وَثَمُودُ وَقَوْمُ لُوطٍ وَأَصْحَٰبُ لْـَٔيْكَةِ أُوْلَٰٓئِكَ ٱلْأَحْزَابُ ﴿١٣﴾

14. None of them but denounced the Messengers, and so My Retribution struck them.

إِن كُلٌّ إِلَّا كَذَّبَ ٱلرُّسُلَ فَحَقَّ عِقَابِ ﴿١٤﴾

15. These are only awaiting a single cry which will not cease.

وَمَا يَنظُرُ هَٰٓؤُلَآءِ إِلَّا صَيْحَةً وَٰحِدَةً مَّا لَهَا مِن فَوَاقٍ ﴿١٥﴾

16. They say: "Our Lord, hasten for us our share before the Day of Reckoning."

وَقَالُوا۟ رَبَّنَا عَجِّل لَّنَا قِطَّنَا قَبْلَ يَوْمِ ٱلْحِسَابِ ﴿١٦﴾

17. Bear patiently with what they say and remember Our servant, David, the mighty one; he was a true penitent.

ٱصْبِرْ عَلَىٰ مَا يَقُولُونَ وَٱذْكُرْ عَبْدَنَا دَاوُۥدَ ذَا ٱلْأَيْدِ إِنَّهُۥٓ أَوَّابٌ ﴿١٧﴾

18. We have subjected the mountains together with him, to glorify in the evening and at daybreak;

إِنَّا سَخَّرْنَا ٱلْجِبَالَ مَعَهُۥ يُسَبِّحْنَ بِٱلْعَشِىِّ وَٱلْإِشْرَاقِ ﴿١٨﴾

19. And the birds were mustered: all obedient to him (David).

وَٱلطَّيْرَ مَحْشُورَةً كُلٌّ لَّهُۥٓ أَوَّابٌ ﴿١٩﴾

20. And We strengthened his kingdom and gave him wisdom and the decisive speech.

وَشَدَدْنَا مُلْكَهُۥ وَءَاتَيْنَٰهُ ٱلْحِكْمَةَ وَفَصْلَ ٱلْخِطَابِ ﴿٢٠﴾

21. Have you heard the news of the enemy when they scaled the sanctuary?

۞ وَهَلْ أَتَىٰكَ نَبَؤُا۟ ٱلْخَصْمِ إِذْ تَسَوَّرُوا۟ ٱلْمِحْرَابَ ﴿٢١﴾

22. When they entered upon David and he was afraid of them. They said: "Do not fear. We are two adversaries, one of us encroached on the other unjustly; so judge between us with justice and do not transgress, and guide us to the Straight Path.

إِذْ دَخَلُوا۟ عَلَىٰ دَاوُۥدَ فَفَزِعَ مِنْهُمْ قَالُوا۟ لَا تَخَفْ خَصْمَانِ بَغَىٰ بَعْضُنَا عَلَىٰ بَعْضٍ فَٱحْكُم بَيْنَنَا بِٱلْحَقِّ وَلَا تُشْطِطْ وَٱهْدِنَآ إِلَىٰ سَوَآءِ ٱلصِّرَٰطِ ﴿٢٢﴾

---

728. A metaphor for power or grandeur.
729. Mentioned four times in the Qur'an, they are probably the people of Madyan.

23. "This is my brother, who has ninety-nine ewes and I have only one. So he said: 'Let me take charge of it,' and he overcame me in the argument."

إِنَّ هَٰذَآ أَخِى لَهُۥ تِسْعٌ وَتِسْعُونَ نَعْجَةً وَلِىَ نَعْجَةٌ وَٰحِدَةٌ فَقَالَ أَكْفِلْنِيهَا وَعَزَّنِى فِى ٱلْخِطَابِ ۝

24. He[730] said: "He has wronged you by asking for your ewe on top of his ewes. Indeed, many partners have encroached one on the other, except for those who believe and do the righteous deeds; and how few they are?" David thought that We had tried him, so he asked forgiveness from his Lord and fell down on his knees and repented.

قَالَ لَقَدْ ظَلَمَكَ بِسُؤَالِ نَعْجَتِكَ إِلَىٰ نِعَاجِهِۦ وَإِنَّ كَثِيرًا مِّنَ ٱلْخُلَطَآءِ لَيَبْغِى بَعْضُهُمْ عَلَىٰ بَعْضٍ إِلَّا ٱلَّذِينَ ءَامَنُوا وَعَمِلُوا ٱلصَّٰلِحَٰتِ وَقَلِيلٌ مَّا هُمْ وَظَنَّ دَاوُۥدُ أَنَّمَا فَتَنَّٰهُ فَٱسْتَغْفَرَ رَبَّهُۥ وَخَرَّ رَاكِعًا وَأَنَابَ ۝

25. So, We forgave him that. Indeed, he has a close relationship with Us and a fair recourse.

فَغَفَرْنَا لَهُۥ ذَٰلِكَ وَإِنَّ لَهُۥ عِندَنَا لَزُلْفَىٰ وَحُسْنَ مَـَٔابٍ ۝

26. O David, We have appointed you a vicegerent on earth; so judge justly among men and do not follow your fancy, lest it lead you away from the Path of Allah. Indeed those who lead others away from the Path of Allah will have a terrible punishment, because they have forgotten the Day of Reckoning.

يَٰدَاوُۥدُ إِنَّا جَعَلْنَٰكَ خَلِيفَةً فِى ٱلْأَرْضِ فَٱحْكُم بَيْنَ ٱلنَّاسِ بِٱلْحَقِّ وَلَا تَتَّبِعِ ٱلْهَوَىٰ فَيُضِلَّكَ عَن سَبِيلِ ٱللَّهِ إِنَّ ٱلَّذِينَ يَضِلُّونَ عَن سَبِيلِ ٱللَّهِ لَهُمْ عَذَابٌ شَدِيدٌ بِمَا نَسُوا يَوْمَ ٱلْحِسَابِ ۝

27. We have not created the heaven and the earth and what is between them in vain. That is the presumption of the unbelievers; so woe betide the unbelievers because of the Fire.

وَمَا خَلَقْنَا ٱلسَّمَآءَ وَٱلْأَرْضَ وَمَا بَيْنَهُمَا بَٰطِلًا ذَٰلِكَ ظَنُّ ٱلَّذِينَ كَفَرُوا فَوَيْلٌ لِّلَّذِينَ كَفَرُوا مِنَ ٱلنَّارِ ۝

28. Or shall We regard those who believe and do the righteous deeds like those who work corruption in the land, or shall We regard the God-fearing like the transgressors?

أَمْ نَجْعَلُ ٱلَّذِينَ ءَامَنُوا وَعَمِلُوا ٱلصَّٰلِحَٰتِ كَٱلْمُفْسِدِينَ فِى ٱلْأَرْضِ أَمْ نَجْعَلُ ٱلْمُتَّقِينَ كَٱلْفُجَّارِ ۝

29. It is a Blessed Book that We have sent down to you, that they may ponder its Verses, and that those possessed of under-standing may remember.

كِتَٰبٌ أَنزَلْنَٰهُ إِلَيْكَ مُبَٰرَكٌ لِّيَدَّبَّرُوٓا ءَايَٰتِهِۦ وَلِيَتَذَكَّرَ أُو۟لُوا ٱلْأَلْبَٰبِ ۝

---

730. David. A possible reference to Nathan's report of a dispute he submitted to David. cf II *Samuel*, 12.

30. And We granted David, Solomon, a blessed servant. Indeed, he was penitent.

وَوَهَبْنَا لِدَاوُدَ سُلَيْمَٰنَ نِعْمَ الْعَبْدُ إِنَّهُ أَوَّابٌ ﴿٣٠﴾

31. When the light-footed horses were presented to him in the evening,

إِذْ عُرِضَ عَلَيْهِ بِالْعَشِيِّ الصَّٰفِنَٰتُ الْجِيَادُ ﴿٣١﴾

32. He said: "I have preferred the love of earthly good to the mention of My Lord, till the sun disappeared behind the veil."

فَقَالَ إِنِّي أَحْبَبْتُ حُبَّ الْخَيْرِ عَن ذِكْرِ رَبِّي حَتَّىٰ تَوَارَتْ بِالْحِجَابِ ﴿٣٢﴾

33. "Bring them back to me." Then he proceeded to wipe their shanks and necks.

رُدُّوهَا عَلَيَّ فَطَفِقَ مَسْحًا بِالسُّوقِ وَالْأَعْنَاقِ ﴿٣٣﴾

34. And We tried Solomon and cast upon his throne a dead body; then he repented.

وَلَقَدْ فَتَنَّا سُلَيْمَٰنَ وَأَلْقَيْنَا عَلَىٰ كُرْسِيِّهِ جَسَدًا ثُمَّ أَنَابَ ﴿٣٤﴾

35. He said: "Lord, forgive me and grant me a kingdom that no one after me will deserve; you are indeed the All-Giver."

قَالَ رَبِّ اغْفِرْ لِي وَهَبْ لِي مُلْكًا لَّا يَنبَغِي لِأَحَدٍ مِّنْ بَعْدِي إِنَّكَ أَنتَ الْوَهَّابُ ﴿٣٥﴾

36. So, We subjected the wind unto him, to blow at his command softly, wherever he wished;

فَسَخَّرْنَا لَهُ الرِّيحَ تَجْرِي بِأَمْرِهِ رُخَاءً حَيْثُ أَصَابَ ﴿٣٦﴾

37. And of the demons every builder and diver;

وَالشَّيَٰطِينَ كُلَّ بَنَّاءٍ وَغَوَّاصٍ ﴿٣٧﴾

38. And others shackled in fetters.

وَآخَرِينَ مُقَرَّنِينَ فِي الْأَصْفَادِ ﴿٣٨﴾

39. "This is Our Bounty; so give or withhold without account."

هَٰذَا عَطَاؤُنَا فَامْنُنْ أَوْ أَمْسِكْ بِغَيْرِ حِسَابٍ ﴿٣٩﴾

40. And he has to Us a close relationship and a fair recourse.

وَإِنَّ لَهُ عِندَنَا لَزُلْفَىٰ وَحُسْنَ مَآبٍ ﴿٤٠﴾

41. And remember Our servant Job when he called out to his Lord: "Satan has visited me with weariness and torture."

وَاذْكُرْ عَبْدَنَا أَيُّوبَ إِذْ نَادَىٰ رَبَّهُ أَنِّي مَسَّنِيَ الشَّيْطَٰنُ بِنُصْبٍ وَعَذَابٍ ﴿٤١﴾

42. "Stamp with your foot, and behold, here is a cool washing-place, and water to drink."

ارْكُضْ بِرِجْلِكَ هَٰذَا مُغْتَسَلٌ بَارِدٌ وَشَرَابٌ ﴿٤٢﴾

43. And We granted to him his family and the like of them also, as a Mercy from Us and a Reminder to people of understanding.

وَوَهَبْنَا لَهُ أَهْلَهُ وَمِثْلَهُم مَّعَهُمْ رَحْمَةً مِّنَّا وَذِكْرَىٰ لِأُولِي الْأَلْبَٰبِ ﴿٤٣﴾

44. "And take with your hand a bundle of twigs and strike with it, and do not break your oath." We have indeed found him steadfast, a blessed servant. He was truly penitent.

وَخُذْ بِيَدِكَ ضِغْثًا فَاضْرِب بِّهِ وَلَا تَحْنَثْ إِنَّا وَجَدْنَٰهُ صَابِرًا نِّعْمَ الْعَبْدُ إِنَّهُ أَوَّابٌ ﴿٤٤﴾

45. And remember Our servants, Abraham, Isaac and Jacob, men of might and perception.

وَاذْكُرْ عِبَدَنَا إِبْرَهِيمَ وَإِسْحَقَ وَيَعْقُوبَ أُولِي الْأَيْدِى وَالْأَبْصَرِ ۝

46. We have favoured them with the pure trait of remembering the Abode.[731]

إِنَّا أَخْلَصْنَهُم بِخَالِصَةٍ ذِكْرَى الدَّارِ ۝

47. They are surely for Us among the well-chosen, the pious.

وَإِنَّهُمْ عِندَنَا لَمِنَ الْمُصْطَفَيْنَ الْأَخْيَارِ ۝

48. And remember Isma'il, Elias and Dhul-Kifl; each was one of the pious.

وَاذْكُرْ إِسْمَعِيلَ وَالْيَسَعَ وَذَا الْكِفْلِ وَكُلٌّ مِّنَ الْأَخْيَارِ ۝

49. This is a Reminder and the God-fearing will surely have a fair resort.

هَذَا ذِكْرٌ وَإِنَّ لِلْمُتَّقِينَ لَحُسْنَ مَثَابٍ ۝

50. Gardens of Eden whereof the gates are wide-open for them.

جَنَّتِ عَدْنٍ مُّفَتَّحَةً لَّهُمُ الْأَبْوَبُ ۝

51. Reclining therein and calling for abundant fruit and beverage.

مُتَّكِئِينَ فِيهَا يَدْعُونَ فِيهَا بِفَكِهَةٍ كَثِيرَةٍ وَشَرَابٍ ۝

52. And they have mates of equal age, averting their gaze.

۞ وَعِندَهُمْ قَصِرَتُ الطَّرْفِ أَتْرَابٌ ۝

53. "This is what you are promised for the Day of Reckoning.

هَذَا مَا تُوعَدُونَ لِيَوْمِ الْحِسَابِ ۝

54. "This is Our provision which will not end.

إِنَّ هَذَا لَرِزْقُنَا مَا لَهُ مِن نَّفَادٍ ۝

55. "That is that, but the aggressors shall have the worst resort.

هَذَا وَإِنَّ لِلطَّغِينَ لَشَرَّ مَثَابٍ ۝

56. "Hell, in which they roast. Wretched is their couch!

جَهَنَّمَ يَصْلَوْنَهَا فَبِئْسَ الْمِهَادُ ۝

57. "That, let them taste it, as boiling water and pus.

هَذَا فَلْيَذُوقُوهُ حَمِيمٌ وَغَسَّاقٌ ۝

58. "And another, of the same kind, manifold.

وَءَاخَرُ مِن شَكْلِهِ أَزْوَجٌ ۝

59. "This is another throng marching with you; no welcome to them, they will roast in the Fire."

هَذَا فَوْجٌ مُّقْتَحِمٌ مَّعَكُمْ لَا مَرْحَبًا بِهِمْ إِنَّهُمْ صَالُوا النَّارِ ۝

60. They say: "No welcome to you; you have offered it to us in advance, and what a wretched resting-place!"

قَالُوا بَلْ أَنتُمْ لَا مَرْحَبًا بِكُمْ أَنتُمْ قَدَّمْتُمُوهُ لَنَا فَبِئْسَ الْقَرَارُ ۝

---

731. Paradise.

61. They say: "Our Lord, whoever has offered this to us, multiply his punishment in the Fire."

قَالُوا رَبَّنَا مَن قَدَّمَ لَنَا هَذَا فَزِدْهُ عَذَابًا ضِعْفًا فِي النَّارِ ﴿٦١﴾

62. And they say: "What is it with us that we do not see men here we used to reckon among the wicked?

وَقَالُوا مَا لَنَا لَا نَرَىٰ رِجَالًا كُنَّا نَعُدُّهُم مِّنَ الْأَشْرَارِ ﴿٦٢﴾

63. "We took them for a laughing-stock, or have our eyes been diverted away from them?"

أَتَّخَذْنَاهُمْ سِخْرِيًّا أَمْ زَاغَتْ عَنْهُمُ الْأَبْصَارُ ﴿٦٣﴾

64. This is perfectly true, the feuding of the people of the Fire.

إِنَّ ذَلِكَ لَحَقٌّ تَخَاصُمُ أَهْلِ النَّارِ ﴿٦٤﴾

65. Say: "I am only a warner and there is no god but Allah, the One, the Conqueror.

قُلْ إِنَّمَا أَنَا مُنذِرٌ وَمَا مِنْ إِلَهٍ إِلَّا اللَّهُ الْوَاحِدُ الْقَهَّارُ ﴿٦٥﴾

66. "The Lord of the heavens and the earth and what is between them, the All-Mighty, the All-Forgiving."

رَبُّ السَّمَوَاتِ وَالْأَرْضِ وَمَا بَيْنَهُمَا الْعَزِيزُ الْغَفَّارُ ﴿٦٦﴾

67. Say: "That (this Qur'an) is great news,

قُلْ هُوَ نَبَأٌ عَظِيمٌ ﴿٦٧﴾

68. "From which you are turning away.

أَنتُمْ عَنْهُ مُعْرِضُونَ ﴿٦٨﴾

69. "I had no knowledge of the Higher Host, when they were disputing among themselves.

مَا كَانَ لِيَ مِنْ عِلْمٍ بِالْمَلَإِ الْأَعْلَىٰ إِذْ يَخْتَصِمُونَ ﴿٦٩﴾

70. "It is only revealed to me that I am a manifest warner."

إِن يُوحَىٰ إِلَيَّ إِلَّا أَنَّمَا أَنَا نَذِيرٌ مُّبِينٌ ﴿٧٠﴾

71. When your Lord said to the angels: "I am going to create a mortal out of clay.

إِذْ قَالَ رَبُّكَ لِلْمَلَائِكَةِ إِنِّي خَالِقٌ بَشَرًا مِّن طِينٍ ﴿٧١﴾

72. "When I have fashioned him and breathed into him of My Spirit, fall prostrate before him."

فَإِذَا سَوَّيْتُهُ وَنَفَخْتُ فِيهِ مِن رُّوحِي فَقَعُوا لَهُ سَاجِدِينَ ﴿٧٢﴾

73. Then all the angels prostrated themselves entirely;

فَسَجَدَ الْمَلَائِكَةُ كُلُّهُمْ أَجْمَعُونَ ﴿٧٣﴾

74. Except for Iblis; he waxed proud and was one of the unbelievers.

إِلَّا إِبْلِيسَ اسْتَكْبَرَ وَكَانَ مِنَ الْكَافِرِينَ ﴿٧٤﴾

75. He said: "O Iblis, what prevented you from prostrating yourself before what I created with My Own Hands? Have you waxed proud or were you one of the exalted?"

قَالَ يَا إِبْلِيسُ مَا مَنَعَكَ أَن تَسْجُدَ لِمَا خَلَقْتُ بِيَدَيَّ أَسْتَكْبَرْتَ أَمْ كُنتَ مِنَ الْعَالِينَ ﴿٧٥﴾

76. He said: "I am better than he; You created me from fire and You created him from clay."

قَالَ أَنَا۠ خَيْرٌ مِّنْهُ خَلَقْتَنِى مِن نَّارٍ وَخَلَقْتَهُ مِن طِينٍ ﴿٧٦﴾

77. (Allah) said: "Get out of here;[732] you are truly accursed.

قَالَ فَٱخْرُجْ مِنْهَا فَإِنَّكَ رَجِيمٌ ﴿٧٧﴾

78. "And My curse shall pursue you till the Day of Judgement."

وَإِنَّ عَلَيْكَ لَعْنَتِى إِلَىٰ يَوْمِ ٱلدِّينِ ﴿٧٨﴾

79. He said: "Lord, give me respite till the day they shall be resuscitated."

قَالَ رَبِّ فَأَنظِرْنِى إِلَىٰ يَوْمِ يُبْعَثُونَ ﴿٧٩﴾

80. (Allah) said: "You are one of those respited,

قَالَ فَإِنَّكَ مِنَ ٱلْمُنظَرِينَ ﴿٨٠﴾

81. "Till the Day of the well-known time."

إِلَىٰ يَوْمِ ٱلْوَقْتِ ٱلْمَعْلُومِ ﴿٨١﴾

82. He (Satan) said: "By Your glory, I will seduce them all,

قَالَ فَبِعِزَّتِكَ لَأُغْوِيَنَّهُمْ أَجْمَعِينَ ﴿٨٢﴾

83. "Except for your sincere servants among them."

إِلَّا عِبَادَكَ مِنْهُمُ ٱلْمُخْلَصِينَ ﴿٨٣﴾

84. (Allah) said: "Truly, and I say the truth;

قَالَ فَٱلْحَقُّ وَٱلْحَقَّ أَقُولُ ﴿٨٤﴾

85. "I will fill Hell with you and those of them who follow you all together."

لَأَمْلَأَنَّ جَهَنَّمَ مِنكَ وَمِمَّن تَبِعَكَ مِنْهُمْ أَجْمَعِينَ ﴿٨٥﴾

86. Say (O Muhammad): "I ask you no wage for it and I am not one of those who pretend.

قُلْ مَا أَسْأَلُكُمْ عَلَيْهِ مِنْ أَجْرٍ وَمَا أَنَا۠ مِنَ ٱلْمُتَكَلِّفِينَ ﴿٨٦﴾

87. "It is only a Reminder to mankind.

إِنْ هُوَ إِلَّا ذِكْرٌ لِّلْعَٰلَمِينَ ﴿٨٧﴾

88. "And you will learn its message after a while."

وَلَتَعْلَمُنَّ نَبَأَهُۥ بَعْدَ حِينٍ ﴿٨٨﴾

Sûrat Az-Zumar, (The Throngs) 39

In the Name of Allah, the Compassionate, the Merciful

1. The sending down of the Book is from Allah, the All-Mighty, the Wise.

تَنزِيلُ ٱلْكِتَٰبِ مِنَ ٱللَّهِ ٱلْعَزِيزِ ٱلْحَكِيمِ ﴿١﴾

2. We have, indeed, sent down the Book to you in truth; so worship Allah professing the religion sincerely to Him.

إِنَّآ أَنزَلْنَآ إِلَيْكَ ٱلْكِتَٰبَ بِٱلْحَقِّ فَٱعْبُدِ ٱللَّهَ مُخْلِصًا لَّهُ ٱلدِّينَ ﴿٢﴾

بِسْمِ ٱللَّهِ ٱلرَّحْمَٰنِ ٱلرَّحِيمِ

---

732. Paradise.

462

3. Sincere religion truly belongs to Allah. Those who took other protectors, apart from Him, say: "We only worship them so as to bring us closer to Allah in rank". Allah surely judges between them with respect to what they differ upon. Allah surely does not guide him who is a thankless liar.

أَلَا لِلَّهِ الدِّينُ الْخَالِصُ وَالَّذِينَ اتَّخَذُوا مِن دُونِهِ أَوْلِيَاءَ مَا نَعْبُدُهُمْ إِلَّا لِيُقَرِّبُونَا إِلَى اللَّهِ زُلْفَى إِنَّ اللَّهَ يَحْكُمُ بَيْنَهُمْ فِي مَا هُمْ فِيهِ يَخْتَلِفُونَ إِنَّ اللَّهَ لَا يَهْدِي مَنْ هُوَ كَذِبٌ كَفَّارٌ ۞

4. Had Allah wanted to take to Himself a child, He would have chosen from what He has created whomever He pleases. Glory be to Him; He is Allah, the One, the Conqueror.

لَوْ أَرَادَ اللَّهُ أَن يَتَّخِذَ وَلَدًا لَاصْطَفَى مِمَّا يَخْلُقُ مَا يَشَاءُ سُبْحَانَهُ هُوَ اللَّهُ الْوَاحِدُ الْقَهَّارُ ۞

5. He created the heavens and the earth in truth. He wraps up the night around the day and He wraps up the day around the night. He has subjected the sun and the moon, each running for an appointed term. He is indeed the All-Mighty, the All-Forgiving.

خَلَقَ السَّمَاوَاتِ وَالْأَرْضَ بِالْحَقِّ يُكَوِّرُ الْلَيْلَ عَلَى النَّهَارِ وَيُكَوِّرُ النَّهَارَ عَلَى الْلَيْلِ وَسَخَّرَ الشَّمْسَ وَالْقَمَرَ كُلٌّ يَجْرِي لِأَجَلٍ مُّسَمًّى أَلَا هُوَ الْعَزِيزُ الْغَفَّارُ ۞

6. He created you from a single soul; then, out of it, He made its mate, and brought down for you of the cattle eight pairs. He creates you in your mothers' bellies, one creation after another, in three shadows of darkness. That indeed is Allah, your Lord. His is the dominion; there is no god but He. How, then, are you diverted?

خَلَقَكُم مِّن نَّفْسٍ وَاحِدَةٍ ثُمَّ جَعَلَ مِنْهَا زَوْجَهَا وَأَنزَلَ لَكُم مِّنَ الْأَنْعَامِ ثَمَانِيَةَ أَزْوَاجٍ يَخْلُقُكُمْ فِي بُطُونِ أُمَّهَاتِكُمْ خَلْقًا مِّنْ بَعْدِ خَلْقٍ فِي ظُلُمَاتٍ ثَلَاثٍ ذَلِكُمُ اللَّهُ رَبُّكُمْ لَهُ الْمُلْكُ لَا إِلَهَ إِلَّا هُوَ فَأَنَّى تُصْرَفُونَ ۞

7. If you disbelieve, Allah does not need you, although He does not approve disbelief in His servants. However, if you give thanks, He will approve that in you. No sinning soul shall bear the burden of another. Then unto your Lord is your return and He will tell you what you used to do. He knows the secrets within the breasts.

إِن تَكْفُرُوا فَإِنَّ اللَّهَ غَنِيٌّ عَنكُمْ وَلَا يَرْضَى لِعِبَادِهِ الْكُفْرَ وَإِن تَشْكُرُوا يَرْضَهُ لَكُمْ وَلَا تَزِرُ وَازِرَةٌ وِزْرَ أُخْرَى ثُمَّ إِلَى رَبِّكُم مَّرْجِعُكُمْ فَيُنَبِّئُكُم بِمَا كُنتُمْ تَعْمَلُونَ إِنَّهُ عَلِيمٌ بِذَاتِ الصُّدُورِ ۞

8. If some adversity touches man, he will call upon his Lord, repenting unto Him; then, if He confers on him a grace of His, he forgets what he was calling for before that and assigns equals to Allah, so as to lead others

۞ وَإِذَا مَسَّ الْإِنسَانَ ضُرٌّ دَعَا رَبَّهُ مُنِيبًا إِلَيْهِ ثُمَّ إِذَا خَوَّلَهُ نِعْمَةً مِّنْهُ نَسِيَ مَا كَانَ يَدْعُو إِلَيْهِ مِن قَبْلُ وَجَعَلَ لِلَّهِ أَندَادًا لِّيُضِلَّ عَن سَبِيلِهِ قُلْ تَمَتَّعْ بِكُفْرِكَ

astray from His Path. Say: "Enjoy your disbelief a little; for you are truly one of the companions of the Fire."

قَلِيلًا إِنَّكَ مِنْ أَصْحَابِ ٱلنَّارِ ۞

9. Is he who worships devoutly in the watches of the night, prostrating himself and standing up, fears the Hereafter and hopes for the Mercy of his Lord [like unto the other]? Say: "Are those who know and those who do not know alike?" Only those possessed of understanding will remember.

أَمَّنْ هُوَ قَـٰنِتٌ ءَانَآءَ ٱلَّيْلِ سَاجِدًا وَقَآئِمًا يَحْذَرُ ٱلْءَاخِرَةَ وَيَرْجُوا۟ رَحْمَةَ رَبِّهِۦ قُلْ هَلْ يَسْتَوِى ٱلَّذِينَ يَعْلَمُونَ وَٱلَّذِينَ لَا يَعْلَمُونَ إِنَّمَا يَتَذَكَّرُ أُو۟لُوا۟ ٱلْأَلْبَـٰبِ ۞

10. Say: "O My servants who have believed, fear your Lord. Those who have been bounteous in this world will have a bounty, and Allah's earth is vast. The steadfast will be paid their wages in full, without reckoning."

قُلْ يَـٰعِبَادِ ٱلَّذِينَ ءَامَنُوا۟ ٱتَّقُوا۟ رَبَّكُمْ لِلَّذِينَ أَحْسَنُوا۟ فِى هَـٰذِهِ ٱلدُّنْيَا حَسَنَةٌ وَأَرْضُ ٱللَّهِ وَٰسِعَةٌ إِنَّمَا يُوَفَّى ٱلصَّـٰبِرُونَ أَجْرَهُم بِغَيْرِ حِسَابٍ ۞

11. Say: "I have been commanded to worship Allah, professing to Him the religion sincerely.

قُلْ إِنِّىٓ أُمِرْتُ أَنْ أَعْبُدَ ٱللَّهَ مُخْلِصًا لَّهُ ٱلدِّينَ ۞

12. "And I have been commanded to be the first of those who submit."

وَأُمِرْتُ لِأَنْ أَكُونَ أَوَّلَ ٱلْمُسْلِمِينَ ۞

13. Say: "I fear if I disobey my Lord, the punishment of a great Day."

قُلْ إِنِّىٓ أَخَافُ إِنْ عَصَيْتُ رَبِّى عَذَابَ يَوْمٍ عَظِيمٍ ۞

14. Say: "Allah alone I worship professing to Him my religion sincerely.

قُلِ ٱللَّهَ أَعْبُدُ مُخْلِصًا لَّهُ دِينِى ۞

15. "Worship, then, what you wish, apart from Him." Say: "Indeed, those who have lost themselves and their families on the Day of Resurrection are the real losers. That is truly the manifest loss."

فَٱعْبُدُوا۟ مَا شِئْتُم مِّن دُونِهِۦ قُلْ إِنَّ ٱلْخَـٰسِرِينَ ٱلَّذِينَ خَسِرُوٓا۟ أَنفُسَهُمْ وَأَهْلِيهِمْ يَوْمَ ٱلْقِيَـٰمَةِ أَلَا ذَٰلِكَ هُوَ ٱلْخُسْرَانُ ٱلْمُبِينُ ۞

16. They shall have over them awnings of fire and under them other awnings. That is what Allah frightens His servants with: "O My servants fear Me, then."

لَهُم مِّن فَوْقِهِمْ ظُلَلٌ مِّنَ ٱلنَّارِ وَمِن تَحْتِهِمْ ظُلَلٌ ذَٰلِكَ يُخَوِّفُ ٱللَّهُ بِهِۦ عِبَادَهُۥ يَـٰعِبَادِ فَٱتَّقُونِ ۞

17. Those who shunned the worship of idols and turned in repentance unto Allah, theirs is the good news. "Announce, then, the good news to My servants."

وَٱلَّذِينَ ٱجْتَنَبُوا۟ ٱلطَّـٰغُوتَ أَن يَعْبُدُوهَا وَأَنَابُوٓا۟ إِلَى ٱللَّهِ لَهُمُ ٱلْبُشْرَىٰ فَبَشِّرْ عِبَادِ ۞

18. Those who hear the Word and follow the fairest of it; those are the ones whom Allah has guided and those are the people of understanding!

19. He upon whom the Word of punishment has been uttered, are you able to deliver from the Fire?

20. But those who fear their Lord will have chambers over which other chambers are built and beneath which the rivers flow. That is Allah's Promise. Allah does not break His Promise.

21. Have you not seen that Allah has sent down water from heaven, then threaded it as springs in the ground. Then He brings out vegetation of various hues through it. Then it withers, and you see it looking yellow; then He turns it into scraps. In that, there surely is a Reminder to people of understanding.

22. Now, what of one whose breast Allah has dilated unto Islam, so that he basks in light from his Lord? Woe betide then the hard-hearted, upon Allah's mention. Those are in manifest error.

23. Allah has sent down the fairest discourse as a Book, both insistent and corroboratory, from which the skins of those who fear their Lord shiver. Then their skins and hearts mellow at the mention of Allah. That is the guidance of Allah whereby He guides whomever He wishes; and he whom Allah leads astray will have no other guide.

24. Is he who wards off with his face the evil punishment on the Day of Resurrection? And it is said then to the wrongdoers: "Taste what you used to earn."

25. Those who preceded them denounced as liars [the Messengers], whereupon punishment afflicted them from whence they did not know.

الَّذِينَ يَسْتَمِعُونَ الْقَوْلَ فَيَتَّبِعُونَ أَحْسَنَهُ أُوْلَئِكَ الَّذِينَ هَدَاهُمُ اللَّهُ وَأُوْلَئِكَ هُمْ أُوْلُوا الْأَلْبَابِ ﴿١٨﴾

أَفَمَنْ حَقَّ عَلَيْهِ كَلِمَةُ الْعَذَابِ أَفَأَنتَ تُنقِذُ مَن فِي النَّارِ ﴿١٩﴾

لَكِنِ الَّذِينَ اتَّقَوْا رَبَّهُمْ لَهُمْ غُرَفٌ مِّن فَوْقِهَا غُرَفٌ مَّبْنِيَّةٌ تَجْرِي مِن تَحْتِهَا الْأَنْهَارُ وَعْدَ اللَّهِ لَا يُخْلِفُ اللَّهُ الْمِيعَادَ ﴿٢٠﴾

أَلَمْ تَرَ أَنَّ اللَّهَ أَنزَلَ مِنَ السَّمَاءِ مَاءً فَسَلَكَهُ يَنَابِيعَ فِي الْأَرْضِ ثُمَّ يُخْرِجُ بِهِ زَرْعًا مُّخْتَلِفًا أَلْوَانُهُ ثُمَّ يَهِيجُ فَتَرَاهُ مُصْفَرًّا ثُمَّ يَجْعَلُهُ حُطَامًا إِنَّ فِي ذَلِكَ لَذِكْرَى لِأُوْلِي الْأَلْبَابِ ﴿٢١﴾

أَفَمَن شَرَحَ اللَّهُ صَدْرَهُ لِلْإِسْلَامِ فَهُوَ عَلَى نُورٍ مِّن رَّبِّهِ فَوَيْلٌ لِّلْقَاسِيَةِ قُلُوبُهُم مِّن ذِكْرِ اللَّهِ أُوْلَئِكَ فِي ضَلَالٍ مُّبِينٍ ﴿٢٢﴾

اللَّهُ نَزَّلَ أَحْسَنَ الْحَدِيثِ كِتَابًا مُّتَشَابِهًا مَّثَانِيَ تَقْشَعِرُّ مِنْهُ جُلُودُ الَّذِينَ يَخْشَوْنَ رَبَّهُمْ ثُمَّ تَلِينُ جُلُودُهُمْ وَقُلُوبُهُمْ إِلَى ذِكْرِ اللَّهِ ذَلِكَ هُدَى اللَّهِ يَهْدِي بِهِ مَن يَشَاءُ وَمَن يُضْلِلِ اللَّهُ فَمَا لَهُ مِنْ هَادٍ ﴿٢٣﴾

أَفَمَن يَتَّقِي بِوَجْهِهِ سُوءَ الْعَذَابِ يَوْمَ الْقِيَامَةِ وَقِيلَ لِلظَّالِمِينَ ذُوقُوا مَا كُنتُمْ تَكْسِبُونَ ﴿٢٤﴾

كَذَّبَ الَّذِينَ مِن قَبْلِهِمْ فَأَتَاهُمُ الْعَذَابُ مِنْ حَيْثُ لَا يَشْعُرُونَ ﴿٢٥﴾

26. And so Allah made them taste disgrace in the present life; but the punishment of the Hereafter is surely greater, if only they knew.

فَأَذَاقَهُمُ ٱللَّهُ ٱلْخِزْىَ فِى ٱلْحَيَوٰةِ ٱلدُّنْيَا وَلَعَذَابُ ٱلْأَخِرَةِ أَكْبَرُ لَوْ كَانُوا يَعْلَمُونَ ﴿٢٦﴾

27. We have given mankind every kind of parable in this Qur'an, that perchance they might remember.

وَلَقَدْ ضَرَبْنَا لِلنَّاسِ فِى هَٰذَا ٱلْقُرْءَانِ مِن كُلِّ مَثَلٍ لَّعَلَّهُمْ يَتَذَكَّرُونَ ﴿٢٧﴾

28. We made it an Arabic Qur'an without any defect that perchance they might be God-fearing.

قُرْءَانًا عَرَبِيًّا غَيْرَ ذِى عِوَجٍ لَّعَلَّهُمْ يَتَّقُونَ ﴿٢٨﴾

29. Allah has given as a parable a man owned by partners who are at odds and a man owned exclusively by one man. Are they equal in status? Praise be to Allah, but most of them do not know.

ضَرَبَ ٱللَّهُ مَثَلًا رَّجُلًا فِيهِ شُرَكَآءُ مُتَشَٰكِسُونَ وَرَجُلًا سَلَمًا لِّرَجُلٍ هَلْ يَسْتَوِيَانِ مَثَلًا ٱلْحَمْدُ لِلَّهِ بَلْ أَكْثَرُهُمْ لَا يَعْلَمُونَ ﴿٢٩﴾

30. You are mortal and they are mortal too.

إِنَّكَ مَيِّتٌ وَإِنَّهُم مَّيِّتُونَ ﴿٣٠﴾

31. Then on the Day of Resurrection, you shall appear before your Lord defending yourself.

ثُمَّ إِنَّكُمْ يَوْمَ ٱلْقِيَٰمَةِ عِندَ رَبِّكُمْ تَخْتَصِمُونَ ﴿٣١﴾

32. Who, then, is more unjust than one who imputes lies to Allah and denounces the Truth as a lie when he hears it? Is not in Hell an abode for the unbelievers?

۞ فَمَنْ أَظْلَمُ مِمَّن كَذَبَ عَلَى ٱللَّهِ وَكَذَّبَ بِٱلصِّدْقِ إِذْ جَآءَهُ أَلَيْسَ فِى جَهَنَّمَ مَثْوًى لِّلْكَٰفِرِينَ ﴿٣٢﴾

33. But he who brings the Truth and believes in it - those are the true God-fearing people.

وَٱلَّذِى جَآءَ بِٱلصِّدْقِ وَصَدَّقَ بِهِ أُوْلَٰئِكَ هُمُ ٱلْمُتَّقُونَ ﴿٣٣﴾

34. They shall have what they wish from their Lord. That is the reward of the beneficent.

لَهُم مَّا يَشَآءُونَ عِندَ رَبِّهِمْ ذَٰلِكَ جَزَآءُ ٱلْمُحْسِنِينَ ﴿٣٤﴾

35. That Allah might remit their worst deeds and reward them their due according to the fairest deeds they used to do.

لِيُكَفِّرَ ٱللَّهُ عَنْهُمْ أَسْوَأَ ٱلَّذِى عَمِلُوا وَيَجْزِيَهُمْ أَجْرَهُم بِأَحْسَنِ ٱلَّذِى كَانُوا يَعْمَلُونَ ﴿٣٥﴾

36. Does not Allah suffice His servant? Yet they frighten you with those apart from Him.[733] Whomever Allah leads astray will have no other guide.

أَلَيْسَ ٱللَّهُ بِكَافٍ عَبْدَهُ وَيُخَوِّفُونَكَ بِٱلَّذِينَ مِن دُونِهِ وَمَن يُضْلِلِ ٱللَّهُ فَمَا لَهُ مِنْ هَادٍ ﴿٣٦﴾

---

733. That is, idols.

37. And whomever Allah guides none will lead astray. Is not Allah All-Mighty, Vengeful?

38. If you ask them: "Who has created the heavens and the earth?", they will reply: "Allah." Say: "Do you see, then? What you call upon, apart from Allah, should Allah wish me ill, will they lift His ill? Or should Allah will a mercy for me, will they withhold His Mercy?" Say: "Allah suffices for me. In Him those who trust should put their trust."

39. Say: "My people, act according to your ability. I am acting; then you will know.

40. "Whoever is visited by punishment will be degraded by it and a lasting punishment will befall him."

41. We have sent the Book upon you for all mankind in truth. He who is well-guided is guided to his own gain, and he who goes astray, will go astray to his loss. You are not their overseer.

42. Allah carries off the souls of men upon their death and the souls of those who are not dead in their sleep. He then holds back those whose death He has decreed and releases the others till an appointed term. Surely, there are in that signs for a people who reflect.

43. Or have they taken intercessors, apart from Allah? Say: "Even if they have no power whatever and no understanding."

44. Say: "To Allah belongs all intercession. His is the dominion of the heavens and the earth. Then unto Him you will be returned."

45. If Allah alone is mentioned, the hearts of those who do not believe in the Hereafter shudder; but if those apart from Him are mentioned, behold, they rejoice.

وَمَن يَهْدِ ٱللَّهُ فَمَا لَهُ مِن مُّضِلٍّ أَلَيْسَ ٱللَّهُ بِعَزِيزٍ ذِى ٱنتِقَامٍ ﴿٣٧﴾

وَلَئِن سَأَلْتَهُم مَّنْ خَلَقَ ٱلسَّمَٰوَٰتِ وَٱلْأَرْضَ لَيَقُولُنَّ ٱللَّهُ قُلْ أَفَرَءَيْتُم مَّا تَدْعُونَ مِن دُونِ ٱللَّهِ إِنْ أَرَادَنِيَ ٱللَّهُ بِضُرٍّ هَلْ هُنَّ كَٰشِفَٰتُ ضُرِّهِ أَوْ أَرَادَنِي بِرَحْمَةٍ هَلْ هُنَّ مُمْسِكَٰتُ رَحْمَتِهِ قُلْ حَسْبِيَ ٱللَّهُ عَلَيْهِ يَتَوَكَّلُ ٱلْمُتَوَكِّلُونَ ﴿٣٨﴾

قُلْ يَٰقَوْمِ ٱعْمَلُوا۟ عَلَىٰ مَكَانَتِكُمْ إِنِّي عَٰمِلٌ فَسَوْفَ تَعْلَمُونَ ﴿٣٩﴾

مَن يَأْتِيهِ عَذَابٌ يُخْزِيهِ وَيَحِلُّ عَلَيْهِ عَذَابٌ مُّقِيمٌ ﴿٤٠﴾

إِنَّآ أَنزَلْنَا عَلَيْكَ ٱلْكِتَٰبَ لِلنَّاسِ بِٱلْحَقِّ فَمَنِ ٱهْتَدَىٰ فَلِنَفْسِهِ وَمَن ضَلَّ فَإِنَّمَا يَضِلُّ عَلَيْهَا وَمَآ أَنتَ عَلَيْهِم بِوَكِيلٍ ﴿٤١﴾

ٱللَّهُ يَتَوَفَّى ٱلْأَنفُسَ حِينَ مَوْتِهَا وَٱلَّتِي لَمْ تَمُتْ فِي مَنَامِهَا فَيُمْسِكُ ٱلَّتِي قَضَىٰ عَلَيْهَا ٱلْمَوْتَ وَيُرْسِلُ ٱلْأُخْرَىٰٓ إِلَىٰٓ أَجَلٍ مُّسَمًّى إِنَّ فِي ذَٰلِكَ لَءَايَٰتٍ لِّقَوْمٍ يَتَفَكَّرُونَ ﴿٤٢﴾

أَمِ ٱتَّخَذُوا۟ مِن دُونِ ٱللَّهِ شُفَعَآءَ قُلْ أَوَلَوْ كَانُوا۟ لَا يَمْلِكُونَ شَيْـًٔا وَلَا يَعْقِلُونَ ﴿٤٣﴾

قُل لِّلَّهِ ٱلشَّفَٰعَةُ جَمِيعًا لَّهُ مُلْكُ ٱلسَّمَٰوَٰتِ وَٱلْأَرْضِ ثُمَّ إِلَيْهِ تُرْجَعُونَ ﴿٤٤﴾

وَإِذَا ذُكِرَ ٱللَّهُ وَحْدَهُ ٱشْمَأَزَّتْ قُلُوبُ ٱلَّذِينَ لَا يُؤْمِنُونَ بِٱلْءَاخِرَةِ وَإِذَا ذُكِرَ ٱلَّذِينَ مِن دُونِهِۦٓ إِذَا هُمْ يَسْتَبْشِرُونَ ﴿٤٥﴾

46. Say: "O Allah, Creator of the heavens and the earth, Knower of the Unseen and the Seen, You shall judge between your servants regarding that whereon they used to differ."

قُلِ ٱللَّهُمَّ فَاطِرَ ٱلسَّمَـٰوَٰتِ وَٱلْأَرْضِ عَـٰلِمَ ٱلْغَيْبِ وَٱلشَّهَـٰدَةِ أَنتَ تَحْكُمُ بَيْنَ عِبَادِكَ فِى مَا كَانُوا۟ فِيهِ يَخْتَلِفُونَ ۝

47. Had the wrongdoers possessed all that is on earth and the like of it too, they would have redeemed therewith themselves from the terrible punishment on the Day of Resurrection, and there would have appeared to them from Allah that which they did not count on.

وَلَوْ أَنَّ لِلَّذِينَ ظَلَمُوا۟ مَا فِى ٱلْأَرْضِ جَمِيعًا وَمِثْلَهُ مَعَهُ لَٱفْتَدَوْا۟ بِهِ مِن سُوٓءِ ٱلْعَذَابِ يَوْمَ ٱلْقِيَـٰمَةِ وَبَدَا لَهُم مِّنَ ٱللَّهِ مَا لَمْ يَكُونُوا۟ يَحْتَسِبُونَ ۝

48. And there would have appeared to them the evils of what they have earned, and what they scoffed at would have afflicted them.

وَبَدَا لَهُمْ سَيِّـَٔاتُ مَا كَسَبُوا۟ وَحَاقَ بِهِم مَّا كَانُوا۟ بِهِ يَسْتَهْزِءُونَ ۝

49. When an injury touches a man, he calls upon Us. Then if We accord him a bounty from Us, he says: "I have been granted it on account of some knowledge." However, it is a mere trial, but most of them do not know.

فَإِذَا مَسَّ ٱلْإِنسَـٰنَ ضُرٌّ دَعَانَا ثُمَّ إِذَا خَوَّلْنَـٰهُ نِعْمَةً مِّنَّا قَالَ إِنَّمَآ أُوتِيتُهُۥ عَلَىٰ عِلْمٍ بَلْ هِىَ فِتْنَةٌ وَلَـٰكِنَّ أَكْثَرَهُمْ لَا يَعْلَمُونَ ۝

50. Thus those who preceded them have said it, but what they had earned did not avail them.

قَدْ قَالَهَا ٱلَّذِينَ مِن قَبْلِهِمْ فَمَآ أَغْنَىٰ عَنْهُم مَّا كَانُوا۟ يَكْسِبُونَ ۝

51. And so the evils of what they had earned smote them, and the evil-doers among these[734] will be smitten by the evils of what they earned; and they will not frustrate Us.

فَأَصَابَهُمْ سَيِّـَٔاتُ مَا كَسَبُوا۟ وَٱلَّذِينَ ظَلَمُوا۟ مِنْ هَـٰٓؤُلَآءِ سَيُصِيبُهُمْ سَيِّـَٔاتُ مَا كَسَبُوا۟ وَمَا هُم بِمُعْجِزِينَ ۝

52. Did they not know that Allah expands the provision to whomever He wishes and constricts it? Surely, there are in that signs to a people who believe.

أَوَلَمْ يَعْلَمُوٓا۟ أَنَّ ٱللَّهَ يَبْسُطُ ٱلرِّزْقَ لِمَن يَشَآءُ وَيَقْدِرُ إِنَّ فِى ذَٰلِكَ لَءَايَـٰتٍ لِّقَوْمٍ يُؤْمِنُونَ ۝

53. Say: "O My servants, who have been excessive against themselves: Do not despair of Allah's Mercy; Allah remits all sins. He is indeed the All-Forgiving, the All-Clement.

۞ قُلْ يَـٰعِبَادِىَ ٱلَّذِينَ أَسْرَفُوا۟ عَلَىٰٓ أَنفُسِهِمْ لَا تَقْنَطُوا۟ مِن رَّحْمَةِ ٱللَّهِ إِنَّ ٱللَّهَ يَغْفِرُ ٱلذُّنُوبَ جَمِيعًا إِنَّهُۥ هُوَ ٱلْغَفُورُ ٱلرَّحِيمُ ۝

---

734. Muhammad's contemporaries.

54. "Return to your Lord and submit to Him before punishment visits you for then you will have no support.

وَأَنِيبُوٓاْ إِلَىٰ رَبِّكُمْ وَأَسْلِمُوا لَهُ مِن قَبْلِ أَن يَأْتِيَكُمُ ٱلْعَذَابُ ثُمَّ لَا تُنصَرُونَ ۝

55. "And follow the fairest of what has been sent down to you from your Lord, before punishment visits you suddenly while you are unaware.

وَٱتَّبِعُوٓاْ أَحْسَنَ مَآ أُنزِلَ إِلَيْكُم مِّن رَّبِّكُم مِّن قَبْلِ أَن يَأْتِيَكُمُ ٱلْعَذَابُ بَغْتَةً وَأَنتُمْ لَا تَشْعُرُونَ ۝

56. "Lest any soul should say: 'Woe betide me for what I have neglected of my duty to Allah and for having been one of the scoffers.'

أَن تَقُولَ نَفْسٌ يَٰحَسْرَتَىٰ عَلَىٰ مَا فَرَّطتُ فِى جَنۢبِ ٱللَّهِ وَإِن كُنتُ لَمِنَ ٱلسَّٰخِرِينَ ۝

57. "Or it should say: 'Had Allah guided me, I would have been one of the God-fearing.'

أَوْ تَقُولَ لَوْ أَنَّ ٱللَّهَ هَدَىٰنِى لَكُنتُ مِنَ ٱلْمُتَّقِينَ ۝

58. "Or it should say, when it sees the punishment: 'If only I had a second chance, then I would be one of the beneficent'."

أَوْ تَقُولَ حِينَ تَرَى ٱلْعَذَابَ لَوْ أَنَّ لِى كَرَّةً فَأَكُونَ مِنَ ٱلْمُحْسِنِينَ ۝

59. Yes indeed! My signs came to you, but you denounced them as lies and waxed proud and were one of the unbelievers.

بَلَىٰ قَدْ جَآءَتْكَ ءَايَٰتِى فَكَذَّبْتَ بِهَا وَٱسْتَكْبَرْتَ وَكُنتَ مِنَ ٱلْكَٰفِرِينَ ۝

60. On the Day of Resurrection, you will see those who told lies against Allah with their faces blackened. Is not there in Hell a resting-place for the arrogant?

وَيَوْمَ ٱلْقِيَٰمَةِ تَرَى ٱلَّذِينَ كَذَبُوا عَلَى ٱللَّهِ وُجُوهُهُم مُّسْوَدَّةٌ أَلَيْسَ فِى جَهَنَّمَ مَثْوًى لِّلْمُتَكَبِّرِينَ ۝

61. And Allah will save the God-fearing on account of their felicitous deeds. No evil will touch them and they will not grieve.

وَيُنَجِّى ٱللَّهُ ٱلَّذِينَ ٱتَّقَوْا بِمَفَازَتِهِمْ لَا يَمَسُّهُمُ ٱلسُّوٓءُ وَلَا هُمْ يَحْزَنُونَ ۝

62. Allah is the Creator of everything and He is the Guardian of everything.

ٱللَّهُ خَٰلِقُ كُلِّ شَىْءٍ وَهُوَ عَلَىٰ كُلِّ شَىْءٍ وَكِيلٌ ۝

63. His are the keys of the heavens and the earth; and those who have disbelieved in Allah's Signs are the losers.

لَّهُۥ مَقَالِيدُ ٱلسَّمَٰوَٰتِ وَٱلْأَرْضِ وَٱلَّذِينَ كَفَرُوا بِـَٔايَٰتِ ٱللَّهِ أُوْلَٰٓئِكَ هُمُ ٱلْخَٰسِرُونَ ۝

64. Say: "Do you, then, command me to worship anyone other than Allah, O ignorant ones?"

قُلْ أَفَغَيْرَ ٱللَّهِ تَأْمُرُوٓنِّى أَعْبُدُ أَيُّهَا ٱلْجَٰهِلُونَ ۝

65. He has in fact revealed to you[735] and those who preceded you: "If you associate

وَلَقَدْ أُوحِىَ إِلَيْكَ وَإِلَى ٱلَّذِينَ مِن قَبْلِكَ لَئِنْ أَشْرَكْتَ

---

735. Muhammad.

any others with Allah, He will frustrate your work and you will certainly be one of the losers."

66. Instead, worship Allah and be one of the thankful.

67. They have not recognized Allah's true measure. The whole earth shall be in His grasp and the heavens shall be rolled up in His Right Hand on the Day of the Resurrection. Glory be to Him, and may He be exalted above what they associate with Him.

68. And the Trumpet shall be blown, so that whoever is in the heavens or on earth shall be made to expire, save him whom Allah wishes. Then it shall be blown another time, and behold, they shall arise, looking out.

69. And the earth shall shine with the light of its Lord and the Book shall be laid down. Then, the Prophets and the witnesses shall be brought forward, and judgement shall be passed justly between them, and they shall not be wronged.

70. Every soul shall be paid in full for what it has done, and He knows best what they do.

71. And the unbelievers shall be driven to Hell in throngs; so that when they have reached it, its gates will be opened and its keepers will say to them: "Have not Messengers from your own people come to you reciting to you the Revelations of your Lord and warning you against the Encounter of this your Day?" They will say: "Yes, indeed"; but the word of punishment has come to pass against the unbelievers.

72. It will be said: "Enter the gates of Hell, dwelling therein forever. Wretched is the dwelling of the arrogant."

لَيَحْبَطَنَّ عَمَلُكَ وَلَتَكُونَنَّ مِنَ ٱلْخَٰسِرِينَ ﴿٦٥﴾

بَلِ ٱللَّهَ فَٱعْبُدْ وَكُن مِّنَ ٱلشَّٰكِرِينَ ﴿٦٦﴾

وَمَا قَدَرُوا۟ ٱللَّهَ حَقَّ قَدْرِهِۦ وَٱلْأَرْضُ جَمِيعًا قَبْضَتُهُۥ يَوْمَ ٱلْقِيَٰمَةِ وَٱلسَّمَٰوَٰتُ مَطْوِيَّٰتٌۢ بِيَمِينِهِۦ ۚ سُبْحَٰنَهُۥ وَتَعَٰلَىٰ عَمَّا يُشْرِكُونَ ﴿٦٧﴾

وَنُفِخَ فِى ٱلصُّورِ فَصَعِقَ مَن فِى ٱلسَّمَٰوَٰتِ وَمَن فِى ٱلْأَرْضِ إِلَّا مَن شَآءَ ٱللَّهُ ۖ ثُمَّ نُفِخَ فِيهِ أُخْرَىٰ فَإِذَا هُمْ قِيَامٌ يَنظُرُونَ ﴿٦٨﴾

وَأَشْرَقَتِ ٱلْأَرْضُ بِنُورِ رَبِّهَا وَوُضِعَ ٱلْكِتَٰبُ وَجِا۟ىٓءَ بِٱلنَّبِيِّۦنَ وَٱلشُّهَدَآءِ وَقُضِىَ بَيْنَهُم بِٱلْحَقِّ وَهُمْ لَا يُظْلَمُونَ ﴿٦٩﴾

وَوُفِّيَتْ كُلُّ نَفْسٍ مَّا عَمِلَتْ وَهُوَ أَعْلَمُ بِمَا يَفْعَلُونَ ﴿٧٠﴾

وَسِيقَ ٱلَّذِينَ كَفَرُوٓا۟ إِلَىٰ جَهَنَّمَ زُمَرًا ۖ حَتَّىٰٓ إِذَا جَآءُوهَا فُتِحَتْ أَبْوَٰبُهَا وَقَالَ لَهُمْ خَزَنَتُهَآ أَلَمْ يَأْتِكُمْ رُسُلٌ مِّنكُمْ يَتْلُونَ عَلَيْكُمْ ءَايَٰتِ رَبِّكُمْ وَيُنذِرُونَكُمْ لِقَآءَ يَوْمِكُمْ هَٰذَا ۚ قَالُوا۟ بَلَىٰ وَلَٰكِنْ حَقَّتْ كَلِمَةُ ٱلْعَذَابِ عَلَى ٱلْكَٰفِرِينَ ﴿٧١﴾

قِيلَ ٱدْخُلُوٓا۟ أَبْوَٰبَ جَهَنَّمَ خَٰلِدِينَ فِيهَا ۖ فَبِئْسَ مَثْوَى ٱلْمُتَكَبِّرِينَ ﴿٧٢﴾

73. And those who feared their Lord will be led into Paradise in throngs. Then, when they have reached it and its gates are opened, [they will enter it] and its keepers will say: "Peace be upon you; you have fared well, so enter it to dwell therein forever."

74. And they will say: "Praise be to Allah Who has been truthful in His Promise to us and has bequeathed upon us the land, wherein we are able to settle in Paradise wherever we wish. Blessed is the wage of the labourers!"

75. And you will see the angels circling around the Throne proclaiming the praise of their Lord. And it will be justly decided between them and it will be said: "Praise be to Allah, the Lord of the Worlds."

Sûrat Ghâfir,
(The Forgiver) 40

In the Name of Allah,
the Compassionate, the Merciful

1. Ha - Mim.

2. The sending down of the Book is from Allah, the All-Mighty, the All-Knowing.

3. The Forgiver of sins, Receiver of repentance, Terrible in retribution, the Bountiful. There is no god but He. Unto Him is the ultimate return.

4. No one disputes concerning the Signs of Allah, except the unbelievers; so do not be deceived by their wandering in the lands.

5. Before them, the people of Noah and the Confederates after them have denounced, and each nation sallied forth against their Messenger to seize him, and they disputed falsely to repudiate therewith the truth. Then I seized them. How, then, was My retribution?

471

6. And thus your Lord's Word against the unbelievers was fulfilled, that they are, indeed, the companions of the Fire.

7. Those who carry the Throne and those around it proclaim the praise of their Lord, believe in Him and ask forgiveness for the believers: "Lord, You have encompassed everything in mercy and knowledge; so forgive those who have repented and followed Your Path, and guard them against the punishment of Hell.

8. "Lord, and admit them into the Gardens of Eden which You have promised them and those who have been righteous, of their fathers, their spouses and their progeny. You are indeed the All-Mighty, the All-Wise.

9. "And guard them against evil deeds. He whom You guard against evil deeds on that Day, You have surely been merciful to; and that is the great triumph."

10. To the unbelievers it shall be announced: "Allah's contempt is greater than your self-contempt, when you were summoned to believe, but you disbelieved."

11. They will say: "Our Lord, You have caused us to be dead twice and brought us to life twice, and so we have confessed our sins. Is there now a way out?"

12. That is because if Allah is called upon alone, you disbelieve; but if others are associated with Him, you believe. Judgement is Allah's, the All-High, the All-Great.

13. It is He Who shows you His Signs and sends down from heaven provision for you; but only he who repents will remember.

14. So, call on Allah professing religion sincerely unto Him, even if the unbelievers should resent it.

15. Exalted in rank, Owner of the Throne, He casts the spirit by His command upon whomever of His servants He wishes, to warn of the Day of the Encounter.

رَفِيعُ ٱلدَّرَجَٰتِ ذُو ٱلۡعَرۡشِ يُلۡقِى ٱلرُّوحَ مِنۡ أَمۡرِهِۦ عَلَىٰ مَن يَشَآءُ مِنۡ عِبَادِهِۦ لِيُنذِرَ يَوۡمَ ٱلتَّلَاقِ ﴿١٥﴾

16. The Day on which they will emerge, nothing of theirs being concealed from Allah. "Whose is the sovereignty today?" "It is Allah's, the One, the Conqueror."

يَوۡمَ هُم بَٰرِزُونَ لَا يَخۡفَىٰ عَلَى ٱللَّهِ مِنۡهُمۡ شَىۡءٌ لِّمَنِ ٱلۡمُلۡكُ ٱلۡيَوۡمَ لِلَّهِ ٱلۡوَٰحِدِ ٱلۡقَهَّارِ ﴿١٦﴾

17. Today, every soul will be rewarded for what it has earned. There is no injustice today. Allah is surely Quick in reckoning.

ٱلۡيَوۡمَ تُجۡزَىٰ كُلُّ نَفۡسٍ بِمَا كَسَبَتۡ لَا ظُلۡمَ ٱلۡيَوۡمَ إِنَّ ٱللَّهَ سَرِيعُ ٱلۡحِسَابِ ﴿١٧﴾

18. Warn them of the Day of Imminence, when the hearts shall come up to the throats. The wrongdoers will have then no intimate friend and no intercessor who will be heeded.

وَأَنذِرۡهُمۡ يَوۡمَ ٱلۡءَازِفَةِ إِذِ ٱلۡقُلُوبُ لَدَى ٱلۡحَنَاجِرِ كَٰظِمِينَ مَا لِلظَّٰلِمِينَ مِنۡ حَمِيمٍ وَلَا شَفِيعٍ يُطَاعُ ﴿١٨﴾

19. He knows what the eyes betray and what the breasts conceal.

يَعۡلَمُ خَآئِنَةَ ٱلۡأَعۡيُنِ وَمَا تُخۡفِى ٱلصُّدُورُ ﴿١٩﴾

20. Allah judges rightly, but those upon whom they call, apart from Him, judge of naught. Allah is the All-Hearing, the All-Seeing.

وَٱللَّهُ يَقۡضِى بِٱلۡحَقِّ وَٱلَّذِينَ يَدۡعُونَ مِن دُونِهِۦ لَا يَقۡضُونَ بِشَىۡءٍ إِنَّ ٱللَّهَ هُوَ ٱلسَّمِيعُ ٱلۡبَصِيرُ ﴿٢٠﴾

21. Have they not journeyed in the land and seen what was the ultimate fate of those who came before them? [They were mightier than they in powers and vestiges they left in the land.] Then Allah seized them because of their sins, and against Allah they had no protector.

۞ أَوَلَمۡ يَسِيرُواْ فِى ٱلۡأَرۡضِ فَيَنظُرُواْ كَيۡفَ كَانَ عَٰقِبَةُ ٱلَّذِينَ كَانُواْ مِن قَبۡلِهِمۡ كَانُواْ هُمۡ أَشَدَّ مِنۡهُمۡ قُوَّةً وَءَاثَارًا فِى ٱلۡأَرۡضِ فَأَخَذَهُمُ ٱللَّهُ بِذُنُوبِهِمۡ وَمَا كَانَ لَهُم مِّنَ ٱللَّهِ مِن وَاقٍ ﴿٢١﴾

22. That is because their Messengers used to come to them with the clear proofs, but they disbelieved. So Allah seized them; He is indeed Strong, Terrible in retribution.

ذَٰلِكَ بِأَنَّهُمۡ كَانَت تَّأۡتِيهِمۡ رُسُلُهُم بِٱلۡبَيِّنَٰتِ فَكَفَرُواْ فَأَخَذَهُمُ ٱللَّهُ إِنَّهُۥ قَوِىٌّ شَدِيدُ ٱلۡعِقَابِ ﴿٢٢﴾

23. We have indeed sent Moses forth with Our Signs and a manifest authority,

وَلَقَدۡ أَرۡسَلۡنَا مُوسَىٰ بِـَٔايَٰتِنَا وَسُلۡطَٰنٍ مُّبِينٍ ﴿٢٣﴾

24. Unto Pharaoh, Haman and Korah[736] but they said: "A lying sorcerer."

إِلَىٰ فِرْعَوْنَ وَهَـٰمَـٰنَ وَقَـٰرُونَ فَقَالُوا سَـٰحِرٌ كَذَّابٌ ﴿٢٤﴾

25. When he brought them the Truth from Us, they said: "Slay the sons of those who have believed with him, but spare their women." However, the cunning of the unbelievers is in error.

فَلَمَّا جَآءَهُم بِٱلْحَقِّ مِنْ عِندِنَا قَالُوا ٱقْتُلُوٓا أَبْنَآءَ ٱلَّذِينَ ءَامَنُوا مَعَهُ وَٱسْتَحْيُوا نِسَآءَهُمْ وَمَا كَيْدُ ٱلْكَـٰفِرِينَ إِلَّا فِى ضَلَـٰلٍ ﴿٢٥﴾

26. And Pharaoh said: "Let me kill Moses, and let him call upon his Lord. I fear that he may change your religion and cause corruption to spread in the land."

وَقَالَ فِرْعَوْنُ ذَرُونِىٓ أَقْتُلْ مُوسَىٰ وَلْيَدْعُ رَبَّهُۥٓ إِنِّىٓ أَخَافُ أَن يُبَدِّلَ دِينَكُمْ أَوْ أَن يُظْهِرَ فِى ٱلْأَرْضِ ٱلْفَسَادَ ﴿٢٦﴾

27. Moses said: "I seek refuge with my Lord and your Lord from every arrogant one who does not believe in the Day of Reckoning."

وَقَالَ مُوسَىٰٓ إِنِّى عُذْتُ بِرَبِّى وَرَبِّكُم مِّن كُلِّ مُتَكَبِّرٍ لَّا يُؤْمِنُ بِيَوْمِ ٱلْحِسَابِ ﴿٢٧﴾

28. Then a believing man of Pharaoh's folk, who kept hidden his belief, said: "Will you kill a man for saying: 'My Lord is Allah', and he has brought you the clear proofs from your Lord? If he is a liar, his lying will recoil upon him, but if he is truthful, you will be smitten with some of what he is promising you. Allah will not guide one who is an extravagant imposter.

وَقَالَ رَجُلٌ مُّؤْمِنٌ مِّنْ ءَالِ فِرْعَوْنَ يَكْتُمُ إِيمَـٰنَهُۥٓ أَتَقْتُلُونَ رَجُلًا أَن يَقُولَ رَبِّىَ ٱللَّهُ وَقَدْ جَآءَكُم بِٱلْبَيِّنَـٰتِ مِن رَّبِّكُمْ وَإِن يَكُ كَـٰذِبًا فَعَلَيْهِ كَذِبُهُۥ وَإِن يَكُ صَادِقًا يُصِبْكُم بَعْضُ ٱلَّذِى يَعِدُكُمْ إِنَّ ٱللَّهَ لَا يَهْدِى مَنْ هُوَ مُسْرِفٌ كَذَّابٌ ﴿٢٨﴾

29. "O my people, yours is the dominion today, supreme in the land; but who will protect us against Allah's Might, if it should smite us?" Pharaoh said: "I do not show you except what I see, and I do not guide except in the path of rectitude."

يَـٰقَوْمِ لَكُمُ ٱلْمُلْكُ ٱلْيَوْمَ ظَـٰهِرِينَ فِى ٱلْأَرْضِ فَمَن يَنصُرُنَا مِنۢ بَأْسِ ٱللَّهِ إِن جَآءَنَا قَالَ فِرْعَوْنُ مَآ أُرِيكُمْ إِلَّا مَآ أَرَىٰ وَمَآ أَهْدِيكُمْ إِلَّا سَبِيلَ ٱلرَّشَادِ ﴿٢٩﴾

30. Then the one who had believed said: "O my people, I fear for you the like of the day of the Confederates.

وَقَالَ ٱلَّذِىٓ ءَامَنَ يَـٰقَوْمِ إِنِّىٓ أَخَافُ عَلَيْكُم مِّثْلَ يَوْمِ ٱلْأَحْزَابِ ﴿٣٠﴾

31. "Like the wont of the people of Noah, 'Ad, Thamud and those who came after them. Allah does not intend wronging the servants.

مِثْلَ دَأْبِ قَوْمِ نُوحٍ وَعَادٍ وَثَمُودَ وَٱلَّذِينَ مِنۢ بَعْدِهِمْ وَمَا ٱللَّهُ يُرِيدُ ظُلْمًا لِّلْعِبَادِ ﴿٣١﴾

---

736. See Surah 28: 76, 79.

32. "And, O my people, I fear for you the Day of Altercation.

وَيَٰقَوْمِ إِنِّى أَخَافُ عَلَيْكُمْ يَوْمَ ٱلتَّنَادِ ﴿٣٢﴾

33. "The Day you will turn away in flight, having no defender against Allah. Whomever Allah leads astray will have no one to guide him.

يَوْمَ تُوَلُّونَ مُدْبِرِينَ مَا لَكُم مِّنَ ٱللَّهِ مِنْ عَاصِمٍ وَمَن يُضْلِلِ ٱللَّهُ فَمَا لَهُۥ مِنْ هَادٍ ﴿٣٣﴾

34. "Joseph brought you the clear proofs before, but you continued to doubt what he brought you. Then, when he perished you said: 'Allah will never send forth a Messenger after him.' This is how Allah leads astray whoever is extravagant and suspicious.

وَلَقَدْ جَآءَكُمْ يُوسُفُ مِن قَبْلُ بِٱلْبَيِّنَٰتِ فَمَا زِلْتُمْ فِى شَكٍّ مِّمَّا جَآءَكُم بِهِۦ حَتَّىٰٓ إِذَا هَلَكَ قُلْتُمْ لَن يَبْعَثَ ٱللَّهُ مِنۢ بَعْدِهِۦ رَسُولاً كَذَٰلِكَ يُضِلُّ ٱللَّهُ مَنْ هُوَ مُسْرِفٌ مُّرْتَابٌ ﴿٣٤﴾

35. "Those who dispute concerning Allah's Signs without any authority given to them - how hateful is that in the sight of Allah and the believers. That is how Allah places a seal on the heart of every arrogant bully."

ٱلَّذِينَ يُجَٰدِلُونَ فِىٓ ءَايَٰتِ ٱللَّهِ بِغَيْرِ سُلْطَٰنٍ أَتَىٰهُمْ كَبُرَ مَقْتًا عِندَ ٱللَّهِ وَعِندَ ٱلَّذِينَ ءَامَنُوا۟ كَذَٰلِكَ يَطْبَعُ ٱللَّهُ عَلَىٰ كُلِّ قَلْبِ مُتَكَبِّرٍ جَبَّارٍ ﴿٣٥﴾

36. And Pharaoh said: "O Haman, build me a tower that I may perchance reach the pathways,

وَقَالَ فِرْعَوْنُ يَٰهَٰمَٰنُ ٱبْنِ لِى صَرْحًا لَّعَلِّىٓ أَبْلُغُ ٱلْأَسْبَٰبَ ﴿٣٦﴾

37. "The pathways of heaven; and then look upon the God of Moses. For I think he is a liar." That is how embellished for Pharaoh was his evil deed and how he was barred from the Path. Pharaoh's guile was only destined to fail.

أَسْبَٰبَ ٱلسَّمَٰوَٰتِ فَأَطَّلِعَ إِلَىٰٓ إِلَٰهِ مُوسَىٰ وَإِنِّى لَأَظُنُّهُۥ كَٰذِبًا وَكَذَٰلِكَ زُيِّنَ لِفِرْعَوْنَ سُوٓءُ عَمَلِهِۦ وَصُدَّ عَنِ ٱلسَّبِيلِ وَمَا كَيْدُ فِرْعَوْنَ إِلَّا فِى تَبَابٍ ﴿٣٧﴾

38. Then he who had believed said: "O my people, follow me and I will guide you to the path of rectitude.

وَقَالَ ٱلَّذِىٓ ءَامَنَ يَٰقَوْمِ ٱتَّبِعُونِ أَهْدِكُمْ سَبِيلَ ٱلرَّشَادِ ﴿٣٨﴾

39. "O my people, this present life is a fleeting pleasure, but the world to come is the abode of permanence.

يَٰقَوْمِ إِنَّمَا هَٰذِهِ ٱلْحَيَوٰةُ ٱلدُّنْيَا مَتَٰعٌ وَإِنَّ ٱلْءَاخِرَةَ هِىَ دَارُ ٱلْقَرَارِ ﴿٣٩﴾

40. "Whoever does an evil deed will only be rewarded its like; but whoever does a righteous deed, whether male or female, being a believer - those shall enter Paradise receiving therein provision without measure.

مَنْ عَمِلَ سَيِّئَةً فَلَا يُجْزَىٰٓ إِلَّا مِثْلَهَا وَمَنْ عَمِلَ صَٰلِحًا مِّن ذَكَرٍ أَوْ أُنثَىٰ وَهُوَ مُؤْمِنٌ فَأُو۟لَٰٓئِكَ يَدْخُلُونَ ٱلْجَنَّةَ يُرْزَقُونَ فِيهَا بِغَيْرِ حِسَابٍ ﴿٤٠﴾

41. "And, O my people, do I call you unto salvation, while you call me unto the Fire?

42. "You call me to disbelieve in Allah and associate with Him that whereof I have no knowledge, while I call you unto the All-Mighty, the All-Pardoner.

43. "No wonder that what you call me unto has no callers in this world, nor in the Hereafter; and that our ultimate return is unto Allah; and that the extravagant are the true companions of the Fire.

44. "You will remember what I am saying to you. I entrust my fate to Allah. Allah is surely Well Aware of the servants."

45. Then, Allah guarded him against the evils of their scheming; and the evil punishment encompassed Pharaoh's folk;

46. The Fire to which they shall be exposed morning and evening. And the Day the Hour shall come to pass, it will be said:[737] "Admit Pharaoh's folk to the worst punishment."

47. And while they dispute in the Fire, the weak will say to those who waxed proud: "We were followers of yours. Will you, then, withhold from us a part of the Fire?"

48. Those who waxed proud will say: "We are truly all in it. Allah has judged between the servants."

49. Those in the Fire will say to the keepers of Hell: "Call on your Lord that He may remit a day of punishment for us."

50. They will reply: "Did not your Messengers bring you clear proofs?" They will say: "Yes indeed." They will reply: "Call then, although the call of the unbelievers is in vain."

---

737. To the angels.

476

51. We shall support Our Messengers and the believers in the present life and on the Day the witnesses shall arise;

52. The Day when their excuses will not profit the wrongdoers, and the curse will be upon them and they will have the worst dwelling.

53. We have indeed given Moses the guidance and bequeathed to the Children of Israel the Book,

54. As a guidance and a reminder to people of understanding.

55. So stand fast; Allah's Promise is true. Seek the forgiveness of your sin and proclaim the praise of your Lord evenings and mornings.

56. As for those who dispute regarding Allah's Signs without any authority given to them, there is nothing in their breasts but the desire for grandeur, which they will never attain. So, seek refuge with Allah; for He is surely the All-Hearing, the All-Seeing.

57. Surely, the creation of the heavens and the earth is greater than the creation of mankind, but most people do not know.

58. The blind and the seeing man are not equal; nor are those who believe and do the righteous deeds and the evil-doer. Little do you remember!

59. The Hour is indeed coming, no doubt about it; but most people do not believe.

60. Your Lord has said: "Call on Me and I will answer you. Those who are too proud to worship Me shall enter Hell totally abased."

61. It is Allah Who made the night for you, to rest in it, and the day to see your way. Allah is truly Bountiful to mankind, but most people do not give thanks.

إِنَّا لَنَنصُرُ رُسُلَنَا وَٱلَّذِينَ ءَامَنُوا۟ فِى ٱلْحَيَوٰةِ ٱلدُّنْيَا وَيَوْمَ يَقُومُ ٱلْأَشْهَـٰدُ ۝

يَوْمَ لَا يَنفَعُ ٱلظَّـٰلِمِينَ مَعْذِرَتُهُمْ ۖ وَلَهُمُ ٱللَّعْنَةُ وَلَهُمْ سُوٓءُ ٱلدَّارِ ۝

وَلَقَدْ ءَاتَيْنَا مُوسَى ٱلْهُدَىٰ وَأَوْرَثْنَا بَنِىٓ إِسْرَٰٓءِيلَ ٱلْكِتَـٰبَ ۝

هُدًى وَذِكْرَىٰ لِأُو۟لِى ٱلْأَلْبَـٰبِ ۝

فَٱصْبِرْ إِنَّ وَعْدَ ٱللَّهِ حَقٌّ وَٱسْتَغْفِرْ لِذَنۢبِكَ وَسَبِّحْ بِحَمْدِ رَبِّكَ بِٱلْعَشِىِّ وَٱلْإِبْكَـٰرِ ۝

إِنَّ ٱلَّذِينَ يُجَـٰدِلُونَ فِىٓ ءَايَـٰتِ ٱللَّهِ بِغَيْرِ سُلْطَـٰنٍ أَتَىٰهُمْ ۙ إِن فِى صُدُورِهِمْ إِلَّا كِبْرٌ مَّا هُم بِبَـٰلِغِيهِ ۚ فَٱسْتَعِذْ بِٱللَّهِ ۖ إِنَّهُۥ هُوَ ٱلسَّمِيعُ ٱلْبَصِيرُ ۝

لَخَلْقُ ٱلسَّمَـٰوَٰتِ وَٱلْأَرْضِ أَكْبَرُ مِنْ خَلْقِ ٱلنَّاسِ وَلَـٰكِنَّ أَكْثَرَ ٱلنَّاسِ لَا يَعْلَمُونَ ۝

وَمَا يَسْتَوِى ٱلْأَعْمَىٰ وَٱلْبَصِيرُ وَٱلَّذِينَ ءَامَنُوا۟ وَعَمِلُوا۟ ٱلصَّـٰلِحَـٰتِ وَلَا ٱلْمُسِىٓءُ ۚ قَلِيلًا مَّا تَتَذَكَّرُونَ ۝

إِنَّ ٱلسَّاعَةَ لَءَاتِيَةٌ لَّا رَيْبَ فِيهَا وَلَـٰكِنَّ أَكْثَرَ ٱلنَّاسِ لَا يُؤْمِنُونَ ۝

وَقَالَ رَبُّكُمُ ٱدْعُونِىٓ أَسْتَجِبْ لَكُمْ ۚ إِنَّ ٱلَّذِينَ يَسْتَكْبِرُونَ عَنْ عِبَادَتِى سَيَدْخُلُونَ جَهَنَّمَ دَاخِرِينَ ۝

ٱللَّهُ ٱلَّذِى جَعَلَ لَكُمُ ٱلَّيْلَ لِتَسْكُنُوا۟ فِيهِ وَٱلنَّهَارَ مُبْصِرًا ۚ إِنَّ ٱللَّهَ لَذُو فَضْلٍ عَلَى ٱلنَّاسِ وَلَـٰكِنَّ أَكْثَرَ ٱلنَّاسِ لَا يَشْكُرُونَ ۝

62. That for you is Allah your Lord, Creator of everything. There is no god but He. How then are you perverted?

ذَٰلِكُمُ ٱللَّهُ رَبُّكُمْ خَٰلِقُ كُلِّ شَىْءٍ لَّآ إِلَٰهَ إِلَّا هُوَ فَأَنَّىٰ تُؤْفَكُونَ ۝

63. Thus as those who used to repudiate Allah's Signs were perverted too.

كَذَٰلِكَ يُؤْفَكُ ٱلَّذِينَ كَانُوا۟ بِـَٔايَٰتِ ٱللَّهِ يَجْحَدُونَ ۝

64. It is Allah Who made the earth a fixed station for you and the sky a high edifice. He fashioned you in a shapely manner and provided you with the good things. That for you is Allah, your Lord; so blessed be Allah, the Lord of the Worlds.

ٱللَّهُ ٱلَّذِى جَعَلَ لَكُمُ ٱلْأَرْضَ قَرَارًا وَٱلسَّمَآءَ بِنَآءً وَصَوَّرَكُمْ فَأَحْسَنَ صُوَرَكُمْ وَرَزَقَكُم مِّنَ ٱلطَّيِّبَٰتِ ذَٰلِكُمُ ٱللَّهُ رَبُّكُمْ فَتَبَارَكَ ٱللَّهُ رَبُّ ٱلْعَٰلَمِينَ ۝

65. He is the Living One; there is no god but He. So call on Him professing sincerely the religion unto Him. Praise be to Allah, the Lord of the Worlds.

هُوَ ٱلْحَىُّ لَآ إِلَٰهَ إِلَّا هُوَ فَٱدْعُوهُ مُخْلِصِينَ لَهُ ٱلدِّينَ ٱلْحَمْدُ لِلَّهِ رَبِّ ٱلْعَٰلَمِينَ ۝

66. Say: "I have been forbidden to worship those you call upon, apart from Allah; since the clear proofs have come to me from my Lord and I have been commanded to submit to the Lord of the Worlds."

۞ قُلْ إِنِّى نُهِيتُ أَنْ أَعْبُدَ ٱلَّذِينَ تَدْعُونَ مِن دُونِ ٱللَّهِ لَمَّا جَآءَنِىَ ٱلْبَيِّنَٰتُ مِن رَّبِّى وَأُمِرْتُ أَنْ أُسْلِمَ لِرَبِّ ٱلْعَٰلَمِينَ ۝

67. It is He Who created you from dust, then from a sperm, then from a clot. Then He brings you out as infants; then allows you to come of age, then become old men. Some of you will pass away before that, but you will attain a fixed term, that perchance you might understand.

هُوَ ٱلَّذِى خَلَقَكُم مِّن تُرَابٍ ثُمَّ مِن نُّطْفَةٍ ثُمَّ مِنْ عَلَقَةٍ ثُمَّ يُخْرِجُكُمْ طِفْلًا ثُمَّ لِتَبْلُغُوٓا۟ أَشُدَّكُمْ ثُمَّ لِتَكُونُوا۟ شُيُوخًا وَمِنكُم مَّن يُتَوَفَّىٰ مِن قَبْلُ وَلِتَبْلُغُوٓا۟ أَجَلًا مُّسَمًّى وَلَعَلَّكُمْ تَعْقِلُونَ ۝

68. It is He Who brings to life and causes to die. Then, if He decrees a certain matter, He only says to it: "Be", and it comes to be.

هُوَ ٱلَّذِى يُحْىِۦ وَيُمِيتُ فَإِذَا قَضَىٰٓ أَمْرًا فَإِنَّمَا يَقُولُ لَهُۥ كُن فَيَكُونُ ۝

69. Have you not observed those who dispute regarding Allah's Signs, how they are perverted?

أَلَمْ تَرَ إِلَى ٱلَّذِينَ يُجَٰدِلُونَ فِىٓ ءَايَٰتِ ٱللَّهِ أَنَّىٰ يُصْرَفُونَ ۝

70. Those who disbelieved in this Book and in what We sent Our Messengers with; they shall surely know.

ٱلَّذِينَ كَذَّبُوا۟ بِٱلْكِتَٰبِ وَبِمَآ أَرْسَلْنَا بِهِۦ رُسُلَنَا فَسَوْفَ يَعْلَمُونَ ۝

71. When the fetters and chains shall be upon their necks and they shall be dragged along.

إِذِ ٱلْأَغْلَٰلُ فِىٓ أَعْنَٰقِهِمْ وَٱلسَّلَٰسِلُ يُسْحَبُونَ ۝

72. In the boiling water; then, in the Fire they will be consumed.

فِى ٱلْحَمِيمِ ثُمَّ فِى ٱلنَّارِ يُسْجَرُونَ ﴿٧٢﴾

73. Then it will be said to them: "Where are those you used to set up as associates,

ثُمَّ قِيلَ لَهُمْ أَيْنَ مَا كُنتُمْ تُشْرِكُونَ ﴿٧٣﴾

74. "Apart from Allah?" They will say: "They strayed away from us. Indeed, we did not call upon anything formerly." Thus Allah leads the unbelievers astray.

مِن دُونِ ٱللَّهِ قَالُوا۟ ضَلُّوا۟ عَنَّا بَل لَّمْ نَكُن نَّدْعُوا۟ مِن قَبْلُ شَيْـًٔا كَذَٰلِكَ يُضِلُّ ٱللَّهُ ٱلْكَٰفِرِينَ ﴿٧٤﴾

75. That is because you used to rejoice on earth in what is other than the truth and because you used to frolic.

ذَٰلِكُم بِمَا كُنتُمْ تَفْرَحُونَ فِى ٱلْأَرْضِ بِغَيْرِ ٱلْحَقِّ وَبِمَا كُنتُمْ تَمْرَحُونَ ﴿٧٥﴾

76. Enter then the gates of Hell, dwelling therein forever. Evil is the dwelling of the arrogant.

ٱدْخُلُوٓا۟ أَبْوَٰبَ جَهَنَّمَ خَٰلِدِينَ فِيهَا فَبِئْسَ مَثْوَى ٱلْمُتَكَبِّرِينَ ﴿٧٦﴾

77. So, bear up patiently; Allah's Promise is true. We will either show you[738] what We are promising them, or We will call you unto Us. Then unto Us they will be brought back.

فَٱصْبِرْ إِنَّ وَعْدَ ٱللَّهِ حَقٌّ فَإِمَّا نُرِيَنَّكَ بَعْضَ ٱلَّذِى نَعِدُهُمْ أَوْ نَتَوَفَّيَنَّكَ فَإِلَيْنَا يُرْجَعُونَ ﴿٧٧﴾

78. Indeed, We have sent Messengers before you. Of some We have told you the tale and of some We did not tell. It is not in any Messenger's power to bring a sign, save by Allah's Leave. Then, when Allah's Decree comes, the issue shall be decided justly; and there and then the seekers of vanity shall perish.

وَلَقَدْ أَرْسَلْنَا رُسُلًا مِّن قَبْلِكَ مِنْهُم مَّن قَصَصْنَا عَلَيْكَ وَمِنْهُم مَّن لَّمْ نَقْصُصْ عَلَيْكَ وَمَا كَانَ لِرَسُولٍ أَن يَأْتِىَ بِـَٔايَةٍ إِلَّا بِإِذْنِ ٱللَّهِ فَإِذَا جَآءَ أَمْرُ ٱللَّهِ قُضِىَ بِٱلْحَقِّ وَخَسِرَ هُنَالِكَ ٱلْمُبْطِلُونَ ﴿٧٨﴾

79. It is Allah Who created for you the cattle, so that some you may ride and some you may eat.

ٱللَّهُ ٱلَّذِى جَعَلَ لَكُمُ ٱلْأَنْعَٰمَ لِتَرْكَبُوا۟ مِنْهَا وَمِنْهَا تَأْكُلُونَ ﴿٧٩﴾

80. And in them, you have other benefits as well; and upon them you may attain any need within your breasts. And upon them and upon the ships you may be borne along.

وَلَكُمْ فِيهَا مَنَٰفِعُ وَلِتَبْلُغُوا۟ عَلَيْهَا حَاجَةً فِى صُدُورِكُمْ وَعَلَيْهَا وَعَلَى ٱلْفُلْكِ تُحْمَلُونَ ﴿٨٠﴾

81. And He shows you His Signs. Which Signs of Allah will you then deny?

وَيُرِيكُمْ ءَايَٰتِهِۦ فَأَىَّ ءَايَٰتِ ٱللَّهِ تُنكِرُونَ ﴿٨١﴾

---

738. Muhammad.

82. Have they not travelled in the land, then, to see what was the fate of those who preceded them? They were more numerous than they and had greater power and influence in the land. Yet what they used to earn availed them nothing.

83. Then, when their Messengers came to them with the clear proofs, they rejoiced in the knowledge they had and were afflicted with that which they used to mock at.

84. But when they saw Our Might, they said: "We believe in Allah alone and disbelieve in that which we used to associate with Him."

85. Yet, their belief, upon seeing Our Might, did not profit them. It is Allah's Way of old regarding His servants; and the unbelievers shall be lost there and then.

Sûrat Fussilat, (Well-Expounded) 41

*In the Name of Allah,
the Compassionate, the Merciful*

1. Ha - Mim.

2. This is a revelation from the Compassionate, the Merciful;

3. A Book whose Verses have been well-expounded, an Arabic Qur'an addressed to a people who know;

4. Bearing good news and warning. Yet most of them have turned away and are unheeding.

5. They say: "Our hearts are shielded against what you call us unto, in our ears is a heaviness and between us and yourself is a veil. So act, we are acting too."

6. Say: "I am only a mortal like you, to whom it is revealed that your God is One God; so head straight towards Him and seek His forgiveness, and woe betide the idolaters;

7. "Those who do not pay the alms, and in the Hereafter they disbelieve."

8. Surely, those who believe and do the righteous deeds shall have an unstinted wage.

9. Say: "Do you really disbelieve in Him Who created the earth in [two days] and assign equals to Him? That is the Lord of the Worlds."

10. And He set up immovable mountains upon it and blessed it, and ordained therein their varied provisions in four days equally to all those who ask.

11. Then He arose to heaven while it was smoke, and He said to it and to the earth: "Come over, willingly or unwillingly." They said: "We come willingly."

12. Then He completed them as seven heavens in two days and assigned to each heaven its proper order. And We adorned the lower heaven with lamps as protection.[739] That is the determination of the All-Mighty, the All-Knowing.

13. If they turn away, then say: "I warn you against a thunderbolt like the thunderbolt of 'Ad and Thamud."

14. When the Messengers came to them from their front and their rear saying: "Do not worship any one but Allah", they said: "Had our Lord wished, He would certainly have sent down angels. Therefore, we disbelieve in the Message you have been sent with."

---

739. From the demons.

قُلْ إِنَّمَا أَنَا بَشَرٌ مِّثْلُكُمْ يُوحَىٰ إِلَيَّ أَنَّمَا إِلَٰهُكُمْ إِلَٰهٌ وَٰحِدٌ فَٱسْتَقِيمُوٓا۟ إِلَيْهِ وَٱسْتَغْفِرُوهُ وَوَيْلٌ لِّلْمُشْرِكِينَ ۝

ٱلَّذِينَ لَا يُؤْتُونَ ٱلزَّكَوٰةَ وَهُم بِٱلْآخِرَةِ هُمْ كَٰفِرُونَ ۝

إِنَّ ٱلَّذِينَ ءَامَنُوا۟ وَعَمِلُوا۟ ٱلصَّٰلِحَٰتِ لَهُمْ أَجْرٌ غَيْرُ مَمْنُونٍ ۝

۞ قُلْ أَئِنَّكُمْ لَتَكْفُرُونَ بِٱلَّذِى خَلَقَ ٱلْأَرْضَ فِى يَوْمَيْنِ وَتَجْعَلُونَ لَهُۥٓ أَندَادًا ذَٰلِكَ رَبُّ ٱلْعَٰلَمِينَ ۝

وَجَعَلَ فِيهَا رَوَٰسِىَ مِن فَوْقِهَا وَبَٰرَكَ فِيهَا وَقَدَّرَ فِيهَآ أَقْوَٰتَهَا فِىٓ أَرْبَعَةِ أَيَّامٍ سَوَآءً لِّلسَّآئِلِينَ ۝

ثُمَّ ٱسْتَوَىٰٓ إِلَى ٱلسَّمَآءِ وَهِىَ دُخَانٌ فَقَالَ لَهَا وَلِلْأَرْضِ ٱئْتِيَا طَوْعًا أَوْ كَرْهًا قَالَتَآ أَتَيْنَا طَآئِعِينَ ۝

فَقَضَىٰهُنَّ سَبْعَ سَمَٰوَاتٍ فِى يَوْمَيْنِ وَأَوْحَىٰ فِى كُلِّ سَمَآءٍ أَمْرَهَا وَزَيَّنَّا ٱلسَّمَآءَ ٱلدُّنْيَا بِمَصَٰبِيحَ وَحِفْظًا ذَٰلِكَ تَقْدِيرُ ٱلْعَزِيزِ ٱلْعَلِيمِ ۝

فَإِنْ أَعْرَضُوا۟ فَقُلْ أَنذَرْتُكُمْ صَٰعِقَةً مِّثْلَ صَٰعِقَةِ عَادٍ وَثَمُودَ ۝

إِذْ جَآءَتْهُمُ ٱلرُّسُلُ مِنۢ بَيْنِ أَيْدِيهِمْ وَمِنْ خَلْفِهِمْ أَلَّا تَعْبُدُوٓا۟ إِلَّا ٱللَّهَ قَالُوا۟ لَوْ شَآءَ رَبُّنَا لَأَنزَلَ مَلَٰٓئِكَةً فَإِنَّا بِمَآ أُرْسِلْتُم بِهِۦ كَٰفِرُونَ ۝

15. As for 'Ad, they waxed proud in the land unjustly and said: "Who is superior to us in strength?" Did they not see that Allah Who created them is superior to them in strength? And they used to repudiate Our Signs.

فَأَمَّا عَادٌ فَٱسْتَكْبَرُوا فِى ٱلْأَرْضِ بِغَيْرِ ٱلْحَقِّ وَقَالُوا مَنْ أَشَدُّ مِنَّا قُوَّةً أَوَلَمْ يَرَوْا أَنَّ ٱللَّهَ ٱلَّذِى خَلَقَهُمْ هُوَ أَشَدُّ مِنْهُمْ قُوَّةً وَكَانُوا بِـَٔايَـٰتِنَا يَجْحَدُونَ ﴿١٥﴾

16. So, We loosed upon them a roaring wind on inauspicious days, so as to make them taste the punishment of disgrace in the present life. However, the punishment of the Hereafter is more disgraceful and they shall not receive support.

فَأَرْسَلْنَا عَلَيْهِمْ رِيحًا صَرْصَرًا فِى أَيَّامٍ نَّحِسَاتٍ لِّنُذِيقَهُمْ عَذَابَ ٱلْخِزْىِ فِى ٱلْحَيَوٰةِ ٱلدُّنْيَا وَلَعَذَابُ ٱلْأَخِرَةِ أَخْزَىٰ وَهُمْ لَا يُنصَرُونَ ﴿١٦﴾

17. But as for Thamud, We extended guidance to them; yet they preferred blindness to guidance, and so the thunderbolt of humiliating punishment seized them on account of what they used to earn.

وَأَمَّا ثَمُودُ فَهَدَيْنَـٰهُمْ فَٱسْتَحَبُّوا ٱلْعَمَىٰ عَلَى ٱلْهُدَىٰ فَأَخَذَتْهُمْ صَـٰعِقَةُ ٱلْعَذَابِ ٱلْهُونِ بِمَا كَانُوا يَكْسِبُونَ ﴿١٧﴾

18. And We delivered those who believed and were God-fearing.

وَنَجَّيْنَا ٱلَّذِينَ ءَامَنُوا وَكَانُوا يَتَّقُونَ ﴿١٨﴾

19. And when the enemies of Allah are mustered unto the Fire, they shall be held in check.

وَيَوْمَ يُحْشَرُ أَعْدَآءُ ٱللَّهِ إِلَى ٱلنَّارِ فَهُمْ يُوزَعُونَ ﴿١٩﴾

20. When they reach it, their hearing, sights and skins shall bear witness against them regarding what they used to do.

حَتَّىٰ إِذَا مَا جَآءُوهَا شَهِدَ عَلَيْهِمْ سَمْعُهُمْ وَأَبْصَـٰرُهُمْ وَجُلُودُهُم بِمَا كَانُوا يَعْمَلُونَ ﴿٢٠﴾

21. And they will say to their skins: "Why did you bear witness against us?" They will say: "Allah Who gave everything speech gave us speech, and He is the One Who created you the first time and unto Him you shall be returned."

وَقَالُوا لِجُلُودِهِمْ لِمَ شَهِدتُّمْ عَلَيْنَا قَالُوا أَنطَقَنَا ٱللَّهُ ٱلَّذِى أَنطَقَ كُلَّ شَىْءٍ وَهُوَ خَلَقَكُمْ أَوَّلَ مَرَّةٍ وَإِلَيْهِ تُرْجَعُونَ ﴿٢١﴾

22. You did not try to hide from the witness that your hearing, sights and skins would bear against you; but you thought that Allah does not know much of what you do.

وَمَا كُنتُمْ تَسْتَتِرُونَ أَن يَشْهَدَ عَلَيْكُمْ سَمْعُكُمْ وَلَا أَبْصَـٰرُكُمْ وَلَا جُلُودُكُمْ وَلَـٰكِن ظَنَنتُمْ أَنَّ ٱللَّهَ لَا يَعْلَمُ كَثِيرًا مِّمَّا تَعْمَلُونَ ﴿٢٢﴾

23. And that thought you entertained regarding your Lord led to your destruction, and so you were numbered among the losers.

وَذَٰلِكُمْ ظَنُّكُمُ ٱلَّذِى ظَنَنتُم بِرَبِّكُمْ أَرْدَىٰكُمْ فَأَصْبَحْتُم مِّنَ ٱلْخَـٰسِرِينَ ﴿٢٣﴾

24. Now if they bear up, then the Fire is their dwelling; and if they seek restoration to favour they will not be among those restored.

فَإِن يَصۡبِرُوا۟ فَٱلنَّارُ مَثۡوًى لَّهُمۡ وَإِن يَسۡتَعۡتِبُوا۟ فَمَا هُم مِّنَ ٱلۡمُعۡتَبِينَ ۝

25. And We have ordained for them companions, who embellished what is in front of them and is behind them. The sentence then was pronounced against them, along with nations which had gone before them, of jinn and men. Truly, they were the losers.

۞ وَقَيَّضۡنَا لَهُمۡ قُرَنَآءَ فَزَيَّنُوا۟ لَهُم مَّا بَيۡنَ أَيۡدِيهِمۡ وَمَا خَلۡفَهُمۡ وَحَقَّ عَلَيۡهِمُ ٱلۡقَوۡلُ فِىٓ أُمَمٍ قَدۡ خَلَتۡ مِن قَبۡلِهِم مِّنَ ٱلۡجِنِّ وَٱلۡإِنسِ إِنَّهُمۡ كَانُوا۟ خَٰسِرِينَ ۝

26. The unbelievers said: "Do not listen to this Qur'an, but babble in reading it, that perchance you might win."

وَقَالَ ٱلَّذِينَ كَفَرُوا۟ لَا تَسۡمَعُوا۟ لِهَٰذَا ٱلۡقُرۡءَانِ وَٱلۡغَوۡا۟ فِيهِ لَعَلَّكُمۡ تَغۡلِبُونَ ۝

27. Truly, We shall make the unbelievers taste a terrible punishment, and We shall reward them for the worst of what they used to do.

فَلَنُذِيقَنَّ ٱلَّذِينَ كَفَرُوا۟ عَذَابًا شَدِيدًا وَلَنَجۡزِيَنَّهُمۡ أَسۡوَأَ ٱلَّذِى كَانُوا۟ يَعۡمَلُونَ ۝

28. That is the reward of Allah's enemies, the Fire wherein they shall have an eternal abode, as a reward for that they used to repudiate Our Signs.

ذَٰلِكَ جَزَآءُ أَعۡدَآءِ ٱللَّهِ ٱلنَّارُ لَهُمۡ فِيهَا دَارُ ٱلۡخُلۡدِ جَزَآءًۢ بِمَا كَانُوا۟ بِـَٔايَٰتِنَا يَجۡحَدُونَ ۝

29. The unbelievers shall say: "Lord, show us both those who led us astray of jinn and men, that we might trample them under our feet and that they may be reckoned among the lowliest of creatures."

وَقَالَ ٱلَّذِينَ كَفَرُوا۟ رَبَّنَآ أَرِنَا ٱلَّذَيۡنِ أَضَلَّانَا مِنَ ٱلۡجِنِّ وَٱلۡإِنسِ نَجۡعَلۡهُمَا تَحۡتَ أَقۡدَامِنَا لِيَكُونَا مِنَ ٱلۡأَسۡفَلِينَ ۝

30. Those who say: "Our Lord is Allah", then are upright, the angels shall descend upon them saying: "Do not fear or grieve, but rejoice in the Paradise which you were promised.

إِنَّ ٱلَّذِينَ قَالُوا۟ رَبُّنَا ٱللَّهُ ثُمَّ ٱسۡتَقَٰمُوا۟ تَتَنَزَّلُ عَلَيۡهِمُ ٱلۡمَلَٰٓئِكَةُ أَلَّا تَخَافُوا۟ وَلَا تَحۡزَنُوا۟ وَأَبۡشِرُوا۟ بِٱلۡجَنَّةِ ٱلَّتِى كُنتُمۡ تُوعَدُونَ ۝

31. "We are your protectors in the present life and in the Hereafter, wherein you shall have whatever your hearts desire and you shall have therein whatever you call for;

نَحۡنُ أَوۡلِيَآؤُكُمۡ فِى ٱلۡحَيَوٰةِ ٱلدُّنۡيَا وَفِى ٱلۡءَاخِرَةِ وَلَكُمۡ فِيهَا مَا تَشۡتَهِىٓ أَنفُسُكُمۡ وَلَكُمۡ فِيهَا مَا تَدَّعُونَ ۝

32. "As hospitality from an All-Forgiving, Merciful One."

نُزُلًا مِّنۡ غَفُورٍ رَّحِيمٍ ۝

33. Who is fairer in speech than one who calls unto Allah and performs the righteous deed and says: "I am one of those who submit."

وَمَنْ أَحْسَنُ قَوْلًا مِّمَّن دَعَا إِلَى اللَّهِ وَعَمِلَ صَٰلِحًا وَقَالَ إِنَّنِي مِنَ الْمُسْلِمِينَ ۝

34. The fair and evil deeds are not equal. Respond with that which is fairer, so that he against whom you have a grudge shall be like an intimate friend.

وَلَا تَسْتَوِى الْحَسَنَةُ وَلَا السَّيِّئَةُ ادْفَعْ بِالَّتِى هِىَ أَحْسَنُ فَإِذَا الَّذِى بَيْنَكَ وَبَيْنَهُ عَدَٰوَةٌ كَأَنَّهُ وَلِىٌّ حَمِيمٌ ۝

35. None shall be accorded this rank except those who have stood fast, and none shall be accorded it except one blessed with great good fortune.

وَمَا يُلَقَّىٰهَآ إِلَّا الَّذِينَ صَبَرُوا وَمَا يُلَقَّىٰهَآ إِلَّا ذُو حَظٍّ عَظِيمٍ ۝

36. And if a temptation of Satan should visit you, then seek refuge with Allah. He is indeed All-Hearing, All-Knowing.

وَإِمَّا يَنزَغَنَّكَ مِنَ الشَّيْطَٰنِ نَزْغٌ فَاسْتَعِذْ بِاللَّهِ إِنَّهُ هُوَ السَّمِيعُ الْعَلِيمُ ۝

37. Of His Signs are the night and the day, the sun and the moon. Do not prostrate yourselves to the sun or to the moon, but prostrate yourselves to Allah Who created them, if it is He you truly worship.

وَمِنْ ءَايَٰتِهِ الَّيْلُ وَالنَّهَارُ وَالشَّمْسُ وَالْقَمَرُ لَا تَسْجُدُوا لِلشَّمْسِ وَلَا لِلْقَمَرِ وَاسْجُدُوا لِلَّهِ الَّذِى خَلَقَهُنَّ إِن كُنتُمْ إِيَّاهُ تَعْبُدُونَ ۝

38. Should they wax proud, then those with your Lord do glorify Him by night and day, without growing weary.

فَإِنِ اسْتَكْبَرُوا فَالَّذِينَ عِندَ رَبِّكَ يُسَبِّحُونَ لَهُ بِالَّيْلِ وَالنَّهَارِ وَهُمْ لَا يَسْئَمُونَ ۩ ۝

39. And of His Signs is that you see the earth desolate but when We send down water upon it, it quivers and swells. Indeed, He Who revived it shall revive the dead. Truly He has power over everything.

وَمِنْ ءَايَٰتِهِ أَنَّكَ تَرَى الْأَرْضَ خَٰشِعَةً فَإِذَآ أَنزَلْنَا عَلَيْهَا الْمَاءَ اهْتَزَّتْ وَرَبَتْ إِنَّ الَّذِى أَحْيَاهَا لَمُحْىِ الْمَوْتَىٰ إِنَّهُ عَلَىٰ كُلِّ شَىْءٍ قَدِيرٌ ۝

40. Those who turn away from Our Signs are not hidden from Us. Is he, then, who is cast in the Fire better than he who comes forward safely on the Day of Resurrection? Do what you please; He is Fully Aware of what you do.

إِنَّ الَّذِينَ يُلْحِدُونَ فِى ءَايَٰتِنَا لَا يَخْفَوْنَ عَلَيْنَا أَفَمَن يُلْقَىٰ فِى النَّارِ خَيْرٌ أَم مَّن يَأْتِى ءَامِنًا يَوْمَ الْقِيَٰمَةِ اعْمَلُوا مَا شِئْتُمْ إِنَّهُ بِمَا تَعْمَلُونَ بَصِيرٌ ۝

41. Nor are those who have disbelieved the Reminder when it came to them [hidden from Us]. It is surely a noble Book,

إِنَّ الَّذِينَ كَفَرُوا بِالذِّكْرِ لَمَّا جَآءَهُمْ وَإِنَّهُ لَكِتَٰبٌ عَزِيزٌ ۝

42. To which falsehood does not come from its front nor from behind it - a revelation sent down from the Wise, Praiseworthy.

لَّا يَأْتِيهِ الْبَٰطِلُ مِن بَيْنِ يَدَيْهِ وَلَا مِنْ خَلْفِهِ تَنزِيلٌ مِّنْ حَكِيمٍ حَمِيدٍ ۝

43. You are not told except what was told to the Messengers before you. Surely, your Lord is a Master of Forgiveness and a Master of Painful Retribution.

مَّا يُقَالُ لَكَ إِلَّا مَا قَدْ قِيلَ لِلرُّسُلِ مِن قَبْلِكَ إِنَّ رَبَّكَ لَذُو مَغْفِرَةٍ وَذُو عِقَابٍ أَلِيمٍ ﴿٤٣﴾

44. Had We made it a foreign Qur'an, they would have said: "If only its verses were well expounded!" What, whether foreign or Arabic, say: "It is for the believers a guidance and a healing; but for those who do not believe, it is a heaviness in their ears, and for them it is a blindness. It is as if, those[740] were called from a distant place."

وَلَوْ جَعَلْنَاهُ قُرْآنًا أَعْجَمِيًّا لَقَالُوا لَوْلَا فُصِّلَتْ ءَايَاتُهُۥ ءَاعْجَمِيٌّ وَعَرَبِيٌّ قُلْ هُوَ لِلَّذِينَ ءَامَنُوا هُدًى وَشِفَاءٌ وَالَّذِينَ لَا يُؤْمِنُونَ فِى ءَاذَانِهِمْ وَقْرٌ وَهُوَ عَلَيْهِمْ عَمًى أُوْلَٰئِكَ يُنَادَوْنَ مِن مَّكَانٍ بَعِيدٍ ﴿٤٤﴾

45. We have given Moses the Book, but it was the subject of controversy. Had it not been for a Word that preceded from your Lord, a decision between them would have been made. Yet they are, with respect to it, in disquieting doubt.

وَلَقَدْ ءَاتَيْنَا مُوسَى الْكِتَابَ فَاخْتُلِفَ فِيهِ وَلَوْلَا كَلِمَةٌ سَبَقَتْ مِن رَّبِّكَ لَقُضِيَ بَيْنَهُمْ وَإِنَّهُمْ لَفِى شَكٍّ مِّنْهُ مُرِيبٍ ﴿٤٥﴾

46. He who performs a righteous deed performs it to his own advantage, and he who perpetrates evil perpetrates it to his loss. Your Lord is not unjust to His servants.

مَّنْ عَمِلَ صَالِحًا فَلِنَفْسِهِۦ وَمَنْ أَسَاءَ فَعَلَيْهَا وَمَا رَبُّكَ بِظَلَّامٍ لِّلْعَبِيدِ ﴿٤٦﴾

47. Upon Him devolves the knowledge of the Hour. No fruit comes out of its bud and no female bears or delivers but with His Knowledge. And on the Day He shall call out to them: "Where are My associates?", they will say: "We proclaim unto You: 'None of us is a witness.' "

۞ إِلَيْهِ يُرَدُّ عِلْمُ السَّاعَةِ وَمَا تَخْرُجُ مِن ثَمَرَاتٍ مِّنْ أَكْمَامِهَا وَمَا تَحْمِلُ مِنْ أُنثَى وَلَا تَضَعُ إِلَّا بِعِلْمِهِۦ وَيَوْمَ يُنَادِيهِمْ أَيْنَ شُرَكَاءِى قَالُوا ءَاذَنَّاكَ مَا مِنَّا مِن شَهِيدٍ ﴿٤٧﴾

48. And what they used to allege formerly will stray away from them and they will realize that they have no escape.

وَضَلَّ عَنْهُم مَّا كَانُوا يَدْعُونَ مِن قَبْلُ وَظَنُّوا مَا لَهُم مِّن مَّحِيصٍ ﴿٤٨﴾

49. Man does not tire of praying for good, but when evil touches him he becomes downcast and despondent.

لَّا يَسْأَمُ الْإِنسَانُ مِن دُعَاءِ الْخَيْرِ وَإِن مَّسَّهُ الشَّرُّ فَيَؤُوسٌ قَنُوطٌ ﴿٤٩﴾

---

740. The unbelievers.

50. And if We let him taste a mercy from Us after some adversity that has visited him, he will say: "This is mine and I do not believe the Hour is coming. If I am returned to my Lord, I will surely have the fairest reward." We shall, then, inform the unbelievers about the things they did and will make them taste an awful punishment.

وَلَئِنْ أَذَقْنَاهُ رَحْمَةً مِّنَّا مِنْ بَعْدِ ضَرَّاءَ مَسَّتْهُ لَيَقُولَنَّ هَذَا لِي وَمَا أَظُنُّ ٱلسَّاعَةَ قَآئِمَةً وَلَئِن رُّجِعْتُ إِلَى رَبِّى إِنَّ لِي عِندَهُ لَلْحُسْنَى فَلَنُنَبِّئَنَّ ٱلَّذِينَ كَفَرُواْ بِمَا عَمِلُواْ وَلَنُذِيقَنَّهُم مِّنْ عَذَابٍ غَلِيظٍ ﴿٥٠﴾

51. If We are gracious to man, he slinks away and turns aside; and if an evil touches him, he is given to constant prayer.

وَإِذَآ أَنْعَمْنَا عَلَى ٱلْإِنسَٰنِ أَعْرَضَ وَنَأَى بِجَانِبِهِۦ وَإِذَا مَسَّهُ ٱلشَّرُّ فَذُو دُعَآءٍ عَرِيضٍ ﴿٥١﴾

52. Say: "What do you think? If it[741] is from Allah and then you disbelieve in it, who is more astray than one who is given to profound contention?"

قُلْ أَرَءَيْتُمْ إِن كَانَ مِنْ عِندِ ٱللَّهِ ثُمَّ كَفَرْتُم بِهِۦ مَنْ أَضَلُّ مِمَّنْ هُوَ فِى شِقَاقٍ بَعِيدٍ ﴿٥٢﴾

53. We shall show them Our Signs in the distant regions and in their own souls, until it becomes clear to them that it is the Truth. Does it not suffice your Lord that He is a Witness of everything?

سَنُرِيهِمْ ءَايَٰتِنَا فِى ٱلْآفَاقِ وَفِى أَنفُسِهِمْ حَتَّى يَتَبَيَّنَ لَهُمْ أَنَّهُ ٱلْحَقُّ أَوَلَمْ يَكْفِ بِرَبِّكَ أَنَّهُ عَلَى كُلِّ شَىْءٍ شَهِيدٌ ﴿٥٣﴾

54. Lo and behold, they are in doubt regarding the Encounter of their Lord. Lo, He truly encompasses everything.

أَلَآ إِنَّهُمْ فِى مِرْيَةٍ مِّن لِّقَآءِ رَبِّهِمْ أَلَآ إِنَّهُ بِكُلِّ شَىْءٍ مُّحِيطٌ ﴿٥٤﴾

Sûrat Ash-Shura, (Consultation) 42

In the Name of Allah,
the Compassionate, the Merciful

بِسْمِ ٱللَّهِ ٱلرَّحْمَٰنِ ٱلرَّحِيمِ

1. Ha - Mim.

حمٓ ﴿١﴾

2. 'Ain - Sin - Qaf.[742]

عٓسٓقٓ ﴿٢﴾

3. Thus Allah, the All-Mighty, the All-Wise reveals to you and to those who preceded you.

كَذَٰلِكَ يُوحِىٓ إِلَيْكَ وَإِلَى ٱلَّذِينَ مِن قَبْلِكَ ٱللَّهُ ٱلْعَزِيزُ ٱلْحَكِيمُ ﴿٣﴾

---

741. The Qur'an.
742. This Surah has two sets of symbols, which is unusual.

4. To Him belongs what is in the heavens or on earth, and He is the All-High, the Great.

لَهُ مَا فِى ٱلسَّمَٰوَٰتِ وَمَا فِى ٱلْأَرْضِ وَهُوَ ٱلْعَلِىُّ ٱلْعَظِيمُ ۞

5. The heavens are almost rent asunder above them; while the angels proclaim the praise of their Lord and ask forgiveness for those on earth. Lo, Allah is truly the All-Forgiving, the Merciful!

تَكَادُ ٱلسَّمَٰوَٰتُ يَتَفَطَّرْنَ مِن فَوْقِهِنَّ وَٱلْمَلَٰئِكَةُ يُسَبِّحُونَ بِحَمْدِ رَبِّهِمْ وَيَسْتَغْفِرُونَ لِمَن فِى ٱلْأَرْضِ أَلَآ إِنَّ ٱللَّهَ هُوَ ٱلْغَفُورُ ٱلرَّحِيمُ ۞

6. Those who have taken other protectors, apart from Him, Allah oversees them and you are not their guardian.

وَٱلَّذِينَ ٱتَّخَذُوا۟ مِن دُونِهِۦٓ أَوْلِيَآءَ ٱللَّهُ حَفِيظٌ عَلَيْهِمْ وَمَآ أَنتَ عَلَيْهِم بِوَكِيلٍ ۞

7. And so, We revealed to you an Arabic Qur'an in order to warn the Mother of the Cities[743] and those around it and to warn of the Day of Forgathering which is undoubted, whereon a group shall be in Paradise and a group shall be in Hell.

وَكَذَٰلِكَ أَوْحَيْنَآ إِلَيْكَ قُرْءَانًا عَرَبِيًّا لِّتُنذِرَ أُمَّ ٱلْقُرَىٰ وَمَنْ حَوْلَهَا وَتُنذِرَ يَوْمَ ٱلْجَمْعِ لَا رَيْبَ فِيهِ فَرِيقٌ فِى ٱلْجَنَّةِ وَفَرِيقٌ فِى ٱلسَّعِيرِ ۞

8. Had Allah wished, He would have made them a single nation, but He admits whom He wishes into His Mercy. Yet, the wrong-doers have no protector or supporter.

وَلَوْ شَآءَ ٱللَّهُ لَجَعَلَهُمْ أُمَّةً وَٰحِدَةً وَلَٰكِن يُدْخِلُ مَن يَشَآءُ فِى رَحْمَتِهِۦ وَٱلظَّٰلِمُونَ مَا لَهُم مِّن وَلِىٍّ وَلَا نَصِيرٍ ۞

9. Or have they taken, apart from Him, other protectors? Surely Allah is the Protector and He revives the dead and has power over everything.

أَمِ ٱتَّخَذُوا۟ مِن دُونِهِۦٓ أَوْلِيَآءَ فَٱللَّهُ هُوَ ٱلْوَلِىُّ وَهُوَ يُحْىِ ٱلْمَوْتَىٰ وَهُوَ عَلَىٰ كُلِّ شَىْءٍ قَدِيرٌ ۞

10. Whatever you disagree upon, unto Allah is the decision thereof. That, then, is Allah, my Lord. In Him I have put my trust, and unto Him I repent.

وَمَا ٱخْتَلَفْتُمْ فِيهِ مِن شَىْءٍ فَحُكْمُهُۥٓ إِلَى ٱللَّهِ ذَٰلِكُمُ ٱللَّهُ رَبِّى عَلَيْهِ تَوَكَّلْتُ وَإِلَيْهِ أُنِيبُ ۞

11. Creator of the heavens and the earth. Of yourselves He has made couples and of the cattle pairs, multiplying you thereby. Nothing is like unto Him; He is the All-Hearing, the All-Seeing.

فَاطِرُ ٱلسَّمَٰوَٰتِ وَٱلْأَرْضِ جَعَلَ لَكُم مِّنْ أَنفُسِكُمْ أَزْوَٰجًا وَمِنَ ٱلْأَنْعَٰمِ أَزْوَٰجًا يَذْرَؤُكُمْ فِيهِ لَيْسَ كَمِثْلِهِۦ شَىْءٌ وَهُوَ ٱلسَّمِيعُ ٱلْبَصِيرُ ۞

---

743. Mecca.

12. To Him belong the keys of the heavens and the earth. He expands the provision to whom He wishes or constricts it. Indeed, He has knowledge of everything.

لَهُۥ مَقَالِيدُ ٱلسَّمَـٰوَٰتِ وَٱلْأَرْضِ يَبْسُطُ ٱلرِّزْقَ لِمَن يَشَآءُ وَيَقْدِرُ إِنَّهُۥ بِكُلِّ شَىْءٍ عَلِيمٌ ﴿١٢﴾

13. He has enacted for you as a religion that which He charged Noah with and that which We revealed to you, and what We charged Abraham, Moses and Jesus with: "Perform the religion and do not diverge therein." Outrageous in the sight of the idolaters is what you call them to. Allah elects unto Himself whomever He pleases and guides to Himself whoever repents.

۞ شَرَعَ لَكُم مِّنَ ٱلدِّينِ مَا وَصَّىٰ بِهِۦ نُوحًا وَٱلَّذِىٓ أَوْحَيْنَآ إِلَيْكَ وَمَا وَصَّيْنَا بِهِۦٓ إِبْرَٰهِيمَ وَمُوسَىٰ وَعِيسَىٰٓ أَنْ أَقِيمُوا۟ ٱلدِّينَ وَلَا تَتَفَرَّقُوا۟ فِيهِ كَبُرَ عَلَى ٱلْمُشْرِكِينَ مَا تَدْعُوهُمْ إِلَيْهِ ٱللَّهُ يَجْتَبِىٓ إِلَيْهِ مَن يَشَآءُ وَيَهْدِىٓ إِلَيْهِ مَن يُنِيبُ ﴿١٣﴾

14. They did not split up except after the Knowledge came to them out of contention among themselves. Yet, but for a Word which preceded from your Lord deferring them until an appointed term, judgement would have been pronounced upon them. Indeed, those to whom the Book was bequeathed, after them, are in disquieting doubt concerning it.

وَمَا تَفَرَّقُوٓا۟ إِلَّا مِنۢ بَعْدِ مَا جَآءَهُمُ ٱلْعِلْمُ بَغْيًۢا بَيْنَهُمْ وَلَوْلَا كَلِمَةٌ سَبَقَتْ مِن رَّبِّكَ إِلَىٰٓ أَجَلٍ مُّسَمًّى لَّقُضِىَ بَيْنَهُمْ وَإِنَّ ٱلَّذِينَ أُورِثُوا۟ ٱلْكِتَـٰبَ مِنۢ بَعْدِهِمْ لَفِى شَكٍّ مِّنْهُ مُرِيبٍ ﴿١٤﴾

15. Therefore, summon and be upright as you were commanded, and do not follow their fancies, but say: "I believe in whatever Book Allah has sent down. I have been commanded to judge justly between you. Allah is our Lord and your Lord; we have our deeds and you have your deeds. There is no dispute between us and you; Allah will gather us together and unto Him is the ultimate return."

فَلِذَٰلِكَ فَٱدْعُ وَٱسْتَقِمْ كَمَآ أُمِرْتَ وَلَا تَتَّبِعْ أَهْوَآءَهُمْ وَقُلْ ءَامَنتُ بِمَآ أَنزَلَ ٱللَّهُ مِن كِتَـٰبٍ وَأُمِرْتُ لِأَعْدِلَ بَيْنَكُمُ ٱللَّهُ رَبُّنَا وَرَبُّكُمْ لَنَآ أَعْمَـٰلُنَا وَلَكُمْ أَعْمَـٰلُكُمْ لَا حُجَّةَ بَيْنَنَا وَبَيْنَكُمُ ٱللَّهُ يَجْمَعُ بَيْنَنَا وَإِلَيْهِ ٱلْمَصِيرُ ﴿١٥﴾

16. Those who argue concerning Allah, after His call was answered, their argument is null and void in the sight of their Lord, and upon them is a scourge, and a terrible punishment awaits them.

وَٱلَّذِينَ يُحَآجُّونَ فِى ٱللَّهِ مِنۢ بَعْدِ مَا ٱسْتُجِيبَ لَهُۥ حُجَّتُهُمْ دَاحِضَةٌ عِندَ رَبِّهِمْ وَعَلَيْهِمْ غَضَبٌ وَلَهُمْ عَذَابٌ شَدِيدٌ ﴿١٦﴾

17. It is Allah Who sent down the Book in truth, and the Balance[744] too. What do you know? Perhaps the Hour is near.

18. Those who do not believe in it ask you to hasten it, whereas the believers are in awe of it and know that it is the Truth. Indeed, those who are in doubt concerning the Hour are in profound error.

19. Allah is kind to His servants, providing for whomever He wishes; and He is the All-Powerful, the All-Mighty.

20. He who wishes the tillage of the Hereafter, We will increase his tillage, and he who wishes the tillage of the present life, We will give him thereof; but in the Hereafter, he will have no share.

21. Or do they have associates who enacted for them as a religion that for which Allah did not give leave? But for the Word of Decision, judgement would have been pronounced upon them. Surely, the wrongdoers will suffer a painful punishment.

22. You see the wrongdoers in awe of what they have earned, although it is bound to catch up with them; but those who believe and do the righteous deeds shall be consigned to the greenest gardens, wherein they have whatever they desire from their Lord. That is the great bounty.

23. That is the good news which Allah announces to His servants who believe, and do the good deeds. Say: "I ask you no reward for it except friendship towards kinsmen." Whoever performs a good deed, We shall increase its goodness. Allah is truly All-Forgiving, Thankful.

اللَّهُ الَّذِى أَنزَلَ الْكِتَٰبَ بِالْحَقِّ وَالْمِيزَانَ وَمَا يُدْرِيكَ لَعَلَّ السَّاعَةَ قَرِيبٌ ۝

يَسْتَعْجِلُ بِهَا الَّذِينَ لَا يُؤْمِنُونَ بِهَا وَالَّذِينَ ءَامَنُوا مُشْفِقُونَ مِنْهَا وَيَعْلَمُونَ أَنَّهَا الْحَقُّ أَلَا إِنَّ الَّذِينَ يُمَارُونَ فِى السَّاعَةِ لَفِى ضَلَٰلٍ بَعِيدٍ ۝

اللَّهُ لَطِيفٌ بِعِبَادِهِ يَرْزُقُ مَن يَشَاءُ وَهُوَ الْقَوِىُّ الْعَزِيزُ ۝

مَن كَانَ يُرِيدُ حَرْثَ الْأَخِرَةِ نَزِدْ لَهُ فِى حَرْثِهِ وَمَن كَانَ يُرِيدُ حَرْثَ الدُّنْيَا نُؤْتِهِ مِنْهَا وَمَا لَهُ فِى الْأَخِرَةِ مِن نَّصِيبٍ ۝

أَمْ لَهُمْ شُرَكَٰؤُا شَرَعُوا لَهُم مِّنَ الدِّينِ مَا لَمْ يَأْذَنۢ بِهِ اللَّهُ وَلَوْلَا كَلِمَةُ الْفَصْلِ لَقُضِىَ بَيْنَهُمْ وَإِنَّ الظَّٰلِمِينَ لَهُمْ عَذَابٌ أَلِيمٌ ۝

تَرَى الظَّٰلِمِينَ مُشْفِقِينَ مِمَّا كَسَبُوا وَهُوَ وَاقِعٌ بِهِمْ وَالَّذِينَ ءَامَنُوا وَعَمِلُوا الصَّٰلِحَٰتِ فِى رَوْضَاتِ الْجَنَّاتِ لَهُم مَّا يَشَاءُونَ عِندَ رَبِّهِمْ ذَٰلِكَ هُوَ الْفَضْلُ الْكَبِيرُ ۝

ذَٰلِكَ الَّذِى يُبَشِّرُ اللَّهُ عِبَادَهُ الَّذِينَ ءَامَنُوا وَعَمِلُوا الصَّٰلِحَٰتِ قُل لَّا أَسْـَٔلُكُمْ عَلَيْهِ أَجْرًا إِلَّا الْمَوَدَّةَ فِى الْقُرْبَىٰ وَمَن يَقْتَرِفْ حَسَنَةً نَّزِدْ لَهُ فِيهَا حُسْنًا إِنَّ اللَّهَ غَفُورٌ شَكُورٌ ۝

---

744. The Balance of right and wrong.

24. Or will they say: "He has imputed falsehood to Allah"? Had Allah willed, He would have put a seal upon your heart. He obliterates falsehood and confirms the Truth by His Words. Surely, He knows the secrets hidden in the breasts.

أَمْ يَقُولُونَ افْتَرَىٰ عَلَى اللَّهِ كَذِبًا فَإِن يَشَإِ اللَّهُ يَخْتِمْ عَلَىٰ قَلْبِكَ وَيَمْحُ اللَّهُ الْبَاطِلَ وَيُحِقُّ الْحَقَّ بِكَلِمَاتِهِ إِنَّهُ عَلِيمٌ بِذَاتِ الصُّدُورِ ﴿٢٤﴾

25. It is He Who accepts the repentance of His servants, pardons the evil deeds and knows what you do.

وَهُوَ الَّذِي يَقْبَلُ التَّوْبَةَ عَنْ عِبَادِهِ وَيَعْفُوا عَنِ السَّيِّئَاتِ وَيَعْلَمُ مَا تَفْعَلُونَ ﴿٢٥﴾

26. And He answers those who believe and do the righteous deeds and increases them of His Bounty; but the unbelievers will suffer a terrible punishment.

وَيَسْتَجِيبُ الَّذِينَ ءَامَنُوا وَعَمِلُوا الصَّالِحَاتِ وَيَزِيدُهُم مِّن فَضْلِهِ وَالْكَافِرُونَ لَهُمْ عَذَابٌ شَدِيدٌ ﴿٢٦﴾

27. Had Allah expanded provision for His servants, they would have exceeded the bounds of injustice in the land; but He sends down in measure whatever He wishes. He is truly Well-Informed about His servants, All-Seeing.

۞ وَلَوْ بَسَطَ اللَّهُ الرِّزْقَ لِعِبَادِهِ لَبَغَوْا فِي الْأَرْضِ وَلَٰكِن يُنَزِّلُ بِقَدَرٍ مَّا يَشَاءُ إِنَّهُ بِعِبَادِهِ خَبِيرٌ بَصِيرٌ ﴿٢٧﴾

28. It is He Who sends the rain down, after they have despaired, and spreads out His Mercy. He is the Protector, the Praiseworthy.

وَهُوَ الَّذِي يُنَزِّلُ الْغَيْثَ مِنْ بَعْدِ مَا قَنَطُوا وَيَنْشُرُ رَحْمَتَهُ وَهُوَ الْوَلِيُّ الْحَمِيدُ ﴿٢٨﴾

29. And of His Signs is the creation of the heavens and the earth and the beasts He has scattered abroad in them; and He is able to gather them together, whenever He wishes.

وَمِنْ ءَايَاتِهِ خَلْقُ السَّمَاوَاتِ وَالْأَرْضِ وَمَا بَثَّ فِيهِمَا مِن دَابَّةٍ وَهُوَ عَلَىٰ جَمْعِهِمْ إِذَا يَشَاءُ قَدِيرٌ ﴿٢٩﴾

30. Whatever calamity might hit you is due to what your hands have earned; yet He pardons much.

وَمَا أَصَابَكُم مِّن مُّصِيبَةٍ فَبِمَا كَسَبَتْ أَيْدِيكُمْ وَيَعْفُوا عَن كَثِيرٍ ﴿٣٠﴾

31. You are not able to thwart Him on earth and you do not have, apart from Allah, any protector or supporter.

وَمَا أَنتُم بِمُعْجِزِينَ فِي الْأَرْضِ وَمَا لَكُم مِّن دُونِ اللَّهِ مِن وَلِيٍّ وَلَا نَصِيرٍ ﴿٣١﴾

32. And of His Signs are ships sailing in the sea like high mountains.

وَمِنْ ءَايَاتِهِ الْجَوَارِ فِي الْبَحْرِ كَالْأَعْلَامِ ﴿٣٢﴾

33. If He wishes, He will calm the wind, and then they will remain motionless upon its surface. In that are signs to every steadfast and thankful person;

إِن يَشَأْ يُسْكِنِ الرِّيحَ فَيَظْلَلْنَ رَوَاكِدَ عَلَىٰ ظَهْرِهِ إِنَّ فِي ذَٰلِكَ لَآيَاتٍ لِّكُلِّ صَبَّارٍ شَكُورٍ ﴿٣٣﴾

490

34. Or destroy them for what they[745] have earned, while pardoning many;

35. That those who dispute concerning Our Signs might know that they have no escape.

36. For whatever you have been given is only the enjoyment of the present life, but what Allah has is better and more enduring for those who believe and put their trust in their Lord;

37. And those who avoid the grave sins and foul acts, and, if angered, will forgive;

38. And those who answer their Lord, and perform the prayer - their affair being a counsel among themselves, and of what We provided them with, they spend;

39. And those who, if they are oppressed, will overcome.

40. The reward of evil is an evil like it, but he who pardons and makes amends, his wage is with Allah. Indeed, He does not like the wrongdoers.

41. He who overcomes after being wronged - upon those there is no reproach.

42. The reproach is surely upon those who wrong mankind and transgress in the land unjustly. To those a painful punishment is in store.

43. But he who bears patiently and forgives - that is a sign of real resolve.

44. Whoever Allah leads astray will have no protector apart from Him; and you will see the wrongdoers when they see the punishment saying: "Is there a way of going back?"

---

745. The passengers.

أَوْ يُوبِقْهُنَّ بِمَا كَسَبُوا وَيَعْفُ عَن كَثِيرٍ ۝

وَيَعْلَمَ الَّذِينَ يُجَادِلُونَ فِي ءَايَـٰتِنَا مَا لَهُم مِّن مَّحِيصٍ ۝

فَمَا أُوتِيتُم مِّن شَىْءٍ فَمَتَـٰعُ الْحَيَوٰةِ الدُّنْيَا وَمَا عِندَ اللَّهِ خَيْرٌ وَأَبْقَىٰ لِلَّذِينَ ءَامَنُوا وَعَلَىٰ رَبِّهِمْ يَتَوَكَّلُونَ ۝

وَالَّذِينَ يَجْتَنِبُونَ كَبَـٰئِرَ الْإِثْمِ وَالْفَوَٰحِشَ وَإِذَا مَا غَضِبُوا هُمْ يَغْفِرُونَ ۝

وَالَّذِينَ اسْتَجَابُوا لِرَبِّهِمْ وَأَقَامُوا الصَّلَوٰةَ وَأَمْرُهُمْ شُورَىٰ بَيْنَهُمْ وَمِمَّا رَزَقْنَـٰهُمْ يُنفِقُونَ ۝

وَالَّذِينَ إِذَا أَصَابَهُمُ الْبَغْيُ هُمْ يَنتَصِرُونَ ۝

وَجَزَٰٓؤُا۟ سَيِّئَةٍ سَيِّئَةٌ مِّثْلُهَا فَمَنْ عَفَا وَأَصْلَحَ فَأَجْرُهُ عَلَى اللَّهِ إِنَّهُ لَا يُحِبُّ الظَّـٰلِمِينَ ۝

وَلَمَنِ انتَصَرَ بَعْدَ ظُلْمِهِ فَأُو۟لَـٰٓئِكَ مَا عَلَيْهِم مِّن سَبِيلٍ ۝

إِنَّمَا السَّبِيلُ عَلَى الَّذِينَ يَظْلِمُونَ النَّاسَ وَيَبْغُونَ فِي الْأَرْضِ بِغَيْرِ الْحَقِّ أُو۟لَـٰٓئِكَ لَهُمْ عَذَابٌ أَلِيمٌ ۝

وَلَمَن صَبَرَ وَغَفَرَ إِنَّ ذَٰلِكَ لَمِنْ عَزْمِ الْأُمُورِ ۝

وَمَن يُضْلِلِ اللَّهُ فَمَا لَهُ مِن وَلِيٍّ مِّنْ بَعْدِهِ وَتَرَى الظَّـٰلِمِينَ لَمَّا رَأَوُا الْعَذَابَ يَقُولُونَ هَلْ إِلَىٰ مَرَدٍّ مِّن سَبِيلٍ ۝

45. You will see them being exposed to it,[746] abject in their humiliation, looking askew. The believers will say: "The losers are truly those who have lost themselves and their families on the Day of Resurrection. Surely, the wrongdoers will suffer lasting punishment."

46. They have no protectors to support them, apart from Allah. Whoever Allah leads astray has no way out.

47. Answer your Lord's Call before a Day comes from Allah that cannot be turned back. Upon that Day you will have no shelter, no disclaimer.

48. Should they turn away, We have not sent you as a guardian to watch over them; incumbent on you is delivering the Message only. Indeed, when We make man taste a mercy from Us, he rejoices in it; but when they are afflicted with a misfortune, on account of what their hands had previously perpetrated, then man is truly thankless.

49. To Allah belongs the dominion of the heavens and the earth. He creates whatever He pleases, and grants whomever He wishes females, and whomever He wishes males.

50. Or He marries them, males and females, and makes whomever He wishes sterile. Indeed, He is All-Knowing, All-Powerful.

51. It is not given to any mortal that Allah should speak to him, except by Revelation or from behind a veil. Otherwise, He sends forth a Messenger who reveals by His Permission whatever He wishes. He is, indeed, All-High, All-Wise.

---

746. The Fire.

52. That is how We revealed to you a Spirit by Our Command. You did not know what the Book is nor what is Belief; but We made it a light, by which We guide whomever We wish of Our servants. You will surely guide unto a Straight Path;

53. The Path of Allah, to Whom belongs whatever is in the heavens or on earth. Lo, unto Allah will all matters ultimately revert.

Sûrat Az-Zukhruf,
(Adornment) 43

In the Name of Allah,
the Compassionate, the Merciful

1. Ha - Mim.

2. By the Manifest Book.

3. We have made it an Arabic Qur'an that perchance you may understand.

4. And, indeed, it is in the Mother of the Book, with Us, lofty and wise.

5. Shall We then divert the Reminder from you mercifully, because you are an extravagant people?

6. How many a Prophet have We sent unto the ancients?

7. But not a Prophet came to them whom they did not mock.

8. So We destroyed a people mightier than they in valour; and the example of the ancients was gone.

9. If you ask them: "Who created the heavens and the earth?", they will certainly say: "The All-Mighty, the All-Knowing created them."

10. He Who made the earth level ground for you and made for you pathways therein, that perchance you may be well-guided;

وَكَذَٰلِكَ أَوْحَيْنَآ إِلَيْكَ رُوحًا مِّنْ أَمْرِنَا مَا كُنتَ تَدْرِى مَا ٱلْكِتَٰبُ وَلَا ٱلْإِيمَٰنُ وَلَٰكِن جَعَلْنَٰهُ نُورًا نَّهْدِى بِهِۦ مَن نَّشَآءُ مِنْ عِبَادِنَا وَإِنَّكَ لَتَهْدِىٓ إِلَىٰ صِرَٰطٍ مُّسْتَقِيمٍ ۝

صِرَٰطِ ٱللَّهِ ٱلَّذِى لَهُۥ مَا فِى ٱلسَّمَٰوَٰتِ وَمَا فِى ٱلْأَرْضِ أَلَآ إِلَى ٱللَّهِ تَصِيرُ ٱلْأُمُورُ ۝

بِسْمِ ٱللَّهِ ٱلرَّحْمَٰنِ ٱلرَّحِيمِ

حمٓ ۝

وَٱلْكِتَٰبِ ٱلْمُبِينِ ۝

إِنَّا جَعَلْنَٰهُ قُرْءَٰنًا عَرَبِيًّا لَّعَلَّكُمْ تَعْقِلُونَ ۝

وَإِنَّهُۥ فِىٓ أُمِّ ٱلْكِتَٰبِ لَدَيْنَا لَعَلِىٌّ حَكِيمٌ ۝

أَفَنَضْرِبُ عَنكُمُ ٱلذِّكْرَ صَفْحًا أَن كُنتُمْ قَوْمًا مُّسْرِفِينَ ۝

وَكَمْ أَرْسَلْنَا مِن نَّبِىٍّ فِى ٱلْأَوَّلِينَ ۝

وَمَا يَأْتِيهِم مِّن نَّبِىٍّ إِلَّا كَانُوا۟ بِهِۦ يَسْتَهْزِءُونَ ۝

فَأَهْلَكْنَآ أَشَدَّ مِنْهُم بَطْشًا وَمَضَىٰ مَثَلُ ٱلْأَوَّلِينَ ۝

وَلَئِن سَأَلْتَهُم مَّنْ خَلَقَ ٱلسَّمَٰوَٰتِ وَٱلْأَرْضَ لَيَقُولُنَّ خَلَقَهُنَّ ٱلْعَزِيزُ ٱلْعَلِيمُ ۝

ٱلَّذِى جَعَلَ لَكُمُ ٱلْأَرْضَ مَهْدًا وَجَعَلَ لَكُمْ فِيهَا سُبُلًا لَّعَلَّكُمْ تَهْتَدُونَ ۝

11. And Who sent down water from heaven in set measure; and so We revived therewith a dead town. Thus you shall be brought forth;

وَٱلَّذِى نَزَّلَ مِنَ ٱلسَّمَاءِ مَاءً بِقَدَرٍ فَأَنشَرْنَا بِهِۦ بَلْدَةً مَّيْتًا كَذَلِكَ تُخْرَجُونَ ﴿١١﴾

12. And Who created all the pairs and made for you such ships and cattle as you can mount.

وَٱلَّذِى خَلَقَ ٱلْأَزْوَاجَ كُلَّهَا وَجَعَلَ لَكُم مِّنَ ٱلْفُلْكِ وَٱلْأَنْعَامِ مَا تَرْكَبُونَ ﴿١٢﴾

13. That you might sit upon their backs, then remember the Grace of your Lord when you are seated thereon and say: "Glory be to Him Who subjected this to us, whereas we were not equal to it.

لِتَسْتَوُۥا عَلَى ظُهُورِهِۦ ثُمَّ تَذْكُرُوا نِعْمَةَ رَبِّكُمْ إِذَا ٱسْتَوَيْتُمْ عَلَيْهِ وَتَقُولُوا سُبْحَانَ ٱلَّذِى سَخَّرَ لَنَا هَذَا وَمَا كُنَّا لَهُۥ مُقْرِنِينَ ﴿١٣﴾

14. "And, surely, unto our Lord we shall return."

وَإِنَّا إِلَى رَبِّنَا لَمُنقَلِبُونَ ﴿١٤﴾

15. They have attributed to Him part of His servants. Man is indeed manifestly thankless.

وَجَعَلُوا لَهُۥ مِنْ عِبَادِهِۦ جُزْءًا إِنَّ ٱلْإِنسَانَ لَكَفُورٌ مُّبِينٌ ﴿١٥﴾

16. Or has He taken for Himself daughters from what He creates, and favoured you with sons?

أَمِ ٱتَّخَذَ مِمَّا يَخْلُقُ بَنَاتٍ وَأَصْفَاكُم بِٱلْبَنِينَ ﴿١٦﴾

17. And when one of them is given the news of what he attributes the like thereof,[747] to the All-Compassionate, his face becomes darkened and he is filled with gloom.

وَإِذَا بُشِّرَ أَحَدُهُم بِمَا ضَرَبَ لِلرَّحْمَنِ مَثَلًا ظَلَّ وَجْهُهُۥ مُسْوَدًّا وَهُوَ كَظِيمٌ ﴿١٧﴾

18. What, one who is brought up in luxury but in the art of disputation is not well-versed?[748]

أَوَمَن يُنَشَّؤُا فِى ٱلْحِلْيَةِ وَهُوَ فِى ٱلْخِصَامِ غَيْرُ مُبِينٍ ﴿١٨﴾

19. And they have made the angels, who are servants of the All-Compassionate, females. What, have they witnessed their creation? Surely, their testimony will be written down and they will be questioned.

وَجَعَلُوا ٱلْمَلَائِكَةَ ٱلَّذِينَ هُمْ عِبَادُ ٱلرَّحْمَنِ إِنَاثًا أَشَهِدُوا خَلْقَهُمْ سَتُكْتَبُ شَهَادَتُهُمْ وَيُسْأَلُونَ ﴿١٩﴾

20. They say: "If the All-Compassionate had willed it, we would not have worshipped them." They have no knowledge of that at all; they are only lying.

وَقَالُوا لَوْ شَاءَ ٱلرَّحْمَنُ مَا عَبَدْنَاهُم مَّا لَهُم بِذَلِكَ مِنْ عِلْمٍ إِنْ هُمْ إِلَّا يَخْرُصُونَ ﴿٢٠﴾

---

747. That is, daughters. Thus are daughters distinguished from boys.
748. To be assigned to God?

21. Or have We given them a Book prior to this one,[749] so that they are clinging to it?

أَمْ ءَاتَيْنَـٰهُمْ كِتَـٰبًا مِّن قَبْلِهِ فَهُم بِهِۦ مُسْتَمْسِكُونَ ﴿٢١﴾

22. No, they say: "We found our fathers upon this course,[750] and we are actually following in their footsteps."

بَلْ قَالُوٓا۟ إِنَّا وَجَدْنَآ ءَابَآءَنَا عَلَىٰٓ أُمَّةٍ وَإِنَّا عَلَىٰٓ ءَاثَـٰرِهِم مُّهْتَدُونَ ﴿٢٢﴾

23. Likewise, We never sent forth a warner to any city before you, but its affluent chiefs have said: "We have found our fathers upon a certain course, and we are actually following in their footsteps."

وَكَذَٰلِكَ مَآ أَرْسَلْنَا مِن قَبْلِكَ فِى قَرْيَةٍ مِّن نَّذِيرٍ إِلَّا قَالَ مُتْرَفُوهَآ إِنَّا وَجَدْنَآ ءَابَآءَنَا عَلَىٰٓ أُمَّةٍ وَإِنَّا عَلَىٰٓ ءَاثَـٰرِهِم مُّقْتَدُونَ ﴿٢٣﴾

24. He said: "What if I were to bring you a more certain guidance than what you found your fathers upon?" They said: "We are definitely disbelievers in what you were sent forth with."

۞ قَـٰلَ أَوَلَوْ جِئْتُكُم بِأَهْدَىٰ مِمَّا وَجَدتُّمْ عَلَيْهِ ءَابَآءَكُمْ قَالُوٓا۟ إِنَّا بِمَآ أُرْسِلْتُم بِهِۦ كَـٰفِرُونَ ﴿٢٤﴾

25. So, We wreaked vengeance upon them. Behold, then, what was the fate of those who deny.

فَٱنتَقَمْنَا مِنْهُمْ فَٱنظُرْ كَيْفَ كَانَ عَـٰقِبَةُ ٱلْمُكَذِّبِينَ ﴿٢٥﴾

26. When Abraham said to his father and his people: "I am certainly quit of what you worship;

وَإِذْ قَالَ إِبْرَٰهِيمُ لِأَبِيهِ وَقَوْمِهِۦٓ إِنَّنِى بَرَآءٌ مِّمَّا تَعْبُدُونَ ﴿٢٦﴾

27. "Except for Him Who created me. He will certainly guide me well."

إِلَّا ٱلَّذِى فَطَرَنِى فَإِنَّهُۥ سَيَهْدِينِ ﴿٢٧﴾

28. And he made it an enduring word in his progeny, that perchance they might repent.

وَجَعَلَهَا كَلِمَةًۢ بَاقِيَةً فِى عَقِبِهِۦ لَعَلَّهُمْ يَرْجِعُونَ ﴿٢٨﴾

29. Yet, I gave these and their fathers some enjoyment, till the Truth and a manifest Messenger came to them.

بَلْ مَتَّعْتُ هَـٰٓؤُلَآءِ وَءَابَآءَهُمْ حَتَّىٰ جَآءَهُمُ ٱلْحَقُّ وَرَسُولٌ مُّبِينٌ ﴿٢٩﴾

30. But when the Truth came to them, they said: "That is sorcery, and we are definitely disbelieving therein."

وَلَمَّا جَآءَهُمُ ٱلْحَقُّ قَالُوا۟ هَـٰذَا سِحْرٌ وَإِنَّا بِهِۦ كَـٰفِرُونَ ﴿٣٠﴾

31. They also said: "If only this Qur'an had been sent down upon some outstanding man from the two cities."[751]

وَقَالُوا۟ لَوْلَا نُزِّلَ هَـٰذَا ٱلْقُرْءَانُ عَلَىٰ رَجُلٍ مِّنَ ٱلْقَرْيَتَيْنِ عَظِيمٍ ﴿٣١﴾

---

749. The Qur'an.
750. *Ummah*, path or creed.
751. Mecca and Ta'if.

32. Do they apportion the Mercy of your Lord? It is We Who have apportioned their livelihood among them in the present life and raised some of them in rank above others; so that some would be subservient to the others. Your Lord's Mercy is better than what they amass.

33. And were it not for fear that mankind would be a single nation, We would have assigned to those who disbelieve in the All-Compassionate, roofs of silver for their houses and stairways upon which they ascend;

34. And portals for their houses and couches upon which they recline;

35. And adornment of gold; but all that is nothing but worldly enjoyment. Yet the Hereafter with your Lord is reserved for the God-fearing.

36. And he who is blind to the remembrance of the All-Compassionate, We shall assign to him a demon, who will be his constant companion.

37. They[752] will certainly bar them from the Path, while they think that they are well-guided.

38. But when he comes to Us, he will say: "Would that between me and you is the distance between East and West." What a wretched companion!

39. Today, it will not avail you, being wrongdoers, that you are partners in punishment.

40. Are you able, then, to make the deaf hear or guide the blind and him who is in manifest error?

أَهُمْ يَقْسِمُونَ رَحْمَتَ رَبِّكَ نَحْنُ قَسَمْنَا بَيْنَهُم مَّعِيشَتَهُمْ فِى ٱلْحَيَوٰةِ ٱلدُّنْيَا وَرَفَعْنَا بَعْضَهُمْ فَوْقَ بَعْضٍ دَرَجَٰتٍ لِّيَتَّخِذَ بَعْضُهُم بَعْضًا سُخْرِيًّا وَرَحْمَتُ رَبِّكَ خَيْرٌ مِّمَّا يَجْمَعُونَ ﴿٣٢﴾

وَلَوْلَآ أَن يَكُونَ ٱلنَّاسُ أُمَّةً وَٰحِدَةً لَّجَعَلْنَا لِمَن يَكْفُرُ بِٱلرَّحْمَٰنِ لِبُيُوتِهِمْ سُقُفًا مِّن فِضَّةٍ وَمَعَارِجَ عَلَيْهَا يَظْهَرُونَ ﴿٣٣﴾

وَلِبُيُوتِهِمْ أَبْوَٰبًا وَسُرُرًا عَلَيْهَا يَتَّكِئُونَ ﴿٣٤﴾

وَزُخْرُفًا وَإِن كُلُّ ذَٰلِكَ لَمَّا مَتَٰعُ ٱلْحَيَوٰةِ ٱلدُّنْيَا وَٱلْءَاخِرَةُ عِندَ رَبِّكَ لِلْمُتَّقِينَ ﴿٣٥﴾

وَمَن يَعْشُ عَن ذِكْرِ ٱلرَّحْمَٰنِ نُقَيِّضْ لَهُۥ شَيْطَٰنًا فَهُوَ لَهُۥ قَرِينٌ ﴿٣٦﴾

وَإِنَّهُمْ لَيَصُدُّونَهُمْ عَنِ ٱلسَّبِيلِ وَيَحْسَبُونَ أَنَّهُم مُّهْتَدُونَ ﴿٣٧﴾

حَتَّىٰٓ إِذَا جَآءَنَا قَالَ يَٰلَيْتَ بَيْنِى وَبَيْنَكَ بُعْدَ ٱلْمَشْرِقَيْنِ فَبِئْسَ ٱلْقَرِينُ ﴿٣٨﴾

وَلَن يَنفَعَكُمُ ٱلْيَوْمَ إِذ ظَّلَمْتُمْ أَنَّكُمْ فِى ٱلْعَذَابِ مُشْتَرِكُونَ ﴿٣٩﴾

أَفَأَنتَ تُسْمِعُ ٱلصُّمَّ أَوْ تَهْدِى ٱلْعُمْىَ وَمَن كَانَ فِى ضَلَٰلٍ مُّبِينٍ ﴿٤٠﴾

---

752. The demons.

41. Were We to carry you off, We would then wreak vengeance upon them;

فَإِمَّا نَذْهَبَنَّ بِكَ فَإِنَّا مِنْهُم مُّنتَقِمُونَ ﴿٤١﴾

42. Or show you that which We have promised. For We certainly have power over them.

أَوْ نُرِيَنَّكَ الَّذِى وَعَدْنَهُمْ فَإِنَّا عَلَيْهِم مُّقْتَدِرُونَ ﴿٤٢﴾

43. Cling then to what was revealed to you; you are certainly upon a Straight Path.

فَاسْتَمْسِكْ بِالَّذِى أُوحِىَ إِلَيْكَ إِنَّكَ عَلَى صِرَطٍ مُّسْتَقِيمٍ ﴿٤٣﴾

44. And it[753] is surely a Reminder to you and to your people; and you shall be questioned.

وَإِنَّهُ لَذِكْرٌ لَّكَ وَلِقَوْمِكَ وَسَوْفَ تُسْئَلُونَ ﴿٤٤﴾

45. Ask those of Our Messengers We sent before you: "Have We ever set up, apart from the All-Compassionate, any other gods to be worshipped?"

وَسْئَلْ مَنْ أَرْسَلْنَا مِن قَبْلِكَ مِن رُّسُلِنَا أَجَعَلْنَا مِن دُونِ الرَّحْمَنِ ءَالِهَةً يُعْبَدُونَ ﴿٤٥﴾

46. We have in fact sent Moses with Our Signs to Pharaoh and his dignitaries. He said: "I am the Messenger of the Lord of the Worlds."

وَلَقَدْ أَرْسَلْنَا مُوسَى بِـَٔايَتِنَا إِلَى فِرْعَوْنَ وَمَلَإِيْهِ فَقَالَ إِنِّى رَسُولُ رَبِّ الْعَلَمِينَ ﴿٤٦﴾

47. But when he brought them Our Signs, lo, they laughed at them.

فَلَمَّا جَآءَهُم بِـَٔايَتِنَا إِذَا هُم مِّنْهَا يَضْحَكُونَ ﴿٤٧﴾

48. Yet, We did not show them a sign but it was greater than its counterpart. Then We seized them with punishment, that perchance they might retract.

وَمَا نُرِيهِم مِّنْ ءَايَةٍ إِلَّا هِىَ أَكْبَرُ مِنْ أُخْتِهَا وَأَخَذْنَهُم بِالْعَذَابِ لَعَلَّهُمْ يَرْجِعُونَ ﴿٤٨﴾

49. And they said (to Moses): "O Sorcerer, call upon your Lord for us, by the pledge He made with you. We shall, then, be well-guided."

وَقَالُوا يَأَيُّهَ السَّاحِرُ ادْعُ لَنَا رَبَّكَ بِمَا عَهِدَ عِندَكَ إِنَّنَا لَمُهْتَدُونَ ﴿٤٩﴾

50. But when We lifted the punishment from them, behold, they broke their pledge.

فَلَمَّا كَشَفْنَا عَنْهُمُ الْعَذَابَ إِذَا هُمْ يَنكُثُونَ ﴿٥٠﴾

51. And Pharaoh called out to his people: "O my people, do I not have the kingdom of Egypt, and these rivers flow beneath me? Do you not see, then?

وَنَادَى فِرْعَوْنُ فِى قَوْمِهِ قَالَ يَقَوْمِ أَلَيْسَ لِى مُلْكُ مِصْرَ وَهَذِهِ الْأَنْهَرُ تَجْرِى مِن تَحْتِى أَفَلَا تُبْصِرُونَ ﴿٥١﴾

52. "Or, am I not better than this weakling who cannot speak clearly?

أَمْ أَنَا خَيْرٌ مِّنْ هَذَا الَّذِى هُوَ مَهِينٌ وَلَا يَكَادُ يُبِينُ ﴿٥٢﴾

---

753. The Qur'an.

53. "Why, then, no bracelets of gold were cast down upon him or angels came with him in company?"

فَلَوْلَا أُلْقِىَ عَلَيْهِ أَسْوِرَةٌ مِّن ذَهَبٍ أَوْ جَآءَ مَعَهُ الْمَلَٰٓئِكَةُ مُقْتَرِنِينَ ﴿٥٣﴾

54. Thus, he incited his people and so they obeyed him. They were, indeed, a sinful people.

فَٱسْتَخَفَّ قَوْمَهُ فَأَطَاعُوهُ إِنَّهُمْ كَانُوا قَوْمًا فَٰسِقِينَ ﴿٥٤﴾

55. Then when they roused Our anger, We wreaked a vengeance upon them and drowned them all.

فَلَمَّآ ءَاسَفُونَا ٱنتَقَمْنَا مِنْهُمْ فَأَغْرَقْنَٰهُمْ أَجْمَعِينَ ﴿٥٥﴾

56. And so, We made them a people gone by, and an example to the others.

فَجَعَلْنَٰهُمْ سَلَفًا وَمَثَلًا لِّلْءَاخِرِينَ ﴿٥٦﴾

57. And when the son of Mary was held up as an example, behold, your people turned away from him.

۞ وَلَمَّا ضُرِبَ ٱبْنُ مَرْيَمَ مَثَلًا إِذَا قَوْمُكَ مِنْهُ يَصِدُّونَ ﴿٥٧﴾

58. They said: "Are our deities better or he?" They only cited it to you disputatiously. Indeed, they are a contentious people.

وَقَالُوٓا ءَأَٰلِهَتُنَا خَيْرٌ أَمْ هُوَ مَا ضَرَبُوهُ لَكَ إِلَّا جَدَلًا بَلْ هُمْ قَوْمٌ خَصِمُونَ ﴿٥٨﴾

59. He was merely a servant whom We favoured and set up as an example to the Children of Israel.

إِنْ هُوَ إِلَّا عَبْدٌ أَنْعَمْنَا عَلَيْهِ وَجَعَلْنَٰهُ مَثَلًا لِّبَنِىٓ إِسْرَٰٓءِيلَ ﴿٥٩﴾

60. Had We wished, We would have made of you angels to be successors on earth.

وَلَوْ نَشَآءُ لَجَعَلْنَا مِنكُم مَّلَٰٓئِكَةً فِى ٱلْأَرْضِ يَخْلُفُونَ ﴿٦٠﴾

61. And it is surely the knowledge of the Hour; so do not doubt it and follow Me. This is a Straight Path.

وَإِنَّهُ لَعِلْمٌ لِّلسَّاعَةِ فَلَا تَمْتَرُنَّ بِهَا وَٱتَّبِعُونِ هَٰذَا صِرَٰطٌ مُّسْتَقِيمٌ ﴿٦١﴾

62. And let not Satan bar you. He is, indeed, a manifest enemy of yours.

وَلَا يَصُدَّنَّكُمُ ٱلشَّيْطَٰنُ إِنَّهُ لَكُمْ عَدُوٌّ مُّبِينٌ ﴿٦٢﴾

63. When Jesus brought the clear proofs, he said: "I have come to you with the Wisdom and to make clear to you part of that whereon you are differing. So fear Allah and obey me.

وَلَمَّا جَآءَ عِيسَىٰ بِٱلْبَيِّنَٰتِ قَالَ قَدْ جِئْتُكُم بِٱلْحِكْمَةِ وَلِأُبَيِّنَ لَكُم بَعْضَ ٱلَّذِى تَخْتَلِفُونَ فِيهِ فَٱتَّقُوا ٱللَّهَ وَأَطِيعُونِ ﴿٦٣﴾

64. "Allah is, indeed, my Lord and your Lord; so worship Him. This is a Straight Path."

إِنَّ ٱللَّهَ هُوَ رَبِّى وَرَبُّكُمْ فَٱعْبُدُوهُ هَٰذَا صِرَٰطٌ مُّسْتَقِيمٌ ﴿٦٤﴾

65. Then the factions among them fell apart. Woe unto the wrongdoers, from the punishment of a painful Day.

فَٱخْتَلَفَ ٱلْأَحْزَابُ مِنۢ بَيْنِهِمْ فَوَيْلٌ لِّلَّذِينَ ظَلَمُوا مِنْ عَذَابِ يَوْمٍ أَلِيمٍ ﴿٦٥﴾

66. Are they only waiting for the Hour to come upon them suddenly, while they are unaware?

هَلْ يَنظُرُونَ إِلَّا ٱلسَّاعَةَ أَن تَأْتِيَهُم بَغْتَةً وَهُمْ لَا يَشْعُرُونَ ﴿٦٦﴾

67. Friends on that Day shall be enemies of one another; except for the God-fearing.

ٱلْأَخِلَّآءُ يَوْمَئِذٍ بَعْضُهُمْ لِبَعْضٍ عَدُوٌّ إِلَّا ٱلْمُتَّقِينَ ﴿٦٧﴾

68. O My servants, today you have no cause to fear nor to grieve.

يَٰعِبَادِ لَا خَوْفٌ عَلَيْكُمُ ٱلْيَوْمَ وَلَا أَنتُمْ تَحْزَنُونَ ﴿٦٨﴾

69. Those who believe in Our Signs and are submissive.

ٱلَّذِينَ ءَامَنُوا۟ بِـَٔايَٰتِنَا وَكَانُوا۟ مُسْلِمِينَ ﴿٦٩﴾

70. "Enter Paradise, you and your spouses joyfully.

ٱدْخُلُوا۟ ٱلْجَنَّةَ أَنتُمْ وَأَزْوَٰجُكُمْ تُحْبَرُونَ ﴿٧٠﴾

71. "Platters and cups of gold shall be passed around them, and therein shall be whatever souls desire and eyes delight in, and in it you shall dwell forever."

يُطَافُ عَلَيْهِم بِصِحَافٍ مِّن ذَهَبٍ وَأَكْوَابٍ وَفِيهَا مَا تَشْتَهِيهِ ٱلْأَنفُسُ وَتَلَذُّ ٱلْأَعْيُنُ وَأَنتُمْ فِيهَا خَٰلِدُونَ ﴿٧١﴾

72. That is the Paradise which you were given as an inheritance for what you used to do.

وَتِلْكَ ٱلْجَنَّةُ ٱلَّتِىٓ أُورِثْتُمُوهَا بِمَا كُنتُمْ تَعْمَلُونَ ﴿٧٢﴾

73. Therein you have abundant fruit from which you will eat.

لَكُمْ فِيهَا فَٰكِهَةٌ كَثِيرَةٌ مِّنْهَا تَأْكُلُونَ ﴿٧٣﴾

74. Indeed, the criminals shall suffer the punishment of Hell forever.

إِنَّ ٱلْمُجْرِمِينَ فِى عَذَابِ جَهَنَّمَ خَٰلِدُونَ ﴿٧٤﴾

75. They will not be relieved and they are in it completely confounded.

لَا يُفَتَّرُ عَنْهُمْ وَهُمْ فِيهِ مُبْلِسُونَ ﴿٧٥﴾

76. We did not wrong them, but they were the wrongdoers themselves.

وَمَا ظَلَمْنَٰهُمْ وَلَٰكِن كَانُوا۟ هُمُ ٱلظَّٰلِمِينَ ﴿٧٦﴾

77. They call out: "O Malik,[754] let your Lord be done with us." He will say: "You are surely staying on".

وَنَادَوْا۟ يَٰمَٰلِكُ لِيَقْضِ عَلَيْنَا رَبُّكَ قَالَ إِنَّكُم مَّٰكِثُونَ ﴿٧٧﴾

78. We brought you the Truth, but most of you were averse to the Truth.

لَقَدْ جِئْنَٰكُم بِٱلْحَقِّ وَلَٰكِنَّ أَكْثَرَكُمْ لِلْحَقِّ كَٰرِهُونَ ﴿٧٨﴾

79. Or had they contrived some scheme. We are certainly contriving too.

أَمْ أَبْرَمُوٓا۟ أَمْرًا فَإِنَّا مُبْرِمُونَ ﴿٧٩﴾

---

754. The keeper of Hell.

80. Or, do they think that We do not hear their secret and their private counsels. Yes, indeed, and Our messengers[755] are in their midst writing down.

أَمْ يَحْسَبُونَ أَنَّا لَا نَسْمَعُ سِرَّهُمْ وَنَجْوَاهُم بَلَى وَرُسُلُنَا لَدَيْهِمْ يَكْتُبُونَ ﴿٨٠﴾

81. Say: "If the All-Compassionate has a child, I would be the first worshipper."

قُلْ إِن كَانَ لِلرَّحْمَٰنِ وَلَدٌ فَأَنَا أَوَّلُ الْعَابِدِينَ ﴿٨١﴾

82. Exalted be the Lord of the heavens and the earth, the Lord of the Throne, above what they describe.

سُبْحَانَ رَبِّ السَّمَاوَاتِ وَالْأَرْضِ رَبِّ الْعَرْشِ عَمَّا يَصِفُونَ ﴿٨٢﴾

83. So leave them to romp and frolic till they encounter their Day which they have been promised.

فَذَرْهُمْ يَخُوضُوا وَيَلْعَبُوا حَتَّىٰ يُلَاقُوا يَوْمَهُمُ الَّذِي يُوعَدُونَ ﴿٨٣﴾

84. It is He Who in heaven is God, and on earth is God; and He is the All-Wise, the All-Knowing.

وَهُوَ الَّذِي فِي السَّمَاءِ إِلَٰهٌ وَفِي الْأَرْضِ إِلَٰهٌ وَهُوَ الْحَكِيمُ الْعَلِيمُ ﴿٨٤﴾

85. Blessed is He Who has the dominion of the heavens and the earth and what is between them, and Who has the knowledge of the Hour, and unto Him you shall be returned.

وَتَبَارَكَ الَّذِي لَهُ مُلْكُ السَّمَاوَاتِ وَالْأَرْضِ وَمَا بَيْنَهُمَا وَعِندَهُ عِلْمُ السَّاعَةِ وَإِلَيْهِ تُرْجَعُونَ ﴿٨٥﴾

86. Those upon whom they call, apart from Him, do not have the power of intercession, except he who bears witness to the Truth knowingly.

وَلَا يَمْلِكُ الَّذِينَ يَدْعُونَ مِن دُونِهِ الشَّفَاعَةَ إِلَّا مَن شَهِدَ بِالْحَقِّ وَهُمْ يَعْلَمُونَ ﴿٨٦﴾

87. If you ask them: "Who creates them?", they will say: "Allah." Why, then, are they perverted?

وَلَئِن سَأَلْتَهُم مَّنْ خَلَقَهُمْ لَيَقُولُنَّ اللَّهُ فَأَنَّىٰ يُؤْفَكُونَ ﴿٨٧﴾

88. And his[756] petition is: "Lord, these are surely a people who do not believe".

وَقِيلِهِ يَا رَبِّ إِنَّ هَٰؤُلَاءِ قَوْمٌ لَّا يُؤْمِنُونَ ﴿٨٨﴾

89. So turn away from them, and say: 'Peace.' For they will certainly come to know.

فَاصْفَحْ عَنْهُمْ وَقُلْ سَلَامٌ فَسَوْفَ يَعْلَمُونَ ﴿٨٩﴾

---

755. The angels.
756. Muhammad.

| Sûrat Ad-Dukhân,
(The Smoke) 44 |
| :---: |

In the Name of Allah,
the Compassionate, the Merciful

1. Ha - Mim.

2. By the Manifest Book.

3. We have sent it down on a blessed night.
We were then admonishing.

4. Therein, every wise matter is determined,

5. As a Command from Us. We have been
sending forth revelations,

6. As a Mercy from your Lord. He is indeed
the All-Hearing, the All-Knowing.

7. The Lord of the heavens and the earth and
what is between them; if you only believe
with certainty.

8. There is no other god but He. He gives life
and causes to die; your Lord and the Lord of
your forefathers.

9. Yet, in doubt, they frolic.

10. Await, then, the Day when heaven shall
bring forth visible smoke;

11. Enveloping the people. This is a painful
punishment,

12. "Our Lord, lift the punishment from us,
for we are true believers."

13. How can there be for them an admonition, when a manifest Messenger has already
come to them?

14. But they turned away from him saying:
"He is a tutored madman."

15. We will lift the punishment a little. Surely,
you are reverting.

16. On the Day when We shall strike the
mightiest blow, then We shall take Our
revenge.

17. In fact, We have tried the people of Pharaoh before them, and a noble Messenger came to them [saying]:

18. "Deliver to me Allah's servants,[757] for I am unto you a faithful Messenger.

19. "Do not rise arrogantly against Allah; for I come to you with a manifest authority.

20. "I seek refuge with my Lord and your Lord, lest you stone me.

21. "And if you do not believe me, then leave me alone."

22. Then he called out to his Lord: "These are indeed a criminal people".

23. (Allah said): "Set out then, with My servants at night; for you are being followed.

24. "Leave the sea behind as still as ever; for they are a drowning host."

25. How many gardens and well-springs did they leave behind?

26. And plantations and a noble station;

27. And prosperity which they thoroughly enjoyed.

28. So it was, and We bequeathed them to another people.

29. Neither the heavens nor the earth cried for them and they were given no respite.

30. And thus We saved the Children of Israel from the demeaning punishment;

31. From Pharaoh; for he was haughty and extravagant.

32. We have indeed chosen them knowingly, above all other peoples;

33. And given them many Signs wherein there was a manifest trial.

---

757. The Children of Israel.

34. Truly, these people[758] will say:

إِنَّ هَٰؤُلَآءِ لَيَقُولُونَ ۝

35. "It is only our first death and we will not be raised from the dead.

إِنْ هِيَ إِلَّا مَوْتَتُنَا ٱلْأُولَىٰ وَمَا نَحْنُ بِمُنشَرِينَ ۝

36. "Bring then back our fathers if you are truthful."

فَأْتُوا بِآبَآئِنَآ إِن كُنتُمْ صَٰدِقِينَ ۝

37. Are they any better than the people of Tubba'[759] and those who preceded them? We destroyed them all; for they were criminals.

أَهُمْ خَيْرٌ أَمْ قَوْمُ تُبَّعٍ وَٱلَّذِينَ مِن قَبْلِهِمْ أَهْلَكْنَٰهُمْ إِنَّهُمْ كَانُوا مُجْرِمِينَ ۝

38. We did not create the heavens and the earth and what is between them in jest.

وَمَا خَلَقْنَا ٱلسَّمَٰوَٰتِ وَٱلْأَرْضَ وَمَا بَيْنَهُمَا لَٰعِبِينَ ۝

39. We only created them in truth, but most of them do not know.

مَا خَلَقْنَٰهُمَآ إِلَّا بِٱلْحَقِّ وَلَٰكِنَّ أَكْثَرَهُمْ لَا يَعْلَمُونَ ۝

40. The Day of Decision is truly their appointed time all together.

إِنَّ يَوْمَ ٱلْفَصْلِ مِيقَٰتُهُمْ أَجْمَعِينَ ۝

41. The Day when no master shall profit a client a whit, and they will not be supported;

يَوْمَ لَا يُغْنِي مَوْلًى عَن مَّوْلًى شَيْئًا وَلَا هُمْ يُنصَرُونَ ۝

42. Except for him upon whom Allah has Mercy. He is indeed the All-Mighty, the Merciful.

إِلَّا مَن رَّحِمَ ٱللَّهُ إِنَّهُ هُوَ ٱلْعَزِيزُ ٱلرَّحِيمُ ۝

43. The Tree of Zaqqum[760] will certainly be

إِنَّ شَجَرَتَ ٱلزَّقُّومِ ۝

44. The food of the sinner.

طَعَامُ ٱلْأَثِيمِ ۝

45. Like molten lead, which boils in the bellies;

كَٱلْمُهْلِ يَغْلِي فِي ٱلْبُطُونِ ۝

46. Like boiling water.

كَغَلْيِ ٱلْحَمِيمِ ۝

47. "Take him and thrust him into the pit of Hell.

خُذُوهُ فَٱعْتِلُوهُ إِلَىٰ سَوَآءِ ٱلْجَحِيمِ ۝

48. "Then pour over his head the agony of the boiling water;

ثُمَّ صُبُّوا فَوْقَ رَأْسِهِ مِنْ عَذَابِ ٱلْحَمِيمِ ۝

49. "Saying: 'Taste, you are truly the mighty and noble one.'

ذُقْ إِنَّكَ أَنتَ ٱلْعَزِيزُ ٱلْكَرِيمُ ۝

50. "That is the punishment which you used to doubt."

إِنَّ هَٰذَا مَا كُنتُم بِهِۦ تَمْتَرُونَ ۝

---

758. Quraysh and their ilk, who questioned Muhammad's prophetic call.
759. Tubba' refers originally to the kings of southern Arabia, in pre-Islamic times.
760. The Tree of Bitterness.

51. However, the God-fearing are in a secure place;

إِنَّ ٱلْمُتَّقِينَ فِى مَقَامٍ أَمِينٍ ۝

52. In gardens and well-springs.

فِى جَنَّٰتٍ وَعُيُونٍ ۝

53. They wear silk and brocade facing each other.

يَلْبَسُونَ مِن سُندُسٍ وَإِسْتَبْرَقٍ مُّتَقَٰبِلِينَ ۝

54. Thus it will be; and We gave them wide-eyed houris in marriage.

كَذَٰلِكَ وَزَوَّجْنَٰهُم بِحُورٍ عِينٍ ۝

55. They call therein for every fruit in perfect security.

يَدْعُونَ فِيهَا بِكُلِّ فَٰكِهَةٍ ءَامِنِينَ ۝

56. They do not taste death therein, except for the first death; and He guards them against the punishment of Hell;

لَا يَذُوقُونَ فِيهَا ٱلْمَوْتَ إِلَّا ٱلْمَوْتَةَ ٱلْأُولَىٰ وَوَقَىٰهُمْ عَذَابَ ٱلْجَحِيمِ ۝

57. As a Bounty from your Lord. That is the great triumph.

فَضْلًا مِّن رَّبِّكَ ذَٰلِكَ هُوَ ٱلْفَوْزُ ٱلْعَظِيمُ ۝

58. We have made it[761] easy in your own tongue, so that they may remember.

فَإِنَّمَا يَسَّرْنَٰهُ بِلِسَانِكَ لَعَلَّهُمْ يَتَذَكَّرُونَ ۝

59. So wait and watch; they are waiting and watching.

فَٱرْتَقِبْ إِنَّهُم مُّرْتَقِبُونَ ۝

Sûrat Al-Jâthiyah, (The Kneeling One) 45

سورة الجاثية

In the Name of Allah, the Compassionate, the Merciful

بِسْمِ ٱللَّهِ ٱلرَّحْمَٰنِ ٱلرَّحِيمِ

1. Ha - Mim.

حم ۝

2. This is the revelation of the Book from Allah, the All-Mighty, All-Wise.

تَنزِيلُ ٱلْكِتَٰبِ مِنَ ٱللَّهِ ٱلْعَزِيزِ ٱلْحَكِيمِ ۝

3. Surely, in the heavens and the earth there are signs for the believers.

إِنَّ فِى ٱلسَّمَٰوَٰتِ وَٱلْأَرْضِ لَءَايَٰتٍ لِّلْمُؤْمِنِينَ ۝

4. And in your creation and the beasts scattered abroad, there are signs for people who are of certain faith.

وَفِى خَلْقِكُمْ وَمَا يَبُثُّ مِن دَآبَّةٍ ءَايَٰتٌ لِّقَوْمٍ يُوقِنُونَ ۝

---

761. The Qur'an.

5. And in the alternation of the night and the day and in what Allah has sent down from heaven as provision, reviving thereby the earth after it was dead and in the disposition of the wind - there are signs for a people who understand.

6. Those are the Signs of Allah which We recite to you in truth. In what discourse other than Allah's and His Signs, then, will they believe?

7. Woe unto every sinful liar;

8. He hears Allah's Signs recited to him, then perseveres in his arrogance as though he did not hear them. Announce to him, then, the good news of a painful punishment.

9. And if he learns about any of Our Signs, he takes them in jest. Such people shall have a demeaning punishment.

10. Behind them is Hell and what they earned will not profit them a whit, nor what they have taken, apart from Allah, as protectors; and they will have a terrible punishment.

11. This is true guidance, and those who have disbelieved in the Signs of their Lord will have the punishment of a painful scourge.

12. It is Allah Who subjected the sea to you, so that ships might sail in it at His Command, and that you might seek some of His Bounty, and that perchance you might give thanks.

13. And He subjected to you what is in the heavens and the earth all together, [as a grace] from Him. There are in that signs for a people who reflect.

14. Tell the believers to forgive those who do not hope for Allah's Days, that He may reward a people for what they used to earn.

وَاخْتِلَٰفِ الَّيْلِ وَالنَّهَارِ وَمَآ أَنزَلَ اللَّهُ مِنَ السَّمَآءِ مِن رِّزْقٍ فَأَحْيَا بِهِ الْأَرْضَ بَعْدَ مَوْتِهَا وَتَصْرِيفِ الرِّيَٰحِ ءَايَٰتٌ لِّقَوْمٍ يَعْقِلُونَ ۝

تِلْكَ ءَايَٰتُ اللَّهِ نَتْلُوهَا عَلَيْكَ بِالْحَقِّ فَبِأَيِّ حَدِيثٍ بَعْدَ اللَّهِ وَءَايَٰتِهِۦ يُؤْمِنُونَ ۝

وَيْلٌ لِّكُلِّ أَفَّاكٍ أَثِيمٍ ۝

يَسْمَعُ ءَايَٰتِ اللَّهِ تُتْلَىٰ عَلَيْهِ ثُمَّ يُصِرُّ مُسْتَكْبِرًا كَأَن لَّمْ يَسْمَعْهَا فَبَشِّرْهُ بِعَذَابٍ أَلِيمٍ ۝

وَإِذَا عَلِمَ مِنْ ءَايَٰتِنَا شَيْـًٔا اتَّخَذَهَا هُزُوًا أُوْلَٰٓئِكَ لَهُمْ عَذَابٌ مُّهِينٌ ۝

مِّن وَرَآئِهِمْ جَهَنَّمُ وَلَا يُغْنِى عَنْهُم مَّا كَسَبُوا۟ شَيْـًٔا وَلَا مَا اتَّخَذُوا۟ مِن دُونِ اللَّهِ أَوْلِيَآءَ وَلَهُمْ عَذَابٌ عَظِيمٌ ۝

هَٰذَا هُدًى وَالَّذِينَ كَفَرُوا۟ بِـَٔايَٰتِ رَبِّهِمْ لَهُمْ عَذَابٌ مِّن رِّجْزٍ أَلِيمٌ ۝

۞ اللَّهُ الَّذِى سَخَّرَ لَكُمُ الْبَحْرَ لِتَجْرِىَ الْفُلْكُ فِيهِ بِأَمْرِهِۦ وَلِتَبْتَغُوا۟ مِن فَضْلِهِۦ وَلَعَلَّكُمْ تَشْكُرُونَ ۝

وَسَخَّرَ لَكُم مَّا فِى السَّمَٰوَٰتِ وَمَا فِى الْأَرْضِ جَمِيعًا مِّنْهُ إِنَّ فِى ذَٰلِكَ لَءَايَٰتٍ لِّقَوْمٍ يَتَفَكَّرُونَ ۝

قُل لِّلَّذِينَ ءَامَنُوا۟ يَغْفِرُوا۟ لِلَّذِينَ لَا يَرْجُونَ أَيَّامَ اللَّهِ لِيَجْزِىَ قَوْمًا بِمَا كَانُوا۟ يَكْسِبُونَ ۝

15. He who does a righteous deed, it is to his own advantage, and he who perpetrates evil, it is to his own loss. Then, unto your Lord you shall be returned.

16. In fact, We gave the Children of Israel the Book, the Judgement and the Prophecy. We provided them with the good things, and preferred them to all the other peoples.

17. And We gave them clear proofs of the Decree, but they did not diverge except when the knowledge came to them, out of spite among themselves. Surely your Lord shall judge between them on the Day of Resurrection, regarding that over which they used to diverge.

18. Then, We set you upon a right course[762] of the Decree; so follow it and do not follow the fancies of those who do not know.

19. They will avail you nothing against Allah; and indeed the wrongdoers are friends of each other, but Allah is the friend of the God-fearing.

20. This[763] is an illumination for mankind, a guidance and mercy unto a people who believe with certainty.

21. What, do those who have perpetrated the evil deeds believe that We shall regard them as equal to those who have believed and done the righteous deeds, whether in their life or death? Evil is their judgement!

22. Allah created the heavens and the earth in truth, so that every soul may be rewarded for what it has earned; and they shall not be wronged.

---

762. *Shari'ah*.
763. The Qur'an.

23. Have you seen him who has taken his fancy as his god and Allah has led him astray knowingly, and set a seal upon his hearing and his heart, and placed a veil upon his sight. Who, then, will guide him besides Allah? Do you not remember?

أَفَرَءَيْتَ مَنِ ٱتَّخَذَ إِلَٰهَهُ هَوَىٰهُ وَأَضَلَّهُ ٱللَّهُ عَلَىٰ عِلْمٍ وَخَتَمَ عَلَىٰ سَمْعِهِ وَقَلْبِهِ وَجَعَلَ عَلَىٰ بَصَرِهِ غِشَٰوَةً فَمَن يَهْدِيهِ مِنۢ بَعْدِ ٱللَّهِ أَفَلَا تَذَكَّرُونَ ﴿٢٣﴾

24. They say: "There is nothing but this our present life. We die and we live and we are only destroyed by time." However, they have no certain knowledge of this; they are only conjecturing.

وَقَالُوا۟ مَا هِىَ إِلَّا حَيَاتُنَا ٱلدُّنْيَا نَمُوتُ وَنَحْيَا وَمَا يُهْلِكُنَآ إِلَّا ٱلدَّهْرُ وَمَا لَهُم بِذَٰلِكَ مِنْ عِلْمٍ إِنْ هُمْ إِلَّا يَظُنُّونَ ﴿٢٤﴾

25. And when Our Signs are clearly recited to them, their only argument is to say: "Bring our fathers back, if you are truthful."

وَإِذَا تُتْلَىٰ عَلَيْهِمْ ءَايَٰتُنَا بَيِّنَٰتٍ مَّا كَانَ حُجَّتَهُمْ إِلَّآ أَن قَالُوا۟ ٱئْتُوا۟ بِـَٔابَآئِنَآ إِن كُنتُمْ صَٰدِقِينَ ﴿٢٥﴾

26. Say: "Allah gives you life, then causes you to die, then musters you unto the Day of Resurrection, which is undoubted. Yet most people do not know."

قُلِ ٱللَّهُ يُحْيِيكُمْ ثُمَّ يُمِيتُكُمْ ثُمَّ يَجْمَعُكُمْ إِلَىٰ يَوْمِ ٱلْقِيَٰمَةِ لَا رَيْبَ فِيهِ وَلَٰكِنَّ أَكْثَرَ ٱلنَّاسِ لَا يَعْلَمُونَ ﴿٢٦﴾

27. To Allah belongs the dominion of the heavens and the earth, and when the Hour shall come, on that Day the negators shall lose.

وَلِلَّهِ مُلْكُ ٱلسَّمَٰوَٰتِ وَٱلْأَرْضِ وَيَوْمَ تَقُومُ ٱلسَّاعَةُ يَوْمَئِذٍ يَخْسَرُ ٱلْمُبْطِلُونَ ﴿٢٧﴾

28. And you will see every nation kneeling; each nation being called unto its Book: "Today, you shall be rewarded for what you used to do.

وَتَرَىٰ كُلَّ أُمَّةٍ جَاثِيَةً كُلُّ أُمَّةٍ تُدْعَىٰٓ إِلَىٰ كِتَٰبِهَا ٱلْيَوْمَ تُجْزَوْنَ مَا كُنتُمْ تَعْمَلُونَ ﴿٢٨﴾

29. "This is Our Book which speaks against you truly. In fact, We used to record what you were doing."

هَٰذَا كِتَٰبُنَا يَنطِقُ عَلَيْكُم بِٱلْحَقِّ إِنَّا كُنَّا نَسْتَنسِخُ مَا كُنتُمْ تَعْمَلُونَ ﴿٢٩﴾

30. As to those who believed and did the righteous deeds, their Lord will admit them into His Mercy. That is the manifest triumph.

فَأَمَّا ٱلَّذِينَ ءَامَنُوا۟ وَعَمِلُوا۟ ٱلصَّٰلِحَٰتِ فَيُدْخِلُهُمْ رَبُّهُمْ فِى رَحْمَتِهِ ذَٰلِكَ هُوَ ٱلْفَوْزُ ٱلْمُبِينُ ﴿٣٠﴾

31. But as for those who disbelieved [they will be asked]: "Were not My Signs recited to you, but you waxed proud and were a criminal people?"

وَأَمَّا ٱلَّذِينَ كَفَرُوٓا۟ أَفَلَمْ تَكُنْ ءَايَٰتِى تُتْلَىٰ عَلَيْكُمْ فَٱسْتَكْبَرْتُمْ وَكُنتُمْ قَوْمًا مُّجْرِمِينَ ﴿٣١﴾

32. And when it was said: "Allah's Promise is true and the Hour is undoubted", you said: "We do not know what the Hour is. We only conjecture and are by no means certain."

وَإِذَا قِيلَ إِنَّ وَعْدَ ٱللَّهِ حَقٌّ وَٱلسَّاعَةُ لَا رَيْبَ فِيهَا قُلْتُم مَّا نَدْرِى مَا ٱلسَّاعَةُ إِن نَّظُنُّ إِلَّا ظَنًّا وَمَا نَحْنُ بِمُسْتَيْقِنِينَ ﴿٣٢﴾

33. Then the evil of their deeds shall appear to them and they will be smitten by that which they used to mock.

وَبَدَا لَهُمْ سَيِّئَاتُ مَا عَمِلُوا۟ وَحَاقَ بِهِم مَّا كَانُوا۟ بِهِ يَسْتَهْزِءُونَ ﴿٣٣﴾

34. And it will be said: "Today We forget you, as you forgot the Encounter of this your day, and your abode is the Fire and you will have no supporters.

وَقِيلَ ٱلْيَوْمَ نَنسَىٰكُمْ كَمَا نَسِيتُمْ لِقَآءَ يَوْمِكُمْ هَٰذَا وَمَأْوَىٰكُمُ ٱلنَّارُ وَمَا لَكُم مِّن نَّٰصِرِينَ ﴿٣٤﴾

35. "That is because you took Allah's Signs in jest and the earthly life lured you." So today they will not be brought out of it and they will not be allowed to repent.

ذَٰلِكُم بِأَنَّكُمُ ٱتَّخَذْتُمْ ءَايَٰتِ ٱللَّهِ هُزُوًا وَغَرَّتْكُمُ ٱلْحَيَوٰةُ ٱلدُّنْيَا فَٱلْيَوْمَ لَا يُخْرَجُونَ مِنْهَا وَلَا هُمْ يُسْتَعْتَبُونَ ﴿٣٥﴾

36. Praise, then, be to Allah, the Lord of the heavens and the Lord of the earth, the Lord of the Worlds.

فَلِلَّهِ ٱلْحَمْدُ رَبِّ ٱلسَّمَٰوَٰتِ وَرَبِّ ٱلْأَرْضِ رَبِّ ٱلْعَٰلَمِينَ ﴿٣٦﴾

37. Unto Him is the grandeur in the heavens and on the earth, and He is the All-Mighty, the All-Wise.

وَلَهُ ٱلْكِبْرِيَآءُ فِى ٱلسَّمَٰوَٰتِ وَٱلْأَرْضِ وَهُوَ ٱلْعَزِيزُ ٱلْحَكِيمُ ﴿٣٧﴾

Sûrat Al-Ahqâf, (The Sand-Dunes) 46

سُورَةُ ٱلْأَحْقَافِ

In the Name of Allah, the Compassionate, the Merciful

بِسْمِ ٱللَّهِ ٱلرَّحْمَٰنِ ٱلرَّحِيمِ

1. Ha - Mim.

حمٓ ﴿١﴾

2. This is the revelation of the Book from Allah, the All-Mighty, the All-Wise.

تَنزِيلُ ٱلْكِتَٰبِ مِنَ ٱللَّهِ ٱلْعَزِيزِ ٱلْحَكِيمِ ﴿٢﴾

3. We have not created the heavens and the earth and what is between them except in truth and for an appointed term. Yet the unbelievers do not heed what they were warned against.

مَا خَلَقْنَا ٱلسَّمَٰوَٰتِ وَٱلْأَرْضَ وَمَا بَيْنَهُمَآ إِلَّا بِٱلْحَقِّ وَأَجَلٍ مُّسَمًّى وَٱلَّذِينَ كَفَرُوا۟ عَمَّآ أُنذِرُوا۟ مُعْرِضُونَ ﴿٣﴾

4. Say: "Have you considered what you call upon,[764] apart from Allah? Show me what they have created of the earth, or whether they have a share of the heavens? Bring me a book before this one or some vestige of knowledge, if you are truthful?"

5. Who is farther astray than he who calls, apart from Allah, upon him who does not answer his call till the Day of Resurrection? They are even heedless of their calling.

6. And when people are mustered, they will be their enemies, and even their worship they will disclaim.

7. And when Our Clear Signs are recited to them, those who have disbelieved will say to the Truth when it comes to them: "This is manifest sorcery."

8. Or do they say: "He invented it?" Say: "If I have invented it, you have no means of helping me against Allah. He knows best what you are expatiating upon. Let Him suffice as a witness between me and you. He is the All-Forgiving, the All-Merciful."

9. Say: "I am not the first of the Messengers and I do not know what will be done with me or with you. I only follow what is revealed to me and I am only a manifest warner."

10. Say: "Have you considered? What if it be from Allah and you disbelieve in it, while a witness from the Children of Israel bears witness to the like of it and believes, whereas you wax proud? Surely, Allah does not guide the wrongdoing people rightly."

---

764. The idols.

11. The unbelievers say to the believers:
"Had it been any good, they would not have
beaten us to it", and since they have not been
guided by it, they will certainly say: "This is
an old fabrication."

وَقَالَ ٱلَّذِينَ كَفَرُوا۟ لِلَّذِينَ ءَامَنُوا۟ لَوْ كَانَ خَيْرًا مَّا سَبَقُونَآ إِلَيْهِ وَإِذْ لَمْ يَهْتَدُوا۟ بِهِۦ فَسَيَقُولُونَ هَٰذَآ إِفْكٌ قَدِيمٌ ۝

12. And before it, there came the Book of
Moses, as a guidance and a mercy; and this is
a corroborating Book in Arabic tongue to
warn the wrongdoers and serve as good
news to the beneficent.

وَمِن قَبْلِهِۦ كِتَٰبُ مُوسَىٰٓ إِمَامًا وَرَحْمَةً وَهَٰذَا كِتَٰبٌ مُّصَدِّقٌ لِّسَانًا عَرَبِيًّا لِّيُنذِرَ ٱلَّذِينَ ظَلَمُوا۟ وَبُشْرَىٰ لِلْمُحْسِنِينَ ۝

13. Indeed, those who say: "Our Lord is
Allah", and then are upright, have no cause
to fear and they shall not grieve.

إِنَّ ٱلَّذِينَ قَالُوا۟ رَبُّنَا ٱللَّهُ ثُمَّ ٱسْتَقَٰمُوا۟ فَلَا خَوْفٌ عَلَيْهِمْ وَلَا هُمْ يَحْزَنُونَ ۝

14. Those are the companions of Paradise
dwelling in it forever, as a reward for what
they used to do.

أُو۟لَٰٓئِكَ أَصْحَٰبُ ٱلْجَنَّةِ خَٰلِدِينَ فِيهَا جَزَآءًۢ بِمَا كَانُوا۟ يَعْمَلُونَ ۝

15. We have commanded man to be kind to
his parents; his mother bore him painfully
and delivered him painfully, his gestation
and weaning totalling thirty months. When
he is fully grown and turns forty years, he will
say: "Lord, inspire me to be thankful for the
favour, with which You have favoured me
and favoured my parents; and to do a
righteous deed, well-pleasing to You. Grant
me righteousness in my progeny; I have truly
repented to You and am one of those who
submit."

وَوَصَّيْنَا ٱلْإِنسَٰنَ بِوَٰلِدَيْهِ إِحْسَٰنًا حَمَلَتْهُ أُمُّهُۥ كُرْهًا وَوَضَعَتْهُ كُرْهًا وَحَمْلُهُۥ وَفِصَٰلُهُۥ ثَلَٰثُونَ شَهْرًا حَتَّىٰٓ إِذَا بَلَغَ أَشُدَّهُۥ وَبَلَغَ أَرْبَعِينَ سَنَةً قَالَ رَبِّ أَوْزِعْنِىٓ أَنْ أَشْكُرَ نِعْمَتَكَ ٱلَّتِىٓ أَنْعَمْتَ عَلَىَّ وَعَلَىٰ وَٰلِدَىَّ وَأَنْ أَعْمَلَ صَٰلِحًا تَرْضَىٰهُ وَأَصْلِحْ لِى فِى ذُرِّيَّتِىٓ إِنِّى تُبْتُ إِلَيْكَ وَإِنِّى مِنَ ٱلْمُسْلِمِينَ ۝

16. Those from whom We accept the best of
what they do and overlook their evil deeds
shall be reckoned among the companions of
Paradise, this being the promise of the truth
which they were promised.

أُو۟لَٰٓئِكَ ٱلَّذِينَ نَتَقَبَّلُ عَنْهُمْ أَحْسَنَ مَا عَمِلُوا۟ وَنَتَجَاوَزُ عَن سَيِّـَٔاتِهِمْ فِىٓ أَصْحَٰبِ ٱلْجَنَّةِ وَعْدَ ٱلصِّدْقِ ٱلَّذِى كَانُوا۟ يُوعَدُونَ ۝

17. But as for him who says to his parents:
"Fie upon you. Do you promise me to be
raised up,[765] while generations have already

وَٱلَّذِى قَالَ لِوَٰلِدَيْهِ أُفٍّ لَّكُمَآ أَتَعِدَانِنِىٓ أَنْ أُخْرَجَ وَقَدْ خَلَتِ ٱلْقُرُونُ مِن قَبْلِى وَهُمَا يَسْتَغِيثَانِ ٱللَّهَ وَيْلَكَ ءَامِنْ

---

765. That is, raised from the dead.

gone before me?" They both call upon Allah to help them: "Woe unto you, have faith. Allah's Promise is true." But he will say: "These are merely legends of the ancients."

18. Those against whom the Decree was pronounced, from among nations which passed away before them, both of jinn and mankind, were truly the losers.

19. To each will be allotted ranks according to what they did, and He will certainly pay them in full for their works, and they shall not be wronged.

20. On the day that the unbelievers shall be exposed to the Fire: "You have squandered your goods in your worldly life and enjoyed them. Today, then, you will be rewarded with the punishment of humiliation, because you used to wax proud on earth, without any right, and because you used to sin."

21. And remember the brother of 'Ad, when he warned his people upon the sand-dunes, warners having gone before him and after him, saying: "Do not worship any one but Allah. I fear for you the punishment of a great Day."

22. They said: "Did you come to divert us from our deities? Bring us then what you are promising us if you are truthful."

23. He said: "Knowledge is only with Allah and I am conveying to you the message I was charged with, but I see that you are an ignorant people."

24. Then, when they saw it[766] as a cloud-burst coming towards their valley, they said: "This is a cloud-burst raining upon us." No, it is what you sought to hasten, a wind wherein is a painful punishment;

إِنَّ وَعْدَ اللَّهِ حَقٌّ فَيَقُولُ مَا هَٰذَا إِلَّا أَسَاطِيرُ الْأَوَّلِينَ ﴿١٧﴾

أُوْلَٰئِكَ الَّذِينَ حَقَّ عَلَيْهِمُ الْقَوْلُ فِي أُمَمٍ قَدْ خَلَتْ مِن قَبْلِهِم مِّنَ الْجِنِّ وَالْإِنسِ إِنَّهُمْ كَانُوا خَاسِرِينَ ﴿١٨﴾

وَلِكُلٍّ دَرَجَاتٌ مِّمَّا عَمِلُوا وَلِيُوَفِّيَهُمْ أَعْمَالَهُمْ وَهُمْ لَا يُظْلَمُونَ ﴿١٩﴾

وَيَوْمَ يُعْرَضُ الَّذِينَ كَفَرُوا عَلَى النَّارِ أَذْهَبْتُمْ طَيِّبَاتِكُمْ فِي حَيَاتِكُمُ الدُّنْيَا وَاسْتَمْتَعْتُم بِهَا فَالْيَوْمَ تُجْزَوْنَ عَذَابَ الْهُونِ بِمَا كُنتُمْ تَسْتَكْبِرُونَ فِي الْأَرْضِ بِغَيْرِ الْحَقِّ وَبِمَا كُنتُمْ تَفْسُقُونَ ﴿٢٠﴾

۞ وَاذْكُرْ أَخَا عَادٍ إِذْ أَنذَرَ قَوْمَهُ بِالْأَحْقَافِ وَقَدْ خَلَتِ النُّذُرُ مِن بَيْنِ يَدَيْهِ وَمِنْ خَلْفِهِ أَلَّا تَعْبُدُوا إِلَّا اللَّهَ إِنِّي أَخَافُ عَلَيْكُمْ عَذَابَ يَوْمٍ عَظِيمٍ ﴿٢١﴾

قَالُوا أَجِئْتَنَا لِتَأْفِكَنَا عَنْ آلِهَتِنَا فَأْتِنَا بِمَا تَعِدُنَا إِن كُنتَ مِنَ الصَّادِقِينَ ﴿٢٢﴾

قَالَ إِنَّمَا الْعِلْمُ عِندَ اللَّهِ وَأُبَلِّغُكُم مَّا أُرْسِلْتُ بِهِ وَلَٰكِنِّي أَرَاكُمْ قَوْمًا تَجْهَلُونَ ﴿٢٣﴾

فَلَمَّا رَأَوْهُ عَارِضًا مُّسْتَقْبِلَ أَوْدِيَتِهِمْ قَالُوا هَٰذَا عَارِضٌ مُّمْطِرُنَا بَلْ هُوَ مَا اسْتَعْجَلْتُم بِهِ رِيحٌ فِيهَا عَذَابٌ أَلِيمٌ ﴿٢٤﴾

---

766. The punishment.

25. Destroying everything at the behest of its Lord. Then when they woke up, there was nothing to be seen except their dwellings. Thus do We reward the criminal people.

26. We had established them firmly in a manner We did not establish you, and We gave them hearing, eye-sight and hearts; but their hearing, eye-sight and hearts availed them nothing, as they repudiated the Signs of Allah; and so they were overwhelmed by that which they used to mock.

27. We have also destroyed the cities surrounding you and expounded the Signs, that perchance they might return.

28. Why, then, were they not supported by those whom they took, apart from Allah, as favourite deities? No, they abandoned them. That was their fabrication and what they used to allege.

29. And when We dispatched towards you a group of jinn to listen to the Qur'an, and they attended to it, they said: "Listen", but when it was finished they returned to their own people to warn them.

30. They said: "O our people, we have heard a Book sent down after Moses, confirming what came before it and guiding to the truth and to a Straight Path.

31. "O our people, respond to the caller[767] unto Allah and believe in him, and He (Allah) will forgive you some of your sins and save you from a painful punishment."

32. He who does not answer the caller unto Allah will not thwart Him on earth and he will not have any protectors apart from Him. Such people are in manifest error.

---

767. Muhammad.

33. Have they not seen that Allah, Who has created the heavens and the earth and has not been wearied by creating them, is Able to raise the dead? Yes indeed, He has power over everything.

أَوَلَمْ يَرَوْا أَنَّ اللَّهَ الَّذِي خَلَقَ السَّمَوَاتِ وَالْأَرْضَ وَلَمْ يَعْيَ بِخَلْقِهِنَّ بِقَادِرٍ عَلَى أَن يُحْيِيَ الْمَوْتَى بَلَى إِنَّهُ عَلَى كُلِّ شَيْءٍ قَدِيرٌ ۝

34. And on the Day that the unbelievers shall be exposed to the Fire [they will be asked]: "Is this not just?" They will say: "Yes indeed, by our Lord." He will then say: "Taste now the punishment for your disbelief."

وَيَوْمَ يُعْرَضُ الَّذِينَ كَفَرُوا عَلَى النَّارِ أَلَيْسَ هَذَا بِالْحَقِّ قَالُوا بَلَى وَرَبِّنَا قَالَ فَذُوقُوا الْعَذَابَ بِمَا كُنتُمْ تَكْفُرُونَ ۝

35. So bear up patiently, as the Constant Messengers[768] bore up, and do not seek to hasten it[769] for them. On that Day they shall see what they were promised, as if they had not lingered except for a single hour of the day. This is a proclamation. Shall any but the sinful people be destroyed?

فَاصْبِرْ كَمَا صَبَرَ أُوْلُوا الْعَزْمِ مِنَ الرُّسُلِ وَلَا تَسْتَعْجِل لَّهُمْ كَأَنَّهُمْ يَوْمَ يَرَوْنَ مَا يُوعَدُونَ لَمْ يَلْبَثُوا إِلَّا سَاعَةً مِّن نَّهَارٍ بَلَاغٌ فَهَلْ يُهْلَكُ إِلَّا الْقَوْمُ الْفَاسِقُونَ ۝

Sûrat Muhammad, (The Prophet) 47

سُورَةُ مُحَمَّدٍ

In the Name of Allah, the Compassionate, the Merciful

بِسْمِ اللَّهِ الرَّحْمَنِ الرَّحِيمِ

1. Those who have disbelieved and barred others from the Path of Allah, He will render their works perverse;

الَّذِينَ كَفَرُوا وَصَدُّوا عَن سَبِيلِ اللَّهِ أَضَلَّ أَعْمَالَهُمْ ۝

2. But those who have believed and done the righteous deeds and believed in what was sent down upon Muhammad, which is the Truth from their Lord, He will remit their sins and set their minds aright.

وَالَّذِينَ ءَامَنُوا وَعَمِلُوا الصَّالِحَاتِ وَءَامَنُوا بِمَا نُزِّلَ عَلَى مُحَمَّدٍ وَهُوَ الْحَقُّ مِن رَّبِّهِمْ كَفَّرَ عَنْهُمْ سَيِّئَاتِهِمْ وَأَصْلَحَ بَالَهُمْ ۝

3. That is because those who have disbelieved have followed falsehood, but those who have believed have followed the truth from their Lord. Thus does Allah frame the parables for mankind.

ذَلِكَ بِأَنَّ الَّذِينَ كَفَرُوا اتَّبَعُوا الْبَاطِلَ وَأَنَّ الَّذِينَ ءَامَنُوا اتَّبَعُوا الْحَقَّ مِن رَّبِّهِمْ كَذَلِكَ يَضْرِبُ اللَّهُ لِلنَّاسِ أَمْثَالَهُمْ ۝

---

768. Noah, Abraham, Moses and Jesus.
769. Punishment.

4. So, when you meet the unbelievers, strike their necks till you have bloodied them, then fasten the shackles. Thereupon, release them freely or for a ransom, till the war is over. So be it. Yet had Allah wished, He would have taken vengeance upon them, but He wanted to test you by one another. Those who die in the Cause of Allah, He will not render their works perverse.

فَإِذَا لَقِيتُمُ الَّذِينَ كَفَرُوا فَضَرْبَ الرِّقَابِ حَتَّى إِذَا أَثْخَنتُمُوهُمْ فَشُدُّوا الْوَثَاقَ فَإِمَّا مَنًّا بَعْدُ وَإِمَّا فِدَاءً حَتَّى تَضَعَ الْحَرْبُ أَوْزَارَهَا ذَلِكَ وَلَوْ يَشَاءُ اللَّهُ لَانتَصَرَ مِنْهُمْ وَلَكِن لِّيَبْلُوَ بَعْضَكُم بِبَعْضٍ وَالَّذِينَ قُتِلُوا فِي سَبِيلِ اللَّهِ فَلَن يُضِلَّ أَعْمَالَهُمْ ۝

5. He shall guide them and set their minds aright;

سَيَهْدِيهِمْ وَيُصْلِحُ بَالَهُمْ ۝

6. And shall admit them into Paradise which He has made known to them.

وَيُدْخِلُهُمُ الْجَنَّةَ عَرَّفَهَا لَهُمْ ۝

7. O believers, if you support Allah, He will support you and steady your footsteps.

يَا أَيُّهَا الَّذِينَ آمَنُوا إِن تَنصُرُوا اللَّهَ يَنصُرْكُمْ وَيُثَبِّتْ أَقْدَامَكُمْ ۝

8. But as to the unbelievers, wretched are they and perverse are their works.

وَالَّذِينَ كَفَرُوا فَتَعْسًا لَّهُمْ وَأَضَلَّ أَعْمَالَهُمْ ۝

9. That is because they despised what Allah has sent down; so He foiled their actions.

ذَلِكَ بِأَنَّهُمْ كَرِهُوا مَا أَنزَلَ اللَّهُ فَأَحْبَطَ أَعْمَالَهُمْ ۝

10. Did they not travel in the land and see what was the fate of those who preceded them? Allah brought utter destruction on them; and the like of this awaits the unbelievers.

۞ أَفَلَمْ يَسِيرُوا فِي الْأَرْضِ فَيَنظُرُوا كَيْفَ كَانَ عَاقِبَةُ الَّذِينَ مِن قَبْلِهِمْ دَمَّرَ اللَّهُ عَلَيْهِمْ وَلِلْكَافِرِينَ أَمْثَالُهَا ۝

11. That is because Allah is the Protector of the believers, but the unbelievers shall have no protector.

ذَلِكَ بِأَنَّ اللَّهَ مَوْلَى الَّذِينَ آمَنُوا وَأَنَّ الْكَافِرِينَ لَا مَوْلَى لَهُمْ ۝

12. Allah shall admit those who believe and do the righteous deeds into gardens beneath which rivers flow; but the unbelievers shall take their pleasure and eat like cattle, and the Fire shall be their abode.

إِنَّ اللَّهَ يُدْخِلُ الَّذِينَ آمَنُوا وَعَمِلُوا الصَّالِحَاتِ جَنَّاتٍ تَجْرِي مِن تَحْتِهَا الْأَنْهَارُ وَالَّذِينَ كَفَرُوا يَتَمَتَّعُونَ وَيَأْكُلُونَ كَمَا تَأْكُلُ الْأَنْعَامُ وَالنَّارُ مَثْوًى لَّهُمْ ۝

13. How many a city that was mightier than your city,[770] which cast you out, have We destroyed, and they had no supporter?

وَكَأَيِّن مِّن قَرْيَةٍ هِيَ أَشَدُّ قُوَّةً مِّن قَرْيَتِكَ الَّتِي أَخْرَجَتْكَ أَهْلَكْنَاهُمْ فَلَا نَاصِرَ لَهُمْ ۝

---

770. Mecca.

14. Is he who relies on a clear proof from his Lord like one whose evil action has been embellished for him? They have simply followed their fancies.

أَفَمَن كَانَ عَلَىٰ بَيِّنَةٍ مِّن رَّبِّهِۦ كَمَن زُيِّنَ لَهُۥ سُوٓءُ عَمَلِهِۦ وَٱتَّبَعُوٓاْ أَهْوَآءَهُم ﴿١٤﴾

15. The likeness of the Garden which the God-fearing have been promised is this: rivers of water not stagnant, rivers of milk whose taste has not changed, rivers of wine delighting its drinkers and rivers of distilled honey. Therein they have every variety of fruit and forgiveness from their Lord too. Are they to be compared with those who dwell in the Fire forever and are given to drink boiling water which will rip up their bowels?

مَّثَلُ ٱلْجَنَّةِ ٱلَّتِى وُعِدَ ٱلْمُتَّقُونَ فِيهَآ أَنْهَٰرٌ مِّن مَّآءٍ غَيْرِ ءَاسِنٍ وَأَنْهَٰرٌ مِّن لَّبَنٍ لَّمْ يَتَغَيَّرْ طَعْمُهُۥ وَأَنْهَٰرٌ مِّنْ خَمْرٍ لَّذَّةٍ لِّلشَّٰرِبِينَ وَأَنْهَٰرٌ مِّنْ عَسَلٍ مُّصَفًّى وَلَهُمْ فِيهَا مِن كُلِّ ٱلثَّمَرَٰتِ وَمَغْفِرَةٌ مِّن رَّبِّهِمْ كَمَنْ هُوَ خَٰلِدٌ فِى ٱلنَّارِ وَسُقُواْ مَآءً حَمِيمًا فَقَطَّعَ أَمْعَآءَهُمْ ﴿١٥﴾

16. There are some of them who listen to you, but as soon as they leave you, they say to those who have been given the Knowledge: "What did he say just now?" Such are those upon whose hearts Allah has set a seal and who have followed their fancies.

وَمِنْهُم مَّن يَسْتَمِعُ إِلَيْكَ حَتَّىٰٓ إِذَا خَرَجُواْ مِنْ عِندِكَ قَالُواْ لِلَّذِينَ أُوتُواْ ٱلْعِلْمَ مَاذَا قَالَ ءَانِفًا أُوْلَٰٓئِكَ ٱلَّذِينَ طَبَعَ ٱللَّهُ عَلَىٰ قُلُوبِهِمْ وَٱتَّبَعُوٓاْ أَهْوَآءَهُمْ ﴿١٦﴾

17. But those who are rightly guided, He increases them in guidance and accords them their piety.

وَٱلَّذِينَ ٱهْتَدَوْاْ زَادَهُمْ هُدًى وَءَاتَىٰهُمْ تَقْوَىٰهُمْ ﴿١٧﴾

18. Do they, then, only expect that the Hour should come upon them suddenly? In fact, its signs have already come. How then, when it comes, will they regain their recollection?

فَهَلْ يَنظُرُونَ إِلَّا ٱلسَّاعَةَ أَن تَأْتِيَهُم بَغْتَةً فَقَدْ جَآءَ أَشْرَاطُهَا فَأَنَّىٰ لَهُمْ إِذَا جَآءَتْهُمْ ذِكْرَىٰهُمْ ﴿١٨﴾

19. So, know that there is no god but Allah, and ask forgiveness for your sins and for the believers, men and women. Allah knows your goings and comings, and your settling down.

فَٱعْلَمْ أَنَّهُۥ لَآ إِلَٰهَ إِلَّا ٱللَّهُ وَٱسْتَغْفِرْ لِذَنۢبِكَ وَلِلْمُؤْمِنِينَ وَٱلْمُؤْمِنَٰتِ وَٱللَّهُ يَعْلَمُ مُتَقَلَّبَكُمْ وَمَثْوَىٰكُمْ ﴿١٩﴾

20. The believers say: "If only a surah is sent down", but when a sound surah is sent down and fighting is mentioned therein, you will see those in whose hearts is a sickness look at you like one who has fainted in the throes of death. Far better for them,

وَيَقُولُ ٱلَّذِينَ ءَامَنُواْ لَوْلَا نُزِّلَتْ سُورَةٌ فَإِذَآ أُنزِلَتْ سُورَةٌ مُّحْكَمَةٌ وَذُكِرَ فِيهَا ٱلْقِتَالُ رَأَيْتَ ٱلَّذِينَ فِى قُلُوبِهِم مَّرَضٌ يَنظُرُونَ إِلَيْكَ نَظَرَ ٱلْمَغْشِىِّ عَلَيْهِ مِنَ ٱلْمَوْتِ فَأَوْلَىٰ لَهُمْ ﴿٢٠﴾

21. Would have been obedience and a fair word! So when the matter is resolved, it would have been better for them to be true to Allah.

طَاعَةٌ وَقَوْلٌ مَّعْرُوفٌ فَإِذَا عَزَمَ ٱلْأَمْرُ فَلَوْ صَدَقُوا ٱللَّهَ لَكَانَ خَيْرًا لَّهُمْ ﴿٢١﴾

22. Would you, perhaps, if you were to rule, spread corruption in the land and sever the bonds of your kin?

فَهَلْ عَسَيْتُمْ إِن تَوَلَّيْتُمْ أَن تُفْسِدُوا فِى ٱلْأَرْضِ وَتُقَطِّعُوا أَرْحَامَكُمْ ﴿٢٢﴾

23. Such are those whom Allah has cursed, and has made them deaf and blotted out their eyesight.

أُوْلَـٰئِكَ ٱلَّذِينَ لَعَنَهُمُ ٱللَّهُ فَأَصَمَّهُمْ وَأَعْمَىٰ أَبْصَـٰرَهُمْ ﴿٢٣﴾

24. Will they not ponder the Qur'an, or are there locks upon their hearts?

أَفَلَا يَتَدَبَّرُونَ ٱلْقُرْءَانَ أَمْ عَلَىٰ قُلُوبٍ أَقْفَالُهَا ﴿٢٤﴾

25. Surely, those who have turned upon their heels after the Guidance was manifested to them, it was Satan who insinuated to them and deluded them.

إِنَّ ٱلَّذِينَ ٱرْتَدُّوا عَلَىٰ أَدْبَـٰرِهِم مِّنۢ بَعْدِ مَا تَبَيَّنَ لَهُمُ ٱلْهُدَى ٱلشَّيْطَـٰنُ سَوَّلَ لَهُمْ وَأَمْلَىٰ لَهُمْ ﴿٢٥﴾

26. That is because they said to those who disliked what Allah has sent down: "We shall obey you in part of the matter'', but Allah knows their secretiveness.

ذَٰلِكَ بِأَنَّهُمْ قَالُوا لِلَّذِينَ كَرِهُوا مَا نَزَّلَ ٱللَّهُ سَنُطِيعُكُمْ فِى بَعْضِ ٱلْأَمْرِ وَٱللَّهُ يَعْلَمُ إِسْرَارَهُمْ ﴿٢٦﴾

27. How, then, will it be when the angels shall carry them off, beating their faces and their buttocks?

فَكَيْفَ إِذَا تَوَفَّتْهُمُ ٱلْمَلَـٰئِكَةُ يَضْرِبُونَ وُجُوهَهُمْ وَأَدْبَـٰرَهُمْ ﴿٢٧﴾

28. That is because they have followed what has angered Allah and were averse to His good pleasure. So He has foiled their works.

ذَٰلِكَ بِأَنَّهُمُ ٱتَّبَعُوا مَا أَسْخَطَ ٱللَّهَ وَكَرِهُوا رِضْوَٰنَهُ فَأَحْبَطَ أَعْمَـٰلَهُمْ ﴿٢٨﴾

29. Or do those in whose hearts is a sickness think that Allah will not bring their rancours to light?

أَمْ حَسِبَ ٱلَّذِينَ فِى قُلُوبِهِم مَّرَضٌ أَن لَّن يُخْرِجَ ٱللَّهُ أَضْغَـٰنَهُمْ ﴿٢٩﴾

30. Had We wished, We would have shown them to you, so that you might know them by their mark. And you shall surely know them by their distorted speech. Allah knows your works.

وَلَوْ نَشَآءُ لَأَرَيْنَـٰكَهُمْ فَلَعَرَفْتَهُم بِسِيمَـٰهُمْ وَلَتَعْرِفَنَّهُمْ فِى لَحْنِ ٱلْقَوْلِ وَٱللَّهُ يَعْلَمُ أَعْمَـٰلَكُمْ ﴿٣٠﴾

31. And We shall test you so as to know who are the fighters among you and who are the steadfast; and We shall test your news.

وَلَنَبْلُوَنَّكُمْ حَتَّىٰ نَعْلَمَ ٱلْمُجَـٰهِدِينَ مِنكُمْ وَٱلصَّـٰبِرِينَ وَنَبْلُوَا۟ أَخْبَارَكُمْ ﴿٣١﴾

32. Indeed, those who have disbelieved and barred (men) from Allah's Path and were at odds with the Messenger, after the Guidance became manifest to them, will not cause Allah any harm, and He will foil their works.

33. O believers, obey Allah and obey the Messenger and do not render your actions vain.

34. Indeed, those who have disbelieved and barred from Allah's Path, then died as unbelievers, Allah will not forgive them.

35. So do not weaken and call for peace, while you have the upper hand and Allah is with you. He will not stint you your actions.

36. Indeed, this present life is but sport and amusement; and if you believe and are God-fearing, He will give you your wages and will not ask you for your possessions.

37. Were He to ask you for them and press you, you will surely be niggardly, and He will bring your rancours to light.

38. There you are; you are called upon to spend freely in Allah's Cause, but some of you are niggardly. Yet he who is niggardly is only niggardly unto himself. Allah is the All-Sufficient and you are the destitute. If you turn back, He will replace you by a people other than you, and they will not be like you at all.

إِنَّ الَّذِينَ كَفَرُوا وَصَدُّوا عَن سَبِيلِ اللَّهِ وَشَاقُّوا الرَّسُولَ مِنۢ بَعْدِ مَا تَبَيَّنَ لَهُمُ الْهُدَىٰ لَن يَضُرُّوا اللَّهَ شَيْـًٔا وَسَيُحْبِطُ أَعْمَالَهُمْ ﴿٣٢﴾

۞ يَٰٓأَيُّهَا الَّذِينَ ءَامَنُوٓا أَطِيعُوا اللَّهَ وَأَطِيعُوا الرَّسُولَ وَلَا تُبْطِلُوٓا أَعْمَالَكُمْ ﴿٣٣﴾

إِنَّ الَّذِينَ كَفَرُوا وَصَدُّوا عَن سَبِيلِ اللَّهِ ثُمَّ مَاتُوا وَهُمْ كُفَّارٌ فَلَن يَغْفِرَ اللَّهُ لَهُمْ ﴿٣٤﴾

فَلَا تَهِنُوا وَتَدْعُوٓا إِلَى السَّلْمِ وَأَنتُمُ الْأَعْلَوْنَ وَاللَّهُ مَعَكُمْ وَلَن يَتِرَكُمْ أَعْمَالَكُمْ ﴿٣٥﴾

إِنَّمَا الْحَيَوٰةُ الدُّنْيَا لَعِبٌ وَلَهْوٌ وَإِن تُؤْمِنُوا وَتَتَّقُوا يُؤْتِكُمْ أُجُورَكُمْ وَلَا يَسْـَٔلْكُمْ أَمْوَٰلَكُمْ ﴿٣٦﴾

إِن يَسْـَٔلْكُمُوهَا فَيُحْفِكُمْ تَبْخَلُوا وَيُخْرِجْ أَضْغَٰنَكُمْ ﴿٣٧﴾

هَٰٓأَنتُمْ هَٰٓؤُلَآءِ تُدْعَوْنَ لِتُنفِقُوا فِى سَبِيلِ اللَّهِ فَمِنكُم مَّن يَبْخَلُ وَمَن يَبْخَلْ فَإِنَّمَا يَبْخَلُ عَن نَّفْسِهِ وَاللَّهُ الْغَنِىُّ وَأَنتُمُ الْفُقَرَآءُ وَإِن تَتَوَلَّوْا يَسْتَبْدِلْ قَوْمًا غَيْرَكُمْ ثُمَّ لَا يَكُونُوٓا أَمْثَٰلَكُم ﴿٣٨﴾

Sûrat Al-Fath,
(The Victory) 48

In the Name of Allah,
the Compassionate, the Merciful

1. We have indeed given you a manifest victory,

2. That Allah may forgive you your former and your latter sins, and complete His Blessing upon you and lead you unto a straight path;

3. And that Allah may give you a mighty victory.

4. It is He Who has sent down the Serenity upon the hearts of the believers that they may increase in faith upon their faith. To Allah belong the hosts of the heavens and the earth; and Allah is All-Knowing and Wise.

5. That He may admit the believers, men and women, into gardens beneath which rivers flow, dwelling therein forever, and that He may remit their sins. That, in Allah's Sight, is a great triumph.

6. And that He may punish the hypocrites, men and women, and the unbelievers, men and women, who think evil thoughts of Allah. Upon them is the evil turn of fortune. Allah is wrathful at them, curses them and has prepared Hell for them; and what a wretched fate!

7. To Allah belong the hosts of the heavens and the earth, and Allah is All-Mighty and Wise.

8. Indeed, We have sent you forth as a witness, a bearer of good news and a warner;

9. That you[771] may believe in Allah and His Messenger, to honour, revere and glorify Him, morning and evening.

---

771. People of Medina.

10. Those who pay you[772] homage are actually paying Allah homage. Allah's Hand is above their hands; so he who breaks his oath only breaks it to his loss, and he who fulfils what he had pledged unto Allah, He will grant him a great wage.

إِنَّ ٱلَّذِينَ يُبَايِعُونَكَ إِنَّمَا يُبَايِعُونَ ٱللَّهَ يَدُ ٱللَّهِ فَوْقَ أَيْدِيهِمْ فَمَن نَّكَثَ فَإِنَّمَا يَنكُثُ عَلَى نَفْسِهِۦ وَمَنْ أَوْفَىٰ بِمَا عَٰهَدَ عَلَيْهُ ٱللَّهَ فَسَيُؤْتِيهِ أَجْرًا عَظِيمًا ﴿١٠﴾

11. The Bedouins who stayed behind[773] will say to you: "Our possessions and our families preoccupied us; so ask forgiveness for us." They say with their tongues what is not in their hearts. Say: "Who can avail you anything against Allah, if He wishes to harm you or He wishes to profit you? No, Allah is Fully Aware of what you do.

سَيَقُولُ لَكَ ٱلْمُخَلَّفُونَ مِنَ ٱلْأَعْرَابِ شَغَلَتْنَآ أَمْوَٰلُنَا وَأَهْلُونَا فَٱسْتَغْفِرْ لَنَا يَقُولُونَ بِأَلْسِنَتِهِم مَّا لَيْسَ فِي قُلُوبِهِمْ قُلْ فَمَن يَمْلِكُ لَكُم مِّنَ ٱللَّهِ شَيْئًا إِنْ أَرَادَ بِكُمْ ضَرًّا أَوْ أَرَادَ بِكُمْ نَفْعًا بَلْ كَانَ ٱللَّهُ بِمَا تَعْمَلُونَ خَبِيرًا ﴿١١﴾

12. "Rather, you thought that the Messenger and the believers will never return to their families; and that was embellished in your hearts and you entertained evil thoughts and were a useless people."

بَلْ ظَنَنتُمْ أَن لَّن يَنقَلِبَ ٱلرَّسُولُ وَٱلْمُؤْمِنُونَ إِلَىٰٓ أَهْلِيهِمْ أَبَدًا وَزُيِّنَ ذَٰلِكَ فِي قُلُوبِكُمْ وَظَنَنتُمْ ظَنَّ ٱلسَّوْءِ وَكُنتُمْ قَوْمًا بُورًا ﴿١٢﴾

13. He who does not believe in Allah and His Messenger, We have, indeed, prepared for the unbelievers a blazing Fire.

وَمَن لَّمْ يُؤْمِنۢ بِٱللَّهِ وَرَسُولِهِۦ فَإِنَّآ أَعْتَدْنَا لِلْكَٰفِرِينَ سَعِيرًا ﴿١٣﴾

14. To Allah belongs the dominion of the heavens and the earth; He forgives whomever He wishes and punishes whomever He wishes. Allah is All-Forgiving and Merciful.

وَلِلَّهِ مُلْكُ ٱلسَّمَٰوَٰتِ وَٱلْأَرْضِ يَغْفِرُ لِمَن يَشَآءُ وَيُعَذِّبُ مَن يَشَآءُ وَكَانَ ٱللَّهُ غَفُورًا رَّحِيمًا ﴿١٤﴾

15. Those who stayed behind will say, when you set out after certain spoils to seize them: "Let us follow you"; intending to change Allah's Words. Say: "You shall not follow us; thus has Allah said already." They will then say: "No, you are jealous of us." Rather, they understand but a little.

سَيَقُولُ ٱلْمُخَلَّفُونَ إِذَا ٱنطَلَقْتُمْ إِلَىٰ مَغَانِمَ لِتَأْخُذُوهَا ذَرُونَا نَتَّبِعْكُمْ يُرِيدُونَ أَن يُبَدِّلُوٓا۟ كَلَٰمَ ٱللَّهِ قُل لَّن تَتَّبِعُونَا كَذَٰلِكُمْ قَالَ ٱللَّهُ مِن قَبْلُ فَسَيَقُولُونَ بَلْ تَحْسُدُونَنَا بَلْ كَانُوا۟ لَا يَفْقَهُونَ إِلَّا قَلِيلًا ﴿١٥﴾

---

772. The Prophet.
773. During the siege [of Mecca] in the year eight of the Hijrah.

16. Say to those who stayed behind: "You shall be called up against a people of great might; you shall fight them or they shall submit. If, then, you obey, He will grant you a fair wage; but if you turn away as you turned away before, He will inflict a painful punishment upon you."

قُل لِّلْمُخَلَّفِينَ مِنَ ٱلْأَعْرَابِ سَتُدْعَوْنَ إِلَىٰ قَوْمٍ أُوْلِى بَأْسٍ شَدِيدٍ تُقَٰتِلُونَهُمْ أَوْ يُسْلِمُونَ فَإِن تُطِيعُوا۟ يُؤْتِكُمُ ٱللَّهُ أَجْرًا حَسَنًا وَإِن تَتَوَلَّوْا۟ كَمَا تَوَلَّيْتُم مِّن قَبْلُ يُعَذِّبْكُمْ عَذَابًا أَلِيمًا ۝

17. The blind are not to blame, nor the cripple is to blame, nor the sick are to blame. Whoever obeys Allah and His Messenger, He will admit him into Gardens beneath which rivers flow; but he who turns away, He will inflict upon him a painful punishment.

لَّيْسَ عَلَى ٱلْأَعْمَىٰ حَرَجٌ وَلَا عَلَى ٱلْأَعْرَجِ حَرَجٌ وَلَا عَلَى ٱلْمَرِيضِ حَرَجٌ وَمَن يُطِعِ ٱللَّهَ وَرَسُولَهُ يُدْخِلْهُ جَنَّٰتٍ تَجْرِى مِن تَحْتِهَا ٱلْأَنْهَٰرُ وَمَن يَتَوَلَّ يُعَذِّبْهُ عَذَابًا أَلِيمًا ۝

18. Allah was well pleased with the believers, when they paid you homage under the tree; so He knew what was in their hearts and sent down the Serenity upon them and rewarded them with a victory near at hand,

۞ لَّقَدْ رَضِىَ ٱللَّهُ عَنِ ٱلْمُؤْمِنِينَ إِذْ يُبَايِعُونَكَ تَحْتَ ٱلشَّجَرَةِ فَعَلِمَ مَا فِى قُلُوبِهِمْ فَأَنزَلَ ٱلسَّكِينَةَ عَلَيْهِمْ وَأَثَٰبَهُمْ فَتْحًا قَرِيبًا ۝

19. And with many spoils for them to seize. Allah is All-Mighty, All-Wise.

وَمَغَانِمَ كَثِيرَةً يَأْخُذُونَهَا وَكَانَ ٱللَّهُ عَزِيزًا حَكِيمًا ۝

20. Allah has promised you many spoils, for you to take, and He has hastened this one[774] and held the hands of people back off you, that it may be a sign to the believers and that He might guide you to a straight path.

وَعَدَكُمُ ٱللَّهُ مَغَانِمَ كَثِيرَةً تَأْخُذُونَهَا فَعَجَّلَ لَكُمْ هَٰذِهِ وَكَفَّ أَيْدِىَ ٱلنَّاسِ عَنكُمْ وَلِتَكُونَ ءَايَةً لِّلْمُؤْمِنِينَ وَيَهْدِيَكُمْ صِرَٰطًا مُّسْتَقِيمًا ۝

21. And another one[775] which you could not take; Allah had besieged it already. Allah has power over everything.

وَأُخْرَىٰ لَمْ تَقْدِرُوا۟ عَلَيْهَا قَدْ أَحَاطَ ٱللَّهُ بِهَا وَكَانَ ٱللَّهُ عَلَىٰ كُلِّ شَىْءٍ قَدِيرًا ۝

22. Had the unbelievers fought you, they would certainly have turned their backs in flight; then they would have found no friend or supporter.

وَلَوْ قَٰتَلَكُمُ ٱلَّذِينَ كَفَرُوا۟ لَوَلَّوُا۟ ٱلْأَدْبَٰرَ ثُمَّ لَا يَجِدُونَ وَلِيًّا وَلَا نَصِيرًا ۝

---

774. The spoils of Khaybar.
775. Mecca.

23. It is Allah's Way which has gone before; and you will never find any alteration of Allah's Way.

24. It is He Who held their hands back from you, and your hands from them in the valley of Mecca, after He gave you victory over them. Allah observed whatever you do.

25. It is they who disbelieved and barred you from the Sacred Mosque, and the offering was prevented from reaching its sacrificial site. Had it not been for some believing men and some believing women, whom you did not know, lest you should trample them and earn thereby the guilt unwittingly, that Allah might thereby admit into His Mercy whomever He wishes. Had they stood apart, We would have inflicted on those of them who disbelieved a painful punishment.

26. When the unbelievers instilled in their hearts fierceness, the fierceness of paganism, Allah then sent down His Serenity upon His Messenger and upon the believers, and imposed on them the word of piety, they being more deserving thereof and worthier. Allah has knowledge of everything.

27. Allah has fulfilled His Messenger's vision in truth: "You shall enter the Sacred Mosque, if Allah wishes, in security, your heads shaved and your hair cut short, without fear." For He knew what you did not know and gave you, prior to that, a victory near at hand.[776]

28. It is He Who sent forth His Messenger with the guidance and the religion of truth, that He may exalt it above every other religion. Allah suffices as Witness.

سُنَّةَ ٱللَّهِ ٱلَّتِي قَدْ خَلَتْ مِن قَبْلُ وَلَن تَجِدَ لِسُنَّةِ ٱللَّهِ تَبْدِيلًا ﴿٢٣﴾

وَهُوَ ٱلَّذِي كَفَّ أَيْدِيَهُمْ عَنكُمْ وَأَيْدِيَكُمْ عَنْهُم بِبَطْنِ مَكَّةَ مِنۢ بَعْدِ أَنْ أَظْفَرَكُمْ عَلَيْهِمْ وَكَانَ ٱللَّهُ بِمَا تَعْمَلُونَ بَصِيرًا ﴿٢٤﴾

هُمُ ٱلَّذِينَ كَفَرُوا۟ وَصَدُّوكُمْ عَنِ ٱلْمَسْجِدِ ٱلْحَرَامِ وَٱلْهَدْيَ مَعْكُوفًا أَن يَبْلُغَ مَحِلَّهُۥ وَلَوْلَا رِجَالٌ مُّؤْمِنُونَ وَنِسَآءٌ مُّؤْمِنَٰتٌ لَّمْ تَعْلَمُوهُمْ أَن تَطَـُٔوهُمْ فَتُصِيبَكُم مِّنْهُم مَّعَرَّةٌۢ بِغَيْرِ عِلْمٍ لِّيُدْخِلَ ٱللَّهُ فِي رَحْمَتِهِۦ مَن يَشَآءُ لَوْ تَزَيَّلُوا۟ لَعَذَّبْنَا ٱلَّذِينَ كَفَرُوا۟ مِنْهُمْ عَذَابًا أَلِيمًا ﴿٢٥﴾

إِذْ جَعَلَ ٱلَّذِينَ كَفَرُوا۟ فِي قُلُوبِهِمُ ٱلْحَمِيَّةَ حَمِيَّةَ ٱلْجَٰهِلِيَّةِ فَأَنزَلَ ٱللَّهُ سَكِينَتَهُۥ عَلَىٰ رَسُولِهِۦ وَعَلَى ٱلْمُؤْمِنِينَ وَأَلْزَمَهُمْ كَلِمَةَ ٱلتَّقْوَىٰ وَكَانُوٓا۟ أَحَقَّ بِهَا وَأَهْلَهَا وَكَانَ ٱللَّهُ بِكُلِّ شَىْءٍ عَلِيمًا ﴿٢٦﴾

لَّقَدْ صَدَقَ ٱللَّهُ رَسُولَهُ ٱلرُّءْيَا بِٱلْحَقِّ لَتَدْخُلُنَّ ٱلْمَسْجِدَ ٱلْحَرَامَ إِن شَآءَ ٱللَّهُ ءَامِنِينَ مُحَلِّقِينَ رُءُوسَكُمْ وَمُقَصِّرِينَ لَا تَخَافُونَ فَعَلِمَ مَا لَمْ تَعْلَمُوا۟ فَجَعَلَ مِن دُونِ ذَٰلِكَ فَتْحًا قَرِيبًا ﴿٢٧﴾

هُوَ ٱلَّذِىٓ أَرْسَلَ رَسُولَهُۥ بِٱلْهُدَىٰ وَدِينِ ٱلْحَقِّ لِيُظْهِرَهُۥ عَلَى ٱلدِّينِ كُلِّهِۦ وَكَفَىٰ بِٱللَّهِ شَهِيدًا ﴿٢٨﴾

---

776. By signing the peace of Hudaibiyah and capturing the settlement of Khaybar.

29. Muhammad is the Messenger of Allah and those who are with him are hard on the unbelievers, merciful towards each other. You will see them kneeling and prostrating themselves, seeking bounty and good pleasure from Allah; their mark is upon their faces, as a trace of their prostration. That is their likeness in the Torah and their likeness in the Gospels; just as a seed which puts forth its shoot, strengthens it and grows stout, then rises straight upon its stalks, delighting the sower, to vex thereby the unbelievers. Allah has promised those who believe and do the righteous deeds forgiveness and a great wage.

مُّحَمَّدٌ رَّسُولُ ٱللَّهِ وَٱلَّذِينَ مَعَهُۥ أَشِدَّآءُ عَلَى ٱلْكُفَّارِ رُحَمَآءُ بَيْنَهُمْ تَرَىٰهُمْ رُكَّعًا سُجَّدًا يَبْتَغُونَ فَضْلًا مِّنَ ٱللَّهِ وَرِضْوَٰنًا سِيمَاهُمْ فِى وُجُوهِهِم مِّنْ أَثَرِ ٱلسُّجُودِ ذَٰلِكَ مَثَلُهُمْ فِى ٱلتَّوْرَىٰةِ وَمَثَلُهُمْ فِى ٱلْإِنجِيلِ كَزَرْعٍ أَخْرَجَ شَطْـَٔهُۥ فَـَٔازَرَهُۥ فَٱسْتَغْلَظَ فَٱسْتَوَىٰ عَلَىٰ سُوقِهِۦ يُعْجِبُ ٱلزُّرَّاعَ لِيَغِيظَ بِهِمُ ٱلْكُفَّارَ وَعَدَ ٱللَّهُ ٱلَّذِينَ ءَامَنُوا۟ وَعَمِلُوا۟ ٱلصَّٰلِحَٰتِ مِنْهُم مَّغْفِرَةً وَأَجْرًا عَظِيمًۢا ﴿٢٩﴾

Sûrat Al-Hujurât, (The Chambers) 49

In the Name of Allah, the Compassionate, the Merciful

بِسْمِ ٱللَّهِ ٱلرَّحْمَٰنِ ٱلرَّحِيمِ

1. O believers, do not advance hastily before Allah and His Messenger, and fear Allah. Allah is indeed All-Hearing, All-Knowing.

يَٰٓأَيُّهَا ٱلَّذِينَ ءَامَنُوا۟ لَا تُقَدِّمُوا۟ بَيْنَ يَدَىِ ٱللَّهِ وَرَسُولِهِۦ وَٱتَّقُوا۟ ٱللَّهَ إِنَّ ٱللَّهَ سَمِيعٌ عَلِيمٌ ﴿١﴾

2. O believers, do not raise your voices above the Prophet's voice and do not be loud in speaking to him, as you speak loudly to one another, lest your works come to grief while you are unaware.

يَٰٓأَيُّهَا ٱلَّذِينَ ءَامَنُوا۟ لَا تَرْفَعُوٓا۟ أَصْوَٰتَكُمْ فَوْقَ صَوْتِ ٱلنَّبِىِّ وَلَا تَجْهَرُوا۟ لَهُۥ بِٱلْقَوْلِ كَجَهْرِ بَعْضِكُمْ لِبَعْضٍ أَن تَحْبَطَ أَعْمَٰلُكُمْ وَأَنتُمْ لَا تَشْعُرُونَ ﴿٢﴾

3. Surely, those who lower their voices in the presence of Allah's Messenger are those whose hearts Allah had tested for piety. They will have forgiveness and a great wage.

إِنَّ ٱلَّذِينَ يَغُضُّونَ أَصْوَٰتَهُمْ عِندَ رَسُولِ ٱللَّهِ أُو۟لَٰٓئِكَ ٱلَّذِينَ ٱمْتَحَنَ ٱللَّهُ قُلُوبَهُمْ لِلتَّقْوَىٰ لَهُم مَّغْفِرَةٌ وَأَجْرٌ عَظِيمٌ ﴿٣﴾

4. Those who call you from behind the Chambers, most of them do not understand.

إِنَّ ٱلَّذِينَ يُنَادُونَكَ مِن وَرَآءِ ٱلْحُجُرَٰتِ أَكْثَرُهُمْ لَا يَعْقِلُونَ ﴿٤﴾

5. Had they waited for you to come out to meet them, it would have been better for them. Allah is All-Forgiving and Merciful.

6. O believers, if a sinner brings you a piece of news, make sure you do not cause some people distress unwittingly, and so regret subsequently what you have done.

7. Know that Allah's Messenger is in your midst. Were he to obey you in much of your affairs, you would suffer hardship; but Allah has endeared belief to you and embellished it in your hearts, and He has made you to hate unbelief, sin and disobedience. Such are the rightly guided.

8. As a Bounty from Allah and a Favour. Allah is All-Knowing and Wise.

9. If two parties of the believers should fight one another, bring them peacefully together; but if one of them seeks to oppress the other, then fight the oppressor until it reverts to Allah's Command. If it reverts, then bring them together in justice and be equitable; for Allah loves the equitable.

10. Surely, the believers are brothers; so bring your two brothers together and fear Allah, so that you may receive Mercy.

11. O believers, let not one people scoff at another people, lest they be better than they; nor women at other women, lest they be better than they. Do not slander yourselves and do not revile each other with false names. Wretched is the name of ungodliness, after belief! He who does not repent, such are the wrongdoers, indeed.

وَلَوْ أَنَّهُمْ صَبَرُوا حَتَّىٰ تَخْرُجَ إِلَيْهِمْ لَكَانَ خَيْرًا لَّهُمْ وَاللَّهُ غَفُورٌ رَّحِيمٌ ۝

يَـٰٓأَيُّهَا ٱلَّذِينَ ءَامَنُوٓا إِن جَآءَكُمْ فَاسِقٌ بِنَبَإٍ فَتَبَيَّنُوٓا أَن تُصِيبُوا قَوْمًۢا بِجَهَـٰلَةٍ فَتُصْبِحُوا عَلَىٰ مَا فَعَلْتُمْ نَـٰدِمِينَ ۝

وَٱعْلَمُوٓا أَنَّ فِيكُمْ رَسُولَ ٱللَّهِ لَوْ يُطِيعُكُمْ فِى كَثِيرٍ مِّنَ ٱلْأَمْرِ لَعَنِتُّمْ وَلَـٰكِنَّ ٱللَّهَ حَبَّبَ إِلَيْكُمُ ٱلْإِيمَـٰنَ وَزَيَّنَهُۥ فِى قُلُوبِكُمْ وَكَرَّهَ إِلَيْكُمُ ٱلْكُفْرَ وَٱلْفُسُوقَ وَٱلْعِصْيَانَ أُوْلَـٰٓئِكَ هُمُ ٱلرَّٰشِدُونَ ۝

فَضْلًا مِّنَ ٱللَّهِ وَنِعْمَةً وَٱللَّهُ عَلِيمٌ حَكِيمٌ ۝

وَإِن طَآئِفَتَانِ مِنَ ٱلْمُؤْمِنِينَ ٱقْتَتَلُوا فَأَصْلِحُوا بَيْنَهُمَا فَإِنۢ بَغَتْ إِحْدَىٰهُمَا عَلَى ٱلْأُخْرَىٰ فَقَـٰتِلُوا ٱلَّتِى تَبْغِى حَتَّىٰ تَفِىٓءَ إِلَىٰٓ أَمْرِ ٱللَّهِ فَإِن فَآءَتْ فَأَصْلِحُوا بَيْنَهُمَا بِٱلْعَدْلِ وَأَقْسِطُوٓا إِنَّ ٱللَّهَ يُحِبُّ ٱلْمُقْسِطِينَ ۝

إِنَّمَا ٱلْمُؤْمِنُونَ إِخْوَةٌ فَأَصْلِحُوا بَيْنَ أَخَوَيْكُمْ وَٱتَّقُوا ٱللَّهَ لَعَلَّكُمْ تُرْحَمُونَ ۝

يَـٰٓأَيُّهَا ٱلَّذِينَ ءَامَنُوا لَا يَسْخَرْ قَوْمٌ مِّن قَوْمٍ عَسَىٰٓ أَن يَكُونُوا خَيْرًا مِّنْهُمْ وَلَا نِسَآءٌ مِّن نِّسَآءٍ عَسَىٰٓ أَن يَكُنَّ خَيْرًا مِّنْهُنَّ وَلَا تَلْمِزُوٓا أَنفُسَكُمْ وَلَا تَنَابَزُوا بِٱلْأَلْقَـٰبِ بِئْسَ ٱلِٱسْمُ ٱلْفُسُوقُ بَعْدَ ٱلْإِيمَـٰنِ وَمَن لَّمْ يَتُبْ فَأُوْلَـٰٓئِكَ هُمُ ٱلظَّـٰلِمُونَ ۝

12. O believers, avoid much suspicion; for some suspicion is a sin. Do not spy and do not backbite one another. Does any of you wish to eat his brother's flesh dead? You would surely hate it. Fear Allah, for Allah is truly Absolving, Merciful.

يَٰٓأَيُّهَا ٱلَّذِينَ ءَامَنُوا۟ ٱجْتَنِبُوا۟ كَثِيرًا مِّنَ ٱلظَّنِّ إِنَّ بَعْضَ ٱلظَّنِّ إِثْمٌ وَلَا تَجَسَّسُوا۟ وَلَا يَغْتَب بَّعْضُكُم بَعْضًا أَيُحِبُّ أَحَدُكُمْ أَن يَأْكُلَ لَحْمَ أَخِيهِ مَيْتًا فَكَرِهْتُمُوهُ وَٱتَّقُوا۟ ٱللَّهَ إِنَّ ٱللَّهَ تَوَّابٌ رَّحِيمٌ ﴿١٢﴾

13. O mankind, We have created you male and female and made you nations and tribes, so that you might come to know one another. Surely the noblest of you in Allah's Sight is the most pious. Allah indeed is All-Knowing, All-Informed.

يَٰٓأَيُّهَا ٱلنَّاسُ إِنَّا خَلَقْنَٰكُم مِّن ذَكَرٍ وَأُنثَىٰ وَجَعَلْنَٰكُمْ شُعُوبًا وَقَبَآئِلَ لِتَعَارَفُوٓا۟ إِنَّ أَكْرَمَكُمْ عِندَ ٱللَّهِ أَتْقَىٰكُمْ إِنَّ ٱللَّهَ عَلِيمٌ خَبِيرٌ ﴿١٣﴾

14. The Bedouins say: "We believe." Say: "You do not believe, but say: 'We submit'; for belief has not yet entered your hearts. If you obey Allah and His Messenger, He will not stint you any of your works. Allah is surely All-Forgiving and Merciful."

۞ قَالَتِ ٱلْأَعْرَابُ ءَامَنَّا قُل لَّمْ تُؤْمِنُوا۟ وَلَٰكِن قُولُوٓا۟ أَسْلَمْنَا وَلَمَّا يَدْخُلِ ٱلْإِيمَٰنُ فِى قُلُوبِكُمْ وَإِن تُطِيعُوا۟ ٱللَّهَ وَرَسُولَهُۥ لَا يَلِتْكُم مِّنْ أَعْمَٰلِكُمْ شَيْـًٔا إِنَّ ٱللَّهَ غَفُورٌ رَّحِيمٌ ﴿١٤﴾

15. Indeed, the believers are those who have believed in Allah and His Messenger, then were not in doubt, but struggled with their possessions and themselves in the Cause of Allah. Those are the truthful ones.

إِنَّمَا ٱلْمُؤْمِنُونَ ٱلَّذِينَ ءَامَنُوا۟ بِٱللَّهِ وَرَسُولِهِۦ ثُمَّ لَمْ يَرْتَابُوا۟ وَجَٰهَدُوا۟ بِأَمْوَٰلِهِمْ وَأَنفُسِهِمْ فِى سَبِيلِ ٱللَّهِ أُو۟لَٰٓئِكَ هُمُ ٱلصَّٰدِقُونَ ﴿١٥﴾

16. Say: "Will you inform Allah about your religion, while Allah knows what is in the heavens and in the earth? Allah has knowledge of everything."

قُلْ أَتُعَلِّمُونَ ٱللَّهَ بِدِينِكُمْ وَٱللَّهُ يَعْلَمُ مَا فِى ٱلسَّمَٰوَٰتِ وَمَا فِى ٱلْأَرْضِ وَٱللَّهُ بِكُلِّ شَىْءٍ عَلِيمٌ ﴿١٦﴾

17. They regard it a favour to you that they have submitted. Say: "Do not regard your submission a favour to me; rather Allah has favoured you when He guided you to belief, if you are really truthful.

يَمُنُّونَ عَلَيْكَ أَنْ أَسْلَمُوا۟ قُل لَّا تَمُنُّوا۟ عَلَىَّ إِسْلَٰمَكُم بَلِ ٱللَّهُ يَمُنُّ عَلَيْكُمْ أَنْ هَدَىٰكُمْ لِلْإِيمَٰنِ إِن كُنتُمْ صَٰدِقِينَ ﴿١٧﴾

18. "Allah knows the secrets of the heavens and the earth, and Allah sees well the things you do."

إِنَّ ٱللَّهَ يَعْلَمُ غَيْبَ ٱلسَّمَٰوَٰتِ وَٱلْأَرْضِ وَٱللَّهُ بَصِيرٌۢ بِمَا تَعْمَلُونَ ﴿١٨﴾

Sûrat Qâf, **50**	سُورَةُ قٓ

In the Name of Allah,
the Compassionate, the Merciful

بِسْمِ ٱللَّهِ ٱلرَّحْمَٰنِ ٱلرَّحِيمِ

1. Qâf.
By the glorious Qur'an.

قٓ ۚ وَٱلْقُرْءَانِ ٱلْمَجِيدِ ﴿١﴾

2. Yet, they marvel that a warner has come to them from among them, and so the un-believers say: "This is a strange thing!

بَلْ عَجِبُوٓا۟ أَن جَآءَهُم مُّنذِرٌ مِّنْهُمْ فَقَالَ ٱلْكَٰفِرُونَ هَٰذَا شَىْءٌ عَجِيبٌ ﴿٢﴾

3. "What, when we are dead and have become dust - that is a far-off return!"

أَءِذَا مِتْنَا وَكُنَّا تُرَابًا ذَٰلِكَ رَجْعٌ بَعِيدٌ ﴿٣﴾

4. We know well what the earth shall swallow up of them; for We have a recording Book.

قَدْ عَلِمْنَا مَا تَنقُصُ ٱلْأَرْضُ مِنْهُمْ ۖ وَعِندَنَا كِتَٰبٌ حَفِيظٌ ﴿٤﴾

5. Yet, they have denounced the Truth when it came to them, and so they are in a confused state.

بَلْ كَذَّبُوا۟ بِٱلْحَقِّ لَمَّا جَآءَهُمْ فَهُمْ فِىٓ أَمْرٍ مَّرِيجٍ ﴿٥﴾

6. Have they not beheld the heaven above them, how We erected it and adorned it, and it has no cracks?

أَفَلَمْ يَنظُرُوٓا۟ إِلَى ٱلسَّمَآءِ فَوْقَهُمْ كَيْفَ بَنَيْنَٰهَا وَزَيَّنَّٰهَا وَمَا لَهَا مِن فُرُوجٍ ﴿٦﴾

7. And the earth We have spread out and set in it immovable mountains; and We cause to grow in it every delightful variety;

وَٱلْأَرْضَ مَدَدْنَٰهَا وَأَلْقَيْنَا فِيهَا رَوَٰسِىَ وَأَنۢبَتْنَا فِيهَا مِن كُلِّ زَوْجٍ بَهِيجٍ ﴿٧﴾

8. As a guidance and reminder to every penitent servant.

تَبْصِرَةً وَذِكْرَىٰ لِكُلِّ عَبْدٍ مُّنِيبٍ ﴿٨﴾

9. And We brought down from heaven blessed water and caused thereby gardens to grow and harvest-grain;

وَنَزَّلْنَا مِنَ ٱلسَّمَآءِ مَآءً مُّبَٰرَكًا فَأَنۢبَتْنَا بِهِۦ جَنَّٰتٍ وَحَبَّ ٱلْحَصِيدِ ﴿٩﴾

10. And tall palm trees with clusters well-knit,

وَٱلنَّخْلَ بَاسِقَٰتٍ لَّهَا طَلْعٌ نَّضِيدٌ ﴿١٠﴾

11. As provision for the servants; and We have revived thereby a dead town. Thus will the Resurrection[777] be.

رِّزْقًا لِّلْعِبَادِ ۖ وَأَحْيَيْنَا بِهِۦ بَلْدَةً مَّيْتًا ۚ كَذَٰلِكَ ٱلْخُرُوجُ ﴿١١﴾

---

777. Or Exodus.

12. Prior to them, the people of Noah, the Companions of al-Rass and Thamud denounced [the Prophets].

كَذَّبَتْ قَبْلَهُمْ قَوْمُ نُوحٍ وَأَصْحَابُ الرَّسِّ وَثَمُودُ ﴿١٢﴾

13. 'Ad, Pharaoh and the brethren of Lot, too;

وَعَادٌ وَفِرْعَوْنُ وَإِخْوَانُ لُوطٍ ﴿١٣﴾

14. And the Companions of the Thicket and the people of Tubba', they all denounced the Messengers and so My Warning was fulfilled.

وَأَصْحَابُ الْأَيْكَةِ وَقَوْمُ تُبَّعٍ كُلٌّ كَذَّبَ الرُّسُلَ فَحَقَّ وَعِيدِ ﴿١٤﴾

15. Were We wearied by the first creation? No, they are in doubt regarding a new creation.

أَفَعَيِينَا بِالْخَلْقِ الْأَوَّلِ بَلْ هُمْ فِي لَبْسٍ مِنْ خَلْقٍ جَدِيدٍ ﴿١٥﴾

16. We have indeed created man, and We know what his soul insinuates to him. We are to him closer than the jugular vein.

وَلَقَدْ خَلَقْنَا الْإِنسَانَ وَنَعْلَمُ مَا تُوَسْوِسُ بِهِ نَفْسُهُ وَنَحْنُ أَقْرَبُ إِلَيْهِ مِنْ حَبْلِ الْوَرِيدِ ﴿١٦﴾

17. When the two angels receive, one sitting on the right, the other on the left;

إِذْ يَتَلَقَّى الْمُتَلَقِّيَانِ عَنِ الْيَمِينِ وَعَنِ الشِّمَالِ قَعِيدٌ ﴿١٧﴾

18. He does not utter a word but is observed by a vigilant observer by his side.

مَا يَلْفِظُ مِنْ قَوْلٍ إِلَّا لَدَيْهِ رَقِيبٌ عَتِيدٌ ﴿١٨﴾

19. The death pang has come in truth. "That is what you were turning away from."

وَجَاءَتْ سَكْرَةُ الْمَوْتِ بِالْحَقِّ ذَلِكَ مَا كُنْتَ مِنْهُ تَحِيدُ ﴿١٩﴾

20. The Trumpet will be blown: "That is the Day of Warning."

وَنُفِخَ فِي الصُّورِ ذَلِكَ يَوْمُ الْوَعِيدِ ﴿٢٠﴾

21. Every soul will come forward with (an angel) driver and (an angel) witness.

وَجَاءَتْ كُلُّ نَفْسٍ مَعَهَا سَائِقٌ وَشَهِيدٌ ﴿٢١﴾

22. "You were oblivious of this; so We lifted your cover from you and your vision today is keen."

لَقَدْ كُنْتَ فِي غَفْلَةٍ مِنْ هَذَا فَكَشَفْنَا عَنْكَ غِطَاءَكَ فَبَصَرُكَ الْيَوْمَ حَدِيدٌ ﴿٢٢﴾

23. His companion (angel) will say: "This is what I have; it is ready."

وَقَالَ قَرِينُهُ هَذَا مَا لَدَيَّ عَتِيدٌ ﴿٢٣﴾

24. (Allah will say): "Cast into Hell every obdurate unbeliever;

أَلْقِيَا فِي جَهَنَّمَ كُلَّ كَفَّارٍ عَنِيدٍ ﴿٢٤﴾

25. "Hinderer of the good, transgressor and doubter;

مَنَّاعٍ لِلْخَيْرِ مُعْتَدٍ مُرِيبٍ ﴿٢٥﴾

26. "Who has set up another god beside Allah. Cast him, then, into the terrible punishment."

الَّذِي جَعَلَ مَعَ اللَّهِ إِلَهًا آخَرَ فَأَلْقِيَاهُ فِي الْعَذَابِ الشَّدِيدِ ﴿٢٦﴾

27. His companion[778] will say: "Our Lord, I did not mislead him; but he was already in profound error."

28. He[779] will say: "Do not dispute before Me; for I had warned you in advance.

29. "No word can be changed before Me, and I am no oppressor of servants."

30. "On the Day We shall say to Hell: 'Are you full?', and it shall respond: 'Is there more to come?'"•

31. Paradise will be brought closer to the God-fearing, not a far distance.

32. "This is what you were promised; to every penitent keeper,[780]

33. "He who fears the Compassionate in the Unseen and comes forward with a penitent heart.

34. "Enter it in peace; that is the Day of Immortality."

35. They will have whatever they desire therein, and We have yet much more.

36. How many a generation mightier than they have We destroyed before them? Search the land, then, is there any escape?

37. In that is a reminder to whoever has a heart or lends an ear, while he witnesses.

38. Indeed, We have created the heavens and the earth and what is between them in six days, and We were not touched by weariness.

39. Bear up with what they say and proclaim the Praise of your Lord before sunrise and before sunset.

قَالَ قَرِينُهُ رَبَّنَا مَا أَطْغَيْتُهُ وَلَٰكِن كَانَ فِى ضَلَٰلٍ بَعِيدٍ ﴿٢٧﴾

قَالَ لَا تَخْتَصِمُوا لَدَىَّ وَقَدْ قَدَّمْتُ إِلَيْكُم بِٱلْوَعِيدِ ﴿٢٨﴾

مَا يُبَدَّلُ ٱلْقَوْلُ لَدَىَّ وَمَا أَنَا۠ بِظَلَّٰمٍ لِّلْعَبِيدِ ﴿٢٩﴾

يَوْمَ نَقُولُ لِجَهَنَّمَ هَلِ ٱمْتَلَأْتِ وَتَقُولُ هَلْ مِن مَّزِيدٍ ﴿٣٠﴾

وَأُزْلِفَتِ ٱلْجَنَّةُ لِلْمُتَّقِينَ غَيْرَ بَعِيدٍ ﴿٣١﴾

هَٰذَا مَا تُوعَدُونَ لِكُلِّ أَوَّابٍ حَفِيظٍ ﴿٣٢﴾

مَّنْ خَشِىَ ٱلرَّحْمَٰنَ بِٱلْغَيْبِ وَجَآءَ بِقَلْبٍ مُّنِيبٍ ﴿٣٣﴾

ٱدْخُلُوهَا بِسَلَٰمٍ ذَٰلِكَ يَوْمُ ٱلْخُلُودِ ﴿٣٤﴾

لَهُم مَّا يَشَآءُونَ فِيهَا وَلَدَيْنَا مَزِيدٌ ﴿٣٥﴾

وَكَمْ أَهْلَكْنَا قَبْلَهُم مِّن قَرْنٍ هُمْ أَشَدُّ مِنْهُم بَطْشًا فَنَقَّبُوا۟ فِى ٱلْبِلَٰدِ هَلْ مِن مَّحِيصٍ ﴿٣٦﴾

إِنَّ فِى ذَٰلِكَ لَذِكْرَىٰ لِمَن كَانَ لَهُۥ قَلْبٌ أَوْ أَلْقَى ٱلسَّمْعَ وَهُوَ شَهِيدٌ ﴿٣٧﴾

وَلَقَدْ خَلَقْنَا ٱلسَّمَٰوَٰتِ وَٱلْأَرْضَ وَمَا بَيْنَهُمَا فِى سِتَّةِ أَيَّامٍ وَمَا مَسَّنَا مِن لُّغُوبٍ ﴿٣٨﴾

فَٱصْبِرْ عَلَىٰ مَا يَقُولُونَ وَسَبِّحْ بِحَمْدِ رَبِّكَ قَبْلَ طُلُوعِ ٱلشَّمْسِ وَقَبْلَ ٱلْغُرُوبِ ﴿٣٩﴾

---

778. His demon.
779. Allah.
780. Of Allah's ordinances.

40. And in the night and in the wake of the prostrations, glorify Him.

وَمِنَ ٱلَّيْلِ فَسَبِّحْهُ وَأَدْبَرَ ٱلسُّجُودِ ۝

41. And listen on the Day the caller shall call out from a nearby place;

وَٱسْتَمِعْ يَوْمَ يُنَادِ ٱلْمُنَادِ مِن مَّكَانٍ قَرِيبٍ ۝

42. The day they shall hear the Cry of Truth: "That is the day of rising again."

يَوْمَ يَسْمَعُونَ ٱلصَّيْحَةَ بِٱلْحَقِّ ذَٰلِكَ يَوْمُ ٱلْخُرُوجِ ۝

43. It is We Who give life and cause to die and unto Us is the ultimate return;

إِنَّا نَحْنُ نُحْىِ وَنُمِيتُ وَإِلَيْنَا ٱلْمَصِيرُ ۝

44. The Day that the earth shall be rent asunder around them, as they hasten forth. That, indeed, is an easy mustering for Us.

يَوْمَ تَشَقَّقُ ٱلْأَرْضُ عَنْهُمْ سِرَاعًا ذَٰلِكَ حَشْرٌ عَلَيْنَا يَسِيرٌ ۝

45. We know better what they say and you are not a tyrant terrorizing them. So, remind, by the Qur'an, him who fears My Warning.

نَّحْنُ أَعْلَمُ بِمَا يَقُولُونَ وَمَا أَنتَ عَلَيْهِم بِجَبَّارٍ فَذَكِّرْ بِٱلْقُرْءَانِ مَن يَخَافُ وَعِيدِ ۝

Sûrat Adh-Dhâriyât,
(The Scattering Winds) 51

In the Name of Allah,
the Compassionate, the Merciful

بِسْمِ ٱللَّهِ ٱلرَّحْمَٰنِ ٱلرَّحِيمِ

1. By the scattering winds, as they scatter:

وَٱلذَّٰرِيَٰتِ ذَرْوًا ۝

2. And the clouds, bearing their burden;

فَٱلْحَٰمِلَٰتِ وِقْرًا ۝

3. And the smoothly cruising ships;

فَٱلْجَٰرِيَٰتِ يُسْرًا ۝

4. And the angels which apportion the Command.

فَٱلْمُقَسِّمَٰتِ أَمْرًا ۝

5. Surely, what you are promised is true;

إِنَّمَا تُوعَدُونَ لَصَادِقٌ ۝

6. And the Judgement shall come to pass.

وَإِنَّ ٱلدِّينَ لَوَٰقِعٌ ۝

7. By the heaven with its many tracks,

وَٱلسَّمَاءِ ذَاتِ ٱلْحُبُكِ ۝

8. You are at variance in what you say.

إِنَّكُمْ لَفِى قَوْلٍ مُّخْتَلِفٍ ۝

9. From it[781] are diverted those who would be diverted.

يُؤْفَكُ عَنْهُ مَنْ أُفِكَ ۝

10. May the imposters perish!

قُتِلَ ٱلْخَرَّٰصُونَ ۝

11. Those who are bemused in their perplexity.

ٱلَّذِينَ هُمْ فِى غَمْرَةٍ سَاهُونَ ۝

---

781. The Qur'an.

12. They ask: "When is the Day of Judgement coming?"

يَسْـَٔلُونَ أَيَّانَ يَوْمُ ٱلدِّينِ ﴿١٢﴾

13. The Day they shall be exposed to the Fire.

يَوْمَ هُمْ عَلَى ٱلنَّارِ يُفْتَنُونَ ﴿١٣﴾

14. "Taste your ordeal; this is what you were trying to hasten."

ذُوقُوا۟ فِتْنَتَكُمْ هَٰذَا ٱلَّذِى كُنتُم بِهِۦ تَسْتَعْجِلُونَ ﴿١٤﴾

15. The God-fearing shall be amidst gardens and springs;

إِنَّ ٱلْمُتَّقِينَ فِى جَنَّٰتٍ وَعُيُونٍ ﴿١٥﴾

16. Availing themselves of what their Lord has given them. Before that time, they were beneficent.

ءَاخِذِينَ مَآ ءَاتَىٰهُمْ رَبُّهُمْ إِنَّهُمْ كَانُوا۟ قَبْلَ ذَٰلِكَ مُحْسِنِينَ ﴿١٦﴾

17. They used to sleep but a short watch of the night;

كَانُوا۟ قَلِيلًا مِّنَ ٱلَّيْلِ مَا يَهْجَعُونَ ﴿١٧﴾

18. And at daybreak, they used to ask for forgiveness,

وَبِٱلْأَسْحَارِ هُمْ يَسْتَغْفِرُونَ ﴿١٨﴾

19. And of their possessions, the beggar and the destitute had a share.

وَفِىٓ أَمْوَٰلِهِمْ حَقٌّ لِّلسَّآئِلِ وَٱلْمَحْرُومِ ﴿١٩﴾

20. In the earth are signs for those of certain faith;

وَفِى ٱلْأَرْضِ ءَايَٰتٌ لِّلْمُوقِنِينَ ﴿٢٠﴾

21. And in your souls too. Do you not see?

وَفِىٓ أَنفُسِكُمْ أَفَلَا تُبْصِرُونَ ﴿٢١﴾

22. In heaven is your provision and what you are promised.

وَفِى ٱلسَّمَآءِ رِزْقُكُمْ وَمَا تُوعَدُونَ ﴿٢٢﴾

23. By the Lord of the heaven and earth; it is certainly true, just as your own speaking is true.

فَوَرَبِّ ٱلسَّمَآءِ وَٱلْأَرْضِ إِنَّهُۥ لَحَقٌّ مِّثْلَ مَآ أَنَّكُمْ تَنطِقُونَ ﴿٢٣﴾

24. Has the tale of Abraham's honoured guests reached you?

هَلْ أَتَىٰكَ حَدِيثُ ضَيْفِ إِبْرَٰهِيمَ ٱلْمُكْرَمِينَ ﴿٢٤﴾

25. When they entered upon him and said: "Peace", he replied: "Peace; you are an unknown people to me."

إِذْ دَخَلُوا۟ عَلَيْهِ فَقَالُوا۟ سَلَٰمًا قَالَ سَلَٰمٌ قَوْمٌ مُّنكَرُونَ ﴿٢٥﴾

26. Then, he went back to his own family and brought a fattened calf.

فَرَاغَ إِلَىٰٓ أَهْلِهِۦ فَجَآءَ بِعِجْلٍ سَمِينٍ ﴿٢٦﴾

27. He offered it to them, saying: "Will you not eat?"

فَقَرَّبَهُۥٓ إِلَيْهِمْ قَالَ أَلَا تَأْكُلُونَ ﴿٢٧﴾

28. So, he conceived a fear of them. They said: "Do not fear", and they announced to him the good news of a clever boy.

فَأَوْجَسَ مِنْهُمْ خِيفَةً قَالُوا لَا تَخَفْ وَبَشَّرُوهُ بِغُلَٰمٍ عَلِيمٍ ۝

29. Then his wife came shouting and she smote her face and said: "I am a barren old woman."

فَأَقْبَلَتِ ٱمْرَأَتُهُۥ فِى صَرَّةٍ فَصَكَّتْ وَجْهَهَا وَقَالَتْ عَجُوزٌ عَقِيمٌ ۝

30. They said: "That is what your Lord has said. He is indeed the Wise, the All-Knowing."

قَالُوا كَذَٰلِكِ قَالَ رَبُّكِ إِنَّهُۥ هُوَ ٱلْحَكِيمُ ٱلْعَلِيمُ ۝

31. He[782] said: "And what is your business, O envoys?"

۞ قَالَ فَمَا خَطْبُكُمْ أَيُّهَا ٱلْمُرْسَلُونَ ۝

32. They said: "We have been sent forth to a criminal people;

قَالُوا إِنَّا أُرْسِلْنَا إِلَىٰ قَوْمٍ مُّجْرِمِينَ ۝

33. "To unleash on them stones of clay,

لِنُرْسِلَ عَلَيْهِمْ حِجَارَةً مِّن طِينٍ ۝

34. "Marked by your Lord for the extravagant.

مُّسَوَّمَةً عِندَ رَبِّكَ لِلْمُسْرِفِينَ ۝

35. "So, we brought out such believers as were therein.

فَأَخْرَجْنَا مَن كَانَ فِيهَا مِنَ ٱلْمُؤْمِنِينَ ۝

36. "But did not find in it except one house of those who have submitted.

فَمَا وَجَدْنَا فِيهَا غَيْرَ بَيْتٍ مِّنَ ٱلْمُسْلِمِينَ ۝

37. "And we left therein a sign for those who fear the painful punishment."

وَتَرَكْنَا فِيهَآ ءَايَةً لِّلَّذِينَ يَخَافُونَ ٱلْعَذَابَ ٱلْأَلِيمَ ۝

38. And in Moses,[783] when We sent him forth to Pharaoh with manifest authority.

وَفِى مُوسَىٰٓ إِذْ أَرْسَلْنَٰهُ إِلَىٰ فِرْعَوْنَ بِسُلْطَٰنٍ مُّبِينٍ ۝

39. He[784] turned away with his retinue and said: "A sorcerer or a madman."

فَتَوَلَّىٰ بِرُكْنِهِۦ وَقَالَ سَٰحِرٌ أَوْ مَجْنُونٌ ۝

40. So, We seized him and his hosts and cast them into the sea; for he was blameworthy.

فَأَخَذْنَٰهُ وَجُنُودَهُۥ فَنَبَذْنَٰهُمْ فِى ٱلْيَمِّ وَهُوَ مُلِيمٌ ۝

41. And in 'Ad, when We loosed upon them the barren wind;

وَفِى عَادٍ إِذْ أَرْسَلْنَا عَلَيْهِمُ ٱلرِّيحَ ٱلْعَقِيمَ ۝

42. It left nothing it came upon, but reduced it to rubble.

مَا تَذَرُ مِن شَىْءٍ أَتَتْ عَلَيْهِ إِلَّا جَعَلَتْهُ كَٱلرَّمِيمِ ۝

43. And in Thamud, when it was said to them: "Enjoy yourselves for a while."

وَفِى ثَمُودَ إِذْ قِيلَ لَهُمْ تَمَتَّعُوا حَتَّىٰ حِينٍ ۝

---

782. Abraham.
783. Is a sign.
784. Pharaoh.

44. Then, they disdained arrogantly the command of their Lord, and so the thunderbolt struck them, while they looked on.

فَعَتَوْا عَنْ أَمْرِ رَبِّهِمْ فَأَخَذَتْهُمُ ٱلصَّٰعِقَةُ وَهُمْ يَنظُرُونَ ۝

45. They were unable to stand upright, and they were not victorious.

فَمَا ٱسْتَطَٰعُوا۟ مِن قِيَامٍ وَمَا كَانُوا۟ مُنتَصِرِينَ ۝

46. And We destroyed the people of Noah before that. They were indeed a sinful people.

وَقَوْمَ نُوحٍ مِّن قَبْلُ إِنَّهُمْ كَانُوا۟ قَوْمًا فَٰسِقِينَ ۝

47. And heaven, We have built it mightily, and We shall surely expand it.

وَٱلسَّمَآءَ بَنَيْنَٰهَا بِأَيْيْدٍ وَإِنَّا لَمُوسِعُونَ ۝

48. And the earth, We have spread it out; and how excellently we smoothed it down!

وَٱلْأَرْضَ فَرَشْنَٰهَا فَنِعْمَ ٱلْمَٰهِدُونَ ۝

49. And of everything, We have created a pair, that perchance you might remember.

وَمِن كُلِّ شَىْءٍ خَلَقْنَا زَوْجَيْنِ لَعَلَّكُمْ تَذَكَّرُونَ ۝

50. Therefore, flee unto Allah. I am to you a manifest warner from Him.

فَفِرُّوٓا۟ إِلَى ٱللَّهِ إِنِّى لَكُم مِّنْهُ نَذِيرٌ مُّبِينٌ ۝

51. And do not set up with Allah another god. I am to you a manifest warner from Him.

وَلَا تَجْعَلُوا۟ مَعَ ٱللَّهِ إِلَٰهًا ءَاخَرَ إِنِّى لَكُم مِّنْهُ نَذِيرٌ مُّبِينٌ ۝

52. Likewise, no Messenger came to those who preceded them but they said: "A sorcerer or a madman."

كَذَٰلِكَ مَآ أَتَى ٱلَّذِينَ مِن قَبْلِهِم مِّن رَّسُولٍ إِلَّا قَالُوا۟ سَاحِرٌ أَوْ مَجْنُونٌ ۝

53. Have they attested to each other concerning him?[785] No, they are an unjust people.

أَتَوَاصَوْا۟ بِهِۦ بَلْ هُمْ قَوْمٌ طَاغُونَ ۝

54. So, turn away from them; you are not to blame.

فَتَوَلَّ عَنْهُمْ فَمَآ أَنتَ بِمَلُومٍ ۝

55. And remind; for the reminder will benefit the believers.

وَذَكِّرْ فَإِنَّ ٱلذِّكْرَىٰ تَنفَعُ ٱلْمُؤْمِنِينَ ۝

56. I have not created the jinn and mankind except to worship Me.

وَمَا خَلَقْتُ ٱلْجِنَّ وَٱلْإِنسَ إِلَّا لِيَعْبُدُونِ ۝

57. I do not desire provision from them, and I do not want them to feed Me.

مَآ أُرِيدُ مِنْهُم مِّن رِّزْقٍ وَمَآ أُرِيدُ أَن يُطْعِمُونِ ۝

---

785. Muhammad.

58. Surely, Allah is the All-Provider, the Mighty One, the Strong.

إِنَّ ٱللَّهَ هُوَ ٱلرَّزَّاقُ ذُو ٱلْقُوَّةِ ٱلْمَتِينُ ﴿٥٨﴾

59. The wrongdoers will have a portion like the portions of their fellows; so let them not rush Me.

فَإِنَّ لِلَّذِينَ ظَلَمُوا ذَنُوبًا مِّثْلَ ذَنُوبِ أَصْحَٰبِهِمْ فَلَا يَسْتَعْجِلُونِ ﴿٥٩﴾

60. Woe unto the unbelievers on that Day which they have been promised.

فَوَيْلٌ لِّلَّذِينَ كَفَرُوا مِن يَوْمِهِمُ ٱلَّذِي يُوعَدُونَ ﴿٦٠﴾

Sûrat At-Tur, (The Mount) 52

سُورَةُ الطُّور

In the Name of Allah, the Compassionate, the Merciful

بِسْمِ ٱللَّهِ ٱلرَّحْمَٰنِ ٱلرَّحِيمِ

1. By the Mount,

وَٱلطُّورِ ﴿١﴾

2. And a Book inscribed,

وَكِتَٰبٍ مَّسْطُورٍ ﴿٢﴾

3. In a rolled-out parchment.

فِي رَقٍّ مَّنشُورٍ ﴿٣﴾

4. And by the inhabited House,

وَٱلْبَيْتِ ٱلْمَعْمُورِ ﴿٤﴾

5. And the upraised roof,

وَٱلسَّقْفِ ٱلْمَرْفُوعِ ﴿٥﴾

6. And the roaring sea,

وَٱلْبَحْرِ ٱلْمَسْجُورِ ﴿٦﴾

7. The punishment of your Lord is surely coming.

إِنَّ عَذَابَ رَبِّكَ لَوَٰقِعٌ ﴿٧﴾

8. No one will be able to avert it.

مَّا لَهُۥ مِن دَافِعٍ ﴿٨﴾

9. On the Day when heaven shall turn round and round;

يَوْمَ تَمُورُ ٱلسَّمَآءُ مَوْرًا ﴿٩﴾

10. And the mountains shall be set in motion.

وَتَسِيرُ ٱلْجِبَالُ سَيْرًا ﴿١٠﴾

11. Woe, on that Day, unto those who denounce;

فَوَيْلٌ يَوْمَئِذٍ لِّلْمُكَذِّبِينَ ﴿١١﴾

12. Those who are stumbling about in confusion.

ٱلَّذِينَ هُمْ فِي خَوْضٍ يَلْعَبُونَ ﴿١٢﴾

13. On the Day they will be driven into the Fire of Hell by force.

يَوْمَ يُدَعُّونَ إِلَىٰ نَارِ جَهَنَّمَ دَعًّا ﴿١٣﴾

14. "This is the Fire which you used to deny.

هَٰذِهِ ٱلنَّارُ ٱلَّتِي كُنتُم بِهَا تُكَذِّبُونَ ﴿١٤﴾

15. "Is this magic or do you not see?

أَفَسِحْرٌ هَٰذَآ أَمْ أَنتُمْ لَا تُبْصِرُونَ ﴿١٥﴾

16. "Burn in it. Bear up or do not bear up; it is the same for you. You are only rewarded for what you used to do."

ٱصْلَوْهَا فَٱصْبِرُوٓا أَوْ لَا تَصْبِرُوا سَوَآءٌ عَلَيْكُمْ إِنَّمَا تُجْزَوْنَ مَا كُنتُمْ تَعْمَلُونَ ﴿١٦﴾

17. The God-fearing are indeed in gardens and bliss,

إِنَّ ٱلْمُتَّقِينَ فِى جَنَّٰتٍ وَنَعِيمٍ ﴿١٧﴾

18. Rejoicing in what their Lord has given them; and their Lord shall guard them against the punishment of Hell, [saying]:

فَٰكِهِينَ بِمَآ ءَاتَىٰهُمْ رَبُّهُمْ وَوَقَىٰهُمْ رَبُّهُمْ عَذَابَ ٱلْجَحِيمِ ﴿١٨﴾

19. "Eat and drink merrily, for what you used to do."

كُلُوا۟ وَٱشْرَبُوا۟ هَنِيٓـًٔا بِمَا كُنتُمْ تَعْمَلُونَ ﴿١٩﴾

20. Reclining on ranged couches, and We shall wed them to wide-eyed houris.

مُتَّكِئِينَ عَلَىٰ سُرُرٍ مَّصْفُوفَةٍ وَزَوَّجْنَٰهُم بِحُورٍ عِينٍ ﴿٢٠﴾

21. And those who have believed and their progeny followed them in belief, We shall join their progeny to them. We shall not deprive them of any of their work; every man shall be bound by what he has earned.

وَٱلَّذِينَ ءَامَنُوا۟ وَٱتَّبَعَتْهُمْ ذُرِّيَّتُهُم بِإِيمَٰنٍ أَلْحَقْنَا بِهِمْ ذُرِّيَّتَهُمْ وَمَآ أَلَتْنَٰهُم مِّنْ عَمَلِهِم مِّن شَىْءٍ كُلُّ ٱمْرِئٍ بِمَا كَسَبَ رَهِينٌ ﴿٢١﴾

22. And We shall supply them with fruit and meat, such as they desire.

وَأَمْدَدْنَٰهُم بِفَٰكِهَةٍ وَلَحْمٍ مِّمَّا يَشْتَهُونَ ﴿٢٢﴾

23. They will exchange therein a cup wherein there is no idle talk or vilification.

يَتَنَٰزَعُونَ فِيهَا كَأْسًا لَّا لَغْوٌ فِيهَا وَلَا تَأْثِيمٌ ﴿٢٣﴾

24. And boys of their own will go round them, as if they were hidden pearls.

۞ وَيَطُوفُ عَلَيْهِمْ غِلْمَانٌ لَّهُمْ كَأَنَّهُمْ لُؤْلُؤٌ مَّكْنُونٌ ﴿٢٤﴾

25. They turn one to another asking each other questions;

وَأَقْبَلَ بَعْضُهُمْ عَلَىٰ بَعْضٍ يَتَسَآءَلُونَ ﴿٢٥﴾

26. They say: "We were formerly in the midst of our families living in awe;

قَالُوٓا۟ إِنَّا كُنَّا قَبْلُ فِىٓ أَهْلِنَا مُشْفِقِينَ ﴿٢٦﴾

27. "Then Allah was gracious to us and guarded us against the torment of the scorching wind.

فَمَنَّ ٱللَّهُ عَلَيْنَا وَوَقَىٰنَا عَذَابَ ٱلسَّمُومِ ﴿٢٧﴾

28. "We used formerly to call on Him; He is the All-Gracious, the Merciful."

إِنَّا كُنَّا مِن قَبْلُ نَدْعُوهُ إِنَّهُۥ هُوَ ٱلْبَرُّ ٱلرَّحِيمُ ﴿٢٨﴾

29. So remind [them]; for you[786] are not, by the Grace of your Lord, a soothsayer or a madman.

فَذَكِّرْ فَمَآ أَنتَ بِنِعْمَتِ رَبِّكَ بِكَاهِنٍ وَلَا مَجْنُونٍ ﴿٢٩﴾

30. Or do they say: "A poet for whom we await an uncertain fate."

أَمْ يَقُولُونَ شَاعِرٌ نَّتَرَبَّصُ بِهِۦ رَيْبَ ٱلْمَنُونِ ﴿٣٠﴾

---

786. That is, Muhammad.

31. Say: "Await, I am indeed with you awaiting."

قُل تَرَبَّصُوا فَإِنِّي مَعَكُم مِّنَ ٱلْمُتَرَبِّصِينَ ۝

32. Or do their minds bid them do this; or are they, rather, an aggressive people?

أَمْ تَأْمُرُهُمْ أَحْلَـٰمُهُم بِهَـٰذَآ أَمْ هُمْ قَوْمٌ طَاغُونَ ۝

33. Or do they say: "He fabricated it"? No, they believe not.

أَمْ يَقُولُونَ تَقَوَّلَهُۥ بَل لَّا يُؤْمِنُونَ ۝

34. Let them bring, then, a discourse like it, if they are truthful.

فَلْيَأْتُوا بِحَدِيثٍ مِّثْلِهِۦٓ إِن كَانُوا صَـٰدِقِينَ ۝

35. Were they created out of nothing, or are they like creators?

أَمْ خُلِقُوا مِنْ غَيْرِ شَىْءٍ أَمْ هُمُ ٱلْخَـٰلِقُونَ ۝

36. Or did they create the heavens and the earth? No, they do not believe with certainty.

أَمْ خَلَقُوا ٱلسَّمَـٰوَٰتِ وَٱلْأَرْضَ بَل لَّا يُوقِنُونَ ۝

37. Or do they possess the treasuries of your Lord; or are they the domineering ones?

أَمْ عِندَهُمْ خَزَآئِنُ رَبِّكَ أَمْ هُمُ ٱلْمُصَيْطِرُونَ ۝

38. Or, do they have a ladder whereon they listen? Let their listener, then, bring a manifest authority.

أَمْ لَهُمْ سُلَّمٌ يَسْتَمِعُونَ فِيهِ فَلْيَأْتِ مُسْتَمِعُهُم بِسُلْطَـٰنٍ مُّبِينٍ ۝

39. Or, does He have the daughters and you have the sons?

أَمْ لَهُ ٱلْبَنَـٰتُ وَلَكُمُ ٱلْبَنُونَ ۝

40. Or, are you asking them a wage; therefore they are weighed down with debt?

أَمْ تَسْـَٔلُهُمْ أَجْرًا فَهُم مِّن مَّغْرَمٍ مُّثْقَلُونَ ۝

41. Or, do they have the knowledge of the Unseen, and so they are writing it down?

أَمْ عِندَهُمُ ٱلْغَيْبُ فَهُمْ يَكْتُبُونَ ۝

42. Or, do they desire to scheme? The unbelievers are truly the objects of scheming.

أَمْ يُرِيدُونَ كَيْدًا فَٱلَّذِينَ كَفَرُوا هُمُ ٱلْمَكِيدُونَ ۝

43. Or, do they have a god other than Allah? Allah be exalted above what they associate!

أَمْ لَهُمْ إِلَـٰهٌ غَيْرُ ٱللَّهِ سُبْحَـٰنَ ٱللَّهِ عَمَّا يُشْرِكُونَ ۝

44. If they see a lump falling down from the sky, they say: "A mass of clouds."

وَإِن يَرَوْا كِسْفًا مِّنَ ٱلسَّمَآءِ سَاقِطًا يَقُولُوا سَحَابٌ مَّرْكُومٌ ۝

45. Leave them, then, till they encounter the Day on which they will be thunderstruck;

فَذَرْهُمْ حَتَّىٰ يُلَـٰقُوا يَوْمَهُمُ ٱلَّذِى فِيهِ يُصْعَقُونَ ۝

46. The Day when their cunning will avail them nothing, and they will not be supported.

يَوْمَ لَا يُغْنِى عَنْهُمْ كَيْدُهُمْ شَيْـًٔا وَلَا هُمْ يُنصَرُونَ ۝

47. And the wrongdoers shall suffer a punishment beyond that; but most of them do not know.

وَإِنَّ لِلَّذِينَ ظَلَمُوا عَذَابًا دُونَ ذَلِكَ وَلَكِنَّ أَكْثَرَهُمْ لَا يَعْلَمُونَ ۝

48. Bear with your Lord's Judgement, for you are in Our thoughts; and proclaim the Praise of your Lord when you arise;

وَاصْبِرْ لِحُكْمِ رَبِّكَ فَإِنَّكَ بِأَعْيُنِنَا وَسَبِّحْ بِحَمْدِ رَبِّكَ حِينَ تَقُومُ ۝

49. And in the night, glorify Him, and at the receding of the stars.

وَمِنَ اللَّيْلِ فَسَبِّحْهُ وَإِدْبَارَ النُّجُومِ ۝

Sûrat An-Najm, (The Star) 53

In the Name of Allah,
the Compassionate, the Merciful

بِسْمِ اللَّهِ الرَّحْمَنِ الرَّحِيمِ

1. By the star when it goes down,

وَالنَّجْمِ إِذَا هَوَى ۝

2. Your Companion[787] has not gone astray or erred,

مَا ضَلَّ صَاحِبُكُمْ وَمَا غَوَى ۝

3. And he does not talk capriciously.

وَمَا يَنطِقُ عَنِ الْهَوَى ۝

4. It[788] is only a Revelation being revealed,

إِنْ هُوَ إِلَّا وَحْيٌ يُوحَى ۝

5. Taught him by a mighty one,[789]

عَلَّمَهُ شَدِيدُ الْقُوَى ۝

6. Possessed of steadfastness. And so he arose,

ذُو مِرَّةٍ فَاسْتَوَى ۝

7. While he was on the highest horizon;

وَهُوَ بِالْأُفُقِ الْأَعْلَى ۝

8. Then, he came closer and hovered around;

ثُمَّ دَنَا فَتَدَلَّى ۝

9. Coming thus within two bows' length or closer.

فَكَانَ قَابَ قَوْسَيْنِ أَوْ أَدْنَى ۝

10. Then (Allah) revealed to His servant what he revealed.

فَأَوْحَى إِلَى عَبْدِهِ مَا أَوْحَى ۝

11. The heart did not deny what it saw.

مَا كَذَبَ الْفُؤَادُ مَا رَأَى ۝

12. Do you, then, dispute with him (Muhammad) concerning what he saw?

أَفَتُمَارُونَهُ عَلَى مَا يَرَى ۝

13. He has indeed seen him (Gabriel) a second time;

وَلَقَدْ رَآهُ نَزْلَةً أُخْرَى ۝

---

787. Muhammad.
788. The Qur'an.
789. The angel Gabriel (Jibril).

14. By the Lotus Tree of the outermost limit.

عِندَ سِدْرَةِ ٱلْمُنتَهَىٰ ﴿١٤﴾

15. Close by it is the Garden of Refuge.

عِندَهَا جَنَّةُ ٱلْمَأْوَىٰ ﴿١٥﴾

16. As the Lotus Tree was covered by that which covers it;

إِذْ يَغْشَى ٱلسِّدْرَةَ مَا يَغْشَىٰ ﴿١٦﴾

17. His gaze did not shift nor did he exceed the bound.

مَا زَاغَ ٱلْبَصَرُ وَمَا طَغَىٰ ﴿١٧﴾

18. He saw some of the Great Signs of his Lord.

لَقَدْ رَأَىٰ مِنْ ءَايَٰتِ رَبِّهِ ٱلْكُبْرَىٰ ﴿١٨﴾

19. Have you, then, seen al-Lat and al-'Uzza?

أَفَرَءَيْتُمُ ٱللَّٰتَ وَٱلْعُزَّىٰ ﴿١٩﴾

20. And Manat, the third one, the other?

وَمَنَوٰةَ ٱلثَّالِثَةَ ٱلْأُخْرَىٰ ﴿٢٠﴾

21. Do you have the male and He has the female?

أَلَكُمُ ٱلذَّكَرُ وَلَهُ ٱلْأُنثَىٰ ﴿٢١﴾

22. That indeed is an unjust division.

تِلْكَ إِذًا قِسْمَةٌ ضِيزَىٰ ﴿٢٢﴾

23. These are mere names you and your fathers have named, for which Allah did not send down any authority. They only follow conjecture and what the souls desire; yet Guidance has come to them from their Lord.

إِنْ هِيَ إِلَّا أَسْمَاءٌ سَمَّيْتُمُوهَا أَنتُمْ وَءَابَاؤُكُم مَّا أَنزَلَ ٱللَّهُ بِهَا مِن سُلْطَٰنٍ إِن يَتَّبِعُونَ إِلَّا ٱلظَّنَّ وَمَا تَهْوَى ٱلْأَنفُسُ وَلَقَدْ جَاءَهُم مِّن رَّبِّهِمُ ٱلْهُدَىٰ ﴿٢٣﴾

24. Or will man have whatever he wishes?

أَمْ لِلْإِنسَٰنِ مَا تَمَنَّىٰ ﴿٢٤﴾

25. For to Allah belongs the last and the first life.

فَلِلَّهِ ٱلْءَاخِرَةُ وَٱلْأُولَىٰ ﴿٢٥﴾

26. How many an angel is there in the heavens whose intercession avails nothing, except after Allah gives leave to whoever He wishes and is well-pleased with.

۞ وَكَم مِّن مَّلَكٍ فِى ٱلسَّمَٰوَٰتِ لَا تُغْنِى شَفَٰعَتُهُمْ شَيْئًا إِلَّا مِنۢ بَعْدِ أَن يَأْذَنَ ٱللَّهُ لِمَن يَشَاءُ وَيَرْضَىٰ ﴿٢٦﴾

27. Those who do not believe in the Hereafter will surely give the angels the names of females.

إِنَّ ٱلَّذِينَ لَا يُؤْمِنُونَ بِٱلْءَاخِرَةِ لَيُسَمُّونَ ٱلْمَلَٰئِكَةَ تَسْمِيَةَ ٱلْأُنثَىٰ ﴿٢٧﴾

28. Yet, they have no knowledge thereof. They only follow conjecture, but conjecture avails nothing regarding truth.

وَمَا لَهُم بِهِۦ مِنْ عِلْمٍ إِن يَتَّبِعُونَ إِلَّا ٱلظَّنَّ وَإِنَّ ٱلظَّنَّ لَا يُغْنِى مِنَ ٱلْحَقِّ شَيْئًا ﴿٢٨﴾

29. So turn away from him who has given up Our Reminder and only desires the present life.

فَأَعْرِضْ عَن مَّن تَوَلَّىٰ عَن ذِكْرِنَا وَلَمْ يُرِدْ إِلَّا ٱلْحَيَوٰةَ ٱلدُّنْيَا ﴿٢٩﴾

30. That is their attainment in knowledge. Your Lord indeed knows better those who have strayed from His Path, and He knows better those who are well-guided.

ذَٰلِكَ مَبْلَغُهُم مِّنَ ٱلْعِلْمِ إِنَّ رَبَّكَ هُوَ أَعْلَمُ بِمَن ضَلَّ عَن سَبِيلِهِ وَهُوَ أَعْلَمُ بِمَنِ ٱهْتَدَىٰ ۝

31. And to Allah belongs whatever is in the heavens and on the earth, that He may reward the evildoers for what they did, and reward the righteous with the fairest reward;

وَلِلَّهِ مَا فِي ٱلسَّمَٰوَٰتِ وَمَا فِي ٱلْأَرْضِ لِيَجْزِيَ ٱلَّذِينَ أَسَٰٓـُٔوا۟ بِمَا عَمِلُوا۟ وَيَجْزِيَ ٱلَّذِينَ أَحْسَنُوا۟ بِٱلْحُسْنَى ۝

32. Those who avoid grave sins and foul acts, except for venial ones. Your Lord's Forgiveness is indeed ample. He knows you very well since He produced you from earth, and while you were still embryos in your mothers' wombs. Do not commend yourselves, He knows very well who is God-fearing.

ٱلَّذِينَ يَجْتَنِبُونَ كَبَٰٓئِرَ ٱلْإِثْمِ وَٱلْفَوَٰحِشَ إِلَّا ٱللَّمَمَ إِنَّ رَبَّكَ وَٰسِعُ ٱلْمَغْفِرَةِ هُوَ أَعْلَمُ بِكُمْ إِذْ أَنشَأَكُم مِّنَ ٱلْأَرْضِ وَإِذْ أَنتُمْ أَجِنَّةٌ فِي بُطُونِ أُمَّهَٰتِكُمْ فَلَا تُزَكُّوٓا۟ أَنفُسَكُمْ هُوَ أَعْلَمُ بِمَنِ ٱتَّقَىٰ ۝

33. Have you considered him who turned away;

أَفَرَءَيْتَ ٱلَّذِى تَوَلَّىٰ ۝

34. Gave a little then held back?[790]

وَأَعْطَىٰ قَلِيلًا وَأَكْدَىٰٓ ۝

35. Does he have the knowledge of the Unseen and is therefore a seer?

أَعِندَهُۥ عِلْمُ ٱلْغَيْبِ فَهُوَ يَرَىٰٓ ۝

36. Has he not been told about what the scrolls of Moses contain?

أَمْ لَمْ يُنَبَّأْ بِمَا فِي صُحُفِ مُوسَىٰ ۝

37. And Abraham who fulfilled his pledge;

وَإِبْرَٰهِيمَ ٱلَّذِى وَفَّىٰٓ ۝

38. That no sinning soul shall bear the burden of another soul;

أَلَّا تَزِرُ وَازِرَةٌ وِزْرَ أُخْرَىٰ ۝

39. And that man will only earn what he strives for;

وَأَن لَّيْسَ لِلْإِنسَٰنِ إِلَّا مَا سَعَىٰ ۝

40. And that his striving shall be witnessed;

وَأَنَّ سَعْيَهُۥ سَوْفَ يُرَىٰ ۝

41. Then he will be rewarded for it the fullest reward;

ثُمَّ يُجْزَىٰهُ ٱلْجَزَآءَ ٱلْأَوْفَىٰ ۝

42. And that unto your Lord is the ultimate return;

وَأَنَّ إِلَىٰ رَبِّكَ ٱلْمُنتَهَىٰ ۝

---

790. The reference is to al-Walid Ibn al-Mughirah, who wanted to bargain his sins away for money; so he made a down payment and withheld the rest of the money.

43. And that He causes people to laugh and to cry;

44. And that He causes some to die and to live;

45. And that He has created the pairs, both male and female;

46. From a sperm when it is emitted;

47. And that upon Him devolves the second creation;

48. And that He gives riches and possessions;

49. And that He is the Lord of Sirius;

50. And that He destroyed the first 'Ad;

51. And Thamud, as well, leaving nothing behind;

52. And the people of Noah before that; for they were more unjust and more domineering;

53. And brought down the subverted city;[791]

54. So, He covered it with what He covered.

55. Which of your Lord's Bounties, then, do you doubt?

56. This is one of the first warnings.

57. The Last Day is imminent;

58. It has, apart from Allah, no discloser.

59. Do you then marvel at this discourse?

60. You laugh and do not cry;

61. While you are fully distracted.

62. Prostrate yourselves before Allah, then, and worship Him.

---

791. That is Sodom, city of Lot.

Sûrat Al-Qamar, (The Moon) 54

In the Name of Allah, the Compassionate, the Merciful

1. The Hour is drawing near and the moon is split asunder.

2. If they see a sign, they turn away and say: "Continued sorcery."

3. They denounced and followed their fancies, while every matter had been settled.

4. And they have received such news as would deter,

5. An outstanding wisdom; so what good are warnings?

6. Turn away from them. On the Day the caller shall call out unto an abominable thing;

7. They will come out of their graves, with their eyes downcast, as if they were swarming locusts,

8. Scrambling towards the caller. The unbelievers will say: "This is a very hard Day."

9. The people of Noah denounced before them; they denounced Our servant as a liar and said: "A madman", and he was rebuffed.

10. So, he called upon his Lord: "I am beaten; so give me support."

11. Thereupon, We opened up the gates of heaven with torrential water;

12. And caused the earth to gush with springs, and so the waters converged in accordance with a foreordained decree.

13. And We carried him along upon a ship made of boards and iron plates;

14. Sailing before Our Very Eyes, as a reward to him who was disbelieved.

15. We have indeed left it as a sign. Is there, then, any one who will remember?

وَلَقَدْ تَرَكْنَاهَا ءَايَةً فَهَلْ مِن مُّدَّكِرٍ ۝

16. How, then, were My Punishment and My Warnings?

فَكَيْفَ كَانَ عَذَابِي وَنُذُرِ ۝

17. And We have made the Qur'an easy to remember. Is there, then, any one who will remember?

وَلَقَدْ يَسَّرْنَا ٱلْقُرْءَانَ لِلذِّكْرِ فَهَلْ مِن مُّدَّكِرٍ ۝

18. 'Ad denounced; how, then, were My Punishment and My Warnings?

كَذَّبَتْ عَادٌ فَكَيْفَ كَانَ عَذَابِي وَنُذُرِ ۝

19. We have loosed upon them a mighty wind, on a day of constant misfortune;

إِنَّا أَرْسَلْنَا عَلَيْهِمْ رِيحًا صَرْصَرًا فِي يَوْمِ نَحْسٍ مُّسْتَمِرٍّ ۝

20. Uprooting people, as though they were the stumps of fallen palm trees.

تَنزِعُ ٱلنَّاسَ كَأَنَّهُمْ أَعْجَازُ نَخْلٍ مُّنقَعِرٍ ۝

21. How, then, were My Punishment and My Warnings?

فَكَيْفَ كَانَ عَذَابِي وَنُذُرِ ۝

22. We have made the Qur'an easy to remember. Is there, then, any one who will remember?

وَلَقَدْ يَسَّرْنَا ٱلْقُرْءَانَ لِلذِّكْرِ فَهَلْ مِن مُّدَّكِرٍ ۝

23. Thamud denounced the warnings as lies.

كَذَّبَتْ ثَمُودُ بِٱلنُّذُرِ ۝

24. So they said: "Shall we follow a lone mortal from among us? We are indeed in error and folly.

فَقَالُوٓا أَبَشَرًا مِّنَّا وَحِدًا نَّتَّبِعُهُ إِنَّآ إِذًا لَّفِي ضَلَلٍ وَسُعُرٍ ۝

25. "Has the Reminder been sent down upon him alone from among us? No, he is an arrogant liar."

أَءُلْقِيَ ٱلذِّكْرُ عَلَيْهِ مِنۢ بَيْنِنَا بَلْ هُوَ كَذَّابٌ أَشِرٌ ۝

26. They will surely know tomorrow who is the arrogant liar.

سَيَعْلَمُونَ غَدًا مَّنِ ٱلْكَذَّابُ ٱلْأَشِرُ ۝

27. We shall send the she-camel as a test for them; so watch them and be patient.

إِنَّا مُرْسِلُوا ٱلنَّاقَةِ فِتْنَةً لَّهُمْ فَٱرْتَقِبْهُمْ وَٱصْطَبِرْ ۝

28. And tell them that the water is to be divided between them, each drinking in turn.

وَنَبِّئْهُمْ أَنَّ ٱلْمَآءَ قِسْمَةٌ بَيْنَهُمْ كُلُّ شِرْبٍ مُّحْتَضَرٌ ۝

29. They called their companion, and so he took charge and hamstrung [her].

فَنَادَوْا صَاحِبَهُمْ فَتَعَاطَىٰ فَعَقَرَ ۝

30. How then were My Punishment and My Warnings?

فَكَيْفَ كَانَ عَذَابِي وَنُذُرِ ۝

31. We released upon them a single cry and they became like the stubble of a corral-builder.

إِنَّآ أَرْسَلْنَا عَلَيْهِمْ صَيْحَةً وَاحِدَةً فَكَانُوا كَهَشِيمِ ٱلْمُحْتَظِرِ ﴿٣١﴾

32. We have, indeed, made the Qur'an easy to remember. Is there, then, any one who will remember?

وَلَقَدْ يَسَّرْنَا ٱلْقُرْآنَ لِلذِّكْرِ فَهَلْ مِن مُّدَّكِرٍ ﴿٣٢﴾

33. The people of Lot denounced the warnings as lies.

كَذَّبَتْ قَوْمُ لُوطٍ بِٱلنُّذُرِ ﴿٣٣﴾

34. We loosed upon them a squall of pebbles, except for the family of Lot whom We saved at dawn,

إِنَّآ أَرْسَلْنَا عَلَيْهِمْ حَاصِبًا إِلَّآ ءَالَ لُوطٍ نَّجَّيْنَٰهُم بِسَحَرٍ ﴿٣٤﴾

35. As a Grace from Us. Thus do We reward those who give thanks.

نِّعْمَةً مِّنْ عِندِنَا كَذَٰلِكَ نَجْزِى مَن شَكَرَ ﴿٣٥﴾

36. He had warned them of Our Onslaught, but they doubted the warnings.

وَلَقَدْ أَنذَرَهُم بَطْشَتَنَا فَتَمَارَوْا بِٱلنُّذُرِ ﴿٣٦﴾

37. And they even solicited of him his guests; so We blotted out their eyesight: "Taste, then, My Punishment and My Warnings."

وَلَقَدْ رَٰوَدُوهُ عَن ضَيْفِهِۦ فَطَمَسْنَآ أَعْيُنَهُمْ فَذُوقُوا عَذَابِى وَنُذُرِ ﴿٣٧﴾

38. Early in the morning, they were visited with implacable punishment.

وَلَقَدْ صَبَّحَهُم بُكْرَةً عَذَابٌ مُّسْتَقِرٌّ ﴿٣٨﴾

39. "Taste, then, My Punishment and My Warnings."

فَذُوقُوا عَذَابِى وَنُذُرِ ﴿٣٩﴾

40. We have, indeed, made the Qur'an easy to remember. Is there, then, any one who will remember?

وَلَقَدْ يَسَّرْنَا ٱلْقُرْآنَ لِلذِّكْرِ فَهَلْ مِن مُّدَّكِرٍ ﴿٤٠﴾

41. The warnings also came to Pharaoh's folk.

وَلَقَدْ جَآءَ ءَالَ فِرْعَوْنَ ٱلنُّذُرُ ﴿٤١﴾

42. They denounced all Our Signs as lies; so We seized them in the manner of One Who is Mighty and Strong.

كَذَّبُوا بِـَٔايَٰتِنَا كُلِّهَا فَأَخَذْنَٰهُمْ أَخْذَ عَزِيزٍ مُّقْتَدِرٍ ﴿٤٢﴾

43. Are your unbelievers better than all those; or have you been exonerated in the Scriptures?

أَكُفَّارُكُمْ خَيْرٌ مِّنْ أُوْلَٰئِكُمْ أَمْ لَكُم بَرَآءَةٌ فِى ٱلزُّبُرِ ﴿٤٣﴾

44. Or do they say: "We are a band which will conquer."

أَمْ يَقُولُونَ نَحْنُ جَمِيعٌ مُّنتَصِرٌ ﴿٤٤﴾

45. The host will certainly be routed and turn their backs in flight.

سَيُهْزَمُ ٱلْجَمْعُ وَيُوَلُّونَ ٱلدُّبُرَ ﴿٤٥﴾

46. No, the Hour shall be their appointment; and the Hour is very grievous and bitter.

بَلِ ٱلسَّاعَةُ مَوْعِدُهُمْ وَٱلسَّاعَةُ أَدْهَىٰ وَأَمَرُّ ﴿٤٦﴾

47. The criminals are indeed in error and blazes;

إِنَّ ٱلْمُجْرِمِينَ فِى ضَلَٰلٍ وَسُعُرٍ ﴿٤٧﴾

48. The day they will be dragged upon their faces into the Fire: "Taste now the touch of Saqar."792

يَوْمَ يُسْحَبُونَ فِى ٱلنَّارِ عَلَىٰ وُجُوهِهِمْ ذُوقُوا۟ مَسَّ سَقَرَ ﴿٤٨﴾

49. Indeed, We have created everything in measure.

إِنَّا كُلَّ شَىْءٍ خَلَقْنَٰهُ بِقَدَرٍ ﴿٤٩﴾

50. Our Command is but one word, like the twinkling of an eye.

وَمَآ أَمْرُنَآ إِلَّا وَٰحِدَةٌ كَلَمْحٍۭ بِٱلْبَصَرِ ﴿٥٠﴾

51. We have destroyed your likes; is there anyone who will remember?

وَلَقَدْ أَهْلَكْنَآ أَشْيَاعَكُمْ فَهَلْ مِن مُّدَّكِرٍ ﴿٥١﴾

52. Everything they have done is recorded in the Scriptures.

وَكُلُّ شَىْءٍ فَعَلُوهُ فِى ٱلزُّبُرِ ﴿٥٢﴾

53. Everything, small or big, is written down.

وَكُلُّ صَغِيرٍ وَكَبِيرٍ مُّسْتَطَرٌ ﴿٥٣﴾

54. The God-fearing are, indeed, amid gardens and rivers;

إِنَّ ٱلْمُتَّقِينَ فِى جَنَّٰتٍ وَنَهَرٍ ﴿٥٤﴾

55. Upon a seat of truth in the presence of an Omnipotent King.

فِى مَقْعَدِ صِدْقٍ عِندَ مَلِيكٍ مُّقْتَدِرٍۭ ﴿٥٥﴾

**Sûrat Ar-Rahmân,
(The All-Compassionate) 55**

*In the Name of Allah,
the Compassionate, the Merciful*

بِسْمِ ٱللَّهِ ٱلرَّحْمَٰنِ ٱلرَّحِيمِ

1. The Compassionate,

ٱلرَّحْمَٰنُ ﴿١﴾

2. Has taught the Qur'an.

عَلَّمَ ٱلْقُرْءَانَ ﴿٢﴾

3. He created man;

خَلَقَ ٱلْإِنسَٰنَ ﴿٣﴾

4. And taught him elocution.

عَلَّمَهُ ٱلْبَيَانَ ﴿٤﴾

5. The sun and the moon move according to a plan.

ٱلشَّمْسُ وَٱلْقَمَرُ بِحُسْبَانٍ ﴿٥﴾

---

792. Another name for Hell.

6. The shrubs[793] and the trees prostrate themselves.

وَٱلنَّجْمُ وَٱلشَّجَرُ يَسْجُدَانِ ۝

7. And the sky, He raised and He set up the balance;

وَٱلسَّمَآءَ رَفَعَهَا وَوَضَعَ ٱلْمِيزَانَ ۝

8. That you may not transgress in the balance.

أَلَّا تَطْغَوْا۟ فِى ٱلْمِيزَانِ ۝

9. Conduct your weighing with equity and do not stint the balance.

وَأَقِيمُوا۟ ٱلْوَزْنَ بِٱلْقِسْطِ وَلَا تُخْسِرُوا۟ ٱلْمِيزَانَ ۝

10. And the earth, He set up for all mankind.

وَٱلْأَرْضَ وَضَعَهَا لِلْأَنَامِ ۝

11. In it are fruit and palm trees in buds;

فِيهَا فَٰكِهَةٌ وَٱلنَّخْلُ ذَاتُ ٱلْأَكْمَامِ ۝

12. And grain in blades and fragrant plants.

وَٱلْحَبُّ ذُو ٱلْعَصْفِ وَٱلرَّيْحَانُ ۝

13. So, which of your Lord's Bounties do you, both,[794] deny?

فَبِأَىِّ ءَالَآءِ رَبِّكُمَا تُكَذِّبَانِ ۝

14. He created man from hard clay, like bricks.

خَلَقَ ٱلْإِنسَٰنَ مِن صَلْصَٰلٍ كَٱلْفَخَّارِ ۝

15. And He created the jinn from tongues of fire.

وَخَلَقَ ٱلْجَآنَّ مِن مَّارِجٍ مِّن نَّارٍ ۝

16. So, which of your Lord's Bounties do you both deny?

فَبِأَىِّ ءَالَآءِ رَبِّكُمَا تُكَذِّبَانِ ۝

17. The Lord of the two Easts and the two Wests.

رَبُّ ٱلْمَشْرِقَيْنِ وَرَبُّ ٱلْمَغْرِبَيْنِ ۝

18. So, which of your Lord's Bounties do you both deny?

فَبِأَىِّ ءَالَآءِ رَبِّكُمَا تُكَذِّبَانِ ۝

19. He unleashed the two seas so as to merge together.

مَرَجَ ٱلْبَحْرَيْنِ يَلْتَقِيَانِ ۝

20. Between them is a barrier which they do not overstep.

بَيْنَهُمَا بَرْزَخٌ لَّا يَبْغِيَانِ ۝

21. So, which of your Lord's Bounties do you both deny?

فَبِأَىِّ ءَالَآءِ رَبِّكُمَا تُكَذِّبَانِ ۝

22. From them both come out pearls and coral.

يَخْرُجُ مِنْهُمَا ٱللُّؤْلُؤُ وَٱلْمَرْجَانُ ۝

23. So, which of your Lord's Bounties do you both deny?

فَبِأَىِّ ءَالَآءِ رَبِّكُمَا تُكَذِّبَانِ ۝

---

793. Or stars (*al-najm*).
794. *Jinn* and humans.

24. To Him belong the seagoing ships towering upon the sea like mountains.

وَلَهُ ٱلْجَوَارِ ٱلْمُنشَـَٔاتُ فِى ٱلْبَحْرِ كَٱلْأَعْلَٰمِ ﴿٢٤﴾

25. So, which of your Lord's Bounties do you both deny?

فَبِأَىِّ ءَالَآءِ رَبِّكُمَا تُكَذِّبَانِ ﴿٢٥﴾

26. Everyone upon it[795] is perishing;

كُلُّ مَنْ عَلَيْهَا فَانٍ ﴿٢٦﴾

27. But the Face of your Lord, full of majesty and nobility, shall abide.

وَيَبْقَىٰ وَجْهُ رَبِّكَ ذُو ٱلْجَلَٰلِ وَٱلْإِكْرَامِ ﴿٢٧﴾

28. So, which of your Lord's Bounties do you both deny?

فَبِأَىِّ ءَالَآءِ رَبِّكُمَا تُكَذِّبَانِ ﴿٢٨﴾

29. Whatever is in the heavens or on the earth petitions Him, and every day He is attending to some new matter.

يَسْـَٔلُهُ مَن فِى ٱلسَّمَٰوَٰتِ وَٱلْأَرْضِ كُلَّ يَوْمٍ هُوَ فِى شَأْنٍ ﴿٢٩﴾

30. So, which of your Lord's Bounties, do you both deny?

فَبِأَىِّ ءَالَآءِ رَبِّكُمَا تُكَذِّبَانِ ﴿٣٠﴾

31. We shall attend to you, O two races?[796]

سَنَفْرُغُ لَكُمْ أَيُّهَ ٱلثَّقَلَانِ ﴿٣١﴾

32. So, which of your Lord's Bounties do you both deny?

فَبِأَىِّ ءَالَآءِ رَبِّكُمَا تُكَذِّبَانِ ﴿٣٢﴾

33. O jinn and human folk, if you can pass through the bounds of the heavens and the earth, pass through them. You will not pass through without some authority.

يَٰمَعْشَرَ ٱلْجِنِّ وَٱلْإِنسِ إِنِ ٱسْتَطَعْتُمْ أَن تَنفُذُوا۟ مِنْ أَقْطَارِ ٱلسَّمَٰوَٰتِ وَٱلْأَرْضِ فَٱنفُذُوا۟ لَا تَنفُذُونَ إِلَّا بِسُلْطَٰنٍ ﴿٣٣﴾

34. So, which of your Lord's Bounties do you both deny?

فَبِأَىِّ ءَالَآءِ رَبِّكُمَا تُكَذِّبَانِ ﴿٣٤﴾

35. A flame of fire and brass will be loosed upon you, so that you will not receive any support.

يُرْسَلُ عَلَيْكُمَا شُوَاظٌ مِّن نَّارٍ وَنُحَاسٌ فَلَا تَنتَصِرَانِ ﴿٣٥﴾

36. So, which of your Lord's Bounties do you both deny?

فَبِأَىِّ ءَالَآءِ رَبِّكُمَا تُكَذِّبَانِ ﴿٣٦﴾

37. When the heaven shall be rent asunder and turned red like pigment.

فَإِذَا ٱنشَقَّتِ ٱلسَّمَآءُ فَكَانَتْ وَرْدَةً كَٱلدِّهَانِ ﴿٣٧﴾

38. So, which of your Lord's Bounties do you both deny?

فَبِأَىِّ ءَالَآءِ رَبِّكُمَا تُكَذِّبَانِ ﴿٣٨﴾

39. On that day, none shall be questioned about his sin, whether a man or a jinn.

فَيَوْمَئِذٍ لَّا يُسْـَٔلُ عَن ذَنۢبِهِۦٓ إِنسٌ وَلَا جَآنٌّ ﴿٣٩﴾

---

795. The earth.
796. Of men and *jinn*.

40. So, which of your Lord's Bounties do you both deny?

فَبِأَيِّ ءَالَآءِ رَبِّكُمَا تُكَذِّبَانِ ۝

41. The criminals shall be known by their marks; then they shall be seized by their forelocks and their feet.

يُعْرَفُ ٱلْمُجْرِمُونَ بِسِيمَٰهُمْ فَيُؤْخَذُ بِٱلنَّوَٰصِى وَٱلْأَقْدَامِ ۝

42. So, which of your Lord's Bounties do you both deny?

فَبِأَيِّ ءَالَآءِ رَبِّكُمَا تُكَذِّبَانِ ۝

43. This is Hell, which the criminals deny.

هَٰذِهِۦ جَهَنَّمُ ٱلَّتِى يُكَذِّبُ بِهَا ٱلْمُجْرِمُونَ ۝

44. They circle between it and between a hot-water cauldron.

يَطُوفُونَ بَيْنَهَا وَبَيْنَ حَمِيمٍ ءَانٍ ۝

45. So, which of your Lord's Bounties do you both deny?

فَبِأَيِّ ءَالَآءِ رَبِّكُمَا تُكَذِّبَانِ ۝

46. But, for him who fears his Lord two gardens [are reserved].

وَلِمَنْ خَافَ مَقَامَ رَبِّهِۦ جَنَّتَانِ ۝

47. So, which of your Lord's Bounties do you both deny?

فَبِأَيِّ ءَالَآءِ رَبِّكُمَا تُكَذِّبَانِ ۝

48. They have numerous branches.

ذَوَاتَآ أَفْنَانٍ ۝

49. So, which of your Lord's Bounties do you both deny?

فَبِأَيِّ ءَالَآءِ رَبِّكُمَا تُكَذِّبَانِ ۝

50. And there are therein two flowing springs.

فِيهِمَا عَيْنَانِ تَجْرِيَانِ ۝

51. So, which of your Lord's Bounties do you both deny?

فَبِأَيِّ ءَالَآءِ رَبِّكُمَا تُكَذِّبَانِ ۝

52. Therein is a pair of every fruit.

فِيهِمَا مِن كُلِّ فَٰكِهَةٍ زَوْجَانِ ۝

53. So, which of your Lord's Bounties do you both deny?

فَبِأَيِّ ءَالَآءِ رَبِّكُمَا تُكَذِّبَانِ ۝

54. Reclining upon couches whose linings are of brocade and the fruits of the two gardens are near at hand.

مُتَّكِئِينَ عَلَىٰ فُرُشٍ بَطَآئِنُهَا مِنْ إِسْتَبْرَقٍ وَجَنَى ٱلْجَنَّتَيْنِ دَانٍ ۝

55. So, which of your Lord's Bounties do you both deny?

فَبِأَيِّ ءَالَآءِ رَبِّكُمَا تُكَذِّبَانِ ۝

56. Therein are maidens lowering their glances and they have not been touched, before them by any man or jinn.

فِيهِنَّ قَٰصِرَٰتُ ٱلطَّرْفِ لَمْ يَطْمِثْهُنَّ إِنسٌ قَبْلَهُمْ وَلَا جَآنٌّ ۝

57. So, which of your Lord's Bounties do you both deny?

فَبِأَىِّ ءَالَآءِ رَبِّكُمَا تُكَذِّبَانِ ۝

58. They are like rubies and coral.

كَأَنَّهُنَّ ٱلْيَاقُوتُ وَٱلْمَرْجَانُ ۝

59. So, which of your Lord's Bounties do you both deny?

فَبِأَىِّ ءَالَآءِ رَبِّكُمَا تُكَذِّبَانِ ۝

60. Shall the reward of beneficence be other than beneficence?

هَلْ جَزَآءُ ٱلْإِحْسَـٰنِ إِلَّا ٱلْإِحْسَـٰنُ ۝

61. So, which of your Lord's Bounties do you both deny?

فَبِأَىِّ ءَالَآءِ رَبِّكُمَا تُكَذِّبَانِ ۝

62. And beneath them[797] are two other gardens.

وَمِن دُونِهِمَا جَنَّتَانِ ۝

63. So, which of your Lord's Bounties do you both deny?

فَبِأَىِّ ءَالَآءِ رَبِّكُمَا تُكَذِّبَانِ ۝

64. Of dark green colour.

مُدْهَآمَّتَانِ ۝

65. So, which of your Lord's Bounties do you both deny?

فَبِأَىِّ ءَالَآءِ رَبِّكُمَا تُكَذِّبَانِ ۝

66. Therein are two gushing springs.

فِيهِمَا عَيْنَانِ نَضَّاخَتَانِ ۝

67. So, which of your Lord's Bounties do you both deny?

فَبِأَىِّ ءَالَآءِ رَبِّكُمَا تُكَذِّبَانِ ۝

68. Therein are fruits, palm trees and pomegranates.

فِيهِمَا فَاكِهَةٌ وَنَخْلٌ وَرُمَّانٌ ۝

69. So, which of your Lord's Bounties do you both deny?

فَبِأَىِّ ءَالَآءِ رَبِّكُمَا تُكَذِّبَانِ ۝

70. Therein are beautiful, virtuous maidens.

فِيهِنَّ خَيْرَٰتٌ حِسَانٌ ۝

71. So, which of your Lord's Bounties do you both deny?

فَبِأَىِّ ءَالَآءِ رَبِّكُمَا تُكَذِّبَانِ ۝

72. Wide-eyed, cloistered in pavilions.

حُورٌ مَّقْصُورَٰتٌ فِى ٱلْخِيَامِ ۝

73. So, which of your Lord's Bounties do you both deny?

فَبِأَىِّ ءَالَآءِ رَبِّكُمَا تُكَذِّبَانِ ۝

74. No man or jinn touched them before.

لَمْ يَطْمِثْهُنَّ إِنسٌ قَبْلَهُمْ وَلَا جَآنٌّ ۝

75. So, which of your Lord's Bounties do you both deny?

فَبِأَىِّ ءَالَآءِ رَبِّكُمَا تُكَذِّبَانِ ۝

---

797. The two gardens.

76. Reclining upon green cushions and superb rugs.

مُتَّكِئِينَ عَلَىٰ رَفْرَفٍ خُضْرٍ وَعَبْقَرِيٍّ حِسَانٍ ﴿٧٦﴾

77. So, which of your Lord's Bounties do you both deny?

فَبِأَيِّ ءَالَآءِ رَبِّكُمَا تُكَذِّبَانِ ﴿٧٧﴾

78. Blessed be the Name of your Lord, full of majesty and splendour.

تَبَٰرَكَ ٱسْمُ رَبِّكَ ذِى ٱلْجَلَٰلِ وَٱلْإِكْرَامِ ﴿٧٨﴾

Sûrat Al-Waqi'ah, (The Happening) 56

سُورَةُ ٱلْوَاقِعَةِ

In the Name of Allah, the Compassionate, the Merciful

بِسْمِ ٱللَّهِ ٱلرَّحْمَٰنِ ٱلرَّحِيمِ

1. When the Happening comes to pass.

إِذَا وَقَعَتِ ٱلْوَاقِعَةُ ﴿١﴾

2. Of its occurrence there is no denial;

لَيْسَ لِوَقْعَتِهَا كَاذِبَةٌ ﴿٢﴾

3. Abasing some, exalting others.

خَافِضَةٌ رَّافِعَةٌ ﴿٣﴾

4. When the earth shall be shaken violently,

إِذَا رُجَّتِ ٱلْأَرْضُ رَجًّا ﴿٤﴾

5. And the mountains shall be reduced to rubble,

وَبُسَّتِ ٱلْجِبَالُ بَسًّا ﴿٥﴾

6. So that they become scattered dust.

فَكَانَتْ هَبَآءً مُّنۢبَثًّا ﴿٦﴾

7. And you shall be three categories:

وَكُنتُمْ أَزْوَٰجًا ثَلَٰثَةً ﴿٧﴾

8. The Companions of the Right - behold the Companions of the Right?

فَأَصْحَٰبُ ٱلْمَيْمَنَةِ مَآ أَصْحَٰبُ ٱلْمَيْمَنَةِ ﴿٨﴾

9. And the Companions of the Left - behold the Companions of the Left?

وَأَصْحَٰبُ ٱلْمَشْـَٔمَةِ مَآ أَصْحَٰبُ ٱلْمَشْـَٔمَةِ ﴿٩﴾

10. And the outstrippers,[798] the outstrippers;

وَٱلسَّٰبِقُونَ ٱلسَّٰبِقُونَ ﴿١٠﴾

11. Those are the favoured ones,

أُوْلَٰٓئِكَ ٱلْمُقَرَّبُونَ ﴿١١﴾

12. In the Gardens of Bliss;

فِى جَنَّٰتِ ٱلنَّعِيمِ ﴿١٢﴾

13. A throng of the ancients,

ثُلَّةٌ مِّنَ ٱلْأَوَّلِينَ ﴿١٣﴾

14. And a small band of the latecomers.

وَقَلِيلٌ مِّنَ ٱلْءَاخِرِينَ ﴿١٤﴾

15. Upon beds interwoven with gold;

عَلَىٰ سُرُرٍ مَّوْضُونَةٍ ﴿١٥﴾

16. Reclining upon them, facing each other.

مُتَّكِئِينَ عَلَيْهَا مُتَقَٰبِلِينَ ﴿١٦﴾

---

798. The Companions of the Right are the blessed; the Companions of the Left, the damned. The outstrippers are the privileged few.

17. While immortal youths go round them,

يَطُوفُ عَلَيْهِمْ وِلْدَٰنٌ مُّخَلَّدُونَ ۝

18. With goblets, pitchers and a cup of limpid drink.

بِأَكْوَابٍ وَأَبَارِيقَ وَكَأْسٍ مِّن مَّعِينٍ ۝

19. Their heads do not ache from it and they do not become intoxicated.

لَّا يُصَدَّعُونَ عَنْهَا وَلَا يُنزِفُونَ ۝

20. And with such fruits as they care to choose;

وَفَٰكِهَةٍ مِّمَّا يَتَخَيَّرُونَ ۝

21. And such flesh of fowl as they desire;

وَلَحْمِ طَيْرٍ مِّمَّا يَشْتَهُونَ ۝

22. And wide-eyed houris,

وَحُورٌ عِينٌ ۝

23. Like hidden pearls;

كَأَمْثَٰلِ ٱللُّؤْلُؤِ ٱلْمَكْنُونِ ۝

24. As a reward for what they used to do.

جَزَآءً بِمَا كَانُوا۟ يَعْمَلُونَ ۝

25. They do not hear therein idle talk or vilification;

لَا يَسْمَعُونَ فِيهَا لَغْوًا وَلَا تَأْثِيمًا ۝

26. Only the greeting: "Peace, peace!"

إِلَّا قِيلًا سَلَٰمًا سَلَٰمًا ۝

27. As for the Companions of the Right; and behold the Companions of the Right?

وَأَصْحَٰبُ ٱلْيَمِينِ مَا أَصْحَٰبُ ٱلْيَمِينِ ۝

28. They are in the midst of thornless Lotus Trees,

فِى سِدْرٍ مَّخْضُودٍ ۝

29. And braided acacias,

وَطَلْحٍ مَّنضُودٍ ۝

30. And extended shade,

وَظِلٍّ مَّمْدُودٍ ۝

31. And overflowing water;

وَمَآءٍ مَّسْكُوبٍ ۝

32. And abundant fruit,

وَفَٰكِهَةٍ كَثِيرَةٍ ۝

33. Neither withheld nor forbidden,

لَّا مَقْطُوعَةٍ وَلَا مَمْنُوعَةٍ ۝

34. And uplifted mattresses.

وَفُرُشٍ مَّرْفُوعَةٍ ۝

35. We have formed them originally;

إِنَّآ أَنشَأْنَٰهُنَّ إِنشَآءً ۝

36. And made them pure virgins,

فَجَعَلْنَٰهُنَّ أَبْكَارًا ۝

37. Tender and unageing,

عُرُبًا أَتْرَابًا ۝

38. For the Companions of the Right;

لِّأَصْحَٰبِ ٱلْيَمِينِ ۝

39. A throng of the ancients,

ثُلَّةٌ مِّنَ ٱلْأَوَّلِينَ ۝

40. And a throng of the latecomers.

وَثُلَّةٌ مِّنَ ٱلْآخِرِينَ ۝

41. As for the Companions of the Left; and what are the Companions of the Left?

وَأَصْحَٰبُ ٱلشِّمَالِ مَا أَصْحَٰبُ ٱلشِّمَالِ ۝

42. Amid searing wind and boiling water;

فِى سَمُومٍ وَحَمِيمٍ ۝

43. And a shadow of thick smoke,

وَظِلٍّ مِّن يَحْمُومٍ ۝

44. Which is neither cool nor bounteous.

45. They lived before that in luxury;

46. And they used to insist upon the Great Blasphemy.

47. They used to say: "What? When we are dead and turn into dust and bones, shall we be raised from the dead?

48. "And our forefathers, too?"

49. Say: "The first and the last,

50. "Shall be gathered upon an appointed, pre-assigned Day.

51. "Then you, erring ones and denouncers,

52. "Shall eat from the Tree of Bitterness,

53. "Filling your bellies therefrom,

54. "And drinking on top of it boiling water,

55. "Lapping it like thirsty camels."

56. That shall be their meal on the Day of Judgement.

57. We have created you, if only you would believe!

58. Have you seen the semen you emit?

59. Do you create it, or are We the Creators?

60. We have decreed death upon you and We would not be outstripped;

61. Had We wanted to change the like of you and form you afresh in a fashion you do not know.

62. You have already known the first fashioning; if only you would remember.

63. Have you seen what you till?

64. Do you sow it yourselves, or are We the Sowers?

65. Had We wished, We would have reduced it to rubble, and so you would have remained wondering:

لَّا بَارِدٍ وَلَا كَرِيمٍ ٤٤

إِنَّهُمْ كَانُوا قَبْلَ ذَلِكَ مُتْرَفِينَ ٤٥

وَكَانُوا يُصِرُّونَ عَلَى الْحِنثِ الْعَظِيمِ ٤٦

وَكَانُوا يَقُولُونَ أَئِذَا مِتْنَا وَكُنَّا تُرَابًا وَعِظَامًا أَئِنَّا لَمَبْعُوثُونَ ٤٧

أَوَ ءَابَاؤُنَا الْأَوَّلُونَ ٤٨

قُلْ إِنَّ الْأَوَّلِينَ وَالْآخِرِينَ ٤٩

لَمَجْمُوعُونَ إِلَى مِيقَاتِ يَوْمٍ مَّعْلُومٍ ٥٠

ثُمَّ إِنَّكُمْ أَيُّهَا الضَّالُّونَ الْمُكَذِّبُونَ ٥١

لَآكِلُونَ مِن شَجَرٍ مِّن زَقُّومٍ ٥٢

فَمَالِئُونَ مِنْهَا الْبُطُونَ ٥٣

فَشَارِبُونَ عَلَيْهِ مِنَ الْحَمِيمِ ٥٤

فَشَارِبُونَ شُرْبَ الْهِيمِ ٥٥

هَذَا نُزُلُهُمْ يَوْمَ الدِّينِ ٥٦

نَحْنُ خَلَقْنَاكُمْ فَلَوْلَا تُصَدِّقُونَ ٥٧

أَفَرَءَيْتُم مَّا تُمْنُونَ ٥٨

ءَأَنتُمْ تَخْلُقُونَهُ أَمْ نَحْنُ الْخَالِقُونَ ٥٩

نَحْنُ قَدَّرْنَا بَيْنَكُمُ الْمَوْتَ وَمَا نَحْنُ بِمَسْبُوقِينَ ٦٠

عَلَى أَن نُّبَدِّلَ أَمْثَالَكُمْ وَنُنشِئَكُمْ فِي مَا لَا تَعْلَمُونَ ٦١

وَلَقَدْ عَلِمْتُمُ النَّشْأَةَ الْأُولَى فَلَوْلَا تَذَكَّرُونَ ٦٢

أَفَرَءَيْتُم مَّا تَحْرُثُونَ ٦٣

ءَأَنتُمْ تَزْرَعُونَهُ أَمْ نَحْنُ الزَّارِعُونَ ٦٤

لَوْ نَشَاءُ لَجَعَلْنَاهُ حُطَامًا فَظَلْتُمْ تَفَكَّهُونَ ٦٥

66. "We are penalized, indeed;

إِنَّا لَمُغْرَمُونَ ۝

67. "No, we are being deprived."

بَلۡ نَحۡنُ مَحۡرُومُونَ ۝

68. Or have you seen the water that you drink?

أَفَرَءَيۡتُمُ ٱلۡمَآءَ ٱلَّذِى تَشۡرَبُونَ ۝

69. Have you brought it down from the clouds or did We send it down?

ءَأَنتُمۡ أَنزَلۡتُمُوهُ مِنَ ٱلۡمُزۡنِ أَمۡ نَحۡنُ ٱلۡمُنزِلُونَ ۝

70. Had We wished, We would have made it bitter; if only you would give thanks.

لَوۡ نَشَآءُ جَعَلۡنَٰهُ أُجَاجٗا فَلَوۡلَا تَشۡكُرُونَ ۝

71. Or did you see the fire which you kindle?

أَفَرَءَيۡتُمُ ٱلنَّارَ ٱلَّتِى تُورُونَ ۝

72. Did you make its timber to grow or were We the Growers?

ءَأَنتُمۡ أَنشَأۡتُمۡ شَجَرَتَهَآ أَمۡ نَحۡنُ ٱلۡمُنشِـُٔونَ ۝

73. We have made it a reminder and a boon to the desert-dwellers.

نَحۡنُ جَعَلۡنَٰهَا تَذۡكِرَةٗ وَمَتَٰعٗا لِّلۡمُقۡوِينَ ۝

74. Glorify, then, the name of your Great Lord.

فَسَبِّحۡ بِٱسۡمِ رَبِّكَ ٱلۡعَظِيمِ ۝

75. No! I swear by the falling of the stars;

۞ فَلَآ أُقۡسِمُ بِمَوَٰقِعِ ٱلنُّجُومِ ۝

76. It is indeed a mighty oath, if only you knew.

وَإِنَّهُۥ لَقَسَمٌ لَّوۡ تَعۡلَمُونَ عَظِيمٌ ۝

77. It is, indeed, a noble Qur'an.

إِنَّهُۥ لَقُرۡءَانٌ كَرِيمٌ ۝

78. In a hidden Book,

فِى كِتَٰبٖ مَّكۡنُونٖ ۝

79. That only the purified shall touch.

لَّا يَمَسُّهُۥٓ إِلَّا ٱلۡمُطَهَّرُونَ ۝

80. A Revelation from the Lord of the Worlds.

تَنزِيلٌ مِّن رَّبِّ ٱلۡعَٰلَمِينَ ۝

81. Are you, then, regarding this discourse, dissimulating?

أَفَبِهَٰذَا ٱلۡحَدِيثِ أَنتُم مُّدۡهِنُونَ ۝

82. And do you make it your livelihood to denounce it as lies?

وَتَجۡعَلُونَ رِزۡقَكُمۡ أَنَّكُمۡ تُكَذِّبُونَ ۝

83. Would that, when the soul leaps to the throat,

فَلَوۡلَآ إِذَا بَلَغَتِ ٱلۡحُلۡقُومَ ۝

84. And you are, then, waiting;

وَأَنتُمۡ حِينَئِذٖ تَنظُرُونَ ۝

85. While We are closer to him[799] than you, but you do not see.

وَنَحۡنُ أَقۡرَبُ إِلَيۡهِ مِنكُمۡ وَلَٰكِن لَّا تُبۡصِرُونَ ۝

86. And would that, not being subject to judgement,

فَلَوۡلَآ إِن كُنتُمۡ غَيۡرَ مَدِينِينَ ۝

---

799. The dead man.

87. You are able to bring them[800] back, if you are truthful!

88. However, if he[801] is one of those who are favoured;

89. Then ease and delight, and Gardens of Bliss are his.

90. But if he is one of the Companions of the Right;

91. Then "Peace upon you", from the Companions of the Right.

92. However, if he is one of those who denounce and err;

93. Then he will be served boiling water,

94. And will be scorched by the Fire.

95. That indeed is the certain Truth.

96. So, glorify the Name of your Lord, the Great One.

Sûrat Al-Hadîd,
(Iron) 57

In the Name of Allah,
the Compassionate, the Merciful

1. Whatever is in the heavens and the earth glorifies Allah. He is the All-Mighty, the Wise.

2. To Him belongs the dominion of the heavens and the earth. He brings to life and causes to die, and He has power over everything.

3. He is the First and the Last, the Outer and the Inner, and He has knowledge of every-thing.

---

800. The souls.
801. The dead man.

4. It is He Who created the heavens and the earth in six days; then He sat upon the Throne. He knows what penetrates into the earth and what comes out of it; what comes down from heaven and ascends to it. He is with you, wherever you are: Allah perceives whatever you do.

5. To Him belongs the dominion of the heavens and the earth, and unto Allah all matters are ultimately referred.

6. He causes the night to phase into the day and the day to phase into the night, and He knows the secrets within the breasts.

7. Believe in Allah and His Messenger and spend freely from what He has bequeathed to you. For those of you who believe and spend freely will have a great wage.

8. What is the matter with you? You do not believe in Allah, although the Messenger calls upon you to believe in your Lord, and He has already taken your covenant, if you are true believers?

9. It is He Who sends down upon His servant manifest Signs, so as to bring you out from the dark shadows into the light. Allah is indeed All-Clement and Merciful towards you.

10. And why is it that you do not spend freely in the Cause of Allah, when to Allah belongs the heritage of the heavens and the earth? Not all those of you who spent freely before the Conquest[802] and have fought are equal. However they are higher in rank than those who spent freely and fought after-wards; and unto each Allah has promised the fairest reward. Allah is Fully Aware of what you do.

---

802. The Conquest of Mecca, 8 AH.

11. Who is he that will lend Allah a fair loan, that He might double it for him; and he will have a generous wage.

12. On the Day that you will see the believers, men and women, with their light beaming in front of them, and in their right hands [the sign]: "Your good news today is Gardens beneath which rivers flow, dwelling therein forever. That indeed is the great triumph."

13. On the Day the hypocrites, men and women, will say to the believers: "Wait for us, so that we may borrow from your light." It will be said: "Go back and seek for yourselves a light." Then a wall will be raised between them both, which has a door. On the inner part thereof is Mercy, and on the opposite side the outer part thereof is punishment.

14. They will call out to them: "Were we not with you?" They will say: "Yes indeed; but you deluded yourselves, you waited long, doubted and were deceived by false hopes, until Allah's Decree came and the deceiver[803] deceived you regarding Allah."

15. Therefore, today no ransom will be taken from you, nor from the unbelievers. The Fire will be your refuge; it will be your master; and what an evil fate!

16. Is it not time that the believers' hearts should bow down at the mention of Allah and the Truth which was sent down, and not to be like those who were given the Book previously, but as time went by, their hearts hardened, and many of them are sinners now?

مَن ذَا ٱلَّذِى يُقْرِضُ ٱللَّهَ قَرْضًا حَسَنًا فَيُضَٰعِفَهُۥ لَهُۥ وَلَهُۥٓ أَجْرٌ كَرِيمٌ ﴿١١﴾

يَوْمَ تَرَى ٱلْمُؤْمِنِينَ وَٱلْمُؤْمِنَٰتِ يَسْعَىٰ نُورُهُم بَيْنَ أَيْدِيهِمْ وَبِأَيْمَٰنِهِم بُشْرَىٰكُمُ ٱلْيَوْمَ جَنَّٰتٌ تَجْرِى مِن تَحْتِهَا ٱلْأَنْهَٰرُ خَٰلِدِينَ فِيهَآ ذَٰلِكَ هُوَ ٱلْفَوْزُ ٱلْعَظِيمُ ﴿١٢﴾

يَوْمَ يَقُولُ ٱلْمُنَٰفِقُونَ وَٱلْمُنَٰفِقَٰتُ لِلَّذِينَ ءَامَنُوا ٱنظُرُونَا نَقْتَبِسْ مِن نُّورِكُمْ قِيلَ ٱرْجِعُوا وَرَآءَكُمْ فَٱلْتَمِسُوا نُورًا فَضُرِبَ بَيْنَهُم بِسُورٍ لَّهُۥ بَابٌ بَاطِنُهُۥ فِيهِ ٱلرَّحْمَةُ وَظَٰهِرُهُۥ مِن قِبَلِهِ ٱلْعَذَابُ ﴿١٣﴾

يُنَادُونَهُمْ أَلَمْ نَكُن مَّعَكُمْ قَالُوا بَلَىٰ وَلَٰكِنَّكُمْ فَتَنتُمْ أَنفُسَكُمْ وَتَرَبَّصْتُمْ وَٱرْتَبْتُمْ وَغَرَّتْكُمُ ٱلْأَمَانِىُّ حَتَّىٰ جَآءَ أَمْرُ ٱللَّهِ وَغَرَّكُم بِٱللَّهِ ٱلْغَرُورُ ﴿١٤﴾

فَٱلْيَوْمَ لَا يُؤْخَذُ مِنكُمْ فِدْيَةٌ وَلَا مِنَ ٱلَّذِينَ كَفَرُوا مَأْوَىٰكُمُ ٱلنَّارُ هِىَ مَوْلَىٰكُمْ وَبِئْسَ ٱلْمَصِيرُ ﴿١٥﴾

۞ أَلَمْ يَأْنِ لِلَّذِينَ ءَامَنُوٓا أَن تَخْشَعَ قُلُوبُهُمْ لِذِكْرِ ٱللَّهِ وَمَا نَزَلَ مِنَ ٱلْحَقِّ وَلَا يَكُونُوا كَٱلَّذِينَ أُوتُوا ٱلْكِتَٰبَ مِن قَبْلُ فَطَالَ عَلَيْهِمُ ٱلْأَمَدُ فَقَسَتْ قُلُوبُهُمْ وَكَثِيرٌ مِّنْهُمْ فَٰسِقُونَ ﴿١٦﴾

---

803. Satan.

17. Know that Allah revives the earth after it is dead. We have expounded the Signs clearly for you, that perchance you might understand.

18. Surely, the men and women who give in charity and who have lent Allah a fair loan will receive its double and they will have a generous wage.

19. And those who believe in Allah and His Messengers are truly the pious and the martyrs in their Lord's Sight. They shall have their wage and their light; but those who disbelieve and deny Our Signs, are truly the Companions of Hell.

20. Know that the present life is but sport and diversion, adornment, boasting among you and rivalry in amassing wealth and children. It is like a rain whose vegetation delighted the unbelievers, then it withered and you see it turning yellow and then it becomes stubble. In the Hereafter there is terrible punishment, forgiveness from Allah and good pleasure. The present life is but the enjoyment of vanity.

21. Vie with one another unto forgiveness from your Lord and a Garden the breadth whereof is like the breadth of the heavens and the earth; it has been prepared for those who believe in Allah and His Messengers. That is Allah's Bounty which He confers upon whoever He pleases. And Allah's is the Great Bounty.

22. Not a disaster befalls in the earth or in yourselves but is in a Book, before We create it. That for Allah is an easy matter.

23. So that you may not grieve for what you missed, and rejoice at what came your way. Allah does not like the conceited and the boastful;

اعْلَمُوٓا أَنَّ اللَّهَ يُحْيِ الْأَرْضَ بَعْدَ مَوْتِهَا قَدْ بَيَّنَّا لَكُمُ الْآيَاتِ لَعَلَّكُمْ تَعْقِلُونَ ۝

إِنَّ الْمُصَّدِّقِينَ وَالْمُصَّدِّقَاتِ وَأَقْرَضُوا اللَّهَ قَرْضًا حَسَنًا يُضَاعَفُ لَهُمْ وَلَهُمْ أَجْرٌ كَرِيمٌ ۝

وَالَّذِينَ ءَامَنُوا بِاللَّهِ وَرُسُلِهِۦٓ أُوْلَٰٓئِكَ هُمُ الصِّدِّيقُونَ وَالشُّهَدَآءُ عِندَ رَبِّهِمْ لَهُمْ أَجْرُهُمْ وَنُورُهُمْ وَالَّذِينَ كَفَرُوا وَكَذَّبُوا بِـَٔايَاتِنَآ أُوْلَٰٓئِكَ أَصْحَابُ الْجَحِيمِ ۝

اعْلَمُوٓا أَنَّمَا الْحَيَوٰةُ الدُّنْيَا لَعِبٌ وَلَهْوٌ وَزِينَةٌ وَتَفَاخُرٌ بَيْنَكُمْ وَتَكَاثُرٌ فِي الْأَمْوَالِ وَالْأَوْلَادِ كَمَثَلِ غَيْثٍ أَعْجَبَ الْكُفَّارَ نَبَاتُهُۥ ثُمَّ يَهِيجُ فَتَرَىٰهُ مُصْفَرًّا ثُمَّ يَكُونُ حُطَامًا وَفِي الْآخِرَةِ عَذَابٌ شَدِيدٌ وَمَغْفِرَةٌ مِّنَ اللَّهِ وَرِضْوَانٌ وَمَا الْحَيَوٰةُ الدُّنْيَآ إِلَّا مَتَاعُ الْغُرُورِ ۝

سَابِقُوٓا إِلَىٰ مَغْفِرَةٍ مِّن رَّبِّكُمْ وَجَنَّةٍ عَرْضُهَا كَعَرْضِ السَّمَآءِ وَالْأَرْضِ أُعِدَّتْ لِلَّذِينَ ءَامَنُوا بِاللَّهِ وَرُسُلِهِۦ ذَٰلِكَ فَضْلُ اللَّهِ يُؤْتِيهِ مَن يَشَآءُ وَاللَّهُ ذُو الْفَضْلِ الْعَظِيمِ ۝

مَآ أَصَابَ مِن مُّصِيبَةٍ فِي الْأَرْضِ وَلَا فِي أَنفُسِكُمْ إِلَّا فِي كِتَابٍ مِّن قَبْلِ أَن نَّبْرَأَهَآ إِنَّ ذَٰلِكَ عَلَى اللَّهِ يَسِيرٌ ۝

لِّكَيْلَا تَأْسَوْا عَلَىٰ مَا فَاتَكُمْ وَلَا تَفْرَحُوا بِمَآ ءَاتَاكُمْ وَاللَّهُ لَا يُحِبُّ كُلَّ مُخْتَالٍ فَخُورٍ ۝

24. Those who are niggardly and bid people to be niggardly. He who turns away, Allah is All-Sufficient, Praiseworthy.

25. We have sent forth Our Messengers with clear proofs and sent down with them the Book and the Balance, so that people might act equitably. We have also sent down iron, which has mighty power and benefits for mankind, and that Allah might know who supports Him and His Messengers invisibly. Allah is indeed Strong and Mighty.

26. We have also sent forth Noah and Abraham and assigned Prophethood and the Book to their progeny. Some of them are well-guided and many of them are sinners.

27. Then, We sent forth in their wake Our Messengers and followed up with Jesus, son of Mary, and We gave him the Gospel and We instilled in the hearts of those who followed him compassion and mercy. As for the monasticism which they invented, for We did not prescribe it for them, seeking thereby to please Allah, they did not observe it properly; so We rewarded those of them who believed, but many of them are sinful.

28. O believers, fear Allah and believe in His Messenger, so that He might show you His Mercy twofold, give you a light by which you might walk about and forgive you. Allah is All-Forgiving, Merciful;

29. That the People of the Book may know that they have no power over anything of Allah's Bounty, and that Bounty is in Allah's Power; He gives it to whoever He pleases. Allah's is the Great Bounty.

الَّذِينَ يَبْخَلُونَ وَيَأْمُرُونَ النَّاسَ بِالْبُخْلِ وَمَن يَتَوَلَّ فَإِنَّ اللَّهَ هُوَ الْغَنِيُّ الْحَمِيدُ ﴿٢٤﴾

لَقَدْ أَرْسَلْنَا رُسُلَنَا بِالْبَيِّنَٰتِ وَأَنزَلْنَا مَعَهُمُ الْكِتَٰبَ وَالْمِيزَانَ لِيَقُومَ النَّاسُ بِالْقِسْطِ وَأَنزَلْنَا الْحَدِيدَ فِيهِ بَأْسٌ شَدِيدٌ وَمَنَٰفِعُ لِلنَّاسِ وَلِيَعْلَمَ اللَّهُ مَن يَنصُرُهُ وَرُسُلَهُ بِالْغَيْبِ إِنَّ اللَّهَ قَوِيٌّ عَزِيزٌ ﴿٢٥﴾

وَلَقَدْ أَرْسَلْنَا نُوحًا وَإِبْرَٰهِيمَ وَجَعَلْنَا فِي ذُرِّيَّتِهِمَا النُّبُوَّةَ وَالْكِتَٰبَ فَمِنْهُم مُّهْتَدٍ وَكَثِيرٌ مِّنْهُمْ فَٰسِقُونَ ﴿٢٦﴾

ثُمَّ قَفَّيْنَا عَلَىٰ ءَاثَٰرِهِم بِرُسُلِنَا وَقَفَّيْنَا بِعِيسَى ابْنِ مَرْيَمَ وَءَاتَيْنَٰهُ الْإِنجِيلَ وَجَعَلْنَا فِي قُلُوبِ الَّذِينَ اتَّبَعُوهُ رَأْفَةً وَرَحْمَةً وَرَهْبَانِيَّةً ابْتَدَعُوهَا مَا كَتَبْنَٰهَا عَلَيْهِمْ إِلَّا ابْتِغَاءَ رِضْوَٰنِ اللَّهِ فَمَا رَعَوْهَا حَقَّ رِعَايَتِهَا فَـَٔاتَيْنَا الَّذِينَ ءَامَنُوا مِنْهُمْ أَجْرَهُمْ وَكَثِيرٌ مِّنْهُمْ فَٰسِقُونَ ﴿٢٧﴾

يَٰٓأَيُّهَا الَّذِينَ ءَامَنُوا اتَّقُوا اللَّهَ وَءَامِنُوا بِرَسُولِهِ يُؤْتِكُمْ كِفْلَيْنِ مِن رَّحْمَتِهِ وَيَجْعَل لَّكُمْ نُورًا تَمْشُونَ بِهِ وَيَغْفِرْ لَكُمْ وَاللَّهُ غَفُورٌ رَّحِيمٌ ﴿٢٨﴾

لِّئَلَّا يَعْلَمَ أَهْلُ الْكِتَٰبِ أَلَّا يَقْدِرُونَ عَلَىٰ شَيْءٍ مِّن فَضْلِ اللَّهِ وَأَنَّ الْفَضْلَ بِيَدِ اللَّهِ يُؤْتِيهِ مَن يَشَاءُ وَاللَّهُ ذُو الْفَضْلِ الْعَظِيمِ ﴿٢٩﴾

Sûrat Al-Mujadilah,
(The Pleading Woman) 58

*In the Name of Allah,
the Compassionate, the Merciful*

1. Allah has heard the words of that woman who disputes with you, concerning her husband, and complains to Allah, while Allah hears you both conversing. Allah is truly All-Hearing, All-Seeing.

2. Those of you who ignore their wives saying: "You are like our mother's back", should know that they are not really their mothers. Their mothers are only those women who gave them birth, and they are certainly making a reprehensible statement and a lie. But Allah is indeed All-Pardoning, All-Forgiving.

3. And those who say of their wives: "You are like our mother's back", then retract what they said, have to free a slave before touching each other. That is what you are admonished, and Allah is Fully Aware of what you do.

4. As for him who does not have the means, he should fast two consecutive months, before they can touch each other; and he who cannot should feed sixty poor persons. That is prescribed that you may believe in Allah and His Messenger and these are the bounds of Allah. The unbelievers shall have a very painful punishment.

5. Those who antagonize Allah and His Messenger shall be abased by Allah, as He abased those who preceded them. We have, indeed, sent down very clear Signs; and the unbelievers shall have a demeaning punishment.

6. On the Day when Allah shall raise them all from the dead, then inform them of what they did. Allah has kept count of it, but they have forgotten it. Allah is a Witness of everything.

يَوْمَ يَبْعَثُهُمُ ٱللَّهُ جَمِيعًا فَيُنَبِّئُهُم بِمَا عَمِلُوٓاْ أَحْصَىٰهُ ٱللَّهُ وَنَسُوهُ وَٱللَّهُ عَلَىٰ كُلِّ شَىْءٍ شَهِيدٌ ۝

7. Have you not considered that Allah knows what is in the heavens and on the earth. No three conspire in secret, but He is the fourth of them; nor five but He is the sixth of them; nor even less than that or more but He is with them wherever they are. Then He shall inform them of what they did on the Day of Resurrection. Allah, indeed, has knowledge of everything.

أَلَمْ تَرَ أَنَّ ٱللَّهَ يَعْلَمُ مَا فِى ٱلسَّمَٰوَٰتِ وَمَا فِى ٱلْأَرْضِ مَا يَكُونُ مِن نَّجْوَىٰ ثَلَٰثَةٍ إِلَّا هُوَ رَابِعُهُمْ وَلَا خَمْسَةٍ إِلَّا هُوَ سَادِسُهُمْ وَلَآ أَدْنَىٰ مِن ذَٰلِكَ وَلَآ أَكْثَرَ إِلَّا هُوَ مَعَهُمْ أَيْنَ مَا كَانُوٓاْ ثُمَّ يُنَبِّئُهُم بِمَا عَمِلُواْ يَوْمَ ٱلْقِيَٰمَةِ إِنَّ ٱللَّهَ بِكُلِّ شَىْءٍ عَلِيمٌ ۝

8. Have you not considered those who were forbidden to converse secretly, then they return to what they were forbidden from and converse secretly in sin and aggression and the disobedience of the Messenger? Then, when they come to you, they greet you with a greeting that Allah never greeted you with. They say within themselves: "If only Allah were to punish us for what we say!" May Hell suffice them; and what a wretched fate!

أَلَمْ تَرَ إِلَى ٱلَّذِينَ نُهُواْ عَنِ ٱلنَّجْوَىٰ ثُمَّ يَعُودُونَ لِمَا نُهُواْ عَنْهُ وَيَتَنَٰجَوْنَ بِٱلْإِثْمِ وَٱلْعُدْوَٰنِ وَمَعْصِيَتِ ٱلرَّسُولِ وَإِذَا جَآءُوكَ حَيَّوْكَ بِمَا لَمْ يُحَيِّكَ بِهِ ٱللَّهُ وَيَقُولُونَ فِىٓ أَنفُسِهِمْ لَوْلَا يُعَذِّبُنَا ٱللَّهُ بِمَا نَقُولُ حَسْبُهُمْ جَهَنَّمُ يَصْلَوْنَهَا فَبِئْسَ ٱلْمَصِيرُ ۝

9. O believers, if you converse secretly among yourselves, do not converse in sin, aggression and disobedience of the Messenger; but converse in righteousness and piety, and fear Allah unto Whom you shall be mustered.

يَٰٓأَيُّهَا ٱلَّذِينَ ءَامَنُوٓاْ إِذَا تَنَٰجَيْتُمْ فَلَا تَتَنَٰجَوْاْ بِٱلْإِثْمِ وَٱلْعُدْوَٰنِ وَمَعْصِيَتِ ٱلرَّسُولِ وَتَنَٰجَوْاْ بِٱلْبِرِّ وَٱلتَّقْوَىٰ وَٱتَّقُواْ ٱللَّهَ ٱلَّذِىٓ إِلَيْهِ تُحْشَرُونَ ۝

10. Conversing in secret is an act of Satan, so as to sadden the believers; but that will not harm them in the least, except with Allah's Leave. Let the believers put their trust in Allah.

إِنَّمَا ٱلنَّجْوَىٰ مِنَ ٱلشَّيْطَٰنِ لِيَحْزُنَ ٱلَّذِينَ ءَامَنُواْ وَلَيْسَ بِضَآرِّهِمْ شَيْئًا إِلَّا بِإِذْنِ ٱللَّهِ وَعَلَى ٱللَّهِ فَلْيَتَوَكَّلِ ٱلْمُؤْمِنُونَ ۝

11. O believers, if you are told: "Make room in assemblies", then make room that Allah may make room for you; and if you are told:

يَٰٓأَيُّهَا ٱلَّذِينَ ءَامَنُوٓاْ إِذَا قِيلَ لَكُمْ تَفَسَّحُواْ فِى ٱلْمَجَٰلِسِ فَٱفْسَحُواْ يَفْسَحِ ٱللَّهُ لَكُمْ وَإِذَا قِيلَ ٱنشُزُواْ فَٱنشُزُواْ يَرْفَعِ

"Sally forth", then sally forth, that Allah may elevate those of you who have believed and those who have been given knowledge many steps. Allah is Fully Aware of what you do.

12. O believers, if you converse privately with the Messenger, then tender a free offering before your secret conversing. That is better for you and purer; but if you do not have the means, then Allah is All-Forgiving, Merciful.

13. Do you dread to make free offerings before your private converse? If you do not do so and Allah pardons you, then perform the prayer, give the alms and obey Allah and His Messenger. Allah is Aware of what you do.

14. Have you not considered those who befriended a people who incurred Allah's Wrath? They are not of you nor of them; and they swear in falsehood knowingly.

15. Allah has prepared for them a terrible punishment. Evil indeed is what they used to do.

16. They took their oaths as a smoke-screen, and so they debarred access to Allah's Path. Theirs, then, is a demeaning punishment.

17. Neither their possessions nor their children shall avail them anything against Allah. Those are the Companions of the Fire, dwelling therein forever.

18. On the Day Allah shall resurrect all and they will swear to Him as they swear to you, thinking that they have something to gain. Indeed, they are the liars.

19. Satan has taken hold of them, and so caused them to forget the mention of Allah. Those are the party of Satan; indeed the party of Satan are the losers.

اللَّهُ الَّذِينَ ءَامَنُوا مِنكُمْ وَالَّذِينَ أُوتُوا الْعِلْمَ دَرَجَاتٍ وَاللَّهُ بِمَا تَعْمَلُونَ خَبِيرٌ ۝

يَاۤأَيُّهَا الَّذِينَ ءَامَنُوٓا إِذَا نَاجَيْتُمُ الرَّسُولَ فَقَدِّمُوا بَيْنَ يَدَىْ نَجْوَىٰكُمْ صَدَقَةً ذَلِكَ خَيْرٌ لَّكُمْ وَأَطْهَرُ فَإِن لَّمْ تَجِدُوا فَإِنَّ اللَّهَ غَفُورٌ رَّحِيمٌ ۝

ءَأَشْفَقْتُمْ أَن تُقَدِّمُوا بَيْنَ يَدَىْ نَجْوَىٰكُمْ صَدَقَاتٍ فَإِذْ لَمْ تَفْعَلُوا وَتَابَ اللَّهُ عَلَيْكُمْ فَأَقِيمُوا الصَّلَوٰةَ وَءَاتُوا الزَّكَوٰةَ وَأَطِيعُوا اللَّهَ وَرَسُولَهُ وَاللَّهُ خَبِيرٌ بِمَا تَعْمَلُونَ ۝

۞ أَلَمْ تَرَ إِلَى الَّذِينَ تَوَلَّوْا قَوْمًا غَضِبَ اللَّهُ عَلَيْهِم مَّا هُم مِّنكُمْ وَلَا مِنْهُمْ وَيَحْلِفُونَ عَلَى الْكَذِبِ وَهُمْ يَعْلَمُونَ ۝

أَعَدَّ اللَّهُ لَهُمْ عَذَابًا شَدِيدًا إِنَّهُمْ سَآءَ مَا كَانُوا يَعْمَلُونَ ۝

اتَّخَذُوٓا أَيْمَانَهُمْ جُنَّةً فَصَدُّوا عَن سَبِيلِ اللَّهِ فَلَهُمْ عَذَابٌ مُّهِينٌ ۝

لَّن تُغْنِيَ عَنْهُمْ أَمْوَالُهُمْ وَلَاۤ أَوْلَادُهُم مِّنَ اللَّهِ شَيْئًا أُوْلَٰٓئِكَ أَصْحَابُ النَّارِ هُمْ فِيهَا خَالِدُونَ ۝

يَوْمَ يَبْعَثُهُمُ اللَّهُ جَمِيعًا فَيَحْلِفُونَ لَهُ كَمَا يَحْلِفُونَ لَكُمْ وَيَحْسَبُونَ أَنَّهُمْ عَلَىٰ شَيْءٍ أَلَاۤ إِنَّهُمْ هُمُ الْكَاذِبُونَ ۝

اسْتَحْوَذَ عَلَيْهِمُ الشَّيْطَانُ فَأَنْسَاهُمْ ذِكْرَ اللَّهِ أُوْلَٰٓئِكَ حِزْبُ الشَّيْطَانِ أَلَاۤ إِنَّ حِزْبَ الشَّيْطَانِ هُمُ الْخَاسِرُونَ ۝

20. Those who antagonize Allah and His Messenger are surely among the lowliest.

21. Allah has written: "I shall certainly vanquish, I and My Messengers." Surely Allah is Strong, All-Mighty.

22. You will not find a people who believe in Allah and the Last Day befriending those who antagonize Allah and His Messenger, even if they are their fathers, their sons, their brothers or their clansmen. Those, Allah has inscribed faith upon their hearts and strengthened them with a spirit from Himself, and He will admit them into Gardens, beneath which rivers flow, dwelling therein forever. Allah is well-pleased with them and they are well-pleased with Him. Those are Allah's Party; surely Allah's Party shall be the prosperous.

Sûrat Al-Hashr,
(The Mustering) 59

In the Name of Allah,
the Compassionate, the Merciful

1. Everything in the heavens and the earth glorifies Allah. He is the All-Mighty, the All-Wise.

2. It is He Who drove out the unbelievers among the People of the Book from their homes at the first mustering. You did not think that they would be driven out, and they thought that their forts would protect them from Allah. Then, Allah seized them from an unexpected quarter and cast terror into their hearts, so that they destroyed their homes with their own hands, as well as the hands of the believers. Reflect, then, O people of perception!

إِنَّ ٱلَّذِينَ يُحَآدُّونَ ٱللَّهَ وَرَسُولَهُ أُوْلَـٰٓئِكَ فِى ٱلۡأَذَلِّينَ ۝

كَتَبَ ٱللَّهُ لَأَغۡلِبَنَّ أَنَا۠ وَرُسُلِىٓ إِنَّ ٱللَّهَ قَوِىٌّ عَزِيزٌ ۝

لَّا تَجِدُ قَوۡمًا يُؤۡمِنُونَ بِٱللَّهِ وَٱلۡيَوۡمِ ٱلۡأَخِرِ يُوَآدُّونَ مَنۡ حَآدَّ ٱللَّهَ وَرَسُولَهُۥ وَلَوۡ كَانُوٓاْ ءَابَآءَهُمۡ أَوۡ أَبۡنَآءَهُمۡ أَوۡ إِخۡوَٰنَهُمۡ أَوۡ عَشِيرَتَهُمۡ أُوْلَـٰٓئِكَ كَتَبَ فِى قُلُوبِهِمُ ٱلۡإِيمَـٰنَ وَأَيَّدَهُم بِرُوحٍ مِّنۡهُ وَيُدۡخِلُهُمۡ جَنَّـٰتٍ تَجۡرِى مِن تَحۡتِهَا ٱلۡأَنۡهَـٰرُ خَـٰلِدِينَ فِيهَا رَضِىَ ٱللَّهُ عَنۡهُمۡ وَرَضُواْ عَنۡهُ أُوْلَـٰٓئِكَ حِزۡبُ ٱللَّهِ أَلَآ إِنَّ حِزۡبَ ٱللَّهِ هُمُ ٱلۡمُفۡلِحُونَ ۝

سُورَةُ الحَشر

بِسۡمِ ٱللَّهِ ٱلرَّحۡمَـٰنِ ٱلرَّحِيمِ

سَبَّحَ لِلَّهِ مَا فِى ٱلسَّمَـٰوَٰتِ وَمَا فِى ٱلۡأَرۡضِ وَهُوَ ٱلۡعَزِيزُ ٱلۡحَكِيمُ ۝

هُوَ ٱلَّذِىٓ أَخۡرَجَ ٱلَّذِينَ كَفَرُواْ مِنۡ أَهۡلِ ٱلۡكِتَـٰبِ مِن دِيَـٰرِهِمۡ لِأَوَّلِ ٱلۡحَشۡرِ مَا ظَنَنتُمۡ أَن يَخۡرُجُواْ وَظَنُّوٓاْ أَنَّهُم مَّانِعَتُهُمۡ حُصُونُهُم مِّنَ ٱللَّهِ فَأَتَىٰهُمُ ٱللَّهُ مِنۡ حَيۡثُ لَمۡ يَحۡتَسِبُواْ وَقَذَفَ فِى قُلُوبِهِمُ ٱلرُّعۡبَ يُخۡرِبُونَ بُيُوتَهُم بِأَيۡدِيهِمۡ وَأَيۡدِى ٱلۡمُؤۡمِنِينَ فَٱعۡتَبِرُواْ يَـٰٓأُوْلِى ٱلۡأَبۡصَـٰرِ ۝

3. Had not Allah decreed dispersion upon them, He would certainly have punished them in the present life, and in the Hereafter, the punishment of the Fire shall be theirs.

وَلَوْلَا أَن كَتَبَ ٱللَّهُ عَلَيْهِمُ ٱلْجَلَاءَ لَعَذَّبَهُمْ فِى ٱلدُّنْيَا وَلَهُمْ فِى ٱلْآخِرَةِ عَذَابُ ٱلنَّارِ ﴿٣﴾

4. That is because they have opposed Allah and His Messenger, and he who opposes Allah will find Allah terrible in retribution.

ذَٰلِكَ بِأَنَّهُمْ شَآقُّوا۟ ٱللَّهَ وَرَسُولَهُۥ وَمَن يُشَآقِّ ٱللَّهَ فَإِنَّ ٱللَّهَ شَدِيدُ ٱلْعِقَابِ ﴿٤﴾

5. Whatever palm trees you cut off or leave standing upon their roots is only by Allah's Leave, and that he might disgrace the sinners.

مَا قَطَعْتُم مِّن لِّينَةٍ أَوْ تَرَكْتُمُوهَا قَآئِمَةً عَلَىٰٓ أُصُولِهَا فَبِإِذْنِ ٱللَّهِ وَلِيُخْزِىَ ٱلْفَٰسِقِينَ ﴿٥﴾

6. Whatever spoils Allah has bestowed on His Messenger from them, you did not send against them any horses or other mounts; but Allah confers on His Messengers authority over whoever He pleases. Allah has power over everything.

وَمَآ أَفَآءَ ٱللَّهُ عَلَىٰ رَسُولِهِۦ مِنْهُمْ فَمَآ أَوْجَفْتُمْ عَلَيْهِ مِنْ خَيْلٍ وَلَا رِكَابٍ وَلَٰكِنَّ ٱللَّهَ يُسَلِّطُ رُسُلَهُۥ عَلَىٰ مَن يَشَآءُ وَٱللَّهُ عَلَىٰ كُلِّ شَىْءٍ قَدِيرٌ ﴿٦﴾

7. And whatever spoils Allah bestows on His Messenger from the inhabitants of the cities belongs to Allah, His Messenger, the kinsmen, the orphans, the destitute and the wayfarers; so that it might not circulate among the rich of you. Whatever the Messenger gives you, take; but whatever he forbids, refrain from. Fear Allah, for Allah is terrible in retribution.

مَّآ أَفَآءَ ٱللَّهُ عَلَىٰ رَسُولِهِۦ مِنْ أَهْلِ ٱلْقُرَىٰ فَلِلَّهِ وَلِلرَّسُولِ وَلِذِى ٱلْقُرْبَىٰ وَٱلْيَتَٰمَىٰ وَٱلْمَسَٰكِينِ وَٱبْنِ ٱلسَّبِيلِ كَىْ لَا يَكُونَ دُولَةً بَيْنَ ٱلْأَغْنِيَآءِ مِنكُمْ وَمَآ ءَاتَىٰكُمُ ٱلرَّسُولُ فَخُذُوهُ وَمَا نَهَىٰكُمْ عَنْهُ فَٱنتَهُوا۟ وَٱتَّقُوا۟ ٱللَّهَ إِنَّ ٱللَّهَ شَدِيدُ ٱلْعِقَابِ ﴿٧﴾

8. Give to the poor Emigrants who were driven out of their homes and their possessions, seeking bounty from Allah and good pleasure and assisting Allah and His Messenger. Those indeed are the truthful ones.

لِلْفُقَرَآءِ ٱلْمُهَٰجِرِينَ ٱلَّذِينَ أُخْرِجُوا۟ مِن دِيَٰرِهِمْ وَأَمْوَٰلِهِمْ يَبْتَغُونَ فَضْلًا مِّنَ ٱللَّهِ وَرِضْوَٰنًا وَيَنصُرُونَ ٱللَّهَ وَرَسُولَهُۥٓ أُو۟لَٰٓئِكَ هُمُ ٱلصَّٰدِقُونَ ﴿٨﴾

9. And those who had already established themselves and embraced their Faith before them[804] love those who emigrated to them; and they do not find in their hearts any need for what had been bestowed upon them and

وَٱلَّذِينَ تَبَوَّءُو ٱلدَّارَ وَٱلْإِيمَٰنَ مِن قَبْلِهِمْ يُحِبُّونَ مَنْ هَاجَرَ إِلَيْهِمْ وَلَا يَجِدُونَ فِى صُدُورِهِمْ حَاجَةً مِّمَّآ أُوتُوا۟ وَيُؤْثِرُونَ عَلَىٰٓ أَنفُسِهِمْ وَلَوْ كَانَ بِهِمْ خَصَاصَةٌ

---

804. That is, the people of Medina, known as *al-Ansar*, or supporters, as against the Meccans known as *al-Mubajirun*, or emigrants.

prefer them to themselves, even if they are in dire need. He is indeed prosperous who is guarded against the avarice of his soul.

10. Those who came after them say: "Our Lord, forgive us and our brothers who preceded us in belief and do not instil in our hearts any rancour towards those who believe. Lord, You are indeed Clement and Merciful."

11. Have you not considered the hypocrites? They say to their brethren who have disbelieved from the People of the Book: "If you are driven out, we will go out with you and we will never obey anyone against you; and should anyone fight you, we will certainly support you." Allah bears witness that they are liars, indeed.

12. If they are driven out, they will not go out with them; and if anyone fights them, they will not support them. Even if they support them, they will turn their backs in flight; then they will not receive any support.

13. You are indeed more terrifying in their hearts than Allah. That is because they are a people who do not understand.

14. They do not fight you all together except in fortified cities or from behind walls. Their prowess is great among themselves. You think they are united, yet their hearts are at variance. That is because they are a people who do not understand.

15. Like those who, shortly before them, tasted the futility of their action. They shall have a painful punishment.

16. Like Satan, when he said to man: "Disbelieve"; then when he disbelieved, he said: "I am quit of you. Indeed, I fear Allah, the Lord of the Worlds."

وَمَن يُوقَ شُحَّ نَفْسِهِ فَأُوْلَٰئِكَ هُمُ ٱلْمُفْلِحُونَ ۞

وَٱلَّذِينَ جَآءُو مِنۢ بَعْدِهِمْ يَقُولُونَ رَبَّنَا ٱغْفِرْ لَنَا وَلِإِخْوَٰنِنَا ٱلَّذِينَ سَبَقُونَا بِٱلْإِيمَٰنِ وَلَا تَجْعَلْ فِى قُلُوبِنَا غِلًّا لِّلَّذِينَ ءَامَنُوا رَبَّنَآ إِنَّكَ رَءُوفٌ رَّحِيمٌ ۞

۞ أَلَمْ تَرَ إِلَى ٱلَّذِينَ نَافَقُوا يَقُولُونَ لِإِخْوَٰنِهِمُ ٱلَّذِينَ كَفَرُوا مِنْ أَهْلِ ٱلْكِتَٰبِ لَئِنْ أُخْرِجْتُمْ لَنَخْرُجَنَّ مَعَكُمْ وَلَا نُطِيعُ فِيكُمْ أَحَدًا أَبَدًا وَإِن قُوتِلْتُمْ لَنَنصُرَنَّكُمْ وَٱللَّهُ يَشْهَدُ إِنَّهُمْ لَكَٰذِبُونَ ۞

لَئِنْ أُخْرِجُوا لَا يَخْرُجُونَ مَعَهُمْ وَلَئِن قُوتِلُوا لَا يَنصُرُونَهُمْ وَلَئِن نَّصَرُوهُمْ لَيُوَلُّنَّ ٱلْأَدْبَٰرَ ثُمَّ لَا يُنصَرُونَ ۞

لَأَنتُمْ أَشَدُّ رَهْبَةً فِى صُدُورِهِم مِّنَ ٱللَّهِ ذَٰلِكَ بِأَنَّهُمْ قَوْمٌ لَّا يَفْقَهُونَ ۞

لَا يُقَٰتِلُونَكُمْ جَمِيعًا إِلَّا فِى قُرًى مُّحَصَّنَةٍ أَوْ مِن وَرَآءِ جُدُرٍۭ بَأْسُهُم بَيْنَهُمْ شَدِيدٌ تَحْسَبُهُمْ جَمِيعًا وَقُلُوبُهُمْ شَتَّىٰ ذَٰلِكَ بِأَنَّهُمْ قَوْمٌ لَّا يَعْقِلُونَ ۞

كَمَثَلِ ٱلَّذِينَ مِن قَبْلِهِمْ قَرِيبًا ذَاقُوا وَبَالَ أَمْرِهِمْ وَلَهُمْ عَذَابٌ أَلِيمٌ ۞

كَمَثَلِ ٱلشَّيْطَٰنِ إِذْ قَالَ لِلْإِنسَٰنِ ٱكْفُرْ فَلَمَّا كَفَرَ قَالَ إِنِّى بَرِىٓءٌ مِّنكَ إِنِّىٓ أَخَافُ ٱللَّهَ رَبَّ ٱلْعَٰلَمِينَ ۞

17. Thereupon, their end together was to be in the Fire, dwelling therein forever. That is the reward of the wrongdoers.

فَكَانَ عَٰقِبَتَهُمَآ أَنَّهُمَا فِى ٱلنَّارِ خَٰلِدَيْنِ فِيهَآ وَذَٰلِكَ جَزَٰٓؤُاْ ٱلظَّٰلِمِينَ ۝

18. O believers, fear Allah and let each soul consider what it has forwarded for the morrow. Fear Allah; He is Aware of what you do.

يَٰٓأَيُّهَا ٱلَّذِينَ ءَامَنُواْ ٱتَّقُواْ ٱللَّهَ وَلْتَنظُرْ نَفْسٌ مَّا قَدَّمَتْ لِغَدٍ وَٱتَّقُواْ ٱللَّهَ إِنَّ ٱللَّهَ خَبِيرٌۢ بِمَا تَعْمَلُونَ ۝

19. Do not be like those who forgot Allah, and so He made them forget themselves. Those are indeed the sinners.

وَلَا تَكُونُواْ كَٱلَّذِينَ نَسُواْ ٱللَّهَ فَأَنسَىٰهُمْ أَنفُسَهُمْ أُوْلَٰٓئِكَ هُمُ ٱلْفَٰسِقُونَ ۝

20. The Companions of the Fire and the Companions of Paradise are not equal. The Companions of Paradise are indeed the winners.

لَا يَسْتَوِىٓ أَصْحَٰبُ ٱلنَّارِ وَأَصْحَٰبُ ٱلْجَنَّةِ أَصْحَٰبُ ٱلْجَنَّةِ هُمُ ٱلْفَآئِزُونَ ۝

21. Had We sent down this Qur'an upon a mountain, you would have seen it bowing down and rent asunder out of the fear of Allah. Those are the parables which We recite to mankind, that perchance they might reflect.

لَوْ أَنزَلْنَا هَٰذَا ٱلْقُرْءَانَ عَلَىٰ جَبَلٍ لَّرَأَيْتَهُ خَٰشِعًا مُّتَصَدِّعًا مِّنْ خَشْيَةِ ٱللَّهِ وَتِلْكَ ٱلْأَمْثَٰلُ نَضْرِبُهَا لِلنَّاسِ لَعَلَّهُمْ يَتَفَكَّرُونَ ۝

22. He is Allah; there is no god but He, the Knower of the Unseen and the Seen. He is the Compassionate, the Merciful.

هُوَ ٱللَّهُ ٱلَّذِى لَآ إِلَٰهَ إِلَّا هُوَ عَٰلِمُ ٱلْغَيْبِ وَٱلشَّهَٰدَةِ هُوَ ٱلرَّحْمَٰنُ ٱلرَّحِيمُ ۝

23. He is Allah. There is no god but He, the King, the Holy, the Peace-Giver, the Faith-Giver, the Overseer, the All-Mighty, the Overlord, the Haughty. May Allah be exalted above what they associate.

هُوَ ٱللَّهُ ٱلَّذِى لَآ إِلَٰهَ إِلَّا هُوَ ٱلْمَلِكُ ٱلْقُدُّوسُ ٱلسَّلَٰمُ ٱلْمُؤْمِنُ ٱلْمُهَيْمِنُ ٱلْعَزِيزُ ٱلْجَبَّارُ ٱلْمُتَكَبِّرُ سُبْحَٰنَ ٱللَّهِ عَمَّا يُشْرِكُونَ ۝

24. He is Allah, the Creator, the Maker, the Fashioner. His are the Beautiful Names; whatever is in the heavens and on the earth glorifies Him. He is the All-Mighty, the Wise.

هُوَ ٱللَّهُ ٱلْخَٰلِقُ ٱلْبَارِئُ ٱلْمُصَوِّرُ لَهُ ٱلْأَسْمَآءُ ٱلْحُسْنَىٰ يُسَبِّحُ لَهُ مَا فِى ٱلسَّمَٰوَٰتِ وَٱلْأَرْضِ وَهُوَ ٱلْعَزِيزُ ٱلْحَكِيمُ ۝

Sûrat Al-Mumtahanah, (The Woman Tested) 60

In the Name of Allah, the Compassionate, the Merciful

1. O believers, do not take My enemy and your enemy for supporters, showing them friendship, when they have disbelieved what has come to you of the Truth. They expel the Messenger and expel you because you have believed in Allah, your Lord. If you have gone out to struggle in My Cause and to seek My Good Pleasure secretly showing them friendship, while I know very well what you conceal and what you reveal. He who does that among you has surely strayed from the Right Path.

2. If they come upon you, they will be enemies of yours and will stretch out their hands and tongues against you with malice, and they wish that you would disbelieve.

3. Your kinsmen or your children will not profit you on the Day of Resurrection. He shall separate you one from the other; and Allah perceives well what you do.

4. You have had a good example in Abraham and those with him, when they said to their people: "We are quit of you and what you worship apart from Allah. We disbelieve in you. Enmity and hatred have arisen between you and us forever, till you believe in Allah alone; except for Abraham's words to his father: 'I will ask forgiveness for you, although I have no power from Allah to do anything for you.' Lord, in You we trust, to You we turn and unto You is the ultimate resort.

563

5. "Lord, do not cause us to be a temptation for those who have disbelieved, and forgive us. Our Lord, You are indeed the All-Mighty, the All-Wise."

6. You had indeed in them a good example; that is for whoever hopes for Allah and the Last Day. Whoever repents, surely Allah is the All-Mighty, All-Praiseworthy.

7. It may be that Allah will establish friendship between you and those of them who were your enemies. Allah is All-Powerful, and Allah is All-Forgiving, All-Merciful.

8. Allah does not forbid you, regarding those who did not fight you and did not drive you out of your homes, to be generous to them and deal with them justly. Allah surely loves the just.

9. Allah only forbids you, regarding those who fought you in religion and drove you out of your homes and assisted in driving you out, to take them for friends. Those who take them for friends are, indeed, the wrongdoers.

10. O believers, if believing women come to you as Emigrants, then test them; Allah knows better their faith. If you find them to be believers, do not send them back to the unbelievers. They are neither lawful to the unbelieving men, nor are those men lawful to them. Give them what they[805] had paid in dowry; and you are not at fault if you marry them, provided you pay them their dowries. Do not hold fast to unbelieving women; demand what you have spent and let them demand what they have spent. That is Allah's Judgement. He judges between you, and Allah is All-Knowing and Wise.

---

805. The unbelieving husbands.

11. If any of your wives desert you to the unbelievers, and you decide to penalize them, then give those [husbands] whose wives have gone away the like of what they have spent, and fear Allah in Whom you believe.

12. O Prophet, if believing women come to you to pay you homage, pledging not to associate anything with Allah, steal, commit adultery, kill their children, come up with a lie they invent between their hands and feet[806] or disobey you in any honourable matter, then accept their homage and ask Allah's Forgiveness for them. Allah indeed is All-Forgiving, All-Merciful.

13. O believers, do not befriend a people against whom Allah is wrathful and who have despaired of the Hereafter, just as the unbelievers have despaired of the dwellers of the tombs.

Sûrat As-Saff,
(The Battle Array) 61

In the Name of Allah,
the Compassionate, the Merciful

1. Everything in the heavens and on the earth glorifies Allah. He is the All-Mighty, the Wise.

2. O believers, why do you profess what you do not practise?

3. It is very hateful in Allah's Sight that you profess what you do not practise.

4. Allah loves those who fight in His Cause arrayed in battle, as though they were a compact structure.

---

806. That is, allege that an illegitimate child is their husband's.

5. When Moses said to his people: "O my people, why do you injure me, although you know that I am Allah's Messenger to you?" When they swerved, Allah caused their hearts to swerve. Allah does not guide the sinful people.

وَإِذْ قَالَ مُوسَىٰ لِقَوْمِهِۦ يَٰقَوْمِ لِمَ تُؤْذُونَنِى وَقَد تَّعْلَمُونَ أَنِّى رَسُولُ ٱللَّهِ إِلَيْكُمْ فَلَمَّا زَاغُوٓا۟ أَزَاغَ ٱللَّهُ قُلُوبَهُمْ وَٱللَّهُ لَا يَهْدِى ٱلْقَوْمَ ٱلْفَٰسِقِينَ ۝

6. And when Jesus, son of Mary, said: "O Children of Israel, I am Allah's Messenger to you, confirming what came before me of the Torah, and announcing the news of a Messenger who will come after me, whose name is Ahmad." Then when he (Ahmad i.e. Mohammad) brought them the clear proofs, they said: "This is manifest sorcery."

وَإِذْ قَالَ عِيسَى ٱبْنُ مَرْيَمَ يَٰبَنِىٓ إِسْرَٰٓءِيلَ إِنِّى رَسُولُ ٱللَّهِ إِلَيْكُم مُّصَدِّقًا لِّمَا بَيْنَ يَدَىَّ مِنَ ٱلتَّوْرَىٰةِ وَمُبَشِّرًۢا بِرَسُولٍ يَأْتِى مِنۢ بَعْدِى ٱسْمُهُۥٓ أَحْمَدُ فَلَمَّا جَآءَهُم بِٱلْبَيِّنَٰتِ قَالُوا۟ هَٰذَا سِحْرٌ مُّبِينٌ ۝

7. And who is a greater wrongdoer than he who imputes falsehood to Allah, when he is summoned to submission (to Allah)?[807] Allah does not guide the wrongdoing people.

وَمَنْ أَظْلَمُ مِمَّنِ ٱفْتَرَىٰ عَلَى ٱللَّهِ ٱلْكَذِبَ وَهُوَ يُدْعَىٰٓ إِلَى ٱلْإِسْلَٰمِ وَٱللَّهُ لَا يَهْدِى ٱلْقَوْمَ ٱلظَّٰلِمِينَ ۝

8. They wish to extinguish Allah's Lights with their mouths, but Allah will perfect His Light, even though the unbelievers might be averse.

يُرِيدُونَ لِيُطْفِـُٔوا۟ نُورَ ٱللَّهِ بِأَفْوَٰهِهِمْ وَٱللَّهُ مُتِمُّ نُورِهِۦ وَلَوْ كَرِهَ ٱلْكَٰفِرُونَ ۝

9. It is He Who sent His Messenger forth with the guidance and the religion of truth, to make it triumph over every religion, even though the idolaters may be averse.

هُوَ ٱلَّذِىٓ أَرْسَلَ رَسُولَهُۥ بِٱلْهُدَىٰ وَدِينِ ٱلْحَقِّ لِيُظْهِرَهُۥ عَلَى ٱلدِّينِ كُلِّهِۦ وَلَوْ كَرِهَ ٱلْمُشْرِكُونَ ۝

10. O believers, shall I show you a trade which will deliver you from a very painful punishment?

يَٰٓأَيُّهَا ٱلَّذِينَ ءَامَنُوا۟ هَلْ أَدُلُّكُمْ عَلَىٰ تِجَٰرَةٍ تُنجِيكُم مِّنْ عَذَابٍ أَلِيمٍ ۝

11. Believe in Allah and His Messenger and struggle in the Cause of Allah with your possessions and yourselves. That is far better for you, if only you knew.

تُؤْمِنُونَ بِٱللَّهِ وَرَسُولِهِۦ وَتُجَٰهِدُونَ فِى سَبِيلِ ٱللَّهِ بِأَمْوَٰلِكُمْ وَأَنفُسِكُمْ ذَٰلِكُمْ خَيْرٌ لَّكُمْ إِن كُنتُمْ تَعْلَمُونَ ۝

12. He will then forgive you your sins and admit you into Gardens, beneath which rivers flow, and into fine dwellings in the Gardens of Eden. That is the great triumph.

يَغْفِرْ لَكُمْ ذُنُوبَكُمْ وَيُدْخِلْكُمْ جَنَّٰتٍ تَجْرِى مِن تَحْتِهَا ٱلْأَنْهَٰرُ وَمَسَٰكِنَ طَيِّبَةً فِى جَنَّٰتِ عَدْنٍ ذَٰلِكَ ٱلْفَوْزُ ٱلْعَظِيمُ ۝

---

807. The Arabic word is *al-Islam*, which means submission to the Will of God.

13. And another thing you love: support from Allah and an imminent victory. So announce the good news to the believers.

وَأُخْرَىٰ تُحِبُّونَهَا نَصْرٌ مِّنَ ٱللَّهِ وَفَتْحٌ قَرِيبٌ وَبَشِّرِ ٱلْمُؤْمِنِينَ ۝

14. O believers, be supporters of Allah, as Jesus, son of Mary, said to the disciples: "Who are my supporters unto Allah?" The disciples replied: "We are Allah's supporters"; and so a group of the Children of Israel believed, while another group disbelieved. Then, We supported those who believed against their foe; and so they were triumphant.

يَٰٓأَيُّهَا ٱلَّذِينَ ءَامَنُوا۟ كُونُوٓا۟ أَنصَارَ ٱللَّهِ كَمَا قَالَ عِيسَى ٱبْنُ مَرْيَمَ لِلْحَوَارِيِّۦنَ مَنْ أَنصَارِىٓ إِلَى ٱللَّهِ قَالَ ٱلْحَوَارِيُّونَ نَحْنُ أَنصَارُ ٱللَّهِ فَـَٔامَنَت طَّآئِفَةٌ مِّنۢ بَنِىٓ إِسْرَٰٓءِيلَ وَكَفَرَت طَّآئِفَةٌ فَأَيَّدْنَا ٱلَّذِينَ ءَامَنُوا۟ عَلَىٰ عَدُوِّهِمْ فَأَصْبَحُوا۟ ظَٰهِرِينَ ۝

Sûrat Al-Jumu'ah, (Friday, or The Congregation) 62

In the Name of Allah,
the Compassionate, the Merciful

بِسْمِ ٱللَّهِ ٱلرَّحْمَٰنِ ٱلرَّحِيمِ

1. Everything in the heavens and on the earth glorifies Allah, the King, the Holy One, the All-Mighty, the All-Wise.

يُسَبِّحُ لِلَّهِ مَا فِى ٱلسَّمَٰوَٰتِ وَمَا فِى ٱلْأَرْضِ ٱلْمَلِكِ ٱلْقُدُّوسِ ٱلْعَزِيزِ ٱلْحَكِيمِ ۝

2. It is He Who has raised up from the common nations[808] a Messenger of their own, reciting to them His Signs, purifying them and teaching them the Book and the wisdom, although they had been in manifest error before that;

هُوَ ٱلَّذِى بَعَثَ فِى ٱلْأُمِّيِّۦنَ رَسُولًا مِّنْهُمْ يَتْلُوا۟ عَلَيْهِمْ ءَايَٰتِهِۦ وَيُزَكِّيهِمْ وَيُعَلِّمُهُمُ ٱلْكِتَٰبَ وَٱلْحِكْمَةَ وَإِن كَانُوا۟ مِن قَبْلُ لَفِى ضَلَٰلٍ مُّبِينٍ ۝

3. And others from them, who had not joined them yet. He is the All-Mighty, the Wise.

وَءَاخَرِينَ مِنْهُمْ لَمَّا يَلْحَقُوا۟ بِهِمْ وَهُوَ ٱلْعَزِيزُ ٱلْحَكِيمُ ۝

4. That is Allah's Bounty which He imparts to whomever He pleases; and to Allah belongs the Great Bounty.

ذَٰلِكَ فَضْلُ ٱللَّهِ يُؤْتِيهِ مَن يَشَآءُ وَٱللَّهُ ذُو ٱلْفَضْلِ ٱلْعَظِيمِ ۝

---

808. Arabic *al-Ummiyyun*, which could also mean the illiterates, or the people with no revealed scripture, as against the People of the Book, or Jews and Christians.

5. The case of those who were loaded with the Torah, then failed to carry it, is similar to an ass which carries learned books. Wretched is the case of the people who have denounced Allah's Signs. Allah does not guide the wrongdoing people.

مَثَلُ ٱلَّذِينَ حُمِّلُوا ٱلتَّوْرَىٰةَ ثُمَّ لَمْ يَحْمِلُوهَا كَمَثَلِ ٱلْحِمَارِ يَحْمِلُ أَسْفَارًا بِئْسَ مَثَلُ ٱلْقَوْمِ ٱلَّذِينَ كَذَّبُوا بِـَٔايَـٰتِ ٱللَّهِ وَٱللَّهُ لَا يَهْدِى ٱلْقَوْمَ ٱلظَّـٰلِمِينَ ۝

6. Say: "O you who have adopted Judaism; if you claim to be Allah's friends, apart from other people, then do wish for death, if you are truthful."

قُلْ يَـٰٓأَيُّهَا ٱلَّذِينَ هَادُوٓا إِن زَعَمْتُمْ أَنَّكُمْ أَوْلِيَآءُ لِلَّهِ مِن دُونِ ٱلنَّاسِ فَتَمَنَّوُا ٱلْمَوْتَ إِن كُنتُمْ صَـٰدِقِينَ ۝

7. Yet, they will never wish it, due to what their hands have advanced. Allah knows well the wrongdoers.

وَلَا يَتَمَنَّوْنَهُۥٓ أَبَدًۢا بِمَا قَدَّمَتْ أَيْدِيهِمْ وَٱللَّهُ عَلِيمٌۢ بِٱلظَّـٰلِمِينَ ۝

8. Say: "The death from which you flee will surely overtake you. Then you will be turned over to Him Who knows the Unseen and the Seen, and He will inform you about what you used to do."

قُلْ إِنَّ ٱلْمَوْتَ ٱلَّذِى تَفِرُّونَ مِنْهُ فَإِنَّهُۥ مُلَـٰقِيكُمْ ثُمَّ تُرَدُّونَ إِلَىٰ عَـٰلِمِ ٱلْغَيْبِ وَٱلشَّهَـٰدَةِ فَيُنَبِّئُكُم بِمَا كُنتُمْ تَعْمَلُونَ ۝

9. O believers, when the call for prayer on the Day of Congregation[809] is sounded, then hasten to the mention of Allah and leave off trading. That is far better for you, if only you knew.

يَـٰٓأَيُّهَا ٱلَّذِينَ ءَامَنُوٓا إِذَا نُودِىَ لِلصَّلَوٰةِ مِن يَوْمِ ٱلْجُمُعَةِ فَٱسْعَوْا إِلَىٰ ذِكْرِ ٱللَّهِ وَذَرُوا ٱلْبَيْعَ ذَٰلِكُمْ خَيْرٌ لَّكُمْ إِن كُنتُمْ تَعْلَمُونَ ۝

10. Then, when prayer is over, spread out throughout the land and seek some of Allah's Bounty, and remember Allah often, that perchance you might prosper.

فَإِذَا قُضِيَتِ ٱلصَّلَوٰةُ فَٱنتَشِرُوا فِى ٱلْأَرْضِ وَٱبْتَغُوا مِن فَضْلِ ٱللَّهِ وَٱذْكُرُوا ٱللَّهَ كَثِيرًا لَّعَلَّكُمْ تُفْلِحُونَ ۝

11. However, when they see trading or sport, they scramble towards it and leave you standing up. Say: "What Allah has in store is far better than sport or trading; and Allah is the Best of providers."

وَإِذَا رَأَوْا تِجَـٰرَةً أَوْ لَهْوًا ٱنفَضُّوٓا إِلَيْهَا وَتَرَكُوكَ قَآئِمًا قُلْ مَا عِندَ ٱللَّهِ خَيْرٌ مِّنَ ٱللَّهْوِ وَمِنَ ٱلتِّجَـٰرَةِ وَٱللَّهُ خَيْرُ ٱلرَّٰزِقِينَ ۝

---

809. Or Friday.

Sûrat Al-Munâfiqûn, (The Hypocrites) 63

In the Name of Allah, the Compassionate, the Merciful

1. When the hypocrites come to you, they say: "We bear witness that you are indeed Allah's Messenger." Allah knows that you are indeed His Messenger and Allah bears witness that the hypocrites are liars.

2. They take their oaths as a shield and so they bar other people from the Path of Allah. Evil is what they used to do.

3. That is because they believed, then disbelieved; and so a seal was set upon their hearts. Therefore, they do not understand at all.

4. If you see them, their bodies please you; and if they speak, you listen to their words, as though they were propped-up wooden logs. They think every cry is aimed at them; they are the enemy, so beware of them. May Allah discomfit them, how they are perverted!

5. If it is said to them: "Come, that the Messenger of Allah may seek forgiveness for you"; they bend their heads and you see them walking away, waxing proud.

6. It is the same for them whether you seek forgiveness for them or you do not seek forgiveness. Allah will not forgive them. Surely, Allah will not guide the sinful people.

7. It is they who say: "Do not spend any money on those[810] who side with Allah's Messenger until they disperse." To Allah belong the treasuries of the heavens and the earth, but the hypocrites do not understand.

---

810. The Meccan Emigrants.

8. They say: "If we return to the City,[811] the mightiest will drive out the lowliest therefrom." Might belongs to Allah, His Messenger and the believers, but the hypocrites do not know.

يَقُولُونَ لَئِن رَّجَعْنَآ إِلَى ٱلْمَدِينَةِ لَيُخْرِجَنَّ ٱلْأَعَزُّ مِنْهَا ٱلْأَذَلَّ وَلِلَّهِ ٱلْعِزَّةُ وَلِرَسُولِهِۦ وَلِلْمُؤْمِنِينَ وَلَٰكِنَّ ٱلْمُنَٰفِقِينَ لَا يَعْلَمُونَ ۝

9. O believers, let not your possessions or children distract you from the remembrance of Allah. Whoever does that - those are the real losers.

يَٰٓأَيُّهَا ٱلَّذِينَ ءَامَنُوا۟ لَا تُلْهِكُمْ أَمْوَٰلُكُمْ وَلَآ أَوْلَٰدُكُمْ عَن ذِكْرِ ٱللَّهِ وَمَن يَفْعَلْ ذَٰلِكَ فَأُو۟لَٰٓئِكَ هُمُ ٱلْخَٰسِرُونَ ۝

10. Spend freely from what We have provided for you, before death overtakes each one of you. Then he will say: "Lord, if only You would reprieve me for a short period, so that I may give in charity and be one of the righteous."

وَأَنفِقُوا۟ مِن مَّا رَزَقْنَٰكُم مِّن قَبْلِ أَن يَأْتِىَ أَحَدَكُمُ ٱلْمَوْتُ فَيَقُولَ رَبِّ لَوْلَآ أَخَّرْتَنِىٓ إِلَىٰٓ أَجَلٍ قَرِيبٍ فَأَصَّدَّقَ وَأَكُن مِّنَ ٱلصَّٰلِحِينَ ۝

11. Allah will not reprieve a single soul when its term comes. Allah is Fully Aware of what you do.

وَلَن يُؤَخِّرَ ٱللَّهُ نَفْسًا إِذَا جَآءَ أَجَلُهَا وَٱللَّهُ خَبِيرٌۢ بِمَا تَعْمَلُونَ ۝

Sûrat At-Taghâbun, (Mutual Exchange) 64

سُورَةُ التَّغَابُنِ

In the Name of Allah, the Compassionate, the Merciful

بِسْمِ ٱللَّهِ ٱلرَّحْمَٰنِ ٱلرَّحِيمِ

1. Everything in the heavens and on the earth glorifies Allah. His is the sovereignty and His is the praise, and He has power over everything.

يُسَبِّحُ لِلَّهِ مَا فِى ٱلسَّمَٰوَٰتِ وَمَا فِى ٱلْأَرْضِ لَهُ ٱلْمُلْكُ وَلَهُ ٱلْحَمْدُ وَهُوَ عَلَىٰ كُلِّ شَىْءٍ قَدِيرٌ ۝

2. It is He Who created you. Some of you are unbelievers, and some believers; and Allah perceives what you do.

هُوَ ٱلَّذِى خَلَقَكُمْ فَمِنكُمْ كَافِرٌ وَمِنكُم مُّؤْمِنٌ وَٱللَّهُ بِمَا تَعْمَلُونَ بَصِيرٌ ۝

3. He created the heavens and the earth in truth, and He fashioned you and shaped well your forms. Unto Him is the ultimate resort.

خَلَقَ ٱلسَّمَٰوَٰتِ وَٱلْأَرْضَ بِٱلْحَقِّ وَصَوَّرَكُمْ فَأَحْسَنَ صُوَرَكُمْ وَإِلَيْهِ ٱلْمَصِيرُ ۝

---

811. Yathrib, Medina.

4. He knows what is in the heavens and on the earth, and He knows what you conceal and what you reveal. Allah knows well the thoughts hidden in the breasts.

5. Has not the news of those who disbelieved formerly come to you, and so they tasted the evil plight of their condition? A painful punishment awaits them.

6. That is because their Messengers used to bring them the clear proofs, but they would say: "Will mortals guide us rightly?" So, they disbelieved and turned their backs and Allah was well content. Allah is All-Sufficient, All-Worthy.

7. The unbelievers claimed that they will not be raised from the dead. Say: "Yes indeed by my Lord, you shall be raised, then you will be informed about what you did. That for Allah is an easy matter."

8. Therefore, believe in Allah, His Messenger and the Light which We sent down. Allah is Aware of what you do.

9. On the Day when He shall gather you for the Day of Forgathering. That is the Day of Mutual Exchange.[812] He who believes in Allah and acts righteously, He will acquit him of his evil actions and admit him into Gardens beneath which rivers flow, dwelling therein forever. That is the great triumph.

10. And those who disbelieved and denounced Our Signs, those are the Companions of the Fire, dwelling therein forever; and what a miserable fate!

11. No disaster befalls but by Allah's Leave. Whoever believes in Allah, He will guide his heart rightly. Allah has knowledge of everything.

يَعْلَمُ مَا فِى ٱلسَّمَٰوَٰتِ وَٱلْأَرْضِ وَيَعْلَمُ مَا تُسِرُّونَ وَمَا تُعْلِنُونَ وَٱللَّهُ عَلِيمٌ بِذَاتِ ٱلصُّدُورِ ﴿٤﴾

أَلَمْ يَأْتِكُمْ نَبَؤُاْ ٱلَّذِينَ كَفَرُواْ مِن قَبْلُ فَذَاقُواْ وَبَالَ أَمْرِهِمْ وَلَهُمْ عَذَابٌ أَلِيمٌ ﴿٥﴾

ذَٰلِكَ بِأَنَّهُۥ كَانَت تَّأْتِيهِمْ رُسُلُهُم بِٱلْبَيِّنَٰتِ فَقَالُوٓاْ أَبَشَرٌ يَهْدُونَنَا فَكَفَرُواْ وَتَوَلَّواْ وَّٱسْتَغْنَى ٱللَّهُ وَٱللَّهُ غَنِىٌّ حَمِيدٌ ﴿٦﴾

زَعَمَ ٱلَّذِينَ كَفَرُوٓاْ أَن لَّن يُبْعَثُواْ قُلْ بَلَىٰ وَرَبِّى لَتُبْعَثُنَّ ثُمَّ لَتُنَبَّؤُنَّ بِمَا عَمِلْتُمْ وَذَٰلِكَ عَلَى ٱللَّهِ يَسِيرٌ ﴿٧﴾

فَـَٔامِنُواْ بِٱللَّهِ وَرَسُولِهِۦ وَٱلنُّورِ ٱلَّذِىٓ أَنزَلْنَا وَٱللَّهُ بِمَا تَعْمَلُونَ خَبِيرٌ ﴿٨﴾

يَوْمَ يَجْمَعُكُمْ لِيَوْمِ ٱلْجَمْعِ ذَٰلِكَ يَوْمُ ٱلتَّغَابُنِ وَمَن يُؤْمِنۢ بِٱللَّهِ وَيَعْمَلْ صَٰلِحًا يُكَفِّرْ عَنْهُ سَيِّـَٔاتِهِۦ وَيُدْخِلْهُ جَنَّٰتٍ تَجْرِى مِن تَحْتِهَا ٱلْأَنْهَٰرُ خَٰلِدِينَ فِيهَآ أَبَدًا ذَٰلِكَ ٱلْفَوْزُ ٱلْعَظِيمُ ﴿٩﴾

وَٱلَّذِينَ كَفَرُواْ وَكَذَّبُواْ بِـَٔايَٰتِنَآ أُوْلَٰٓئِكَ أَصْحَٰبُ ٱلنَّارِ خَٰلِدِينَ فِيهَا وَبِئْسَ ٱلْمَصِيرُ ﴿١٠﴾

مَآ أَصَابَ مِن مُّصِيبَةٍ إِلَّا بِإِذْنِ ٱللَّهِ وَمَن يُؤْمِنۢ بِٱللَّهِ يَهْدِ قَلْبَهُۥ وَٱللَّهُ بِكُلِّ شَىْءٍ عَلِيمٌ ﴿١١﴾

---

812. When the inhabitants of Paradise would have defrauded the inhabitants of Hell, according to al-Tabari.

12. Obey Allah and obey the Messenger. If you turn away, it is only incumbent on Our Messenger to deliver the manifest message.

وَأَطِيعُوا۟ اللَّهَ وَأَطِيعُوا۟ الرَّسُولَ فَإِن تَوَلَّيْتُمْ فَإِنَّمَا عَلَىٰ رَسُولِنَا الْبَلَـٰغُ الْمُبِينُ ۝

13. Allah, there is no god but He; and in Allah let the believers put their trust.

اللَّهُ لَآ إِلَـٰهَ إِلَّا هُوَ وَعَلَى اللَّهِ فَلْيَتَوَكَّلِ الْمُؤْمِنُونَ ۝

14. O believers, in the midst of your wives and children, there is an enemy of yours, so beware of them. Yet, if you pardon, overlook and forgive, surely Allah is All-Forgiving, All-Merciful.

يَـٰٓأَيُّهَا الَّذِينَ ءَامَنُوٓا۟ إِنَّ مِنْ أَزْوَٰجِكُمْ وَأَوْلَـٰدِكُمْ عَدُوًّا لَّكُمْ فَاحْذَرُوهُمْ وَإِن تَعْفُوا۟ وَتَصْفَحُوا۟ وَتَغْفِرُوا۟ فَإِنَّ اللَّهَ غَفُورٌ رَّحِيمٌ ۝

15. Your possessions and children are surely a temptation, and with Allah is a great reward.

إِنَّمَآ أَمْوَٰلُكُمْ وَأَوْلَـٰدُكُمْ فِتْنَةٌ وَاللَّهُ عِندَهُۥٓ أَجْرٌ عَظِيمٌ ۝

16. So, fear Allah as much as you can, listen, obey and spend freely. That is best for you. He who is guarded against the avarice of his soul - those are the prosperous.

فَاتَّقُوا۟ اللَّهَ مَا اسْتَطَعْتُمْ وَاسْمَعُوا۟ وَأَطِيعُوا۟ وَأَنفِقُوا۟ خَيْرًا لِّأَنفُسِكُمْ وَمَن يُوقَ شُحَّ نَفْسِهِۦ فَأُو۟لَـٰٓئِكَ هُمُ الْمُفْلِحُونَ ۝

17. If you lend Allah a fair loan, He will multiply it for you and forgive you. Allah is All-Grateful, All-Clement;

إِن تُقْرِضُوا۟ اللَّهَ قَرْضًا حَسَنًا يُضَـٰعِفْهُ لَكُمْ وَيَغْفِرْ لَكُمْ وَاللَّهُ شَكُورٌ حَلِيمٌ ۝

18. Knower of the Unseen and the Seen, the All-Mighty, the Wise.

عَـٰلِمُ الْغَيْبِ وَالشَّهَـٰدَةِ الْعَزِيزُ الْحَكِيمُ ۝

Sûrat At-Talâq, (The Divorce) 65

سُورَةُ الطَّلَاقِ

In the Name of Allah, the Compassionate, the Merciful

بِسْمِ اللَّهِ الرَّحْمَـٰنِ الرَّحِيمِ

1. O Prophet, if you divorce your women, divorce them when they have completed their menstrual period. Calculate the period and fear Allah, your Lord. Do not drive them out of their homes, and let them not go out, unless they have committed a manifest foul act. Those are the bounds of Allah. He who transgresses the bounds of Allah has surely wronged himself. You do not know, Allah may perhaps bring about something new after that.

يَـٰٓأَيُّهَا النَّبِىُّ إِذَا طَلَّقْتُمُ النِّسَآءَ فَطَلِّقُوهُنَّ لِعِدَّتِهِنَّ وَأَحْصُوا۟ الْعِدَّةَ وَاتَّقُوا۟ اللَّهَ رَبَّكُمْ لَا تُخْرِجُوهُنَّ مِنۢ بُيُوتِهِنَّ وَلَا يَخْرُجْنَ إِلَّآ أَن يَأْتِينَ بِفَـٰحِشَةٍ مُّبَيِّنَةٍ وَتِلْكَ حُدُودُ اللَّهِ وَمَن يَتَعَدَّ حُدُودَ اللَّهِ فَقَدْ ظَلَمَ نَفْسَهُۥ لَا تَدْرِى لَعَلَّ اللَّهَ يُحْدِثُ بَعْدَ ذَٰلِكَ أَمْرًا ۝

2. Then, when they have reached their term, retain them honourably or part with them honourably, calling two just witnesses from among yourselves. Administer the witnessing to Allah Himself. By that is exhorted whoever believes in Allah and the Last Day. He who fears Allah, He will grant him a way out;

3. And He will provide for him from sources he could never conceive. He who puts his trust in Allah, Allah will be sufficient unto him. Allah shall attain His goal. Allah has meted out a measure for everything.

4. As for those of your women who have despaired of menstruation, if you are in doubt, then their term shall be three months; and those too who have not menstruated yet. As to those women with child, their term shall be upon delivering their burden. He who fears Allah, Allah will grant him relief in his affair.

5. That is Allah's Command, which He has sent down to you; and he who fears Allah, He will acquit him of his sins and amplify his reward.

6. Put them up where you are lodged, according to your means, and do not badger them so as to make life difficult for them. If they are with child, support them until they deliver their burden; and if they suckle for you, then pay them their wages. Confer with each other honourably; but if you are at odds, let another woman suckle him.

7. Let the man of means spend out of his means, and he whose provision has been constricted, spend out of what Allah gave him. Allah does not charge any soul except with what He gave it. Allah will cause relief to follow every hardship.

فَإِذَا بَلَغْنَ أَجَلَهُنَّ فَأَمْسِكُوهُنَّ بِمَعْرُوفٍ أَوْ فَارِقُوهُنَّ بِمَعْرُوفٍ وَأَشْهِدُوا ذَوَىْ عَدْلٍ مِّنكُمْ وَأَقِيمُوا الشَّهَـٰدَةَ لِلَّهِ ذَٰلِكُمْ يُوعَظُ بِهِۦ مَن كَانَ يُؤْمِنُ بِاللَّهِ وَالْيَوْمِ الْـَٔاخِرِ وَمَن يَتَّقِ اللَّهَ يَجْعَل لَّهُۥ مَخْرَجًا ۝

وَيَرْزُقْهُ مِنْ حَيْثُ لَا يَحْتَسِبُ وَمَن يَتَوَكَّلْ عَلَى اللَّهِ فَهُوَ حَسْبُهُۥٓ إِنَّ اللَّهَ بَٰلِغُ أَمْرِهِۦ قَدْ جَعَلَ اللَّهُ لِكُلِّ شَىْءٍ قَدْرًا ۝

وَالَّٰٓـِٔى يَئِسْنَ مِنَ الْمَحِيضِ مِن نِّسَآئِكُمْ إِنِ ارْتَبْتُمْ فَعِدَّتُهُنَّ ثَلَٰثَةُ أَشْهُرٍ وَالَّٰٓـِٔى لَمْ يَحِضْنَ وَأُولَٰتُ الْأَحْمَالِ أَجَلُهُنَّ أَن يَضَعْنَ حَمْلَهُنَّ وَمَن يَتَّقِ اللَّهَ يَجْعَل لَّهُۥ مِنْ أَمْرِهِۦ يُسْرًا ۝

ذَٰلِكَ أَمْرُ اللَّهِ أَنزَلَهُۥٓ إِلَيْكُمْ وَمَن يَتَّقِ اللَّهَ يُكَفِّرْ عَنْهُ سَيِّـَٔاتِهِۦ وَيُعْظِمْ لَهُۥٓ أَجْرًا ۝

أَسْكِنُوهُنَّ مِنْ حَيْثُ سَكَنتُم مِّن وُجْدِكُمْ وَلَا تُضَآرُّوهُنَّ لِتُضَيِّقُوا عَلَيْهِنَّ وَإِن كُنَّ أُولَٰتِ حَمْلٍ فَأَنفِقُوا عَلَيْهِنَّ حَتَّىٰ يَضَعْنَ حَمْلَهُنَّ فَإِنْ أَرْضَعْنَ لَكُمْ فَـَٔاتُوهُنَّ أُجُورَهُنَّ وَأْتَمِرُوا بَيْنَكُم بِمَعْرُوفٍ وَإِن تَعَاسَرْتُمْ فَسَتُرْضِعُ لَهُۥٓ أُخْرَىٰ ۝

لِيُنفِقْ ذُو سَعَةٍ مِّن سَعَتِهِۦ وَمَن قُدِرَ عَلَيْهِ رِزْقُهُۥ فَلْيُنفِقْ مِمَّآ ءَاتَىٰهُ اللَّهُ لَا يُكَلِّفُ اللَّهُ نَفْسًا إِلَّا مَآ ءَاتَىٰهَا سَيَجْعَلُ اللَّهُ بَعْدَ عُسْرٍ يُسْرًا ۝

8. How many a city transgressed arrogantly the Command of its Lord and His Messengers; and so We brought it to account severely and punished it with an abominable punishment.

وَكَأَيِّن مِّن قَرْيَةٍ عَتَتْ عَنْ أَمْرِ رَبِّهَا وَرُسُلِهِ فَحَاسَبْنَاهَا حِسَابًا شَدِيدًا وَعَذَّبْنَاهَا عَذَابًا نُّكْرًا ۝

9. And so it tasted the bane of its deed and the outcome of its deed was perdition.

فَذَاقَتْ وَبَالَ أَمْرِهَا وَكَانَ عَاقِبَةُ أَمْرِهَا خُسْرًا ۝

10. Allah has prepared for them a terrible punishment. So fear Allah, O people of understanding who have believed. Allah has sent down to you, as a reminder,

أَعَدَّ اللَّهُ لَهُمْ عَذَابًا شَدِيدًا فَاتَّقُوا اللَّهَ يَا أُولِي الْأَلْبَابِ الَّذِينَ آمَنُوا قَدْ أَنزَلَ اللَّهُ إِلَيْكُمْ ذِكْرًا ۝

11. A Messenger, reciting to you the Signs of Allah fully clarified; so as to bring those who have believed and done the righteous deeds from the shadows of darkness to light. He who believes in Allah and does the righteous deed, Allah will admit him into Gardens, beneath which rivers flow, dwelling therein forever. Allah has assigned to him a fair provision.

رَّسُولًا يَتْلُو عَلَيْكُمْ آيَاتِ اللَّهِ مُبَيِّنَاتٍ لِّيُخْرِجَ الَّذِينَ آمَنُوا وَعَمِلُوا الصَّالِحَاتِ مِنَ الظُّلُمَاتِ إِلَى النُّورِ وَمَن يُؤْمِن بِاللَّهِ وَيَعْمَلْ صَالِحًا يُدْخِلْهُ جَنَّاتٍ تَجْرِي مِن تَحْتِهَا الْأَنْهَارُ خَالِدِينَ فِيهَا أَبَدًا قَدْ أَحْسَنَ اللَّهُ لَهُ رِزْقًا ۝

12. It is Allah Who created seven heavens and of the earth like thereof. The Decree descends among them all, that you might know that Allah has power over everything and that Allah has encompassed everything in knowledge.

اللَّهُ الَّذِي خَلَقَ سَبْعَ سَمَاوَاتٍ وَمِنَ الْأَرْضِ مِثْلَهُنَّ يَتَنَزَّلُ الْأَمْرُ بَيْنَهُنَّ لِتَعْلَمُوا أَنَّ اللَّهَ عَلَى كُلِّ شَيْءٍ قَدِيرٌ وَأَنَّ اللَّهَ قَدْ أَحَاطَ بِكُلِّ شَيْءٍ عِلْمًا ۝

Sûrat At-Tahrim,
(The Prohibition) 66

In the Name of Allah,
the Compassionate, the Merciful

بِسْمِ اللَّهِ الرَّحْمَٰنِ الرَّحِيمِ

1. O Prophet, why do you prohibit what Allah has made lawful to you, seeking thereby the good pleasure of your wives? Allah is All-Forgiving, Merciful.

يَا أَيُّهَا النَّبِيُّ لِمَ تُحَرِّمُ مَا أَحَلَّ اللَّهُ لَكَ تَبْتَغِي مَرْضَاتَ أَزْوَاجِكَ وَاللَّهُ غَفُورٌ رَّحِيمٌ ۝

2. Allah has prescribed to you the absolution of your oaths. Allah is your Master and He is the All-Knowing, the Wise.

قَدْ فَرَضَ اللَّهُ لَكُمْ تَحِلَّةَ أَيْمَانِكُمْ وَاللَّهُ مَوْلَاكُمْ وَهُوَ الْعَلِيمُ الْحَكِيمُ ۝

3. And when the Prophet confided to one of his wives a certain matter;[813] and she divulged it, and Allah disclosed it to him too, he made known part of it, but withheld the other part. Then, when he told her about it, she said: "Who told you this?" He said: "The All-Knowing, All-Informed told me."

4. If you two[814] repent unto Allah, then your hearts will have certainly inclined; but if you band together against him, then Allah is his Master. Gabriel, the righteous among the believers and the angels thereupon are his supporters, too.

5. Perhaps, his Lord will, if he divorces you, give him in exchange wives better than you, submissive, believing, obedient, penitent, devout, fasting, either previously married or virgins.

6. O believers, guard yourselves and your families against a Fire whose fuel is people and stones; its overseers are harsh, terrible angels who do not disobey what Allah commands, but will do what they are commanded.

7. O believers, do not give excuses today; for you are only rewarded for what you used to do.

8. O believers, turn to Allah in sincere repentance, that your Lord might perchance acquit you of your evil deeds and admit you into Gardens, beneath which rivers flow, on a day when Allah will not disgrace the Prophet and those who have believed with him. Their light flickering before them and in their right hands, they will say: "Our Lord, perfect for us our light and forgive us; You have indeed power over everything."

---

813. His eating of honey.
814. The two wives of the Prophet.

9. O Prophet, struggle with the unbelievers and the hypocrites, and deal harshly with them. Their refuge shall be Hell, and what an evil resort!

بَيَأَيُّهَا ٱلنَّبِيُّ جَٰهِدِ ٱلْكُفَّارَ وَٱلْمُنَٰفِقِينَ وَٱغْلُظْ عَلَيْهِمْ وَمَأْوَىٰهُمْ جَهَنَّمُ وَبِئْسَ ٱلْمَصِيرُ ﴿٩﴾

10. Allah gave as an instance of the unbelievers the wife of Noah and the wife of Lot. They were under two of Our righteous servants, then they betrayed them. Nothing availed them against Allah and it was said to them: "Enter you two the Fire with the other entrants."

ضَرَبَ ٱللَّهُ مَثَلًا لِّلَّذِينَ كَفَرُوا۟ ٱمْرَأَتَ نُوحٍ وَٱمْرَأَتَ لُوطٍ كَانَتَا تَحْتَ عَبْدَيْنِ مِنْ عِبَادِنَا صَٰلِحَيْنِ فَخَانَتَاهُمَا فَلَمْ يُغْنِيَا عَنْهُمَا مِنَ ٱللَّهِ شَيْـًٔا وَقِيلَ ٱدْخُلَا ٱلنَّارَ مَعَ ٱلدَّٰخِلِينَ ﴿١٠﴾

11. Allah has given as an instance of believers the wife of Pharaoh, when she said: "Lord, build for me, with You, a house in Paradise and deliver me from Pharaoh and his work, and deliver me from the wrong-doing people."

وَضَرَبَ ٱللَّهُ مَثَلًا لِّلَّذِينَ ءَامَنُوا۟ ٱمْرَأَتَ فِرْعَوْنَ إِذْ قَالَتْ رَبِّ ٱبْنِ لِى عِندَكَ بَيْتًا فِى ٱلْجَنَّةِ وَنَجِّنِى مِن فِرْعَوْنَ وَعَمَلِهِ وَنَجِّنِى مِنَ ٱلْقَوْمِ ٱلظَّٰلِمِينَ ﴿١١﴾

12. And Mary, daughter of Imran, who guarded her womb, and so We breathed into it of Our Spirit; and she believed in the truth of her Lord's Words and His Books and was one of the pious.

وَمَرْيَمَ ٱبْنَتَ عِمْرَٰنَ ٱلَّتِىٓ أَحْصَنَتْ فَرْجَهَا فَنَفَخْنَا فِيهِ مِن رُّوحِنَا وَصَدَّقَتْ بِكَلِمَٰتِ رَبِّهَا وَكُتُبِهِ وَكَانَتْ مِنَ ٱلْقَٰنِتِينَ ﴿١٢﴾

Sûrat Al-Mulk, (The Sovereignty) 67

سُورَةُ الملك

In the Name of Allah, the Compassionate, the Merciful

بِسْمِ ٱللَّهِ ٱلرَّحْمَٰنِ ٱلرَّحِيمِ

1. Blessed be He in Whose hands is the sovereignty and He has power over everything.

تَبَٰرَكَ ٱلَّذِى بِيَدِهِ ٱلْمُلْكُ وَهُوَ عَلَىٰ كُلِّ شَىْءٍ قَدِيرٌ ﴿١﴾

2. He Who created death and life so as to test you as to whoever of you is fairer in action. He is the All-Mighty, the All-Forgiving.

ٱلَّذِى خَلَقَ ٱلْمَوْتَ وَٱلْحَيَوٰةَ لِيَبْلُوَكُمْ أَيُّكُمْ أَحْسَنُ عَمَلًا وَهُوَ ٱلْعَزِيزُ ٱلْغَفُورُ ﴿٢﴾

3. He Who has created seven stratified heavens. You do not see any discrepancy in the creation of the Compassionate. So fix your gaze, do you see any cracks?

ٱلَّذِى خَلَقَ سَبْعَ سَمَٰوَٰتٍ طِبَاقًا مَّا تَرَىٰ فِى خَلْقِ ٱلرَّحْمَٰنِ مِن تَفَٰوُتٍ فَٱرْجِعِ ٱلْبَصَرَ هَلْ تَرَىٰ مِن فُطُورٍ ﴿٣﴾

4. Then, fix your gaze again and again, and your gaze will recoil back to you discomfited and weary.

ثُمَّ ٱرْجِعِ ٱلْبَصَرَ كَرَّتَيْنِ يَنقَلِبْ إِلَيْكَ ٱلْبَصَرُ خَاسِئًا وَهُوَ حَسِيرٌ ۝

5. We have adorned the lower heaven with lamps, and We turned them into missiles launched against the devils; and We have prepared for them the punishment of the Fire.

وَلَقَدْ زَيَّنَّا ٱلسَّمَاءَ ٱلدُّنْيَا بِمَصَابِيحَ وَجَعَلْنَاهَا رُجُومًا لِّلشَّيَاطِينِ وَأَعْتَدْنَا لَهُمْ عَذَابَ ٱلسَّعِيرِ ۝

6. And to those who have disbelieved in their Lord, the punishment of Hell is reserved; and what an evil resort!

وَلِلَّذِينَ كَفَرُوا بِرَبِّهِمْ عَذَابُ جَهَنَّمَ وَبِئْسَ ٱلْمَصِيرُ ۝

7. When they are cast into it, they hear its heavy breathing, as it boils over.

إِذَآ أُلْقُوا فِيهَا سَمِعُوا لَهَا شَهِيقًا وَهِيَ تَفُورُ ۝

8. It almost bursts with rage. Every time a new throng is cast into it, its keepers ask them: "Has no warner come to you?"

تَكَادُ تَمَيَّزُ مِنَ ٱلْغَيْظِ كُلَّمَآ أُلْقِيَ فِيهَا فَوْجٌ سَأَلَهُمْ خَزَنَتُهَآ أَلَمْ يَأْتِكُمْ نَذِيرٌ ۝

9. They will say: "Yes indeed; a warner came to us but we disbelieved and said: 'Allah did not send down anything; you are simply in grave error.'

قَالُوا بَلَىٰ قَدْ جَآءَنَا نَذِيرٌ فَكَذَّبْنَا وَقُلْنَا مَا نَزَّلَ ٱللَّهُ مِن شَيْءٍ إِنْ أَنتُمْ إِلَّا فِي ضَلَالٍ كَبِيرٍ ۝

10. And they will also say: "Had we listened or reasoned, we would not be among the Companions of the Fire."

وَقَالُوا لَوْ كُنَّا نَسْمَعُ أَوْ نَعْقِلُ مَا كُنَّا فِيٓ أَصْحَابِ ٱلسَّعِيرِ ۝

11. So, they will confess their sin. Away, then, with the Companions of the Fire!

فَٱعْتَرَفُوا بِذَنبِهِمْ فَسُحْقًا لِّأَصْحَابِ ٱلسَّعِيرِ ۝

12. Indeed, those who fear their Lord unseen will be accorded forgiveness and a great reward.

إِنَّ ٱلَّذِينَ يَخْشَوْنَ رَبَّهُم بِٱلْغَيْبِ لَهُم مَّغْفِرَةٌ وَأَجْرٌ كَبِيرٌ ۝

13. Conceal your words or proclaim them, He knows very well the secrets of the breasts.

وَأَسِرُّوا قَوْلَكُمْ أَوِ ٱجْهَرُوا بِهِ إِنَّهُ عَلِيمٌ بِذَاتِ ٱلصُّدُورِ ۝

14. Does He not know what He has created, though He is the All-Subtle, the All-Informed?

أَلَا يَعْلَمُ مَنْ خَلَقَ وَهُوَ ٱللَّطِيفُ ٱلْخَبِيرُ ۝

15. It is He Who made the earth level for you; so stroll through its regions and eat of His provision. Unto Him is the Resurrection.

هُوَ ٱلَّذِي جَعَلَ لَكُمُ ٱلْأَرْضَ ذَلُولًا فَٱمْشُوا فِي مَنَاكِبِهَا وَكُلُوا مِن رِّزْقِهِ وَإِلَيْهِ ٱلنُّشُورُ ۝

16. Are you sure that He Who is in heaven will not cause the earth to cave in upon you? Behold how it quakes!

ءَأَمِنتُم مَّن فِى ٱلسَّمَآءِ أَن يَخْسِفَ بِكُمُ ٱلْأَرْضَ فَإِذَا هِىَ تَمُورُ ﴿١٦﴾

17. Or are you sure that He Who is in heaven will not let loose upon you a squall of pebbles? Then you shall know how My Warning sounds.

أَمْ أَمِنتُم مَّن فِى ٱلسَّمَآءِ أَن يُرْسِلَ عَلَيْكُمْ حَاصِبًا فَسَتَعْلَمُونَ كَيْفَ نَذِيرِ ﴿١٧﴾

18. Those who preceded you have disbelieved. How then was My abomination?

وَلَقَدْ كَذَّبَ ٱلَّذِينَ مِن قَبْلِهِمْ فَكَيْفَ كَانَ نَكِيرِ ﴿١٨﴾

19. Have they not considered the birds above them spreading their wings and folding them? They are only held up by the Compassionate. He is the Perceiver of everything.

أَوَلَمْ يَرَوْا۟ إِلَى ٱلطَّيْرِ فَوْقَهُمْ صَٰٓفَّٰتٍ وَيَقْبِضْنَ مَا يُمْسِكُهُنَّ إِلَّا ٱلرَّحْمَٰنُ إِنَّهُۥ بِكُلِّ شَىْءٍ بَصِيرٌ ﴿١٩﴾

20. Or who is this who is a sentinel for you to protect you against the Compassionate? The unbelievers are simply in error.

أَمَّنْ هَٰذَا ٱلَّذِى هُوَ جُندٌ لَّكُمْ يَنصُرُكُم مِّن دُونِ ٱلرَّحْمَٰنِ إِنِ ٱلْكَٰفِرُونَ إِلَّا فِى غُرُورٍ ﴿٢٠﴾

21. Or who is this who will provide for you, if He withholds His provision? Rather they have persisted in arrogance and aversion.

أَمَّنْ هَٰذَا ٱلَّذِى يَرْزُقُكُمْ إِنْ أَمْسَكَ رِزْقَهُۥ بَل لَّجُّوا۟ فِى عُتُوٍّ وَنُفُورٍ ﴿٢١﴾

22. Is he who walks prone upon his face better guided, or he who walks upon a Straight Path?

أَفَمَن يَمْشِى مُكِبًّا عَلَىٰ وَجْهِهِۦٓ أَهْدَىٰٓ أَمَّن يَمْشِى سَوِيًّا عَلَىٰ صِرَٰطٍ مُّسْتَقِيمٍ ﴿٢٢﴾

23. Say: "It is He Who originated you and created for you hearing, sight, and hearts. How little do you give thanks?"

قُلْ هُوَ ٱلَّذِىٓ أَنشَأَكُمْ وَجَعَلَ لَكُمُ ٱلسَّمْعَ وَٱلْأَبْصَٰرَ وَٱلْأَفْـِٔدَةَ قَلِيلًا مَّا تَشْكُرُونَ ﴿٢٣﴾

24. Say: "It is He Who scattered you abroad in the land, and unto Him you shall be mustered."

قُلْ هُوَ ٱلَّذِى ذَرَأَكُمْ فِى ٱلْأَرْضِ وَإِلَيْهِ تُحْشَرُونَ ﴿٢٤﴾

25. They say: "When is this promise to be fulfilled, if you are truthful?"

وَيَقُولُونَ مَتَىٰ هَٰذَا ٱلْوَعْدُ إِن كُنتُمْ صَٰدِقِينَ ﴿٢٥﴾

26. Say: "Knowledge is with Allah; I am only a manifest warner."

قُلْ إِنَّمَا ٱلْعِلْمُ عِندَ ٱللَّهِ وَإِنَّمَآ أَنَا۠ نَذِيرٌ مُّبِينٌ ﴿٢٦﴾

27. When they see it[815] close at hand, the faces of the unbelievers become grim, and it will be said to them: "That is what you used to boast about."

فَلَمَّا رَأَوْهُ زُلْفَةً سِيئَتْ وُجُوهُ ٱلَّذِينَ كَفَرُوا وَقِيلَ هَٰذَا ٱلَّذِى كُنتُم بِهِۦ تَدَّعُونَ ۝

28. Say: "Have you considered, what if Allah destroyed me and those with me or had Mercy on us, who will protect the unbelievers from a painful punishment?"

قُلْ أَرَءَيْتُمْ إِنْ أَهْلَكَنِىَ ٱللَّهُ وَمَن مَّعِىَ أَوْ رَحِمَنَا فَمَن يُجِيرُ ٱلْكَٰفِرِينَ مِنْ عَذَابٍ أَلِيمٍ ۝

29. Say: "He is the Compassionate, we believe in Him, and in Him we put our trust. You will then know who is in manifest error."

قُلْ هُوَ ٱلرَّحْمَٰنُ ءَامَنَّا بِهِۦ وَعَلَيْهِ تَوَكَّلْنَا فَسَتَعْلَمُونَ مَنْ هُوَ فِى ضَلَٰلٍ مُّبِينٍ ۝

30. Have you considered who, if your water drains away, will bring you pure running water?

قُلْ أَرَءَيْتُمْ إِنْ أَصْبَحَ مَآؤُكُمْ غَوْرًا فَمَن يَأْتِيكُم بِمَآءٍ مَّعِينٍ ۝

Sûrat Al-Qalam, (The Pen) 68

 سُورَةُ الْقَلَمِ

In the Name of Allah, the Compassionate, the Merciful

بِسْمِ ٱللَّهِ ٱلرَّحْمَٰنِ ٱلرَّحِيمِ

1. Nûn.
By the pen and what they inscribe,

نٓ وَٱلْقَلَمِ وَمَا يَسْطُرُونَ ۝

2. You are not (O Muhammad), by the Grace of your Lord, a madman.

مَآ أَنتَ بِنِعْمَةِ رَبِّكَ بِمَجْنُونٍ ۝

3. You will have a wage which is unstinted;

وَإِنَّ لَكَ لَأَجْرًا غَيْرَ مَمْنُونٍ ۝

4. And you are truly a man of noble character.

وَإِنَّكَ لَعَلَىٰ خُلُقٍ عَظِيمٍ ۝

5. You shall see and they shall see,

فَسَتُبْصِرُ وَيُبْصِرُونَ ۝

6. Which of you is the demented one.

بِأَييِّكُمُ ٱلْمَفْتُونُ ۝

7. Surely, your Lord knows better who has strayed from His Path and He knows better the well-guided.

إِنَّ رَبَّكَ هُوَ أَعْلَمُ بِمَن ضَلَّ عَن سَبِيلِهِۦ وَهُوَ أَعْلَمُ بِٱلْمُهْتَدِينَ ۝

8. So do not obey the unbelievers.

فَلَا تُطِعِ ٱلْمُكَذِّبِينَ ۝

9. They wished that you would dissimulate, so that they might dissimulate too.

وَدُّوا لَوْ تُدْهِنُ فَيُدْهِنُونَ ۝

---

815. The punishment.

10. And do not obey every lowly swearer of oaths;

وَلَا تُطِعْ كُلَّ حَلَّافٍ مَّهِينٍ ﴿١٠﴾

11. Backbiter, going around, bearing calumny;

هَمَّازٍ مَّشَّآءٍ بِنَمِيمٍ ﴿١١﴾

12. Hinderer of good, aggressor, wicked;

مَّنَّاعٍ لِّلْخَيْرِ مُعْتَدٍ أَثِيمٍ ﴿١٢﴾

13. Coarse, on top of that, and quarrelsome;

عُتُلٍّ بَعْدَ ذَٰلِكَ زَنِيمٍ ﴿١٣﴾

14. Because he has wealth and children.[816]

أَن كَانَ ذَا مَالٍ وَبَنِينَ ﴿١٤﴾

15. If Our Verses are recited to him, he says: "Legends of the ancients."

إِذَا تُتْلَىٰ عَلَيْهِ ءَايَٰتُنَا قَالَ أَسَٰطِيرُ الْأَوَّلِينَ ﴿١٥﴾

16. We shall brand him upon the muzzle.

سَنَسِمُهُ عَلَى الْخُرْطُومِ ﴿١٦﴾

17. We have tested you, just as We tested the Companions of the Garden when they swore to pluck its fruit in the morning,

إِنَّا بَلَوْنَٰهُمْ كَمَا بَلَوْنَآ أَصْحَٰبَ الْجَنَّةِ إِذْ أَقْسَمُوا لَيَصْرِمُنَّهَا مُصْبِحِينَ ﴿١٧﴾

18. Without any reservations.

وَلَا يَسْتَثْنُونَ ﴿١٨﴾

19. Then a night-stalker from your Lord visited them while they were asleep.

فَطَافَ عَلَيْهَا طَآئِفٌ مِّن رَّبِّكَ وَهُمْ نَآئِمُونَ ﴿١٩﴾

20. And so it (the Garden) became black like a cropped-off field.

فَأَصْبَحَتْ كَالصَّرِيمِ ﴿٢٠﴾

21. Thereupon they called out to each other in the morning:

فَتَنَادَوْا مُصْبِحِينَ ﴿٢١﴾

22. "Go forth to your tillage, if you would crop it off."

أَنِ اغْدُوا عَلَىٰ حَرْثِكُمْ إِن كُنتُمْ صَٰرِمِينَ ﴿٢٢﴾

23. So, they set out whispering to each other:

فَانطَلَقُوا وَهُمْ يَتَخَٰفَتُونَ ﴿٢٣﴾

24. "Let no destitute person enter it today with you around."

أَن لَّا يَدْخُلَنَّهَا الْيَوْمَ عَلَيْكُم مِّسْكِينٌ ﴿٢٤﴾

25. And they proceeded next morning angrily, fully determined.

وَغَدَوْا عَلَىٰ حَرْدٍ قَٰدِرِينَ ﴿٢٥﴾

26. When they saw it, they said: "We have surely gone astray.

فَلَمَّا رَأَوْهَا قَالُوٓا إِنَّا لَضَآلُّونَ ﴿٢٦﴾

27. "Rather we are dispossessed."

بَلْ نَحْنُ مَحْرُومُونَ ﴿٢٧﴾

28. The most reasonable of them said: "Did I not tell you, if only you glorify."

قَالَ أَوْسَطُهُمْ أَلَمْ أَقُل لَّكُمْ لَوْلَا تُسَبِّحُونَ ﴿٢٨﴾

---

816. The reference is to a Qurashite, al-Walid Ibn al-Mughirah, an enemy of the Prophet.

29. They said: "Glory to our Lord, we were indeed wrongdoers."

قَالُوا سُبْحَٰنَ رَبِّنَآ إِنَّا كُنَّا ظَٰلِمِينَ ﴿٢٩﴾

30. Then, they turned to one another, reproaching each other.

فَأَقْبَلَ بَعْضُهُمْ عَلَىٰ بَعْضٍ يَتَلَٰوَمُونَ ﴿٣٠﴾

31. They said: "Woe betide us; we have indeed been domineering.

قَالُوا يَٰوَيْلَنَآ إِنَّا كُنَّا طَٰغِينَ ﴿٣١﴾

32. "Maybe our Lord will give us a better substitute for it.[817] We are truly turning to our Lord."

عَسَىٰ رَبُّنَآ أَن يُبْدِلَنَا خَيْرًا مِّنْهَآ إِنَّآ إِلَىٰ رَبِّنَا رَٰغِبُونَ ﴿٣٢﴾

33. Such is the punishment; but the punishment of the Hereafter is greater, if only they knew.

كَذَٰلِكَ ٱلْعَذَابُ وَلَعَذَابُ ٱلْءَاخِرَةِ أَكْبَرُ لَوْ كَانُوا يَعْلَمُونَ ﴿٣٣﴾

34. Surely, for the God-fearing there are Gardens of Bliss with their Lord.

إِنَّ لِلْمُتَّقِينَ عِندَ رَبِّهِمْ جَنَّٰتِ ٱلنَّعِيمِ ﴿٣٤﴾

35. Shall We consider those who submit like those who are criminals?

أَفَنَجْعَلُ ٱلْمُسْلِمِينَ كَٱلْمُجْرِمِينَ ﴿٣٥﴾

36. What is the matter with you; how do you judge?

مَا لَكُمْ كَيْفَ تَحْكُمُونَ ﴿٣٦﴾

37. Or do you have a Book in which you study?

أَمْ لَكُمْ كِتَٰبٌ فِيهِ تَدْرُسُونَ ﴿٣٧﴾

38. Wherein there is whatever you choose.

إِنَّ لَكُمْ فِيهِ لَمَا تَخَيَّرُونَ ﴿٣٨﴾

39. Or do you have solemn oaths binding upon Us till the Day of Resurrection? You shall have in fact whatever you judge.

أَمْ لَكُمْ أَيْمَٰنٌ عَلَيْنَا بَٰلِغَةٌ إِلَىٰ يَوْمِ ٱلْقِيَٰمَةِ إِنَّ لَكُمْ لَمَا تَحْكُمُونَ ﴿٣٩﴾

40. Ask them: "Who among them is a guarantor of that?"

سَلْهُمْ أَيُّهُم بِذَٰلِكَ زَعِيمٌ ﴿٤٠﴾

41. Or do they have associates? Let them, then, produce their associates, if they are truthful.

أَمْ لَهُمْ شُرَكَآءُ فَلْيَأْتُوا بِشُرَكَآئِهِمْ إِن كَانُوا صَٰدِقِينَ ﴿٤١﴾

42. On the Day when nothing shall be concealed and they shall be called upon to prostrate themselves, but will not be able to.

يَوْمَ يُكْشَفُ عَن سَاقٍ وَيُدْعَوْنَ إِلَى ٱلسُّجُودِ فَلَا يَسْتَطِيعُونَ ﴿٤٢﴾

---

817. The Garden.

43. Their eyes shall be cast down, disgrace overwhelming them, although they were called to prostrate themselves while they were in a sound condition.

خَٰشِعَةً أَبْصَٰرُهُمْ تَرْهَقُهُمْ ذِلَّةٌ وَقَدْ كَانُوا۟ يُدْعَوْنَ إِلَى ٱلسُّجُودِ وَهُمْ سَٰلِمُونَ ۝

44. So, leave Me alone with those who disbelieve this discourse. We shall draw them out whence they do not know.

فَذَرْنِى وَمَن يُكَذِّبُ بِهَٰذَا ٱلْحَدِيثِ سَنَسْتَدْرِجُهُم مِّنْ حَيْثُ لَا يَعْلَمُونَ ۝

45. And I will give them respite; My cunning is certain.

وَأُمْلِى لَهُمْ إِنَّ كَيْدِى مَتِينٌ ۝

46. Or will you ask them for remuneration? They are surely burdened with debts.

أَمْ تَسْـَٔلُهُمْ أَجْرًا فَهُم مِّن مَّغْرَمٍ مُّثْقَلُونَ ۝

47. Or are they in possession of the Unseen, and so they are writing it down?

أَمْ عِندَهُمُ ٱلْغَيْبُ فَهُمْ يَكْتُبُونَ ۝

48. Bear up with your Lord's Judgement, then, and do not be like the Man of the Whale,[818] when he called out fully distressed.

فَٱصْبِرْ لِحُكْمِ رَبِّكَ وَلَا تَكُن كَصَاحِبِ ٱلْحُوتِ إِذْ نَادَىٰ وَهُوَ مَكْظُومٌ ۝

49. Had not a Grace from his Lord been meted out to him, he would have been cast out in the wilderness, fully despised.

لَّوْلَا أَن تَدَٰرَكَهُ نِعْمَةٌ مِّن رَّبِّهِ لَنُبِذَ بِٱلْعَرَآءِ وَهُوَ مَذْمُومٌ ۝

50. But his Lord chose him and made him one of the righteous.

فَٱجْتَبَٰهُ رَبُّهُ فَجَعَلَهُ مِنَ ٱلصَّٰلِحِينَ ۝

51. The unbelievers will almost strike you down with their glances, on hearing the Reminder,[819] and will say: "He is truly possessed."

وَإِن يَكَادُ ٱلَّذِينَ كَفَرُوا۟ لَيُزْلِقُونَكَ بِأَبْصَٰرِهِمْ لَمَّا سَمِعُوا۟ ٱلذِّكْرَ وَيَقُولُونَ إِنَّهُۥ لَمَجْنُونٌ ۝

52. It is only a Reminder to all the Worlds.

وَمَا هُوَ إِلَّا ذِكْرٌ لِّلْعَٰلَمِينَ ۝

Sûrat Al-Hâqqah, (The Certain Hour) 69

In the Name of Allah,
the Compassionate, the Merciful

بِسْمِ ٱللَّهِ ٱلرَّحْمَٰنِ ٱلرَّحِيمِ

1. The Certain Hour;

ٱلْحَآقَّةُ ۝

2. And what is the Certain Hour?

مَا ٱلْحَآقَّةُ ۝

---

818. Jonah.
819. The Qur'an.

3. If only you knew what the Certain Hour is.

وَمَآ أَدْرَىٰكَ مَا ٱلْحَآقَّةُ ۝

4. The people of Thamud and 'Ad have disbelieved in the Great Calamity.

كَذَّبَتْ ثَمُودُ وَعَادٌ بِٱلْقَارِعَةِ ۝

5. As to the people of Thamud, they were destroyed by the overwhelming Cry;

فَأَمَّا ثَمُودُ فَأُهْلِكُوا بِٱلطَّاغِيَةِ ۝

6. But 'Ad were destroyed by a violent, gusty wind,

وَأَمَّا عَادٌ فَأُهْلِكُوا بِرِيحٍ صَرْصَرٍ عَاتِيَةٍ ۝

7. Which He unleashed upon them for seven nights and eight days in succession; so you could see the people during that time prostrate, as though they were the stumps of hollow palm trees.

سَخَّرَهَا عَلَيْهِمْ سَبْعَ لَيَالٍ وَثَمَٰنِيَةَ أَيَّامٍ حُسُومًا فَتَرَى ٱلْقَوْمَ فِيهَا صَرْعَىٰ كَأَنَّهُمْ أَعْجَازُ نَخْلٍ خَاوِيَةٍ ۝

8. Do you see now any vestige of them?

فَهَلْ تَرَىٰ لَهُم مِّن بَاقِيَةٍ ۝

9. Then Pharaoh came, and those before him, and the Overturned Cities, steeped in sin.

وَجَآءَ فِرْعَوْنُ وَمَن قَبْلَهُ وَٱلْمُؤْتَفِكَٰتُ بِٱلْخَاطِئَةِ ۝

10. They disobeyed the Messenger of their Lord and so He seized them with an overpowering grip.

فَعَصَوْا رَسُولَ رَبِّهِمْ فَأَخَذَهُمْ أَخْذَةً رَّابِيَةً ۝

11. Indeed, when the water rose, We carried you along in the cruising ship.

إِنَّا لَمَّا طَغَا ٱلْمَآءُ حَمَلْنَٰكُمْ فِي ٱلْجَارِيَةِ ۝

12. So as to make it a reminder for you and to be grasped by an attentive ear.

لِنَجْعَلَهَا لَكُمْ تَذْكِرَةً وَتَعِيَهَآ أُذُنٌ وَٰعِيَةٌ ۝

13. Then when the Trumpet shall be blown a single time;

فَإِذَا نُفِخَ فِي ٱلصُّورِ نَفْخَةٌ وَٰحِدَةٌ ۝

14. And the earth and the mountains shall be lifted and then crushed with a single blow.

وَحُمِلَتِ ٱلْأَرْضُ وَٱلْجِبَالُ فَدُكَّتَا دَكَّةً وَٰحِدَةً ۝

15. Then, on that Day the terrible Calamity shall come to pass;

فَيَوْمَئِذٍ وَقَعَتِ ٱلْوَاقِعَةُ ۝

16. And the heavens shall be rent asunder, so that on that Day it shall be tottering;

وَٱنشَقَّتِ ٱلسَّمَآءُ فَهِيَ يَوْمَئِذٍ وَاهِيَةٌ ۝

17. And the angels shall be ranged around its borders, eight of whom will be carrying above them, on that Day, the Throne of your Lord.

وَٱلْمَلَكُ عَلَىٰ أَرْجَآئِهَا وَيَحْمِلُ عَرْشَ رَبِّكَ فَوْقَهُمْ يَوْمَئِذٍ ثَمَٰنِيَةٌ ۝

18. On that Day, you shall be paraded, not a whit of your deeds will be concealed.

‏يَوْمَئِذٍ تُعْرَضُونَ لَا تَخْفَىٰ مِنكُمْ خَافِيَةٌ ۝‏

19. As for him who has been given his book in his right hand, he shall say: "Come along, read my book.

‏فَأَمَّا مَنْ أُوتِىَ كِتَٰبَهُۥ بِيَمِينِهِۦ فَيَقُولُ هَآؤُمُ ٱقْرَءُوا۟ كِتَٰبِيَهْ ۝‏

20. "I knew I was going to meet my reckoning."

‏إِنِّى ظَنَنتُ أَنِّى مُلَٰقٍ حِسَابِيَهْ ۝‏

21. Therefore, he is in a well-pleasing condition;

‏فَهُوَ فِى عِيشَةٍ رَّاضِيَةٍ ۝‏

22. Living in a lofty Garden;

‏فِى جَنَّةٍ عَالِيَةٍ ۝‏

23. Whose clusters are close at hand.

‏قُطُوفُهَا دَانِيَةٌ ۝‏

24. "Eat and drink merrily for what you did in the days gone by."

‏كُلُوا۟ وَٱشْرَبُوا۟ هَنِيٓـًٔا بِمَآ أَسْلَفْتُمْ فِى ٱلْأَيَّامِ ٱلْخَالِيَةِ ۝‏

25. But as for him who is given his book in his left hand, he shall say: "Would that I had never been given my book,

‏وَأَمَّا مَنْ أُوتِىَ كِتَٰبَهُۥ بِشِمَالِهِۦ فَيَقُولُ يَٰلَيْتَنِى لَمْ أُوتَ كِتَٰبِيَهْ ۝‏

26. "And that I did not know what my account is;

‏وَلَمْ أَدْرِ مَا حِسَابِيَهْ ۝‏

27. "Would that it had been the final death blow.

‏يَٰلَيْتَهَا كَانَتِ ٱلْقَاضِيَةَ ۝‏

28. "My wealth has not availed me;

‏مَآ أَغْنَىٰ عَنِّى مَالِيَهْ ۝‏

29. "And my authority has vanished from me."

‏هَلَكَ عَنِّى سُلْطَٰنِيَهْ ۝‏

30. [It will be said:] "Take him and shackle him;

‏خُذُوهُ فَغُلُّوهُ ۝‏

31. "Then let him roast in Hell.

‏ثُمَّ ٱلْجَحِيمَ صَلُّوهُ ۝‏

32. "Then, in a chain whose length is seventy cubits, tie him up.

‏ثُمَّ فِى سِلْسِلَةٍ ذَرْعُهَا سَبْعُونَ ذِرَاعًا فَٱسْلُكُوهُ ۝‏

33. "He certainly did not believe in Allah, the Sublime.

‏إِنَّهُۥ كَانَ لَا يُؤْمِنُ بِٱللَّهِ ٱلْعَظِيمِ ۝‏

34. "And did not urge feeding the destitute.

‏وَلَا يَحُضُّ عَلَىٰ طَعَامِ ٱلْمِسْكِينِ ۝‏

35. "Therefore, today he shall have no intimate friend, here;

‏فَلَيْسَ لَهُ ٱلْيَوْمَ هَٰهُنَا حَمِيمٌ ۝‏

36. "And no food except foul pus;

وَلَا طَعَامٌ إِلَّا مِنْ غِسْلِينٍ ﴿٣٦﴾

37. "Which only the sinners will eat."

لَّا يَأْكُلُهُۥٓ إِلَّا ٱلْخَٰطِـُٔونَ ﴿٣٧﴾

38. No; I swear by what you see;

فَلَآ أُقْسِمُ بِمَا تُبْصِرُونَ ﴿٣٨﴾

39. And what you do not see.

وَمَا لَا تُبْصِرُونَ ﴿٣٩﴾

40. It is the speech of a noble Messenger;

إِنَّهُۥ لَقَوْلُ رَسُولٍ كَرِيمٍ ﴿٤٠﴾

41. And it is not the speech of a poet. How little do you believe!

وَمَا هُوَ بِقَوْلِ شَاعِرٍ قَلِيلًا مَّا تُؤْمِنُونَ ﴿٤١﴾

42. Nor the speech of a soothsayer; how little do you remember.

وَلَا بِقَوْلِ كَاهِنٍ قَلِيلًا مَّا تَذَكَّرُونَ ﴿٤٢﴾

43. It is the Revelation from the Lord of the Worlds.

تَنزِيلٌ مِّن رَّبِّ ٱلْعَٰلَمِينَ ﴿٤٣﴾

44. Had he[820] imputed to Us falsely some statements;

وَلَوْ تَقَوَّلَ عَلَيْنَا بَعْضَ ٱلْأَقَاوِيلِ ﴿٤٤﴾

45. We would have seized him by the right arm;

لَأَخَذْنَا مِنْهُ بِٱلْيَمِينِ ﴿٤٥﴾

46. Then cut off his great artery.

ثُمَّ لَقَطَعْنَا مِنْهُ ٱلْوَتِينَ ﴿٤٦﴾

47. None of you would have restrained Us from him.

فَمَا مِنكُم مِّنْ أَحَدٍ عَنْهُ حَٰجِزِينَ ﴿٤٧﴾

48. Surely, it[821] is a Reminder for the God-fearing.

وَإِنَّهُۥ لَتَذْكِرَةٌ لِّلْمُتَّقِينَ ﴿٤٨﴾

49. And We know that some of you will denounce it as lies.

وَإِنَّا لَنَعْلَمُ أَنَّ مِنكُم مُّكَذِّبِينَ ﴿٤٩﴾

50. And it is surely a source of grief for the unbelievers;

وَإِنَّهُۥ لَحَسْرَةٌ عَلَى ٱلْكَٰفِرِينَ ﴿٥٠﴾

51. And it is surely the certain truth.

وَإِنَّهُۥ لَحَقُّ ٱلْيَقِينِ ﴿٥١﴾

52. So, glorify the Name of your Lord, the Sublime.

فَسَبِّحْ بِٱسْمِ رَبِّكَ ٱلْعَظِيمِ ﴿٥٢﴾

---

820. Muhammad.
821. The Qur'an.

Sûrat Al-Ma'ârij,
(The Ways of Ascent) 70

بِسۡمِ ٱللَّهِ ٱلرَّحۡمَٰنِ ٱلرَّحِيمِ

In the Name of Allah,
the Compassionate, the Merciful

1. A questioner asked about an imminent punishment,

سَأَلَ سَآئِلٌ بِعَذَابٍ وَاقِعٍ ۝١

2. Of the unbelievers, that none can avert;

لِّلۡكَٰفِرِينَ لَيۡسَ لَهُۥ دَافِعٌ ۝٢

3. From Allah, Lord of the Ways of Ascent.

مِّنَ ٱللَّهِ ذِى ٱلۡمَعَارِجِ ۝٣

4. Unto Him the angels and the Spirit[822] ascend on a Day the duration thereof is fifty thousand years.

تَعۡرُجُ ٱلۡمَلَٰٓئِكَةُ وَٱلرُّوحُ إِلَيۡهِ فِى يَوۡمٍ كَانَ مِقۡدَارُهُۥ خَمۡسِينَ أَلۡفَ سَنَةٍ ۝٤

5. Bear up patiently then.

فَٱصۡبِرۡ صَبۡرًا جَمِيلًا ۝٥

6. They think it is distant;

إِنَّهُمۡ يَرَوۡنَهُۥ بَعِيدًا ۝٦

7. But We think it is close.

وَنَرَىٰهُ قَرِيبًا ۝٧

8. On the Day when heaven will be like molten brass;

يَوۡمَ تَكُونُ ٱلسَّمَآءُ كَٱلۡمُهۡلِ ۝٨

9. And the mountains like tufted wool.

وَتَكُونُ ٱلۡجِبَالُ كَٱلۡعِهۡنِ ۝٩

10. And no friend shall ask an intimate friend.

وَلَا يَسۡـَٔلُ حَمِيمٌ حَمِيمًا ۝١٠

11. They shall be made to see each other. The criminal wishes that he would be redeemed from the punishment of that day by his sons;

يُبَصَّرُونَهُمۡ يَوَدُّ ٱلۡمُجۡرِمُ لَوۡ يَفۡتَدِى مِنۡ عَذَابِ يَوۡمِئِذٍ بِبَنِيهِ ۝١١

12. His spouse and his brother;

وَصَٰحِبَتِهِۦ وَأَخِيهِ ۝١٢

13. And his clan, who gives him refuge;

وَفَصِيلَتِهِ ٱلَّتِى تُـٔۡوِيهِ ۝١٣

14. And every one on earth; then that he might save him.

وَمَن فِى ٱلۡأَرۡضِ جَمِيعًا ثُمَّ يُنجِيهِ ۝١٤

15. No, it is truly a blazing fire;

كَلَّآ إِنَّهَا لَظَىٰ ۝١٥

16. Which strips off the scalps.

نَزَّاعَةً لِّلشَّوَىٰ ۝١٦

17. It summons him who has turned his back and fled;

تَدۡعُواْ مَنۡ أَدۡبَرَ وَتَوَلَّىٰ ۝١٧

---

822. Gabriel (Jibril).

18. And amassed wealth and hoarded it.

وَجَمَعَ فَأَوْعَىٰ ﴿١٨﴾

19. Man was truly created apprehensive.

۞ إِنَّ ٱلْإِنسَٰنَ خُلِقَ هَلُوعًا ﴿١٩﴾

20. When misfortune visits him, he is frightened;

إِذَا مَسَّهُ ٱلشَّرُّ جَزُوعًا ﴿٢٠﴾

21. But when good fortune visits him, he is avaricious.

وَإِذَا مَسَّهُ ٱلْخَيْرُ مَنُوعًا ﴿٢١﴾

22. Except for those who pray;

إِلَّا ٱلْمُصَلِّينَ ﴿٢٢﴾

23. Those who are constantly at prayer;

ٱلَّذِينَ هُمْ عَلَىٰ صَلَاتِهِمْ دَآئِمُونَ ﴿٢٣﴾

24. And those who have set aside a fixed portion of their wealth,

وَٱلَّذِينَ فِىٓ أَمْوَٰلِهِمْ حَقٌّ مَّعْلُومٌ ﴿٢٤﴾

25. For the beggar and the destitute.

لِّلسَّآئِلِ وَٱلْمَحْرُومِ ﴿٢٥﴾

26. And those who believe firmly in the Day of Judgement;

وَٱلَّذِينَ يُصَدِّقُونَ بِيَوْمِ ٱلدِّينِ ﴿٢٦﴾

27. And those who fear the punishment of their Lord.

وَٱلَّذِينَ هُم مِّنْ عَذَابِ رَبِّهِم مُّشْفِقُونَ ﴿٢٧﴾

28. The punishment of their Lord cannot be averted;

إِنَّ عَذَابَ رَبِّهِمْ غَيْرُ مَأْمُونٍ ﴿٢٨﴾

29. And those who guard their private parts;

وَٱلَّذِينَ هُمْ لِفُرُوجِهِمْ حَٰفِظُونَ ﴿٢٩﴾

30. Except from their wives or what their right hands possess; for they are not therein blameworthy.

إِلَّا عَلَىٰٓ أَزْوَٰجِهِمْ أَوْ مَا مَلَكَتْ أَيْمَٰنُهُمْ فَإِنَّهُمْ غَيْرُ مَلُومِينَ ﴿٣٠﴾

31. He who seeks [pleasure] beyond that - those are the transgressors.

فَمَنِ ٱبْتَغَىٰ وَرَآءَ ذَٰلِكَ فَأُوْلَٰٓئِكَ هُمُ ٱلْعَادُونَ ﴿٣١﴾

32. And those who honour their trusts and their pledges;

وَٱلَّذِينَ هُمْ لِأَمَٰنَٰتِهِمْ وَعَهْدِهِمْ رَٰعُونَ ﴿٣٢﴾

33. And those who stand by their testimonies;

وَٱلَّذِينَ هُم بِشَهَٰدَٰتِهِمْ قَآئِمُونَ ﴿٣٣﴾

34. And those who observe their prayer;

وَٱلَّذِينَ هُمْ عَلَىٰ صَلَاتِهِمْ يُحَافِظُونَ ﴿٣٤﴾

35. All those shall be in Gardens, well-honoured.

أُوْلَٰٓئِكَ فِى جَنَّٰتٍ مُّكْرَمُونَ ﴿٣٥﴾

36. What is it with the unbelievers stretching their necks towards you?

فَمَالِ ٱلَّذِينَ كَفَرُوا۟ قِبَلَكَ مُهْطِعِينَ ﴿٣٦﴾

37. From the right and the left banding together?

عَنِ ٱلْيَمِينِ وَعَنِ ٱلشِّمَالِ عِزِينَ ﴿٣٧﴾

38. Does everyone of them hope to enter the Garden of Bliss?

أَيَطْمَعُ كُلُّ امْرِئٍ مِّنْهُمْ أَن يُدْخَلَ جَنَّةَ نَعِيمٍ ﴿٣٨﴾

39. Not at all. We have created them from what they know.

كَلَّا إِنَّا خَلَقْنَاهُم مِّمَّا يَعْلَمُونَ ﴿٣٩﴾

40. No; I swear by the Lord of the East and the West that We are Capable,

فَلَا أُقْسِمُ بِرَبِّ الْمَشَارِقِ وَالْمَغَارِبِ إِنَّا لَقَادِرُونَ ﴿٤٠﴾

41. Of replacing them by many who are better than they; and We shall not be outstripped.

عَلَى أَن نُّبَدِّلَ خَيْرًا مِّنْهُمْ وَمَا نَحْنُ بِمَسْبُوقِينَ ﴿٤١﴾

42. So leave them to romp and play till they meet their Day, which they have been promised.

فَذَرْهُمْ يَخُوضُوا وَيَلْعَبُوا حَتَّى يُلَاقُوا يَوْمَهُمُ الَّذِي يُوعَدُونَ ﴿٤٢﴾

43. The Day they will come out of the tombs hastily, as though they are hurrying towards their idols;

يَوْمَ يَخْرُجُونَ مِنَ الْأَجْدَاثِ سِرَاعًا كَأَنَّهُمْ إِلَى نُصُبٍ يُوفِضُونَ ﴿٤٣﴾

44. Their eyes cast down; overwhelmed by humiliation. That is the Day which they were promised.

خَاشِعَةً أَبْصَارُهُمْ تَرْهَقُهُمْ ذِلَّةٌ ذَٰلِكَ الْيَوْمُ الَّذِي كَانُوا يُوعَدُونَ ﴿٤٤﴾

Sûrat Nûh,
(Noah) 71

سُورَةُ نُوحٍ

In the Name of Allah,
the Compassionate, the Merciful

بِسْمِ اللَّهِ الرَّحْمَٰنِ الرَّحِيمِ

1. We have indeed sent Noah forth to his people saying: "Warn your people before a painful punishment afflicts them."

إِنَّا أَرْسَلْنَا نُوحًا إِلَى قَوْمِهِ أَنْ أَنذِرْ قَوْمَكَ مِن قَبْلِ أَن يَأْتِيَهُمْ عَذَابٌ أَلِيمٌ ﴿١﴾

2. He said: "O my people, I am truly a manifest warner to you;

قَالَ يَا قَوْمِ إِنِّي لَكُمْ نَذِيرٌ مُّبِينٌ ﴿٢﴾

3. "That you should worship Allah and fear Him, and obey me.

أَنِ اعْبُدُوا اللَّهَ وَاتَّقُوهُ وَأَطِيعُونِ ﴿٣﴾

4. "Then, He will forgive you your sins and reprieve you till an appointed term. Allah's term cannot be deferred, once it comes; if only you knew."

يَغْفِرْ لَكُم مِّن ذُنُوبِكُمْ وَيُؤَخِّرْكُمْ إِلَى أَجَلٍ مُّسَمًّى إِنَّ أَجَلَ اللَّهِ إِذَا جَاءَ لَا يُؤَخَّرُ لَوْ كُنتُمْ تَعْلَمُونَ ﴿٤﴾

5. He said: "Lord, I have called my people night and day;

قَالَ رَبِّ إِنِّى دَعَوْتُ قَوْمِى لَيْلًا وَنَهَارًا ۝

6. "But my call only increased them in defection.

فَلَمْ يَزِدْهُمْ دُعَآءِىٓ إِلَّا فِرَارًا ۝

7. "In fact, every time I called them, so that You might forgive them, they put their fingers in their ears, wrapped themselves up in their clothes, persisted and waxed very proud.

وَإِنِّى كُلَّمَا دَعَوْتُهُمْ لِتَغْفِرَ لَهُمْ جَعَلُوٓاْ أَصَٰبِعَهُمْ فِىٓ ءَاذَانِهِمْ وَٱسْتَغْشَوْاْ ثِيَابَهُمْ وَأَصَرُّواْ وَٱسْتَكْبَرُواْ ٱسْتِكْبَارًا ۝

8. "Then, I called them publicly;

ثُمَّ إِنِّى دَعَوْتُهُمْ جِهَارًا ۝

9. "Then, I proclaimed to them and spoke to them in secret.

ثُمَّ إِنِّىٓ أَعْلَنتُ لَهُمْ وَأَسْرَرْتُ لَهُمْ إِسْرَارًا ۝

10. "I said to them: 'Ask forgiveness from your Lord; He is truly All-Forgiving.

فَقُلْتُ ٱسْتَغْفِرُواْ رَبَّكُمْ إِنَّهُ كَانَ غَفَّارًا ۝

11. "'He will then loose heavens upon you in torrents;

يُرْسِلِ ٱلسَّمَآءَ عَلَيْكُم مِّدْرَارًا ۝

12. "And provide you with wealth and sons, and allot for you gardens, and allot for you rivers.

وَيُمْدِدْكُم بِأَمْوَٰلٍ وَبَنِينَ وَيَجْعَل لَّكُمْ جَنَّٰتٍ وَيَجْعَل لَّكُمْ أَنْهَٰرًا ۝

13. "'What is the matter with you? Why do you not show reverence towards Allah?

مَّا لَكُمْ لَا تَرْجُونَ لِلَّهِ وَقَارًا ۝

14. "'Although, He created you in stages.

وَقَدْ خَلَقَكُمْ أَطْوَارًا ۝

15. "'Do you not see how He created for you seven heavens superposed upon one an-other?

أَلَمْ تَرَوْاْ كَيْفَ خَلَقَ ٱللَّهُ سَبْعَ سَمَٰوَٰتٍ طِبَاقًا ۝

16. "'And placed the moon therein as a light and made the sun a lamp?

وَجَعَلَ ٱلْقَمَرَ فِيهِنَّ نُورًا وَجَعَلَ ٱلشَّمْسَ سِرَاجًا ۝

17. "'And Allah caused you to grow out of the earth;

وَٱللَّهُ أَنۢبَتَكُم مِّنَ ٱلْأَرْضِ نَبَاتًا ۝

18. "'Then, He will cause you to return to it and bring you out.

ثُمَّ يُعِيدُكُمْ فِيهَا وَيُخْرِجُكُمْ إِخْرَاجًا ۝

19. "'And Allah has made the earth a vast expanse for you;

وَٱللَّهُ جَعَلَ لَكُمُ ٱلْأَرْضَ بِسَاطًا ۝

20. "'So that you might follow therein broad pathways.'»

لِتَسْلُكُواْ مِنْهَا سُبُلًا فِجَاجًا ۝

589

21. Noah said: "Lord, they have disobeyed me and followed one whose wealth and children only increased him in perdition;

22. "And they devised a mighty plot.

23. "And they said: 'Do not forsake your gods; do not forsake Wadd, Suwa', Yaghuth, Ya'uq or Nasr.'[823]

24. "They have led many astray. Hence, increase not the wrongdoers except in greater error."

25. Because of their sins, they were drowned, and were hurled into the Fire. Then, they did not find, apart from Allah, any supporters.

26. And Noah said: "Lord, do not leave of the unbelievers a single dweller upon the earth.

27. "Surely, if You leave them alone, they will lead Your servants astray and will not beget any but unbelieving libertines.

28. "Lord, forgive me and my parents, and whoever enters my house as a believer and all the believers, men and women; and do not increase the wrongdoers except greater perdition."

Sûrat Al-Jinn, (The Jinn) 72

In the Name of Allah, the Compassionate, the Merciful

1. Say: "It was revealed to me that a company of jinn listened; then they said: 'We have indeed heard a wonderful Qur'an;

2. "'It guides to rectitude; so we believed in it, and we shall never associate anyone with our Lord;

قَالَ نُوحٌ رَّبِّ إِنَّهُمْ عَصَوْنِي وَٱتَّبَعُوا۟ مَن لَّمْ يَزِدْهُ مَالُهُۥ وَوَلَدُهُۥٓ إِلَّا خَسَارًا ﴿٢١﴾

وَمَكَرُوا۟ مَكْرًا كُبَّارًا ﴿٢٢﴾

وَقَالُوا۟ لَا تَذَرُنَّ ءَالِهَتَكُمْ وَلَا تَذَرُنَّ وَدًّا وَلَا سُوَاعًا وَلَا يَغُوثَ وَيَعُوقَ وَنَسْرًا ﴿٢٣﴾

وَقَدْ أَضَلُّوا۟ كَثِيرًا وَلَا تَزِدِ ٱلظَّٰلِمِينَ إِلَّا ضَلَٰلًا ﴿٢٤﴾

مِّمَّا خَطِيٓـَٰٔتِهِمْ أُغْرِقُوا۟ فَأُدْخِلُوا۟ نَارًا فَلَمْ يَجِدُوا۟ لَهُم مِّن دُونِ ٱللَّهِ أَنصَارًا ﴿٢٥﴾

وَقَالَ نُوحٌ رَّبِّ لَا تَذَرْ عَلَى ٱلْأَرْضِ مِنَ ٱلْكَٰفِرِينَ دَيَّارًا ﴿٢٦﴾

إِنَّكَ إِن تَذَرْهُمْ يُضِلُّوا۟ عِبَادَكَ وَلَا يَلِدُوٓا۟ إِلَّا فَاجِرًا كَفَّارًا ﴿٢٧﴾

رَّبِّ ٱغْفِرْ لِي وَلِوَٰلِدَيَّ وَلِمَن دَخَلَ بَيْتِيَ مُؤْمِنًا وَلِلْمُؤْمِنِينَ وَٱلْمُؤْمِنَٰتِ وَلَا تَزِدِ ٱلظَّٰلِمِينَ إِلَّا تَبَارًا ﴿٢٨﴾

سُورَةُ الْجِنِّ

بِسْمِ ٱللَّهِ ٱلرَّحْمَٰنِ ٱلرَّحِيمِ

قُلْ أُوحِيَ إِلَيَّ أَنَّهُ ٱسْتَمَعَ نَفَرٌ مِّنَ ٱلْجِنِّ فَقَالُوٓا۟ إِنَّا سَمِعْنَا قُرْءَانًا عَجَبًا ﴿١﴾

يَهْدِىٓ إِلَى ٱلرُّشْدِ فَـَٔامَنَّا بِهِۦ وَلَن نُّشْرِكَ بِرَبِّنَآ أَحَدًا ﴿٢﴾

---

823. These were some of the deities of the pagan Arab tribes before Islam.

3. "'And that He, may our Lord's Majesty be exalted, has not taken a consort or a son;

وَأَنَّهُ تَعَـٰلَىٰ جَدُّ رَبِّنَا مَا ٱتَّخَذَ صَـٰحِبَةً وَلَا وَلَدًا ۝

4. "'And that our fools used to speak impertinently of Allah;

وَأَنَّهُ كَانَ يَقُولُ سَفِيهُنَا عَلَى ٱللَّهِ شَطَطًا ۝

5. "'And that we thought that neither mankind nor the jinn will impute to Allah any falsehood;

وَأَنَّا ظَنَنَّا أَن لَّن تَقُولَ ٱلْإِنسُ وَٱلْجِنُّ عَلَى ٱللَّهِ كَذِبًا ۝

6. "'And that some individual humans used to seek refuge with some men of the jinn, and so they increased them in perversion;

وَأَنَّهُ كَانَ رِجَالٌ مِّنَ ٱلْإِنسِ يَعُوذُونَ بِرِجَالٍ مِّنَ ٱلْجِنِّ فَزَادُوهُمْ رَهَقًا ۝

7. "'And that they thought, as you thought, that Allah will not raise anybody from the dead;

وَأَنَّهُمْ ظَنُّوا۟ كَمَا ظَنَنتُمْ أَن لَّن يَبْعَثَ ٱللَّهُ أَحَدًا ۝

8. "'And that we reached out to heaven, but we found it filled with mighty guards and comets;

وَأَنَّا لَمَسْنَا ٱلسَّمَآءَ فَوَجَدْنَـٰهَا مُلِئَتْ حَرَسًا شَدِيدًا وَشُهُبًا ۝

9. "'And that we used to sit around it eavesdropping; but whoever listens now will find a comet in wait for him;

وَأَنَّا كُنَّا نَقْعُدُ مِنْهَا مَقَـٰعِدَ لِلسَّمْعِ فَمَن يَسْتَمِعِ ٱلْـَٔانَ يَجِدْ لَهُۥ شِهَابًا رَّصَدًا ۝

10. "'And that we do not know whether ill was intended for whoever is on earth, or whether their Lord intended rectitude for them;

وَأَنَّا لَا نَدْرِىٓ أَشَرٌّ أُرِيدَ بِمَن فِى ٱلْأَرْضِ أَمْ أَرَادَ بِهِمْ رَبُّهُمْ رَشَدًا ۝

11. "'And that some of us are righteous and some are less than that for we were of diverse persuasions;

وَأَنَّا مِنَّا ٱلصَّـٰلِحُونَ وَمِنَّا دُونَ ذَٰلِكَ كُنَّا طَرَآئِقَ قِدَدًا ۝

12. "'And that we knew that we will not thwart Allah on earth, and that we will not thwart Him by flight;

وَأَنَّا ظَنَنَّآ أَن لَّن نُّعْجِزَ ٱللَّهَ فِى ٱلْأَرْضِ وَلَن نُّعْجِزَهُۥ هَرَبًا ۝

13. "'And that when we heard the Guidance, we believed in it; for he who believes in his Lord need not fear to be stinted or over-burdened;

وَأَنَّا لَمَّا سَمِعْنَا ٱلْهُدَىٰٓ ءَامَنَّا بِهِۦ فَمَن يُؤْمِنۢ بِرَبِّهِۦ فَلَا يَخَافُ بَخْسًا وَلَا رَهَقًا ۝

14. "'And that some of us are submitting and some are diverging'. Those who have submitted have surely sought rectitude."

وَأَنَّا مِنَّا ٱلْمُسْلِمُونَ وَمِنَّا ٱلْقَـٰسِطُونَ فَمَنْ أَسْلَمَ فَأُو۟لَـٰٓئِكَ تَحَرَّوْا۟ رَشَدًا ۝

15. But those who have diverged, have been firewood for Hell;

وَأَمَّا ٱلْقَٰسِطُونَ فَكَانُوا۟ لِجَهَنَّمَ حَطَبًا ﴿١٥﴾

16. And that had they followed the Right Path, We would have given them abundant water to drink;

وَأَلَّوِ ٱسْتَقَٰمُوا۟ عَلَى ٱلطَّرِيقَةِ لَأَسْقَيْنَٰهُم مَّآءً غَدَقًا ﴿١٦﴾

17. So as to test them thereby. He who refrains from the mention of his Lord, He will afflict him with terrible punishment;

لِّنَفْتِنَهُمْ فِيهِ وَمَن يُعْرِضْ عَن ذِكْرِ رَبِّهِ يَسْلُكْهُ عَذَابًا صَعَدًا ﴿١٧﴾

18. And that mosques are Allah's; so do not call, besides Allah, upon anyone else;

وَأَنَّ ٱلْمَسَٰجِدَ لِلَّهِ فَلَا تَدْعُوا۟ مَعَ ٱللَّهِ أَحَدًا ﴿١٨﴾

19. And that when the servant of Allah[824] got up calling on Him, they almost set upon him in throngs.

وَأَنَّهُۥ لَمَّا قَامَ عَبْدُ ٱللَّهِ يَدْعُوهُ كَادُوا۟ يَكُونُونَ عَلَيْهِ لِبَدًا ﴿١٩﴾

20. Say: "I only call upon my Lord, and I do not associate with Him anyone else."

قُلْ إِنَّمَآ أَدْعُوا۟ رَبِّى وَلَآ أُشْرِكُ بِهِۦٓ أَحَدًا ﴿٢٠﴾

21. Say: "I have no power to harm or guide you rightly."

قُلْ إِنِّى لَآ أَمْلِكُ لَكُمْ ضَرًّا وَلَا رَشَدًا ﴿٢١﴾

22. Say: "No one shall protect me from Allah, and I will not find, apart from Him, any refuge;

قُلْ إِنِّى لَن يُجِيرَنِى مِنَ ٱللَّهِ أَحَدٌ وَلَنْ أَجِدَ مِن دُونِهِۦ مُلْتَحَدًا ﴿٢٢﴾

23. "Except for a proclamation from Allah and His Messages. He who disobeys Allah and His Messenger, for him the Fire of Hell is in store. Therein they shall dwell forever."

إِلَّا بَلَٰغًا مِّنَ ٱللَّهِ وَرِسَٰلَٰتِهِۦ وَمَن يَعْصِ ٱللَّهَ وَرَسُولَهُۥ فَإِنَّ لَهُۥ نَارَ جَهَنَّمَ خَٰلِدِينَ فِيهَآ أَبَدًا ﴿٢٣﴾

24. Until, when they see what they are promised, they will then know certainly who is weaker in supporters and is fewer in numbers.

حَتَّىٰٓ إِذَا رَأَوْا۟ مَا يُوعَدُونَ فَسَيَعْلَمُونَ مَنْ أَضْعَفُ نَاصِرًا وَأَقَلُّ عَدَدًا ﴿٢٤﴾

25. Say: "I do not know whether what you are promised is near, or whether my Lord shall extend it for a period.

قُلْ إِنْ أَدْرِىٓ أَقَرِيبٌ مَّا تُوعَدُونَ أَمْ يَجْعَلُ لَهُۥ رَبِّىٓ أَمَدًا ﴿٢٥﴾

26. "Knower of the Unseen, He does not disclose His Unseen to anyone."

عَٰلِمُ ٱلْغَيْبِ فَلَا يُظْهِرُ عَلَىٰ غَيْبِهِۦٓ أَحَدًا ﴿٢٦﴾

---

824. Muhammad.

27. Except for any Messenger He is well-pleased with. He then will dispatch watchmen before him and behind him;

إِلَّا مَنِ ٱرْتَضَىٰ مِن رَّسُولٍ فَإِنَّهُۥ يَسْلُكُ مِنۢ بَيْنِ يَدَيْهِ وَمِنْ خَلْفِهِۦ رَصَدًا ٢٧

28. So as to know that they have delivered the Messages of their Lord. And He encompasses whatever they have and numbers everything.

لِّيَعْلَمَ أَن قَدْ أَبْلَغُوا۟ رِسَٰلَٰتِ رَبِّهِمْ وَأَحَاطَ بِمَا لَدَيْهِمْ وَأَحْصَىٰ كُلَّ شَىْءٍ عَدَدًۢا ٢٨

Sûrat Al-Muzzammil, (The Enwrapped) 73

بِسْمِ ۞ سُورَةُ الْمُزَّمِّلِ ۞

In the Name of Allah, the Compassionate, the Merciful

بِسْمِ ٱللَّهِ ٱلرَّحْمَٰنِ ٱلرَّحِيمِ

1. O enwrapped one,[825]

يَٰٓأَيُّهَا ٱلْمُزَّمِّلُ ١

2. Keep vigil throughout the night, except for a little while;

قُمِ ٱلَّيْلَ إِلَّا قَلِيلًا ٢

3. Half of it, or a little less;

نِّصْفَهُۥ أَوِ ٱنقُصْ مِنْهُ قَلِيلًا ٣

4. Or add a little thereto and chant the Qur'an loudly.

أَوْ زِدْ عَلَيْهِ وَرَتِّلِ ٱلْقُرْءَانَ تَرْتِيلًا ٤

5. Indeed, We shall deliver unto you a weighty discourse.

إِنَّا سَنُلْقِى عَلَيْكَ قَوْلًا ثَقِيلًا ٥

6. Surely, the early hours of the night are more onerous and more amenable to straight talk.

إِنَّ نَاشِئَةَ ٱلَّيْلِ هِىَ أَشَدُّ وَطْـًٔا وَأَقْوَمُ قِيلًا ٦

7. You have during the day a long-drawn business.

إِنَّ لَكَ فِى ٱلنَّهَارِ سَبْحًا طَوِيلًا ٧

8. Remember the name of your Lord and devote yourself fully to Him.

وَٱذْكُرِ ٱسْمَ رَبِّكَ وَتَبَتَّلْ إِلَيْهِ تَبْتِيلًا ٨

9. He is the Lord of the East and the West; there is no god but He, so take Him as your Guardian.

رَّبُّ ٱلْمَشْرِقِ وَٱلْمَغْرِبِ لَآ إِلَٰهَ إِلَّا هُوَ فَٱتَّخِذْهُ وَكِيلًا ٩

10. And bear up with what they say, and forsake them graciously.

وَٱصْبِرْ عَلَىٰ مَا يَقُولُونَ وَٱهْجُرْهُمْ هَجْرًا جَمِيلًا ١٠

---

825. That is, Muhammad, who used to be "wrapped up" when revelation was imparted to him by the Angel Gabriel.

11. And let Me deal with those who deny and live in luxury; and give them a little respite.

12. We have indeed shackles and a blazing Fire;

13. And food upon which they choke and painful punishment.

14. On the Day when the earth and the mountains shall tremble, and the mountains shall turn into heaps of sand.

15. We have sent unto you a Messenger, bearing witness against you, just as We had sent unto Pharaoh a Messenger.

16. Then Pharaoh disobeyed the Messenger; so We seized him with terrible force.

17. So, how will you guard, if you disbelieve, against a Day which will make the children white with fear?

18. The heavens shall be rent asunder thereby. His Promise is a thing accomplished.

19. This is truly a reminder; so that he who wishes may follow unto his Lord a path.

20. Your Lord knows that you keep vigil a little less than two-thirds of the night and a half or a third thereof, together with a group of your followers. Allah determines the measure of the night and the day; He knows that you will not keep it all, and so He has absolved you. Read, then, what you can of the Qur'an. He knows that there will be, among you, sick people and others who journey in the land, seeking part of Allah's Bounty, and still others who fight for the Cause of Allah. Recite, then, what you can of it, perform the prayer, give the alms and lend Allah a fair loan. Whatever good you forward for your soul's sake, you shall find it with Allah growing into a greater good and a greater wage. Seek Allah's Forgiveness; Allah is indeed All-Forgiving, All-Merciful.

وَذَرْنِي وَالْمُكَذِّبِينَ أُوْلِي النَّعْمَةِ وَمَهِّلْهُمْ قَلِيلًا ﴿١١﴾

إِنَّ لَدَيْنَا أَنكَالًا وَجَحِيمًا ﴿١٢﴾

وَطَعَامًا ذَا غُصَّةٍ وَعَذَابًا أَلِيمًا ﴿١٣﴾

يَوْمَ تَرْجُفُ الْأَرْضُ وَالْجِبَالُ وَكَانَتِ الْجِبَالُ كَثِيبًا مَّهِيلًا ﴿١٤﴾

إِنَّا أَرْسَلْنَا إِلَيْكُمْ رَسُولًا شَاهِدًا عَلَيْكُمْ كَمَا أَرْسَلْنَا إِلَى فِرْعَوْنَ رَسُولًا ﴿١٥﴾

فَعَصَى فِرْعَوْنُ الرَّسُولَ فَأَخَذْنَاهُ أَخْذًا وَبِيلًا ﴿١٦﴾

فَكَيْفَ تَتَّقُونَ إِن كَفَرْتُمْ يَوْمًا يَجْعَلُ الْوِلْدَانَ شِيبًا ﴿١٧﴾

السَّمَاءُ مُنفَطِرٌ بِهِ كَانَ وَعْدُهُ مَفْعُولًا ﴿١٨﴾

إِنَّ هَٰذِهِ تَذْكِرَةٌ فَمَن شَاءَ اتَّخَذَ إِلَى رَبِّهِ سَبِيلًا ﴿١٩﴾

۞ إِنَّ رَبَّكَ يَعْلَمُ أَنَّكَ تَقُومُ أَدْنَى مِن ثُلُثَيِ الَّيْلِ وَنِصْفَهُ وَثُلُثَهُ وَطَائِفَةٌ مِّنَ الَّذِينَ مَعَكَ وَاللَّهُ يُقَدِّرُ الَّيْلَ وَالنَّهَارَ عَلِمَ أَن لَّن تُحْصُوهُ فَتَابَ عَلَيْكُمْ فَاقْرَءُوا مَا تَيَسَّرَ مِنَ الْقُرْآنِ عَلِمَ أَن سَيَكُونُ مِنكُم مَّرْضَى وَءَاخَرُونَ يَضْرِبُونَ فِي الْأَرْضِ يَبْتَغُونَ مِن فَضْلِ اللَّهِ وَءَاخَرُونَ يُقَاتِلُونَ فِي سَبِيلِ اللَّهِ فَاقْرَءُوا مَا تَيَسَّرَ مِنْهُ وَأَقِيمُوا الصَّلَاةَ وَءَاتُوا الزَّكَاةَ وَأَقْرِضُوا اللَّهَ قَرْضًا حَسَنًا وَمَا تُقَدِّمُوا لِأَنفُسِكُم مِّنْ خَيْرٍ تَجِدُوهُ عِندَ اللَّهِ هُوَ خَيْرًا وَأَعْظَمَ أَجْرًا وَاسْتَغْفِرُوا اللَّهَ إِنَّ اللَّهَ غَفُورٌ رَّحِيمٌ ﴿٢٠﴾

Sûrat Al-Muddathir, (The Enrobed) 74

*In the Name of Allah,
the Compassionate, the Merciful*

1. O enrobed one,

2. Arise and warn.

3. Glorify your Lord,

4. And purify your garments,

5. And abandon abomination.

6. Do not give in expectation of increased return,

7. And for the sake of your Lord, persevere.

8. Then, when the Trumpet is sounded;

9. It is then a hard Day,

10. For the unbelievers, not an easy one.

11. Leave Me with him whom I created alone,

12. And gave him abundant wealth,

13. And children as witnesses;

14. And I smoothed things for him.

15. Nevertheless, he is eager that I increase him.

16. He has been an obdurate disbeliever in Our Signs.[826]

17. I will exhaust him increasingly.

18. He reflected and reckoned.

19. May he perish how he reckoned!

20. Again, may he perish how he reckoned!

21. Then he considered;

---

826. The reference is to al-Walîd Ibn al-Mughîrah, an enemy of Islam.

22. Then he frowned and turned pale.

ثُمَّ عَبَسَ وَبَسَرَ ﴿٢٢﴾

23. Then he turned back and waxed proud,

ثُمَّ أَدْبَرَ وَٱسْتَكْبَرَ ﴿٢٣﴾

24. Saying: "This indeed is nothing but sorcery recounted;

فَقَالَ إِنْ هَٰذَآ إِلَّا سِحْرٌ يُؤْثَرُ ﴿٢٤﴾

25. "This is only the discourse of mortals."

إِنْ هَٰذَآ إِلَّا قَوْلُ ٱلْبَشَرِ ﴿٢٥﴾

26. I will roast him in Saqar.[827]

سَأُصْلِيهِ سَقَرَ ﴿٢٦﴾

27. If only you knew what is Saqar.

وَمَآ أَدْرَىٰكَ مَا سَقَرُ ﴿٢٧﴾

28. It leaves nothing or spares nothing,

لَا تُبْقِى وَلَا تَذَرُ ﴿٢٨﴾

29. Scorching mankind.

لَوَّاحَةٌ لِّلْبَشَرِ ﴿٢٩﴾

30. Upon it stand nineteen guards.

عَلَيْهَا تِسْعَةَ عَشَرَ ﴿٣٠﴾

31. We have only made angels the guardians of the Fire; and We have not fixed their number except as a temptation for those who have disbelieved; so that those who received the Book[828] might be certain and those who have believed increase in belief; and that those who received the Book and the believers together may not doubt; and that those in whose hearts there is a sickness together with the unbelievers [might say]: "What did Allah mean by this allegory?" Thus Allah leads those whom He wishes astray and guides those whom He wishes rightly. None knows the hosts of your Lord except He. It is only a reminder for mankind.

وَمَا جَعَلْنَآ أَصْحَٰبَ ٱلنَّارِ إِلَّا مَلَٰٓئِكَةً وَمَا جَعَلْنَا عِدَّتَهُمْ إِلَّا فِتْنَةً لِّلَّذِينَ كَفَرُوا لِيَسْتَيْقِنَ ٱلَّذِينَ أُوتُوا ٱلْكِتَٰبَ وَيَزْدَادَ ٱلَّذِينَ ءَامَنُوٓا إِيمَٰنًا وَلَا يَرْتَابَ ٱلَّذِينَ أُوتُوا ٱلْكِتَٰبَ وَٱلْمُؤْمِنُونَ وَلِيَقُولَ ٱلَّذِينَ فِى قُلُوبِهِم مَّرَضٌ وَٱلْكَٰفِرُونَ مَاذَآ أَرَادَ ٱللَّهُ بِهَٰذَا مَثَلًا كَذَٰلِكَ يُضِلُّ ٱللَّهُ مَن يَشَآءُ وَيَهْدِى مَن يَشَآءُ وَمَا يَعْلَمُ جُنُودَ رَبِّكَ إِلَّا هُوَ وَمَا هِىَ إِلَّا ذِكْرَىٰ لِلْبَشَرِ ﴿٣١﴾

32. By the moon;

كَلَّا وَٱلْقَمَرِ ﴿٣٢﴾

33. And the night when it recedes;

وَٱلَّيْلِ إِذْ أَدْبَرَ ﴿٣٣﴾

34. And the morning when it lights up.

وَٱلصُّبْحِ إِذَآ أَسْفَرَ ﴿٣٤﴾

35. Surely it is one of the great ordeals,

إِنَّهَا لَإِحْدَى ٱلْكُبَرِ ﴿٣٥﴾

36. A warning to mankind;

نَذِيرًا لِّلْبَشَرِ ﴿٣٦﴾

---

827. One of the names of Hell.
828. The People of the Book, or Christians and Jews.

37. To whoever of you wishes to advance or retreat.

لِمَن شَآءَ مِنكُمْ أَن يَتَقَدَّمَ أَوْ يَتَأَخَّرَ ۝

38. Every soul is a hostage to what it has earned;

كُلُّ نَفْسٍ بِمَا كَسَبَتْ رَهِينَةٌ ۝

39. Except for the Companions of the Right;

إِلَّآ أَصْحَبَ ٱلْيَمِينِ ۝

40. In Gardens, they will ask,

فِى جَنَّتٍ يَتَسَآءَلُونَ ۝

41. Concerning the criminals:

عَنِ ٱلْمُجْرِمِينَ ۝

42. "What drove you into Saqar?"

مَا سَلَكَكُمْ فِى سَقَرَ ۝

43. They will say: "We were not among those who prayed,

قَالُوا لَمْ نَكُ مِنَ ٱلْمُصَلِّينَ ۝

44. "And we were not among those who fed the destitute;

وَلَمْ نَكُ نُطْعِمُ ٱلْمِسْكِينَ ۝

45. "And we used to romp with the rompers;

وَكُنَّا نَخُوضُ مَعَ ٱلْخَآئِضِينَ ۝

46. "And we used to deny the Day of Judgement;

وَكُنَّا نُكَذِّبُ بِيَوْمِ ٱلدِّينِ ۝

47. "Till the Certainty came to us."

حَتَّىٰ أَتَىٰنَا ٱلْيَقِينُ ۝

48. But the intercession of the intercessors will avail them nothing.

فَمَا تَنفَعُهُمْ شَفَعَةُ ٱلشَّفِعِينَ ۝

49. Why are they turning away from the Reminder?[829]

فَمَا لَهُمْ عَنِ ٱلتَّذْكِرَةِ مُعْرِضِينَ ۝

50. As though they were startled asses,

كَأَنَّهُمْ حُمُرٌ مُّسْتَنفِرَةٌ ۝

51. Fleeing from a lion?

فَرَّتْ مِن قَسْوَرَةٍ ۝

52. Rather, each one of them wishes to be given scrolls unrolled.

بَلْ يُرِيدُ كُلُّ ٱمْرِئٍ مِّنْهُمْ أَن يُؤْتَىٰ صُحُفًا مُّنَشَّرَةً ۝

53. No, they do not fear the Hereafter.

كَلَّا بَل لَّا يَخَافُونَ ٱلْآخِرَةَ ۝

54. No, it is indeed a Reminder.

كَلَّا إِنَّهُ تَذْكِرَةٌ ۝

55. So that he who wishes might remember it

فَمَن شَآءَ ذَكَرَهُ ۝

56. But they will only remember if Allah wishes. He is worthy to be feared and worthy to forgive.

وَمَا يَذْكُرُونَ إِلَّا أَن يَشَآءَ ٱللَّهُ هُوَ أَهْلُ ٱلتَّقْوَىٰ وَأَهْلُ ٱلْمَغْفِرَةِ ۝

---

829. The Qur'an.

Sûrat Al-Qiyamah, (The Resurrection) 75

بِسۡمِ ٱللَّهِ ٱلرَّحۡمَٰنِ ٱلرَّحِيمِ

In the Name of Allah,
the Compassionate, the Merciful

1. No! I swear by the Day of Resurrection;

2. No! I swear by the reproachful soul.

3. Does man think that We will not put his bones back together?

4. Yes indeed; We are Able to straighten his fingertips.

5. Rather, man wishes to continue his profligacy in front of Him.

6. He asks: "When is the Day of Resurrection coming?"

7. Then, when the sight is dazzled;

8. And the moon is eclipsed;

9. And the sun and moon are joined together;

10. Man will say on that Day: "Where is the escape?"

11. No, there shall be no escape;

12. Unto your Lord is the ultimate resort.

13. Man shall be informed on that Day about what he has advanced or deferred.

14. Rather, man against himself shall be a witness;

15. Even if he makes excuses.

16. Do not wag your tongue with it[830] to hurry on with it.

17. It is incumbent upon Us to put it together and to recite it.

18. Then, when We recite it, follow its recitation.

لَآ أُقۡسِمُ بِيَوۡمِ ٱلۡقِيَٰمَةِ ﴿١﴾

وَلَآ أُقۡسِمُ بِٱلنَّفۡسِ ٱللَّوَّامَةِ ﴿٢﴾

أَيَحۡسَبُ ٱلۡإِنسَٰنُ أَلَّن نَّجۡمَعَ عِظَامَهُ ﴿٣﴾

بَلَىٰ قَٰدِرِينَ عَلَىٰٓ أَن نُّسَوِّيَ بَنَانَهُ ﴿٤﴾

بَلۡ يُرِيدُ ٱلۡإِنسَٰنُ لِيَفۡجُرَ أَمَامَهُ ﴿٥﴾

يَسۡـَٔلُ أَيَّانَ يَوۡمُ ٱلۡقِيَٰمَةِ ﴿٦﴾

فَإِذَا بَرِقَ ٱلۡبَصَرُ ﴿٧﴾

وَخَسَفَ ٱلۡقَمَرُ ﴿٨﴾

وَجُمِعَ ٱلشَّمۡسُ وَٱلۡقَمَرُ ﴿٩﴾

يَقُولُ ٱلۡإِنسَٰنُ يَوۡمَئِذٍ أَيۡنَ ٱلۡمَفَرُّ ﴿١٠﴾

كَلَّا لَا وَزَرَ ﴿١١﴾

إِلَىٰ رَبِّكَ يَوۡمَئِذٍ ٱلۡمُسۡتَقَرُّ ﴿١٢﴾

يُنَبَّؤُاْ ٱلۡإِنسَٰنُ يَوۡمَئِذٍۭ بِمَا قَدَّمَ وَأَخَّرَ ﴿١٣﴾

بَلِ ٱلۡإِنسَٰنُ عَلَىٰ نَفۡسِهِۦ بَصِيرَةٌ ﴿١٤﴾

وَلَوۡ أَلۡقَىٰ مَعَاذِيرَهُۥ ﴿١٥﴾

لَا تُحَرِّكۡ بِهِۦ لِسَانَكَ لِتَعۡجَلَ بِهِۦٓ ﴿١٦﴾

إِنَّ عَلَيۡنَا جَمۡعَهُۥ وَقُرۡءَانَهُۥ ﴿١٧﴾

فَإِذَا قَرَأۡنَٰهُ فَٱتَّبِعۡ قُرۡءَانَهُۥ ﴿١٨﴾

---

830. The Qur'an.

19. Then, it is incumbent upon Us to expound it clearly.

ثُمَّ إِنَّ عَلَيْنَا بَيَانَهُ ﴿١٩﴾

20. No indeed, you love the present life;

كَلَّا بَلْ تُحِبُّونَ ٱلْعَاجِلَةَ ﴿٢٠﴾

21. And forsake the Hereafter.

وَتَذَرُونَ ٱلْآخِرَةَ ﴿٢١﴾

22. On that Day, faces shall be radiant,

وُجُوهٌ يَوْمَئِذٍ نَّاضِرَةٌ ﴿٢٢﴾

23. Looking upon their Lord.

إِلَىٰ رَبِّهَا نَاظِرَةٌ ﴿٢٣﴾

24. And faces, on that Day, shall be scowling;

وَوُجُوهٌ يَوْمَئِذٍ بَاسِرَةٌ ﴿٢٤﴾

25. Thinking that a disaster shall be wreaked upon them.

تَظُنُّ أَن يُفْعَلَ بِهَا فَاقِرَةٌ ﴿٢٥﴾

26. No indeed, when (the soul) reaches the breast-bones,

كَلَّا إِذَا بَلَغَتِ ٱلتَّرَاقِيَ ﴿٢٦﴾

27. And it is said: "Who shall be the charmer?"

وَقِيلَ مَنْ رَاقٍ ﴿٢٧﴾

28. And he[831] thinks that that was the parting;

وَظَنَّ أَنَّهُ ٱلْفِرَاقُ ﴿٢٨﴾

29. And leg is intertwined with leg;

وَٱلْتَفَّتِ ٱلسَّاقُ بِٱلسَّاقِ ﴿٢٩﴾

30. Unto your Lord shall be the resort.

إِلَىٰ رَبِّكَ يَوْمَئِذٍ ٱلْمَسَاقُ ﴿٣٠﴾

31. For he[832] did not believe nor pray;

فَلَا صَدَّقَ وَلَا صَلَّىٰ ﴿٣١﴾

32. But rather denied and turned away.

وَلَٰكِن كَذَّبَ وَتَوَلَّىٰ ﴿٣٢﴾

33. Then, he went to his own folk in a swagger.

ثُمَّ ذَهَبَ إِلَىٰ أَهْلِهِ يَتَمَطَّىٰ ﴿٣٣﴾

34. Woe be to you and woe;

أَوْلَىٰ لَكَ فَأَوْلَىٰ ﴿٣٤﴾

35. Then, woe be to you and woe!

ثُمَّ أَوْلَىٰ لَكَ فَأَوْلَىٰ ﴿٣٥﴾

36. Does man think that he shall be left untended?

أَيَحْسَبُ ٱلْإِنسَانُ أَن يُتْرَكَ سُدًى ﴿٣٦﴾

37. Was he not a drop of sperm released?

أَلَمْ يَكُ نُطْفَةً مِّن مَّنِيٍّ يُمْنَىٰ ﴿٣٧﴾

38. Then, he was a leech; then He created and fashioned (him);

ثُمَّ كَانَ عَلَقَةً فَخَلَقَ فَسَوَّىٰ ﴿٣٨﴾

39. Making of him a couple, male and female.

فَجَعَلَ مِنْهُ ٱلزَّوْجَيْنِ ٱلذَّكَرَ وَٱلْأُنثَىٰ ﴿٣٩﴾

40. Is not that One Able to quicken the dead?

أَلَيْسَ ذَٰلِكَ بِقَادِرٍ عَلَىٰ أَن يُحْيِيَ ٱلْمَوْتَىٰ ﴿٤٠﴾

---

831. Abu Jahl, an inveterate enemy of Islam who persecuted the Prophet and his followers in Mecca.
832. Abu Jahl.

Sûrat Al-Insân, (Man) 76

بِسْمِ اللَّهِ الرَّحْمَنِ الرَّحِيمِ

*In the Name of Allah,
the Compassionate, the Merciful*

1. Has there come upon man a period of time when he was not a noteworthy thing?

هَلْ أَتَىٰ عَلَى الْإِنسَٰنِ حِينٌ مِّنَ الدَّهْرِ لَمْ يَكُن شَيْئًا مَّذْكُورًا ۝

2. We have indeed created man from a mixed sperm to test him; and so We made him capable of hearing and sight.

إِنَّا خَلَقْنَا الْإِنسَٰنَ مِن نُّطْفَةٍ أَمْشَاجٍ نَّبْتَلِيهِ فَجَعَلْنَٰهُ سَمِيعًا بَصِيرًا ۝

3. We have guided him upon the path, either as thankful or thankless.

إِنَّا هَدَيْنَٰهُ السَّبِيلَ إِمَّا شَاكِرًا وَإِمَّا كَفُورًا ۝

4. We have prepared for the unbelievers chains and fetters and a blazing Fire.

إِنَّا أَعْتَدْنَا لِلْكَٰفِرِينَ سَلَٰسِلَا۟ وَأَغْلَٰلًا وَسَعِيرًا ۝

5. The pious will surely drink from a cup whose mixture is camphor,

إِنَّ الْأَبْرَارَ يَشْرَبُونَ مِن كَأْسٍ كَانَ مِزَاجُهَا كَافُورًا ۝

6. A spring from which the servants of Allah shall drink, making it gush abundantly.

عَيْنًا يَشْرَبُ بِهَا عِبَادُ اللَّهِ يُفَجِّرُونَهَا تَفْجِيرًا ۝

7. They fulfil their vows and fear a Day whose evil is rampant.

يُوفُونَ بِالنَّذْرِ وَيَخَافُونَ يَوْمًا كَانَ شَرُّهُۥ مُسْتَطِيرًا ۝

8. And they give food, despite their love of it, to the destitute, the orphan and the captive.

وَيُطْعِمُونَ الطَّعَامَ عَلَىٰ حُبِّهِۦ مِسْكِينًا وَيَتِيمًا وَأَسِيرًا ۝

9. [They say:] "We only feed you for the sake of Allah; We do not want from you any reward or gratitude.

إِنَّمَا نُطْعِمُكُمْ لِوَجْهِ اللَّهِ لَا نُرِيدُ مِنكُمْ جَزَآءً وَلَا شُكُورًا ۝

10. "We fear from our Lord a dark and dreadful Day."

إِنَّا نَخَافُ مِن رَّبِّنَا يَوْمًا عَبُوسًا قَمْطَرِيرًا ۝

11. But Allah will guard them against the evil of that Day and give them radiance and joy.

فَوَقَىٰهُمُ اللَّهُ شَرَّ ذَٰلِكَ الْيَوْمِ وَلَقَّىٰهُمْ نَضْرَةً وَسُرُورًا ۝

12. And reward them for their forbearance, with a garden and silk.

وَجَزَىٰهُم بِمَا صَبَرُوا۟ جَنَّةً وَحَرِيرًا ۝

13. Therein, they shall recline upon couches, and they shall see therein neither [blazing] sun nor bitter cold.

مُّتَّكِئِينَ فِيهَا عَلَى الْأَرَآئِكِ لَا يَرَوْنَ فِيهَا شَمْسًا وَلَا زَمْهَرِيرًا ۝

14. And its shades shall be close to them and its fruit-bunches shall be brought down.

وَدَانِيَةً عَلَيْهِمْ ظِلَٰلُهَا وَذُلِّلَتْ قُطُوفُهَا تَذْلِيلًا ۝

15. And cup-bearers shall go round them with vessels of silver and goblets of glass,

وَيُطَافُ عَلَيْهِم بِـَانِيَةٍ مِّن فِضَّةٍ وَأَكْوَابٍ كَانَتْ قَوَارِيرَا۟ ﴿١٥﴾

6. Goblets of silver which they measured exactly.

قَوَارِيرَا۟ مِن فِضَّةٍ قَدَّرُوهَا تَقْدِيرًا ﴿١٦﴾

17. And they are given therein to drink a cup whose mixture is ginger.

وَيُسْقَوْنَ فِيهَا كَأْسًا كَانَ مِزَاجُهَا زَنجَبِيلًا ﴿١٧﴾

18. A spring therein is called Salsabil.

عَيْنًا فِيهَا تُسَمَّىٰ سَلْسَبِيلًا ﴿١٨﴾

19. And there go round them immortal boys; when you see them, you will think that they are scattered pearls.

۞ وَيَطُوفُ عَلَيْهِمْ وِلْدَٰنٌ مُّخَلَّدُونَ إِذَا رَأَيْتَهُمْ حَسِبْتَهُمْ لُؤْلُؤًا مَّنثُورًا ﴿١٩﴾

20. If you look there, you will see bliss and a vast kingdom.

وَإِذَا رَأَيْتَ ثَمَّ رَأَيْتَ نَعِيمًا وَمُلْكًا كَبِيرًا ﴿٢٠﴾

21. Upon them are green silk garments and brocade; and they have been adorned with silver bracelets, and their Lord has given them a pure potion.

عَٰلِيَهُمْ ثِيَابُ سُندُسٍ خُضْرٌ وَإِسْتَبْرَقٌ وَحُلُّوٓا۟ أَسَاوِرَ مِن فِضَّةٍ وَسَقَىٰهُمْ رَبُّهُمْ شَرَابًا طَهُورًا ﴿٢١﴾

22. "This indeed has been your reward, and your endeavour has been appreciated."

إِنَّ هَٰذَا كَانَ لَكُمْ جَزَآءً وَكَانَ سَعْيُكُم مَّشْكُورًا ﴿٢٢﴾

23. We have indeed sent down the Qur'an upon you as a revelation;

إِنَّا نَحْنُ نَزَّلْنَا عَلَيْكَ ٱلْقُرْءَانَ تَنزِيلًا ﴿٢٣﴾

24. So bear up with your Lord's Judgement and do not obey any sinful or thankless one of them.

فَٱصْبِرْ لِحُكْمِ رَبِّكَ وَلَا تُطِعْ مِنْهُمْ ءَاثِمًا أَوْ كَفُورًا ﴿٢٤﴾

25. And mention the Name of your Lord morning and evening.

وَٱذْكُرِ ٱسْمَ رَبِّكَ بُكْرَةً وَأَصِيلًا ﴿٢٥﴾

26. And for part of the night, prostrate yourself to Him and glorify Him all night long.

وَمِنَ ٱلَّيْلِ فَٱسْجُدْ لَهُ وَسَبِّحْهُ لَيْلًا طَوِيلًا ﴿٢٦﴾

27. Those people love the present world and leave behind them a burdensome Day.

إِنَّ هَٰٓؤُلَآءِ يُحِبُّونَ ٱلْعَاجِلَةَ وَيَذَرُونَ وَرَآءَهُمْ يَوْمًا ثَقِيلًا ﴿٢٧﴾

28. We have created them and fastened their joints well; and if We wish We would change their likes completely.

نَّحْنُ خَلَقْنَٰهُمْ وَشَدَدْنَآ أَسْرَهُمْ وَإِذَا شِئْنَا بَدَّلْنَآ أَمْثَٰلَهُمْ تَبْدِيلًا ﴿٢٨﴾

29. This indeed is a reminder; so he who wishes will follow, unto his Lord, a path.

إِنَّ هَٰذِهِۦ تَذْكِرَةٌ فَمَن شَآءَ ٱتَّخَذَ إِلَىٰ رَبِّهِۦ سَبِيلًا ﴿٢٩﴾

30. Yet, you do not wish unless Allah wishes. Allah is truly All-Knowing and Wise.

وَمَا تَشَآءُونَ إِلَّا أَن يَشَآءَ ٱللَّهُ إِنَّ ٱللَّهَ كَانَ عَلِيمًا حَكِيمًا ۝

31. He admits into His Mercy whomever He wishes; and for the wrongdoers He has prepared a painful punishment.

يُدْخِلُ مَن يَشَآءُ فِى رَحْمَتِهِۦ وَٱلظَّٰلِمِينَ أَعَدَّ لَهُمْ عَذَابًا أَلِيمًا ۝

Sûrat Al-Mursalât,
(The Dispatched Ones) 77

سورة المرسلات

In the Name of Allah,
the Compassionate, the Merciful

بِسْمِ ٱللَّهِ ٱلرَّحْمَٰنِ ٱلرَّحِيمِ

1. By those dispatched[833] in succession;

وَٱلْمُرْسَلَٰتِ عُرْفًا ۝

2. And by the tempestuous winds;

فَٱلْعَٰصِفَٰتِ عَصْفًا ۝

3. And by those who spread out;

وَٱلنَّٰشِرَٰتِ نَشْرًا ۝

4. And the dividing distinguishers;

فَٱلْفَٰرِقَٰتِ فَرْقًا ۝

5. And by those who deliver a reminder;

فَٱلْمُلْقِيَٰتِ ذِكْرًا ۝

6. As an excuse or a warning.

عُذْرًا أَوْ نُذْرًا ۝

7. Indeed, what you are promised shall come to pass.

إِنَّمَا تُوعَدُونَ لَوَٰقِعٌ ۝

8. When the stars have been extinguished;

فَإِذَا ٱلنُّجُومُ طُمِسَتْ ۝

9. And the heavens have been rent asunder;

وَإِذَا ٱلسَّمَآءُ فُرِجَتْ ۝

10. And when the mountains are blown to pieces;

وَإِذَا ٱلْجِبَالُ نُسِفَتْ ۝

11. And when the Messengers have been assigned a term;

وَإِذَا ٱلرُّسُلُ أُقِّتَتْ ۝

12. To what day have they been deferred?

لِأَىِّ يَوْمٍ أُجِّلَتْ ۝

13. Unto the Day of Decision,

لِيَوْمِ ٱلْفَصْلِ ۝

14. If only you knew what is the Day of Decision.

وَمَآ أَدْرَىٰكَ مَا يَوْمُ ٱلْفَصْلِ ۝

15. Woe betide, on that Day, those who denounce.

وَيْلٌ يَوْمَئِذٍ لِّلْمُكَذِّبِينَ ۝

833. The angels.

16. Have We not destroyed the ancients?

أَلَمْ نُهْلِكِ الْأَوَّلِينَ ۝

17. Then, We shall send after them the latter folk.

ثُمَّ نُتْبِعُهُمُ الْآخِرِينَ ۝

18. Thus We deal with the criminals.

كَذَٰلِكَ نَفْعَلُ بِالْمُجْرِمِينَ ۝

19. Woe betide, on that Day, those who denounce.

وَيْلٌ يَوْمَئِذٍ لِّلْمُكَذِّبِينَ ۝

20. Have We not created them from base water?

أَلَمْ نَخْلُقكُّم مِّن مَّآءٍ مَّهِينٍ ۝

21. That We laid in a secure place;

فَجَعَلْنَٰهُ فِى قَرَارٍ مَّكِينٍ ۝

22. Until an appointed term.

إِلَىٰ قَدَرٍ مَّعْلُومٍ ۝

23. We determined, and what excellent determiners were We!

فَقَدَرْنَا فَنِعْمَ الْقَٰدِرُونَ ۝

24. Woe, on that Day, betide those who denounce.

وَيْلٌ يَوْمَئِذٍ لِّلْمُكَذِّبِينَ ۝

25. Have We not made the earth a receptacle,

أَلَمْ نَجْعَلِ الْأَرْضَ كِفَاتًا ۝

26. Containing the living and the dead;

أَحْيَآءً وَأَمْوَٰتًا ۝

27. And created in it towering mountains and given you pure water to drink.

وَجَعَلْنَا فِيهَا رَوَٰسِىَ شَٰمِخَٰتٍ وَأَسْقَيْنَٰكُم مَّآءً فُرَاتًا ۝

28. Woe betide, on that Day, those who denounce!

وَيْلٌ يَوْمَئِذٍ لِّلْمُكَذِّبِينَ ۝

29. Go forth to what you used to denounce as lies.

انطَلِقُوٓا۟ إِلَىٰ مَا كُنتُم بِهِۦ تُكَذِّبُونَ ۝

30. Go forth to a three-pronged shade;

انطَلِقُوٓا۟ إِلَىٰ ظِلٍّ ذِى ثَلَٰثِ شُعَبٍ ۝

31. Which neither shades nor avails against the flames.

لَّا ظَلِيلٍ وَلَا يُغْنِى مِنَ اللَّهَبِ ۝

32. It[834] shoots forth sparks as huge as a castle;

إِنَّهَا تَرْمِى بِشَرَرٍ كَالْقَصْرِ ۝

33. Which look like golden camel-herds.

كَأَنَّهُۥ جِمَٰلَتٌ صُفْرٌ ۝

34. Woe betide, on that Day, those who denounce.

وَيْلٌ يَوْمَئِذٍ لِّلْمُكَذِّبِينَ ۝

---

834. Hell.

35. This is a Day on which they shall not speak;

هَٰذَا يَوْمُ لَا يَنطِقُونَ ۝

36. And they will not be permitted to make excuses.

وَلَا يُؤْذَنُ لَهُمْ فَيَعْتَذِرُونَ ۝

37. Woe betide, on that Day, those who denounce.

وَيْلٌ يَوْمَئِذٍ لِّلْمُكَذِّبِينَ ۝

38. This is the Day of Decision; We have gathered you together with the ancients.

هَٰذَا يَوْمُ ٱلْفَصْلِ جَمَعْنَٰكُمْ وَٱلْأَوَّلِينَ ۝

39. So, if you have any schemes, then scheme against Me.

فَإِن كَانَ لَكُمْ كَيْدٌ فَكِيدُونِ ۝

40. Woe betide, on that Day, those who denounce.

وَيْلٌ يَوْمَئِذٍ لِّلْمُكَذِّبِينَ ۝

41. The God-fearing shall dwell amid shades and springs,

إِنَّ ٱلْمُتَّقِينَ فِى ظِلَٰلٍ وَعُيُونٍ ۝

42. And fruits of the kind they desire.

وَفَوَٰكِهَ مِمَّا يَشْتَهُونَ ۝

43. Eat and drink merrily, for what you used to do.

كُلُوا۟ وَٱشْرَبُوا۟ هَنِيٓئًا بِمَا كُنتُمْ تَعْمَلُونَ ۝

44. That is how We reward the beneficent.

إِنَّا كَذَٰلِكَ نَجْزِى ٱلْمُحْسِنِينَ ۝

45. Woe betide, on that Day, those who denounce:

وَيْلٌ يَوْمَئِذٍ لِّلْمُكَذِّبِينَ ۝

46. "Eat and enjoy yourselves a little; you are indeed criminals."

كُلُوا۟ وَتَمَتَّعُوا۟ قَلِيلًا إِنَّكُم مُّجْرِمُونَ ۝

47. Woe betide, on that Day, those who denounce.

وَيْلٌ يَوْمَئِذٍ لِّلْمُكَذِّبِينَ ۝

48. If they are told to bow down, they will not bow down.

وَإِذَا قِيلَ لَهُمُ ٱرْكَعُوا۟ لَا يَرْكَعُونَ ۝

49. Woe betide, on that Day, those who denounce.

وَيْلٌ يَوْمَئِذٍ لِّلْمُكَذِّبِينَ ۝

50. What discourse will they believe in after this?

فَبِأَىِّ حَدِيثٍ بَعْدَهُ يُؤْمِنُونَ ۝

Sûrat An-Naba', **(The Tidings) 78**	سُورَةُ النَّبَا

In the Name of Allah,
the Compassionate, the Merciful

بِسۡمِ ٱللَّهِ ٱلرَّحۡمَٰنِ ٱلرَّحِيمِ

1. What are they asking each other about?

عَمَّ يَتَسَآءَلُونَ ۝

2. About the great tidings,

عَنِ ٱلنَّبَإِ ٱلۡعَظِيمِ ۝

3. Concerning which they are disputing.

ٱلَّذِى هُمۡ فِيهِ مُخۡتَلِفُونَ ۝

4. Indeed; they will certainly know.

كَلَّا سَيَعۡلَمُونَ ۝

5. Then, indeed; they will certainly know.

ثُمَّ كَلَّا سَيَعۡلَمُونَ ۝

6. Have We not made the earth as a couch for you?

أَلَمۡ نَجۡعَلِ ٱلۡأَرۡضَ مِهَٰدًا ۝

7. And the mountains as pegs?

وَٱلۡجِبَالَ أَوۡتَادًا ۝

8. And created you in pairs?

وَخَلَقۡنَٰكُمۡ أَزۡوَٰجًا ۝

9. And made your sleep a period of rest?

وَجَعَلۡنَا نَوۡمَكُمۡ سُبَاتًا ۝

10. And made the night as a garment?

وَجَعَلۡنَا ٱلَّيۡلَ لِبَاسًا ۝

11. And made the day a source of livelihood?

وَجَعَلۡنَا ٱلنَّهَارَ مَعَاشًا ۝

12. And built above you seven mighty [heavens]?

وَبَنَيۡنَا فَوۡقَكُمۡ سَبۡعًا شِدَادًا ۝

13. And created a shining lamp?

وَجَعَلۡنَا سِرَاجًا وَهَّاجًا ۝

14. And brought down from the rain-clouds abundant water?

وَأَنزَلۡنَا مِنَ ٱلۡمُعۡصِرَٰتِ مَآءً ثَجَّاجًا ۝

15. To bring forth thereby grain and vegetation?

لِنُخۡرِجَ بِهِۦ حَبًّا وَنَبَاتًا ۝

16. And luxuriant gardens?

وَجَنَّٰتٍ أَلۡفَافًا ۝

17. The Day of Decision is a term appointed.

إِنَّ يَوۡمَ ٱلۡفَصۡلِ كَانَ مِيقَٰتًا ۝

18. The Day the Trumpet is sounded and you will come in throngs.

يَوۡمَ يُنفَخُ فِى ٱلصُّورِ فَتَأۡتُونَ أَفۡوَاجًا ۝

19. And the heavens are opened up and turn into wide portals.

وَفُتِحَتِ ٱلسَّمَآءُ فَكَانَتۡ أَبۡوَٰبًا ۝

20. And the mountains are set in motion and turn into a mirage.

وَسُيِّرَتِ ٱلۡجِبَالُ فَكَانَتۡ سَرَابًا ۝

21. Hell is, indeed, lying in ambush;

إِنَّ جَهَنَّمَ كَانَتۡ مِرۡصَادًا ۝

22. A refuge for the transgressors;

لِّلطَّٰغِينَ مَـَٔابًا ۝

23. Tarrying therein for ages;

24. Wherein, they do not taste any coolness or fresh drinks,

25. Except for boiling water and freezing hail;

26. As an appropriate reward.

27. Indeed, they did not expect any reckoning;

28. And denounced Our Signs as lies.

29. Everything We have enumerated fully in a Book.

30. So taste. We will only increase your punishment.

31. The God-fearing will score a victory,

32. Gardens and vineyards,

33. And round-breasted mates,

34. And a brim-full cup.

35. Therein, they do not hear any idle talk or denunciation.

36. A reward from your Lord, a sufficient gift;

37. The Lord of the heavens and the earth and what lies between them; the Compassionate to Whom they do not have the power to speak.

38. The Day when the Spirit[835] and the angels shall stand in line; none shall speak except him whom the Compassionate has allowed and has spoken the truth.

39. That will be the True Day; he who wishes will return unto his Lord penitently.

40. Indeed, We have warned you of an imminent punishment, on the Day when man will see what his hands have done, and the unbeliever will say: "O, would that I have been mere dust."

---

835. Gabriel.

| Sûrat An-Nâzi'ât, (The Snatchers) 79 | سُورَةُ النَّازِعَاتِ |

*In the Name of Allah,
the Compassionate, the Merciful*

بِسْمِ اللَّهِ الرَّحْمَنِ الرَّحِيمِ

1. By those who snatch violently,

وَالنَّازِعَاتِ غَرْقًا ۝

2. And those who draw out lightly,

وَالنَّاشِطَاتِ نَشْطًا ۝

3. And those who glide smoothly,

وَالسَّابِحَاتِ سَبْحًا ۝

4. And those who outstrip suddenly,

فَالسَّابِقَاتِ سَبْقًا ۝

5. And those who conduct an affair.

فَالْمُدَبِّرَاتِ أَمْرًا ۝

6. On the Day that the first blast shall reverberate.

يَوْمَ تَرْجُفُ الرَّاجِفَةُ ۝

7. Followed by the succeeding blast.

تَتْبَعُهَا الرَّادِفَةُ ۝

8. Hearts on that Day shall be throbbing;

قُلُوبٌ يَوْمَئِذٍ وَاجِفَةٌ ۝

9. Their sights downcast.

أَبْصَارُهَا خَاشِعَةٌ ۝

10. They will say: "Shall we then be restored to the original condition?

يَقُولُونَ أَءِنَّا لَمَرْدُودُونَ فِي الْحَافِرَةِ ۝

11. "Shall we, after we were shrivelled bones?"

أَءِذَا كُنَّا عِظَامًا نَخِرَةً ۝

12. They will say: "That indeed was a losing turn."

قَالُوا تِلْكَ إِذًا كَرَّةٌ خَاسِرَةٌ ۝

13. Then, it will be only a single blast;

فَإِنَّمَا هِيَ زَجْرَةٌ وَاحِدَةٌ ۝

14. And they will be back upon the surface of the earth.

فَإِذَا هُم بِالسَّاهِرَةِ ۝

15. Have you heard Moses' story?

هَلْ أَتَاكَ حَدِيثُ مُوسَى ۝

16. When his Lord called out to him in the sacred valley, Tuwa?

إِذْ نَادَاهُ رَبُّهُ بِالْوَادِ الْمُقَدَّسِ طُوًى ۝

17. Go forth to Pharaoh; indeed, he has waxed arrogant.

اذْهَبْ إِلَى فِرْعَوْنَ إِنَّهُ طَغَى ۝

18. Say: "Do you wish to be cleansed?

فَقُلْ هَل لَّكَ إِلَى أَن تَزَكَّى ۝

19. "And that I might lead you to your Lord, so that you might fear [Him]?"

وَأَهْدِيَكَ إِلَى رَبِّكَ فَتَخْشَى ۝

20. Thereupon he (Moses) showed him the great sign;

فَأَرَاهُ الْآيَةَ الْكُبْرَى ۝

21. But he (Pharaoh) denounced and disobeyed.

فَكَذَّبَ وَعَصَى ﴿٢١﴾

22. Then, he turned back striving.

ثُمَّ أَدْبَرَ يَسْعَى ﴿٢٢﴾

23. He summoned (his people) and proclaimed.

فَحَشَرَ فَنَادَى ﴿٢٣﴾

24. He said: "I am truly your supreme lord."

فَقَالَ أَنَا رَبُّكُمُ الْأَعْلَى ﴿٢٤﴾

25. Then Allah seized him with the punishment of the last world and the first.

فَأَخَذَهُ اللَّهُ نَكَالَ الْآخِرَةِ وَالْأُولَى ﴿٢٥﴾

26. Surely, there is in that a lesson to him who fears.

إِنَّ فِي ذَلِكَ لَعِبْرَةً لِمَن يَخْشَى ﴿٢٦﴾

27. Are you, then, stronger in constitution than the heaven He has erected?

أَأَنتُمْ أَشَدُّ خَلْقًا أَمِ السَّمَاءُ بَنَاهَا ﴿٢٧﴾

28. He raised its vault and levelled it off.

رَفَعَ سَمْكَهَا فَسَوَّاهَا ﴿٢٨﴾

29. He dimmed its night and lighted its day.

وَأَغْطَشَ لَيْلَهَا وَأَخْرَجَ ضُحَاهَا ﴿٢٩﴾

30. Then, the earth, He flattened.

وَالْأَرْضَ بَعْدَ ذَلِكَ دَحَاهَا ﴿٣٠﴾

31. From it, He brought out its water and its pasture.

أَخْرَجَ مِنْهَا مَاءَهَا وَمَرْعَاهَا ﴿٣١﴾

32. And the mountains, He established firmly,

وَالْجِبَالَ أَرْسَاهَا ﴿٣٢﴾

33. As a source of enjoyment for you and your cattle.

مَتَاعًا لَكُمْ وَلِأَنْعَامِكُمْ ﴿٣٣﴾

34. Then, when the Great Calamity shall come;

فَإِذَا جَاءَتِ الطَّامَّةُ الْكُبْرَى ﴿٣٤﴾

35. On the Day that man will remember what he has done;

يَوْمَ يَتَذَكَّرُ الْإِنسَانُ مَا سَعَى ﴿٣٥﴾

36. And Hell shall be exhibited to whoever can see.

وَبُرِّزَتِ الْجَحِيمُ لِمَن يَرَى ﴿٣٦﴾

37. Then, as to him who has transgressed,

فَأَمَّا مَن طَغَى ﴿٣٧﴾

38. And preferred the present life;

وَآثَرَ الْحَيَاةَ الدُّنْيَا ﴿٣٨﴾

39. Hell, indeed, is the refuge.

فَإِنَّ الْجَحِيمَ هِيَ الْمَأْوَى ﴿٣٩﴾

40. But as to him who fears the station of his Lord, and forbids his soul from passion;

وَأَمَّا مَنْ خَافَ مَقَامَ رَبِّهِ وَنَهَى النَّفْسَ عَنِ الْهَوَى ﴿٤٠﴾

41. Then, Paradise is the refuge.

فَإِنَّ الْجَنَّةَ هِيَ الْمَأْوَى ﴿٤١﴾

42. They ask you about the Hour: "When shall it come?"

يَسْأَلُونَكَ عَنِ السَّاعَةِ أَيَّانَ مُرْسَاهَا ﴿٤٢﴾

43. How far are you from remembering it?

فِيمَ أَنتَ مِن ذِكْرَاهَآ ۝

44. Unto your Lord it will come to rest.

إِلَىٰ رَبِّكَ مُنتَهَىٰهَآ ۝

45. You are only a warner unto him who fears it.

إِنَّمَآ أَنتَ مُنذِرُ مَن يَخْشَىٰهَا ۝

46. They are, on the Day that they will see it, as though they only tarried an evening or a forenoon.

كَأَنَّهُمْ يَوْمَ يَرَوْنَهَا لَمْ يَلْبَثُوٓا۟ إِلَّا عَشِيَّةً أَوْ ضُحَىٰهَا ۝

Sûrat 'Abasa, (He Frowned) 80

In the Name of Allah, the Compassionate, the Merciful

بِسْمِ ٱللَّهِ ٱلرَّحْمَٰنِ ٱلرَّحِيمِ

1. He[836] frowned and turned his back;

عَبَسَ وَتَوَلَّىٰٓ ۝

2. When the blind man[837] came to him.

أَن جَآءَهُ ٱلْأَعْمَىٰ ۝

3. How do you know? Perhaps he might cleanse himself.

وَمَا يُدْرِيكَ لَعَلَّهُۥ يَزَّكَّىٰٓ ۝

4. Or remember, and then remembrance might profit him.

أَوْ يَذَّكَّرُ فَتَنفَعَهُ ٱلذِّكْرَىٰٓ ۝

5. As for him who has grown wealthy,

أَمَّا مَنِ ٱسْتَغْنَىٰ ۝

6. You attend to him closely;

فَأَنتَ لَهُۥ تَصَدَّىٰ ۝

7. And it does not bother you if he does not cleanse himself.

وَمَا عَلَيْكَ أَلَّا يَزَّكَّىٰ ۝

8. Yet he who comes to you running,

وَأَمَّا مَن جَآءَكَ يَسْعَىٰ ۝

9. While fearful,

وَهُوَ يَخْشَىٰ ۝

10. You do not take any notice of him.

فَأَنتَ عَنْهُ تَلَهَّىٰ ۝

11. Yet, it[838] is only a reminder,

كَلَّآ إِنَّهَا تَذْكِرَةٌ ۝

12. Whoever wishes will remember it;

فَمَن شَآءَ ذَكَرَهُۥ ۝

13. In scrolls highly honoured,

فِى صُحُفٍ مُّكَرَّمَةٍ ۝

14. Lifted up and purified,

مَّرْفُوعَةٍ مُّطَهَّرَةٍ ۝

---

836. Muhammad.
837. 'Abdullah Ibn Umm Maktum, a poor man anxious to learn the Qur'an, who importuned the Prophet.
838. The Qur'an.

15. By the hands of scribes,

بِأَيْدِى سَفَرَةٍ ﴿١٥﴾

16. Honourable and pious.

كِرَامٍ بَرَرَةٍ ﴿١٦﴾

17. May man perish! How thankless he is!

قُتِلَ الْإِنسَٰنُ مَآ أَكْفَرَهُ ﴿١٧﴾

18. Of what did He create him?

مِنْ أَىِّ شَىْءٍ خَلَقَهُ ﴿١٨﴾

19. Of a sperm, He created him and determined him.

مِن نُّطْفَةٍ خَلَقَهُ فَقَدَّرَهُ ﴿١٩﴾

20. Then He smoothed his path;

ثُمَّ السَّبِيلَ يَسَّرَهُ ﴿٢٠﴾

21. Then He caused him to die and entombed him;

ثُمَّ أَمَاتَهُ فَأَقْبَرَهُ ﴿٢١﴾

22. Then, if He wishes, He will raise him from the dead.

ثُمَّ إِذَا شَآءَ أَنشَرَهُ ﴿٢٢﴾

23. No indeed; he did not fulfil what He commanded him.

كَلَّا لَمَّا يَقْضِ مَآ أَمَرَهُ ﴿٢٣﴾

24. Let man consider his nourishment.

فَلْيَنظُرِ الْإِنسَٰنُ إِلَىٰ طَعَامِهِ ﴿٢٤﴾

25. We have poured the water abundantly;

أَنَّا صَبَبْنَا الْمَآءَ صَبًّا ﴿٢٥﴾

26. Then, We split the earth wide open;

ثُمَّ شَقَقْنَا الْأَرْضَ شَقًّا ﴿٢٦﴾

27. Then caused the grain to grow therein,

فَأَنۢبَتْنَا فِيهَا حَبًّا ﴿٢٧﴾

28. Together with vines and green vegetation;

وَعِنَبًا وَقَضْبًا ﴿٢٨﴾

29. And olives and palm trees;

وَزَيْتُونًا وَنَخْلًا ﴿٢٩﴾

30. And gardens with dense trees,

وَحَدَآئِقَ غُلْبًا ﴿٣٠﴾

31. And fruits and grass,

وَفَٰكِهَةً وَأَبًّا ﴿٣١﴾

32. For your enjoyment and that of your cattle.

مَّتَٰعًا لَّكُمْ وَلِأَنْعَٰمِكُمْ ﴿٣٢﴾

33. Then, when the Deafening Blast shall sound;

فَإِذَا جَآءَتِ الصَّآخَّةُ ﴿٣٣﴾

34. On the Day, when man shall run away from his brother,

يَوْمَ يَفِرُّ الْمَرْءُ مِنْ أَخِيهِ ﴿٣٤﴾

35. His mother and his father,

وَأُمِّهِ وَأَبِيهِ ﴿٣٥﴾

36. His consort and his sons.

وَصَٰحِبَتِهِ وَبَنِيهِ ﴿٣٦﴾

37. To every one of them on that Day is a business sufficing him.

لِكُلِّ امْرِئٍ مِّنْهُمْ يَوْمَئِذٍ شَأْنٌ يُغْنِيهِ ﴿٣٧﴾

38. Some faces, on that Day, will be bright,

وُجُوهٌ يَوْمَئِذٍ مُّسْفِرَةٌ ۝

39. Laughing and joyful;

ضَاحِكَةٌ مُّسْتَبْشِرَةٌ ۝

40. And other faces, on that Day, will be covered with dust,

وَوُجُوهٌ يَوْمَئِذٍ عَلَيْهَا غَبَرَةٌ ۝

41. Enveloped in smoke.

تَرْهَقُهَا قَتَرَةٌ ۝

42. Those are the unbelievers, the profligate.

أُوْلَٰٓئِكَ هُمُ ٱلْكَفَرَةُ ٱلْفَجَرَةُ ۝

**Sûrat At-Takwir,
(The Coiling Up) 81**

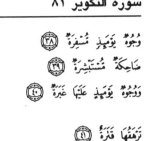

*In the Name of Allah,
the Compassionate, the Merciful*

بِسْمِ ٱللَّهِ ٱلرَّحْمَٰنِ ٱلرَّحِيمِ

1. When the sun shall be coiled up;

إِذَا ٱلشَّمْسُ كُوِّرَتْ ۝

2. And when the stars shall be scattered about;

وَإِذَا ٱلنُّجُومُ ٱنكَدَرَتْ ۝

3. And when the mountains shall be set in motion;

وَإِذَا ٱلْجِبَالُ سُيِّرَتْ ۝

4. And when the pregnant camels shall be discarded;

وَإِذَا ٱلْعِشَارُ عُطِّلَتْ ۝

5. And when the beasts shall be corralled;

وَإِذَا ٱلْوُحُوشُ حُشِرَتْ ۝

6. And when the seas shall rise mightily;

وَإِذَا ٱلْبِحَارُ سُجِّرَتْ ۝

7. And when souls shall be paired off;

وَإِذَا ٱلنُّفُوسُ زُوِّجَتْ ۝

8. And when the buried infant shall be asked:

وَإِذَا ٱلْمَوْءُۥدَةُ سُئِلَتْ ۝

9. "For what sin was she killed?"

بِأَيِّ ذَنۢبٍ قُتِلَتْ ۝

10. And when the scrolls shall be unrolled;

وَإِذَا ٱلصُّحُفُ نُشِرَتْ ۝

11. And when heaven shall be scraped off;

وَإِذَا ٱلسَّمَآءُ كُشِطَتْ ۝

12. And when Hell shall be stoked;

وَإِذَا ٱلْجَحِيمُ سُعِّرَتْ ۝

13. And when Paradise shall be brought near;

وَإِذَا ٱلْجَنَّةُ أُزْلِفَتْ ۝

14. Then each soul shall know what it had brought forth.

عَلِمَتْ نَفْسٌ مَّآ أَحْضَرَتْ ۝

15. No, I swear by the alternating stars,

فَلَآ أُقْسِمُ بِٱلْخُنَّسِ ۝

16. Which circle then hide;

ٱلْجَوَارِ ٱلْكُنَّسِ ۝

17. And the night when it recedes;

وَٱلَّيْلِ إِذَا عَسْعَسَ ۝

18. And the morning when it breaks,

وَٱلصُّبْحِ إِذَا تَنَفَّسَ ﴿١٨﴾

19. It is truly the discourse of a noble Messenger;[839]

إِنَّهُ لَقَوْلُ رَسُولٍ كَرِيمٍ ﴿١٩﴾

20. Who has power, with the Lord of the Throne, and is highly placed;

ذِى قُوَّةٍ عِندَ ذِى ٱلْعَرْشِ مَكِينٍ ﴿٢٠﴾

21. Obeyed, then trustworthy.

مُّطَاعٍ ثَمَّ أَمِينٍ ﴿٢١﴾

22. Your Companion[840] is not mad;

وَمَا صَاحِبُكُم بِمَجْنُونٍ ﴿٢٢﴾

23. He saw him[841] upon the luminous horizon.

وَلَقَدْ رَءَاهُ بِٱلْأُفُقِ ٱلْمُبِينِ ﴿٢٣﴾

24. He is not, regarding the Unseen, niggardly;

وَمَا هُوَ عَلَى ٱلْغَيْبِ بِضَنِينٍ ﴿٢٤﴾

25. And it is not the discourse of a devil, accursed.

وَمَا هُوَ بِقَوْلِ شَيْطَانٍ رَّجِيمٍ ﴿٢٥﴾

26. Where, then, will you go?

فَأَيْنَ تَذْهَبُونَ ﴿٢٦﴾

27. It is only a Reminder to all mankind;

إِنْ هُوَ إِلَّا ذِكْرٌ لِّلْعَالَمِينَ ﴿٢٧﴾

28. To whoever of you who wishes to reform their ways.

لِمَن شَاءَ مِنكُمْ أَن يَسْتَقِيمَ ﴿٢٨﴾

29. But you will not wish unless Allah, the Lord of the Worlds, wishes.

وَمَا تَشَاءُونَ إِلَّا أَن يَشَاءَ ٱللَّهُ رَبُّ ٱلْعَالَمِينَ ﴿٢٩﴾

**Sûrat Al-Infitâr,
(The Cleaving Asunder) 82**

*In the Name of Allah,
the Compassionate, the Merciful*

بِسْمِ ٱللَّهِ ٱلرَّحْمَٰنِ ٱلرَّحِيمِ

1. When the heavens are cleft asunder,

إِذَا ٱلسَّمَاءُ ٱنفَطَرَتْ ﴿١﴾

2. And when the stars are scattered [about].

وَإِذَا ٱلْكَوَاكِبُ ٱنتَثَرَتْ ﴿٢﴾

3. And when the seas are blown open;

وَإِذَا ٱلْبِحَارُ فُجِّرَتْ ﴿٣﴾

4. And when the tombs are strewn around;

وَإِذَا ٱلْقُبُورُ بُعْثِرَتْ ﴿٤﴾

5. Then each soul shall know what it advanced and what it deferred.

عَلِمَتْ نَفْسٌ مَّا قَدَّمَتْ وَأَخَّرَتْ ﴿٥﴾

---

839. Gabriel.
840. Muhammad.
841. Gabriel.

6. O man, what deluded you concerning your Munificent Lord,

يَٰٓأَيُّهَا ٱلْإِنسَٰنُ مَا غَرَّكَ بِرَبِّكَ ٱلْكَرِيمِ ⑥

7. Who created you, fashioned you and made you well-wrought.

ٱلَّذِى خَلَقَكَ فَسَوَّىٰكَ فَعَدَلَكَ ⑦

8. In whichever form He wished, He put you together.

فِىٓ أَىِّ صُورَةٍ مَّا شَآءَ رَكَّبَكَ ⑧

9. No, but you deny the Judgement;

كَلَّا بَلْ تُكَذِّبُونَ بِٱلدِّينِ ⑨

10. Yet over you stand watchers,

وَإِنَّ عَلَيْكُمْ لَحَٰفِظِينَ ⑩

11. Noble recorders,

كِرَامًا كَٰتِبِينَ ⑪

12. Who know what you do.

يَعْلَمُونَ مَا تَفْعَلُونَ ⑫

13. The pious shall, indeed, be in Bliss.

إِنَّ ٱلْأَبْرَارَ لَفِى نَعِيمٍ ⑬

14. And the profligate shall be in Hell;

وَإِنَّ ٱلْفُجَّارَ لَفِى جَحِيمٍ ⑭

15. Burning therein on the Day of Judgement.

يَصْلَوْنَهَا يَوْمَ ٱلدِّينِ ⑮

16. And they shall never be far away from it.

وَمَا هُمْ عَنْهَا بِغَآئِبِينَ ⑯

17. If only you knew what is the Day of Judgement?

وَمَآ أَدْرَىٰكَ مَا يَوْمُ ٱلدِّينِ ⑰

18. Again, if only you knew what is the Day of Judgement?

ثُمَّ مَآ أَدْرَىٰكَ مَا يَوْمُ ٱلدِّينِ ⑱

19. A Day when no soul shall avail another soul anything, and the Command on that day shall be Allah's.

يَوْمَ لَا تَمْلِكُ نَفْسٌ لِّنَفْسٍ شَيْئًا ۖ وَٱلْأَمْرُ يَوْمَئِذٍ لِّلَّهِ ⑲

Sûrat Al-Mutaffifîn,
(The Skimpers) 83

سُورَةُ المُطَفِّفِينَ

In the Name of Allah,
the Compassionate, the Merciful

بِسْمِ ٱللَّهِ ٱلرَّحْمَٰنِ ٱلرَّحِيمِ

1. Woe to the skimpers,

وَيْلٌ لِّلْمُطَفِّفِينَ ①

2. Who, when they measure for themselves from others exact full measure;

ٱلَّذِينَ إِذَا ٱكْتَالُوا۟ عَلَى ٱلنَّاسِ يَسْتَوْفُونَ ②

3. But when they measure or weigh for others actually skimp.

وَإِذَا كَالُوهُمْ أَو وَّزَنُوهُمْ يُخْسِرُونَ ③

4. Do not those people think that they will be resuscitated,

أَلَا يَظُنُّ أُو۟لَٰٓئِكَ أَنَّهُم مَّبْعُوثُونَ ④

5. On a Great Day?

لِيَوْمٍ عَظِيمٍ ۝

6. A Day when mankind will stand before the Lord of the Worlds.

يَوْمَ يَقُومُ ٱلنَّاسُ لِرَبِّ ٱلْعَٰلَمِينَ ۝

7. Not at all; the book of the profligate is locked up in the Underworld.

كَلَّا إِنَّ كِتَٰبَ ٱلْفُجَّارِ لَفِى سِجِّينٍ ۝

8. If only you knew what is the Underworld.

وَمَا أَدْرَىٰكَ مَا سِجِّينٌ ۝

9. A book inscribed.

كِتَٰبٌ مَّرْقُومٌ ۝

10. Woe betide, on that Day, those who denounce;

وَيْلٌ يَوْمَئِذٍ لِّلْمُكَذِّبِينَ ۝

11. Those who deny the Day of Judgement.

ٱلَّذِينَ يُكَذِّبُونَ بِيَوْمِ ٱلدِّينِ ۝

12. Yet, only a sinful aggressor denies it.

وَمَا يُكَذِّبُ بِهِ إِلَّا كُلُّ مُعْتَدٍ أَثِيمٍ ۝

13. When Our Signs are recited to him, he says: "Mere legends of the ancients."

إِذَا تُتْلَىٰ عَلَيْهِ ءَايَٰتُنَا قَالَ أَسَٰطِيرُ ٱلْأَوَّلِينَ ۝

14. Not at all; their hearts are overwhelmed with what they were earning.

كَلَّا بَلْ رَانَ عَلَىٰ قُلُوبِهِم مَّا كَانُوا۟ يَكْسِبُونَ ۝

15. Not at all; surely on that Day they shall be screened off from their Lord.

كَلَّا إِنَّهُمْ عَن رَّبِّهِمْ يَوْمَئِذٍ لَّمَحْجُوبُونَ ۝

16. Then, they shall roast in Hell.

ثُمَّ إِنَّهُمْ لَصَالُوا۟ ٱلْجَحِيمِ ۝

17. Then it will be said to them: ‹This is what you used to deny."

ثُمَّ يُقَالُ هَٰذَا ٱلَّذِى كُنتُم بِهِۦ تُكَذِّبُونَ ۝

18. No indeed; the book of the pious is in the Higher World.

كَلَّا إِنَّ كِتَٰبَ ٱلْأَبْرَارِ لَفِى عِلِّيِّينَ ۝

19. And if only you knew what is the Higher World;

وَمَا أَدْرَىٰكَ مَا عِلِّيُّونَ ۝

20. A book inscribed,

كِتَٰبٌ مَّرْقُومٌ ۝

21. Witnessed by those well-favoured.

يَشْهَدُهُ ٱلْمُقَرَّبُونَ ۝

22. The pious are indeed in Bliss;

إِنَّ ٱلْأَبْرَارَ لَفِى نَعِيمٍ ۝

23. Upon couches gazing round.

عَلَى ٱلْأَرَائِكِ يَنظُرُونَ ۝

24. You will recognize in their faces the glow of bliss.

تَعْرِفُ فِى وُجُوهِهِمْ نَضْرَةَ ٱلنَّعِيمِ ۝

25. They are given to drink from a sealed wine;

يُسْقَوْنَ مِن رَّحِيقٍ مَّخْتُومٍ ۝

26. Whose seal is musk. Over that, let the competitors compete;

خِتَٰمُهُۥ مِسْكٌ وَفِى ذَٰلِكَ فَلْيَتَنَافَسِ ٱلْمُتَنَٰفِسُونَ ۝

27. And its mixture is from Tasnim;[842]

28. A spring from which the well-favoured drink.

29. The criminals used to laugh at the believers;

30. And if they pass by them they would wink at one another.

31. And if they go back to their families, they would go back jeering,

32. And if they see them, they would say: "These are indeed in error."

33. Yet, they were not sent to watch over them.

34. But, today, the believers shall laugh at the unbelievers.

35. Upon couches, they gaze round.

36. Have the unbelievers been rewarded for what they used to do?

وَمِزَاجُهُۥ مِن تَسْنِيمٍ ۝

عَيْنًا يَشْرَبُ بِهَا ٱلْمُقَرَّبُونَ ۝

إِنَّ ٱلَّذِينَ أَجْرَمُوا۟ كَانُوا۟ مِنَ ٱلَّذِينَ ءَامَنُوا۟ يَضْحَكُونَ ۝

وَإِذَا مَرُّوا۟ بِهِمْ يَتَغَامَزُونَ ۝

وَإِذَا ٱنقَلَبُوٓا۟ إِلَىٰٓ أَهْلِهِمُ ٱنقَلَبُوا۟ فَكِهِينَ ۝

وَإِذَا رَأَوْهُمْ قَالُوٓا۟ إِنَّ هَـٰٓؤُلَآءِ لَضَآلُّونَ ۝

وَمَآ أُرْسِلُوا۟ عَلَيْهِمْ حَـٰفِظِينَ ۝

فَٱلْيَوْمَ ٱلَّذِينَ ءَامَنُوا۟ مِنَ ٱلْكُفَّارِ يَضْحَكُونَ ۝

عَلَى ٱلْأَرَآئِكِ يَنظُرُونَ ۝

هَلْ ثُوِّبَ ٱلْكُفَّارُ مَا كَانُوا۟ يَفْعَلُونَ ۝

Sûrat Al-Inshiqâq,
(The Rending Asunder) 84

بِسْمِ ٱللَّهِ ٱلرَّحْمَـٰنِ ٱلرَّحِيمِ

In the Name of Allah,
the Compassionate, the Merciful

1. When the heaven is rent asunder;

2. And hearkens to its Lord and is judged.

3. And when the earth is spread out;

4. And casts out what is within it and is voided;

5. And hearkens to its Lord and is judged.

6. O man, you strive unto your Lord and you shall meet Him.

إِذَا ٱلسَّمَآءُ ٱنشَقَّتْ ۝

وَأَذِنَتْ لِرَبِّهَا وَحُقَّتْ ۝

وَإِذَا ٱلْأَرْضُ مُدَّتْ ۝

وَأَلْقَتْ مَا فِيهَا وَتَخَلَّتْ ۝

وَأَذِنَتْ لِرَبِّهَا وَحُقَّتْ ۝

يَـٰٓأَيُّهَا ٱلْإِنسَـٰنُ إِنَّكَ كَادِحٌ إِلَىٰ رَبِّكَ كَدْحًا فَمُلَـٰقِيهِ ۝

---

842. A spring in Paradise.

7. As for him who will be given his book in his right hand;

فَأَمَّا مَنْ أُوتِيَ كِتَبَهُ بِيَمِينِهِ ۞

8. He shall be called to an easy reckoning,

فَسَوْفَ يُحَاسَبُ حِسَابًا يَسِيرًا ۞

9. And shall go back to his people well-pleased.

وَيَنقَلِبُ إِلَى أَهْلِهِ مَسْرُورًا ۞

10. But as for him who is given his book behind his back;

وَأَمَّا مَنْ أُوتِيَ كِتَبَهُ وَرَآءَ ظَهْرِهِ ۞

11. He shall call out: "Perdition!"

فَسَوْفَ يَدْعُوا ثُبُورًا ۞

12. And burn in Hell-fire.

وَيَصْلَى سَعِيرًا ۞

13. He was, indeed, in the midst of his people, living happily.

إِنَّهُ كَانَ فِي أَهْلِهِ مَسْرُورًا ۞

14. He supposed that he will never go back.

إِنَّهُ ظَنَّ أَن لَّن يَحُورَ ۞

15. No, indeed, his Lord was observing him.

بَلَى إِنَّ رَبَّهُ كَانَ بِهِ بَصِيرًا ۞

16. No, I swear by the twilight,

فَلَا أُقْسِمُ بِالشَّفَقِ ۞

17. And by the night and what it brings forth,

وَالَّيْلِ وَمَا وَسَقَ ۞

18. And by the moon when it is full,

وَالْقَمَرِ إِذَا اتَّسَقَ ۞

19. That you will mount stage by stage.

لَتَرْكَبُنَّ طَبَقًا عَن طَبَقٍ ۞

20. What is the matter with them that they will not believe?

فَمَا لَهُمْ لَا يُؤْمِنُونَ ۞

21. And if the Qur'an is recited to them, they will not prostrate themselves?

وَإِذَا قُرِئَ عَلَيْهِمُ الْقُرْءَانُ لَا يَسْجُدُونَ ۩ ۞

22. Yet, the unbelievers are denouncing;

بَلِ الَّذِينَ كَفَرُوا يُكَذِّبُونَ ۞

23. And Allah knows better what they are thinking in secret.

وَاللَّهُ أَعْلَمُ بِمَا يُوعُونَ ۞

24. So announce to them the good news of a very painful punishment;

فَبَشِّرْهُم بِعَذَابٍ أَلِيمٍ ۞

25. Except for those who believe and do the righteous deeds. They will have an unstinted wage.

إِلَّا الَّذِينَ ءَامَنُوا وَعَمِلُوا الصَّالِحَاتِ لَهُمْ أَجْرٌ غَيْرُ مَمْنُونٍ ۞

Sûrat Al-Burûj, (The Constellations) 85

سُورَةُ البُرُوجِ

In the Name of Allah,
the Compassionate, the Merciful

بِسْمِ اللَّهِ الرَّحْمَٰنِ الرَّحِيمِ

1. By the heaven of the many constellations;

وَالسَّمَاءِ ذَاتِ الْبُرُوجِ ①

2. And by the Promised Day;

وَالْيَوْمِ الْمَوْعُودِ ②

3. And by every witness and what is witnessed.

وَشَاهِدٍ وَمَشْهُودٍ ③

4. Perish the companions of the Pit,

قُتِلَ أَصْحَابُ الْأُخْدُودِ ④

5. The fire well-stoked;

النَّارِ ذَاتِ الْوَقُودِ ⑤

6. While they sat around it,

إِذْ هُمْ عَلَيْهَا قُعُودٌ ⑥

7. And were witnessing what they did to the believers.

وَهُمْ عَلَىٰ مَا يَفْعَلُونَ بِالْمُؤْمِنِينَ شُهُودٌ ⑦

8. They did not begrudge them except that they believed in Allah, the All-Mighty, the All-Praiseworthy;

وَمَا نَقَمُوا مِنْهُمْ إِلَّا أَن يُؤْمِنُوا بِاللَّهِ الْعَزِيزِ الْحَمِيدِ ⑧

9. To Whom belongs the dominion of the heavens and the earth. Allah is Witness of everything.

الَّذِي لَهُ مُلْكُ السَّمَاوَاتِ وَالْأَرْضِ وَاللَّهُ عَلَىٰ كُلِّ شَيْءٍ شَهِيدٌ ⑨

10. Surely, those who have tempted the believers, men and women, then did not repent, will suffer the punishment of Hell; and theirs is the punishment of burning.

إِنَّ الَّذِينَ فَتَنُوا الْمُؤْمِنِينَ وَالْمُؤْمِنَاتِ ثُمَّ لَمْ يَتُوبُوا فَلَهُمْ عَذَابُ جَهَنَّمَ وَلَهُمْ عَذَابُ الْحَرِيقِ ⑩

11. Surely, those who have believed and done the righteous deeds shall have Gardens beneath which rivers flow. That is the great triumph.

إِنَّ الَّذِينَ آمَنُوا وَعَمِلُوا الصَّالِحَاتِ لَهُمْ جَنَّاتٌ تَجْرِي مِن تَحْتِهَا الْأَنْهَارُ ذَٰلِكَ الْفَوْزُ الْكَبِيرُ ⑪

12. The vengeance of your Lord is surely terrible.

إِنَّ بَطْشَ رَبِّكَ لَشَدِيدٌ ⑫

13. It is He Who originates and brings back;

إِنَّهُ هُوَ يُبْدِئُ وَيُعِيدُ ⑬

14. And He is the All-Forgiving, the All-Friendly;

وَهُوَ الْغَفُورُ الْوَدُودُ ⑭

15. Lord of the glorious Throne;

ذُو الْعَرْشِ الْمَجِيدُ ⑮

16. Doer of what He wills.

17. Have you heard the story of the hosts?

18. Of Pharaoh and Thamud.

19. Yet, the unbelievers continue to denounce.

20. While Allah, from behind them, is All-Embracing.

21. Yet, it is a glorious Qur'an,

22. In a Well-Preserved Tablet.

**Sûrat At-Tariq,
(The Night-Visitor) 86**

*In the Name of Allah,
the Compassionate, the Merciful*

1. By the heavens and the night-visitor.

2. If only you knew what is the night-visitor,

3. The piercing star.

4. Every soul has a watcher;

5. So let man consider what he was created from.

6. He was created from flowing water;

7. Emanating from what lies between the loins and the breast-bones.

8. Surely, He has the power to bring him back,

9. When the consciences of men shall be tested.

10. Then, he will have no power and no supporter.

11. And by the heaven which alternates;

12. And the earth which is split up.

13. It is indeed a decisive discourse;

14. And it is no joking matter.

وَمَا هُوَ بِٱلْهَزْلِ ﴿١٤﴾

15. They are indeed scheming mightily,

إِنَّهُمْ يَكِيدُونَ كَيْدًا ﴿١٥﴾

16. And I am scheming mightily.

وَأَكِيدُ كَيْدًا ﴿١٦﴾

17. So, give the unbelievers some respite. Respite them slowly.

فَمَهِّلِ ٱلْكَٰفِرِينَ أَمْهِلْهُمْ رُوَيْدًا ﴿١٧﴾

Sûrat Al-A'la, (The Most High) 87

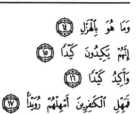

In the Name of Allah, the Compassionate, the Merciful

1. Glorify the name of your Lord, the Most High;

سَبِّحِ ٱسْمَ رَبِّكَ ٱلْأَعْلَى ﴿١﴾

2. Who created and fashioned well;

ٱلَّذِى خَلَقَ فَسَوَّىٰ ﴿٢﴾

3. And Who fore-ordained and guided rightly;

وَٱلَّذِى قَدَّرَ فَهَدَىٰ ﴿٣﴾

4. And Who brought out the pasture;

وَٱلَّذِىٓ أَخْرَجَ ٱلْمَرْعَىٰ ﴿٤﴾

5. Then turned it into greenish-black straw.

فَجَعَلَهُ غُثَآءً أَحْوَىٰ ﴿٥﴾

6. We shall make you recite; so you will not forget;

سَنُقْرِئُكَ فَلَا تَنسَىٰ ﴿٦﴾

7. Except what Allah wishes. He certainly knows what is proclaimed and what is hidden.

إِلَّا مَا شَآءَ ٱللَّهُ إِنَّهُ يَعْلَمُ ٱلْجَهْرَ وَمَا يَخْفَىٰ ﴿٧﴾

8. And We shall ease your travel on an easy course.

وَنُيَسِّرُكَ لِلْيُسْرَىٰ ﴿٨﴾

9. So remind, if the reminder will avail.

فَذَكِّرْ إِن نَّفَعَتِ ٱلذِّكْرَىٰ ﴿٩﴾

10. He who fears shall remember;

سَيَذَّكَّرُ مَن يَخْشَىٰ ﴿١٠﴾

11. And the most wretched shall refrain from it;

وَيَتَجَنَّبُهَا ٱلْأَشْقَى ﴿١١﴾

12. He who shall roast in the great Fire,

ٱلَّذِى يَصْلَى ٱلنَّارَ ٱلْكُبْرَىٰ ﴿١٢﴾

13. Then, he will neither die therein nor live.

ثُمَّ لَا يَمُوتُ فِيهَا وَلَا يَحْيَىٰ ﴿١٣﴾

14. He who cleanses himself shall prosper;

قَدْ أَفْلَحَ مَن تَزَكَّىٰ ﴿١٤﴾

15. Remembering his Lord's Name and praying.

وَذَكَرَ ٱسْمَ رَبِّهِ فَصَلَّىٰ ﴿١٥﴾

16. No, you prefer the present life;

بَلْ تُؤْثِرُونَ ٱلْحَيَوٰةَ ٱلدُّنْيَا ۝

17. Whereas the Hereafter is better and more lasting.

وَٱلْءَاخِرَةُ خَيْرٌ وَأَبْقَىٰ ۝

18. That, indeed, is in the ancient scrolls,

إِنَّ هَٰذَا لَفِى ٱلصُّحُفِ ٱلْأُولَىٰ ۝

19. The scrolls of Abraham and Moses.

صُحُفِ إِبْرَٰهِيمَ وَمُوسَىٰ ۝

**Sûrat Al-Ghâshiyah,
(The Overwhelming Day) 88**

سُورَةُ ٱلْغَاشِيَةِ

*In the Name of Allah,
the Compassionate, the Merciful*

بِسْمِ ٱللَّهِ ٱلرَّحْمَٰنِ ٱلرَّحِيمِ

1. Have you heard the story of the Overwhelming Day?

هَلْ أَتَىٰكَ حَدِيثُ ٱلْغَٰشِيَةِ ۝

2. Faces on that Day shall be downcast,

وُجُوهٌ يَوْمَئِذٍ خَٰشِعَةٌ ۝

3. Labouring and toiling;

عَامِلَةٌ نَّاصِبَةٌ ۝

4. Roasting in a scorching fire;

تَصْلَىٰ نَارًا حَامِيَةً ۝

5. Given to drink from a boiling spring.

تُسْقَىٰ مِنْ عَيْنٍ ءَانِيَةٍ ۝

6. They will have no nourishment except from poisonous cactus,

لَّيْسَ لَهُمْ طَعَامٌ إِلَّا مِن ضَرِيعٍ ۝

7. Which neither fattens nor appeases hunger.

لَّا يُسْمِنُ وَلَا يُغْنِى مِن جُوعٍ ۝

8. Faces on that Day shall be blissful,

وُجُوهٌ يَوْمَئِذٍ نَّاعِمَةٌ ۝

9. Well-pleased with their endeavour;

لِّسَعْيِهَا رَاضِيَةٌ ۝

10. In a lofty Garden;

فِى جَنَّةٍ عَالِيَةٍ ۝

11. Wherein no idle talk is heard;

لَّا تَسْمَعُ فِيهَا لَٰغِيَةً ۝

12. Wherein is a flowing spring;

فِيهَا عَيْنٌ جَارِيَةٌ ۝

13. Wherein are upraised couches;

فِيهَا سُرُرٌ مَّرْفُوعَةٌ ۝

14. And cups ranged round,

وَأَكْوَابٌ مَّوْضُوعَةٌ ۝

15. And cushions in rows,

وَنَمَارِقُ مَصْفُوفَةٌ ۝

16. And carpets spread out.

وَزَرَابِىُّ مَبْثُوثَةٌ ۝

17. Will they, then, not consider the camels, how they were created?

أَفَلَا يَنظُرُونَ إِلَى ٱلْإِبِلِ كَيْفَ خُلِقَتْ ۝

18. And heaven, how it was raised up?

وَإِلَى ٱلسَّمَاءِ كَيْفَ رُفِعَتْ ﴿١٨﴾

19. And the mountains, how they were hoisted?

وَإِلَى ٱلْجِبَالِ كَيْفَ نُصِبَتْ ﴿١٩﴾

20. And the earth, how it was levelled.

وَإِلَى ٱلْأَرْضِ كَيْفَ سُطِحَتْ ﴿٢٠﴾

21. So, exhort, you are a mere exhorter;

فَذَكِّرْ إِنَّمَا أَنتَ مُذَكِّرٌ ﴿٢١﴾

22. You are not supposed to dominate them;

لَّسْتَ عَلَيْهِم بِمُصَيْطِرٍ ﴿٢٢﴾

23. Except for him who turns away and disbelieves;

إِلَّا مَن تَوَلَّىٰ وَكَفَرَ ﴿٢٣﴾

24. Then Allah will punish him in the most terrible way.

فَيُعَذِّبُهُ ٱللَّهُ ٱلْعَذَابَ ٱلْأَكْبَرَ ﴿٢٤﴾

25. Indeed, unto Us is their return;

إِنَّ إِلَيْنَآ إِيَابَهُمْ ﴿٢٥﴾

26. Then, upon Us rests their reckoning.

ثُمَّ إِنَّ عَلَيْنَا حِسَابَهُم ﴿٢٦﴾

Sûrat Al-Fajr, (The Dawn) 89

سُورَةُ الْفَجْرِ

In the Name of Allah,
the Compassionate, the Merciful

بِسْمِ ٱللَّهِ ٱلرَّحْمَٰنِ ٱلرَّحِيمِ

1. By the dawn,

وَٱلْفَجْرِ ﴿١﴾

2. And by the ten nights;

وَلَيَالٍ عَشْرٍ ﴿٢﴾

3. And the even and the odd;

وَٱلشَّفْعِ وَٱلْوَتْرِ ﴿٣﴾

4. And the night, when it runs its course.

وَٱلَّيْلِ إِذَا يَسْرِ ﴿٤﴾

5. Is there in that an oath for a man of acumen?

هَلْ فِي ذَٰلِكَ قَسَمٌ لِّذِي حِجْرٍ ﴿٥﴾

6. Have you not seen how your Lord dealt with 'Ad?

أَلَمْ تَرَ كَيْفَ فَعَلَ رَبُّكَ بِعَادٍ ﴿٦﴾

7. Iram[843] of the many pillars;

إِرَمَ ذَاتِ ٱلْعِمَادِ ﴿٧﴾

8. The like of which was not created in the land?

ٱلَّتِي لَمْ يُخْلَقْ مِثْلُهَا فِي ٱلْبِلَٰدِ ﴿٨﴾

9. And Thamud, who burrowed the rock in the valley?

وَثَمُودَ ٱلَّذِينَ جَابُوا ٱلصَّخْرَ بِٱلْوَادِ ﴿٩﴾

10. And Pharaoh of the many tent-pegs?[844]

وَفِرْعَوْنَ ذِي ٱلْأَوْتَادِ ﴿١٠﴾

---

843. The ancient city of 'Ad in central Arabia.
844. A metaphor for power or grandeur.

11. Who waxed arrogant in the land;

ٱلَّذِينَ طَغَوْا۟ فِى ٱلْبِلَٰدِ ۝

12. And compounded corruption in it.

فَأَكْثَرُوا۟ فِيهَا ٱلْفَسَادَ ۝

13. Then your Lord unloosed upon them a scourge of punishment.

فَصَبَّ عَلَيْهِمْ رَبُّكَ سَوْطَ عَذَابٍ ۝

14. Your Lord is, indeed, Ever-Observant.

إِنَّ رَبَّكَ لَبِٱلْمِرْصَادِ ۝

15. As for man, whenever his Lord tests him, honouring him and favouring him with bounties, he says: "My Lord has honoured me."

فَأَمَّا ٱلْإِنسَٰنُ إِذَا مَا ٱبْتَلَىٰهُ رَبُّهُۥ فَأَكْرَمَهُۥ وَنَعَّمَهُۥ فَيَقُولُ رَبِّىٓ أَكْرَمَنِ ۝

16. But when He tests him, straitening his provision, he says: "My Lord has despised me."

وَأَمَّآ إِذَا مَا ٱبْتَلَىٰهُ فَقَدَرَ عَلَيْهِ رِزْقَهُۥ فَيَقُولُ رَبِّىٓ أَهَٰنَنِ ۝

17. Not at all; you do not actually honour the orphan;

كَلَّا ۖ بَل لَّا تُكْرِمُونَ ٱلْيَتِيمَ ۝

18. And do not advocate the feeding of the destitute;

وَلَا تَحَٰٓضُّونَ عَلَىٰ طَعَامِ ٱلْمِسْكِينِ ۝

19. And you devour the inheritance greedily;

وَتَأْكُلُونَ ٱلتُّرَاثَ أَكْلًا لَّمًّا ۝

20. And you love wealth ardently.

وَتُحِبُّونَ ٱلْمَالَ حُبًّا جَمًّا ۝

21. No; when the earth is demolished completely.

كَلَّآ إِذَا دُكَّتِ ٱلْأَرْضُ دَكًّا دَكًّا ۝

22. And your Lord comes, together with the angels, in rows upon rows;

وَجَآءَ رَبُّكَ وَٱلْمَلَكُ صَفًّا صَفًّا ۝

23. And Hell is brought forth on that Day. Then man will remember on that Day; but wherefrom will remembrance come to him?

وَجِا۟ىٓءَ يَوْمَئِذٍ بِجَهَنَّمَ ۚ يَوْمَئِذٍ يَتَذَكَّرُ ٱلْإِنسَٰنُ وَأَنَّىٰ لَهُ ٱلذِّكْرَىٰ ۝

24. He will say: "Would that I had advanced something for (this) my life!"

يَقُولُ يَٰلَيْتَنِى قَدَّمْتُ لِحَيَاتِى ۝

25. On that Day, none shall punish like His punishment;

فَيَوْمَئِذٍ لَّا يُعَذِّبُ عَذَابَهُۥٓ أَحَدٌ ۝

26. And none shall bind with fetters like His.

وَلَا يُوثِقُ وَثَاقَهُۥٓ أَحَدٌ ۝

27. O quiescent soul,

يَٰٓأَيَّتُهَا ٱلنَّفْسُ ٱلْمُطْمَئِنَّةُ ۝

28. Return unto your Lord well-pleased and well-pleasing;

ٱرْجِعِىٓ إِلَىٰ رَبِّكِ رَاضِيَةً مَّرْضِيَّةً ۝

29. And join the ranks of My servants;

فَٱدْخُلِى فِى عِبَٰدِى ۝

30. And enter My Paradise.

وَٱدْخُلِى جَنَّتِى ۝

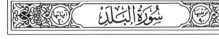

Sûrat Al-Balad, (The City) 90

In the Name of Allah, the Compassionate, the Merciful

1. No; I swear by this city.[845]

2. And you[846] are a resident of this city.

3. And by the begetter and what he begot;

4. We have, indeed, created man to toil.

5. Does he think that none shall have power over him?

6. He says: "I have squandered a large sum of money."

7. Does he think that no one saw him?

8. Have We not given him two eyes,

9. A tongue and two lips,

10. And guided him onto the two high-ways?[847]

11. Yet he did not brave the rocky pass.

12. If only you knew what is the rocky pass.

13. The freeing of a slave;

14. Or feeding, upon a day of famine,

15. An orphan near of kin;

16. Or a destitute man in dire need;

17. Then, being one of those who believe, command steadfastness to each other and command compassion.

18. Those are the Companions of the Right;

19. But those who disbelieve in Our Signs are the Companions of the Left;

20. A fire will close in on them.

---

845. Mecca.
846. Muhammad.
847. Of right and wrong.

Sûrat Ash-Shams, (The Sun) 91	سُورَةُ الشَّمْسِ

In the Name of Allah,
the Compassionate, the Merciful

بِسْمِ ٱللَّهِ ٱلرَّحْمَٰنِ ٱلرَّحِيمِ

1. By the sun and its forenoon brightness,

وَٱلشَّمْسِ وَضُحَىٰهَا ﴿١﴾

2. And the moon when it follows it,

وَٱلْقَمَرِ إِذَا تَلَىٰهَا ﴿٢﴾

3. And the day when it exhibits its light,

وَٱلنَّهَارِ إِذَا جَلَّىٰهَا ﴿٣﴾

4. And the night when it obscures it;

وَٱلَّيْلِ إِذَا يَغْشَىٰهَا ﴿٤﴾

5. And by the heaven and Him Who erected it;

وَٱلسَّمَاءِ وَمَا بَنَىٰهَا ﴿٥﴾

6. And the earth and Him Who spread it out,

وَٱلْأَرْضِ وَمَا طَحَىٰهَا ﴿٦﴾

7. And the soul and Him Who fashioned it well,

وَنَفْسٍ وَمَا سَوَّىٰهَا ﴿٧﴾

8. Inspiring it to profligacy and piety.

فَأَلْهَمَهَا فُجُورَهَا وَتَقْوَىٰهَا ﴿٨﴾

9. Prosperous shall be he who purifies it,

قَدْ أَفْلَحَ مَن زَكَّىٰهَا ﴿٩﴾

10. And ruined he who corrupts it.

وَقَدْ خَابَ مَن دَسَّىٰهَا ﴿١٠﴾

11. Thamud have denounced, due to their arrogance,

كَذَّبَتْ ثَمُودُ بِطَغْوَىٰهَا ﴿١١﴾

12. When their most vicious citizen emerged.

إِذِ ٱنۢبَعَثَ أَشْقَىٰهَا ﴿١٢﴾

13. Then Allah's Messenger said to them: "Beware of Allah's she-camel and her drinking time."

فَقَالَ لَهُمْ رَسُولُ ٱللَّهِ نَاقَةَ ٱللَّهِ وَسُقْيَىٰهَا ﴿١٣﴾

14. They called him a liar and hamstrung her; whereupon their Lord destroyed them for their sins and settled the matter;

فَكَذَّبُوهُ فَعَقَرُوهَا فَدَمْدَمَ عَلَيْهِمْ رَبُّهُم بِذَنۢبِهِمْ فَسَوَّىٰهَا ﴿١٤﴾

15. And He does not fear its sequel.

وَلَا يَخَافُ عُقْبَىٰهَا ﴿١٥﴾

Sûrat Al-Layl,
(The Night) 92

In the Name of Allah,
the Compassionate, the Merciful

1. By the night when it darkens,

2. And the day when it lights up,

3. And by Him Who created the male and the female,

4. Your striving is manifold.

5. As for him who gives in charity and fears Allah,

6. And believes in the fairest reward;

7. We shall lead him onto the easiest course.

8. But as for him who is niggardly and has grown complacent,

9. And disbelieves in the fairest reward;

10. We shall lead him into the hardest course.

11. What will his wealth avail him, if he perishes?

12. Ours is simply to guide;

13. And Ours is the Last Day and the First.

14. So, I have warned you to beware of a blazing Fire;

15. Which none except the most vicious will roast in;

16. He who denounces and turns away.

17. But the most pious shall be spared it;

18. He who gives his wealth in self-purification;

19. And none receives a favour from him, for the sake of a reward;

20. Except seeking the Face of his Lord, the Most High.

21. And he will surely be well-pleased.

Sûrat Ad-Duha, (The Forenoon) 93

In the Name of Allah, the Compassionate, the Merciful

1. By the forenoon;

2. And the night when it falls calmly;

3. Your Lord did not forsake you or scorn you.

4. Surely, the Last Day is better for you than the First.

5. Your Lord shall surely give you [of His Bounty]; and so you shall be well-pleased.

6. Did He not find you an orphan, and then gave you refuge?

7. And found you in error, and then guided you?

8. And found you in need, and then enriched you?

9. As for the orphan, you shall not oppress him;

10. And as for the beggar, you shall not drive him away;

11. And as for your Lord's Favour, you shall proclaim it.

Sûrat Ash-Sharh, (The Dilation) 94

In the Name of Allah, the Compassionate, the Merciful

1. Did We not dilate your breast;

2. And lift from you your burden;

3. Which had weighed down your back?

4. Did We not exalt your name?

5. Surely, along with hardship is ease.

6. Surely, along with hardship is ease.

إِنَّ مَعَ ٱلْعُسْرِ يُسْرًا ۝

7. So when you have finished, toil on;

فَإِذَا فَرَغْتَ فَٱنصَبْ ۝

8. And unto your Lord, incline.

وَإِلَىٰ رَبِّكَ فَٱرْغَب ۝

Sûrat At-Tîn,
(The Fig) 95

سُورَةُ التِّينِ

In the Name of Allah,
the Compassionate, the Merciful

بِسْمِ ٱللَّهِ ٱلرَّحْمَٰنِ ٱلرَّحِيمِ

1. By the fig and the olive,

وَٱلتِّينِ وَٱلزَّيْتُونِ ۝

2. And by Mount Sinai,

وَطُورِ سِينِينَ ۝

3. And by this secure City;

وَهَٰذَا ٱلْبَلَدِ ٱلْأَمِينِ ۝

4. We have created man in the best of shapes;

لَقَدْ خَلَقْنَا ٱلْإِنسَٰنَ فِي أَحْسَنِ تَقْوِيمٍ ۝

5. Then brought him to the lowest ebb;

ثُمَّ رَدَدْنَٰهُ أَسْفَلَ سَٰفِلِينَ ۝

6. Except for those who have believed and done the righteous deeds; they shall have an unstinted wage.

إِلَّا ٱلَّذِينَ ءَامَنُوا وَعَمِلُوا ٱلصَّٰلِحَٰتِ فَلَهُمْ أَجْرٌ غَيْرُ مَمْنُونٍ ۝

7. What then causes you to deny the Judgement?

فَمَا يُكَذِّبُكَ بَعْدُ بِٱلدِّينِ ۝

8. Is not Allah the Best of Judges?

أَلَيْسَ ٱللَّهُ بِأَحْكَمِ ٱلْحَٰكِمِينَ ۝

Sûrat Al-'Alaq,
(The Clot) 96

سُورَةُ العَلَقِ

In the Name of Allah,
the Compassionate, the Merciful

بِسْمِ ٱللَّهِ ٱلرَّحْمَٰنِ ٱلرَّحِيمِ

1. Read, in the Name of your Lord, Who created:

ٱقْرَأْ بِٱسْمِ رَبِّكَ ٱلَّذِي خَلَقَ ۝

2. He created man from a clot.

خَلَقَ ٱلْإِنسَٰنَ مِنْ عَلَقٍ ۝

3. Read, by your Most Generous Lord,

ٱقْرَأْ وَرَبُّكَ ٱلْأَكْرَمُ ۝

4. Who taught by the pen.

ٱلَّذِي عَلَّمَ بِٱلْقَلَمِ ۝

5. He taught man what he did not know.

عَلَّمَ ٱلْإِنسَٰنَ مَا لَمْ يَعْلَمْ ۝

6. Yet, man will, indeed, wax arrogant;

كَلَّا إِنَّ ٱلْإِنسَٰنَ لَيَطْغَىٰ ۝

7. For he thinks himself self-sufficient.

أَن رَّءَاهُ ٱسْتَغْنَىٰ ۝

8. Surely, unto your Lord is the ultimate return.

إِنَّ إِلَىٰ رَبِّكَ ٱلرُّجْعَىٰ ﴿٨﴾

9. Have you considered him[848] who forbids,

أَرَءَيْتَ ٱلَّذِى يَنْهَىٰ ﴿٩﴾

10. A servant when he prays?

عَبْدًا إِذَا صَلَّىٰ ﴿١٠﴾

11. Have you considered whether he was well-guided?

أَرَءَيْتَ إِن كَانَ عَلَى ٱلْهُدَىٰ ﴿١١﴾

12. Or commanded piety?

أَوْ أَمَرَ بِٱلتَّقْوَىٰ ﴿١٢﴾

13. Have you considered whether he was lying and back-tracking?

أَرَءَيْتَ إِن كَذَّبَ وَتَوَلَّىٰ ﴿١٣﴾

14. Does he not know that Allah perceives?

أَلَمْ يَعْلَم بِأَنَّ ٱللَّهَ يَرَىٰ ﴿١٤﴾

15. No; if he will not desist, We shall take him by the forelock,

كَلَّا لَئِن لَّمْ يَنتَهِ لَنَسْفَعًۢا بِٱلنَّاصِيَةِ ﴿١٥﴾

16. A lying, erring forelock.

نَاصِيَةٍ كَاذِبَةٍ خَاطِئَةٍ ﴿١٦﴾

17. Let him then call his company.

فَلْيَدْعُ نَادِيَهُ ﴿١٧﴾

18. We shall call the guards of Hell.

سَنَدْعُ ٱلزَّبَانِيَةَ ﴿١٨﴾

19. No; do not obey him. Prostrate yourself and come closer.

كَلَّا لَا تُطِعْهُ وَٱسْجُدْ وَٱقْتَرِب ۩ ﴿١٩﴾

Sûrat Al-Qadr, (The Power) 97

سُورَةُ القَدْرِ

In the Name of Allah, the Compassionate, the Merciful

بِسْمِ ٱللَّهِ ٱلرَّحْمَٰنِ ٱلرَّحِيمِ

1. We have sent it[849] down on the Night of Power.

إِنَّا أَنزَلْنَٰهُ فِى لَيْلَةِ ٱلْقَدْرِ ﴿١﴾

2. If only you knew what is the Night of Power.

وَمَآ أَدْرَىٰكَ مَا لَيْلَةُ ٱلْقَدْرِ ﴿٢﴾

3. The Night of Power is better than a thousand months.

لَيْلَةُ ٱلْقَدْرِ خَيْرٌ مِّنْ أَلْفِ شَهْرٍ ﴿٣﴾

4. The angels and the Spirit[850] descend thereon by the Leave of their Lord with every Command.

تَنَزَّلُ ٱلْمَلَٰٓئِكَةُ وَٱلرُّوحُ فِيهَا بِإِذْنِ رَبِّهِم مِّن كُلِّ أَمْرٍ ﴿٤﴾

5. It is peace, till the break of dawn.

سَلَٰمٌ هِىَ حَتَّىٰ مَطْلَعِ ٱلْفَجْرِ ﴿٥﴾

---

848. Abu Jahl.
849. The Qur'an.
850. Gabriel.

Sûrat Al-Bayyinah,
(The Clear Proof) 98

بِسْمِ اللَّهِ الرَّحْمَٰنِ الرَّحِيمِ

In the Name of Allah,
the Compassionate, the Merciful

لَمْ يَكُنِ الَّذِينَ كَفَرُوا مِنْ أَهْلِ الْكِتَابِ وَالْمُشْرِكِينَ مُنفَكِّينَ حَتَّىٰ تَأْتِيَهُمُ الْبَيِّنَةُ ﴿١﴾

1. The unbelievers, among the people of the Book and the idolaters, would not desist till the clear proof comes to them;

رَسُولٌ مِّنَ اللَّهِ يَتْلُو صُحُفًا مُّطَهَّرَةً ﴿٢﴾

2. A Messenger from Allah reciting purified scrolls,

فِيهَا كُتُبٌ قَيِّمَةٌ ﴿٣﴾

3. Wherein are valuable books.

وَمَا تَفَرَّقَ الَّذِينَ أُوتُوا الْكِتَابَ إِلَّا مِنْ بَعْدِ مَا جَاءَتْهُمُ الْبَيِّنَةُ ﴿٤﴾

4. Those who were given the Book did not diverge except after the clear proof came to them.

وَمَا أُمِرُوا إِلَّا لِيَعْبُدُوا اللَّهَ مُخْلِصِينَ لَهُ الدِّينَ حُنَفَاءَ وَيُقِيمُوا الصَّلَاةَ وَيُؤْتُوا الزَّكَاةَ وَذَٰلِكَ دِينُ الْقَيِّمَةِ ﴿٥﴾

5. And they were only commanded to worship Allah, professing the religion sincerely to Him as upright believers, to perform the prayers and give the alms. That is the religion of truth.

إِنَّ الَّذِينَ كَفَرُوا مِنْ أَهْلِ الْكِتَابِ وَالْمُشْرِكِينَ فِي نَارِ جَهَنَّمَ خَالِدِينَ فِيهَا أُولَٰئِكَ هُمْ شَرُّ الْبَرِيَّةِ ﴿٦﴾

6. The unbelievers, among the People of the Book and the idolaters, shall be in the Fire of Hell, dwelling therein forever. Those are the worst of creatures.

إِنَّ الَّذِينَ آمَنُوا وَعَمِلُوا الصَّالِحَاتِ أُولَٰئِكَ هُمْ خَيْرُ الْبَرِيَّةِ ﴿٧﴾

7. Those who have believed and did the righteous deeds - those are the best of creatures.

جَزَاؤُهُمْ عِندَ رَبِّهِمْ جَنَّاتُ عَدْنٍ تَجْرِي مِن تَحْتِهَا الْأَنْهَارُ خَالِدِينَ فِيهَا أَبَدًا رَّضِيَ اللَّهُ عَنْهُمْ وَرَضُوا عَنْهُ ذَٰلِكَ لِمَنْ خَشِيَ رَبَّهُ ﴿٨﴾

8. Their reward with their Lord will be Gardens of Eden, beneath which rivers flow, dwelling therein forever. Allah is well-pleased with them and they are well-pleased with Him. That is the lot of whoever fears his Lord.

Sûrat Az-Zalzalah,
(The Earthquake) 99

سُورَةُ الزَّلْزَلَةِ

In the Name of Allah,
the Compassionate, the Merciful

بِسْمِ اللَّهِ الرَّحْمَٰنِ الرَّحِيمِ

1. When the earth shall quake violently,

إِذَا زُلْزِلَتِ الْأَرْضُ زِلْزَالَهَا ﴿١﴾

2. And the earth shall bring forth its burdens;

وَأَخْرَجَتِ الْأَرْضُ أَثْقَالَهَا ﴿٢﴾

3. And man shall say: "What is happening to it?"

وَقَالَ الْإِنسَٰنُ مَا لَهَا ﴿٣﴾

4. On that Day, it shall relate its tales;

يَوْمَئِذٍ تُحَدِّثُ أَخْبَارَهَا ﴿٤﴾

5. That its Lord has inspired it.

بِأَنَّ رَبَّكَ أَوْحَىٰ لَهَا ﴿٥﴾

6. On that Day, men shall emerge in clusters to see their works.

يَوْمَئِذٍ يَصْدُرُ النَّاسُ أَشْتَاتًا لِيُرَوْا أَعْمَالَهُمْ ﴿٦﴾

7. Then whoever has done an atom's weight of good shall find it;

فَمَن يَعْمَلْ مِثْقَالَ ذَرَّةٍ خَيْرًا يَرَهُ ﴿٧﴾

8. And whoever has done an atom's weight of evil shall find it.

وَمَن يَعْمَلْ مِثْقَالَ ذَرَّةٍ شَرًّا يَرَهُ ﴿٨﴾

Sûrat Al-'Adiyât,
(The Chargers) 100

سُورَةُ الْعَادِيَاتِ

In the Name of Allah,
the Compassionate, the Merciful

بِسْمِ اللَّهِ الرَّحْمَٰنِ الرَّحِيمِ

1. By the snorting chargers;

وَالْعَادِيَاتِ ضَبْحًا ﴿١﴾

2. And the strikers of fire, as they run;

فَالْمُورِيَاتِ قَدْحًا ﴿٢﴾

3. And the raiders at dawn;

فَالْمُغِيرَاتِ صُبْحًا ﴿٣﴾

4. Raising thereon clouds of dust;

فَأَثَرْنَ بِهِ نَقْعًا ﴿٤﴾

5. Plunging therein through a throng.

فَوَسَطْنَ بِهِ جَمْعًا ﴿٥﴾

6. Man is truly thankless unto his Lord;

إِنَّ الْإِنسَٰنَ لِرَبِّهِ لَكَنُودٌ ﴿٦﴾

7. And he is a witness thereof.

وَإِنَّهُ عَلَىٰ ذَٰلِكَ لَشَهِيدٌ ﴿٧﴾

8. He is indeed a passionate lover of earthly goods.

وَإِنَّهُ لِحُبِّ الْخَيْرِ لَشَدِيدٌ ﴿٨﴾

9. Does he not know that when what is in the graves is scattered around?

﴿٩﴾ ۞ أَفَلَا يَعْلَمُ إِذَا بُعْثِرَ مَا فِى ٱلْقُبُورِ

10. And what is within the breasts is brought out?

﴿١٠﴾ وَحُصِّلَ مَا فِى ٱلصُّدُورِ

11. Their Lord is, surely, Well-Informed about them on that Day.

﴿١١﴾ إِنَّ رَبَّهُم بِهِمْ يَوْمَئِذٍ لَّخَبِيرٌۢ

Sûrat Al-Qari'ah, (The Clatterer) 101

﴿سُورَةُ الْقَارِعَةِ﴾

In the Name of Allah, the Compassionate, the Merciful

بِسْمِ ٱللَّهِ ٱلرَّحْمَٰنِ ٱلرَّحِيمِ

1. The Clatterer![851]

﴿١﴾ ٱلْقَارِعَةُ

2. What is the Clatterer?

﴿٢﴾ مَا ٱلْقَارِعَةُ

3. If only you knew what is the Clatterer.

﴿٣﴾ وَمَآ أَدْرَىٰكَ مَا ٱلْقَارِعَةُ

4. The Day that men shall be like scattered butterflies;

﴿٤﴾ يَوْمَ يَكُونُ ٱلنَّاسُ كَٱلْفَرَاشِ ٱلْمَبْثُوثِ

5. And the mountains like tufted wool.

﴿٥﴾ وَتَكُونُ ٱلْجِبَالُ كَٱلْعِهْنِ ٱلْمَنفُوشِ

6. As for him whose scales shall be weighty,

﴿٦﴾ فَأَمَّا مَن ثَقُلَتْ مَوَٰزِينُهُۥ

7. He shall enjoy a well-pleasing life.

﴿٧﴾ فَهُوَ فِى عِيشَةٍ رَّاضِيَةٍ

8. But as for him whose scales are light,

﴿٨﴾ وَأَمَّا مَنْ خَفَّتْ مَوَٰزِينُهُۥ

9. His mother shall be the Pit.

﴿٩﴾ فَأُمُّهُۥ هَاوِيَةٌ

10. And if only you knew what it is.

﴿١٠﴾ وَمَآ أَدْرَىٰكَ مَا هِيَهْ

11. A blazing Fire.

﴿١١﴾ نَارٌ حَامِيَةٌۢ

---

851. That is, the Day of Judgement when the clatter of milling crowds fills the air.

<table>
<tr><td>

Sûrat At-Takâthur,
(Covetousness) 102

</td><td>

سُورَةُ التَّكَاثُرِ

</td></tr>
</table>

In the Name of Allah,
the Compassionate, the Merciful

بِسْمِ اللَّهِ الرَّحْمَٰنِ الرَّحِيمِ

1. Covetousness has distracted you,

أَلْهَىٰكُمُ التَّكَاثُرُ ۝

2. Till you visited the graveyards.

حَتَّىٰ زُرْتُمُ الْمَقَابِرَ ۝

3. No; you shall surely know.

كَلَّا سَوْفَ تَعْلَمُونَ ۝

4. Again, no; you shall surely know.

ثُمَّ كَلَّا سَوْفَ تَعْلَمُونَ ۝

5. No; if only you knew with certainty,

كَلَّا لَوْ تَعْلَمُونَ عِلْمَ الْيَقِينِ ۝

6. You would surely have perceived Hell.

لَتَرَوُنَّ الْجَحِيمَ ۝

7. Then, you will have perceived it with visual certainty.

ثُمَّ لَتَرَوُنَّهَا عَيْنَ الْيَقِينِ ۝

8. Then, on that Day, you will surely be questioned about the Bliss.

ثُمَّ لَتُسْأَلُنَّ يَوْمَئِذٍ عَنِ النَّعِيمِ ۝

<table>
<tr><td>

Sûrat Al-'Asr,
(The Aeon) 103

</td><td>

سُورَةُ الْعَصْرِ

</td></tr>
</table>

In the Name of Allah,
the Compassionate, the Merciful

بِسْمِ اللَّهِ الرَّحْمَٰنِ الرَّحِيمِ

1. By the aeon,[852]

وَالْعَصْرِ ۝

2. Man is, indeed, a prey to perdition,

إِنَّ الْإِنْسَانَ لَفِي خُسْرٍ ۝

3. Except for those who believe, do the righteous deeds, urge each other to seek the truth and urge each other to be steadfast.

إِلَّا الَّذِينَ آمَنُوا وَعَمِلُوا الصَّالِحَاتِ وَتَوَاصَوْا بِالْحَقِّ وَتَوَاصَوْا بِالصَّبْرِ ۝

---

852. Or time.

632

Sûrat Al-Humazah,
(The Backbiter) 104

سُورَةُ الهُمَزَة

*In the Name of Allah,
the Compassionate, the Merciful*

بِسْمِ اللَّهِ الرَّحْمَنِ الرَّحِيمِ

1. Woe unto every backbiter and slanderer,

وَيْلٌ لِّكُلِّ هُمَزَةٍ لُّمَزَةٍ ۝

2. Who amasses wealth and counts it diligently.

الَّذِى جَمَعَ مَالًا وَعَدَّدَهُ ۝

3. He thinks that his wealth will make him immortal.

يَحْسَبُ أَنَّ مَالَهُ أَخْلَدَهُ ۝

4. Not at all; he shall be cast into the Smasher.

كَلَّا لَيُنۢبَذَنَّ فِى الْحُطَمَةِ ۝

5. And if only you knew what is the Smasher.

وَمَا أَدْرَىٰكَ مَا الْحُطَمَةُ ۝

6. It is Allah's kindled Fire,

نَارُ اللَّهِ الْمُوقَدَةُ ۝

7. Which attains even the hearts.

الَّتِى تَطَّلِعُ عَلَى الْأَفْـِٔدَةِ ۝

8. Upon them it is closing in;

إِنَّهَا عَلَيْهِم مُّؤْصَدَةٌ ۝

9. On pillars stretched out.

فِى عَمَدٍ مُّمَدَّدَةٍ ۝

Sûrat Al-Fîl,
(The Elephant) 105

سُورَةُ الفِيل

*In the Name of Allah,
the Compassionate, the Merciful*

بِسْمِ اللَّهِ الرَّحْمَنِ الرَّحِيمِ

1. Have you not seen how your Lord dealt with the Companions of the Elephant?

أَلَمْ تَرَ كَيْفَ فَعَلَ رَبُّكَ بِأَصْحَابِ الْفِيلِ ۝

2. Did He not turn their cunning into perdition?

أَلَمْ يَجْعَلْ كَيْدَهُمْ فِى تَضْلِيلٍ ۝

3. And send upon them swarms of birds;

وَأَرْسَلَ عَلَيْهِمْ طَيْرًا أَبَابِيلَ ۝

4. Hurling upon them stones of clay;

تَرْمِيهِم بِحِجَارَةٍ مِّن سِجِّيلٍ ۝

5. And so He reduced them to munched blades of grass.

فَجَعَلَهُمْ كَعَصْفٍ مَّأْكُولٍ ۝

Sûrat Quraysh, (Quraysh) 106

سُورَةُ قُرَيْشٍ

In the Name of Allah,
the Compassionate, the Merciful

بِسْمِ ٱللَّهِ ٱلرَّحْمَنِ ٱلرَّحِيمِ

1. For Quraysh's customary journey,

لِإِيلَٰفِ قُرَيْشٍ ①

2. The journey of the winter and summer,

إِۦلَٰفِهِمْ رِحْلَةَ ٱلشِّتَآءِ وَٱلصَّيْفِ ②

3. Let them worship the Lord of this House,

فَلْيَعْبُدُوا رَبَّ هَٰذَا ٱلْبَيْتِ ③

4. Who has fed them when they were hungry and secured them against fear.

ٱلَّذِىٓ أَطْعَمَهُم مِّن جُوعٍ وَءَامَنَهُم مِّنْ خَوْفٍۭ ④

Sûrat Al-Mâ'ûn, (Benefaction) 107

سُورَةُ ٱلْمَاعُونَ

In the Name of Allah,
the Compassionate, the Merciful

بِسْمِ ٱللَّهِ ٱلرَّحْمَنِ ٱلرَّحِيمِ

1. Have you seen him who denies the Judgement?

أَرَءَيْتَ ٱلَّذِى يُكَذِّبُ بِٱلدِّينِ ①

2. It is the one who pushes the orphan around,

فَذَٰلِكَ ٱلَّذِى يَدُعُّ ٱلْيَتِيمَ ②

3. And does not urge the feeding of the destitute.

وَلَا يَحُضُّ عَلَىٰ طَعَامِ ٱلْمِسْكِينِ ③

4. Woe unto those who pray;

فَوَيْلٌ لِّلْمُصَلِّينَ ④

5. Those who are oblivious of their prayer;

ٱلَّذِينَ هُمْ عَن صَلَاتِهِمْ سَاهُونَ ⑤

6. Those who dissimulate;

ٱلَّذِينَ هُمْ يُرَآءُونَ ⑥

7. And forbid benefaction.

وَيَمْنَعُونَ ٱلْمَاعُونَ ⑦

Sûrat Al-Kawthar, (Abundance) 108

سُورَةُ ٱلْكَوْثَرِ

In the Name of Allah,
the Compassionate, the Merciful

بِسْمِ ٱللَّهِ ٱلرَّحْمَنِ ٱلرَّحِيمِ

1. We have surely given you abundance;

إِنَّآ أَعْطَيْنَٰكَ ٱلْكَوْثَرَ ①

2. So pray to your Lord and offer in sacrifice.

فَصَلِّ لِرَبِّكَ وَٱنْحَرْ ②

3. Indeed, your chief hater is the real childless.[853]

إِنَّ شَانِئَكَ هُوَ ٱلْأَبْتَرُ ③

---

853. The reference is to al-'Aas Ibn Wa'il, who chided Muhammad upon the death of his son.

<table>
<tr><td>

**Sûrat Al-Kâfirûn,
(The Unbelievers) 109**

</td><td>

سُوۡرَةُ الۡكَافِرُوۡنَ

</td></tr>
</table>

*In the Name of Allah,
the Compassionate, the Merciful*

بِسۡمِ اللّٰهِ الرَّحۡمٰنِ الرَّحِيۡمِ

1. Say: "O unbelievers,

قُلۡ يٰۤاَيُّهَا الۡكٰفِرُوۡنَ ۝

2. "I do not worship what you worship,

لَاۤ اَعۡبُدُ مَا تَعۡبُدُوۡنَ ۝

3. "Nor do you worship what I worship;

وَلَاۤ اَنۡتُمۡ عٰبِدُوۡنَ مَاۤ اَعۡبُدُ ۝

4. "Nor do I worship what you have worshipped,

وَلَاۤ اَنَا عَابِدٌ مَّا عَبَدۡتُّمۡ ۝

5. "Nor do you worship what I worship.

وَلَاۤ اَنۡتُمۡ عٰبِدُوۡنَ مَاۤ اَعۡبُدُ ۝

6. "You have your religion and I have mine."

لَكُمۡ دِيۡنُكُمۡ وَلِيَ دِيۡنِ ۝

<table>
<tr><td>

**Sûrat An-Nasr,
(The Support) 110**

</td><td>

سُوۡرَةُ النَّصۡرِ

</td></tr>
</table>

*In the Name of Allah,
the Compassionate, the Merciful*

بِسۡمِ اللّٰهِ الرَّحۡمٰنِ الرَّحِيۡمِ

1. When Allah's Support and victory come,

اِذَا جَآءَ نَصۡرُ اللّٰهِ وَالۡفَتۡحُ ۝

2. And you see people entering Allah's religion in throngs;

وَرَاَيۡتَ النَّاسَ يَدۡخُلُوۡنَ فِىۡ دِيۡنِ اللّٰهِ اَفۡوَاجًا ۝

3. Then, magnify the Praise of your Lord and seek His Forgiveness. He is indeed All-Forgiving.

فَسَبِّحۡ بِحَمۡدِ رَبِّكَ وَاسۡتَغۡفِرۡهُ اِنَّهٗ كَانَ تَوَّابًا ۝

<table>
<tr><td>

**Sûrat Al-Masad,
(The Fibre) 111**

</td><td>

سُوۡرَةُ الۡمَسَدِ

</td></tr>
</table>

*In the Name of Allah,
the Compassionate, the Merciful*

بِسۡمِ اللّٰهِ الرَّحۡمٰنِ الرَّحِيۡمِ

1. Perish the hands of Abu Lahab,[854] and may he perish too;

تَبَّتۡ يَدَاۤ اَبِىۡ لَهَبٍ وَّتَبَّ ۝

2. Neither his wealth nor what he has earned will avail him anything.

مَاۤ اَغۡنٰى عَنۡهُ مَالُهٗ وَمَا كَسَبَ ۝

---

854. Uncle of the Prophet and an inveterate enemy of Islam in the early days.

3. He will roast in a flaming fire,

سَيَصْلَىٰ نَارًا ذَاتَ لَهَبٍ ۞

4. And his wife will be a carrier of fire-wood,

وَٱمْرَأَتُهُ حَمَّالَةَ ٱلْحَطَبِ ۞

5. She shall have a rope of fibre around her neck.

فِى جِيدِهَا حَبْلٌ مِّن مَّسَدٍ ۞

**Sûrat Al-Ikhlâs,
(Sincerity) 112**

*In the Name of Allah,
the Compassionate, the Merciful*

بِسْمِ ٱللَّهِ ٱلرَّحْمَٰنِ ٱلرَّحِيمِ

1. Say: "He is Allah, the only One,

قُلْ هُوَ ٱللَّهُ أَحَدٌ ۞

2. "Allah, the Everlasting.

ٱللَّهُ ٱلصَّمَدُ ۞

3. "He did not beget and is not begotten,

لَمْ يَلِدْ وَلَمْ يُولَدْ ۞

4. "And none is His equal."

وَلَمْ يَكُن لَّهُ كُفُوًا أَحَدٌ ۞

**Sûrat Al-Falaq,
(The Daybreak) 113**

*In the Name of Allah,
the Compassionate, the Merciful*

بِسْمِ ٱللَّهِ ٱلرَّحْمَٰنِ ٱلرَّحِيمِ

1. Say: "I seek refuge with the Lord of the Daybreak,

قُلْ أَعُوذُ بِرَبِّ ٱلْفَلَقِ ۞

2. "From the evil of what He has created,

مِن شَرِّ مَا خَلَقَ ۞

3. "And the evil of the darkness when it gathers,

وَمِن شَرِّ غَاسِقٍ إِذَا وَقَبَ ۞

4. "And the evil of those who blow into knotted reeds,[855]

وَمِن شَرِّ ٱلنَّفَّٰثَٰتِ فِى ٱلْعُقَدِ ۞

5. "And from the evil of the envious when he envies."

وَمِن شَرِّ حَاسِدٍ إِذَا حَسَدَ ۞

---

855. Witches or sorceresses.

Sûrat An-Nâs, (The People) 114	سُورَةُ النَّاسِ

In the Name of Allah,
the Compassionate, the Merciful

بِسْمِ ٱللَّهِ ٱلرَّحْمَٰنِ ٱلرَّحِيمِ

1. Say: "I seek refuge with the Lord of the people,

قُلْ أَعُوذُ بِرَبِّ ٱلنَّاسِ ﴿١﴾

2. "The King of the people;

مَلِكِ ٱلنَّاسِ ﴿٢﴾

3. "The God of the people,

إِلَٰهِ ٱلنَّاسِ ﴿٣﴾

4. "From the evil of the slinking whisperer,[856]

مِن شَرِّ ٱلْوَسْوَاسِ ٱلْخَنَّاسِ ﴿٤﴾

5. "Who whispers in the breasts of people,

ٱلَّذِى يُوَسْوِسُ فِى صُدُورِ ٱلنَّاسِ ﴿٥﴾

6. "Both jinn and men."

مِنَ ٱلْجِنَّةِ وَٱلنَّاسِ ﴿٦﴾

---

856. Satan.

Index

entering with permission - 352
entering those of the Prophet - 426
Hud - 157, 216-231, 372
Hudaibiyah, peace of - 521n
Hunayn - 188
hunting - 108, 122
hypocrites - 94, 102, 103, 118n, 181, 193, 198, 399,
428, 518, 553, 561
Iblis - 10, 370, 431, 461
Ibn al Ashraf, Ka'b - 90n
Ibn Harithah, Zayd - 424n
Ibn Shurayq, al-Akhnas - 36n
Ibn Thabit, Zayd - 1
Ibn Umm Maktum, Abdullah - 609n
Ibn Wa'il, al 'Aas - 634n
Idolaters - 185-186, 266, 333, 399n, 410, 428, 481, 488,
629
Idols - 122, 326, 334, 396n, 400, 464, 509n
Idris - 305, 328
Imminence, Day of - 473
Immortality, Day of - 527
'Imran (father of Mary) - 58, 576
indecencies - 153, 159, 273, 351
infidels (*kafirun*) - 2
inheritance - 32n, 82, 86, 107
intercession - 93, 467
iqra' (read) - 1
Iram - 621
Iron rods - 333
Isaac - 3, 25, 65, 105, 137, 225, 232, 235, 255, 305, 237,
401, 452, 460
Islam - 56, 65, 108, 143, 465
al-Islam - 566n
Isma'il - 23-25, 28n, 65, 105, 137, 255, 305, 328, 460
Israel
    see Jacob
Israelites - 44n
    see also Children of Israel
Izhar - 396n
Jacob - 3, 24, 65, 105, 137, 225, 232, 235, 239, 241n,
301, 305, 327, 401, 460
Jahiliyah - 116n
Jericho - 12n
Jerusalem - 12n, 47n
Jesus - 25, 65, 104, 137
    Allah's conversation with - 126
    birth of - 60, 303
    charged with religion - 488
    death of - 61, 104
    son of Mary - 3, 17, 46, 60, 115, 120, 344, 420, 498,

555, 566-567
    strengthened with the Holy Spirit - 17, 46
Jews - 13, 21, 22, 88, 105, 115, 119, 121, 188, 276, 333
    forbidden food for - 146
    not to be taken as friends - 116
    status in the Qur'an - 1, 2-3
Jibril - 1
Jinn - 143, 379, 381, 430, 454, 512, 531
    creation of the - 140, 258, 543
    and men - 141, 144, 154, 172, 230, 286, 417, 483,
    511, 544, 637
    worship of the - 433
Job - 3, 105, 137, 328, 459
John the Baptist - 3, 59, 137, 302, 328
Jonah - 105, 137, 215, 328n, 453, 582n
Joseph - 137, 231-244, 475
    and his brothers - 231-242
Joshua - 296n
Judaism - 568
Judgement, Day of - 46n, 259, 370, 447, 462, 529, 549,
587, 597, 613, 614
al-Judi mountain - 222
Justice - 90, 273, 523, 564
Ka'ba, sacred shrine of the - 1, 2, 23n, 26n, 66, 123,
334
    see also Sacred House
Kafirun (infidels)
Kalam Allah (Word of God) - 1
Karoon - 396, 402
Khaybar - 520n, 521n
killing by mistake - 95
kingship - 46, 57
Knowledge - 488, 578
Korah - 396n, 474
Last Abode - 397
Last Day - 6, 13, 23, 31, 119, 188, 191, 538, 559, 564,
625, 626
al-Lat, pagan god - 536
al-Lawh al-Mahfouz - 441n
legislation, Islamic - 2
life
    and death - 346
    present - 206, 554
Lot - 3, 137, 159-160, 326-327, 383, 401, 402, 453
    people of - 194n, 226-227, 260, 336, 374, 526, 541
    wife of - 160, 261, 383, 402, 576
Lotus Trees - 536, 548
Madyan - 194, 457n
    see Midian
Magians - 333

بسم الله الرحمن الرحيم

AL - AZHAR AL - SHARIF

ISLAMIC RESEARCH ACADEMY

GENERAL DEPARTMENT

For Research, Writting & Translation

الأزهــــر الشريف

مجمــع البحـوث الاسـلامية

الادارة العـــامـة

للبحـوث والتأليف والترجمــة

Messrs. Garnet Publishing limited.

with reference to your letter

dated, 5 July, 2000, In respect of your

request that this department may review your

book titled: An Interpretation of the Qur'án

English translation of the meanings

A Bilingual Edition.

Translated by Majid Fakhry.

After having reviewed this book as requested

we have the pleasure to declare that we

have no objection to approve this book and

Put it in Circulation or introduced for

republication.

Tran. department.   Dir. General.

Diaa El deen   El sayyed El Eraky

10٥

٢٠

نموذج رقم « ١٧ »

بسم الله الرحمن الرحيم

AL - AZHAR AL - SHARIF
ISLAMIC RESEARCH ACADEMY
GENERAL DEPARTMENT
For Research, Writting & Translation

الأزهـــر الشريف
مجمـع البحـوث الاسلامية
الادارة العـــامة
للبحـــوث والتأليف والترجمـة

السـيد / الأستاذ محمود بن الحاج
دار ناريس للطباعة والنشر

السـلام عليـكم ورحمـة اللـه وبـركاته ــ وبعـد :

فبناء على الطلب الخاص بفحص ومراجعة كتاب : ترجمة معاني القرآن الكريم
وبلـغتـ الهنجاريـة من تأليف : احلام من جدتري ، بالكلمة بتعليـ به

نفيد بان الكتاب المذكور ليس فيه ما يتعارض مع العقيدة الاسلامية ولا مانع
من طبعــه ونشـره على نفقتكم الخـاصة .

مع التـأكيد على ضرورة العنـاية التامة بكتـابة الآيات القـرآنية والأحاديث
النبوية الشريفة والالتزام بتسليم ٥ خمس نسخ لمكتبة الأزهر الشريف بعد الطبـع .

واللـــه المـــوفق ،،،

والسـلام عليـكم ورحمـة اللـه وبركاته ،،،

إدارة لبرجمة
حصار لتم محمد

تحريرا في ٦ / ١٨ / ١٤٠١ هـ
الموافق ٩ / ١٦ / ٨٢ م

مـدير عـام
ادارة البحوث والتأليف والترجمة